Cost Management

A Strategic Emphasis

SECOND EDITION

Cost Management

A Strategic Emphasis

Edward J. Blocher
University of North Carolina at Chapel Hill
Kenan-Flagler Business School

Kung H. Chen
University of Nebraska
School of Accountancy

Thomas W. Lin
University of Southern California
Leventhal School of Accounting

McGraw-Hill Irwin

Boston   Burr Ridge, IL   Dubuque, IA   Madison, WI   New York   San Francisco   St. Louis
Bangkok   Bogotá   Caracas   Kuala Lumpur   Lisbon   London   Madrid   Mexico City
Milan   Montreal   New Delhi   Santiago   Seoul   Singapore   Sydney   Taipei   Toronto

McGraw-Hill Higher Education

*A Division of The **McGraw-Hill** Companies*

COST MANAGEMENT: A STRATEGIC EMPHASIS

Published by McGraw-Hill/Irwin, an imprint of The McGraw-Hill Companies, Inc. 1221
Avenue of the Americas, New York, NY, 10020. Copyright ©2002, 1999, by The McGraw-Hill Companies, Inc.

Some ancillaries, including electronic and print components, may not be available to customers outside the
United States.

This book is printed on acid-free paper.

3 4 5 6 7 8 9 0 QWV/QWV 0 9 8 7 6 5 4 3

ISBN 0072404302

Publisher: *Brent Gordon*
Senior sponsoring editor: *Stewart Mattson*
Developmental editor: *Erin Cibula*
Marketing manager: *Richard Kolasa*
Senior project managers: *Kelly L. Delso and Jean Hamilton*
Senior production supervisor: *Lori Koetters*
Senior designer: *Jennifer McQueen*
Cover images: *©2001 Photodisc, Inc. All rights reserved.*
Interior design: *Joel Davies/Z Graphics*
Photo research coordinator: *David A. Tietz*
Photo researcher: *Sarah Evertson*
Senior supplement coordinator: *Carol Loreth*
New media: *Anthony Sherman*
Compositor: *Precision Graphics*
Typeface: *10.5/12 Goudy*
Printer: *Quebecor World Versailles Inc*
www.mhhe.com

Material from the Certified Management Accountant Examination by the Institute of Certified Management
Accountants, is reprinted and/or adapted with permission.

INTERNATIONAL EDITION ISBN 0-07-112302-4

Library of Congress Cataloging-in-Publication Data

Blocher, Edward.
    Cost management : a strategic emphasis / Edward J. Blocher, Kung H. Chen, Thomas
W. Lin.—2nd ed.
        p. cm.
    Includes indexes.
    ISBN 0-07-240430-2 (alk. paper)
    1. Cost accounting. 2. Managerial accounting. I. Chen, Kung H. II. Lin, W. Thomas.
III. Title.

HF5686.C8 B559 2002
658.15'52—dc21

2001030667

To our wives: Sandy, Mary, and Angela

And children: Joseph and David
Robert and Melissa
Bill and Margaret

Edward J. Blocher   is Professor of Accounting at the Kenan-Flagler Business School at the University of North Carolina. He received his bachelor's degree in economics from Rice University, his MBA degree from Tulane University, and his PhD in accounting from the University of Texas at Austin. He has been a faculty member at the University of North Carolina since 1976. He has also been on the faculty of Northwestern University.

Professor Blocher is an active member of the American Accounting Association, where he presents workshops on cost management and founded the section on Artificial Intelligence and Expert Systems. He is also active in the American Institute of CPAs, where he has served on two task forces.

While he is involved in a number of accounting organizations, Professor Blocher has been the most continuously active in the Institute of Management Accountants. He is a Certified Management Accountant (CMA), has taught review courses for the CMA exam, and has served on the Institute's national education committee. He remains active in the Institute's Raleigh-Durham chapter, where he has served in many positions.

Professor Blocher is the author of a book on analytical procedures (Prentice Hall) and a research monograph on management fraud (Institute of Management Accountants), and is a coauthor of monographs published by the American Accounting Association and the American Institute of CPAs. He is also author or coauthor of several articles appearing in various journals, including *The Accounting Review, Management Accounting, Journal of Cost Management, Journal of Accountancy, Accounting and Business Research, Accounting, Organizations and Society*, and *Auditing: A Journal of Practice and Theory*.

Putting research and teaching into practice is important to Professor Blocher, who has worked closely with other firms and organizations in developing products, publications, and teaching materials. He was the principal designer of an accounting analysis system for Prentice Hall Professional Software and has worked with Blue Cross and Blue Shield of North Carolina, the American Institute of CPAs, KPMG Peat Marwick, Grant Thornton, and the Chancellor's Office at the University of North Carolina at Chapel Hill, among others.

Kung H. Chen   is the Steinhardt Foundation Professor of Accounting and the Director of Graduate Programs in the School of Accountancy at the University of Nebraska–Lincoln. A graduate of National Taiwan University, he has his MBA degree from West Virginia University and a PhD from the University of Texas–Austin.

Professor Chen has published his research in various journals, including *The Accounting Review, Encyclopedia of Accounting, Internal Auditor, Journal of Business Finance & Accounting, Behavioral Research in Accounting, Journal of Accounting Literature, Advances in Accounting, Financial Management*, and *International Journal of Accounting*, and has presented research papers to audiences in several countries including the United States, New Zealand, Japan, Taiwan, Korea, and China.

Thomas W. Lin is the Accounting Circle Professor of Accounting at the Leventhal School of Accounting at the University of Southern California. He received his BA in business administration from National Taiwan University, MBA from National Chengchi University in Taiwan, MS in accounting and information systems from UCLA, and a PhD in accounting from The Ohio State University. He has experience as a management accountant and a systems analyst and has been an assistant to the president of a multinational plastics firm and a computer auditor of an international accounting firm.

Professor Lin has published five books and over 70 papers in various journals, including *The Accounting Review, Journal of Management Accounting Research, Journal of Accountancy, Journal of Business Finance and Accounting, Advances in Accounting, Journal of Information Systems, IS Audit & Control Journal,* and *Auditing: A Journal of Practice and Theory.* He has presented seminars on new developments in cost management in North America and Asia.

Professor Lin has worked with many companies, including KPMG Peat Marwick, PricewaterhouseCoopers, Times Mirror, Carnation, Western Refuse and Hauling, City of Chino, Formosa Plastics, Intex Plastics, Zee Toys, FCB Taiwan California Bank, and General Bank. He is active in the American Accounting Association and the Institute of Management Accountants. A Certified Management Accountant (CMA), he was awarded a Certificate of Distinguished Performance by the Institute of Certified Management Accountants.

The authors have taught cost management for a number of years. For the last five years, they have taught an American Accounting Association workshop, Teaching Strategic Cost Management.

Over the past 12 years, we have seen a dramatic shift in the way educators and practitioners view the field of cost accounting. This changing view is the result of an increasingly competitive environment due to the introduction of new manufacturing and information technologies, the focus on the customer, and the growth of worldwide markets. Accounting information plays a vital role in determining the most appropriate strategic direction for the organization. In particular, cost information is a critical type of information needed for effective management. For this reason, the role of the cost accountant has expanded. Once viewed as technical experts in accounting methods and procedures, accountants are now participants on multifunctional management teams. Procedural cost accounting methods are important, but equally important is knowing how and when to apply them for more effective decision making. Employers today are looking for accounting professionals who understand the business environment and can interpret important cost information in ways that contribute to the firm's success.

Our text, *Cost Management: A Strategic Emphasis*, addresses these changing needs. Our goal in writing this book is **to better prepare students to understand the critical role that cost management information plays in the overall success of an organization.** To do this, we have presented cost and management accounting in an entirely new way: first, by organizing the topics according to the functions of management and, second, by presenting the topics in conjunction with the basic concepts of strategy. Throughout the text, you will discover a running theme: **How does the topic we are discussing help the firm more effectively compete in its industry?** This organization helps students gain an understanding of how learning cost accounting techniques can better serve the company as a whole.

WHY THE STRATEGIC EMPHASIS?

In taking a strategic emphasis, *Cost Management* considers the long-term competitive success of the firm. Management reports that focus only on short-term financial results will not suffice. Each successful firm maintains a competitive advantage based on a unique strategy. The strategy identifies the critical success factors that the firm must achieve. These success factors include financial measures such as profit or sales growth and non-financial measures such as new product development, product quality, and customer satisfaction. Only by succeeding at these critical success factors will the firm maintain its strategic competitive advantage. The role of cost management is to identify, measure, collect, analyze, and report information on these critical factors reliably and in a timely manner. Cost management information provides the critical information the manager needs to develop and implement successful strategies.

For more than a decade, educators and cost management practitioners have called for a strategic emphasis in cost management and accounting education. In addition, the Accounting Education Change Commission, the American Institute of Certified Public Accountants (AICPA), the American Accounting Association (AAA), and many of the large accounting firms have called for change in accounting education—change to reflect the broader responsibilities of the practicing accountant. The expectation is very clear now that the accountant must be knowledgeable about business and be able to effectively work as part of a management team for the success of the firm or organization.

An example of the forces behind these changes is a survey of 800 management accountants commissioned by the Institute of Management Accountants (IMA), completed in 1996, and updated in 1999. The *Practice Analysis of Management Accounting* revealed the changing expectations that top managers have for management accountants. Instead of financial reporting specialists only, managers now expect management accountants to develop and interpret information that will help the firm succeed. For example, a respondent from ITT automotive indicated that management accountants need to be far more knowledgeable about the operations of the business.

The IMA has taken additional steps to recognize the importance of strategy. It has changed the name of its journal from *Management Accounting* to *Strategic Finance* and has added a certification program in financial management. These moves are intended to show clearly that the expectations for the management accountant have gone beyond technical accounting material to include financial and strategic analysis.

Another example is a recent study sponsored by the AAA, the AICPA, the IMA, and the Big-5 accounting firms, Accounting Education: Charting the Course Through a Perilous Future, by W. Steve Albrecht and Robert J. Sack. This study revealed that accounting educators and practitioners expect accounting students to be better prepared for assisting companies and organizations in strategic planning, financial analysis, and business consulting.

GOALS OF COST MANAGEMENT: A STRATEGIC EMPHASIS

This evolution in the field of cost accounting has created a need for contemporary teaching materials that **help students make the connection between learning basic accounting methods and serving the overall needs of the company.** Our specific goals in writing this book are to help students do the following:

1. Understand how a firm or organization chooses its competitive strategy, including the identification and measurement of critical success factors.

2. Learn how cost management methods and practices are used to help the firm succeed.

3. Understand and apply appropriate cost management methods in each of the four management functions:
   a. Strategic management.
   b. Planning and decision making.
   c. Preparation of financial reports.
   d. Management and operational control.

4. See the effect of the contemporary business environment on cost management methods and practices, including the global business environment, new manufacturing and information technologies, the increasing focus on the customer, new management organizational forms, and other social, ethical, political, and cultural considerations.

5. Understand the role of cost management in the firm's use of contemporary management techniques such as total quality management, benchmarking, continuous improvement, activity-based management, reengineering, the theory of constraints, mass customization, target costing, life-cycle costing, and the balanced scorecard.

WELCOME TO STUDENTS

We have written this book to help you understand more about management and the role of cost management in helping a firm or organization succeed. Unlike many books that attempt to teach you about accounting, we seek to teach you about management and how managers use our area of accounting, cost management, to make better decisions and improve their companies.

An important aspect of cost management is the strategic focus. By *strategy*, we mean the long-term plan the firm has developed to compete successfully. Any firm or organization must have a competitive edge. For some firms, it is low cost and for others it might be high quality or unique product features. We know in these competitive times that a firm does not succeed by being ordinary. In contrast, it develops a strategy that will set it apart from competitors and ensure its attractiveness to customers. Why is strategy so important in cost management? Because in accounting and other areas of management, firms are becoming more focused on adding value for the customer or shareholder. Cost management helps an organization provide the added value.

Every chapter and every problem in the text have larger issues: How does this firm compete? And thus, what type of cost management information does it need? We do not present a cost management method simply for you to become proficient at it. We want you to know why, when, and how it is used. We believe that a proper understanding of cost management practices and methods is essential for a good manager, and we believe that you will agree.

ORGANIZATION AND CONTENT DIFFERENCES

Along with the important traditional cost management methods and procedures, this text includes relevant discussions of strategy. This unique strategic emphasis is integrated in the text in three ways:

1. **Strategic framework.** The book is organized to emphasize the role of cost management information in each management function. In this way, each cost management method is clearly linked not only to the firm's overall strategy but also to the management function that uses the method. Each part of the book develops the role of cost management information in each of the four management functions:
    a. Strategic Management—Parts I and II
    b. Planning and Decision Making—Part III
    c. Product Costing and Financial Reporting—Part IV
    d. Operational Control and Management Control—Parts V and VI, respectively
2. **Early coverage of basic strategic concepts.** The introductory chapters develop important strategic concepts that are then used throughout the book. These chapters explain how firms compete and the nature of the key measures that managers must use to gain and maintain a competitive advantage.
3. **Running theme: How does this topic contribute to the firm's success?** A key feature of the book is that the strategic theme is used to integrate the individual chapters into a coherent whole in which each of the parts contributes to the overall strategic emphasis. For example, most chapters start with an explanation of the strategic role of the chapter topic in cost management.

The following chart demonstrates how these three differentiating aspects of the book are applied to three different types of chapters: (1) a chapter covering a traditional topic that is usually presented in a procedural manner, (2) a chapter covering a contemporary topic that involves a significant advancement of a traditional cost management method, and (3) a chapter covering strategic topics such as contemporary management methods used to enhance the firm's competitiveness.

Key Differences in Each Chapter

Chapter 1: Cost Management: An Overview

This chapter introduces the central theme of the book, the strategic role of cost management. It describes the contemporary business environment and explains how it has affected the role of cost management. The strategic role of cost management is then linked to the development of 10 new management techniques, including total quality management, target costing, and the balanced scorecard.

Chapter 2: Strategic Analysis and Strategic Cost Management

This chapter explains how firms develop strategies to succeed. The concepts of strategy and how a firm develops a competitive one are presented using Michael Porter's framework: cost leadership and differentiation. Coverage includes an introduction to the concept of critical success factors, the strategic role of the balanced scorecard, and an explanation of value-chain analysis.

Chapter 3: Basic Cost Concepts

This topic can often seem to be a glossary of somewhat related concepts. In contrast, the basic cost terms and concepts are presented in this book as they relate to the four management functions to emphasize the use of the terms in actual cost management methods and practices. This organization emphasizes the role of cost management in each of the four management functions and thus provides increased motivation for learning the terms since it is clear from the start how they will be used later in the book.

Chapter 4: Activity-Based Costing and Management

Activity-based costing is presented thoroughly in this chapter, including value-added and non-value-added activities; activity-based management; applications in manu-

	Strategic Framework: Organization by Management Function	Strategic Concepts: Covered Early in the Book	Strategic Theme: Integrated Throughout the Book
	Traditional Topic		
Job Costing (Chapter 12)	Cost management systems such as job order costing have an important role in the management function: preparing financial reports for both internal and external use. This management function is covered in Part IV of the book, with Chapter 12 as the introductory chapter.	The coverage of strategy in Chapter 2 provides a good foundation that explains why job order costing can add value and competitiveness for a company. The chapter explains the business purpose of job costing, linking it to the firm's strategy, as developed in Chapter 2.	Chapter 12 begins with an explanation of the different costing systems, including job order costing, with the objective of showing the business purpose of the different systems.
	Contemporary Topic		
Activity-Based Costing and Management (Chapter 4)	Activity-based costing is covered early in the book, in Part II, Contemporary Cost Management Concepts, because the activity approach to cost management is a critical feature of many management methods and practices. For example, early coverage of activity-based costing means that we can more effectively integrate activity-based costing into the later chapters on cost estimation, cost-volume-profit, decision making, and customer profitability analysis.	The early coverage of strategy allows us to explain the importance of contemporary topics such as activity-based costing in the context of the firm's critical success factors. For example, activity-based costing is most important for firms that compete on price/low cost and have somewhat complex sales/production processes.	Activity-based costing is a critical cost management method for firms that compete on cost leadership and have complex manufacturing environments. The chapter begins with an explanation of the contemporary manufacturing environment and explains how activity-based costing is used to improve management decision making.
	Strategic Topics		
Target Costing, Theory of Constraints, and Life-Cycle Costing (Chapter 5)	Target costing, life-cycle costing, and the theory of constraints are three contemporary management techniques that are used to enhance the competitiveness of the firm. The topics deal directly with the first management function of strategic management and are covered in Part II, Contemporary Cost Management Concepts.	Since strategic management, including the topics of Chapter 5, is the most important of the management functions, we cover it at the beginning of the book in Parts I and II.	Each topic in Chapter 5 is presented from the perspective of how the method can help the firm become more successful, that is, how it can best achieve its strategy.

facturing, marketing, and administration; and applications in service firms and not-for-profit organizations. The topic is motivated by reference to the contemporary manufacturing environment (JIT, robotics, and FMS) and the limitations of volume-based costing.

Chapter 5: Target Costing, Theory of Constraints, and Life-Cycle Costing

This chapter explains several new cost management topics: target costing, the theory of constraints, life-cycle costing, and strategic pricing. An organizing theme is the life cycle of the product from both a cost and a sales perspective. From the cost perspective, the cost life-cycle of the product begins with the upstream activities of research, development, and testing; then manufacturing; and finally the downstream activities of delivery, support, and service. Target costing is developed for the upstream activities while the theory of constraints is developed for the manufacturing phase, and life-cycle costing looks at the entire cost life cycle. In addition, strategic pricing is explained as a method for managing the product's costs from the time the product is introduced, to the growth in its market, to its removal from the market.

Chapter 6: Total Quality Management

The entire chapter is devoted to total quality management. The types of quality conformance, the different costs of quality, and the means to detect defects are covered extensively. A special feature of the chapter is an extensive section on cost of quality reports, including the cost of quality matrix.

Chapter 7: Cost Estimation

This chapter integrates the strategic theme in both the chapter's text and its problem material. The emphasis is on the role of cost estimation and on the choice of estimation method. The presentation of each method explains the expected reliability and accuracy of the method as a basis for understanding its proper use in management accounting practice. Special emphasis is given to regression analysis; it is the most reliable and accurate of the estimation methods.

Chapter 8: Cost-Volume-Profit Analysis

This chapter begins with the strategic role of cost-volume-profit analysis and then covers two different methods: the equation and the ratio methods, each developed for breakeven in units or dollars. The strategic theme is emphasized in an extensive section on sensitivity analysis, which includes a discussion of operating leverage and its use in analyzing a firm's strategy. A unique section develops a cost-volume-profit analysis when using activity-based costing.

Chapter 9: Strategy and the Master Budget

A unique aspect of this chapter is the full development of the budgeting process, from the formulation of the budget committee to the review and approval of the final budget as well as the ethical and behavioral issues that arise during the budget process.

Chapter 10: Decision Making with Relevant Costs and Strategic Analysis

This chapter goes beyond the typical focus of determining relevant costs. It includes a discussion of the importance of taking a strategic approach in using relevant cost analysis, using several examples. Particular emphasis is on managerial incentives in decision making and the strategic role of profitability analysis, both with single and with multiple products and limited resources.

Chapter 11: Capital Budgeting

The strategic focus is an integral part of this chapter. The coverage is complete and thorough, including all current methods, the tax effects, and the techniques for project evaluation and review. A unique aspect of the chapter is the careful treatment of the determination of cash flows using each of the capital budgeting methods.

Chapter 12: Job Costing

Rather than simply present the procedural aspects of this method, the discussion has been expanded to include an explanation of why a firm would choose to use the job costing method. It addresses how the design of the cost system and the choice of a system such as job order costing fit the firm's strategic objectives. The different costing methods are explained, and there is a discussion of when and why each is used.

Chapter 13: Process Costing

Continuing the discussion of cost systems from Chapter 12, this chapter explains the business context in which the process costing method is used. The procedural aspects of the method are then carefully developed. Several actual examples are used to demonstrate how the method fits different operating conditions.

Chapter 14: Cost Allocation: Service Departments and Joint Product Costs

The chapter considers the traditional issues of cost allocation among production and service departments and that involve joint production processes. The coverage is objective based; it begins with strategic, implementation, and ethical issues involved in cost allocation. The development of the procedural aspects is comprehensive. Examples show the complete cost allocation cycle: the allocation of costs to department, the reallocation of costs for service departments to production departments, and the allocation to products.

Chapter 15: The Flexible Budget and Standard Costing: Direct Materials and Direct Labor and Chapter 16: Standard Costing: Factory Overhead

These two chapters begin with an introduction to the use of standard costing within the management function of operational control. Particular emphasis is placed on the strategic role of standard costing and on which firms use it and why. A unique aspect of the chapter is the careful development of the determination of cost standards in practice, considering new manufacturing environments and using benchmarking and activity analysis.

Chapter 17: Managing Marketing Effectiveness, Productivity, and Customer Profitability

The critical success factors for most firms include both the productivity of operations and the effectiveness of sales and marketing. The presentation of productivity is a natural follow-up to the standard costing material presented in Chapters 15 and 16. A unique aspect of the presentation is its unified approach; it presents the different forms of analysis in a way that clearly demonstrates how they are interrelated and can be integrated. Similarly, a special feature of the sales and marketing analysis is the unified approach. All variances are shown in an integrated manner.

Chapter 18: Management Control and Strategic Performance Measurement

The emphasis is on strategic business units (SBUs) and how their managers are motivated, evaluated, and rewarded to contribute most effectively to the firm's success. We consider two types of strategic business units in this chapter, one evaluated on cost only and the other evaluated based on the profitability of the SBU. Unique aspects of this chapter include the use of the balanced scorecard, the role of outsourcing for cost SBUs, the development of the principal-agent model, the explanation of the role of the sales life cycle in management control, and a special section on determining which type of SBU a firm should use based on its competitive strategy.

Chapter 19: Strategic Investment Units and Transfer Pricing

Return on investment for investment centers is a topic that is often criticized for its failure to provide a strategic motivation and evaluation of managers. We have addressed this by presenting both the limitations and contributions of return on investment for a strategic business unit and new ways in which strategic business units are evaluated, including the use of economic value added and the balanced scorecard.

The second topic of the chapter, transfer pricing, is treated in a very up-to-date manner, including international taxation, an increasingly important issue for multinational companies.

Chapter 20: Management Compensation and Business Valuation

Two of the emerging issues in cost management are covered in this chapter. Executive compensation is an important part of the strategy of most firms because of the increasing competition for top executives. Our coverage presents the strategic objectives as well as many of the operational issues of implementing compensation plans, including the different types of bonus plans, tax issues, and financial reporting issues. The valuation of the firm has become increasingly important, both as a way to evaluate the firm's management and as a basis for investors to assess the company's value. Several of the common valuation methods are covered.

UPDATES TO THE SECOND EDITION

The focus of the revision of the second edition is to improve on what we have. The improvements are in additional and better problem material and updates for current changes in management accounting practice, particularly the following:

- A significant increase in the number of end-of-chapter problems, especially adapted CMA exam problems.
- A significant increase in the number of examples and problems involving service industries, particularly in hospital cost management.
- An update on the emerging concepts of strategy and their relevance for cost management (Chapter 2).
- Clarification of the relationships between and among strategic positioning, the value chain, and the balanced scorecard (Chapter 2).
- A significant increase in the number of examples and problems involving the theory of constraints, including a new appendix covering advanced topics (Chapter 5).
- Use of regression analysis as an analytical tool not only in analyzing cost behavior (Chapter 7) but also in sensitivity analysis (Chapter 8), management control (Chapter 18), and executive compensation (Chapter 20).
- Integration of activity-based costing through the text by using examples and problem material in Chapters 8, 9, 10 and 17.
- A new appendix to Chapter 10 that covers the use of linear programming in product mix decisions; Excel Solver is used to simplify the solution method, and Excel screens are presented to follow the use of Solver.
- Extensive integration of spreadsheet-based solution methods in the text and problem material, including the use of the following:
  - Excel Solver to solve linear programming problems (Chapter 10) and reciprocal cost allocation problems (Chapter 14).
  - Excel regression to solve linear regression problems.
  - Spreadsheets to perform sensitivity analysis in cost-volume-profit analysis.
  - Spreadsheets to prepare process cost reports.
  - Actual Excel screens to illustrate the use of methods that make the replication of the examples and problems easier following the illustrated Excel commands.
- Expanded coverage of operation costing in Chapter 12.
- An appendix on spoilage, rework, and scrap is added to Chapter 12.
- Discussion with illustrations on cost reconciliation in Chapter 13.
- The use of Excel Solver to solve reciprocal service allocation problems in Chapter 14.

- More comprehensive development of the role of the balanced scorecard in management performance evaluation (Chapter 18).
- New real-world stories in each chapter reflect business and management practices and concerns in recent years. For example, Chapter 20 includes an update on current practices and issues regarding executive stock options; Chapter 19 covers the concept of intangible assets, and Chapter 2 discusses the development of the euro.

IMPORTANT PEDAGOGICAL DIFFERENCES

CHAPTER OPENERS. These learning objectives and vignettes relate real-world companies, such as Amazon.com and Coca-Cola, to the cost management concepts covered in the chapter.

COST MANAGEMENT IN ACTION. This feature placed in each chapter gives students the opportunity to reflect on the topics introduced in the chapter and to check their understanding. Comments on each feature at the end of the chapter enables students to check their answers.

Part I Introduction to Cost Management

COST MANAGEMENT IN ACTION

How Can Dell Retain Its Glitter?

Dell Computer was one of the biggest success stories of the last decade of the twentieth century. From 1995–2000, its stock price significantly outperformed that of its key rivals, Hewlett-Packard, IBM, Compaq, Intel, and Cisco Systems. *Business Week* chose CEO Michael Dell as one of the Top Executives of the Year in 1999. Dell succeeded in all dimensions of company performance: profit growth, stock price gains, operating efficiency and speed, and customer service. These successes paid big dividends for the company, which more than doubled its sales in two years. Its stock price had almost a 100 percent average annual price increase throughout the 1990s—the best performing stock of the

decade. But trouble is ahead. For the quarter ended July 2000*, Dell's sales increases fell nearly to the industry average. Perhaps this is due to Dell's dependence on the PC market, which is showing signs of a slowdown. What should Dell do in this situation—stick with its strategy of dominance in the mail-order PC market or look to a new strategy of some kind? How might any of the contemporary management techniques just described in the text help—and how?

*For current financial information about Dell, see http://yahoo.marketguide.com/.

Source: "The Top Executives," *Business Week*, January 11, 1999, p. 74.

REAL WORLD EXAMPLES. These boxed elements highlight actual companies and business practices to illustrate how cost accounting is practiced in the real world.

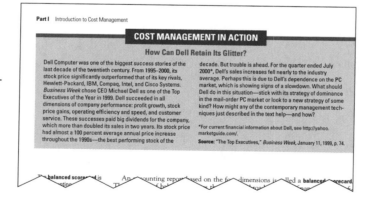

in the industry), rapid product innovation, slow growth in total market demand, or significant overcapacity in the industry. How intense is the overall industry rivalry facing the firm?

- **Pressure from substitute products.** Will the presence of readily substitutable products increase the intensity level of the firm's competition?

How Does the Motion Picture Industry Compete?

Think about this for a minute. Which competitive strategy—cost leadership or differentiation—would you as a producer of movies for theatres and television choose to be most profitable and successful? Clearly what brings a moviegoer to one film rather than another is not the price since most newly released feature films have the same ticket price in a given area. In contrast, the promise of entertainment—a differentiating feature—attracts the consumer.

Edgard Bronfman, Jr., CEO of Seagram and head of Universal Studios, has complained that the studios cannot charge a

cost-based ticket price although films differ greatly in production cost, for example, from $200 million for *Titanic* to $3 million for *The Full Monty*. If ticket prices were to follow costs, *Titanic* would have been priced at almost $20, but *The Full Monty* would have cost only about a quarter.

Source: "If Tickets Reflected the Cost of Movies," *Business Week*, April 20, 1998.

38

Problem Material. The end-of-chapter material was designed to promote better understanding of the strategic role of the cost management methods and practices presented in that chapter. We have taken great care to develop problems and cases that effectively demonstrate the strategic issues presented in the chapter. Types of problem material include **self-study problems** (with answers provided at the end of the chapter), **questions** to test comprehension of key concepts, and **exercises and problems** for more comprehensive practice of important concepts and procedures. A variety of exercises and problems that deal with emerging strategic, international, service, and ethics issues are included. These problems are marked appropriately for easy identification.

 Strategy   *International*   *Service* *Ethics*

A spreadsheet icon indicates problems that, by their nature, should be solved using a spreadsheet developed by the student. We do not provide a solution template for the student to complete but rely on the student to learn by developing the spreadsheet from scratch. The solutions manual for these problems presents the solution in Excel.

SUPPORT MATERIALS

Web Resources. This book is supported by a dynamic website located at http://www.mhhe.com/business/accounting/blocher2e. The site contains information about the book, the authors, and additional on-line resources designed for both students and instructors. Be sure to check out the interactive spreadsheets created by Peggy Hussey (Northern Kentucky University). These are downloadable spreadsheet applications to use with selected end-of-chapter problems. We invite you to visit the site often to stay current or to give us feedback.

PowerWeb. PowerWeb is a database of on-line cost management articles updated weekly. It also provides exercises and teaching suggestions for instructors. PowerWeb password cards are automatically shrink-wrapped with each new copy of the text. *NEW!*

Especially for Students

Cases and Readings in Strategic Cost Management. (ISBN 0072498838) This supplement contains a host of value-added resources. It includes an extensive set of longer cases pertaining to a variety of important topics. These case scenarios put students in situations that allow them to think strategically and to apply concepts that they have learned in the course. Key readings have been chosen to give students more background into the evolution of strategic cost management topics.

Study Guide. (ISBN 0072405066) Prepared by Roger Doost (Clemson University), this booklet reviews the highlights of each chapter and includes a variety of self-study questions for student review. Every chapter includes short-answer questions organized by learning objective, multiple-choice questions, and thorough exercises. Suggested answers to all questions and exercises are included.

Check Figures. Prepared by the authors, this list of answers allows students to check their work. Simply download the list from the website (www.mhhe.com/blocher2e).

Instructor Support

Instructor's Manual. (ISBN 0072405082) Written by the authors, this helpful guide includes lecture outlines, teaching tips, and ideas for additional class discussion. Suggested teaching notes are also provided to accompany the *Cases & Readings in Strategic Cost Management* booklet.

Solutions Manual. (ISBN 0072405090) The authors prepared this booklet that contains fully worked solutions to questions, exercises, and problems from the text. All solutions have been carefully reviewed for accuracy by a number of outside sources. The electronic format of the solutions manual is available for downloading from the website.

Solutions Transparencies. (ISBN 0072405147) Solutions to all problems are available on transparencies for classroom presentations.

Test Bank. (ISBN 0072405163) This test bank, prepared by the authors, is designed to help instructors create exams consistent with the text's strategic emphasis. Each chapter includes true/false and multiple-choice questions, short problems, and extended problems requiring strategic thinking.

Computerized Test Bank. (ISBN 0072405120) This computerized version of the manual test bank is an advanced feature generator from Brownstone Research Group. It allows instructors to create exams, add and edit questions, save and reload multiple choice tests, insert instructions to students, and select questions based on type or objective. The computerized test bank also provides an on-line testing program and a versatile grade book. It is available in Windows format.

Ready Shows. (ISBN 0072408022) Prepared by the authors and Jon A. Booker and Charles W. Caldwell, Tennessee Technological University. Ready Shows use Power-Point software to illustrate chapter concepts making lecture presentations more interesting. Order the Ready Shows on CD-ROM or simply download them from the website (www.mhhe.com/blocher2e).

ACKNOWLEDGMENTS

In writing this book, we were fortunate to have received extensive feedback from a number of accounting educators. We want to thank our colleagues for their careful and complete review of our work. The comments that we received were invaluable in helping us to shape the manuscript. We believe that this collaborative development process helped us to create a text that will truly meet the needs of today's students and instructors. We are sincerely grateful to the following individuals for their participation in the process:

Adnan Abdeen, California State University at Los Angeles; Vidya N. Awasthi, Seattle University; Charles D. Bailey, University of Central Florida; Progyan Basu, Howard University; Mohamed E. Bayou, University of Michigan at Dearborn; Jerome V. Bennett, University of South Carolina at Spartanburg; Susan C. Borkowski, LaSalle University; Bruce Bradford, Fairfield University; Gregory P. Cermignano, Widener University; Kimberly Charland, Kansas State University; Peter Clarke, University College Dublin; Bob Cluskey, Tennessee State University; G. R. Cluskey Jr., Bradley University; Michael Cornick, University of North Carolina at Charlotte; Roger K. Doost, Clemson University; Jerry W. Ferry, University of North Alabama; Lila H. Greco, Orange County Community College; Susan Hamlen, SUNY at Buffalo; Jan Heier, Auburn University at Montgomery; Dick Houser, Northern Arizona University; Mohamed E. A. Hussein, University of Connecticut; Michele E. Johnson,

University of Sioux Falls; Thomas Kam, Hawaii Pacific University; David Keys, Northern Illinois University; Zafar U. Khan, Eastern Michigan University; Larry N. Killough, Virginia Polytechnic Institute and State University; Leslie Kren, University of Wisconsin-Milwaukee; Lawrence D. Lewis, Gonzaga University; Gregory K. Lowry, Troy State University; David Marcinko, SUNY-Albany; Kevin McNelis, New Mexico State University; Theodore J. Mock, University of Southern California; Fred Nordhauser, University of Texas at San Antonio; Marilyn Okleshen, Mankato State University; Khursheed Omer, University of Houston Downtown; David Pariser, West Virginia University; Diane D. Pattison, University of San Diego; Shirley Polejewski, University of St. Thomas; Anthony H. Presutti Jr., Miami University; Leo A. Ruggle, Mankato State University; Sajay Samuel, University of Connecticut; Ali Sedaghat, Loyola College in Maryland; Douglas Sharp, Wichita State University; Melkote K. Shivaswamy, Ball State University; Kenneth P. Sinclair, Lehigh University; James C. Stallman, University of Missouri-Columbia; Louis Stewart, New York University; Jane Stoneback, Central Connecticut State University; Nathan Stuart, Indiana Univeristy; Sandra Weber, Truman State University; Stacey Whitecotton, Arizona State University; and Martin G. H. Wu, New York University

Finally, we are most appreciative of the outstanding assistance and support provided by the professionals of McGraw-Hill/Irwin: Stewart Mattson, our sponsoring editor, for his guidance; our developmental editor, Erin Cibula, for her invaluable suggestions; Rich Kolasa, our marketing manager, for his significant promotional efforts; Kelly Delso and Jean Hamilton, our project managers, for their attention to detail; Jennifer McQueen, for the outstanding presentation of the text; Carol Loreth, our supplements coordinator, for her timeliness and accuracy in delivering the support material; and Tony Sherman, our media producer, for his technical expertise in delivering our online material. An added thanks to Nina McGuffin for her development work.

Ed Blocher
Kung Chen
Tom Lin

BRIEF CONTENTS

CONTENTS

*Bold entries highlighted in blue refer to important discussions of strategy and strategic cost management topics.

xxi

CHAPTER 8

CHAPTER 9

Contents

Contents

Contents

Cost Management

A Strategic Emphasis

Cost Management

An Overview

After studying this chapter you should be able to . . .

1 Explain the use of cost management information in each of the four functions of management and in different types of organizations, with emphasis on the strategic management function

2 Explain how the contemporary business environment has influenced cost management

3 Explain the contemporary management techniques and how they have influenced cost management

4 Describe the professional environment of the management accountant, including professional organizations, professional certifications, and professional ethics

5 Understand the principles and rules of professional ethics and explain how to apply them

Talk about a success story! Wal-Mart has grown from its first discount store in 1962 to become the world's largest retailer. It has accomplished this through the day-to-day attention to its clear business mission: "We exist to provide value to the customer." It achieves this mission through a strategy that involves the extensive use of technology, and opportunity-oriented management style that values change and experimentation, a focus on friendly customer service, and aggressive efforts to grow the business globally.[1] This chapter shows how companies use these strategic initiatives and other important contemporary management techniques to make them more competitive and successful. For example, a section of the chapter on the global business environment shows how the worldwide liberalization of trade has helped firms like Wal-Mart succeed (to illustrate that success, Wal-Mart's sales outside the United States increased from 0 to 13.8 percent of total sales in a relatively short period, 1993 to 1999). Another section explains the increased importance of the customer; many business leaders now argue that business and other organizations have moved from a "product" orientation to a "consumer" orientation. As evidence of his

---

[1]   For more about the Wal-Mart success story, see the Wal-Mart website at www.wal-mart.com, James C. Collins and Jerry I. Porras, *Built to Last* (New York: Harper Business, 1994); Sam Walton and John Huey, *Sam Walton: Made in America* (New York: Doubleday, 1992); and Mike Ballard and Frederick W. Langrehr, "What CPAs Can Learn from Wal-Mart," *Journal of Accountancy,* November 1992, p. 101.

focus on the customer, Sam Walton once led 100,000 Wal-Mart employees at a mid-1980s teleconference in the following:

> Now, I want you to raise your right hand. . . . I want you to repeat after me: From this day forward, I solemnly promise and declare that every time a customer comes within 10 feet of me, I will smile, look him in the eye, and greet him, so help me Sam.[2]

A key element in implementing Wal-Mart's Strategy was to set ambitious goals. Already a company with $44 billion in sales in 1992, it projected annual sales of more than $100 billion by 2000. In the 2000 fiscal year, Wal-Mart had net sales of $165 billion—almost a four-fold increase, a compound eight-year growth rate of about 18%!

This book is about how managers build a successful company as those at Wal-Mart have done. Everyone wants to be a winner, and so it is in business and accounting. We are interested in how the management accountant can play a key role in making a firm or organization successful. Now you might be asking, Don't we have to know what you mean by *success*? Absolutely! A firm must define clearly what it means by success in its mission statement. Then it must develop a roadmap to accomplish that mission, which we call *strategy*. In Wal-Mart's case, the mission was to achieve customer value, and the strategy involved the extensive use of technology, a management structure that welcomed change, and a constant focus on customer service. Recognize also that Wal-Mart, by succeeding in its mission and strategy, has build an enormous amount of wealth for its shareholders. Currently, the company's market value (number of shares outstanding times share price) is approximately $230 billion.

Because we are interested in how the management accountant can help a company be successful, we take a strategic approach throughout the book, beginning with an introduction to strategy in chapter 2. The key idea is that success comes from developing and implementing an effective strategy aided by management accounting methods. These management accounting methods are covered in this text chapter by chapter; we discuss them because we know they have helped companies succeed. Before considering these management accounting methods, we need to introduce some basic concepts related to management accounting, the most basic of which is the concept of cost management information.

> The most successful man in life is the man who has the best information.
> BENJAMIN DISRAELI, A NINETEENTH-CENTURY
> PRIME MINISTER OF ENGLAND

LEARNING OBJECTIVE 1 ▶

Explain the use of cost management information in each of the four functions of management and in different types of organizations with emphasis on the strategic management function.

As Disraeli knew in the nineteenth century, having the best information is the key to success. In today's business environment, the development and use of information—especially cost management information—is a critical factor in the effective management of a firm or organization. As the business environment has changed, the role of cost management information has expanded to serve all management functions.

THE USES OF COST MANAGEMENT

Cost management information is the information the manager needs to effectively manage the firm or not-for-profit organization.

Cost management information is a broad concept. It is the information the manager needs to effectively manage the firm or not-for-profit organization and includes both *financial information* about costs and revenues as well as relevant *nonfinancial information* about productivity, quality, and other key success factors for the firm.[3]

Financial information alone can be misleading, because it tends to have a short-term focus, what we earned last month, for example. For competitive success, a firm

---

[2] Walton and Huey, *Sam Walton: Made in America*, p. 223

[3] *Cost* is often defined as the use of a resource that has a financial consequence. In this text, we use the broader concept of cost management information that includes nonfinancial information as well as financial information.

Short-Term Financial Focus vs. Long Term Value

If the management accountant were to focus on financial information only, how would he or she explain the success of a company like eBay? eBay has relatively few physical assets on the balance sheet, and the income statement looks mediocre, and yet its stock price shows it to be a better investment than some firms have more assets and earnings. Investors are apparently betting on the long-term success of the firm, based on the popularity of its website and its customer loyalty. These strategic factors do not appear on the income statement or balance sheet. In fact, it is estimated that 30 percent–70 percent of stock prives are associated with factors that are not in the financial statements. Like these investors, the management accountant needs to focus on the measures that drive long-term success, and not just financial factors.

Source: "New Math for a New Econonmy," by Alan A. Webber, *Fast Company,* January-February 2000, pp. 214–224; "eBay: Bidding for Web Domination," by Amy Stone, *Business Week,* January 11, 2001.

needs to focus on longer-term factors, such as product and manufacturing advances, product quality, and customer loyalty. Emphasis on financial information alone could lead managers to stress cost reduction (a financial measure) while ignoring or even lowering quality standards (a nonfinancial measure). This decision could be a critical mistake, leading to the loss of customers and market share in the long term. Internationally known business consultants, such as W. Edwards Deming, Peter Drucker, and others, point out the importance of considering nonfinancial and long-term measures of operating performance if a firm is to compete successfully. A central theme of this book, then, is that cost management information includes the information—both financial and nonfinancial and both short term and long-term that managers need to lead their firms to competitive success.

Management accountants develop cost management information for which a firm's controller is responsible. The controller, who reports to the firm's chief financial officer (CFO), has a number of other duties, including financial reporting, maintaining financial systems, and other reporting functions (to industry organizations, governmental units, etc.), as illustrated in Exhibit 1–1. The CFO has the overall responsibility for the

Exhibit 1–1 A Typical Organization Chart Showing the Functions of the Controller

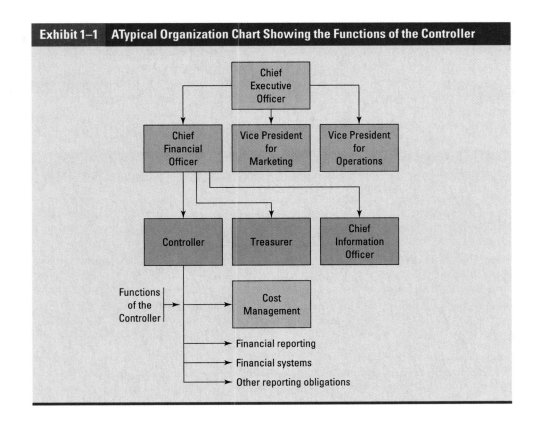

financial function; the treasurer manages investor and creditor relationships, and the chief information officer (CIO) manages the firm's use of information technology, including computer systems and communications.

In contrast to the cost management function, the financial reporting function involves preparing financial statements for *external users* such as investors and government regulators. These financial accounting reports require compliance with external certain requirements. Cost management information is developed for use *within* the firm to facilitate management and is not required to meet those requirements. The main focus of cost management information therefore must be *usefulness* and *timeliness;* the focus of financial reports must be *accuracy* and *compliance* with reporting requirements. However, strict adherence to accuracy often compromises the usefulness and timeliness of the information. The function of the financial systems department is to develop and maintain the financial reporting system and related systems such as payroll, financial security systems, and tax preparation. The challenge for the controller is to reconcile these different and potentially conflicting roles.[4]

The Four Functions of Management

The management accountant develops cost management information for the CFO and other managers to use to manage the firm and make more competitive and successful. Cost management information is provided for each of the four major management functions: (1) strategic management, (2) planning and decision making, (3) management and operational control, and (4) preparation of financial statements. The most important function is **strategic management,** which is the development of a sustainable competitive position in which the firm's competitive advantage provides continued success. A strategy is a set of goals and specific action plans that, if achieved, provide the desired competitive advantage. Strategic management involves identifying and implementing these goals and action plans. Next, management is responsible for **planning and decision making,** which involves budgeting and profit planning, cash flow management, and other decisions related to the firm's operations, such as deciding when to lease or buy a facility, when to repair or replace a piece of equipment, when to change a marketing plan, and when to begin new product development.

The third area of responsibility, control, consists of two functions, operational control and management control, involving top- and mid-level managers. **Operational control** takes place when mid-level managers (e.g., plant managers, product managers, regional managers) monitor the activities of operating-level managers and employees (e.g., production supervisors and various department heads). In contrast, **management control** is the evaluation of mid-level managers by upper-level managers (the controller or the CFO).

Strategic management is the development of a sustainable competitive position.

Planning and decision making involves budgeting and profit planning, cash flow management, and other decisions related to operations.

Operational control exists when mid-level managers monitor the activities of operating-level managers and employees.

Management control is the evaluation of mid-level managers by upper-level managers.

Cost Management Information Is Needed for Each of the Four Management Functions

1. **Strategic Management.** Cost management information is needed to make sound strategic decisions regarding choice of products, manufacturing methods, marketing techniques and channels, and other long-term issues.

2. **Planning and Decision Making.** Cost management information is needed to support recurring decisions regarding replacing equipment, managing cash flow, budgeting raw materials purchases, scheduling production, and pricing.

3. **Management and Operational Control.** Cost management information is needed to provide a fair and effective basis for identifying inefficient operations and to reward and support the most effective managers.

4. **Preparation of Financial Statements.** Cost management information is needed to provide accurate accounting for inventory and other assets, in compliance with reporting requirements, for the preparation of financial reports and for use in the three other management functions.

---

[4] A history of cost management is provided by Robert S. Kaplan, "The Evolution of Management Accounting," *The Accounting Review,* July 1984, pp. 390–418.

In the fourth function, **preparation of financial statements,** management complies with the reporting requirements of relevant groups (such as the Financial Accounting Standards Board) and relevant federal government authorities (for example, the Internal Revenue Service and the Securities and Exchange Commission).[5] The financial statement information also serves the other three management functions, because this information is often an important part of planning and decision making, control, and strategic management.

Preparation of financial statements. requires management to comply with the financial reporting requirements of regulatory agencies.

Strategic Management and Strategic Cost Management

Effective strategic management is critical to the success of the firm or organization and is thus a pervasive theme of this book. The growing pressures of global competition, technological innovation, and changes in business processes have made cost management much more critical and dynamic than ever before. Managers must think *competitively;* doing so requires a strategy.

Strategic thinking involves anticipating changes; products and production processes are designed to accommodate expected changes in customer demands. Flexibility is important. The ability to make fast changes is critical as a result of the demand of the new management concepts of e-commerce, speed to market, and agile manufacturing. Product life cycles—the time from the introduction of a new product

Why Strategy? Managers Tell Us Why

Our unique approach in this book is to demonstrate cost management from a strategic emphasis. Every cost management method we cover is linked to the firm's strategy, that is, how the method helps the firm to be successful. Why emphasize the strategic approach? Managers tell us why . . .

- A 1999 survey of 300 management accountants by the Institute of Management Accountants (the IMA is the main professional organization for those in cost management) showed that the accountants viewed themselves as broad finance professionals whose most important work activities, that is, "those that will be most critical to their company's success in three years," were the following:

  - Long-term strategic planning.
  - Financial and economic analysis.
  - Customer and product profitability.
  - Computer systems and operations.
  - Process improvement.

These results show an important shift in the management accounting profession to strategic analysis, cost management information, and nonfinancial as well as financial information. This represents a move away from financial reporting only.

- The principal journal for the profession, *Management Accounting,* changed its name to *Strategic Finance* in April 1999. As noted in the IMA 1999 survey, managers now view accountants in the cost management function as finance professionals having an integral, strategic role in a firm's management. The work of accountants, no longer score-keepers only, is better described as "strategic finance."

- The American Institute of Certified Public Accountants (AICPA), another key professional organization for accountants, has also recognized the change in the profession. The AICPA uses the term *new finance* to refer to the growing focus on strategy and "business partnership" for accountants who work within firms.

- Robert Half International, and executive recruitment firm, reported a 1999 survey of 1,400 CFOs of companies with more than 20 employees. CFOs expect that at least 40 percent of their work will be nonfinancial by the year 2004, indicating a greater need for business strategy and analysis but less need for financial reporting.

- The business press generally has set new and more strategic expectations for accountants. An example is the recent *Business Week* article, "Up From Bean Counter: The Role of the CFO Is Expanding to Strategist, Venture Capitalist, and Chief Negotiator." The title tells it all!

Sources: "Counting More, Counting Less: Transformations in the Management Accounting Profession," report of a research project conducted by Gary Siegel and James E. Sorensen for the Institute of Management Accountants, August 1999; AICAP website (www.aicpa.org), "Center for Excellence in Financial Management"; *The CPA Letter,* July/August 1999, p. 8: Marcia Vickers, "Up From Bean Counter: The Role of the CFO Is Expanding to Strategist, Venture Capitalist, and Chief Negotiator," *Business Week,* August 28, 2000, pp. 119–120. Also the report of interviews and focus groups of dozens of accountants, businesspeople, and professors regarding the current and desired state of accounting education: W. Steve Albrecht and Robert J. Sack, "Accounting Education: Charting the Course through a Perilous Future," *Accounting Education Series Number 16* (American Accounting Association, 2000).

---

[5] The professional groups are identified and explained at the end of this chapter.

to its removal from the market—is expected to become shorter and shorter. Success in the recent past days or months is no longer a measure of ultimate success; the manager must be "driving" the firm by using the windshield, not the rear-view mirror.

The strategic emphasis also requires creative and integrative thinking, that is, the ability to identify and solve problems from a cross-functional view. The business functions are often identified as marketing, production, finance, and accounting/controllership. Instead of viewing a problem as a production problem, a marketing problem, or a finance and accounting problem, cross-functional teams view it from an integrative approach that combines skills from all functions simultaneously. The integrative approach is necessary in a dynamic and competitive environment. The firm's attention is focused on satisfying the customers' needs; all of the firm's resources, *from all functions*, are directed to that goal.

Because strategic issues are increasing in importance to management, cost management has moved from a traditional role of product costing and operational control to a broader, strategic focus: strategic cost management. **Strategic cost management** is the development of cost management information to facilitate the principal management function, strategic management.

> **Strategic cost management** is the development of cost management information to facilitate the principal management function, strategic management.

Types of Organizations

Cost management information is useful in a wide range of organizations: business firms, governmental units, and not-for-profit organizations. Business firms are usually categorized by industry, the main categories being merchandising, manufacturing, and service. Merchandising firms purchase goods for resale. Merchandisers that sell to other merchandisers are called *wholesalers*; those selling directly to consumers are called *retailers*. Examples of merchandising firms are the large retailers, such as Sears, Wal-Mart, and Amazon.com.

Manufacturing firms use raw materials, labor, and manufacturing facilities and equipment to produce products. They sell these products to merchandising firms or to other manufacturers as raw materials to make other products. Examples of manufacturers are General Motors, IBM, and Cisco Systems.

Service firms provide a service to customers that offers convenience, freedom, safety, or comfort. Common services include transportation, health care, financial services (banking, insurance, accounting), personal services (physical training, hair styling), and legal services. In the United States, service industries are growing at a much faster rate than is manufacturing or merchandising, in part because of the increased demand for leisure and convenience and society's increased complexity.

Governmental and not-for-profit organizations provide services, much like the firms in service industries. However, these organizations provide the services for which no direct relationship exists between the amount paid and the services provided. Instead, both the nature of these services and the customers to receive them are determined by government or philanthropic organizations. The resources are provided by governmental units and/or charities. The services provided by these organizations are often called *public goods* to indicate that no typical market exists for them. Public goods have a number of unique characteristics, such as the impracticality of limiting consumption to a single customer (clean water and police and fire protection are provided for *all* residents).

Most firms and organizations use cost management information. For example, manufacturing firms use it to manage production costs. Similarly, retail firms such as Wal-Mart use cost management information to manage stocking, distribution, and customer service. Firms in the service industries, such as those providing financial services or other professional services, use cost management information to identify the most profitable services and to manage the costs of providing those services.

Cost management information is used in a wide variety of ways. Whatever the business a firm must know the cost of new products or services, the cost of making improvements in existing products or services, and the cost of finding a new way to produce the products or provide the services. Cost management information is used to determine prices, to change product or service offerings to improve profitability, to update manufacturing facilities in a timely fashion, and to determine new marketing methods or distribution channels. For example, manufacturers such as Hewlett-Packard study the cost implications of design options for each new product. The design study includes analysis of projected manufacturing costs as well as costs to be incurred after the product is completed, which include service and warranty costs. Service and warranty costs are often called *downstream costs* because they occur after manufacturing. By analyzing both manufacturing and downstream costs, Hewlett-Packard is able to determine whether product enhancements might cause manufacturing and downstream costs to be out of line with expected increases in customer value and revenue for that feature.

Both large and small firms, in all types of industries use cost management information. A firm's degree of reliance on cost management depends on the nature of its competitive strategy. Many firms compete on the basis of being the low-cost provider of the industry's goods or services; for these firms, cost management is critical. Other firms, such as cosmetics, fashion, and pharmaceutical firms, compete on the basis of product leadership, in which the unusual or innovative features of the product make the firm successful. For these firms, the critical management concern is maintaining product leadership through product development and marketing. The role of cost management is to support the firm's strategy by providing the information managers that need to succeed in their product development and marketing efforts, such as the expected cost of adding a new product feature, the defect rate of a new part, or the reliability of a new manufacturing process.

Not-for-profit and governmental organizations also must have a strategy to accomplish their mission and satisfy their constituents. Historically, governmental units and not-for-profit agencies have tended to focus on their responsibility to spend in approved ways rather than to spend in efficient and effective ways. Increasingly, however, these types of organizations are using cost management for efficient and effective use of their financial resources. For not-for-profit organizations especially, being able to predict the effect of an anticipated budget cut or increase on planned service levels is important. Cost management information usually serves as a starting point in assessing the effect of changing funding levels on activities and services. For example, the funding of Durham Service Corps, a nonprofit provider of educational services, was cut by approximately 30 percent in a recent period. By studying of its cost structure, the agency was able to project a cutback in service of approximately 50 percent based on the fact that a significant proportion of its costs (for facilities and administration) was not directly involved in providing the educational services and could not be reduced. Therefore, the cuts had to come from costs for classroom teachers. Thus, the analysis of the organization's cost structure explains why a 30 percent change in the budget had a greater effect on direct services.

THE CONTEMPORARY BUSINESS ENVIRONMENT

Many changes in the business environment in recent years have caused significant modifications in cost management practices. The primary changes are (1) increase in global competition, (2) advances in manufacturing technologies, (3) advances in information technologies, the Internet, and e-commerce (4) greater focus on the customer, (5) new forms of management organization, and (6) changes in the social, political, and cultural environment of business.

◀**LEARNING OBJECTIVE 2**

Explain how the contemporary business environment has influenced cost management.

The Global Business Environment

A key development that drives the extensive changes in the contemporary business environment is the growth of international markets and trade. Businesses and not-for-profit organizations, as well as consumers and regulators, are all significantly affected

Going Global: The Growing Importance of Worldwide Markets

The following table indicates the percentage of sales coming from outside the home market for the listed companies.

	1993	1999
General Electric	16.5%	30.1%
Wal-Mart	0.0	13.8
McDonald's	46.9	61.5
Nokia	85.0	97.6
Toyota	44.6	49.5

Source: Standard & Poor's, Company reports.

by the rapid growth of economic interdependence and increased competition from other countries. The North American Free Trade Agreement (NAFTA), the World Trade Organization (WTO), the European Union (EU), and the growing number of alliances among large multinational firms clearly indicate that the opportunities for growth and profitability lie in global markets. Most consumers benefit as low-cost, high-quality goods are traded worldwide. Managers and business owners know the importance of pursuing sales and production activities in foreign countries, and investors benefit from the increased opportunities for investment in foreign firms.

The increasing competitiveness of the global business environment means that firms increasingly need cost management information to be competitive. Firms need financial and nonfinancial information about doing business and competing effectively in other countries.

Manufacturing Technologies

To remain competitive in the face of the increased global competition, firms around the world are adopting new manufacturing technologies. These include just-in-time inventory methods to reduce the cost and waste of maintaining large levels of raw materials and unfinished product. Also, many firms are adopting the methods applied in Japanese manufacturing that have produced significant cost and quality improvements through the use of quality teams and statistical quality control. Other manufacturing changes include flexible manufacturing techniques developed to reduce setup times and allow fast turnaround of customer orders. A key competitive edge in what is called *speed-to-market* is the ability to deliver the product or service faster than the competition.

Another main area of manufacturing process change is the gradual *increase in facilities costs relative to the costs of materials and labor* to make the product. Firms that once viewed facilities costs as uncontrollable and focused their attention on managing labor and materials costs have now redirected their attention to controlling facilities costs.

The New Economy: Use of Information Technology, the Internet, and E-Commerce

Perhaps the most fundamental of all business changes in recent years has been the increasing use of information technology, the Internet, and e-commerce. Called the *new economy*, is reflected in the rapid growth if Internet-based firms (the "dot-com's" such as Amazon, eBay, and Etrade) and the increased use of the Internet for communications, sales, and business data processing. These technologies have fostered the growing strategic focus in cost management by reducing the time required for record keeping (Internet firms such as netledger.com offer complete financial record keeping services over the Internet) and expanding the individual manager's access to information within the firm, the industry, and the business environment around the world.

The Global Competition in Wireless Communications

The communications industry offering products that are dramatically changing the way people talk to one another. International Data Corp. estimates that one-third of the U.S. population and more than one-half of the populations of Europe and Japan use some form of wireless communication. Global giants such as Nokia, Motorola, and Ericsson provide the products, and other global giants such as Sprint, AT&T and Verizon (United States), Vodaphone (United Kingdom), Deutsche Tekekom (Germany), Telecom (France), and NTT DoCoMo (Japan) provide the wireless services to what is expected to be 1 billion global customers within the next several years. The new wireless products and services are expected to push the growth of e-commerce and to provide

entirely new services, such as wireless medical sensors that will alert doctors to medical emergencies. The cost management issues related to these products and services are emerging. How can the technologies be used to reduce the cost of providing such products and services? How can the wireless tools be used to provide a new competitive edge for established firms? Management accountants, as strategic partners, will be expected to have the expertise to assist managers in resolving these issues.

Source: "Wireless in Cyberspace," *Business Week,* special section May 29, 2000, pp. 136–64; and "Deutsche Telekom's Wireless Wager," *Business Week,* August 7, 2000, pp. 31–34.

Focus on the Customer

A key change in the business environment is increased *consumer expectation* for product functionality and quality. The result has been a shorter product life cycle, as firms seek to add new features and new products as quickly as possible, thereby increasing the overall intensity of competition.

In past years, a business typically succeeded by focusing on only a relatively small number of products with limited features and by organizing production into long, low-cost, and high-volume production runs aided by assembly-line automation. The new business process focuses instead on customer satisfaction. Producing value for the customer changes the orientation of managers from low-cost production of large quantities to *quality, service, timeliness of delivery, and the ability to respond to the customer's desire for specific features.* Today the critical success factors (discussed later) are all customer oriented. Cost management practices are also changing; cost management reports now include specific measures of customer preferences and customer satisfaction.

Management Organization

Management organization has changed in response to the changes in marketing and manufacturing. Because of the focus on customer satisfaction and value, the emphasis has shifted from financial and profit-based measures of performance to customer-related, nonfinancial performance measures such as quality, time to delivery, and service. Similarly, the hierarchical command-and-control type of organization is being replaced by a more flexible organizational form that encourages teamwork and coordination among business functions. In response to these changes, cost management practices are also changing to include reports that are useful to cross-functional teams of managers; the reports reflect the multifunctional roles of these teams and include a variety of operating and financial information: product quality, unit cost, customer satisfaction, and production bottlenecks, for example.

The changes in manufacturing, marketing, and management in organizations are summarized in Exhibit 1–2.

Social, Political, and Cultural Considerations

In addition to changes in the business environment, significant changes have taken place in the social, political, and cultural environments that affect business. Although the nature and extent of these changes vary a great deal from country to country, they include a more ethnically and racially diverse workforce, a renewed sense of ethical responsibility among managers and employees, and an increased deregulation of business by the federal government.

Exhibit 1–2	Comparison of Prior and Contemporary Business Environments	
	Prior Business Environment	**Contemporary Business Environment**
	Manufacturing	
Basis of competition	Economies of scale, standardization	Quality, functionality, customer satisfaction
Manufacturing process	High volume, long production runs, significant levels of in-process and finished inventory	Low volume, short production runs, focus on reducing inventory levels and other non-value-added activities and costs
Manufacturing technology	Assembly line automation, isolated technology applications	Robotics, flexible manufacturing systems, integrated technology applications connected by networks
Required labor skills	Machine-paced, low-level skills	Individually and team-paced, high-level skills
Emphasis on quality	Acceptance of a normal or usual amount of waste	Goal of zero defects
	Marketing	
Products	Relatively few variations, long product life cycles	Large number of variations, short product life cycles
Markets	Largely domestic	Global
	Management Organization	
Type of information recorded and reported	Almost exclusively financial data	Financial and operating data, the firm's strategic success factors
Management organizational structure	Hierarchical, command and control	Network-based organization forms, teamwork focus—employee has more responsibility and control, coaching rather than command and control
Management focus	Emphasis on the short term, short-term performance measures and compensation, concern for sustaining the current stock price, short tenure and high mobility of top managers	Emphasis on the long term, focus on critical success factors, commitment to the long-term success of the firm, including adding shareholder value

The new business environment requires firms to be flexible and adaptable and to place greater responsibility in the hands of a more highly skilled workforce. Additionally, the changes tend to focus the firm on factors *outside* the production of its product or provision of its service on the ultimate consumer and the global society in which the consumer lives.

THE STRATEGIC FOCUS OF COST MANAGEMENT

The competitive firm incorporates the emerging and anticipated changes in the contemporary environment of business into its business planning and practices. The competitive firm is customer driven, uses advanced manufacturing technologies when appropriate, anticipates the effect of changes in regulatory requirements and customer tastes, and recognizes its complex social, political, and cultural environment. Guided by strategic thinking, the management accountant focuses on the factors that make the company successful rather than costs and other financial measures. We are reminded of the story of the Scottish farmer who had prize sheep to take to market. When asked why his sheep were always superior to those of his neighbors, the farmer responded, "While they're weighing their sheep, I'm fattening mine."[6] Similarly, cost

---

[6]   Sheep farmer story adapted from IEEE, *Spectrum*, January 1992, p. 25.

management focuses not on the measurement per se but on the *identification of those measures that are critical* to the firm's success. Robert Kaplan's classification of the phases of the development of cost management systems describes this shift in focus:[7]

Stage 1. Cost management systems are basic transaction reporting systems.

Stage 2. As they develop into the second stage, cost management systems focus on external financial reporting. The objective is reliable financial reports; accordingly, the usefulness for cost management is limited.

Stage 3. Cost management systems track key operating data and develop more accurate and relevant cost information for decision making; cost management information is developed.

Stage 4. Strategically relevant cost management information is an integral part of the system.

The first two stages of cost system development focus on the management accountant's measurement and reporting role, and the third stage shifts to operational control. In the fourth stage, the ultimate goal, the management accountant is viewed as an integral part of management, not as a reporter but as a full business partner, with the skills of identifying, summarizing, and reporting the critical factors necessary for the firm's success. **Critical success factors (CSFs)** are measures of those aspects of the firm's performance that are essential to its competitive advantage and, therefore to its success. Many of these critical success factors are financial, but many, are nonfinancial. The unique factors for any given firm depend on the nature of the competition it faces.

CONTEMPORARY MANAGEMENT TECHNIQUES

Managers commonly use the following tools to implement the firm's broad strategy and to facilitate the achievement of success on critical success factors: benchmarking, total quality management, continuous improvement (*kaizen*), activity-based costing, reengineering, the theory of constraints, mass customization, target costing, life-cycle costing, and the balanced scorecard.

Benchmarking

Benchmarking is a process by which a firm identifies its critical success factors, studies the best practices of other firms (or other units within a firm) for achieving these critical success factors, and then implements improvements in the firm's processes to match or beat the performance of those competitors. Benchmarking was first implemented by Xerox Corporation in the late 1970s.[8] Today many firms use benchmarking, and some of these firms are recognized as leaders, and therefore benchmarks, in selected areas (see Exhibit 1–3).

Benchmarking efforts are facilitated today by cooperative networks of noncompeting firms that exchange benchmarking information. For example, the Continuous Improvement Center of the Institute of Management Accountants (IMA) helps organizations benchmark and thereby improve their financial processes. The IMA program includes access to a benchmark database, assistance in assessing CSFs, assistance to firms in implementing improvement opportunities, and recognition that honors firms that achieve outstanding levels of continuous improvement. The American Institute of CPAs (AICPA) has partnered with Hackett Benchmarking and Research Group (www.hackettbenchmarking.com/aicpa/home.htm) to provide finance-related

Critical success factors (CSFs) are measures of those aspects of the firm's performance that are essential to its competitive advantage and, therefore, to its success.

◀**LEARNING OBJECTIVE 3**

Explain the contemporary management techniques and how they have influenced cost management.

Benchmarking is a process by which a firm identifies its critical success factors, studies the best practices of other firms (or other units within a firm) for achieving these critical success factors, and then implements improvements in the firm's processes to match or beat the performance of those competitors.

---

[7] Robert S. Kaplan, "The Four-Stage Model of Cost System Design," *Management Accounting*, February 1990, pp. 22–26.

[8] R. C. Camp, *Benchmarking: The Search for Industry Best Practices that Lead to Superior Performance* (Milwaukee, Wis.: American Society for Quality Control Press, 1989); and Alexandra Biesada, "Strategic Benchmarking," *Financial World*, September 29, 1992, pp. 30–58.

Exhibit 1–3	Leading Firms in Selected Critical Success Factors

Customer Service	Innovation and Product Development	Quality	Corporate Social Responsibility	Labor Relationships and Employee Retraining
L.L. Bean	3M	Toyota	Merck	Ford
FedEx	Apple Computer	Motorola	Johnson & Johnson	IBM
Wal-Mart	Hewlett-Packard	IBM	General Electric	Johnson & Johnson
Nordstrom	Sony	Xerox	Ford	Lucent
Home Depot	Nokia	Ford	Ben & Jerry's	Hewlett-Packard
Amazon.com				

Sources: "Beg, Borrow, and Benchmark," *Business Week*, November 30, 1992, pp. 74–75; James C. Collins and Jerry I. Porras, *Built to Last* (New York: Harper Business, 1994); and "The Best Corporate Reputations in America," *The Wall Street Journal*, September 23, 1999, p. B-1.

benchmarks for AIPCA members who are corporate financial managers. The International Benchmarking Clearinghouse (www.apqc.org) also assists firms in strategic benchmarking.

Total Quality Management

> **Total quality management (TQM)** is a technique by which management develops policies and practices to ensure that the firm's products and services exceed customers' expectations.

Total quality management (TQM) is a technique by which management develops policies and practices to ensure that the firm's products and services exceed customers' expectations. This approach includes increased product functionality, reliability, durability, and serviceability. Cost management is used to analyze the cost consequences of different design choices for TQM and to measure and report the many aspects of quality including, for example, production breakdowns and production defects, wasted labor or raw materials, the number of service calls, and the nature of the complaints, warranty costs, and product recalls.

TQM efforts can build brand loyalty and help the company improve product quality and competitiveness quickly. For example, Hewlett-Packard has instituted a policy of taking back products returned by customers to retailers—something many computer manufacturers do only reluctantly. This policy builds retailer and customer loyalty, and it provides Hewlett-Packard an early warning of product problems.[9]

Continuous Improvement

> Whether you think you can or whether you think you can't—you're right.
>
> HENRY FORD

> **Continuous improvement** (the Japanese word is *kaizen*) is a management technique by which managers and workers commit to a program of continuous improvement in quality and other critical success factors.

Henry Ford realized that the right attitude is important to success. That belief is what continuous improvement is all about. **Continuous improvement** (the Japanese word is *kaizen*) is a management technique by which managers and workers commit to a program of continuous improvement in quality and other critical success factors. Its origin is attributed to Japanese manufacturers who pursue quality tirelessly. Continuous improvement is very often associated with benchmarking and total quality management as firms seek to identify other firms as models to learn how to improve their critical success factors.

---

[9] "The Printer King Invades Home PCs," *Business Week*, August 21, 1995, pp. 74–75.

The Importance of Speed: A Tale of Two Companies.

One company, Dell Corporation, is a global manufacturer of PCs. Its success at the end of the 20th century was extraordinary. In the period 1996–1999, Dell's common stock outperformed that of IBM, Cisco Systems, Hewlett-Packard, Microsoft, and Intel. Most important, this happened during a period of increasing price pressures and lower unit profits in the industry. It succeeded by reducing manufacturing time dramatically so that customers could expect their mail-order computers to arrive in a few days in comparison to the weeks that customers of other mail-order PC makers had to wait. As Michael Dell, chairman and CEO of Dell Computer, said, "Speed is everything in this business. We're setting the pace for the industry":

- Speed in order taking: Orders are confirmed to customers in 5 minutes.

- Speed in manufacturing; An order received by 9 A.M. Monday is shipped by 9 P.M. Tuesday.

- Speed in collection: Within 24 hours, phone and Web orders are collected in cash; in contrast, rival manufactur-

ers that sell through dealers wait from a month or more to collect on sales.

- Speed in resupply: Circuit boards are restocked at the Austin, Texas, plant from suppliers in Mexico within 15 hours of an order.

Dell's speed reduces manufacturing costs and inventory holding costs as well as providing a key value for customers.

The second company, VF Corporation, a clothing manufacturer, helped its customers (such as Wal-Mart and J.C. Penney) forecast demand and proper stocking levels on its fastest moving items. It provides this service by linking the computers of the manufacturer and retailing customer. Using this technology, VF was able to restock its customers' shelves much faster, sometimes overnight.

Sources: "Whirlwind on the Web," *Business Week,* April 7, 1997, p. 132–136; and "Just Get It to the Stores on Time," *Business Week,* March 6, 1995, p. 66–67.

Activity-Based Costing and Management

Many firms have found that they can improve planning, product costing, operational control, and management control by using **activity analysis** to develop a detailed description of the specific activities performed in the firm's operations. The activity analysis provides the basis for activity-based costing and activity-based management. **Activity-based costing (ABC)** is used to improve the accuracy of cost analysis by improving the tracing of costs to products or to individual customers. **Activity-based management (ABM)** uses activity analysis to improve operational control and management control. ABC and ABM are key strategic tools for many firms, especially those with complex operations.

Reengineering

Reengineering is a process for creating competitive advantage in which a firm reorganizes its operating and management functions, often with the result that jobs are modified, combined, or eliminated. It has been defined as the "fundamental rethinking and radical redesign of business processes to achieve dramatic improvements in critical, contemporary measures of performance, such as cost, quality, service, and speed."[10] Under the pressure of global competition, many firms look to reengineering as a way to reduce the cost of management and operations and as a basis for careful reanalysis of the firm's strategic competitive advantage. Cost management supports the reengineering effort by providing the relevant information.

The Theory of Constraints

The **theory of constraints (TOC)** is a strategic technique to help firms effectively improve a very important critical success factor: cycle time, the rate at which raw materials are converted to finished products.[11] TOC helps identify and eliminate bottlenecks—

Activity analysis is used to develop a detailed description of the specific activities performed in the firm's operations.

Activity-based costing (ABC) is used to improve the accuracy of cost analysis by improving the tracing of costs to products or to individual customers.

Activity-based management (ABM) uses activity analysis to improve operational control and management control.

Reengineering is a process for creating competitive advantage in which a firm reorganizes its operating and management functions, often with the result that jobs are modified, combined, or eliminated.

The **theory of constraints (TOC)** is a strategic technique to help firms effectively improve the rate at which raw materials are converted to finished products.

---

10   The definition is provided by Michael Hammer and James Champy, *Re-Engineering the Corporation* (New York: Harper Press, 1993). Another useful reference is the book by Roy Harmon and Leroy D. Peterson, *Re-Inventing the Factory* (New York: Free Press, 1990).

11   Two of the best sources for descriptions of the theory of constraints are the following books: E. Goldratt and J. Cox, *The Goal* (New York: Free Press, 1986); and E. Goldratt, *The Theory of Constraints* (New York: North River Press, 1990).

places where partially completed products tend to accumulate as they wait to be processed—in the production process.

In the competitive global marketplace common to most industries, the ability to be faster than competitors is often a critical success factor. Many managers argue that the focus on speed in the TOC approach is crucial. They consider speed in product development, product delivery, and manufacturing to be paramount as global competitors find ever higher customer expectations for rapid product development and prompt delivery. Many Internet firms, including sellers of computer products, clothing, and other consumer goods, are finding that promise of prompt delivery is sometimes the only way to make a sale since competition has forced all competing firms to provide excellent quality products and services.

In many industries, the speed of product development and the ability to meet a rapidly growing market demand for a product are critical to the firm's profitability. For example, in the computer software industry, often the firm that reaches the market first with a high-quality system captures the market. This was true of Netscape's Navigator and Intuit's Quicken. An example of what can happen when speed is not paramount comes from IBM Corporation. In the early 1990s, IBM developed popular new computers, the Thinkpad notebook and the Aptiva desktop computer, but initially lacked the manufacturing and distribution resources to meet the demand. The rising demand was then met by Compaq and other manufacturers, which were better prepared.

Bottlenecks can appear in areas other than manufacturing, such as purchasing and distribution. Firms are adopting global strategies for sourcing materials and distributing product. Such strategies involve global dispersion of plant operations and increasing reliance on transportation, especially air transport. In North Carolina, a global transpark facility is under development to provide North Carolina manufacturers and others who locate near this facility the ability to source materials, assemble products, and distribute products worldwide in 48 hours. Efforts are under way to develop freighters that will cut the time of transatlantic voyages in half.[12] With these innovations, firms located nearby will continue to set a new, higher standard for global competition.

Mass Customization

Increasingly, many manufacturing and service firms find that customers expect products and services to be developed for each customer's unique needs. For example, a particular bicycle customer might expect the product to be designed to fit his or her height, weight, and usage requirements. Or Dell and Gateway computer manufacturers will assemble a computer based on the customer's exact specifications. Many firms have found that they can compete successfully with a strategy that targets customers' unique needs. In **mass customization,** marketing and production processes are designed to handle the increased variety that results from this type of business.[13] This redesign involves a larger number of smaller production runs in manufacturing and specially designed marketing and service functions. The greater variety and complexity of production under mass customization increases a portion of production costs, although the costs of marketing and servicing the product might be reduced. Mass customization can be an effective way for a firm to compete in an industry in which the price and quality expectations of many consumers are met by existing manufacturers. It does this by distinguishing itself through providing a fast, customized service. The growth of mass customization is, in effect, another indication of the increased attention given to satisfying the customer.

> **Mass customization** is a management technique in which marketing and production processes are designed to handle the increased variety that results from delivering customized products and services to customers.

---

[12] "Warp Speed on the High Seas," *Business Week*, September 18, 1995, pp. 155–56.

[13] Find out more about mass customization in articles by James H. Gilmore, "Reengineering for Mass Customization," *Journal of Cost Management*, Fall 1993, pp. 22–29; and Joseph P. Pine II, Bart Victor, and Andrew C. Boynton, "Making Mass Customization Work," *Harvard Business Review*, September–October 1993, pp. 108–19.

Target Costing

Target costing is a tool that has resulted directly from the intensely competitive markets in many industries.[14] **Target costing** determines the desired cost for a product on the basis of a given competitive price, such that the product will earn a desired profit. Cost is thus determined by price. The firm using target costing must often adopt strict cost-reduction measures or redesign the product or manufacturing process in order to meet the market price and remain profitable.

Target cost = Market-determined price − Desired profit

Target costing forces the firm to become more competitive, and, like benchmarking, it is a common strategic form of analysis in intensely competitive industries where even small price differences attract consumers to the lower-priced product. The computer software industry is a good example of the application of target costing. Competing software producers often sell at a market-determined price level (sometimes a price set by the industry leader) and try to differentiate their product in terms of the quality and quantity of new features in each upgrade or new version of the software. The automobile industry follows a similar pattern.

Margin note: **Target costing** determines the desired cost for a product on the basis of a given competitive price so that the product will earn a desired profit.

Life-Cycle Costing

Life-cycle costing is a management technique used to identify and monitor the costs of a product throughout its life cycle. The life cycle consists of all steps from product design and purchase of raw materials to delivery and service of the finished product. The steps include (1) research and development; (2) product design, including prototyping, target costing, and testing; (3) manufacturing, inspecting, packaging, and warehousing; (4) marketing, promotion, and distribution; and (5) sales and service. Cost management has traditionally focused only on costs incurred at the third step, manufacturing. Thinking strategically, management accountants now manage the product's full life cycle of costs, including upstream and downstream costs as well as manufacturing costs. This expanded focus means that they pay careful attention, especially to product design, since design decisions lock in most subsequent life-cycle costs.

Margin note: **Life-cycle costing** is a management technique used to identify and monitor the costs of a product throughout its life cycle.

The Balanced Scorecard

Strategic information using critical success factors provides a road map for the firm to use to chart its competitive course and serves as a benchmark for competitive success. Financial measures such as profitability reflect only a partial, and frequently only a short-term, measure of the firm's progress. Without strategic information, the firm is likely to stray from its competitive course and to make strategically wrong product decisions, for example, choosing the wrong products or the wrong marketing and distribution methods.

To emphasize the importance of using strategic information, *both financial and nonfinancial*, accounting reports of a firm's performance are now often based on critical success factors in four different dimensions. One dimension is financial; the other three dimensions are nonfinancial:

1. **Financial performance.** Measures of profitability and market value, among others, as indicators of how well the firm satisfies its owners and shareholders.

2. **Customer satisfaction.** Measures of quality, service, and low cost, among others, as indicators of how well the firm satisfies its customers.

3. **Internal business processes.** Measures of the efficiency and effectiveness with which the firm produces the product or service.

4. **Innovation and learning.** Measures of the firm's ability to develop and utilize human resources to meet its strategic goals now and into the future.

---

[14] A useful reference for target costing is the book by Y. Monden and M. Sakurai (eds.), *Japanese Management Accounting: A World Class Approach to Profit Management* (Cambridge, Mass.: Productivity Press, 1993).

COST MANAGEMENT IN ACTION

How Can Dell Retain its Glitter?

Dell Computer was one of the biggest success stories of the last decade of the twentieth century. From 1995 to 2000, its stock price significantly outperformed that of its key rivals, Hewlett-Packard, IBM, Compaq, Intel, and Cisco Systems. *Business Week* chose CEO Michael Dell as one of the Top Executives of the Year in 1999. Dell succeeded in all dimensions of company performance: profit growth, stock price gains, operating efficiency and speed, and customer service. These successes paid big dividends for the company, which more than doubled its sales in two years. Its stock price had almost a 100 percent average annual price increase throughout the 1990s—the best performing stock of the decade! But trouble is ahead. For the quarter ended July

2000*, Dell's sales increases fell nearly to the industry average. Perhaps this is due to Dell's dependence on the PC market, which is showing signs of a slowdown. What should Dell do in this situation—stick with its strategy of dominance in the mail-order PC market or look to a new strategy of some kind? How might any of the contemporary management techniques just described in the text help?

*For current financial information about Dell, see http://yahoo.market guide.com/.

Sources: "The Top Executives, *Business Week,* January 11, 1999, p. 74.

(Refer to comments on Cost Management in Action at end of chapter.)

The **balanced scorecard** is an accounting report that includes the firm's critical success factors in four areas: (1) financial performance, (2) customer satisfaction, (3) internal business processes, and (4) innovation and learning.

An accounting report based on the four dimensions is called a **balanced scorecard.** The concept of balance captures the intent of broad coverage, financial and nonfinancial, of all factors that contribute to the firm's success in achieving its strategic goals. The balanced scorecard provides a basis for a more complete analysis than is possible with financial data alone. The use of the balanced scorecard is thus a critical ingredient of the overall approach that firms take to become and remain competitive.

THE PROFESSIONAL ENVIRONMENT OF COST MANAGEMENT

> An organization's ability to learn, and to translate that learning into action rapidly, is the ultimate competitive advantage.
>
> JACK WELCH

LEARNING OBJECTIVE 4▶

Describe the professional environment of the management accountant, including professional organizations, professional certifications, and professional ethics

Jack Welch, the former chairman of General Electric, understands the importance of continuous learning in business. His words apply equally well to the management accountant. Management accountants must continuously improve their technical and other skills and maintain a constant high level of professionalism, integrity, and objectivity about their work. Many professional organizations, such as the Institute of Management Accountants (IMA) and the American Institute of CPAs (AICPA), encourage their members to earn relevant professional certifications, participate in professional development programs, and continually reflect on the professional ethics they bring to their work.

Professional Organizations

The professional environment of the management accountant is influenced by two types of organizations: one that sets guidelines and regulations regarding management accounting practices and one that promotes the professionalism and competence of management accountants.

The first group of organizations includes a number of federal agencies, such as the Internal Revenue Service, which sets product costing guidelines for tax purposes, and the Federal Trade Commission (FTC), which, to foster competitive practices and protect trade, restricts pricing practices and requires that prices in most circumstances be justified on the basis of cost. In addition, the Securities and Exchange Commission (SEC) provides guidance, rules, and regulations regarding financial reporting.

Where to Look for Information on Professional Organizations

American Institute of CPAs (AICPA): http://www.aicpa.org/

Federal Trade Commission (FTC): http://www.ftc.gov/

Financial Executives Institute (FEI): http://www.fei.org

Institute of Internal Auditors (IIA): http://www.rutgers.edu/Accounting/raw/iia

Institute of Management Accountants (IMA): http://www.imanet.org

Internal Revenue Service (IRS): http://www.irs.ustreas.gov/prod/coverhtml

Securities and Exchange Commission (SEC): http://www.sec.gov/

Society of Management Accountants (SMAC, Canada): http://www.cma-Canada.org/

The Chartered Institute of Management Accountants (CIMA, UK): www.cima.org.uk

American Accounting Association Management Accounting Section (MAS):
http://rutgers.edu/accounting/raw/aaa/aaamas

Consortium for Advanced Manufacturing (CAM-I): http://cam-i.org.

In the private sector, the Financial Accounting Standards Board (FASB), an independent organization, and the AICPA supply additional guidance regarding financial reporting practices. The AICPA also provides educational opportunities in the form of newsletters, magazines, professional development seminars, and technical meetings for management accountants.

Congress established the Cost Accounting Standards Board (CASB) in 1970 (Public Law 91–379), which operates under the Office of Federal Procurement Policy "to make, promulgate, amend and rescind cost accounting standards and interpretations thereof designed to achieve uniformity and consistency in the cost accounting standards governing measurement, assignment, and allocation of cost to contracts with the United States federal government." The CASB's objective is to achieve uniformity and consistency in the cost accounting standards used by government suppliers in order to reduce the incidence of fraud and abuse. Twenty standards cover a broad range of issues in cost accounting.

Another group of organizations supports the growth and professionalism of management accounting practice. The Institute of Management Accountants (IMA) is the principal organization devoted primarily to management accountants in the United States. The IMA provide magazines, newsletters, research reports, management accounting practice reports, professional development seminars, and monthly technical meetings that serve the broad purpose of providing continuing education opportunities for management accountants. In the United Kingdom, the Chartered Institute of Management Accountants (CIMA) performs a similar role, as does the Society of Management Accountants (SMA) in Canada, the Spanish Management Accounting Association, the French Accounting Association, and the Institutes of Chartered Accountants in Ireland, Australia, Scotland, and India. Similar organizations are present in most other countries around the world.

In areas related to the management accounting function, the Financial Executives Institute (FEI) provides services much like those provided by the IMA for financial managers, including controllers and treasurers.

Because one of the management control responsibilities of the management accountant is to develop effective systems to detect and prevent errors and fraud in the accounting records, the management accountant commonly has strong ties to the control-oriented organizations such as the Institute of Internal Auditors (IIA).

Even if you're on the right track, you'll get run over if you just sit there.

WILL ROGERS

Professional Certifications

The role of professional certification programs is to provide a distinct measure of experience, training, and performance capability for the management accountant. Certification is one way in which the management accountant shows professional achievement and stature. Three types of certification are relevant for management accountants. The first is the Certified Management Accountant (CMA) designation administered by the Institute of Management Accountants, which is achieved by passing a qualifying exam and satisfying certain background and experience requirements. The exam covers four areas of knowledge relevant to the practice of management accounting: (1) economics, finance, and management; (2) financial accounting and reporting; (3) management analysis and reporting; and (4) decision analysis and information systems. The material required for part (3) of the exam is covered throughout this book; portions of parts (1), (2), and (4) are also covered.

The second relevant certification is the Certified Financial Manager (CFM) program of the IMA. This program is intended for the broader responsibilities of the financial manager, such as those of the chief financial officer. The exam includes topics related to corporate financial management in addition to the topics covered on the CMA exam.

The third certification is the Certified Public Accountant (CPA) designation. Like the CMA and CFM, the CPA is earned by passing a qualifying exam, which the AICPA prepares and grades, and by satisfying certain background, education, and experience requirements. Unlike the CMA, which is an international designation, the CPA certificate is awarded and monitored in the United States by each state which has its own set of criteria. While the CPA designation is critical for those accountants who practice auditing, the CMA is widely viewed as the most relevant for those dealing with cost management issues.[15] Many countries have certificates that are equivalent to the CPA.

Loyalty Is Out, and Life-Long Learning Is In

A sociological study of mid-managers in eight large companies in the early 1990s found that these managers were on the whole rather complacent about the layoffs and downsizings occurring in their companies. Through further study, the principal researcher, Charles Heckscher, found that these managers had a high degree of loyalty to the company and an almost paternalistic view of the company: top management would do the right thing for the company and its employees. Moreover, when the managers were put into two groups—one for high-performing companies and one for low-performing companies—additional insights emerged. The managers of low-performing firms had surprisingly little knowledge of their firm's business and little understanding of the business functions (marketing, operations,...) outside their own area of expertise. In contrast, the managers from the successful firms were more likely to be able to explain clearly the firm's business and strategy.

Mr. Heckscher's conclusion from the study was that managers in the coming years need to focus more on maintaining their skills and adding value for the firm. Loyalty is out, and life-long learning (becoming a professional manager) is in.

Source: "If Loyalty Is Out, then What's in?" *New York Times,* January 29, 1995, p. F-21.

Integrative Skills Can Get You Ahead

While assigned as an internal auditor of a large manufacturing company, Joellyn Willis tried her best to add value to her company. Having prior experience in cost accounting, she was able to assist plant managers with difficult operational problems in addition to performing her internal audit assignments. She viewed her work as an opportunity to apply all of her skills and experience to improve the firm's operations. She is now vice president of operations at the company.

Source: *The Wall Street Journal,* September 8, 1998, p. B-4.

---

[15] A fourth type of certification, the Certified Cost Analyst (CCA), is sponsored by the Institute of Cost Analysis. As with the others, its requirements include a qualifying exam and eight years of experience in cost analysis. The orientation of this exam and certification is accounting for federal contractors, especially defense contractors.

Professional Ethics

Ethics is an important aspect of the management accountant's work and profession. Professional ethics can be summed up as the commitment of the management accountant to provide a useful service for management. This commitment means that the management accountant has the competence, integrity, confidentiality, and objectivity to serve management effectively.

◄LEARNING OBJECTIVE 5

Understand the principles and rules of professional ethics and explain how to apply them.

The IMA Code of Ethics

The ethical behavior of the management accountant is guided by the code of ethics of the Institute of Management Accountants (IMA). The IMA code of ethics specifies *minimum* standards of behavior that are intended to guide the management accountant and to inspire a very high overall level of professionalism. By complying with these standards, management accountants enhance their profession and facilitate the development of a trusting relationship in which managers and others can confidently rely on their work.

The IMA code of ethics contains four main sections: (1) competence, (2) confidentiality, (3) integrity, and (4) objectivity (Exhibit 1–4). The standard of competence requires the management accountant to develop and maintain the skills necessary for her or his area of practice and to continually reassess the adequacy of those skills as the firm grows and becomes more complex. The standard of confidentiality requires adherence to the firm's policies regarding communication of data to protect its trade secrets

---

Exhibit 1–4   Institute of Management Accountants Code of Ethics

Competence

- Maintain an appropriate level of professional competence by ongoing development of knowledge and skills.
- Perform professional duties in accordance with relevant laws, regulations, and technical standards.
- Prepare complete and clear reports and recommendations after appropriate analyses of relevant and reliable information.

Confidentiality

- Refrain from disclosing confidential information acquired in the course of the work except when authorized, unless legally obligated to do so.
- Inform subordinates as appropriate regarding the confidentiality of information acquired in the course of the work and monitor one's activities to assure the maintenance of that confidentiality.
- Refrain from using or appearing to use confidential information acquired in the course of the work for unethical or illegal advantage either personally or through third parties.

Integrity

- Avoid actual or apparent conflicts of interest and advise all appropriate parties of any potential conflict.
- Refrain from engaging in any activity that would prejudice one's ability to carry out his or her duties ethically.
- Refuse any gift, favor, or hospitality that would influence or would appear to influence one's actions.
- Refrain from either actively or passively subverting the attainment of the organization's legitimate and ethical objectives.
- Recognize and communicate professional limitations or other constraints that would preclude responsible judgment or successful performance of an activity.
- Communicate unfavorable as well as favorable information and professional judgments or opinions.
- Refrain from engaging in or supporting any activity that would discredit the profession.

Objectivity

- Communicate information fairly and objectively.
- Disclose fully all relevant information that could reasonably be expected to influence an intended user's understanding of the reports, comments, and recommendations presented.

Source: Statement on Management Accounting No. 1C, "Standards of Ethical Conduct for Management Accountants;" (Montvale, N.J.: Institute of Management Accountants, June 1, 1983), pp. 1–2.

A Value-Based Approach to Global Competition Is Good Strategy

At least some firms have found that an ethical, value-based approach can be effective in competing in the global marketplace. For example, British Petroleum Co. (BP), takes a strong interest in the social and economic welfare of the cities and towns where it does business. This includes job training programs and support of small businesses in South Africa, the use of computer technology in Vietnam to help control flooding, and the financing of forest replanting in Turkey. In Colombia, BP recycles its waste material into bricks for local homebuilding, and in Zambia it supplies materials and equipment for medical doctors. Have these efforts hurt BP's bottom line—global earnings? To the contrary, BP's CEO John Browne says, "These efforts have nothing to do with charity, and everything to do with our long-term self-interest." BP's earnings in the last six years appear to prove the point; profits have increased more than four times, and shareholders' return has been in excess of 30 percent annually.

Similarly, in 1982 Johnson & Johnson (J&J) turned what could have been a catastrophe for the firm into a strategic success when its Tylenol product was found to have some contaminants resulting in a number of deaths in the Chicago area. J&J rapidly removed all Tylenol products from the entire U. S. market at a cost of $100 million and mobilized a large communication effort to warn users of the dangers of the product. In part because of these efforts and adherence to its corporate Credo, which states that J&J assumes responsibility for its product and its employees, the company has succeeded in earning broad public support and confidence (see Exhibit 1-3), which has contributed significantly to its competitive advantage. Compare J&J's handling of the Tylenol problem with the response by Firestone and Ford to the tire problems on Explorers in 1999–2000. How many product recalls are handled as promptly and completely as in the J&J case? J&J's corporate Credo, an inspiring statement, can be accessed on the firm's home page (www.jnj.comn/home.html); it is provided in a number of different languages. Motorola, Inc. also has a comprehensive code of business conduct. See it at www.motorola.com/code/code.html.

Source: "Globalism Doesn't Have to Be Cruel," *Business Week,* February 9, 1998, p. 26; Francis J. Aguilar and Arvind Bhambri, "Johnson & Johnson (A)," Harvard Business School Case No. 384-053.

and other confidential information. Integrity refers to behaving in a professional manner (e.g., refraining from activities that would discredit the firm or profession, such as unfair hiring practices) and to avoiding conflicts of interest (e.g., not accepting a gift from a supplier or customer). Finally, objectivity refers to the need to maintain impartial judgment (e.g., not developing analyses to support a decision that the management accountant knows is not correct).

How to Apply the Code of Ethics

Handling situations in which an ethical issue arises can be very challenging and frustrating. Using the following step-by-step approach can be helpful:

First, the management accountant must consider the ethical principles or standards that might apply in the situation: competence, integrity, confidentiality, and objectivity. Also important is keeping in mind the broad objective of the code of ethics, which is to maintain management's confidence in the profession. The management accountant must consider how the resolution of the situation would affect a manager's trust and reliance on her or him and on other management accountants.

Second, the management accountant should discuss the situation with a superior. If the superior is part of the situation, the management accountant should seek out the person or persons *within the firm* who have the equivalent or higher level of responsibility, such as a manager in the firm's human resources department or a member of the audit committee. In keeping with the standard of confidentiality, the accountant does not communicate such problems outside the firm except as indicated in the fourth step.

Third, if the ethical conflict cannot be resolved and the matter is significant, the management accountant might have to resign from the firm and communicate the reasons to the appropriate management level.

Fourth, the management accountant must, if resigning, consider his or her responsibility to communicate the matter outside the firm to regulatory authorities or to the firm's external auditor.

SUMMARY OF LEARNING OBJECTIVES

The central theme of this book is that cost management information includes all the information that managers need to manage effectively to lead their firms to competitive success. Cost management information includes both financial and nonfinancial information critical to the firm's success. The specific role of cost management in the firm differs depending on the firm's competitive strategy, its type of industry and organization (manufacturing firm, service firm, merchandising firm, not-for-profit organization, or governmental organization), and the management function to which cost management is applied (the functions are strategic management, planning and decision making, management and operational control, and preparation of financial statements).

Changes in the business environment have altered the nature of competition and the types of techniques managers use to succeed in their businesses. These changes include (1) an increase in global competition, (2) advances in manufacturing technologies, (3) advances in information technologies, the Internet, and e-commerce, (4) a greater focus on the customer, (5) new forms of management organization, and (6) changes in the social, political, and cultural environment of business.

Of particular importance are the changes in business, especially the increase in global competition and the changes in management techniques, that have created the need for a new, strategic approach to management and to cost management. Cost management can assist the firm in using the new management techniques: benchmarking, total quality management, continuous improvement, activity-based costing and management, reengineering, the theory of constraints, mass customization, target costing, life-cycle costing, and the balanced scorecard.

A variety of professional organizations supports management accounting, including the Institute of Management Accountants (IMA), the American Institute of Certified Public Accountants (AICPA), and the Financial Executives Institute (FEI), among others. Several relevant certification programs recognize competence and experience in management accounting; they include the Certified Management Accountant (CMA) and the Certified Financial Manager (CFM) programs of the IMA and the Certified Public Accountant (CPA) program of the AICPA.

The management accountant is responsible to the firm and to the public for maintaining a high standard of performance, as set forth in the IMA code of professional ethics. The professional ethics standards of the management accountant include competence, integrity, objectivity, and confidentiality.

KEY TERMS

Activity analysis 15

Activity-based costing (ABC) 15

Activity-based management (ABM) 15

Balanced scorecard 18

Benchmarking 13

Continuous improvement 14

Cost management information 4

Critical success factors (CSFs) 13

Life-cycle costing 17

Management control 6

Mass customization 16

Operational control 6

Planning and decision making 6

Preparation of financial statements 7

Reengineering 15

Strategic cost management 8

Strategic management 6

Target costing 17

Theory of constraints (TOC) 15

Total quality management (TQM) 14

COMMENTS ON COST MANAGEMENT IN ACTION

How can Dell Retain Its Glitter?

Dell Corporation lost some of its glitter in the 2000–2001 period, but its key business measures were solid. For example, sales growth was expected to remain at 30 percent or better—a performance that would delight most firms. Dell might want to rethink its strategy, however; some possible areas of new focus include the very low-cost home PC market, which Dell had left to others. Its foreign sales were low (18 percent of total sales) relative to other PC manufacturers whose foreign sales are as much as 50 percent of total sales. What other possible strategic initiatives can you think of?

Already a world-class user of advanced manufacturing methods (outsourcing and low-cost manufacturing), perhaps Dell should consider other new management techniques such as continuous improvement to reduce manufacturing and other costs throughout the product life cycle. This approach might draw attention to downstream costs such as selling and distribution costs for which opportunities for improvement might exist. As price competition becomes more intense, Dell can use target costing to further reduce manufacturing, distribution, and service costs by identifying low-cost product designs that contain desired product features.

Source: Gary Mc Williams, "Dell Looks for Ways to Rekindle the Fire It Had as an Upstart," *The Wall Street Journal*, August 31, 2000,

SELF-STUDY PROBLEM

(For solution, please turn to the end of the chapter.)

An Ethical Problem

An ethical situation involving potential manipulation of accounting earnings occurred in Bausch & Lomb's (B&L) contact lens unit. Apparently, B&L used inappropriate accounting methods to inflate year-end sales. The story, as reported by *Business Week* (December 19, 1994, pp. 108–110), is as follows:

September 1993: Independent contact lens distributors say B&L asks them to buy 4 to 6 months' worth of inventory. B&L says buildup supports a new marketing program, but distributors say uneven results leave them with 4 to 12 months' inventory in early December.

December 13, 1993: B&L calls a meeting and tells distributors to take additional inventories ranging from one to two years' worth or face cutoff. B&L says the buildup is needed for programs aimed at getting high-volume accounts to buy from distributors rather than from the company.

December 24, 1993: Insisting that lenses be ordered by December 24, B&L rushes out shipments. That tactic adds sales of $25 million, but distributors say B&L gave verbal assurances that the distributors would pay for lenses only when sold. B&L says small payments were set through June, when balances were due.

June 15, 1994: With the new promotions lagging, less than 10 percent of the inventory is sold—or paid for. When the final payments fall due, most distributors refuse to pay. Meanwhile, B&L continues to sell directly to some high-volume accounts at prices below what the distributors paid.

October 1994: With the majority of the inventory unsold, B&L takes most back. Distributors pay sharply discounted prices for the rest. B&L's third-quarter revenues drop 10 percent, to $449 million, and earnings plummet 86 percent, to $7.7 million, as a result of inventory reduction efforts and price cuts.

Required   What are the ethical issues in this case?

QUESTIONS

1-1 Give four examples of firms you believe would be significant users of cost management information and explain why.

1-2 Give three examples of firms you believe would *not* be significant users of cost management information and explain why.

1-3 What does the term *cost management* mean? Who in the typical firm or organization is responsible for cost management?

1-4 Name three professional cost management organizations and explain their roles and objectives.

1-5 What type of professional certification is most relevant for the management accountant and why?

1-6 List the four functions of management. Explain what type of cost management information is appropriate for each.

1-7 Which is the most important function of management? Explain why?

1-8 Identify the different types of business firms and other organizations that use cost management information, and explain how the information is used.

1-9 Name a firm or organization you know of that you are reasonably sure uses strategic cost management and explain why it does so.

1-10 As firms move to the Internet for sales and customer service, how do you expect their competitive strategies will change?

1-11 As firms move to the Internet for sales and customer service, how do you expect their need for cost management information will change?

1-12 What are some factors in the contemporary business environment that are causing changes in business firms and other organizations? How are the changes affecting the way those firms and organizations use cost management information?

1-13 Contrast past and present business environments with regard to the following aspects: basis of competition, manufacturing processes and manufacturing technology, required labor skills, emphasis on quality, number of products, number of markets, types of cost management information needed, management organizational structure, and management focus.

1-14 Name the 10 contemporary management techniques and describe each briefly.

EXERCISES

1-15 **ROBERT HALF SURVEY, NEW SKILLS FOR THE CFO**   A number of firms in the Thomasville–High Point area of North Carolina are either directly or indirectly involved in furniture manufacturing. Paul Descoll, the CFO of one of these firms, Thomasville Furniture Industries, was asked to respond to the recent survey of 1,400 CFOs by Robert Half International, Inc. The survey projected large increases in hiring for new finance and accounting professionals in firms throughout the United States. The survey also reported that the CFOs expected in the coming years to see far greater emphasis placed on business strategy and less placed on financial report preparation as part of the finance function. They predicted that computer technologies would continue to affect the finance function by reducing the time and effort involved in processing transactions and by transferring the focus to the interpretation and use of the information available from the computer systems.

Required   What do you think the implications of the Robert Half survey are for finance and accounting professionals? As the top financial manager of a large manufacturing company, what do you think CFO Descoll had to say about the role of finance and accounting professionals?

25

1–16   STRATEGY, ETHICS, REAL ESTATE SERVICES   As a management accountant in a small real estate services firm, you have become aware of a strategic initiative in your firm to promote its services to a new class of customers. Currently, most of your firm's customers lease space in large office buildings where they might occupy three or more floors of the building. Your firm provides maintenance, security and cleaning services for the office space leased by these customers. The strategic initiative you have discovered is to seek out smaller firms that occupy as small a space as a few thousand square feet. You know that most of these smaller firms are now serviced in a haphazard manner, with part-time help for which turnover is very high; some of the smaller office buildings might not employ security of any kind. You expect that the demand for your company's services among firms of this smaller size will be good, but you are worried about the profitability of these new customers. In fact, although you cannot prove it with hard numbers, you are sure that this new strategy will cause big losses for your firm. You have not been consulted about this new strategy by the firm's owners because you are not viewed as part of the management decision-making team. You would like very much, however, to be more involved in the company's strategy development and decision making.

Required   What should you do or say about this new strategic initiative?

Strategy

1–17   THE THEORY OF CONSTRAINTS, MANUFACTURING VS. RETAIL   Manufacturing firms such as Fed Ex, General Motors, and General Electric utilize the concept of the theory of constraints and emphasize speed of throughput in their manufacturing operations.

Required   Discuss whether the concept of throughput in the theory of constraints is appropriate for retail and service industries. Take as a specific example the Wal-Mart chain of retail stores. How would or could you, apply this management technique to Wal-Mart?

PROBLEMS

1–18   CONTEMPORARY MANAGEMENT TECHNIQUES   Tim Johnson is a news reporter and feature writer for *The Wall Street Review*, an important daily newspaper for financial managers. Tim's assignment is to develop a feature article on target costing, including interviews with chief financial officers and operating managers. Tim has a generous travel budget for research into company history, operations, and market analysis for the firms he selects for the article.

Required

1. Tim has asked you to recommend industries and firms that would be good candidates for the article. What would you advise? Explain your recommendations.

2. Assume that Tim's assignment is a feature article on life-cycle costing. Answer as you did for requirement 1.

3. Assume that Tim's assignment is a feature article on the theory of constraints. Answer as you did for requirement 1.

1–19   PROFESSIONAL ORGANIZATIONS AND CERTIFICATION   Ian Walsh has just been hired as a management accountant for a large manufacturing firm near his hometown of Canton, Ohio. The firm manufactures a wide variety of plastic products for the automobile industry, the packaging industry, and other customers. At least initially, Ian's principal assignments have been to develop product costs for new product lines. His cost accounting professor has suggested to Ian that he begin to consider professional organizations and professional certifications that will help him in his career.

Required   Which organizations and certifications would you suggest for Ian, and why?

1–20 BALANCED SCORECARD Johnson Industrial Controls, Inc. (JIC), is a large manufacturer of specialized instruments used in automated manufacturing plants. JIC has grown steadily over the past several years on the strength of technological innovation in its key product lines. The firm now employs 3,500 production employees and 450 staff and management personnel in six large plants located across the United States. In the past few years, the growth of sales and profits has declined sharply, because of the entrance into the market of new competitors. As part of a recent strategic planning effort, JIC identified its key competitive strengths and weaknesses. JIC management believe that the critical strengths are in the quality of the product and that the weakness in recent years has been in customer service, particularly in meeting scheduled deliveries. The failure to meet promised delivery dates can be quite costly to JIC's customers, because it is likely to delay the construction or upgrading of the customers' plants and therefore delay the customers' production and sales.

JIC's management believes that the adoption of the balanced scorecard for internal reporting might help the firm become more competitive.

Required
1. Explain how the balanced scorecard might help a firm like JIC.
2. Develop a brief balanced scorecard for JIC. Give some examples of the items that might be included in each of these four parts of the scorecard: (a) customer satisfaction, (b) financial performance, (c) manufacturing and business processes, and (d) human resources.

1-21 BANKING, STRATEGY, SKILLS A large U.S.–based commercial bank with global operations recently initiated a new program for recruiting recent college graduates into the financial function of the bank. These new hires will initially be involved in a variety of financial functions, including transactions processing, control, risk management, business performance reporting, new business analysis, and financial analysis. Recognizing that they are competing with many other banks for the relatively small number of qualified graduates, the firm has assigned you to develop a skills statement to be used in college recruiting as well as an in-house training program for new hires. You have some old training manuals and recruiting guides to assist you, but your boss advises you not to use them but to start with a fresh page. The reason for developing new materials is that the bank recently reorganized based on new management methods. You dumped all of those materials in the back of a file cabinet and began to develop the skills statement and training program.

Required
1. Briefly explain 8 to 10 critical success factors for this bank. Consider how a bank of this size remains competitive and successful.
2. Develop a one-page outline of the skill statement and training program that your boss requested. Be brief and specific about the proper job description of a new employee in the finance area of the bank.

1-22 CONSULTING, SKILLS A consulting firm offering a broad range of services will soon visit your college to recruit graduates. This firm has more than 20,000 professional staff in 275 offices of 11 different countries. Most of its clients are large corporations in a variety of different industries. Because of the opportunity for the experience and travel, you are very interested in getting a job with this firm. You have an interview in two weeks, and you're planning to do some research about the firm and the job to be as well prepared as you can be for the interview.

Required Write a brief, one-half page statement of what you think the job description for this employer is. What skills would you need to succeed as a consultant in this firm.

Service

Strategy

1–23 **ACTIVITY ANALYSIS IN A BANK**   Mesa Financial is a small bank located in west Texas. As a small bank, Mesa has a rather limited range of services: mortgage loans, installment (mostly auto) loans, commercial loans, checking and savings accounts, and certificates of deposit. Mesa's management has learned that activity analysis could be used to study the efficiency of the bank's operations.

Required

1. Explain how activity analysis might help a bank like Mesa.

2. Give six to eight examples of activities you would expect to identify in Mesa's operations.

International

Strategy

1–24 **STRATEGY, INTERNATIONAL**   In the mid-1980s, Toyota and General Motors formed a strategic alliance to jointly manufacture certain engine parts in an old General Motors plant in Fremont, California. For Toyota, the expected benefit was to gain experience in working with U.S. suppliers, trade groups, and employee groups. Such experience would be useful if Toyota later built its own manufacturing plants in the United States. For General Motors, the expected benefit was to obtain firsthand experience with the Japanese carmaker's manufacturing and management techniques as a basis for potential improvements in General Motors's own management methods.

Required

1. Identify and explain the critical success factors for both Toyota and General Motors that provided the motivation for the strategic alliance at Fremont.

2. What are some of the risks for Toyota and for General Motors in this alliance?

Ethics

1–25 **ETHICS, PRODUCT QUALITY**   HighTech, Inc., manufacturers computer chips and components. HighTech has just introduced a new version of its memory chip, which is far faster than the previous version. Because of high product demand for the new chip, the testing process has been thorough but hurried. As the firm's chief of operations, you discover after the chip has been on the market for a few months and is selling very well that it has a minor fault that will cause hard-to-discover failures in certain, very unusual circumstances.

Required   Now that you know of the chip's faults, what should you disclose and to whom should you disclose it?

Strategy

1–26 **STRATEGY, DAIMLERCHRYSLER**   DaimlerChrysler is one of the largest global automakers, has the premier auto brand, Mercedes, which has a very strong position both in the European and worldwide markets. It also has Chrysler products that are strong in the United States and have a presence worldwide. Most recently, DaimlerChrysler extended its global reach to Asia with significant investments in the Japanese automaker Mitsubishi Motors and the Korean automaker, Hyundai. The move into Asia is prompted in part by increasing competition and price pressure in the luxury car market where Mercedes has a strong position. The Mitsubishi and Hyundai investments are expected to provide DaimlerChrysler access to new technologies and markets.

Required

1. Briefly explain Daimler's strategy as reflected by its recent acquisitions. How would you compare this strategy to that of other large automakers?

2. What are the risks of this strategy?

(Hint: To improve your answer, research the company using the business press such as *The Wall Street Journal, Business Week,* or *Fortune,* or the websites Yahoo.com (Finance) and Businessweek.com.

SOLUTION TO SELF-STUDY PROBLEM

An Ethical Problem

As reported, B&L apparently made several direct efforts to improperly inflate earnings through forced sales to distributors. The ethical principles involved are integrity and objectivity, both of which have been violated in this case.

Strategic Analysis and Strategic Cost Management

2

After studying this chapter, you should be able to . . .

1 Explain competitive strategy and show how the contemporary business environment influences strategy

2 Identify the two principal types of competitive strategy

3 Demonstrate how a firm identifies its own competitive strategy, including determining its critical success factors, and how it designs a strategic cost information system

4 Explain value-chain analysis and show how it is used to better understand a firm's competitive advantage

5 Understand the implications of strategic analysis for cost management

Amazon.com typifies successful competition in the new economy far more than any other form. Some would say that Amazon invented the Internet retailing business model that all other dot-coms are struggling to copy. Amazon understands well the strategy (i.e., business model) of developing and maintaining customer loyalty, which is the key to success in retail e-business and implements it effectively.[1] Walter Mossberg, technology commentator for *The Wall Street Journal*, puts it this way:

> While Amazon.com is price competitive, it didn't get to be the Web's largest retailer, with 23 million customers, by having the lowest prices on all items all the time. It doesn't guarantee to match or beat others' prices. Instead, Amazon has won the loyalty of millions by building an online store that is friendly, easy to use, and inspires a sense of confidence and community among its customers. People trust Amazon, partly because it knows their tastes and does what it promises. For me, and apparently many

---

[1]   See Frederick F. Reichheld and Phil Schefter, "E-Loyalty: Your Secret Weapon on the Web," *Harvard Business Review*, July–August 2000, pp. 105–113.

others, it wouldn't be worth roaming all over the Web to save a few bucks shopping elsewhere.[2]

LEARNING OBJECTIVE 1 ▶

Explain competitive strategy and show how the contemporary business environment influences strategy.

The amazing thing about Amazon is that it created such a successful strategy for e-commerce at a time when there was no model to use as a guide. This chapter is an introduction to strategy, that is, how firms like Amazon develop a competitive advantage. One of the ideas we will see in the chapter is that some firms have achieved success on the basis of a low-cost/low-price competitive advantage; others succeed because of superior customer service. We would conclude from Mossberg's comments, that Amazon.com relies on customer service and loyalty rather than low price only. It is important to understand how a firm competes to be able to develop useful cost management information. If Amazon.com's strategy is to build customer loyalty, it follows that its management accountant should develop and maintain relevant, timely, and accurate information about the firm's progress and prospects in meeting this goal.

HOW A FIRM SUCCEEDS: THE COMPETITIVE STRATEGY

A **strategy** is a set of policies, procedures, and approaches to business that produce long-term success.

A firm succeeds by finding a sustainable, long-term **strategy,** that is, a set of policies, procedures, and approaches to business that produce long-term success. Finding a strategy begins with determining the purpose and long-range direction, and therefore the mission, of the company. Exhibit 2–1 lists excerpts from the mission statements of several companies. The mission is developed into specific performance objectives, which are then implemented by specific corporate strategies, that is, specific actions to achieve the objectives that will fulfill the mission. See the Sara Lee corporate strategy in Exhibit 2–2. Note that Sara Lee's broad mission statement is explained in terms of more specific objectives, which are in turn operationalized through specific corporate strategies.

Firms have responded to the changes in business in many ways, including reengineering operational processes, downsizing the workforce, outsourcing service func-

---

Exhibit 2–1   Mission Statements of Selected Companies

Ford Motor Company (www.ford.com)
To be a low-cost producer of the highest-quality products and services that provide the best customer value.

General Electric (www.ge.com)
To become the most competitive enterprise in the world by being number one or number two in market share in every business the company is in.

IBM (www.ibm.com)
To be the most successful information-technology company in the world.

Motorola (www.motorola.com)
To complete the picture at home—integrating broadband with wireless services.

Johnson & Johnson (www.jnj.com)
To alleviate pain and disease.

United Parcel Service (www.ups.com)
To move at the speed of business.

Walt Disney (Disney.com)
To make people happy.

Merck (www.merck.com)
To preserve and improve human life.

Sara Lee (www.saralee.com)
To build leadership brands in three highly focused global businesses: Food and Beverage, Intimates and Underwear, and Household Products. Our primary purpose is to create long-term shareholder value.

---

[2]   Walter S. Mossberg, "Amazon.com Still Remains a Web Shopping Model," *The Wall Street Journal,* September 21, 2000, p. B-1. Amazon is also featured in "Can Amazon Make It?" *Business Week,* July 10, 2000, pp. 38–43; "The Amazon Question," *The Industry Standard,* July 10–17, 2000, pp. 58–61; and "This Race Isn't Even Close," by Timothy J. Mullaney, *Business Week,* December 18, 2000, pp. 208–210.

Exhibit 2–2	Sara Lee Corporate Strategy

Management Philosophy

Sara Lee Corporation is committed to the principle of decentralized management.

The company is organized into a large number of discrete profit centers, each led by an operating executive with a high degree of authority and accountability for the performance of that business.

Operating executives are selected and developed based on their ability to succeed in this entrepreneurial environment. Success at Sara Lee Corporation is measured by performance, and the company makes use of numerous reward systems to motivate management to achieve an outstanding level of performance.

This management philosophy is a defining and enduring attribute of Sara Lee Corporation.

Lines of Business

Sara Lee Corporation is a global consumer packaged goods company with more than $20 billion in annual revenues and divided into three highly focused global businesses: Food and Beverage, Intimates and Underwear, and Household Products.

Progress

Sara Lee Corporation has a 20-year history of delivering record sales and profits. One reason is that we set aggressive goals for ourselves and empower management to achieve them.

Financial Goals

We believe that the key drivers of increased shareholder value are Sara Lee's ability to grow profits, generate high returns on capital employed in our business and maintain a strong financial position. These value drivers—earnings growth, profitability and financial strength—are the basis for the goals that guide our financial management.

- **Earnings Growth:**   Real growth in earnings per share of 8% to 10% per year
- **Profitability:**   Return on invested capital above 20%
- **Financial Strength:**   Cash flow to total debt greater than 40%

Source: Sara Lee Corporation (www.saralee.com).

Exhibit 2–3	Cost Management Focus in Prior and Contemporary Business Environments

	Prior Business Environment	Contemporary Business Environment
Cost management focus	Financial reporting and cost analysis; common emphasis on standardization and standard costs; the accountant as functional expert and financial scorekeeper	Cost management as a tool for the development and implementation of business strategy; the accountant as business partner

tions, and developing smaller, more efficient, and more socially responsible organizational policies and structures. They have attempted to become more adaptable as the pace of change increases.

Firms also are beginning to use cost management to support their strategic goals. Cost management has shifted away from a focus on the stewardship role: product costing and financial reporting. The new focus is on a management-facilitating role: developing cost and other information to support the management of the firm and the achievement of its strategic goals. Before the changes in business processes, a focus on detailed methods for product costing and control at the departmental level was appropriate for the high-volume, standardized, infrequently changing manufacturing processes of that time. Now a firm's cost accounting system must be more dynamic to deal with the more rapidly changing environment and the increasing diversity of products and manufacturing processes. The cost management system must be able to assist management in this dynamic environment by facilitating strategic management. The contemporary business environment focuses on critical success factors, including both financial and nonfinancial factors (Exhibit 2–3).

Strategic Measures of Success

The strategic cost management system develops strategic information, including both financial and nonfinancial information. In the past, firms tended to focus primarily on financial performance measures, such as growth in sales and earnings, cash flow, and stock price. In contrast, firms in the contemporary business environment use strategic management to focus primarily on strategic measures of success, many of which are nonfinancial measures of operations, such as market share, product quality, customer satisfaction, and growth opportunities (see Exhibit 2–4). The financial measures show the impact of the firm's policies and procedures on the firm's *current financial position* and, therefore, its *current* return to the shareholders. In contrast, the nonfinancial factors show the firm's *current and potential competitive position* as measured from at least three additional perspectives: (1) the customer, (2) internal business processes, and (3) innovation and learning (i.e., human resources). Additional perspectives include community and social impact, governmental relations, and ethical or professional management behavior. Strategic financial and nonfinancial measures of success are also commonly called *critical success factors* (CSFs).

Without strategic information, the firm is likely to stray from its competitive course, to make strategically wrong manufacturing and marketing decisions: to choose the wrong products or the wrong customers. Some of the consequences of a lack of strategic information are shown in Exhibit 2–5.

Exhibit 2–4   Financial and Nonfinancial Measures of Success
Critical Success Factors

Financial Measures of Success	Nonfinancial Measures of Success
Sales growth	**Customer Measures**
Earnings growth	Market share and growth in market share
Dividend growth	Customer service
Bond and credit ratings	On-time delivery
Cash flow	Customer satisfaction
Increase in stock price	Brand recognition
	Positions in favorable markets
	Internal Business Processes
	High product quality
	Manufacturing innovation
	High manufacturing productivity
	Cycle time
	Yield and reduction in waste
	Learning and Innovation (Human Resources)
	Competence and integrity of managers
	Morale and firmwide culture
	Education and training
	Innovation in new products and manufacturing methods

Exhibit 2–5   Consequences of Lack of Strategic Information

Decision making based on guesses and intuition only

Lack of clarity about direction and goals

Lack of a clear and favorable perception of the firm by customers and suppliers

Incorrect investment decisions; choosing products, markets, or manufacturing processes inconsistent with strategic goals

Inability to effectively benchmark competitors, resulting in lack of knowledge about more effective competitive strategies

Failure to identify most profitable products, customers, and markets

DEVELOPING A COMPETITIVE STRATEGY: STRATEGIC POSITIONING

The concept of competitive strategy developed by Michael Porter identifies two main types of competitive strategies: cost leadership and differentiation. A firm conducts a three-step strategic competitive analysis to identify its competitive strategy.[3]

◀**LEARNING OBJECTIVE 2**

Identify the two principal types of competitive strategy.

A Framework for Strategic Competitive Analysis

In developing a sustainable competitive position, each firm purposefully or as a result of market forces arrives at one of the two competitive strategies: cost leadership or differentiation.

Cost Leadership

Cost leadership is a strategy in which a firm outperforms competitors in producing products or services at the lowest cost. The cost leader makes sustainable profits at lower prices, thereby limiting the growth of competition in the industry through its success at price wars and undermining the profitability of competitors, which must meet the firm's low price. The cost leader normally has a relatively large market share and tends to avoid niche or segment markets by using the price advantage to attract a large portion of the broad market. While most firms make strong efforts to reduce costs, the cost leader may focus almost exclusively on cost reduction, thereby ensuring a significant cost and price advantage in the market.

Cost advantages usually result from productivity in the manufacturing process, in distribution, or in overall administration. For example, technological innovation in the manufacturing process and labor savings from overseas production are common routes to competitive productivity. Firms known to be successful at cost leadership are typically very large manufacturers and retailers, such as Wal-Mart, Texas Instruments, and Compaq.

A potential weakness of the cost leadership strategy is the tendency to cut costs in a way that undermines demand for the product or service, for example, by deleting key features. The cost leader remains competitive only so long as the consumer sees that the product or service is (at least nearly) equivalent to competing products that cost somewhat more.

Cost leadership is a competitive strategy in which a firm succeeds in producing products or services at the lowest cost in the industry.

Differentiation

The **differentiation** strategy is implemented by creating a perception among consumers that the product or service is unique in some important way, usually by being of higher quality. This perception allows the firm to charge higher prices and outperform the competition in profits without reducing costs significantly. Most industries, including automobile, consumer electronics, and industrial equipment, have differentiated firms. The appeal of differentiation is especially strong for product lines for which the perception of quality and image is important, as in cosmetics, jewelry, and automobiles. Tiffany, Bentley, Rolex, Maytag, and Mercedes-Benz are good examples of firms that stress differentiation.

A weakness of the differentiation strategy is the firm's tendency to undermine its strength by attempting to lower costs or by ignoring the necessity to have a continual and aggressive marketing plan to reinforce the perceived difference. If the consumer begins to believe that the perceived difference is not significant, lower-cost rival products will appear more attractive.

Differentiation is a competitive strategy in which a firm succeeds by developing and maintaining a unique value for the product as perceived by consumers.

---

[3]   This section is adapted from Michael Porter, *Competitive Advantage* (New York: Free Press, 1985), chap. 1, except that we, for simplicity, omit a third strategy, focus. The Porter concept of competitive strategy is widely used. Another common view of competitive strategy is that of the Boston Consulting Group (B. D. Henderson, *Henderson on Corporate Strategy* [Cambridge, Mass.: Abt Books, 1979]). For a discussion of the Boston Consulting Group's view and that of others, see the chapter appendix.

Which Is It: Cost Leadership or Differentiation? General Motors and Calvin Klein

GENERAL MOTORS: IMAGE OR PRICE?

Leaders in the automobile industry, among the most competitive industries in the world, struggle to determine an effective strategy. It's not easy, as recent events at General Motors (GM) illustrated when the automaker pressed its dealers to stop price cutting and push brand value and image instead. GM exerted control over local dealers' pricing/selling strategy by in part reducing the money it set aside for dealers to use in local ads. The dealers, and some analysts, were infuriated by GM's move, believing that "the reality is that this is a price-driven market." (Merrill Lynch & Co. auto analyst Nicholas Lobaccaro). GM's response was that brand value is what creates market share and profits, although it can take time to do so. The incident shows that the development of a strategy, either cost leadership or differentiation, is a difficult and controversial process.

For another view of competition in the auto industry, see p. 44, "Global Automakers' Winning Strategy."

CALVIN KLEIN: SAK'S FIFTH AVENUE OR COSTCO?

For many, the name Calvin Klein (CK) is synonymous with expensive clothing and accessories, super models, and fashion shows. It has an image of quality and style. In reality, a significant amount of CK products are sold by discount retailers such as Costco. How can this be? The answer is that the 58-year-old designer, Calvin Klein, licensed a manufacturer, Warnaco Group, Inc. (among others), to produce his products. Under the arrangement, CK receives a royalty based on Warnaco's sales. As it turns out, Warnaco found that it could be more successful with the brand through a broad strategy of sales to a number of retailers, including discounters. Recently, thinking that this strategy would hurt his brand, Mr. Klein has tried to separate himself from the Warnaco deal.

Source: "GM Dealers Aren't Buying It," *Business Week*, February 8, 1999, pp. 46–47; and "Behind a Bitter Suit Filed by Calvin Klein Lies Grit of Licensing," *The Wall Street Journal*, June 1, 2000, p. 1.

Exhibit 2–6   Distinctive Aspects of the Two Competitive Strategies

Aspect	Cost Leadership	Differentiation
Strategic target	Broad cross-section of the market	Broad cross-section of the market
Basis of competitive advantage	Lowest cost in the industry	Unique product or service
Product line	Limited selection	Wide variety, differentiating features
Production emphasis	Lowest possible cost with high quality and essential product features	Innovation in differentiating products
Marketing emphasis	Low price	Premium price and innovative, differentiating features

Source: A. A. Thompson and A. J. Strickland, *Strategic Management,* 10th ed. (New York: McGraw-Hill, 1998).

Other Strategic Issues

A firm succeeds, then, by adopting and effectively implementing one of the strategies explained earlier (and summarized in Exhibit 2–6). Recognize that although one strategy is generally dominant, a firm is most likely to employ both of the strategies at the same time. However, a firm following both strategies is likely to succeed only if it achieves one of them significantly. A firm that does not achieve at least one strategy is not likely to be successful. This situation is what Michael Porter calls "getting stuck in the middle." A firm that is stuck in the middle is not able to sustain a competitive advantage. This often happens when a successfully differentiated firm attempts to diversify outside its area of expertise in which it can compete most effectively. An example is Intel Corp., whose stock price was hurt by projections of lower than expected revenues for the third quarter of 2000. Some investors apparently were concerned that the company's focus on new product lines—home networking equipment and Internet access chips, among others—had taken the firm away from its core business of making chips for personal computers.[4]

Another common way for a company to get stuck in the middle arises from its normal progression from one type of strategy to another as it grows. Often, a firm begins small and succeeds through effective differentiation or focus. Then, as it grows and its product or service matures in the marketplace, the firm begins to focus on cost leadership as the principal way to succeed. A firm must be careful to identify these stages in its growth and appropriately adapt its corporate strategies to them.

Critical Success Factors and SWOT Analysis

Identifying a sustainable competitive strategy for a given firm can be described as a three-step process. (Step 1 is discussed in this section; steps 2 and 3 in the following two sections.)

> **Step 1.** Obtain a strategic analysis of the firm using SWOT (strengths, weaknesses, opportunities, and threats) analysis. What are these elements for the firm? Determine the firm's overall strategy (cost or differentiation) and its critical success factors.

SWOT analysis is a systematic procedure for identifying a firm's critical success factors: its *internal* strengths and weaknesses and its *external* opportunities and threats. Strengths are skills and resources that the firm has more abundantly than other firms. Skills or competencies that the firm employs especially well are called **core competencies.** The concept of core competencies is important because it points to areas of significant competitive advantage for the firm; core competencies can be used as the building blocks of the firm's overall strategy. In contrast, weaknesses represent a lack of important skills or competencies relative to the presence of those resources in competing firms.

◀**LEARNING OBJECTIVE 3**

Demonstrate how a firm identifies its own competitive strategy, including determining its critical success factors, and how it designs a strategic cost information system.

SWOT analysis is a systematic procedure for identifying a firm's critical success factors: its internal strengths and weaknesses and its external opportunities and threats.

Skills or competencies that the firm employs especially well are called **core competencies.**

Retailing and the Internet: What's the Right Strategy?

In his recent book, Bill Gates provides some useful thoughts on how the Internet will affect retail business and other service providers. In his chapter "The Middleman Must Add Value," he says:

> The Internet is a great tool for helping customers find the best deal they can. It is reasonably easy for consumers to jump from one retail Web site to another to find the best prices on some goods.... The Web will provide more value in areas where matching buyers and sellers is more difficult, such as services, or where markets are small or dispersed. How does a consumer easily find a used product—car, computer, stereo— with certain capabilities and a certain price range? People trying to buy or sell hard-to-find items of any kind, such as antiques, parts for older equipment, or specialty items, will benefit. The GAP, for instance, is finding that the most frequent customers of its online clothing store are people looking for sizes that are not normally stocked in physical stores.... For service

industries, the Internet requires you to be either a high-volume, low-cost provider or a high-touch, customer-service provider. For the high-volume, low-cost model you use Internet technology to create a self-service approach. You make a lot of information available to customers and you drive a lot of traffic and transactions through your Internet site offering the best price. Because only a few companies in any market will be the high-volume players, most companies will have to find ways to use the Internet not just to reduce costs, but also to deliver new services.

Based on Bill Gates's comments, it seems that the Internet can help a company achieve either a cost leadership or a differentiation strategy and that the determination of this strategy depends on whether the firm can achieve very high volumes or satisfy unique and special customer requirements.

Source: Bill Gates: *Business @ The Speed of Thought* (New York: Warner Books, 1999) p. 9.

---

[4]   See "Intel Drops Plans for New Chip, Heightening Strategy Concerns," *The Wall Street Journal*, October 2, 2000.

Strengths and weaknesses are most easily identified by looking inside the firm at its specific resources:

- **Product lines.** Are the firm's products innovative? Are the product offerings too wide or too narrow? Are there important and distinctive technological advances?

- **Management.** What is the level of experience and competence?

- **Research and development.** Is the firm ahead of or behind competitors? What is the outlook for important new products and services?

- **Manufacturing.** How competitive, flexible, productive, and technologically advanced are the current manufacturing processes? What plans are there for improvements in facilities and processes?

- **Marketing.** How effective is the overall marketing approach, including promotion, selling, and advertising?

- **Strategy.** How clearly defined, communicated, and effectively implemented is corporate strategy?

Opportunities and threats are identified by looking outside the firm. Opportunities are important favorable situations in the firm's environment. Demographic trends, changes in regulatory matters, and technological changes in the industry might provide significant advantages or disadvantages for the firm. For example, the gradual aging of the U.S. population represents an advantage for firms that specialize in products and services for the elderly. In contrast, threats are major unfavorable situations in the firm's environment. These might include the entrance of new competitors or competing products, unfavorable changes in government regulations, and technological change that is unfavorable to the firm.

Opportunities and threats can be identified most easily by analyzing the industry and the firm's competitors:

- **Barriers to entry.** Do certain factors, such as capital requirements, economies of scale, product differentiation, and access to selected distribution channels, protect the firm from newcomers? Do other factors, including the cost of buyer switching, government regulations and policies that favor the firm, and educational and licensing restrictions, restrict competition? To what degree is the firm protected from competition from new entrants to the industry?

- **Intensity of rivalry among competitors.** Intense rivalry can be the result of high entry barriers, specialized assets (and therefore limited flexibility for a firm in the industry), rapid product innovation, slow growth in total market demand, or significant overcapacity in the industry. How intense is the overall industry rivalry facing the firm?

- **Pressure from substitute products.** Will the presence of readily substitutable products increase the intensity level of the firm's competition?

How Does the Motion Picture Industry Compete?

Think about this for a minute. Which competitive strategy—cost leadership or differentiation—would you as a producer of movies for theatres and television choose to be most profitable and successful? Clearly what brings a moviegoer to one film rather than another is not the price since most newly released feature films have the same ticket price in a given area. In contrast, the promise of entertainment—a differentiating feature—attracts the consumer.

Edgard Bronfman, Jr., CEO of Seagram and head of Universal Studios, has complained that the studios cannot charge a cost-based ticket price although films differ greatly in production cost, for example, from $200 million for *Titanic* to $3 million for *The Full Monty*. If ticket prices were to follow costs, *Titanic* would have been priced at almost $20, but *The Full Monty* would have cost only about a quarter.

Source: "If Tickets Reflected the Cost of Movies," *Business Week*, April 20, 1998.

- **Bargaining power of customers**. The greater the bargaining power of the firm's customers, the greater the level of competition facing the firm. Bargaining power of customers is likely higher if switching costs are relatively low and if the products are not differentiated.

- **Bargaining power of suppliers.** The greater the bargaining power of a firm's suppliers, the greater the overall level of competition facing the firm. The bargaining power of suppliers is higher when a few large firms dominate the group of suppliers and when these suppliers have other good outlets for their products.

SWOT analysis guides the strategic analysis by focusing attention on the strengths, weaknesses, opportunities, and threats critical to the company's success. By carefully identifying the critical success factors in this way, executives and managers can discover differences in viewpoints. For example, what some managers might view as a strength others might view as a weakness. SWOT analysis therefore also serves as a means for obtaining greater understanding and perhaps consensus among managers regarding the factors that are crucial to the firm's success. In addition, a careful consideration of its CSFs will lead to the identification of the firm's appropriate overall strategy. The ultimate objectives of the SWOT analysis, then, are to identify the overall strategy and the CSFs of the firm and to begin to develop a consensus among executives and managers regarding them.

Cost, Quality, and Time   Many firms find that a consideration of critical success factors yields a renewed focus on the three key factors: cost, quality, and speed of product development and product delivery. Increasingly, firms find that they must compete effectively on each of these three factors.[5] Consumer expectations are very high for quality, cost, and speed. Retail businesses such as Wal-Mart and Home Depot succeed

---

Globalization, Strategy, and Exchange Rates: The Euro

Since January 1999, the euro has been used as the common currency of many European countries. For the first 20 months following its introduction, the euro steadily lost about 25 percent in its value relative to the U.S. dollar, creating two types of strategic issues for U.S. and European firms.* One issue is that the falling euro has meant a higher cost for U.S. goods in euro countries, which has caused problems for U.S. exporters, especially for smaller firms. For example, Hatteras Yacht Company of New Bern, North Carolina, has lost some sales of its large boats to European customers. Other compa-

---

*The Economic and Monetary Union (EMU) of Europe has 15 member countries: Austria, Belgium, Denmark, Finland, France, Germany, Greece, Ireland, Italy, Luxembourg, the Netherlands, Portugal, Spain, Sweden, and the United Kingdom. As of October 2000, all of these countries except Denmark, Sweden, and the United Kingdom had adopted the euro. The EMU is the long-term project for the economic unification of Europe. A major milestone in this effort was the creation of the euro, the new single currency for Europe, on January 1, 1999, by fixing exchange rates for adopting countries. For more information, see http://europa.eu.int/euro/; see also, "Euro's Drop Is Hardest for the Smallest," *The Wall Street Journal*, October 2, 2000, International Section, p. 1; and "As Euro Falls, U.S. Firms Don't Pounce," *The Wall Street Journal*, September 18, 2000, p. A25.

nies, such as Vermeer Manufacturing Company (of Pella, Iowa), maker of agricultural and industrial machines, have adopted dealer incentives to reduce the effect of the euro's change on its European customers. Larger firms, such as McDonald's, have for many years protected overseas profits by hedging the exchange rates, that is, buying and selling overseas currencies at fixed prices to guarantee a given exchange rate in its business transactions. Of course, the issue is reversed if the dollar were falling relative to the euro, producing an advantage for the U.S. exporter.

The second strategic issue is that the falling euro causes those holding U.S. dollars to favor purchases in these European countries. This means that U.S. firms have the opportunity to make strategically beneficial investments in European companies at a favorable net cost, considering the exchange rate. The message is that firms, small or large, with a significant global component to their business must plan strategically for dealing with the effects of changing exchange rates on their business.

---

[5]   This point is made in Robin Cooper's concept of the confrontation strategy based on quality, price, and functionality (Robin Cooper, *When Lean Enterprises Collide* [Boston: Harvard Business School Press, 1995]).

by providing high-quality goods at low prices in a timely manner. Suppliers to these firms expect to meet very high standards of quality (including inspections by the retailer at the manufacturer's plant) and to meet increasingly demanding delivery terms, in many cases delivering product directly to the retail location, bypassing any warehousing operation. Cost, time, and quality are discussed in greater detail in Part Two.

Measures for Critical Success Factors

The second step in the process of identifying a competitive strategy follows the identification of the firm's CSFs.

> **Step 2.** Develop relevant and reliable measures for the CSFs identified in the first step.

Developing measures for the CSFs involves a careful study of the firm's business processes. Product development, manufacturing, marketing, management, and financial functions are investigated to determine in which specific ways these functions contribute to the firm's success. The objective at this step is to determine the specific measures that will allow the firm to monitor its progress toward achieving its strategic goals. Exhibit 2–7 lists sample CSFs and ways in which they might be measured.

Success Through Focus on Time: Toyota Motor Company

When a fire in the manufacturing plant of a supplier destroyed the main source of brake parts for Toyota in 1997, experts expected Toyota's own manufacturing plants to be down for several days or weeks waiting for a new source for the critical parts. Because Toyota has developed a close-knit family of suppliers over the years, however, it was able to use this large support system of 36 suppliers (including a sewing machine company that had never made car parts) to replace the lost manufacturing capacity within five days, a remarkably fast recovery. Toyota clearly showed that it could avoid the risk of relying on suppliers, as in this case, by building a loyal network of a closely knit family of suppliers that would come to Toyota's aid in a crisis. All the members of the "family" knew how important it was to recover Toyota production as quickly as possible.

Source: "Toyota's Fast Rebound after Fire at Supplier Shows Why It Is Tough," *The Wall Street Journal*, May 8, 1997, p. 1.

CEO Strategies for Success

The Gallop Organization recently surveyed chief executive officers, presidents, and owners of firms with 100 or more employees, asking what was most important in their firms for competitive advantage and success. The results follow:

Critical Success Factor	Percentage Choosing This Factor as Most Important
Customer service	27%
Product (or service) quality	25
Operating efficiency	18
Communication and information technology	9
Flexibility and adaptability	9
Innovation	7
Speed to market	2
Don't know	3

These responses tell us not only what the heads of these firms view as critical success factors but also something about the firms' strategies. Some of these CSFs, such as customer service, speed to market, and innovation, are consistent with the differentiation strategy; operating efficiency is consistent, however, with the cost leadership strategy. The other CSFs could be associated with either type of strategy.

Source: *USA Today*, August 18, 1999, p. 1.

Exhibit 2–7	Measuring Critical Success Factors

Critical Success Factor	How to Measure the CSF
Financial Factors	
• Profitability	Earnings from operations, earnings trend
• Liquidity	Cash flow adequacy, trend in cash flow, interest coverage, asset turnover, inventory turnover, receivables turnover
• Sales	Level of sales in critical product groups, sales trend, percent of sales from new products, sales forecast accuracy
• Market value	Share price
Customer Factors	
• Customer satisfaction	Customer returns and complaints, customer survey
• Dealer and distributor	Coverage and strength of dealer and distributor channel relationships
• Marketing and selling	Trends in sales performance, training, market research activities
• Timeliness of delivery	On-time delivery performance, time from order to customer receipt
• Quality	Customer complaints, warranty expense
Internal Business Processes	
• Quality	Number of defects, number of returns, customer survey, amount of scrap, amount of rework, field service reports, warranty claims, vendor quality defects
• Productivity	Cycle time (from raw materials to finished product); labor efficiency; machine efficiency; amount of waste, rework, and scrap
• Flexibility	Setup time, cycle time
• Equipment readiness	Downtime, operator experience, machine capacity, maintenance activities
• Safety	Number of accidents, effects of accidents
Learning and Innovation	
• Product innovation	Number of design changes, number of new patents or copyrights, skills of research and development staff
• Timeliness of new product	Number of days over or under the announced ship date
• Skill development	Number of training hours, amount of skill performance improvement
• Employee morale	Employee turnover, number of complaints, employee survey
• Competence	Rate of turnover; training; experience; adaptability; financial and operating performance measures
Other Factors	
• Governmental relations	Number of violations, community service activities

Information Systems for Critical Success Factors: The Balanced Scorecard

The final step in identifying competitive advantage follows the development of measures for the firm's CSFs.

Step 3. Develop an information system in the form of a balanced scorecard for supporting the firm's overall strategy and for reporting critical success factors to appropriate managers.

A starting point in developing the strategic information system is to consider the firm's competitive strategy. For example, if its strategy is cost leadership, the information system should record and report concise quantitative information that will assist in cost control. This involves monitoring the manufacturing and service operations where the costs are incurred. The methods used to provide this type of information are explained in Part Five.

On the other hand, if the firm's strategy is to succeed through product differentiation, the information system should focus on activities related to coordination and performance evaluation at the management level where product design and enhancement decisions are made. The methods used to provide this type of information are explained in Part Six of the book. These ideas are summarized in Exhibit 2–8.

Once the focus of the information system has been determined based on the firm's strategy, the relevant critical success factors are measured, collected, and reported, often in the form of a balanced scorecard. It serves as an action plan, a basis for implementing the strategy expressed in the CSFs. Because of its broad, strategic role, the balanced scorecard includes all of the firm's critical success factors, which, as noted in Exhibits 2–4 and 2–7, are typically shown in four areas: (1) financial performance, (2) customer satisfaction, (3) internal business processes, and (4) learning and innovation. Each group of CSFs in the balanced scorecard summarizes the firm's performance for that strategic objective (see Exhibit 2–9).

The design of the balanced scorecard, as for any information system, should consider management requirements for the information, including its timelines, accuracy, confidentiality, and appropriate organizational level within the firm to address the selected critical success factor. For example, if the organization structure is based on relatively autonomous teams, the balanced scorecard should focus on team performance when appropriate. Alternatively, in the hierarchical organization, the balanced scorecard should have upward and downward information flows within the hierarchy, and the CSFs should be linked within the hierarchy.

Exhibit 2–10 illustrates how a corporate-level CSF such as quality (as measured in part by warranty return rate) can be linked to CSFs at each level in the hierarchy of manufacturing management.[6] At the corporate level, the CEO and board of directors are concerned with the warranty return rate; the vice president of manufacturing deals with specific CSFs, each of which can be linked to the reduction of the warranty

Exhibit 2–8	Effects of Competitive Strategy on Required Skills, Reporting Systems, and Cost Management Systems		
Strategy	**Required Skills and Resources**	**Organization and Reporting Requirements**	**Strategic Cost Management System for This Strategy is Found in**
Cost leadership	Substantial capital investment and access to capital Process engineering skills Intense supervision of labor Products designed for ease of manufacture	Tight cost control Frequent, detailed control reports Structured organization and policies Incentives based on meeting strict quantitative targets	Part Five: Operational Control
Differentiation	Strong marketing abilities Product engineering Corporate reputation for quality or technological leadership Long tradition in the industry or unique skills drawn from other businesses	Strong coordination among functions: research, product development, manufacturing, and marketing	Part Six: Management Control

Source: Michael E. Porter, *Competitive Advantage* (New York: Free Press, 1985), p. 40.

---

[6] M. E. Beischel and K. R. Smith, "Linking the Shop Floor to the Top Floor," *Management Accounting*, October 1991, p. 27.

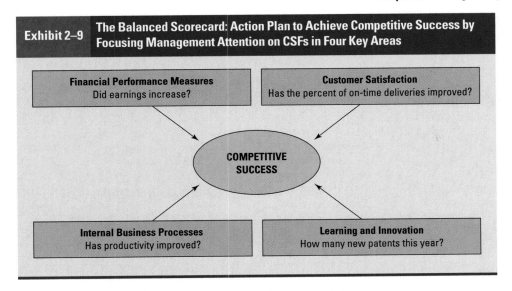

Exhibit 2–9 The Balanced Scorecard: Action Plan to Achieve Competitive Success by Focusing Management Attention on CSFs in Four Key Areas

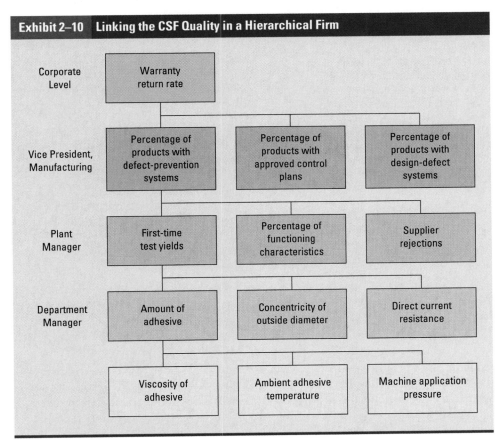

Exhibit 2–10 Linking the CSF Quality in a Hierarchical Firm

return rate, for example, the percentage of products with defect-prevention systems. Similarly, the plant managers have CSFs that can be linked to those of the manufacturing vice president. In the same manner, operations on the shop floor can be linked to the overall corporate CSF of reducing warranty returns.

A final consideration is that the development and reporting of CSFs must be linked to the firm's financial objectives. For example, if quality is a corporate goal, making the warranty return rate a relevant quality-related CSF, the strategic information system should develop relevant information about the costs and benefits of

Global Automakers' Winning Strategy

Competitive advantage in the global sales of autos has produced some high drama in recent years as the world's largest automakers seek to increase their global reach. In one such transaction, Ford Motor Co. purchased Britain's Rover Group Ltd. from Bayerische Motoren Werke AG (BMW). In 1994, BMW had purchased Rover, a well-known maker of luxury autos and SUVs, with the intention of achieving firmwide economies of scale and meeting the tightening European fuel-economy standards. BMW spent billions of dollars trying to improve manufacturing efficiency at Rover and trying to develop a coherent brand strategy for the Rover line that linked effectively with BMW's fleet at that

time. The unsuccessful efforts led to the sale of the Rover line to Ford.

Ford hopes that the Rover brand will fit well with its corporate strategy: to build profits from up-scale brands based on a low-volume, high-margin business. The Rover SUV is expected to sell to more affluent customers than Ford's current SUVs. The brand should also complement Ford's current luxury brands, Jaguar, Volvo, and Aston Martin.

Source: " Ford Grabs Prize as Losses Force BMW to Sell Rover," *Business Week*, March 17, 2000; and "The World Is Not Always Your Oyster," *Business Week*, October 30, 1995, p. 132.

Sustainable Development and the Balanced Scorecard at Royal Dutch/Shell

Royal Dutch/Shell Companies (Shell) uses a version of the balanced scorecard concept to define its business strategy and to report its performance in achieving this strategy. Shell is a global company operating in 135 countries with almost 100,000 employees, delivering a wide variety of products in the oil, chemical, and related industries. The firm's strategy is based on the principle of sustainable development, which in broad terms means that it is dedicated to developing natural capital, promoting economic prosperity, and developing social capital in all the countries in which it operates. Using the balanced scorecard, this broad principle is implemented by measuring and improving critical success factors grouped into four categories (the CSF list is partial):

- Economic measures.
    - —Crude oil prices.
    - —Operating profit.
    - —Total debt ratio.
    - —Net income.
- Environmental measures.
    - —Greenhouse gas emissions.
    - —Carbon dioxide emissions.

- —Emissions of nitrogen oxides.
- —Total number of spills of oil and chemical products.
- Social measures.
    - —Number of countries using procedures to ensure equal employment opportunities.
    - —Gender diversity, by management level.
    - —Number of countries screening against the use of child labor.
    - —Number of health and safety incidents.
- Shell employees and partners/business integrity and business principles.
    - —Number of reported cases of bribery.
    - —Number of countries with a screening process for compliance with Shell business principles.
    - —Number of responses to the "Tell Shell" program.

These CSFs were reported in the Shell 2000 annual report; many were verified by independent auditors.

Source: The Royal Dutch/Shell Group of Companies Annual Report 2000; and its website, www.shell.com.

reducing the warranty return rate. One element to consider is what net impact will the warranty return rate have on short- and long-term earnings. The strategic management of the firm requires managers to attend to CSFs and monitor their progress in achieving strategic goals by watching short- and long-term profitability goals and using the strategic information system.

Value-chain analysis is a strategic analysis tool used to identify where value to customers can be increased or costs reduced and to better understand the firm's linkages with suppliers, customers, and other firms in the industry.

VALUE-CHAIN ANALYSIS

Value-chain analysis is a strategic analysis tool used to better understand the firm's competitive advantage, to identify where value to customers can be increased or costs reduced, and to better understand the firm's linkages with suppliers, customers, and other firms in the industry. The activities include all steps necessary to provide a competitive product or service to the customer. For a manufacturer, this starts with product development and new product testing, then to raw materials purchases and manufacturing, and finally sales and service (Exhibit 2–11). For a service firm, the activities begin with the concept of the service and its design, purpose, and demand and then moves to the set of activities that provide the service to create a satisfied customer. Although the value chains are sometimes more difficult to describe for a service firm or a not-for-profit organization because they might have no physical flow to visualize, the approach is applied in all types of firms. A firm might break its operations into dozens or hundreds of activities; in this chapter, it is sufficient to limit the analysis to no more than six to eight activities.

The term *value chain* is used because each activity is intended to add value to the product or service for the customer. Management can better understand the firm's competitive advantage and strategy by separating its operations according to activity. If the firm succeeds by cost leadership, for example, management should determine whether each individual activity in the value chain is consistent with that overall strategy. A careful consideration of each activity should also identify those activities in which the firm is most and least competitive.

The value-chain analysis focuses on the product's total value chain, from its design to its manufacture to its service after the sale. The underlying concept of the analysis is that each individual firm occupies a selected part or parts of this entire value chain.

The determination of which part or parts of the value chain to occupy is a strategic analysis based on the consideration of comparative advantage for the individual firm, that is, where the firm can best provide value to the ultimate consumer at the lowest possible cost. For example, some firms in the computer-manufacturing industry focus on the manufacture of chips (Texas Instruments) while others primarily manufacture processors (Intel), hard drives (Seagate and Western Digital), or monitors (Sony). Some manufacturers (IBM, Compaq) combine purchased and manufactured components to manufacture the complete computer; others (Dell, Gateway) depend primarily

◀**LEARNING OBJECTIVE 4**

Explain value-chain analysis and show how it is used to better understand a firm's competitive advantage.

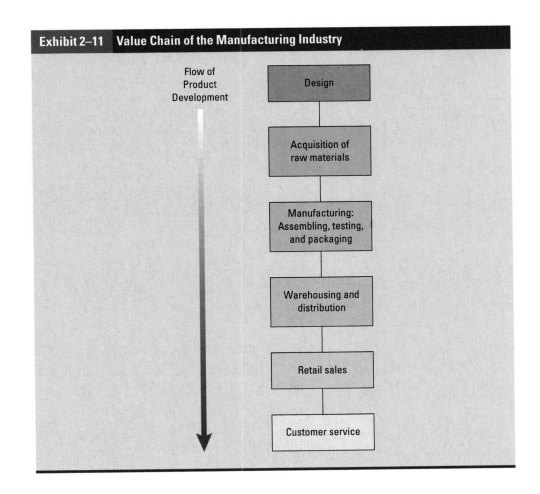

Exhibit 2–11   Value Chain of the Manufacturing Industry

on purchased components. In the sport-shoe industry, Reebok manufactures its shoes and sells them to large retailers; Nike concentrates on design, sales, and promotion, contracting out all manufacturing. In effect, each firm establishes itself in one or more parts of the value chain on the basis of a strategic analysis of its competitive advantage.

Value-chain analysis has three steps:

Step 1: Identify the Value-Chain Activities

> **Value activities** are activities that firms in the industry must perform in the process of converting raw material to final product, including customer service.

The firm identifies the specific **value activities** that firms in the industry must perform in the processes of designing, manufacturing, and providing customer service. Some firms are involved in a single activity or a subset of the total activities. For example, some firms only manufacture while others distribute and sell the product. See the value chain for the computer-manufacturing industry in Exhibit 2–12.

The development of a value chain differs depending on the type of industry. For example, the focus in a service industry is on operations and on advertising and promotion rather than on raw materials and manufacturing (an example of a service industry value chain is shown in self-study problem 1 at the end of the chapter). The activities also should be determined at a relatively detailed level of operations, that is, at the level of business unit or process just large enough to be managed as a separate business activity (in effect, the output of the process has a market value). For example, the completion of a chip or computer board is likely to be an activity (the output has a market), but packaging the chip or board is not likely to be an activity in a value-chain analysis.

Step 2: Identify the Cost Driver(s) at Each Value Activity

A *cost driver* is any factor that changes the level of total cost.[7] The objective in this step is to identify activities for which the firm has a current or potential cost advan-

Exhibit 2–12	Value Chain for the Computer-Manufacturing Industry*	
Step in the Value Chain	**Activities**	**Expected Output of Activities**
Step 1: Design	Performing research and development	Completed product design
Step 2: Raw materials acquisition	Mining, developing, and refining	Silicon, plastic, various metals
Step 3: Materials assembled into components	Converting raw materials into components and parts used to manufacture the computer	Desired components and parts
Stage 1	Converting, assembling, finishing, testing, and grading	Chips, processors, other basic components
Stage 2		Boards, higher-level components
Step 4: Computer manufacturing	Final assembling, packaging, and shipping the final product	Completed computers
Step 5: Wholesaling, warehousing, and distribution	Moving products to retail locations and warehouses, as needed	Rail, truck, and air shipments
Step 6: Retail sales	Making retail sale	Cash receipts
Step 7: Customer service	Processing returns, inquiries, and repairs	Serviced and restocked computers

*Although only seven activities are shown here for simplicity, the value chain for a manufacturer such as Compaq likely has dozens or perhaps hundreds of activities.

---

[7] The difference between a value activity and a cost driver activity is that the value activity is a higher level of aggregation; in effect, one or more cost drivers are likely to be involved in any one value activity.

tage. For instance, an insurance agency might find that an important cost driver is maintaining the records on customers' accounts. This strategic cost driver information can lead the agency to look for ways to reduce or outsource these costs, possibly by hiring an outside computer-service firm to handle the data processing tasks in order to reduce overall costs and maintain or improve competitiveness.

Step 3: Develop a Competitive Advantage by Reducing Cost or Adding Value

In this step, the firm determines the nature of its current and potential competitive advantage by studying the value activities and cost drivers identified earlier. In doing so, the firm must consider the following:

1. **Identify competitive advantage (cost leadership or differentiation).** The analysis of value activities can help management better understand the firm's strategic competitive advantage and its proper positioning in the overall industry value chain. For example, in the computer industry, certain firms (e.g., Hewlett-Packard) focus primarily on innovative design while others (e.g., Texas Instruments and Compaq) focus on low-cost manufacturing.

2. **Identify opportunities for added value.** The analysis of value activities can help identify activities in which the firm can add significant value for the customer. For example, food-processing plants and packaging plants are now commonly located near their largest customers to provide faster and cheaper delivery. Similarly, large retailers such as Wal-Mart use computer-based technology to coordinate with suppliers to efficiently and quickly restock each of its stores. In banking, ATMs (automated teller machines) were introduced to provide improved customer service and to reduce processing costs. Banks have begun to develop on-line computer technologies to further enhance customer service and to provide an opportunity to reduce processing costs further.

3. **Identify opportunities for reduced cost.** A study of its value activities and cost drivers can help a firm determine those parts of the value chain for which it is *not* competitive. For example, firms in the information technology business, such as Flextronics International Ltd., Solectron Corp., and SCI Systems, Inc., have become large suppliers of parts and subassemblies for computer manufacturers and other information technology manufacturers such as Hewlett-Packard, Sony, Compaq, and Cisco Systems Inc. The brand-name manufacturers have found that outsourcing some of the manufacturing to firms such as Flextronics reduces total cost and can improve speed and competitiveness.

4. **Exploit linkages among activities in the value chain.** The decision to provide an activity internally or to outsource it is sometimes influenced by the way that activity is affected by another activity in the value chain. For example, Iowa Beef Processors moved its processing plants to be near the feedlots in the southwest and midwest states, thereby saving transportation costs and reducing the loss in weight that the animals usually suffered during transportation. Firms such as Otis Elevator and Whirlpool Corporation have found that it is important to provide customer service internally since service representatives are sources of valuable information from customers; they can feed information regarding product weaknesses and desirable new features to product designers and manufacturing managers in a timely manner.

Additionally, value-chain linkages can explain the desirability of recent corporate mergers, such as ABC with Disney and NationsBank with Bank of America, or the acquisition of the investment bank Donaldson Lufkin & Jenrette Inc. by Credit Suisse Group of Switzerland. The combination of the firms provides greater access to global markets and a more desirable bundle of products and services for customers. Similarly, the Swiss food giant Nestle recently entered a joint venture with British-owned Haagen-Dazs to sell ice cream worldwide; the joint venture provides access for the Haagen-Dazs brand to convenience stores to which Nestle already supplies its own ice cream products.

In summary, value-chain analysis supports the firm's strategic competitive advantage by facilitating the discovery of opportunities for adding value for the customers and/or by reducing the cost to provide the product or service.

Value-Chain Analysis in Computer Manufacturing

The computer industry offers excellent opportunities to show value-chain analysis in action. The Computer Intelligence Company (CIC), a disguised representation of an actual company, manufactures computers for small businesses in the Raleigh–Durham, North Carolina, area. CIC has an excellent reputation for service and reliability as well as a growing list of customers. The manufacturing process consists primarily of assembling components purchased from various electronics firms plus a small amount of metalworking and finishing. The manufacturing operations cost $250 per unit. The purchased parts cost CIC $500, of which $300 is for parts that CIC could manufacture in its existing facility for $190 in materials for each unit plus an investment in labor and equipment that would cost $55,000 per month. CIC is considering whether to make or continue to buy these parts.

CIC can contract out to another Durham firm, JBM Enterprises, the marketing, distributing, and servicing of its units. This would save CIC $175,000 in monthly materials and labor costs. The cost of the contract would be $130 per machine sold for

---

How Firms Find Ways to Add Value and Reduce Cost

AMTRAK ADDS VALUE

Amtrak (National Railroad Passenger Corporation) provides passenger rail service throughout the United States and in parts of Canada. In a recent interview, Barbara Richardson, executive vice president, explains how the company decided to add value to the Acela Express, the United States' first 150 mph train:

> We learned some valuable lessons while we've reengineered our brand. For one thing, simply creating a new product and repackaging it isn't enough. New names, new colors, or new advertising images won't make you competitive. Acela potentially could gain us about 3 million additional customers in the Northeast alone. So we had to think at a much deeper level about what we wanted to convey. We should not only have to look different, we would have to act different. Our solution? Redesign our whole way of doing business to create an across-the-board, consistent service strategy to provide a seamless travel experience. We researched each step that customers take, from when they begin planning a trip to when they arrive at their final destinations. We made things such as ticket purchasing simpler, and we made our posted signs consistent from station to station.

GROUP-PURCHASING ORGANIZATIONS IN HOSPITALS REDUCE COST

Hospitals spend significant amounts for supplies and equipment, not only to purchase them but also to maintain the purchasing activity. Many hospitals have found that they can reduce spending significantly by contracting out all purchasing to group-purchasing organizations (GPOs) such as Premier, Inc., Amerinet, or Novation. As a GPO, Premier utilizes the economies of bulk purchasing for savings of 5% or more on commodity items and savings of 25% or more for high-tech equipment. Under increasing cost pressure, hospitals find such arrangements are helping them become more profitable. The six largest GPOs now handle contracts for more than 80 percent of the nation's acute-care hospitals. The downside of these arrangements is that they can restrict the hospital's access to innovative new products. GPO-approved vendors do not provide them.

Source: Lucy McCauley, "Relaunch," *Fast Company*, July 2000, p. 134. Reprinted from the July 2000 issue of *Fast Company* Magazine. All rights reserved. To subscribe, please call 800-542-6029 or visit www.fastcompany.com.

COST MANAGEMENT IN ACTION

Automakers and Parts Manufacturing: Spin Off the Parts?

Recently, both General Motors and Ford Motor Company have spun off their parts units, Delphi Automotive Systems and Visteon, respectively. Delphi and Visteon are now able to do business with other automakers. For example, Delphi makes instrument panels for Mercedes trucks. The stock market reacted to the news of these spin-offs enthusiastically. Why? What do you see as the potential costs and/or benefits?

(Refer to comments on Cost Management in Action at end of chapter.)

the average of 600 units sold per month. CIC uses value-chain analysis to study the effect of these options on its strategy and costs. The analysis is summarized in Exhibit 2–13.

The value-chain analysis in Exhibit 2–13 shows that CIC can save $108,000 per month ($355,000 – $247,000) by choosing option 2; thus, from a cost advantage, it

Value-Chain Analysis to Help Find Downstream Profits: U-Haul, Boeing, and General Electric

Some firms are finding that their traditional core business is under continuing profit pressure and that the route to profitability is to expand downstream. A good example is U-Haul, which, under intense price competition from Ryder and Hertz-Penske in the truck rental business, adopted the strategy of charging low rental rates to build volume and to simultaneously expand downstream by advancing the sale of its accessories: boxes, insurance, packaging materials, and other moving supplies. U-Haul barely broke even on truck rentals but was profitable on the accessory and other down-stream business. It effectively redefined the truck rental busi-ness by looking downstream for the profits.

Manufacturers such as Boeing and General Electric also use the value-chain concept to find profits downstream. For exam-ple, Boeing offers a number of products and services in addition to the aircraft it manufactures: financing, local parts supply, ground maintenance, logistics management, and pilot training. In the cyclical industry in which it operates, Boeing can find profits from them during the slack manufacturing times.

General Electric has connected its locomotive manufacturing business to its financing unit, GE Capital, to provide customer financing for not only locomotives but also boxcars and other rail assets. Other GE units profit by refurbishing and reselling boxcars and by developing advanced rail tracking systems. In effect, GE finds providing a broad range of services to the locomotive customer more profitable than manufacturing only.

Sources: Orit Gadiesh and James L. Gilbert, "Profit Pools: A Fresh Look at Strategy," *Harvard Business Review,* May–June 1998, pp. 139–47; and Richard Wise and Peter Baumgartner, "Go Downstream: The New Profit Imperative in Manufacturing," *Harvard Business Review,* September–October 1999, pp. 133–41.

Exhibit 2–13   Value-Chain Analysis for CIC Manufacturing Company

Value Activity	Option 1: Continue Current Operations	Option 2: Manufacture Components and Contract Out Marketing, Distributing, and Servicing Functions
Acquiring raw materials	CIC is not involved at this step in the value chain.	CIC is not involved at this step in the value chain.
Manufacturing computer chips and other parts	CIC is not involved at this step in the value chain; the cost of these parts is $200 to CIC.	CIC is not involved at this step in the value chain; the cost of these parts is $200 to CIC.
Manufacturing components, some of which CIC can make	CIC purchases $300 of parts for each unit.	CIC manufactures these parts for $190 per unit plus monthly costs of $55,000.
Assembling	CIC's costs are $250.	CIC's costs are $250.
Marketing, distributing, and servicing	CIC's costs are $175,000 per month.	CIC contracts out servicing to JBM Enterprises for $130 per unit sold.
Summary of Costs that Differ between Options		
	1. Unit costs for purchased components: $300 2. Monthly costs for marketing, distributing, and servicing: $175,000	1. Unit costs for manufacturing components ($190) plus cost of JBM contract ($130): $320 2. Monthly costs for labor and equipment: $55,000
	Total relevant costs for this option (assuming 600 units sold per month): $300 × 600 + $175,000 = $355,000 per month	Total relevant costs for this option (assuming 600 units sold per month): $320 × 600 + $55,000 = $247,000 per month

Note: Items in color are value-chain activities in which CIC operates.

prefers option 2. However, CIC also must consider its strategic competitive position. If its customers rely on CIC primarily for its service and reliability, then contracting out the marketing, distributing, and servicing functions is unwise; CIC should retain control over these critical success factors. Moreover, by moving to a strategy of making rather than buying the components, CIC is moving in the direction of competing on cost leadership with other computer manufacturers. It is unlikely that CIC can succeed at cost leadership because of its relatively small size and the presence of effective competitors already in this part of the value chain (IBM, Compaq, Dell, and Gateway, to name a few). Thus, option 2 pulls CIC away from its proven competitive advantage of emphasis on customer service. From a strategic view, option 1 is preferred, even though the costs are higher.[8] The value-chain analysis provides a useful framework for studying CIC's options and determining where it can reduce costs and where it can compete most effectively on the value chain.

This chapter has discussed three strategic cost management resources: strategic positioning, value-chain analysis, and the balanced scorecard. We can see the broad perspective in which the three strategic resources are linked in a comprehensive strategic analysis. The first, strategic positioning, is used (with SWOT analysis and the identification of CSFs) to develop the firm's strategy, that is, the policies, procedures, and approaches that will lead it to competitive success. The second, value-chain analysis, builds on the strategy developed in the first step by breaking it down into detailed activities. This provides the firm a way to better understand its strategy and, in particular, to identify activities that are (or are not) contributing to the firm's overall success. The final step, the use of the balanced scorecard, provides a way to implement the detailed strategy developed through strategic positioning and value-chain analysis by providing the measures and processes for evaluating the firm's achievement of the CSFs needed for success. The balanced scorecard provides even more; as a reflection of the firm's strategy, it is a concrete and dynamic basis for continual reassessment of the firm's strategy. Thus, a feedback loop exists from the balanced scorecard to strategic positioning as illustrated in Exhibit 2–14. Because of its key role in performance evaluation, we encounter the balanced scorecard again in Chapter 18.

STRATEGIC COST MANAGEMENT IN NOT-FOR-PROFIT ORGANIZATIONS

Strategic cost management is likely to serve a somewhat different role in not-for-profit or governmental organizations than in for-profit organizations. These organizations must satisfy funding authorities, political leaders, and the general public as to their effectiveness and efficiency. The balanced scorecard can be used to monitor and evaluate the organization's performance on the key internal processes (e.g., efficiency

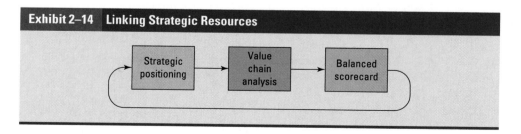

Exhibit 2–14 Linking Strategic Resources

Strategic positioning → Value chain analysis → Balanced scorecard

---

[8] The options facing CIC can also be viewed as two separate outsourcing decisions, one for the manufacture of components and the other for marketing, distributing, and servicing. Both favor outsourcing. The manufacturing decision favors outsourcing for a savings of $11,000 ($300 × 600 – $190 × 600 – $55,000), and the marketing, distributing, and servicing decision favors outsourcing for a savings of $97,000 ($175,000 – $130 × 600).

measures such as pounds of trash removed), customer satisfaction measures (with the public and political leaders as the customers), key financial measures (e.g., credit rating, fund balance), and human resources measures.

Additionally, value-chain analysis can be used to determine at what points costs can be reduced or value added in the organization's value chain. In contrast to the acquisition of raw materials or the process of advertising and promotion, the first step in the value chain for a not-for-profit or governmental organization is likely to be to develop a statement of the organization's broad social mission, including the specific public needs served. The second step is to develop resources for the organization, including both personnel and facilities. The third and fourth steps are to operate the organization and deliver its service to the public, respectively.

IMPLICATIONS OF STRATEGIC ANALYSIS FOR COST MANAGEMENT

Changes in the business environment have transformed the role of cost management. The introduction of new manufacturing and information technologies, the focus on the customer, the increase and growth of worldwide markets, and other changes require firms to develop strategic information systems to effectively maintain their competitive advantage in the industry. This means that cost management must provide appropriate types of information that have not been provided under traditional cost accounting systems.

◀ **LEARNING OBJECTIVE 5**

Understand the implications of strategic analysis for cost management.

First is a need for information that addresses the strategic objectives of the firm. Reports that focus only on operational issues, such as those often summarized in financial reports, no longer suffice. The critical success factors to which the firm must attend are diverse, and many of them relate to long-term issues such as new-product development, quality, customer relations, and other CSFs. Only by succeeding at these CSFs can the firm maintain its competitive advantage. The role of cost management then must be to identify, collect, measure, and report information on the CSFs reliably and in a timely manner. Many of the CSFs are nonfinancial measures, such as delivery speed, cycle time, and customer satisfaction. The cost manager is thus involved in developing both the financial and nonfinancial information reported in the balanced scorecard.

Second, the efforts to sustain a competitive advantage require long-term plans. SWOT analysis and value-chain analysis are used to identify the firm's strategic position in the industry, and the balanced scorecard is used to maintain that position. Success in the short term is no longer a measure of ultimate success since long-term success requires strategic, long-term planning and action.

Third, the strategic approach requires integrative thinking, that is, the ability to identify and solve problems from a cross-functional view. Instead of viewing a problem as a marketing problem, a production problem, or a finance and accounting problem, the integrative approach utilizes skills from many functions simultaneously, very often in a team setting. The integrative approach is necessary because the firm's attention is focused on satisfying the customers' needs, and all of the firm's resources, from all different functions, are directed to this goal.

Spurred by the increasing importance of strategic issues in management, cost management has adopted a strategic focus. The role of cost management has become that of a strategic partner, no longer simply a function of record keeping and reporting.

SUMMARY

The use of cost management facilitates a firm's strategic management. The management accountant has moved from a procedural, stewardship role to more of a strategic facilitation role, to a business partnership role in the firm. Michael Porter's work in strategic management explains the fundamentals of how firms compete. This grounding in the competitive environment of the firm determines the cost management role. That is, knowing how a firm competes and identifying its critical success factors are necessary to know how the firm's cost management system should be designed.

The two main types of competitive strategy are cost leadership and differentiation. Cost leadership is a strategy that relies on lowest-cost production and distribution; differentiation relies on outstanding quality or product features. Critical success factors are the specific, measurable aspects of the firm's products and operations, such as speed of service, safety of the workplace, and customer satisfaction, which, when achieved, lead to successful competition.

Three important strategic management techniques are SWOT analysis, the balanced scorecard, and value-chain analysis. SWOT analysis is a technique for identifying a firm's strategy and critical success factors based on an identification of its strengths, weaknesses, opportunities, and threats in the business environment. Value-chain analysis is a technique for determining the firm's strategic competitive advantage and for assisting the management accountant in identifying opportunities for reducing cost and/or adding value to the firm's products and services. The balanced scorecard is a cost management report that summarizes the critical success factors for management.

The implication of strategic analysis is that the management accountant must also adopt a strategic focus, that is, develop integrative skills for working with teams of operations, marketing, and other managers in the organization to lead the company to competitive success.

APPENDIX A

More about Strategy

Strategy is a complex topic for which there are many views. On a very basic level, some view strategy as the firm's broad purpose or direction (very much as we have used the concept of mission in the chapter); others see it as a way to determine a competitive position. Our approach, using Michael Porter's framework, is to use the latter view as a way to determine competitive positioning.[1]

The Boston Consulting Group (BCG) framework can be viewed as a mission-based approach, which argues that each firm or unit has one of the following three missions: to build, harvest, or hold. The *build mission* focuses the firm on revenue growth and market share; earnings and other goals are secondary. The *harvest mission* implies a short-term focus on increasing current earnings and cash flows. The *hold strategy* seeks to protect the firm's current competitive position.[2]

Again, our approach in this text is based on strategy as competitive positioning, for which Michael Porter's work is the key resource. Others have extended and clarified his concepts in important ways, as has Porter himself.[3] His 1996 extension of the orig-

---

[1] The distinction between strategy as mission and strategy as competitive positioning is handled very well by Robert Simons, *Levers of Control* (Cambridge Mass.: Harvard Business School Press, 1995), chap. 1; and John K. Shank and Vijay Govindarajan, *Strategic Cost Management* (New York: Free Press, 1993), chap. 5. See also Porter, *Competitive Advantage*.

[2] For more on the BCG approach, see "The Product Portfolio," *Perspectives* (Boston, Mass.: The Boston Group, Inc, 1970); B. D. Henderson, *Henderson on Corporate Strategy*. (Cambridge, Mass.: Abt Books, 1979); and Shank and Govindarajan, *Strategic Cost Management*.

[3] For Porter's follow-up on his framework, see Michael E. Porter, "What Is Strategy?" *Harvard Business Review*, November–December 1996, p. 61. For extensions and clarifications of the framework, see Shank and Govindarajan, *Strategic Cost Management*; Robert Simons, *Performance Measurement and Control Systems for Implementing Strategy* (Upper Saddle River, N.J.: Prentice Hall, 2000); Simons, *Levers of Control*; and Michael Treacy and Fred Wiersma, *The Discipline of Market Leaders* (Reading, MA: Addison-Wesley, 1995). A useful integration of the different concepts of strategy is presented by Kim Langfield-Smith, "Management Control Systems and Strategy: A Critical Review," *Accounting, Organizations and Society*, February 1997, pp. 207–232.

inal framework added a number of concepts. First, he advised managers not to confuse the concepts of operational effectiveness and strategy. Second, he added three new concepts of strategy: needs based, variety based, and access based. He explains and provides examples of each type.

Those who argue that, for many firms, cost leadership and differentiation are not separate strategies but must be achieved simultaneously take a somewhat different approach. Richard D'Aveni and Robert Gunther were among the first to advance this view or what they called *hypercompetition*. Similarly, Robin Cooper argued that, in an environment of lean competition, many firms compete simultaneously on cost, product features, and quality; he called this competition *confrontation*. These views have had an important influence on how managers think about strategy and choose strategies to employ. For example, Cooper shows how the confrontation strategy is consistent with the observed increased usage of target costing in certain industries.[4]

The most recent concept was advanced by Arnoldo Hax and Dean Wilde in what they called the *delta model*.[5] It adds the concept of competition via economic dominance, as shown in the competitive strategies of Microsoft, Intel, and Cisco Systems, and focus on customer economics, as shown by Saturn. To summarize, a comprehensive discussion of strategy goes beyond the goals of this text. The references here provide additional readings that present a deeper discussion of the different views of strategy.

KEY TERMS

Core competencies	37	SWOT analysis	37
Cost leadership	35	Value activities	46
Differentiation	35	Value-chain analysis	44
Strategy	32		

COMMENTS ON COST MANAGEMENT IN ACTION

Automakers and Parts Manufacturing: Spin Off the Parts?

The consensus of analysts and the business press is that Ford and General Motors were wise to spin off their parts manufacturing units, Visteon and Delphi, respectively. The reasons can be tied to a value-chain analysis of the automakers. The first reason is that the parts manufacturers are more cost efficient at operating the specialized design teams and manufacturing processes for these parts than the automakers. A second reason is that the spin off allows each automaker to look for the best technology at the best price by shopping around to other parts manufacturers. A third reason is that the spin off allows the automaker to reduce its total capital requirement and investment risk by divesting itself from the fixed costs associated with operating the parts units.

The new approach is consistent with another development in auto design, modular manufacturing, in which suppliers provide not just parts but entire sections of the car: the interior, the chassis, and so on. Automakers argue that handling the complexity of manufacturing today's auto is easier if the manufacturing is broken down into modules using the specialty design and manufacturing skills of these suppliers.

---

[4] Richard D'Aveni and Robert Gunther, *Hypercompetition: Managing the Dynamics of Strategic Maneuvering* (New York: Free Press, 1994); Robin Cooper, *When Lean Enterprises Collide: Competition through Confrontation* (Cambridge, Mass.: Harvard Business School Press, 1995); and Robin Cooper, "Costing Techniques to Support Corporate Strategy: Evidence from Japan," *Management Accounting Research*, 1996, pp. 219–46.

[5] Arnoldo C. Hax and Dean L. Wilde II, "The Delta Model: Adaptive Management for a Changing World," *Sloan Management Review*, Winter 1999, pp. 11–28.

The spin-off is a win-win strategy as well, since Delphi and Visteon will be able to compete more effectively for business from other automakers and to independently develop their technologies and manufacturing expertise.

Sources: "Maybe What's Good for GM Is Good for Ford," *Business Week*, April 24, 2000, p. 60; "GM: Modular Plants Won't Be a Snap," *Business Week*, November 9, 1998, pp. 168–72; and "Souping Up the Supply Chain," *Business Week*, August 31, 1998, pp. 110–12

SELF-STUDY PROBLEMS

(For solutions, please turn to the end of the chapter.)

1. Value-Chain Analysis

Jack Smith, a consultant for the Waynesboro Bulls AA baseball team, has been asked to complete a value-chain analysis of the franchise with a particular focus on a comparison with a nearby competing team, the Durham Buffaloes. Jack has been able to collect selected cost data as follows for each of the six steps in the value chain. Single-ticket prices range from $4.50 to $8.00, and average paying attendance is approximately 2,200 for Waynesboro and 5,000 for Durham.

Average Cost per Person at Scheduled Games

Waynesboro Bulls	Activities in the Value Chain	Durham Buffaloes
$ 0.45	Advertising and general promotion expenses	$ 0.50
0.28	Ticket sales: At local sporting goods stores and the ballpark	0.25
0.65	Ballpark operations	0.80
0.23	Management compensation	0.18
0.95	Players' salaries	1.05
0.20	Game-day operations: security, special entertainment, and game-day promotions	0.65
$2.76	Total cost	$3.43

Required   Analyze the value chain to help Jack better understand the nature of the competition between the Bulls and the Buffaloes and to identify opportunities for adding value and/or reducing cost at each activity.

Ethics

2. Competitive Strategy, Ethics

Frank Sills, the CEO and founder of Enviro-Wear, is facing the first big challenge to his young company. He began the company on the principle of environmental consciousness in the manufacture of sports and recreation wear. His idea was to develop clothing that would appeal to active people concerned about quality, waste in manufacturing and packaging, and the environmental impact of manufacturing the goods they purchased. Starting with a small shop in Zebulon, North Carolina, Frank was able to develop his small business through strategic alliances with mail-order merchandisers and through effective public relations about his environmentally concerned processes. A special advantage for the young firm was Frank's knowledge of accounting and his prior experience as a CPA in a national public accounting firm and as the controller of a small manufacturing firm. He is also a certified management accountant.

Enviro-Wear had reached $25,000,000 in sales in its sixth year when a disastrous set of events put the firm and its prospects in a tailspin. A news reporter overheard one of the key sales managers telling jokes about the poor quality of the firm's clothing, and the story spread quickly. At the same time, rumors (largely unfounded) spread that the firm was not really as environmentally conscious in its manufacturing and packaging as it claimed. The result was an immediate decline in sales; some retailers even returned goods.

Frank intends to fire the manager and publicly deny any association with the manager's comments and to defend the firm's environmental record.

Required

1. On the basis of Porter's analysis of strategic competitive advantage, what type of competitive strategy has Enviro-Wear followed? What type of strategy should it follow in the future?

2. What are the ethical issues involved in the case? How would you resolve them?

QUESTIONS

2–1 Identify and explain the two types of competitive strategy.

2–2 Identify three or four well-known firms that succeed through cost leadership.

2–3 Identify three or four well-known firms that succeed through product differentiation.

2–4 How are the three strategic resources—strategic positioning, the value chain, and the balanced scorecard—linked in a comprehensive strategic analysis?

2–5 Explain the process of identifying a competitive advantage for a firm.

2–6 What is the meaning of "getting stuck in the middle" in the context of competitive strategy? How does such a situation arise?

2–7 What is SWOT analysis? For what is it used?

2–8 What is the role of the cost manager regarding nonfinancial performance measures such as delivery speed and customer satisfaction?

2–9 Explain the difference between short-term and long-term performance measures, and give two or three examples of each.

2–10 What is a critical success factor? What is its role in strategic management and in cost management?

2–11 Identify four or five potential critical success factors for a manufacturer of industrial chemicals. Explain why you consider those factors critical for the firm to be successful.

2–12 Identify four or five potential critical success factors for a large savings and loan institution.

2–13 Identify four or five potential critical success factors for a small chain of retail jewelry stores.

2–14 Identify four or five potential critical success factors for a large retail discount store that features a broad range of consumer merchandise.

2–15 Identify four or five potential critical success factors for a small auto-repair shop.

2–16 What is a balanced scorecard? What is its primary objective?

2–17 Contrast using the balanced scorecard with using only financial measures of success.

2–18 What are the implications of strategic analysis for cost management?

2–19 Explain the uses of value-chain analysis.

EXERCISES

2–20 **SPECIAL ORDER, STRATEGY** Joel Deaine, CEO of Deaine Enterprises, Inc. (DEI), is considering a special offer to manufacture a new line of women's clothing for a large department store chain. DEI has specialized in designer women's clothing sold in small, upscale retail clothing stores throughout the

Strategy

country. To protect the very elite brand image, DEI has not sold clothing to the large department stores. The current offer, however, might be too good to turn down. The department store is willing to commit to a large order, which would be very profitable to DEI, and the order would be renewed automatically for two more years, presumably to continue after that point.

Required Analyze the choice Joel faces based on a competitive analysis.

Strategy

2–21 STRATEGY, COMPETITIVE ADVANTAGE In the mid-1970s, a large retailer of auto parts, Best Parts, Inc. (BPI), was looking for ways to invest an accumulation of excess cash. BPI's success was built on a carefully developed inventory control system that guaranteed the availability of a desired part on demand 99 percent of the time and within one business day for the remaining 1 percent. The speed and quality of service set BPI apart from other parts dealers, and the business continued to grow.

On the advice of close friends and consultants, BPI's owner and CEO decided to invest a significant portion of the excess cash in a small chain of gift and craft stores in shopping malls.

Required Determine BPI's competitive advantage (cost leadership or differentiation) in the auto-parts business. Assess whether this competitive advantage will or will not facilitate success in the new venture.

PROBLEMS

Service

2–22 STRATEGY, BALANCED SCORECARD, HEALTH CARE Consumers, employers, and governments at all levels are very concerned about the rising costs of health care. As a result, health care systems nationwide are experiencing an ongoing demand to improve the efficiency of their operations. The health care industry faces significant challenges due to changing patient needs, reduced reimbursement, and the fierce competitive environment. The industry is experiencing consolidations through systemwide mergers and acquisitions as a way to streamline operating costs. Patients and payors are demanding a one-stop shopping approach. While improving operations is necessary, the quality of the health care delivered must not be jeopardized. The Medical University of Greenbelt is feeling the impact of the increasing penetration of its market by managed-care companies. As a result, management has been asked to develop a strategic plan to ensure that its funding sources will continue to meet the demands of its patients.

Because it is an academic medical center, the Medical University of Greenbelt's mission encompasses three components: clinical care, education, and research. Management must consider these competing objectives in the proposed plan:

1. What should the Medical University of Greenbelt's strategy emphasize?

2. Do you think a balanced scorecard could help ensure the success of the Medical University of Greenbelt? What advantages does a balanced scorecard have over a traditional approach?

3. Determine four or five critical success factors for each of the four areas within the balanced scorecard. Remember that in addition to patients, its employees, employers, suppliers/distributors, other training entities, community, and payors are considered customers.

4. What types of challenges will management face in implementing a balanced scorecard? How can employee buy-in be increased?

2–23 STRATEGIC POSITIONING Fowler's Farm is a 1,000-acre dairy and tobacco farm located in Chatham County, near Pittsboro, North Carolina. Jack

Strategy

Fowler, the owner, has been farming since 1982. He initially purchased 235 acres and has made the following purchases since then: 300 acres in 1985, 150 acres in 1988, dairy equipment and buildings worth $350,000 in 1988, and 315 acres in 1998. The cost of farmland has inflated over the years so that, although Jack has a total investment of $1,850,000, the land's current market value is $2,650,000. The current net book value of his buildings and equipment is $300,000, with an estimated replacement cost of $1,250,000. Current price pressures on farm commodities have affected Fowler's Farm as well as others across the country. Jack has watched as many of his neighbors either have quit farming or have been consolidated into larger, more profitable farms.

Fowler's Farm consists of three different operating segments: dairy farming, tobacco, and corn and other crops intended for livestock feed. The dairy farm consists of 198 milk-producing cows that are grazed on 250 acres of farmland. The crop farm consists of the remaining acreage that covers several types of terrain and has several types of soil. Some of the land is high and hilly, some of it is low and claylike, and the rest is humus-rich soil. Jack determines the fertilizer mix for the type of soil and type of crop to be planted by rules of thumb based on his experience.

The farm equipment used consists of automated milking equipment, six tractors, two tandem-axle grain bed trucks, and numerous discs, plows, wagons, and assorted tractor and hand tools. The farm has three equipment storage barns, an equipment maintenance shed, and a 90,000-bushel grain elevator/drier. The equipment and buildings have an estimated market value of $1,500,000.

Jack employs five full-time farmhands, a mechanic, and a bookkeeper and has contracted part-time accounting/tax assistance with a local CPA firm in Pittsboro. All employees are salaried; the farmhands and the bookkeeper make $25,000 a year, and the mechanic makes $32,000 annually. The CPA contract costs $15,000 a year.

In 2000, the farm produced 256,000 gallons of raw milk, 23,000 bushels of tobacco, and 75,300 bushels of corn. Jack sells the tobacco by contract and auction at the end of the harvest. The gross income in 2000 was $1,345,000, providing Jack a net income after taxes of $233,500.

Jack's daughter Kelly has just returned from college. She knows that the farm is a good business but believes that the use of proper operating procedures and cost management systems could increase profitability and improve efficiency, allowing her father to have more leisure time. She also knows that her father has always run the farm from his experience and "rules of thumb" and is wary of scientific concepts and management principles. For example, he has little understanding of the accounting procedures of the farm, has not participated in the process, and has adopted few, if any, methods to maintain control over inventories and equipment. He has trusted his employees to maintain the farm appropriately without using any accounting or operating procedures over inventories or equipment, preventive maintenance schedules, or scientific application of crop rotation or livestock management.

Required Identify and describe briefly the competitive strategy for Fowler's Farm and explain your choice.

2–24 VALUE CHAIN ANALYSIS

Required Develop a value chain of six to nine activities for Fowler's Farm based on problem 2–23.

2–25 THE BALANCED SCORECARD

Required Develop a balanced scorecard with three or more groups of CSFs for Fowler's Farm based on problem 2–23. Explain your choice of groups and identify four to five CSFs in each group. Make sure that your CSFs are quantitative and can be measured.

Strategy

2–26   STRATEGIC POSITIONING   Tartan Corporation has been manufacturing high-quality home lighting systems for more than 80 years. The company's first products in the 1920s—the classic line—were high-quality floor lamps and table lamps made of the highest-quality materials with features that other manufacturers did not attempt: multiple switches, adjustable heights, and stained glass. In the 1950s and 1960s, the company introduced a number of new products that were in demand at the time, including track lighting and lava lamps, which became the company's Modern line. In keeping with its brand image, Tartan ensured that these new products also met the highest standards of quality in the industry. A new customer style emerged in the 1960s and 1970s, which resulted in another new line of products, contemporary. It was followed in more recent years by two new product lines, Margaret Stewart and Western.

Jess Jones, the company's chief financial officer, had become concerned about the performance of some of the product lines in recent years. Although total sales were growing at an acceptable rate, approximately 10 percent per year, the sales mix was changing significantly, as shown in the following product line sales report. Jess was particularly concerned about the Classic line because of its sharp drop in sales and its high costs. Because of the high level of craftsmanship required for the Classic line, it always had higher than average costs for labor and materials. Furthermore, attracting and retaining the highly skilled workers necessary for this product line were becoming more and more difficult. The workers in the Classic line in 2000 were likely to be older and very loyal employees who were paid well because of their skill and seniority. These workers displayed the highest level of workmanship in the company and, some would argue, in the entire industry. Few newer employees seemed eager to learn the skills required in this product line.

Moreover, manufacturing capacity was experiencing an increasing strain. The sharper than expected increase in sales for the Western styles had created a backlog of orders for them, and plant managers had been scrambling to find the plant capacity to meet the demand. Some plant supervisors suggested shutting down the Classic line to make capacity for the Western line. Some managers of the Margaret Stewart line argued the same thing. However, eliminating the Classic line would make obsolete about $233,000 worth of raw materials inventory that is used only in the manufacture of Classic line products.

Tom Richter, the firm's sales manager, acknowledged that sales of the Classic line were more and more difficult to find and that demand for the new styles was increasing. He also noted that the sales of these products reflected significant regional differences. The Western line was popular in the south and west, and the Contemporary, Modern, and Stewart styles were popular nationally. The Classic line tended to have strong support only in the northeast states. In some sales districts in these states, Classic sales represent a relatively high proportion of total sales.

Kelly Arnold, the firm's CEO, is aware of these concerns and has decided to set up a task force to consider the firm's options and strategy in regard to these problems.

Product Line Sales Report

	Classic	Contemporary	Margaret Stewart	Modern	Western
1990	20%	33%	5%	40%	2%
1995	16	35	11	34	4
1999	14	33	14	33	6
2000	9	31	18	31	11

Required   Describe Tartan's competitive strategy. On the basis of this competitive strategy, what recommendation would you make to the task force?

2–27 VALUE CHAIN ANALYSIS

Required   Develop a value chain of six to eight items for Tartan Corporation described in problem 2–26. Why would the value chain be useful to a firm like Tartan?

2–28 THE BALANCED SCORECARD

Required   Develop a balanced scorecard with three or more groups of CSFs for Tartan Corporation described in problem 2–26. Explain your choice of groups and identify four to five CSFs in each group. Make sure that your CSFs are quantitative and can be measured.

2–29 STRATEGIC ANALYSIS   Jim Hargreave's lifelong hobby is racing small sailboats. Jim has been successful both at the sport and in the design of new equipment to be used on small sailboats to make them easier to sail and more effective in racing. Jim is now thinking about starting a mail-order business in his garage to sell products he favors as well as some he has designed himself. He plans to contract out most of the manufacturing for the parts and equipment to machine shops and other small manufacturers in his area.

Strategy

Required   Develop a strategic analysis for Jim's new business plan. What should be his competitive position; that is, how should he choose to compete in the existing market for sailboat supplies and equipment? How is he likely to use cost management information in building his business?

2–30 STRATEGIC ANALYSIS   Consider the following companies, each of which is your consulting client:

Service

1. Performance Bicycles, a mail-order company that supplies bicycles, parts, and bicycling equipment and clothing.

2. The Oxford Omni, a downtown hotel that primarily serves convention and business travelers.

3. The Orange County Public Health Clinic, which is supported by tax revenues of Orange County and public donations.

4. The Harley-Davidson motorcycle company.

5. The Merck pharmaceutical company.

6. St. Sebastian's College, a small, private liberal arts college.

Required   Determine each client's competitive strategy and related critical success factors.

2–31 STRATEGIC ANALYSIS, THE COMPUTER INDUSTRY   Compaq Corporation and Hewlett-Packard (HP) are two significant competitors in the computer industry, although they have somewhat different product lines and quite different approaches to competition. Both have a reputation for the highest-quality product and innovation. However, the ways they compete reflect some important differences. Compaq sustains competitive advantage by developing products with competitive functionality and quality while maintaining low cost. These products compete directly with those of other manufacturers in basic functionality. In contrast, HP puts the greatest focus on innovation; its products are innovative. These differences lead to differences in manufacturing and marketing practices. Compaq emphasizes low-cost manufacturing, high volume, and relatively few plant locations; HP has a larger number of small plants and a focus on product development and innovation rather than cost. In research and development, Compaq looks for ways to improve value and lower cost for standard products while HP spends its R&D dollar on developing new and innovative products. Although the product life cycle in both firms is relatively short, that of HP is somewhat shorter. Because HP tends to lead in product development, it moves on to new and advanced products when competitors catch up.

International

Strategy

Required

1. Identify and describe the competitive strategies of HP and Compaq.

2. Using Exhibit 2–12, which shows the value chain for the computer-manufacturing industry, identify where HP and Compaq fit in the industry. Which steps of the value chain are most important to HP? To Compaq?

3. How would your answer in requirement 2 differ if you were to assume that HP and Compaq operated exclusively in one country, the United States? What does your answer say about the importance of global issues in competitive analysis?

Strategy

2–32 STRATEGIC ANALYSIS, THE CAMERA INDUSTRY Olympus, Kodak, Canon, and other firms in the market for low-cost cameras have experienced significant changes in recent years. The rate of introduction of new products has increased significantly. Entirely new products, such as the digital camera, are coming down in cost, so they are likely to be a factor in the low-cost segment of the market in the coming years. Additionally, product life cycles have fallen from several years to several months. The new products in this market are introduced at the same price as the products they replace, but the new products have some significant advances in functionality, such as integrated flash, zoom lens, and "red-eye" reduction. Thus, there are price points at which the customer expects to purchase a camera of a given functionality. In effect, the camera manufacturers compete to supply distinctive and therefore competitive functionality at the same cost as that of the previous models.

The manufacturing process for Olympus, one of the key firms in the industry, is representative of the others. Olympus makes extensive use of suppliers for components of the camera. Working closely with the suppliers, not only in a supplier's manufacturing process but also in the supplier's design of the parts, ensures the quality of the parts. Each supplier is, in effect, part of a team that includes the other suppliers and Olympus's own design and manufacturing operations.

Required

1. How does this type of competition differ from the Porter framework of cost leadership and differentiation?

2. Develop a value chain for Olympus camera company. What are the opportunities for cost reduction and/or value enhancement for Olympus?

Strategy

2–33 STRATEGIC ANALYSIS, THE BALANCED SCORECARD, AND VALUE-CHAIN ANALYSIS; THE PACKAGING INDUSTRY Dana Packaging Company is a large producer of paper and coated-paper containers with sales worldwide. The market for Dana's products has become very competitive in recent years because of the entrance of two large European competitors. In response, Dana has decided to enter new markets where the competition is less severe. The new markets are principally the high end of the packaging business for products that require more technological sophistication and better materials. Food and consumer products companies use these more advanced products to enhance the appeal of their high-end products. In particular, more sturdy, more colorful, more attractive, and better-sealing packaging has some appeal in the gourmet food business, especially in coffees, baked goods, and some dairy products. As a consequence of the shift, Dana has had to reorient its factory to produce the smaller batches of product associated with this new line of business. This change has required additional training for plant personnel and some upgrading of factory equipment to reduce setup time.

Dana's manufacturing process begins with pulp paper, which it produces in its own mills around the world. Some of the pulp material is purchased from recycling operators when price and availability are favorable. The pulp paper is then converted into paperboard, which is produced at Dana's own plants or purchased at times from outside vendors. In most cases, the paperboard plants are located near the pulp mills. At this point in the manufacturing process, the paperboard might be coated with a plastic material, a special embossing, or some other feature. This process is done at separate plants owned by Dana. On occasion, but infrequently when Dana's plants are very busy, the coating and embossing process is outsourced to other manufacturers. The final step in the process is filling the containers with the food product or consumer product. This step is done exclusively at Dana-owned plants. Dana has tried to maintain a high reputation for the quality of the filling process, stressing safety, cleanliness, and low cost to its customers.

Required

1. Describe Dana Company's new strategic competitive position.

2. Develop a value chain for Dana. What are its opportunities for cost reduction and/or value enhancement?

3. Dana's management is considering the use of a balanced scorecard for the firm. For each of the four areas within the balanced scorecard, list two or three examples of measurable critical success factors that should be included.

2–34 **VALUE-CHAIN ANALYSIS**

Required Develop a value chain for the airline industry. Identify areas in which any given airline might find a cost advantage by modifying the value chain in some way. Similarly, identify areas of the value chain in which the airline might be able to develop additional value for the airline customer. For example, consider ways the ticketing operation might be reconfigured for either cost or value-added advantage.

2–35 **VALUE-CHAIN ANALYSIS** Sheldon Radio manufactures yacht radios, navigational equipment, and depth-sounding and related equipment from a small plant near New Bern, North Carolina. One of Sheldon's most popular products, making up 40 percent of its revenues and 35 percent of its profits, is a marine radio, model VF4500, which is installed on many of the new large boats produced in the United States. Production and sales average 500 units per month. Sheldon has achieved its success in the market through excellent customer service and product reliability. The manufacturing process consists primarily of the assembly of components purchased from various electronics firms plus a small amount of metalworking and finishing. The manufacturing operations cost $110 per unit. The purchased parts cost Sheldon $250, of which $130 is for parts that Sheldon could manufacture in its existing facility for $80 in materials for each unit plus an investment in labor and equipment that would cost $35,000 per month.

Sheldon is considering outsourcing the marketing, distributing, and servicing for its units to another North Carolina firm, Brashear Enterprises. This would save Sheldon $125,000 in monthly materials and labor costs. The cost of the contract would be $105 per radio.

Required

1. Prepare a value-chain analysis for Sheldon to assist in deciding whether to purchase or manufacture the parts and whether to contract out the marketing, distributing, and servicing of the units.

2. Should Sheldon (a) continue to purchase the parts or manufacture them and (b) continue to provide the marketing, distributing, and servicing or outsource these activities to Brashear? Explain your answer.

Strategy

2–36 STRATEGY, ETHICS The tire business is becoming increasingly competitive as new manufacturers from Southeast Asia and elsewhere enter the global marketplace. At the same time, customer expectations for performance, tread life, and safety continue to increase. An increasing variety of vehicles, from the small and innovative gas/electric vehicles to the large SUVs, place more demands on tire designers and on tire manufacturing flexibility. Established brands such as Goodyear and Firestone must look to new ways to compete and maintain profitability.

Required

Ethics

1. Is the competitive strategy of a global tire maker cost leadership or differentiation? Explain your answer.
2. What are the ethical issues, if any, for tire manufacturers?

2–37 STRATEGY, VALUE CHAIN In the late 1990s, the bike maker Cannondale Corp. faced a variety of key strategic issues. One was the firm's continued dependence on Shimano Inc. of Japan to supply many parts for its bikes, particularly the derailleur, brakes, and crankset. A particularly troublesome aspect of this situation was that Shimano's high-quality and highly innovative parts were relatively expensive. Cannondale wished to reduce its dependency on these outsourced parts. A second issue was the increasing competition from Trek Bicycle Corp and Specialized Bicycle Components Inc. for bicycles in the upper-end range of the market where Cannondale competed. Cannondale had built a successful business on the basis of high quality and innovative products. Its customers were bicyclists who expected the highest quality and most advanced features. Industry analysts predicted consolidation in the industry for manufacturers that use Shimano parts but cannot differentiate their products effectively; these bicycle makers will likely be forced to compete on price.

Required

1. Consider the use of Shimano parts as one aspect of the value chain for Cannondale. Describe Cannondale's current strategy. How should this strategy change, if at all, to compete effectively with Trek and Specialized?
2. Should Cannondale continue to outsource Shimano parts? Why or why not?

SOLUTIONS TO SELF-STUDY PROBLEMS

1. Value-Chain Analysis

The cost figures Jack has assembled suggest that the two teams' operations are generally quite similar, as expected in AA baseball. However, an important difference is the amount the Durham team spends on game-day operations, more than three times that of the Waynesboro Bulls. That difference has, in part, built a loyal set of fans in Durham where gate receipts average more than twice that of Waynesboro ($28,500 versus $12,350). The Buffaloes appear to have found an effective way to compete by drawing attendance to special game-day events and promotions.

To begin to compete more effectively and profitably, Waynesboro might consider additional value-added services, such as game-day activities similar to those offered in Durham. Waynesboro's costs per person are somewhat lower than Durham's, but its cost savings are probably not enough to offset the loss in revenues.

On the cost side, the comparison with Durham shows little immediate promise for cost reduction; Waynesboro spends on the average less than Durham in every category except management compensation. Perhaps this also indicates that instead of reducing costs, Waynesboro should spend *more* on fan development. The next step in

Jack's analysis might be to survey Waynesboro fans to determine the level of satisfaction and to identify desired services that are not currently provided.

2. Competitive Strategy, Ethics

1. Enviro-Wear's strategy to this point is best described as a differentiation strategy, with which Frank has been able to succeed by differentiating his products as environmentally sound. This approach has appealed to a sufficient number of sportswear customers, and Enviro-Wear has grown accordingly. However, given the unfortunate jokes made by the sales manager and the rumors, the differentiation strategy is unlikely to continue to work; the offense of the jokes and the disclosure of some discrepancies in the manufacturing methods will likely undermine the appeal of environmentally sound manufacturing. Frank must work quickly to maintain differentiation, perhaps through a quick response that effectively shows the firm's commitment to quality and environmental issues. If that fails, he should quickly decide what change in strategy is necessary for the firm to survive and continue to succeed. He should consider a new strategy, perhaps based on cost leadership. The cost leadership strategy would bring the company into competition with different types of firms, and Frank must determine whether Enviro-Wear could successfully compete in that type of market.

2. This case has a number of ethical issues that are especially important to Frank as a CPA and a CMA with previous experience in public accounting practice. He should try to identify and understand the different options and the ethical aspects of the consequences of each option. For example, should Frank deny all charges against the company? Should he undertake an investigation to determine what his other sales managers think (do they have the same view as the offensive sales manager)? Do the firm's manufacturing processes really live up to the claimed quality and environmental standards? The relevant ethical issue requires communicating unfavorable as well as favorable information and disclosing fully all relevant information that could reasonably be expected to influence a consumer's understanding of the situation. To disguise or mislead consumers and others would conflict with the professional standards with which Frank is very familiar.

Also at issue is whether it is appropriate to fire the offensive sales manager. Most would probably agree that the firing is appropriate since the sales manager has publicly put himself at odds with the firm's strategic goals. However, others might want to consider the consequences of the firing and its fairness to the employee.

Basic Cost Concepts

3

After studying this chapter, you should be able to . . .

1 Explain the cost driver concepts at the activity, volume, structural, and executional levels

2 Explain the cost concepts used in product and service costing

3 Demonstrate how costs flow through the accounts

4 Prepare an income statement for both a manufacturing firm and a merchandising firm

5 Explain the cost concepts related to the use of cost information in planning and decision making

6 Explain the cost concepts related to the use of cost information for management and operational control

Maker of such well-known brands as Tide detergent and Crest toothpaste, Procter & Gamble (P&G) is recognized as one of the leading consumer products companies in the world. It has achieved success through product excellence and continuous improvement.[1] One key area of continuous improvement is the firm's emphasis on cost reduction through product and process simplification. To accomplish this, P&G uses a concept that we study in this chapter: the influence of product and process complexity on overall costs. In the early 1990s, P&G had as many as 50 different varieties of some of its brands, including different size containers, flavors, and so on. In addition to variety, the number of trade promotions, discounts, rebates, and coupons that affected P&G's net price were complex. The high complexity in products and pricing increased manufacturing costs, inventory holding costs, selling and distribution costs, customer service costs, administrative and accounting costs, and other operating costs. Over a period of five years, P&G reduced its product variety by one-half, and its profits surged. P&G's message for consumer products companies is to compete with the best but watch out for product and process complexity!

The importance of product simplification to P&G is also reflected by its recent strategic decision not to complete a merger with the drug makers American Home Products Corp. and Warner-Lambert Co. At first glance, the marriage of these three powerful firms might seem to offer a good way to achieve market dominance and economies of scale. On second thought, however, would P&G's capabilities in developing and marketing consumer brands such as Tide detergent be a competitive advantage in developing and marketing drugs? The technologies and expertise from product development to product marketing and distribution are quite different. Moreover, P&G has established an enviable reputation as a consumer-goods company, but it does not have a reputation as a health-focused company (as, for example, does John-

---

[1] For further information on P&G's strategy and continuous improvement efforts, see James C. Collins and Jerry I. Porras, *Built to Last* (New York: Harper Collins, 1994); and "Make it Simple," *Business Week*, September 9, 1996, pp. 96–104. For additional background on P&G's merger decision, see "P&G's Cold Feet May Have Averted a Misstep," *Business Week*, February 7, 2000, p. 42; and "Procter and Gamble: Just Say No to Drugs," *Business Week*, October 9, 2000, p. 128.

son & Johnson). The firm is not likely to maintain a dual image. In fact, a successful strategy normally requires a single focused image in the marketplace, and the merger would dilute and confuse P&G's already excellent reputation as a consumer-products company. Again, simplicity and clarity of strategy are winners.

This chapter explains the importance of the key cost concepts used throughout the text. Of the four groups of key concepts, the first group consists of the basic concepts and relationships among cost objects and cost drivers (e.g., complexity as a cost driver and P&G's products as the cost objects). Each of the remaining three groups includes concepts related to the three management functions: product and service costing, planning and decision making, and management and operational control. The concepts related to the management function of strategic management are covered in Chapter 2.[2]

COST DRIVERS, COST POOLS, AND COST OBJECTS

LEARNING OBJECTIVE 1 ▶

Explain the cost driver concepts at the activity, volume, structural, and executional levels.

A **cost driver** is any factor that causes a change in the cost of an activity.

A critical first step in achieving a competitive advantage is to identify the key cost drivers in the firm or organization. A **cost driver** is any factor that has the effect of changing the level of total cost. For a firm that competes on the basis of cost leadership, management of the key cost drivers is essential. For example, to achieve its low-cost leadership in manufacturing P&G carefully watches the design and manufacturing factors that drive the costs of its products. It makes design improvements when necessary, and the manufacturing plants are designed and automated for the highest efficiency in using materials, labor, and equipment. For firms that are not cost leaders, the management of cost drivers may not be so critical, but attention to the key cost drivers contributes directly to the firm's success. For example, because an important cost driver for retailers is loss and damage to merchandise, most of them establish careful procedures for handling, displaying, and storing it.

A **cost** is incurred when a resource is used for some purpose.

A firm incurs a **cost** when it uses a resource for some purpose. For example, a company producing kitchen appliances has costs of materials (such as sheet metal and bolts for the enclosure), costs of manufacturing labor, and other costs. Often costs are collected into meaningful groups called **cost pools**. Individual costs can be grouped in many different ways, and therefore a cost pool can be defined in many different ways, including by type of cost (labor costs in one pool, material costs in another), by source (department 1, department 2, and so on), or by responsibility (manager 1, manager 2, and so on). For example, an assembly department or a product engineering department might be treated as a cost pool.

Cost pools are the meaningful groups into which costs are often collected.

A **cost object** is any product, service, customer, activity, or organizational unit to which costs are assigned for some management purpose. Products, services, and customers are generally cost objects; manufacturing departments are considered either cost pools or cost objects, depending on whether management's main focus is on the costs for the products or for the manufacturing departments. The concept of cost objects is a broad concept. It also includes groups of products, services, departments, and customers; suppliers; telephone service providers; and so on. Any item to which costs can be traced and that has a key role in management strategy can be considered a cost object.

A **cost object** is any product, service, customer, activity, or organizational unit to which costs are assigned for some management purpose.

Cost Assignment and Cost Allocation: Direct and Indirect Costs

Cost assignment is the process of assigning costs to cost pools or from cost pools to cost objects.

Cost assignment is the process of assigning costs to cost pools or from cost pools to cost objects. A **direct cost** can be conveniently and economically traced directly to a cost pool or a cost object. For example, the cost of materials required for a particular product is a direct cost because it can be traced directly to the product.

The materials cost is accumulated in cost pools (manufacturing departments) and

A **direct cost** can be conveniently and economically traced directly to a cost pool or a cost object.

---

[2] Useful information on cost terms is also available in the IMA's *Statement on Management Accounting No. 2*, "Management Accounting Terminology" (Montvale, N.J.: Institute of Management Accountants, June 1, 1983).

then is traced to each product manufactured, which is a cost object. Similarly, an airline's cost of preparing a passenger's meal is a direct cost that can be traced to each passenger (the cost object). For a direct cost, the cost driver is the number of units of that object, for example, the number of cartons of Tide produced by P&G, or the number of passengers on Flight 617 for Delta Airlines. Total direct cost increases directly in proportion to the number of cartons or passengers.

In contrast, there is no convenient or economical way to trace an **indirect cost** from the cost or cost pool to the cost pool or cost object. That is, the indirect cost is caused by two or more cost pools or objects but cannot be conveniently or economically traced directly to any one. The cost of supervising manufacturing employees and the cost of handling materials are good examples of costs that generally cannot be traced to individual products and therefore are indirect costs for the products. Similarly, the cost of fueling an aircraft is an indirect cost when the cost object is the individual airline customer since the aircraft's use of fuel cannot be traced directly to that customer. In contrast, if the cost object for the airline is the flight, the cost of fuel is a direct cost that can be traced directly to the aircraft's use of fuel for that flight.

> An **indirect cost** has *no* convenient or economical trace from the cost or cost pool to the cost pool or cost object.

Since indirect costs cannot be traced to the cost pool or cost object, the assignment for indirect costs is made by using cost drivers. For example, if the cost driver for materials handling cost is the number of parts, the total cost of materials handling can be assigned to each product on the basis of its total number of parts relative to the total number of parts in all other products. The result is that costs are assigned to the cost pool or cost object that caused the cost in a manner that is fairly representative of the way the cost is incurred. For example, a product with a large number of parts should bear a larger portion of the cost of materials handling than a product with fewer parts. Similarly, a department with a large number of employees should bear a large portion of the cost of supervision provided for all departments.

The assignment of indirect costs to cost pools and cost objects is called **cost allocation,** a form of cost assignment in which direct tracing is not possible, so cost drivers are used instead. The cost drivers used to allocate costs are often called **allocation bases.** The relationships between costs, cost pools, cost objects, and cost drivers in appliance manufacturing are illustrated in Exhibit 3–1 and Exhibit 3–2. This simplified example includes two cost objects (dishwasher, washing machine), two cost pools (assembly department, packing department), and five cost elements (electric motor, materials handling, supervision, packing material, and final product inspection). The electric motor is traced to the assembly department and from there directly to the two products. Similarly, the packing material is traced directly to the packing department and from there directly to the two products. In contrast, since the cost of final inspection has no cost pool, it is traced directly to each of the two products. The two indirect costs, supervision and materials handling, are allocated to the two cost pools (assembly and packing departments) and are then allocated from the cost pools to the products (the allocation bases are shown in Exhibit 3–2).

> **Cost allocation** is the assignment of indirect costs to cost pools and cost objects.
>
> **Allocation bases** are the cost drivers used to allocate costs.

Replacing Indirect Costs with Direct Costs in the Textile Industry: Pluma, Inc.

Pluma, Inc., of Eden, North Carolina, manufactures textile products including fleece and jersey active wear. The firm recently announced cost-cutting measures including the elimination of 90 to 100 jobs involving indirect manufacturing activities such as machine repair and maintenance, human resources, and materials handling. The measures were taken to make Pluma more cost competitive. Those whose positions were eliminated were offered direct labor positions, that is, jobs in activities directly involved in manufacturing the firm's products.

This case illustrates that a high level of indirect costs can be a sign of poor cost management. The indirect costs are necessary for the manufacturing process but do not add value directly to the product. A firm such as Pluma does well to continually review the nature and extent of its indirect costs to determine whether some of the indirect activities causing them can be deleted and to focus on the direct activities that provide benefit to the customer.

Source: "Pluma to Cut Indirect Jobs to Reduce Annual Labor Costs," *Greensboro News and Record,* October 14, 1998.

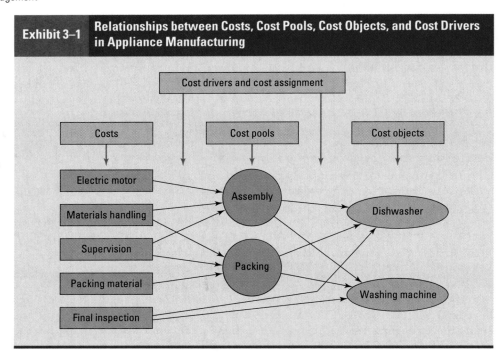

Exhibit 3–1 Relationships between Costs, Cost Pools, Cost Objects, and Cost Drivers in Appliance Manufacturing

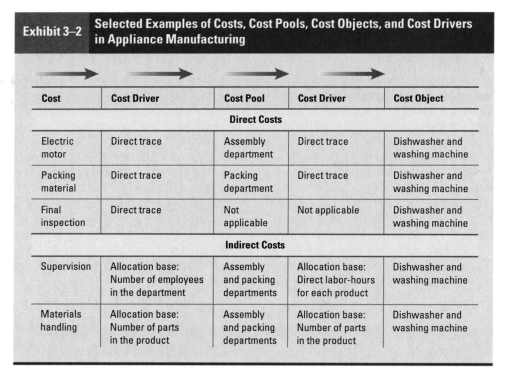

Exhibit 3–2 Selected Examples of Costs, Cost Pools, Cost Objects, and Cost Drivers in Appliance Manufacturing

Cost	Cost Driver	Cost Pool	Cost Driver	Cost Object
Direct Costs				
Electric motor	Direct trace	Assembly department	Direct trace	Dishwasher and washing machine
Packing material	Direct trace	Packing department	Direct trace	Dishwasher and washing machine
Final inspection	Direct trace	Not applicable	Not applicable	Dishwasher and washing machine
Indirect Costs				
Supervision	Allocation base: Number of employees in the department	Assembly and packing departments	Allocation base: Direct labor-hours for each product	Dishwasher and washing machine
Materials handling	Allocation base: Number of parts in the product	Assembly and packing departments	Allocation base: Number of parts in the product	Dishwasher and washing machine

Direct and Indirect Materials Costs

Direct materials cost includes the cost of materials in the product or other cost object (less purchase discounts but including freight and related charges) and usually a reasonable allowance for scrap and defective units (e.g., if a part is stamped from strip steel, the material lost in the stamping is ordinarily included as part of the product's direct materials).[3]

> **Direct materials cost** includes the cost of the materials in the product and a reasonable allowance for scrap and defective units.

---

[3] For additional information about the nature of direct materials cost, see *Statement on Management Accounting No. 4E,* "Practices and Techniques: Definition and Measurement of Direct Material Cost" (Montvale, N.J.: Institute of Management Accountants, June 3, 1986).

On the other hand, the cost of materials used in manufacturing that are not part of the finished product are **indirect materials cost.** Examples include supplies used by manufacturing employees, such as rags and small tools, or materials required by the machines, such as lubricant.[4]

Direct and Indirect Labor Costs

Direct labor cost includes the labor used to manufacture the product or to provide the service plus some portion of nonproductive time that is normal and unavoidable, such as coffee breaks and personal time. Other types of nonproductive labor that are discretionary and planned, such as downtime, training, and setup time, usually are included not as direct labor but as indirect labor.[5]

Indirect labor costs provide a support role for manufacturing. Examples of indirect labor costs include supervision, quality control, inspection, purchasing and receiving, materials handling, janitorial labor, downtime, training, and cleanup. Note that an element of labor can sometimes be both direct and indirect, depending on the cost object; for example, labor for the maintenance and repair of equipment might be direct to the manufacturing department where the equipment is located but indirect to the products manufactured in that department.

Although these examples of direct and indirect costs are from a manufacturing setting, the concepts also apply to service companies. For example, in a restaurant where the cost object is each meal served, the food and food preparation costs are direct costs, but the costs of purchasing, handling, and storing food items are indirect costs. Similarly, in professional services firms such as law firms or accounting firms, the professional labor and materials costs for providing client service are direct costs, but the costs of research materials, nonprofessional support staff, and training professional staff are indirect costs.

Other Indirect Costs

In addition to labor and materials, other types of indirect costs are necessary to manufacture the product or provide the service. They include the costs of facilities, the equipment used to manufacture the product or provide the service, and any other support equipment, such as that used for materials handling.

All indirect costs—for indirect materials, indirect labor, and other indirect items—are commonly combined into a single cost pool called **overhead.** In a manufacturing firm, it is called **factory overhead.**

Indirect materials cost refers to the cost of materials used in manufacturing that are not physically part of the finished product.

Direct labor cost includes the labor used to manufacture the product or to provide the service.

Indirect labor cost includes supervision, quality control, inspection, purchasing and receiving, and other manufacturing support costs.

All indirect costs are commonly combined into a single cost pool called **overhead** or, in a manufacturing firm, **factory overhead.**

Costs, Cost Pools, Cost Objects, and Cost Drivers at Pennsylvania Blue Shield

Costs	1st-Stage Cost Drivers	Activity Cost Pools	2nd-Stage Cost Drivers	Product Costs
• Personal service	– Number of people	• Claims processing	– Volume	• Podiatry
• Facilities & occupancy	– Square footage	• Beneficiary services		• Med Surg
• Data processing	– Hours	• Financial services	– Hours	• Dental
• Supplies & forms	– Resource usage			• Med Special
• Postage	– Unit times			• EMC
				• OCR
				• Paper

Source: Angela Norkiewicz, "Nine Steps to Implementing ABC," *Management Accounting,* April 1994, pp. 28–33.

---

[4]   For cost-benefit reasons, direct materials that are a very small part of materials cost, such as glue and nails, are sometimes not traced to each product but are included instead in indirect materials.

[5]   For additional information about the nature of direct labor cost, see *Statement on Management Accounting No. 4C,* "Practices and Techniques: Definition and Measurement of Direct Labor Cost," (Montvale, N.J.: Institute of Management Accountants, June 13, 1985).

Prime costs refer to direct materials and direct labor that are sometimes considered together.

Conversion cost refers to direct labor and overhead combined into a single amount.

The three types of costs—direct materials, direct labor, and overhead—are sometimes combined for simplicity and convenience. Direct materials and direct labor are sometimes considered together and called **prime costs**. Similarly, direct labor and overhead are often combined into a single amount called **conversion cost**. The labor component of total manufacturing costs for many firms that have highly automated operations is relatively low, and these firms often choose to place their strategic focus on materials and facilities/overhead costs by combining labor costs with overhead.

Types of Cost Drivers

Most firms, especially those following the cost leadership strategy, use cost management to maintain or improve their competitive position. Cost management requires a good understanding of how the total cost of a cost object changes as the cost drivers change. The four types of cost drivers are activity based, volume based, structural, and executional. Activity-based cost drivers are developed at a detailed level of operations and are associated with a given manufacturing activity (or activity in providing a service), such as machine setup, product inspection, materials handling, or packaging. In contrast, volume-based cost drivers are developed at an aggregate level, such as an output level for the number of units produced or the number of direct labor-hours used in manufacturing. Structural and executional cost drivers involve strategic and operational decisions that affect the relationship between these cost drivers and total cost.

Activity-Based Cost Drivers

Activity-based cost drivers are identified by using activity analysis, a detailed description of the specific activities performed in the firm's operations. The description includes each step in manufacturing the product or in providing the service. For each activity, a cost driver is developed to explain how the costs incurred for that activity change. For example, the activities and cost drivers for a bank are illustrated in Exhibit 3–3. The total cost to the bank is affected by the cost driver for each activity.

The detailed description of the firm's activities helps the firm achieve its strategic objectives by enabling it to develop more accurate costs for its products and/or ser-

Exhibit 3–3	Bank Activities and Cost Drivers
Activity	**Cost Driver**
Provide ATM service	Number of ATM transactions
Provide cashier service	Number of banking customers using cashier service
Open and close customer accounts	Number of accounts opened or closed
Advise customers on banking services	Number of customers advised
Issue traveler's checks	Number of requests for checks
Update customer account balances via computer	Number of accounts updated
Investigate unusual transactions	Number of transactions investigated; depends on management policy and procedure
Periodically test controls over cash and transactions processing	Number of tests; based on company policy and driven in part by number of new employees and prior experience with fraud and theft
Prepare applications for new loans (car, home, commercial, . . .)	Number of loan applications prepared
Process loan applications	Number of loan applications processed
Prepare approved loans and disburse funds	Number of loans approved
Mail customer statements	Number of accounts
Process interbank transfers of funds	Number of transfers
Respond to customer inquiries	Number of inquiries

vices. The activity analysis also helps improve operational and management control in the firm since performance at the detailed level can be monitored and evaluated, for example, by (1) identifying which activities are contributing value to the customer and which are not and (2) focusing attention on those activities that are most costly or that differ from expectations. These two benefits are achieved by activity-based costing and activity-based management, which are explained in Chapter 4.

Volume-Based Cost Drivers

Many types of costs are volume based, such as direct materials and direct labor. Total cost for a volume-based cost has a nonlinear relationship with the volume-based cost driver, which is the number of units of output for the product or service. As illustrated in Exhibit 3–4, at low values for the cost driver, costs increase at a decreasing rate, due in part to factors such as more efficient use of resources and higher productivity through learning. The pattern of increasing costs at a decreasing rate is often referred

---

Activities and Cost Drivers in Customer Service: Building Supplies and Services

Local businesses involved in constructing, remodeling, and repairing residential and commercial buildings rely on a variety of local distributors of building supplies, such as electrical and plumbing parts. These local distributors often also sell, rent, and service construction equipment.

Mahany Welding Supply distributes welding supplies and compressed gases in the greater Rochester, New York, area. Its selling and customer service costs include the costs of seven employees and a delivery truck, among others. Five of the seven employees are involved in sales or delivery and other activities; two perform the bookkeeping and accounting functions. An activity analysis completed by Mahany developed the following activities and cost drivers for the firm:

Activity	Cost Driver
Sales	Actual hours of salesperson's time
Purchasing	Number of invoices
Collections	Amount of sales dollars
Error checking	Number of invoices

Warehousing	Amount of sales dollars
Order filling	Amount of actual time
Billing	Number of invoices
Bookkeeping	Number of invoices
Advertising	Amount of sales dollars
Telephone	Amount of sales dollars
Legal and accounting	Number of employees; number of customers
Insurance	Amount of sales dollars
Rent and utilities	Amount of sales dollars

These cost drivers can be used in assigning the costs in each activity to selected products, customers, or personnel. The assigned costs are then the basis for determining the profitability of the products and customers and for assessing the profit contribution of each of the five employees involved in selling.

Source: Michael Krupnicki and Thomas Tyson, "Using ABC to Determine the Cost of Servicing Customers," *Management Accounting,* December 1997, pp. 40–46.

Exhibit 3–4 Total Cost and the Effect of Capacity Limits

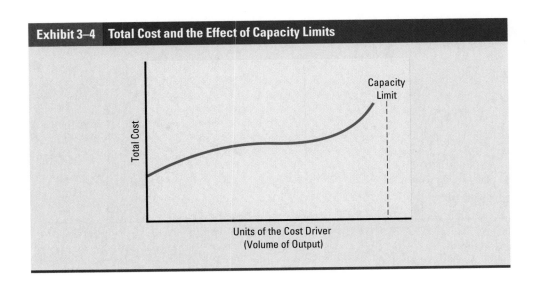

to as *increasing marginal productivity*, which means that the inputs are used more productively or more efficiently as manufacturing output increases.

At higher levels of the cost driver, costs begin to increase at an increasing rate, due in part to inefficiency associated with operating nearer the limit of capacity; the less efficient resources are now being used, overtime may be required, and so on. This cost behavior in the higher levels of the cost driver is said to satisfy the *law of diminishing marginal productivity*.

The nonlinear cost relationships depicted in Exhibit 3–4 present some difficulties in estimating costs and in calculating total costs since linear, algebraic relationships cannot be used. Fortunately, we are often interested in only a relatively small range of activity for the cost driver. For example, we might know in a certain instance that the *volume-based* cost driver will fall somewhere between 3,500 and 3,600 units of product output. We observe that within this range, the total cost curve is approximately linear. The range of the cost driver in which the actual value of the cost driver is expected to fall and for which the relationship is assumed to be approximately linear is called the **relevant range**.

> The **relevant range** is the range of the cost driver in which the actual value of the cost driver is expected to fall and for which the relationship is assumed to be approximately linear.

This simplification process is illustrated in Exhibit 3–5 and Exhibit 3–6. Exhibit 3–5 shows the curved actual total cost line and the relevant range of 3,500 to 3,600 units; Exhibit 3–6 shows the linear approximation of actual total cost; within the relevant range, the behavior of total cost approximates that shown in Exhibit 3–5. Note that the cost line above 3,600 and below 3,500 in Exhibit 3–6 is in red to indicate that this portion of the line is not used to approximate total cost because it is outside the relevant range.

Fixed and Variable Costs

> **Variable cost** is the change in total cost associated with each change in the quantity of the cost driver.

> **Fixed cost** is the portion of the total cost that does not change with a change in the quantity of the cost driver within the relevant range.

Total cost is made up of variable costs and fixed costs. **Variable cost** is the change in total cost associated with each change in the quantity of the cost driver. Common examples of variable costs are costs of direct materials and direct labor. In contrast, **fixed cost** is that portion of the total cost that does not change with a change in the quantity of the cost driver within the relevant range. *Total* fixed costs and *unit* variable costs are expected to remain approximately constant within the relevant range. Fixed cost is illustrated as the horizontal dashed line at $3,000 in Exhibit 3–7. Variable cost is $1 per unit, total cost is the upward-sloping line, and total variable cost is the difference between total cost and fixed cost. Total cost of $6,500 at 3,500 units is made up of fixed cost ($3,000) plus total variable cost (3,500 × $1 = $3,500); similarly, total cost at 3,600 units is $6,600 ($3,000 fixed cost plus 3,600 × $1 = $3,600 variable cost).

Fixed costs include many indirect costs, especially facility costs (depreciation or rent, insurance, taxes on the plant building, and so on), production supervisors' salaries, and other manufacturing support costs that do not change with the number of units pro-

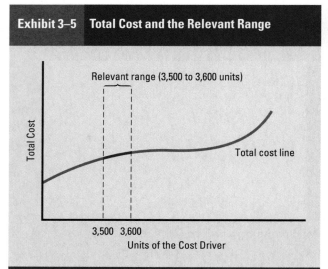

Exhibit 3–5 Total Cost and the Relevant Range

Relevant range (3,500 to 3,600 units)

Total Cost

Total cost line

3,500 3,600
Units of the Cost Driver

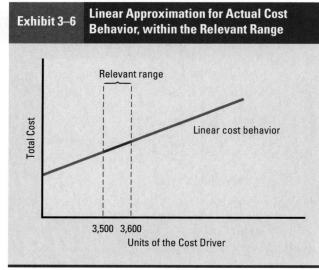

Exhibit 3–6 Linear Approximation for Actual Cost Behavior, within the Relevant Range

Relevant range

Total Cost

Linear cost behavior

3,500 3,600
Units of the Cost Driver

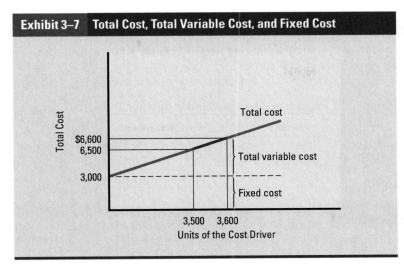

Exhibit 3–7   Total Cost, Total Variable Cost, and Fixed Cost

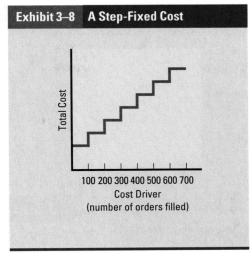

Exhibit 3–8   A Step-Fixed Cost

duced. However, some indirect costs are variable since they change with the number of units produced. An example is lubricant for machines. The term **mixed cost** is used to refer to total cost that includes costs for both variable and fixed components as illustrated.

The determination of whether a cost is variable depends on the nature of the cost object. In manufacturing firms, the cost object is typically the product. In service firms, however, the cost object is often difficult to define because the service can have a number of qualitative as well as quantitative dimensions. Let's develop cost objects for one type of service firm, a hospital, which could use a number of measures of output including the number of patients served, the number successfully treated, and so on. However, a common approach in hospitals is to use the number of patient-days since this measure most closely matches the way the hospital incurs costs.

It has often been said that all costs are variable in the long run; that is, with enough time, any cost can be changed. Thus, fixed costs do not vary *in the short run*. However, although time can be considered a cost driver as implied, we most often consider volume-based cost drivers from an operational perspective; that is, the cost driver is the number of units of output (sometimes labor-hours or machine-hours). Variable costs therefore are those for which total cost changes with changes in the level of output (or labor-hours or machine-hours).

> **Mixed cost** is the term used to refer to total cost when total cost includes both variable and fixed cost components.

Step Costs

A cost is said to be a **step cost** when it varies with the cost driver but does so in discrete steps (Exhibit 3–8). Step costs are characteristic of certain clerical tasks, such as order filling and claims processing. For example, if a warehouse clerk can fill 100 orders in a day, 10 clerks will be needed to process approximately 1,000 orders; as demand exceeds 1,000 orders, an eleventh clerk must be added. The steps correspond to specific levels of the cost driver for which an additional clerk is required; in effect, each step corresponds to one additional clerk. The steps will be relatively narrow if clerks are added for relatively small increases in the cost driver; the steps will be wider for large increases.

The management accountant's determination of whether a cost should be treated as a variable, fixed, or step cost is based on a consideration of how the choice affects the use of the information.

> A cost is said to be a **step cost** when it varies with the cost driver but in discrete steps.

Unit Cost and Marginal Cost

Unit cost (or **average cost**) is the total manufacturing costs (materials, labor, and overhead) divided by units of output. It is a useful concept in setting prices and in evaluating product profitability, but it can be subject to some misleading interpretations. To properly interpret unit cost, we must distinguish *unit variable* costs, which do not change as output changes, from *unit fixed costs*, which do change as output changes.

> **Unit cost** (or **average cost**) is the total manufacturing cost (materials, labor, and overhead) divided by units of output.

For example, a driver's cost per mile is likely lower for a person who keeps a car for 200,000 miles than it is for a person who keeps a car for only 40,000 miles because the fixed costs are spread over more miles. These relationships are illustrated graphically in Exhibit 3–9. The management accountant is careful in using the terms *average cost* and *unit cost* because of the potential for misleading interpretations.

Illustration of Total Fixed Cost and Variable Cost per Unit

	Fixed Cost		Variable Cost	
Units of output	10,000	20,000	10,000	20,000
Per unit	$ 10	$ 5	$ 8	$ 8
Total	100,000	100,000	80,000	160,000

Marginal cost is the additional cost incurred as the cost driver increases by one unit.

The term **marginal cost** is used to describe the additional cost incurred as the cost driver increases by one unit. Under the assumption of linear cost within the relevant range, the concept of marginal cost is equivalent to the concept of unit variable cost.

Structural and Executional Cost Drivers

Structural cost drivers are strategic in nature and involve plans and decisions that have a long-term effect with regard to issues such as scale, experience, technology, and complexity.

Structural and executional cost drivers are used to facilitate strategic and operational decision making.[6] **Structural cost drivers** are strategic in nature because they involve plans and decisions that have long-term effects. Issues such as the following should be considered:

1. **Scale.** How much should be invested? How large should the firm become? Larger firms have lower overall costs as a result of economies of scale. For example, a retail firm such as Wal-Mart or The Gap must determine how many new stores to open in a given year to achieve its strategic objectives and compete effectively as a retailer.

2. **Experience.** How much prior experience does the firm have in its current and planned products and services? The more experience, the lower the development, manufacturing, and distribution costs are likely to be. For example, a manufacturer such as Hewlett-Packard uses existing manufacturing methods as much as possible for new products to reduce the time and cost necessary for workers to become proficient at manufacturing the new product. Additionally, health care management firms such

Survey of Practice: Cost Classification in U.S. Firms

A survey of 350 U.S. manufacturing firms provides the following results regarding how these firms treat selected indirect cost categories (the data show the percentage of the firms treating each type of indirect cost as a variable, step, or fixed cost).

Activity	Variable	Step Cost	Fixed	Other
Setup labor	49%	20%	12%	19%
Material handling labor	40	29	15	16
Quality control labor	28	30	25	17
Repairs and maintenance	23	36	24	17
Tooling	24	27	25	24
Energy	21	36	23	20
Supervision	3	22	58	17
Engineering	5	18	61	16
Data processing	2	12	69	17
Building occupancy	1	5	77	17
Taxes and insurance	1	9	74	16
Depreciation—machinery and equipment	1	6	78	15
Work-in-process inventory carrying cost	19	25	24	32

Source: Il-Woon Kim and Ja Song, "Accounting Practices in Three Countries," *Management Accounting,* August 1990, p. 28.

---

[6] See John K. Shank and Vijay Govindarajan, *Strategic Cost Analysis* (New York: Free Press, 1993), pp. 20–22; and D. Riley, "Competitive Cost Based Investment Strategies for Industrial Companies," *Manufacturing Issues* (New York: Booz, Allen, Hamilton, 1987).

as Columbia/HCA use their knowledge of experience-related cost drivers to reduce the time and cost necessary to improve the profitability of newly acquired hospitals.

3. **Technology.** What process technologies are used in designing, manufacturing, and distributing the product or service? New technologies can reduce these costs significantly. For example, manufacturers such as Procter & Gamble use computer technology to monitor the quantities of its products that its customers (typically, large retailers) have on hand so that it can promptly restock these products as needed. Technological innovation at Intel has lowered the cost of computing dramatically by improving the capability of microprocessors used in personal computers. While the capability of the microprocessors has increased exponentially, their manufacturing costs per unit have not changed significantly. This example of Moore's law describes the costs of digital technology falling (by one-half) every 18 to 24 months.

4. **Complexity.** What is the firm's level of complexity? How many different products does the firm have? As noted in the opening discussion of Procter & Gamble, firms with

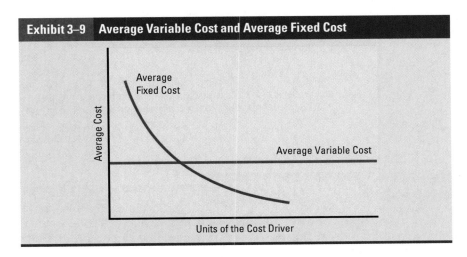

Exhibit 3–9   Average Variable Cost and Average Fixed Cost

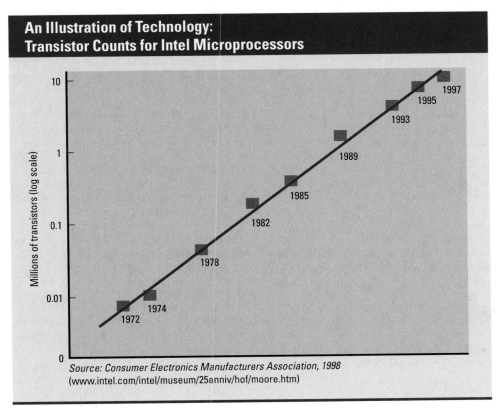

An Illustration of Technology: Transistor Counts for Intel Microprocessors

Source: Consumer Electronics Manufacturers Association, 1998
(www.intel.com/intel/museum/25anniv/hof/moore.htm)

Cost Accounting Practices at Iowa Select Farms

Steve Weiss, chief financial officer of Iowa Select Farms, reported on accounting practices in the pork production industry at the 1998 Pork Financial Management Conference. He indicated the types of variable and fixed costs in the industry and the cost drivers of each. Notice that in this context, the cost of labor is fixed because employees are paid on a fixed salary basis; the only way that labor costs change is to change salary or benefits (listed under fixed cost drivers). The cost object in this case is the number of pigs.

- Variable costs
    - —Feed
    - —Medications
    - —Transportation
    - —Manure
- Variable cost drivers
    - —Feed efficiency matrix
    - —Death/Cull loss
    - —Input costs
    - —Maintenance protocols
    - —Herd health
    - —Medication cost
    - —Distances
    - —Trucking costs
    - —Feed/Water efficiency
- Fixed costs
    - —Labor
    - —Facility costs
        Depreciation
        Lease/Contract
        Utilities
        Insurance
        Property taxes
        Supplies
- Fixed cost drivers
    - —Salary
    - —Benefits
    - —Employment taxes
    - —Bonus plans
    - —Staffing levels

Source: Steve Weiss, "Cost Accounting," paper presented at the 1998 Pork Financial Management Conference (www.iowaselect.com/ind_cost.html)

COST MANAGEMENT IN ACTION

Product Complexity in Consumer Goods Manufacturing

In the mid-1990s, a large consumer goods manufacturer moved its customer base from department and specialty stores to mass merchandising. This strategic change required it to reconsider the complexity of its product lines (numbers of different products, patterns, and colors). The firm approached a large consulting firm to help it identify the nature of the complexity and some desired solutions.

The consulting firm observed the following:

1. As many as 10 different vendors provided certain purchased items.

2. Of the firm's customers after the strategic shift, 98 percent were responsible for only 7 percent of sales volume.

3. The wide variety of pricing discounts and promotional programs added complexity to the accounts receivable collection process because of increased disputes over customers' balances.

4. Seventy-five percent of the firm's volume involved products with five color combinations.

5. Customers' demands for fast delivery of new orders had caused a shift in manufacturing to smaller batch sizes and more frequent equipment setups. Thus, total setup-related costs increased.

As a consultant to the consumer goods manufacturer, what changes would you make in its operations and cost management practices?

(Refer to comments on Cost Management in Action at the end of the chapter.)

many products have higher costs of scheduling and managing the production process, as well as the upstream costs of product development and the downstream costs of distribution and service. These firms often use activity-based costing to better identify the costs and therefore the profitability of their different products, suppliers, and customers.

Strategic analyses using structural cost drivers help the firm improve its competitive position. These analyses include value-chain analysis and activity-based management. Value-chain analysis can help the firm assess the long-term consequences of its current or planned commitment to a structural cost driver. For example, the growth in size and capability of parts manufacturers for automakers should cause the automakers to reassess whether they should outsource the manufacture of certain parts.

Executional cost drivers are factors the firm can manage in short-term, operational decision making to reduce costs. They include the following:

1. **Workforce involvement.** Are the employees dedicated to continual improvement and quality? This workforce commitment will lower costs. Firms with strong employee relationships, such as Federal Express, can reduce operating costs significantly.

2. **Design of the production process.** Can the layout of equipment and processes and the scheduling of production be improved? Speeding up the flow of product through the firm can reduce costs. Innovators in manufacturing technology, such as Motorola and Allen-Bradley, can reduce manufacturing costs significantly.

3. **Supplier relationships.** Can the cost, quality, or delivery of materials and purchased parts be improved to reduce overall costs? Wal-Mart and Toyota, among other firms, maintain a low-cost advantage partially by agreements with their suppliers that they will provide products or parts that meet the companies' explicit requirements as to their quality, timeliness of delivery, and other features.

Plant managers study executional cost drivers to find ways to reduce costs. Such studies are done as a part of operational control, which is covered in Part Five.

> **Executional cost drivers** are factors the firm can manage in the short term to reduce costs, such as workforce involvement, design of the production process, and supplier relationships.

COST CONCEPTS FOR PRODUCT AND SERVICE COSTING

Accurate information about the cost of products and services is important in each management function: strategic management, planning and decision making, management and operational control, and financial statement preparation. The cost accounting systems to provide this information are explained in this section.

> ◀ **LEARNING OBJECTIVE 2**
> *Explain the cost concepts used in product and service costing.*

Cost Accounting for Products and Services

Cost accounting systems for the firms that manufacture products and for the merchandising firms that resell those products differ significantly. Merchandising firms include both retailers, which sell the final product to the consumer, and wholesalers, which distribute the product to retailers. Service firms often have little or no inventory, so their costing systems are relatively simple.

Product Costs and Period Costs

Product inventory for both manufacturing and merchandising firms is treated as an asset on their balance sheets. So long as the inventory has market value, it is considered an asset until the inventory is sold; then the cost of the inventory is transferred to the income statement as **cost of goods sold,** an expense. This is the life cycle of product cost, from design and manufacture (or purchase and stocking, in the merchandising firm) to sales and service, that is, from asset on the balance sheet to expense on the income statement.

> **Cost of goods sold** is the cost of the product transferred to the income statement when inventory is sold.

Product costs for a manufacturing firm include *only* the costs necessary to complete the product:

1. **Direct materials.** The materials used to manufacture the product, which become a physical part of it.
2. **Direct labor.** The labor used to manufacture the product.
3. **Factory overhead.** The indirect costs for materials, labor, and facilities used to support the manufacturing process.

Product costs for a merchandising firm include the cost to purchase the product plus the transportation costs paid by the retailer or wholesaler to get the product to the location from which it will be sold or distributed.

> **Product costs** for a manufacturing firm include *only* the costs necessary to complete the product: direct materials, direct labor, and factory overhead.

All other expenditures for managing the firm and selling the product are expensed in the period in which they are incurred; for that reason, they are called **period costs.** These costs are expensed because there is no expectation that they will produce future value; in contrast, the sale of inventory will produce future earnings. Period costs primarily include the general, selling, and administrative costs that are necessary

> **Period costs** are all nonproduct expenditures for managing the firm and selling the product.

Furniture Manufacturing Costs: Variable/Fixed, Direct/Indirect, and Product/Period Costs

The manufacture of dining table sets is used to provide examples of costs for each cost concept: variable/fixed, direct/indirect, and product/period. The furniture manufacturer for these dining table sets has organized its manufacturing by product line: dining table sets, upholstered chairs, sofas, bedroom furniture, end tables, and outdoor furniture. Each product line has its own manufacturing team although much of the equipment in the plant is shared among product lines (e.g., multiple product lines use the table saws). The company owns its retail sales outlets, each of which offers all of the firm's products. The cost object in this illustration is the *product line* for dining table *sets* (*not* each dining set produced).

VARIABLE/FIXED, DIRECT/INDIRECT, AND PRODUCT/PERIOD COSTS FOR THE <u>PRODUCT LINE</u>, DINING TABLE SETS

	Product Cost		Period (Nonproduct) Cost
	Direct	**Indirect**	
Variable	Wood and fabric	Power for table saws	Sales commissions for sales
Fixed	Salary of manufacturing supervisor	Depreciation on table saws	Insurance and depreciation on company-owned sales outlets

Notes

1. Both nonproduct costs and product costs can be direct or indirect to the cost object. However, while it is very common to distinguish between direct and indirect product costs, it is not common to distinguish between direct and indirect nonproduct costs.

2. This illustration is based on the *cost object*, the product line for dining table *sets*. The examples would not change if we had chosen instead to have the cost object be *each set* manufactured except that the manufacturing supervisor's salary would no longer be a direct fixed product cost. It would become an *indirect* fixed product cost because the salary can be traced to the product line but not to each table set manufactured.

LEARNING OBJECTIVE 3▶

Demonstrate how costs flow through the accounts.

for the management of the company but are *not* involved directly or indirectly in the manufacturing process (or in the purchase of the products for resale). Advertising costs, data processing costs, and executive and staff salaries are good examples of period costs. In a manufacturing or a merchandising firm, period costs are also sometimes referred to as *operating expenses* or *selling and administrative expenses*. In a service firm, these costs are often referred to as *operating expenses*.

Manufacturing, Merchandising, and Service Costing

The cost flows in manufacturing, retail, and service firms are illustrated in Exhibits 3–10, 3–11, 3–12a, and 3–12b. The left-hand side of Exhibit 3–10 presents a graphic representation of the flows of costs for a manufacturing firm. The first step of the manufacturing process is to purchase materials. The second step involves adding the three cost elements—materials used, labor, and overhead—to work in process. In the third step, as production is completed, the production costs that have been accumulating in the Works in Process account are transferred to the Finished Goods Inventory account and from there to the Cost of Goods Sold account when the products are sold.

In the merchandising firm, shown on the right-hand side of Exhibit 3–10, the process is somewhat simpler. It purchases merchandise and places it in the Product Inventory account. When sold, it is transferred to the Cost of Goods Sold account. The merchandising and manufacturing firms in Exhibit 3–10 are shown side by side to emphasize the difference: The merchandising firm purchases inventory but the manufacturing firm manufactures inventory using materials, labor, and overhead.

Manufacturing firms use three inventory accounts: (1) **Materials Inventory**, where the cost of the supply of materials used in the manufacturing process is kept; (2) **Work-in-Process Inventory**, which contains all costs put into manufacture of products that are started but not complete at the financial statement date; and (3) **Finished Goods Inventory**, which holds the cost of goods that are ready for sale. Each account has its own beginning and ending balances.

Materials Inventory keeps the cost of the supply of materials used in the manufacturing process or to provide the service.

Work-in-Process Inventory contains all costs put into the manufacture of products that are started but not complete at the financial statement date.

Finished Goods Inventory holds the cost of goods that are ready for sale.

Exhibit 3–10 **Cost Flows in Manufacturing and Merchandising Firms**

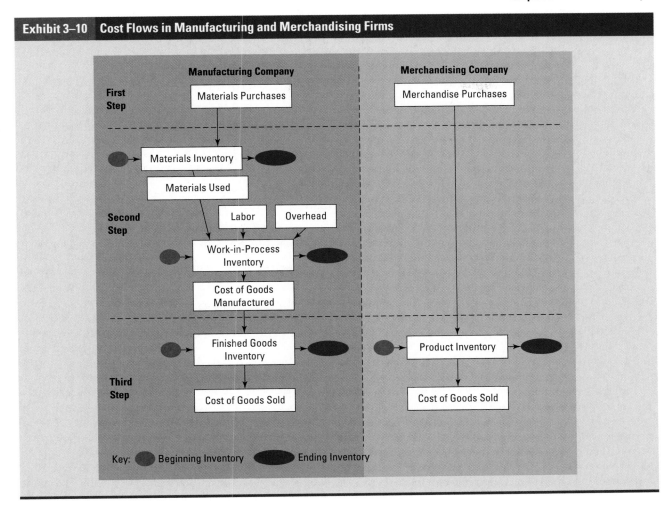

An inventory formula relates the inventory accounts, as follows:

Beginning inventory + Cost added = Cost transferred out + Ending Inventory

The terms *cost added* and *cost transferred out* have different meanings, depending on which inventory account is being considered:

Inventory Account	Cost Added	Cost Transferred Out
Materials Inventory	Purchases of materials	Cost of materials used in production
Work-in-Process Inventory	1. Cost of materials used	Cost of goods manufactured, for products completed this period
	2. Labor cost	
	3. Overhead cost	
Finished Goods Inventory	Costs of goods manufactured	Cost of goods sold

The inventory formula is a useful concept to show how materials, labor, and overhead costs flow into Work-in-Process Inventory, then into Finished Goods Inventory, and finally into Cost of Goods Sold. Exhibit 3–11 illustrates the effects of the cost flows on the accounts involved when the manufacturing firm converts materials into finished products and then sells them and when the merchandising firm sells merchandise inventory.

The illustration in Exhibit 3–11 shows the accounts for a manufacturing company that begins the period with $10 in Materials Inventory, $10 in Work-in-Process Inventory, and $20 in Finished Goods Inventory. During the period, it

Exhibit 3–11 **Account Relationships for Manufacturing and Merchandising Companies**

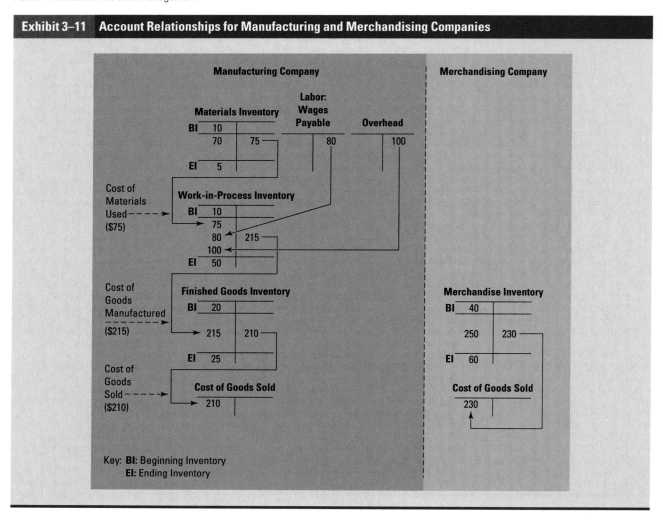

Key: **BI:** Beginning Inventory
EI: Ending Inventory

LEARNING OBJECTIVE 4▶

Prepare an income statement for both a manufacturing firm and a merchandising firm.

Cost of Goods Manufactured is the cost of goods finished and transferred out of the Work-in-Process Inventory account this period.

purchases $70 of materials, uses $75 of materials and $80 of direct labor, and spends $100 for factory overhead. Also during the period, $215 of goods are completed and transferred from the Work-in-Process Inventory account to the Finished Goods Inventory account, and $210 of goods are sold. These events leave ending inventories of $5 in the materials account, $50 in the work-in-process account, and $25 in the finished goods account. The merchandising company purchased merchandise of $250 and made sales of $230, and its Merchandise Inventory account increases from $40 to $60.

Exhibit 3–12a shows how the accounting relationships are then finally represented in the income statements for the two types of firms. Note that the manufacturing firm requires a two-part calculation for cost of goods sold: the first part combines the cost flows affecting the Work-in-Process Inventory account to determine the amount of **Cost of Goods Manufactured**, that is, the cost of the goods finished and transferred out of work in process during this period. The second part combines the cost flows for the Finished Goods Inventory account to determine the amount of the cost of the goods sold and net income, assuming $50 of selling expense for the manufacturing firm and $40 of operating expense for the merchandising firm.

Exhibit 3–12b shows the relatively simple income statement for a service firm with $300 in sales, $60 in materials costs, $40 in labor costs, and $100 in other operating expenses for an operating income of $100.

Exhibit 3–12a Statements for Manufacturing and Merchandising Firms

Manufacturing, Inc
Statement of Cost of Goods Manufactured
For the Year Ended December 31, 2001

(No need for a Cost of Goods Manufactured Statement for Merchandising Inc.)

Direct Materials		
Beginning Inventory	$ 10	
Purchases	70	
Direct Materials Available	$ 80	
Ending Direct Materials Inventory	5	
Direct Materials Used		$ 75
Direct Labor		80
Factory Overhead		100
Total Manufacturing Cost		$255
Add: Beginning Work-in-Process Inventory		10
Total Manufacturing Cost to Account for		265
Less: Ending Work-in-Process Inventory		50
Cost of Goods Manufactured		$215

Manufacturing, Inc.
Income Statement
For the Year Ended December 31, 2001

Sales		$300
Cost of Goods Sold		
Beginning Finished Goods Inventory	$ 20	
Cost of Goods Manufactured	215	
Cost of Goods available for sale	235	
Ending Finished Goods Inventory	25	210
Gross Margin		90
Selling and Administrative expenses		50
Net Income		$ 40

Merchandising, Inc.
Income Statement
For the Year Ended December 31, 2001

Sales		$300
Cost of Goods Sold		
Beginning Finished Goods Inventory	$ 40	
Purchases	250	
Cost of Goods available for sale	$290	
Ending Finished Goods Inventory	60	230
Gross Margin		$ 70
Operating Expenses		40
Net Income		$ 30

Exhibit 3–12b Income Statement for a Service Firm

SERVICE, INC.
Income Statement
For the Year Ended December 31, 2001

Revenues		$300
Operating Expenses		
Materials	$ 60	
Labor	40	
Other Operating Expenses	100	200
Operating Income		$100

COST CONCEPTS FOR PLANNING AND DECISION MAKING

◄LEARNING OBJECTIVE 5

Explain the cost concepts related to the use of cost information in planning and decision making.

To facilitate management decision making and planning, the management accountant provides relevant, timely, and accurate information at a reasonable cost. Relevance is the most critical of the decision-making concepts; timeliness, accuracy, and cost are unimportant if the information is irrelevant.

Relevant Cost

A **relevant cost** has two properties: (1) it *differs for each decision option* and (2) it will be *incurred in the future.*

The concept of relevant cost arises when the decision maker must choose between two or more options. To determine which option is best, the decision maker must determine which option offers the highest benefit, usually in dollars. Thus, the decision maker needs information on relevant costs. A **relevant cost** has two properties: (1) it *differs for each decision option* and (2) it will be *incurred in the future.* If a cost is the same for each option, including it in the decision only wastes time and increases the possibility for simple errors. Costs that have already been incurred or committed are irrelevant because there is no longer any discretion about them.

Differential Cost

A **differential cost** is a cost that differs for each decision option and is therefore relevant.

A **differential cost** is a cost that differs for each decision option and is therefore relevant for the decision maker's choice. A differential cost arises either as the direct cost of selecting an option (the purchase cost of a new machine is the direct effect of replacing an old machine) or as the indirect cost associated with the choice (replacing a machine creates a difference in certain costs, such as those for maintenance or electric power).

Opportunity Cost

Opportunity cost is the benefit lost when choosing one option precludes receiving the benefits from an alternative option.

Opportunity cost is the benefit lost when choosing one option precludes receiving the benefits from an alternative option. If the management accountant ranks the monetary outcomes of the alternative options, it is possible to calculate the opportunity cost of the option chosen by determining the maximum alternative benefit that would have been obtained if the choice had been some alternative use. For example, if a sales manager chooses to forgo an order from a new customer to ensure that a current customer's order is filled on time, the potential profit from the lost order is the manager's *opportunity cost* for this decision. Ensuring the loyalty of an existing customer has a difficult-to-quantify but significant long-term value, but the short-term loss of the new order, while quantifiable, is not so important.

Sunk Cost

Sunk costs are costs that have been incurred or committed in the past and are therefore irrelevant.

Sunk costs are costs that have been incurred or committed in the past and are therefore irrelevant because the decision maker no longer has discretion over them. For example, if a company purchased a new machine without warranty that failed the next day, the purchase price is *irrelevant* for the present decision to replace or to repair the machine. Only future costs are relevant, and the purchase price of the recently acquired machine has no effect on future costs.

An important additional issue related to sunk costs must be considered. There is apparently an inherent bias for decision makers to include sunk costs as relevant to the analysis. Studies by psychologists Kahneman and Tversky found that decision makers are more willing to invest money to "recover" sunk costs than to invest the money to earn the same net return. Similarly, a study by Whyte found that decision makers tend to escalate commitments to sunk costs. The practical implication of these findings is that the management accountants must be particularly careful to develop information for decision makers that separates sunk costs from differential future costs.[7]

Attributes of Cost Information for Decision Making

Accuracy

The experienced decision maker does *not* use accounting information without considering the potential for inaccuracy. Inaccurate data can mislead, resulting in potentially costly mistakes. A primary way to ensure accurate data for decision making is to

---

[7] Daniel Kahneman and Amos Tversky, "Prospect Theory: An Analysis of Decisions under Risk," *Econometrica*, March 1979, pp. 263–91; and Glen Whyte, "Escalating Commitment to a Course of Action: A Reinterpretation," *Academy of Management Review*, 1986, pp. 311–21.

design and monitor an effective system of internal accounting controls. The system of **internal accounting controls** is a set of policies and procedures that restrict and guide activities in the processing of financial data with the objective to prevent or detect errors and fraudulent acts.

The accuracy of the accounting data and the design of the system of internal accounting controls are the responsibility of the controller, who is assisted by external and internal auditors. The external auditor periodically evaluates the control environment and makes recommendations for improved effectiveness; the internal auditor provides an ongoing monitoring role.

Timeliness

Cost management information must be available to the decision maker in a timely manner to facilitate effective decision making. The cost of delay can be significant in many decisions, such as in filling rush orders that may be lost if the necessary information is not timely. The cost of identifying quality defects *early* in a manufacturing process can be far less than the cost of materials and labor wasted until the defect is detected later in the process.

Cost and Value of Cost Information

Thinking of cost management information as having a certain cost and value emphasizes that the management accountant is an information specialist, very much like other financial professionals, such as tax advisers, financial planners, and consultants. The management accountant provides an information service that has both a preparation cost and a value to the user. The preparation costs for cost management information should be controlled as should any other service provided within the firm. These preparation costs are likely influenced by the desired accuracy, timeliness, and level of aggregation; when increased accuracy, timeliness, and detail are desired, the preparation costs are higher.

COST CONCEPTS FOR MANAGEMENT AND OPERATIONAL CONTROL

A crucial role for cost management information is to provide a basis for motivating and rewarding managers' and employees' efforts and effectiveness. Key cost concepts applicable for this management function include controllability and risk preferences.

Controllability

A cost is said to be **controllable** if the manager or employee has discretion in choosing to incur it or can significantly influence its amount within a given, usually short, period of time. For example, the shop supervisor ordinarily *cannot* control rent expense and insurance on the plant facility nor would the division manager ordinarily have discretion over the amount of corporate-level administrative costs. In contrast, employees typically have control over the labor and materials used in their work area. Costs such as advertising and maintenance ordinarily are within the scope of the product or division manager's control.

There are two views of the importance of controllability in the context of employee and manager motivation. One view holds that the manager or employee should be responsible only for the costs that he or she controls. This view is consistent with the argument that to hold managers responsible for changes in costs beyond their control is unfair and unmotivating. The second view is that many "uncontrollable" costs, such as corporate-level administrative costs, are in fact controllable by all managers *taken as a whole*; thus, to include these costs on the managers' costs reports sends a clear message that the firm benefits when managers manage these costs properly.

> The system of **internal accounting controls** is a set of policies and procedures that restrict and guide activities in the processing of financial data with the objective to prevent or detect errors and fraudulent acts.

> ◄**LEARNING OBJECTIVE 6**
>
> *Explain the cost concepts related to the use of cost information for management and operational control.*

> A cost is said to be **controllable** if the manager or employee has discretion in choosing to incur it or can significantly influence its amount within a given, usually short, period of time.

Teaching Risk Taking at Trilogy Software, Inc.

Trilogy Software, Inc., an Austin, Texas, developer of software that helps companies manage product pricing, sales plans, and commissions, is in a stiff head-on competition with rivals Siebel Systems, Inc., and SAP AG. Joe Liemandt, CEO of Trilogy, understands the importance of managers in his company taking risks if Trilogy is to be successful. To prepare managers for risk taking and innovation, he put all new hires through an intense training program that divided them into groups to compete to develop new products and services. Everyone was rewarded with a trip to Las Vegas following the training period. In Las Vegas, to motivate and reward risk taking, Liemandt provided $2,000 cash to each recruit willing to bet that

money at the casinos in Las Vegas. Winners kept their winnings, but losers had to pay back the money to Trilogy in monthly deductions of $400 from their paychecks. Thirty-six of 300 recruits chose to take the bet. Whether winner or loser, all 36 came out ahead. One of the thirty-six, a loser, said, "We are known [at Trilogy] as risk takers, an important attribute in the high-tech world." These 36 are known as the "L2K Club" for "lost $2,000" although one of the 36 actually won $72,000. One employee says, "Joe knows every L2K pretty well."

Source: "How Trilogy Software Trains Its Raw Recruits to Be Risk Takers," *The Wall Street Journal,* September 21, 1998, p. 1.

The Effect of Risk Preferences on Motivation and Decision Making

A manager's risk preferences are important in management and operational control because they can have unexpected and undesirable effects on his or her behavior. Assume that a manager must make a decision for which each option has a different outcome and some outcomes are more certain to happen than others. **Risk preferences** describe the way individuals differentially view decision options because they place a weight on *certain* outcomes that differs from the weight they place on *uncertain* outcomes. The risk associated with uncertain outcomes can be undesirable (or desirable) to the decision maker regardless of the value of the outcome itself. It is necessary to separate the value of the outcome from the positive or negative weight associated with the risk due to uncertainty. For example, people commonly dislike risk and thus prefer a certain $50 over a 50–50 chance at $100. People who prefer risk, on the other hand, would choose to have the chance to win the $100.

Many managers are risk averse; that is, they seek to avoid options with high risk and would choose an option with lower expected value if it had less risk. Other managers are risk prone; they seek risky projects that promise some chance of a high benefit, although the projects may have a significant risk of low benefit. These differences in risk preferences can significantly affect motivation under different supervision and reward techniques. For example, the risk-averse manager is most likely to be highly motivated by supervision that rewards the reduced risk; the opposite is likely true for the risk-prone manager.

Moreover, risk preferences can interfere with proper decision making. For example, a risk-averse manager might choose not to take a risky action that top management would take (for example, to install a costly new machine that would probably reduce operating costs) because of the personal consequences that a potentially unfavorable outcome would have for the manager. For proper motivation and decision making, management and operational control systems should be designed to reduce the negative effects of risk preferences.

> **Risk preferences** describe the way individuals differentially view decision options because they place a weight on *certain* outcomes that differs from the weight they place on *uncertain* outcomes.

SUMMARY

The management accountant must understand a number of important concepts to be an effective information professional: There are several important concepts for the management accountant, which Chapter 3 presents in four groups: (1) cost objects, cost drivers, and cost pools, (2) product and service costing for the preparation of financial statements, (3) planning and decision making, and (4) operational and management control. Group 1 includes concepts that are important in all management functions, while groups 2, 3, and 4 are three of the four management functions. Concepts for the fourth management function, strategic management, are covered in Chapter 2.

The first group of concepts includes the four types of cost drivers: activity based, volume based, structural, and executional. Activity-based cost drivers are at the detail level of operations: equipment setup, materials handling, and clerical or other tasks. In contrast, volume-based cost drivers are at the aggregate level: usually the number of units produced. Structural cost drivers involve plans and decisions having long-term effects; executional cost drivers have short-term decision frames. The most important volume-based concepts are variable costs, which change according to a change in the level of the cost driver, and fixed costs, which do not. Direct costs are defined as costs that can be traced directly to a cost object in contrast to indirect costs, which cannot.

The important concepts in product costing are product costs, which are the costs—of direct materials, direct labor, and indirect manufacturing (called *overhead*) required for the product and production process. Nonproduct costs (also called *period costs*) are the selling, administrative, and other costs not involved in manufacturing. The inventory formula is used to determine the cost of materials used in production, the cost of goods manufactured, and the cost of goods sold for a given period.

The most important concept in planning and decision making is relevant cost—a cost that differs for each option and will occur in the future. When considering options, the management accountant considers relevant costs. All past costs (also called *sunk costs*) are irrelevant because they will not change regardless of the option chosen.

The two key concepts in management and operational control are controllability and risk preferences. Distinguishing controllable costs from other costs is important because managers should be evaluated only on the basis of controllable costs; evaluation, even in part, on the basis of costs a manager cannot control can be negatively motivating. It is also important for the management accountant to recognize in the development of cost management systems that managers tend to be relatively risk averse, which can cause them to make decisions that are not consistent with top management's objectives.

KEY TERMS

COMMENTS ON COST MANAGEMENT IN ACTION

Product Complexity in Consumer Goods Manufacturing

The consultant's observations indicate that the manufacturer was incurring large costs in operations, distribution, and administration due to the high level of complexity in its products. Maintaining relationships with 10 vendors for a single item contributed to high purchasing and stocking costs. Similarly, most of the firm's volume was made up of products with five color combinations, causing manufacturing, warehousing, shipping, and selling costs to be high relative to products with fewer color combinations. The high product variety also required smaller batch production and more frequent setups, which increased manufacturing costs. The variety of different customers, prices, and promotional programs increased manufacturing, shipping, and customer service costs as well as accounting costs related to customer invoices and account balances.

The solution? The firm reduced complexity by reducing the number of customers; the value of each customer was reviewed, and some with low value were not continued. The firm also developed a review process for proposed products or new variations on existing products to ensure their likely profitability. Furthermore, the firm reduced the complexity of equipment setups so that it could meet customers' demands for smaller batch sizes without increasing overall costs. As a result of the reduced complexity, overall profit margins improved. The manufacturer had found a way to deal with the cost consequences of its strategic initiative.

The firm also adopted new cost management practices that included nonfinancial measures such as setup time and frequency, percent of orders shipped on time, percent of orders made on a just-in-time basis, and the number of vendors for the top 20 commodity raw materials items. In addition, the firm began to calculate and regularly review customer profitability by type of market and customer size.

Source: Frank A. J. Gonsalves and Robert G. Eiler, "Managing Complexity through Performance Measurement," *Management Accounting*, August 1996, pp. 34–39.

SELF-STUDY PROBLEM

(For solution, please turn to the end of the chapter.)

The following data pertain to Spartan Products Company:

Sales revenue	$1,000,000
Direct materials inventory, Jan. 1, 2001	20,000
Direct labor—Wages	350,000
Depreciation expense—Plant and equipment	80,000
Indirect labor—Wages	5,000
Heat, light, and power—Plant	12,000
Supervisor's salary—Plant	40,000
Finished goods inventory, Jan. 1, 2001	35,000
Work-in-Process inventory, Dec. 31, 2001	25,000
Supplies—Administrative office	6,000
Property taxes—Plant	13,000
Finished goods inventory, Dec. 31, 2001	40,000
Direct materials inventory, Dec. 31, 2001	30,000
Sales representatives' salaries	190,000
Work-in-Process inventory, Jan. 1, 2001	35,000
Direct materials purchases	100,000
Supplies—Plant	4,000
Depreciation—Administrative office	30,000

Required Prepare a statement of cost of goods manufactured and an income statement for Spartan Products Company for the year ended December 31, 2001, similar to the one in Exhibit 3–12a.

QUESTIONS

3–1   For what particular management function is relevant cost information needed?

3–2   Distinguish between direct and indirect costs and give several examples of each.

3–3   Are all direct costs variable? Explain.

3–4   Are all fixed costs indirect? Explain.

3–5   Define *cost driver*.

3–6   What is the difference between variable and fixed costs?

3–7   Explain step costs and give an example.

3–8   Define *relevant range* and explain its use.

3–9   What is a conversion cost? What are prime costs?

3–10 Why might the term *average cost* be misleading?

3–11 How do total variable costs, total fixed costs, average variable costs, and average fixed costs react to changes in the cost driver?

3–12 What does the term *marginal cost* mean?

3–13 Distinguish between product costs and period costs.

3–14 Explain the difference between cost of goods sold and cost of goods manufactured.

3–15 What are the three types of inventory in a manufacturing firm?

3–16 Cost management information should be relevant, timely, and accurate. Which of these attributes is most important? Why?

3–17 What is a relevant cost?

3–18 Define *differential cost*, *opportunity cost*, and *sunk cost*.

3–19 Should managers be responsible for the costs they cannot control directly? Why or why not?

3–20 What problem can arise if the firm and its employees have different risk preferences? What can be done about this problem?

EXERCISES

3–21 **CLASSIFICATION OF COSTS**   The following costs were taken from the accounting records of the Barnwell Manufacturing Company:

1. State income taxes
2. Insurance on the manufacturing facilities
3. Supplies used in manufacturing
4. Wages for employees in the assembly department
5. Wages for employees who deliver the product
6. Interest on notes payable
7. Materials used in the production process
8. Rent for the sales outlet in Sacramento
9. Electricity for manufacturing equipment
10. Depreciation expense on delivery trucks
11. Wages for the sales staff
12. Factory supervisors' salaries
13. Company president's salary
14. Advertising expense

Required   Classify each item as either a product cost or a period cost. Classify all product costs as direct or indirect, assuming that the cost object is each unit of product manufactured.

3–22   CLASSIFICATION OF COSTS   Following is a list of costs from Oakland Company, a furniture manufacturer:

1. Wood used in chairs
2. Salaries of inspectors
3. Lubricant used in machinery
4. Factory rent
5. Wages of assembly workers
6. Workers' compensation insurance
7. Sandpaper
8. Fabric used for upholstery
9. Property taxes
10. Depreciation on machinery

Required   Classify each cost as direct or indirect assuming that the cost object is each item manufactured. Also indicate whether each cost is a variable or fixed cost.

3–23   CLASSIFICATION OF COSTS IN A GROCERY

Required   Identify the cost objects in a medium to large-size grocery store. What are the cost pools? The cost drivers?

Service

Strategy

3–24   VARIABLE COSTS, CHANGE IN BUDGET   The Community Help Center provides clothing and canned food to needy people in the community. Of the Help Center's costs, 40 percent are fixed and 60 percent are variable. Because of rising unemployment in the community, monetary contributions are down by 20 percent this year. The center's budget was $100,000 last year.

Required   What will be the percentage of change in the amount of services the Help Center can provide this year?

3–25   AVERAGE AND TOTAL COSTS   The Business Students Association wants to have a Christmas dance for its members. The cost of renting a nightclub is $250, and the cost of refreshments will be $1 per person.

Required

1. What is the total cost if 100 people attend? What is the average cost?
2. What is the total cost if 200 people attend? What is the average cost?
3. Explain why average total cost differs with changes in total attendance.

Service

Strategy

3–26   COST CLASSIFICATION   Fran McPhair Dance Studios is a chain of 45 wholly owned dance studios that offer private lessons in ballroom dancing. The studios are located in various cities throughout the southern and southeastern states. McPhair offers a set of 12 private lessons; students may pay for the lessons one at a time, but each student is required to enroll for at least a 12-lesson plan. The 20-, 40-, and 100-lesson plans offer savings. Each dance instructor is paid a small salary plus a commission based on the number of dance lessons provided.

Required

1. McPhair's owner is interested in a strategic analysis of the business. The owner wants to understand why overall profitability has declined slightly in the most recent year while other studios in the area seem to be doing well. What is the proper cost object to begin this analysis? Explain your choice.

2. For each of the cost elements determine the cost classification from the following list for the cost object you chose in requirement 1. (In some cases, two or more classifications apply.)

Cost Elements

1. Each dancing instructor's salary.
2. Manager's salary.
3. Music tapes used in instruction.
4. Utilities for the studio.
5. Part-time studio receptionist.
6. Planning and development materials sent from the home office.
7. Free lessons given by each studio as a promotion.
8. Regional TV and radio advertisements placed several times a year.

Cost Classifications

a. Direct
b. Indirect
c. Variable
d. Fixed
e. Controllable by studio manager
f. Uncontrollable by studio manager

3–27 **ACTIVITIES AND COST DRIVERS IN A HOSPITAL**   Greenbelt Hospital has the following activities in its value chain of providing service to each inpatient admission:

1. Schedule patient.
2. Verify insurance.
3. Admit patient.
4. Prepare patient's room.
5. Review doctor's report.
6. Feed patient.
7. Order tests.
8. Move to/from laboratory.
9. Administer lab tests.
10. Order pharmaceuticals.
11. Complete patient report.
12. Check patient's vital signs.
13. Prepare patient for operation.
14. Move to/from operating room.
15. Operate.
16. Collect charges.
17. Discharge patient.
18. Bill insurance.

Required   Assume that the cost object is the individual patient. Determine the appropriate cost driver(s) for each activity.

3–28 **FIXED, VARIABLE, AND MIXED COSTS**   Adams Manufacturing's five manufacturing departments had the following operating and cost information for the two most recent months of activity:

	May 2000	June 2000
Units produced	10,000	20,000
Costs in each department		
Department A	$10,000	$10,000
Department B	25,000	50,000
Department C	35,000	45,000
Department D	18,000	64,000
Department E	22,000	44,000

Required   Identify whether the cost in each department is fixed, variable, or mixed.

3–29 **RELEVANT, DIFFERENTIAL, AND OPPORTUNITY COSTS**   Jackson Farm Tools, Inc., has two options for repairing its office space, which received extensive wind damage in a recent storm.

	Option 1	Option 2
Cost 1	$ 8,000	$ 8,000
Cost 2	6,420	2,500
Cost 3	16,000	0
Cost 4	20,400	40,800
Total cost	$50,820	$51,300

Required   Identify the relevant differential and opportunity costs in this situation.

3–30 **MILITARY CONTRACTS AND DIRECT VS. INDIRECT COSTS**   In contracts with the U.S. government, direct costs are reimbursable. Indirect costs can be a problem however, when a contract is terminated because the approved cost assignment procedures are no longer appropriate.

The determination of whether a cost is direct of indirect can be critical in some situations. To understand the problem, consider this typical case. A contractor enters into a multiyear, fixed-price development contract with the military. The job requires a significant investment in inspection equipment that the contractor uses only for the military contract. Equipment cost is not treated as a direct cost, however, because governmental cost standards require depreciation costs of all similar assets to be treated consistently, either as direct or indirect costs. Thus, the inspection equipment must be treated as an indirect cost. Because the equipment is an indirect cost, its cost cannot be fully recovered until the project is completed. If the contract is terminated early, only a portion of the cost of the inspection equipment can be recovered.

Required   How do you think this issue should be resolved?

3–31 **BASIC COST TERMS**   Following are descriptions of costs for a small-town cafe (column A) and cost types (column B). The cost object is each meal served.

A—Costs

1. Cost of part-time workers (seasonal fluctuations in breakfast and lunch trade)
2. Rent of the cafe building
3. Cost of full-time workers
4. Cost of utilities (telephone, gas, electric, and trash)
5. Cost of a leased gas-powered grill
6. Cost of cooking ingredients

B—Cost Types

a. Variable cost
b. Step cost
c. Fixed cost

Required   Match each cost in column A to a cost type in column B.

3–32 OPPORTUNITY COST AND RELEVANT COSTS   Emilio is a marketing specialist in Saltillo, Mexico. He has applied for admission to the University of Mexico's MBA program. If accepted, he will resign and move to Mexico City. The relevant data are as follows:

Emilio's annual salary in Saltillo	$34,000
Annual tuition and fees	6,000
Annual book and supply expense	700
Monthly living expenses in Saltillo	800
Monthly living expenses in Mexico City	1,200
Monthly auto expenses (auto required in both cities)	350
Cost of two business suits purchased just prior to resigning	600
Moving expenses	400

Required   Calculate Emilio's opportunity cost of earning an MBA degree if it will take him 12 months to complete the program.

3–33 COST CLASSIFICATION   The XYZ company sells computer accessories using sales representatives. The sales department incurs the following types of costs during each fiscal quarter:

1. Sample product mailed to prospective customers
2. Phone charges for sales representatives calling on customers
3. Repair of faulty products under warranty
4. Travel expenses on business trips
5. Copying expenses
6. Salaries paid to sales representatives
7. Computer time charged to the sales department

Required   Determine whether the listed costs are controllable or uncontrollable by the sales manager or the general manager. Use the following classifications:

a. Controllable by sales manager
b. Uncontrollable by sales manager
c. Controllable by general manager
d. Uncontrollable by general manager

3–34 DIFFERENTIAL COSTS   A nonprofit health organization is studying two methods to increase the number of children in the area who receive measles immunization. The first method involves hiring an educator at $25,000 annual salary. In addition, the educator's expenses, including materials, would be $40,000.

Service

The second method being considered is to strictly enforce an existing law requiring all schoolchildren to be immunized as they enroll for kindergarten. For this program, a staff would be hired to review all necessary paperwork, to send home notices if a child is not in compliance, and to do whatever follow-up work is necessary. Two clerical workers at a total cost of $35,000, including benefits, would be needed to accomplish the task. Cost of supplies and other materials to support the new staff in their jobs would be $15,000.

Required   The health organization must choose between the methods.

1. What are the relevant costs in the decision?
2. What other information might be important?

PROBLEMS

International

3–35 PRODUCT COSTS AND PERIOD COSTS Galletas Americanas is a cookie company in Guadalajara, Mexico, that produces and sells high-quality American-style cookies. The owner wants to identify the various costs incurred each year to be able to plan and control the business costs. Galletas Americanas's costs are the following (in thousands of pesos):

Utilities for the bakery	1,600
Paper used in packaging product	70
Salaries and wages in the bakery	15,000
Cookie ingredients	27,000
Bakery labor and fringe benefits	1,000
Administrative costs	800
Bakery equipment maintenance	600
Depreciation of bakery plant and equipment	1,500
Uniforms	300
Insurance for the bakery	600
Rent for administration offices	13,200
Advertising	1,500
Boxes, bags, and cups used in the bakery	700
Manager's salary	10,000
Overtime premiums	2,000
Idle time	400

Required

1. What is the total amount of product and period costs?

2. Assume that Galletas is planning to expand its business into the United States and Canada, initially targeting the United States. This expansion will not require additional baking facilities, but labor and materials costs will increase, and advertising costs and packaging costs will increase substantially. Also, U.S. authorities will require certain documentation and inspections that will be an added cost for Galletas.

   a. Which of the additional costs are product costs?

   b. Which costs are relevant for the decision whether to expand into the United States?

3–36 COST OF GOODS MANUFACTURED The following information pertains to the Piper Company:

Prime costs	$150,000
Conversion costs	170,000
Direct materials used	65,000
Beginning work in process	75,000
Ending work in process	62,000

Required Determine the cost of goods manufactured.

3–37 EXECUTIONAL COST DRIVERS, INTERNET RETAILER Assume that you are a consultant for a start-up Internet retailer, Bikes.com, which provides a variety of bicycle parts and accessories in a convenient and effective customer service approach. The firm operates from an office building and nearby warehouse located in Danville, Virginia. Currently, the firm has 10 permanent administrative staff, 6 customer service representatives who respond to customer inquiries, and 12 employees who pick, pack, and ship customer orders. All orders are placed over the firm's website. An 800 telephone number is available for customer service. The firm's sales increased at about 20 percent per year in the last two years, a decline from the 50 percent rate in its first three years of operation. Management is concerned that the decline will delay the firm's first expected profit, which had been projected to occur in the next two years. The firm is privately held and has been financed with a combination of bank loans, personal investments of top managers, and venture capital funding.

Required What specific executional cost drivers are important in this business? How should the firm use them to improve its sales rate?

3–38 STRUCTURAL COST DRIVERS

Case A. Food Fare is a small chain of restaurants that has developed a loyal customer base by providing fast-food items with more choices (e.g., how the hamburger should be cooked; self-serve toppings) and a more comfortable atmosphere. The menu has a small number of popular items, including several different hamburgers, grilled chicken sandwiches, and salads. Recently, to broaden its appeal, Food Fare added barbecue, seafood, and steak to its menu.

Case B. Gilman Heating and Air Conditioning, Inc., provides a broad range of services to commercial and residential customers, including installation and repair of several different brands of heating and air conditioning systems. Gilman has a fleet of 28 trucks, each operated by one or more service technicians, depending on the size of a job. A recurrent problem for Gilman has been coordinating the service teams during the day to determine the status of a job and the need for parts not kept in the service vehicle as well as to identify which team to send on emergency calls. Gilman's service area is spread over an urban/rural area of approximately 20 square miles. The company has developed cost and price sheets so that the service technicians accurately and consistently price the service work they perform.

Required For each case, identify the important structural cost drivers for the company and the related strategic issues that it should address to be competitive.

3–39 COST OF GOODS MANUFACTURED AND SOLD Allure Company produces
women's clothing. During 2000, the company incurred the following costs:

Factory rent	$265,000
Direct labor	325,000
Utilities—Factory	88,000
Purchases of direct materials	465,000
Indirect materials	70,000
Indirect labor	35,000

Inventories for the year were as follows:

	January 1	December 31
Direct materials	$ 90,000	$ 50,000
Work in process	40,000	85,000
Finished goods	115,000	95,000

Required
1. Prepare a statement of cost of goods manufactured.
2. Calculate cost of goods sold.

3–40   **COST OF GOODS MANUFACTURED**   The following data pertain to Wheeler Company for the year ended December 31, 2001:

	December 31, 2000	December 31, 2001
Purchases of direct materials		$70,000
Direct labor		30,000
Indirect labor		10,000
Factory insurance		12,000
Depreciation—Factory and equipment		13,000
Repairs and maintenance—Factory and equipment		5,000
Marketing expenses		49,000
General and administrative expenses		30,000
Direct materials inventory	$40,000	47,000
Work-in-process inventory	37,000	35,000
Finished goods inventory	18,000	20,000

Sales in 2001 were $400,000.

Required   Prepare a schedule of cost of goods manufactured and an income statement for Wheeler Company similar to those in Exhibit 3–12a.

3–41   **COST OF GOODS MANUFACTURED, INCOME STATEMENT**   Consider the following information for American Marine Craft, Inc. for the year ended December 31, 2000:

Depreciation expense—Administrative office	$ 32,000
Depreciation expense—Plant and equipment	65,000
Direct labor—Wages	435,000
Direct materials inventory, Dec. 31, 2000	18,000
Direct materials inventory, Jan. 1, 2000	18,000
Direct materials purchases	144,000
Finished goods inventory, Dec. 31, 2000	28,000
Finished goods inventory, Jan. 1, 2000	15,000
Heat, light, & power—Plant	36,000
Indirect labor	25,000
Property taxes—Plant	34,000
Sales representatives' salaries	145,000
Sales revenue	1,500,000
Supervisor's salary	56,000
Supplies—Administrative office	6,000
Supplies—Plant	23,000
Work-in-Process inventory, Dec. 31, 2000	12,000
Work-in-Process inventory, Jan. 1, 2000	23,000

Required   Prepare a statement of cost of goods manufactured and an income statement for American Marine Craft for the year ended December 31, 2000, similar to the one in Exhibit 3–12a.

3–42   **COST OF GOODS MANUFACTURED, CALCULATING UNKNOWNS**   The following information was taken from the accounting records of Ross Manufacturing Company. Unfortunately, some of the data were destroyed by a computer malfunction.

	Case A	Case B
Sales	$80,000	$?
Finished goods inventory, Jan. 1, 2001	15,000	8,000
Finished goods inventory, Dec. 31, 2001	16,000	?
Cost of goods sold	?	23,000
Gross margin	25,000	3,000
Selling and administrative expenses	?	1,000
Net income	10,000	2,000
Work in process, Jan. 1, 2001	?	14,000
Direct material used	6,000	8,000
Direct labor	15,000	9,000
Factory overhead	20,000	?
Total manufacturing costs	?	25,000
Work in process, Dec. 31, 2001	6,000	?
Cost of goods manufactured	?	26,000

Required   Calculate the unknowns indicated by question marks.

3–43   **COST OF GOODS MANUFACTURED, INCOME STATEMENT**   Norton Industries, a manufacturer of cable for the heavy construction industry, closes its books and prepares financial statements at the end of each month. The statement of cost of goods sold for April 2000 follows:

Norton Industries
Statement of Cost of Goods Sold
For the Month Ended April 30, 2000
($000 omitted)

Inventory of finished goods, March 31	$ 50
Cost of goods manufactured	790
Cost of goods available for sale	$840
Less inventory of finished goods, April 30	247
Cost of goods sold	$593

Additional Information

- Of the utilities, 80 percent relates to manufacturing the cable; the remaining 20 percent relates to the sales and administrative functions.
- All rent is for the office building.
- Property taxes are assessed on the manufacturing plant.
- Of the insurance, 60 percent is related to manufacturing the cable; the remaining 40 percent is related to the sales and administrative functions.
- Depreciation expense includes the following:

Manufacturing plant	$20,000
Manufacturing equipment	30,000
Office equipment	4,000
	$54,000

- The company manufactured 7,825 tons of cable during May 2000.
- The inventory balances at May 31, 2000, follow:
- Direct materials inventory $ 23,000
- Work-in-process inventory   220,000
- Finished goods inventory   175,000

Norton Industries
Preclosing Account Balances
May 31, 2000
($000 omitted)

Cash and marketable securities	$ 54
Accounts and notes receivable	210
Direct materials inventory (4/30/00)	28
Work-in-process inventory (4/30/00)	150
Finished goods inventory (4/30/00)	247
Property, plant, and equipment (net)	1,140
Accounts, notes, and taxes payable	70
Bonds payable	600
Paid-in capital	100
Retained earnings	930
Sales	1,488
Sales discounts	20
Other revenue	2
Purchases of direct materials	510
Direct labor	260
Indirect factory labor	90
Office salaries	122
Sales salaries	42
Utilities	135
Rent	9
Property tax	60
Insurance	20
Depreciation	54
Interest expense	6
Freight-in for materials purchases	15

Required   Based on Exhibit 3–12, prepare the following:
1. Statement of cost of goods manufactured for Norton Industries for May 2000.

2. Income statement for Norton Industries for May 2000.

(CMA adapted)

Strategy

3–44 RISK AVERSION AND DECISION MAKING   John Smith is the production manager of Elmo's Glue Company. Because of limited capacity, the company can produce only one of two possible products. Product A is a space-age bonding formula that has a 15 percent probability of making a $1,000,000 profit and an 85% chance of generating a $200,000 profit. Product B is a reformulated household glue that has a 100 percent chance of making a $310,000 profit. John has the responsibility to choose between the two products. Assume that he is more risk averse than Elmo's top management. He receives a bonus of 20 percent of the profit from his department.

Required
1. Which product will John choose? Why?

2. Is this the product Elmo's top management would choose? Why or why not?

3. How can Elmo's change its reward system so that John makes decisions that are consistent with top management's wishes?

Strategy

3–45 RISK AVERSION, STRATEGY   John Holt is the production supervisor for ITEXX, a manufacturer of plastic parts, with customers in the automobile and consumer products industries. On a Tuesday morning, one of ITEXX's sales managers asked John to reschedule his manufacturing jobs for the rest of the week to accommodate the manager's special order from a new customer. The customer required fast turnaround, which meant not only delaying the current production schedule but also running all three production shifts for the remainder of the week. This would make it impossible to complete the regularly scheduled maintenance on the equipment that John had planned for mid-week. The sales manager was determined to get the new customer, which could mean an important increase in overall sales and output at the plant. However, John worried not only about the delay of the current jobs but also about the chance that the maintenance delay would cause one of the machines to fail, which would back up the orders in the plant for at least a week, meaning a substantial delay for the new order as well as those currently scheduled.

Required How do you think John should resolve this problem? What is a good policy for handling such issues in the future?

SOLUTION TO SELF-STUDY PROBLEM

SPARTAN PRODUCTS COMPANY
Statement of Cost of Goods Manufactured
For the Year Ended December 31, 2001

Direct materials		
Direct materials inventory, Jan. 1, 2001	$ 20,000	
Purchases of direct materials	100,000	
Total direct materials available	$120,000	
Direct materials inventory, Dec. 31, 2001	30,000	
Direct materials used		$ 90,000
Direct labor		350,000
Factory overhead		
Heat, light, and power—Plant	12,000	
Supplies—Plant	4,000	
Property taxes—Plant	13,000	
Depreciation expense—Plant and equipment	80,000	
Indirect labor	5,000	
Supervisor's salary—Plant	40,000	
Total factory overhead		154,000
Total manufacturing costs		$594,000
Add: Beginning work-in-process inventory, Jan. 1, 2001		35,000
Total manufacturing costs to account for		$629,000
Less: Ending work-in-process, Dec. 31, 2001		25,000
Cost of goods manufactured		$604,000

SPARTAN PRODUCTS COMPANY
Income Statement
For the Year Ended December 31, 2001

Sales revenue		$1,000,000
Cost of goods sold		
Finished goods inventory, Jan. 1, 2001	$ 35,000	
Cost of goods manufactured	604,000	
Total goods available for sale	$639,000	
Finished goods inventory, Dec. 31, 2001	40,000	
Cost of goods sold		599,000
Gross margin		$401,000
Selling and administrative expenses		
Sales representatives' salaries	190,000	
Supplies—Administrative office	6,000	
Depreciation expense—Administrative office	30,000	
Total selling and administrative expenses		226,000
Net income		$175,000

4

Activity-Based Costing and Management

After studying this chapter, you should be able to . . .

1   Describe the key features of contemporary manufacturing techniques

2   Explain why traditional costing systems tend to distort product costs

3   Describe an activity-based costing system and its benefits, limitations, and two-stage allocation procedures

4   Compute product costs under a traditional costing system and an activity-based costing system

5   Describe an activity-based management system and value-added and non-value-added activities

6   Explain how activity-based costing systems are used in the manufacturing industry

7   Describe how activity-based costing systems are used in marketing and administrative activities

8   Demonstrate how activity-based costing systems are used in service and not-for-profit organizations

9   Relate activity-based costing to strategic cost management

10 Identify key factors for a successful ABC/ABM implementation

Dow Chemical, an international Fortune 100 company, began to shift its strategy from diversification to specialization in its core business of chemicals and plastics in 1993 to ensure its success in highly competitive markets. Dow identified its corporate goal as setting the competitive standard by supplying the optimum combination of cost and quality to provide the highest value to its customers. Dow began using the activity-based costing (ABC) and activity-based management (ABM) cost management techniques at that time to help implement its new strategy in achieving the company goal.[1]

ABC/ABM provided Dow managers the information that enabled them to truly understand the costs of products and customer relationships and to guide their decisions such as pricing, product mix, product design, and process restructuring. Dow also integrated ABC into its budget process and tracked activities as well as costs with its enterprise resource planning system.

ABC/ABM have added value for Dow. The company had total assets of $26 billion and net sales of $19 billion at the end of 1999. This chapter will show how companies use ABC/ABM cost management techniques to make them more competitive and successful.

Since the early 1980s, many other U.S. companies, such as IBM, Hewlett-Packard, Allen-Bradley, Westinghouse, General Motors, General Electric, Eastman Kodak, and Lockheed, have adopted advanced manufacturing technologies to meet global competition. The modernization of U.S. factories has increased quality and lowered costs. Along with these changes, cost management practices and manufacturing processes have changed and improved.

While describing various techniques used in the contemporary manufacturing environment, this chapter identifies the major problems associated with cost accounting in providing accurate and relevant cost information. It also discusses ABC including its benefits and limitations. ABC helps firms reduce distortions caused by traditional costing systems and provides more accurate product costs. It offers a clear view of how a firm's diverse products, services, and activities contribute in the long run to the bottom line.

The chapter also describes ABM and ABC/ABM applications in manufacturing, marketing, administrative, service, and not-for-profit organizations. ABM focuses on

---

[1] For more about the Dow Chemical success story, see its website at www.dow.com; also see James W. Damitio, Gary W. Hayes, and Philip L. Kintzele, "Integrating ABC and ABM at Dow Chemical," *Management Accounting Quarterly*, Winter 2000, pp. 22–26.

managing activities to promote business efficiency and effectiveness and to increase both the value received by customers and the firm's profits.

ABC/ABM systems have been developed and implemented at many companies in addition to Dow, such as General Motors, Data Technologies, Hewlett-Packard, Advanced Micro Devices, Avery International, Cal Electronic Circuits, General Electric, Eastman Kodak, Siemens Electric Motor Works, John Deere Component Works, Merck, Tektronix, Texas Instruments, Alexandria Hospital, Union Pacific Railroad, Amtrak, Data Services, AT&T, Fireman's Fund, American Express, Caterpillar, and Naval Supply System Command.

ABC and ABM are closely tied to strategic cost management. They provide managers more meaningful information for answering strategic questions such as these:

- What are the potential impacts on pricing and product-line decisions if a firm switches from the traditional costing system to an activity-based costing system?

- What are potential cost savings if a firm uses ABM to identify and eliminate non-value-added activities to achieve its low-cost strategy?

- How can ABC/ABM help a firm achieve its competitive strategy of high performance and short lead time in delivering its products?

- How can ABC/ABM help a firm analyze its major customer profitability and develop a customer-focused strategy?

THE CONTEMPORARY MANUFACTURING ENVIRONMENT

LEARNING OBJECTIVE 1 ▶

Describe the key features of contemporary manufacturing techniques.

At the end of the twentieth century, an increasing number of national and international companies made changes in their manufacturing plants. In attempts to reduce costs, increase productivity, improve product quality, and increase flexibility in response to customer needs, these companies have adopted some or all of the following innovative approaches: (1) just-in-time (JIT) manufacturing systems using kanban and work cells tools, (2) various automation techniques such as robots, computer-aided design (CAD), and computer-aided manufacturing (CAM), and (3) integration approaches such as flexible manufacturing systems (FMS) and computer-integrated manufacturing (CIM) to improve manufacturing productivity.

The Just-in-Time System

A **just-in-time (JIT) system** is a comprehensive production and inventory system that purchases or produces materials and parts only as needed and just in time to be used at each stage of the production process.

A **just-in-time (JIT) system** is a comprehensive production and inventory management system that purchases or produces materials and parts only as needed and just in time to be used at each stage of the production process. JIT is a philosophy that can be applied to all aspects of business, including purchasing, production, and delivery. Its goals are to purchase materials and parts just in time to be placed into manufacturing processes and to produce and deliver products just in time to be sold profitably. JIT focuses on eliminating waste, reducing inventories, developing a strong supplier relationship, increasing employee involvement, and developing customer-focused programs. The degree of coordination needed to implement effective JIT manufacturing systems highlights existing problems such as bottlenecks, inventory shrinkage, and unreliable suppliers. JIT helps organizations to become more efficient and better managed, and to earn more profits than their competitors.

Because the JIT environment allows only small inventory buffers, each organizational unit must maintain close communication with other units, customers, and outside vendors. This constant exchange of information enables quick identification of any inefficiencies. Problems concealed in traditional inventory, such as inadequate product or process quality or obsolescence, become evident when JIT is implemented.

Many companies, such as General Motors, Intel, and Westinghouse, have used JIT successfully to cut inventories, improve production efficiency, and raise product quality. For example, Oregon Cutting Systems (OCS), a $250 million company headquartered in Portland, manufactures steel products for cutting saws, timber-harvesting

---

JIT Helps Harley-Davidson

Harley-Davidson used JIT to save more than $22 million within one year by reducing work-in-process inventory. Under the JIT, it manufactures only enough parts to satisfy one day's production and ships these high-quality goods to the job site. JIT reduces working capital requirements for warehousing surplus parts and permits much better quality control.

Source: William T. Turk, "Management Accounting Revitalized: The Harley-Davidson Experience," *Journal of Cost Management,* Winter 1990, pp. 28–39.

---

equipment, and sporting equipment. OCS developed its own version of JIT, called a *zero inventory production system*, that has three major components: (1) JIT manufacturing to improve supplier relationship, smooth the production line, and reduce setup time and inventory; (2) continual improvement to upgrade quality and reduce waste; and (3) employee development and empowerment to promote their personal commitments to the company.

OCS began implementing JIT in the early 1980s; within five years, it had managed to reduce defects by 80 percent and cut scrap and rework by 50 percent. Other results were also remarkable. For example, at one Canadian plant, setup times were reduced from 390 minutes to 1 minute 40 seconds, space requirements were reduced by 40 percent, lead times were cut from 21 days to 3 days, and inventory was reduced by 50 percent.[2]

JIT is not just for manufacturers. Service and retailing firms, such as banks, insurance companies, hospitals, department stores, and accounting firms can also apply it. In nonmanufacturing applications, JIT focuses management's attention on non-value-added processes and just-in-time delivery and service.

Kanban

In Japanese, *kanban* means "card." Workers use a set of control cards to signal the need for materials and products to move from one operation to the next in an assembly line. Kanban is used with JIT to greatly reduce lead times, decrease inventory, and improve productivity by linking all production operations in a smooth, uninterrupted flow.[3]

Kanban is a set of control cards used to signal the need for materials and products to move from one operation to the next in an assembly line.

Kanban is essentially a communication system; it can be a card, a label, a box or bin, a series of in trays, or a number of squares painted or taped on the factory floor or work surface. Its purpose is to inform the previous step in the process to make a part. The kanban card typically contains information identifying the part, its descriptive name, how many of each part should accompany the card, the delivery location, the reorder point on the shelf stack, and the turnaround time negotiated between the internal customer and producer or the plant and an external subcontractor.[4]

Under a kanban system, the previous process or step cannot send parts or components to the subsequent step unless that downstream process or step requests them by means of a kanban card. The subsequent step controls the amount produced. Thus, no overproduction occurs, priority in production becomes obvious, and control of inventory becomes easier.

Work Cells

Work cells are small groups of related manufacturing processes organized in clusters to assemble parts of finished products. Major characteristics of work cells are (1) organizing related manufacturing processes in clusters, (2) placing similar operations together,

Work cells are small groups of related manufacturing processes organized in clusters to assemble parts of finished products.

---

[2] Jack C. Bailes and Ilene K. Kleinsorge, "Cutting Waste with JIT," *Management Accounting,* May 1992, pp. 28–32.

[3] Bruce R. Neumann and Pauline R. Jaouen, "Kanban, ZIPS, and Cost Accounting: A Case Study," *Journal of Accountancy,* August 1986, pp. 132–41.

[4] Richard B. Kitney, "Production Systems with Pull," *CMA Magazine,* July–August 1994, pp. 22–24.

Dell Computer Uses JIT to Minimize Its Inventories

Dell Computer Corporation uses JIT to minimize the need for computer inventories. The firm builds computers to customers' specifications after the orders are received, decreasing its inventories. Dell keeps 35 days of inventory on hand compared to 110 days for Compaq Computer Corporation.

Source: "The Computer Is in the Mail (Really)," *Business Week,* January 23, 1995, pp. 76–77.

---

(3) grouping all production activities from the raw materials stage to the finished goods stage in the same cell, and (4) providing easy visual control so that when a line slowdown or stoppage occurs, feedback is immediate.

Automation

Automation involves replacing human effort with machines. Its goal is to increase efficiency and effectiveness. Factory automation has become a necessity for many industries. The most popular forms are robots, computer-aided design, and computer-aided manufacturing.

Robots

A **robot** is a computer-programmed and controlled machine that performs repetitive activities.

More companies are using robots than ever before. A **robot** is a computer-programmed and controlled machine that performs repetitive activities. By using robots, companies have increased their capacity, decreased the time to manufacture a part (by using more efficient routings), and consequently reduced late orders. Companies are achieving major cost savings with automation by decreasing direct labor costs and tooling costs.

Computer-Aided Design and Manufacturing

Computer-aided design (CAD) is the use of computers in product development, analysis, and design modification to improve the quality and performance of the product.

Computer-aided manufacturing (CAM) is the use of computers to plan, implement, and control production.

Computer-aided design (CAD) is the use of computers in product development, analysis, and design modification to improve the quality and performance of the product. **Computer-aided manufacturing (CAM)** is the use of computers to plan, implement, and control production. General Motors, Ford, and Chrysler use CAM to produce cars. It dispatches production orders to electronic machine tools, robots, and other automated work stations.

In the factories of the future, more companies will use CAD and CAM to respond to changing consumer tastes more quickly. These innovations allow companies to significantly reduce the time necessary to bring their products from the design process to the distribution stage.

A **flexible manufacturing system (FMS)** is a computerized network of automated equipment that produces one or more groups of parts or variations of a product in a flexible manner.

Integration

Automation requires a relatively large investment in computers, computer programming, machines, and equipment. Many firms add automation equipment gradually, one process at a time. To improve efficiency and effectiveness continuously, firms must integrate people and equipment into the smoothly operating teams that have become a vital part of manufacturing strategy. Flexible manufacturing systems (FMS) and computer-integrated manufacturing (CIM) are two integration approaches.

A **flexible manufacturing system (FMS)** is a computerized network of automated equipment that produces one or more groups of parts or variations of a product in a flexible manner. It uses robots and computer-controlled materials-handling systems to link several stand-alone, numerically controlled machines in switching from one production run to another.

Computer-integrated manufacturing (CIM) is a manufacturing system that totally integrates all office and factory functions within a company via a computer-based information network to allow hour-by-hour manufacturing management.

Computer-integrated manufacturing (CIM) is a manufacturing system that totally integrates all office and factory functions within a company via a computer-based information network to allow hour-by-hour manufacturing management.

The major characteristics of modern manufacturing companies that are adopting FMS and CIM are production of high-quality products and services, low inventories, high degrees of automation, quick cycle time, increased flexibility, and advanced information technology. These innovations shift the focus from large production volumes necessary to absorb fixed overhead to a new emphasis on marketing efforts, engineering, and product design. Every world-class manufacturing company needs a world-class cost management system to be able to produce high-quality accounting information for more effective management decisions.

Managers use financial information to judge the impact of their decisions on company profits. Accurate and relevant cost information is an important key to an enterprise's survival, growth, and ability to make profits in this highly competitive environment. Therefore, having a suitable cost system enables a company to evaluate both the profitability of its products and the effects of the resource allocation decisions on profit. It also can be used for planning and control.

LIMITATIONS OF TRADITIONAL COSTING SYSTEMS

The traditional, volume-based costing systems are useful when direct labor and materials are the predominant factors of production, when technology is stable, and when the range of products is limited. Traditional costing systems measure the resources consumed in proportion to the number of individual products produced. However, many organizational resources accompanying the revolution in the business world, such as setup or materials-handling costs for activities and transactions, are unrelated to the physical volume of units produced. Consequently, traditional costing systems do a poor job of attributing the expenses of these support resources to the production and sale of individual products. The expenses typically are allocated to products using unit- or volume-based cost drivers, such as direct labor-hours, direct materials costs, direct labor costs, machine-hours, or units produced. The product costs generated by such allocations are distorted because products do not consume most support resources in proportion to their production volumes.

◀**LEARNING OBJECTIVE 2**

Explain why traditional costing systems tend to distort product costs.

Traditional costing systems do not reflect the way specific activities in an automated plant cause variations in major cost categories. Product costs typically have been monitored in three categories: direct materials, direct labor, and factory overhead. Traditional costing systems were developed when the labor component dominated total manufacturing costs; that is, products requiring the highest labor input drove most of the production costs. Hence, the focus of these systems was on measuring and controlling direct labor costs.

Factory overhead, defined as the sum of all production costs that cannot be directly identified with any product line (the sum of all indirect costs), was traditionally not a major cost element. It includes expenses such as factory maintenance, utilities, insurance, and supervisory salaries. In the contemporary manufacturing environment, most expenditures associated with factory automation now are included in the Factory Overhead account: new equipment depreciation and insurance, salaries for technicians and product engineers, and research and development. As a result, the percentage of total manufacturing costs related to direct labor has consistently decreased, with a corresponding increase in fixed overhead costs.

The major limitation of traditional costing systems is the use of volume-based cost drivers to calculate plantwide or departmental rates. These rates produce inaccurate product costs when a large share of factory overhead costs is not volume based and when firms produce a diverse mix of products with different volumes, sizes, and complexities.

Volume-Based Plantwide and Departmental Rates

The traditional costing system uses either a single plantwide overhead rate or several departmental overhead rates based on output volume to allocate factory overhead cost to products or services. A plantwide rate assumes that, in proportion to the cost driver (e.g., direct labor-hours) used, all products or services benefit from the overhead costs incurred. The departmental rates method uses a separate volume-based cost driver to calculate a predetermined overhead rate (e.g., one uses direct labor-hours and the other uses machine-hours) for each department. Therefore, product costs are more likely than the plantwide rate to reflect different usages in departments. Still, departmental rates do not consider the varying costs of different processes or activities within a department.

Traditional costing systems often allocate overhead to products using volume-based cost drivers such as direct labor-hours or dollars. Firms usually adopt a plantwide overhead rate that results from dividing total budgeted overhead costs by total budgeted direct labor costs. Only a decade ago, overhead rates of 150 percent of direct labor costs were fairly typical. Now overhead rates of 600 percent or even 1,000 percent in highly automated plants are common. As products move through a plant, they are charged overhead costs based on the plantwide rate times the cost of direct labor required by each product.

Such overhead cost allocations in a factory using automation can cause serious distortions. To allocate overhead based on direct labor cost, we must assume that products with higher direct labor contents are responsible for more overhead costs, so they need to be charged higher overhead allocations. In automated environments, however, overhead allocations based on direct labor systematically overstate the costs of products with high direct labor content and understate the costs of other products that utilize more automated processes. Also, because fixed manufacturing costs are associated with groups of products, allocation of factory overhead to any individual product becomes more difficult.

For example, Dole Company has two factories Alpha and Beta. Alpha is a highly automated factory; Beta is a labor-intensive factory. The company has budgeted the following information for the year:

	Alpha	Beta	Total
Budgeted overhead amount	$400,000	$200,000	$600,000
Budgeted number of labor-hours	10,000	50,000	60,000
Budgeted number of machine-hours	20,000	4,000	24,000

Assume that the company uses a single plantwide labor-hour overhead rate as the cost driver for overhead allocation. The single predetermined overhead rate is computed as follows:

$$\frac{\text{Budgeted overhead amount}}{\text{Budgeted number of labor-hours}} = \frac{\$600,000}{60,000} = \$10 \text{ per labor-hour}$$

Old Costing System Distorted Product Costs at Hewlett-Packard

The old product costing system at Hewlett-Packard (HP) used the volume-based labor cost as the cost driver for all nonmaterial costs regardless of the actual cost drivers. On average, labor costs were only 2 percent of total costs, so it was unlikely that they were the major cause of most other costs. The result of using labor cost was significant cost distortion: Products with higher labor costs were overcosted and products with lower labor costs were undercosted. Managers did not have confidence in the product cost predictions using this old labor-based system.

Therefore, HP decided to switch to an activity-based costing system. It measured cost behavior as part of its companywide implementation of activity-based costing. HP used detailed engineering analysis to revise its accounting system at many of its manufacturing sites.

Source: Mike Mertz and Aelene Hardy, "ABC Puts Accountants on Design Team at HP," *Management Accounting,* September 1993, pp. 22–27.

During the first month of the year, the company has the following information for its two products, Widget and Gidget:

	Alpha	Beta
Widget		
Number of labor-hours	500	4,000
Number of machine-hours	800	200
Gidget		
Number of labor-hours	500	1,000
Number of machine-hours	1,200	400

Using the labor-hour-based plantwide overhead rate, the company applied factory overhead costs to the two products as follows:

	Widget	Gidget
Alpha		
$10 × 500	$ 5,000	
$10 × 500		$ 5,000
Beta		
$10 × 4,000	40,000	
$10 × 1,000		10,000
Total overhead applied	$45,000	$15,000

To obtain more accurate product-costing information, assume that Dole Company decides to use two cost drivers, i.e., two separate departmental overhead rates for overhead costs, with a machine-hour-based rate for Alpha and a labor-hour-based rate for Beta. The departmental predetermined overhead cost driver rates are calculated as follows:

$$\textbf{Alpha Overhead Rate}$$

$$\frac{\text{Budgeted overhead amount}}{\text{Budgeted number of machine-hours}} = \frac{\$400,000}{20,000} = \$20 \text{ per machine-hour}$$

$$\textbf{Beta Overhead Rate}$$

$$\frac{\text{Budgeted overhead amount}}{\text{Budgeted number of labor-hours}} = \frac{\$200,000}{50,000} = \$4 \text{ per labor-hour}$$

Using departmental overhead rates, the factory overhead cost assigned to the two products follows:

	Widget	Gidget
Alpha: (cost driver: machine-hours)		
$20 × 800	$16,000	
$20 × 1,200		$24,000
Beta: (cost driver: labor-hours)		
$4 × 4,000	16,000	
$4 × 1,000		4,000
Total overhead applied	$32,000	$28,000

The preceding calculations show that the applied overhead costs with the single plantwide overhead cost driver rate are $13,000 ($45,000 – $32,000) higher for Widget and $13,000 ($15,000 – $28,000) lower for Gidget than had the firm used the two departmental overhead rates. Gidget requires considerably more machine-hours than Widget, but the overhead cost allocation to products with the single plantwide overhead cost driver rate does not consider these differences. Use of departmental rates causes product cost to more accurately reflect the different amount of labor and the different types of machinery and labor involved in producing the two products.

Departmental rates, however, do not consider the varying overhead costs of different processes or activities within a department because some factory overhead costs are not volume based. For example, machine setup cost, product design cost, purchase ordering cost, and materials handling cost are not directly related to either direct labor-hours or machine-hours. The traditional volume-based plantwide and departmental cost driver rate overhead allocation methods can lead to inaccurate product costing.

Volume, Size, and Diversity Complexity

The distortions from unit- or volume-based product cost systems are most severe in firms producing a diverse mix of products. Products that differ in volume, size, and complexity consume support resources in significantly different amounts. As product diversity increases, the amount of resources required for handling and support activities also increases, thereby increasing the distortion of reported product costs by traditional cost systems.

Cooper demonstrates how traditional costing systems overcost large-size, high-volume products and undercost small-size, low-volume products when product diversity exists within the same operation.[5]

Traditional costing systems using unit- or volume-based cost drivers can cause distorted inventory measurement (even if they are perfectly within financial accounting standards). This distortion, in turn, can cause undesirable strategic results, such as wrong product-line decisions, unrealistic pricing, and ineffective resource allocations.

In summary, the traditional cost system is appropriate for firms that have few similar products or services with homogeneous production processes or customers. However, when firms have a variety of products or services with heterogeneous production processes or customers, the traditional cost system distorts product cost information because the cost system (1) is designed to value inventory in the aggregate, not to relate product cost information, (2) uses a common departmental or plantwide cost driver, such as direct labor-hours or dollars (now a small portion of overall production costs) to distribute factory overhead to products, (3) deemphasizes long-term product analysis (when fixed costs become variable costs), and (4) causes managers who are aware of distortions in the traditional system to make intuitive, imprecise adjustments to the traditional cost information without understanding their complete effect.

ACTIVITY-BASED COSTING

An evaluation of the profitability of different product lines requires that factory overhead costs be traced to the finished products because of the relative importance of factory overhead. However, because factory overhead costs are related only indirectly to finished products, management accountants have devised a new way to apply such costs to individual products: activity-based costing.

Activities, Resources, Cost Drivers, Resource Cost Drivers, and Activity Cost Drivers

Before discussing activity-based costing, several important terms need to be defined: *activity, resource, cost driver, resource cost driver,* and *activity cost driver.*

An **activity** is work performed within an organization.[6] It is also an aggregation of actions performed within an organization useful for purposes of activity-based costing.

An **activity** (composed of actions, movements, or work sequences) is work performed within an organization.

---

[5] Robin Cooper, "The Rise of Activity-Based Costing—Part One: What Is an Activity-Based Cost System?" *Journal of Cost Management,* Summer 1988, pp. 45–54.

[6] Norm Raffish and Peter B. B. Turney, "Glossary of Activity-Based Management," *Journal of Cost Management,* Fall 1991, pp. 53–63. Other definitions from this glossary also are used in this chapter.

For example, moving inventory is a warehousing activity. Activities are composed of actions, movements, or work sequences.

A **resource** is an economic element applied or used to perform activities. Salaries and materials, for example, are resources used in performing activities.

As defined in Chapter 3, a *cost driver* is any factor that causes a change in the cost of an activity. It is also a measurable factor used to assign costs to activities and from activities to other activities, products, or services.[7] The two types of cost drivers are resource cost drivers and activity cost drivers.

A **resource cost driver** is a measure of the amount of resources consumed by an activity. It is the cost driver used to assign a resource cost consumed by an activity to a particular cost pool. An example of a resource cost driver is the percentage of total square feet required to perform an activity.

An **activity cost driver** measures how much of an activity a cost object uses. It is used to assign cost pool costs to cost objects. An example is machine hours required for the activity of running machines to produce product X.

> A **resource** is an economic element applied or used to perform activities.
>
> A **resource cost driver** is a measure of the amount of resources consumed by an activity.
>
> An **activity cost driver** measures how much of an activity a cost object uses.

What Is Activity-Based Costing?

As defined earlier, *activity-based costing* (ABC) is a costing approach that assigns costs to products, services, or customers based on the consumption of resources caused by activities. The premise of this costing approach is that a firm's products or services are the results of activities performed and that the required activities use resources incurring costs. Resources are assigned to activities, and activities are assigned to cost objects based on the activities' use. ABC recognizes the causal relationships of cost drivers to activities.

ABC assigns factory overhead costs to cost objects such as products or services by identifying the resources and activities as well as their costs and amounts needed to produce output. A cost driver calculates the resource cost of a unit of activity, and then each resource cost is assigned to the product or service by multiplying the cost of each activity by the amount of each activity consumed in a given period.

Activity-based costing is a system that maintains and processes financial and operating data about a firm's resources based on activities, cost objects, cost drivers, and activity performance measures. It also assigns costs to activities and cost objects.

◄**LEARNING OBJECTIVE 3**

Describe an activity-based costing system and its benefits, limitations, and two-stage allocation procedures.

Cost Drivers at Cal Electronic Circuits, Inc.

Cal Electronic Circuits, Inc., uses 10 cost drivers to produce printed circuit boards (PCB):

1. Number of setups.
2. Number of holes drilled in PCB.
3. Number of layers in PCB.
4. Number of drill sizes required.
5. Number of images per panel in PCB.
6. PCB length and width.
7. Number of parts per panel.
8. Number of engineering hours.
9. Lot size.
10. Volume of chemical waste.

Source: John Lee, "Activity Based Costing at Cal Electronic Circuits," *Management Accounting,* October 1990, pp. 36–38.

---

[7] *Statement No. 4T,* "Implementing Activity-Based Costing" (Institute of Management Accountants, 1993) p. 34. Cost drivers reflect the consumption of costs by activities and the consumption of activities, products, or services.

Two-Stage Allocation Procedures

A **two-stage allocation** assigns a firm's resource costs, namely factory overhead costs, to cost pools and then to cost objects.

A **two-stage allocation** assigns a firm's resource costs, namely factory overhead costs, to cost pools and then to cost objects based on the cost objects' use of those resources. Traditional costing systems first assign factory overhead costs to plant or departmental cost pools or cost centers and then to production outputs (see Exhibit 4–1). This traditional two-stage allocation procedure, however, distorts reported product or service costs considerably. Especially in the second stage, the traditional costing system assigns factory overhead costs from plant or departmental cost pools to outputs using volume-based or unit-level cost drivers, such as direct labor- and machine-hours, direct materials costs, direct labor costs, and output units. Because many factory overhead resources are not used in proportion to the number of output units produced, the traditional system can provide highly inaccurate measures of the costs of support activities used by individual products or services.

An activity-based costing system differs from traditional costing systems by modeling the usage of a firm's resources on activities performed by these resources and then linking the cost of these activities to cost objects such as products, customers, or services (see Exhibit 4–2). In particular, the activity-based costing system more accurately measures the cost of activities that are not proportional to the volume of outputs produced.

Under an activity-based costing system, the first-stage allocation is a resource cost assignment process by which factory overhead costs are assigned to activity cost pools or groups of activities called activity centers by using appropriate resource cost drivers.

The second-stage allocation is an activity cost assignment process by which the costs of activities are assigned to cost objects using appropriate activity cost drivers, which measure the demands a cost object places on an activity.

An activity-based costing system differs from traditional costing systems in two ways: First, the ABC system defines cost pools as activities or activity centers rather than production plant or department cost centers. Second, the cost drivers that the ABC system uses to assign activity costs to cost objects are activity cost drivers based on cause-and-effect relationships. The traditional approach uses a single volume-based cost driver that often bears little or no relationship to either the resource cost or the cost object.

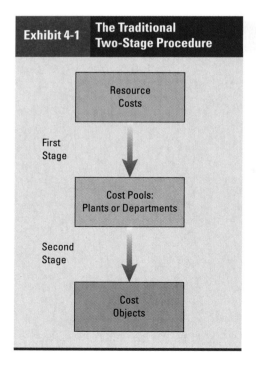

Exhibit 4-1   **The Traditional Two-Stage Procedure**

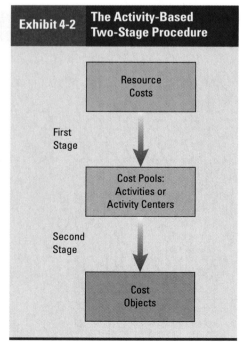

Exhibit 4-2   **The Activity-Based Two-Stage Procedure**

These modifications to the two-stage allocation procedure allow an activity-based costing system to report more accurate costs than traditional costing systems because it clearly identifies the costs of the different activities being performed. It also assigns the costs of those activities to output cost objects using measures that represent the types of demands individual output products or services make on those activities.

When Is an Activity-Based Costing System Needed?

An activity-based costing system provides better costing information and can help management manage efficiently and understand the system's competitive advantages, strengths, and weaknesses. In the past, an activity-based costing system was implemented only when (1) the cost of measuring the activities and their costs decreased, perhaps because of computerized scheduling systems on the production floor, (2) stronger competition increased the cost of erroneous pricing, and (3) product diversity was high in volume, size, or complexity.[8] In fact, all firms should use the ABC system when the benefits of such a system exceed the costs of implementing it.

An activity-based costing system has the most impact, according to Kaplan and Cooper,[9] on firms that (1) have areas with large, increasing expenses and (2) that have numerous products, services, customers, processes, or a combination of these. An example is a plant that produces standard and custom products, high-volume and low-volume products, and mature and new products. Another example is a firm that reserves small and larger orders, offers standard and customized deliveries, and has some customers that demand frequent changes in their delivery requirements and others who make no such demands.

According to a recent survey conducted by the Cost Management Group of the Institute of Management Accountants, more than half (54 percent) of responding companies that have tried ABC are using it for decision-making outside the accounting function. Of those companies using ABC, 89 percent say that it is worth the implementation costs. Who tries ABC? The survey indicated that the higher the potential for cost distortions, the more motivated an organization is to adopt ABC. It also reported that adopting firms had a higher percentage of overhead costs to total production costs. Based on questions relating to competition, cost-reduction efforts, and basis for pricing decisions, ABC adopting firms ranked decision usefulness of the firm's cost information higher than non-ABC firms.[10]

A recent ABC survey by ABC Technologies, Inc. reported that the top four objectives of adopting ABC were product/service costing (58 percent), process analysis (51 percent), performance management (49 percent), and profitability assessment (39 percent).[11]

Steps in Designing an Activity-Based Costing System

The three major steps in designing an activity-based costing system are to (1) identify resource costs and activities, (2) assign resource costs to activities, and (3) assign activity costs to cost objects.

Step 1: Identify Resource Costs and Activities

The first step in designing an ABC system is to conduct an activity analysis to identify resource costs. These costs are incurred to perform various activities. Most resource costs are held in the subaccounts of the general ledger; examples are materials, supplies,

---

[8]   Robin Cooper, "The Rise of Activity-Based Costing—Part Two: When Do I Need an Activity-Based Cost System?" *The Journal of Cost Management*, Fall 1988, pp. 41–48.

[9]   Robert S. Kaplan and Robin Cooper, *Cost and Effects: Using Integrated Cost Systems to Drive Profitability and Performance* (Boston, Mass.: Harvard Business School Press, 1997) pp. 100–101.

[10]   Kip R. Krumwiede, "ABC: Why It's Tried and How It Succeeds," *Strategic Finance*, April 1998, pp. 32–38.

[11]   Mohan Nair, "Activity-Based Costing: Who's Using It and Why?" *Management Accounting Quarterly*, Spring 2000, pp. 29–33.

purchasing, materials handling, warehousing, office space, furniture and fixtures, buildings, equipment, utilities, salaries and benefits, engineering, and accounting.

An *activity analysis* identifies and describes the work an organization performs. Activity analysis includes gathering data from existing documents and records and using survey questionnaires, observation, and ongoing interviews of key personnel. ABC project team members typically ask each key employee or manager questions such as these:

- What work or activities do you do?
- How much time do you spend performing these activities?
- What resources are required to perform these activities?
- Which operational data best reflect the performance of the activities?
- What value does the activity have for the organization?

The team also collects activity data by observing the work performed and listing the activities involved.

Manufacturing processes have four levels of activities:

A unit-level activity is performed for each unit of production.

1. A **unit-level activity** is performed for each unit of production every time the unit of production is produced. Examples of unit-level (volume-based or unit-based) activities include using direct materials, using direct labor-hours, inserting a component, inspecting every item, and running machines.

A batch-level activity is performed for each batch of products rather than for each unit of production.

2. A **batch-level activity** is performed for each batch or group of products rather than for each unit of production. Batch-level activities are performed every time a batch of product is produced. Examples of batch-level activities are setting up machines, placing purchase orders, scheduling production, inspecting every batch, and handling materials.

A product-sustaining activity is performed to support the production of a specific product.

3. A **product-sustaining activity** is performed to support the production of a specific product. Examples of product-sustaining activities include designing products, administering parts, issuing engineering change orders, and expediting.

A facility-sustaining activity is performed to support the production of products in general.

4. A **facility-sustaining activity** is performed to support the production of products in general.[12] Examples of facility-sustaining activities include providing security, safety, maintenance, and plant management, calculating plant depreciation, and paying property taxes.

Step 2: Assign Resource Costs to Activities

Activities drive the cost of resources used. Resource cost drivers are used to assign resource costs to activities. An important criterion for choosing a good resource cost driver is the cause-and-effect relationship. Typical resource cost drivers include the number of (1) meters of utilities; (2) employees for payroll-related activities; (3) setups for a machine activity; (4) moves in a materials-handling activity; (5) machine-hours for a machine-running activity; and (6) square feet for a janitorial cleaning activity.

Although the company's general ledger is a good starting point to find information about the cost of resources used to perform activities, most general ledger systems report the costs of different resources, such as indirect labor, electricity, equipment, and supplies, but do not report the cost of activities performed. New accounting systems are needed to obtain and record this information.

The cost of the resources can be assigned to activities by direct tracing or estimation. Direct tracing requires measuring the actual usage of resources by activities. For example, power used to operate a machine can be traced directly to that machine's operation by observing its meter usage.

If direct measurement is not available, department managers and supervisors are asked to estimate the percentage of time (or effort) that employees spend on each identified activity.

---

[12]   Robin Cooper, "Cost Classification in Unit-Based and Activity-Based Manufacturing Cost Systems," *Journal of Cost Management*, Fall 1990, pp. 4–14.

For example, at AT&T's New River Valley Works, multiple resource cost drivers are used to allocate different costs of resources to activity center cost pools (different shops). Factory overhead at the New River Valley plant is allocated as shown in Exhibit 4–3.[13]

Exhibit 4–3	**Resource Cost Drivers at AT&T New River Valley Plant**
Resources	**Resource Cost Drivers**
Personnel	Number of workers in shop
Storeroom	Number of "picks" used by shop
Engineers	Time worked in or for shop
Materials management	Time worked in or for shop
Accounting	Time worked in or for shop
Research and development	New codes developed for production
Quality	Time worked in or for shop
Utilities	Square-footage

Based on information in F. B. Green, Felix Amenkhienan, and George Johnson, "Performance Measures and JIT," *Management Accounting,* February 1991, p. 53.

Activities and Cost Drivers at Siemens Electric Motor Works	
Cost Driver	**Activity Level**
Direct labor-hours	Unit
Machine-hours	Unit
Direct materials dollars	Unit
Value added	Unit
Number of product orders	Batch
Number of special components	Batch

Source: Robin Cooper, "Cost Classification in Unit-Based and Activity-Based Manufacturing Cost Systems," *Journal of Cost Management,* Fall 1990, pp. 4–14.

Sample Resource Cost Drivers at Hughes Aircraft

For years, Hughes Aircraft allocated service department costs to operating departments using the number of employees as the primary resource cost driver because of its simplicity. In 1991, the company adopted activity-based costing to improve its costing system. Hughes Aircraft uses the following service departments and resource cost drivers:

Service Department (Resources)	Allocation Bases (Resource Cost Drivers)
Human resources	Number of employees Number of new hires Training hours
Security	Square footage
Data processing	Lines printed CPU minutes Storage units

Source: Jack Haedicke and David Feil, "Hughes Aircraft Sets the Standard for ABC," *Management Accounting,* February 1991, pp. 29–33.

---

[13] F. B. Green, Felix Amenkhienan, and George Johnson, "Performance Measures and JIT," *Management Accounting,* February 1991, pp. 50–53.

Step 3: Assign Activity Costs to Cost Objects

Once the cost activities are known, the cost per unit of activity must be measured. This is done by measuring the cost per unit of output produced by the activity. Appropriate comparisons over time and with other organizations can then be used to determine the efficiency (productivity) of these activities.

Outputs are the cost objects for which activities are performed. Typical outputs for a cost system are products, services, customers, projects, or business units. For example, in an insurance company, the outputs could be the individual products or services offered to customers, the customers themselves, the insurance agents, or the divisions that are receiving benefits from corporate resources.

Activity cost drivers are used to assign activity costs to the cost objects. Typical activity cost drivers are purchase orders, receiving reports, inspection reports or hours, parts stored, payments, direct labor-hours, machine-hours, and setups and manufacturing cycle time.

For example, John Deere Component Works started its ABC system in 1985 with eight activities (cost pools) and activity cost drivers as shown in Exhibit 4–4.[14]

Activity cost drivers should explain why an activity's costs go up or down. Once the cost of each activity and what drives it are known, activity cost drivers can be used to determine which products are consuming activities. Cost is allocated in proportion to the activity cost drivers used by each product or product line.

Exhibit 4–4	Activity Cost Drivers at John Deere Component Works	
Activity	**Level**	**Activity Cost Driver**
Materials purchasing	Unit	Material cost
Direct labor support	Unit	Direct labor cost
Machine operation	Unit	Machine-hours
Setup	Batch	Setup hours
Production order	Batch	Number of orders
Materials handling	Batch	Number of loads
Parts administration	Product	Number of parts
General and administrative	Facility	Amount of value added

Source: Robin Cooper and Robert S. Kaplan, *The Design of Cost Management Systems: Solution Manual and Teaching Notes* (Englewood Cliffs, N.J.: Prentice Hall, 1991), p. 310.

Cost Driver Selection Process at Hewlett-Packard's Surface Mount Center

At HP's Surface Mount Center in Boise, the ABC system has been fully operational since early 1993. This facility manufactures about 50 different electronic circuit boards for internal HP customers. The center's accounting, production, and engineering staffs jointly conducted an intense analysis of the production process and cost behavior patterns to select cost drivers. This combination of accounting and engineering analysis helped management choose cost drivers.

Source: C. Mike Merz and A. Hardy, "ABC Puts Accountants on Design Team at HP," *Management Accounting,* September 1993, pp. 22–27.

---

[14] Robin Cooper and Robert S. Kaplan, *The Design of Cost Management Systems* (Englewood Cliffs, N.J.: Prentice Hall, 1991), pp. 291–310.

Benefits and Limitations of an Activity-Based Costing System

Benefits

Activity-based costing helps reduce distortions caused by traditional cost allocations. It provides a clear view of how the mix of a firm's diverse products, services, and activities contributes to the bottom line in the long run.

Major benefits of the activity-based costing are the following:

1. ABC provides more accurate and informative product costs, which lead to more accurate product profitability measurements and to better-informed strategic decisions about pricing, product line, customer market, and capital expenditure.

2. ABC provides more accurate measurements of activity-driving costs, which helps managers improve product and process value by making better product design decisions, controlling costs better, and fostering various value-enhancement projects.

3. ABC provides managers easier access to relevant costs for making business decisions, enabling them to take a more competitive position.

Limitations

Although activity-based costing provides better tracing of costs to individual products than traditional systems, managers should be aware of its limitations before using it to calculate product costs:

1. **Allocations.** Even if activity data are available, some costs probably require allocations to departments and products based on arbitrary volume measures because finding a specific activity that causes the incurrance of the costs might not be practical. Examples are some of the facility-sustaining costs, such as cleaning the factory and managing the production process.

2. **Omission of costs.** ABC omits from the analysis some costs identified with specific products. Activities that cause such costs include marketing, advertising, research and development, product engineering, and warranty claims. The additional costs simply would be traced to individual products and added to the manufacturing costs to determine the total product cost. Traditionally, marketing and administrative costs have not been included in product costs because of the generally accepted accounting principles involved in financial reporting requirements that they be included in period costs.

3. **Expense and time.** An ABC system is very expensive to develop and implement and is very time consuming. Like most innovative management or accounting systems, ABC usually requires more than a year for successful development and implementation.

Comparison of Traditional and Activity-Based Costing Systems

An activity-based costing system traces costs to products through activities. Factory overhead costs are assigned to homogeneous cost pools or activity centers rather than to departments. Activity center costs are assigned to products or services. The process

Differences between Traditional Costing and Activity-Based Costing Systems

Traditional	Activity-Based Costing
Uses from one to three volume-based cost drivers	Uses activity-based multiple cost drivers (including both volume based and nonvolume based)
Assigns overhead costs first to departments and then to products or services	Assigns overhead costs first to activities and then to products or services
Focuses on management responsibility for costs within departments	Focuses on processes and activities for cross-functional problem solving

has three steps. First, costs traced to the same or similar resource drivers are assigned to the same cost pool or activity center. Second, an overhead rate is calculated for each activity center based on a selected activity cost driver. Finally, the overhead costs are assigned to each product by multiplying the specific overhead rate by the amount of the activity cost driver consumed by that product. The major differences between the traditional costing and the activity-based costing system lie in the second and third steps.

Illustration of System Comparison

LEARNING OBJECTIVE 4▶

Compute product costs under a traditional costing system and an activity-based costing system.

The following example contrasts steps 2 and 3 of the traditional costing system, using direct labor-hours as the cost driver, with the activity-based costing system, using both volume-based and nonvolume-based cost drivers.

Northern High-Tech, Inc., successfully produces and sells two types of quality printers, the deluxe and the regular. Assume that the company has the following financial and cost data for the two products:

	Deluxe	Regular
Production volume	5,000	15,000
Selling price	$400.00	$200.00
Unit direct material and labor costs	$200.00	$80.00
Direct labor-hours	25,000	75,000

The company's management accountant has identified the following activities, budgeted cost pools, and activity drivers:

Activity	Budgeted Cost Pool	Activity Cost Driver
Engineering	$ 125,000	Engineering hours
Setups	300,000	Number of setups
Machine running	1,500,000	Machine-hours
Packing	75,000	Number of packing orders
Total	$2,000,000	

These are the actual activity units or transactions for each product:

	Activity Consumption		
Activity Cost Driver	Deluxe	Regular	Total
Engineering hours	5,000	7,500	12,500
Number of setups	200	100	300
Machine-hours	50,000	100,000	150,000
Number of packing orders	5,000	10,000	15,000

Traditional Costing Analysis   In the traditional costing approach, the factory overhead (OH) is allocated on the basis of direct labor-hours (DLH) as the cost driver:

Total DLH: 25,000 + 75,000 = 100,000

Overhead rate per DLH: $2,000,000/100,000 = $20

OH assigned to deluxe: $20 × 25,000 = $500,000

Deluxe OH cost per unit: $500,000/5,000 = $100

OH assigned to regular: $20 × 75,000 = $1,500,000

Regular OH cost per unit: $1,500,000/15,000 = $100

Exhibit 4–5 presents a product profitability analysis under the traditional costing system.

Activity-Based Costing Analysis   In the activity-based costing approach, the cost driver rate for each activity cost driver—that is, the activity rate—is calculated as follows:

(1) Activity Cost Driver	(2) Cost	(3) Activity Consumption	(4) = (2)/(3) Activity Rate
Engineering hours	$ 125,000	12,500	$ 10
Number of setups	300,000	300	1,000
Machine-hours	1,500,000	150,000	10
Number of packing orders	75,000	15,000	5

Factory overhead costs are assigned to both products, as shown by these calculations:

Deluxe Printer

(1) Activity Cost Driver	(2) Activity Rate	(3) Number of Activities	(4) = (2) × (3) Total OH	(5) Unit OH
Engineering hours	$ 10	5,000	$ 50,000	$ 10
Number of setups	1,000	200	200,000	40
Machine-hours	10	50,000	500,000	100
Number of packing orders	5	5,000	25,000	5

Regular Printer

(1) Activity Cost Driver	(2) Activity Rate	(3) Number of Activities	(4) = (2) × (3) Total OH	(5) Unit OH
Engineering hours	$ 10	7,500	$ 75,000	$ 5.00
Number of setups	1,000	100	100,000	6.67
Machine-hours	10	100,000	1,000,000	66.67
Number of packing orders	5	10,000	50,000	3.33

Exhibit 4–6 presents a product profitability analysis under the activity-based costing system and Exhibit 4–7 compares product costs and profit margins under the two costing systems.

Exhibit 4–5   Product Profitability Analysis under the Traditional Costing System

	Deluxe	Regular
Unit selling price	$400	$200
Unit product cost		
Direct material and labor	$200	$ 80
Factory overhead	100	100
Cost per unit	$300	$180
Product margin	$100	$ 20

Exhibit 4–6   Product Profitability Analysis under the ABC Costing System

		Deluxe		Regular
Unit selling price		$400		$200.00
Unit product cost				
Direct material and labor		$200		$80.00
Factory overhead				
Engineering	$ 10		$ 5.00	
Setups	40		6.67	
Machine running	100		66.67	
Packing	5	155	3.33	81.67
Cost per unit		355		161.67
Product margin		$ 45		$ 38.33

115

Exhibit 4–7	Comparison of Alternative Costing Approaches		
	Allocation Method		
	(1) **Traditional**	**(2)** **ABC**	**(1) – (2)** **Difference**
Deluxe			
Total overhead	$ 500,000	$ 775,000	$(275,000)
Unit OH cost	100	155	(55)
Unit margin	100	45	55
Regular			
Total overhead	$1,500,000	$1,225,000	$ 275,000
Unit OH cost	100	81.67	18.33
Unit margin	20	38.33	(18.33)

COST MANAGEMENT IN ACTION

Competition Pressure, High Overhead Costs, and Product Diversity at Whirlpool

In the last decade of the twentieth century, Whirlpool Corporation, an internationally known manufacturer of home appliances, faced increasing competition, higher overhead, and more product diversity. Its managers needed reliable information to evaluate strategic options and promote manufacturing excellence. Specifically, they wanted more accurate unit product costs for the following objectives:

1. Identification of profitable products.
2. Analysis of competitiveness.
3. Cost reduction.

4. Analysis of investments.
5. Budget development.
6. Analysis for make-or-buy decisions.

Whirlpool's top management hired consultants from KPMG Peat Marwick. What do you think the consultants suggested for the firm? What changes did Whirlpool make in its cost management practices?

(Refer to Comments on Cost Management in Action at the end of the chapter.)

Remember that one major limitation of the traditional costing system is that it generally undercosts complex low-volume products and overcosts high-volume products. The activity-based costing system presents a more accurate measurement pattern of overhead consumption. The preceding comparison shows that the traditional product costing system can significantly undercost the deluxe printer (a low-volume product) and overcost the regular printer (a high-volume product) compared with the actual overhead consumption. Consequently, traditional product costing can cause distorted inventory measurement, incorrect product-line decisions, unrealistic pricing, ineffective resource allocations, misplaced strategic focus, misidentified critical success factors, and lost competitive advantage.

ACTIVITY-BASED MANAGEMENT

What Is Activity-Based Management?

LEARNING OBJECTIVE 5▶

Describe an activity-based management system and value-added and non-value-added activities.

After implementing activity-based costing, firms often adopt activity-based management. Broadly speaking, activity-based management increases both the value that customers receive and the profits to the firm.[15] More specifically, *activity-based management (ABM)* is the management of activities to improve the value received by the

---

[15]   Peter B. B. Turney, "Activity-Based Management," *Management Accounting*, January 1992, pp. 20–25.

customer and to increase the firm's profit from providing this value.[16] ABM draws on ABC as its major source of information.

Major advantages of the ABM approach include the following:

1. ABM measures the effectiveness of the key business processes and activities and identifies how they can be improved to reduce costs and to increase value to customers.

2. ABM improves management focus by allocating resources to key value-added activities, customers, and products, and maintains the firm's competitive advantage by using continuous-improvement methods.

Activity-based management uses cost driver analysis, activity analysis, and performance measurement. **Cost driver analysis** includes examining, quantifying, and explaining the effects of cost drivers. Its purpose is to search for the root causes of activity costs. Tools used in cost driver analysis include benchmarking, cause-and-effect diagrams, and Pareto analysis.

As discussed in Chapter 1, *benchmarking* is the search for the best practices within and across industries to identify ways to improve a firm's performance of a task, activity, or process. A **cause-and-effect diagram** maps out a list of causes that affect an activity, process, stated problem, or desired outcome. Because the shape of the diagram is simi-

Cost driver analysis examines, quantifies, and explains the effects of cost drivers.

A **cause-and-effect diagram** maps out a list of causes that affect an activity, process, stated problem, or a desired outcome.

Activity-Based Management at Stockham Valve and Fittings

Stockham Valve and Fittings implemented activity-based management and was able to accomplish the following:

- Produce parts at the lowest cost.
- Design parts to minimize manufacturing costs.
- Modify equipment to reduce costs.
- Increase prices of products priced below ABC cost and drop unprofitable products.

Source: Peter B. B. Turney, "Activity-Based Management," *Management Accounting,* January 1992, pp. 20–25.

The Role of ABC/ABM Tools

Critical Questions	ABC/ABM Tools
What do we do?	Activity analysis, cause-and-effect diagram, Pareto analysis
How much does it cost?	Activity-based costing
How well do we do it?	Performance measurement
How can we do it better?	Benchmarking, using just-in-time processes, performing process redesign, eliminating non-value-added activities

---

General Motors' Parts Suppliers Eliminate Non-Value-Added Activities

General Motors Corporation uses ABC/ABM to force its parts suppliers to cut their costs and prices by eliminating these non-value-added activities: (1) overproducing, (2) overstocking, (3) moving, (4) processing in too many steps, (5) waiting, (6) reworking, (7) idling equipment, (8) idling space, and (9) making a product with features not required by customers.

Source: Joe Cyr, "Waste Removal—Now," *CMA Magazine,* June 1993, p. 23.

---

[16]   Raffish and Turney, "Glossary of Activity-Based Management," p. 57.

lar to a fishbone, it is also called a *fishbone diagram*. **Pareto analysis** is a management tool that shows that 20 percent of a set of important cost drivers are responsible for 80 percent of the total cost incurred. These tools are discussed in more detail in Chapter 6.

Recall that *activity analysis* identifies and describes the activities in an organization. Interviews, questionnaires, observation, and a review of documentation are ways to collect information to be used in this analysis.

Performance measurement identifies items that indicate the work performed and the results achieved by an activity, process, or organizational unit. Performance measures should be both financial and nonfinancial. Examples of financial performance measures are the cost per unit of output, return on sales, and gross cost of every department's value-added and non-value-added activities. Nonfinancial performance measures evaluate customers, manufacturing processes, and human resources. Examples of nonfinancial performance measures are the number of customer complaints, the results of customer satisfaction surveys, the number of defective parts or outputs, the number of output units, the amount of cycle time, the frequency of on-time delivery, the number of employee suggestions, and results of employee morale surveys.

Cooper and Kaplan have classified ABM applications in two groups: operational ABM and strategic ABM.[17] Operational ABM—doing things right or performing activities more efficiently—seeks to enhance efficiency and asset utilization and to lower costs. Operational ABM applications include management techniques such as activity management, business process reengineering, total quality management, and performance measurement.

Strategic ABM—doing the appropriate things or choosing the appropriate activities to perform—attempts to alter the demand for activities to increase profitability while assuming, as a first approximation, that activity efficiency remains constant. For example, strategic ABM encompasses shifting the mix of demand for activities from unprofitable applications by reducing the need for unprofitable activities. Strategic ABM applications include process design, product-line and customer mix, supplier relationships, customer relationships (pricing, order size, delivery, packaging, etc.), market segmentation, and distribution channels.

Value-Added and Non-Value-Added Activities

Activity-based management seeks to identify activities that can be eliminated and to ensure that necessary activities are carried out efficiently. To improve operations, management must search for unnecessary or inefficient activities, determine the cost drivers for the activities, and reduce the level of those cost drivers or eliminate them entirely. A major task of activity analysis is to identify value-added and non-value-added activities.

Summary of Value-Added and Non-Value-Added Activities

Activity	Value Added	Non-Value Added
Designing product	X	
Setting up		X
Waiting		X
Moving		X
Processing	X	
Reworking		X
Repairing		X
Storing		X
Inspecting		X
Delivering product	X	

[17] Kaplan and Cooper, *Cost and Effects: Using Integrated Cost Systems to Drive Profitability and Performance*, p. 4.

Daton Technologies Identifies Value Added and Non-Value-Added Activities

Daton Technologies uses five questions to classify activities as value added or non-value added:

1. Is the activity of value to an external customer?
2. Is the activity required to meet corporate rules?
3. Is the activity required for sound business practices?
4. Is the activity of value to an internal customer?
5. Is the activity a waste?

   The company classifies positive answers to the first two questions under value-added activities and to the last three questions under non-value-added activities. Try to eliminate any activity in question 5. For questions 3 and 4, the company tries to improve the activity or reduce the frequency. Otherwise, try to eliminate that activity. Examples of value-added activities in Daton Technologies are making extrusion runs, shipping, designing parts, and making tools. Examples of non-value-added activities are setup, inspection, regrind, and process returns.

   Source: Neal R. Pemberton, Logan Arumugam, and Nabil Hassan, "ABM at Daton Technologies: From Obstacles to Opportunities," *Management Accounting,* March 1996, pp. 20–27.

Exhibit 4–8	Television News Broadcasting Firm's Value-Added and Non-Value-Added Activities

A *value-added activity* is one that, if eliminated, would affect the accuracy and effectiveness of the newscast and decrease total viewers as well as ratings for that time slot.

1. **Activities that augment accuracy**
   - Verification of story sources and acquired information.
2. **Activities that augment effectiveness**
   - Efficient electronic journalism to ensure effective taped segments.
   - Newscast story order planned so that viewers can follow from one story to the next.
   - Field crew time used to access the best footage possible.
   - Meaningful news story writing.
   - Contents of the newscast planned so that viewers get the best possible package of stories.

A *non-value-added activity* is one that, if eliminated, would not affect the accuracy and effectiveness of the newscast. Therefore, the activity contributes nothing to the quest for viewer retention and improved ratings.

1. **Activities that generate excess**
   - Developing stories from beginning to end but not using them in a newscast.
   - Assigning more than one person to develop each process of the same news story.
2. **Activities that augment delay (downtime)**
   - Newscast not completed on time because some step in the process was inefficient.
   - Too many employees on a particular shift with not enough work to go around.

A **value-added activity** is an activity that contributes to customer value and satisfaction or satisfies an organizational need. Examples include designing products, processing by direct labor, adding direct materials, machining, and delivering products.

A **non-value-added activity** does not contribute to customer value or to the organization's needs. Examples include setting up, moving, waiting, repairing, inspecting, and storing.

Exhibit 4–8 presents an example of a television news broadcasting firm's value-added and non-value-added activities.

> A **value-added activity** is an activity that contributes to customer value and satisfaction or satisfies an organizational need.
>
> A **non-value-added activity** does not contribute to customer value or to the organization's needs.

MANUFACTURING INDUSTRY APPLICATIONS

◀ **LEARNING OBJECTIVE 6**

Explain how activity-based costing systems are used in manufacturing industry.

Activity-based costing initially was developed for manufacturing industry applications. Many manufacturing companies, such as Hewlett-Packard and Advanced Micro Devices, have implemented activity-based costing and management systems successfully.

ABC at Hewlett-Packard

The Roseville Network Division (RND) of Hewlett-Packard (HP) was one of the first divisions to use activity-based costing. Because RND's products were increasing in number and decreasing in length of product life, the design of new products and their production processes was especially important to the division's success. The costing system it had been using, however, did not provide information that managers could use to compare the production costs of different designs.

RND's new costing system focused on the costs of each production process: the different activities of the division. The ABC system started with only two cost drivers, direct labor-hours and number of insertions; now it has nine cost drivers, as shown in Exhibit 4–9.

Engineering managers at RND were pleased with the activity-based costing system that greatly influenced the design of new products. For example, once it became clear that manual insertion was three times as expensive as automatic insertion, designs were modified to include more automatic insertion. The system clearly had the desired effect of influencing the behavior of product designers.[18]

ABC at Advanced Micro Devices

Advanced Micro Devices (AMD), a major semiconductor manufacturer, performed its first activity-based costing project at a test and assembly facility in Penang, Malaysia. The new ABC system identified significant product cost distortions (high-volume, simple products were overcosted by 20 to 30 percent, and low-volume, complex products were undercosted by 600 to 700 percent). ABC provided AMD management a more accurate basis for setting transfer prices between manufacturing and the divisions.

Some of the key non-volume-based cost drivers included (1) line items (for production scheduling and setup activities), (2) quality problems that were encountered (for some process-sustaining activities), and (3) a product's drop below a certain point for yield and quality improvement activities.

The high total of expenses driven by these non-volume-based costs underscored the inaccuracies in the old system that allocated all expenses to products using labor- and machine-hours.

The success of the project was described by the director of finance, who stated, "ABC provided AMD with a cost system solution which will enable and support AMD's strategy of managing profitable growth."[19]

Exhibit 4–9 Cost Drivers at HP's Roseville Network Division	
Cost Driver	**Activity Level**
Number of axial insertions	Unit
Number of radical insertions	Unit
Number of DIP insertions	Unit
Number of manual insertions	Unit
Number of test hours	Unit
Number of solder joints	Unit
Number of boards	Product
Number of parts	Product
Number of slots	Product

Source: Robin Cooper and Peter B. B. Turney, "Internally Forced Activity-Based Cost Systems," in *Measures for Manufacturing Excellence*, ed. R. S. Kaplan (Boston: Harvard Business School Press, 1990), p. 17.

---

[18]   Robin Cooper and Peter B. B. Turney, "Internally Forced Activity-Based Cost Systems," in *Measures for Manufacturing Excellence*, ed. R. S. Kaplan (Boston: Harvard Business School Press, 1990).

[19]   Robin Cooper, Robert Kaplan, Lawrence Maisel, Eileen Morrissey, and Ronald Oehm, *Implementing Activity-Based Cost Management: Moving from Analysis to Action—Implementing Experiences at Eight Companies* (Montvale, N.J.: Institute of Management Accountants, 1992), p. 56.

Traditional Costing System Distorted Product Costs at Xi'an Electronics in China

Xi'an Electronics produces special electronics with more than 250 products that have in excess of 600 specifications. Researchers collected data for 25 of the company's products during July and December 1997 and grouped them into two product categories, high volume and low volume. They found that the unit conversion cost (direct labor and overhead) was 29.58 percent higher under traditional costing (using direct labor hours as the cost driver) than ABC (using 30 cost drivers) for high-volume products and was 45.95 percent lower under traditional costing than ABC for low-volume products. Their findings show that traditional costing overestimates the costs of high-volume products and underestimates the costs of low-volume products.

Source: Pingxin Wang, Qinglu Jin, and Dagang Ke, "Activity-Based Costing and Its Application in Chinese Enterprises," *China Accounting and Finance Review,* March 2000, pp. 138–55.

Exhibit 4–10	Cost Drivers for Marketing Activities

Marketing Activity Cost Pool	Cost Driver
Advertising	Sales units or dollars
	Number of sales calls
Selling	Sales dollars
	Number of orders obtained
Order filling, shipping, warehousing	Weight of shipped product
	Number, weight, or size of units ordered
	Units of shipped product
General office (e.g., credit and collection)	Number of customer orders
	Number of invoice lines

Source: Ronald J. Lewis, "Activity-Based Costing for Marketing," *Management Accounting,* November 1991, pp. 34–35.

MARKETING AND ADMINISTRATIVE APPLICATIONS

Activity-based costing can also be applied to administrative activities, such as accounting, data processing, personnel, quality assurance, printing and duplicating, security, maintenance, and administrative services, and marketing activities, such as advertising, selling, order filling, shipping, warehousing, and credit and collection processing. To apply ABC to marketing activities, management accountants trace marketing costs to activity cost pools; then they trace them to product lines and territories to measure profitability. Exhibit 4–10 presents examples of cost drivers for marketing activities.[20]

ABC product costing can be extended to customer profitability analysis. All customers are not created equal. It is not unusual for ABC customer profitability analysis to find that 80 percent of a firm's profit comes from 20 percent of its customers. The primary focus of this analysis is on selling, general, and administrative costs. It analyzes activities and identifies proper cost drivers for them. Customer profitability analysis can answer the following questions:

1. Which of our customers generates the largest profit?
2. Does a large customer always generate more profit than a small customer?
3. Should we serve a particular class of customers, or should we do business with all types of customers?
4. What types of customer should we market to? What types should we not market to?

◀ **LEARNING OBJECTIVE 7**

Describe how activity-based costing systems are used in marketing and administrative activities.

---

[20]   Ronald J. Lewis, "Activity-Based Costing for Marketing," *Management Accounting*, November 1991, pp. 33–36.

Robotics Distributor Identified Activities and Cost Drivers for Sales and Administration

Robotics Distributor is the U.S. distributor for industrial robots imported from Japan. The product line consists of robots for applications in the areas of welding, materials handling, dispensing, and cutting. Recently, the company began using activity-based costing for sales and administration costs. It identified the following major activities and cost drivers:

Activities	Cost Drivers
Application engineering	Number of proposals
Engineering design	Number of bookings
Documentation	Number of bookings
Sales administration	Number of customers
Marketing	Number of customers
Sales	Number of customers
Customer support administration	Spare parts
Integrator support	Number of integrator customers
Transplant support	Revenue dollars
Finance	Revenue dollars

Using ABC, the monthly operating income of selling the standard robotic product line increased by almost $150,000, validating management's concerns about the previous allocation method. This information facilitated strategic decision making about product line emphasis.

Source: David Bukovinsky, Hans Sprohge, and John Talbott, "Activity-Based Costing for Sales and Administrative Costs: A Case Study," *The CPA Journal,* April 2000, pp. 70–72.

AT&T turned to ABC after its breakup into smaller, more focused business units. The breakup and price deregulation made understanding and managing costs, rather than simply allocating them, critical for AT&T. As a result, AT&T managers implemented an activity-based costing system to help them understand the activities driving their business.

The business billing center was selected for the ABC pilot project. Its activities included monitoring billing records; editing checks; validating data; correcting errors; and printing, sorting, and dispatching invoices to business customers. A cross-functional team prepared a flowchart of the business operations that identified the relationships between resources and activities, between activities and processes, and between process outputs and services provided to each customer.

The cost of services provided to different customers was determined by identifying activity and cost driver consumption characteristics. The firm selected several cost drivers, including customers tested, change requests, service orders, customer locations, bill resolution groups, printer hours, and pages printed.

AT&T managers found the ABC model developed in the pilot study useful in helping the firm manage costs and improve its internal operating processes, supplier relationships, and customer satisfaction.[21]

SERVICE AND NOT-FOR-PROFIT APPLICATIONS

Although ABC has been applied mainly to manufacturing companies, it also can be useful for service and not-for-profit organizations. Numerous companies have developed and implemented ABC systems, including Alexandria Hospital; Union Pacific

LEARNING OBJECTIVE 8▶

Demonstrate how activity-based costing systems are used in service and not-for-profit organizations.

[21] Terrence Hobdy, Jeff Thomson, and Paul Sharman, "Activity-Based Management at AT&T," *Management Accounting,* April 1994, pp. 35–39.

Railroad; Amtrak Auto-Ferry Service; Data Services, Inc.;[22] Fireman's Fund;[23] American Express;[24] US Postal Service;[25] and DSL Client Services.[26]

Service and most not-for-profit organizations have many characteristics that distinguish them from manufacturing companies. Outputs often are more difficult to define, service request activity is less predictable, and overhead and indirect costs are difficult to relate to product or service outputs.

Illustration of Comparison of Traditional and ABC Systems for a Service Firm

Suppose that the accounting firm of Achuck, Buniel & Hinckley performs two audits this week. Both audits have required a total of 100 professional labor-hours. The firm pays $25 per hour to each of its audit staff members. In the first audit, the audit team spent much time researching material, faxing documents, and making long-distance phone calls to complete the engagement, but the second audit required fewer of these activities.

Traditional Costing System

The traditional direct labor-based costing system uniformly assigns the cost of activities to the cost object, in this case an audit. One cost driver, professional labor-hours, is used to allocate overhead. If professional labor-hour is the only method of overhead allocation, the audit that is resource intensive would be undercosted and the audit that is less resource intensive would be overcosted.

Total labor dollars for the week (DL)	$5,000
Total overhead costs for the week (OH)	$8,000
Overhead allocation rate = OH/DL	160% per DL

Under the traditional costing system, therefore, total overhead cost is allocated to each audit by multiplying total labor costs by the overhead allocation rate:

	(1) DL Hours	(2) DL Rate	(3) = (1) × (2) DL Cost	(4) OH Rate	(3) × (4) Applied OH
Audit 1	100	$25/hour	$2,500	160%	$4,000
Audit 2	100	$25/hour	$2,500	160%	$4,000

As you can see, under the traditional costing system, both audits have the same overhead cost of $4,000, although audit 1 is more resource intensive than audit 2. Therefore, under the traditional costing system, audit 1 is undercosted and audit 2 is overcosted. To determine costing more accurately, the ABC system should be used.

Activity-Based Costing System

An activity-based costing system focuses on activities as the fundamental cost objects. This example has one cost pool and one cost driver per activity.

---

[22] William Rotch, "Activity-Based Costing in Service Industries," *Journal of Cost Management*, Summer 1990, pp. 4–14.

[23] Michael Crane and John Meyer, "Focusing on True Costs in a Service Organization," *Management Accounting*, February 1993, pp. 41–45.

[24] David A. Carlson and S. Mark Young, "Activity-Based Total Quality Management at American Express," *Journal of Cost Management*, Spring 1993, pp. 48–58.

[25] Terrell L. Carter, Ali M. Sedaghat, and Thomas D. Williams, "How ABC Changed the Post Office," *Strategic Finance*, February 1998, pp. 28–32.

[26] Barbara Gauharou, "Activity-Based Costing at DSL Client Services," *Management Accounting Quarterly*, Summer 2000, pp. 4–11.

Distorted Medicare Reimbursements with Inappropriate Cost Drivers

Hospitals must annually complete a Medicare cost report to be eligible for government reimbursement for services rendered to Medicare patients. This cost information is used to determine values of Medicare reimbursement parameters. This same cost information often is used as the basis for determining the charges for privately insured patients. For inpatient care costs, Medicare requires that all operating costs pertaining to patient care be allocated to patients based only on the number of days a patient spends in the hospital (patient-days). Thus, Medicare cost reporting does not explicitly consider the possibility of multiple cost drivers.

In a recent study, Huang and Kirby noted that patient care costs can be attributed to at least two cost drivers: (1) the number of patient-days and (2) the number of patients admitted. Patient-day costs include costs of meals, laundry, and basic nursing care; admission costs include costs for taking patients' history upon admission, preparing patients for surgery, intensively tending to them immediately following surgery, preparing rooms for new patients, and handling medical coding and billing. Patient-days are a unit-level cost driver, and admissions are a batch-level cost driver.

Using publicly available data, Huang and Kirby compared the results of current Medicare reimbursement procedures, which use a single volume-based, unit-level cost driver (patient-days), with the results that would be obtained if Medicare reimbursements were based on two cost drivers: a unit-level cost driver (patient-days) and a batch-level cost driver (number of admissions). Their study results suggest that Medicare is potentially overcharged by between $66 million and $1.98 billion per year for hospital patient care! The main reason is that Medicare patients tend to be older and have a much longer average length of hospitalization than private insurance patients do. Because Medicare reimbursements consider only patient-days, Medicare is charged for a disproportionately large share of admitted patients.

Source: Yuchang Huang and Alison L. Kirby, "Distorted Medicare Reimbursements: The Effect of Cost Accounting Choices," *Journal of Management Accounting Research,* Fall 1994, pp. 128–43.

Activities	OH Costs	Cost Drivers	Indirect Cost Application Rate	Total Activities
Direct labor		Number of hours	$25 an hour	200
Copying/faxing	$ 900	Number of copies/faxes	$0.10 a copy/fax	9,000
Long-distance calls	1,600	Number of calls made	$10 a call	160
Research/information services	4,500	Number of calls	$50 a call	90
Data processing	1,000	Number of pages	$10 a page	100
Total	$8,000			

Audit 1 is more resource intensive; more photocopies, long-distance calls, information service calls, and data processing were done to complete the audit.

Activity	Amount	Rate		Applied OH
Copying/faxing	5,000 copies	$0.10 a copy	=	$ 500
Long-distance calls	100 calls	$10 a call	=	1,000
Research/information services	80 calls	$50 a call	=	4,000
Data processing	70 pages	$10 a page	=	700
			Total =	**$6,200**

In contrast, audit 2 is less resource intensive. The breakdown of activities is

Activity	Amount	Rate		Applied OH
Copying/faxing	4,000 copies	$0.10 a copy	=	$ 400
Long-distance calls	60 calls	$10 a call	=	600
Research/information services	10 calls	$50 a call	=	500
Data processing	30 pages	$10 a page	=	300
			Total =	**$1,800**

ABC for E-Retailing

Activity-based costing can be applied to measure and manage e-retailing business. For example, four of the following e-retailing activities (2, 5, 7, and 9) are unique to e-business.

E-Retailing Activities	Cost Drivers
1. Service routine customers	1. E-mail and phone inquiries
2. Electronic customer order processing	2. Time (hardware and software depreciation)
3. Service customer issues	3. E-mail and phone inquiries
4. Merchandise inventory selection and management	4. Number of new products
5. Imaging and annotation	5. Number of changes to inventory database
6. Purchasing and receiving	6. Number of orders
7. Virtual storefront optimization	7. Time (hours dedicated to Web page development)
8. Customer acquisition and retention	8. Number of targeted customers
9. Customer acquisition and retention/revenue share (i.e., affiliate) marketing	9. Number of affiliate links
10. Information systems support	10. Number of desktop machines
11. Business/administration support	11. Number of predominant drivers
12. Business/production support	12. Number of product categories
13. Facility/administration maintenance	13. Square footage in the administrative area
14. Facility/production maintenance	14. Square footage in the production area

Source: Thomas L. Zeller, "Measuring and Managing E-Retailing with Activity-Based Costing," *Journal of Cost Management,* January/February 2000, pp. 17–30.

The engagements clearly are costed more accurately under the ABC system than the traditional costing system.

ACTIVITY-BASED COSTING AND STRATEGIC COST MANAGEMENT

◀**LEARNING OBJECTIVE 9**

Relate activity-based costing to strategic cost management.

Activity-based costing is closely tied to strategic cost management. ABC assigns costs to products or customers according to the resources they consume. It shows how activities consume resources and how products or customers trigger activities. ABC describes a firm as a series of activities whose performance is designed to satisfy customer needs. It provides information for managers to use to manage activities to improve competitiveness and to achieve strategic goals.

Activities are determined by strategic choices. Successful firms put their resources into those activities that lead to the greatest strategic benefit. ABC/ABM helps managers understand the relation between the firm's strategy and the activities and resources needed to implement the strategy.

Cost leadership is a business strategy for achieving competitive advantage. ABC/ABM is critical to this strategy because it identifies key activities, drivers, and ways to improve processes to reduce cost. Providing superior customer value is another business strategy for achieving competitive advantage. ABC/ABM can help managers identify value-enhancement opportunities; develop a customer strategy; support a technological leadership strategy; and establish a pricing strategy by identifying and analyzing key activities, processes, cost drivers, and improvement methods.

Specifically, ABC/ABM provides answers to these strategic cost management questions:

- How do a firm's cost structures and profits compare to those of its competition?

- How does switching from traditional costing to an ABC costing system impact pricing, product design, process design, manufacturing technology, and product-line decisions ?

- What are the cost effects on different products when a firm adopts a new strategy, for example, a change from mass production of standardized products to the production of small lots of customized products?
- What behavior changes occur for the product designers when a firm selects a cost driver to encourage the use of common components instead of many specialized components?
- Could the production process of a particular product be changed to reduce its unit cost?
- Has a firm adopted the most profitable distribution system for its product?
- How would changes in activities and components affect the suppliers and customers in the value chain?
- How will changes in a firm's processes impact the bottom line?
- What are the potential cost savings if a firm uses ABM to identify and eliminate non-value-added activities to achieve its low-cost strategy?
- How can ABC/ABM help a firm make changes to achieve its competitive strategy of high performance and short lead time in delivery of its products?

IMPLEMENTATION ISSUES

LEARNING OBJECTIVE 10 ▶

Identify key factors for a successful ABC/ABM implementation.

A number of factors play an important role in implementing ABC/ABM. For a successful ABC/ABM implementation, management accountants, engineers and manufacturing and operating managers must cooperate to form a design team. They must identify activities and cost drivers, both financial and nonfinancial. The basic information necessary to implement these cost system changes is usually not available because most companies do not collect it.

To obtain the information necessary for new cost management and measurement systems, employees directly involved in operating activities must be interviewed. They can provide information from implementing these activities on a daily basis. Each operating and support department should be carefully studied to analyze its multiple activities. This process allows the identification of cost pools of homogeneous cost drivers that are responsible for each cost category. For example, a quality control department could have three cost pools: inspection of incoming materials (cost driver: purchase orders), inspection of work in process (cost driver: setups), and inspection of finished goods (cost driver: cost of goods sold).

Understanding the production process and identifying cost drivers require a significant amount of persistent effort. In some cases, companies may decide that their particular manufacturing environment does not require such sophisticated cost and performance measurement systems. The effort to redesign cost systems is rewarded for organizations that have high product diversity, various cost drivers, multiple channels of distribution, a wide range of batch sizes and good cost/benefit.

The following are six ways to successfully implement ABC/ABM:

Implementing Strategy	Justification
Involve management and employees in creating an ABC system	Allows them to become familiar with ABC/ABM. They could then be more willing to implement the system because they feel included and share in ownership of the new system.
Maintain a parallel system	Allows individuals to adapt gradually to the ABC/ABM system. Abruptly changing cost systems can confuse and frustrate management and employees.
Use ABC/ABM on a job that will succeed	Shows how and why the process works. Successfully completing one job enables individuals to see the benefits of ABC/ABM more clearly.
Keep the initial ABC/ABM design simple	Avoids overwhelming users and holds costs down; also reduces implementation time.
Create desired incentives	Reassures employees that they will be properly evaluated in accordance with their performance.
Educate management	Uses seminars to educate management about ABC/ABM to enable them to understand the concept and appreciate the benefits. Management becomes aware of the activities that drive the business.

Shields and McEwen conducted a survey of 143 companies in 1993, showing that 75 percent had received a financial benefit from implementing ABC.[27] Using the results of their survey, Shields and McEwen developed seven factors for a successful ABC implementation: (1) top management support; (2) linkage to competitive strategy, stressing quality and JIT/speed; (3) linkage to performance evaluation and compensation; (4) training; (5) nonaccounting ownership (the belief by nonaccountants that the ABC system is of practical use to people throughout the company, not just to the accounting department); (6) adequate resources; and (7) consensus and clarity of the ABC objectives. The main reason for unsuccessful implementation was that many companies overemphasized the architectural and software design of ABC systems and failed to pay adequate attention to other issues.

SUMMARY

Over the past decade, an increasing number of national and international companies have made changes in their manufacturing plants. In attempts to reduce costs, increase productivity, improve product quality, and increase flexibility in response to customer needs, these companies have begun to use some or all of these innovative approaches: (1) just-in-time manufacturing systems with kanban and work cells tools; (2) various automation techniques, such as robots, computer-aided design, and computer-aided manufacturing; and (3) integration approaches such as flexible manufacturing systems and computer-integrated manufacturing to improve manufacturing productivity.

One major limitation of traditional costing systems is the use of a single plantwide factory overhead rate, such as direct labor-hours, or volume-based departmental rates, such as machine-hours and direct materials cost, by firms with diverse products, processes, and volume. These rates produce inaccurate product costs.

Activity-based costing (ABC) assigns costs to products or services based on their consumption of identifiable activities. This system is based on the premise that a firm's products or services result from performing activities and that the required activities incur costs. After activities are assigned to resources, activities are assigned to cost objects according to their use. ABC recognizes the causal relationships of cost drivers to activities.

ABC systems use a two-stage procedure to assign costs to products. The first-stage allocation is a resource cost assignment process by which factory overhead costs are assigned to activity cost pools or groups of activities called *activity centers* by using appropriate resource cost drivers. The second-stage allocation is an activity cost assignment process by which the costs of activities are assigned to products or services using appropriate activity cost drivers.

Activity-based costing helps to reduce distortions caused by traditional costing systems and obtains more accurate product costs. It provides a clear view of how a firm's diverse products, services, and activities contribute to the bottom line in the long run. Developing and implementing an ABC system is expensive and time consuming. Management accountants should be involved as team players in helping their firms develop and implement successful ABC systems.

Activity-based management (ABM) focuses on improving business efficiency and effectiveness and increasing not only the value received by customers but also the firm's profits.

Manufacturing, marketing, and administrative organizations as well as service and not-for-profit groups have successfully applied ABC and ABM.

Activity-based costing is closely tied to strategic cost management. Managers can have more meaningful information to determine the potential impacts on pricing, product design, process design, manufacturing technology, and product

---

[27] Michael D. Shields and Michael A. McEwen, "Implementing Activity-Based Costing Systems Successfully," *Journal of Cost Management*, Winter 1996, pp. 15–22.

127

line decisions by switching from traditional costing systems to an activity-based costing system.

Numerous factors play important roles in implementing ABC/ABM. To be successful, management accountants need to cooperate with engineers and manufacturing and operating managers to form a design team. Activities and cost drivers need to be identified; both financial and nonfinancial performance indicators are required.

KEY TERMS

Activity   106

Activity cost driver   107

Batch-level activity   110

Cause-and-effect diagram   117

Computer-aided design (CAD)   102

Computer-aided manufacturing (CAM)   102

Computer-integrated manufacturing (CIM)   102

Cost driver analysis   117

Facility-sustaining activity   110

Flexible manufacturing system (FMS)   102

Just-in-time (JIT) system   100

Kanban   101

Non-value added activity   119

Pareto analysis   118

Performance measurement   118

Product-sustaining activity   110

Resource   107

Resource cost driver   107

Robot   102

Two-stage allocation   108

Unit-level activity   110

Value added activity   119

Work cells   101

COMMENTS ON COST MANAGEMENT IN ACTION

Competition Pressure, High Overhead Costs, and Product Diversity at Whirlpool

In the 1990 production year, Whirlpool's Evansville, Indiana, plant began as an ABC pilot project for all product lines. The plant's implementation team consisted of two full-time Whirlpool employees with accounting backgrounds and experience in production and operations. KPMG Peat Marwick provided an ABC consultant who acted only as an adviser. The implementation of the ABC pilot program took approximately 16 weeks of full-time work.

Whirlpool used the following steps to implement the ABC pilot project:

1. Develop an activities dictionary.
2. Identify respondents for an activity survey.
3. Conduct activity-work survey sessions.
4. Validate responses with follow-up interviews.
5. Enter people-related time and dollars into Whirlpool's structured productivity analysis system (SPANS), (its database that includes nonfinancial cost drivers), and generate activity reports.
6. Download SPANS into the ABC system.
7. Enter expenses (i.e., general ledger data) into the ABC system.
8. Define activity centers.
9. Define and assign resource cost drivers.
10. Define and assign activity cost drivers.
11. Develop activity cost driver quantities.
12. Generate product-costing reports.
13. Validate results.

Using ABC information, Whirlpool found that volume and complexity affected product costing at the plant. It now uses ABC cost data to analyze make-or-buy decisions. Managers have found that the ABC cost information is more accurate and useful in planning cost-reduction strategies and making decisions about outsourcing than traditional systems. Whirlpool also uses the ABC data to manage costs by setting priorities for developing and improving cost-reduction plans. For example, it used the ABC system to demonstrate and quantify the cost savings to be gained from using bar codes to record the receipt of inventory.

In addition to realizing these benefits, Whirlpool found that maintaining its ABC system is not expensive; it now requires only about 120 hours per year to maintain.

Source: Cynthia B. Greeson and Mehmet C. Kocakulah, "Implementing an ABC Pilot at Whirlpool," *Journal of Cost Management*, March/April 1997, pp. 16–21.

SELF-STUDY PROBLEM

(For the solution, please turn to the end of the chapter.)

Traditional Cost vs. ABC

Carter Company uses a traditional two-stage cost allocation system. The first stage assigns all factory overhead costs to two production departments, A and B, based on machine-hours. The second stage uses direct labor-hours to allocate overhead to individual products, deluxe and regular.

During 2001, the company has a total factory overhead cost of $1,000,000. The number of machine-hours used in production departments A and B were 4,000 and 16,000, respectively. The number of direct labor-hours in production departments A and B were 20,000 and 10,000, respectively.

The following information relates to products deluxe and regular for the month of January 2001:

Cost Drivers	Deluxe	Regular
Units produced and sold	200	800
Unit cost of direct materials	$100	$50
Hourly direct labor wage rate	$25	$20
Direct labor-hours in department A per unit	2	2
Direct labor-hours in department B per unit	1	1

Carter Company is considering implementing an activity-based costing system. Its management accountant has collected this information for activity cost analysis:

Activity	Cost Driver	OH Rate	Driver Consumption Deluxe	Driver Consumption Regular
Material movement	Number of production runs	$ 20	150	200
Machine setups	Number of setups	800	25	50
Inspections	Number of units	30	200	800
Shipment	Number of shipments	20	50	100

Required

1. Calculate the unit cost for each product under the existing traditional costing system.

2. Calculate the unit cost for each product if the proposed ABC system is adopted.

QUESTIONS

4–1 Define the following terms: *just-in-time system, kanban, work cells, robots, computer-aided design, computer-aided manufacturing, flexible manufacturing systems,* and *computer-integrated manufacturing*.

4–2 Explain how a traditional costing system using either a plantwide overhead rate or a volume-based departmental rate can produce distorted product costs.

4–3 What does *product diversity* mean?

4–4 What is activity-based costing, and how can it improve an organization's costing system?

4–5 What is the first-stage procedure in tracing costs to products when using an activity-based costing system?

4–6 What is the second-stage procedure in tracing costs to products when using an activity-based costing system?

4–7 What type of company needs an activity-based costing system?

4–8 What four general levels of activities can be identified in a company?

4–9 Give three examples of unit-level activities.

4–10 Give three examples of batch-level activities.

4–11 Give three examples of product-sustaining activities.

4–12 Give three examples of facility-sustaining activities.

4–13 Why do product costing systems using a single, volume-based cost driver tend to overcost high-volume products? What undesirable strategic effects can such product cost distortion have?

4–14 What is activity-based management?

4–15 Give three examples of value-added activities in an organization type that you choose.

4–16 Give three examples of non-value-added activities in an organization type that you choose.

4–17 How can activity-based costing and management be used in service organizations?

EXERCISES

4–18 **JUST-IN-TIME SYSTEM** Fontana Machinery Company has lost its market share in recent years. At an executive meeting, the company president asked the controller to recommend a cost reduction and productivity improvement tool. The controller suggested the adoption of a just-in-time inventory management system.

Required

1. Describe a JIT system.

2. What are the roles of kanban and work cells in a JIT system?

3. The use of JIT is likely to affect the amount of working capital required by Fontana Machinery Company. Give two examples showing that adoption of a JIT system will reduce the company's working capital.

4–19 **JUST-IN-TIME SYSTEM** Pasadena Electronic Appliance Company has lost its market share in recent years. At an executive meeting, the company president asked the controller to recommend a cost reduction and productivity improvement tool. The controller reported that many companies—large and small—have employed a just-in-time (JIT) system with great success. He had read about companies that had successfully adopted JIT such as Goodyear, Westinghouse, General Motors, Black and Decker, and Intel. The controller suggested that the company adopt a JIT system.

Required

1. Describe a JIT system.
2. What are the main benefits of adopting a JIT system?
3. What are the key elements for the successful operation of a JIT system?

4–20 ACTIVITY LEVELS

Service

Required   Au's is a small hamburger shop at a nearby university. Classify its costs as unit-level, batch-level, product-sustaining, or facility-sustaining activity costs:

1. Bread
2. Cook's wages
3. Store rent
4. Beef
5. Catsup
6. Advertising
7. Cheese
8. Utilities
9. Server's wages
10. Napkins and bags

4–21 ACTIVITY LEVELS AND COST DRIVERS

Required

1. Classify each of the following activities as a unit-level, batch-level, product-sustaining, or facility-sustaining activity:
   a. Machine operation
   b. Machine setup
   c. Production scheduling
   d. Materials receipt
   e. Existing products support
   f. New product introduction
   g. Machine maintenance
   h. Product characteristics modification
   i. Parts administration
   j. Product redesign
   k. Direct labor support
   l. Materials handling
2. Identify a proper cost driver for each activity in requirement 1.

4–22 ACTIVITY LEVELS AND COST DRIVERS

Required

1. Classify each of the following activities as a unit-level, batch-level, product-sustaining, or facility-sustaining activity:
   a. Product design
   b. Production scheduling
   c. Materials ordering
   d. Parts administration
   e. Materials receipt
   f. General and administrative services
   g. Machine setups
   h. Plant administration
   i. Custodial service
   j. Vendor certification
2. Identify a proper cost driver for each activity in requirement 1.

4–23 COST DRIVERS

Service

Required

1. Identify a cost driver for each of these activities for the U.S. Postal Service:
   a. Selling to major customers
   b. Responding to customer concerns
   c. Maintaining Priority Mail program
   d. Accepting bulk mail
   e. Distributing mail
   f. Administering rules to customers

   2. Identify a cost driver for each of the activities for an electric utility company:

     a. Installing electricity in homes

     b. Installing electricity in commercial firms

     c. Installing new electric lines for a community

     d. Responding to calls that installation has not been successful

     e. Repairing electricity in homes

     f. Repairing common electric lines

4–24 TRADITIONAL COSTING VS. ABC Many companies recognize that their cost systems are inadequate for today's powerful global competition. Managers in companies selling multiple products are making important product decisions based on distorted cost information. This happens because most traditional cost systems focused on inventory valuation. To elevate the level of management information, current literature suggests that companies should have as many as three cost systems for (1) inventory valuation, (2) operational control, and (3) activity-based costing.

Required

   1. Discuss why the traditional cost system, developed to value inventory, distorts product cost information.

   2. Identify the purpose and characteristics of each of the following cost systems:

     a. Inventory valuation

     b. Operational control

     c. Activity-based costing

   3. Describe the benefits that management can expect from activity-based costing.

   4. List the steps that a company using a traditional cost system would take to implement activity-based costing.

   (CMA Adapted)

4–25 ACTIVITY-BASED COSTING Shieh Company has identified the following overhead cost pools and cost drivers:

Cost Pools	Activity Costs	Cost Driver	Driver Consumption
Machine setup	$180,000	Setup hours	1,500
Materials handling	50,000	Pounds of materials	12,500
Electric power	20,000	Kilowatt-hours	20,000

The following cost information pertains to the production of products X and Y:

	X	Y
Number of units produced	4,000	20,000
Direct materials cost ($)	$20,000	$25,000
Direct labor cost ($)	$12,000	$20,000
Number of setup hours	100	120
Pounds of materials used	500	1,500
Kilowatt-hours	1,000	2,000

Required Use the activity-based costing approach to calculate the unit cost for each product.

4–26 TRADITIONAL COSTING VS. ABC   Get Well Soon Hospital has a hospitalwide overhead rate based on direct labor-hours. The intensive care unit (ICU) applies overhead using machine-hours. Its budgeted cost and operating data follow:

Service

Budgeted information

Hospital total overhead	$5,360,000
Hospital total direct labor-hours	80,000
Machine-hours for ICU	30,000

Cost Driver Information for ICU

Cost Pool	Budget Cost	Budget Level for Cost Driver	OH Rate	Cost Drivers
Beds	$2,100,000	700	$3,000	Number of beds
Equipment	175,000	3,500	50	Number of monitors
Personnel	180,000	2,000	90	Number of staff

For the month of March, Get Well's intensive care unit recorded the following data:

3,600 direct labor-hours

5,800 machine-hours

60 beds were occupied

330 monitors were used

170 staff worked

Required

1. Calculate Get Well's ICU overhead costs for the month of March using
    a. The hospitalwide rate
    b. The ICU departmentwide rate
    c. The cost drivers for the ICU department
2. Explain the differences and determine which overhead assignment method is more appropriate.

4–27 DISTORTION OF PRODUCT COSTS   Junghans Computer Company has two product lines, computer A and computer B. Overall, company profit has declined in the last six months. According to the controller, computer A costs $500 to manufacture and is a high-volume product. Competitors produce a similar computer with an average market price of $380 that has cut into Junghans' sales volume for computer A. On the other hand, the company makes a large profit margin from sales of computer B because it costs only $400 to produce and sells for $750. The marketing vice president suggests shifting the sales mix in favor of computer B. Unfortunately, computer B is more complicated to make and few are produced.

Strategy

Required   Do you think that Junghans' marketing strategy should focus its sales on the computer A? Or is it better to focus on computer B as suggested by the marketing vice president? Provide analysis for your answer.

4–28 VALUE-ADDED AND NON-VALUE-ADDED ACTIVITIES

Service

Required

1. Classify each hospital radiology activity as a value-added or non-value-added activity:
    a. Receive patients
    b. Load film and take X-ray
    c. Develop X-ray
    d. Interpret X-rays taken
    e. Counsel patients
    f. Provide service to patients
    g. Repair equipment
    h. Test newly installed equipment

2. Classify each hospital nursing activity as a value-added or non-value-added activity:

   a. Update patients' records

   b. Attend to patients

   c. Coordinate lab/radiology/pharmacy

   d. Coordinate housekeeping

   e. Wait for the attending physician to arrive

   f. Attend continuing education courses

4–29   VALUE-ADDED AND NON-VALUE-ADDED ACTIVITIES

Required

1. Classify each of the following warehouse activities as a value-added or non-value-added activity.

   a. Receive goods   d. Move goods to stores

   b. Inspect goods   e. Expedite goods

   c. Move goods to warehouse   f. Manage employees

2. Classify each of the following engineering activities as a value-added or non-value-added activity.

   a. Develop the bill of materials   f. Design tooling

   b. Maintain the bill of materials   g. Provide training

   c. Develop routing   h. Perform management
                                               supervision
   d. Maintain routing

   e. Perform capacity studies

4–30   VALUE-ADDED AND NON-VALUE-ADDED ACTIVITIES

Required   Classify each of Best Keyboard Company's ordering activities as a value-added or non-value-added activity.

1. Receive call or place call

2. Fill out order form

3. Enter order data into computer

4. Print order form

5. Deliver order form to supervisor

6. Obtain supervisor's approval

7. Forward order form to vice president

8. Obtain vice president's final approval

9. Send copy of order form to accounting department

10. Make accounting department entry

11. Deliver the order form to warehouse

12. Box and load order

13. Call UPS for shipping

PROBLEMS

4–31   JUST-IN-TIME SYSTEM

AgriCorp manufactures farm equipment sold by a network of distributors throughout the United States. A majority of the distributors are also repair centers for AgriCorp equipment and depend on AgriCorp's Service Division to provide a timely supply of parts.

In an effort to reduce the Service Division's inventory costs, Richard Bachman, division manager, implemented a just-in-time inventory program on June 1, 2000, the beginning of the company's fiscal year. The program has been in place for a year, and Richard has asked the division controller, Janice Grady, to determine the effect that the program has had on the Service Division's financial performance. Janice has been able to document the following results of just-in-time implementation for the Service Division:

- Average inventory declined from $550,000 to $150,000.

- Projected annual insurance costs of $80,000 declined 60 percent due to the lower average inventory.

- An 8,000 square-foot warehouse previously rented to store raw materials, was not used at all during the year. The division paid $11,200 annual rent for the warehouse. After JIT implementation, it was able to sublet three-quarters of the building to several tenants at $2.50 per square foot; the balance of the space remained idle.

- Two warehouse employees whose services were no longer needed were transferred on June 1, 2000, to the Purchasing Department to assist in coordinating the just-in-time program. The annual salary expense for these two employees totaled $38,000 and continued to be charged to the indirect labor portion of fixed overhead.

- Despite the use of overtime to manufacture 7,500 spare parts, the Service Division lost the sale of 3,800 parts because of stock outs. The overtime premium incurred amounted to $5.60 per part manufactured. The use of overtime to fill spare parts orders was immaterial prior to June 1, 2000.

Prior to the decision to implement the just-in-time inventory program, the Service Division had completed its 2000–01 fiscal budget. Its pro forma income statement, without any adjustments for just-in-time inventory, follows. AgriCorp's incremental borrowing rate for inventory is 9 percent after income taxes. All AgriCorp budgets are prepared using an effective tax rate of 40 percent.

AGRICORP SERVICE DIVISION
Pro Forma Income Statement
For the Year Ending May 31, 2001
($000 omitted)

Sales (280,000 spare parts)		$6,160
Cost of goods sold		
Variable	$2,660	
Fixed	1,120	3,780
Gross profit		$2,380
Selling and administrative expense		
Variable	$ 700	
Fixed	555	1,255
Operating income		$1,125
Other income		75
Income before interest and		
income taxes		$1,200
Interest expense		150
Income before income taxes		$1,050
Income taxes		420
Net income		$ 630

Required

1. Calculate the after-tax cash savings (loss) for AgriCorp's Service Division that resulted during the 2000–01 fiscal year from the adoption of the just-in-time inventory program.

2. Identify and explain the factors, other than financial, that a company should consider before implementing a just-in-time program.

(CMA Adapted)

4–32 COST POOLS AND COST DRIVERS Supertech Corporation is a computer manufacturing company that applies the just-in-time system to its production flow. The following costs are budgeted for December:

Direct materials and parts	$400,000
Engineering design	60,000
Depreciation—building	50,000
Depreciation—machine	40,000
Electrical power	30,000
Insurance	20,000
Property taxes	15,000
Machine maintenance—labor	10,000
Machine maintenance—materials	9,000
Natural gas (for heating)	8,000
Packaging	7,000
Inspection of finished goods	6,000
Setup wages	5,000
Receiving	4,000
Inspection of direct materials	3,000
Purchasing	2,000
Custodial labor	1,000

Required Separate these costs into cost pools and identify the cost driver of each cost pool.

4–33 TRADITIONAL COSTING VS. ABC Robertson Company manufactures laser printers. It uses these overhead (OH) cost drivers:

OH Cost Pool	Cost Driver	OH Cost	Budgeted Level for Cost Driver	Budgeted OH Rate
Quality control	Number of inspections	$50,000	1,000	$50
Machine repetitions	Number of repetitions	100,000	1,000	100
Accounts receivable	Number of invoices	650	25	26
Other OH cost	Number of direct labor-hours	30,000	3,000	10

Robertson has an order for 500 laser printers; production requirements for this order follow:

Number of inspections	25
Number of repetitions	200
Number of invoices processed	250
Number of direct labor-hours	300

Required

1. What is the total overhead cost assigned to the 500 units using an activity-based costing method?
2. What is the cost per laser printer?
3. If Robertson expressed its overhead rate in direct labor-hours, how much overhead would it apply to the entire order for laser printers?
4. Would you recommend the use of ABC or the direct labor-based method to this company? Why?

Strategy

4–34 ACTIVITY-BASED COSTING, VALUE CHAIN ACTIVITIES Hoover Company uses activity-based costing and provides this information:

Manufacturing Activity Area	Cost Driver Used as Application Base	Conversion Cost per Unit of Base
Materials handling	Number of parts	$ 0.45
Machinery	Number of machine-hours	51.00
Assembly	Number of parts	2.85
Inspection	Number of finished units	30.00

Assume that 75 units of a component for packaging machines have been manufactured. Each unit required 105 parts and 3 machine-hours. Direct materials cost $600 per finished unit. All other manufacturing costs are classified as conversion costs.

Required

1. Compute the total manufacturing costs and the unit costs of the 75 units.

2. Suppose that the costs of upstream activities for the company's internal value chain, such as research and development and product design, are analyzed and applied to this component at $180 per unit. Moreover, similar analyses are conducted of downstream activities, such as distribution, marketing, and customer service. The downstream costs applied to this component are $1,050 per unit. Compute the full product cost per unit, including upstream, manufacturing, and downstream activities. What are strategic implications of this new cost result?

3. Explain to Hoover Company the usefulness of calculating the total value-chain cost and of breaking it down by different value-creating activities.

4–35 TRADITIONAL COSTING VS. ABC The controller for California Cooking Oil Company has established these overhead cost pools and cost drivers:

Overhead Cost Pool	Budgeted Overhead	Cost Driver	Estimated Cost Driver Level
Machine setups	$100,000	Number of setups	100
Materials handling	80,000	Number of barrels	8,000
Quality control	200,000	Number of inspections	1,000
Other overhead cost	100,000	Machine-hours	10,000
Total	$480,000		

An order of 500 barrels of cooking oil has used

Machine setups	6 setups
Materials handling	500 barrels
Quality inspections	20 times
Machine-hours	1,000 hours

Required

1. If California uses a single cost driver system based on machine-hours, how much total overhead is applied to an order of 500 barrels?

2. How much overhead is assigned to each barrel of cooking oil under the single cost driver system?

3. If California uses a multiple cost driver system based on total overhead cost, will the total overhead applied for 500 barrels be the same as in requirement 1? If not, compute the total overhead cost under a multiple cost driver system.

4. How big is the difference in the overhead cost per barrel under the single cost driver system and a multiple cost driver system?

Strategy

EXCEL

4–36 TRADITIONAL COSTING VS. ABC Elteha Chemical Company produces three products:

Product A with annual sales of 1,000 units

Product B with annual sales of 3,000 units

Product C with annual sales of 500 units

The company allocates the overhead costs based on direct labor dollars and computes total unit costs for each product as follows:

	Product A	Product B	Product C
Direct materials	$ 50.00	$ 60.00	$ 65.00
Direct labor	20.00	20.00	10.00
Factory overhead*	116.00	116.00	58.00
Total	$186.00	$196.00	$133.00

*Factory overhead budget

Machine setups	$ 8,000
Materials handling	100,000
Hazardous material control	250,000
Quality control	75,000
Other overhead costs	60,000
Total	$493,000

Direct labor dollars budgeted

Product A	$1,000 \times \$20.00 =$	$20,000
Product B	$3,000 \times \$20.00 =$	60,000
Product C	$500 \times \$10.00 =$	5,000
Total		$85,000

Predetermined overhead rate $= \$493,000 / \$85,000$

$= \$5.80$

The target and actual selling prices are

	Product A	Product B	Product C
Product cost	$186.00	$196.00	$133.00
Target price (150%)	279.00	294.00	199.50
Actual price	280.00	250.00	300.00

Required

1. Is product B the least profitable and is product C the most profitable?

2. The controller, who conducted research about product costing, suggested that each product absorbed the following proportion of each cost driver:

		Product		
Overhead	Cost Driver	A	B	C
Machine setup	Number of setups	20%	50%	30%
Materials handling	Weight of direct materials	40	25	35
Hazardous control	Number of inspections	25	45	30
Quality control	Number of inspections	30	35	35
Other overhead	Direct labor-hours	20	70	10

Given these percentages, what is the new product cost for the three products based on the activity-based costing system that the controller would like to switch to?

3. What is the new target price for each product based on 150 percent of the new costs under the ABC system? Compare this price with the actual selling price and comment on the result. Assuming that you are a

manager of Elteha Chemical, describe what actions you would take based on the information provided by the activity-based unit costs.

4–37 TRADITIONAL COSTING Madison, Inc., manufactures box radios in three different styles:

Elite box radio, annual sales 8,000 units

Standard box radio, annual sales 12,000 units

Junior box radio, annual sales 10,000 units

Madison uses a traditional volume-based costing system in applying factory overhead using direct-labor dollars. The cost of each product follows:

	Elite	Standard	Junior
Direct materials	$ 29.25	$19.50	$9.75
Direct labor			
1.0 × $13.50 =	13.50		
0.8 × $13.50 =		10.80	
0.6 × $13.50 =			8.10
Factory overhead	75.38	45.90	34.43
Total	$118.13	$76.20	$52.28

Predetermined overhead rate = 425%

Direct labor budget per annual sales

Elite radio	8,000 × $13.50	=	$108,000
Standard radio	12,000 × $10.80	=	129,600
Junior radio	10,000 × $8.10	=	81,000
Total			$318,600

Factory overhead

Engineering and design	$ 400,799	
Quality control	238,312	
Machinery	557,869	Predetermined rate
Miscellaneous overhead	157,070	$1,354,050 = 4.25
Total	$1,354,050	$ 318,600

Madison's retail price for radios is usually marked up at 175 percent of its full cost.

	Elite	Standard	Junior
Product cost	$118.13	$ 76.20	$ 52.28
Target price	206.73	133.35	91.49
Actual price	150.95	133.35	110.50

Madison has noticed that it is able to charge more for junior box radios with no effect on sales, but it has had to lower its price on the elite radio to sell it.

Required

1. According to this information, what is Madison's most profitable product?

2. What is its least profitable product?

4–38 ACTIVITY-BASED COSTING (Continuation of 4–37) Madison's controller has been researching activity-based costing and has decided to switch to it. A special study determined that Madison's three radio models are responsible for these proportions of each cost driver:

 *Strategy*

	Elite	Standard	Junior
Engineering and design	25%	50%	25%
Quality control	20	30	50
Machinery	35	10	55
Miscellaneous overhead	25	59	16

Required

1. Use the data in Problems 4–37 and 4–38 to develop unit product costs for each of the three products using activity-based costing.

2. Compare and explain unit cost differences between traditional costing and activity-based costing.

3. Calculate the activity-based costing target prices for Madison's three products using its pricing formula. Compare and explain differences between new target prices with actual selling prices and target prices based on traditional costing.

4. What are the implications for Madison's pricing strategy?

4–39   TEAM PROJECT ASSIGNMENT, ACTIVITY ANALYSIS

Required   This is a group assignment. Each group is to select a real-world organization and conduct an activity analysis of one of its processes such as sales and collection, purchase and payment, college admissions, student enrollment, warehousing, or bank deposits. Your written report should include the following:

1. Organization name, background information, persons contacted or interviewed.

2. Descriptions of activities and cost drivers in this process.

3. Process inputs, outputs, and performance measures.

4. Value- and non-value-added activities.

5. Suggested improvements.

Ethics

4–40   ETHICS, COST SYSTEM SELECTION   Aero Dynamics manufacturers airplane parts and engines for a variety of military and civilian aircraft. The company is the sole provider of rocket engines for the U.S. military that it sells for full cost plus a 5 percent markup.

Aero Dynamics's current cost system is a traditional direct labor-hour-based overhead allocation system. Recently, the company conducted a pilot study using the activity-based costing system. The study shows that the new ABC system, while more accurate and timely, will result in the assignment of lower costs to the rocket engines and higher costs to the company's other products. Apparently, the current (less accurate) direct labor-based costing system over-costs the rocket engines and undercosts the other products. On hearing of this, top management has decided to scrap the plans to adopt the ABC system because its rocket engine business with the military is a significant part of its business, and the reduced cost would lower the price and, thus, the profit for this part of Aero Dynamics's business.

Required   As the management accountant participating in this ABC pilot study project, what is your responsibility when you learn that top management has decided to cancel the plans for the ABC system? Can you ignore your professional ethics code in this case? What would you do?

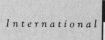

International

4–41   LIBRARY RESEARCH, INTERNATIONAL ABC

Required   Go to your library or use the database of a business periodical to select one article describing an application of the activity-based costing system by a company or companies outside the United States. Your written report should include the following:

1. Title, source, and the abstract (if provided) of the article.

2. Description of the application situation, cost drivers used, and benefits and problems encountered in applying the ABC system.

4–42 TRADITIONAL COSTING VS. ABC Gorden Company produces a variety of electronic equipment. One of its plants produces two dot-matrix printers, the superior and the regular. At the beginning of the year 2001, the following data were prepared for this plant:

Strategy

	Superior	Regular
Quantity	50,000	400,000
Selling price	$475.00	$300.00
Unit prime cost	$180.00	$110.00
Unit overhead cost	$20.00	$130.00

The unit overhead cost is calculated using the predetermined overhead application rate based on direct labor-hours.

Upon examining the data, the manager of marketing was particularly impressed with the per-unit profitability of the superior printer and suggested that more emphasis be placed on producing and selling this product. The plant supervisor objected to this strategy, arguing that the cost of the superior printer was understated. He argued that overhead costs could be assigned more accurately by using multiple cost drivers that reflected each product's consumption. To convince top management that multiple rates could produce a significant difference in product costs, he obtained the following projected information from the controller for the preceding production output:

			Activity Consumption	
Overhead Activity	Cost Driver	Pool Rate*	Superior	Regular
Setups	Number of setups	$2,800	200	100
Machine costs	Machine-hours	100	100,000	400,000
Engineering	Engineering-hours	40	45,000	120,000
Packing	Packing orders	20	50,000	200,000

*Cost per unit of cost driver

Required

1. Using the projected data based on traditional costing, calculate gross profit percentage, gross profit per unit, and total gross profit for each product.

2. Using the pool rates, calculate the overhead cost per unit for each product. Using this new unit cost, calculate gross profit percentage, gross profit per unit, and total gross profit for each product.

3. In view of the outcome in requirement 2, evaluate the suggestion of the manager of marketing to switch the emphasis to the superior model.

4. How does ABC add to Gorden's competitive advantage?

4–43 TRADITIONAL COSTING VS. ABC Hairless Company manufactures a variety of electric shavers used by men and women. The company's plant is partially automated; however, some manual labor is employed. The company uses the activity-based cost system. This cost driver information is used in the product-costing system:

Overhead Cost Pool	Budgeted Overhead Cost	Budgeted Level for Cost Driver	Cost Driver	Overhead Rate
Machine depreciation/maintenance	$27,000	140,400	Machine-hours	$5.20
Factory depreciation/utilities/insurance	30,000	117,000	Machine-hours	3.90
Product design	42,000	504,000	Hours in design	12.00
Material purchasing/storage	147,000	980,000	Raw materials	15% cost

Two current product orders have these requirements:

	15,000 Men's Shavers	20,000 Women's Shavers
Direct labor-hours	24	12
Raw materials cost	29,400	25,725
Hours in design	15	37.5
Machine-hours	50	40

Required

1. What is the total overhead that should be assigned to each product order?

2. What is the overhead cost per shaver?

3. Compute the predetermined overhead rate if the direct labor budget allows for 1,015 hours of direct labor.

4. Compute the total overhead cost assigned to each production order using the predetermined rate.

5. What is the overhead cost per shaver using the predetermined rate?

Strategy

4–44 TRADITIONAL COSTING VS. ABC   The current manufacturing costing system of Auer Corporation has two direct cost categories (direct materials and direct labor). Indirect manufacturing costs are applied to products using a single indirect cost pool. The indirect manufacturing cost application base is number of direct labor-hours; the indirect cost rate is $120 per direct labor-hour.

Auer Corporation is changing from a labor-based to a machine-based manufacturing approach at its aircraft components plant. The plant manager has set up five activity areas, each with its own supervisor and budget responsibility. Pertinent data follow:

Activity Area	Cost Driver Used as Indirect Cost Application Base	Cost per Unit of Application Base
Materials handling	Number of parts	$ 0.70
Lathe work	Number of turns	0.35
Milling	Number of machine-hours	15.00
Grinding	Number of parts	0.60
Shipping	Number of orders shipped	2,180.00

Information technology has advanced to the point where all the necessary data for budgeting in these five activity areas are automatically collected.

The two job orders processed under the new system at the aircraft components plant had the following characteristics:

	Job Order 101	Job Order 102
Direct materials cost per job	$45,300	$5,700
Direct labor cost per job	$16,800	$1,400
Number of direct labor-hours per job	420	35
Number of parts per job	1,500	600
Number of turns per job	80,000	15,000
Number of machine-hours per job	750	70
Number of job orders shipped	1	1
Number of units in each job order	450	20

Required

1. Compute the per-unit manufacturing cost of each job under the existing manufacturing costing system; that is, indirect costs are collected in a single cost pool with direct labor-hours as the application base.

2. Assume that Auer adopts an ABC system. Indirect costs are applied to products using separate indirect cost pools for each of the five activity

areas (materials handling, lathe work, milling, grinding, and shipping). The application base and rate for each activity area are described in the problem. Compute the per-unit manufacturing cost of each job under the ABC approach.

3. Compare the per-unit cost figures for job orders 101 and 102 computed in requirements 1 and 2. Why do they differ? Why might these differences be strategically important to Auer Corporation? How does ABC add to Auer's competitive advantage?

4-45 **TRADITIONAL COSTING VS. ABC** Modern Lighting Inc. manufactures and sells lighting fixtures. The company has two main product lines, ceiling fixtures and luxury pendants. Its products are sold through industry and wholesale suppliers. Due to intense competition, the company has two main problems. First, the price of the high-volume product, ceiling fixture, is often higher than that of competitors' products, so the company lost a significant number of sales. Second, the number of sales of units of the high-profit margin of the luxury pendant also decreased. During the recent executive meeting, the vice president of marketing was particularly impressed with the luxury pendant's per-unit profitability and suggested placing more emphasis on producing and selling it. The plant manager objected to this strategy, arguing that the cost of the ceiling fixture was understated. He argued that overhead costs could be allocated more accurately by using multiple cost drivers that better reflect each product's consumption of overhead activity resources.

Strategy

Because the president did not know whose suggestion to accept, the company hired a consultant to solve these problems. The company's existing cost accounting was the traditional direct labor cost-based system. This system allocated the overhead cost to products on the basis of $1.9267 per direct labor dollar. To control manufacturing costs, the consultant recommended the use of an ABC system to allocate factory overhead costs. The following exhibits provide the data that the consultant used.

Exhibit 1. Product Characteristics

Product	Annual Production Units	Unit Material Cost	Unit Direct Labor Cost	Unit Selling Price
Luxury pendant	4,000	$20	$8	$70
Ceiling fixture	40,000	10	5	40

Exhibit 2. ABC Activity Pools and Cost Drivers

Cost Pools/Activities	Cost Drivers
Machine operation	Machine-hours
Support labor overhead	Direct labor costs
Machine setup	Setup hours
Assembly	Number of parts
Inspection	Inspection hours

Exhibit 3. Estimated Overhead Costs and Activity Consumption Information

		Activity Consumption Levels		
Cost Pools/Activities	Overhead Costs	Total Activity	Luxury Pendants	Ceiling Fixtures
Machine operation	$160,000	10,000	1,500	8,500
Support labor	70,000	232,000	32,000	200,000
Machine setup	68,000	2,500	1,000	1,500
Assembly	88,500	402,500	192,500	210,000
Inspection	60,500	4,000	1,600	2,400
Total	$447,000			

The consultant explained why these cost drivers were appropriate:

- The overhead incurred by machine operation does not depend on the direct labor-hours. Rather, the cost should be allocated to the products on the basis of consumed machine-hours.

- The support labor included any allowance for benefits, break periods and costs related to the supervising and engineering staff. This overhead was indirect to the products but was related to the direct labor costs.

- The setup overhead was generated by changing the job to be run and should be related to the setup hours rather than the direct labor hours.

- The assembly overhead was generated by placing parts in a product. The more parts needed, the higher the overhead costs. Therefore, the correct cost driver should be the parts.

- The inspection overhead was incurred by checking the finished goods. The appropriate cost driver should be the hours spent on the inspection.

Required

1. Using the traditional costing system, calculate the unit manufacturing costs of the two products.

2. Using the activity-based costing system, calculate the unit manufacturing costs of the two products.

3. Under ABC, is the luxury pendant as profitable as the vice president of marketing thinks it is under the existing costing system?

4. Evaluate the marketing vice president's suggestion to shift the sales mix in favor of the luxury pendant units.

5. Give several reasons for the differences between the results for the two different costing systems.

Strategy

4–46 TRADITIONAL COSTING VS. ABC   ADAH Enterprises is in the pharmaceutical industry. It produces three drugs: Diomycin, Homycin, and Addolin belonging to the analgesic (pain-killer) family of medication. Since its inception four years ago, ADAH has used a traditional direct labor-hour-based system to allocate overhead cost to its products.

Eme Akpaffiong, the president of ADAH Enterprises, has just read about activity-based costing in *Management Accounting*. With some curiosity and interest, she has requested that her financial controller, Tak Ho, prepare a comprehensive example showing ADAH's costing system under both traditional costing and activity-based costing.

ADAH has the following budget information for the year:

	Diomycin	Homycin	Addolin
Cost of direct materials	$205,000	$265,000	$258,000
Cost of direct labor	250,000	234,000	263,000
Number of direct labor-hours	7,200	6,500	2,000
Number of capsules manufactured	750,000	500,000	300,000

ADAH has identified the following activities as cost drivers and has allocated them to total overhead cost of $200,000 as follows:

Activity	Cost Driver	Estimated Overhead Cost	Estimated Cost Driver Volume
Machine setup	Setup hours	$ 16,000	1,700
Plant management	Workers	38,000	1,200
Supervision of direct labor	Direct labor-hours	47,000	1,150
Quality inspection	Inspection-hours	48,000	1,050
Expediting production orders	Customers serviced	51,000	650
Total amount of overhead estimated		$200,000	

Tak provides the following justification for selecting the cost drivers:

Setup Hours. The cost driver of setup hours was used for the following reasons: the same product takes about the same amount of setup time regardless of size of batch. For different products, however, the setup time varies.

Number of Workers. Plant management includes plant maintenance and corresponding managerial duties that make production possible. This activity depends on the number of workers. The more workers involved, the higher the cost.

Supervision of Direct Labor. Supervisors spend their time supervising direct workers. Thus, the amount of time they spend on each product is proportional to the direct labor-hours worked.

Quality Inspection. Inspection involves testing a number of units in a batch. The time varies for different products but is the same for all similar products.

Number of Customers Serviced. The need to expedite production increases as the number of customers served by the company increases. Thus, the number of customers served by ADAH is a good product-sustaining measure of expediting production orders.

ADAH gathered the following information about the cost driver volume for each product:

	Diomycin	Homycin	Addolin
Machine setup	300	600	800
Plant management	200	400	600
Supervision of direct labor	200	300	650
Quality inspection	150	200	700
Expediting production orders	50	100	500

Required

1. Use the traditional direct labor-hour costing system to calculate the unit cost of each product.

2. Use the activity-based cost system to calculate the unit cost of each product.

3. The two cost systems provide different results; give several reasons for this. Why might these differences be strategically important to ADAH Enterprises? How does ABC add to ADAH's competitive advantage?

4. Briefly describe five major uses of ABC in the pharmaceutical industry.

4-47 TRADITIONAL COSTING VS. ABC Alaire Corporation manufactures several different printed circuit boards; two of the boards account for the majority of the company's sales. The first product, a television (TV) circuit board, has been a standard in the industry for several years. The market for this board is competitive and price sensitive. Alaire plans to sell 65,000 of the TV boards in 2001 at $150 per unit. The second product, a personal computer (PC) circuit board, is a recent addition to Alaire's product line. Because it incorporates the latest technology, it can be sold at a premium price. The 2001 plans include the sale of 40,000 PC boards at $300 per unit.

 *Strategy*

Alaire's management group is meeting to discuss strategies for 2001. The current topic of conversation is how to spend the sales and promotion dollars for 2001 year. The sales manager believes that the market share for the TV board could be expanded by concentrating Alaire's promotional efforts in this area. In response to this suggestion, the production manager said, "Why don't you go after a bigger market for the PC board? The cost sheets that I get show the contribution from the PC board is more than double the contribution from the TV board. I know we get a premium price for the PC board; selling it should help overall profitability."

Alaire's current traditional costing system shows these data for TV and PC boards:

	TV Board	PC Board
Direct materials	$80	$140
Direct labor	1.5 hours	4 hours
Machine time	.5 hour	1.5 hours

145

The current traditional costing system uses three types of factory overhead: variable factory, materials handling, and machine time. Variable factory overhead is applied on the basis of direct labor-hours. For 2001, it is budgeted at $1,120,000 and 280,000 direct labor-hours. The hourly rates for machine time and direct labor are $10 and $14, respectively. Alaire applies a materials-handling charge at 10 percent of direct materials cost, which is not included in variable factory overhead. Total 2001 expenditures for direct materials are budgeted at $10,600,000.

The company conducted an activity analysis and collected the following information for 10 activities:

Budgeted Overhead Costs		Cost Driver	Annual Activity for Cost Driver
Materials-related overhead			
Procurement	$ 400,000	Number of parts	4,000,000
Production scheduling	220,000	Number of boards	110,000
Packaging and shipping	440,000	Number of boards	110,000
	$1,060,000		
Variable overhead			
Machine setup	$ 446,000	Number of setups	278,750
Hazardous waste disposal	48,000	Pounds of waste	16,000
Quality control	560,000	Number of inspections	160,000
General supplies	66,000	Number of boards	110,000
	$1,120,000		
Manufacturing overhead			
Machine insertion	$1,200,000	Number of insertions	3,000,000
Manual insertion	4,000,000	Number of insertions	1,000,000
Wave soldering	132,000	Number of boards	110,000
	$5,332,000		

Required per Unit	TV Board	PC Board
Parts	25	55
Machine insertions	24	35
Manual insertions	1	20
Machine setups	2	3
Hazardous waste	0.02 lb.	0.35 lb.
Inspections	1	2

Ed Welch, Alaire's controller, believes that before the management group proceeds with the discussion about allocating sales and promotional dollars to individual products, it might be worthwhile to look at these products on the basis of the activities involved in their production. As Ed explained to the group, "Activity-based costing integrates the cost of all activities, known as cost drivers, into individual product costs rather than including these costs in overhead pools." He prepared the preceding information to help the management group understand this concept.

"Using this information," Ed explained, "we can calculate an activity-based cost for each TV board and each PC board and then compare it to the standard cost we have been using. The only cost that remains the same for both cost methods is the cost of direct materials. The cost drivers will replace the direct labor, machine time, and overhead costs in the old standard cost figures."

Required

1. Identify at least four general advantages associated with activity-based costing.

2. On the basis of Alaire's current volume-based costing system and its cost data (direct materials, direct labor, materials-handling charge, variable overhead, and machine time overhead) given in the problem, calculate the total contribution margin expected in 2001 for Alaire Corporation's (a) TV board and (b) PC board.

3. On the basis of activity-based costs, calculate the total contribution margin expected in 2001 for Alaire Corporation's (a) TV board and (b) PC board.

4. Explain how the comparison of the results of the two costing methods might affect the sales, pricing, and promotion decisions made by Alaire Corporation's management group.

(CMA Adapted)

4-48 TRADITIONAL COSTING VS. ABC   Coffee Bean, Inc. (CBI) processes and distributes a variety of different brands of coffee. The company buys coffee beans from around the world and roasts, blends, and packages them for resale. CBI currently has 15 different coffees that it offers to gourmet shops in one-pound bags. The major cost is direct materials; however, a substantial amount of factory overhead is incurred in the predominantly automated roasting and packing process. The company uses relatively little direct labor.

 *Strategy*

Some of the coffees are very popular and sell in large volumes; a few of the newer brands have very low volumes. CBI prices its coffee at full product cost, including allocated overhead, plus a markup of 30 percent. If its prices for certain coffees are significantly higher than the market, CBI lowers its prices. The company competes primarily on the quality of its products, but customers are price conscious as well.

Data for the 2001 budget include factory overhead of $3,000,000, which has been allocated by its current costing system on the basis of each product's direct labor cost. The budgeted direct labor cost for 2001 totals $600,000. Budgeted purchases and use of direct materials (mostly coffee beans) will total $6,000,000.

The budgeted direct costs for one-pound bags of two of the company's products are as follows:

	Mona Loa	Malaysian
Direct materials	$4.20	$3.20
Direct labor	0.30	0.30

CBI's controller believes that the its traditional product costing system could be providing misleading cost information. She has developed this analysis of the 2001 budgeted factory overhead costs:

Activity	Cost Driver	Budgeted Activity	Budgeted Cost
Purchasing	Purchase orders	1,158	$ 579,000
Materials handling	Setups	1,800	720,000
Quality control	Batches	720	144,000
Roasting	Roasting-hours	96,100	961,000
Blending	Blending-hours	33,600	336,000
Packaging	Packaging-hours	26,000	260,000
Total factory overhead cost			$3,000,000

Data regarding the 2001 production of Mona Loa and Malaysian coffee follow. There will be no beginning or ending direct materials inventory for either of these coffees.

	Mona Loa	**Malaysian**
Budgeted sales	100,000 pounds	2,000 pounds
Batch size	10,000 pounds	500 pounds
Setups	3 per batch	3 per batch
Purchase order size	25,000 pounds	500 pounds
Roasting time	1 hour per 100 pounds	1 hour per 100 pounds
Blending time	0.5 hour per 100 pounds	0.5 hour per 100 pounds
Packaging time	0.1 hour per 100 pounds	0.1 hour per 100 pounds

Required

1. Using Coffee Bean, Inc.'s current traditional product costing system

    a. Determine the company's predetermined overhead rate using direct labor cost as the single cost driver.

    b. Determine the full product costs and selling prices of one pound of Mona Loa coffee and one pound of Malaysian coffee.

2. Using an activity-based costing approach, develop a new product cost for one pound of Mona Loa coffee and one pound of Malaysian coffee. Allocate all overhead costs to the 100,000 pounds of Mona Loa and the 2,000 pounds of Malaysian. Compare the results with those in requirement 1.

3. What are the implications of the activity-based costing system with respect to CBI's pricing and product mix strategies? How does ABC add to CBI's competitive advantage?

    (CMA Adapted)

Strategy

4–49   CUSTOMER PROFITABILITY ANALYSIS   ABC costing can be extended to customer profitability analysis. The primary focus of this analysis is selling, general, and administrative costs. The analysis investigates activities and selects proper cost drivers for them. Boston Company's top management decided to analyze the profitability of two major customers: Customer A and Customer B. The company's existing cost system allocates customer service fees to individual customers based on sales dollars. The current charge rate for service fees is 17.5% of sales.

During a recent executive meeting, the company controller presented the following profitability of the two customers:

	Customer Profitability Analysis	
Existing Cost System	**Customer A**	**Customer B**
Sales	$80,000	$80,000
Product cost	(50,000)	(48,000)
Service fees (17.5% of sales)	(14,000)	(14,000)
Gross margin	$16,000	$18,000
Gross margin %	20%	22.5%

Upon examining the data, the marketing vice president was particularly impressed with Customer B's gross margin percentage and suggested that more emphasis be placed on selling to and servicing this customer. The operations manager objected to this strategy, arguing that the service fee to this customer is understated. He stated that service fees could be allocated more accurately by using multiple cost drivers that better reflect each product's consumption of service activity resources. To convince top management that this activity-based costing could produce a significant difference in service fees, he obtained the following information from the controller:

Calculation of ABC Service Costs

Value-Added Activities	Total Estimated Annual Expense	Cost Driver Defined	Estimated Annual Cost Driver Units
Requisitions handling	$3,000,000	Requisitions	300,000
Warehouse	1,050,000	Carton lines	700,000
Pick packing	660,000	Lines (pick pack)	600,000
Data entry	630,000	Carton lines	700,000
Delivery charge		Actual freight cost	

Distribution Services Activities for Customers A and B

	Customer A	Customer B
Annual revenue	$80,000	$80,000
Requisitions	300	700
Requisition lines (all pick-packing)	900	2,100
Freight cost to ship orders	$2,850	$4,650

Required

1. Using the activity-based costing data presented, compute the total cost and gross margin percentage for each customer.

2. Is serving Customer B as profitable as the marketing vice president thinks it is under the existing costing system?

3. Evaluate the marketing vice president's suggestion to shift the customer mix in favor of Customer B.

4–50 ACTIVITY-BASED COSTING Miami Valley Architects Inc. provides a wide range of engineering and architectural consulting services through its three branch offices in Columbus, Cincinnati, and Dayton, Ohio. The company allocates resources and bonuses to the three branches based on the net income reported for the period. The following presents the results of performance for the year 2000 ($ in thousands):

Service

	Columbus	Cincinnati	Dayton	Total
Sales	$1,500	$1,419	$1,067	$3,986
Less: Direct labor	382	317	317	1,016
Direct materials	281	421	185	887
Overhead	710	589	589	1,888
Net income	$ 27	$ 92	$ (24)	$ 195

Miami Valley accumulates overhead items in one overhead pool and allocates it to the branches based on direct labor dollars. For 2000, this predetermined overhead rate was $1,859 for every direct labor dollar incurred by an office. The overhead pool includes rent, depreciation, and taxes, regardless of which office incurred the expense. This method forces the offices to absorb a portion of the overhead incurred by the other offices.

Management is concerned with the results of the 2000 performance reports. During a review of the overhead, many overhead items were clearly not correlated to the movement in direct labor dollars as previously assumed. Management decided that applying overhead based on activity-based costing and direct tracing where possible should provide a more accurate picture of the profitability of each branch.

An analysis of the overhead revealed that the following dollars for rent, utilities, depreciation, and taxes could be traced directly to the office that incurred the overhead ($ in thousands):

	Columbus	Cincinnati	Dayton	Total
Direct overhead	$180	$270	$177	$627

149

Activity pools and their corresponding cost drivers were determined from the accounting records and staff surveys as follows:

General administration	$ 409,000
Project costing	48,000
Accounts payable/receiving	139,000
Accounts receivable	47,000
Payroll/Mail sort & delivery	30,000
Personnel recruiting	38,000
Employee insurance processing	14,000
Proposals	139,000
Sales meetings/Sales aids	202,000
Shipping	24,000
Ordering	48,000
Duplicating costs	46,000
Blueprinting	77,000
	$1,261,000

	Volume of Cost Drivers by Location		
Cost Driver	**Columbus**	**Cincinnati**	**Dayton**
Direct labor dollar	382,413	317,086	317,188
Timesheet entries	6,000	3,800	3,500
Vendor invoices	1,020	850	400
Client invoices	588	444	96
Employees	23	26	18
New hires	8	4	7
Insurance claims filed	230	260	180
Proposals	200	250	60
Contracted sales	1,824,439	1,399,617	571,208
Projects shipped	99	124	30
Purchase orders	135	110	80
Copies duplicated	162,500	146,250	65,000
Blueprints	39,000	31,200	16,000

Required (Round all answers to thousands):

1. What overhead costs should be assigned to each branch based on ABC concepts?

2. What is the contribution of each branch before subtracting the results obtained in requirement 1?

3. What is the profitability of each branch office using ABC?

4. Evaluate the concerns of management regarding the traditional cost technique currently used.

(Adapted from Beth M. Chaffman, CPA, and John Talbott, CMA, IMA Management Accounting Campus Report)

SOLUTION TO SELF-STUDY PROBLEM

Traditional Costing vs. ABC

1. Traditional costing system

Stage 1 Allocation

Total overhead allocated to Department A

$1,000,000 × (4,000/20,000) = $200,000

Total overhead allocated to Department B

$1,000,000 × (16,000/20,000) = $800,000

Stage 2 Allocation

	(Per Unit Cost)	
	Deluxe	**Regular**
Overhead allocated to		
Department A		
($200,000/20,000) × 2 =	$ 20	
($200,000/20,000) × 2 =		$20
Department B		
($800,000/10,000) × 1 =	80	
($800,000/10,000) × 1 =		80
Total	$100	$100

Product cost per unit:

	Deluxe	**Regular**
Direct materials	$100	$ 50
Direct labor		
$25 × (2 + 1) =	75	
$20 × (2 + 1) =		60
Factory overhead	100	100
Unit cost	$275	$210

2. ABC system

	Deluxe	**Regular**
Overhead allocated to		
Material movement		
$20 × 150 =	$ 3,000	
$20 × 200 =		$ 4,000
Machine setups		
$800 × 25 =	20,000	
$800 × 50 =		40,000
Inspections		
$30 × 200 =	6,000	
$30 × 800 =		24,000
Shipment		
$20 × 50 =	1,000	
$20 × 100 =		2,000
Total	$30,000	$70,000
Unit overhead cost	$150	$ 87.50
Product cost per unit		
Direct materials	$100	$ 50
Direct labor	75	60
Factory overhead	150	87.50
Unit cost	$325	$197.50

Note that the traditional costing system overcosts the high-volume regular product and undercosts the low-volume deluxe product.

5

Target Costing, Theory of Constraints, and Life-Cycle Costing

After studying this chapter, you should be able to . . .

1 Explain how to use target costing to facilitate strategic management

2 Apply the theory of constraints to strategic management

3 Describe how life-cycle costing facilitates strategic management

4 Outline the objectives and techniques of strategic pricing

Courtesy of Toyota Motor Manufacturing North America, Inc.

Having two of the world's best selling cars, the Camry and the Corolla, as well as a number of other popular models, Toyota is among the world's most successful automakers. The reason for Toyota's success is that it is able to consistently produce high-quality cars with attractive features at competitive prices. Target costing, a method Toyota pioneered in the 1960s, is one method it uses to achieve high quality and desirable features at a competitive price.[1] Target costing is a design approach in which cost management plays a large part, as we will see in this chapter. Using target costing, a company designs a product to achieve a desired profit while satisfying the customer's expectations for quality and product features. The balancing of costs, features, and quality takes place throughout the design, manufacturing, sale, and service of the car but has the strongest influence in the first phase, design. When design alternatives are being examined and selected, Toyota has the maximum flexibility for choosing options that affect manufacturing and all other product costs such as customer service and warranty work.

Once the design is complete and manufacturing has begun, the cost consequences of the choice of features and manufacturing methods are set until the next model change. As a result, the development of a good, cost-effective design is critical. Target costing places a strong focus on using the design process to improve the product and reduce its cost. And Toyota is well known for its focus on design. A very good example is the redesign of the Camry in 1996. Two elements of the redesign were to make the running lamps part of the headlamp assembly and to make the front grill part of the bumper, which would save time and materials in manufacturing and produce a more crash-resistant bumper—a win/win for Toyota and the car buyer!

Target costing is the first of the four cost management methods we study in this chapter; the others are the theory of constraints, life-cycle costing, and strategic pricing. A common element of the four methods is that each looks at the product from the point of view of the product life cycle. Two significantly different views of the product life cycle are the *cost* life cycle and the *sales* life cycle.

The **cost life cycle** is the sequence of activities within the firm that begins with research and development followed by design, manufacturing (or providing the service),

> The **cost life cycle** is the sequence of activities within the firm that begins with research and development followed by design, manufacturing, marketing/distribution, and customer service.

---

[1] A. Taylor III, "How Toyota Defies Gravity," *Fortune*, December 1997, pp. 100–8; Takao Tanaka, "Target Costing at Toyota," *Journal of Cost Management*, Spring 1993, pp. 4–11; Durward K. Sobek II, Allen C. Ward, and Jeffry K. Liker, "Toyota's Principles of Set-Based Concurrent Engineering," *Sloan Management Review*, Winter 1999, pp. 67–83; "More Camry for Less Cash," *Business Week*, November 18, 1996, p. 186; and "Toyota Motor Corporation: Target Costing System," Harvard Business School Case No. 9-197-031 (May 30, 1997).

The **sales life cycle** is the sequence of phases in the product's or service's life in the market from the introduction of the product or service to the market, growth in sales, and finally maturity, decline, and withdrawal from the market.

marketing/distribution, and customer service. It is the life cycle of the product or service from the viewpoint of costs incurred. The cost life cycle is illustrated in Exhibit 5–1.[2] The **sales life cycle** is the sequence of phases in the product's or service's life in the market from the introduction of the product or service to the market, the growth in sales, and finally maturity, decline, and withdrawal from the market. Sales are at first small, peak in the maturity phase, and decline thereafter, as illustrated in Exhibit 5–2.

Important strategic cost management issues arise in each activity of the cost or sales life cycle. The three methods helpful in analyzing the cost life cycle are target costing, the theory of constraints, and life-cycle costing. Target costing is used for determining profitable product designs early in the cost life cycle. The theory of constraints is a method for improving speed and reducing costs in manufacturing during the middle of the cost life cycle. Life-cycle costing is used throughout the cost life cycle to minimize overall cost. The fourth cost management method, strategic pricing, applies when the firm has a number of products at different phases of the sales life cycle. Strategic pricing is used in this case to determine the product price and to plan product development activities for each product according to its phase in the sales life cycle.

The four methods are commonly used by manufacturing firms, where new product development, manufacturing speed, and efficiency are important. Because a product

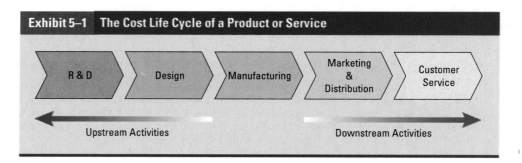

Exhibit 5–1   The Cost Life Cycle of a Product or Service

R & D → Design → Manufacturing → Marketing & Distribution → Customer Service

← Upstream Activities   Downstream Activities →

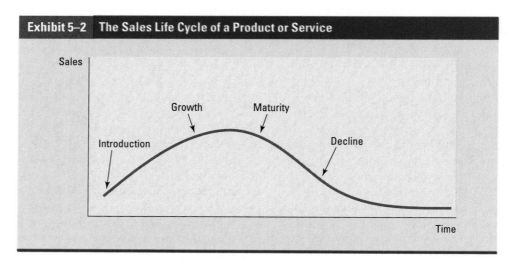

Exhibit 5–2   The Sales Life Cycle of a Product or Service

Sales

Introduction — Growth — Maturity — Decline

Time

---

2   The *cost life cycle* also is called a *value chain* by many writers to emphasize that each activity must add value for the ultimate consumer [Michael Porter, *Competitive Advantage* (New York: Free Press, 1985)]. Note that this concept of the value chain differs from that introduced in Chapter 2. Chapter 2 describes the industry-level value chain; the cost life-cycle concept in this chapter describes the firm-level value chain. We use the broader concept of the industry-level value chain in Chapter 2 to facilitate the strategic focus in that chapter. For a discussion of the two types of value chains, see Joseph G. San Miguel, "Value Chain Analysis for Assessing Competitive Advantage," *Management Accounting Guideline Number 41* (The Society of Management Accountants of Canada, 1996); and Mike Partridge and Lew Perren, "Assessing and Enhancing Strategic Capability: A Value-Driven Approach," *Management Accounting* (UK), June 1994, pp. 28–29.

with clear physical characteristics is involved, applications in manufacturing firms are more intuitive and easily understood. However, each method can also be used in service firms. For example, a local government could use the theory of constraints to speed the process of billing residents for water services (and to reduce the processing cost) or to speed the operations for processing and depositing the collections from these residents.

TARGET COSTING

> Our policy is to reduce the price, extend the operations, and improve the article. You will notice that the reduction of price comes first. We have never considered costs as fixed. Therefore we first reduce the price to the point where we believe more sales result. Then we go ahead and try to make the prices. We do not bother about the costs. The new price forces the costs down. The more usual way is to take the costs and then determine the price, and although that method may be scientific in the narrow sense; it is not scientific in the broad sense, because what earthly use is it to know the cost if it tells you that you cannot manufacture at a price at which the article can be sold? But more to the point is the fact that although one may calculate what a cost is, and of course all of our costs are carefully calculated, no one knows what a cost ought to be. One of the ways of discovering is to name a price so low as to force everybody in the place to the highest point of efficiency. The low price makes everybody dig for profits. We make more discoveries concerning manufacturing and selling under this forced method than by any method of leisurely investigation.
>
> HENRY FORD, *MY LIFE AND MY WORK*, 1923

Henry Ford's thinking would fit well in today's corporate boardrooms, where global competition, increased customer expectations, and competitive pricing in many industries have forced firms to look for ways to reduce costs year after year at the same time producing products with increased levels of quality and functionality. Ford is describing a technique called *target costing*, in which the firm determines the allowable (i.e., "target") cost for the product or service, given a competitive market price, so the firm can earn a desired profit:

◀ **LEARNING OBJECTIVE 1**
Explain how to use target costing to facilitate strategic management.

Target cost = Competitive price − Desired profit

The firm has two options for reducing costs to a target cost level:

1. By integrating new manufacturing technology, using advanced cost management techniques such as activity-based costing, and seeking higher productivity.

2. By redesigning the product or service. This method is beneficial for many firms because it recognizes that design decisions account for much of total product life-cycle costs.[3] By careful attention to design, significant reductions in total cost are possible. This approach to target costing is associated primarily with Japanese manufacturers.[4]

---

[3] The Westinghouse Corporate Services Council estimates that 85 percent of a product's life-cycle cost is determined in the design phase (Karlos A. Artto, "Life Cycle Cost Concepts and Methodologies," *Journal of Cost Management*, Fall 1994, pp. 28–32); see also "Implementing Target Costing," *Management Accounting Guideline Number 28* (The Society of Management Accountants of Canada, 1994). The portion of life-cycle costs that is determined in the design stage is sometimes referred to as a *locked-in* or *designed-in* cost to emphasize that, after the design is complete, it is difficult to reduce these costs.

[4] Robin Cooper and Regine Slagmulder, *Target Costing and Value Engineering* (Portland, Ore.: Productivity Press, 1997).

Target Costing at Ford Motor Company

Ford Motor Company knew that the real opportunities for cutting costs were in the design phase, according to Jim Harbor, an industry analyst. Ford's engineers and factory workers were asked how to trim costs from the manufacture of the 1997 Taurus model. Some of the suggestions and the per car savings follow:

- A new, integrated bracket for the air conditioner ($4).
- Recycled instead of new plastic in splash shields (45 cents).

- Elimination of a plastic part from the wiring harness behind the instrument panel (10 cents).
- Redesigned door hinge pins ($2).
- Plastic moldings for the moon roof instead of metal moldings ($7.85).
- Antilock circuits no longer installed in cars without the system ($1).

Source: "How Ford Cut Costs on the 1997 Taurus, Little by Little," *The Wall Street Journal,* July 18, 1996.

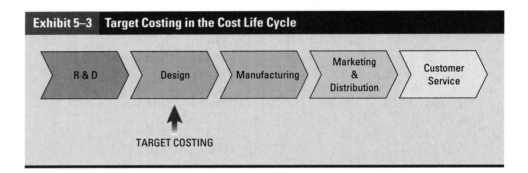

Exhibit 5–3   Target Costing in the Cost Life Cycle

Many firms employ both options: efforts to achieve increased productivity gains and target costing to determine low-cost design. Some managers argue that, unlike programs for productivity improvement, target costing provides a more distinct goal, a specific cost level. Because the goal is more definite, it appears more achievable and therefore more motivating.

Many auto manufacturers, software developers, and other consumer product manufacturers must also determine in the design process the number and types of features to include in periodic updates of a product using cost and market considerations. Target costing, based on analysis of functionality/cost trade-offs, is an appropriate management tool for these firms. With its positioning in the early, upstream phases of the cost life cycle, target costing can clearly help a firm reduce total costs (see Exhibit 5–3).

Japanese industry and a growing number of firms worldwide are using target costing. The Cadillac division at General Motors Corporation; Toyota; Honda Motor Company; Compaq Computer Inc.; Intel, Inc.; and many others are using target costing. Many firms find it difficult to compete successfully on cost leadership or differentiation alone; they must compete on both price and functionality.[5] Target costing is a very useful way to manage the needed trade-off between functionality and cost.

Implementing a target costing approach involves five steps:

1. Determine the market price.
2. Determine the desired profit.
3. Calculate the target cost at market price less desired profit.
4. Use value engineering to identify ways to reduce product cost.
5. Use kaizen costing and operational control to further reduce costs.

The first three steps require no additional explanation. The following sections explain the fourth and fifth steps: the use of value engineering and of kaizen costing and operational control.

[5] Robin Cooper, *When Lean Enterprises Collide* (Boston: Harvard Business School Press, 1995); see also the discussion of hypercompetition in the Appendix to Chapter 2.

Target Costing and Design in the Auto Industry

Many global automakers use target costing and focus on design to speed the development of new products and to improve the features and quality of their products while keeping costs in check.

HONDA MOTOR COMPANY

In the redesign of its popular Civic, Honda looked for ways to improve customer satisfaction while reducing costs. The changes that resulted included integrating the dashboard clock into the radio display, simplifying the trunk hinge, and redesigning the bumper, dashboard, and other parts to have fewer pieces, which cut manufacturing costs.

FORD MOTOR COMPANY

Ford has a new product design program, the Ford Product Development System, to speed the development of new vehicles and to improve the quality and cost-effectiveness of the designs. The system uses a Web-based tool for allowing Ford engineers around the world to collaborate on design efforts; in a recent example, 4,500 engineers in the United States, the United Kingdom, and Germany used the tool. Ford also uses computer-aided design software developed by Structural Dynamics Research Corp. to speed its design process, improve the cost-effectiveness of the designs, and reduce the cost of developing product prototypes.

BMW

BMW has cut its development time for new cars in half through the use of computer-aided design software.

PORSCHE

The manufacturing time for the 911 Carrera was cut from 120 hours to 60 hours through the use of computer-aided design and computer-aided engineering.

DAIMLERCHRYSLER

The U.S. unit of DaimlerChrysler uses the rare metal palladium in catalytic converters to reduce auto emissions, as do many other automakers. The price of the metal, whose principal source is Russia, was stable until political and economic changes there disrupted the supply and caused the price of the metal to jump tenfold. Engineers at the U.S. unit are working to find new ways to meet pollution control standards that do not rely on this rare metal.

Source: Gregory L. White, "Russian Maneuvers Are Making Palladium Ever More Precious," *The Wall Street Journal,* March 6, 2000, p. 1; Gina Imperato, "SDRC Want You to Go Faster," *Fast Company,* October 1999, pp. 90–92; "Hot Wheels," *Business Week,* September 15, 1997, pp. 56–57; Steve Hamm and Marcia Stepanek, "From Reengineering to E-Engineering," *Business Week E-Biz,* March 22, 1999, p. EB15; and "Honda's Civic Lesson," *Business Week,* September 18, 1995.

Value Engineering

Value engineering is used in target costing to reduce product cost by analyzing the trade-offs between different types of product functionality (different types of product features) and total product cost. An important first step in value engineering is to perform a consumer analysis during the design stage of the new or revised product. The consumer analysis identifies critical consumer preferences that define the desired functionality for the new product.

The type of value engineering used depends on the product's functionality. For one group of products—including automobiles, computer software, and many consumer electronic products such as cameras and audio and video equipment—functionality can be added or deleted relatively easily. These products have frequent new models or updates, and customer preferences change frequently. The manufacturer in effect chooses the particular bundle of features to include with each new model of the product. For automobiles, this can mean new performance and new safety features; for computer software, it might mean the ability to perform certain new tasks or analyses.

In contrast, for another group of products, the functionality must be designed into the product rather than added on. These are best represented by specialized equipment and industrial products such as construction equipment, heavy trucks, and specialized medical equipment. In contrast to the first group, customer preferences here are rather stable.

Target costing is more useful for products in the first group because the firm has some discretion about a larger number of features. A common type of value engineering employed in these firms is **functional analysis,** a process of examining the performance and cost of each major function or feature of the product. The objective of the analysis is to determine a desired balance of performance and cost. An overall desired level of achievement of performance for each function is obtained while keeping the cost of all functions below the target cost.

Value engineering is used in target costing to reduce product cost by analyzing the trade-offs between different types of product functionality and total product cost.

Functional analysis is a common type of value engineering in which the performance and cost of each major function or feature of the product is examined.

COST MANAGEMENT IN ACTION

Why Go Abroad (to Latin America)? Compaq, Ericsson, Cisco, Ford, Volkswagen

In competitive industries such as computers, consumer electronics, and autos, manufacturers continuously look for ways to reduce cost and increase value throughout the value chain. Because of intense pricing pressures and increased customer expectations, target costing methods can help identify and analyze the options for competitive advantage. Going abroad is the solution for many firms but for different reasons. We look at the practices in two industries: consumer electronics and computer products, and automakers.

CONSUMER ELECTRONICS AND COMPUTER PRODUCTS

Computer and electronics companies including Compaq, Ericsson, and Cisco Systems have outsourced manufacturing to plants operated by contract manufacturers in Mexico, such as Flextronics International, Ltd., Solectron Corp., and SCI Systems. Cisco, for example, owns relatively few manufacturing plants, opting instead to contract out its manufacturing needs. Why is this an advantage to these three companies?

GLOBAL AUTOMAKERS

Ford, Volkswagen, DaimlerChrysler, General Motors, Renault, and Peugeot have invested in these new manufacturing plants in Mexico and Brazil. Why?

Automaker	Investment in Plants	Country
Ford	$1.9 billion	Brazil
Volkswagen	$1.5 billion	Mexico
Renault	$1.4 billion	Brazil
DaimlerChrysler	$815 million	Brazil
PSA Peugeot Citreon	$600 million	Brazil
General Motors	$600 million	Brazil

(Refer to Comments on Cost Management in Action at the end of the chapter.)

Benchmarking is often used at this step to determine which features give the firm a competitive advantage. In a release of new software, for example, each desired feature of the updated version is reviewed against the cost and time required for its development. The objective is an overall bundle of features for the software that achieves the desired balance of meeting customer preferences while keeping costs below targeted levels. In another example, auto manufacturers must decide which performance and safety features to add to the new model. This decision is based on consumer analysis and a functional analysis of the feature's contribution to consumer preferences compared to its cost. For instance, improved safety air bags could be added, but target cost constraints could delay an improved sound system until a later model year.

Design analysis is the common form of value engineering for products in the second group, industrial and specialized products. The design team prepares several possible designs of the product, each having similar features with different levels of performance and different costs. Benchmarking and value chain analysis help guide the design team in preparing designs that are both low cost and competitive. The design team works with cost management personnel to select the one design that best meets customer preferences while not exceeding the target cost.

A useful comparison of different target costing and cost-reduction strategies in three Japanese firms, based on the field research of Robin Cooper, is illustrated in Exhibit 5–4. Note that the different market demands for functionality result in different cost-reduction approaches. Where customers' expectations for functionality are increasing, as for Nissan and Olympus, there is more significant use of target costing. In contrast, at Komatsu, the emphasis is on value engineering and productivity improvement. Note also that firms such as Nissan, which use both internal and external sourcing for parts and components, use target costing at both the product level and the component level. The overall product-level target cost is achieved when targeted costs for all components are achieved.[6]

Other cost-reduction approaches include cost tables and group technology. **Cost tables** are computer-based databases that include comprehensive information about the firm's cost drivers. Cost drivers include, for example, the size of the product, the materials used in its manufacture, and the number of features. Firms that manufacture

Design analysis is a common form of value engineering in which the design team prepares several possible designs of the product, each having similar features with different levels of performance and different costs.

Cost tables are computer-based databases that include comprehensive information about the firm's cost drivers.

---

[6]   Ibid. Also see Robin Cooper and Regine Slagmulder, "Develop Profitable New Products with Target Costing," *Sloan Management Review*, Summer 1999, pp. 23–33.

Exhibit 5–4	Target Costing in Three Japanese Firms			
Firm/Industry	**Functionality**	**Cost Reduction Approach**	**Strategy**
Olympus/Cameras	Increasing rapidly; is designed in	Target costing using value engineering; the concept of distinctive functionality for the **price point,** plus supportive functionality	Heavy focus on managing functionality, like Nissan, but more so; importance of price points
Nissan/Auto	Rapidly increasing; easy to add or delete functionality	**Value engineering** by product and by each component of each product; then increase price or reduce functionality	Prices are set by desired customers' expectations about functionality; after functionality is set, target cost is used to find savings, especially from suppliers
Komatsu/Construction equipment	Static; must be designed in	**Design analysis** to determine alternative designs. **Functional analysis** to develop cost/functionality trade-offs. **Productivity programs** to reduce the remaining costs	Primary focus is on cost control rather than redesign or functionality analysis

Design Analysis Using Artificial Intelligence: Ford Motor, Procter & Gamble, and General Electric

Artificial intelligence (AI) is the study of human knowledge and thought processes to improve human performance and decision making. It is now being used in software that integrates expert knowledge into computer-based design tools to improve product functionality while reducing manufacturing cost. Large firms such as Ford Motor Co., Procter & Gamble, and General Electric are using it in their design shops.

One such software system is **Innovation Workbench** that alerts the designer to contradictions or conflicts in design objectives. The expertise in the software works with these contradictions to develop novel design approaches for the engineers to consider. For example, in designing a new vacuum cleaner with the contradicting objectives of "works powerfully" and "easy to push," the software developed the idea of pulsation, that is, cycling the suction power on and off at rapid intervals. The machine was therefore easy to push during the "off" part of the cycle, and the suction power could be very powerful during the "on" part of the cycle.

Another AI system, **BizWorks,** predicts pending problems in manufacturing by analyzing data from many sensors in the factory. For example, Myers Industries, Inc., a manufacturer of plastic products, uses BizWorks to predict when the firm's large injection-molding systems are about to turn out defective products or when a customer's order is in danger of being late.

These AI systems are particularly helpful when manufacturing plants are seeking to reduce cycle time and/or move to a mass customization strategy because they help the plants deal with the inherent complexity in the manufacturing process.

Source: Otis Port, "Thinking Machines," *Business Week,* August 7, 2000, pp. 78–86; and "Artificial Imagination," *Business Week,* March 18, 1996.

parts of different size from the same design (pipe fittings, tools, and so on) use cost tables to show the difference in cost for parts of different sizes and different types of materials.

Group technology is a method of identifying similarities in the parts of products a firm manufactures so the same parts can be used in two or more products, thereby reducing costs. Large manufacturers of diverse product lines, such as in the automobile industry, use group technology in this way. A point of concern in the use of group technology is that it reduces manufacturing costs but might increase service and warranty costs if a failed part is used in many different models. The combination of group technology and total quality management can, however, result in lower costs in both manufacturing and service/warranty.

> **Group technology** is a method of identifying similarities in the parts of products a firm manufactures so the same part can be used in two or more products, thereby reducing costs.

Target Costing and Kaizen

The fifth step in target costing is to use Continuous Improvement (kaizen) and operational control to further reduce costs. Kaizen occurs at the manufacturing stage so that the effects of value engineering and improved design are already in place; the

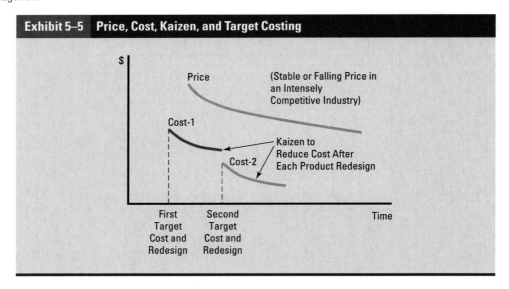

Exhibit 5–5   Price, Cost, Kaizen, and Target Costing

role for cost reduction at this phase is to develop new manufacturing methods (such as flexible manufacturing systems) and to use new management techniques such as operational control (Chapters 15, 16, and 17), total quality management (Chapter 6), and the theory of constraints (next section) to further reduce costs. *Kaizen* means *continual* improvement, that is, the ongoing search for new ways to reduce costs in the manufacturing process of a product with a given design and functionality.

Exhibit 5–5 shows the relationship between target costing and kaizen. Price is assumed to be stable or decreasing over time for firms for which target costing is appropriate because of intense competition on price, product quality and product functionality. These firms respond to the competitive pressure by periodically redesigning their products using target costing to simultaneously reduce the product price and improve their value. Consider the two points in Exhibit 5–5 labeled first and second target cost. The time period between product redesigns is approximately the product's *sales life cycle*. In the time between product redesigns, the firm uses kaizen to reduce product cost in the manufacturing process by streamlining the supply chain and improving both manufacturing methods and productivity programs. Thus, target costing and kaizen are complementary methods used to continually reduce cost and improve value.

Example of the Use of Target Costing in Health Product Manufacturing

Health Products International, Inc. (HPI), is conducting a value engineering project by making a target costing analysis of a major product, a hearing aid. HPI sells a reliable second-generation hearing aid (HPI-2) for $750 (cost of $650) and has obtained 30 percent of this market worldwide at a profit of $100 per aid. However, a competitor recently introduced a new third-generation hearing aid that incorporates a computer chip that improves performance considerably and increases the price to $1,200. Through consumer analysis, HPI has determined that cost-conscious consumers will stay with HPI, which will maintain its market share as long as its price does not exceed $600. HPI must meet the new lower price and maintain its current rate of profit ($100 per unit) by redesigning the hearing aid and/or the manufacturing process.

The target cost for the new aid is $600 − $100 = $500, a reduction in cost of $150 ($650 − $500) from the current model. Because the product has no add-on features, HPI decides to use design analysis with the following alternatives for changes and related savings per unit:

Alternative A. Reduce research and development expenditures ($50), replace the microphone unit with one of nearly equivalent sensitivity ($30), replace toggle power switch with a cheaper and almost as reliable slide switch ($30), replace the current inspection procedure with an integrated quality review process at each assembly station ($40). Total savings: $150.

Alternative B. Replace the amplifier unit with one having slightly less power, not expected to be a noticeable difference for most users ($50), replace the microphone unit with one of nearly equivalent sensitivity ($30), replace toggle power switch with a cheaper and almost as reliable slide switch ($30), replace the current inspection procedure with an integrated quality review process at each assembly station ($40). Total savings: $150.

Alternative C. Increase research and development activity to develop the new third-generation computer chip type of hearing aid (HPI-3, *increase* of $40). Replace the amplifier unit with one of slightly less power, not expected to be a noticeable difference for most users ($50), replace the microphone unit with one of nearly equivalent sensitivity ($30), replace toggle power switch with a cheaper and almost as reliable slide switch ($30), replace the current inspection procedure with an integrated quality review process at each assembly station ($40), renegotiate contract with supplier of plastic casing ($20), replace plastic earpiece material with material of slightly lower quality but well within the user's expectations for 6 to 10 years of use ($20). Net savings: $150.

After a review of its alternatives, HPI chose alternative C, primarily because it included an increase in research and development expenditures that would enable the firm at some future time to compete in the market for the new type of hearing aid. Manufacturing and marketing managers agreed that the design changes proposed in all the options would not significantly alter the market appeal of the current product. Key managers also determined that this alternative was strategically important because the new technology, while only a fraction of the market now, could be dominant in the next 10 to 15 years as prices come down on the new units and user awareness of the benefits of the computer chip become more well known.

THE THEORY OF CONSTRAINTS

Remember that time is money.

BENJAMIN FRANKLIN

Benjamin Franklin must be right. Most strategic initiatives undertaken by firms today focus on improving the speed of their operations throughout the cost life cycle. Why is speed so important? For many companies, it is a competitive edge. Customers expect quick response to inquiries and fast delivery of the product. Shorter sales life cycles in many industries mean that manufacturers are working to reduce product development time. Some of the most successful business models of recent years, such as those of Dell Computer and Amazon.com, are built on speed. Amazon's website states when the product will be shipped; many times this is within 24 hours. In addition, an important new business magazine, *Fast Company*, addresses, in part, the increased interest in speed.

In this part of the chapter, we present one of the key methods used to improve speed, the theory of constraints (TOC), a technique used to improve speed in the manufacturing process. Before looking closely at TOC, we consider the issue of how speed is measured and improved throughout the cost life cycle, as illustrated in Exhibit 5–6. The measures are defined in different ways by different firms, depending on the nature of the firm's operations. For example, manufacturing **cycle time** (or *lead time* or *throughput time*) is commonly defined as follows:

Cycle time = Amount of time between the receipt of a customer order and the shipment of the order

◀LEARNING OBJECTIVE 2

Apply the theory of constraints to facilitate strategic management.

Cycle time is the amount of time between the receipt of a customer order and the shipment of the order.

Exhibit 5–6   Measures of Speed and How to Improve It

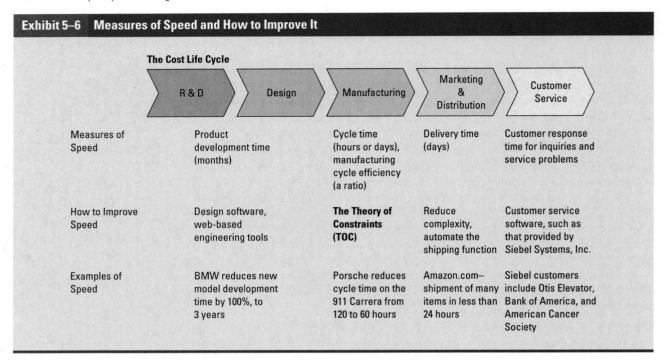

The Cost Life Cycle	R & D	Design	Manufacturing	Marketing & Distribution	Customer Service
Measures of Speed		Product development time (months)	Cycle time (hours or days), manufacturing cycle efficiency (a ratio)	Delivery time (days)	Customer response time for inquiries and service problems
How to Improve Speed		Design software, web-based engineering tools	**The Theory of Constraints (TOC)**	Reduce complexity, automate the shipping function	Customer service software, such as that provided by Siebel Systems, Inc.
Examples of Speed		BMW reduces new model development time by 100%, to 3 years	Porsche reduces cycle time on the 911 Carrera from 120 to 60 hours	Amazon.com— shipment of many items in less than 24 hours	Siebel customers include Otis Elevator, Bank of America, and American Cancer Society

Depending on the firm's operations and objectives, the start of the cycle time can also be defined as the time a production batch is scheduled, the time the raw materials are ordered, or the time that production on the order is started. The finish time of the cycle can also be defined as the time that production is completed or the time the order is ready for shipping. A remarkable success story is Porsche reducing the cycle time for the production of the 911 Carrera from 120 hours to 60 hours.

Another useful measure is **manufacturing cycle efficiency (MCE)**:

> **Manufacturing cycle efficiency (MCE)** is the ratio of processing time to total cycle time.

$$MCE = \frac{\text{Processing time}}{\text{Total cycle time}}$$

MCE separates total cycle time into the time required for each of the various activities: processing (value-adding work on the product), inspection, materials handling, waiting, and so on. Most firms would like to see their MCE close to 1, which reflects less time wasted on moving, waiting, inspecting, and other non-value-adding activities.

The theory of constraints (TOC) was developed by Goldratt and Cox to help managers reduce cycle times and operating costs.[7] Prior to TOC, managers often devoted efforts to improve efficiency and speed *throughout* the manufacturing process instead of focusing attention on just those activities that were constraints (i.e., bottlenecks) in the process. **Constraints** are activities that slow a product's total cycle time. Goldratt and Cox use as an example a troop of boy scouts on a hike; the slowest hiker is the constraint and sets the overall pace for the troop. Manufacturers have learned that increased efficiency and speed with activities that are not constraints could be dysfunctional. Unnecessary efficiency is likely to result in the buildup of work-in-process inventory for activities prior to the constraint (just as the scouts would be

> **Constraints** are those activities that slow the product's cycle time.

[7]   E. Goldratt and J. Cox, *The Goal* (New York: Free Press, 1986); and E. Goldratt, *The Theory of Constraints* (New York: North River Press, 1990). See also Thomas Corbett, *Throughout Accounting* (New York: North River Press, 1998); and "Measuring the Cost of Capacity," *Management Accounting Guideline Number 42* (The Society of Management Accountants of Canada, 1996). An alternative to TOC is demand flow technology; see "American Standard Wises Up," *Business Week*, November 18, 1996, pp. 70–74.

"bunched up" behind the slowest scout) and to divert attention and resources from the actual slow-down cycle time. TOC has turned the attention to improving speed at the constraints, which causes a decrease in the overall cycle time.

Example of the Use of the Theory of Constraints Analysis in Health Product Manufacturing

To illustrate the use of TOC and its five steps, we again consider Healthcare Products International, Inc. (HPI). Suppose that HPI is currently manufacturing both the second generation (HPI-2) and third generation (HPI-3) of hearing aids. The prices for the HPI-2 and HPI-3 are competitive at $600 and $1,200, respectively, and are not expected to change. Because of manufacturing delays and increasing cycle times, HPI has a backlog of orders for both the HPI-2 and the HPI-3. Its monthly number of orders for the HPI-2 is 3,000 units and for the HPI-3 is 1,800 units. New customers are told that they may have to wait three weeks or more for their orders. Management is concerned about the need to improve speed in the manufacturing process and is planning to use TOC.

Steps in the Theory of Constraints Analysis

TOC analysis has five steps:

1. Identify the constraint.
2. Determine the most profitable product mix given the constraint.
3. Maximize the flow through the constraint.
4. Add capacity to the constraint.
5. Redesign the manufacturing process for flexibility and fast cycle time.

The theory of constraints (TOC) is a method for identifying and managing constraints in the manufacturing process so as to speed up the flow of product through the plant. Because of management concern, the company decides to perform TOC analysis.

Step 1: Identify the Constraint

The management accountant works with manufacturing managers and engineers to identify any constraint in the manufacturing process by developing a **flow diagram** of the work done. The flow diagram shows the sequence of processes and the amount of time each requires. The five processes for HPI follow, and their flow diagram is shown in Exhibit 5–7.

> A **flow diagram** is a flowchart of the work done that shows the sequence of processes and the amount of time required for each.

Process 1. Assemble earpiece.

Process 2. Test and program computer chip (product HPI-3 only).

Process 3. Install other electronics.

Process 4. Perform final assembly and test.

Process 5. Pack and ship.

The raw materials cost for the units are $300 for the HPI-2 and $750 for the HPI-3 ($450 for the computer chip and $300 for other electronics).

The constraint is identified by using the flow diagram to analyze the total time required for each process given the current level of demand. Exhibit 5–8 shows a summary of the data for this analysis, including the number of employees available for each process and the total time available per month for all employees (assuming a 40-hour workweek in which 30 hours are available for work and 10 hours are used for breaks, training, etc.). HPI processes are very specialized, and employees are able to work only within their assigned process. Moreover, because of the specialized skills required, HPI has difficulty maintaining adequate staffing in all processes except process 5, pack and ship.

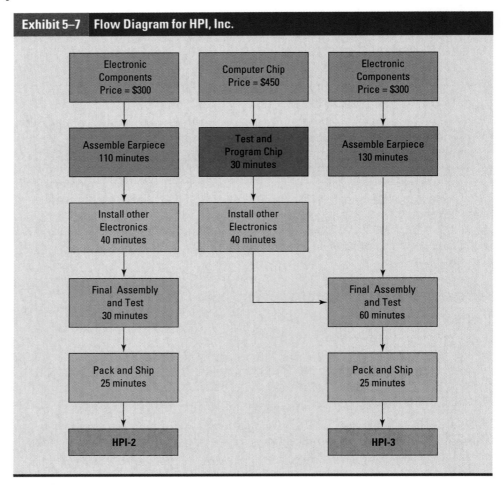

Exhibit 5–7   Flow Diagram for HPI, Inc.

Electronic Components Price = $300 → Assemble Earpiece 110 minutes → Install other Electronics 40 minutes → Final Assembly and Test 30 minutes → Pack and Ship 25 minutes → **HPI-2**

Computer Chip Price = $450 → Test and Program Chip 30 minutes → Install other Electronics 40 minutes → Final Assembly and Test 60 minutes

Electronic Components Price = $300 → Assemble Earpiece 130 minutes → Final Assembly and Test 60 minutes → Pack and Ship 25 minutes → **HPI-3**

Step 1 in Exhibit 5–8 shows the total time required in each process given the current level of demand. Each of the five processes except process 4 has slack time. Therefore, the constraint occurs with process 4, perform final assembly and test. Because of inadequate time (900 hours too few) available in this process, HPI will not be able to meet the total demand for HPI-2 and HPI-3 and will delay some orders or perhaps not fill them at all. HPI must now determine which orders to fill and which not to fill. This takes us to the second step of TOC.

Step 2: Determine the Most Profitable Product Mix Given the Constraint

The most profitable product mix is the combination of products that maximizes total profits for both products. Should we produce all 3,000 units of HPI-2 and whatever we can of HPI-3, or should we produce all 1,800 units of HPI-3 and whatever we can of HPI-2? Or some other mix? The step 2 analysis in Exhibit 5–8 provides the answer.

To determine the most profitable product mix, we first determine the most profitable product, given the constraint. TOC measures product profitability using the **throughput margin,** which is the product price less materials cost (includes the costs of all materials used, purchased components, and materials-handling costs). All other manufacturing costs are excluded in determining profitability because they are assumed to be fixed and will not change regardless of which product mix is chosen.[8] Step 2 in Exhibit 5–8 shows that throughput margins for the HPI-2 and HPI-3 are

Throughput margin is a TOC measure of product profitability; it equals price less materials cost, including all purchased components and materials handling costs.

---

[8]   Note that TOC analysis assumes that factory labor is not a direct and variable cost but is a fixed cost. This assumption applies well to the types of manufacturers for which TOC is most applicable: those with a highly automated production process in which labor is a small, unchanging part of the total cost.

Exhibit 5–8	Summary of Key Data for HPI, Inc., TOC Analysis

Product	Demand	Price	Materials Cost
HPI-2	3,000	$ 600	$ 300
HPI-3	1,800	1,200	750

Minutes Required for Each Product

Process	HPI-2	HPI-3	Number of Employees	Hours Available
1: Assemble earpiece	110	130	80	9,600
2: Test and program computer chip	0	30	16	1,920
3: Install other electronics	40	40	30	3,600
4: Perform final assembly and test	30	60	20	2,400
5: Pack and ship	25	25	18	2,160

Step 1: Identify the Constraint (the process for which total hours required for the given demand exceeds available hours)

	HPI-2	HPI-3	Total Hours	Hours Available	Slack Hours
Process 1: Assemble earpiece (3000 × 110/60)	5,500	3,900	9,400	9,600	200
Process 2: Test and program chip	0	900	900	1,320	420
Process 3: Install other electronics	2,000	1,200	3,200	3,600	400
Process 4: Perform final assembly and test	1,500	1,800	3,300	2,400	(900)
Process 5: Pack and ship	1,250	750	2,000	2,160	160

Step 2: Identify Most Profitable Product Mix

	HPI-2	HPI-3
Price	$600.00	$1,200.00
Materials cost	300.00	750.00
Throughput margin	$300.00	$ 450.00
Constraint time	30	60
Throughput per minute	$ 10.00	$ 7.50

	HPI-2	HPI-3	Total
Demand in hours	3,000	1,800	
Units of product	3,000	900	
Throughput per minute	$ 10.00	$ 7.50	
Total throughput	$30,000	$6,750	$36,750
Unmet demand	—	900	
Hours used	1,500	900	2,400 hrs

$300 and $450, respectively. Although HPI-3 has the higher margin, the profitability analysis is not complete without considering the time required by the constraint, final assembly, and test for each product. Since HPI-3 takes twice as much time in final assembly and test as HPI-2 (60 versus 30 minutes), we can produce twice as many HPI-2 models for each HPI-3 produced. In effect, the relevant measure of profitability is throughput margin *per minute of time in final assembly and test,* that is, a throughput per minute of $10 for HPI-2 and $7.50 for HPI-3. This means that each minute that final assembly and test is used to produce HPI-2 earns $10 while each minute used to produce HPI-3 earns only $7.50. HPI-2 is the most profitable product when final assembly and test is the constraint.

The best product mix is determined in the final section of Exhibit 5–8. HPI produces all demand for HPI-2 since it is the most profitable product. Then HPI determines the remaining capacity in final assembly (2,400 − [3,000 × (30/60)] = 900 hours; each HPI-2 requires 30/60 hours) and use that capacity to produce as many units of HPI-3 as possible (900/[60/60] = 900 units of HPI-3; each unit requires 60/60 hours). The best product mix is therefore 3,000 units of HPI-2 and 900 units of HPI-3 for a total throughput margin of $36,750.

Step 3: Maximize the Flow through the Constraint

In this step, the management accountant looks for ways to speed the flow through the constraint by simplifying the process or improving the product design, among others (see Exhibit 5–9).

The **drum-buffer-rope system** is a system for balancing the flow of production through a constraint, thereby reducing the amount of inventory at the constraint and improving overall productivity.

An important tool for managing product flow in step 3 is the **drum-buffer-rope (DBR) system,** which is a system for balancing the flow of production through a constraint, illustrated in Exhibit 5–10 for Health Products International, Inc. The DBR system works for HPI as follows. In the DBR system, all production flows are synchronized to the drum (the constraint), process 4. The rope is the sequence of processes prior to and including the constraint. The objective is to *balance the flow of production* through the rope by carefully timing and scheduling activity for processes 1 through 3. The buffer is a minimum amount of work-in-process input for process 4 that is maintained to ensure that process 4 is kept busy.

Step 4: Add Capacity to the Constraint

As a longer-term measure to relieve the constraint and improve cycle time, management should consider adding capacity to the constraints by adding new or improved machines and/or additional labor.

Step 5: Redesign the Manufacturing Process for Flexibility and Fast Cycle Time

The most complete strategic response to the constraint is to redesign the manufacturing process, including the introduction of new manufacturing technology, deletion of some hard-to-manufacture products, and redesign of some products for greater ease of manufacturing. Simply removing one or more minor features on a given product might speed up the production process significantly. The use of value engineering as

---

Exhibit 5–9   Maximize Flow through the Constraint

To maximize the flow through a constraint:

1. Simplify the operation:
   - Simplify the product design.
   - Simplify the manufacturing process.
2. Look for quality defects in raw materials that might be slowing things down.
3. Reduce setup time.
4. Reduce other delays due to unscheduled and non-value-added activities, such as inspections or machine breakdowns.
5. Simplify the constraint by removing all activities from it that do not reduce the function of the operation.

Focus on Cycle Time at the IRS and Boozer Lumber Co.

To improve its operations and reduce costs, the Internal Revenue Service (IRS) applied activity analysis and cycle time measures to its various operations. For example, it now calculates and monitors cycle time and cycle efficiency for many of its processing activities.

Boozer Lumber Co. is a small lumber company in Columbia, South Carolina, which provides roof trusses and other products and services to the construction industry. Recently it adapted the production of trusses to accommodate the increased demand for more complex roof structures. The increased complexity of the product created constraints in the manufacturing process that were not immediately apparent to the company's managers. The machine operators were

unfamiliar with the new designs, which were difficult to manufacture, resulting in a dramatic increase in machine setup time. The solution came when Bob Jones, owner of the company, read Goldratt and Cox's novel, *The Goal.* A quick investigation identified the setup for roof trusses as being a constraint in the business, and the company employed experts to speed up the process using an automated system. Within two years, profits had improved enough that the company's 20 managers received a total of $800,000 in bonuses.

Sources: John B. MacArthur, "Cost Management at the IRS," *Management Accounting,* November 1996, pp. 42–46; and "Theory in Novel Spurs Turnaround for Lumber Firm," *Greensboro News and Observer,* August 24, 1999.

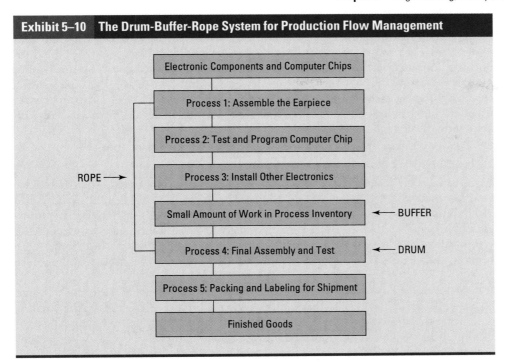

| **Exhibit 5–10** | **The Drum-Buffer-Rope System for Production Flow Management** |

Exhibit 5–11   **Summary of the Five Steps of TOC Analysis**

Step 1: Identify the Constraint

Use a flow diagram. The constraint is a resource that limits production to less than market demand.

Step 2: Determine the Most Profitable Profit Mix Given Constraint

Make product mix decision: Based on capacity available at the constraint, find the most profitable product mix.

Step 3: Maximize the Flow through the Constraint

1. Maximize flow through the constraint (see Exhibit 5–9)
   - Reduce setups.
   - Reduce setup time.
   - Focus on throughput rather than efficiency.
2. Use the drum-buffer-rope system: Maintain a small amount of work in process (buffer) and insert materials only when needed (drum) by the constraint, given lead times (rope).
3. Coordinate resources to keep the constraint busy without building up work in process.

Step 4: Add Capacity on the Constraint

Invest in additional capacity if it will increase throughput more than the cost of the investment.

Do not invest to increase capacity until steps 2 and 3 are complete. Instead, maximize the productivity of the process through the constraint with existing capacity.

Step 5: Redesign the Manufacturing Process for Flexibility and Fast Cycle Time

Consider a redesign of the product or production process to achieve faster throughput.

---

described earlier might help at this point. The five steps of TOC analysis are summarized in Exhibit 5–11.

Theory of Constraints Reports

When a firm focuses on improving cycle time, eliminating constraints, and improving speed of delivery, the performance evaluation measures also focus on these critical success factors. A common approach is to report throughput margin as well as selected operating data in a *theory of constraints report*. An example of this report used by a manufacturer of automotive glass is shown in Exhibit 5–12. Note in the exhibit that window styles H and B are the most profitable because they have far higher throughput margin based on the binding constraint, hours of furnace time. The throughput margin per hour is $3,667 and $2,370 for styles H and B, respectively; in contrast, the throughput margin per hour for styles C and A is less than $1,000. TOC reports are useful for identifying the most profitable product and for monitoring success in achieving the critical success factors.

ABC and the Theory of Constraints

Firms using such cost management methods as target costing and the theory of constraints commonly employ activity-based costing (ABC). ABC is used to assess the profitability of products, just as TOC was used in the previous illustration. The difference is that TOC takes a short-term approach to profitability analysis while ABC costing develops a long-term analysis. The TOC analysis has a short-term focus because of its emphasis only on materials-related costs, but ABC includes all product costs.

On the other hand, unlike TOC, ABC does not explicitly include the resource constraints and capacities of production activities. Thus, ABC cannot be used to determine the short-term best product mix, as for the auto window manufacturer in Exhibit 5–12. ABC and TOC are thus *complementary* methods; ABC provides a comprehensive analysis of cost drivers and accurate unit costs as a basis for strategic decisions about long-term pricing and product mix. In contrast, TOC provides a useful method for improving the short-term profitability of the manufacturing plant through short-term product mix adjustments and through attention to production constraints. The differences between ABC and TOC are outlined in Exhibit 5–13.[9]

Exhibit 5–12	The TOC Report for an Auto Glass Manufacturer			
	Theory of Constraints Report: Throughput Margin for Four Auto Window Styles			
			March 19X2	
	Style C	Style A	Style H	Style B
Window size	0.77	.073	7.05	4.95
Sales volume	High	Moderate	High	Moderate
Units in unfilled orders	1,113	234	882	23
Average lead time (days)	16	23	8	11
Market price	$2.82	$6.68	$38.12	$24.46
Direct production costs				
Materials	0.68	0.64	5.75	4.02
Scrap allowance	0.06	0.05	0.42	0.34
Material handling	0.12	0.12	1.88	1.61
Subtotal	.86	.81	8.05	5.97
Throughput margin	$1.96	$5.87	$30.07	$18.49
Furnace hours per unit	.0062	.0061	.0082	.0078
Throughput margin per hour	$316	$962	$3,667	$2,370

Source: R. J. Campbell, "Pricing Strategy in the Automotive Glass Industry," *Management Accounting*, July 1989, pp. 26–34.

---

[9] For a comparison of TOC and ABC, see Jay S. Holmen, "ABC vs. TOC: It's a Matter of Time," *Management Accounting*, January 1995, pp. 37–40; Robert Kee, "Integrating Activity-Based Costing with the Theory of Constraints to Enhance Production-Related Decision Making," *Accounting Horizons*, December 1995, pp. 48–61; and Robin Cooper and Regine Stagmulder, "Integrating Activity-Based Costing and the Theory of Constraints," *Management Accounting*, February 1999, p. 2.

Exhibit 5–13 Comparison of the TOC and ABC Costing Methods

	TOC	ABC
Main objective	**Short-term focus;** throughput margin analysis based on materials and materials-related costs	**Long-term focus;** analysis of all product costs, including materials, labor, and overhead
Resource constraints and capacities	Included explicitly; a principal focus of TOC	Not included explicitly
Cost drivers	No direct utilization of cost drivers	Develop an understanding of cost drivers at the unit, batch, product, and facility levels
Major use	Optimization of production flow and short-term product mix	Strategic pricing and profit planning

Exhibit 5–14 Life-Cycle Costing in the Cost Life Cycle

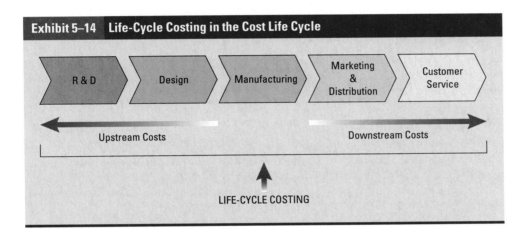

LIFE-CYCLE COSTING

Typically, product or service costs are measured and reported for relatively short periods, such as a month or a year. Life-cycle costing provides a long-term perspective because it considers the entire cost life cycle of the product or service (see Exhibit 5–14). It therefore provides a more complete perspective of product costs and product or service profitability. For example, a product that is designed quickly and carelessly, with little investment in design costs, could have significantly higher marketing and service costs later in the life cycle. Managers are interested in the total cost, over the entire life cycle, not manufacturing costs only. Total cost over the product's life cycle often is broken down into three components: upstream costs, manufacturing costs, and downstream costs:

Upstream Costs

Research and development

Design: Prototyping, testing, and engineering

Manufacturing Costs

Purchasing

Direct manufacturing costs

Indirect manufacturing costs

Downstream Costs

Marketing and distribution: packaging, shipping, samples, promotion, and advertising

Service and warranty: recalls, service, product liability, customer support

◀**LEARNING OBJECTIVE 3**

Describe how life-cycle costing facilitates strategic management.

While cost management methods have tended to focus only on manufacturing costs, upstream and downstream costs can account for a significant portion of total life-cycle costs, especially in certain industries:

Industries with High Upstream and Downstream Costs

Pharmaceuticals

Auto manufacturing

Industries with High Upstream Costs

Computer software

Specialized industrial and medical equipment

Industries with High Downstream Costs

Retail

Perfumes, cosmetics, and toiletries

Upstream and downstream costs are managed in a number of ways including improved relationships with suppliers and distributors; the most crucial way is the design of the product and the manufacturing process. Value-chain analysis, as explained in Chapter 2, can also provide a useful way to identify upstream and downstream linkages for a manufacturing or service firm (see Exhibit 5–15).

The Importance of Design

As managers consider upstream and downstream costs, decision making at the design stage is critical. Although the costs incurred at the design stage could account for only a very small percentage of the total costs over the entire product life cycle, design stage decisions commit a firm to a given production, marketing, and service plan. Therefore, they lock in most of the remaining life-cycle costs.

The critical success factors at the design stage include the following:

Reduced time to market. In a competitive environment where the speed of product development and the speed of delivery are critical, efforts to reduce time to market have the first priority.

Reduced expected service costs. By careful, simple design and the use of modular, interchangeable components, the expected service costs can be greatly reduced.

Improved ease of manufacture. To reduce production costs and speed production, the design must be easy to manufacture.

Process planning and design. The plan for the manufacturing process should be flexible, allowing for fast setups and product changeovers, using agile manufactur-

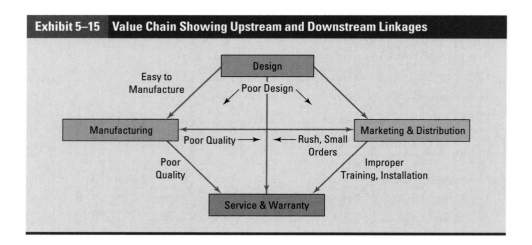

Exhibit 5–15   Value Chain Showing Upstream and Downstream Linkages

ing concepts, computer-integrated manufacturing, computer-assisted design, and concurrent engineering.

The four common design methods are basic engineering, prototyping, templating, and concurrent engineering. See Exhibit 5–16. **Basic engineering** is the method by which product designers work independently from marketing and manufacturing to develop a design from specific plans and specifications. An advantage of this approach is that it can be quick and less costly than the others. The disadvantage is that because basic engineering is independent from marketing and production, the product might be inappropriate for the market (hard to sell and/or service) or might be difficult and costly to manufacture. This method has high downstream costs as a result.

Prototyping is a method by which functional models of the product are developed and tested by engineers and trial customers. A good example of prototyping is the beta testing of software products by customers of the software vendor to provide a trial run of a new software system. The direct cost of prototyping can be high when significant materials and labor are needed to prepare the prototype products. On the other hand, it has great potential for reducing downstream costs since the feedback from the engineers and trial-run customers is used to improve the product and/or the production process.

Templating is a method in which an existing product is scaled up or down to fit the specifications of the desired new product. An example is the Big Mac, Biggie, Double, or Whopper hamburger sandwiches that are derived from simple sandwiches.

Basic engineering is the method in which product designers work independently from marketing and manufacturing to develop a design from specific plans and specifications.

Prototyping is a method in which functional models of the product are developed and tested by engineers and trial customers.

Templating is a method in which an existing product is scaled up or down to fit the specifications of the desired new product.

Exhibit 5–16	Characteristics of the Four Design Methods			
Design Method	**Design Speed**	**Design Cost**		**Downstream Costs**
Basic engineering	Fast	Depends on desired complexity and functionality; should be relatively low		Can be very high because marketing and production are not integral to the design process
Prototyping	Slow	Significant; materials, labor, and time		Potentially can reflect a significant reduction
Templating	Fast	Modest		Unknown; can have costly unexpected results if the scaling does not work in the market or in production
Concurrent engineering	Continuous	Significant; design is an integral, ongoing process		Can result in greatest reduction

Life-Cycle Cost Issues at Porsche, Ford, and General Motors

UPSTREAM COSTS: PORSCHE'S ENGINEERING BECOMES A PROFITABLE BUSINESS

The German automaker Porsche contracts out the services of its elite engineering talent. Porsche has more engineers—2,300—than it needs to develop its own new models. The quality of its engineers attracts other automakers—Opel, DaimlerChrysler, and even the motorcycle company Harley-Davidson—to contract for the engineers' services. The key life-cycle benefits to Porsche are that the extra income from outsourcing the engineers helps make the firm profitable, and, most important, that the firm can afford to retain some of the best engineering talent in the world.

DOWNSTREAM COSTS: GM AND FORD ARE BUYING FRANCHISED DEALERSHIPS AND GOING ONLINE

Noticing that the price of automobiles to consumers is 25 percent or more higher than the price to the dealers, Ford and GM are making efforts to reduce costs to consumers and to streamline the distribution of cars. One initiative in this direction is their effort to purchase franchised dealerships. GM has set a goal of acquiring up to 10 percent of them. A second initiative is to develop Internet sites for direct sales to consumers. An important aspect of the latter initiative is the ability to speed the delivery of cars directly to the consumer. GM has set a goal of reducing the order-to-delivery time from up to eight weeks (in 1999) to 4 to 11 days in 2003.

Sources: "That Van You're Driving May Be Part Porsche," *Business Week,* December 27, 1999, p. 72; "Meet Your Local GM Dealer: GM," *Business Week,* October 11, 1999, p. 48; "GM Retools to Sell Custom Cars Online," *Wall Street Journal,* February 2, 2000, p. B23; "Car Power: Special Report," *Business Week,* October 23, 2000, pp. 72–82.

Concurrent engineering,
or *simultaneous engineering,* is an important new
method that integrates
product design with manu-
facturing and marketing
throughout the product's
life cycle.

Templating is a fast and low-cost design method; the impact on downstream costs depends on how well the scaling works and whether the production costs and market reaction are as expected.

Concurrent engineering, or *simultaneous engineering,* is an important new development in the design of products that is replacing the basic engineering approach in which product designers work in isolation on specialized components of the overall design project. In contrast, concurrent engineering relies on an integrated approach, in which the engineering/design process takes place *throughout the cost life cycle* using cross-functional teams. Information is solicited from and used at each phase of the value chain to improve the product design. For example, customer feedback in the service phase is used directly in the product design. Software developers and other manufacturers are increasingly using product design in a very flexible manner; they incorporate improvements in the product continuously. Some experts argue that this approach has saved firms as much as 20 percent of total product cost.

Examples of the Use of Life-Cycle Costing in a Software Firm

As an example of applying life-cycle costing, consider software developer Analytical Decisions, Inc. (ADI), that provides specialized software for banks and other financial institutions to use to analyze loan loss reserves and to plan loan portfolios. ADI has two products, ADI–1 for large banks and ADI–2 for small banks and savings and loans. Each product is updated annually, with an occasional special update during the year. Each update improves the product's functionality in some significant way.

Initially, ADI analyzed profitability by using the accounting software widely used in the industry, which provided the report shown in Exhibit 5–17. This analysis shows both products to be quite profitable, even in the presence of heavy R&D and selling costs; ADI–1 shows a somewhat higher gross margin (72%; $3,260,000/$4,500,000) than ADI–2 (60%; $1,495,000/$2,500,000). However, the analysis is incomplete since most of ADI's costs (R&D and selling) are not included in the product comparison. Because ADI's systems designers and programmers work in project teams, determining how the R&D costs should be assigned to the two products is relatively simple. Similarly, because ADI's sales and customer-service efforts are logged by product, these costs also can be traced, as shown in Exhibit 5–18.

The life-cycle cost analysis clearly identifies ADI–2 as the more profitable of the two products because ADI–1 incurs the bulk of the R&D and selling costs. Moreover, the revised analysis provides a basis for ADI management to seek possible cost reductions. For example, the ratio of research and development, selling and service costs to sales dollars is much higher for ADI–1 (67%; $3,000,000/$4,500,000) than for ADI–2 (40%; $1,000,000/$2,500,000). Management should investigate whether these higher costs are due to the nature of the different customers or quality problems in ADI–1. Management can use this breakdown of costs throughout the product's life cycle to identify opportunities for cost savings.

Exhibit 5–17	Product-Line Income Statement for Analytical Decisions, Inc.		
	ADI–1	**ADI–2**	**Total**
Sales	$4,500,000	$2,500,000	$7,000,000
Cost of sales	1,240,000	1,005,000	2,245,000
Gross margin	$3,260,000	$1,495,000	$4,755,000
Research and development			2,150,000
Selling and service			1,850,000
Income before tax			$ 755,000

Exhibit 5–18	Life-Cycle Costing for Analytical Decisions, Inc.		
	ADI–1	**ADI–2**	**Total**
Sales	$4,500,000	$2,500,000	$7,000,000
Cost of sales	1,240,000	1,005,000	2,245,000
Gross margin	$3,260,000	$1,495,000	$4,755,000
Less:			
Research and development	1,550,000	600,000	2,150,000
Selling and service	1,450,000	400,000	1,850,000
Net income before tax	$ 260,000	$ 495,000	$ 755,000

STRATEGIC PRICING FOR PHASES OF THE SALES LIFE CYCLE

Strategic pricing depends on the position of the product or service in the sales life cycle. As the sales life cycle becomes shorter (only months in some industries such as consumer electronics), the analysis of the sales life cycle becomes increasingly important.[10] In contrast to the cost life cycle just described, the sales life cycle refers to the phase of the product's or service's sales in the market, from introduction of the product or service to decline and withdrawal from the market. (Exhibit 5–2 illustrates the phases of the sales life cycle.)

◀**LEARNING OBJECTIVE 4**

Outline the objectives and techniques of strategic pricing.

Phase 1: Introduction. The first phase involves little competition, and sales rise slowly as customers become aware of the new product or service. Costs are relatively high because of high R&D expenditures and capital costs for setting up production facilities and marketing efforts. Prices are relatively high because of product differentiation and the high costs at this phase. Product variety is limited.

Phase 2: Growth. Sales begin to increase rapidly as does product variety. The product continues to enjoy the benefits of differentiation. Competition increases, and prices begin to soften.

Phase 3: Maturity. Sales continue to increase but at a decreasing rate. The number of competitors and of product variety decline. Prices soften further, and differentiation is no longer important. Competition is based on cost given competitive quality and functionality.

Phase 4: Decline. Sales and prices decline, as do the number of competitors. Control of costs and an effective distribution network are key to continued survival.

In the first phase, the focus of management is on design, differentiation, and marketing. The focus shifts to new product development and pricing strategy as competition develops in the second phase. In the third and fourth phases, management's attention turns to cost control, quality, and service as the market continues to become more competitive. Thus, the firm's strategy for the product or service changes over the sales life cycle from differentiation in the early phases to cost leadership in the final phases.

Similarly, the strategic pricing approach changes over the product or service life cycle. In the first phase, pricing is set relatively high to recover development costs and to take advantage of product differentiation and the new demand for the product. In the second phase, pricing is likely to stay relatively high as the firm attempts to build

---

[10] Manash R. Ray, "Cost Management for Product Development," *Journal of Cost Management,* Spring 1995, pp. 52–64; "Product Life Cycle Management," *Management Accounting Guideline Number 29* (The Society of Management Accountants of Canada, 1994); and "Product Value Analysis: Strategic Analysis over the Entire Product Life Cycle," *Journal of Cost Management,* May/June 1999, pp. 22–29.

Strategic Pricing and New Product Development Using the Sales Life Cycle: Palm, Elcho, and Gateway

STRATEGIC PRICING AT PALM, INC.

Palm, Inc., provides innovative handheld computing devices used in organization, e-mail, sales data entry, wireless Internet access, and other applications. Palm introduces a number of new products each year, and each new model offers greater functionality than the ones before it. As the new handheld models are introduced at competitive prices, the prices on older models are reduced, and Palm has profitable markets in each of the different life-cycle phases for these products.

NEW PRODUCT DEVELOPMENT AT ELCHO PAINT COMPANY

Elcho Paint Co., which specializes in plastic coatings for automotive and other applications, is a $90 million business that relies heavily on new product development. Approximately one-third of Elcho's 540 employees work in research and technical service. Elcho uses sales life-cycle analysis to plan new product development by grouping its products into product families that represent different generations of a particular application. This helps Elcho to ensure that it continues to offer its customers up-to-date products in each product family. This

approach also assists in product costing by facilitating the tracing of research and development costs (using ABC costing) to the product families and to the individual products.

NEW PRODUCT DEVELOPMENT AT GATEWAY, INC.

Gateway, Inc., manufacturer of computer products, is aware of analysts' forecasts that computer sales and prices are expected to slow in the coming five years because of market saturation. Like other manufacturers, Gateway has begun to seek new sources of revenue by offering financing programs, developing software, providing training classes, and offering Internet and other computer services. Training courses, in particular, have been very profitable for Gateway, realizing 90 percent profit margins.

Sources: Mehmet C. Kocakulah, Dorn Fowler, and Brian L. McGuire, "Implementing an ABC System to Stay Competitive: A Case Study," *Journal of Cost Management,* March/April 2000, pp. 15–19; "Pocketful of Savings," *Business Week,* April 17, 2000, p. 10; and "How PC Makers Are Reprogramming Themselves," *Business Week,* October 30, 2000, p. 64.

Use of Target Costing, Life-Cycle Costing, and Strategic Pricing in New Zealand, the United Kingdom, and the United States

A recent survey of management accountants at the largest firms in New Zealand, the United Kingdom, and the United States revealed a good deal of consistency in the use and perceived usefulness of these three key life-cycle methods among the countries. The only difference was in the response to the perceived usefulness of target costing; U.S. respondents viewed this method as somewhat more valuable than did respondents from the other two countries. Because these are new techniques, the respondents indicated as expected that each method is more useful than actually used. There is also an apparent greater appreciation for strategic pricing relative to the two other methods. Perhaps this simply reflects the fact that the term *strategic pricing* was defined somewhat broadly in the study as "the use of cost data based on strategic and marketing information to develop and identify superior strategies that will sustain a competitive advantage." The following table reports the findings of respondents of large firms (124 from New Zealand, 63 from the United Kingdom, and 127 from the United States).

Cost Management Method	Survey Question	New Zealand	United Kingdom	United States
Target costing	Is method used?*	3.12	3.16	2.90
	Is method helpful?†	3.83	3.40	**4.35**
Life-cycle costing	Is method used?	2.60	2.43	2.60
	Is method helpful?	3.38	3.58	3.76
Strategic pricing	Is method used?	4.63	4.73	4.36
	Is method helpful?	5.32	5.38	5.62

*Survey responses were scored as follows: 1 means "used not at all"; 7 means "used to a great extent"; these scores are the average responses for the number of respondents in each country.

†Survey responses were scored as follows: 1 means "not at all helpful"; 7 means "helpful to a great extent."

Source: C. Guilding, K. S. Cravens, and M. Tayles, "An International Comparison of Strategic Management Accounting Practices," *Management Accounting Research,* 11, 2000, pp. 113–35.

Life-Cycle Costing vs. Strategic Pricing at Olympus Camera, Nissan, and Corning

Some firms, such as Olympus Camera, use life-cycle costing to plan expected cost reductions. That is, the product might not be profitable initially, but with an expectation that upstream and downstream costs as well as manufacturing costs will be reduced later, Olympus expects the product to become profitable eventually. For example, the cost reductions in manufacturing can come about as a result of

kaizen costing. Other firms, such as Nissan and Corning, use strategic pricing to plan prices and costs so that the product is profitable over the entire sales life cycle.

As the sales life cycle of products becomes shorter, as it has in many industries, the use of strategic pricing becomes more important and useful.

Exhibit 5–19	**Critical Success Factors, Strategic Pricing, and Research and Development at the Four Stages of the Sales Life Cycle for a Manufacturer of Computer Processors**			
Computer Processor	**Sales Life-Cycle Phase**	**Critical Success Factors**	**Strategic Pricing**	**Research and Development**
Z300	Introduction	Differentiation, innovation, performance	Price is set relatively high because of demand and differentiation	Expenditures are very high to develop differentiation, innovation, and performance
Y300	Growth	Development of financial resources and manufacturing capacity to sustain growth; development of distribution channels and marketing	As above	Expenditures are high to maintain differentiation, innovation, and performance
X300	Maturity	Effective cost control, quality, service; development of new product features	Target costing is used; price is set by a competitive market	Value engineering is used to determine value/cost relationships through target costing
W300	Decline	Control of costs and effective distribution; reduction of capacity; timing of divest/spin-off	Low price is set	None

profitability in the growing market. In the latter phases, pricing becomes more competitive, and target costing and life-cycle costing methods are used as the firm becomes more a price taker than a price setter and makes efforts to reduce upstream (for product enhancements) and downstream costs.

Example of the Use of the Sales Life Cycle in Computer Manufacturing

Exhibit 5–19 summarizes the relationship between life-cycle phases, critical success factors, and desired pricing for a manufacturer of computer processors. The firm makes four processors: the Z300, Y300, X300, and W300. The Z300 is a very fast processor; the Y300 and X300 are somewhat slower, and the W300 is the slowest.

SUMMARY

The strategic cost management concepts introduced in the preceding chapters are extended here. First, we discuss four cost management methods used to analyze the product or service's life cycle: target costing, the theory of constraints, life-cycle costing, and strategic pricing. Target costing is a tool for analyzing the cost structure to help management identify the proper design features and manufacturing methods to allow the firm to meet a competitive price. The five steps in target costing are (1) determine the market price, (2) determine the desired profit, (3) calculate the target cost (market price less desired profit), (4) use value engineering to identify ways to reduce product cost, and (5) use kaizen costing and operational control to further reduce costs.

The theory of constraints (TOC) is a tool that assists managers in identifying bottlenecks (constraints) and scheduling production to maximize throughput and profits. TOC analysis has five steps: (1) identify the constraint, (2) determine the most efficient product mix given the constraint, (3) maximize the flow through the constraint, (4) add capacity to the constraint, and (5) redesign the manufacturing process for flexibility and fast throughput.

Life-cycle costing assists managers in minimizing total cost over the product's or service's entire life cycle. Life-cycle costing brings a focus to the upstream activities (research and development, engineering) and downstream activities (marketing, distribution, service), as well as the manufacturing and operating costs that cost systems focus on. Especially important is a careful consideration of the effects of design choices on downstream costs. The four common design methods: (1) basic engineering in which engineering is done separately from marketing and production, (2) prototyping in which a working model of the product is developed for testing, (3) templating in which a new product is developed from the design of a similar existing product, and (4) concurrent engineering, that integrates marketing, manufacturing, and design to continually improve a product's design.

Strategic pricing helps management determine the price of the product or service as it moves through the different phases of its sales life cycle.

APPENDIX A

Using the Flow Diagram to Identify Constraints

This chapter has illustrated the use of the flow diagram to identify the constraint when there are two or more products being produced through a common set of processes, with no specific completion time. The flow diagram can also be used when there is a single product or project and a specific completion time. In the latter case, which is illustrated in this appendix, the flow diagram is used to identify the processes that must be finished on time for the product or project to be completed on time.

To illustrate, suppose that a small pharmaceutical firm, Skincare Products, Inc. (SPI), manufactures an insect repellent with sun screen. To produce a batch of product, the firm mixes the active and inert ingredients in a large vat. Because of Food and Drug Administration requirements, SPI provides three inspections: (1) the raw materials it receives, (2) the mix of raw materials during the mixing process, and (3) the final product. The first and second inspections check the materials for correct chemical content and potency; the third inspection focuses on correct weight or item count. The manufacturing process has six processes, which are illustrated in Exhibit 5–20:

Process 1: Receive and inspect raw materials

Process 2: Mix raw materials

Process 3: Perform second inspection

Process 4: Fill and package

Process 5: Perform third inspection

Process 6: Attach labels

Exhibit 5–20 is a flow diagram of the work done that shows the sequence of processes and the amount of time required for each. The flow diagram is used to identify the constraints. Computer techniques do this for large networks, but the constraints for a smaller one such as Exhibit 5–20 can be identified by visual inspection.

Exhibit 5–20   Flow Diagram for Skincare Products, Inc.

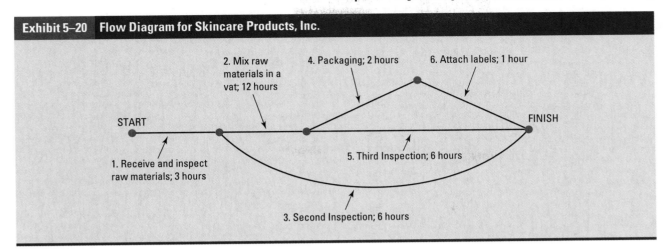

As defined earlier, a *constraint* is any process that delays the entire manufacturing process. The amount of the delay is often called *slack time*. Processes that can be delayed without delaying the finish time for the entire process are called *nonconstraints* or simply *slack* processes since the processes have some slack time in which to be completed. The constraints for SPI are as follows:

Process 1: Receive and inspect raw materials; required time, 3 hours

Process 2: Mix raw materials in vat; required time, 12 hours

Process 5: Perform third inspection; required time, 6 hours

The total time for the entire manufacturing process cannot be less than the total time of these three processes added together (3 + 12 + 6 = 21 hours) since these processes must follow in sequence and cannot overlap. The remaining processes—3, 4, and 6— are not constraints and can be delayed one or more hours without delaying the entire production process. The amount of the delay can be determined as follows. Process 3 requires 6 hours and must be finished while processes 2 and 5 are being completed, but because processes 2 and 5 require 18 hours (12 + 6) and process 3 requires only 6 hours, process 3 has 12 hours (18 – 6) of slack to be finished. Similarly, since processes 4 and 6 together require only 3 hours (2 hours plus 1 hour, respectively) and must be completed during process 5 (which requires 6 hours), in effect 3 hours of slack exist for processes 4 and 6 combined. Often the constraint processes (1, 2, and 5 in this case) are called critical processes since they cannot be delayed without delaying the entire batch of product. Also, the sequence of critical processes is often called the critical path.

KEY TERMS

COMMENTS ON COST MANAGEMENT IN ACTION

Why Go Abroad (to Latin America)? Compaq, Ericsson, Cisco, Ford, and Volkswagen

In competitive industries such as computers, consumer electronics, and automobiles, manufacturers continuously look for ways to reduce cost and increase value throughout the value chain. These industries have chosen to locate extensive manufacturing operations and/or partners in Latin America to reduce cost and to benefit from innovative manufacturing methods and facilities. Wage costs are lower and, using target costing and value engineering, manufacturing processes are built around modular manufacturing methods that reduce the number of parts in the product, speeding the manufacturing process and reducing costs.

CONSUMER ELECTRONICS AND COMPUTER PRODUCTS

Why is outsourcing manufacturing to plants in Mexico an advantage to Cisco, Ericsson, and Compaq? The contract manufacturers' manufacturing experience and technology give them a cost advantage. Flextronics and the other contract manufacturers also can focus on the manufacturing process rather than the entire product value chain. Moreover, they gain economies of scale by manufacturing similar products for different clients. The use of contract manufacturing is an important part of the strategy for Compaq and the others to achieve target costs while maintaining product leadership in design and customer service.

GLOBAL AUTOMAKERS

New manufacturing plants in Mexico and Brazil provide a number of global automakers innovative manufacturing processes as well as access to reduced costs for labor and other operations. The new plants utilize modular design/assembly approaches that significantly reduce the number of parts in the vehicle by combining parts into subassemblies provided by their suppliers. The plant becomes an automated assembler of these subassemblies, saving time and cost.

An additional benefit of the Latin American location for both electronics firms and automakers is that it substantially reduces transportation time and costs for shipments to major markets in North America relative to manufacturing plants located in Asia or other parts of the world.

Sources: Jonathan Friedland and Gary McWilliams, "How a Need for Speed Turned Guadalajara into a High-Tech Hub," *The Wall Street Journal*, March 2, 2000, p. 1; and "Car Power: Special Report," *Business Week*, October 23, 2000, pp. 72–82.

SELF-STUDY PROBLEM

(For the solution, please turn to the end of the chapter.)

Best Brand Lighting, Inc.

Best Brand Lighting, Inc. (BBL) manufactures lighting fixtures. The two major markets for BBL products are major retailers, including Home Depot, Wal-Mart, and Kmart, and specialty lighting stores. The former sell primarily to homeowners, and the latter primarily to electrical contractors.

Although its standard sizes and models typically are sold to the large retailers, BBL sells its products with more specialized features and sizes only to the specialty stores. Thus, the design and manufacturing costs of the products going to the specialty stores are slightly higher. The products in both markets have similar sales life cycles of about two years.

Because of the difference in consumers, BBL has a larger marketing cost for the products sold to the large retailers—advertising in major media to attract homeowners. In contrast, the marketing for the specialty shops consists mainly of catalogs and advertisements in trade publications resulting in a lower overall marketing cost. The sales policies also differ somewhat for the two markets. Sales to specialty stores are priced higher but include significant discounts and attractive return policies. In contrast, sales to the major retailers have restrictive return policies and offer little, if any, discount.

BBL management is interested in an in-depth analysis of the profitability of its two markets. As a first step, it has asked for the average costs and other data for all BBL products:

	Major Retailers	Specialty Stores
Design costs	$ 0.80	$ 1.10
Manufacturing costs	5.20	5.90
Marketing costs	0.95	0.10
Returns	0.05	0.95
Discounts	0.10	0.95
Average price	10.55	12.50
Total market ($000) in BBL's sales region	188,000	32,000
Current unit sales	56,000	14,000

Required   Using the methods discussed in this chapter, analyze BBL's two market segments. What questions would you want to ask management and which fact-finding studies would be appropriate to support this analysis?

QUESTIONS

5–1   Explain the two methods for reducing total product costs to achieve a desired target cost. Which is more common in the consumer electronics industries? In the specialized equipment manufacturing industries?

5–2   What does the term *sales life cycle* mean? What are the phases of the sales life cycle? How does it differ from the cost life cycle?

5–3   Do pricing strategies change over the different phases of the sales life cycle? Explain how.

5–4   Do cost management practices change over the product's sales life cycle? Explain how.

5–5   What is target costing? What types of firms use it?

5–6   What is life-cycle costing? Why is it used?

5–7   Name the five steps of the theory of constraints and explain the purpose of each. Which is the most important step and why?

5–8   What does the term *constraint* mean in the theory of constraint analysis?

5–9   What is the role of the flow diagram in the theory of constraints analysis?

5–10 What are the different methods of product engineering used in product design and life-cycle costing?

5–11 What does the concept of *value engineering* mean? How is it used in target costing?

5–12 What is the main difference between activity-based costing and the theory of constraints? When is it appropriate to use each one?

5–13 For what types of firms is the theory of constraints analysis most appropriate and why?

5–14 For what types of firms is target costing most appropriate and why?

5–15 For what types of firms is life-cycle costing most appropriate and why?

5–16 Explain the difference in intended application between strategic pricing and life-cycle costing.

EXERCISES

5–17 TARGET COSTING MaxiDrive manufactures a wide variety of parts for recreational boating, including a gear and driveshaft part for high-powered outboard boat engines. Original equipment manufacturers such as Mercury and Honda purchase the components for use in large, powerful outboards. The part sells for $610, and sales volume averages 25,000 units per year. Recently, MaxiDrive's major competitor reduced the price of its equivalent unit to $550. The market is very competitive, and MaxiDrive realizes it must meet the new price or lose significant market share. The controller has assembled these cost and usage data for the most recent year for MaxiDrive's production of 25,000 units:

	Standard Cost	Actual Quantity	Actual Cost
Materials	$6,500,000		$7,000,000
Direct labor	2,500,000		2,625,000
Indirect labor	2,500,000		2,400,000
Inspection (hours and cost)	—	1,000	350,000
Materials handling (number of purchases and cost)	—	3,450	485,000
Machine setups (number and cost)	—	1,500	725,000
Returns and rework (number of times and cost)	—	500	130,000
			$13,365,000

Required
1. Calculate the target cost for maintaining current market share and profitability.
2. Can the target cost be achieved? How?

Strategy

5–18 TARGET COSTING Optical Specialists Inc. (OSI) manufactures specialized equipment for polishing optical lenses. There are two models—one (L–25) principally used for fine eyewear and the other (BL–10) for lenses used in binoculars, cameras, and similar equipment.

The manufacturing cost of each unit is calculated using activity-based costing, for these manufacturing cost pools:

Cost Pools	Allocation Base	Costing Rate
Materials handling	Number of parts	$2.35 per part
Manufacturing supervision	Hours of machine time	$12.50 per hour
Assembly	Number of parts	$3.25 per part
Machine setup	Each setup	$88.50 per setup
Inspection and testing	Logged hours	$35.00 per hour
Packaging	Logged hours	$11.50 per hour

OSI currently sells the BL–10 model for $1,250 and the L–25 model for $725. Manufacturing costs and activity usage for the two products follow:

	BL–10	L–25
Direct materials	$135.00	$66.00
Number of parts	98	65
Machine hours	12	7
Inspection time	1.5	1
Packing time	1	0.75
Setups	2	1

Required

1. Calculate the product cost and product margin for each product.

2. A new competitor has entered the market for lens-polishing equipment with a superior product at significantly lower prices, $750 for the BL–10 model and $550 for the L–25 model. To try to compete, OSI has made some radical improvements in the design and manufacturing of its two products. The materials costs and activity usage rates have been decreased significantly:

	BL–10	L–25
Direct materials	$105.00	$57.00
Number of parts	53	41
Machine hours	9	3
Inspection time	0.5	0.25
Packing time	1	0.5
Setups	1	1

Calculate the total product costs with the new activity usage data. Can OSI make a profit with the new costs, assuming that it must meet the price set by the new competitor?

3. What cost management method might be useful to OSI at this time, and why?

5–19 DETERMINING THE IMPACT OF EVALUATING LOCAL CONSTRAINTS   Jim Gordon Nunes is a manufacturing manager at Perkins, Inc., with direct responsibility for the assembly department. Jim's department is the second of four manufacturing operations:

$$\text{Receiving} \rightarrow \text{Assembly} \rightarrow \text{Heat Treatment} \rightarrow \text{Shipping}$$

He has just finished a class in the theory of constraints and is now doing his best to reduce the time and increase the flow through his department. He is the only Perkins manager trying to do this.

Required   Explain the likely outcome of Jim's actions and how you would have attempted to improve the throughput at Perkins, Inc.

5–20 LIFE-CYCLE COSTING   Matt Simpson owns and operates Quality Craft Rentals, which offers canoe rentals and shuttle service on the Nantahala River. Customers can rent canoes at one station, enter the river there, and exit at one of two designated locations to catch a shuttle that returns them to their vehicles at the station they entered. Following are the costs involved in providing this service each year:

	Fixed Costs	Variable Costs
Canoe maintenance	$ 2,300	$2.50
Licenses and permits	3,000	0
Vehicle leases	5,400	0
Station lease	6,920	0
Advertising	6,000	0.50
Operating costs	21,000	0.50

Quality Craft Rentals began business three years ago with a $21,000 expenditure for a fleet of 30 canoes. These are expected to last seven more years, at which time a new fleet must be purchased.

Required   Matt is happy with the steady rental average of 6,400 per year. For this number of rentals, what price should he charge per rental for the business to make a 20 percent life-cycle return on investment?

5–21 MATCHING MARKET CHARACTERISTICS WITH SALES LIFE-CYCLE STAGES

Activities and Market Characteristics	Sales Life-Cycle Stage
Decline in sales	_____
Advertising	_____
Boost in production	_____
Stabilized profits	_____
Competitors' entrance into market	_____
Market research	_____
Market saturation	_____
Start production	_____
Product testing	_____
Termination of product	_____
Large increase in sales	_____

Required Insert the appropriate life-cycle stage in the space provided after each activity.

PROBLEMS

Service

5–22 TARGET COSTING IN A SERVICE FIRM Alert Alarm Systems installs home security systems. Two of its systems, the ICU 100 and the ICU 900, have these characteristics:

Design Specifications	ICU 100	ICU 900	Cost Data
Video cameras	1	3	$150/ea.
Video monitors	1	1	$75/ea.
Motion detectors	5	8	$15/ea.
Floodlights	3	7	$8/ea.
Alarms	1	2	$15/ea.
Wiring	700 ft.	1,100 ft.	$0.10/ft.
Installation	16 hrs.	26 hrs.	$20/hr.

The ICU 100 sells for $810 installed, and the ICU 900 sells for $1,520 installed.

Required
1. What are the current profit margins on both systems?
2. Alert's management believes that it must drop the price on the ICU 100 to $750 and on the ICU 900 to $1,390 to remain competitive in the market. Recalculate profit margins for both products at these price levels.
3. Describe two ways that Alert could cut its costs to get the profit margins back to their original levels.

Strategy

5–23 TARGET COSTING, STRATEGY Benchmark Industries manufactures large workbenches for industrial use. Wayne Garrett, Benchmark's vice president for marketing, has concluded from his market analysis that sales are dwindling for the standard table because of aggressive pricing by competitors. This table sells for $875 whereas the competition sells a comparable table in the $800 range. Wayne has determined that dropping the price to $800 is necessary to regain the firm's annual market share of 10,000 tables. Cost data based on sales of 10,000 tables follow:

	Budgeted Amount	Actual Amount	Actual Cost
Direct materials	400,000 sq. ft.	425,000 sq. ft.	$2,700,000
Direct labor	85,000 hrs.	100,000 hrs.	1,000,000
Machine setups	30,000 hrs.	30,000 hrs.	300,000
Mechanical assembly	320,000 hrs.	320,000 hrs.	4,000,000

Required

1. Calculate the current cost and profit per unit.

2. How much of the current cost per unit is attributable to non-value-added activities?

3. Calculate the new target cost per unit for a sales price of $800 if the profit per unit is maintained.

4. What strategy do you suggest for Benchmark to attain the target cost calculated in requirement 3?

5–24 **TARGET COSTING; HEALTH CARE**   MD Plus is a health maintenance organization (HMO) located in North Carolina. Unlike the traditional fee-for-service model that determines the payment according to the actual services used or costs incurred, MD Plus receives a fixed, prepaid amount from subscribers. The per member per month (PMPM) rate is determined by estimating the health care cost per enrollee within a geographic location. The average health care coverage in North Carolina sells for $115 per month. Because individuals are demanding quality care at reasonable rates, MD Plus must contain its costs to remain competitive. A major competitor, Doctors Nationwide, is entering the North Carolina market with a monthly premium of $109. MD Plus wants to maintain its current market penetration and hopes to increase its enrollees in 2002. The latest data on the number of enrollees and the associated costs follow:

Age	Number of Actual Enrollees in 2001	Number of Projected Enrollees in 2002	Actual Cost in 2001
Less than 1 year	45,000	47,250	$ 3,825,000
1–4	80,500	84,525	6,842,500
5–14	95,000	99,750	8,075,000
15–19	40,000	42,000	3,400,000
20–24	125,000	131,250	10,625,000
25–34	150,000	157,500	12,750,000
35–44	57,000	59,850	4,845,000
45–54	63,000	66,150	5,355,000
55–64	100,000	105,000	8,500,000
65–74	93,000	97,650	7,905,000
75–84	38,000	39,900	3,230,000
85 years and older	29,000	30,450	2,465,000
Total	915,500	961,275	$77,817,500

Required

1. Calculate the target cost required for MD Plus to maintain its current market share and profitability in 2001.

2. Because of rising inflation, MD Plus will charge $125 in 2002 while Doctors Nationwide will increase its premium by $15. Expenses for MD Plus are expected to increase by 6.8 percent in 2002. Based on the projected enrollees, calculate the target cost.

3. Identify the critical success factors for MD Plus. How can the HMO maintain its market share?

5–25 **TARGET COST; WAREHOUSING**   Johnson Supply, a wholesaler, has determined that its operations have three primary activities: purchasing, warehousing, and distributing. The firm reports the following pertinent operating data for the year just completed:

Activity	Cost Driver	Quantity of Cost Driver	Cost per Unit of Cost Driver
Purchasing	Number of purchasing orders	1,000	$100 per order
Warehousing	Number of moves	8,000	20 per move
Distributing	Number of shipments	500	80 per shipment

Johnson buys 100,000 units at an average unit cost of $5 and sells them at an average unit price of $10. The firm also has a fixed operating cost of $50,000 for the year.

Johnson's customers are demanding a 10 percent discount for the coming year. The company expects to sell the same amount if the demand for price reduction can be met. Johnson's suppliers, however, are willing to give only a 2 percent discount.

Required   Johnson has estimated that it can reduce the number of purchasing orders to 800 and can decrease the cost of each shipment $5 with minor changes in its operations. Any further cost saving must come from reengineering the warehousing processes. What is the maximum cost (i.e., target cost) for warehousing if the firm desires to earn the same amount of profit next year?

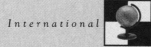

International

Strategy

5–26   TARGET COSTING; INTERNATIONAL   Harpers, Ltd., is a U.K. manufacturer of casual shoes for men and women. It has sustained strong growth in the U.K. market in recent years due to its close attention to fashion trends. Harpers' shoes also have a good reputation for quality and comfort. To expand the business, Harpers is considering introducing its shoes to the U.S. market, where comparable shoes sell for an average of $90 wholesale, more than $16 above what Harpers charges in the United Kingdom (average price, 46 pounds). Management has engaged a marketing consultant to obtain information about what features U.S. consumers seek in shoes if they desire different features. Harpers also has obtained information on the approximate cost of adding these features:

Features Desired in the United States	Cost to Add (in U.S. $)	Importance Rating (5 is most important)
Colorfast material	$4.50	3
Lighter weight	6.75	5
Extra-soft insole	3.00	4
Longer-wearing sole	3.00	2

The current average manufacturing cost of Harpers' shoes is 35 pounds (approximately $56 U.S.), which provides an average profit of $11\frac{1}{4}$ pounds ($18 U.S.) per pair sold. Harpers would like to maintain this profit margin; however, the firm recognizes that the U.S. market requires different features and that shipping and advertising costs would increase approximately $10 U.S. per pair of shoes.

Required

1. What is the target manufacturing cost for shoes to be sold in the United States?

2. Which features, if any, should Harpers add for shoes to be sold in the United States?

3. Critically evaluate Harpers' decision to begin selling shoes in the United States.

5–27   THEORY OF CONSTRAINTS   Precision Engineering Inc. (PEC) is a small manufacturer of precision tools used to construct research equipment for engineering departments at colleges and universities. It sells its two main products, PEC-1 and PEC-2, for $200 and $250, respectively. Due to increasing demand and shortage of specialized labor, PEC has found it increasingly difficult to meet the current weekly demand of 40 units of PEC-1 and 15 units of PEC-2. The following flow diagram shows the manufacturing requirements for the two products and the three types of materials required. Material A is used in PEC-1 only, Material C is used in PEC-2 only, and Material B is used in both PEC-1 and PEC-2.

The amount of weekly labor available for the four manufacturing operations follows:

Receiving and testing materials: 2,000 minutes

Machining (for Material A only): 3,500 minutes

Assembly: 2,000 minutes

Final assembly and testing: 3,500 minutes

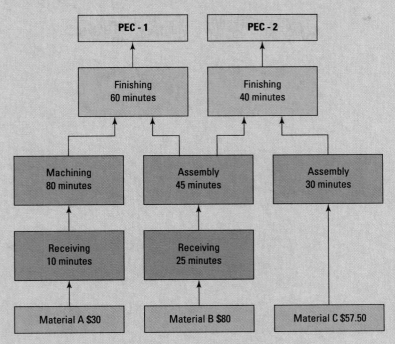

Assume that the labor for each operation is specialized and cannot be moved from one activity to another, that all operations except receiving and testing require a high level of skill, and that PEC cannot increase the capacity on these operations in the short run.

Required What is the best production plan for PEC? Why?

5–28 **THEORY OF CONSTRAINTS; STRATEGY** Hartsook Furniture Co. is a small but fast-growing manufacturer of living room furniture. Its two principal products are end tables and sofas. The flow diagram for the manufacturing at Hartsook follows. Hartsook's manufacturing involves five processes: cutting the lumber, cutting the fabric, sanding, staining, and assembly. One employee cuts fabric and one does the staining. These are relatively skilled workers who could be replaced only with some difficulty. Two workers cut the lumber, and two others perform the sanding operation. There is some skill to these operations, but it is less critical than for staining and fabric cutting. Assembly requires the lowest skill level and is currently done by one full-time employee and a group of part timers who provide a total of 175 hours of working time per week. The other employees work a 40-hour week, with 5 hours off for breaks, training, and personal time. Assume a four-week month and that by prior agreement, none of the employees can be switched from one task to another. The current demand for Hartsook's products and sales prices are as follows, although Hartsook expects demand to increase significantly in the coming months if it is able to successfully obtain the order from a motel chain that it is negotiating.

	End Tables	Sofas
Price	$300	$500
Current demand (units per month)	300	180

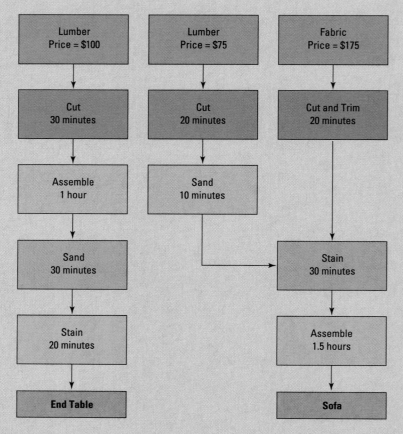

Required

1. What is the most profitable production plan for Hartsook? Explain your answer with supporting calculations.
2. How would you apply the five steps of the theory of constraints to Hartsook's manufacturing operations? What would you recommend for each step?

5–29 **THEORY OF CONSTRAINTS**   Industrial Products Company (IPC) produces a variety of chemicals, primarily adhesives, lubricants, and polymers for industrial use by manufacturers to produce plastics and other compounds. Don Leo, the production vice president, has been informed of a disturbing trend of increasing customer complaints regarding late deliveries from the Canton, Kentucky, plant. The Canton plant is one of the firm's newest and most modern plants and is dedicated to the manufacture of two products, Polymer 1 and Polymer 2. Don has downloaded some incomplete recent information about the Canton plant onto his laptop; he plans to analyze the information in the hour or so he has before his next meeting of the IPC executive committee. He is concerned that some comments will be made about the problems at Canton, and he wants to have an idea of how to respond. Because IPC views Polymer 1 and Polymer 2 as very promising in terms of both sales and profit potential, the news of these problems is likely to spark some comment. The data downloaded by Don is as follows:

Activity	Number of Hours Required for Each Product		Number of Hours Available per Week
	Polymer 1	**Polymer 2**	
Filtering	?	?	320
Stripping	?	?	320
Reacting	3.0	5.0	320

Final filtering	2.0	1.0	160
Mixing	?	?	320
Other information			
Current sales demand (per week)	60	40	
Price	$105	$150	

Don has sketched the following flow diagram for the Canton plant. He believes it is relatively accurate because of his frequent contact with the plant.

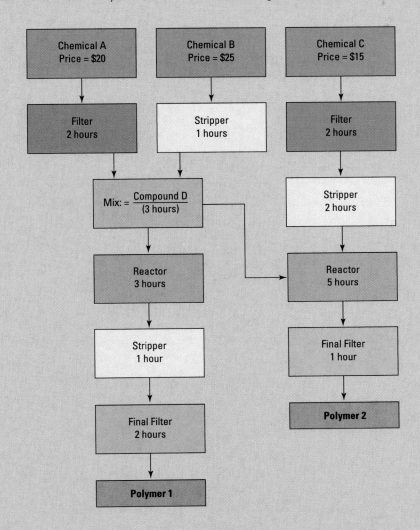

Required   Prepare a short set of notes that Don can use in the executive meeting if questions come up about the problems at the Canton plant.

5–30   **THEORY OF CONSTRAINTS**   Bakker Industries sells three products (611, 613, and 615) that it manufactures in four departments. Both labor and machine time are applied to products in each of the four departments. The machine-processing and labor skills required in each department prohibit switching either machines or labor from one department to another. However, Bakker has a good supply of both full-time and part-time labor and does not expect hiring or retention of employees to be a problem. Because of the availability of part-time labor, Bakker considers labor a variable cost and includes it in the calculation of throughput margin.

Bakker's management is planning its production schedule for the next several months. Some machines will be out of service for extensive overhauling.

Available machine times by department for each of the next six months are as follows:

	Department			
	1	**2**	**3**	**4**
Normal machine capacity in machine-hours	3,500	3,500	3,000	3,500
Capacity of machines being repaired, in machine-hours	500	400	300	200
Available capacity in machine hours	3,000	3,100	2,700	3,300

Labor and machine specifications per unit of product follow:

		Department			
Product	**Labor and Machine Time**	**1**	**2**	**3**	**4**
611	Direct labor-hours	2	3	3	1
	Machine-hours	2	1	2	2
613	Direct labor-hours	1	2	0	2
	Machine-hours	1	1	0	2
615	Direct labor-hours	2	2	1	1
	Machine-hours	2	2	1	1

The Sales Department's forecast of product demand over the next six months is as follows:

Product	**Monthly Sales**
611	500 units
613	400 units
615	1,000 units

Bakker's inventory levels will not increase or decrease during the next six months. The unit price and cost data valid for the next six months follow:

	Product		
	611	**613**	**615**
Price	$196	$123	$167
Direct materials	7	13	17
Direct labor			
Department 1	12	6	12
Department 2	21	14	14
Department 3	24	—	16
Department 4	9	18	9
Variable overhead	27	20	25
Fixed overhead	15	10	32
Variable selling	3	2	4

Required

1. Determine whether Bakker can meet the monthly sales demand for the three products. What department is a constraint, if any?

2. What monthly production schedule would be best for Bakker Industries?

(CMA adapted)

Ethics

5–31 **LIFE-CYCLE COSTING**   Tim Waters, the COO of BioDerm, has asked his cost management team for a product-line profitability analysis for his firm's two products, Xderm and Yderm. The two skin care products require a large amount of research and development and advertising. After receiving the following statement from BioDerm's auditor, Tim concludes that Xderm is the more profitable product and that perhaps cost-cutting measures should be applied to Yderm.

	Xderm	Yderm	Total
Sales	$3,000,000	$2,000,000	$5,000,000
Cost of goods sold	(1,900,000)	(1,600,000)	(3,500,000)
Gross profit	$1,100,000	$ 400,000	$1,500,000
Research and development			(900,000)
Selling expenses			(100,000)
Profit before taxes			$ 500,000

Required

1. Explain why Tim may be wrong in his assessment of the relative performances of the two products.

2. Suppose that 80 percent of the R&D and selling expenses are traceable to Xderm. Prepare life-cycle income statements for each product and calculate the return on sales. What does this tell you about the importance of accurate life-cycle costing?

3. Consider again your answers in requirements 1 and 2 with the following additional information. R&D and selling expenses are substantially higher for Xderm because it is a new product. Tim has strongly supported development of the new product, including the high selling and R&D expenses. He has assured senior managers that the Xderm investment will pay off in improved profits for the firm. What are the ethical issues, if any, facing Tim as he reports to top management on the profitability of the firm's two products?

5–32 **LIFE-CYCLE COSTING**   Starcom Communications Technologies, Inc., has introduced a new phone so small that it can be carried in a wallet. Starcom invested $400,000 in research and development for the technology and another $800,000 to design and test the prototypes. It predicts a four-year life cycle for this phone and has gathered this cost data for it:

	Monthly Fixed Costs	Variable Costs
Manufacturing costs	$25,000	$20
Marketing costs	20,000	5
Customer service costs	3,000	8
Distribution costs	5,000	15
Sales predictions:		
For price of $150—average annual sales of 20,000 units.		
For price of $180—average annual sales of 15,000 units.		
For price of $225—average annual sales of 12,000 units.		

If the price of a wallet phone is $225, Starcom must increase its research and development costs by $100,000 and the prototyping costs by $400,000 to improve the model for the higher price. Fixed customer service costs would also increase by $500 per month and variable distribution costs would increase by $5 per unit to improve the customer service and distribution at the $225 level. At the lowest price level of $150, fixed marketing costs would be reduced by $5,000 per month because the low price would be the principal selling feature.

Required

1. Determine the life-cycle costs for each pricing decision.

2. What price for the wallet phone's life cycle will produce the most profit for Starcom?

5–33 LIFE-CYCLE COSTING The following revenue and cost data are for Turner Manufacturing's two radial saws. The TM 200 is for the commercial market and the TM 800 is for industrial customers. Both products are expected to have three-year life cycles.

	TM200		
	1999	**2000**	**2001**
Revenue			
Costs	$ 500,000	$2,000,000	$2,500,000
Research and development	1,000,000	0	0
Prototypes	300,000	50,000	0
Marketing	60,000	320,000	475,000
Distribution	80,000	120,000	130,000
Manufacturing	20,000	800,000	1,000,000
Customer service	0	60,000	85,000
Income	$(960,000)	$ 650,000	$ 810,000

	TM800		
	Year 1	**Year 2**	**Year 3**
Revenue			
Costs	$ 900,000	$1,800,000	$2,000,000
Research and development	1,150,000	0	0
Prototypes	550,000	30,000	10,000
Marketing	124,000	200,000	260,000
Distribution	170,000	300,000	410,000
Manufacturing	85,000	600,000	700,000
Customer service	0	20,000	10,000
Income	$(1,179,000)	$ 650,000	$ 610,000

Required

1. How would a product life-cycle income statement differ from this calendar-year income statement?

2. Prepare a three-year life-cycle income statement for both products. Which product appears to be more profitable?

3. Prepare a schedule showing each cost category as a percentage of total annual costs. Pay particular attention to the research and development and customer service categories. What do you think this indicates about the profitability of each product over the three-year life cycle?

5–34 LIFE-CYCLE COSTING, HEALTH CARE, DISCOUNTING Cure-all, Inc., has developed a drug that will diminish the effects of aging. Cure-all has spent $1,000,000 on research and development and $2,108,000 for clinical trials. Once the drug is approved by the FDA, which is imminent, it will have a five-year sales life cycle. Laura Russell, Cure-all's chief financial officer, must determine the best alternative for the company among three options. The company can choose to manufacture, package, and distribute the drug; outsource only the manufacturing; or sell the drug's patent. Laura has compiled the following annual cost information for this drug if the company were to manufacture it:

Cost Category	Fixed Costs	Variable Cost per Unit
Manufacturing	$5,000,000	$68.00
Packaging	380,000	20.00
Distribution	1,125,000	6.50
Advertising	2,280,000	12.00

Management anticipates a high demand for the drug and has benchmarked $235 per unit as a reasonable price based on other drugs that promise similar results. Management expects sales volume of 3,000,000 units over five years.

If Cure-all chooses to outsource the manufacturing of the drug while continuing to package, distribute, and advertise it, the manufacturing costs would result in fixed costs of $1,500,000 and variable cost of $80. For the sale of the patent, Cure-all would receive $300,000,000 now and $25,000,000 at the end of every year for the next five years.

Required   Determine the best option for Cure-all. Support your answer.

5-35   **MANUFACTURING CYCLE EFFICIENCY**   Waymouth Manufacturing operates a contract manufacturing plant in Dublin, Ireland. The plant produces a variety of electronics products and components to manufacturers around the world. Cycle time is a critical success factor for Waymouth, which has developed a number of measures of manufacturing speed. The company has studied the matter and found that competitive contract manufacturers have manufacturing cycle efficiency (MCE) times of about 40 percent. When last measured, Waymouth's MCE was 35 percent.

Some key measures from the most recent month's production, averaged over all the jobs during that period, are as follows:

Activity	Average Number of Hours
New product development	30 hours
Materials handling	3
Order setup	6
Machine maintenance	3
Order scheduling	1
Inspection of completed order	5
Packaging and move to storage or ship	2
Manufacturing assembly	23
Order taking and verification	3
Raw materials receipt and stocking	6
Inspection of raw materials	2

Required   Determine the MCE time for the most recent month. What can you infer from the MCE time that you calculated?

5-36   **CONSTRAINT ANALYSIS, FLOW DIAGRAMS (APPENDIX)**   Silver Aviation assembles small aircraft for commercial use. The majority of its business is with small freight airlines serving areas whose airports do not accommodate larger planes. The remainder of Silver's customers are commuter airlines and individuals who use planes in their businesses, such as the owners of larger ranches. Silver recently expanded its market into Central and South America, and the company expects to double its sales over the next three years.

To schedule work and track all projects, Silver uses a flow diagram. The diagram for the assembly of a single cargo plane is shown in Exhibit 1. The diagram shows four alternative paths with the critical path being *ABGEFJK*. Bob Peterson, president of Coastal Airlines, recently placed an order with Silver Aviation for five cargo planes. During contract negotiations, Bob agreed to a delivery time of 13 weeks (five work days per week) for the first plane with the balance of the planes being delivered at the rate of one every four weeks. Because of problems with some of the aircraft that Coastal is currently using, Bob contacted Grace Vander, sales manager for Silver Aviation, to ask about improving the delivery date of the first cargo plane. Grace replied that she believed the schedule could be shortened by as much as 10 work days or two weeks, but the cost of assembly would increase as a result. Bob said he would be willing to consider the increased costs, and they agreed to meet the following day to review a revised schedule that Grace would prepare.

Exhibit 1

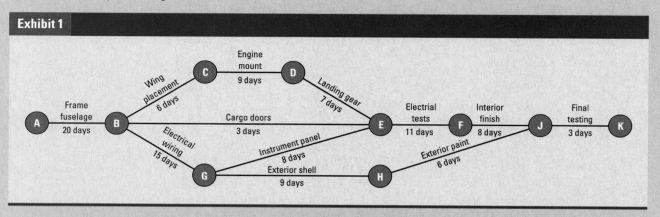

Exhibit 2   Crash Cost Listing

	Activity	Expected Activity Times		Direct Cost		Added Crash Cost Per Reduced Day
		Regular	Crash	Regular	Crash	
AB	Frame fuselage	20 days	16 days	$12,000	$16,800	$1,200
BC	Wing placement	6	5	3,600	5,000	1,400
CD	Engine mount	9	7	6,600	8,000	700
DE	Landing gear	7	5	5,100	6,700	800
BE	Cargo doors	3	3	1,400	1,400	—
BG	Electrical wiring	15	13	9,000	11,000	1,000
GE	Instrument panel	8	6	5,700	8,300	1,300
EF	Electrical tests	11	10	6,800	7,600	800
GH	Exterior shell	9	7	4,200	5,200	500
FJ	Interior finish	8	7	3,600	4,000	400
HJ	Exterior paint	6	5	3,600	4,000	400
JK	Final testing	3	2	3,500	4,400	900
				$65,100	$82,400	

Exhibit 3

Activity Crashed	Additional Cost per Day	Total Direct Cost
		$65,100
HJ by one day	$400	65,500
FJ by one day	400	65,900
GH by two days	500	66,900
CD by two days	700	68,300
EF by one day	800	69,100
DE by two days	800	70,700
BG by one day	1,000	71,700

Because Silver Aviation previously assembled aircraft on an accelerated basis, the company has a list of crash costs for this purpose. Grace used the data shown in Exhibit 2 to develop a plan to cut 10 working days from the schedule at a minimum increase in cost to Coastal Airlines. Upon completing her plan, she reported to Bob that Silver would be able to cut 10 working days from the schedule for an associated increase in cost of $6,000. Grace's Exhibit 3 shows accelerated assembly schedule for the cargo plane starting from the regularly scheduled days and cost.

Required

1. Explain why Grace's plan is unsatisfactory.

2. Revise the accelerated assembly schedule so that Coastal Airlines will take delivery of the first plane two weeks ahead of schedule at the least incremental cost to Coastal.

3. Calculate the incremental costs that Bob will have to pay for this revised accelerated delivery.

(CMA adapted)

5–37 **PRODUCTION PLANNING AND CONTROL STRATEGY**   This is a story about manufacturing performance at one plant of a large company. It begins with Kristen Reynolds, a relatively new plant manager, coming to visit Bryan Simpkins, the plant's head of manufacturing. Kristen and Bryan work for ITR Incorporated, a manufacturer of lighting fixtures with plants located in six countries and worldwide sales. The plant that Kristen and Bryan manage is located in Canada near Hamilton, Ontario. It is the one plant in ITR's system that focuses on custom orders that require special materials, setup, and assembly. The other five plants supply ITR's high-volume, standardized products. Because of changes in the residential and commercial construction industries, the demand for custom orders at the Ontario plant has been increasing steadily. Unfortunately, it has not been filling these orders as quickly as Kristen would like. Many solid customers are waiting days or weeks longer for their orders than they did a year ago; moreover, some ITR sales people have begun to be evasive when customers ask how soon their orders can be filled. Kristen does not know how this is affecting sales or customer goodwill.

> **Kristen** "Hi, Bryan. It's good to see you. I hope all is well with you and the family."
>
> **Bryan** "Going great—though I just learned that Jimmy will have to have braces on his teeth. I don't even want to think of how much that will cost."
>
> **Kristen** "Hey, I've been through that too. No fun. (pause) Bryan, I haven't visited the plant operations in some time. Would you take me for a quick tour?"
>
> **Bryan** "Let's go."

Bryan and Kristen first visit an operation where a skilled worker is operating a machine that molds a metal frame on which multiple light fixtures will later be installed. They watch as the worker (name badge says Ed) completes the last of a batch of 15 frames. Kristen asks how long this batch took him, and he says 82 minutes. "I know this exactly because I have productivity standards to meet, and I must record my time on all jobs. My standard is 6 minutes per item, so I beat my goal." Ed then examines each frame and finds that one has a bad twist and must be rejected; this takes about 10 minutes. He then pushes a button near the machine that calls another worker to remove the defective frame. Meanwhile, Ed loads the 14 good ones on a cart and moves them to the next manufacturing station. Bryan and Kristen note that many frames are already waiting at the next station.

The worker who was called to remove the defective frame tags it, writes up the potential cause(s) for the defect, and then moves the frame to the area of the plant designated for scrap and rework. Kristen and Bryan look at the defect report and note that it indicates two possibilities which will be studied further by another worker assigned to the scrap and rework area. The two possibilities are poor-quality materials, as determined by apparent weaknesses in portions of the framing material and poor work quality (Ed could have damaged the frame accidentally by banging it against one of the roof support beams located next to his work area). Kristen and Bryan note that Ed's workstation area is indeed pretty cramped.

They move to another workstation, which has no operator. By asking a worker at the adjacent station, they determine that the station is down because the machine needs repair. "Joe usually works that station, but he is helping out in the shipping department until his machine is repaired."

They move to another workstation that looks very busy. An order marked "urgent" is waiting at this station, while Dan, the operator, quickly finishes another order. Bryan asks Dan why he has not started the urgent order, and Dan explains that he cannot afford to stop the machine and set it up for another order. This would cost him some time that would lower his productivity on the current job. Dan explains that it is important that he get the items done in the current order quickly, within a standard level of productivity, or production supervisors will be coming to call. Dan says he sees the urgent sign and is working quickly to get to it. He says he might even delay lunch to start it.

To investigate some of the things they observed, Kristen and Bryan next visit the purchasing department. Here they find that the frame material Ed used was purchased from a relatively new vendor at an unbelievably low price. The purchasing department manager approved the purchase because other purchases in the month had gone over budget and this was a way to help meet the budget. The budget is a predetermined amount that the purchasing department is expected to spend each month. Plant policy requires an investigation of any large variances from the budget.

Now, Kristen and Bryan inquire about Joe's machine. A check at the job scheduler's desk shows that the workstation had been in use constantly for the last few weeks. Joe said that he noticed a funny noise but had not reported it because he had some jobs to finish and his productivity is measured by how quickly he finished them. His time between jobs is not measured, but doing jobs quickly is important. Bryan asks the job scheduler why Ed's work area is so crowded since there appears to be plenty of room elsewhere in the plant. The job scheduler says that he is not sure, but that it probably has to do with the fact that each production department is charged a certain amount of plant overhead based on the amount of square feet of space that department occupies. Thus, the department manager for whom Ed works is likely to have reduced the space as much as possible to reduce these overhead charges.

As the story ends, Bryan and Kristen are looking for an answer to how urgent orders are scheduled and moved through the plant.

Required   Consider the manufacturing processes observed in ITR's Ontario plant. What recommendations do you think Bryan and Kristen should make?

SOLUTION TO SELF-STUDY PROBLEM

Best Brand Lighting, Inc.

A thorough analysis will require a good deal more inquiry of management and fact finding than is available from the limited information provided earlier, but a few useful observations can be made.

1.   Encourage BBL to consider increasing the effort put into design to reduce manufacturing costs and to reduce the relatively high rate of product returns in the speciality segment. The cost of design appears low relative to manufacturing and downstream costs, especially in the specialty segment. Inquire about which types of

design approaches are being used. Urge BBL to adopt concurrent engineering–based methods, especially because of the relatively short market life cycles in the industry.

2. Consider additional analysis of pricing. Because of BBL's strong acceptance in the specialty segment and because the differentiation strategy is likely to be important in that segment, a price increase might yield higher profits with little or no loss in market share.

Cost leadership appears to be the appropriate strategy in the major retail segment; inquire what methods the company is using to reduce overall product costs in this segment.

Also, investigate further the rate of customer returns for each product. Is this due to design problems or problems in sales management?

3. Consider a further analysis of marketing expenses. Would an increase in marketing effort in the major retailer segment improve sales in this segment?

4. Consider the need to perform a detailed analysis by product category within each market segment. A detailed analysis might uncover important information about opportunities to reduce cost and add value within the products' value chain.

5. Because of the relatively short sales life cycles, consider whether target costing could be used effectively at BBL. How intense is the level of competition in the industry, and to what extent are trade-offs made between functionality and price in the development and introduction of each new product? If the level of competition is very intense, and trade-offs between functionality and price are key strategic decisions, target costing should be a useful management tool.

6. Investigate the costing system. Is it activity-based? How accurate are the cost figures that it develops?

Total Quality Management

6

After studying this chapter, you should be able to . . .

1 Define *quality* and *total quality management,* and devise guidelines for implementing total quality management

2 Distinguish between the two types of conformance and explain their effects on workers' behavior

3 Identify four major categories of quality costs

4 Prepare and interpret cost of quality reports

5 Describe methods commonly used to identify significant quality problems and their causes

6 Identify distinct characteristics of total quality management in service organizations

7 Explain the relationships between total quality management and productivity

8 Describe the role of management accountants in total quality management and the challenges they face

> You can't turn quality on like a spigot. It's a culture, a lifestyle within a company.
>
> FORD ENGINEER

For decades, management experts in the United States, including W. Edwards Deming and J. M. Juran, urged manufacturers to "design in" quality at the beginning of the process, not to "inspect-in" quality at the end of the production line. The quality call to arms mainly fell on deaf ears in the United States, but not in Japan. More than 30 years ago, Juran predicted that a focus on quality would help turn Japan into an economic powerhouse. By the 1970s and 1980s, Japan was grabbing market shares with better, lower-priced products. They used Deming's and Juran's ideas to slash the cost of quality to as little as 5 percent of total production costs while the cost at U.S. factories was 50 percent, or 10 times as high.[1]

Juran's prediction proved true. In the late 1970s and the early 1980s, many U.S. firms had a rude awakening. Many U.S. executives realized, for the first time, that *Made in the U.S.A.* no longer stood for the best that was available. Once a term of mockery, *Made in Japan* became a term synonymous with quality. U.S. executives, especially those working for firms employing the traditional management techniques that had paid off so well a scant 20 years earlier, found themselves searching frantically for answers and desperately seeking to remain competitive.

U.S. auto manufacturers realized in the late 1970s that Japanese auto manufacturers were somehow able to sell automobiles that performed better, had far fewer defects, and cost less than those made in the United States and still earn high returns. Likewise, when Hewlett-Packard tested the quality of more than 300,000 new computer chips in the early 1980s, it found those made by Japanese manufacturers had zero defects per thousand. Those made by U.S. manufacturers had 11 to 19 defects per thousand. After 1,000 hours of use, the failure rate of U.S. chips was 27 times higher than those of the Japanese chips. Many industry and government leaders in the United States saw the handwriting on the wall: Get quality or lose the race.[2]

The world had changed. Global competition gave consumers abundant choices and they became more cost and value conscious, demanding high-quality products and services. Market shares and operating profits of firms that failed to pay attention to quality eroded substantially and threatened the continuation of the firms' operations.

The 1980s became a decade of remarkable changes for many U.S. firms. Consumers have witnessed major efforts by U.S. manufacturers to improve quality. Many

[1] N. Gross, M. Stepanek, O. Port, and J. Carey, "Will Bugs Eat Up the U.S. Lead in Software?" *Businessweek*, December 6, 1999.

[2] James R. Evans and William M. Lindsay, *The Management and Control of Quality*, 3rd ed. (New York: West Publishing Co., 1996), p. 7.

firms in the United States have engaged in relentless efforts in the last two decades to improve the quality of their products and services. Manufacturers in the United States and other countries have made tremendous progress in quality improvement in the last decade, and continuous improvements have become a way of life for many firms and organizations.

In 1987, Congress established the Malcolm Baldrige National Quality Award to enhance the competitiveness of U.S. businesses by promoting quality awareness, recognizing quality and performance achievements, and publicizing successful performance strategies of U.S. organizations in the areas of manufacturing, service, small business, and—added in 1999—education and health care. Seven broad categories make up the criteria: leadership, strategic planning, customer and market focus, information and analysis, human resource focus, process management, and business results. The fierce competition to win the award is evidence of the importance these firms place on being recognized for their quality operations.[3] Simply applying for the award requires substantial investments in both time and money; the odds of winning are slim. Although no more than three awards are given each year, more than 680 organizations had applied and only 37 had received the award as of November 2000. Some firms have won the award twice.[4]

The Malcolm Baldrige National Quality Award program has helped applicants, award winners, and many other U.S. businesses and organizations to become more competitive. Studies by the National Institute of Standards and Technology, university researchers, and government and business organizations have found that incorporating the Baldrige quality performance concepts pays off in increased productivity, satisfied employees and customers, and improved profitability for both the companies and their investors. In each year since 1995, the hypothetical "Baldrige Stock Index," made up of publicly traded U.S. companies that have received the Malcolm Baldrige National Quality Award, has outperformed the Standard & Poor's 500 by almost three to one. In a recent study of 600 quality award-winning firms including the Baldrige, state, and other quality award programs and a control group, Singhal and Hendricks found that the award-winning companies significantly outperformed the control group in many aspects of their business, including the value of their common stock, operating income, sales, return on sales, and asset growth. Saccomano reported in her study that companies with effective total quality management (TQM) programs had higher stock prices, sales, and income.[5] Agus and Hassan found that long-term TQM adopters had better financial performance than companies that had implemented TQM more recently.[6]

Worldwide, ISO 9000 has become a certification sought after by global companies to gain the stamp of approval on the quality of their products and services.

ISO 9000 is a set of guidelines for quality management and quality standards developed by the International Organization for Standardization in Geneva, Switzerland. More than 90 countries have adopted it. ISO 9000 certification has become a seal of

ISO 9000 is a set of guidelines for quality management and quality standards developed by the International Organization for Standardization in Geneva, Switzerland.

---

[3] Each applicant undergoes a rigorous examination process that takes 300 to 1,000 hours over six months after the applicant completes a detailed self-assessment. The examination process includes visits and reviews by an independent board of examiners primarily from business and quality experts in the private sector of achievements and improvements in every aspect of the organization's business, from strategic planning to human resources to customer satisfaction and performance and business results. Each applicant receives a detailed report on its strengths and opportunities for improvement.

[4] Winners include 3M, ADAC Laboratories, Ames Rubber Corporation, Armstrong, AT&T, BI, Cadillac, Corning, Custom Research, Dana, Eastman Chemical, Federal Express, Globe Metallurgical, Granite Rock Co., GTE, IBM, Marlow, Merrill Lynch, Milliken, Motorola, Solectron, STMicroelectronics, Sunny Fresh Foods, Texas Instruments, Ritz-Carlton, Trident, Wainwright, Wallace, Westinghouse, Xerox, and Zytec.

[5] Ann Saccomano, "TQM Works Over Time," *Traffic World*, 1998, p. 37.

[6] A. Agus and Z. Hassan, "Exploring the Relationship between the Length of Total Quality Management Adoption and Financial Performance: An Empirical Study in Malaysia," *International Journal of Management*, September 2000, pp. 323–33.

quality since the revised standards became effective in 1987. Many firms and organizations require all their suppliers to be ISO 9000 certified.

To become ISO 9000 certified, a firm must prove that it is following ISO 9000 operating procedures; these include inspecting production processes, maintaining equipment, training workers, testing products, and dealing with customer complaints. An independent test company audits the firm's operations and makes recommendations concerning certification.

Recognizing the high cost of failing to meet quality standards and the benefit from being recognized as having high-quality products or services has also prompted firms to improve the quality of their products and services.

The cost of quality can be substantial; on average, it is 20 to 25 percent of sales for many U.S. firms.[7] One consultant, estimates that 40 percent of the cost of doing business in the service sector can be attributed to poor quality.[8] On the other hand, firms with quality products or services gain sales and earn high profits. Attaining high quality and continuous improvement in the quality of products and services has become a way of life for most, if not all, organizations. Pursuing quality has become a

How Have U.S. Firms Done so Far?

In a survey of U.S. business, *The Economist* reports that U.S. firms have made tremendous progress in quality improvement. In 1994, AT&T became the first U.S. company to win Japan's prestigious Deming Prize for quality control. Many other U.S. firms have introduced vigorous quality-raising initiatives and have discovered their own versions of the Japanese *kaizen*, or continuous quality improvement. Six Sigma programs that aim to reduce manufacturing defects to 3.4 per million have become part of quality lore. Many firms, including General Electric, Motorola, and Hewlett-Packard, have not only installed Six Sigma programs in their own factories and offices but also demanded that their suppliers implement similar programs. Some management consultants believe that for U.S. firms, quality is now old hat. They preach that it is time to take quality for granted and move on to the next new idea.

Source: "American Business Survey," *The Economist,* September 16, 1995, p. 5.

No Excuses at the Navy

When results are not as expected, many people blame bad luck. Some organizations, though, cannot afford to have bad luck. These organizations manage complex, high-risk technologies that must have everything occur as specified with no room for deviation. For them, a bit of bad luck threatens far more than a dip in the quarterly profits, and any role that luck might play must be removed completely.

Launching an airplane from an aircraft carrier requires flinging of the airplane into the air by one of the carrier's four steam-powered catapults. The airplane is held in place while its pilot applies full thrust, then the catapult is released, and the plane accelerates to 180 miles per hour in just over two seconds. Less than a minute later, the next catapult in line slingshots its own load off the deck, then the next, and the next, so that a group of 20 planes is airborne in less than 15 minutes. In readying each airplane for its launch, the catapult petty officer must calculate and set the steam pressure, taking into account the weight of the plane and the wind speed, while the crew must check for fuel leaks and other problems. A tiny bit of bad luck—a sudden wind shift, a last-minute mechanical breakdown, a miscommunication between pilot and catapult crew—could send an airplane—and perhaps its pilot, too—to the bottom of the ocean.

Launching a plane often takes place on a deck that is wet, slick with oil in places, and rocking back and forth to the rhythm of the waves. To further complicate matters, a number of other shipboard operations are being performed at the same time, including performing maintenance on the planes, fueling and arming them, moving them around a crowded deck, and parking them. Despite the many ways that things could go wrong, flight deck operations are generally smooth and accidents are quite rare.

Source: Robert Pool, "In the Zero Luck Zone," *Forbes ASAP,* November 27, 2000, pp. 85–91.

---

[7]   Michael R. Ostrega, "Return on Investment through Cost of Quality," *Journal of Cost Management,* Summer 1991, pp. 37–77; Richard K. Youde, "Cost of Quality Reporting: How We See It," *Management Accounting,* January 1992, pp. 33–38.

[8]   Ted Wolf, "Becoming a 'Total Quality' Controller," *The Small Business Controller,* Spring 1992, pp. 24–27.

global revolution affecting every facet of business. Quality reduces costs, increases customer satisfaction, and induces and maintains long-term success and profitability.

This chapter explains total quality management, defines quality and measurement of quality costs, illustrates the preparation of quality reports, examines approaches to detecting causes of deviations in quality, and explores decisions to investigate quality defects.

QUALITY AND STRATEGIC COST MANAGEMENT

In the last two decades, the CEOs of many firms have come to realize that a strategy driven by quality improvements can lead to significant market advantages, improved profitability, and long-term prosperity. The line between planning for quality improvements and planning a standard business strategy has become increasingly blurred. Whether a firm competes through a strategy of cost leadership or product differentiation, quality issues permeate every aspect of its operations. A firm choosing to compete through low prices is not choosing to produce low-quality products. Its low-priced products must meet customers' expectations. Similarly, a differentiation strategy will not be successful if the firm fails to build quality into its products. The guiding principles underlying most quality-improvement programs are to satisfy customers' needs and to meet or exceed customers' expectations. This is also the goal of a strategic plan to gain competitive advantage.

Quality is significant for other reasons, too. Quality costs often are substantial portions of sales revenues. In many organizations, few other factors have as much effect on costs and the bottom line. It is not surprising, therefore, that the current trend is to integrate planning for quality improvements with business strategic planning, recognizing that quality drives the success of the organization.

PIMS Associates, Inc., examined more than 1,200 companies to determine the impact of product quality on corporate performance and found that

- Product quality and profitability are closely related.
- Businesses that offer premium-quality products and services are more likely to have large market shares.
- Quality relates positively to a higher return on investment.[9]

Exhibit 6–1 shows that a firm with improved quality has several strategic competitive advantages and enjoys higher profitability and a higher return on investment. Firms can reap many benefits from improved quality. Improved quality decreases product returns. Lower returns decrease warranty cost and repair expenses. Improved quality lowers inventory levels for raw materials, components, and finished products because the firm has more reliable manufacturing processes and schedules. Improved product quality also lowers manufacturing costs as the firm reduces or eliminates rework and increases productivity. Customers are likely to perceive quality products as having higher values. Perceived high values allow the firm to command higher prices and enjoy a larger market share. Higher prices and greater market shares increase revenues and profits. Improved quality also decreases cycle time. Faster cycle times speed deliveries, and prompt delivery makes happy customers, creates new demand, and increases market shares. Higher revenues and lower costs boost net income and increase the firm's return on investment. Focus on quality also expands the firm's opportunity and decreases its competitive threats.

Cost, quality, and time are among the critical factors in successful strategies. Having quality products allows firms that compete on differentiation to be effective in sustaining their strategy. A firm with low costs and quality products provides its customers with products equal to or better in quality at lower prices. Only with quality products can the firm truly be a cost leader.

---

[9] Evans and Lindsay, *The Management and Control of Quality*, pp. 18–19.

| Exhibit 6–1 | Results of Improved Quality on Profitability and Return on Investment |

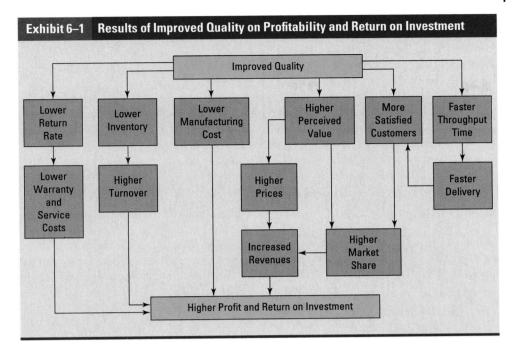

TOTAL QUALITY MANAGEMENT

To survive and be successful in today's global competitive environment, firms must manufacture quality products and provide quality services. A pollster of automotive products, J. D. Power observes that quality is becoming the price of entry for automotive marketers. Consumers everywhere have come to demand high-quality products. Firms must produce quality products and provide quality services to survive, maintain market shares, and earn desired returns. Having quality products and services also enhances and secures competitive advantages of the firm. But what is quality?

◀**LEARNING OBJECTIVE 1**

*Define **quality** and **total quality management**, and devise guidelines for implementing total quality management.*

The Meaning of Quality

There are many definitions of quality, and people often view it differently because of differences in their roles in the production-marketing-consumption chain and in their expectations for products or services. In simpler times, many CEOs perceived quality as a characteristic revealed by "I know it when I see it." Such an approach to quality provides no clear guideline for meeting it and makes quality management very difficult.

The ultimate test of a quality product or service is whether the product or service meets or exceeds customers' expectations. The requirements to meet or exceed customers' expectations then serve as specifications for operations throughout the organization. All individuals, departments, or subdivisions of an organization must strive for conformity to specifications that meet or surpass customer expectations.

Not all customers have the same expectations for a product or service. All 3/8-inch drill bits can drill 3/8-inch holes. Nevertheless, a firm can manufacture a 3/8-inch drill bit that costs $3 apiece for home use and an industrial-strength drill bit that costs $15. The specifications and quality expectations for the less expensive drill bit are not the same as those for the more expensive one. The industrial strength drill bit is designed for heavy, continuous use and can be used for, say, 100 hours before it needs to be replaced. A drill bit for home use, on the other hand, is not designed for continuous use for long hours and has a shorter expected life of, say, 10 hours.

Each can be a quality product if it meets its respective specifications and customers' expectations. A product is a **quality** product if it conforms with a design that meets or exceeds the expectations of customers at a competitive price they are willing to pay.

A **quality** product or service meets or exceeds customers' expectations at a competitive price they are willing to pay.

Expectations for services also differ. A tourist does not expect the same services from a Motel 6 as from a Ritz-Carlton Hotel, although both provide rooms for tourists. A mechanic performs quality service by changing a car's oil as specified: draining old oil, installing a new oil filter, lubricating the chassis, and adding clean new oil. The service is a quality service even if the mechanic used a regular oil, not a new synthesized oil that improves engine performance, if the customer asked for a regular, not a deluxe, oil change. The mechanic has failed to deliver a quality service, however, if the new oil filter falls off the next morning due to improper installation or if the refill is four or six quarts of oil instead of the five quarts specified by the manufacturer. Conformity to specifications determines the quality service of the job.

Characteristics of Total Quality Management

Total quality management (TQM) is the unyielding and continually improving effort by everyone in the firm to understand, meet, and exceed the expectations of customers.[10] Although each organization is most likely to develop its own approach to total quality management to suit its particular culture and management style, certain characteristics are common to most TQM systems. These characteristics are as follows:

- Focusing on satisfying the customer.
- Striving for continuous improvement.
- Fully involving the entire work force.
- Actively supporting and involving top management.
- Using unambiguous and objective measures.
- Recognizing quality achievements in a timely manner.
- Continuously providing training on total quality management.

Exhibit 6–2 describes the critical factors for successful total quality management.

Focus on the Customer

TQM begins by identifying the firm's customers; determining their needs, requirements, and expectations; and then doing whatever it takes to satisfy them. A firm's customers are both external and internal. External customers are the ultimate recipients of the firm's products or services. Internal customers are all individuals or subunits within the firm involved in manufacturing the product or providing the services. At some stage, everyone in a process or organization is a customer or supplier to someone else, either inside or outside the organization.

The TQM process begins by identifying the requirements and expectations of external customers. These requirements and expectations are the bases for specifications for each of a succession of internal customer/suppliers and for the external suppliers to the firm.

A manufacturing firm translates the identified expectations and requirements of external customers into supplier specifications for each successive internal customer/supplier, including design requirements, part characteristics, manufacturing operations, production and external vendor requirements, and selling requirements. A firm can serve its ultimate, external customer better if the firm fully meets all requirements of each internal customer.[11] Ford used this approach to develop and manufacture the Taurus, and in 1993, the Taurus overtook the Honda Accord as the top-selling car in America.

Strive for Continuous Improvement (Kaizen)

The Coca-Cola Company believes that quality is not a destination; it is a way of life. Coca-Cola Company states: "We know we will never arrive; there is no finish."

---

[10] Ibid., p. 17.

[11] Ibid., p. 5.

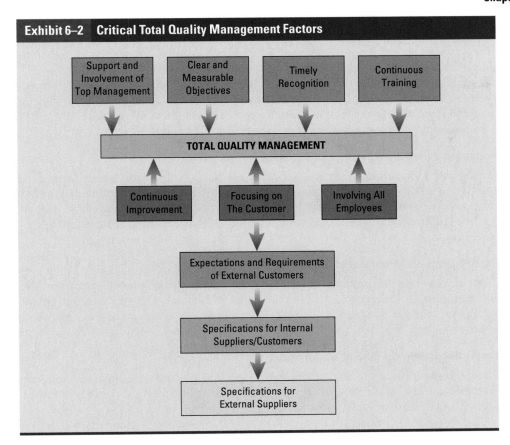

Exhibit 6–2   Critical Total Quality Management Factors

Support and Involvement of Top Management · Clear and Measurable Objectives · Timely Recognition · Continuous Training → **TOTAL QUALITY MANAGEMENT** ← Continuous Improvement · Focusing on The Customer · Involving All Employees → Expectations and Requirements of External Customers → Specifications for Internal Suppliers/Customers → Specifications for External Suppliers

---

Quality Principles in the Coca-Cola Company

The continuous dominance of Coca-Cola as the number one brand in the global soft-drink market is no accident. Coca-Cola believes that

- Quality is the result of focused hard work and diligence; it is not an accident.
- Quality is a way of life; a job worth doing is worth doing right the first time.

- Excellence is the goal and nothing less is acceptable.
- Quality is not a destination; it's a way of life and continuous effort. There is no finish.

Source: "Coca-Cola: A Taste for Quality," The Coca-Cola Company. As cited in James R. Evans and William M. Lindsay, *The Management and Control of Quality* (New York: West Publishing, 1996), p. 12.

Taguchi and Wu believe that continuous quality improvement and cost reduction (kaizen) are necessary to remain competitive in today's global marketplace.[12] "With competitors forever trying to outperform us and customers exhibiting ever-changing expectations, a firm can never reach the ideal quality standard." The processes described in Exhibit 6–2 never end; firms need to continuously update specifications for both internal customers/suppliers and external suppliers to better serve external customers.

Full Involvement of the Entire Work Force

A firm can meet the requirements of its external customers only if each of the internal customers/suppliers in the process satisfies the requirements of the downstream customer. A breakdown in the process, no matter how insignificant, leads to a defective product or service and an unsatisfied customer. Top management must encourage

---

[12] G. Taguchi and Y. Wu, *Introduction to Off-Line Quality Control* (Nagoya, Japan: Central Japan Quality Control Association, 1980).

everyone in the firm, from clerical employees, factory workers, accountants, and engineers to professionals and managers to be actively involved and participate in the firm's efforts to continuously improve quality. Employee involvement can range from simple information sharing, dialogue, group problem solving, all the way to total self-direction. One proven effective approach for employee involvement is **quality (control) circles** or **quality circles** (QCs) for short. A quality circle is a small group of employees from the same work area that meets regularly to identify and solve work-related problems and to implement and monitor solutions to the problems.

Quality circle is a small group of employees from the same work area that meet regularly to identify and solve work-related problems and to implement and monitor solutions to the problems.

Active Support and Involvement of Top Management

Management personnel from the CEO to subdivision managers must participate actively in quality improvements. They also need to demonstrate their dedication to total quality to employees at every level, all vendors and suppliers to the firm, all customers, and the community at every opportunity so that everyone is aware of the primary importance of total quality in every aspect of the firm's operations.

Unambiguous and Measurable Objectives

Clear objectives make progress visible. Measurable objectives forge efforts toward the common goal. To ensure success of total quality management, a firm must set unambiguous and measurable objectives and develop effective measurement and supporting system.

Timely Recognition of Quality Achievement

Timely recognition of the quality achievements of people and subunits is the best way to emphasize the firm's continuous striving for better quality and to ensure efforts toward total quality at every level.

Continuing Education

The race to total quality is never over. Mandatory continuing education and training of employees at all levels is necessary to achieve the culture change and continuous focus required in a total quality management environment.

TQM Implementation Guidelines

A firm cannot implement a successful TQM program overnight. Superficial copying techniques adopted by successful TQM firms such as quality circles, teamwork, kaizen, does not make a TQM firm. It took Japanese companies more than 20 years to approach and surpass the quality level of many U.S. firms. It will take any organization serious about achieving TQM several years of concerted and dedicated efforts by all its members to become a world-class quality firm.

The implementation of TQM is not an easy task and is time consuming. The Institute of Management Accountants (IMA) believes that a typical organization takes three to five years to move from traditional management to TQM. Most likely, the firm will not see many tangible benefits in the early years of implementation, although some specific projects along the way can quickly yield high returns.

Drawing from the experiences of winners of the Malcolm Baldrige award for effectively managing quality, IMA has devised an 11-phase process lasting three years to establish TQM.[13] Throughout the process, the full and genuine involvement of all employees is essential to a successful TQM implementation.

Year One—Preparation and Planning

- Create quality council and staff.
- Conduct executive-quality training programs.

---

[13] "Managing Quality Improvements," *Statement on Management Accounting No. 4-R* (Montvale, N.J.: Institute of Management Accountants, 1993), pp. 10–11.

- Conduct quality audits.
- Prepare gap analysis.
- Develop strategic quality improvement plans.

Year Two—Training and Implementation

- Conduct employee communication and training programs.
- Establish quality teams.
- Create a measurement system and set goals.

Year Three—Assessment, Review, and Revise

- Revise compensation/appraisal/recognition systems.
- Launch external initiatives with suppliers.
- Review and revise.

Create Quality Council and Staff

Most companies have found that successful implementation of TQM requires unwavering and active leadership from the CEO and senior managers. TQM is an undertaking that needs cooperation and the best efforts of all units of the organization. Without management support, a quality improvement program is likely to fail. As Shilliff and Motiska point out, "Every member of the [quality] team is important, but the most important member is the chief executive officer or top management. Without top management's wholehearted support, guidance, and direction, the quality program is doomed to mediocrity or eventual failure."[14]

However, the CEO or top management alone cannot bring forth all the desired benefits from TQM. Only with support from all managers in the top echelon can TQM attain the most desirable results. The necessary leadership often takes the form of an executive-level quality council. The quality council should include the top management team with the CEO chairing the council. The council's primary function is to develop quality mission and vision statements, companywide goals, and a long-term strategy.

Conduct Executive Quality Training Programs

To ensure senior management's unwavering and continuous support of TQM, the firm needs to conduct executive-quality training programs. The primary function of the program is to (1) raise senior management's awareness of the need for a systematic focus on and continuous support of quality improvement, (2) create a common knowledge base on total quality, and (3) establish reasonable expectations and goals. Conducting executive-quality training programs also helps avoid misunderstandings and miscommunication as the change effort progresses.[15]

COST MANAGEMENT IN ACTION

What Is the Most Effective Way to Implement TQM?

Total quality management (TQM) is a key strategic and operational issue for most firms, as their customers continue to have higher expectations for product and service quality. Because it involves most if not all the activities in the firm, the implementation of TQM is usually a complex and difficult process. The full implementation of TQM may take several years. The IMA has identified implementation guidelines that can assist managers in the process. Some firms such as General Electric, Allied Signal, and Weyerhaeuser take additional steps to ensure the success of their quality initiatives. What do you think these additional steps might include?

---

[14] Karl A. Shilliff and Paul J. Motiska, *The Team Approach to Quality* (Milwaukee: ASQC Quality Press, 1992), p. xi.

[15] Ibid., p. 11.

Conduct Quality Audits

A quality audit assesses the firm's quality practices and analyzes the quality performance of the best practices, including those of other companies. Conducting a quality audit enables the firm to identify the company's strengths and weaknesses, develops a long-term strategic quality improvement plan, and identifies which quality improvement opportunities will yield the greatest return to the company in both the short and long terms.

Prepare Gap Analysis

A *gap analysis* is a type of benchmarking that determines the gap in practices between the best in class and a specific firm. Following a quality audit that identifies the strengths and weaknesses of the firm's quality programs, a gap analysis identifies target areas for quality improvements and provides a common objective database for the firm to develop its strategic quality improvement.

Develop Strategic Quality Improvement Plans

The gap analysis results and the goal for quality improvement serve as bases for developing both short-term (one-year) and long-range (three-to-five-year) strategic plans for setting priorities in quality improvements. The initial plan should be limited and specific and have the potential of yielding high, measurable quality benefits.

Conduct Employee Communication and Training Programs

Employee training programs serve as a communication tool to convey management's commitment to total quality and provide employees with necessary skills to achieve total quality; they play critical roles in successful quality improvement programs. In 1996, GE launched a $200 million quality improvement program to slash its defects to four per million. GE began by training 200 "master black belts" who became full-time quality teachers.[16]

Establish Quality Teams

A cross-functional quality team includes members from a variety of employee and management teams and functional units. The cross-functional quality team oversees the continuous improvement efforts and quality task forces throughout the organization and coordinates work to optimize the quality efforts, ensure adequate resources, and resolve issues.

Team members from throughout the organization should include individuals who can identify specific quality requirements and quality costs. Typical team members are product managers, engineers, production workers, customer service representatives, and management accountants.

Once established, quality teams become the main forces behind quality incentives, implementation and monitoring of quality programs, and continuous improvement. One major function of a quality team is to involve all employees in quality programs.

Create a Measurement System and Set Goals

A crucial factor for TQM success is having measures that truly reflect the needs and expectations of customers, both internal and external. A good measurement system that helps TQM often entails developing a new accounting system, because a traditional accounting system often divides and spreads important quality data among myriad accounts. A good measurement system for TQM should also enable all employees to know at all times the progress being made toward total quality and the additional improvements needed.

As an integral part of the firm's financial performance evaluation system, a traditional accounting system can impede quality improvement. All employees of the

---

[16] *The Wall Street Journal*, April 25, 1996, p. A4.

organization must understand that the measurements generated by a TQM system are tools for improvement, not punishment. A separate measurement system also facilitates TQM by reducing the concerns that the effect of expenditures for quality improvement will have on short-term operating results.

Revise Compensation/Appraisal/Recognition Systems

Reward and recognition are the best means to reinforce the emphasis on TQM. Moreover, a proper reward and recognition structure based on quality measures can be a very powerful stimulus to promote TQM in a company (see Chapter 20). Efforts and progress will most likely be short lived if the firm makes no change to its compensation/appraisal/recognition system.

Launch External Initiatives with Suppliers

A supplier is as much a part of the company's operations as one of its divisions. Suppliers that fail to deliver goods as specified can doom a firm's efforts to provide only quality products or services. TQM efforts should include the entire business system that extends from raw materials to the final customer. The following are among the practices successful TQM firms use to ensure having quality suppliers:

- Reducing the supplier base. A reduced supplier base reduces variations in quality, increases supplier commitment, and improves the efficient use of the firm's resources.
- Selecting suppliers based not only on price and their capability and willingness to improve quality, cost, delivery, and flexibility but also on their dedication to continuous improvement.
- Forming long-term relationships with suppliers as working partners.
- Specifying precise supplier expectations and ensuring suppliers' consistent delivery.[17]

Review and Revise

All employees, led by the quality council and quality team, should review quality progress and reassess quality improvement efforts at least annually. Again, as many firms, including Coca Cola, stated, there is no finish line in quality improvement.

TYPES OF CONFORMANCE

Quality involves conformance with the specifications for the product or service that meet or exceed customer requirements and expectations. Conformance, however, can differ among individuals or firms, as it did at Sony, as we describe in the next section.

Goalpost Conformance

Goalpost conformance is conformance to a quality specification expressed as a specified range around the target. The target is the ideal or desirable outcome of the operation.

For example, the target for a production process to manufacture 0.5-inch sheet metal is 0.5-inch thickness for all sheet metal manufactured. Recognizing that meeting the target every time in manufacturing is difficult, a firm often specifies a tolerance range. A firm that specifies a tolerance of ±0.05 inch meets the quality standard if the thickness of its products is between 0.55 inch and 0.45 inch.

A goalpost conformance is a **zero-defects conformance.** Management expects the production process to have all output within the specified range of variations, thus achieving zero-defect conformance. Exhibit 6–3 depicts the goalpost conformance specifications for the sheet metal.

◄ **LEARNING OBJECTIVE 2**

Distinguish between the two types of conformance and explain their effects on workers' behavior.

Goalpost conformance (zero-defects conformance) is conformance to a quality specification expressed as a specified range around the target.

---

[17] Ibid., p. 17.

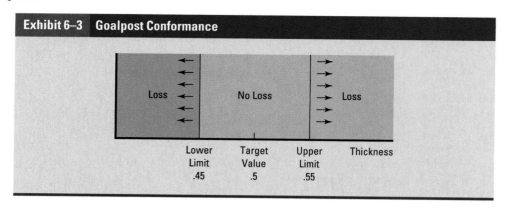

Exhibit 6–3 Goalpost Conformance

Loss	No Loss	Loss	Thickness

Lower Limit .45   Target Value .5   Upper Limit .55

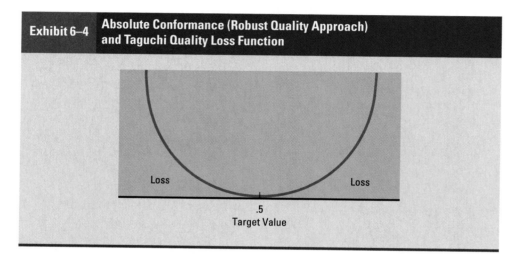

Exhibit 6–4 Absolute Conformance (Robust Quality Approach) and Taguchi Quality Loss Function

Loss   Loss

.5
Target Value

Absolute Quality Conformance

Absolute quality conformance or the **robust quality approach** requires all products or services to meet the target value *exactly* with no variation. The requirement for an absolute conformance requires all sheet metal to have a thickness of 0.5 inch, not 0.5 inch ±0.05 inch or even 0.5 inch ±0.0005 inch. Exhibit 6–4 depicts the robust quality conformance approach.

Any variation from the target value is less than ideal and has potential economic consequences. Robustness in quality is the result of meeting exact targets consistently, not from always staying within tolerance. A firm incurs a cost of variability whenever a product deviates from its target value; greater losses occur with larger variations.

Goalpost or Absolute Conformance?

Goalpost conformance assumes that the firm incurs no quality or failure cost or loss if quality measures fall within the specified limits. The firm incurs quality costs or losses only when the measure is outside the limits. Alternatively, absolute conformance views quality costs or losses as a continuously increasing function starting from the target value. Quality costs, hidden or out of pocket, occur any time the quality measure deviates from its target value.

Which of these two approaches, goalpost or absolute conformance, is better? Perhaps we can find an answer in the experience Sony had in two of its plants that manufacture color televisions.[18]

Absolute quality conformance (robust quality approach) requires all products or services to meet the target value exactly with no variation.

---
[18] Evans and Lindsay, *The Management and Control of Quality*, p. 244.

The two Sony plants manufacture the same television sets and follow the same specification for color density. The two plants, however, use different types of quality conformance. The San Diego plant uses goalpost conformance, and the Tokyo plant adopts absolute conformance. On examining the operating data of a period, Sony found that all the units produced at the San Diego plant fell within the specifications (zero defect), but some of those manufactured at the Japanese plant did not. The quality of the Japanese units, however, was more uniform around the target value, while the quality of the San Diego units was uniformly distributed between the lower and upper limits of the specification, the goalpost, as depicted in Exhibit 6–5.

The average quality cost (loss) per unit of the San Diego plant was $0.89 higher than that of the Japanese plant. One reason for the higher quality cost for units produced at the San Diego plant was the need for more frequent field service. Customers are more likely to complain when the density is farther away from the target value. For a firm having long-term profitability and customer satisfaction as its goals, absolute conformance is the better approach.

Taguchi Quality Loss Function

Genichi Taguchi and Y. Wu proposed the absolute quality conformance approach as an *off-line* quality control.[19] Before engaging in manufacturing or servicing, this approach pays more attention to such activities as the design and the manufacturing or operation processes to facilitate manufacturing the product or providing the service. Taguchi believes that these dimensions need to be perfected before manufacturing the product.

Taguchi and Wu recognize that any variation from the exact specifications entails a cost or loss to the firm, as shown in Exhibit 6–4. The cost or loss can be depicted by a quadratic function.

The **Taguchi quality loss function** depicts the relationship between the total loss to a firm due to quality defects and the extent of quality defects. Overall, the loss grows larger as the variation increases (as a quadratic function): the total loss increases as the magnitude of a quality characteristic of the product or service moves farther away from the target value. A quadratic function means that when the deviation from the target

Taguchi quality loss function depicts the relationship between the total loss to a firm due to quality defects and the extent of quality defects.

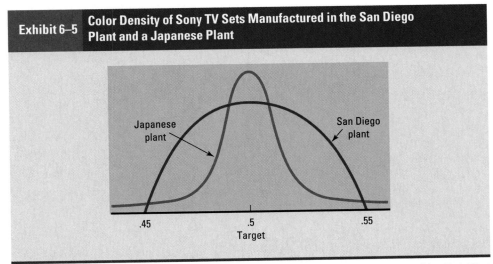

| Exhibit 6–5 | **Color Density of Sony TV Sets Manufactured in the San Diego Plant and a Japanese Plant** |

Source: James R. Evans and William M. Lindsay, *The Management and Control of Quality*, 3rd ed. (New York: West Publishing Co., 1996), p. 245.

19   Taguchi and Wu, *Introduction to Off-Line Quality Control*. See also Evans and Lindsay, *The Management and Control of Quality*, pp. 243–48; and Thomas L. Albright and Harold P. Roth, "The Measurement of Quality Costs: An Alternative Paradigm," *Accounting Horizon*, June 1992, pp. 15–27.

value doubles, the loss quadruples. For instance, if a deviation of 0.1 from the target value has a loss of $4, then a $16 loss occurs when the deviation doubles, or is 0.2 from the target value.

Deviations from the quality standard increase total costs including manufacturing, service, and other hidden quality costs. Examples of the costs due to poor quality or failure to meet the absolute conformance standard are rework, warranty repair or replacement, additional production costs, and loss on disposal. The hidden quality losses include customer dissatisfaction, loss of future business, loss of market share, additional engineering costs, additional management costs, and additional inventory. The exact nature of the loss function for different quality characteristics can differ.

Quality Loss Function

Taguchi believes that a quadratic function provides a good approximation of losses. Losses increase at twice the rate of deviations from the target value; larger deviations from target cause increasingly larger losses. A general expression of the loss function, $L(x)$, for a quality characteristic of a product or service with the observed value of x is

$$L(x) = k(x - T)^2$$

where: x = an observed value of the quality characteristic
T = the target value of the quality characteristic
k = the cost coefficient, determined by the firm's failure costs

k is a constant that is estimated based on the total production and service costs and hidden costs to the firm due to deviation of the quality characteristic from the target value. The value of k for a quality characteristic can be determined using this relationship:

$$k = \frac{\text{Total quality cost}}{(\text{Tolerance allowed})^2}$$

Say, for example, that a firm has determined that no customer will accept sheet metal deviating more than 0.05 inch from the target value in thickness, that the target thickness is 0.5 inch, and that the cost to the firm is $5,000 for each rejection by a customer. The $5,000 cost to the firm includes repair or replacement, processing, service costs, and other costs due to customer dissatisfaction. Then

$$k = \frac{\$5,000}{0.05^2}$$

$$k = \$2,000,000$$

If the actual thickness of a unit is 0.47, then the estimated total loss for the unit is

$$L(0.47) = \$2,000,000(0.47 - 0.5)^2 = \$1,800$$

If, however, the thickness is 0.46, then the estimated total loss from the deviation increases to $3,200.

$$L(0.46) = \$2,000,000(0.46 - 0.5)^2 = \$3,200$$

Total Loss and Average Loss

The loss just calculated is the loss from having one unit with the observed quality characteristic. The total loss for all the units manufactured during a period is the sum of the losses for each unit that varied from the standard.

Alternatively, the total loss due to variations in the quality characteristic can be determined by multiplying the average loss per unit by the total number of units manufactured. The average loss per unit is the expected loss due to variations in the quality characteristic. Exhibit 6–6 shows the results of operations in two plants identified as A and B.

Exhibit 6–6	Total Quality Loss					
x Measured Thickness	L(x) Quality Loss	Plant A Probability	Weighted Loss	Plant B Probability	Weighted Loss
0.43	$9,800	0	$ 0	0.02	$196
0.46	3,200	0.20	640	0.03	96
0.48	800	0.20	160	0.15	120
0.50	0	0.20	0	0.60	0
0.52	800	0.20	160	0.15	120
0.54	3,200	0.20	640	0.03	96
0.57	9,800	0	0	0.02	196
Expected loss			$1,600		$824

The output from plant A spreads equally over the range from 0.46 to 0.54 with no unit falling outside the tolerance limits. The output from plant B concentrates near the specified target value, but not all units lie within the tolerance limits.

Albright and Roth show that the expected, or average, loss per unit can be determined using variance and the square of the mean deviation from the target value as follows:[20]

$$EL(x) = k(\sigma^2 + D^2)$$

where:

$EL(x)$ = expected or average loss for quality characteristic x
σ^2 = variance of the variation about the target value[21]
D = the deviation of the mean value of the quality characteristic from the target, or $D = \bar{x} -$ Target value

The variance is 0.0008 for plant A[22] and 0.000412 for plant B. The value of D is 0 for both plants. Thus,

Plant A: $EL(x) = \$2,000,000(0.0008 + 0) = \$1,600$
Plant B: $EL(x) = \$2,000,000(0.000412 + 0) = \$824$

Notice the similarity in the quality characteristic between plant A and those observed in the Sony plant in San Diego: all units are within the specified tolerance limits and spread somewhat evenly between the specified tolerance limits. The quality characteristic of plant B is similar to those observed in the Sony plant in Japan: not all units lie within the tolerance limit, but most units cluster around the target value. Some units, however, fall outside the tolerance limits. Plant B, like the Sony plant in Japan, incurs a smaller average cost per unit. Even though all units of plant A

---

[20] Albright and Roth, "The Measurement of Quality Costs," p. 23.

[21] Variance, σ^2, is computed as follows:

$$\sigma^2 = \Sigma(x - \bar{x})^2 f(x)$$

where, x = quality characteristic, e.g. measured thickness in Exhibit 6–6.

$\bar{x}$ = mean value of quality characteristics, $\bar{x} = \Sigma x f(x)$

$f(x)$ = probability for observing quality characteristics, x, each value of $f(x)$ lies between 0 and 1, and all value of $f(x)$ sum to 1.

[22] For plant A,

$\bar{x} = \Sigma x f(x) = 0.46 \times 0.20 + 0.48 \times 0.20 + 0.50 \times 0.20 + 0.52 \times 0.20 + 0.54 \times 0.20 = 0.50$

and, $\sigma^2 = (0.46 - 0.50)^2 \times 0.20 + (0.48 - 0.50)^2 \times 0.20 + (0.50 - 0.50)^2 \times 0.20 + (0.52 - 0.50)^2 \times 0.20$
$+ (0.54 - 0.50)^2 \times 0.20 = 0.0008$

are within the tolerance limits while some units of plant B are outside the limits, plant B has a much lower expected loss than that of plant A. The firm can expect a lower cost for plant B than for plant A.

Using Quality Loss Function for Tolerance Determination

Another use of the Taguchi quality loss function is to set tolerances for an operation. Assume that in the sheet metal example, the cost to the firm is only $300 if the firm repairs the product that failed before shipping. The firm can determine the tolerances as follows:

$$\$300 = \$2,000,000(\text{tolerance})^2$$

Solve the equation,

$$\text{Tolerance} = 0.0122$$

Because it is less expensive to rework or repair before shipment, the specification should be set at 0.5 ±0.0122.

Alternatively, the tolerance can be determined as shown below.

$$\text{Tolerance} = T_0\sqrt{C_1/C_2}$$

where, T_0 = current (or customer) tolerance

C_2 = manufacturer's cost when the product failed to meet customer's specification

C_1 = manufacturer's cost to rework or scrap the unit before shipping

For example, in the example above the external failure cost for the metal manufacturer expects, or C_2, is $5,000; the cost to the firm, or C_1, is $300 if the firm repairs, reworks, or scraps the defective unit before shipping; and the customer's tolerance is 0.05. The firm should then set the tolerance at,

$$\text{Tolerance} = \$0.05\sqrt{\$300/\$5,000} = 0.0122$$

LEARNING OBJECTIVE 3▶

Identify four major categories of quality costs.

Costs of quality are costs of activities associated with the prevention, identification, repair, and rectification of poor quality and opportunity costs from lost production time and sales as a result of poor quality.

COSTS OF QUALITY

Costs of quality are costs of activities associated with the prevention, identification, repair, and rectification of poor quality and opportunity costs from lost production time and sales as a result of poor quality. Traditionally, quality costs had been limited to the costs of inspections and testing of finished units. Other costs of poor quality were included as overhead and not identified as quality costs.

Firms have discovered that in addition to manufacturing costs, quality costs include costs associated with supporting functions such as product design, purchasing, public relations, and customer services. Joseph Juran classifies costs of quality into four categories: prevention, appraisal, internal failure, and external failure. A main criterion in Juran's classification of quality costs is the time when quality costs are incurred. Exhibit 6–7 illustrates the components of quality costs.

Quality Is Free

Quality is not only free, but also helps firms make a profit. Every penny a company does not spend on doing things wrong, over, or instead of, becomes a penny right on its bottom line. In these days of "who knows what is going to happen to our business tomorrow," there are not many ways left to increase profits. If managers concentrate on making quality products or services, they can probably increase the firm's profit by an amount equal to 5 to 10 percent of sales. That is a lot of money for free.

Source: Philip Crosby, *Quality Is Free* (New York: McGraw-Hill, 1979).

Exhibit 6–7	**Components of Quality Costs**

Prevention Cost	**Appraisal Cost**
Training	Raw materials inspection
Instructor fees	Work-in-process inspection
Training equipment	Finished goods inspection
Tuition for external training	Test equipment
Training wages and salaries	Acquisition
Planning and execution	Salaries and wages
Salaries	Maintenance
Cost of preventive equipment	**External Failure Cost**
Cost of meetings	Sales returns and allowance due to quality deficiency
Promotion	Warranty cost
Awards	Contribution margin of cancelled sales orders due to quality deficiency
Printing	Contribution margin of lost sales orders due to perceived unsatisfactory quality
Product redesign	
Process improvement	
Quality circle	
Internal Failure Cost	
Scrap	
Rework	
Loss due to downgrades	
Reinspection costs	
Loss due to work interruptions	

Prevention Costs

Prevention costs are expenditures incurred to keep quality defects from occurring. Prevention costs include the following:

- **Quality training costs.** Expenditures for internal and external training programs for employees to ensure proper manufacturing, delivering, and servicing of products and services and to improve quality. These costs include salaries and wages for time spent in training, instruction costs, clerical staff expenses and miscellaneous supplies, and costs expended to prepare handbooks and instructional manuals.

- **Quality planning costs.** Wages and overhead for quality planning and quality circles, new procedure designs, new equipment designs to enhance quality, reliability studies, and supplier evaluations.

- **Equipment maintenance costs.** Costs incurred to install, calibrate, maintain, repair, and inspect production instruments, processes, and systems.

- **Supplier assurance costs.** Costs incurred to ensure deliveries of materials, components, and services that meet the firm's quality standards including selection, evaluation, and training of suppliers to conform with the requirements of TQM.

- **Information systems costs.** Costs expended for developing data requirements and measurement, auditing, and reporting of quality.

- **Product redesign and process improvement.** Costs incurred to evaluate and improve product designs and operating processes to simplify manufacturing processes or to reduce or eliminate quality problems.

- **Quality circle.** Costs incurred to establish and operate quality control circles to identify quality problems and to offer solutions to improve the quality of products and services.

Prevention costs are costs incurred to keep quality defects from occurring.

Typically, as prevention costs increase, other costs of quality decrease. By far the best way a firm can spend its cost of quality money is to invest in preventive actions. Prevention costs eliminate or reduce quality problems and are likely the only value-added costs among costs of quality. Usually, prevention costs are voluntary or discretionary costs and are the most cost-effective way to improve quality.

Appraisal Costs

Appraisal (detection) costs are incurred in the measurement and analysis of data to ascertain whether products and services conform to specifications.

Appraisal (detection) costs are incurred in the measurement and analysis of data to find out whether products and services conform to specifications. These costs are incurred during production and prior to sales to ensure that materials, components, and work meet quality standards. Firms incur appraisal costs to identify defective items and to ensure that all units meet or exceed customer requirements. Incurring these costs does not reduce the errors or keep defects from happening again; it only detects defective units before they are delivered to customers. Appraisal costs include the following:

- **Test and inspection costs.** Costs incurred to test and inspect incoming materials, work in process, and finished goods or services.
- **Test equipment and instruments.** Expenditures incurred to acquire, operate, or maintain facilities, software, machinery, and instruments for testing or appraising the quality of products, services, or processes.
- **Quality audits.** Salaries and wages of all personnel involved in appraising the quality of products and services and other expenditures incurred during quality appraising.
- **Laboratory acceptance testing.**
- **Field evaluation and testing.**
- **Information costs.** Costs to prepare and verify quality reports.

Internal Failure Costs

Internal failure costs are incurred as a result of poor quality found through appraisal prior to delivery to customers.

Internal failure costs are incurred as a result of poor quality found through appraisal prior to delivery to customers. These costs are not value added and are never necessary. These are some internal failure costs:

- **Costs of corrective action.** Costs for time spent to find the cause of failure and to correct the problem.
- **Rework and scrap costs.** Materials, labor, and overhead costs for scrap, rework, and reinspection.
- **Process costs.** Costs expended to redesign the product or processes, unplanned machine downtime for adjustment, and lost production due to process interruption for repair or rework.
- **Expediting costs.** Costs incurred to expedite manufacturing operations due to time spent for repair or rework.
- **Reinspect and retest costs.** Salaries, wages, and expenses incurred during reinspection or retesting of reworked or repaired items.
- **Lost contributions due to increased demand on constraint resources.** Constraint resources spent on defective units increase cycle time and reduce total output. Contributions not earned from units not produced because of the unavailability of the constraint resources reduce the operating income of the firm.

External Failure Costs

External failure costs are incurred to rectify quality defects after unacceptable products or services reach the customer and lost profit opportunities caused by the unacceptable products or services delivered.

External failure costs are costs incurred to rectify quality defects after unacceptable products or services reach the customer and costs of profits lost from missed opportunities as a result of the unacceptable products or services delivered. These costs include the following:

- **Repair or replacement costs.** Repair or replacement of returned goods.
- **Costs to handle customer complaints and returns.** Salaries and administrative overhead for a customer service department; allowance or discount granted for poor quality and freight charges.
- **Product recall and product liability costs.** Administrative costs to handle product recalls, repairs, or replacements; legal costs; and settlements resulting from legal actions.
- **Lost sales due to unsatisfactory products and customer ill will.** Lost contribution margins on canceled orders, lost sales, and decreased market shares.
- **Costs to restore reputation.** Costs of marketing activities to minimize damages from tarnished reputation and to restore the firm's image and reputation.

External failure costs are non-value-added costs and are likely the most expensive costs among costs of quality. In many instances, the largest external failure costs to a firm are opportunity costs that are neither reported by nor available through the firm's accounting system. Without conscientious special efforts to seek out the information, the magnitude of external failure cost may go unnoticed.

The goal of measuring the cost of quality is to eliminate external failure costs, minimize appraisal and internal failure costs, and invest effectively in prevention costs.

Conformance and Nonconformance Costs

Quality expert Philip Crosby believes that there are no quality problems, only product design, materials, labor, and manufacturing problems that lead to poor quality. Crosby proposes that quality costs have two components: the price of conformance and the price of nonconformance.[23] Prevention and appraisal costs are **costs of conformance** because they are incurred to ensure that products or services meet customers' expectations. Internal failure costs and external failure costs are **costs of nonconformance.** They are costs incurred and opportunity costs because of rejection of products or services. The cost of quality is the sum of conformance and nonconformance costs.

Prevention costs are usually the lowest and the easiest among the four costs of quality for management to control. Internal and external failure costs are among the

> **Costs of conformance** are prevention costs and appraisal costs.
>
> **Costs of nonconformance** are internal failure costs and external failure costs.

How Much Does External Failure Cost?

Ford Motor Company unveiled the 2001 model of its best-selling sport-utility vehicle, the Ford Explorer, in late 2000. Yet, three months after the redesigned Explorer, which offers a host of new safety features, began rolling off the assembly line not a single one of the 5,000 built was in dealer showrooms. Instead, they were parked outside factories in St. Louis and Louisville while Ford engineers pored over them looking for defects. Jacques Nasser, CEO of the Ford Motor Company, ordered factory managers to hold off on shipping the new Explorer until engineers had the opportunity to catch any problems.

When asked by financial analysts to comment on the cost of delay and repairing defects, Nasser responded, "Pick a number. It is over $1 billion." The delay was expensive, but

Ford executives say the cost of fixing warranty claims later would be far higher. One defect caught by engineers was an internal steering-column switch that might have led motorists to start the engine in the "drive" position. Left uncorrected, this problem had the potential of resulting in big-time safety recalls. What was the root cause of the problem? It was traced to a supplier who used too much solder on a $1 circuit board. "When you get to the bottom of it, they are that trivial," says a company official of such glitches. "But when you let them escape, they are just huge."

Source: Muller, N., "Putting the Explorer under the Microscope" *Business Week,* February 12, 2001. p. 40.

---

[23] Philip B. Crosby, *Quality without Tears* (New York: McGraw-Hill, 1984), p. 86.

most expensive costs of quality, especially external failure costs. In a typical scenario, the cost of prevention may be $0.10 per unit, the cost of testing and replacing poor quality parts or components during production may be $5, the cost of reworking or reassembling may be $50, and the cost of field repair and other external costs may be $5,000.

External failure costs can be rather substantial. For instance, Firestone Tire Company was forced to recall and replace 6.5 million ATX tires in 2000. In the first two months of the recall, the firm spent more than $500 million of out-of-pocket cost and suffered sales decreases of more than 40 percent. The price of its stock fell to less than half of the value prior to the recall. With the damage to its reputation, lost prospective business, and the legal and liability costs in the years to come, the firm's future is, to say the least, not very bright. Although well-known for quality products for more than a century, some industry experts speculate that Firestone might not even survive this debacle, which could be attributed to a quality problem limited to only one of its many factories around the world.

Better prevention of poor quality clearly reduces all other costs of quality. With fewer problems in quality, less appraisal is needed because the products are made right the first time. Fewer defective units also reduce internal and external failure costs as repairs, rework, and recalls decrease. By spending more on prevention, companies spend less due to internal or external failures. The savings alone can be substantial. Meanwhile, the firm enjoys higher perceived values of its products, increased sales and market share, and improved earnings and returns on investments.

Theoretically, a firm with a completely successful prevention effort incurs neither appraisal costs nor internal or external failure costs. It is easier to *design* and *build* quality in rather than to *inspect* or *repair* quality in. Appraisal costs decrease as quality improves.[24] Nonconformance costs, however, decrease at a much faster rate than prevention costs increase.

REPORTING QUALITY COSTS

LEARNING OBJECTIVE 4▶

Prepare and interpret cost of quality reports.

The purpose of reporting quality cost is to make management aware of its magnitude and to provide a baseline against which the impact of quality improvement activities could be measured. Tasks for reporting quality costs include data definitions, identification of data sources, data collection, and preparation and distribution of quality cost reports.

Data Definition, Sources, and Collection

The first step in generating a quality cost report is to define quality cost categories and identify quality costs within each category. The preceding discussion described common quality cost categories; however, definitions of cost categories can vary among firms. Firms must clearly state operational definitions of all quality costs, and every member of the team needs to have a clear understanding of the firm's quality cost categories. One important step in identifying quality costs is to ask users and suppliers to identify specific costs incurred because of poor quality.

Ideally, each quality cost should have its own account so that quality cost information is readily observable, not buried in a myriad of accounts. These quality cost accounts then become the source of quality cost information.

Cost of Quality Report

A report on cost of quality is useful only if its recipients understand, accept, and can use the content of the report. Reports can be prepared in many ways. Each firm should

---

[24] One reason is that once suppliers have been tested, screened, and monitored, a firm spends much less time verifying compliance than it would otherwise.

select and design a reporting system that (1) can be integrated into its information system and (2) promotes TQM. Among considerations in establishing a quality cost report system are proper stratifications of quality cost reports by product line, department, plant, or division, and the time periods of the reports. Firms also often express costs of quality in percentages of net total sales.

A cost of quality matrix, as illustrated in Exhibit 6–8, is a convenient and useful tool in reporting quality costs. With columns for functions or departments and rows for categories of quality costs, a cost of quality matrix enables each department to identify and recognize the effects of its actions on the cost of quality and to pinpoint areas of high-quality costs. The matrix can contain dollar amounts (actual or estimate) or relative percentages of the amounts in a base period. The base period can be the amount in the first year of implementing the TQM program, preselected benchmark amounts, or other appropriate amounts that management decides to use for monitoring progress.

Analyzing Quality Costs in Formosa Plastics Group

Formosa Plastics Group developed an analytical program to evaluate its quality costs. In its corporate manual, the firm specifies these quality costs based on the ratio of

- Total quality cost to sales revenue and cost of goods sold.
- External failure cost to sales revenue.
- Total failure cost to sales revenue.

- Voluntary cost (prevention and appraisal costs) to sales revenue.
- Total quality cost to direct labor hours.
- Total quality cost to plant assets.

Source: Thomas P. Edmonds, Bor-Yi Tsay, and Wen-Wei Lin, "Analyzing Quality Costs," *Management Accounting,* November 1989, p. 29.

Exhibit 6–8 Cost of Quality Matrix

	Design Engineering	Purchasing	Production	Finance	Accounting	Other	Totals
Prevention costs							
Quality planning							
Training							
Other							
Appraisal costs							
Test and Inspect							
Instruments							
Other							
Internal failure costs							
Scrap							
Rework							
Other							
External failure costs							
Returns							
Recalls							
Other							
Totals							

Source: James R. Evans and William M. Lindsay, *The Management and Control of Quality,* 3rd ed. (New York: West Publishing Co., 1996), p. 303.

| **Exhibit 6–9** | **Cost of Quality Report** |

	Year 2		Year 0		Percent Change
Prevention Costs					
Training	$ 90,000		$ 20,000		350%
Quality planning	86,000		20,000		330
Other quality improvement	60,000		40,000		50
Supplier evaluation	40,000		30,000		33
Total	$ 276,000	3.07%	$ 110,000	1.38%	151
Appraisal Costs					
Testing	120,000		100,000		20
Quality performance measurement	100,000		80,000		25
Supplier monitoring	60,000		10,000		500
Customer surveys	30,000		10,000		200
Total	$ 310,000	3.44%	$ 200,000	2.5%	55
Internal Failure Costs					
Rework and reject	55,000		150,000		(63)
Reinspection and testing	35,000		30,000		(16)
Equipment failure	30,000		50,000		(40)
Downtime	20,000		50,000		(60)
Total	$ 140,000	1.56%	$ 280,000	3.5%	(50)
External Failure Costs					
Product liability insurance	70,000		250,000		(72)
Warranty repairs	100,000		120,000		(17)
Customer losses (estimated)	600,000		1,400,000		(57)
Total	$ 770,000	8.56%	$1,770,000	22.13%	(56)
Total quality costs	$1,496,000	16.62%	$2,360,000	29.50%	(37)
Total Sales	$9,000,000	100%	$8,000,000	100%	

Illustration of a Cost of Quality Report

Exhibit 6–9 illustrates a cost of quality report.[25] Bally Company is a small midwestern manufacturing company with annual sales of approximately $50 million. The firm operates in a highly competitive environment and has been experiencing increasing cost and quality pressures from new and existing competitors. The report shows that the external failure costs for such items as warranty claims, customer dissatisfaction, and market share loss accounted for 75 percent of the total cost of quality in year 0.

To be competitive and to regain market shares, Bally began a corporatewide three-year TQM process. The firm started with substantial increases in prevention and appraisal expenditures. The investment started to pay off in year 2. The internal failure, external failure, and total quality costs have all decreased.

Exhibit 6–9 compares the current year's quality costs to those of a base year. Alternative bases for comparisons can be the budgeted amounts, flexible budget costs, or long-range goals. A cost of quality report also should include output measures whenever possible.

PROBLEM FINDING

LEARNING OBJECTIVE 5▶

Describe methods commonly used to identify significant quality problems and their causes.

To achieve total quality management, firms need to identify and understand truly significant quality problems when they occur. Many helpful tools to identify significant quality problems are available, including control charts, histograms, Pareto diagrams,

---

[25]   Adapted from *IMA Statement No. 4R*.

brainstorming, and cause-and-effect diagrams. These tools are most effective if management accountants take a proactive role throughout the process.

Control Charts

A **control chart** plots successive observations of an operation taken at constant intervals to determine whether all observations fall within the specified range for the operation. The operation can be a machine, workstation, individual worker, work cell, part, or process that affects quality. Intervals can be time periods, batches, production runs, or other demarcations of the operation.

A typical control chart has a horizontal axis representing time intervals, batch numbers, or production runs, and a vertical axis denoting a measure of conformance to the quality specification. The vertical measure also has a specified allowable range of variations, which are referred to as *upper* and *lower limits*, respectively. Exhibit 6–10 contains control charts for manufacturing 1/8-inch drill bits in three workstations.

Say that a firm has determined that all drill bits must be within 0.0005 inch of the specified diameter. All units from workstation A are within the specified range (±0.0005"), and no further investigation is necessary. Three units from workstation B are outside the specified range and suggest out-of-control occurrences. Management should investigate the cause of the aberration to prevent further failure of the quality standard. Although all units manufactured by workstation C are within the specified range acceptable to the firm, management may want to launch an investigation

A **control chart** plots successive observations of an operation taken at constant intervals.

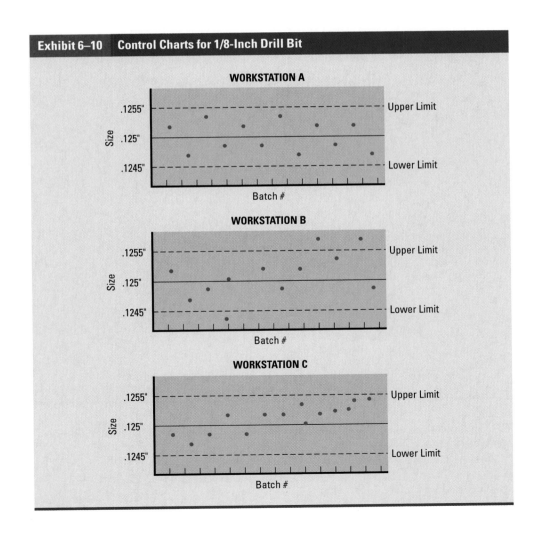

Exhibit 6–10 Control Charts for 1/8-Inch Drill Bit

because the trend suggests that in the future, the operation will most likely produce drill bits outside the specified range if the trend continues.[26]

A process is in *statistical control* if no sample observation is outside the established limits, all observations are randomly distributed with no apparent patterns or runs, and an approximately equal number of observations are above and below the center line with most points nearing the center line. A process may be out of control if the observations show trends, cycles, clusters, or sudden shifts hugging the center line or the control limits. Many sophisticated statistical techniques are available to help determine whether a process is in or out of control.[27]

Control charts are useful in establishing a state of statistical control, monitoring processes, and identifying causes of quality variations. Posting control charts in a common area facilitates early detection of quality problems, promotes awareness of workers on the quality status of their products or services, and encourages active participation in efforts to raise quality. Ittner and Larcker find that firms in the computer industry that use quality control devices such as control charts have higher performance than firms not using them.[28]

Histogram

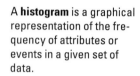

A **histogram** is a graphical representation of the frequency of attributes or events in a given set of data.

A **histogram** is a graphical representation of the frequency of attributes or events in a given set of data. Patterns or variations that are often difficult to see in a set of numbers become clear in a histogram. Exhibit 6–11 contains a histogram of factors that contribute to the quality problems identified by a firm that makes chocolate mousse.

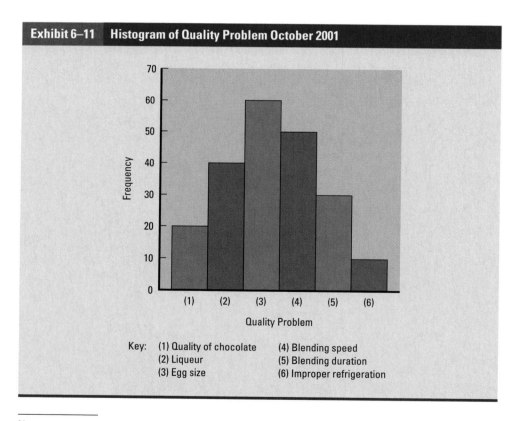

Exhibit 6–11   Histogram of Quality Problem October 2001

Key: (1) Quality of chocolate   (4) Blending speed
       (2) Liqueur   (5) Blending duration
       (3) Egg size   (6) Improper refrigeration

---

[26] Using it in this manner, the control chart is often referred to as a *run chart*. A run chart shows the trend of observations over time.

[27] Evans and Lindsay, *The Management and Control of Quality*, pp. 697–98.

[28] Chris Ittner and David Larcker, "The Performance Effects of Process Management Techniques," *Management Science*, 1997, pp 522–34.

The firm has experienced uneven quality in one line of chocolate mousse. The firm identifies six factors: substandard chocolate, improper liqueur mixture, uneven egg size, uneven blending speed, variant blending time, and improper refrigeration after production. It identified 210 batches as having poor quality. The histogram in Exhibit 6–11 suggests that variations in egg size may be the largest contributor to the quality problem, followed by uneven speed in blending ingredients.

Pareto Diagram

A **Pareto diagram** is a histogram of factors contributing to the quality problem, ordered from the most to the least frequent. Joseph Juran observed in the 1950s that a few causes usually account for most of the quality problems, thus the name Pareto.[29] In Exhibit 6–12 we present a Pareto diagram of the chocolate mousse quality problem.

A Pareto diagram not only ranks the relative size of quality problems but also provides a useful visual aid. Often we also draw a cumulative curve as shown in Exhibit 6–12. Using a Pareto diagram, management can separate the few major causes of quality problems from the many trivial ones and identify areas that contribute most of the quality problems. Then management can focus its efforts on areas that are likely to have the greatest amount of quality improvement. For example, the cumulative line in Exhibit 6–12 shows that improper egg size and erratic blending speed account for 110 quality problems in manufacturing the chocolate mousse. Pareto diagrams are especially useful in making an initial analysis of quality problems identified by a control chart as being outside the specified range.

A **Pareto diagram** is a histogram of the frequency of factors contributing to the quality problem, ordered from the most to the least frequent.

Exhibit 6–12	Pareto Diagram of Quality Problem October 2001

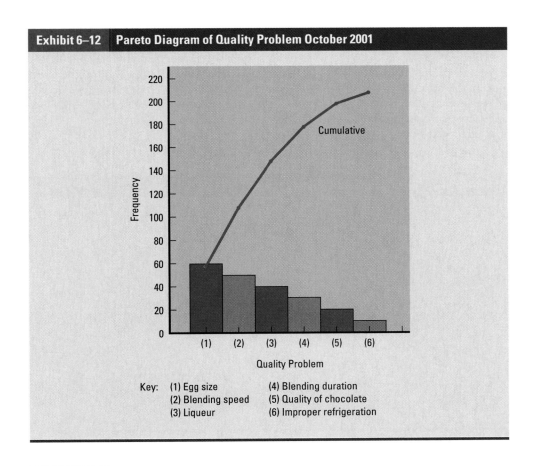

Key: (1) Egg size   (4) Blending duration
      (2) Blending speed   (5) Quality of chocolate
      (3) Liqueur   (6) Improper refrigeration

---

[29] Vilfredo Pareto, a nineteenth-century Italian economist, observed that 80 percent of the wealth in Milan was owned by 20 percent of its residents.

Brainstorming

The ancient Greeks used brainstorming, which was revived by Alex Osborn in the 1940s, as a way to elicit ideas from a group of people in a short time.[30] Brainstorming can identify problems, find causes of a problem, and develop a solution to a quality problem.

A relaxed yet structured group session with members from a variety of backgrounds and responsibilities is conducive to effective brainstorming. Some basic rules for productive brainstorming follow:

1. No criticism of anyone's ideas by word or by gesture.
2. Once an idea has been put forth, there should be no further discussion of that idea during the session, except for clarification.
3. No idea is dumb or silly.
4. Each team member can introduce only one idea at a time.
5. Until most of the members have presented an idea, no member can introduce more than one idea.
6. No single individual should dominate the session.
7. No accusations of blame should occur during the session.[31]

Cause-and-Effect Diagram

The cause-and-effect, or Ishikawa, diagram organizes a chain of causes and effects to sort out root causes and identify relationships between causes and effects. Karou Ishikawa discovered that the number of factors which could influence a process or lead to a problem overwhelmed most plant personnel. To cope with myriad factors, in 1943 he developed cause-and-effect diagrams as an organizing aid.[32] Because of its shape, a fishbone diagram is another name for this diagram.

A cause-and-effect or fishbone diagram consists of a spine, ribs, and bones. At the right end of the horizontal spine is the quality problem at hand. The spine itself connects causes to the effect, the quality problem. Each branch or rib pointing into the spine describes a main cause of the problem. Bones pointing to each rib are contributing factors to the cause. Look at Exhibit 6–13 to see the general structure of a cause-and-effect diagram.

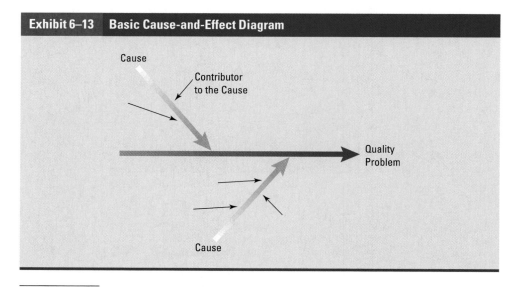

Exhibit 6–13   Basic Cause-and-Effect Diagram

[30] A. F. Osborn, *Applied Imagination* (New York: Scribner's, 1963).

[31] Howard Gitlow, Alan Oppenheim, and Rosa Oppenheim, *Quality Management* (Burr Ridge, Ill.: Irwin, 1995), p. 309.

[32] Karou Ishikawa, *Guides to Quality Control*, 2nd ed. (Tokyo: Asian Productivity Organization, 1986).

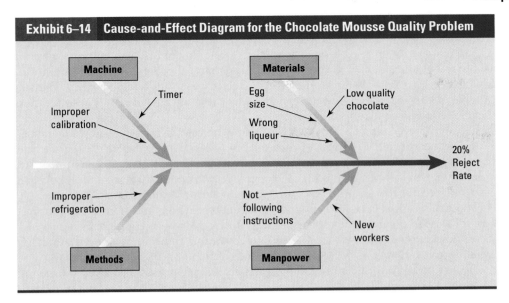

Exhibit 6–14   Cause-and-Effect Diagram for the Chocolate Mousse Quality Problem

Typical main causes for quality problems in manufacturing operations are

- Machines
- Materials
- Methods
- Manpower

Some users refer to the four main categories as *4M*. In Exhibit 6–14, you can see a cause-and-effect diagram for the quality problems in the manufacturing of chocolate mousse.

The two basic types of cause-and-effect diagrams are *dispersion analysis* and *process classification*. A dispersion analysis identifies and classifies causes for a specific quality problem (as previously illustrated for the chocolate mousse problem). A process classification diagram identifies key factors that may have contributed to the poor quality at each step of the process or flow. A process analysis is used when a series of events, steps, or processes creates a problem and it is not clear which one is the major cause of the problem.

TOTAL QUALITY MANAGEMENT IN SERVICE ORGANIZATIONS

◀**LEARNING OBJECTIVE 6**

Identify distinct characteristics of total quality management in service organizations.

Service is an integral part of all corporations and organizations. Service firms and organizations such as law firms, cleaning services, beauty shops, and hospitals provide services to customers or clients. Quality of service is of the utmost importance to service firms or organizations. After all, they rely on services to generate most or all of their revenues. Quality of service is also very important to merchandising or manufacturing corporations. Merchandising and manufacturing firms have contacts with customers both before and after the sale. Even though the cost of providing quality services is usually only a fraction of the total cost in a merchandising or manufacturing firm, quality of service can have significant effects on retaining customers and attracting new ones. A customer unhappy with the quality of service most likely will not come back. A customer who received a rude treatment by a firm's receptionist may take the business elsewhere. A customer not satisfied with the help of a customer service representative could look for alternative sources of supply next time. As Peter F. Drucker points out for service jobs in merchandising or manufacturing firms, "Quality is a condition and a restraint. It is external rather than in itself performance. It has to be built into the process."[33] Reichheld and Sasser report that companies can

---

[33]   Peter F. Drucker, *Managing for the Future* (New York: Truman Tolby Book, 1993), p. 105.

increase their profits by almost 100 percent if they retain just 5 percent more of their customers.[34]

Services are intangible outputs. A good service exists mostly in a customer's mind. While the goal in manufacturing is uniformity, the goal of services is customization. Medical doctors tailor their services to the need of each individual patient. Barbers provide quality service if they cut hair the way their customers want. Customization makes setting specifications difficult.

Furthermore, a service is not complete until the customer receives it. A manufacturing firm can recall a product of poor quality to repair or replace it. A service firm that rendered poor-quality service often can offer only apologies or reparations. An automaker, for example, can recall cars to replace a defective brake system. Rarely can a surgeon recall the patient to undo an operation wrongly executed.

These differences between service and manufacturing organizations make it necessary for service organizations to ensure that only qualified personnel can render services, that all personnel receive continuous education and training, and that quality is built into every step of the services provided to clients and customers.

Quality costs for services also include prevention and appraisal, as well as internal failure and external failure costs. However, the likely astronomical cost of service failures and the irreversibility of service outputs add the importance of prevention in total quality management of services.

Total Quality Management and Public Schools

The business world has known about total quality management (TQM) for years and has witnessed its successful implementation by Japanese companies. This popular business technique, designed to create and instill quality in companies' products and services, is now transcending the border from the business world into the educational arena. At Brooklyn's George Westinghouse Vocational & Technical High School, for example, students are participating in an educational experiment learning and using TQM. With help from corporate sponsors such as Ricoh, IBM, and Xerox, students use TQM principles in their electronics classes (finishing repairs before deadlines and with few mistakes) and receive feedback from the companies on their work. The school administration also uses TQM in its efforts to improve attendance and parental involvement.

Although there are differences between business and education, educators are applying TQM principles to their environment—and with initial success. Westinghouse is not alone in its use of TQM for reform. The number of U.S. public school districts using TQM has increased at a rapid pace in the last few years. The schools adopt a variety of TQM principles to create improvements specific to their particular needs. For example, in keeping with TQM's emphasis on gathering data to identify and help solve problems, Westinghouse teachers and administrators monitor attendance and test scores to pinpoint problems. They then use the information to brainstorm with students to resolve truancy and classroom failures. Other TQM principles at work at Westinghouse include using scatter diagrams to illustrate the relationship between two variables (e.g., how skipping homework leads to poor test grades), benchmarking (using a survey approach developed by Xerox to trace low attendance at parent-teacher events to scheduling conflicts);

and cause-and-effect diagrams (using prompter students to make wake-up calls to classmates, thus decreasing tardiness).

School officials in Hillsborough County, Florida, implement a districtwide quality improvement mission. "Pinellas went 100 percent with a quality boot camp and invested an incredible amount of money," said Jodie Lamb, supervisor for staff development. "We wanted to just focus on the characteristics of a quality organization, focusing on building relationships, helping folks feel empowered, increasing their level of trust in the organization." Faculty and staff members established mission statements, values, and school rules. Principals and teachers serve as trainers.

TQM is not just practiced by teachers and administrators. Student-developed vision and mission statements, goals, and objectives are pinned to classroom bulletin boards and taped to walls. Even prekindergarten teachers trained at mandatory "quality boot camps" talk with children about why they are in school and what it means to be a high-performing student. "Businesses have been asking education to produce workers that are team players, problem solvers that can collaborate together," Sue Boyd, principal at Azalea Elementary School, the recipient of 2000 Governor's Sterling Award on quality education, said. "What this actually means is students are trained in that model. It's not just one child hitting the mark as a student. It extends beyond the classroom into the community, how we all get to the mark of excellence performance."

Sources: For further reading, see "Total Quality Management: Now, It's a Class Act," *Business Week,* October 31, 1994; and Pamela G. Leavy, "Total Quality Management Stressed in Public Schools," *The Tampa Bay Business Journal,* September 15, 2000, p. 22.

---

[34] Frederick F. Reichheld and W. Earl Sasser, Jr., "Zero Defections: Quality Comes to Services," *Harvard Business Review,* September–October 1990, pp. 105–12.

TOTAL QUALITY AND PRODUCTIVITY

A common misconception is that improvements in quality decrease productivity. The reasoning behind this misconception is that quality improvement requires additional input efforts. Because productivity measures the relationship between output and input resources, an effort that requires additional input resources with no increase in output decreases productivity. Managers could believe that materials, labor-hours, and other resources spent on rework, repair, or other activities to improve quality consume additional resources with no increase in output.

◀**LEARNING OBJECTIVE 7**

Explain the relationships between total quality management and productivity.

Studies have shown, however, that improvements in quality lead to *increases* in productivity.[35] The belief that quality improvement and productivity have an inverse relationship could have grown out of the misperception that all units, once manufactured, are good outputs, whatever the quality or required subsequent spending to rectify poor-quality products. A firm's accounting system may not include resources expended on rework or repair in the manufacturing cost of the unit. Rather, repair or rework costs are treated as manufacturing overheads to be shared by all products and units. The term *hidden factory* sometimes refers to the use of facilities and resources for repairs, rework, retests, and other remedial work for poor-quality products. They are hidden because these accounts are often included as part of the total manufacturing overhead shared by all.

Furthermore, many actions or decisions taken to achieve total quality management improve productivity. A simple and easy-to-make product design decreases defects and, at the same time, increases productivity. A decision to streamline the manufacturing process to reduce the chance for error also can increase productivity because it eliminates unnecessary operations.

In their study, Leonard and Sasser found many examples of quality improvement leading to increased productivity, including these:

- Installation of a new clean room to reduce contaminants on printed circuit boards increased output by almost 35 percent.

- Elimination of rework stations at one manufacturing factory for televisions forced workers to find and solve their own quality problems. As a result, the firm experienced an increase in production rates per direct labor-hour. The firm also saved money on rework and rework stations.

- Efforts to do it right the first time and every time by a firm increase not only its manufacturing productivity but also its sales productivity. Sales personnel no longer have to spend time processing returned defective products.[36]

Total Quality Management and Activity-Based Costing

An activity-based accounting system is ideally suited to total quality management. An activity-based costing/activity-based management system facilitates implementation of TQM in two ways. First, it identifies cost with activities and thus increases the visibility of costs of quality. Costs of activities that are results of poor quality become clear to the organization. Traditional accounting systems, in contrast, focus on organizational functions such as production, sales, and administrations. Management is likely not aware of the cost of quality without undertaking a special effort to gather data pertaining to cost of quality.

Second, organizations that use an ABC/ABM system most likely already have much of the cost information needed to implement TQM. A firm with a good ABC/ABM system in place needs only to identify costs and activities relating to costs of quality and quality improvement and classify these costs according to the cost of

[35] Frank S. Leonard and W. Earl Sasser, "The Incline of Quality," *Harvard Business Review*, September–October 1982, pp. 163–71; and Y. K. Shetty, "Corporate Response to Productivity Challenges," *National Productivity Review*, Winter 1984–85, pp. 7–14.

[36] Leonard and Sasser, "The Incline of Quality," pp. 163–71.

quality categories that the firm chooses to use. Firms with traditional accounting systems require additional analyses to identify and measure cost of quality and to prepare cost of quality-reports. Additional tasks and costs of obtaining the necessary cost measures can discourage management from implementing TQM.

Just-in-Time Systems and Total Quality Management

A just-in-time system necessitates a strong emphasis on quality. Defective materials, parts, or components most certainly bring production to grinding halts for JIT firms that operate with no inventory. These firms expect the required materials, parts, or components to be delivered when the processes expect them. If materials or components from upstream suppliers or departments are of low quality, the downstream departments must interrupt their work either to spend time processing them or to wait for new materials or components that meet the quality specifications to arrive. Delays or interruptions defeat JIT systems. To achieve a true JIT operation, a company strongly depends on its suppliers' ability to provide defect-free parts. A company must work closely with its suppliers so that all purchased materials and components meet its quality standard.

THE CHALLENGE OF TOTAL QUALITY MANAGEMENT TO MANAGEMENT ACCOUNTANTS

LEARNING OBJECTIVE 8▶

Describe the role of management accountants in total quality management and the challenges they face.

The role of management accountants in total quality management includes gathering all relevant quality information, participating actively in all phases of the quality program, and reviewing and disseminating quality cost reports. A quality management system developed without active involvement of management accountants could fail to realize its potential. Too often a firm includes quality costs in diverse and scattered accounts for products, marketing, engineering, and services. The impact of these costs and benefits disappears as the firm allocates account balances. As a result, the firm pays scant attention to quality costs and quality results on financial performance.

With their training and expertise in analyzing, measuring, and reporting information, management accountants can help design and conduct comprehensive quality information-gathering, measurement, and reporting systems. Management accountants can improve total quality management further by integrating the quality cost information into the existing management reporting and measurement systems. This integration facilitates the constant and continuous attention to improving quality by making measurement, reporting, and evaluation of quality a regular, routine activity rather than a special effort that will be dropped when the fad is over. A management accountant should be completely involved in all quality improvement activities of the enterprise. The IMA described these activities of an involved management accountant:

- Ensure full representation of management accountants on the main quality control committees and quality improvement teams.
- Make the company fully aware of the competitive benchmarks, competitive gaps, customers' retention rate, and cost of quality.
- Participate actively in identifying areas of greatest quality improvement opportunities and needs.
- Develop quality measures to monitor and assess ongoing progress toward quality goals.
- Be involved closely in vendor-rating decisions.
- Review and evaluate quality control effectiveness and the value of training courses for quality control personnel and human resources staff.
- Gather and continually review scrap and recovery costs.[37]

---

[37] *IMA Statement No. 4R*, p. 9.

To meet the challenges of total quality management, management accountants must have a clear understanding of TQM methodology. They must be able to design, create, or modify information systems that measure and monitor quality and evaluate progress toward total quality as expected of each organizational unit and of the total enterprise. The following are some of the tasks:

- Determine which accounts contain significant data for TQM.
- Reorganize and restructure the existing accounting system to provide accurate and complete quality cost data.
- Revise the chart of accounts to reflect each quality cost category.

A traditional accounting system often fails to associate costs with activities. As a result, quality teams do not have the necessary information readily available to focus on quality problems. A management accountant needs to relate quality costs to activities so that quality teams can focus their efforts appropriately to ensure the success of the TQM effort. One approach is to apply techniques from activity-based costing to TQM so that cost drivers for quality costs are identified clearly (see Chapter 4).

Content of cost of quality reports can vary widely, depending on the organization and its operating characteristics. Management accountants need to ensure that the measurement and reporting process meets the following criteria:

- Addresses the need of the internal customers.
- Includes all relevant cost of quality measures including both financial and non-financial measures.
- Adjusts measures to reflect quality and business challenges.
- Adapts measures as the need changes.
- Is simple and easy to use, execute, and monitor.
- Provides fast and timely feedback to users and managers.
- Fosters improvement rather than just monitoring.
- Motivates and challenges team members to strive for the highest quality gains.[38]

SUMMARY

In today's global competition, with short product life cycles and rapidly changing technologies and consumer tastes, firms can sustain long-term survival and profitability only by manufacturing quality products and rendering quality services.

Providing quality is the best strategy for maintaining long-term profitability. Businesses offering quality products and services usually have large market shares; studies show that quality is positively and significantly related to a higher return on investment.

A quality product or service meets or exceeds a customer's expectations at a price the customer is willing to pay. To achieve quality products or services, many firms adopt *total quality management,* which requires continuous efforts by everyone in an organization to understand, meet, and exceed the expectations of both internal and external customers.

Approaches to conform to quality specifications include goalpost or zero-defect conformance, which meets the quality standard within the specified range of the target, and absolute or robust quality conformance, which meets the specification exactly at the target value.

Four common categories for quality costs are prevention, appraisal, internal failure, and external failure. Prevention and appraisal costs are costs of conformance; and internal and external failure costs are costs of nonconformance.

---

[38] Ibid., p. 31.

Cost of quality reports should enable each department to identify and recognize the effects of its actions on the cost of quality and to pinpoint areas of high-quality costs. In generating a quality cost report, accountants define quality cost categories and identify all quality costs within each category. Ideally, each quality cost should have its own account so that its information is not buried in, or aggregated with, other accounts.

Tools that identify quality problems and are used to find solutions to those problems include control charts, histograms, Pareto diagrams, brainstorming, and cause-and-effect (fishbone or Ishikawa) diagrams. A control chart is a graph that depicts successive observations of an operation taken at constant intervals; it is often used to identify or discover quality problems. Both histograms and Pareto diagrams depict graphically the frequency of quality problems or observations. A Pareto diagram orders quality problems from the largest to the smallest. Brainstorming is a useful way to elicit ideas in identifying quality problems, finding causes of a quality problem, or developing solutions to a quality problem. The cause-and-effect (fishbone or Ishikawa) diagram graphically represents a chain of causes and effects that lead to a quality problem. It is a useful way to sort out root causes and to identify relationships between causes or factors and the quality problem.

Organizations with quality services conform their performance standards with the needs and requirements of their customers. Although quality costs for a service organization or function include prevention, appraisal, internal failure, and external failure costs, service organizations pay the most attention to training and building quality into every step of service rendered because poor quality service usually cannot be recalled or replaced.

Improved quality increases productivity. Evidence has shown that the common misconception of inverse relationships between quality improvement and productivity is a result of including all units, regardless of quality, as good output.

Management accountants, with training and expertise in analyzing, measuring, and reporting information, can help design and conduct comprehensive quality information gathering, measurement, and reporting.

KEY WORDS

Absolute quality conformance   208
Appraisal costs   214
Control chart   219
Costs of conformance   215
Costs of nonconformance   215
Costs of quality   212
External failure costs   214
Goalpost conformance (zero-defects conformance)   207
Histogram   220
Internal failure costs   214
ISO 9000   198
Pareto diagram   221
Prevention costs   213
Quality   201
Quality circle   204
Taguchi quality loss function   209

COMMENTS ON COST MANAGEMENT IN ACTION

To Implement TQM, Get a Black Belt

Companies such as General Electric, Weyerhauser, and Allied Signal are training their managers in quality management. The program is designed for business unit managers, quality managers, and engineers. First used by Motorola in 1986, these training programs provide an intense curriculum in measurement and statistical tools, cost management, team-building, and leadership. Successful candidates are awarded a green belt after months of training, which prepares them to lead their business units to Six Sigma goals in quality defects. Black belt and master black belt status is available for those who have more intensive training.

The key idea is to integrate Six Sigma thinking throughout the organization, and to provide the training so that local managers will be able to lead their units to success. Some firms have even extended the idea to include their business partners. For example, Cascade DieCasting in High Point, N.C., sent four of its managers off for Six Sigma training at the request of a major customer, Black and Decker.

Source: "This Kind of Black Belt Can Help You Score Some Points at Work," by Hal Lancaster, *The Wall Street Journal*, September 14, 1999, pB1.

SELF-STUDY PROBLEMS

(For solution, please turn to the end of the chapter.)

1. Cost of Quality Improvement

An automobile manufacturer plans to spend $1 billion to improve the quality of a new model. The manufacturer expects the quality improvement program to eliminate the need for recall and reduce the costs for warranty repairs. The firm's experience had been, on average, 1.5 recalls for each new model at the cost of $300 per vehicle per recall. The average cost per recall, if one is needed is expected to increase by 10 percent for the new model. Costs for other warranty repairs will decrease from $200 to $80 per unit. Sales of the new model were expected to be 400,000 units without the quality improvement program. The firm believes that the well-publicized quality improvement program will increase the total sales to 650,000 units. If there is a profit of $5,000 per unit, is the $1 billion expenditure justified?

2. Taguchi Quality Loss Function

Marlon Audio Company manufactures cassette tapes. The desired speed of its model SF2000 is 2 inches per second. Any deviation from this value distorts pitch and tempo resulting in poor sound quality. The firm sets the quality specification to 2 ±0.25 because an average customer is likely to complain and return the tape if the speed is off by 0.25 inch per second. The cost per return is $36. The repair cost before the tape is shipped, however, is only $3 per tape.

Required

1. Compute $L(x)$ if x is 2.12 inches.
2. Estimate the tolerance for the firm to minimize its cost.

3. Cost of Quality Report

Coolquietude Electric Instruments manufacturers fans for mini and micro computers. As a first step to focus on quality improvements, the firm has compiled the following operating data for the year just completed (in thousands):

Line inspection	$ 55
Training	120
Returns	100
Warranty repairs	68
Preventive equipment maintenance	20
Recalls	157
Design engineering	67
Scrap	30
Downtime	40
Product-testing equiment	88
Product liability insurance	20
Supplier evaluation	15
Reworks	35
Inspection and testing of incoming materials	25
Litigation costs to defend allegation of defective products	240

Required Prepare a cost of quality report and classify the costs as prevention, appraisal, internal failure, and external failure.

QUESTIONS

6–1 Define *quality*.

6–2 What are the reasons that the cost of poor quality reached an epidemic level before U.S. companies were motivated to do something about the problem in the 1980s?

6–3 What is TQM? At what point can a firm consider its effort to achieve total quality management complete?

6–4 What are the Malcolm Baldrige Award and an ISO 9000 certificate? Why do many firms in the United States seek them?

6–5 What are the core principles of total quality management?

6–6 Why is continuous quality improvement essential to achieve TQM and critical to an organization's success and competitive position?

6–7 Describe the processes for an effective implementation of TQM.

6–8 What are the purposes of conducting a quality audit?

6–9 What is gap analysis?

6–10 Why is it often necessary to revise a firm's compensation and appraisal systems when implementing TQM?

6–11 Describe goalpost conformance.

6–12 Discuss the difference between goalpost conformance and absolute quality conformance.

6–13 Taguchi argues that being within specification limits is not enough to be competitive in today's global economy. Do you agree? Why?

6–14 What is the likely cost to a firm when its product or service does not conform to customers' expectations for features or performance?

6–15 Name three types of costs associated with each of the following cost categories:
   a. Prevention
   b. Appraisal
   c. Internal failure
   d. External failure

6–16 Which of the following cost categories tend to increase during the early years of TQM? Which of them tend to decrease over the years due to successful total quality management? Why?
   a. Prevention
   b. Appraisal
   c. Internal failure
   d. External failure

6–17 What is cost of conformance? Nonconformance?

6–18 Many organizations found that investments in prevention and appraisal usually resulted in major cost savings in other areas. Explain this phenomenon.

6–19 What functions does cost of quality reporting play in a quality improvement program?

6–20 Name and briefly describe three methods that companies use to identify quality problems.

6–21 What is an Ishikawa diagram? What is its primary purpose?

6–22 What are the main causes of quality problems in a typical cause-and-effect diagram for manufacturing operations?

6–23 What is a Pareto chart? What is its function?

6–24 What are similarities and distinct characteristics in TQM for manufacturing and service firms?

6–25 What are the relationships between quality and productivity? Do efforts at productivity improvement help or hurt quality? Do quality improvement efforts help or hurt productivity? Why?

6–26 What roles do management accountants play in TQM?

6–27 How can management accountants meet the challenges of TQM?

EXERCISES

6–28 **PARETO DIAGRAM** The following causes of absenteeism for a fellow student are for the year just completed:

Cause of Absenteeism	Occurrences
Personal illness	12
Child's illness	26
Car broke down	8
Personal emergency	32
Overslept	9
Unexpected visitor	11

Required Construct a Pareto diagram.

6–29 **HISTOGRAM GRAPH** Genova Company classifies its costs of quality into four categories. The costs of quality as a percentage of cost of goods sold for the last three years are

	2003	2002	2001
Prevention costs	2.00%	4.00%	1.00%
Appraisal costs	1.50	2.50	3.00
Internal failure costs	14.00	23.00	27.00
External failure costs	12.00	18.00	31.00

Required

1. Prepare a histogram that shows the costs of quality trends as a percentage of costs of goods sold.

2. Comment on the trends in cost of quality over the three-year period from 2001 to 2003.

3. What cost of quality can the firm expect as a percentage of its cost of goods sold in 2004?

6–30 **QUALITY COST CLASSIFICATION**

Required Classify each of the following costs into types of quality cost:

1. Materials, labor, and overhead costs of scrapped units.

2. Engineering time spent to determine the causes of failures to meet product specification.

3. Wages and salaries for the time spent by workers to gather quality measurements.

4. Information systems costs expended to develop data requirements.

5. Clerical staff expenses to coordinate training programs.

6. Salaries for members of problem-solving teams.

7. Payment to settle a product liability lawsuit.

6–31   QUALITY COST CLASSIFICATION

Required   Identify the quality cost category for each of the following costs:

1. Materials, labor, and overhead costs spent on reworks for returned items.

2. Unplanned machine downtime to correct a mal-alignment.

3. Wages and salaries for the time spent by workers to analyze quality measurements.

4. Overtime premiums resulting from unplanned machine downtime.

5. Maintenance costs for measurement instruments.

6. Reengineering costs for operation processes.

7. Salaries and ancillary costs to conduct reliability studies.

8. Costs spent on implementing process control plans.

9. Costs spent to respond to complaints filed by federal regulation agencies.

10. Express freight premiums for returning products to customers.

6–32   COST OF QUALITY IMPROVEMENT   PIM Industries, Inc. manufactures electronics components. Each unit costs $30 before the final test. The final test rejects, on average, 5% of the 50,000 units manufactured per year. The average rejection rate of other firms in the same industry is 3%. A consultant has determined that poor lighting is the most likely cause of this high rejection rate. It would cost $100,000 to install adequate lighting (plus added $5,000 annual operating cost) in the assembly department, which would be useful for 5 years. With adequate lighting, the firm should be able to have a rejection rate at the industry average.

Required   Should the firm install the lighting?

6–33   COST OF QUALITY IMPROVEMENT   Office Pro sells office supplies to major corporations and institutions. Customers such as educational, religious, and not-for-profit institutions, and governmental agencies are exempt from sales tax. The firm estimates that it spends $600,000 each year by not collecting sales tax from customers who are not entitled to be exempt from sales tax. The firm can hire three auditors to check the certification of each customer claiming sales-tax exemption and reduce the cost by 90 percent. The firm estimates that each auditor will cost $80,000, including salary, benefits, and expenses. In addition, the annual cost for necessary office space and equipment for the auditors is approximately $100,000.

Required   What is the cost to the firm to reduce the errors by 90 percent?

6–34   TAGUCHI COST COEFFICIENT   Solidtronic Inc., an OEM manufacturer, has a product specification of 75 ± 5. The cost for warranty services is estimated at $500 per unit.

Required   What is the value of k, the cost coefficient, in the Taguchi loss function?

6–35   ESTIMATE TOTAL COST USING TAGUCHI LOSS FUNCTION

Required   Use the data given in 6–34 to calculate the estimated total cost when the measured quality characteristic is 78.

6–36   AVERAGE COST PER UNIT USING TAGUCHI LOSS FUNCTION   Use the data given in 6–34.

Required   What is the expected loss (cost) per unit if the manufacturing process is centered on the target specification with a standard deviation of 2?

6–37 **TAGUCHI COST COEFFICIENT** Flextronchip, an OEM manufacturer, has a third generation chip for cell phones with a specification of 0.2 ± 0.0002 mm for the distance between two adjacent pins. The loss due to a defective chip is $20.

Required Compute the value of k in the Taguchi loss function.

6–38 **EXPECTED LOSS USING TAGUCHI FUNCTION** Use the data from Flextronchip given in 6–37.

The firm has taken a sample of 100 chips from the production process. The results are shown below.

Measurement	Frequency
0.1996	2
0.1997	5
0.1998	12
0.1999	11
0.2000	45
0.2001	10
0.2002	8
0.2003	5
0.2004	2

Required Calculate the quality loss for each of the observed measurements and the expected loss for the production process.

6–39 **EXPECTED LOSS USING TAGUCHI FUNCTION** Use the data from Flextronchip given in 6–37 and 6–38. Determine the variance and calculate the expected loss using the calculated variance.

6–40 **USING TAGUCHI FUNCTION TO DETERMINE TOLERANCE** The desired distance for Flextronchip customers is 0.2 mm between two adjacent pins. Any deviation from this value causes interference. The process of handling complaints costs the firm at least $50 per chip. The engineers of the firm expect the average customer will be likely to complain when the distance is off the target by at least 0.0003. At the factory, the adjustment can be made at a cost of $1.60, which includes the labor to make the adjustment and additional testing.

Required What should the tolerance be before an adjustment is made at the factory?

PROBLEMS

6–41 **QUALITY COST CLASSIFICATION** A partial list of Josephson Manufacturing Company's activities during the past year includes the following:

a. Materials for repairs of goods under warranty.

b. Inspection of goods repaired under warranty.

c. Customer returns.

d. Canceled sales orders due to unsatisfactory products previously delivered to its customers.

e. Maintenance costs for testing equipment.

f. Inspecting finished goods.

g. Time spent to determine courses needed for quality training.

h. Debugging software before production.

i. Technical help to resolve a customer's production problems that could have been caused by bugs in the software shipped with the firm's equipment.

j. Supervision of testing personnel.

233

Required

1. Classify each cost using one of the following categories: prevention cost, appraisal cost, internal failure cost, external failure cost, or not a quality cost.

2. Identify conformance and nonconformance costs in the list of activities.

6–42 QUALITY COST CLASSIFICATION

Required   Classify these following items into types of cost of quality:

1. Warranty repairs
2. Scrap
3. Allowance granted due to blemish
4. Contribution margins of lost sales
5. Tuition for quality courses
6. Raw materials inspections
7. Work-in-process inspection
8. Shipping cost for replacements
9. Recalls
10. Attorney's fee for unsuccessful defense of complaints about quality
11. Inspection of reworks
12. Overtime caused by reworking
13. Machine maintenance
14. Tuning of testing equipment

6–43 COST OF QUALITY CATEGORY   The management of Brooks Company thinks that its total costs of quality can be reduced by increasing expenditures in certain key costs of quality categories. Management has identified the following costs of quality:

Cost of Quality	Costs
Rework	$6,000
Recalls	15,000
Reengineering efforts	9,000
Repair	12,000
Replacements	12,000
Retesting	5,000
Supervision	18,000
Scrap	9,000
Training	15,000
Testing of incoming materials	7,000
Inspection of work in process	18,000
Downtime	10,000
Product liability insurance	9,000
Quality audits	5,000
Continuous improvement	1,000
Warranty repairs	15,000

Required

1. Classify these costs into the four cost of quality categories.
2. Determine the total dollars being spent on each category.
3. Based on the company's expenditures by cost of quality categories, on which cost category should the company concentrate its efforts to decrease its overall costs of quality?

6–44   COST OF QUALITY REPORT   Buster Company manufactures custom-designed milling machines and incurred the following cost of quality in 2000 and 2001:

	2001	2000
Rework	$200,000	$250,000
Quality manual	40,000	50,000
Product design	300,000	270,000
Testing	80,000	60,000
Retesting	50,000	90,000
Product recalls	360,000	500,000
Field service	230,000	350,000
Disposal of defective units	90,000	85,000

The sales in each of the two years totaled $6,000,000. The firm's cost of goods sold is typically one-third of net sales.

Required

1. Prepare a cost of quality report that classifies the firm's costs under the proper cost of quality category.

2. Calculate the ratio of each cost of quality category to sales in each of the two years. Comment on the trends in cost of quality between 2000 and 2001.

3. Give three examples of nonfinancial measures that Buster Company might want to monitor as part of a total quality management effort.

6–45   PREPARING A COST OF QUALITY REPORT   Tarheel Company incurred these costs of quality:

	2000	2001
Calibration	$ 75,000	$100,000
Product design	150,000	175,000
Product liability	125,000	75,000
Product recalls	400,000	200,000
Retesting	250,000	200,000
Rework	325,000	100,000
Testing	50,000	150,000
Training	75,000	100,000
Warranty repairs	150,000	75,000

Required   Prepare a cost of quality report that classifies each of these costs under the proper cost of quality category. Indicate whether the costs are increasing or decreasing and by how much.

6–46   QUALITY COST REPORT   Scrabbling Enterprises is a pioneer in designing and producing scrabbling devices. SE's products were brilliantly designed, but management neglected the manufacturing process; as a consequence, quality problems have been chronic. When customers complained about defective units, SE simply sent a repairperson or replaced the defective unit with a new one. Recently, several competitors introduced similar products that lack these quality problems, causing SE's sales to decline. The firm's market share declined from 60 to 40 percent in 2000.

To rescue the situation, SE embarked on an intensive campaign to strengthen its quality control at the beginning of 2001. These efforts met with some success; the downward slide in sales was reversed, and the firm's market share increased from 40 percent in 2000 to 45 percent in 2001. To help monitor the company's progress, costs relating to quality and quality control were compiled for the previous year (2000) and for the first full year of the quality campaign (2001). The costs, which do not include the lost sales due to a reputation for poor quality, appear in thousands:

	2001	2000
Product recalls	$ 600	$3,500
Systems development	680	120
Inspection	2,770	1,700
Net cost of scrap	1,300	800
Supplies used in testing	40	30
Warrranty repairs	2,800	3,300
Rework labor	1,600	1,400
Statistical process control	270	—
Customer returns of defective goods	200	3,200
Cost of testing equipment	390	270
Quality engineering	1,650	1,080
Downtime due to quality problems	1,100	600

Required

1. Prepare a quality cost report for both 2000 and 2001. Carry percentage computations to two decimal places.

2. Prepare a histogram showing the distribution of the various quality costs by category.

3. Write an analysis to accompany the reports you have prepared in requirements 1 and 2 on the effectiveness of the changes the firm made in the last year.

4. Suppose that the firm has just learned that its major competitor has reduced its price by 20 percent. SE can afford to lower its price only if it can cut costs. A sales manager suggests that the firm can reduce quality engineering and inspection work until the market stabilizes. The manager also points out that reduced inspections will decrease the net cost of scrap and losses of downtime due to quality problems. Do you agree?

6-47 **QUALITY COST REPORT**   Carrie Lee, the president of Lee Enterprises, was concerned about the result of her company's new quality control efforts. "Maybe the emphasis we've placed on upgrading our quality control system will pay off in the long run, but it doesn't seem to be helping us much right now. I thought improved quality would give a real boost to sales, but sales have remained flat at about $10,000,000 for the last two years."

Lee Enterprises has seen its market share decline in recent years because of increased foreign competition. An intensive effort to strengthen the quality control system was initiated a year ago (on January 1, 2001) in the hope that better quality would strengthen the company's competitive position and reduce warranty and servicing costs. These costs (in thousands) relate to quality and quality control over the last two years:

	2001	2000
Warranty repairs	$140	$420
Rework labor	200	140
Supplies used in testing	6	4
Depreciation of testing equipment	34	22
Warranty replacements	18	60
Field servicing	120	180
Inspection	120	76
Systems development	106	64
Disposal of defective products	76	54

Net cost of scrap	124	86
Product recalls	82	340
Product testing	160	98
Statistical process control	74	—
Quality engineering	80	56

Required

1. Prepare a quality cost report that contains data for both 2000 and 2001. Carry percentage computations to two decimal places.

2. Prepare a histogram showing the distribution of the various quality costs by category.

3. Prepare a written evaluation to accompany the reports you have prepared in requirements 1 and 2. This evaluation should discuss the distribution of quality costs in the company, changes in this distribution that you detect have taken place over the last year, and any other information you believe would be useful to management.

4. A member of the management team believes that employees will be more conscientious in their work if they are held responsible for mistakes. He suggests that workers should do rework on their own time and that they also should pay for disposal of defective units and the cost of scraps. The proposal estimates that the firm can save another $400,000 in quality costs and the employees are less likely to make as many errors. Should the firm implement the proposal?

(CMA Adapted)

6–48 **COST OF QUALITY PROGRAM, NONFINANCIAL INFORMATION** International Tractor (IT) manufactures tractor parts. A major customer has just warned IT that if it does not improve its quality, it will lose the firm's business. Duane Smith, IT's controller, must develop a cost of quality program. He seeks your advice on classifying each of the following items as (i) a prevention cost, (ii) an appraisal cost, (iii) an internal failure cost, or (iv) an external failure cost:

a. Cost of tractor parts returned to International Tractor.

b. Costs of having to rework defective parts detected by the engineering quality assurance team.

c. Cost of inspecting the products on the production line by the IT quality inspectors.

d. Labor cost of product designer at IT whose job is to design products that will not break under extreme pressure.

e. Payment for employees who visit customers with complaints.

Required

1. Classify the five individual items into one of the four categories.

2. Give two examples of nonfinancial performance measures that IT can use to monitor its total quality control effort.

3. Recommend an effective TQM implementation procedure to meet the customer's demand.

6–49 **RELEVANT COSTS AND QUALITY IMPROVEMENT** Lightening Bulk Company is a moving company specializing in transporting large items worldwide. The firm has an 85 percent on-time delivery rate. Twelve percent of the items are misplaced and the remaining 3 percent are lost in shipping. On average, the firm incurs an additional $60 per item to track down and deliver misplaced items. Lost items cost the firm about $300 per item. Last year the firm shipped 5,000 items with an average freight bill of $200 per item shipped.

The firm's manager is considering investing in a new scheduling and tracking system costing $150,000 per year. The new system is expected to reduce misplaced items to 1 percent and lost items to 0.5 percent. Furthermore, the firm expects the total sales to increase by 10 percent with the improved service. The average contribution margin is 40 percent.

Required

1. Should the firm install the new tracking system?
2. What other factors does the firm's manager need to consider in making the decision?
3. Upon further investigation, the manager discovered that 80 percent of the misplaced or lost items either originated in or were delivered to the same country. What is the maximum amount the firm should spend to reduce the problems in that country by 90 percent?

6–50 **QUALITY IMPROVEMENT, RELEVANT COST ANALYSIS**   Worrix Corporation manufactures and sells 3,000 premium quality multimedia projectors at $12,000 per unit each year. At the current production level, the firm's manufacturing costs include variable costs of $2,500 per unit and annual fixed costs of $6,000,000. Additional selling, administrative, and other expenses, not including 15 percent sales commissions, are $10,000,000 per year.

The new model, introduced a year ago, has experienced a flickering problem. On average the firm reworks 40 percent of the completed units and still has to repair under warranty 15 percent of the units shipped. The additional work required for rework and repair causes the firm to add additional capacity with annual fixed costs of $1,800,000. The variable costs per unit are $2,000 for rework and $2,500, including transportation cost, for repair.

The chief engineer, Patti Mehandra, has proposed a modified manufacturing process that will almost entirely eliminate the flickering problem. The new process will require $12,000,000 for new equipment and installation and $3,000,000 for training. Patti believes that current appraisal costs of $600,000 per year and $50 per unit can be eliminated within one year after the installation of the new process. The firm currently inspects all units before shipment. Furthermore, warranty repair cost will be only $1,000 for no more than 5 percent of the units shipped.

Worrix believes that none of the fixed costs of rework or repair can be saved and that a new model will be introduced in three years. The new technology will most likely render the current equipment obsolete.

The accountant estimates that repairs cost the firm 20 percent of its business.

Required

1. What are the additional costs of choosing the new process?
2. What are the benefits of choosing the new process?
3. Should Worrix use the new process?
4. What factors should be considered before making the final decision?
5. A member of the board is very concerned about the substantial amount of additional funds needed for the new process. Because the current model will be replaced in about three years, the board member suggests that the firm should take no action and the problem will go away in three years. Do you agree?

6–51 **TAGUCHI LOSS FUNCTION**   Duramold specializes in manufacturing molded plastic panels to be fitted on car doors. The blueprint specification for the thickness of a high-demand model calls for 0.1875 ±0.0025 inch. It costs $120 to manufacture and $150 to scrap a part that does not meet the specifications. The thickness measure for the unit just completed is 0.1893 inch.

Required Use the Taguchi loss function to determine

1. The value of k.
2. The amount of loss for the unit.

6–52 TAGUCHI LOSS FUNCTION Use the data from problem 6–51 for Duramold. The firm can eliminate the uneven thickness by adding a production worker at the critical production point for $6 per unit.

Required At what tolerance should the panel be manufactured?

6–53 TAGUCHI LOSS FUNCTION An electronic component has an output voltage specification of 125 ±5 millivolts. The loss to the firm for a component that does not meet the specification is $200. The output voltage for a sample unit is 122 millivolts.

Required Use the Taguchi loss function to determine

1. The value of k.
2. The amount of loss.

6–54 TAGUCHI LOSS FUNCTION Use the data for problem 6–53. The firm can adjust the output voltage at the factory by changing a resistor at a cost of $12.

Required At what voltage should the electronic component be manufactured?

6–55 TAGUCHI LOSS FUNCTION North Platt Machinery Company manufactures a shaft that must fit inside a sleeve. The firm has just received an order of 50,000 units from Southernstar Exploration Company for $80 per unit. North Platt can manufacture the shaft at $50 per unit. Southernstar desires the diameter of the shaft to be 1.275 cm. The diameter of the shaft must not be less than 1.25 cm, in order to fit properly inside the sleeve. To be able to insert the shaft into a sleeve without the use of force, the diameter cannot be larger than 1.30 cm. A defective shaft is discarded and a replacement has to be shipped via express freight to locations around the world. North Platt estimates that the average cost of handling and shipping a replacement shaft will be approximately $70. Shown below are the diameters from a sample of 80 shafts manufactured during a trial run.

Diameter	Number of Unit	Diameter	Number of Unit	Diameter	Number of Unit
1.232	1	1.273	6	1.292	2
1.240	2	1.274	7	1.292	1
1.250	3	1.275	18	1.294	4
1.258	2	1.276	8	1.298	2
1.262	2	1.277	5	1.300	2
1.270	3	1.280	2	1.304	1
1.272	6	1.288	2	1.320	1

Required Use the Taguchi loss function to determine

1. The expected losss
2. The tolerance in diameter that the amount should set for the shaft.

6–56 ANALYZING COST OF QUALITY REPORT Bergen Inc. produces telephone equipment at its Georgia plant. In recent years, the company's market share has been eroded by stiff competition from Asian and European competitors. Price and product quality are the two key areas in which companies compete in this market.

Jerry Holman, Bergen's president, decided to devote more resources to the improvement of product quality after learning that his company's products had been ranked fourth in product quality in a 1998 survey of telephone equipment users. He believed that Bergen could no longer afford to ignore the importance of product quality. Jerry set up a task force that he headed to implement a formal quality improvement program. Included on the task force were representatives from engineering, sales, customer service, production, and accounting because Jerry believed that this is a companywide program and all employees should share the responsibility for its success.

After the first task force meeting, Sheila Haynes, manager of sales, asked Tony Reese, production manager, what he thought of the proposed program. Tony replied, "I have reservations. Quality is too abstract to be attaching costs to it and then to be holding you and me responsible for cost improvements. I like to work with goals that I can see and count! I don't like my annual bonus to be based on a decrease in quality costs; there are too many variables that we have no control over!"

Bergen's quality improvement program has been in operation for 18 months, and the following cost report was recently issued.

As they were reviewing the report, Sheila asked Tony what he thought of the quality program now. "The work is really moving through the production department," replied Reese. "We used to spend time helping the customer service department solve their problems, but they are leaving us alone these days. I have no complaints so far. I'll be anxious to see how much the program increases our bonuses."

Cost of Quality Report by Quarter
(in thousands)

	June 30, 2000	September 30, 2000	December 31, 2000	March 31, 2001	June 30, 2001	September 30, 2001
Prevention costs						
Machine maintenance	$ 215	$ 215	$ 202	$ 190	$ 170	$ 160
Training suppliers	5	45	25	20	20	15
Design reviews	20	102	111	100	104	95
	$ 240	$ 362	$ 338	$ 310	$ 294	$ 270
Appraisal costs						
Incoming inspection	$ 45	$ 53	$ 57	$ 36	$ 34	$ 22
Final testing	160	160	154	140	115	94
	$ 205	$ 213	$ 211	$ 176	$ 149	$ 116
Internal failure costs						
Rework	$ 120	$ 106	$ 114	$ 88	$ 78	$ 62
Scrap	68	64	53	42	40	40
	$ 188	$ 170	$ 167	$ 130	$ 118	$ 102
External failure costs						
Warranty repairs	$ 69	$ 31	$ 24	$ 25	$ 23	$ 23
Customer returns	262	251	122	116	87	80
	$ 331	$ 282	$ 146	$ 141	$ 110	$ 103
Total quality cost	$ 964	$1,027	$ 862	$ 757	$ 671	$ 591
Total production cost	$4,120	$4,540	$4,380	$4,650	$4,580	$4,510

Required

1. Identify at least three factors that should be present for an organization to successfully implement a quality improvement program.

2. By analyzing the cost of quality report presented, determine whether Bergen's quality improvement program has been successful. List specific evidence to support your answer.

3. Discuss why Tony Reese's current reaction to the quality improvement program is more favorable than his initial reaction.

4. Jerry Holman believed that the quality improvement program was essential and that Bergen could no longer afford to ignore the importance of product quality. Discuss how Bergen could measure the opportunity cost of not implementing the quality improvement program.

(CMA Adapted)

6–57 **EXPECTED QUALITY COST, CONFIDENCE INTERVAL, AND SAMPLE SIZE (REQUIRES CHAPTER 7)** Paragon Manufacturing produces small motors for assembly in handheld tools such as chain saws and circular saws. The company recently began manufacturing a new motor, model EZ3, and forecasts an annual demand of 200,000 units for this model.

Each model EZ3 requires a housing manufactured to precise engineering specifications. Paragon purchases these housings, which are not subject to quality control inspection before entering the production process; however, Paragon performance-tests the entire motor after final assembly. During pilot production runs of the new motor, several of the housings had wrong sizes and were rejected. If the housings were too shallow, they could not be assembled correctly; if they were too deep, the motor would not operate properly.

Ross Webster, Paragon's production manager, gathered the following information during the pilot production runs.

- When housings were rejected during assembly because they were too shallow, they were replaced with new housings. This change in housings required nine minutes of additional direct labor for each affected unit.

- The units that were rejected during performance testing because the housings were too deep had to be torn down and reassembled with new housings. This operation required 1 hour and 15 minutes of additional direct labor for each affected unit.

- The supplier of the housings is willing to take back the defective housings but will refund only one-half of the price. In the future, if Paragon inspects the housings before they enter the assembly process, the supplier will refund the full price of all rejected housings.

- The costs of model EZ3 follow:

Materials*	$ 44
Direct labor (3 hrs. @ $12/hr.)	36
Variable overhead ($18/hr.)	54
Total costs	$134

*Includes $7.00 for housing.

- The majority of the rejections experienced during the pilot runs were related to the housings. Ross's estimate of the probability of rejections for a lot of 800 housings follows:

Rejection during Assembly		Rejection during Performance Testing	
Quantity	Probability	Quantity	Probability
90	0.40	50	0.50
70	0.30	40	0.15
50	0.20	20	0.15
30	0.10	10	0.20

241

If Paragon decides to inspect the housings prior to assembly, Ross must select the appropriate sample size by using the following two formulas. The estimated sample size (formula 1) must be modified by the second formula (final sample size) because Ross will be sampling without replacement.

Formula 1

$$nc = C^2 pq/a^2$$

Formula 2

$$nf = \frac{nc}{1 + \dfrac{nc}{N}}$$

where:

nc = first estimate of sample size
nf = final sample size
C = confidence coefficient
p = maximum rejection rate
q = $1 - p$
a = precision level
N = number of items in the population

Required

1. Determine the maximum amount that Paragon Manufacturing would be willing to spend annually to implement quality control inspection of the housings before assembly begins.

2. For the purpose of quality control inspection, determine the sample size that Ross should select from a lot of 800 housings if the desired level is 95.5 percent (confidence coefficient 2.00) with a precision of 1 percent and rejections not to exceed 1 percent.

3. Without prejudice to your answer in requirement 2, for quality control inspection purposes, assume that the sample size is 240 housings and the desired level is 95.5 percent (confidence coefficient 2.00) with a precision of 1 percent and rejections not to exceed 1 percent. Determine whether Ross should accept or reject a lot if there are

   a. Two defective housings in the sample.

   b. Three defective housings in the sample.

   Explain your answer in each situation.

(CMA Adapted)

SOLUTION TO SELF-STUDY PROBLEMS

1. Cost of Quality Improvement

Cost of the quality improvement program		$1,000,000,000
Savings from eliminating recalls	$300 × 110% × 1.5 × 500,000 = $247,500,000	
Decreases in warranty repair cost	($200 − $80) × 500,000 = 60,000,000	
Profit from increased sales	(650,000 − 500,000) × $5,000 = 750,000,000	1,057,500,000
Increase in Profit from the Quality Improvement Program		$ 57,500,000

2. Taguchi Quality Loss Function

1. $\$36 = k (0.25)^2$
   $k = \$576$
   $L(x = 2.12) = \$576(2.12 - 2.0)^2 = \$8.2944$
2. $\$3 = \$576(\text{tolerance})^2$
   Tolerance = 0.0722
   Therefore, the specification should be set at 2 inches ±0.0722 inch.

Yes, the increase in profit and decrease in cost exceed the $1 billion cost of quality improvement.

3.   Cost of Quality Report

Coolquietude Electric Instruments
Cost of Quality Report
For the Year 2001

Prevention costs	
Training	$ 120
Design engineering	67
Preventive equipment maintenance	20
Supplier evaluation	15
Total prevention costs	$ 222
Appraisal costs	
Line inspection	$ 55
Product-testing equipment	88
Inspection and testing of incoming materials	25
Total appraisal costs	$ 168
Internal failure costs	
Scrap	$ 30
Downtime	40
Reworks	35
Total internal failure costs	$ 105
External failure costs	
Returns	$ 100
Warranty repairs	68
Recalls	157
Product liability insurance	20
Litigation costs	240
Total external failure costs	$ 585
Total cost of quality	$1,080

Cost Estimation

7

After studying this chapter, you should be able to . . .

1   Understand the strategic role of cost estimation

2   Apply the six steps of cost estimation

3   Use each of the cost estimation methods: the high-low method, work measurement, and regression analysis

4   Explain the data requirements and implementation problems of the cost estimation methods

5   Use learning curves in cost estimation when learning is present

6   Use statistical measures to evaluate a regression analysis

AP/Wide World Photos.

LEARNING OBJECTIVE 1

Understand the strategic role of cost estimation.

Cost management information is critical in cost planning and decision making (planning for a new product or plant expansion and making other decisions). However, a basic requirement for cost effective planning is to use *accurate cost estimates* in the planning process. This chapter shows the methods to use to develop accurate estimates.

Cost estimation is particularly important for the construction industry. Large construction projects are often obtained on the basis of competitive bids. The contractors that bid on these projects must have accurate cost estimation methods to win their share of the bids and to be profitable. Cost estimation methods for contractors develop detailed analyses of the material and labor costs that are directly traceable to the project, as well as projections of the indirect costs, preferably using activity analysis as described in Chapter 4.

Cost estimation for construction contractors is such a critical aspect of these firms' success that a number of consultants and software developers have created tools and techniques to assist the contractors in cost estimation. The American Society of Professional Estimators (www.aspenational.com) and other professional organizations provide education and opportunities for professional development for cost managers involved in construction cost estimation. A number of consultants (e.g., Cost Concepts, Inc., www.costconcepts.com; and Davis Langdon Adamson Associates, www.adamsonassociates.com/) and software providers (e.g., LUQS International Inc, www.luqs.com; and Prosoft Inc., www.prosoftinc.com) provide additional services.

One of the world's largest construction firms is Daewoo Construction Corp. of Korea, which has residential, commercial, and civil construction offices and construction projects in 30 countries throughout Asia, North America, and other parts of the world (http://www.dwconst.co.kr/english/e_main.htm). Daewoo's corporate mission is to build "a creative company to lead global construction through technology and quality excellence." One critical part of the implementation of that corporate mission is the use of world-class cost estimation.

STRATEGIC ROLE OF COST ESTIMATION

The strategic cost literature suggests that management accountants should actively participate in early strategic decision making. Their contributions at early stages are likely to be in the form of predictions of (1) costs of alternative activities, processes, or organizational forms—both of the firm and its competitors, (2) financial and operational impacts of alternative strategic choices, and (3) costs (dollars and time) of alternative implementation strategies. If management accountants do not fill this role, others will.[1]

---

[1] Dale W. Jalinski and Frank H. Selto, "Integration of Accounting and Strategy: A Longitudinal Field Study," working paper, University of Colorado at Boulder, July 1995.

As Jalinski and Selto indicate, a critical starting point for strategic cost management is having accurate cost estimates. The strategic approach is forward looking, and thus cost estimation is an essential element of it. **Cost estimation** is the development of a well-defined relationship between a cost object and its cost drivers for the purpose of predicting the cost.

Cost estimation facilitates strategic management in two important ways. First, it helps predict future costs using previously identified activity-based, volume-based, structural, or executional cost drivers. Second, cost estimation helps identify the key cost drivers for a cost object and which of these cost drivers are most useful in predicting cost.

Using Cost Estimation to Predict Future Costs

Strategic management requires accurate cost estimates for many applications, including these:

1. To facilitate strategic positioning analysis. Cost estimates are particularly important for firms competing on the basis of cost leadership. Cost estimates guide management in determining which contemporary management techniques, such as target costing or total quality management, the firm should employ to succeed in its chosen strategy.

2. To facilitate value-chain analysis. Cost estimates help the firm identify potential opportunities for cost reduction by reconfiguring the value chain. For example, cost estimates are useful in determining whether overall costs and value to the product can be improved by manufacturing one of its components in-house or by purchasing it from a supplier.

3. To facilitate target costing and life-cycle costing. Cost estimates are an integral part of target costing and life-cycle costing. Management uses cost estimates of different product designs as part of the process of selecting the particular design that provides the best trade-off of value to the customer versus manufacturing and other costs. Similarly, cost estimates are used to determine the minimum expected life-cycle cost for a product or service.

Cost Estimation for Different Types of Cost Drivers

The cost estimation methods explained in this chapter can be used for any of the four types of cost drivers: activity based, volume based, structural, or executional. The relationships between costs and activity-based or volume-based cost drivers often are best fit by the linear cost estimation methods explained in this chapter because these relationships are at least approximately linear within the relevant range of the firm's operations.

Structural cost drivers involve plans and decisions that have a long-term and therefore strategic impact on the firm. Such decisions include manufacturing experience, scale of product, product or production technology, and product or production complexity. Technology and complexity issues often lead management to use activity-based costing and linear estimation methods. In contrast, experience and scale often require nonlinear methods. As a cost driver, experience represents the reduction in

---

Up the Ladder of Success for Management Accountants

A recent survey of 400 companies identified the mix of personal and business skills these companies required of finance professionals. Of the four most highly prized professional skills, two included skills directly related to cost estimation: trend analysis and forecasting. The other profes-sional skills were information technology and budgeting. The most highly prized personal skills included leadership, inter-personal strengths, communication, and problem solving.

Source: "Up the Ladder of Success," *The Journal of Accountancy,* November 2000, p. 24.

unit cost due to learning. The effect on total cost of experience is nonlinear: that is, costs decrease with increased manufacturing experience. The learning effect is explained in Appendix A to the chapter. Similarly, the relationship between the structural cost driver, scale, and total cost is nonlinear. *Scale* is the term used to describe the manufacture of similar products that differ in size—for example, pipe valves of different capacity. A common effect of scale is that total manufacturing cost increases more rapidly than the increase in the size of the product. For example, the manufacture of a 22-inch industrial valve requires more than twice the cost of an 11-inch valve. The relationship between manufacturing cost and valve size can be predicted by a mathematical estimation model called the *power law* that is used in industrial engineering.[2]

Using Cost Estimation to Identify Cost Drivers

Often the most practical way to identify cost drivers is to rely on the judgment of product designers, engineers, and manufacturing personnel. Those who are most knowledgeable about the product and production processes have the most useful information on cost drivers. Cost estimation sometimes plays a discovery role and at other times a collaborative role to validate and confirm the judgments of the designers and engineers. For example, Hewlett-Packard uses cost estimation to confirm the usefulness of cost drivers selected by teams of engineers and production personnel.[3]

SIX STEPS OF COST ESTIMATION

The six steps of cost estimation are to (1) define the cost object for which the related costs are to be estimated, (2) determine the cost drivers, (3) collect consistent and accurate data on the cost object and the cost drivers, (4) graph the data, (5) select and employ an appropriate estimation method, and (6) evaluate the accuracy of the cost estimate.

◀**LEARNING OBJECTIVE 2**
Apply the six steps of cost estimation.

Step 1: Define the Cost Object to Be Estimated

Although it might seem elementary, defining the particular cost to be estimated requires care. For example, if the goal is to estimate product costs to improve product pricing, the relevant cost objects are the products manufactured in the plant; product cost is relevant for pricing. In contrast, if the goal is to reward the managers most effective at reducing cost, the most appropriate cost objects are the individual manufacturing departments in the plant since costs are most directly controllable by department managers.

Step 2: Determine the Cost Drivers

Cost drivers are the causal factors used in the estimation of the cost. Some examples of estimated costs and their related cost drivers follow:

Cost to Be Estimated	Cost Driver
Fuel expense for auto	Miles driven
Heating expense for a building	Temperature to be maintained in the building
Maintenance cost in a manufacturing plant	Machine-hours, labor-hours
Product design cost	Number of design elements, design changes

Identifying cost drivers is the most important step in developing the cost estimate. A number of relevant drivers might exist, and some might not be immediately obvious.

---

2 Based on information in Phillip F. Ostwald, *Cost Estimating for Engineering and Management* (Englewood Cliffs, N.J.: Prentice Hall, 1974).

3 Based on information from Mike Merz and Arlene Hardy, "ABC Puts Accountants on Design Team at HP," *Management Accounting*, September 1993, pp. 22–27.

Fuel expense for a large delivery truck, for example, might be primarily a function of miles traveled, but it is also affected by the average weight delivered, the number of hours of operation, and the nature of the delivery area.

Step 3: Collect Consistent and Accurate Data

Once the cost drivers have been selected, the management accountant collects data on the cost object and cost drivers. The data must be consistent and accurate. *Consistent* means that each period of data is calculated on the same accounting basis and that all transactions are properly recorded in the period in which they occurred.

The accuracy of the data depends on the nature of the source. Sometimes data developed within the firm are very reliable, as a result of management policies and procedures to ensure accuracy. Accuracy also varies among external sources of data, including governmental sources, trade and industry publications, universities, and other sources. The choice of cost drivers requires trade-offs between the relevance of the drivers and the consistency and accuracy of the data.

Step 4: Graph the Data

The objective of graphing data is to identify unusual patterns. Any shift or nonlinearity in the data must be given special attention in developing the estimate. For example, a week's downtime to install new equipment causes unusual production data for that week; such data should be excluded when developing a cost estimate. Any unusual occurrences can be detected easily by studying a graph.

Step 5: Select and Employ the Estimation Method

The three estimation methods presented in the next section of the chapter differ in their ability to provide superior accuracy in cost estimation relative to the cost of the expertise and resources required. The management accountant chooses the method with the best precision/cost trade-off for the estimation objectives.

Step 6: Assess the Accuracy of the Cost Estimate

A critical final step in cost estimation is to consider the potential for error when the estimate is prepared. This involves considering the completeness and appropriateness of cost drivers selected in step 2, the consistency and accuracy of data selected in step 3, the study of the graphs in step 4, and the precision of the method selected in step 5.

COST ESTIMATION METHODS

LEARNING OBJECTIVE 3▶

Use each of the cost estimation methods: the high-low method, work measurement, and regression analysis.

The three estimation methods are (1) the high-low method, (2) work measurement, and (3) regression analysis. The methods are listed from least to most accurate. However, the cost and effort in employing the methods are inverse to this sequence; the high-low method is the easiest and least costly, and the regression analysis method is both the most accurate and most costly, requiring more time, data collection, and expertise (see Exhibit 7–1). In choosing the best estimation method, management accountants must consider the level of accuracy desired and any limitations on cost, time, and effort.[4]

---

[4] A fourth estimation method, the *account classification method,* is used when the management accountant's information for cost estimation purposes is limited to the balances in the financial statement accounts. In this case, the accountant simply chooses for each cost account (rent, labor, materials, etc.) whether the costs in the account are fixed (e.g., rent expense) or variable (e.g., manufacturing direct labor). A difficulty with this method is that the costs in most accounts are mixed (e.g., the manufacturing labor account includes both direct and indirect labor, and thus both variable and fixed costs) and cannot be classified as simply fixed or variable. Because of the limited use of this method and the availability of much better methods, we do not consider it any further.

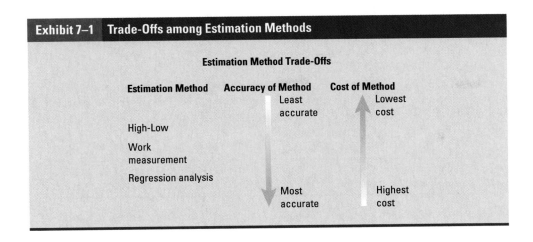

Exhibit 7-1 Trade-Offs among Estimation Methods

Estimation Method Trade-Offs

Estimation Method	Accuracy of Method	Cost of Method
High-Low	Least accurate	Lowest cost
Work measurement		
Regression analysis	Most accurate	Highest cost

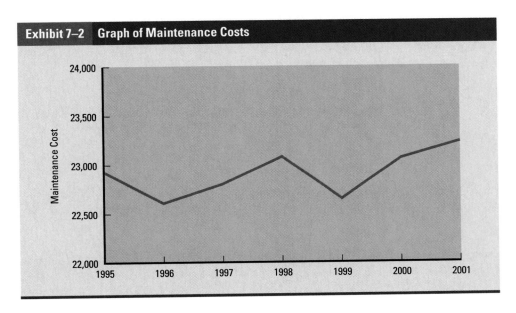

Exhibit 7-2 Graph of Maintenance Costs

Ben Garcia's Data on Maintenance Costs

To illustrate the three methods, we use the example of a management accountant named Ben Garcia who is developing cost estimates of maintenance costs for a large manufacturing company. Garcia has the following data on maintenance costs:

	1995	1996	1997	1998	1999	2000	2001
Maintenance cost ($)	22,843	22,510	22,706	23,030	22,413	22,935	23,175

As a first step, Garcia graphs the data (Exhibit 7–2) and observes that maintenance costs are increasing, although not steadily. Based only on the graphs, he also predicts that maintenance costs will be between $23,000 and $23,500 in the coming year, 2002. Since this prediction is rough and he wants to improve its accuracy, he turns to the cost estimation methods, beginning with the high-low method.

High-Low Method

The **high-low method** uses algebra to determine a *unique* estimation line between representative high and low points in the data. The high-low method accomplishes two important objectives for Garcia. First, it adds a degree of quantitative precision to the estimate, which is based on a unique cost line rather than a rough estimate based on a

The **high-low method** uses algebra to determine a *unique* estimation line between representative low and high points in the data.

view of the graph. Second, it permits him to add additional information that might be useful in predicting maintenance costs. For example, he knows that total maintenance costs are likely to include both variable and fixed costs. The fixed cost portion is the planned (preventive) maintenance that is performed regardless of the plant's volume of activity. Also, a part of maintenance cost varies with the number of operating hours; more operating hours mean more wear on the machines and thus more maintenance costs. Garcia collects the additional information, operating hours, as follows:

	1995	1996	1997	1998	1999	2000	2001
Total operating hours	3,451	3,325	3,383	3,614	3,423	3,410	3,500
Maintenance costs ($)	22,843	22,510	22,706	23,030	22,413	22,935	23,175

To use the high-low method, Garcia enters the data into a graph, as shown in Exhibit 7–3, and then selects two points from the data, one representative of the lower points and the other representative of the higher points. Often these can be simply the lowest and highest points in the data. However, if either the highest or lowest point is a great distance from the other points around it, a biased estimation can result. Both points must be representative of the data around them.

The high-low estimate is represented as follows:

$$Y = a + b \times H$$

where: Y = the value of the estimated maintenance cost
H = the cost driver, the number of hours of operation for the plant
a = a fixed quantity that represents the value of Y when H = zero
b = the slope of the line. In the plant maintenance example, it is the unit variable cost for maintenance

To obtain the high and low points, Garcia draws a freehand line through the data to help select the high and low points (try this yourself on Exhibit 7–3). He then

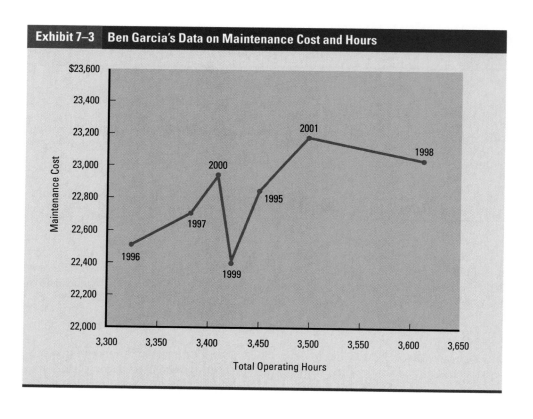

Exhibit 7–3   Ben Garcia's Data on Maintenance Cost and Hours

chooses a high and a low point reasonably close to the freehand line. Suppose that he has chosen the points for 1996 and 1998. Then he calculates the value for b:

$$b = \text{Variable cost per hour}$$

$$= \frac{\text{Difference between } \textbf{costs} \text{ for high and low points}}{\text{Difference for the value of the } \textbf{cost driver} \text{ for the high and low points}}$$

$$b = \frac{\$23,030 - \$22,510}{3,614 - 3,325} = \$1.80 \text{ per hour}$$

Next, the value for a (the fixed quantity) can be calculated using either 1996 or 1998 data:

Using 1998 Data
$$a = Y - (b \times H) = \$23,030 - \$1.80 \times 3,614 = \$16,525$$

Using 1996 data gives the same value for a because fixed cost is the same at both levels of operating hours; only total variable costs for the two levels differ:

Using 1996 Data
$$a = Y - (b \times H) = \$22,510 - \$1.80 \times 3,325 = \$16,525$$

So the estimation equation using the high-low method is

$$Y = \$16,525 + \$1.80 \times H$$

This equation can be used to estimate maintenance cost for 2002. Suppose that 3,600 operating hours are expected in 2002. Then maintenance costs are estimated as follows:

$$\text{Maintenance cost in 2002} = \$16,525 + \$1.80 \times 3,600$$

$$= \$23,005$$

Management accountants find the high-low equation useful for estimating *total costs* but not the amount of fixed costs alone. The reason is that the estimate applies only to the *relevant range* of the cost driver used to develop the estimate, the range from 3,325 to 3,614 hours. The value of a, a measure that is relevant at zero hours only, is too far from the relevant range to be properly interpreted as a fixed cost. Its role is to serve only as the constant part of the estimation equation used to *predict total cost.*

The key advantage of the high-low method is to provide a precise mathematical cost equation. However, the high-low method is limited; it can represent only the best possible line for the two selected points, and the selection of the two points requires judgment. The next two methods, work measurement and regression, are more accurate because they use statistical estimation, which provides greater mathematical precision. By including estimation error directly in the analysis, they also provide useful measures of their estimation accuracy. The accuracy of the high-low method can be evaluated only subjectively; work measurement and regression have objective, quantitative measures of their estimation accuracy.

Work Measurement

Work measurement is a statistical cost estimation method that makes a detailed study of some production or service activity to measure the time or input required per unit of output. For example, work measurement is applied to manufacturing operations to determine the labor and/or materials needed to manufacture the part or subassembly completed in that operation. In the nonmanufacturing context, the method is used to measure the time required to complete certain tasks, such as processing receipts or processing bills for payment.

Although a variety of work measurement methods is used in practice, the most common is **work sampling,** a statistical method that makes a series of measurements

Work measurement is a statistical cost estimation method that makes a detailed study of some production or service activity to measure the time or input required per unit of output.

Work sampling is a statistical method that makes a series of measurements about the activity under study.

about the activity under study. These measurements are analyzed statistically to obtain estimates of the time and/or materials the activity requires.

As an example, suppose that Kupper Insurance Company provides insurance coverage for automobile drivers. The cost of processing claims has increased significantly in recent years, and the firm is studying that cost. A careful statistical analysis including data for several different employees and several types of claims, is completed over a three-week period. The mean processing time is found to be 18 minutes, and the range is such that 95 percent of the claims required between 14 and 22 minutes. On the basis of this study, Kupper is able to estimate processing costs more accurately and to evaluate the processing clerks more effectively and more fairly. For example, if a given claims-processing clerk requires 24 minutes on average per claim, that clerk likely needs training or supervision because this amount of time is outside the 95 percent likelihood range. Kupper considers the work measurement to be an ongoing activity and continues to sample the processing times throughout the year and to make adjustments to estimated times as needed.

Regression Analysis

Regression analysis is a statistical method for obtaining the unique cost estimating equation that best fits a set of data points.	**Regression analysis** is a statistical method for obtaining the unique cost-estimating equation that best fits a set of data points. Regression analysis fits the data by *minimizing the sum of the squares* of the estimation errors. Each error is the distance measured from the regression line to one of the data points. Because regression analysis systematically minimizes the estimation errors in this way, it is called **least squares regression.**

Least squares regression, which minimizes the sum of the squares of the estimation errors, is widely viewed as one of the most effective methods for estimating costs.

A regression analysis has two types of variables. The **dependent variable** is the cost to be estimated.[5] The **independent** variable is the cost driver used to estimate the amount of the dependent variable. When one cost driver is used, the analysis is called a *simple regression analysis.* When two or more cost drivers are used, it is called *multiple regression.*

The **dependent variable** is the cost to be estimated.

The **independent variable** is the cost driver used to estimate the value of the dependent variable.

The regression equation has both an intercept and a slope term, much like the high-low method. In addition, the amount of the estimation error is considered explicitly in the regression estimate, which is

$$Y = a + bX + e$$

where: Y = the amount of the *dependent variable,* the cost to be estimated

a = a *fixed quantity,* also called the *intercept* or *constant term,* which represents the amount of Y when $X = 0$

X = the value for the *independent variable,* the cost driver for the cost to be estimated; there may be one or more cost drivers

b = the *unit variable cost,* also called the *coefficient* of the independent variable, that is, the increase in Y (cost) for each unit increase in X (cost driver)

e = the regression *error,* which is the distance between the regression line and the data point

To illustrate the method, Exhibit 7–4A and the accompanying table show three months of data on supplies expense and production levels. (To simplify the presentation, only three data points are used; applications of regression usually involve 12 or more data points.) The management accountant's task is to estimate supplies expense for month 4, in which the production level is expected to be 125 units.

Month	Supplies Expense *(Y)*	Production Level *(X)*
1	$250	50 units
2	310	100
3	325	150
4	?	125

---

[5]   Although the dependent variable is a cost in most of the cases we consider, the dependent variable also could be a revenue or some other type of financial or operating data.

Exhibit 7–4A	Supplies Expense Data for Regression Application

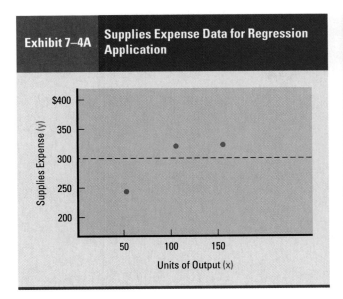

Exhibit 7–4B	The Regression Line for Supplies Expense with Units of Output as the Cost Driver (i.e., independent variable)

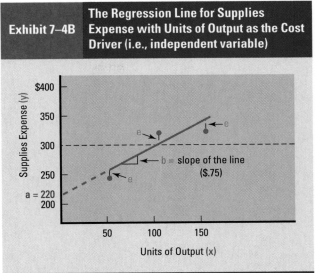

The regression for the data is determined by a statistical procedure that finds the unique line through the three data points that minimizes the sum of the squared error distances. The regression line (see Exhibit 7–4B) is[6]

$$Y = \$220 + \$0.75\,X$$

And the estimated value for supplies expense in month 4 is

$$Y = \$220 + \$0.75 \times 125 = \$313.75$$

Regression analysis gives management accountants an objective, statistically precise method to estimate supplies expense. Its principal advantage is a unique estimate that produces the least estimation error for the data. On the other hand, since the errors are squared to find the best fitting line, the regression analysis can be influenced strongly by unusual data points called **outliers,** with the result that the estimation line is not representative of most of the data. Such a situation is illustrated in Exhibit 7–5. To prevent this type of distortion, management accountants often prepare a graph of the data prior to using regression and determine whether any outliers are present. Each outlier is reviewed to determine whether it is due to a data-recording error, normal operating condition, or a unique and unrecurring event. Guided by the objective of developing the regression that is most representative of the data, the accountant then decides whether to correct or remove the outlier.

Outliers are unusual data points that strongly influence a regression analysis.

Choosing the Dependent Variable

Development of a regression analysis begins with the choice of the cost object, the dependent variable. The dependent variable might be at a very aggregate level, such as total maintenance costs for the entire firm, or at a detail level, such as maintenance costs for each plant or department. The choice of aggregation level depends on the objectives for the cost estimation, data availability and reliability, and cost/benefit considerations. When a key objective is accuracy, a detailed level of analysis often is preferred.

Choosing the Independent Variables (Cost Drivers)

To identify the independent variables, management accountants consider all financial, operating, and other economic data that might be relevant for estimating the dependent

---

[6] The derivation of the intercept ($220) and coefficient ($0.75) for this regression line is beyond the scope of this text, but it can be found in textbooks on basic probability and statistics such as that by Sheldon Ross, *Introductory Statistics* (New York: McGraw Hill, 1996). Appendix B to this chapter also has a technical reference on regression analysis.

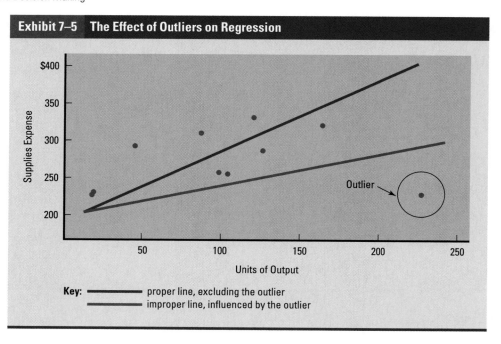

Exhibit 7–5 The Effect of Outliers on Regression

Key: ———— proper line, excluding the outlier
———— improper line, influenced by the outlier

Exhibit 7–6 Independent Variables for Selected Dependent Variables
Types of Independent Variables: Financial, Operating, Economic, and Other

Selected Dependent Variables	Financial Data	Operating Data	Economic Indicators	Other
• Sales	• Selling expense	• Store size • Store type	• Price level index • Index of local economic conditions	• Dummy variable for change in credit policy
• Labor expense	• Wage rates • Sales	• Hours worked • Dummy variable for change in labor mix • Number of employees	• Index of local wage rates	• Trend variable • Dummy variable for significant pay rate change
• Utilities expense	• Sales	• Average daily temperature • Dummy variable for change in thermostat setting • Number of hours store is open		• Dummy variable for significant change in utility rate • Trend variable
• General expenses: office salaries and supplies, telephone, printing and duplicating, and repairs	• Sales • Total expense • Net fixed assets	• Store type • Store size • Number of employees	• Index of local price level	• Age of store • Dummy variable for change in office automation

variable. The goal is to choose variables that (1) are relevant; that is, they change when the dependent variable changes, and (2) do not duplicate other independent variables. As an example, Exhibit 7–6 presents some dependent and independent variables that might be appropriate for the study of costs in a chain of retail stores.

Most often the data in a regression analysis are numerical amounts in dollars or units. Another type of variable, called a **dummy variable,** represents the presence or absence of a condition. For example, dummy variables can be used to indicate season-

A **dummy variable** is used to represent the presence or absence of a condition.

254

ality. If the management accountant is estimating costs of production, and if production is always high in March, a dummy variable with a value of 1 for March and 0 for the other months could be used.

Evaluating a Regression Analysis

In addition to a cost estimate, regression analysis also provides quantitative measures of its precision and reliability. *Precision* refers to the accuracy of the estimates from the regression, and *reliability* indicates whether the regression reflects actual relationships among the variables, that is, is it likely to continue to predict accurately? These measures can aid management accountants in assessing the usefulness of the regression. Three key measures are explained here. These and other statistical measures are explained more fully in Appendix B.

1. *R*-squared, also called the *coefficient of determination*.
2. The *t*-value.
3. The standard error of the estimate (*SE*).

R-squared and the *t*-value are used to measure the reliability of the regression, the standard error is a useful measure of the precision, or accuracy, of the regression.

R-squared is a number between zero and 1 and is often described as a measure of the explanatory power of the regression; that is, the degree to which changes in the dependent variable can be predicted by changes in the independent variables. A more reliable regression is one that has an *R*-squared close to 1. When viewed graphically, regressions with high *R*-squared show the data points lying near the regression line; in low *R*-squared regressions, the data points are scattered about, as demonstrated in Exhibit 7–7A (high *R*-squared) and 7–7B (low *R*-squared). Most regression analyses involving financial data have *R*-squared values above 0.5, and many have values in the 0.8 to 0.9 range.[7]

The **t-value** is a measure of the reliability of each independent variable. *Reliability* is the degree to which an independent variable has a valid, stable, long-term relationship with the dependent variable. A relatively small *t*-value (generally, the *t*-value should be more than 2) indicates little or no relationship between the independent and dependent variables. A variable with a low *t*-value should be removed from the regression to simplify the model and because it can lead to less accurate cost estimates.

When two or more independent variables exist, the presence of a low *t*-value for one or more of these variables is a possible signal of what is called **multicollinearity,**

R-squared is a number between zero and 1 and often is described as a measure of the explanatory power of the regression, that is, the degree to which changes in the dependent variable can be predicted by changes in the independent variable(s).

The **t-value** is a measure of the reliability of each independent variable, that is, the degree to which an independent variable has a valid, stable, long-term relationship with the dependent variable.

Multicollinearity means that two or more independent variables are highly correlated with each other.

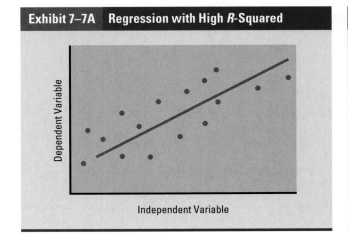

Exhibit 7–7A   Regression with High *R*-Squared

Dependent Variable / Independent Variable

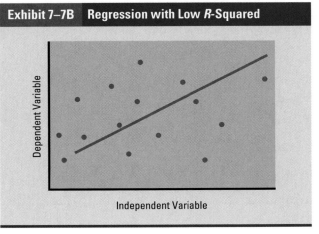

Exhibit 7–7B   Regression with Low *R*-Squared

Dependent Variable / Independent Variable

---

[7] The square root of *R*-squared, or simply *R*, is called the *correlation coefficient* and is interpreted in the same manner as *R*-squared. The correlation coefficient is a number between −1 and +1; a value near zero is interpreted as a lack of relationship between the independent and dependent variables. When *R* is positive, the relationship is direct; that is, when one variable increases, so does the other. When *R* is negative, the relationship is inverse; that is, when one variable increases, the other decreases.

Correlation means that a given variable tends to change predictably in the same (or opposite) direction for a given change in the other, correlated variable.

which means that two or more independent variables are highly correlated with each other. As suggested by the name, independent variables are supposed to be independent of each other, not correlated. **Correlation** among variables means that a given variable tends to change predictably in the same (or opposite) direction for a given change in the other variable. For example, the number of machine-hours used in manufacturing is correlated with the number of labor-hours because both are affected by the same factor, the number of units produced. Moreover, because a common trend tends to affect many types of financial data, accounting and operating data are commonly highly correlated.

The effect of multicollinearity is that the regression is less reliable and the estimates less accurate. Thus, when a management accountant has reason to believe that two or more of the variables in the equation are correlated and the *t*-values are relatively low, additional regressions that remove one or more of these independent variables should be considered.

The **standard error of the estimate (*SE*)** is a measure of the accuracy of the regression's estimates.

The **standard error of the estimate (*SE*)** is a measure of the accuracy of the regression's estimates. It is a range around the regression estimate in which we can be reasonably sure that the unknown actual value will fall. For example, if the regression estimate is $4,500 and the *SE* is $500, there is reasonable confidence that the unknown actual value lies in the range $4,500 +/− $500, that is, between $4,000 and $5,000.[8]

Because it is used to measure a confidence range, the *SE* must be interpreted by its relationship to the average size of the dependent variable. If the *SE* is small relative to the dependent variable, the precision of the regression can be assessed as relatively good. How small the *SE* value must be for a favorable precision evaluation is a matter of judgment, but a threshold of approximately 5 to 10 percent of the average of the dependent variable can be used. The confidence ranges for two regressions are illustrated in Exhibit 7–8A (good precision) and 7–8B (relatively poor precision).

Note that in Exhibits 7–8A and 7–8B the *SE* value increases as points on the regression line move farther in either direction from the mean of the independent variable. This is consistent with the concept of the relevant range. The estimate is most accurate near the mean of the independent variable and less accurate the farther it is from the mean.

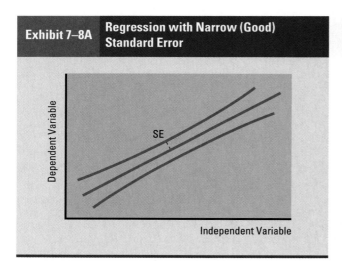

Exhibit 7–8A   **Regression with Narrow (Good) Standard Error**

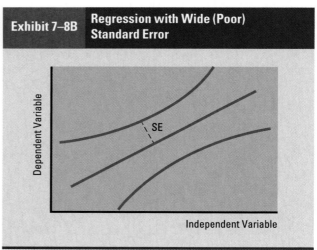

Exhibit 7–8B   **Regression with Wide (Poor) Standard Error**

---

[8]   The standard error of the estimate provides a quantitative measure of the confidence one has with the accuracy of the estimate. See Appendix B for a more detailed explanation. An excellent discussion of the standard error and other regression measures, including a spreadsheet illustration, is provided in Adel M. Novin, "Applying Overhead: How to Find the Right Bases and Rates," *Management Accounting*, March 1992, pp. 40–43.

Applications of Regression Analysis

Regression analysis is used for cost estimation and a wide variety of financial management functions that the management accountant is likely to encounter. Five functions (and references for additional reading) are given here.

PREDICTING OVERHEAD COSTS

Regression is used to identify the best of several alternative overhead applications bases. (G. R. Cluskey Jr., Mitchell H. Raiborn, and Doan T. Modianos, "Multiple-Cost Flexible Budgets and PC-Based Regression Analysis," *Journal of Cost Management,* July–August 2000, pp. 35–47; and Adel M. Novin, "Applying Overhead: How to Find the Right Bases and Rates," *Management Accounting,* March 1992, pp. 40–43.)

REAL ESTATE APPRAISAL

Regression is used to estimate the value of commercial real estate properties using a variety of financial, operating, and general economic independent variables. (Stephen T. Crosson, Charles G. Dannis, and Thomas G. Thibodeau, "Regression Analysis: A Cost-Effective Approach for the Valuation of Commercial Property," *Real Estate Finance,* Winter 1996.)

IDENTIFYING AND SOLVING QUALITY CONTROL PROBLEMS

Regression analysis is used to supplement engineering analyses of defects. The approach is found to be particularly useful when production cannot be delayed to test individual machines and processes; the regression uses plant data to predict the likely cause of the defects. (Henry L. LeFevre, "Using Plant Data for Regression Analysis," *Quality,* April 1987, pp. 35–38.)

COLLEGE AND PROFESSIONAL FOOTBALL SCORES

Regression analysis has been used to predict the winning margins in football games based on key independent variables such as the number of turnovers. Researchers find better regressions (reliability and precision) for college and university games than for professional football games. (G. Wagner and V. Oliver, "College and Professional Football Scores: A Multiple Regression Analysis," *American Economist,* Spring 1987, pp. 33–38.)

SELECTING TARGETS FOR MERGERS AND ACQUISITIONS

Regression analysis has been used to estimate the value of companies that are potential merger or acquisition targets. The value of the approach is to corroborate other valuation methods, such as those based on net present value. (William P. Flaherty, "Using Regression Analysis to Price the Best Targets," *Mergers and Acquisitions,* April 1991, pp. 47–51.)

Using Regression to Estimate Maintenance Costs

We continue the case developed earlier, Ben Garcia's estimation of maintenance costs. Following the six steps outlined in the first section of the chapter, Garcia defined the cost object and the relevant cost driver as maintenance cost and operating hours, respectively. He also collected and graphed the data (Exhibit 7–3). The next step is to solve the regression using regression software such as the Excel spreadsheet program, with the following findings (Y represents maintenance cost and H represents operating hours):

$$Y = \$15{,}843 + \$2.02 \times H$$

Garcia expects approximately 3,600 operating hours in 2002, so the amount of maintenance cost for 2002 is estimated to be

$$Y = \$15{,}843 + \$2.02 \times 3{,}600 = \$23{,}115$$

The statistical measures are
R-squared = .461
t-value = 2.07
Standard error of the estimate = \$221.71
Ratio of SE to the mean of the dependent variable = 0.98%

Garcia notes that R-squared is less than 0.5, the t-value is greater than 2.0, and the SE is approximately 1 percent of the mean of the dependent variable. The SE and t-values are very good. However, since the R-squared is low, Garcia asks his accounting assistant, Kim Jan, to review the regression.

Jan looks at the regression and the related graphs and comments immediately that in 1999 maintenance cost dropped significantly, and operating hours experienced a modest drop. Garcia observes that the drop in 1999 was probably due to the unusually

---

COST MANAGEMENT IN ACTION

Using Regression to Estimate the Value of Commercial Real Estate

Regression analysis is commonly used as one means to estimate the value of commercial real estate properties. It is used for two key types of properties: income-producing properties, such as apartment buildings and office buildings, and nonincome-producing properties, such as warehouses and

manufacturing plants. Identify what you think are the two or three key independent variables for estimating the value for each type of property. (Refer to Comments on Cost Management in Action at the end of the chapter.)

poor economic conditions that year; thus, output was reduced and operating hours and maintenance fell accordingly. Recalling that dummy variables can be used to correct for isolated variations and seasonal or other patterns, Jan suggests that Garcia run the regression again with a dummy variable having a value of 1 in 1999 and a value of zero otherwise (the symbol D represents the dummy variable). The new regression is as follows:

$$Y = \$16,467 + \$1.856 \times H - \$408.638 \times D$$

With the revised regression, the estimate of maintenance costs for 2002 is as follows (assuming no unusual unfavorable event in 2002, and thus $D = 0$):

$$Y = \$16,467 + \$1.856 \times 3,600 - \$408.638 \times 0$$

$$= \$23,149$$

The statistical measures are as follows:

R-squared = .772

t-values:

Hours: 2.60

Dummy variable: 22.33

Standard error of the estimate (SE) = \$ 161.27

Ratio of SE to the mean of the dependent variable = 0.71%

Garcia observes that the inclusion of the dummy variable improves R-squared, the t-values, and the SE of the regression. For this reason, he should rely on the estimate from the latter regression.

Using Spreadsheet Software for Regression Analysis

Suppose that WinDoor Inc. is developing a regression cost equation for the indirect costs in its plant. WinDoor manufactures windows and doors used in home construction; both products are made in standard and custom sizes. Occasionally, a very large order substantially increases the direct and indirect costs in a given month. The indirect costs primarily consist of supplies, quality control and testing, overtime, and other indirect labor. Regression is to be used to budget indirect costs for the coming year, primarily for cash management purposes. The management accountant, Charlotte Williams, knows from prior years that both direct labor-hours and machine-hours in the plant are good independent variables for estimating indirect costs. She gathers the data in Exhibit 7–9 for the most recent 12 months.

Williams develops the regression for these data using a spreadsheet program, Excel. To use Excel, she selects the **Regression** option from the Tools/Data Analysis menu, then selects the X and Y ranges for the independent and dependent variables, and obtains the regression results in Exhibit 7–10 (where L represents labor-hours and M represents machine-hours):

$$Y = \$35,070 + \$5.090 \times L + \$40.471 \times M$$

Exhibit 7–9   Indirect Costs, Labor- and Machine-Hours for WinDoor Inc.

Date	Total Indirect Costs	Direct Labor-Hours	Machine-Hours
June 2000	$274,500	26,940	2,009
July	320,000	35,690	3,057
August	323,200	32,580	3,523
September	219,900	24,580	1,856
October	232,100	19,950	2,168
November	342,300	34,330	3,056
December	427,800	43,180	3,848
January 2001	231,000	21,290	1,999
February	257,300	28,430	2,290
March	248,700	24,660	1,894
April	248,400	27,870	2,134
May	338,400	31,940	3,145

Exhibit 7–10   Excel Regression Results for WinDoor Data, Showing Regression Dialog Box

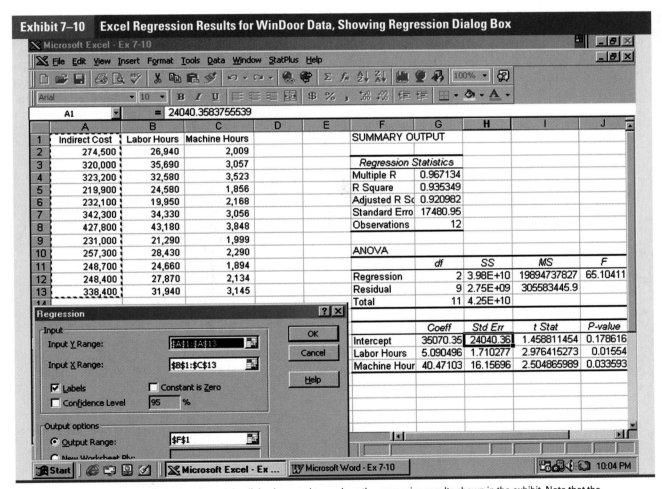

This exhibit shows both the regression results and the dialog box used to produce the regression results shown in the exhibit. Note that the independent variables (X Range) and dependent variable (Y Range) are entered into the dialog box. Labels are used in the top row of each column of data. The output is presented in the cells to the right and below the selected cell, F1.

The dialog box is accessed by choosing **Data Analysis** under the Tools menu in Excel. If you do not find Data Analysis there, you must install it using **Add-Ins. . .,** which is also under the Tools menu. After selecting **Add-Ins. . .,** choose to install **Analysis ToolPak,** which contains data analysis and regression.

The statistical measures follow:

    R-squared = .935

    t-values:

        Labor-hours: 2.976

        Machine-hours: 2.505

    Standard error of the estimate (SE) = \$17,480

    Ratio of SE to mean of the dependent variable = 6.05%

The regression satisfies our statistical criteria: R-squared is relatively high, and the t-values and SE are good. Thus, WinDoor can use the regression for estimates with a reasonable degree of confidence.

DATA REQUIREMENTS AND IMPLEMENTATION PROBLEMS

LEARNING OBJECTIVE 4▶

Explain the data requirements and implementation problems of the cost estimation methods.

To develop a cost estimate using regression or any other estimation method, management accountants must consider those aspects of data collection that can significantly affect precision and reliability. Three main issues are (1) data accuracy, (2) time period choice, and (3) nonlinearity.

Data Accuracy

All methods previously explained rely on the accuracy of the data used in the estimation. Whether it be financial data, operating data, or economic indicators (examples shown in Exhibit 7–6), management must carefully consider the source of the data and its reliability. If the source is inside the firm (usually financial and operating data), management can develop reporting requirements to ensure the accuracy of the data. For external economic data, management determines the reliability of data by considering the source. For example, trade and industry associations commonly provide industry and economic data for association members; by reputation, some providers are more reliable than others. Economic data are available from the U.S. government, local and state governments, and research firms and universities; some have better reputations for accuracy than do others. Management accountants must determine how much to rely on the data used in the estimation method.

Selecting the Time Period

1. **Mismatched time periods.** The data for each variable must be from the same time period. Mixing biweekly and monthly data is a problem, as is using data for sales based on the calendar month and for wages expense based on four consecutive weekly periods. Difficulties also arise when supplies are purchased in one period but used in the next.

2. **Length of time period.** The period can vary from daily to weekly or annually. If the period is too short, the chance of mismatch increases because of recording lags or errors. On the other hand, if the period is too long, important short-term relationships in the data might be averaged out, and the regression will not have much explanatory power. Moreover, a longer period reduces the number of data points needed to improve the precision and reliability of the regression. Management accountants must determine which time period best satisfies the competing objectives for a reliable and precise regression.

Nonlinearity Problems

Nonlinearity causes other problems to arise because of certain time-series patterns to the data. These patterns are trend, seasonality, shift, outliers, and fixed costs.

1. **Trend and/or seasonality.** A common characteristic of accounting data is a significant trend that results from changing prices and/or seasonality that can affect the

Cost Estimation at Chrysler and Texas Instruments

Daimler-Chrysler's U.S. manufacturing unit uses cost estimation methods to project the cost of materials to be used in manufacturing its products. The consumer price index (CPI) is a significant predictor variable in the Chrysler method. Unfortunately, the consumer price index is systematically in error, sometimes by as much as 100%. One reason is that the official U.S. government statistics on prices fail to consider important changes in consumer buying patterns, improvements in the quality of products, and improvements in the functionality of products. For example, a product can cost a little more than it did a few years ago, but its quality and functionality make it a bargain relative to the prior year's product; the relevant price may have really dropped significantly. Consumers also could have moved on to other products. Thus, Chrysler's ability to accurately predict its materials costs is limited by the inaccuracy of the CPI, which is an important input in the estimation method.

Similarly, Texas Instruments, Inc. (TI), relies on industrial production statistics from the U.S. government in projecting revenues in its different product lines. These statistics are biased because they rely on electricity consumption to measure industrial production, an approach termed "prehistoric" by TI's chief economist, Vladi Catto. Other distortions arise because of confusing and inconsistent means used to measure imports and exports, and biases in measuring capacity utilization and productivity in U.S. factories. Firms such as TI and Chrysler find developing accurate estimates of costs and revenues to be difficult when key economic indicators are unreliable.

For further reading, see "The Real Truth about the Economy," *Business Week,* November 7, 1994, pp. 110–118.

Exhibit 7–11	Adjusting for Trend and Seasonality Using First Difference or a Price Index		
		Price Index Adjustment	
Supplies Expense	First Difference	Hypothetical Price Index for Supplies Expense	Supplies Expense Adjusted for Price Index
$250	—	1.00	$250/1.00 = $250
310	$60	1.08	310/1.08 = 287
325	15	1.12	325/1.12 = 290

precision and reliability of the estimate. When trend or seasonality is present, a linear regression is not a good fit to the data, and the management accountant should use a method to deseasonalize or to detrend a variable. The most common methods to do this follow:

- Use of a price change index to adjust the values of each variable to some common time period.
- Use of a decomposition technique that extracts the seasonal, cyclical, and trend components of the data series.[9]
- Use of a trend variable. A **trend variable** takes on values of 1, 2, 3, . . . for each period in sequence.
- Replacement of the original values of each of the variables with the first differences. **First difference** for each variable is the difference between each value and the succeeding value in the time series.

You can see the index approach and the first difference approach in Exhibit 7–11 using the supplies expense data from Exhibit 7–2.

Trend is present in virtually all financial time series data used in management accounting because of inflation and growth in the economy. Thus, it is a pervasive issue in the proper development of a regression analysis.

A **trend variable** is a variable that takes on values of 1, 2, 3,...for each period in sequence.

First difference for each variable is the difference between each value and the succeeding value in the time series.

---

[9] An explanation of the decomposition of time series is beyond the scope of this introductory material. Decomposition is presented in basic texts on probability and statistics, such as S. Ross, *Introductory Statistics.*

   2. Outliers. As mentioned earlier, when an error in the data or an unusual or nonrecurring business condition affects operations for a given period, the result might be a data point that is far from the others, an outlier. Because outliers can significantly decrease the precision and reliability of the estimate, they should be corrected or adjusted (using, for example, a dummy variable) if it is clear that they are unusual or nonrecurring.

   3. Data Shift. In contrast to the outlier, if the unusual business condition is long lasting, such as the introduction of new production technology or other permanent change, the average direction of the data has a distinct shift that should be included in the estimate. One way to handle this is to use a dummy variable to indicate the periods before and after the shift.

SUMMARY

Cost estimation is one of the most important activities the management accountant performs in supporting the firm's strategy. It has an important role in developing a strategic competitive position as well as in using value-chain analysis, target costing, and other planning and evaluation contexts within cost management.

To use cost estimation effectively, the management accountant develops and evaluates a cost-estimating model in six steps: (1) define the cost object, (2) determine the cost drivers, (3) collect consistent and accurate data, (4) graph the data, (5) select and apply a cost estimation method, and (6) evaluate the accuracy of the cost estimate.

This chapter presents three estimation methods. The high-low method develops a unique estimation equation using algebra and the representative low and high points in the data. Two statistical methods, work measurement and regression analysis, also are presented. Work measurement is a study of a work activity to measure the time or input required per unit of output. Regression analysis obtains a unique best-fitting line for the data. The chapter's focus is on the proper interpretation of the three key measures of the precision and reliability of the regression: R-squared, the t-value, and the standard error of the estimate.

In applying any cost estimation method management accountants consider the three main implementation problems: (1) inaccurate data, (2) mismatched data from different time periods and time periods that are too short or too long , and (3) nonlinearity in the data.

The most reliable and accurate method available to the management accountant is regression analysis, which can be solved using spreadsheet software such as Microsoft Excel. An advantage of regression analysis is that its results include quantitative and objective measures of the reliability and accuracy of the regression estimate.

APPENDIX A

Learning Curve Analysis

LEARNING OBJECTIVE 5▶

Use learning curves in cost estimation when learning is present.

One prominent example of nonlinear cost behavior is a cost influenced by learning. When an activity has a certain labor component and repetition of the same activity or operation makes the labor more proficient, the task is completed more quickly with the same or a higher level of quality. Learning can occur in a wide variety of ways, from the individual level as new employees gain experience, to the aggregate level in which a group of employees experiences improvement in productivity. We consider the latter instance in this appendix.

A **learning curve analysis** is a systematic method for estimating costs when learning is present.

Costs are affected by learning in a wide variety of contexts, especially in large-scale production settings, such as the manufacture of airplanes and ships. In each case, we can model the expected improvement in productivity and use this information in the estimation of future costs. A **learning curve analysis** is a systematic method for estimating costs when learning is present.

One of the first well-documented applications of learning curves occurred in the World War II aircraft industry.[1] Studies showed that the total time to manufacture two airplanes declined by approximately 20 percent of the total time without learning. In other words, the average *per-unit* time to build the first two units was 80 percent of the time for the first unit. For example, if the time to build the first unit is 20 hours, the *average* time to build the first two units is 16 hours (20 × 0.8), or a total of 32 hours (16 × 2) for two units. Without learning, it would take 40 hours (20 × 2). The **learning rate** is the percentage by which average time (or total time) falls from previous levels as output doubles. In this example, the rate is 80 percent. The unit cost behavior of the learning curve is illustrated in Exhibit 7–12.

Additional evidence of the practical importance of learning curves is the common reference to start-up costs in corporate annual reports and the financial press. A commonly accepted business principle is that new products and production processes have a period of low productivity followed by increasing productivity. Thereafter, the rate of improvement in productivity tends to decline over time until it reaches some equilibrium level where it remains relatively stable until another change in the product line or production process occurs.[2]

> The **learning rate** is the percentage by which average time (or total time) falls from previous levels as output doubles.

Learning Curves in Software Development

SofTech, Inc., is a vendor of software for financial analysts. SofTech's development staff recently changed its development language, T-Base, to a new language, Z-Base, which permits faster development and provides certain object-oriented programming benefits. Now SofTech is calculating the learning time needed for its programmers to

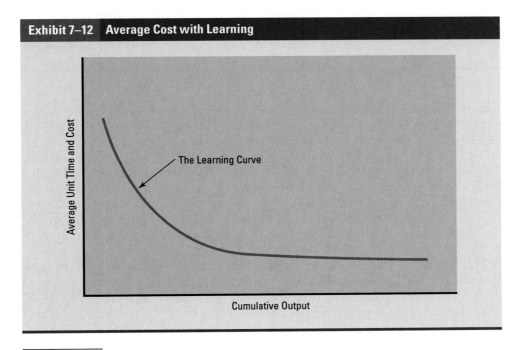

Exhibit 7–12   Average Cost with Learning

The Learning Curve

Average Unit Time and Cost

Cumulative Output

---

[1]   Frank J. Andress, "The Learning Curve as a Production Tool," *Harvard Business Review*, January–February 1954; and Harold Asher, "Cost Quality Relationships in the Airframe Industry," Report R–291 (Santa Monica, CA: The RAND Corporation, July 1956).

[2]   As in the World War II airplane production example, the common learning rate is approximately 80 percent. Two conventional models are used in learning curve analysis. One measures learning on the basis of average unit cost, the other on the basis of marginal cost. Both models are conceptually and mathematically similar, although the average cost model tends to lead to lower unit costs. The average cost model is the more common, and for clarity and simplicity, it is the only model we present here. For a full explanation and comparison of the two models, see J. Chen and R. Manes, "Distinguishing the Two Forms of the Constant Percentage Learning Curve Model," *Contemporary Accounting Research*, Spring 1985, pp. 242–52.

Applications of Learning Curves

Learning curve analysis is commonly used to improve cost estimates in situations when learning is likely to occur. Three example applications (and sources discussing the sources involved) follow.

SEMICONDUCTOR PRODUCTION

Costs of computer memory chips have continued to fall in recent years. One reason, among many, involves improved techniques in making the chips that have reduced the waste in manufacturing the silicon wafers. Learning curves are widely used in the industry to measure the improvement in yield, which in one study showed the learning rate to be about 72 percent. (Harald Gruber, "The Yield Factor and the Learning Curve in Semiconductor Production," *Applied Economics*, August 1994, pp. 837–44.)

AIRCRAFT GUIDANCE SYSTEMS

As discussed in the text, one of the earliest applications of the learning curve was in aircraft manufacturing. The British firm Above & Beyond, Ltd., continues this tradition by using the learning curve to estimate the reduction in costs for its development of guidance systems for space shuttles. The firm's engineers estimate the learning rate to be about 87 percent. (G. J. Steven, "The Learning Curve: From Aircraft to Spacecraft?" *Management Accounting* (London), May 1999, pp. 64–65.)

PROJECT MANAGEMENT

When projects involve repetitive operations, the learning curve is applicable, as this study illustrates. (Jean-Pierre Amor and Charles J. Teplitz, "An Efficient Approximation for Project Composite Learning Curves," *Project Management Journal*, September 1998, pp. 28–42.)

Exhibit 7–13	Softech, Inc.'s Learning Curve for Z-Base	
Cumulative Output	**Average Time**	**Total Time**
500 lines	100 hours	100 hours
1,000 lines	$100 \times .8 = 80$ hours	$80 \times 2 = 160$ hours
2,000 lines	$80 \times .8 = 64$ hours	$64 \times 4 = 256$ hours
4,000 lines	$64 \times .8 = 51.2$ hours	$51.2 \times 8 = 409.6$ hours

come up to speed in the new language. These estimates are important because programming costs have increased 10 percent to $65 per hour in the past year and are expected to rise as quickly in the coming years. For purposes of this analysis, SofTech estimates the learning rate for Z-Base to be 80 percent and the initial time for coding 500 lines of good code in Z-Base to be 100 hours. The time and related cost required for developing the first 4,000-line application in Z-Base can be determined by using the learning curve; see Exhibit 7–13.

Learning rates are obtained by reviewing and analyzing historical data. The methods vary from the simple high-low method to regression analysis based on fitting a nonlinear relationship to the historical data.[3]

Note that the learning curve has a more general application than we present here. For example, the learning rate can be derived and applied for any set increment in output, not only the output-doubling assumption shown here. However, since the 80 percent with output-doubling approach is commonly used, it is the model presented here.

---

[3] For example, to estimate the parameters of the model, *a* and *b*, using the high-low method, select two appropriate points and determine the learning equation for each point. Then substitute *a* for *b* and take the log of both sides of the new equation. Then solve for *b*. To determine the learning rate necessary to achieve a given level of output within a certain time limitation, use the methods described in Patrick B. McKenzie, "An Alternative Learning Curve Formula," *Issues in Accounting Education*, Fall 1987, pp. 383–88; and C. Carl Pegels, "Start Up or Learning Curves—Some New Approaches," *Decision Sciences*, October 1976, pp. 705–13. Software can be used to facilitate the use of learning curves. Examples include CURV1, a product of Production Technology, an industrial engineering consulting firm (www.protech-ie.com/curv1.htm) and an Excel add-in Foresee. See Charles D. Bailey, "Estimation of Production Costs and Labor Hours Using an Excel Add-in," *Management Accounting Quarterly*, Summer 2000, pp. 25–31; www.bus.ucf.edu/bailey.

Learning Helps Quality at Chrysler
The learning effect can help a firm improve quality as well as productivity. For example, Chrysler achieved higher levels of quality for the second year of production on the new car, the Prowler. Reporters for the magazine *Car and Driver* indicated that the new Prowler seemed more solid. When asked about this, Plymouth officials reported that the difference was not due to design changes but to the increasing expertise of the assembly line workers. **Source:** "The Prowler Gets More Growl," *Car and Driver,* April 1998, p. 25.

Note also that a learning rate of *1 is equivalent to no learning. A learning rate of .5 is best interpreted as the maximum learning rate* because the total time for actual production equals the time for a single unit. Thus, the learning rate is always a number greater than .5 and less than 1. Actual case studies reveal that the learning rate most often falls near .8.

What Decisions Are Influenced by Learning?

Because the productivity of labor is a vital aspect of any production process, learning curve analysis can be an important way to improve the quality of a wide range of decisions. For example, when product prices are based in part on costs, learning curves could be used to determine a life-cycle plan for a new product for product pricing. Moreover, learning curves would be helpful in these areas:

1. **The make-or-buy decision (Chapter 10).** When the cost to make a part is affected by learning, the analysis can be used to more accurately reflect the total cost over time of the make option.

2. **Preparation of bids for production contracts; life-cycle costing (Chapter 5).** Learning curves play an important role in ensuring that the contract cost estimates are accurate over the life of the contract.

3. **Cost-volume-profit analysis (Chapter 8).** The determination of a breakeven point might be significantly influenced by the presence of learning.[4] Failing to consider learning causes overstatement of the actual number of units required for breakeven.

4. **Development of standard product costs (Chapters 15 and 16).** When learning occurs, standard costs change over time, and the appropriate labor costs must be adjusted on a timely basis.[5]

5. **Capital budgeting (Chapter 11).** Learning curves capture cost behavior more accurately over the life of the capital investment by including the expected improvements in labor productivity due to learning.

6. **Budgeting production levels and labor needs (Chapter 9).** Another useful application of learning curves is the development of the annual or quarterly production plan and related labor requirement budget. When the activity or operation is affected by learning, the production and labor budgets should be adjusted accordingly.

7. **Management control (Chapters 18 and 19).** The use of learning curves is important in properly evaluating managers when costs are affected by learning. The evaluation should recognize the pattern of relatively higher costs at the early phase of the product life cycle.

---

[4]   Edward V. McIntyre, "Cost-Volume-Profit Analysis Adjusted for Learning," *Management Science*, October 1977, pp. 149–60.

[5]   Jackson F. Gillespie, "An Application of Learning Curves to Standard Costing," *Management Accounting*, September 1981, pp. 63–65.

Limitations of Learning Curve Analysis

Although learning curve analysis can significantly enhance the ability to predict costs when learning occurs, three inherent limitations and problems are associated with the use of this method.

The first and key limitation of using learning curves is that the approach is most appropriate for labor-intensive contexts that involve repetitive tasks performed for long production runs for which repeated trials improve performance, or learning. When the production process is designed to maximize flexibility and very fast set-up times for manufacturing machinery using robotics and computer controls as many manufacturers now do, the manufacturing setting requires relatively little repetitive labor and consequently relatively little opportunity for learning.

A second limitation is that the learning rate is assumed to be constant (average labor time decreases at a fixed rate as output doubles). In actual applications, the decline in labor time might not be constant. For example, the learning rate could be 80 percent for the first 20,000 units, 90 percent for the next 35,000 units, and 95 percent thereafter. Such differences indicate the need to update projections based on the observed progression of learning.

Third, a carefully estimated learning curve might be unreliable because the observed change in productivity in the data used to fit the model was actually associated with factors other than learning. For example, the increase in productivity might have been due to a change in labor mix, a change in product mix, or some combination of other related factors. In such cases, the learning model is unreliable and produces inaccurate estimates of labor time and cost.

APPENDIX B

> For which of you, intending to build a tower, sitteth not down first, and counteth the cost, whether he may have sufficient to finish?
>
> BIBLE, AUTHORIZED VERSION, LUKE 14:28

Regression Analysis

LEARNING OBJECTIVE 6▶

Use statistical measures to evaluate a regression analysis.

This appendix uses an example to explain the development of a regression estimate and the related statistical measures. Then we interpret the statistical measures to assess the precision and reliability of the regression.

The Regression Estimate

To illustrate the manner in which a regression estimate is obtained, we use the data in Exhibit 7–4. Recall that regression analysis finds the unique line through the data that minimizes the sum of the squares of the errors, where the error is measured as the difference between the values predicted by the regression and the actual values for the dependent variable. In this example, the dependent variable, supplies expense (Y), is estimated with a single independent variable, production level (X). The regression for the three data points is

$$Y = a + b \times X = \$220 + \$0.75 \times X$$

The intercept term, labeled a, and the coefficient of the independent variable, labeled b, are obtained from a set of calculations performed by spreadsheet programs and are described in basic textbooks on probability and statistics. The calculations themselves are beyond the scope of this text. Our focus is on the derivation and interpretation of the statistical measures that tell management accountants something about the reliability and precision of the regression.

Statistical Measures

The statistical measures of the reliability and precision of the regression are derived from an analysis of the variance of the dependent variable. *Variance* is a measure of the degree to which the values of the dependent variable vary about its mean. The term *analysis of variance* is used because the regression analysis is based on a separation of the total variance of the dependent variable into error and explained components. The underlying concept is that in predicting individual values for the dependent variable, the regression is *explaining changes (i.e., variance) in the dependent variable* associated with changes in the independent variable. The variance in the dependent variable that is not explained is called the residual, or *error variance*. Thus, the regression's ability to correctly predict changes in the dependent variable is a key measure of its reliability and is measured by the proportion of explained to error variances. Based on the data in Exhibit 7–4, Exhibit 7–14 shows how the variance measures are obtained.

The first two columns of Exhibit 7–14 show the data for the independent (X) and dependent (Y) variables. Column (3) shows the mean of the dependent variable (YM), and column (4) the regression prediction (YE) for each of the points. The last three columns indicate the three variance measures. Column (5) shows the total variance, or variance of the dependent variable, measured as the difference between each data point and the mean of the dependent variable (Y – YM). Column (6) shows the variance explained by the regression (YE – YM), and column (7) shows the error variance, (Y – YE). The measures in these last three columns are squared and summed to arrive at the desired values for *total* variance, explained variance, and error variance, respectively. The sum of the error and explained variance terms equals total variance. These terms are illustrated in Exhibit 7–15 and the values calculated in Exhibit 7–16.

The three variance terms are the basic elements of the statistical analysis of the regression. This is best illustrated in the analysis of variance table in Exhibit 7–16. The **analysis of variance table** separates the total variance of the dependent variable into both error and explained components. The first two columns of the table show the type and amount of variance for each of the three variance terms. The third column shows the **degrees of freedom** for each component, which represents the number of independent choices that can be made for that component. Thus, the number of degrees of freedom for the explained variance component is always equal to the number of independent variables, and the total degrees of freedom is always equal to the number of data points less 1. The error degrees of freedom equal the total less the explained degrees of freedom.

The fourth column, **mean squared variance**, is the ratio of the amount of the variance of a component (in the second column) to the number of degrees of freedom (in the third column).

The analysis of variance table serves as a useful basis to discuss the key statistical measures of the regression. Of the six principal measures in Exhibit 7–17, one measure refers to the precision of the regression and five measures refer to the reliability of the regression. *Precision* refers to the ability of the regression to provide accurate estimates—how close the regression's estimates are to the unknown true value. *Reliability*

The **analysis of variance table** separates the total variance of the dependent variable into both error and explained variance components.

The **degrees of freedom** for each component of variance represent the number of independent choices that can be made for that component.

Mean squared variance is the ratio of the amount of variance of a component to the number of degrees of freedom for that component.

Exhibit 7–14	Variance Components for Regression Analysis					
1	2	3	4	5	6	7
Dependent Variable Y	Independent Variable X	Mean of Y (YM)	Regression Prediction for Y (YE)	Total Variance of Y (T) = (Y – YM)	Regression Variance (R) = (YE – YM)	Error Variance (E) = (Y – YE)
250	50	295	257.5	(45)	(37.5)	(7.5)
310	100	295	295.0	15	0.0	15.0
325	150	295	332.5	30	37.5	(7.5)

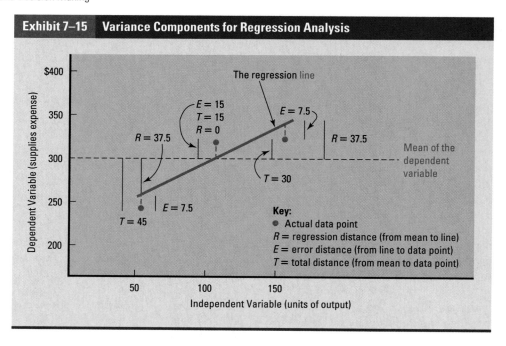

Exhibit 7–15   Variance Components for Regression Analysis

Exhibit 7–16   Analysis of Variance Table for Regression Analysis

Source of Variance	Variance of Each Component of the Regression (also called *sum of squares*)	Degrees of Freedom	Mean Squared Variance
Explained (regression)	$37.5^2 + 0^2 + 37.5^2 = 2,812.5$	1	2,812.5
Error	$7.5^2 + 15^2 + 7.5^2 = 337.5$	1	337.5
Total	$(45)^2 + (15)^2 + (30)^2 = 3,150.0$	2	1,575.0

Exhibit 7–17   Six Key Statistical Measures

Precision
1.   Precision of the regression (measured by the standard error of the estimate)

Reliability
2.   Goodness of fit (*R*-squared)
3.   Statistical reliability (*F*-statistic)
4.   Statistical reliability for each independent variable (*t*-value)
5.   Reliability of precision (rank-order correlation)
6.   Nonindependence of errors (Durbin-Watson statistic)

refers to the confidence the user can have that the regression is valid; that is, how likely the regression is to continue to provide accurate predictions over time and for different levels of the independent variables.

After explaining each of the statistical measures, we summarize the explanations in Exhibit 7–20.

Precision of the Regression

The standard error of the estimate (*SE*) is a useful measure of the accuracy of the regression's estimates. The standard error is interpreted as a range of values around the regression estimate such that we can be approximately 67 percent confident the actual value lies in this range (see Exhibits 7–8A and 7–8B). An inverse relationship, and therefore a trade-off, exists between the confidence level and the width of the interval. The value of the *SE* for a given regression can be obtained directly from the analysis of variance table as follows:

$$SE = \sqrt{\text{Mean square error}}$$
$$= \sqrt{337.5} = 18.37$$

The precision and accuracy of the regression improve as the variance for error is reduced and as the number of data points increases, as illustrated in the preceding formula for *SE*.

The standard error of the estimate can also be used to develop confidence intervals for the accuracy of the prediction, as illustrated in Exhibits 7–8A and B. A **confidence interval** is a range around the regression line within which the management accountant can be confident the actual value of the predicted cost will fall. A 67 percent confidence interval is determined by taking the regression line and identifying a range that is 1 standard error distance on either side of the regression line; a 95 percent confidence interval would be determined from 2 standard error distances. Confidence intervals are useful and precise tools for management accountants to describe the degree of precision obtained from the regression.

A **confidence interval** is a range around the regression line within which the management accountant can be confident the actual value of the predicted cost will fall.

Goodness of Fit (*R*-squared)

R-squared (also called the *coefficient of determination*) is a direct measure of the explanatory power of the regression. It measures the percent of variance in the dependent variable that can be explained by the independent variable. *R*-squared is calculated in Exhibit 7–16:

$$R^2 = \frac{\Sigma \text{ of squares (explained)}}{\Sigma \text{ of squares (total)}}$$
$$= \frac{2,812.5}{3,150} = .892$$

The explanatory power of the regression improves as the explained sum of squares increases relative to the total sum of squares. A value close to 1 reflects a good-fitting regression with strong explanatory power.

Statistical Reliability

The **F-statistic** is a useful measure of the statistical reliability of the regression. Statistical reliability asks whether the relationship between the variables in the regression actually exists or whether the correlation between the variables an accident of the data at hand. If only a small number of data points are used, it is possible to have a relatively high *R*-squared (if the regression is a good fit to the data points), but this offers relatively little confidence that an actual stable relationship exists.

The larger the *F*, the lower the risk that the regression is statistically unreliable. The determination of an acceptable *F*-value depends on the number of data points, but the required *F*-value decreases as the number of data points increase. Most regres-

The **F-statistic** is a useful measure of the statistical reliability of the regression.

Learning and Regression in Heart Transplants

A recent study used both learning curves and multiple regression to examine the effect of learning on the cost of heart transplants. Based on a study of 71 heart transplant patients, the study found evidence of a learning rate of approximately 95 percent. The cost of the surgery for the 50th heart transplant patient was predicted to be less than one-half the cost of the surgery for the first patient!

Source: John R. Woods et al., "The Learning Curve and the Cost of Heart Transplantation," *Health Services Research*, June 1992, pp. 219–39.

sion software programs show the F-value and the related risk score, which should be less than approximately 5 percent. The F-statistic can be obtained from the analysis of variance table as follows (because in part of the small number of data points, this F-value has a relatively high risk score of 21 percent):

$$F = \frac{\text{Mean square (explained)}}{\text{Mean square (errors)}}$$

$$= \frac{2,812.5}{337.5} = 8.333$$

The R-squared value and the F-statistic usually tell the same story; that is, they are both favorable or unfavorable. However, if the regression used a very large number of data points (a few hundred or more), it is possible to have a good score for the F-statistic but a poor fit based on the R-squared value. The number of data points in such a case is so large that the mean square error is very small (and therefore F is large) although the sum of squares for error is large, and therefore R-squared is poor. In this case, management accountants should interpret the regression as having statistical reliability (it is not by chance), but having perhaps little practical reliability (goodness of fit). That is, the management accountant can be relatively confident that there is a poor regression. The reverse is true for very small samples. The implication is that R-squared and the F-statistic must be interpreted carefully when the sample size is either very small or very large.

Statistical Reliability for Each of the Independent Variables (*t*-value)

The t-value is a measure of the reliability of each independent variable and as such, it has an interpretation very much like that of the F-statistic. The t-value equals the ratio of the coefficient of the independent variable to the standard error of the coefficient for that independent variable. The standard error of the coefficient is not the same as the standard error of the estimate, but it is interpreted in the same way. However, the SE cannot be obtained directly from the analysis of variance table. For the data in Exhibit 7–14, the value of the standard error for the coefficient is .2598.[6] The t-value is thus

$$t = .75/.2598 = 2.8868$$

A t-value larger than 2.0 indicates that the independent variable is reliable at a risk level of approximately 5 percent and is therefore a reliable independent variable to include in the regression. Regression software shows the 95 percent confidence range for the coefficient of each of the independent variables. The range of the standard error of the estimate should be relatively small. A small range provides confidence in the accuracy of the coefficient's value.

Reliability of Precision (Nonconstant Variance)

Nonconstant variance is the condition when the variance of the errors is not constant over the range of the independent variable.

For certain sets of data, the standard error of the estimate varies over the range of the independent variable. The variance of the errors is not constant over the range of the independent variable. This is the case, for example, when the relationship between the independent and dependent variables becomes less stable over time. This type of behavior is illustrated in Exhibit 7–18.

If there is non-constant variance, the SE value provided by the regression is not uniformly accurate over the range of the independent variable. To detect nonconstant variance, we calculate the rank-order correlation between the position of the data and the size of the error. The **rank-order correlation** is a statistic that measures the degree to

The **rank-order correlation** is a statistic that measures the degree to which two sets of numbers tend to have the same order or rank.

---

6   The standard error of the coefficient is calculated as follows:

$$\text{Standard error} = SE/(\text{Std. deviation of the independent variable})$$

$$= \frac{18.37}{\sqrt{(50-100)^2 + (100-100)^2 + (150-100)^2}} = .2598$$

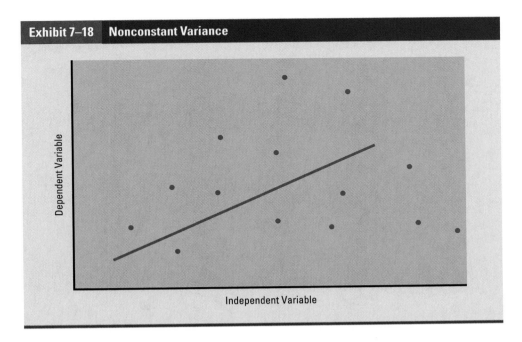

Exhibit 7–18 Nonconstant Variance

which two sets of numbers tend to have the same order, or rank. A relatively high rank-order correlation is evidence of nonconstant variance. For the data in Exhibit 7–14, the Spearman rank-correlation coefficient is .125, a relatively small correlation that indicates little evidence of nonconstant variance. The calculation of rank-order correlation is beyond the scope of this introductory chapter but can be found in many statistics texts.

To fix the problem of nonconstant variance, management accountants should transform the dependent variable with the log or square root to see whether this improves the behavior of the errors. If it does not fix the condition, management accountants should be very cautious in interpreting the *SE* value.

Nonindependent Errors (Durbin-Watson Statistic)

A key assumption of regression is that the relationship between the independent and dependent variables is linear. If the data are nonlinear because of seasonality or a cyclical pattern, for example, the errors are systematically related to each other, that is, are not independent. This assumption is violated frequently because financial data are often affected by trend, seasonality, and cyclical influences. The relationship between the variables might also be inherently nonlinear, as when learning occurs or a multiplicative rather than an additive relationship exists (such as predicting payroll costs from hours worked and wage rates). Then the regression is unreliable and subject to greater than expected estimation errors. One type of nonlinearity (nonindependence of errors) is illustrated in Exhibit 7–19.

A common method that detects nonlinearity is the **Durbin-Watson (DW) statistic.** It is calculated from the amount and change of the errors over the range of the independent variable. The DW value falls between zero and 4.0; with 20 or more data points, a value of DW between approximately 1.0 and 3.0 indicates little chance of a nonlinearity as described earlier; values less than 1.0 or greater than 3.0 should indicate the need to study the data and to choose appropriate fixes if necessary.

The problem of nonindependent errors usually can be fixed by deseasonalizing the data, using a dummy variable for seasonality, or using an index to remove the trend. Alternatively, what may be required is to convert a multiplicative relationship to an equivalent additive (that is, linear) relationship by taking the logarithm of the independent and dependent variables. The statistical measures, their indicators, and ways to fix the underlying conditions are summarized in Exhibit 7–20.

The Durbin-Watson statistic is a measure of the extent of nonlinearity in the regression.

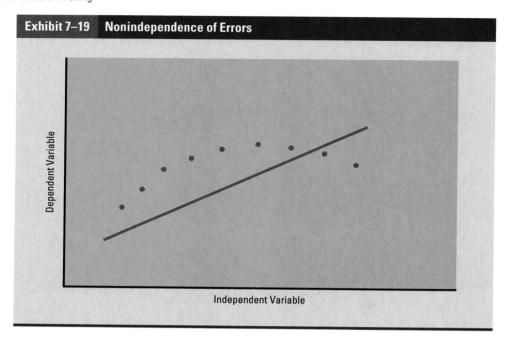

Exhibit 7–19   Nonindependence of Errors

Independent Variable

(y-axis label: Dependent Variable)

Exhibit 7–20   Summary of Statistical Measures

Measure Concerns	Statistical Measure	What Is an OK Value?*	What Is the Right Fix If Not OK?	Consequence If Not Fixed
Reliability— Goodness of fit	R-squared	Should be approximately .75 or better	• Add or delete independent variables • If DW is poor, could need transforms (lag, log, first differences, . . .) • Correct measurement errors in the data, for example, cutoff errors, or reporting lags	• Inaccurate estimates
Statistical reliability for the regression	F-statistic	Depends on sample size	• Increase sample size • Other changes as suggested for reliability—goodness of fit	• Inaccurate estimates
Statistical reliability for the independent variables	t-value	Should be greater than 2.0	• Delete or transform the independent variable	• Inaccurate estimates
Precision of the regression	Standard error of the estimates (SE)	Should be small relative to the dependent variable	• Same considerations as for reliability—goodness of fit above	• Inaccurate estimates
Reliability of precision (non constant variance)	Rank-order correlation	Should be small	• Square root or log transform the dependent variable • Add a dummy variable	• SE is unreliable
Reliability— Potential nonlinearity (nonindependence of errors)	Durbin-Watson statistic (DW)	Between 2.0 and 3.0	*For certain series:* • Deseasonalize • Detrend • Use dummy variable for shift *For nonlinear relationship* • Log transform • Some other nonlinear transform	• Inaccurate estimates • SE is unreliable

*The values shown here are useful for a wide range of regressions. The exact values for a specific regression depend on a number of factors including the sample size and the number of independent variables. A recent study of regression analysis applied to 20 different overhead cost accounts showed that most of the R-squared values fall between .83 and .93. The values for the standard error of the estimates averaged 12 percent of the mean of the dependent variable, with most falling between 5 percent and 20 percent. See G. R. Cluskey Jr., Mitchell H. Raiborn, and Doan T. Modianos, "Multiple-Cost Flexible Budgets and PC-Based Regression Analysis," *Journal of Cost Management,* July–August 2000, pp. 35–47.

Multiple Linear Regression

Although the previous discussion illustrated simple linear regression (one independent variable), the same concerns are applicable for two or more independent variables. One additional concern arises with multiple independent variables: multicollinearity, which exists when two or more of the independent variables are significantly correlated. Multicollinearity can be detected by reviewing the correlation values given in the output of the regression. Multicollinearity violates the regression assumption that the independent variables are independent and that the relationships are linear and additive. When present, multicollinearity can show good values of R-squared, but it also can lead management accountants to overestimate the degree of reliability actually present in the regression. Thus, multicollinearity does not so much degrade the estimation performance of the regression as it distorts the confidence that management accountants should have in the regression.

KEY TERMS

COMMENTS ON COST MANAGEMENT IN ACTION

Using Regression to Estimate the Value of Commercial Real Estate

ESTIMATING REAL ESTATE VALUES FOR APARTMENT BUILDINGS AND OFFICE BUILDINGS

As expected, real estate appraisers performing regression analysis to appraise the value of an apartment building or an office building use as the dominant independent variable the property's past, current, and expected future net operating income (NOI). That is, the chief determinant of the value of the property is its ability to produce cash flows and profits. Other variables regarding the property include its size (as measured by the number of units, number of square feet, number of two-bedroom and one-bedroom apartments, etc.), its age, and the relevant vacancy rate in the property and in the submarket area where it is located. Since the regression analysis is usually built from actual sales numbers over a period of time, these appraisers also use a trend variable to tie the sales price of the property to the year it was sold.

ESTIMATING REAL ESTATE VALUES FOR WAREHOUSES AND MANUFACTURING PLANTS

Similarly, real estate appraisers have developed regression analyses for warehouses and manufacturing plants using their size, age, and location. The NOI variable is usually not relevant. They also use a trend variable to distinguish sales of properties in different years. For example, an analysis of sales value (per square foot) of industrial properties in the Los Angeles area in the early 1990s showed a significant trend variable (−$2.83 per square foot per year); the coefficient on the trend variable was negative because prices were falling during that period. A significant size variable (−$2.43 per square foot, per 100,000 square feet of space) indicated that larger buildings had on average lower sales prices per square foot. Age was also a factor, the coefficient being −$0.41 per square foot per year of age. The location variable was also significant, showing that properties in certain counties in the Los Angeles area (Orange County, San Bernadino, etc.) were predicted to have as much as a $2.32 difference in value per square foot.

Sources: Stephen T. Crosson, Charles G. Dannis, and Thomas G. Thibodeau, "Regression Analysis: A Cost-Effective Approach for the Valuation of Commercial Property," *Real Estate Finance*, Winter 1996; Maxwell O. Ramsland Jr. and Daniel E. Markham, "Market-Supported Adjustments Using Multiple Regression Analysis," *The Appraisal Journal*, April 1998, pp. 181–91; and Stephen C. Kincheloe, "Linear Regression Analysis of Economic Variables in the Sales Comparison and Income Approaches," *The Appraisal Journal*, October 1993.

SELF-STUDY PROBLEMS

(For solutions, please turn to the end of the chapter.)

1. Using the High-Low Method

Hector's Delivery Service uses four small vans and six pickup trucks to deliver small packages in the Charlotte, North Carolina, metropolitan area. Hector spends a considerable amount of money on the gas, oil, and regular maintenance of his vehicles, which is done at a variety of service stations and repair shops. To budget his vehicle expenses for the coming year, he gathers data on his expenses and number of deliveries for each month of the current year.

	Total Vehicle Expenses	Total Deliveries
January	$145,329	5,882
February	133,245	5,567
March	123,245	5,166
April	164,295	6,621
May	163,937	6,433
June	176,229	6,681
July	180,553	7,182
August	177,293	6,577
September	155,389	5,942
October	150,832	5,622
November	152,993	5,599
December	201,783	7,433

Required Use the high-low estimation method to determine the relationship between the number of deliveries and the cost of maintaining the vehicles.

2. Using Regression Analysis

George Harder is the Imperial Foods Company's plant manager of one of the processing plants. George is concerned about the increase in plant overhead costs in recent months. He has collected data on overhead costs for the past 24 months and has decided to use regression to study the factors influencing these costs. He has also collected data on materials cost, direct labor-hours, and machine-hours as potential independent variables to use in predicting overhead.

George runs two regression analyses on these data, with the following results:

	Regression 1 (labor-hours only)	Regression 2 (labor-hours and machine-hours)
R-squared	.65	.58
Standard error	$12,554	$13,793
Standard error as a percent of the dependent variable	12%	14%
t-values		
Materials cost	2.0	−1.6
Labor-hours	4.5	3.8
Machine-hours		1.4

Required   Which of the two regressions is better and why?

3. Using Both High-Low and Regression

John Meeks Company is a medium-size manufacturing company with plants in three small mid-Atlantic towns. The company makes plastic parts for automobiles and trucks, primarily door panels, exterior trim, and related items. The parts have an average cost of $5 to $20. The company has a steady demand for its products from both domestic and foreign automakers and has experienced growth in sales averaging between 10 and 20 percent over the last 8 to 10 years.

Currently, management is reviewing the incidence of scrap and waste in the manufacturing process at one of its plants. Meeks defines scrap and waste as any defective unit that is rejected for lack of functionality or another aspect of quality. The plants have a number of different inspection points, and failure or rejection can occur at any inspection point. The number of defective units is listed in the following table; management estimates the cost of this waste in labor and materials to be approximately $10 per unit.

An unfavorable trend appears to exist with regard to defects, and management has asked you to investigate and estimate the defective units in the coming months. A first step in your investigation is to identify the cost drivers of defective parts, to understand what causes them, and to provide a basis on which to estimate future defects. For this purpose, you have obtained these recent data on the units produced, the units shipped, and the cost of sales since these numbers are easily available and relatively reliable on a monthly basis:

	Units Produced (000s)	Cost of Sales (000s)	Units Shipped (000s)	Defective Units
Jan 2000	55	689	50	856
Feb	58	737	53	1,335
Mar	69	886	64	1,610
Apr	61	768	56	1,405
May	65	828	60	1,511
Jun	69	878	64	1,600
Jul	75	962	70	1,570
Aug	81	1052	76	1,910
Sep	70	1104	80	2,011
Oct	79	1224	89	2,230
Nov	82	1261	92	2,300
Dec	70	1020	74	1,849

continued

continued

Jan 2001	67	850	62	1,549
Feb	72	916	67	1,669
Mar	85	1107	80	2,012
Apr	75	968	70	1,756
May	81	1037	76	1,889
Jun	85	1103	80	1,650
Jul	92	1208	87	2,187
Aug	100	1310	95	2,387
Sep	91	1380	101	2,514
Oct	101	1536	111	2,787
Nov	105	1580	115	2,310
Dec	88	1270	92	2,311

Required   Use the high-low method and regression analysis to estimate the defective units in the coming months and to determine which method provides the best fit for this purpose.

QUESTIONS

7–1   Define *cost estimation* and explain its purpose in each of the management functions.

7–2   Explain the assumptions used in cost estimation.

7–3   List the three methods of cost estimation. Explain the advantages and disadvantages of each.

7–4   Explain the implementation problems in cost estimation.

7–5   What are the six steps in cost estimation? Which one is the most important? Why?

7–6   Contrast the use of regression analysis and the high-low method to estimate costs.

7–7   How is cost estimation used in activity-based costing?

7–8   Explain how to choose the dependent and independent variables in regression analysis.

7–9   What are nonlinear cost relationships? Give two examples.

7–10   List four advantages of regression analysis.

7–11   Explain what dummy variables are and how they are used in regression analysis.

7–12   How do we know when high correlation exists? Is high correlation the same as cause and effect?

7–13   What does the coefficient of determination (R-squared) measure?

7–14   Cost Classification: Match each cost described here to the appropriate cost behavior pattern shown in the graphs (a) through (l).

   1.   The cost of lumber used to manufacture wooden kitchen tables.

   2.   The cost of order fillers in a warehouse. When demand increases, the number is increased, and when demand falls off, the number is decreased.

   3.   The salary of the plant's quality control inspector, who inspects each batch of products.

   4.   The cost of water and sewer service to the manufacturing plant. The local municipality charges a fixed rate per gallon for usage up to 10,000 gallons, and a higher charge per gallon for usage above that point.

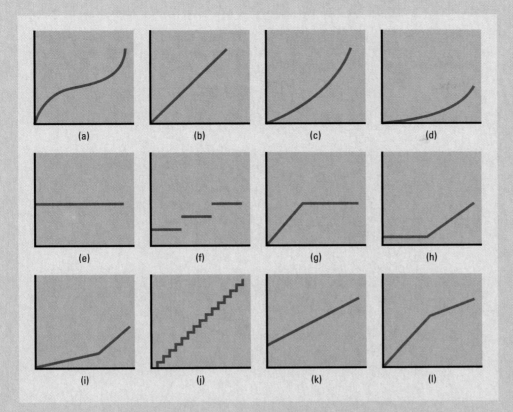

5. The cost of an Internet connection of $23 per month.

6. The cost of an Internet connection of $10 per month plus $2 per hour of usage above 10 hours.

7. The cost to make copies of a given document at a printing shop, which reduces the per-copy charge for customers who make more than 100 copies of the document.

8. The total cost of manufacturing a new camera over its entire life cycle.

9. To discourage excess usage and to level the demand, especially in peak load times, the local electric utility increases the per-kilowatt-hour charge for each additional 5,000 kilowatt-hours' usage.

10. A clothing store in the SunnyVale Mall pays a fixed rental charge of $1,000 per month plus 2 percent of gross sales receipts.

11. The cost of repair for a machine used in manufacturing.

12. A shoe store in the SunnyVale Mall pays 6 percent of gross sales receipts, up to a maximum of $3,000 per month as a rental charge.

EXERCISES

7–15 COST RELATIONSHIPS   CompuCo hired Daffner & Associates to design a new computer-aided manufacturing facility that is to produce 250 computers per month. The variable costs for each computer are $450 and the fixed costs total $62,250 per month.

Required   What is the average cost per unit if the facility normally expects to operate at 90 percent of capacity?

7–16   COST RELATIONSHIPS   The following costs are for Optical View Inc., a contact lens manufacturer:

Output in Units	Fixed Costs	Variable Costs	Total Costs
250	$4,750	$ 7,500	$12,250
300	4,750	9,000	13,750
350	4,750	10,500	15,250
400	4,750	12,000	16,750

Required

1.   Graph total cost, total variable costs, and total fixed costs.

2.   Graph the per-unit total cost, per-unit variable cost, and per-unit fixed cost.

3.   Discuss the behavior of the fixed, variable, and total cost.

7–17   COST ESTIMATION, AVERAGE COST   Maribeth's Cafe bakes croissants that it sells to local restaurants and grocery stores in the Raleigh, North Carolina, area. The average costs to bake the croissants are $0.55 for 500 and $0.50 for 600.

Required   If the cost function for croissants is linear, what will be the average cost to bake 560?

Service

7–18   COST ESTIMATION USING GRAPHS, SERVICE   Lawson Advertising Agency is trying to persuade Kansas City Sailboards Company to spend more money on advertising. The agency's argument is that a positive linear relationship exists between advertising and sales in the sailboard industry. Sue Lawson presents these data taken from industry data for stores similar in size and market share to Kansas City Sailboards:

Advertising Expense	Annual Sales
$2,500	$ 95,000
3,000	110,000
3,500	124,000
4,000	138,000
4,500	143,000
5,000	147,000
5,500	150,000

Required

1.   Graph annual sales and advertising expense.

2.   Do the data prove Sue's point?

7–19   COST ESTIMATION, HIGH-LOW METHOD   Ethan Manufacturing Inc. produces floor mats for automobiles. The owner, Joseph Ethan, has asked you to assist him in estimating his maintenance costs. Together, you and Joseph determine that the single best cost driver for maintenance costs is machine-hours. These data are from the previous fiscal year for maintenance expense and machine-hours:

Month	Maintenance Expense	Machine-Hours
1	$2,600	1,690
2	2,760	1,770
3	2,910	1,850

4	3,020	1,870
5	3,100	1,900
6	3,070	1,880
7	3,010	1,860
8	2,850	1,840
9	2,620	1,700
10	2,220	1,100
11	2,230	1,300
12	2,450	1,590

Required What is the cost equation for maintenance cost using the high-low method?

PROBLEMS

7–20 COST ESTIMATION, HIGH-LOW METHOD Bob Schmitz Company specializes in the purchase, renovation, and resale of older homes. Bob Schmitz employs several carpenters and painters to do the work for him. It is essential for him to have accurate cost estimates so he can determine total renovation costs before he purchases a piece of property. If estimated renovation costs plus the purchase price of a house are higher than its estimated resale value, the house is not a worthwhile investment.

Bob has been using the home's interior square feet for his exterior paint cost estimations. Recently he decided to include the number of openings—the total number of doors and windows in a house—as a cost driver. Their cost is significant because they require time-consuming preparatory work and careful brushwork. The rest of the house usually is painted either by rollers or spray guns, which are relatively efficient ways to apply paint to a large area. Bob has kept careful records of these expenses on his last 12 jobs:

House	Square Feet	Openings	Cost
1	2,600	13	$3,300
2	3,010	15	3,750
3	2,800	12	3,100
4	2,850	12	3,150
5	4,050	19	4,700
6	2,700	13	3,250
7	2,375	11	2,800
8	2,450	11	2,800
9	2,600	10	2,875
10	3,700	16	4,100
11	2,650	13	3,200
12	3,550	16	3,950

Required

1. Using the high-low cost estimation technique, determine the cost of painting a 3,200-square-foot house with 14 openings. Also determine the cost for a 2,400-square-foot house with 8 openings.

2. Plot the cost data against square feet and against openings. Which variable is a better cost driver? Why?

7–21 COST ESTIMATION, MACHINE REPLACEMENT, ETHICS SpectroGlass Company manufactures glass for office buildings in Arizona and Southern California. As a result of age and wear, a critical machine in the production process has begun to produce quality defects. SpectroGlass is considering replacing the old machine with a new machine either brand A or brand B. The

Ethics

International

manufacturer of each machine has provided SpectroGlass these data on the cost of operation of its machine at various levels of output:

Output (square yards)	Machine A Estimated Total Costs	Machine B Estimated Total Costs
4,000	$ 54,600	$ 70,000
7,000	78,800	100,000
9,000	90,300	115,000
14,000	114,900	137,000
16,000	132,400	146,000
24,000	210,000	192,000

Required

1. If SpectroGlass's output is expected to be 22,000 square yards, which machine should it purchase? At 15,000 square yards?

2. As a cost analyst at Spectroglass, you have been assigned to complete requirement 1. A production supervisor comes to you to say that the nature of the defect is really very difficult to detect and that most customers will not notice it, so he questions replacing it. He suggests that you modify your calculations to justify keeping the present machine to keep things the way they are and save the company some money. What do you say?

3. Assume that brand A is manufactured in Germany and brand B is manufactured in Canada. As a U.S.–based firm, what considerations are important to SpectroGlass, in addition to those already mentioned in your answer to requirement 1?

7–22   COST ESTIMATION, HIGH-LOW METHOD   Antelope Park Amoco (APA) in Antelope Park, Alaska, has noticed that utility bills are substantially higher the colder the average monthly temperature is. The only thing in the shop that uses natural gas is the furnace. Because of prevailing low temperatures, the furnace is used every month of the year (though less in the summer months and very little in August). Everything else in the shop runs on electricity, and electricity use is fairly constant throughout the year.

For a year, APA has been recording the average daily temperature and the cost of its monthly utility bills for natural gas and electricity.

	Average Temperature	Utility Cost
January	31°F	$760
February	41	629
March	43	543
April	44	410
May	46	275
June	50	233
July	53	220
August	60	210
September	50	305
October	40	530
November	30	750
December	20	870

Required   Use the high-low method to estimate utility cost for the upcoming months of January and February. The forecast for January is a near record average temperature of 10°F; temperatures in February are expected to average 40°F.

7–23 to 7–27 REGRESSION ANALYSIS Problems 7–23 through 7–27 are based on Armer Company, which is accumulating data to use in preparing its annual profit plan for the coming year. The cost behavior pattern of the maintenance costs must be determined. The accounting staff has suggested the use of linear regression to derive an equation for maintenance hours and costs. Data regarding the maintenance hours and costs for the last year and the results of the regression analysis follow:

	Hours of Activity	Maintenance Costs
January	480	$ 4,200
February	320	3,000
March	400	3,600
April	300	2,820
May	500	4,350
June	310	2,960
July	320	3,030
August	520	4,470
September	490	4,260
October	470	4,050
November	350	3,300
December	340	3,160
Sum	4,800	$43,200
Average	400	3,600

Average cost per hour ($43,200/4,800) = $9.00

a (intercept)	684.65
b coefficient	7.2884
Standard error of the estimate	34.469
R-squared	.99724
t-value for *b*	60.105

Required (7–23) If Armer Company uses the high-low method of analysis, the equation for the relationship between hours of activity and maintenance cost follows:

a. $y = 400 + 9.0x$

b. $y = 570 + 7.5x$

c. $y = 3,600 + 400x$

d. $y = 570 + 9.0x$

e. None of the above

(CMA Adapted)

Required (7–24) Based on the data derived from the regression analysis, 420 maintenance hours in a month mean that maintenance costs should be budgeted at

a. $3,780

b. $3,461

c. $3,797

d. $3,746

e. None of the above

(CMA Adapted)

Required (7–25)   The coefficient of determination for Armer's regression equation for the maintenance activities is

  a. 34.469/49.515

  b. .99724

  c. square root of .99724

  d. $(.99724)^2$

  e. None of the above

(CMA Adapted)

Required (7–26)   The percent of the total variance that can be explained by the regression equation is

  a. 99.724%

  b. 69.613%

  c. 80.982%

  d. 99.862%

  e. None of the above

(CMA Adapted)

Required (7–27)   At 400 hours of activity, Armer management can be approximately two-thirds confident that the maintenance costs will be in the range of

  a. $3,550.50–$3,649.53

  b. $3,551.37–$3,648.51

  c. $3,586.18–$3,613.93

  d. $3,565.54–$3,634.47

  e. None of the above

(CMA Adapted)

7–28   REGRESSION ANALYSIS   Whittenberg Distributors, a major retailing and mail-order operation, has been in business for the past 10 years. During that time, its mail-order operations have grown from a sideline to represent more than 80 percent of the company's annual sales. Of course, the company has suffered growing pains. At times, overloaded or faulty computer programs resulted in lost sales, and scheduling temporary workers to augment the permanent staff during peak periods has always been a problem.

Peter Bloom, manager of mail-order operations, has developed procedures for handling most problems. However, he is still trying to improve the scheduling of temporary workers to take customer telephone orders. Under the current system, Peter keeps a permanent staff of 60 employees who handle the base telephone workload and supplements this staff with temporary workers as needed. The temporary workers are hired on a daily basis; he determines the number needed for the next day the afternoon before based on his estimate of the upcoming telephone volume.

Peter has decided to try regression analysis to improve the hiring of temporary workers. By summarizing the daily labor hours into weekly totals for the past year, he determined the number of workers used each week. In addition, he listed the number of orders processed each week. After entering the data into a spreadsheet, Peter ran two regressions. Regression 1 related the total number of workers (permanent staff plus temporary workers) to the number of orders received. Regression 2 related only temporary workers to the number of orders received. The output of these analyses follows:

$$\text{Regression model: } W = a + b \times T$$

where: W = workers; T = telephone orders

	Regression 1	Regression 2
a	21.938	−46.569
b	.0043	.0051
Standard error of the estimate	3.721	3.295
t-value	1.95	2.04
Coefficient of determination	.624	.755
Durbin Watson statistic	1.33	1.67

Required

1. Peter Bloom estimates that Whittenberg Distributors will receive 12,740 orders during the second week of December.

   a. Predict the number of temporary workers needed for this week using regression 1. Round your answer to the nearest whole number.

   b. Using regression 2, predict the number of temporary workers needed during this week. Round your answer to the nearest whole number.

2. Which of the two regression analyses appears to be better? Explain your answer.

3. Describe at least three ways that Peter Bloom could improve his analysis to make better predictions than either of these regression results provides.

(CMA Adapted)

7–29 REGRESSION ANALYSIS, EVALUATING REGRESSION EQUATIONS   Hascup Appliances Inc. manufactures and sells a line of washers and dryers throughout the western United States. Linda McElroy, a financial analyst for Hascup, has been tracking the expenditures experienced in advertising campaigns and in factory rebates. Linda believes that the level of advertising expenses and/or factory rebates can be used to forecast sales. Linda believes that linear regression is the proper tool and has developed the regression equations shown in the following table based on 18 months of accumulated data. The notation used in the equations are as follows:

S = total monthly sales dollars
A = monthly advertising expenditures
R = monthly rebate costs

	Equation 1	Equation 2	Equation 3
Equation	$S = 87,780 + 22.95A$	$S = 91,940 + 95.85R$	$S = 230 + 22.68A + 94.16R$
R-squared	.462	.337	.804
Standard error of the estimate	$32,180	$34,830	$22,390

Required

1. If Hascup Appliances is projecting advertising expenditures of $19,000 and factory rebates of $8,700 for the next month, calculate next month's expected sales using equation 1.

2. Based on equation 3, determine expected sales if Hascup spends $5,000 on factory rebates and $10,000 on advertising.

3. Identify the regression equation that Hascup Appliances should choose to predict sales and explain why.

(CMA Adapted)

7–30 REGRESSION ANALYSIS   United States Motors Inc. (USMI) manufactures automobiles and light trucks and distributes them for sale to consumers through franchised retail outlets. As part of the franchise agreement, dealerships must provide monthly financial statements following the USMI accounting procedures manual. USMI has developed the following financial profile of an average dealership that sells 1,500 new vehicles annually.

Strategy

Average Dealership Financial Profile
Composite Income Statement

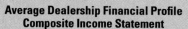

Sales	$30,000,000
Cost of goods sold	24,750,000
Gross profit	$ 5,250,000
Operating costs	
Variable expenses	862,500
Mixed expenses	2,300,000
Fixed expenses	1,854,000
Operating income	$ 233,500

USMI is considering a major expansion of its dealership network. The vice president of marketing has asked Jack Snyder, corporate controller, to develop some measure of the risk associated with the addition of these franchises. Jack estimates that 90 percent of the mixed expenses shown are variable for purposes of this analysis. He also suggested performing regression analyses on the various components of the mixed expenses to more definitively determine their variability.

Required

1. Calculate the composite dealership profit if 2,000 units are sold.

2. Assume that regression analyses were performed on the separate components of the mixed expenses and that a coefficient of determination value of .60 was determined as applicable to aggregate mixed expenses over the relevant range.

   a. Define the term *relevant range*.

   b. Explain the significance of an *R*-squared value of .60 to USMI's analysis.

   c. Describe the limitations that may exist in applying the composite-based relationships to specific new dealerships that have been proposed.

   d. Define the *standard error of the estimate*.

3. The regression equation that John Snyder developed to project annual sales of a dealership has an *R*-Squared of 60 percent and a standard error of the estimate of $4,500,000. If the projected annual sales for a dealership total $28,500,000, determine the approximate 95 percent confidence range for John's prediction of sales.

4. What is the strategic role of regression analysis for USMI?

(CMA Adapted)

Service

7–31   COST ESTIMATION, REGRESSION ANALYSIS   A local realty company has purchased a regression program to help estimate the sale prices of homes. The realtors have run three different regressions using as the independent variables (1) the number of square feet, (2) the number of bedrooms, and (3) both the number of square feet and of bedrooms. The data and the results from their regression analyses are

House	Square Feet	Bedrooms	Selling Price
1	2,300	3	$ 76,000
2	3,700	4	150,000
3	2,700	3	114,000
4	2,500	3	86,000
5	4,000	5	176,000
6	2,600	3	89,000
7	2,300	2	80,000
8	1,800	2	84,000

9	3,500	5	140,000
10	3,300	4	146,000
11	2,900	3	110,000
12	3,000	4	112,000
			mean = $113,583

Regression using square feet only

Intercept: −24,425.67
Coefficient of the independent variable: 47.86 ($t = 9.23$)
R-squared: .8949
Standard error of the estimate: $11,117.31
F-statistic: 85.21 ($p<.01$)
Durbin-Watson statistic: 2.63

Regression using bedrooms only

Intercept: 17,160.31
Coefficient of the independent variable: 28,221.38 ($t = 5.32$)
R-squared: .7389
Standard error of the estimate: $17,528.19
F-statistic: 28.30 ($p<.01$)
Durbin-Watson statistic: 2.64

Regression using both square feet and bedrooms:

Intercept: −25,246.42
Coefficients:
   Square feet: 49.65 t-values: 3.66
   Bedrooms: −1262.48   −.14
R-squared: .8952
Standard error of the estimate: $11,705.28
F-statistic: 38.44 ($p<.01$)
Durbin-Watson statistic: 2.61

Required
1. Which is the best regression? Why?
2. What other potentially relevant cost drivers might you consider?

7–32 **COST ESTIMATION, HIGH-LOW METHOD, REGRESSION ANALYSIS** Clothes for U is a large merchandiser of apparel for budget-minded families. Management recently became concerned about the amount of inventory carrying costs and transportation costs between warehouses and retail outlets. As a starting point in further analyses, Gregory Gonzales, the controller, wants to test different forecasting methods and then use the best one to forecast quarterly expenses for 2002. The relevant data for the previous three years follows:

Quarter	Warehouse and Transportation Expense ($000)
1/1999	$12,500
2	11,300
3	11,600
4	13,700
1/2000	12,900
2	12,100
3	11,700
4	14,000
1/2001	13,300
2	12,300
3	12,100
4	14,600

The results of a simple regression analysis using all 12 data points yielded an intercept of $11,854.55 and a coefficient for the independent variable of $126.22 ($R$-squared = .19, t = 1.5, SE = 974).

Required

1. Calculate the quarterly forecasts for 2002 using the high-low method and regression analysis. Recommend which method Gregory should use.

2. How does your analysis in requirement 1 change if Clothes for U is involved in global sourcing of products for its stores?

7-33 **COST ESTIMATION, REGRESSION ANALYSIS** Plantworld is a large nursery and retail store specializing in house and garden plants and supplies. Jean Raouth, the assistant manager, is in the process of budgeting monthly supplies expense for 2002. She assumes that in some way supplies expense is related to sales, either in units or in dollars. She has collected these data for sales and supplies expenses for June 1999 through December 2001, and has estimated sales for 2002:

Date	Supplies Expense	Sales Units	Sales Dollars
Jun 1999	$2,745	354	$2,009
Jul	3,200	436	2,190
Aug	3,232	525	1,878
Sep	2,199	145	1,856
Oct	2,321	199	2,168
Nov	3,432	543	1,899
Dec	4,278	1,189	2,463
Jan 2000	2,310	212	1,999
Feb	2,573	284	2,190
Mar	2,487	246	1,894
Apr	2,484	278	2,134
May	3,384	498	2,100
Jun	2,945	224	1,874
Jul	2,758	312	2,265
Aug	3,394	485	2,435
Sep	2,254	188	1,893
Oct	2,763	276	2,232
Nov	3,245	489	2,004
Dec	4,576	1,045	2,109
Jan 2001	2,103	104	2,195
Feb	2,056	167	2,045
Mar	4,874	1,298	2,301
Apr	2,784	398	1,893
May	2,345	187	2,345
Jun	2,912	334	2,094
Jul	2,093	264	1,934
Aug	2,873	333	1,783
Sep	2,563	143	1,977
Oct	2,384	245	1,857
Nov	2,476	232	2,189
Dec	2,364	322	2,093
Jan 2002 (estimated)		435	1,567
Feb		234	1,923
Mar		123	1,894
Apr		446	1,276
May		1,200	1,576

Jun	1,789	2,593
Jul	475	2,453
Aug	584	2,736
Sep	1,103	1,598
Oct	220	1,576
Nov	876	2,398
Dec	834	1,783

Required

1. Develop the regression that Jean should use based on these data and using the regression procedure in Excel or an equivalent regression software program. Evaluate the reliability and precision of the regression you have chosen.

2. What are the predicted monthly figures for supplies expense for 2002?

7–34 LEARNING CURVES The Air Force Museum Foundation has commissioned the purchase of 16 Four F Sixes, pre–World War II aircraft. They will be built completely from scratch to the exact specifications used for the originals. As further authentication, the aircraft will be made using the technology and manufacturing processes available when the originals were built. Each of the 16 will be flown to Air Force and aviation museums throughout the country for exhibition. Aviation enthusiasts can also visit the production facility to see exactly how such aircraft were built in 1938.

Soren Industries wants to bid on the aircraft contract and asked for and received certain cost information about the Four F Sixes from the Air Force. The information includes some of the old cost data from the builders of the original aircraft. The available information is for the total accumulated time as the first, eighth, and thirty-second aircraft, respectively, were completed.

Output	Total Hours
1	250
8	1,458
32	4,724

Required

1. If Soren Industries expects that the time spent per unit will be the same as it was in 1938, how many hours will it take to build the 16 aircraft for the Air Force Museum Foundation?

2. What is the role of learning curves in Soren Industries' business for contracts such as this?

7–35 LEARNING CURVES Ben Matthews and David Everhart work for a landscaping company in Twin Cities, Oklahoma. Their principal job is to lay railroad ties to line the sidewalks around apartment complexes and to install flower boxes. The first time Ben and David undertook one of these projects, they spent 17 hours. Their goal by the end of the summer was to be able to finish an apartment complex in 8 hours, one working day. They performed eight of these jobs and had an 80 percent learning curve. Assume that all apartment complexes are approximately the same size.

Required Did they reach their goal? If not, what would the learning rate have to have been for them to have accomplished their goal?

7–36 LEARNING CURVES Emotional Headdress (EH) is a Des Moines, Iowa, manufacturer of avant garde hats and headwear. On March 11, 2001, the company purchased a new machine to aid in producing various established product lines. Production efficiency on the new machine increases with the workforce experience. It has been shown that as cumulative output on the new machine increases, average labor time per unit decreases up to the production of at least 3,200 units. As EH's cumulative output doubles from a base of 100 units produced, the average labor time per unit declines by 15 percent. EH's production varies little from month to month and averages 800 hats per month.

Emotional Headdress has developed a new style of men's hat, the Morrisey, to be produced on the new machine. One hundred Morrisey hats can be produced in a total of 25 labor-hours. All other direct costs to produce each Morrisey hat are $16.25, excluding direct labor cost. EH's direct labor cost per hour is $15. Fixed costs are $8,000 per month, and EH has the capacity to produce 3,200 hats per month.

Required

1. Emotional Headdress wishes to set the selling price for a Morrisey hat at 125 percent of the hat production cost. At the production level of 100 units, what is the selling price?

2. The company has received an order for 1,600 Morrisey hats from Smiths, Inc. Smiths is offering $20 for each hat. Should the company accept Smiths' order and produce the 1,600 hats? Explain.

Strategy

7–37 LEARNING CURVES Hauser Company, a family-owned business, engineers and manufactures a line of mopeds and dirt bikes under the trade-name Trailite. The company has been in business for almost 20 years and has maintained a profitable share of the recreational vehicle market due to its reputation for high-quality products. In addition, Hauser's engineering department has kept the company in the forefront by incorporating the latest technology in the Trailite bikes. Most subassembly work for the bikes is subcontracted to reliable vendors. However, the final assembly and inspection of all products is performed at Hauser's plant. Hauser recently developed a new braking system for the Trailite Model-500 dirt bike. Because of the company's current availability of production capacity, Jim Walsh, production manager, recommended that the first lot of the new braking system be manufactured in-house rather than by subcontractors. This 80-unit production run has now been completed. The cumulative average labor-hours per unit for the braking system was 60 hours. Hauser's experience with similar products indicates that a learning curve of 80 percent is applicable and that the learning factor can be expected to extend through the fourth production run. Hauser's direct labor cost is $14.50 per direct labor-hour. Its management must decide whether to continue producing the braking system in its own plant or to subcontract this work. Joyce Lane, Hauser's purchasing agent, has received a proposal from MACQ, a company specializing in component assembly. MACQ has done work in the past for Hauser and has proved to be efficient and reliable. The terms of MACQ's proposal are negotiable, and before beginning discussions with them, Joyce has decided to conduct some relevant financial analysis.

Required

1. Hauser Company has an immediate requirement for a total of 1,000 units of the braking system. Determine Hauser's future direct labor costs to produce the required braking system units if it manufactures the units in-house.

2. A consultant has advised Joyce that the learning rate for this application might be closer to 75 percent. What is the effect on projected costs of using a 75 percent learning curve as opposed to an 80 percent learning curve?

3. What conditions in a manufacturing plant, if present, would offset the potential benefits of the learning curve? What is the strategic role of learning curve analysis for Hauser Company?

(CMA Adapted)

7–38 REGRESSION ANALYSIS Pilot Shop is a catalog business providing a wide variety of aviation products to pilots throughout the world. Maynard Shephard, the recently hired assistant controller, has been asked to develop a cost function to forecast shipping costs. The previous assistant controller had forecast shipping department costs each year by plotting cost data against direct labor-hours for the most recent 12 months and visually fitting a straight line through the points. The results were not satisfactory.

After discussions with the shipping department personnel, Maynard decided that shipping costs could be more closely related to the number of orders filled. He based his conclusion on the fact that 10 months ago the shipping department added some automated equipment. Furthermore, he believes that using linear regression analysis will improve the forecasts of shipping costs. Cost data for the shipping department have been accumulated for the last 25 weeks. He ran two regression analyses of the data, one using direct labor-hours, and one using the number of cartons shipped. The information from the two linear regressions follows:

	Regression 1	Regression 2
Equation	$SC = 804.3 + 15.68DL$	$SC = 642.9 + 3.92NR$
R-squared	.365	.729
Standard error of the estimate	2.652	1.884
t-value	1.89	3.46

where: SC = total shipping department costs
DL = total direct labor-hours
NR = number of cartons shipped

Required

1. Identify which cost function (regression 1 or regression 2) that Pilot Shop should adapt for forecasting total shipping department cost and explain why.

2. If Pilot Shop projects that 600 orders will be filled the coming week, calculate the total shipping department cost using the regression you selected in requirement 1.

3. Explain two or three important limitations of the regression you selected in requirement 1, and identify one or two ways to address the limitations. Specifically include in your discussion the effect, if any, of the global nature of Pilot Shop's business.

(CMA Adapted)

7–39 REGRESSION ANALYSIS Danzer Company manufactures a line of lawn care products distributed primarily through landscaping companies and is in the process of developing its marketing strategy for the upcoming fiscal year. As in the past, the marketing strategy focuses on quality and customer service. Danzer employs linear regression to forecast sales by region. The marketing department has prepared the following regression models for the midwestern, the southern, and the eastern regions using actual sales data from the past 10 years. In general terms, the midwest region is characterized by rapid growth in recent years, while the eastern region is characterized by slow to little growth based on long-term relationships with nurseries, arboretums, and research units at local universities where new ideas are tested.

S_t = forecasted sales for the region in time period t

S_{t+1} = actual sales for the region in time period $t-1$

Howard Todesco, president of Danzer Company, and Frank Mulrooney, vice president of marketing, wonder whether the results of the regression analysis can be relied on to develop the company's marketing strategy. The results of the analysis indicate that they should recommend to the board of directors that Danzer drop the eastern region; however, they read recently that the economy of the eastern states in general, and the market for lawn care products specifically, is entering a period of rejuvenation.

	Midwestern Region	Southern Region	Eastern Region
Equation	$S_t = \$400 + 1.12 S_{t-1}$	$S_t = \$445\,1 + 1.06\, S_{t-1}$	$S_t = \$510 + 0.985\, S_{t-1}$
R-squared	.9025	.8649	.9216
Standard error of the estimate	$495,000	$480,000	$500,000
Calculated t-statistic for the regression coefficient	3.64	3.88	3.70

Required

1. Evaluate the three regressions in terms of precision and reliability.

2. Identify the basic assumptions underlying regression analysis.

3. If actual sales for the eastern region total $2,200,000 in the current year, calculate the sales forecast for the coming year.

4. Discuss the strategic issues that are important to whether Danzer Company's board of directors should accept a recommendation to drop the eastern region.

(CMA Adapted)

7–40 **REGRESSION ANALYSIS: CROSS-SECTIONAL ANALYSIS; CALCULATION OF A REGRESSION EQUATION**   Jim Manzano is the general partner of an investment group that owns a number of commercial and industrial properties, including a chain of 15 convenience stores located in the greater metropolitan area of Cleveland, Ohio. Jim is concerned about the recent increase in inventory theft and waste (he calls it "spoilage") in his stores. Spoilage has increased by more than 20 percent in each of the past two years. In some stores, the main reason is theft; in others, it is damage and vandalism; and in still others, merchandise actually does spoil and must be thrown out. Jim has collected data on spoilage at each of his stores in the recent month and is looking for patterns of spoilage relative to store size (measured by square feet of floor space, number of employees, and total sales) and to the location of the store (location 1 is an area where few arrests for theft, disorderly conduct, or vandalism are made, and location 3 is for areas with high arrests). Jim is not sure, but he suspects, based on his experience managing convenience stores, that a relationship exists among these factors. A colleague told him that a type of regression called "cross-sectional" regression would suit his needs. The cross-sectional regression takes data from a single time period and determines predictions for the dependent variable at different cost objects (in this case, different stores). The objective of the cross-sectional regression is to compare the actual known value for the dependent variable to the predicted value as a basis for assessing the reasonableness of the actual value. This approach is often used in cases similar to Jim's in which the accuracy or reasonableness of the reported dependent variable is a concern. In effect, the cross-sectional regression develops a model that represents the overall patterns in all the data, and the unusual stores will be identified by the largest error terms in the regression. The following data are for the most recent month's operations:

Store Number	Inventory Spoilage	Square Footage	Number of Employees	Location	Sales
1	$ 1,512	2,400	8	1	$ 312,389
2	3,005	3,900	10	2	346,235
3	1,686	3,200	12	1	376,465
4	1,908	3,400	12	1	345,723
5	2,384	3,750	9	2	453,983
6	4,806	4,800	10	3	502,984
7	2,253	3,500	8	1	325,436
8	1,443	3,000	10	1	253,647
9	3,755	5,550	15	2	562,534
10	1,023	2,250	15	1	287,364
11	1,552	2,500	9	1	198,374
12	2,119	3,500	16	2	333,984
13	5,506	7,500	15	3	673,345
14	3,034	5,700	16	2	588,947
15	772	2,200	8	1	225,364
Totals	$36,758	57,150	173		$5,786,774

Required

1. Using Excel or an equivalent software program, prepare a regression analysis that predicts inventory spoilage at each of the 15 stores. Use any of the four potential independent variables (or a combination) you think appropriate and explain your answer. Also evaluate the precision and reliability of the regression you select.

2. Using the regression equation you developed in requirement 1, determine which of the 15 stores might have inventory spoilage that is out of line relative to the entire chain of stores. Explain your choice.

7–41 REGRESSION ANALYSIS IN TAX COURT CASES   Since at least the late 1960s, the court systems in the United States and elsewhere have accepted regression analysis as evidence in court cases. In many instances, however, because of limitations or errors in developing the regression analysis, tax courts question or deny the regression evidence. A study was performed recently to determine the factors in the regression analysis that the court considered in determining whether regression evidence was admissible.

Required   What factors regarding the development of a regression analysis do you suspect the tax courts considered in determining the acceptability of a regression analysis as evidence?

SOLUTIONS TO SELF-STUDY PROBLEMS

1.   Using the High-Low Method

Begin by graphing the data to determine whether there are any unusual (i.e., seasonal) patterns or outliers in Exhibit 7–21.

The graph shows no unusual patterns or outliers, so the high-low estimate can be determined directly from the low point (March) and the high point (December) as follows:

To determine the slope of the line (unit variable cost)

$$(\$201{,}783 - \$123{,}245)/(7{,}433 - 5{,}166) = \$34.644 \text{ per delivery}$$

To determine the intercept

$$\$201{,}783 - 7{,}433 \times \$34.644 = -\$55{,}726$$

$$\$123{,}245 - 5{,}166 \times \$34.644 = -\$55{,}726$$

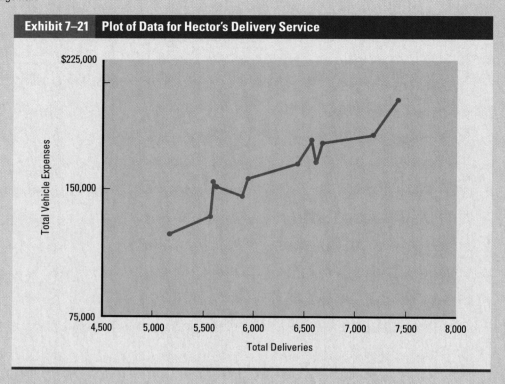

Exhibit 7–21 Plot of Data for Hector's Delivery Service

The estimation equation is

$$\text{Vehicle costs} = -\$55,726 + \$34.644 \times \text{Number of deliveries/Month}$$

Note that the intercept is a negative number, which simply means that the relevant range of 5,166 to 7,433 deliveries is so far from the zero point (where the intercept is) that the intercept cannot be properly interpreted as a fixed cost. The estimation equation therefore is useful only within the relevant range of approximately 5,000 to 7,500 deliveries and should not be used to estimate costs outside that range.

2. Using Regression Analysis

All relevant criteria favor the first regression based on higher R-squared and t-values and lower standard error. Moreover, the sign on the materials cost variable in regression 2 is negative, which is difficult to explain. This variable should have a direct relationship with overhead; thus, the sign of the variable should be positive. The reason for the improvement of regression 1 over regression 2 might be that machine-hours are highly correlated with either materials costs, labor-hours, or both, thus causing multicollinearity. By excluding machine-hours as an independent variable, George reduced or removed the multicollinearity, and the regression improved as a result. He should therefore use regression 1.

3. Using Both High-Low and Regression

Begin by graphing the data for the number of defective units, as shown in Exhibit 7–22. The objective is to identify any unusual patterns that must be considered in developing an estimate.

Exhibit 7–22 shows that the number of defective units varies considerably from month to month and that a steady increase has occurred over the past two years. Knowing that the production level also has been increasing (as measured either by cost of sales, units produced, or units shipped), we now want to determine whether the relationship between defects and production level (Exhibit 7–23) has changed.

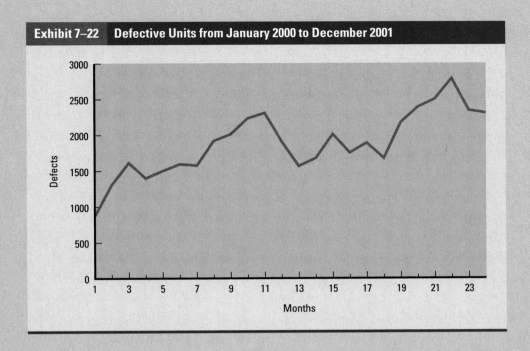

Exhibit 7–22   Defective Units from January 2000 to December 2001

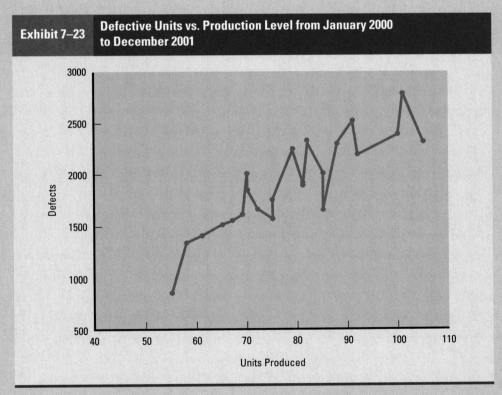

Exhibit 7–23   Defective Units vs. Production Level from January 2000 to December 2001

We begin with units produced as the independent variable, since it should have the most direct relationship with defects; the other independent variables can be tried later. The second graph (Exhibit 7–23) makes clear that a relationship exists between units produced and the number of defects.

The next step is to quantify this relationship with the high-low method and regression analysis. We begin with the high-low analysis. For Exhibit 7–23, we identify February 2000 and December 2001 as representative low and high periods, respectively.

We calculate the high-low estimate as follows (these two points are not the absolute lowest and highest points, but they produce a line that is representative of the data):

$$\text{slope} = (2{,}311 - 1{,}335)/(88 - 58) = 32.533$$

And

$$\text{Intercept} = 2{,}311 - 32.533 \times 88 = 1{,}335 - 32.533 \times 58 = -552$$

Thus, the estimation equation is

$$\text{Number of defects} = -552 + 32.533 \times \text{Production level}$$

The high-low estimate is subject to the limitations of subjectivity in the choice of high and low points and because it uses only those two data points to develop the estimate. Regression is thus performed to provide a more precise estimate. Thus, the next step is to obtain a regression analysis from the previous data and to assess the precision and reliability of the regression estimate. The regression can be completed with a spreadsheet program or any of a number of available software systems. The results for three regression analyses are presented in Exhibit 7–24. The dependent variable in each case is the number of defective units.

Regression 1 has the following independent variables: cost of sales, units shipped, and units produced. R-squared and SE are OK, but we observe that all three t-values are less than 2.0, indicating unreliable independent variables. Because a priori we expect correlation among these variables and because of the low t-values, we suspect multicollinearity among these variables. To reduce the effect of multicollinearity, we try regression 2, which removes the variable units shipped since that variable is likely to be least associated with defective units and has among the lowest of the t-values. R-squared for regression 2 is essentially the same as for regression 1, although SE improves very slightly, and the t-value for cost of sales is now OK. The results of regression 3, with the cost of sales variable only, show that SE and the t-value improve again while R-squared is unchanged. Because it has the best SE and t-values, and a very good R-squared, the third regression is the best choice.

Exhibit 7–24   Regressions for the Number of Defects

Intercept	Coefficient of Independent Variable	t-value for Independent Variable	R-squared	Standard Error of the Estimate
Regression 1				
103.20			.883	161
	−38.974 (units shipped)	−.44		
	−2.849 (units produced)	−.38		
	4.702 (cost of sales)	.72		
Regression 2				
92.24			.881	158
	−2.230 (units produced)	−.309		
	1.837 (cost of sales)	4.54		
Regression 3				
43.95			.881	155
	1.720 (cost of sales)	12.77		

Cost-Volume-Profit Analysis

8

After studying this chapter, you should be able to . . .

1 Explain cost-volume-profit (CVP) analysis, the CVP model, and the strategic role of CVP analysis

2 Apply CVP analysis for breakeven planning

3 Apply CVP analysis for revenue and cost planning

4 Apply CVP analysis for activity-based costing

5 Employ sensitivity analysis to more effectively use CVP analysis when actual sales are uncertain

6 Adapt CVP analysis for multiple products

7 Apply CVP analysis in service firms and not-for-profit organizations

8 Identify the assumptions and limitations of CVP analysis and their effect on the proper interpretation of the results

AP/Wide World Photos.

For some companies, just about each product or service is new and different. This is true for SFX Entertainment, Inc. (www.sfx.com), the world's largest provider of live entertainment events. SFX produces live entertainment, mostly musical entertainment, in more than 70 locations. Each show offers a new opportunity for SFX to be profitable, but careful planning is necessary to achieve success. A key part of this planning for SFX is to use cost-volume-profit analysis, the topic of this chapter. SFX uses cost-volume-profit (CVP) analysis to project estimated profits for each live event, given the company's projections about attendance; that is, CVP analysis shows the relationship between volume of attendance and the event's related costs and profits.

Some of SFX's events are planned on a fixed-fee basis; that is, the entertainer is paid a fixed amount for the performance that is not tied to attendance. Other events are planned so that the entertainer receives a payment based on the audience number. The fixed-fee arrangement is somewhat riskier for SFX because it bears the risk of low attendance and therefore low profits or losses; of course, the upside is that SFX does well if attendance is high. In contrast, the entertainer paid on the basis of attendance shares some of the risk.

For fixed-fee events, SFX uses attendance projections and cost-volume-profit analysis to carefully project costs and profits and to plan levels of advertising and other expenses. This type of planning is critical for SFX's overall success and profitability.

COST-VOLUME-PROFIT ANALYSIS

Cost-volume-profit (CVP) analysis is a method for analyzing how various operating decisions and marketing decisions will affect net income.

Cost-volume-profit (CVP) analysis is a method for analyzing how operating decisions and marketing decisions affect net income based on an understanding of the relationship between variable costs, fixed costs, unit selling price, and the output level. CVP analysis has many applications:

- Setting prices for products and services.
- Introducing a new product or service.
- Replacing a piece of equipment.
- Deciding whether to make or buy a given product or service.
- Performing strategic what-if analyses.

CVP analysis is based on an explicit model of the relationships between its three factors—costs, revenues, and profits—and how they change in a predictable way as the volume of activity changes. The CVP model is

$$\text{Profit} = \text{Revenues} - \text{Total costs}$$

or equivalently, since total costs include both fixed and variable cost elements:

$$\text{Revenues} = \text{Fixed costs} + \text{Variable costs} + \text{Profit}$$

Now, replacing revenues with the number of units sold times price, and replacing variable cost with unit variable cost times the number of units sold, the CVP model is

$$\text{Units sold} \times \text{Price} = \text{Fixed cost}$$
$$+ \text{Units sold} \times \text{Unit variable cost}$$
$$+ \text{Profit}$$

For easier use, the model is commonly shown in a symbolic form

where: Q = units sold
v = unit variable cost
f = total fixed cost
p = unit selling price
N = operating profit (profits *exclusive* of unusual or nonrecurring items and income taxes)

$$p \times Q = f + v \times Q + N$$

Contribution Margin and Contribution Income Statement

Effective use of the CVP model requires an understanding of three additional concepts: the contribution margin, the contribution margin ratio, and the contribution income statement. The contribution margin is both a unit and a total concept. The **unit contribution margin** is the difference between unit sales price and unit variable cost:

The **unit contribution margin** is the difference between unit sales price and unit variable cost and is a measure of the increase in profit for a unit increase in sales.

The **total contribution margin** is the unit contribution margin multiplied by the number of units sold.

$$p - v = \text{Unit contribution margin}$$

The unit contribution margin measures the increase in profit for a unit increase in sales. If sales are expected to increase by 100 units, profits should increase by 100 times the contribution margin. The **total contribution margin** is the unit contribution margin multiplied by the number of units sold.

For example, suppose that Household Furnishings, Inc. (HFI), a manufacturer of home furnishings, is interested in developing a new product, a wooden TV table, that would be priced at $75 and would have variable costs of $35 per unit. The investment would require new fixed costs of $5,000 per month. HFI wants to achieve an increase in operating profit of at least $48,000 per year. The data for HFI are summarized in Exhibit 8–1.

Exhibit 8–1	Data for Household Furnishings, Inc. (HFI):TV Table		
	Per Unit	**Monthly**	**Annual**
Fixed cost		$ 5,000	$ 60,000
Desired operating profit		4,000	48,000
Revenue	$75		
Variable cost	35		
Planned production		250 units	3,000 units
Planned sales		250 units	3,000 units

Exhibit 8–2	Contribution Income Statement for Household Furnishings, Inc.						
	2000		**2001**				
	Amount	**Percent**	**Amount**	**Percent**	**Change**	**Notes**	
Sales	$180,000	100.00%	$195,000	100.00%	$15,000		
Variable costs	84,000	46.67	91,000	46.67	7,000		
Contribution margin	$ 96,000	53.33%	$104,000	53.33%	$ 8,000	0.5333 is the contribution margin rate	
Fixed costs	60,000		60,000		0		
Profit	$ 36,000		$ 44,000		$ 8,000	$8,000 = 0.5333 × $15,000	

The unit contribution margin for each table would be $40 ($75 – $35). Using the unit contribution margin, we see that if HFI expects to sell 3,000 tables per year, it can expect to increase total contribution margin by $120,000 ($40 × 3,000) and operating profit by $60,000 ($120,000 – $60,000 fixed cost), which is $12,000 higher than the desired increase in operating profit of $48,000.

A measure of the profit contributions per sales dollar is the **contribution margin ratio,** which is the ratio of the unit contribution margin to unit sales price $(p - v)/p$. The contribution margin ratio for HFI's proposed TV table is 0.533 = ($75 – $35)/$75. The ratio identifies the amount of increase (or decrease) in profits caused by a given increase (or decrease) in sales dollars. What is the effect on profits of an increase of $15,000 in sales? We can quickly calculate that profits will increase by $8,000 ($15,000 × 0.5333).

A useful way to show the information developed in CVP analysis is to use the contribution income statement. The **contribution income statement** begins with revenues and subtracts variable and fixed costs to obtain the total contribution margin and net income, respectively. In contrast, the conventional income statement that we prepared in Chapter 3 begins with revenues and subtracts product costs and nonproduct costs to obtain gross margin and net income, respectively. Exhibit 8–2 shows the contribution income statement for HFI for the years 2000 (2,400 units sold) and 2001 (2,600 units sold). Note that the sales increase of 200 units and $15,000 caused an $8,000 increase in profits as predicted by the contribution margin and contribution margin ratio. The key advantage of the contribution income statement is that it provides an easy and accurate prediction of the effect of a change in sales on profits. This is not possible with the conventional income statement, which does not separate variable and fixed costs.

> The **contribution margin ratio** is the ratio of the unit contribution margin to unit sales price $(p - v)/p$.

> The **contribution income statement** focuses on variable costs and fixed costs, in contrast to the conventional income statement in Chapter 3, which focuses on product costs and nonproduct costs.

STRATEGIC ROLE OF CVP ANALYSIS

CVP analysis has an important role in a firm's strategic management. For example, it is important in using both life-cycle costing and target costing. In life-cycle costing, CVP analysis is used in the early stages of the product's cost life cycle to determine whether the product is likely to achieve the desired profitability. Similarly, CVP analysis can assist in target costing at these early stages by showing the effect on profit of alternative product designs at expected sales levels.

In addition, CVP analysis can be used at later phases of the life cycle, during manufacturing planning, to determine the most cost-effective manufacturing process. Such manufacturing decisions include when to replace a machine, what type of machine to buy, when to automate a process, and when to outsource a manufacturing operation. CVP analysis is also used in the final stages of the cost life cycle to help determine the best marketing and distribution systems. For example, CVP analysis can be used to determine whether paying salespeople on a salary basis or a commission basis is more cost effective. Similarly, it can help to assess the desirability of a discount program or a promotional plan. Some of the strategic questions answered by CVP analysis are outlined in Exhibit 8–3.

CVP analysis also has a role in strategic positioning. A firm that has chosen to compete on cost leadership needs CVP analysis primarily at the manufacturing stage of the cost life cycle. The role of CVP analysis here is to identify the most cost-effective manufacturing methods, including automation, outsourcing, and total quality management. In contrast, a firm following the differentiation strategy needs CVP

Exhibit 8–3	**Strategic Questions Answered by CVP Analysis**

1. What is the expected level of profit at a given sales volume?
2. What additional amount of sales is needed to achieve a desired level of profit?
3. What will be the effect on profit of a given increase in sales?
4. What is the required funding level for a governmental agency, given desired service levels?
5. Is the forecast for sales consistent with forecasted profits?
6. What additional profit would be obtained from a given percentage reduction in unit variable costs?
7. What increase in sales is needed to make up a given decrease in price to maintain the present profit level?
8. What sales level is needed to cover all costs in a sales region or product line?
9. What is the required amount of increase in sales to meet the additional fixed charges from a proposed plant expansion?
10. What additional sales are needed to improve profits by a desired amount?

The High Cost of Low Loyalty

Recent studies on the cost of obtaining and serving customers over the entire product life cycle have highlighted the very high cost to acquire customers in some industries. Some estimates show that increasing the customer retention rate by a modest 5 percent can improve profits by as much as 95 percent. One study showed that the cost to acquire a customer averaged between $50 and $80 in three industries: consumer electronics/appliances, groceries, and apparel. The years to breakeven for each customer varied from approximately one year in the apparel industry to more than four years in the consumer electronics/appliance industry. These firms are careful to use breakeven analysis to study all phases of the product life cycle for a new product or a marketing promotion.

In Internet-based retailing, breakeven analysis can be particularly important: It costs 20 to 40 percent more for e-tailers to acquire customers than for brick-and-mortar retailers.

However, the cost of serving the customers, the downstream costs, are significantly lower for e-tailers than for other retailers. The bottom line—customer retention and customer loyalty are critical for e-tailers. This is the lesson learned by the most successful ones, including Dell, Amazon.com, and eBay and by other Internet-based businesses such as America Online. For example, Amazon.com has a strong reputation for good customer service, including its one-click ordering. eBay has taken special steps to ensure the reliability of its transactions and to prevent fraud. The competitive strategy for these firms is to differentiate themselves from others by providing superior customer service. Customers appreciate these efforts and respond with their loyalty.

Source: Frederick F. Reichheld and Phil Schefter, "E-Loyalty: Your Secret Weapon on the Web," *Harvard Business Review*, July–August 2000, pp. 105–13.

analysis in the early phases of the cost life cycle to assess the profitability of new products and the desirability of new features for existing products.

CVP ANALYSIS FOR BREAKEVEN PLANNING

◀ **LEARNING OBJECTIVE 2**

Apply CVP analysis for breakeven planning.

> We first survey the plot, then draw the model;
> And when we see the figure of the house,
> Then we must rate the cost of the erection;
> Which, if we find outweighs ability,
> What do we then but draw anew the model.
> WILLIAM SHAKESPEARE, HENRY IV, PART II, ACT 1

The starting point in many business plans is to determine the **breakeven point,** the point at which revenues equal total costs and profit is zero. This point can be determined by using CVP analysis. The CVP model is solved by inserting known values for v, p, and f, setting N equal to zero, and then solving for Q. We can solve for Q in two ways: the equation method and the contribution margin method. Each method can determine the breakeven point in units sold or sales dollars.

The **breakeven point** is the point at which revenues equal total cost and profit is zero.

Equation Method: For Breakeven in Units

The equation method uses the CVP model directly. For example, the equation for the analysis of HFI's sale of TV tables is

$$\$75 \times Q = \$5,000 + \$35 \times Q$$

Solving for Q, we determine that the breakeven point is $Q = 125$ TV tables per month (1,500 units per year).

$$(\$75 - \$35) \times Q = \$5,000$$

$$Q = \$5,000/(\$75 - \$35)$$

$$Q = \$5,000/\$40 = 125 \text{ units per month}$$

The contribution to profit per TV table is measured directly by the unit contribution margin, $p - v$, which is $40 per table. So, since at sales of 125 units the profit is zero, at 126 units the profit is $40 (one unit past breakeven at $40), at 127 units the profit is $2 \times \$40 = \$80$, and so on. Using the unit contribution margin gives us a quick way to determine the change in profit for a change in sales units. At the 128-unit level, profit is

Sales: 128 units at $75/unit	$9,600
Less:	
Variable costs: 128 at $35/unit	4,480
Contributing margin costs	$5,120
Fixed costs	5,000
Total profit	$ 120

Equation Method: For Breakeven in Dollars

Sometimes units sold, unit variable cost, and sales price are not known, or it is impractical to determine them. For example, suppose that a firm has many products and is interested in finding the overall breakeven level for all products taken together. It is not practical to find the breakeven in units for each product, but it is possible to find the breakeven in sales dollars for all products. We use the equation method in a revised form, where Y is the breakeven point in *sales dollars*:

$$Y = (v/p) \times Y + f + N$$

Breakeven Analysis in Community Banking

In a competitive business such as community banking, management carefully plans to ensure the profitability of new products and services. New locations of a branch bank in a supermarket represent a key part of some community banks' growth strategy. To make this decision, banks must determine the amount of funds and fees that a specific supermarket location will generate and then determine the expected revenues and expenses from that funding level. This analysis requires estimates of the direct expenses of opening and maintaining the branch as well as the interest expense on funds developed at the branch and any increase in indirect expenses caused by opening the branch. The analysis often shows that the branch will not be profitable unless its fee income is relatively high. The following analysis shows how projections of deposits, interest revenue and expense, and direct and indirect expense can be used to project the amount of fee revenue needed for breakeven; in this example, the required fee revenue is $125,000 per year.

BREAKEVEN ANALYSIS: BRANCH BANK, SUPERMARKET LOCATION

Average Deposits, First Year of Operations (projected)		
Gross funds		$7,500,000
Less: Nonearning funds		250,000
Net funds provided		$7,250,000
Projected Income Statement, First Year of Operation *		
Interest revenue from new funds		$ 525,000
Fee revenue (required for breakeven)		**125,000**
Total revenue		$ 650,000
Expenses		
Interest expense	345,000	
Direct expenses	200,000	
Indirect expenses	105,000	650,000
Net income		$ 0

*Projections for direct and indirect expense amounts and for interest revenue and expense are based on the expense and revenue experience of similar branch banks, given the projected funding level.

Source: Tom Flynn, "The Supermarket Branch Revisited," *Banking Journal,* October 1997, (www.banking.com/aba/community_1097.asp).

Using algebra, we can see that this model is equivalent to the model used earlier for breakeven in units, except that Q is replaced by Y/p (i.e., sales in dollars = $Y = Q \times p$). Continuing with the HFI data in Exhibit 8–1, assume that we do not know that price is $75 and that unit variable cost is $35; instead, we know only total variable cost ($210,000) and total sales ($450,000). We can obtain the ratio, $v/p = 0.4667$ ($210,000/$450,000), and solve for monthly breakeven:

$$Y = 0.4667 \times Y + \$5,000$$

$$Y = \$9,375 \text{ per month}$$

Contribution Margin Method

A convenient method for calculating the breakeven point is to use the equation in its equivalent algebraic form (derived by solving the model for Q):

$$Q = \text{Fixed costs/Unit contribution margin}$$

$$= f/(p - v)$$

The contribution margin method (so-called because the contribution margin is the denominator of the ratio) produces the same result as the equation method:

$$Q = (\$5,000)/(\$75 - \$35) = 125 \text{ units per month}$$

The contribution margin method can also be used to obtain breakeven in dollars, using the contribution margin ratio (replacing $p \times Q$ with Y and solving for Y)

$$Y = \frac{F + N}{(p - v)/p}$$

where:

$$(p - v)/p = \text{the contribution margin ratio}$$
$$N = 0 \text{ in this case}$$

For the HFI example, the contribution margin ratio is 0.5333 and

$$Y = \$5{,}000/0.5333 = \$9{,}375$$

Some people find the equation method easier to use, and others prefer to use the contribution margin method. Use the method with which you are most comfortable. Both methods produce the same results.

Breakeven Analysis: Hemp Production in Manitoba

Hemp, an agricultural product, is a natural fiber that has many industrial and commercial uses, including handbags, backpacks, hats, paper, rope, industrial fabrics, and clothing (www.hempsisters.com). In some areas of the world, particularly Australia and Canada, hemp is viewed as a potentially significant new opportunity for agricultural production, and business and agricultural leaders are studying the strategic issues involved in making further investments in the crop. For example, an agricultural analysis by the Manitoba, Canada, department of agriculture carefully estimates the breakeven for the production of hemp.

Based on estimates made in 1998, a farmer interested in producing hemp must receive a price of at least $ 0.55 per pound to break even on farming for hemp. This analysis is shown in the following table and assumes seed price of $4 per lb, a 20-pound per acre seeding rate, and a crop yield of 400 pounds per acre. The analysis ignores the costs associated with investment in land and machinery on the assumption that these costs remain the same whether or not the farmer grows hemp. All figures are in Canadian dollars.

ESTIMATED OPERATING COSTS PER ACRE FOR THE PRODUCTION OF HEMP

Seed	$80.00
Fertilizer	38.15
Chemicals	10.00
Fuel	11.00
Machinery operating costs	15.00
Crop insurance	6.00
Other costs	7.50
Land taxes	5.50
Licensing fee	15.00
Sampling and analytical fees	15.00
Drying costs	3.57
Cleaning costs	5.00
Interest on operating costs	7.44
Total operating costs	$219.16

We solve for breakeven price per pound:
Revenue per acre = Total operating cost per acre

$$p \times 400 \text{ lb.} = \$219.16$$

$$p = \$ 0.55 \text{ /lb}$$

Source: "Industrial Hemp for Manitoba," http://www.gov.mb.ca/agriculture/crops/hemp/bko04s00.html). Currently hemp is illegal in the United States because it contains a very small amount of THC, the active ingredient in marijuana.

CVP Graph and the Profit-Volume Graph

The **CVP graph** illustrates how the levels of revenues and total costs change over different levels of output.

The **profit-volume graph** illustrates how the level of profits changes over different levels of output.

Breakeven analysis is illustrated graphically in Exhibit 8–4. It shows the CVP graph at the top and the profit-volume graph beneath. The **CVP graph** illustrates how the levels of revenues and total costs change over different levels of output. Note in the CVP graph that at output levels lower than 125 units, the revenue line falls below the cost line, resulting in losses. In contrast, all points above the 125-unit level show profits.

The **profit-volume graph** at the lower portion of the exhibit illustrates how the level of profits changes over different levels of output. At 125 units, profits are zero, and positive profits appear for output levels greater than 125. The slope of the profit-volume line is the unit contribution margin; therefore, the profit-volume graph can be used to read directly how total contribution margin, and therefore profits, change as the output level changes.

Summary of Breakeven Methods

The Equation Methods

1. Breakeven in units (Q = sales in units)

$$p \times Q = v \times Q + f + N$$

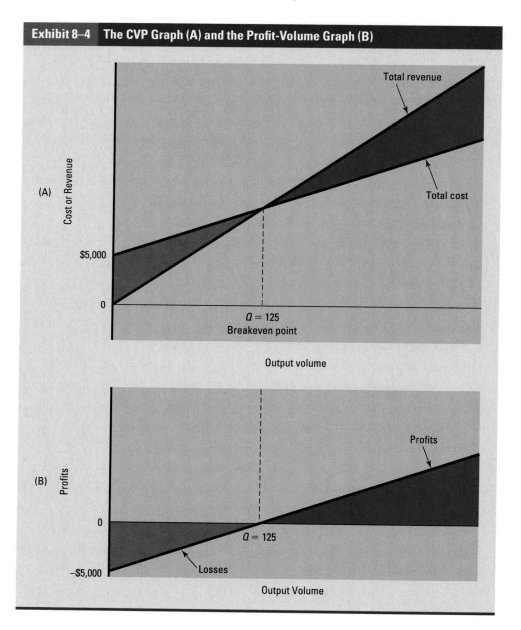

Exhibit 8–4 The CVP Graph (A) and the Profit-Volume Graph (B)

2. Breakeven in dollars (Y = sales in dollars)

$$Y = (v/p) \times Y + f + N$$

The Contribution Margin Methods

3. Breakeven in units =

$$\frac{(f + N)}{(p - v)}$$

4. Breakeven in dollars =

$$\frac{(f + N)}{(p - v)/p}$$

CVP ANALYSIS FOR REVENUE AND COST PLANNING

CVP analysis can be used to determine the level of sales needed to achieve a desired level of profit. The two possible objectives are revenue planning and cost planning.

◀**LEARNING OBJECTIVE 3**

Apply CVP analysis for revenue and cost planning.

Revenue Planning

CVP analysis assists managers in revenue planning to determine the revenue required to achieve a desired profit level. For example, if HFI's management needs to know the sales volume necessary to achieve $48,000 in annual profits, we substitute $60,000 for fixed costs and $48,000 for desired profit; the solution in units is

$$Q = \frac{f + N}{p - v} = \frac{\$60,000 + \$48,000}{\$75 - \$35} = 2,700 \text{ units per year}$$

The solution in sales dollars is

$$p \times Q = \$75 \times 2,700 = \$202,500 \text{ per year}$$

Cost Planning

For cost planning decisions, the manager knows the value of Q and the desired profit but needs to find the value of the required variable cost or fixed cost. Two examples follow.

Examples of CVP in Revenue Planning and Cost Planning

REVENUE PLANNING: PUBLIC RELATIONS CONSULTING FIRM

Paulette J. Robinson, president of a McLean, Virginia, consulting firm, uses breakeven analysis to assess the potential profitability of potential consulting engagements. She has found that the opportunities for new clients exceed her capacity to provide services without growing the business and adding staff. Wishing to maintain the size of the business and to cut down on her 20-hour days, seven days a week, she used breakeven analysis to choose which engagements to keep and which to decline based on the projected contribution of each engagement. This helps Paulette achieve her strategy of maintaining a balance between her work and personal time.

COST PLANNING: REGIONAL DENTAL PRACTICE

Katherine G. Collier, owner of a $1.3 million-grossing dental practice in Baltimore, uses breakeven analysis to evaluate the profitability of her business as the volume of patients

increases. In a recent instance, the analysis convinced her that a planned expansion of her practice to an additional medical office was not likely to be profitable, and she canceled the expansion plans.

COST PLANNING: A PIZZA FRANCHISE

Christopher Lau saved his money from cooking, serving, and delivering pizzas with the dream of owning a franchise of the locally popular Blackjack Pizza Restaurant. Christopher used his knowledge as a business student to study the cost-volume relationships in the pizza business. He concluded that he needed to gross about $8,000 per week, or about 1,217 pies a week to break even given his planned investment in a Blackjack franchise.

Sources: Kevin D. Thompson, "Planning for Profit," *Black Enterprise*, April 1993, pp. 93–94; and "The Pizza Franchise Was His Dream; Then the 'Unfathomable,'" *Wall Street Journal*, June 23, 1999, p. 1.

Trade-offs between Fixed and Variable Costs

To facilitate target costing, CVP analysis is used to determine the most cost-effective trade-off between different types of costs. To continue with the HFI example, assume sales of 2,700 units per year. Management is now considering the purchase of a new piece of production machinery that will reduce variable costs but also increase fixed costs by $2,250 per month. How much must unit variable costs fall to maintain the current level of profit, assuming that sales volume and all other factors remain the same?

Q = 2,700 units
p = $75
v = an unknown (previously $35)
f = $5,000 + $2,250 = $7,250 per month ($87,000 per year)
N = $48,000

Now, instead of solving for Q (which is given as 2,700 units), we solve for v, as follows:

$$Q = \frac{f+N}{p-v}$$

$$p-v = \frac{(f+N)}{Q}$$

$$v = p - \frac{(f+N)}{Q}$$

$$v = \$75 - (\$87,000 + \$48,000)/2,700 = \$25$$

In effect, for sales and profits to remain unchanged with the increase in fixed costs, unit variable costs must fall from $35 to $25.

Sales Commissions and Salaries

Another cost planning use of CVP analysis is to determine the most cost-effective means to manage downstream costs such as selling costs. To illustrate, HFI management is reviewing sales salaries and commissions and finds that $1,000 of the monthly $5,000 fixed costs is for sales salaries, that $7.50 of the $35.00 of unit variable cost is a 10 percent sales commission, and that $27.50 of variable cost is not commission based. Suppose that the salespeople are asking for a $450 increase in salary. Management responds that the salaries can be raised only if the commission rate is decreased. How much must management reduce the commission rate to keep profits the same, assuming that sales volume and all other factors remain unchanged?

With the proposed changes in variable and fixed costs to accommodate the new salary and commission plan, fixed costs increase by $450 per month and variable costs decrease as a result of the decrease in the commission rate, r:

v = Commission rate × Sales price
  + Other noncommission-based unit variable costs

$v = r \times \$75 + \$27.50$

And:

f = Current monthly fixed costs + Increase in monthly salary

$f = \$5,000 + 450 = \$5,450$ per month, or $65,400 per year

Now we use the CVP model to solve for v:

$$Q = \frac{f+N}{p-v}$$

$$v = p - \frac{f+N}{Q}$$

and substituting for v and f with $N = \$48,000$ and $Q = \$2,700$ as before:

$$r \times \$75.00 + \$27.50 = \$75.00 - (\$65,400.00 + \$48,000.00)/2,700$$

$$r = 0.0733$$

In this situation, the manager must reduce the commission rate from 10 to 7.33 percent to keep profits the same and pay an additional monthly salary of $450 to the salespeople.

Including Income Taxes in CVP Analysis

The manager's decisions about costs and prices usually must include income taxes because taxes affect the amount of profit for a given level of sales. In the HFI example if we assume that the average tax rate is 20 percent, to achieve the desired annual *after-tax* profit of $48,000, HFI must generate before-tax profits of at least $60,000 [$48,000/(1 − .2)]. Thus, when taxes are considered, the CVP model is as follows, where the average tax rate is t:

$$Q = \frac{f + \dfrac{N}{(1-t)}}{(p-v)}$$

or

$$Q = \frac{\$60,000 + \$48,000/(1 - 0.2)}{\$75 - \$35} = 3,000 \text{ units per year}$$

This amount is an increase of 300 units over the 2,700 units required for the before-tax profit level.

CVP ANALYSIS FOR ACTIVITY-BASED COSTING

The conventional approach to CVP analysis is to use a volume-based measure, that is, a measure based on units of product manufactured and sold. The preceding discussion has assumed a volume-based approach. An alternative approach is activity-based costing. Activity-based costing identifies cost drivers for detailed-level indirect cost activities, such as machine setup, materials handling, inspection, and engineering. In contrast, the volume-based approach combines the costs of these activities and treats them as fixed costs since they do not vary with output volume.

◄**LEARNING OBJECTIVE 4**
Apply CVP analysis for activity-based costing.

Activity-based costing provides a more accurate determination of costs because it separately identifies and traces indirect costs to products rather than combining them in a pool of fixed costs as the volume-based approach does. Returning to the HFI example, we show how CVP analysis can be adapted when activity-based costing is used.

The conventional, volume-based CVP analysis provides:

$$Q = (\$60,000 + 48,000)/(\$75 - \$35) = 2,700 \text{ units}$$

How does the activity-based CVP analysis work? Suppose that the cost accounting staff has been able to trace approximately $10,000 of last year's fixed costs to batch-level activities such as machine setup and inspection. This estimate was made when the firm was operating at 100 batches per year. These costs can be traced directly to each batch, although not to each unit of output. The staff has also learned that this year's production of 3,000 units is to be produced in batches of 30 units, so 100 batches will be produced again this year. We assume that batch-level costs increase in proportion to an increase in the number of batches produced during the year; that is, $100 per batch ($10,000/100). The activity-based CVP model is thus developed in the following way.

First, we define new terms for fixed cost: $f = f^{\text{VB}} + f^{\text{AB}}$, where:

f^{VB} = the volume-based fixed costs, the portion of fixed costs that *do not* vary with the activity cost driver, $50,000 ($60,000 − $10,000)

f^{AB} = the portion of fixed costs that do vary with the activity cost driver, $10,000; we assume that $10,000 is necessary for 3,000 units of output, requiring 100 production batches of 30 units each

Second, we define the following terms:

v^{AB} = the cost per batch for the activity-based cost driver, $10,000/100 = $100 per batch

b = the number of units in a batch, 30 units (3,000/100)

v^{AB}/b = the cost per unit of product for batch-related costs when the batch is size b; v^{AB}/b = $3.33 ($100.00/30)

Third, the CVP model for activity-based costing is

$$Q = \frac{f^{VB} + N}{p - v - (v^{AB}/b)}$$

Fourth, substituting data from the HFI example,

$$Q = \frac{\$50,000 + \$48,000}{\$75 - \$35 - \$100/30} = 2,673 \text{ units}$$

$$= 89.1 \text{ batches } (2,673/30)$$

This method assumes that we hold batch size constant and vary the number of batches as the total volume changes. The number of batches must be a whole number, however. In this case, 90 batches are required for the 2,673 units; 89 batches of 30 units each (89 × 30 = 2,670 units) plus one additional batch. The analysis should be recalculated for exact breakeven using 90 batches as follows, where the cost of 90 batches is 90 × $100 per batch = $9,000:

$$Q = \frac{\$50,000 + \$9,000 + \$48,000}{\$75 - \$35} = 2,675 \text{ units}$$

The solution for the activity-based model is slightly lower than for the volume-based model (2,675 units versus 2,700 units) because the ABC method allows for lower total batch-level costs. Instead of a fixed batch-level cost of $10,000 under the volume-based approach, the ABC method allows the batch-level costs to decrease (or increase) as volume decreases (or increases).

To illustrate the effect of batch size on the solution, suppose that production is scheduled in smaller batches of 20 units and that batch costs continue to be $100 each. How many units must be sold now to earn $48,000? The answer is 2,800 units and 140 batches, as shown here. Note that the cost of batch-level activities has now increased substantially, from $10,000 for 100 batches to $14,000 for 140 batches.

$$Q = (\$50,000 + \$48,000)/(\$75 - \$35 - \$100/20)$$

$$= 2,800 \text{ units}$$

or

$$= 140 \text{ batches } (2,800/20) \text{ of 20 units each}$$

We also could determine this from the following, using $14,000 for total batch level costs:

$$Q = \frac{\$50,000 + \$14,000 + \$48,000}{\$75 - \$35} = 2,800 \text{ units}$$

Notice that the number of units to achieve breakeven increases when the batch size is decreased. This is due directly to the increase in the total batch-level costs as batch size is decreased. CVP analysis based on activity-based costing can provide a more precise analysis of the relationships among volume, costs, and profits by considering batch-level costs.[1]

SENSITIVITY ANALYSIS OF CVP RESULTS

CVP analysis becomes an important strategic tool when managers use it to determine the sensitivity of profits (or breakeven) to possible changes in costs or sales volume. If costs, prices, or volumes can change significantly, the firm's strategy might also have to change. For example, if there is a risk that sales levels will fall below projected levels, management would be prudent to reduce planned investments in fixed costs (i.e., investments to increase production capacity). The additional capacity will not be needed if sales fall, but it would be difficult to reduce the fixed costs in the short term. **Sensitivity analysis** is the name for a variety of methods that examine how an amount changes if factors involved in predicting that amount change. Sensitivity analysis is particularly important when a great deal of uncertainty exists about the potential level of future sales volumes, prices, or costs. We present three of the most common methods for sensitivity analysis: (1) what-if analysis using the contribution margin and contribution margin ratio, (2) the margin of safety, and (3) operating leverage.[2]

◀**LEARNING OBJECTIVE 5**

Employ sensitivity analysis to more effectively use CVP analysis when actual sales are uncertain.

Sensitivity analysis is the name for a variety of methods used to examine how an amount will change if factors involved in predicting that amount change.

What-if Analysis of Sales: Contribution Margin and Contribution Margin Ratio

What-if analysis is the calculation of an amount given different levels for a factor that influences that amount. It is a common approach to sensitivity analysis when uncertainty is present. Many times it is based on the contribution margin and the contribution margin ratio. For example, the contribution margin ($40) and contribution margin ratio (0.5333) for HFI provide a direct measure of the sensitivity of HFI's profits to changes in volume. Each unit change in volume affects profits by $40; each dollar change in sales affects profits by $0.5333. Use of a spreadsheet such as Excel and tools such as data tables, scenarios, and goal-seek can facilitate the analysis.[3] An example of a data table for HFI is shown in Exhibit 8–5; units sold, fixed cost, and price are held constant, and we examine the effect of changes in unit variable cost on profits.

What-if-analysis is the calculation of an amount given different levels for a factor that influences that amount.

Exhibit 8–5	What-If Sensitivity Analysis for HFI, Inc.				
Units Sold	**Unit Variable Cost**	**Fixed Cost**	**Price**	**Profit**	
1,500	$30	$60,000	$75	7,500	
1,500	35	60,000	75	—	
1,500	40	60,000	75	−7,500	
1,500	45	60,000	75	−15,000	

[1] See the discussion of CVP analysis for activity-based costing in Lawrence M. Metzger, "The Power to Compete: The New Math of Precision Management," *The National Public Accountant*, May 1993, pp. 14–32.

[2] Other approaches to sensitivity analysis go beyond the coverage of this text and include analytical methods and spreadsheet simulation methods; see Jimmy E. Hilliard and Robert A. Leitch, "Breakeven Analysis of Alternatives under Uncertainty," *Management Accounting*, March 1977, pp. 53–57; and David R. Fordham and S. Brooks Marshall, "Tools for Dealing with Uncertainty," *Management Accounting*, September 1997, pp. 38–43.

[3] Data tables, scenarios, and goal-seek are functions of Microsoft Excel. Use of these tools in what-if analysis is explained in Stephanie M. Bryant, "Hey, What If...?" *Journal of Accountancy*, June 2000, pp. 35–45.

Margin of Safety

The **margin of safety** measures the potential effect of a change in sales on profits and is calculated as follows:

$$\text{Margin of safety} = \text{Planned sales} - \text{Breakeven sales}$$

Returning to the HFI example, assume that the planned number of sales of TV tables is 3,000 units per year; since the breakeven quantity is 1,500 units, the margin of safety is

$$\text{Margin of safety in units} = 3,000 - 1,500 = 1,500 \text{ units}$$

or

$$\text{Margin of safety in sales dollars} = 1,500 \times \$75 = \$112,500$$

The margin of safety also can be used as a ratio, a percentage of sales:

$$\text{Margin of safety ratio} = \text{Margin of safety/Planned sales}$$

$$= 1,500/3,000 = .5$$

The **margin of safety ratio** is a useful measure for comparing the risk of two alternative products or for assessing the risk in any given product. The product with a relatively low margin of safety ratio is the riskier of the two products and therefore usually requires more of management's attention.

Operating Leverage

Changes in the contemporary manufacturing environment include improved production techniques through automation, work-flow enhancements, and other techniques. As these changes take place, the nature of CVP analysis also changes. For example, in a fully automated production environment, labor costs are less important, and variable costs consist primarily of materials costs. In some settings, such as the manufacture of certain electrical parts and components, the materials cost is also relatively low so that fixed costs are very high relative to total cost. In this context, CVP analysis can play a crucial strategic role because profits are more sensitive to the number of units manufactured and sold. In other manufacturing operations, with low fixed costs and relatively high variable costs, profits are less sensitive to changes in sales, and CVP is relatively less important.

Consider two firms: One has relatively low fixed costs and relatively high unit variable costs (a labor-intensive firm), and the other has relatively high fixed costs and relatively low variable costs (a fully automated firm). Sample data for two such firms are shown in Exhibit 8–6.

These two situations are compared in Exhibit 8–7A (relatively high fixed costs) and Exhibit 8–7B (relatively low fixed costs). Note that the breakeven point is the same in each case, 50,000 units. However, if we examine the profit at 25,000 units above breakeven or the loss at 25,000 units below breakeven, a strong contrast emerges. For

Exhibit 8–6	Contrasting Data for Fully Automated and Labor-Intensive Firms	
	Fully Automated: **High Fixed Cost**	**Labor Intensive:** **Low Fixed Cost**
Fixed cost/year	$500,000	$150,000
Variable cost/unit	2	9
Price	12	12
Contribution margin	10	3

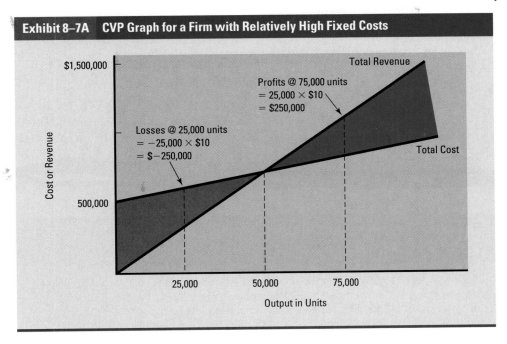

Exhibit 8–7A CVP Graph for a Firm with Relatively High Fixed Costs

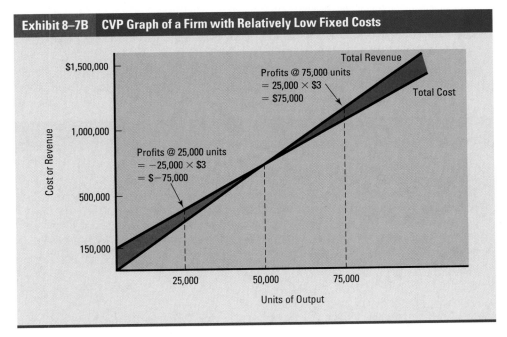

Exhibit 8–7B CVP Graph of a Firm with Relatively Low Fixed Costs

the firm with relatively high fixed costs (Exhibit 8–7A), the loss at 25,000 units is relatively large, $250,000, while the profit at 75,000 units is also relatively large, $250,000. In contrast, when fixed costs are low (Exhibit 8–7B), the loss at 25,000 units is only $75,000 and the profit at 75,000 units is only $75,000.

Clearly, a firm with high fixed costs is riskier because profits are very strongly affected by the level of activity. High profits are earned beyond breakeven, but high losses result from falling below breakeven. In this context, CVP analysis is particularly important in planning the use of new manufacturing technologies that have the potential to change the relationship between fixed and variable costs.

The potential effect of the risk that sales will fall short of planned levels, as influenced by the relative proportion of fixed to variable manufacturing costs, can be measured by **operating leverage**, which is the ratio of the contribution margin to profit. For the HFI data (Exhibit 8–2), the operating leverage for 2000 is as follows:

$$\text{Operating leverage} = \text{Contribution margin/Profit}$$
$$= \$96,000/\$36,000 = 2.667$$

Operating leverage of 2.667 means that since HFI's sales increased 8.33 percent ($15,000/$180,000) from 2000 to 2001, profits should increase by 22.22 percent (2.667 × 8.33%). A quick calculation demonstrates that profit has increased by 22.22 percent ($8,000/$36,000).

A higher value for operating leverage indicates a higher risk in the sense that a given change in sales will have a relatively greater impact on profits. When sales volume is

---

Operating Leverage and Corporate Strategy at Goodyear Tire and Rubber

Learning hard lessons from intensive foreign competition in the 1980s, many large U.S. manufacturers trimmed their manufacturing capacity. When demand surged in the 1990s, they did not expand their plants, but achieved the additional capacity by using overtime labor and machine utilization approaching 24 hours a day, every day. The additional variable costs of overtime labor, expensive overnight materials shipments, high employee turnover, and skyrocketing machine repair and maintenance costs were judged to be a better strategy than the commitment to hard-to-lose fixed costs required to expand capacity. The automotive industry was especially affected, as was Goodyear Tire and Rubber, Inc., and Intermet Corp, a manufacturer of auto parts.

Source: "Just-in-Time Manufacturing Is Working Overtime," *Business Week,* November 6, 1999, p. 36.

Operating Leverage at Chrysler Corporation

Chrysler management announced that a planned new luxury car would not be built. The economics were just not there. When asked about the number of cars needed to break even on the planned new car (Codename LX), however, management acknowledged a relatively small number, about 30,000 vehicles. The reason for the low breakeven is that Chrysler adds manufacturing capacity only in response to proven demand. Chrysler president Robert Lutz explained that in comparison to Ford, Chrysler has similar labor and materials cost. The big difference is in the per-unit fixed costs, where Lutz thinks Chrysler is $1,000 to $1,500 lower than Ford.

Source: "The Car Chrysler Didn't Build," *Forbes,* August 12, 1996, pp. 89–90.

Operating Leverage in the Computer Industry: Microprocessors and Software

In many industries, growth in demand for a product or service often leads to price inflation. In contrast, high-tech industries, such as those that manufacture microprocessors or semiconductors and those that develop software, find that rising demand can actually drive prices down. This happens because being competitive in the semiconductor industry or in mainstream software products requires a very large investment. The fixed costs of the investment and the capacity to produce the chips or the programs are very high while the variable costs of producing them are relatively low. As demand rises, the per-unit fixed costs fall, and thus the trend to concentration in the industry and the ever-falling prices.

Source: "Cover Story: The Computer Industry," *Business Week,* March 31, 1997, p. 64.

Sensitivity Analysis in a Graphical Format: Fuel Cell Technology

Sometimes showing the results of a sensitivity analysis in the form of a graph is useful. The U.S. Department of Energy has used this approach to study the decision to adopt fuel cell technology for generating electricity by such large users as the Pittsburgh International Airport, AT&T Research Laboratory in Morristown, New Jersey, and Kirkland Air Force Base in New Mexico. Fuel cell technology converts natural gas to electricity in a clean and efficient manner. Fuel cells are cost effective when the cost of natural gas is relatively low and the cost of other sources of electricity is relatively high. The study produced a breakeven analysis and related sensitivity analysis showing that a breakeven line can be determined (see the following) to clearly identify the preferred technology (fuel cell or conventional sources of electricity) based on variations in the cost of natural gas and conventional electricity.

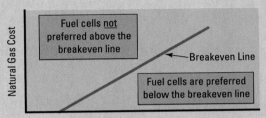

The breakeven line as shown is determined by solving the equation that sets total cost of one technology equal to that of the other. The two axes in the graph are the unit variable costs for each alternative.

To illustrate, using the data from Exhibit 8–6, we solve the equation that sets total cost of the automated factory equal to

that of the labor-intensive factory. The fixed costs and volume level are assumed, and the equation is solved for the variable cost of each alternative as a function of the variable cost of the other alternative (where Y = unit variable cost for the automated factory and X = unit variable cost for the labor-intensive factory, volume = 50,000 units, and the remaining data are from Exhibit 8–6):

$$\text{Total cost of automated} = \text{Total cost of labor-intensive}$$
$$\text{factory} \qquad\qquad \text{factory}$$

$$Y \times 50,000 + \$500,000 = X \times 50,000 + \$150,000$$

$$Y = X - 7$$

The sensitivity graph for these data follows. The labor-intensive factory favors the area above the line and the automated factory favors the area below the line.

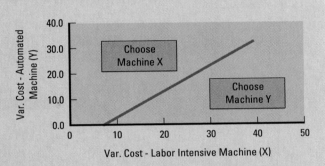

Source: Pacific Northwest National Laboratory, "Federal Technology Alerts: Natural Gas Fuel Cells," U.S. Department of Energy, November 1995 (www.pnl.gov/fta/5_nat.htm).

COST MANAGEMENT IN ACTION

How Does American Airlines Handle the Cost of Growth?

American Airlines is one of the largest and most successful airlines in the world. It has been a powerful competitor in the industry, setting prices and competitive standards by developing key innovations such as frequent flyer programs, supersaver fares, and integrated reservation systems. A key aspect of American's success is its ability to control costs in an industry that has rapidly moved to cost leadership after its deregulation some years ago. Robert Crandall, long-time CEO of American, once said, "The market is telling all the traditional airlines that they must compete in a low cost, low

price world. . . . This business is intensely, vigorously, bitterly, savagely competitive."

American has targeted improvements in its direct costs by hedging fuel costs, developing innovative salary and wage structures for flight crews and other employees, and redesigning on-board service activities. The average wage cost per seat mile at American has decreased over time. How does American create improvements in the more difficult-to-manage indirect costs of providing its service? (Refer to Comments on Cost Management in Action at the end of the chapter.)

---

strong, a high level of leverage is desirable, but when sales begin to fall, a lower level of leverage is preferable. Each firm chooses the level of operating leverage that is consistent with its competitive strategy. For example, a firm with a dominant position in its market might choose a high level of leverage to exploit its advantage. In contrast, a weaker firm might choose the less risky low-leverage strategy.

CVP ANALYSIS WITH MULTIPLE PRODUCTS

LEARNING OBJECTIVE 6▶

Adapt CVP analysis for multiple products.

One simplifying assumption made in the chapter to this point is to develop the CVP model for only a single product. How does the analysis change if we must deal with two or more products? What if the two or more products share the same fixed costs? Can we still calculate a breakeven value for each product? This section adapts the CVP model to answer questions such as these.

Our adaptation of the CVP model requires one key assumption: The sales of the product will *continue at the same sales mix.* That is, the sales of each product will remain at the same proportion of total sales. The mix can be determined in either sales units or sales dollars; the important point is that it must remain constant.

Assuming a constant sales mix allows us to treat the two or more products as one combined product mix by computing a weighted-average contribution margin. The weighted-average contribution margin is used to determine the total sales necessary to attain the desired operating result.

To illustrate, we use the example of Windbreakers, Inc., which sells light-weight sport/recreational jackets. Windbreakers has three products, calm (to wear in a light breeze) Windy, and Gale (for wear in harsher weather). Relevant information for these products is in Exhibit 8–8. The total fixed costs for the period are expected to be $168,000.

From this information, we can calculate the weighted-average contribution margin ratio as follows, using the ratio of sales relative to total sales for each product.

$$0.5(0.2) + 0.4(0.25) + 0.1(0.1) = 0.21$$

= Weighted-average contribution margin ratio

The breakeven point for all three products can be calculated as follows:

$$Y = \$168,000/0.21 = \$800,000$$

This means that for Windbreakers to breakeven, $800,000 of all three products must be sold in the same proportion as last year's sales mix. The sales for each product are as follows:

For calm	0.5($800,000) = $400,000	(13,334 jackets at $30)
For windy	0.4($800,000) = 320,000	(10,000 jackets at $32)
For gale	0.1($800,000) = 80,000	(2,000 jackets at $40)
Total	$800,000	

The sale of jackets in the correct sales mix produces exactly the breakeven contribution method of $168,000:

$$\$6(13,334) + \$8(10,000) + \$4(2,000) = \$168,000$$

The solution relies on the assumed constant sales mix for the products involved. If the sales mix changes, the analysis must be revised. As new sales mix, price, or cost

Exhibit 8–8	Sales and Cost Data for Windbreakers, Inc.			
	Calm	**Windy**	**Gale**	**Total**
Last period's sales	$750,000	$600,000	$150,000	$1,500,000
Percent of sales	50	40	10	100%
Price	$ 30	$ 32	$ 40	
Unit variable cost	24	24	36	
Contribution margin	$ 6	$ 8	$ 4	
Contribution margin ratio	0.20	0.25	0.10	

information becomes available, the breakeven analysis should be recomputed. Note also that this solution is based on an assumed constant sales mix in *dollars*. When the sales mix is given in dollars, as in this case, the contribution margin *ratio* is used to obtain the breakeven in *dollars*, as is consistent with the breakeven formula presented earlier (use the contribution margin for breakeven in units, the contribution margin ratio for breakeven in dollars). Similarly, when the sales mix is constant in *units*, the contribution margin *per unit* is used to obtain the breakeven in *units*.

For practicality, this approach is also best utilized with a small number of products. With a large number of products, the best approach is to approximate the overall contribution margin ratio (perhaps by product group or by knowledge of mark-up rates) and determine the overall breakeven in sales in this manner. Moreover, when a small number of products are involved, the question arises about the most profitable product mix, as it does in Chapter 5 with the theory of constraints. In this case, adapting the CVP analysis to the theory of constraints by focusing on the time in the constraint rather than total volume can be useful.[4]

CVP ANALYSIS FOR NOT-FOR-PROFIT ORGANIZATIONS AND SERVICE FIRMS

◀ **LEARNING OBJECTIVE 7**

Apply CVP analysis in not-for-profit organizations and service firms.

Not-for-profit organizations and service firms can also use CVP analysis. To illustrate, consider a small mental health agency experiencing financial difficulty. Orange County Mental Health Center's financial support comes from the county, whose funding is falling because of a recession in the local economy. As a result, the county commissioners have set an across-the-board budget cut of about 5 percent for the new fiscal year. The center's funding was $735,000 last year and is projected to be approximately $700,000 next year. Its director figures that variable costs (including medications, handout publications, and some administrative costs) amount to approximately $10 per visit for the almost 300 patients who regularly see counselors at the center. All other costs are fixed, including salaries for the counselors, record-keeping costs, and facilities costs. How will the budget cuts affect the level of services the center provides?

To answer this question, we must determine precisely the center's activity with the associated fixed and variable costs. Although we could define activity in a variety of ways, we choose the number of patient visits as a logical measure of the center's activity. The director estimates 13,000 to 14,000 patient visits occurred last year. With this information, we can develop the cost equation illustrated in Exhibit 8–9. We assume 13,500 visits last year and that unit variable costs are constant at $10 per visit in the range of 10,000 to 14,000 visits per year; total variable costs were therefore $135,000 ($10 × 13,500) last year. We determine total fixed costs for last year:

$$\text{Funding} = \text{Total cost}$$

$$= \text{Total fixed costs} + \text{Total variable costs}$$

$$\$735,000 = \text{Total fixed costs} + \$135,000$$

$$\text{Total fixed costs} = \$600,000$$

Now the director can analyze the effect of the budget change on the center's service levels. At the $700,000 budget level expected for next year, the activity level is approximately 10,000 visits. Total cost of $700,000 less fixed cost of $600,000 leaves variable costs of $100,000; thus, $100,000/$10 = 10,000 visits. The director can now see that the approximate 5 percent cut in the budget is expected to result in an approximate 26 percent drop in patient contact [(13,500 − 10,000)/13,500].

---

[4] This technique is demonstrated in Robert Luther and Brian O'Donovan, "Cost-Volume-Profit Analysis and the Theory of Constraints," *Journal of Cost Management*, September–October, 1998, pp. 16–21.

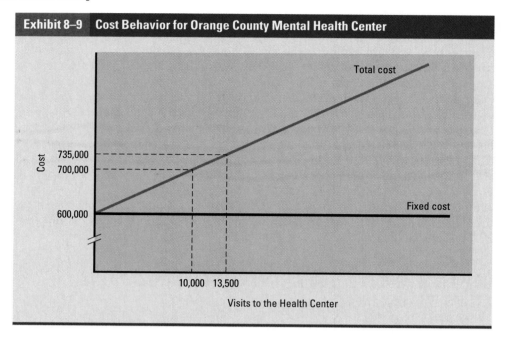

Exhibit 8–9   Cost Behavior for Orange County Mental Health Center

Although the county commissioners might have expected that the center's activity would be reduced by approximately 5 percent with the budget cut, the actual contraction in services is much more severe (26 percent). This occurs because fixed costs are expected to remain constant in the new budget year, but expected savings from reducing activity levels will be less than the effect on the activity itself. The county commissioners should realize that the mental health center's costs are predominantly fixed costs, and therefore budget cuts will affect services more than expected.

As demonstrated earlier, service firms can also use CVP analysis; for example, in the airline industry or the medical care industry. Airline firms use CVP to identify profitable new routes and to manage variable costs to meet reduced revenues in times of fare wars in the industry. Similarly, firms that specialize in home health care, nursing homes, or outpatient care use CVP analysis to identify profitable new services and to help analyze the costs of delivering existing services.

BEHAVIORAL ISSUES IN USING CVP ANALYSIS

Occasionally a behavioral issue arises when using CVP analysis. As our example of the county mental health clinic illustrates, understanding cost-volume behavior may be necessary to appropriately decide issues regarding the use of public funds.

Behavioral issues arise because of the uncertainty in the factors of the CVP model—price, expected sales level, variable costs, and fixed costs. As we saw in Chapter 3, the presence of uncertainty means that risk-averse decision makers may be biased in their efforts to avoid unfavorable consequences. For example, a CVP analysis might indicate that a new product should be introduced because its breakeven point produces a reasonably high margin of safety; the firm would therefore wish to introduce the product. However, if significant uncertainty exists about the product's expected sales and if the choice is made by a risk-averse manager whose compensation and reputation are likely to be adversely affected in the event of poor sales, the manager might choose not to introduce the product, which is contrary to the firm's objectives. When uncertainty is significant in a CVP analysis, management must be aware of the bias resulting from risk aversion.

ASSUMPTIONS AND LIMITATIONS OF CVP ANALYSIS

Linearity and the Relevant Range

The CVP model assumes that revenues and total costs are linear over the relevant range of activity. Although actual cost behavior is not linear, we use the concept of the relevant range introduced in Chapter 3 so that within a given limited range of output, total costs are expected to increase at an approximately linear rate. The caution for the manager is therefore to remember that the calculations performed within the context of a given CVP model should not be used outside the relevant range.

◄**LEARNING OBJECTIVE 8**

Identify the assumptions and limitations of CVP analysis and their effect on the proper interpretation of the results.

Step Costs

As illustrated in Exhibit 8–10, the cost behavior under examination may be so "lumpy" (step costs) that an approximation via a relevant range is unworkable. Although CVP analysis can be done, it becomes somewhat more cumbersome. Exhibit 8–10 illustrates a situation with a price of $18, a unit variable cost of $10, an initial fixed cost of $100,000, and an incremental fixed cost of another $100,000 when output exceeds 10,000 units. The expenditure of the additional fixed cost provides capacity for up to 30,000 units. A CVP analysis requires that the manager determine the breakeven point for each range (below and above the point at 10,000 units). For these data, we find no breakeven below the 10,000 unit level of output, but the breakeven point can be obtained for the upper range as follows:

$$Q = f/(p - v) = \$200,000/(\$18 - \$10) = 25,000 \text{ units}$$

Thus, losses will be incurred up to the 25,000-unit level, and the additional investment in capacity will be necessary to achieve this production and sales level. Of potential concern to the manager is the relatively narrow range of profitability, between 25,000 and 30,000 units. Therefore, additional analysis might be advisable to better determine the extent of demand for the product and the cost of extending capacity beyond 30,000 units.

Identifying Fixed and Variable Cost for CVP Analysis

In CVP analysis it is not always easy to identify the dollar figures used for fixed costs and unit variable cost. So next we discuss how to differentiate fixed from variable costs.

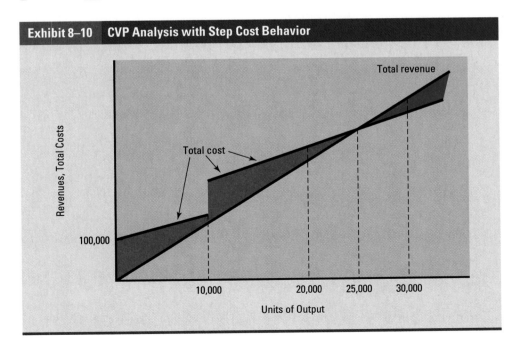

Exhibit 8–10   CVP Analysis with Step Cost Behavior

Fixed Costs to Include

Suppose that management wants to calculate the breakeven point for a new product for Household Furnishings, Inc. The new product is a computer table designed for easy assembly and intended for the low-price end of the market. Is the cost of the president's salary a relevant fixed cost for this calculation? It is not because the president's salary does not change whether HFI introduces the computer table; it is a fixed cost for the corporation, but it is irrelevant for the analysis of the short-term profitability of the new product.

In a short-term analysis, relevant fixed costs are those expected to change with the introduction of the new product. These include costs of any new production facilities, salaries of new production personnel, and similar costs.

If a new product does not require any new fixed costs because existing capacity, facilities, and personnel can handle the added production, what is the breakeven point? For a *short-term analysis*, the breakeven point is zero since the new product must cover no new fixed costs. That is, each product sold, beginning with the first, contributes to profit in the excess of price over variable cost. In contrast, for a *long-term analysis* of breakeven, all current and expected future fixed costs associated with the production, distribution, and sale of the product are relevant. Moreover, for a long-term analysis, the methods discussed in Chapter 11 could also be used, including the discounting of future cash flows. Failure to do so when considering breakeven over two or more years can lead to an unwarranted favorable bias to the analysis since discounting future cash flows reduces the value of these amounts, especially when relatively high discount rates are applicable.[5]

The Period in Which the Cost Was Incurred

The fixed costs in a CVP analysis can include the expected cash outflows for fixed costs in the period for which breakeven is expected; alternatively, they can include the fixed costs as determined by accrual accounting. The cash flow fixed costs include all cash outflows for insurance, taxes, and salaries but exclude the noncash items such as depreciation, amortization of patents, and other noncash expenses. The advantage of the cash flow approach is its focus on the company's cash needs.

An accrual accounting approach to determine the amount of fixed costs includes all costs normally expensed in the income statement, including depreciation, amortization, and accrued expenses. The advantage of this approach is that it ties the CVP analysis to the income statement. In choosing between these two approaches, a manager considers the relative benefits of information most relevant for cash flows or for accrual net profit.[6]

Breakeven for Cash Flows: Internet Retailer

Following a decline in the market for Internet stocks in the spring of 2000, a number of Internet retailers found financing their operations to be difficult. Those that had raised funds before the stock price decline were in a better position to maintain their operations and planned activities. We can calculate a cash breakeven point for those firms based on a predicted rate of sales growth and the current use of cash. For those firms not able to achieve a breakeven in a short number of months, additional financing is necessary.

Some firms and their cash breakeven dates follow:

Firm	Breakeven
Amazon.com	Late 2002
Drugstore.com	2003
BarnesandNoble.com	Fall 2002
Fogdog	Mid-2002

Source: "Building the Perfect E-tailer," *Business Week*, October 23, 2000, p. EB34.

---

[5]   Mark Freeman and Kerrie Freeman make this point in "Considering the Time Value of Money in Breakeven Analysis," *Management Accounting* (London), January 1993, pp. 50–52.

[6]   Some useful references for cash flow and accrual breakeven analysis are Bipin Ajikkya, Rowland Atiase, and Linda Bamber, "Absorption versus Direct Costing: Income Reconciliation and Cost-Volume-Profit Analysis," *Issues in Accounting Education*, Fall 1986, pp. 268–81; and David Solomons, "Breakeven Analysis under Absorption Costing," *The Accounting Review*, July 1968, pp. 447–52.

Unit Variable Costs

In measuring unit variable cost, the management accountant must be careful to include all relevant variable costs, not only production costs but also selling and distribution costs. Thus, expense for commissions is properly included as a unit variable cost. Any transportation or warehousing costs, if they change with level of output, are relevant.

SUMMARY

This chapter develops CVP analysis, a linear model of the relationships between costs, revenues, and output levels. The analysis is used for breakeven planning, revenue planning, and cost planning.

Breakeven planning determines the output level at which profits are zero. Breakeven analysis is used in planning and budgeting to assess the desirability of current and potential products and services. CVP analysis is also used in revenue planning to determine the sales needed to achieve a desired profit level by adding desired profit to the breakeven equation. In cost planning, CVP analysis is used to find the required reduction in costs to meet desired profits or to find the required change in fixed cost for a given change in variable cost (or vice versa).

Two additional concepts—activity-based costing and sensitivity analysis—enhance revenue and cost planning. Activity-based costing breaks fixed costs into batch- and unit-related costs, so CVP analyses can be performed at either (or both) the batch or unit level.

Sensitivity analysis is useful because profits of firms with relatively high fixed costs are more sensitive to changes in the level of sales. The sensitivity, or risk, of changes in sales levels is measured by the margin of safety and operating leverage.

With two or more products, the use of CVP analysis requires the assumption of a constant sales mix between them, and the weighted-average contribution margin is used to calculate the breakeven point.

Not-for-profit and service firms also use breakeven analysis. We presented the example of a municipal health agency's use of breakeven analysis to predict the effects of changing funding levels on its operations.

A number of behavioral issues and limitations must be considered in using breakeven analysis. For example, since uncertainties regarding the projections involved in the analysis likely exist, considering whether risk-averse managers will use the analysis in the manner corporate management intends is important. In using breakeven analysis, we also assume that fixed costs and unit variable cost do not change, although we are able to handle special situations such as those involving step costs, as illustrated in the chapter.

KEY TERMS

Breakeven point   301

Contribution income statement   299

Contribution margin ratio   299

Cost-volume-profit (CVP) analysis   298

CVP graph   304

Margin of safety   310

Margin of safety ratio   310

Operating leverage   312

Profit-volume graph   304

Sensitivity analyisis   309

Total contribution margin   298

Unit contribution margin   298

What-if analysis   309

COMMENTS ON COST MANAGEMENT IN ACTION

How Does American Airlines Handle the Cost of Growth?

American Airlines' indirect costs, including the cost of the aircraft, airport facilities costs, and other indirect costs, are more difficult to manage because they do not respond quickly to changes in the volume of business. American's strategy therefore is to operate at a relatively low level of operating leverage. In terms of investment in aircraft, this means that American keeps a small number of aircraft relative to the number of required flights. In terms of airport facilities, American concentrates on locations with profitable flights. Elizabeth Bailey, an expert in the industry, observed, "Those airlines in trouble are in trouble by and large because they leveraged themselves in the 1980s. American didn't leverage itself in that crazy way." By keeping its leverage and fixed costs low, as well as reducing its direct costs, American is in a better position to meet the industry price wars.

Sources: "Stuck," *Business Week*, November 15, 1993; and "Bob Crandall: An American Gladiator," *Business Week*, April 27, 1998, p. 44.

SELF-STUDY PROBLEM

(For solution, please turn to the end of the chapter.)

The following data refer to a single product, the TECHWHIZ, made by the Markdata Computer Company:

Sales price = $5,595

Materials cost (including purchased components) = $899

Direct labor cost = $233

Facilities cost (for a highly automated plant mainly includes rent, insurance, taxes, and depreciation) = $2,352,000 per year

Required

1. What is the unit contribution margin?
2. What is the breakeven point in units and dollars?
3. What is the desired level of sales if the company plans to increase fixed costs by 5 percent (to improve product quality and appearance) and achieve a desired before-tax profit of $200,000?
4. If the company's income tax rate is 22 percent, what unit sales are necessary to achieve an after-tax profit of $150,000?

QUESTIONS

8–1   What is the underlying relationship in CVP analysis?

8–2   When might it be better to find the breakeven point in sales dollars rather than in units?

8–3   What is the contribution margin ratio and how is it used?

8–4   What are the basic assumptions of CVP analysis?

8–5   Why might the percentage budget cut for a not-for-profit agency not equal the resultant change in the activity level?

8–6   If a new product does not require any new fixed costs because the company utilizes the existing capacity of facilities and personnel, what is the breakeven point?

8–7   Is CVP analysis used in profit planning, cost planning, or revenue planning?

8–8   Why does the issue of taxes not affect the calculation of the breakeven point?

8–9 Why is CVP analysis important in planning the use of new manufacturing technologies?

8–10 What type of risk does sensitivity analysis address?

8–11 Explain the four methods for calculating the breakeven point.

8–12 What is the margin of safety, and for what is it used?

8–13 What is operating leverage, and for what is it used?

8–14 How are step costs treated in CVP analysis?

8–15 Desired before-tax net income equals the desired after-tax net income multiplied by _____?

8–16 How is CVP analysis used to calculate the breakeven point for multiple products?

8–17 Why do management accountants use sensitivity analysis?

EXERCISES

8–18 **MAKE OR BUY, TWO MACHINES** Calista Company manufactures electronic equipment. It currently purchases the special switches used in each of its products from an outside supplier. The supplier charges Calista $2 per switch. Calista's CEO is considering purchasing either machine X or machine Y so the company can manufacture its own switches. The projected data are

	Machine X	Machine Y
Annual fixed cost	$135,000	$204,000
Variable cost per switch	0.65	0.30

Required

1. For each machine, what is the minimum number of switches that Calista must make annually for total costs to equal outside purchase cost?

2. What is the most profitable alternative for producing 200,000 switches per year?

3. What volume level would produce the same total costs regardless of the machine purchased?

8–19 **OPERATING LEVERAGE** These sales and cost data (000s) are for two companies in the transportation industry:

	Company A		Company B	
	Amount	Percent of sales	Amount	Percent of sales
Sales	$100,000	100%	$100,000	100%
Variable costs	60,000	60	30,000	30
Contribution margin	$ 40,000	40%	$ 70,000	70%
Fixed costs	15,000		40,000	
Net income	$ 25,000		$ 30,000	

Required

1. Calculate the operating leverage for each company. If sales increase, which company benefits more? How do you know?

2. Assume that sales rise 10 percent in the next year. Calculate the percentage increase in profit for each company. Are the results what you expected?

8–20   CHANGE IN FIXED COSTS   Riley Company manufactures high-level computer monitors. Following is a summary of its basic cost and revenue data:

	Per Unit	Percent of Sales
Sales price	$400	100%
Variable costs	240	60
Unit contribution margin	$160	40%

Assume that Riley is currently selling 500 computer monitors per month totaling $200,000. The sales manager believes that a $15,000 increase in the advertising budget would increase monthly sales by $50,000.

Required   Should the advertising budget be increased? Explain your answer.

8–21   CVP ANALYSIS   Puppy Inc., maker of quality dog houses, has experienced a steady growth in sales over the past five years. Since his business has grown, Tomas Tomassino, the president of Puppy Inc., believes he needs an aggressive advertising campaign next year to maintain the company's growth. To prepare for the growth, the chief accountant prepared the following data for the current year for the president:

Variable costs per dog house	
Direct labor	$ 20.00
Direct materials	10.25
Variable overhead	4.50
Total variable costs	$ 34.75
Fixed costs	
Manufacturing	$ 28,000
Selling	35,000
Administrative	60,000
Total fixed costs	$ 123,000
Selling price per dog house	$ 60.00
Expected sales (30,000 units)	$1,800,000
Tax rate: 40%	

Required

1.   If costs and sales prices remain the same, what is the projected income for the coming year?

2.   What is the breakeven point in units for the coming year?

3.   Tomas has set the sales target at 32,000 dog houses. He foresees an additional selling expense of $12,000 for advertising and expects all other costs to remain constant. What will be the net income if the additional $12,000 is spent on advertising?

4.   What will be the new breakeven point if an additional $12,000 is spent on advertising?

5.   If the additional $12,000 is spent for advertising the next year, what is the required sales level in units to equal the current year's net income?

8–22   MULTIPLE PRODUCT CVP ANALYSIS   Reader's Retreat is a small book store that rents space in a neighborhood shopping mall for $19,200 a year. Its utilities add another $7,800 yearly. The total staff salaries and benefits projected for next year equal $56,000. Reader's Retreat also spends $900 on advertising and $2,400 on professional services. Other overhead expenses total $11,500.

Jamie Davis, the company's owner, would like to make a $40,000 profit after taxes next year, when her tax rate will be 33 percent. The store sells hardbound books, paperback books, and magazines. The average cost of each category of items and Reader's markup on cost is $12.00 and 50 percent, hardbacks; $2.40 and 60 percent, paperbacks; and $1.90 and 60 percent, magazines.

In past years, 70 percent of the store's sales revenue came from hardback books, 20 percent from paperbacks, and the remaining 10 percent from magazines.

Required

1. What is the contribution margin of each sales item?
2. What are the store's projected fixed costs for next year?
3. What is the breakeven point for Reader's Retreat to achieve zero profit?
4. What sales level will the store need to reach the target after-tax profit?

8–23 THE ROLE OF INCOME TAXES   In 2001, Triad Company had fixed costs of $200,000 and variable costs of 80 percent of total sales revenue, earned $70,000 of net income after taxes, and had an income tax rate of 30 percent.

Required   Determine (1) before-tax operating income, (2) total contribution margin, (3) total sales, and (4) breakeven point in dollar sales.

8–24 CVP ANALYSIS WITH TAXES   Jeffrey Company produces and sells socks. Variable costs are $3 per pair, and fixed costs for the year total $75,000. The selling price is $5 per pair.

Required   Calculate the following:

1. The breakeven point in units.
2. The breakeven point in sales dollars.
3. The units required to make a before-tax profit of $10,000.
4. The sales in dollars required to make a before-tax profit of $8,000.
5. The sales units and sales dollars required to make an after-tax profit of $12,000 given a tax rate of 40 percent.

8–25 CHANGE IN PRICE, FIXED COSTS   Refer to the data in problem 8–20. Assume again that Riley Company is currently selling 500 computer monitors per month. To increase sales, the manager wants to cut the sales price by $40 per unit and increase the advertising budget by $15,000. Management believes that unit sales will increase by 50 percent if these two steps are followed. Fixed costs are $50,000 per month.

Required

1. Should the Riley Company follow this new strategy?
2. Prepare a comparative income statement to prove your results.

8–26 BUDGET CUTS   Student Health Services Pharmacy provides certain medications to students free of charge. Currently, 40 percent of the pharmacy's costs are fixed; the other 60 percent are variable. The pharmacy's budget was $200,000 last year, but the university recently cut this year's budget by 20 percent.

 Service

Required   What is the percentage decrease in the amount of services the pharmacy can provide this year?

8–27 MULTIPLE PRODUCTS CVP   Jordan Company can produce two types of carpet cleaners, the Brighter and Elegance. The data on the two machines is as follows:

	Brighter	Elegance
Sales volume in units	1,000	1,200
Unit sales price	$200	$250
Unit variable cost	120	120
Unit contribution margin	$ 80	$130

The number of machine-hours to produce Brighter is 1 and to produce Elegance is 2. Total fixed costs for the manufacture of both products are $132,000. Demand is high enough to keep the plant operating at full capacity; machine time is insufficient to fill all 1,000 orders for Brighter and 1,200 orders for Elegance.

Required

1. Using a spreadsheet, determine the breakeven point for Jordan Company, assuming that the sales mix remains constant in sales dollars.

2. Which of the two products do you think is more profitable? Why?

PROBLEMS

Strategy

8–28 CVP ANALYSIS, STRATEGY Frank's Western Wear is a western hat retailer in Dallas, Texas. Although Frank's carries numerous styles of western hats, each hat has approximately the same price and invoice (purchase) cost, as shown in the following table. Sales personnel receive large commissions to encourage them to be more aggressive in their sales efforts. Currently, the Dallas economy is really humming, and sales growth at Frank's has been great. The business is very competitive, however, and Frank has relied on his knowledgeable and courteous staff to attract and retain customers who otherwise might go to other western wear stores. Because of the rapid growth in sales, Frank is also finding the management of certain aspects of the business, such as restocking of inventory and hiring and training new salespeople, more difficult.

Sales price	$ 30.00
Per unit variable expenses	
Invoice cost	15.50
Sales commissions	4.50
Total per unit variable costs	$ 20.00
Total annual fixed expenses	
Advertising	$ 20,000
Rent	25,000
Salaries	105,000
Total fixed expenses	$150,000

Required

1. Calculate the annual breakeven point in unit sales and dollar sales.

2. If Frank's sells 20,000 hats, what is its net income or loss?

3. If Frank's sells 25,000, what is its margin of safety and margin of safety ratio?

4. Frank is considering the elimination of sales commissions completely and increasing salaries by $82,000 annually. What would be the new breakeven point in units? What would be the net income or loss if 20,000 hats are sold with the new salary plan?

5. Identify and discuss the strategic issues in the decision to eliminate sales commissions (see requirement 4). How do these strategic concerns affect Frank's decision?

8–29 MULTIPLE PRODUCTS Most businesses sell several products at varying prices. The products often have different unit variable costs. Thus, the total profit and the breakeven point depend on the proportions in which the products are sold. Sales mix is the relative contribution of sales among various products sold by a firm. Assume that the sales of Hycel, Inc., are the following for a typical year:

Product	Units Sold	Sales Mix
A	8,000	80%
B	2,000	20
Total	10,000	100%

Assume the following unit selling prices and unit variable costs:

Product	Selling Price	Variable Cost per Unit	Unit Contribution Margin
A	$ 90	$70	$ 20
B	140	95	45

Fixed costs are $200,000 per year.

Required

1. Determine the breakeven point in units.
2. Determine the number of units required for a before-tax net profit of $40,000.

8–30 CVP ANALYSIS   Lewis & Clark Company, a canoe manufacturer, has a projected income for 2001 as follows:

Sales (10,000 units)		$6,000,000
Operating expenses		
Variable expenses	$4,500,000	
Fixed expenses	450,000	
Total expenses		4,950,000
Net income		$1,050,000

Required

1. Determine the breakeven point in units.
2. Using the contribution margin ratio, determine the breakeven in sales revenue.
3. Determine the required sales in dollars to earn an income of $1,400,000.
4. What is the breakeven point in units if the variable cost increases by 10 percent?

8–31 MULTIPLE PRODUCT CVP ANALYSIS   Neptune Company recently acquired the technology needed to produce small, standard, and super marine bilge pumps. Budgeted fixed costs for the manufacture of all three products total $425,000. The *budgeted* sales by product and in total for the coming year are as follows:

	Small		Standard		Super	
	Amount	Percent	Amount	Percent	Amount	Percent
Sales	$175,000	100%	$400,000	100%	$250,000	100%
Variable costs	120,000	69	100,000	25	125,000	50
Contribution	$ 55,000	31%	$300,000	75%	$125,000	50%

Actual sales for the year were not as planned; the following lists sales by product:

Small	$400,000
Standard	225,000
Super	200,000
	$825,000

Required

1. Prepare a contribution income statement for the year based on actual sales data.
2. Compute the breakeven sales dollars for the year based on both budgeted and actual sales, assuming that the sales mix remains constant in sales dollars.

3. The company president knows that total actual sales were $825,000 for the year, the same as budgeted. Because she had seen the budgeted income statement, she was expecting a nice profit from producing the bilge pumps. Explain to her what happened.

8–32 CVP ANALYSIS, TAXES Sunshine Company produces and sells dolls. It projects the following revenue and costs for production and sales:

Sales price per unit	$ 10.00
Variable production costs per unit	1.50
Fixed production costs (total)	170,000
Variable selling costs per unit	2.50
Fixed selling costs (total)	145,000

Required

1. Determine the breakeven point in units and dollars.
2. What is Sunshine's pretax profit at 60,000 units?
3. Sunshine is subject to a tax rate of 30 percent. If the president wants to make an after-tax profit of $25,000, how many units must the company produce and sell?
4. What must sales be (in units) to produce a before-tax profit equal to 20 percent of sales? Include a short income computation to prove your answer.
5. Sunshine Company is considering an alternate strategy to reduce fixed production costs by $70,000. However, this would cause variable production costs to increase to $2.50 per unit. What is the number of units at which the company is indifferent as to the original production strategy and the new strategy?

8–33 CVP ANALYSIS, TAXES Elmire Company produces and sells watches. It projects the following information for next year:

Sales price per unit	$ 60
Variable production cost per unit	30
Fixed production costs (total)	200,000
Variable selling costs per unit	5
Fixed selling costs (total)	150,000

Required

1. Determine the breakeven point in units and dollars.
2. How many units does the company need to sell to earn a pretax profit of $150,000?
3. What will Elmire's pretax profit be at 40,000 units?
4. Elmire is subject to a tax rate of 40 percent. If the CEO wants an after-tax profit of $150,000, how many units must it sell?
5. Elmire is considering an alternate strategy to reduce fixed production costs by $50,000. However, this would cause variable production costs to increase to $35 per unit. What is the number of units at which the company is indifferent as to the original production strategy and the new strategy?
6. Prepare a CVP graph based on the original data.

Service

8–34 CVP ANALYSIS IN A PROFESSIONAL SERVICE FIRM A local CPA firm, Bidwell and Hope, has been asked to bid on a contract to perform audits for three counties in its home state. Should the firm be awarded the contract, it must hire two new staff members at salaries of $30,000 each to handle the additional workload. (Existing staff are fully scheduled.) The managing partner is convinced that obtaining the contract will lead to additional new profit-oriented clients from the respective counties. Expected new work (excluding the three counties) is 800 hours at an average billing rate of $38.50. Other relevant information follows about the firm's annual revenues and costs:

Firm volume in hours (normal)	30,750
Fixed costs	$470,000
Variable costs	$3.90/hr

Should the firm win the contract, these audits will require 900 hours of expected work.

Required

1. If the managing partner's expectations are correct, what is the lowest bid the firm can submit and still expect to increase annual net income?

2. If the contract is obtained at a price of $40,000, what is the minimum number of hours of new business in addition to the county work that must be obtained for the firm to break even on total new business?

(Adapted, R. Shockley)

8–35 **CVP ANALYSIS, ACTIVITY-BASED COSTING, TAXES** Sports Plus, Inc., produces software for personal computers. The company's main product is Swing!, a golf training program. The total variable cost of the product is $10. Fixed manufacturing expenses are $60,000 per month, and the price of the product is $300. In the coming year, the company plans to spend $100,000 for advertising and $50,000 for research and development. Because this proprietorship is managed from a personal residence, it incurs no other fixed costs. The federal and state tax rate for the proprietor is 40 percent. The company expects 6,000 units of sales for the next year.

Required

1. Determine the breakeven point for the coming year in number of units.

2. Suppose that 20 percent of the manufacturing fixed costs are batch-level costs from testing and packaging. Because of the nature of the testing process, all production has the same batch size of 20 units.

3. Determine the number of units required for the coming year to cover a 100 percent increase in advertising expenses and a $12,000 after-tax profit per month.

8–36 **CVP ANALYSIS** Maria Ramirez operates a feedlot on a farm near Gretna, Nebraska. She buys steers that weigh about 700 pounds, feeds them, and sells them when they reach approximately 1,200 pounds. Her annual fixed expenses follow:

Annual Fixed Costs	
Land (100 acres at $20 each)	$2,000
Silo	1,000
Tractor	500
Feedwagon	200
Chopper	200
Silage wagons	200
Barn and fence	500
Total fixed costs	$4,600

Variable costs to purchase and feed each 700-pound steer follow:

Purchase price	$700
Corn or sorghum	30
Silage	60
Medicine implants	10
Miscellaneous	64
Total variable costs	$864

All steers are sold on a per-pound basis.

Required

1. What is the breakeven selling price per pound if 200 steers are bought and sold per year?

2. What is the breakeven number of steers if Maria can contract a price of $76 per hundredweight (pounds)?

3. What is the selling price per pound needed for 200 steers assuming a $20,000 before-tax profit?

Service

8–37 CVP ANALYSIS The nonprofit Cardiac Diagnostic Screening Center (CDSC) is contemplating purchasing a blood gases analysis machine at a cost of $750,000. Useful life for this machine is 10 years. The screening center currently serves 5,000 patients per year, 30 percent of whom need blood gases analysis data as part of their diagnostic tests. The blood samples are presently sent to a private laboratory that charges $85 per sample. In-house variable expenses are estimated to be $40 per sample if CDSC purchases the analysis machine.

Required

1. Determine the indifference point between purchasing the machine or using the private laboratory.

2. Determine how many additional patients would be needed so that CDSC would be indifferent between purchasing the analysis machine and the $85 lab charge.

3. Determine the amount of the private laboratory charge so that CDSC would be indifferent as to purchasing the analysis machine or using the private laboratory, assuming the current service level of 5,000 patients per year.

Strategy

8–38 CVP ANALYSIS Headlines Publishing Company (HPC) specializes in international business news publications. Its principal product is *HPC-Monthly*, which is mailed to subscribers the first week of each month. A weekly version, called *HPC-Weekly*, is also available to subscribers over the Web at a higher cost. Sixty percent of HPC's subscribers are nondomestic customers. The company experienced a fast growth in subscribers in its first few years of operation, but sales have begun to slow in recent years as new competitors have entered the market. HPC has the following cost structure and sales revenue for its subscription operations on a yearly basis. All costs and all subscription fees are in U.S. dollars.

Fixed Cost		
$306,000 per month		

Variable Costs		
Mailing	$ 0.60	per issue
Commission	3.00	per subscription
Administrative	1.50	per subscription

Sales Mix Information	
HPC-Weekly	20 percent
HPC-Monthly	80 percent

Selling Price

HPC-Weekly	$47 per subscription
HPC-Monthly	$19 per subscription

Required   Use these data to determine the following:

1. Contribution margin for weekly and monthly subscriptions.

2. Contribution margin ratio for weekly and monthly subscriptions.

3. HPC's breakeven point in sales units and sales dollars.

4. HPC's breakeven point to reach a target before-tax profit of $75,000.

5. What are the critical success factors for HPC? For its domestic subscribers? For its international subscribers? How can CVP analysis be used to make HPC more competitive?

8-39 CVP ANALYSIS   Peter Farrow is considering opening a franchise CD store in a new shopping mall that has just been completed. Based on historical data from other franchise stores and a careful market study, he is confident that the store can achieve monthly sales of $180,000. Variable costs (excluding rent) will be approximately 70 percent of sales dollars. Rent payable to the mall owners will be 7 percent of sales or $11,000, whichever is higher. Initial cost of the franchise is $25,000, paid for in one lump sum. Monthly fixed costs, totaling $33,000, consist of

Strategy

Installment loan for leasehold improvements	$ 800
Salaried employees (4 at $2,750)	11,000
Owner's salary	15,000
Franchise fee	4,000
Insurance, property taxes, etc.	2,200
Total fixed costs	$33,000

Peter is aware that a department store with a large discount CD department is also considering moving into the mall directly opposite the location he is considering. He knows that he will select his merchandise carefully and will offer top-notch customer service, but a new store would take some of his business. If the department store moves in, he calculates that his sales would decline by at least 10 but not more than 18 percent. A decline of even 10 percent would require him to reduce the cost of salaried employees to $10,000 by replacing one full-time employee with part-time help. Peter considers a 15 percent minimum annual return on his initial investment in the franchise as the minimal return necessary to justify opening the store.

Required

1. Determine the sales volume per month necessary to achieve the desired return, assuming that the competing department store does *not* rent space in the mall.

2. Determine the breakeven sales volume, assuming that the competing department store does move into the mall and sales are reduced by (a) 10 percent and (b) 18 percent.

3. Should Peter open the store? What additional analysis should he undertake?

4. Assume a sales volume decrease of 18 percent. How far below $32,000 would Peter have to reduce fixed costs to break even? Is it likely that he would be able to do this?

(Adapted, R. Shockley)

329

Ethics

8–40 CVP ANALYSIS, COMMISSIONS, ETHICS Marston Corporation manufactures pharmaceutical products sold through a network of sales agents in the United States and Canada. The agents are currently paid an 18 percent commission on sales; that percentage was used when Marston prepared the following budgeted income statement for the fiscal year ending June 30, 2001.

MARSTON CORPORATION
Budgeted Income Statement
For the Year Ending June 30, 2001
($000 omitted)

Sales		$26,000
Cost of goods sold		
Variable	$11,700	
Fixed	2,870	14,570
Gross profit		$11,430
Selling and administrative costs		
Commissions	$ 4,680	
Fixed advertising cost	750	
Fixed administrative cost	1,850	7,280
Operating income		$ 4,150
Fixed interest cost		650
Income before income taxes		$ 3,500
Income taxes (40 percent)		14,00
Net income		$ 2,100

Since the completion of the income statement, Marston has learned that its sales agents are requiring a 5 percent increase in their commission rate (to 23 percent) for the upcoming year. As a result, Marston's president has decided to investigate the possibility of hiring its own sales staff in place of the network of sales agents and has asked Tom Markowitz, Marston's controller, to gather information on the costs associated with this change.

Tom estimates that Marston must hire eight salespeople to cover the current market area, at an average annual payroll cost for each employee of $80,000, including fringe benefits expense. Travel and entertainment expense is expected to total $600,000 for the year, and the annual cost of hiring a sales manager and sales secretary will be $150,000. In addition to their salaries, the eight salespeople will each earn commissions at the rate of 10 percent. The president believes that Marston also should increase its advertising budget by $500,000.

Required

1. Determine Marston Corporation's breakeven point in sales dollars for the fiscal year ending June 30, 2001, if the company hires its own sales force and increases its advertising costs.

2. If Marston continues to sell through its network of sales agents and pays the higher commission rate, determine the estimated volume in sales dollars for the fiscal year ending June 30, 2001, that would be required to generate the same net income as projected in the budgeted income statement.

3. Describe the general assumptions underlying breakeven analysis that limit its usefulness.

4. What is the indifference point in sales for the firm to either accept the agents' demand or adopt the proposed change? Which plan is better for the firm?

5. Assume that total sales for the year ending June 30, 2002, will remain approximately the same as for the year ending June 30, 2001. Would

you, as the head of the sales agents' union, demand an increase in commission rate?

6. What are the ethical issues, if any, that Tom should consider before adopting the new program?

(CMA Adapted)

8-41   CVP ANALYSIS, DIFFERENT PRODUCTION PLANS   The PTO Division of Galva Manufacturing Company produces power take-off units for the farm equipment business. The PTO Division, headquartered in Peoria, has a newly renovated, automated plant in Peoria and an older, less-automated plant in Moline. Both plants produce the same power take-off units for farm tractors that are sold to most domestic and foreign tractor manufacturers.

The PTO Division expects to produce and sell 192,000 power take-off units during the coming year. The division production manager has the following data available regarding the unit costs, unit prices, and production capacities for the two plants.

- All fixed costs are based on a normal year of 240 work days. When the number of work days exceeds 240, variable manufacturing costs increase by $3 per unit in Peoria and $8 per unit in Moline. Capacity for each plant is 300 working days.

- Galva Manufacturing charges each of its plants a per-unit fee for administrative services such as payroll, general accounting, and purchasing because management considers these services to be a function of the work performed at the plants. For each plant at Peoria and Moline, the fee is $6.50 and represents the variable portion of general and administrative expense.

Wishing to maximize the higher unit profit at Moline, PTO's production manager has decided to manufacture 96,000 units at each plant. This production plan results in Moline's operating at capacity and Peoria's operating at its normal volume. Galva's corporate controller is not happy with this plan because she does not believe it represents optimal usage of PTO's plants.

	Peoria	**Moline**
Selling price	$150.00	$ 150.00
Variable manufacturing cost	72.00	88.00
Fixed manufacturing cost	30.00	15.00
Commission (5 percent)	7.50	7.50
General and administrative expense	25.50	21.00
Total unit cost	$131.50	$ 131.50
Unit profit	$ 15.00	$ 18.50
Production rate per day	400 units	320 units

Required

1. Determine the annual breakeven units for each PTO plant.

2. Determine the operating income that would result from the division production manager's plan to produce 96,000 units at each plant.

3. Determine the optimal production plan to produce the 192,000 units at PTO's plants in Peoria and Moline and the resulting operating income for the PTO Division. Be sure to support the plan with appropriate calculations.

(CMA Adapted)

Strategy

8-42 CVP ANALYSIS, BID PRICING Marcus Fibers Inc. specializes in the manufacture of synthetic fibers that the company uses in many products such as blankets, coats, and uniforms for police and firefighters. Marcus has been in business since 1975 and has been profitable each year since 1983. The company uses a standard cost system and applies overhead on the basis of direct labor-hours.

Marcus recently received a request to bid on the manufacture of 800,000 blankets scheduled for delivery to several military bases. The bid must be stated at full cost per unit plus a return on full cost of no more than 9 percent after income taxes. *Full cost* has been defined as all variable costs of manufacturing the product, a reasonable amount of fixed overhead, and a reasonable incremental administrative cost associated with the manufacture and sale of the product. The contractor has indicated that bids in excess of $25 per blanket are not likely to be considered.

To prepare the bid for the 800,000 blankets, Andrea Lightner, cost management analyst, has gathered the following information concerning the costs associated with the production of the blankets.

Raw material per pound of fibers	$ 1.50
Direct labor per hour	$ 7.00
Direct machine costs per blanket*	$ 10.00
Variable overhead per direct-labor hour	$ 3.00
Fixed overhead per direct labor-hour	$ 8.00
Incremental administrative costs per 1,000 blankets	$2,500.00
Special fee per blanket‡	$ 0.50
Material usage	6 pounds per blanket
Production rate	4 blankets per direct labor hour
Effective tax rate	40 percent

*Direct machine costs consist of items, such as special lubricants, replacement needles used in stitching, and maintenance costs, that are not included in the normal overhead rates.

‡Marcus recently developed a new blanket fiber at a cost of $750,000. To recover this cost, it adds a $0.50 fee to the cost of each blanket using the new fiber. To date, the company has recovered $125,000. Andrea knows that this fee does not fit within the definition of full cost because it is not a cost to manufacture the product.

Required

1. Calculate the minimum price per blanket that Marcus Fibers could bid without reducing the company's net income.

2. Using the *full cost* criteria and the maximum allowable return specified, calculate the bid price per blanket for Marcus Fibers.

3. Without prejudice to your answer to requirement 2, assume that the price per blanket that Marcus calculated using the cost-plus criteria specified is higher than the maximum allowed bid of $25 per blanket. Discuss the strategic factors that the company should consider before deciding whether to submit a bid at the maximum acceptable price of $25 per blanket.

(CMA Adapted)

8-43 CVP ANALYSIS, PROBABILITY ANALYSIS Don Masters and two colleagues are considering the opening of a law office in a large metropolitan area to make inexpensive legal services available to people who cannot otherwise afford these services. They intend to provide easy access for their clients by having the office open 360 days per year, 16 hours each day from 7:00 A.M. to 11:00 P.M. A lawyer, paralegal, legal secretary, and clerk-receptionist would staff the office for each of the two 8-hour shifts.

To determine the feasibility of the project, Don hired a marketing consultant to assist with market projections. The consultant's results show that if the firm spends $500,000 on advertising the first year, the number of new clients expected each day would have the following probability distribution:

Number of New Clients per Day	Probability
20	.10
30	.30
55	.40
85	.20

Don and his associates believe these numbers to be reasonable and are prepared to spend the $500,000 on advertising. Other pertinent information about the operation of the office follows.

The only charge to each new client would be $30 for an initial consultation. The firm will accept all cases that warrant further legal work on a contingency basis with the firm earning 30 percent of any favorable settlements or judgments. Don estimates that 20 percent of new client consultations will result in favorable settlements or judgments averaging $2,000 each. He does not expect repeat clients during the first year of operations.

The hourly wages for the staff are projected to be $25 for the lawyer, $20 for the paralegal, $15 for the legal secretary, and $10 for the clerk-receptionist. Fringe benefit expense will be 40 percent of the wages paid. A total of 400 hours of overtime is expected for the year; this will be divided equally between the legal secretary and the clerk-receptionist positions. Overtime will be paid at one and one-half times the regular wage, and the fringe benefit expense will apply to the full wage.

Don has located 6,000 square feet of suitable office space that rents for $28 per square foot annually. Associated expenses will be $22,000 for property insurance and $32,000 for utilities. The group must purchase malpractice insurance expected to cost $180,000 annually.

The initial investment in office equipment will be $60,000; this equipment has an estimated useful life of four years. The cost of office supplies has been estimated to be $4 per expected new client consultation.

Required

1. Determine how many new clients must visit the law office that Don and his colleagues are considering for the venture to break even its first year of operations.

2. Using the probability information provided by the marketing consultant, determine whether it is feasible for the law office to achieve breakeven operations.

3. Explain how Don and his associates could use sensitivity analysis to assist in this analysis.

(CMA Adapted)

8–44 CVP ANALYSIS, STRATEGY, CRITICAL SUCCESS FACTORS Garner Strategy Institute (GSI) presents executive-level training seminars nationally. Eastern University (EU) has approached GSI to present 40 one-week seminars during 2002. This activity level represents the maximum number of seminars that GSI is capable of presenting annually. GSI staff would present the weeklong seminars in various cities throughout the United States and Canada.

Terry Garner, GSI's president, is evaluating three financial options for the revenues from Eastern: accept a flat fee for each seminar, receive a percentage of Eastern's "profit before tax" from the seminars, and form a joint venture to share costs and profits.

Strategy

Estimated costs for the 2002 seminar schedule follow.

	Garner Strategy Institute	Eastern University
Fixed costs		
Salaries and benefits	$200,000	N/A*
Facilities	48,000	N/A*
Travel and hotel	0	$210,000
Other	70,000	N/A*
Total fixed costs	$318,000	$210,000
Variable costs		Per Participant
Supplies and materials	0	$47
Marketing	0	18
Other site costs	0	35

*Eastern's fixed costs are excluded because the amounts are not considered relevant for this decision (i.e., they will be incurred whether the seminars are presented). Eastern does not include these costs when calculating the "profit before the tax" for the seminars.

EU plans to charge $1,200 per participant for each one-week seminar. It will pay all variable promotion, site costs, and materials costs.

Required

1. Assume that the seminars are handled as a joint venture by GSI and EU to pool costs and revenues.

   a. Determine the total number of seminar participants needed to break even on the total costs for this joint venture. Show supporting computations.

   b. Assume that the joint venture has an effective income tax rate of 30 percent. How many seminar participants must the joint venture enroll to earn a net income of $169,400? Show supporting computations.

2. Assume that GSI and EU do not form a joint venture, but that GSI is an independent contractor for EU. EU offers two payment options to GSI: a flat fee of $9,500 for each seminar, or a fee of 40 percent of EU's "profit before tax" from the seminars. Compute the minimum number of participants needed for GSI to prefer the 40 percent fee option over the flat fee. Show supporting computations.

3. What are the strategic and implementation issues for GSI to consider in deciding whether to enter into the joint venture? For Eastern?

(CMA Adapted)

Strategy

8-45 CVP ANALYSIS, STRATEGY, ABC COSTING, UNCERTAINTY Omni Graphics is a small manufacturer of electronic products for computers with graphics capabilities. The company has succeeded by being very innovative in product design. As a spin-off of a large electronics manufacturer (ElecTech), Omni management has extensive experience in both marketing and manufacturing in the electronics industry. A long list of equity investors is betting that the firm will really take off because of the growth of specialized graphic software and the increased demand for computers with enhanced graphics capability. A number of market analysts say, however, that the market for the firm's products is somewhat risky, as it is for many high-tech start-ups because of the number of new competitors entering the market, and Omni's unproven technology.

Omni's main product is a circuit board (CB3668) used in computers with enhanced graphics capabilities. Prices vary depending on the terms of sale and the size of the purchase; the average price for the CB3668 is $100. If the firm is able to take off, it might be able to raise prices, but it might have to reduce the price because of increased competition. The firm expects to sell 150,000 units in the coming year, and sales are expected to increase in the following years. The future for Omni looks very bright indeed, but it is new and has not developed a strong financial base. Cash flow management is a critical feature of the firm's financial management, and top management must watch cash flow numbers closely.

At present, Omni is manufacturing the CB3668 in a plant leased from ElecTech using some equipment purchased from ElecTech. Omni manufactures about 70 percent of the parts in this circuit board.

Omni management is considering a significant reengineering project to significantly change the plant and manufacturing process. The project's objective is to increase the number of purchased parts (to about 55%) and to reduce the complexity of the manufacturing process. This would also permit Omni to remove some leased equipment and to sell some of the most expensive equipment in the plant.

The per unit manufacturing costs for 150,000 units of CB3668 follow:

	Current Manufacturing Cost	Proposed Manufacturing Costs
Materials and purchased parts	$ 6.00	$15.00
Direct labor	12.50	13.75
Variable overhead	25.00	30.00
Fixed overhead	40.00	20.00
Manufacturing information for CB3668		
Number of setups	3,000	2,300
Batch size	50	50
Cost per setup	$300	N/A*
Machine hours	88,000	55,000

*N/A: Not available, but time permitting, management wants to determine the cost per setup.

General, selling, and administrative costs are $10 per unit and $1,250,000 fixed; these costs are not expected to differ for either the current or the proposed manufacturing plan.

Required

1. Explain briefly (a) what Omni's strategy is (b) what you think it should be and (c) why.

2. Compute the contribution margin and volume-based breakeven in units for CB3668, both before and after the proposed reengineering project.

3. For the current manufacturing plan only, compute an activity-based breakeven analysis in units for CB3668, assuming that setup costs are the firm's only batch level cost. Also assume that Omni will keep the batch size fixed at 50 units and that the number of batches will vary as the volume level changes. Interpret the difference between the volume-based and activity-based breakeven points.

4. Determine the number of sales units at which Omni would be indifferent as to the current manufacturing plan or the proposed plan.

5. Should Omni undertake the proposed reengineering plan? Using a spreadsheet, support your answer with sensitivity analysis and a discussion of short-term and long-term considerations.

8–46 **NEW MANUFACTURING FACILITY, STRATEGY** Julius Brooks, plant manager for ICL, Inc., a manufacturer of auto parts, has been successful in recent years because of the very high quality of his products and the speed of delivery. A growing market for ICL is automakers who want it to participate in the design

Strategy

of the car and to design certain parts. The ICL design team supervised by Julius has developed an excellent reputation among the automakers for quality designs, which have reduced warranty and service costs for the automakers. The result has been that a substantial part of the plant's revenues are now from design work, and sometimes ICL subcontracts the actual manufacturing to other manufacturers. Nevertheless, competitors continue to cut prices, and Julius is finding it more difficult to cut costs to meet the competition. Working with top management, he has helped design a new, automated factory located in Georgia to take advantage of the tax breaks allowed by the State of Georgia and the local community.

Required   Discuss the strategic aspects of the plan for the new factory.

Strategy

8–47   CVP ANALYSIS, ABC COSTING   Precision Bicycle Company (PBC) is a high-end manufacturer of bicycles. Its products are sold in specialty retail bike stores throughout the United States and Canada. This year's expected production is 10,000 units, but demand in the bicycle market has fluctuated in recent years so that PBC is also predicting that the actual production/sales figure could be anywhere between 7,000 and 15,000 bikes. To control quality, PBC currently makes most of the parts for its bikes, including the rear brake. PBC's accountant reports the following costs for making the 10,000 rear brake assemblies:

	Per-Unit Costs	Costs for 10,000 Units
Direct materials	$10.00	$100,000
Direct manufacturing labor	6.00	60,000
Variable manufacturing overhead (power and utilities)	3.00	30,000
Inspection, setup, materials handling	2.00	20,000
Machine lease	3.40	34,000
Allocated fixed plant administration, taxes, and insurance	6.00	60,000
Total costs		$304,000

An outside vendor has offered to supply PBC up to 20,000 brake assemblies for $25 each. The following additional information is available:

- Inspection, setup, and materials-handling costs vary directly with the number of batches in which the bikes are produced. PBC produces brakes in batches of 1,000 units.

- PBC's machine lease costs are for the equipment used to make the brakes. If PBC buys all brakes from the outside vendor, it will be able to cancel the lease and avoid this cost.

Required   Assume that if PBC purchases the brake assemblies from the outside supplier, the facility where it currently makes them will remain idle for at least the next year. At that point, PBC might consider leasing the space or using it for an alternative use. Should PBC accept the outside supplier's offer? Support your answer using CVP analysis. Include an assessment of the strategic issues facing PBC that might affect your answer.

SOLUTION TO SELF-STUDY PROBLEM

Breakeven Analysis

1. Unit contribution margin = $5,595 - $899 - $233 = $4,463
2. Breakeven

    In units:

    $$Q = (f + N)/(p - v)$$

    $$Q = \$2,352,000/\$4,463 = 527 \text{ units}$$

    In dollars:

    $$pQ = \$5,595 \times 527 = \$2,948,565$$

    Or

    $$p \times Q = \frac{(f + N)}{(p - v)/p} = \frac{\$2,352,000}{0.797676} = \$2,948,565$$

3. New level of fixed costs = $2,352,000(1 + .05) = $2,469,600

    Breakeven:

    $$Q = (f + N)/(p - v)$$

    $$Q = (\$2,469,600 + \$200,000)/(\$4,463)$$

    $$= 599 \text{ units}$$

4. Incorporate a tax rate of 22 percent and desired profit of $150,000:

    $$Q = [\$2,352,000 + (\$150,000)/(1 - 0.22)]/\$4,463 = 570 \text{ units}$$

Strategy and the Master Budget

9

After studying this chapter, you should be able to . . .

1 Describe the role of a budget in planning, communicating, motivating, controlling, and evaluating performance

2 Discuss the importance of strategy and its role in budgeting; identify factors common to successful budgets

3 Outline the budgeting process

4 Prepare a master budget and explain the interrelationships among its components

5 Identify unique budgeting characteristics of service and not-for-profit organizations and of organizations operating in international settings

6 Apply zero-base, activity-based, and kaizen budgeting

7 Discuss the roles of ethics and behavioral concerns in budgeting

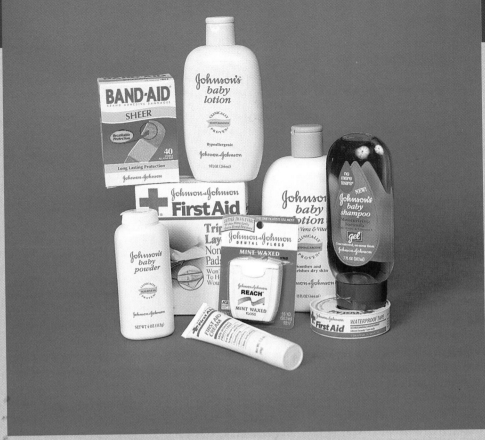

Johnson & Johnson, one of the largest manufacturers of health care products and providers of related services for the consumer, pharmaceutical, and professional markets in the world, started as a small manufacturer of health and well-being–related products in New Jersey in 1887.[1] Today, it has more than 99,000 employees and more than 190 operating companies in 51 countries and sells its products in more than 175 countries. Surveys conducted over the years by *Business Week, Forbes, Fortune*, and others repeatedly have ranked Johnson & Johnson as one of the most innovative, well-managed, and admired firms in the world. Its employees and job applicants consider the firm to be among the best to work for.

How does Johnson & Johnson do it? It relies on a comprehensive formal planning, budgeting, and control system in formulating and implementing strategy, coordinating and monitoring operations, and reviewing and evaluating performances. Johnson & Johnson is organized on the principles of decentralized management with its Executive Committee as the principal management group responsible for the entire firm's operation. Executive Committee members also serve as worldwide chairmen of group operating committees. These committees oversee and coordinate the activities of domestic and international companies related to each of the consumer, pharmaceutical, and professional segments of business. Operating management of each company reports directly, or through a line executive, to a group operating committee. Consistent with its policy of decentralization, each operational manager is responsible for all aspects of her or his unit including budget preparation, revisions, and implementation. Every January, each operating company reviews and revises its 5- and 10-year plans from the previous year and its mission statement and prepares the budget for the

---

[1] For more information about the company, see its website: /www.JJ.com/.

coming year and a two-year plan. The budgeting process is not completed until the approval of the profit plan in December.[2]

This chapter discusses the budgeting processes and techniques that many successful companies such as Johnson & Johnson use as part of their management processes.

Know when to spend, and when to spare. And you need not be busy, and you'll never be bare.

JAMES KELLY, *SCOTTISH PROVERBS*, 1721,

If you don't know where you're going, you'll end up somewhere else.

YOGI BERRA

Harold S. Geneen, the legendary CEO of ITT for nearly two decades, relied on the numbers to manage the firm's more than 250 profit centers.[3] Like many successful executives, he believed that a well-managed firm implemented the planned strategy and operations to achieve the planned results. Growth and long-term profitability are results of good planning and implementation. Seldom does a firm get more than the expected. Under Geneen's management, ITT grew from a relatively unknown company to an international conglomerate in manufacturing, telecommunication, oil, services, and other businesses.

Business continually deals with the future and uncertainty. Planning is a process of charting the future course in this uncertain and dynamic world to attain desired goals. Good planning helps managers attain goals, recognize opportunities, and minimize the negative effects of unavoidable events. Successful organizations are the result of careful planning and diligent implementation. Conversely, failure to plan often results in compromising goals and can lead to financial disaster. The budget is one aspect of planning used by many organizations, for profit, not for profit, large or small, service or manufacturing.

ROLE OF A BUDGET

LEARNING OBJECTIVE 1▶

Describe the role of a budget in planning, communicating, motivating, controlling, and evaluating performance.

A **budget** is an organization's operation plan; it identifies the resources and commitments required to fulfill the organization's goals for the period identified.

Budgeting is the process of preparing a budget.

A **budget** is an organization's operation plan; it identifies the resources and commitments required to fulfill the organization's goals for the period identified. A budget includes both financial and nonfinancial aspects of the planned operations. The budget for a period is both a guideline for operation and a projection of the operating results for the budgeted period. The process of preparing a budget is called **budgeting**.

Budgets and the budgeting process are intertwined with all aspects of management. In addition to being a plan of operations, a budget plays an important role in allocating resources, coordinating operations including identifying constraints and communicating and authorizing actions, motivating and guiding implementation, providing guidelines for controlling operations and managing cash flows, and furnishing criteria for evaluating performance.

In preparing a budget, a firm's management needs to be forward looking in assessing future situations as they pertain to the firm's strategic goals. Budget preparations allow management time to work out any problems the company might face in the

---

[2] A description of the budgeting process at Johnson & Johnson can be found in Robert Simon, "Planning, Control, and Uncertainty: A Process View," in William J. Bruns, Jr., and Robert S. Kaplan, eds., *Accounting and Management: Field Study Perspectives*. (Boston: Harvard University Press, 1987), pp. 339–62. A case study, Codman & Shurtleff, Inc. (Harvard Business School: 187–081), describes the budgeting process of a subsidiary of Johnson & Johnson.

[3] Harold S. Geneen, *Managing* (New York: Avon Books, 1984), chap. 9, "The Numbers."

How Can Moviemakers Keep Their Heads (Budgets) above Water?

A common sport when a movie is released is to speculate about the amount by which the project exceeded its budget. Why do moviemaking budgets often get out of hand? Doesn't the movie industry worry about budgets and profitability like other corporations and industries?

According to Bill Mechanic, chairman of Twentieth Century Fox, the industry learned a good deal regarding budget management from the making of *Titanic*. "We learned some lessons making *Titanic*....We have tightened up our budget controls, made sure we had more representatives on the set. Making movies for a budget is about planning and execu-

tion, and we have learned a great deal about that." Mechanic noted that having more accounting systems in place to keep track of where and why money is spent helps achieve effective cost control. As he put it, "You start to treat this like a real business...we all knew the budget [for *Titanic*] was a bit soft. It would have helped some if we had known ahead of time what we were really in for."

Source: "Online Original: Q & A with Bill Mechanic of Twentieth Century Fox," *Business Week*, January 12, 1998.

coming periods. This extra time enables the firm to minimize the adverse effects that anticipated problems could have on operations. Because all divisions are not likely to think alike and have the same plan for their operations, completion of a budget for all units of an organization also mandates coordinating operations among all budgeted units and synchronizing the operating activities of various departments. Use of budgets helps firms to run smoother operations and achieve better results.

The budget also can help managers identify current and potential bottlenecks in operations. Critical resources can then be mustered to ease any bottlenecks and prevent them from becoming obstacles to attaining budgetary goals.

A budget is a formal expression of plans for future actions. In many organizations, budgets are the only formal expression of future plans. A budget also serves as a communication device through which top management defines its plans and goals for the period so that other managers and employees have access to this information. The operation plan of a budget allows each division to know what it needs to do to satisfy its obligations to other divisions. The manufacturing division knows, for example, that it needs to complete the production of a given product before a certain date if the marketing division budget calls for delivery of that product to a customer on that date. Budgets prescribe what performance the organization expects of all divisions and all employees for the period.

A budget also is a motivating device. With clearly delineated expected results for the budget period, employees know what is expected of them; this in turn sustains morale and motivates people to work to attain the budgeted goals. The budget of an organization that employs participative budgeting involving all or most personnel to formulate all or part of it often can further motivate employees to attain the budgeted goals because the employees identify the budget as their own.

During operations, budgets serve as frames of reference. They become guidelines for operations, criteria for monitoring and controlling activities, and authorizations for actions. An organization's success requires that all of its subunits carry out their operations as planned. Budgets spell out the expected operations of each unit and subdivision and enable them to coordinate activities. The authorization function of budgets is especially important for government and not-for-profit organizations because budgeted amounts often serve both as approval of activities and as a ceiling for expenditures.

At the end of an operating period, a firm's budget also serves as a basis for evaluating its performance. The budget represents the specific results expected of the firm's divisions and employees for the period against which actual operating results can be measured.

Budgets and budgeting processes also perform many other functions. Covaleski and Dirsmith state that budgeting systems accomplish many purposes beyond achieving planning and control. Budgeting systems are at once forms and sources of power, and they serve as a political advocacy device used by both budgeters and budgetees in the internal resource allocation process.[4]

STRATEGY, THE LONG-TERM PLAN, AND THE MASTER BUDGET

LEARNING OBJECTIVE 2▶

Discuss the importance of strategy and its role in budgeting; identify factors common to successful budgets.

Importance of Strategy in Budgeting

A firm's strategy is the path it chooses for attaining its long-term goals and missions. It is the starting point in preparing its plans and budgets. American Express Company considers itself a personal financial services company. Corporate financial services such as investment banking do not fit into the firm's strategic course and therefore have been removed from its operations. B. F. Goodrich Company determined in the early 1980s that for competitive reasons, it would not stay in the automobile tire business and focused its strategy on other rubber products. Finally, Varity Corporation, a leading maker of diesel engines and automotive parts, decided not to be in the farm equipment business, even though its farm equipment manufacturing subsidiary, Massey-Ferguson, accounted for nearly 90 percent of its total revenue. Again, for competitive reasons, the firm made the strategic decision to leave the farm equipment business. Subsequent budgets of these firms reflect those strategic decisions.

The process of determining a firm's strategy begins by assessing external factors that affect operations and evaluating internal factors that can be its strengths and weaknesses. External factors typically include competition, technological, economic, political, regulatory, social, and environmental factors. A careful examination of such factors can help the organization identify opportunities, limitations, and threats. An organization's internal factors include operating characteristics such as financial strength, managerial expertise, functional structure, and organizational culture. Matching the organization's strengths with its identified opportunities and threats enables it to form its strategy. Exhibit 9–1 shows the development of a firm's product strategy.[5]

The importance of strategy in planning and budgeting cannot be overemphasized. A budget without inputs from the organization's strategic plan usually starts with the previous year's numbers, but a budget that starts with the strategic plan begins with the organization's goals and objectives and builds a budget to achieve them. Without a good strategy, an organization might not be able to take full advantage of its opportunities and its strengths. Repeatedly missed opportunities can lead an organization to stagnate. In the worst cases, an inappropriate strategy or lack of one eventually leads to the demise of organizations.

In the late 1960s and early 1970s, U.S. auto manufacturers decided not to develop compact and subcompact automobiles; thus, they did not plan and budget the necessary resources for developing and manufacturing such vehicles. This strategy later proved to be a costly mistake, and automakers suffered for almost 20 years because of this strategic decision. They did not begin to recover until the early 1990s.

Motorola suffered from a similar strategic mistake in the late 1990s. Motorola, which once dominated the wireless communication markets in the United States and most of the world, lost its dominating and very profitable position when it decided to continue pushing for analog technologies and invested only minimum amounts in digital technologies in the early 1990s.

The success stories of many business firms are stories of the value of good strategy. Wal-Mart stores took advantage of its experience in operating stores in medium-size towns and expanded nationally into these markets, becoming first in the nation

---

4   Mark A. Covaleski and Mark W. Dirsmith, "Dialectic Tension, Double Reflexivity and the Everyday Accounting Researcher: On Using Qualitative Methods," *Accounting, Organizations and Society* 5(6): 545.

5   Adapted from Robert N. Anthony and Vijay Govindarajan, *Management Control System,* 8th ed. (Burr Ridge, IL: Irwin, 1995), p. 265.

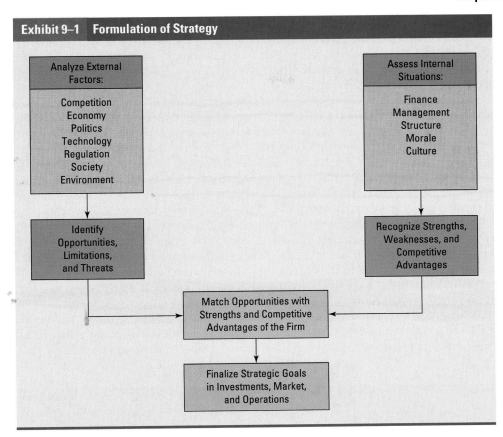

Exhibit 9–1   Formulation of Strategy

among retail stores. American Express, B. F. Goodrich, and Varity all have enjoyed appreciations in their stock returns greater than the S&P 500 since adopting their new strategies.

Strategic Goals and Long-Term Objectives

Long-range planning, the capital budget, and the master budget implement a strategy. Strategy provides the framework within which a long-range plan is developed. The organization's **long-range plan** identifies the actions required during the typical 5- to 10-year period covered by the plan to attain the firm's strategic goal. For instance, B. F. Goodrich accomplished its strategic goal of leaving the automobile tire business by gradually phasing out its automobile tire manufacturing operations. Varity chose to liquidate Massey-Ferguson by downsizing and diversification. To divest its investment banking business, American Express Company decided in January 1994 to infuse more than $1 billion into its investment banking arm, Lehman Brothers Inc. The capital infusion lifted the subsidiary's credit rating and American Express was able to sell Lehman Brothers Inc. in May 1994. These actions required long-range planning and coordination for the organizations to attain the goals set forth in their strategies.

Long-range planning often entails **capital budgeting,** which is a process for evaluating and choosing among an organization's proposed long-range major projects such as the purchase of new equipment, construction of a new factory, and addition of new products. A capital budget is a plan for major expenditures that have long-term effects on the organization. Capital budgets are prepared to bring an organization's capabilities into line with the needs of its long-range plan and long-term sales forecast. An organization's capacity is a result of capital investments made in prior budgeting periods. The resources required and activities planned for the current period's capital budgeting must be included in the budget.

> **Long-range plan** is a plan that identifies which actions are required during the 5- to 10-year period covered by the plan to attain the firm's strategic goal.

> **Capital budgeting** is a process for evaluating an organization's proposed long-range major projects.

Short-Term Objectives and the Master Budget

Long-term objectives and plans, operating results of past periods, and expected future operating and environmental factors including economic, industry, and marketing conditions give rise to short-term objectives. These, in turn, serve as the basis for preparing the master budget for a period.

A **master budget** translates the organization's strategy and long-term objectives into action steps and is a plan of operations for a specific period for the budget unit. The period is usually short, a year, a quarter, or a month. A master budget sets specific goals for all of the organization's major operations and provides a detailed plan for acquisitions and commitments of financial resources during the budget period. The plan of operations is based on the goals of the organization's strategic and long-range plans, expected future events, and the recent actual operating results. Exhibit 9–2 illustrates the relationship between strategic goals, objectives, budgets, operations, and controls.

Because a master budget commits limited resources to attain the goals set for the organization for the period, such commitments must be made with a clear idea of where the organization is heading. The master budget must be consistent, therefore, with the goals prescribed in the organization's strategic and long-range plans.

A master budget differs from a long-range plan in at least two respects: A master budget is a short-term operating plan that typically covers a period of no more than one year; a long-term plan extends over a longer period, such as three to five years.[6] In addition, the focal point of a master budget is a responsibility center; a long-range plan is most likely structured along strategic business units, programs, activities, or product lines.

> A **master budget** is a plan of operations for a business unit during a specific period.

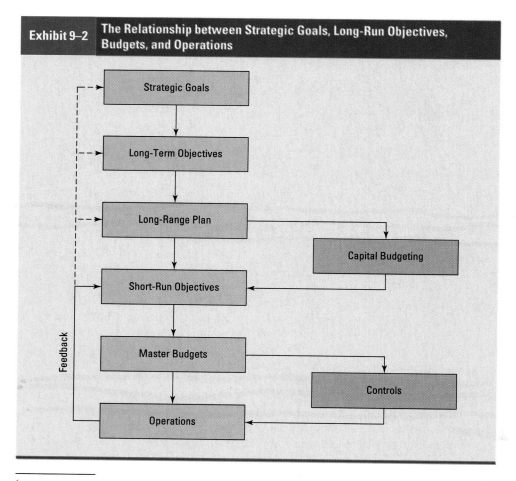

Exhibit 9–2   The Relationship between Strategic Goals, Long-Run Objectives, Budgets, and Operations

---

[6]   It is not unusual for businesses with two distinct seasons to have two operating budgets within a year. For example, many sports teams have two operating budgets for a year.

The operating results of recent years—including the expected results of the year that is about to end—impose limitations on the courses of action available to the organization in preparing a master budget. The expected future events simultaneously shape the set of actions from which a firm can choose to attain its goals. Both the operating results of recent years and the expected future events can affect a firm's strategic goals and long-range plans.

A master budget is also a comprehensive financial summarization of the organization's budgets and plans for operating activities of its subunits for the next year. It comprises operating budgets and financial budgets. **Operating budgets** are plans that identify needed resources and the way that these resources will be acquired for all day-to-day activities such as sales and services, production, purchasing, marketing, and research and development. Examples of operating budgets include production budgets, purchase budgets, personnel budgets, and sales promotion budgets. **Financial budgets** are plans that identify sources of funds for the budgeted operation and the uses for these funds during a period to carry out the budget activities. Financial budgets usually include budgets for cash inflows and outflows, operating incomes, and financial position. Thus, a master budget includes all planned activities and results of both operating and financing decisions for activities that will occur during the next operating period. Together, an organization's operating and financial budgets communicate the needed resources and the availability of these resources, its operating plans and those of its subunits, its expectations, and the criteria against which its performance and that of all subunits will be assessed.

Operating budgets are plans that identify resources needed in operating activities and the acquisition of these resources.

Financial budgets identify sources and uses of funds for the budgeted operations to achieve the expected operating results for the period.

Common Factors of Successful Budgets

No single characteristic can define a successful budget. Many factors are, however, common to successful budgets. Most important among them is that managers accepted and supported the budget.

A successful budget often becomes a personalized budget of the people who have the responsibility for carrying it out. They feel it is *their* budget, not a detached, impersonal institutional budget. They own the budget and are the ones who bring the budgeted goal to fruition.

A budget is more likely to be successful if employees perceive it as a planning and coordinating tool to help them to do a better job, not as a pressure device to squeeze the last drop of their energy out of them. Nor is a budget likely to be an asset when it is viewed as a tool for management to use to place blame.

A successful budget is a motivating device that helps people work toward the goal and the improvement of the organization; it is never used as an excuse for not doing things strategically important to the organization. The expression *not in the budget* never crops up in an organization with a successful budget.

These factors are discussed in more detail later in the chapter. Finally, a successful budget contains technically correct and reasonably accurate numbers. A budget will not be accepted and thus will not do the job intended if it is not technically correct. A budget with inaccurate numbers will fail to gain the confidence of the people affected by it and will be rendered useless.

BUDGETING PROCESS

The budgeting process can range from the informal simple process a small firm uses that takes only days to complete to the elaborate, lengthy procedure a large firm or the federal government employs that requires several months or even more than a year to complete. Regardless of the budgeting process an organization uses, its top management has the ultimate responsibility for the budgets and seeing that management at all levels understands and supports them.

Budgeting processes usually include the formation of a budget committee; determination of the budget period; specification of budget guidelines; preparation of the initial budget proposal; budget negotiation, review, and approval; and budget revision.

◄**LEARNING OBJECTIVE 3**
Outline the budgeting process.

Budget Committee

A budget committee composed of members of senior management oversees all budget matters. A typical budget committee includes the chief executive officer or one or more vice presidents, heads of strategic business units, and the chief financial officer. The size of the committee depends on such factors as the size of the organization, number of people involved in budget matters, extent of organizational units' participation in the budget processes, and the chief executive officer's management style. In some organizations, the chief executive officer makes all budget decisions and there is no committee.

The budget committee is the highest authority in an organization for all matters related to the budget. The committee sets or approves the overall budget goals for all major business units, directs and coordinates budget preparation, resolves conflicts and differences that may arise during budget preparation, approves the final budget, monitors operations as the year unfolds, and reviews the operating results at the end of the period. The budget committee also approves major revisions of the budget during the period.

Budget Period

Budgets usually are prepared for a set time period, most commonly one year. Although a firm's budget period can be independent of its fiscal year, the budget year for most organizations coincides with their fiscal year. Synchronizing budget periods with the organization's fiscal period facilitates comparisons of actual operating results with the budgeted amounts. Many companies break the budget period into subperiods and have quarterly or monthly budgets.

An increasing number of companies are using a continuous budget. A **continuous (rolling) budget** is a budget system that has in effect a budget for a set number of months, quarters, or years at all times. Thus, as a month or quarter ends, the original budget is updated based on the newly available information, and the budget for a new month or quarter is added. Advances in information technology and availability of easy-to-use budgeting and planning software facilitate the continuous updating of budgets and have greatly increased the number of firms that use continuous budgets. Many companies no longer view their budgets as cast in stone at the start of a fiscal year but as living documents revised on an ongoing basis throughout the year.

Johnson & Johnson uses a continuous budget and prepares two annual budgets each year, one for each of the next two years. Each year, the second-year budget is revised and updated based on the information that has become available since the last budget preparation period. This second-year budget then becomes the master budget for the coming period and a new second-year budget is prepared. In addition, Johnson & Johnson prepares 5- and 10-year budgets.

In practice, firms seldom have a budget for only one year. The budgets for the years beyond the coming year, however, usually contain only the essential operating data. Advantages of this system include a longer strategic perspective for managers that allows them more time to make operating decisions and the opportunity to assess the accuracy of forecasts.

A popular continuous budgeting system is to have in place 4 quarterly or 12 monthly budgets at all times. A survey showed that 15 percent of firms maintained 4 quarterly budgets; another 5 percent had 12 monthly budgets.[7] In addition to having a constant budget period at all times, continuous budgets yield other benefits. Managers of firms using continuous budgets are more likely to adopt a perspective that looks at operations beyond the immediate future at all times, not just once a year as the budget is prepared. Firms using continuous budgets are also more likely to have

> A **continuous (rolling) budget** is a budgeting system that has in effect a budget for a set number of months, quarters, or years at all times.

---

[7] William P. Cress and James B. Pettijohn, "A Survey of Budget-Related Planning and Control Policies and Procedures," *Journal of Accounting Education*, Fall 1985, pp. 61–78.

Effective Rolling Budget

One budgeting technique that has gained increasing popularity in recent years is rolling forecasts and budgets. The heightened uses of this budgeting approach is a result of progress in information technology and the widespread practice of quarterly reporting for many public companies. A firm can enjoy substantial benefits from adopting such a budgeting approach. A forecast made and a budget prepared or revised on a quarterly basis can obviously incorporate the most recent changes in operating factors, market trends, and economic variables.

John Fanning of World Class Finance, KPMG Consulting, points out that firms need to heed three caveats to attain an effective use of a rolling forecast approach. First, the firm needs to ensure that the overall volume of information required is reasonable. The amount of detail required needs to be substantially reduced so that the overall effort required is no more than that needed under the traditional approach despite the greater frequency of projections. Second, senior management needs to be actively involved and provide critical input to the process. Projections based on a superficial overview will not suffice and consequent budget revisions will most likely be perfunctory. The re-forecasts and re-budgets must be based on a thorough analysis of the changes in operating variables and the marketplace in which the firm operates. Third, care must be taken to ensure that adopting the re-forecasting and rolling budget does not reinforce the concentration on financial measures and result in the exclusion of other critical operating measures.

Source: John Fanning, "Budgeting in the 21st Century," *Management Accounting* (British), November 1999.

up-to-date budgets because the preparation of a budget for a new quarter or month often leads to revision of the existing budget.

Budget Guidelines

An organization forms its budget guidelines for the coming period based on its strategic goals and long-term plan. One responsibility of the budget committee is to provide these initial budget guidelines that set the tone for the budget and govern its preparation. All responsibility centers (or budget units) follow the initial budget guidelines in preparing their budgets. In addition, the budget committee also needs to consider developments that have occurred since the adoption of the strategic plan; the general outlook of the economy and the market; the organization's goal for the budgeting period; specific corporate policies such as mandates for downsizing, reengineering, and special promotions; and the operating results of the year to date.

Initial Budget Proposal

Based on the initial budget guidelines, each responsibility center prepares its initial budget proposal. A budget unit needs to consider a number of internal factors in preparing an initial budget proposal:

- Changes in availability of equipment or facilities.
- Adoption of new manufacturing processes.
- Changes in product design or product mix.
- Introduction of new products.
- Changes in expectations or operating processes of other budget units that the budget unit relies on for its input materials or other operating factors.
- Changes in other operating factors or in the expectations or operating processes in those other budget units that rely on the budget unit to supply them components.

External factors to consider in forming an initial budget proposal include the following:

- Changes in the labor market.
- Availability of raw materials or components and their prices.
- The industry's outlook for the near term.
- Competitors' actions.

Budget Negotiation

The superior of budget units examines the initial budget proposal to determine whether it is within the budget guidelines. The superior also verifies whether the budget goals can be reasonably attained and are in line with the goals of the units at the next level up and that the budgeted operations are consistent with those of other budget units, including all units directly and indirectly affected. These reviews identify needed changes to the original budget and are made according to negotiations between the budget unit and its superior. Negotiations occur at all levels of the organization. They are perhaps the core of the budgeting process and take up the bulk of the budget preparation time.

Review and Approval

As budget units approve their budgets, the budgets go through the successive levels of the organization until they reach the final level, when the combined unit budgets become the organization's budget. The budget committee reviews the budget for consistency with the budget guidelines, attainment of the desired short-term goals, and fulfillment of the strategic plan. The budget committee gives final approval, and the chief executive officer then approves the entire budget and submits it to the board of directors.

Revision

Procedures for budget revision vary from one organization to another. Once a budget has been approved, some organizations allow it to be revised only under special circumstances; other organizations, such as firms adopting continuous budget systems, build in quarterly or monthly revisions.

For organizations that allow budget revisions only under special circumstances, obtaining approval to modify a budget can be difficult. Not all events, however, unfold as predicted in a budget. Strictly implementing a budget as prescribed even when the actual events differ significantly from those expected certainly is not a desirable behavior. In such cases, managers should be encouraged not to rely on the budget as the absolute guideline in operations.

Systematic, periodic revision of the approved budget or the use of a continuous budget can be an advantage in dynamic operations because the updated budget provides better operating guidelines. Regular budget revision, however, could encourage responsibility centers not to prepare their budgets with due diligence. Organizations with systematic budget revisions need to ensure that revisions are allowed only if circumstances have changed significantly and are beyond the control of the budget unit or the organization.

Why Paramount Pictures Prepares Budgets

- To determine whether a project will lose money or make a profit (negative or positive cash flow).
- To compute the impact of certain planned decisions or of market changes on an existing budget.
- To validate business decisions already taken.
- To set targets/management objectives.
- To determine tax rates, cash borrowing needs, and so on.

Source: Stephen P. Taylor, senior vice president, finance, Paramount Pictures, at the University of Southern California, November 14, 1991.

MASTER BUDGET

The master budget is the comprehensive budget for the period and consists of many interrelated budgets including both operating and financial budgets. Preparation of a master budget starts with a review of the firm's strategic goals, long-term objectives, and long-range plan. Some firms refer to the process of preparing a master budget as *profit planning* or *targeting*. The process is not complete until the top management accepts the projected financial statements for the budget period. Projected financial statements include the income statement, balance sheet, and cash flow statement. Some organizations refer to these budgeted financial statements as *pro forma financial statements*. Exhibit 9–3 delineates the relationships among components of a master budget.

◀**LEARNING OBJECTIVE 4**

Prepare a master budget and explain the interrelationships among components.

Strategic Planning and Budgeting

The master budget is the document an organization relies on as it carries out its strategic plan to meet its goals. The master budget for the period is prepared following the budget guidelines; this is the organization's operating plan and budget.

Budgeting for Sales

A firm attains its desired goals through sales. Almost all activities of a firm emanate from efforts to attain sales goals and sales growth. The importance of having the best sales budget for a firm cannot be overemphasized.

Exhibit 9–3   The Master Budget

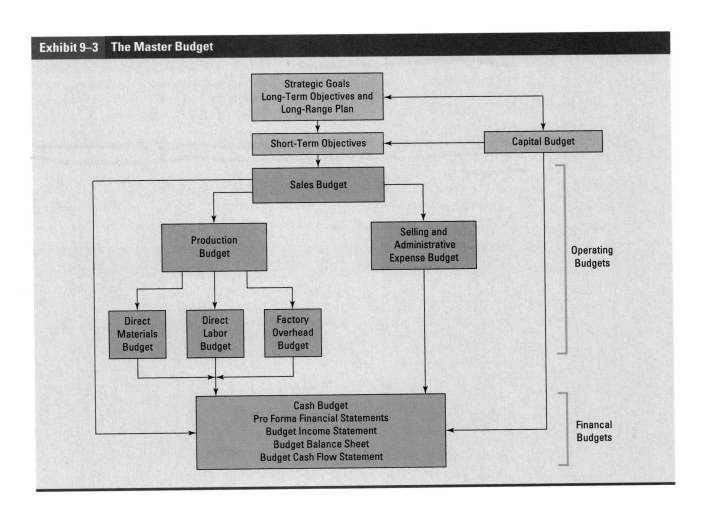

Sales Forecast

A sales forecast estimates future sales of the firm's products and is the starting point in preparing sales budgets for the period. An accurate sales forecast enhances the usefulness of the budget as a planning and control tool.

Sales forecasting by its nature is subjective. To reduce subjectivity in forecasts, many firms generate several independent sales forecasts as a standard procedure. A firm can, for example, have its market research unit, the manager of its business unit, and the sales department of its budget unit prepare a sales forecast. As a result, the volume of sales in the sales budget would be the one that all parties agree is the most likely prediction.

The following are among the factors that should be considered in sales forecasting:

- Current sales levels and sales trends of the past few years.
- General economic and industry conditions.
- Competitors' actions and operating plans.
- Pricing policies.
- Credit policies.
- Advertising and promotional activities.
- Unfilled back orders.

Many sales forecasting tools are available.[8] Among them are trend analysis and econometric models. A *trend analysis* can range from a simple visual plotting of past data on a graph to a sophisticated time-series model. An advantage of trend analysis is that all the data needed can be obtained easily from the firm's records because it uses only past data. History, however, never repeats itself exactly. Forecast adjustments for future events that could cause results to deviate from the historical trend are needed.

Econometric models such as regression or time-series analyses incorporate past sales data and other factors that affect sales. A firm may use an econometric model that includes, for example, national and regional economic indicators, unemployment rates, consumer-confidence indexes, and age-group distributions. The advantages of using econometric models in forecasting include objectivity, verifiability, and explicit measures of reliability.

The use of econometric models has become more common in recent years partly because of the wider availability of powerful, inexpensive computers and user-friendly software. No model, however, can replace human judgment, no matter how complete or sophisticated it might be. A combination of experienced judgment and analyses often leads to a better forecast than does relying on only one technique or the other.

Effect of Inaccurate Sales Forecast

At the end of its fiscal year on July 29, 2000, Cisco reported $1.2 billion in inventory. The firm reported in early February 2001 that it had inventories of $2.5 billion—an increase of more than 100 percent in six months, despite the fact that Cisco's sales grew 25 percent during that same period. The increase in inventory led Cisco's suppliers to suffer a similar fate. The inventory of Solectron, one of Cisco's major suppliers, went up from $1.8 billion in February 2000 to $4.5 billion at year-end. Flextronics, another supplier to Cisco, reports increases in inventories from $470 million at the end of 1999 to $1.73 billion at the end of 2000. Much of Solectron's and Flextronics' inventory is intended for Cisco. "Cisco's (sales) forecasts were wrong,...and these guys are feeling its pain." At a cost of 1 percent per month, the increases in inventory added tremendous financial burdens to these firms and increased Cisco's costs.

Source: Fortune, March 5, 2001, p. 42.

---

[8]   Chapter 7 discusses quantitative techniques useful in sales forecasting in more detail.

Sales Budget

A **sales budget** shows expected sales in units at their expected selling prices. Preparation of the sales budget for a period usually starts with the firm's forecasted sales level, production capacity, and long-term and short-term objectives.[9]

A sales budget is the cornerstone of budget preparation because a firm can complete the plan for other activities only after it identifies the expected sales level. A manufacturing firm cannot complete its production schedule without knowing the number of units it must produce, and the number of units to be produced can be ascertained only after the firm knows the number of units budgeted to be sold for the period. Once the number of units to be sold and produced has been determined, the units of materials to be purchased, the number of employees needed for the operation, and the required factory overheads can be determined. Expected selling and administrative expenses also are determined by the desired sales level.

Exhibit 9–4 illustrates the sales budget for Kerry Industrial Company for 2002 fiscal year. After examining its sales forecast for the coming year, operating results of the year to date, strategic goals, long-range plans for the firm and the product, and the budget guidelines, Kerry sets the sales levels shown and a selling price of $30 per unit.

Production Budget

The production budget follows the sales budget. A **production budget** is a plan for acquiring and combining the resources needed to carry out the manufacturing operations that allow the firm to satisfy its sales goals and have the desired amount of inventory at the end of the budget period. The total number of units to be produced depends on the

> A **sales budget** shows expected sales in units at their expected selling prices.

> A **production budget** is a plan for acquiring and combining the resources needed to carry out the manufacturing operations that allow the firm to satisfy its sales goals and have the desired amount of inventory at the end of the budget period.

Budgeting at Borg-Warner Automotive

The Muncie, Indiana, plant of Borg-Warner Automotive drives its budget with cost targets by product line and department. The initial step in its budgeting processes is to develop sales estimates for the coming year. Current costs then provide baselines. From there the firm incorporates basic assumptions, such as inflation, planned product and process changes, and special program costs, to arrive at a base budget. Before completing the budgeting processes, operating managers work with accounting to fine-tune assumptions and incorporate other goals and objectives.

Source: George F. Hanks, Michael A. Freid, and Jack Huber, "Shifting Gears at Borg-Warner Automotive," *Management Accounting,* February 1994, p. 28.

Exhibit 9–4 Sales Budget

KERRY INDUSTRIAL COMPANY
Sales Budget
For the Quarter Ended June 30, 2002

	April	May	June	Quarter
Sales in units	20,000	25,000	35,000	80,000
Selling price per unit	× 30	× 30	× 30	× 30
Total sales	$600,000	$750,000	$1,050,000	$2,400,000

---

[9]   Determination of sales levels and preparation of the sales budget for the period might not occur at the same time in some firms. When the sales budget includes marketing plans to attain sales, the sales budget and the firm's marketing plan must be prepared at the same time.

budgeted sales, the desired amount of finished goods ending inventory, and the units of finished goods beginning inventory as described in the following:

$$\underset{\text{(in units)}}{\text{Budgeted production}} = \underset{\text{(in units)}}{\text{Budgeted sales}} + \underset{\text{(in units)}}{\text{Desired ending inventory}} - \underset{\text{(in units)}}{\text{Beginning inventory}}$$

Selecting the desired ending inventory for a period requires balancing opposing goals. On one hand, a firm does not want to lose sales because of insufficient inventory. On the other hand, having an excessive amount of inventory on hand is costly. Thus, the organization must determine how quickly it can increase production if demand warrants and then set its desired production and inventory levels accordingly. For a firm using a just-in-time system, for example, the desired ending as well as the beginning inventory will be a small amount or zero.

Other factors that affect a production budget include company policies regarding stabilizing production versus flexible production schedules that minimize finished inventories, conditions of production equipment, availability of production resources such as materials and laborers, and experience with production yields and quality.

To illustrate, Kerry expects to have 5,000 units on hand at the beginning of the quarter, April 1. The firm's operation guideline requires the inventory on hand at the end of each month to be 30 percent of the following month's predicted sales. Kerry therefore has a production budget to manufacture 22,500 units in April as calculated here.

1. Determine the desired amount of ending inventory (April 30):

Expected sales in May	25,000	units
× Desired percentage of the next month's sales to be on hand April 30	× 30%	
Desired ending inventory on April 30	7,500	units

2. Calculate the production units budgeted for April:

Number of sales units budgeted for April	20,000	units
+ Desired ending inventory	+ 7,500	units
Total number of units needed in April	27,500	units
− Beginning inventory on hand on April 1	− 5,000	units
Number of production units budgeted for April	22,500	units

Exhibit 9–5 shows Kerry's production budget for the first quarter of 2002. This budget is based on the sales budget in Exhibit 9–4 and the expected sales of 40,000 units in July. Kerry expects its total sales in May 2002 to be 25,000 units. The desired ending inventory on April 30, therefore, is 7,500 units as shown in step 1 below. Step 2 shows the calculation that determines the number of units to be manufactured in April.

Exhibit 9–5	**Production Budget**			

KERRY INDUSTRIAL COMPANY
Production Budget
For the Quarter Ended June 30, 2002

	April	May	June	Quarter
Budgeted sales in units	20,000	25,000	35,000	80,000
Add: Desired ending inventory of finished units	7,500	10,500	12,000	12,000
Total units needed	27,500	35,500	47,000	92,000
Less: Beginning inventory of finished units	5,000	7,500	10,500	5,000
Budgeted production in units	22,500	28,000	36,500	87,000

Most of the quarterly amounts are simply the sums of the appropriate monthly figures. For example, in Exhibit 9–5 the budgeted sales for the quarter, 80,000 units, is the sum of the budgeted sales in April (20,000 units), May (25,000 units), and June (35,000 units). The desired amount of *ending finished inventory* of the quarter, however, is the desired ending inventory of *June*, the end of the quarter, not the sum of the desired ending amount in each of the three months. The amount of *beginning inventory* of the quarter is the beginning inventory of the first month of the quarter. These two *amounts* refer to specific times in the quarter, not the amount for the entire period.

The production manager reviews the production budget to ascertain that the firm can attain the budgeted level of production with the facilities available, keeping in mind the other activities scheduled for the same period. If the production level exceeds the maximum capacity available, management can either revise the budgeted sales level or find alternatives to satisfy the demand. If the available capacity exceeds the budgeted production level, management might want to find alternative uses for the idle capacity or schedule other activities such as preventive maintenance and trial runs of new production processes. This ability to coordinate sales needs and production activities is another benefit of having a budget that allows firms to identify mismatches between capacity and output.

The sales budget for the quarter shows that Kerry expects to have increasing sales. When sales vary over periods, management can either change the production level as needed, as Kerry did in the previous budget, or maintain a stable production level. With a total of 87,000 units to be produced during the quarter, Kerry may set the production level at 29,000 units per month.

Maintaining a constant production level enables the firm to keep a constant employment level. The current trend, however, is away from maintaining a constant production level. Use of new manufacturing technology and adoption of just-in-time operations in recent years have forced an increasing number of firms to adjust production activity to changes in sales volume, not to keep it steady.

Direct Materials Usage and Purchases

The information in the production budget becomes the basis for preparing several other budgets for the period. The first is the **direct materials usage budget** (Exhibit 9–6), which shows the amount of direct materials required for production and their budgeted cost. The last line of the production budget (Exhibit 9–5) shows the number of units of its only product that Kerry Industrial Company plans to manufacture in April: 22,500 units. This amount becomes line 1 of Exhibit 9–6, Kerry's direct materials usage budget. This budget shows that production of one unit requires 3 pounds of aluminum alloy for a total of 67,500 pounds (line 3) to produce the 22,500 units planned. The remainder of the direct materials usage budget (Exhibit 9–6, part B) identifies the cost of direct materials for the budget period, but it can be completed after Kerry prepares the second budget, its direct materials purchase budget (Exhibit 9–7). A direct materials purchase budget shows the amount of direct materials (in units and cost) to be purchased during the period to meet production needs.

Kerry prepares its direct materials purchase budget to identify the purchases that it must make to ensure that it has sufficient direct materials available to meet production needs and to maintain the amount of direct materials ending inventory required by the firm's operation guidelines. Line 3 of Exhibit 9–6 shows that the firm needs 67,500, 84,000, and 109,500 pounds of aluminum alloy to meet the production budget for April, May, and June, respectively. In addition, operation guidelines require an ending direct materials inventory of 10 percent of the next period's production. Ending inventory of aluminum alloy for April is 8,400 pounds (line 2 of Exhibit 9–7, which is 10% of May's production need of 84,000 pounds; see line 3 of Exhibit 9–6). The sum of lines 1 and 2 (Exhibit 9–7) identifies the total amount of direct materials needed for April, 75,900 pounds. The firm expects to have 7,000 pounds (March's ending inventory) as the beginning balance in April; this amount must be subtracted from the amount to

A **direct materials usage budget** shows the direct materials required for production and their budgeted cost.

Exhibit 9–6 Direct Materials Usage Budget

KERRY INDUSTRIAL COMPANY
Direct Materials Usage Budget
For the Quarter Ended June 30, 2002

Line	Item	April	May	June	Quarter	Calculation
A.	**Production Requirement**					
1.	Budgeted production	22,500	28,000	36,500	87,000	
2.	Pounds of aluminum alloy for one unit of product	× 3	× 3	× 3	× 3	
3.	Total pounds of aluminum alloy needed in production	67,500	84,000	109,500	261,000	
B.	**Cost of Direct Materials**					
4.	Pounds of aluminum alloy from beginning inventory	7,000	8,400	10,950	7,000	
5.	Cost per pound	$ 2.40	$ 2.45	$ 2.50	$ 2.40	
6.	Total cost of aluminum alloy beginning inventory	$ 16,800	$ 20,580	$ 27,375	$ 16,800	(4) × (5)
7.	Total cost of aluminum alloy purchases	168,805	216,375	284,310	669,490	Ex.* 9–7
8.	Total cost of aluminum alloy available	$185,605	$236,955	$311,685	$686,290	(6) + (7)
9.	Desired ending inventory of aluminum alloy in units	8,400	10,950	10,800	10,800	Ex. 9–7
10.	Cost per unit	$ 2.45	$ 2.50	$ 2.60	$ 2.60	Ex. 9–7
11.	Aluminum alloy ending inventory	$ 20,580	$ 27,375	$ 28,080	$ 28,080	(9) × (10)
12.	Total cost of aluminum alloy used in production	$165,025	$209,580	$283,605	$658,210	(8) − (11)

*Ex. = Exhibit

Exhibit 9–7 Direct Materials Purchase Budget

KERRY INDUSTRIAL COMPANY
Direct Materials Purchase Budget
For the Quarter Ended June 30, 2002

Line		April	May	June	Quarter
1.	Total direct materials needed in production (from part A of Exhibit 9–6)	67,500	84,000	109,500	261,000
2.	Add: Desired direct materials ending inventory	8,400	10,950	10,800	10,800
3.	Total direct materials needed	75,900	94,950	120,300	271,800
4.	Less: Direct materials beginning inventory	7,000	8,400	10,950	7,000
5.	Total direct materials purchases	68,900	86,550	109,350	264,800
6.	Purchase price per pound	$ 2.45	$ 2.50	$ 2.60	
7.	Total cost for direct materials purchases	$168,805	$216,375	$284,310	$669,490

buy. Thus, Kerry must purchase 68,900 pounds in April (line 5). These steps summarize the calculations in Exhibit 9–7:

Total amount of direct materials needed in production for April	Line 1
+ Amount of direct materials required in ending inventory at end of April	+ Line 2
Total amount of direct materials needed for April	Line 3
− Amount of April direct materials beginning inventory (left on March 31)	− Line 4
Direct materials to be purchased for April	Line 5

Kerry's purchasing department estimates the cost of aluminum alloy to be $2.45 per pound in April, for a total cost of $168,805 for the 68,900 pounds it must purchase.

Following the procedure just described, the firm completes the purchase budgets for May and June. June's direct materials ending inventory of 10,800 pounds is determined based on the 36,000 units to be manufactured in July (3 pounds per unit × 36,000 = 108,000 pounds; 10% × 108,000 = 10,800 pounds).

At the beginning of April, Kerry has on hand 7,000 pounds of the direct material, which cost $2.40 per pound, for a total cost of $16,800 (Exhibit 9–6, line 6). Using the FIFO inventory valuation, Kerry's cost of ending inventory in April is the last purchase price, which is $2.45 per pound, or $20,580 (line 11). The total cost of the direct materials for the period—April—is $165,025 (line 12), which is the total cost of the direct materials available (line 8, $185,605) less the ending inventory (line 11, $20,580).

Direct Labor Budget

The production budget also serves as the basis for preparing the direct labor budget. A firm's labor force must include sufficient skilled employees required to produce the finished goods scheduled for the period. The direct labor budget enables the personnel department to plan for direct labor and to avoid emergency hiring or labor shortages and the need to lay off workers. Erratic labor employment can decrease employees' sense of loyalty, increase their insecurity, and lead to inefficiency.

Many firms have stable employment policies or labor contracts that prevent them from hiring and laying off employees in direct proportion to their production needs. A direct labor budget enables the firm to identify circumstances when it can either reschedule production or plan temporary employee reassignments to perform other tasks. Manufacturing cells common to many firms that adopt new manufacturing technologies can use the direct labor budget to plan for maintenance, minor repair, installation, testing, learning to use new equipment, or other activities.

A company usually prepares a direct labor budget for each type of labor needed in production. Kerry has two skill levels, skilled and semiskilled. The production process uses 0.5 hour of semiskilled labor and 0.2 hour of skilled labor. The hourly wages are $8 and $12 for semiskilled and skilled laborers, respectively. Exhibit 9–8 illustrates the direct labor budget for the first quarter of 2002.

Factory Overhead Budget

The factory overhead budget includes all production costs other than direct materials and direct labor. Unlike direct materials and direct labor, which tend to vary in direct proportion with the number of units manufactured, manufacturing overhead costs include costs that do not vary in direct proportion with the units manufactured but with the facilities the firm has and the way the production is performed. Examples include costs of facilities and costs that vary with the batch size and number of setups in production. Manufacturing overhead also includes fixed costs, such as salaries of production supervisors and factory depreciation expenses.

Budgeting for factory overhead costs requires forecasting the number of units to be produced, determining the way in which production is to be performed, and incorporating external factors that affect factory overhead. Many firms separate the factory overhead budget into variable and fixed overhead items. All factory overhead costs

Exhibit 9–8   Direct Labor Budget

KERRY INDUSTRIAL COMPANY
Direct Labor Budget
For the Quarter Ended June 30, 2002

Line	Labor	April	May	June	Quarter
	Semiskilled				
1.	Budgeted production	22,500	28,000	36,500	87,000
2.	Semiskilled direct labor-hours per unit	× 0.5	× 0.5	× 0.5	× 0.5
3.	Total semiskilled direct labor-hours needed	11,250	14,000	18,250	43,500
4.	Hourly wage rate of semiskilled labor	$ 8	$ 8	$ 8	$ 8
5.	Total wages for semiskilled labor	$ 90,000	$112,000	$146,000	$348,000
	Skilled				
6.	Budgeted production	22,500	28,000	36,500	87,000
7.	Skilled direct labor-hours per unit	× 0.2	× 0.2	× 0.2	× 0.2
8.	Total skilled direct labor-hours needed	4,500	5,600	7,300	17,400
9.	Hourly wage for skilled labor	$ 12	$ 12	$ 12	$ 12
10.	Total wages for skilled labor	$ 54,000	$ 67,200	$ 87,600	$208,800
	Total				
11.	Total direct manufacturing labor-hour (3) + (8)	15,750	19,600	25,550	60,900
12.	Total cost for direct manufacturing labor (5) + (10)	$144,000	$179,200	$233,600	$556,800

other than those that vary in direct proportion to the units manufactured are treated as fixed costs. Such practices are justified because nonvariable factory overhead costs usually remain the same within a given range of production activities. Exhibit 9–9 shows Kerry's factory overhead costs budget for the first quarter of 2002.

Cost of Goods Manufactured and Sold Budget

The cost of goods manufactured and sold budget reports the total and per-unit budgeted production cost in each period. Exhibits 9–5 through 9–9 provide the data needed to complete this budget. Exhibit 9–10 shows the cost of goods manufactured and sold budget for the first quarter of 2002 prepared by Kerry Industrial Company. The company's finished goods inventory on April 1 is assumed to have a unit cost of $18.

Two items in this budget appear in other budgets for the same period. The income statement budget uses the cost of goods sold to determine the gross margin of the period, and the balance sheet includes the finished goods ending inventory in total assets. These two financial statements are shown later.

Merchandise Purchase Budget

A merchandising firm does not have a production budget. Instead, the manufacturing firm's production budget, as illustrated in Exhibit 9–5, is replaced by a merchandise purchase budget.

A merchandise purchase budget of a firm shows the amount of merchandise it needs to purchase during the period.

A firm's **merchandise purchase budget** shows the amount of merchandise it needs to purchase during the period. The basic format of a merchandise purchase budget is the same as the production budget. Instead of budgeted production as shown in Exhibit 9–5, however, the last items in a merchandise purchase budget are *budgeted purchases*.

Exhibit 9–9   Factory Overhead Budget

KERRY INDUSTRIAL COMPANY
Factory Overhead Budget
For the Quarter Ended June 30, 2002

	Rate per DLH*	April	May	June	Quarter
Total direct labor-hours		15,750	19,600	25,550	60,900
Variable factory overhead					
Supplies	$0.12	$ 1,890	$ 2,352	$ 3,066	$ 7,308
Indirect labor	1.00	15,750	19,600	25,550	60,900
Fringe benefits	3.00	47,250	58,800	76,650	182,700
Power	0.20	3,150	3,920	5,110	12,180
Maintenance	0.08	1,260	1,568	2,044	4,872
Total variable factory overhead	$4.40	$ 69,300	$ 86,240	$112,420	$267,960
Fixed factory overhead					
Depreciation		$ 30,000	$ 30,000	$ 40,000	$100,000
Factory insurance		2,500	2,500	2,500	7,500
Property taxes		900	900	900	2,700
Supervision		8,900	8,900	8,900	26,700
Power		1,250	1,250	1,250	3,750
Maintenance		750	750	750	2,250
Total fixed factory overhead		$ 44,300	$ 44,300	$ 54,300	$142,900
Total factory overhead		$113,600	$130,540	$166,720	$410,860

*Direct labor-hour.

Exhibit 9–10   Cost of Goods Manufactured and Sold Budget

KERRY INDUSTRIAL COMPANY
Cost of Goods Manufactured and Sold Budget
For the Quarter Ended June 30, 2002

	April	May	June	Quarter
Direct materials (Line 12, Exhibit 9–6)	$165,025	$209,580	$283,605	$ 658,210
Direct labor (Line 12, Exhibit 9–8)	144,000	179,200	233,600	556,800
Total factory overhead (Exhibit 9–9)	113,600	130,540	166,720	410,860
Total cost of goods manufactured	$422,625	$519,320	$683,925	$1,625,870
Finished goods beginning inventory	90,000	140,875	194,745	90,000
Total cost of goods available for sale	$512,625	$660,195	$878,670	$1,715,870
Finished goods ending inventory	140,875	194,745	224,852	224,852
Cost of goods sold	$371,750	$465,450	$653,818	$1,491,018

Selling and General Administrative Expense Budget

The selling and general administrative expense budget contains all nonmanufacturing expenses expected in the budget period. Exhibit 9–11 shows Kerry Industrial Company's selling and general administrative expense budget for the first quarter of 2002. This budget is important as a guideline for operations. However, using this budget to evaluate performance must be done carefully, because many items in it are discretionary expenditures and have mostly long-term impacts.

Exhibit 9–11	Selling and General Administrative Expense Budget

KERRY INDUSTRIAL COMPANY
Selling and General Administrative Expense Budget
For the Quarter Ended June 30, 2002

	April	May	June	Quarter
Selling expenses				
Variable selling expense				
Sales commissions	$ 30,000	$ 37,500	$ 52,500	$120,000
Delivery expenses	2,000	2,500	3,500	8,000
Bad debts expenses	9,000	11,250	15,750	36,000
Total variable selling expense	$ 41,000	$ 51,250	$ 71,750	$164,000
Fixed selling expense				
Sales salary	$ 8,000	$ 8,000	$ 8,000	$ 24,000
Advertising	50,000	50,000	50,000	150,000
Delivery expenses	6,000	6,000	6,000	18,000
Depreciation	20,000	20,000	20,000	60,000
Total fixed selling expense	$ 84,000	$ 84,000	$ 84,000	$252,000
Total selling expense	$125,000	$135,250	$155,750	$416,000
General administrative expenses (all fixed)				
Administrative salaries	$ 25,000	$ 25,000	$ 25,000	$ 75,000
Accounting and data processing	12,000	12,000	12,000	36,000
Depreciation	7,000	7,000	7,000	21,000
Other administrative expenses	6,000	6,000	6,000	18,000
Total administrative expense	$ 50,000	$ 50,000	$ 50,000	$150,000
Total selling and administrative expense	$175,000	$185,250	$205,750	$566,000

For example, a manager could cut expenditures for customer service from $200,000 to $50,000 to improve earnings and to show that he or she has good control of expenses. The manager's incentive is a reward in the form of a bonus or promotion resulting from the likely short-term result of this expenditure reduction. The customer service reduction probably will not have any immediate effect on sales but will most likely have negative consequences for the firm in the future. Hence, firms must be wary of taking a short-term perspective when preparing a selling and administrative expense budget.

Cash Budget

> A **cash budget** brings together the anticipated effects of all budgeted activities on cash.

Having an adequate amount of cash on hand at all times is crucial for a business's survival and capturing opportunities. A **cash budget** brings together the anticipated effects of all budgeted activities on cash. It also delineates the expected cash receipts and disbursements during the budget period. By preparing a cash budget, management can ensure having sufficient cash on hand to carry out its planned activities, arrange financing in advance to avoid the high costs of emergency borrowing, and plan investments to earn the highest possible return from any excess cash on hand. For smaller firms and those with seasonal business, the cash budget is especially critical to ensuring smooth operations and avoiding crises. The critical importance of having adequate cash to meet all operation needs leads many firms to consider cash budgets among the most important element of their master budget.

A cash budget includes all items that affect cash flows and pulls data from almost all parts of the master budget. In preparing a cash budget, a firm reviews all budgets to identify all revenues, expenses, and other transactions that affect cash.

A cash budget generally includes three major sections:

1. Cash available
2. Cash disbursements
3. Financing

The cash available section details the sources of cash for operations to use. In general, an organization's two sources of cash are the cash balance at the beginning of the budget period and cash collections during that period. Cash collections include cash collected from sales and accounts and notes receivable. Factors that could affect cash sales and cash collections of accounts include the firm's sales levels, credit policy, and collection experience.

A firm can engage in nonroutine transactions that generate cash. Examples are selling operating assets such as equipment or a building, or nonoperating assets such as land purchased for the site of a factory that the firm no longer intends to build. All proceeds from such sales should be included in the cash available section.

The cash disbursements section lists *all* payments, including those for purchases of direct materials and supplies, wages and salaries, operating expenses, interest expenses, and taxes. The difference between cash available and cash disbursements is the *ending cash balance* before financing.

A firm must arrange for additional funds if its cash balance is expected to fall below the desired minimum balance set by management. On the other hand, when the firm expects to have a significant amount of excess cash, it must determine how to invest the excess. Return, liquidity, and risk must be weighed for alternative investments. Both the additional funding and planned investments are included in the financing section.

Exhibit 9–12 shows the cash budget of the Kerry Industrial Company for the quarter ended June 30, 2002. In addition to reviewing Exhibits 9–4 through 9–11 to identify items that affect cash, management must gather additional information about the firm's operating characteristics and policies to complete the cash budget. The following are examples of such items and policies for Kerry:

1. The firm has a policy to maintain a minimum cash balance of $50,000. It expects to have $75,000 cash on hand on April 1.
2. The firm expects 70 percent of its sales to be cash sales. The other sales are made to Kerry's customers that have open accounts. The firm also estimates that 40 percent of the cash customers use credit cards for their purchases. The bank charges a 3 percent service fee to process credit card charges.
3. Kerry sends statements to its customers on the first of each month with terms of 2/10, n/eom.[10] It is paid for 80 percent of the accounts within the month; it receives 60 percent of these payments within the discount period. Fifteen percent of the accounts send in their checks the following month. Kerry has a 5 percent bad debt rate on its accounts receivable.
4. The typical term for Kerry's purchases of direct materials is n/30. The firm pays 60 percent of its purchases in the month of the purchase and the remainder in the following month. In addition, Kerry estimates that, on June 30, 2002, the balance of office supplies will be $38,906 and the sales tax yet to remit will be $7,812.
5. All expenses and wages are paid as incurred.
6. Total sales were $400,000 in February and $450,000 in March.
7. The firm purchased a total of $155,000 direct materials in March.
8. Equipment purchased in January for $200,000 will be delivered in May, terms COD.
9. The firm has a revolving 30-day account at 1 percent per month with the First National Bank for all temporary financing needs. The account must be drawn in increments of $50,000 with repayment occurring no sooner than 30 days.

---

[10] Customers who pay within 10 days receive a 2 percent discount on the total amount due. The payment is due on or before the end of the month.

Exhibit 9–12   Cash Budget

KERRY INDUSTRIAL COMPANY
Cash Budget
For the Quarter Ended June 30, 2002

	April	May	June	Quarter
Cash Available				
Cash balance, beginning	$ 75,000	$ 84,781	$ 91,916	$ 75,000
Cash collections				
Cash from cash sales[a]	$252,000	$315,000	$ 441,000	$1,008,000
Credit card sales[a]	162,960	203,700	285,180	651,840
Collections of accounts:				
Within cash discount period[b]	63,504	84,672	105,840	254,016
After the cash discount:				
From prior month's sales[c]	43,200	57,600	72,000	172,800
From sales two months earlier[d]	18,000	20,250	27,000	65,250
Total cash collections	$539,664	$681,222	$ 931,020	$2,151,906
Total cash available	$614,664	$766,003	$1,022,936	$2,226,906
Cash Disbursement				
Purchases of direct materials				
Current month purchases[e]	$101,283	$129,825	$ 170,586	$ 401,694
Last month's purchases[f]	62,000	67,522	86,550	216,072
Total payment for direct materials purchases	$163,283	$197,347	$ 257,136	$ 617,766
Direct labor wages	$144,000	$179,200	$ 233,600	$ 556,800
Factory overheads	$ 83,600	$100,540	$ 126,720	$ 310,860
Operating expenses				
Sales commissions	$ 30,000	$ 37,500	$ 52,500	$ 120,000
Sales salary	8,000	8,000	8,000	24,000
Administrative salaries	25,000	25,000	25,000	75,000
Delivery expenses	8,000	8,500	9,500	26,000
Advertising	50,000	50,000	50,000	150,000
Accounting and data processing	12,000	12,000	12,000	36,000
Other selling and general administrative expenses	6,000	6,000	6,000	18,000
Total payment for operating expenses	$139,000	$147,000	$ 163,000	$ 449,000
Equipment purchase		$200,000		$ 200,000
Total cash disbursement	$529,883	$824,087	$ 780,456	$2,134,426
Cash balance before financing	$ 84,781	$ (58,084)	$ 242,480	$ 92,480
Financing				
First National Bank		$150,000		$ 150,000
Payment to First National Bank				
Principal			(150,000)	(150,000)
Interest			(1,500)	(1,500)
Total financing		$150,000	$ (151,500)	$ (1,500)
Cash balance	$ 84,781	$ 91,916	$ 90,980	$ 90,980

[a]*April*
Total cash sales in April: $600,000 × 0.7 = $420,000
Cash paying customers are $420,000 × 0.6 = $252,000
Collections from credit card sales: $420,000 × 0.4 × 0.97 = $162,960

May
Total cash sales in May: $750,000 × 0.7 = $525,000
Cash paying customers are $525,000 × 0.6 = $315,000
Collections from credit card sales: $525,000 × 0.4 × 0.97 = $203,700

June
Total cash sales in June: $1,050,000 × 0.7 = $735,000
Cash paying customers are $735,000 × 0.6 = $441,000
Collections from credit card sales: $735,000 × 0.4 × 0.97 = $285,180

[b]For April from sales in March: $450,000 × 0.3 × 0.8 × 0.6 × 0.98 = $63,504
For May from sales in April: $600,000 × 0.3 × 0.8 × 0.6 × 0.98 = $84,672

For June from sales in May: $750,000 × 0.3 × 0.8 × 0.6 × 0.98 = $105,840
[c]For April from sales in March: $450,000 × 0.3 × 0.8 × 0.4 = $43,200
For May from sales in April: $600,000 × 0.3 × 0.8 × 0.4 = $57,600
For June from sales in May: $750,000 × 0.3 × 0.8 × 0.4 = $72,000
[d]For April from sales in February: $400,000 × 0.3 × 0.15 = $18,000
For May from sales in March: $450,000 × 0.3 × 0.15 = $20,250
For June from sales in April: $600,000 × 0.3 × 0.15 = $27,000
[e]For April for purchases in April: $168,805 × 0.6 = $101,283
For May for purchases in May: $216,375 × 0.6 = $129,825
For June for purchases in June: $284,310 × 0.6 = $170,586
[f]For April for purchases in March: $155,000 × 0.4 = $62,000
For May for purchases in April: $168,805 × 0.4 = $67,522
For June for purchases in May: $216,375 × 0.4 = $86,550

Budget Income Statement

The budget income statement shows the profit a firm can expect from its budgeted operations. Management assesses actions to take when the budgeted income for the period falls short of the goal. In such cases, the budget is revised to incorporate the effect of action(s) to be taken to improve the operating outcome. Once the budget income statement has been approved, it becomes the benchmark against which the performance of the period is to be evaluated. Exhibits 9–4, 9–10, and 9–11 provide information needed to prepare the budget income statement for the period in Exhibit 9–13.

Budget Balance Sheet

The last step in a budget preparation cycle usually is to prepare the budget balance sheet. The starting point in preparing the budget balance sheet is the budgeted balance sheet at the end of the current operating period, which is the beginning of the budget period. Exhibit 9–14 presents the budget balance sheet as of March 31, 2002, the end of Kerry Industrial Company's current operating period.

In preparing the budget balance sheet, the firm incorporates effects of operations during the budget period into the budgeted balance sheet at the end of the current period (see Exhibit 9–14). Exhibit 9–15 shows the budget balance sheet at the end of the budget period.

For example, the amount of cash in Exhibit 9–15, $90,980, is taken from the ending cash balance of the cash budget of the period (Exhibit 9–12). The ending balance of raw materials, $28,080, is from Exhibit 9–6. The gross amount for building and equipment, $964,000, is the sum of the beginning balance in the Building and Equipment account reported in Exhibit 9–14, $764,000, and the purchase of new equipment during the budget period, $200,000, as shown in the cash budget for May and, again, for the quarter (Exhibit 9–12).

BUDGETING IN SERVICE FIRMS AND NOT-FOR-PROFIT ORGANIZATIONS

Budgeting is not a mere accounting procedure. Several other issues are of concern in budgeting. Each firm or organization should consider the specific conditions surrounding its operations. For example, service firms and not-for-profit organizations have different considerations than those of the manufacturing and merchandising

◀**LEARNING OBJECTIVES 5**

Identify unique budgeting characteristics of service and not-for-profit organizations and of organizations operating in international settings.

Exhibit 9–13   Budget Income Statement

KERRY INDUSTRIAL COMPANY
Budget Income Statement
For the Quarter Ended June 30, 2002

	April	May	June	Quarter
Sales (Exhibit 9–4)	$600,000	$750,000	$1,050,000	$2,400,000
Cost of goods sold (Exhibit 9–10)	371,750	465,450	653,818	1,491,018
Gross margin	$228,250	$284,550	$ 396,182	$ 908,982
Selling and general administrative expenses (Exhibit 9–11)	175,000	185,250	205,750	566,000
Net operating income	$ 53,250	$ 99,300	$ 190,432	$ 342,982
Less: Interest expense (Exhibit 9–12)			1,500	1,500
Income before taxes	$ 53,250	$ 99,300	$ 188,932	$ 341,482
Less: Income taxes (30%)	15,975	29,790	56,680	102,445
Net income	$ 37,275	$ 69,510	$ 132,252	$ 239,037

Exhibit 9–14 Budget Balance Sheet

KERRY INDUSTRIAL COMPANY
Budget Balance Sheet
March 31, 2002

Assets

Current assets			
Cash		$ 75,000	
Accounts receivable		153,000	
Raw materials inventory		16,800	
Finished goods inventory		90,000	
Office supplies		3,500	
Total current assets			$338,300
Plant, property, and equipment			
Land		$ 40,000	
Buildings and equipment	$764,000		
Less: Accumulated depreciation	168,000	596,000	
Total plant, property, and equipment			636,000
Total assets			$974,300

Liabilities and Stockholders' Equity

Current liabilities			
Accounts payable		$ 62,000	
Sales tax payable		4,500	
Total liabilities			$ 66,500
Stockholders' equity			
Common stock		$303,300	
Retained earnings		604,500	
Total stockholders' equity			907,800
Total liabilities and stockholders' equity			$974,300

firms discussed earlier. This section examines special concerns in budgeting for service firms and not-for-profit organizations as well as several budgeting approaches.

Budgeting in Service Industries

The budgeting procedures are primarily the same for service and manufacturing or merchandising firms. A service firm carefully plans how to secure the resources required to render its services and fulfill its budgeted goals, just as a manufacturing firm plans its manufacturing activities and acquires materials, labor, and other resources for its budgeted sales. The budgets for service firms differ from those of manufacturing or merchandising firms primarily in the absence of production or merchandise purchase budgets and their ancillary budgets. The focal point of a service organization's budgeting is personnel planning. A service firm must ensure that it has personnel with the appropriate skills to perform the services required for the budgeted service revenue.

As an example, AccuTax, Inc., provides tax services to small firms and individuals. It expects to have these total revenues from preparing tax returns:

Tax returns for business firms		$1,200,000
Individual tax returns		
Simple tax forms	$300,000	
Complicated tax forms	500,000	800,000
Total revenues		$2,000,000

Exhibit 9–15 **Budget Balance Sheet**

KERRY INDUSTRIAL COMPANY
Budget Balance Sheet
June 30, 2002

Assets

Current assets			
Cash (Exhibit 9–12)		$ 90,980	
Accounts receivable[a]		333,000	
Raw materials inventory (Exhibit 9–6)		28,080	
Finished goods inventory (Exhibit 9–10)		224,852	
Office supplies		38,906	
Total current assets			$ 715,818
Plant, property, and equipment			
Land (Exhibit 9–14)		$ 40,000	
Buildings and equipment	$964,000		
Less: Accumulated depreciation[b]	349,000	615,000	
Total plant, property, and equipment			655,000
Total assets			$1,370,818

Liabilities and Stockholders' Equity

Current liabilities			
Accounts payable (Exhibits 9–7 and 9–12)[c]		$113,724	
Sales tax payable		7,812	
Income tax payable (Exhibit 9–13)		102,445	
Total liabilities			$ 223,981
Stockholders' equity			
Common stock (Exhibit 9–14)		$303,300	
Retained earnings (Exhibits 9–13 and 9–14)[d]		843,537	
Total stockholders' equity			1,146,837
Total liabilities and stockholders' equity			$1,370,818

[a]June Sales:

Total credit sales in June	$1,050,000 × 0.30 = $315,000	
Allowance for bad debts	$315,000 × 0.05 = 15,750	
Total net accounts receivable from sales in June		$299,250
May Sales:		
Total credit sales in May	$750,000 × 0.30 = $225,000	
Allowance for bad debts	$225,000 × 0.05 = 11,250	
Total net accounts receivable as of May 31	$213,750	
Collections in June	$225,000 × 0.80 = 180,000	
Remaining accounts receivable from May sales		33,750
Accounts receivable, June 30, 2002		$333,000
[b]Accumulated depreciation, March 31, 2002 (Exhibit 9–14)		$168,000
Depreciation expenses:		
Factory (Exhibit 9–9)	$100,000	
Selling (Exhibit 9–11)	60,000	
General administrative (Exhibit 9–11)	21,000	
Total depreciation expense for the quarter ended June 30, 2002		181,000
Accumulated depreciation, June 30, 2002		$349,000
[c]Direct materials purchases in June, 2002 (Exhibit 9–7)		$284,310
Payments (Exhibit 9–12)		170,586
Accounts payable, June 30, 2002		$113,724
[d]Retained earnings, March 31, 2002 (Exhibit 9–14)		$604,500
Net income for the quarter ended June 30, 2002 (Exhibit 9–13)		239,037
Retained earnings, June 30, 2002		$843,537

The firm charges $100 per hour for services rendered to business firms, $50 per hour for services rendered to individuals with complicated tax matters, and $30 per hour for services rendered to individuals with simple tax returns. The firm therefore needs to budget the following:

Staff hours to serve business firms	$1,200,000 ÷ $100 = 12,000
Staff hours to serve individual taxpayers	
Simple tax forms	$300,000 ÷ $30 = 10,000
Complicated tax forms	$500,000 ÷ $50 = 10,000
Total service hours budgeted	32,000

Suppose, however, that most of the AccuTax, Inc., staff have the skills necessary to provide services to business firms. The higher wage rate for these highly skilled staff, when paid for completing individual returns that draw considerably less in revenue, causes the firm's earnings to drop. The budget projections, if followed, would have led to hiring a staff mix better suited for the expected work.

Many firms in service industries consider people to be their principal assets often called *human capital*. A service organization with a good budgeting system can avoid short-term fluctuations in staff levels and achieve higher productivity from personnel than can a firm without a budget system.

Budgeting in Not-for-Profit Organizations

The objectives of not-for-profit organizations such as governments, state universities or colleges, secondary and primary schools, charity organizations, museums, and foundations are different from those of for-profit organizations. Non-profit organizations have no single bottom-line amount, such as operating income, that is recognized as the ultimate criterion in budgeting.

A not-for-profit organization's objective is to provide services efficiently and effectively as mandated in its charter, yet within the amount of expenditure allowed. With no clear standard by which to measure performance in delivering services, and with a clear mandate not to exceed budgeted expenditures, the master budget of a not-for-profit organization often becomes the means to plan and document *authorization for expenditures*. In effect, the budget for a not-for-profit organization often becomes the source of power and the limitations of the budgeted unit.

How Should a Service Firm Prepare Its Budget?

Tom McCarthy, a consultant in hotel management, suggests six points for an effective budgeting process for the marketing departments of firms in the lodging industry.

1. Develop the budget from a zero base. Do not approve a budget item, because it has always been recommended and approved in the past. All expenditures should be examined with a fresh look and without any preconceived notion.

2. Develop the budget on a need basis. Write the marketing plan first, then cost out each strategy/action step to build the total budget.

3. Budget for the entire year. Those without an annual budget often spend too much early in the year when there seems to be plenty of money and end up not having funds for important expenditures later in the year.

4. Look at the entire marketing budget as a whole. Do not treat sales, advertising, merchandising, and public rela-

tions budgets as separate and apart from each other when deciding the best use of each marketing dollar.

5. "Fight it out/turn it over. At Marriott, we had a great budgeting system. Each department fought it out for the approval of the budget before the year began. Some of those battles were pretty tough, but once you had agreement from your supervisor, the budget was turned over to you for your control throughout the year. . . . No more running to the boss for approvals on a piecemeal basis."

6. Implement and control the budget. A good budget is a futile exercise and all is for naught if the budget is not followed and controlled.

Source: Tom McCarthy, "Take a Fresh Look at Budgeting," *Lodging Hospitality,* 54 (8).

A not-for-profit organization begins its budget preparation by estimating the total revenues for the budget period. Because these organizations often do not have the option to increase revenues by increasing marketing activities, they must decide how best to allocate limited resources to competing activities and subunits. The budget must show that the organization can at least break even at the estimated amount of revenue.[11] Once approved, the budget shows the resources the organization plans to use to perform its activities. Revisions are seldom made during the budget period, and the organization's operations usually follow the budget.

BUDGETING IN INTERNATIONAL SETTINGS

Firms operating in an international setting must pay attention to the specific environment(s) in which they operate. A multinational company (MNC) faces several unique budgeting issues that arise because of cultural and language differences, dissimilar political and legal environments, fluctuating monetary exchange rates, and discrepancies in the inflation rates of different countries, among others. An operating procedure acceptable in one country may be against the law in another country. Also, fluctuating currency exchange rates and different inflation rates must be incorporated into the budget because changes in these rates affect the MNC's budgeted purchasing power, operating income, and cash flows.

Subsidiaries or subdivisions of a multinational firm often have their own budgets. They must follow the firm's budget procedure and coordinate their budgets with other divisions of the firm because all budgets must be approved by the MNC's budget committee. A subsidiary of an international firm in Belgium, for example, must negotiate its budget with the European headquarters in Geneva, Switzerland; then the budgets must be ultimately approved by corporate headquarters in New York City.

ALTERNATIVE BUDGETING APPROACHES

Many alternative approaches to budget preparation have been proposed over the years. These approaches, when used properly, can greatly improve budget effectiveness. Those that have been proven to be useful by many firms or organizations include zero-based, activity-based, and kaizen budgeting.

Zero-Base Budgeting

Zero-base budgeting is a budgeting process that requires managers to prepare budgets from ground zero. A typical budgeting process is an incremental process and starts with the budget and the likely operating results for the current period. The process assumes that most, if not all, current activities and functions will continue into the budget period. The primary focus in a typical budgeting process is on changes to the current operating budget.

In contrast, a zero-base budgeting process allows no activities or functions to be included in the budget unless managers can justify their need. Zero-base budgeting requires managers or budgeting teams to perform in-depth reviews and analyses of all budget items. Such a budgeting process encourages managers to be aware of activities or functions that have outlived their usefulness or have been a waste of resources. A tight, efficient budget often results from zero-base budgeting.

Zero-base budgeting has drawn considerable attention since the 1970s. Although its popularity has faded since its heyday, many organizations, especially government and not-for-profit organizations, still use it.

A good budgeting process should follow the fundamental concept of zero-base budgeting; namely, regular, periodic review of all activities and functions. The amount of

◀ **LEARNING OBJECTIVE 6**

Apply zero-base, activity-based, and kaizen budgeting.

Zero-base budgeting is a budgeting process that requires managers to prepare budgets from ground zero.

---

[11] The budget for the federal government of the United States is an exception.

An Alternative to Zero-Base Budgeting

Ewing Kauffman dealt with creeping expenses by insisting that managers start budgeting at an expense level 10 percent lower than that of the current year. They had to justify adding the 10 percent before they could add any more expense for the coming year. The practice worked well enough for Kauffman, who went on to own the Kansas City Royals and to found Ewing Marion Kauffman Foundation.

Source: *Inc.,* December 1995, p. 13.

work and time needed to complete zero-base budgeting, however, makes it impossible for an organization to review and examine all of its activities from the zero-budget level every year. As an alternative, many organizations schedule zero-base budgeting periodically or perform zero-base budgeting for different divisions each year. For example, the highway department of a state government could adopt rotating five-year zero-base budgeting. All divisions of the department would be subject to in-depth review of their activities every fifth year, with the process applying to different divisions each year. Organizations with considerable turnover at middle or senior levels are good candidates for using zero-based budgeting. Management turnover decreases resistance and reduces or eliminates parochial knowledge on which previous budgets are based.

Activity-Based Budgeting

Activity-based budgeting (ABB) is a budgeting process that focuses on costs of activities or cost drivers necessary for production and sales.

Activity-based budgeting (ABB) is a budgeting process that focuses on costs of activities or cost drivers necessary for operations. ABB segregates costs into homogeneous cost pools based on cost drivers that result from activity-based costing (ABC).[12] Thus, ABB begins by separating all budget costs into homogeneous cost pools such as unit, batch, product, and facility. Criteria for inclusion in a cost pool is that the costs in that pool vary in similar proportions when the level of activity changes. A firm that uses ABC already has separated its costs into such cost pools. The accuracy of the cost pools for the budget period, however, needs to be reviewed before employing them in budgeting, especially when a firm has experienced inexplicable variances.

Exhibit 9–16 contrasts traditional budgeting with ABB. Traditional costing systems focus on the cost elements of objects, such as materials, labor, and manufacturing overhead, and assign an operation's costs and expenses of resources to outputs via

Exhibit 9–16	Traditional vs. Activity-Based Budgeting	
	Traditional Budgeting	**Activity-Based Budgeting**
Budgeting unit	Expressed as the cost of functional areas or spending categories	Expressed as the cost of performing activities
Focus on	Input resources	Value-added activities
Orientation	History	Continuous improvement
Roles of suppliers and customers	Does not formally consider suppliers and customers in budgeting	Coordinates with suppliers and considers the needs of customers in budgeting
Control objective	Maximizes managers' performances	Synchronize activities
Budget base	Cost behavior patterns: variable and fixed costs	Utilized and unutilized capacity

---

[12] Chapter 4 discusses activity-based costing in detail.

cost pools using volume drivers. Aggregations of resource costs into cost pools obscure relationships between resource consumption and output and complicate decisions regarding resource utilizations and output levels or selections. As a result, traditional cost systems emphasize the allocation of past costs and expenses to products via a simplified method, such as labor-hours, machine-hours, units of materials used, and output units. The obscure and complicated relationship between costs and outputs under traditional cost systems makes it difficult to ascertain the effects of changes that, in turn, cause budgets under traditional costing systems to be mere applications of past costs to future periods.

An activity-based budgeting system prepares budgets based on the costs to perform various activities and links resource consumption to activities. An ABB system strives to define a clear relationship between resource consumption and output; this clear relationship among activities, cost, and output enables managers to examine the effects of resource demands when changes are made, for example, to the products offered, product design, product mix, manufacturing processes, market share, and customer mix. ABB directs attention to the expected costs to perform various activities. Budgeting systems under ABC can easily incorporate future-oriented cost data and make the budget relevant for the target period.

ABB facilitates continuous improvement. The process in preparing a budget under ABB highlights opportunities for cost reduction and elimination of wasteful activities. ABB facilitates identification of value-added activities and elimination of non-value-added activities. In contrast, history often is the underlying theme in a traditional budget. Resources for a function usually are provided for in a traditional budget unless the organization has experienced difficulties.

A traditional budget confines its activities within the organization and seldom reaches beyond the firm's loading docks. The firm treats the activities of its suppliers or customers as given conditions to the budget. In contrast, a successful ABB requires coordinating closely with suppliers and meeting the needs of customers.

As a control tool, a traditional budget focuses on minimizing variances and maximizing responsibility units' performances. The primary objective for control in ABB is to coordinate and synchronize activities of the entire firm to serve customers.

Kaizen (Continuous Improvement) Budgeting

Chapter 1 noted that continuous improvement (kaizen) has become a common practice for firms operating in today's globally competitive environment. **Kaizen budgeting** is a budgeting approach that explicitly demands continuous improvement and incorporates

> **Kaizen budgeting** is a budgeting approach that explicitly demands continuous improvement and incorporates all expected improvements in the resultant budget.

Activity-Based Budgeting at Digital Semiconductor

Digital Semiconductor, a strategic business unit of Digital Corporation, designed and manufactured Alpha microprocessors and other semiconductor products. In May 1998, Intel acquired the unit, which was experiencing rapid major technology changes, facing major investment decisions, and feeling increasing pressure to improve its performance. The deteriorating financial condition of its parent company (DEC) only made the situation worse. Digital Semiconductor adopted activity-based budgeting (ABB) to gain a better understanding of its cost structure and to establish reasonable product projections.

Digital Semiconductor's adoption of ABB evolved from the firm's activity-based costing and followed the firm's value chain, providing cost and accounting data by activity and beneficiary of those activities across functional areas of the firm.

The successful installation of an ABC and, subsequently, an ABB system at Digital Semiconductor significantly improved the assignment of costs and clearly identified value-added and non-value-added activities. As a result, management gained better understanding of activity-cost drivers and cost projections. ABB influenced managers to focus on the amount of activities rather than the amount of budget spending. This, in turn, changed managers' behaviors. Product design, manufacturing, and finance managers were able to communicate better using the common language of ABB. Fabrication, assembly, and test operations were managed more effectively as the cost of department and division activities became clear.

Source: Richard J. Block and Lawrence P. Carr, "Activity-Based Budgeting at Digital Semiconductor," *Journal of Cost Management,* November/December 1999, pp. 11–20.

all expected improvements in the resulting budget. A kaizen budgeting process bases budgets on the desired future operating processes rather than the continuation of the current practices as is often the case in traditional budgeting. A kaizen budget reflects all changes from the continuous improvement.

Kaizen budgeting begins by analyzing current practices to identify areas for improvement and determine expected changes needed to attain the desired improvement(s). Budgets are prepared based on improved practices or procedures. As a result, budgeted costs often are lower than those in the preceding period, and the firm expects to be able to manufacture products or render services at a lower cost. Kaizen budgeting mandates, for example, a 10 percent decrease in a product's manufacturing cost for the budget period. The cost to manufacture a product that previously required labor costs of $500 has a budgeted manufacturing labor cost of $450 in a kaizen budget.

Kaizen budgeting is not limited to internal improvements. Many firms expect and demand continuous improvements of their suppliers and explicitly incorporate consequent effects on costs and delivery schedules of parts and components in budgeted production cost and manufacturing schedules. For example, Citizen Watch demands its suppliers to decrease their costs a minimum of 3 percent per year and includes this decrease in the budget. Suppliers keep any cost savings in excess of 3 percent.[13]

A kaizen budget decrease is not the same as the budget cuts we often see firms or governments make when facing a budget crunch because of diminishing profits, decreasing sales, or declining tax revenues. A budget cut often is a reluctant passive response to a mandate that is accomplished by reducing productive activities or services. In contrast, kaizen budgeting promotes active engagement in reforming or altering practices. A decrease in cost in a kaizen budget is a result of performing the same activity more efficiently and with higher quality; it is not a result of arbitrarily eliminating activities or components.

COMPUTER SOFTWARE IN BUDGETING AND PLANNING

Budget preparation is a laborious, time-consuming process requiring intensive coordination, number crunching, and reconciliation. This is one reason that a budget, once completed, tends to remain as unchanging as a statue. A budget that is not changed once prepared and the painstakingly slow processes most likely required to revise a budget can no longer keep up with the needs of companies operating in rapidly changing business conditions.

Spreadsheet programs such as Microsoft Excel and similar programs can help ease the burden of number crunching and reduce detail work done manually in preparing or revising a budget. However, the usefulness of spreadsheets in budgeting and planning varies greatly with the abilities of the firm's programmers who develop the spreadsheet-based budgeting and planning module as well as the comfort of others using the program. Furthermore, spreadsheet modules often lack the ability to coordinate the budgets of various divisions and render a fragmented budgeting process.

Many integrated budgeting and planning programs now available integrate strategic planning, budgeting, management reporting, sensitivity analysis, and financial consolidations into one package. The online architecture of most of these programs makes it easy to involve more people in the budgeting and planning processes, provide instant feedback, and allow constant updates of budgets in response to changing circumstances.[14] The online budgeting-planning capability facilitates communication and enables firms to use both top-down and bottom-up budgeting approaches.

---

[13] Robin Cooper, *Citizen Watch Company, Ltd.*, Harvard Business School case 9–194–033. © 1993 by the President and Fellows of Harvard College.

[14] For example, Comshare Inc.'s Comshare MPC; Hyperion Solution Corporation's Hyperion Planning; Cognos Inc.'s Cognos Finance 5.0; OutlookSoft Corp.'s Everest; and Adaytum Software Inc.'s e.Planning. Enterprise software including those by Oracle, Peoplesoft, SAP, and J.D. Edwards also offer extensive budgeting and planning capability.

Executives and division managers can easily access the same application simultaneously while working on the same budget. The real-time capability eliminates the need to e-mail ideas, changes, and results back and forth. Top management can provide budget guidelines, goals, and objectives, and departmental managers and field personnel can enter their contributions and budget requests directly into the application.

A computer-based budgeting and planning system can also aid sensitivity analyses. Executives can pose what-if questions and the system will analyze the effects of changes and generate the results quickly.[15] For example, Amway Corp. uses its planning software to test changes in strategic assumptions and different budget scenarios, such as a new hiring plan, a new pricing schedule, a change in the cost of materials, a

---

Better Budget at Fujitsu

Fujitsu Computer Products of America, the San Jose, California–based manufacturer of mass data storage products such as disk drives and tapes, decided in 1997 that its traditional planning and budgeting processes were a waste of time. Kevin T. Parker, senior vice president in charge of finance and administration, explains that "there was a tremendous amount of effort put into the administrative aspects of budgeting, distributing spreadsheets and collecting information. The process took so long that by the time we had completed our critical assumptions, such as expected market growth, they no longer were valid."

Fujitsu's department managers budgeted at the detail level before the company had agreed on strategic objectives. Department managers forecast product availability and customer expectations independent of each other and then kicked them upstairs for review. The budgets would go through many churns, traveling up and down the corporate ladder until they were final. This circuitous routine took two months, an exceptionally long period of time in the fast-paced computer industry. Says Parker, "We were being overtaken by events. Something had to give."

Enter KPMG, a Big Five accounting firm. KPMG benchmarked Fujitsu's system against other Silicon Valley companies and reengineered its processes. Following the suggestion of KPMG, Fujitsu replaced its Excel spreadsheet with software links to the firm's enterprise resource planning (ERP) software. The company installed Pillar from Hyperion to link information generated by its ERP programs to provide a front-end planning database and an analytic tool.

The process was arduous and expensive. The result, however, justified the effort. Fujitsu's budget is no longer an exercise in reading tea leaves. Instead, the firm uses a monthly rolling budget that enables its financial managers to measure real performance. Says Parker, "We used to predict something but had no capability to measure it. For example, we'd project a revenue increase of X percent in a particular geographic region or product line, but since we couldn't measure this we couldn't use the information strategically." Furthermore, the system allows for more careful analysis and planning. Parker explains, "I can do a wide range of specific planning scenarios using Pillar. Say I want to know what will

happen to our financial stream if I delay a product introduction for 30 days. Pillar will tell me."

The new system reaped dividends for Fujitsu in 1999, when it became apparent that its disk drive business was headed for a period of oversupply. Parker entered the information into the Pillar program, which advised the company to hold back on hiring and other capital investment plans during the period. The firm changed its budget to accommodate the suggestions.

The system provided other benefits that more than paid for its implementation. As a result of the change, Fujitsu's management now works as a team and, using the enterprise planning software tools, determines strategic and tactical assumptions before doing any detailed planning. The team discusses product launches, customer and competitive issues, pricing assumptions, and target market shares; documents that information; and then brings in competitive analyses—before reaching overall planning objectives. When it is completed, the strategic plan goes to Fujitsu's product-line and sales managers, who are required to create a forecast and tactics to support the corporate objectives. Their observations are rolled together and measured to ensure that they conform to the original target. If a forecast and tactic fall short, Fujitsu's financial managers make corrective changes before the budget is approved.

Moreover, unsupported assumptions are no longer repeated up and down the management ladder. Fujitsu's process now encompasses one up-and-down cycle. The new system eliminates multi-iterative budgets that waste time and rarely reconcile them and replace them with continuous plans owned by department managers, not finance. As a result, its planning and budgeting process takes about 10 to 15 days compared with six to eight weeks under the previous system. Because managers spend less time on budgeting, they devote more time to understanding Fujitsu's individual businesses. In the past, there wasn't enough time left over after the budgeting process, Parker says. Although Fujitsu is a very large corporation (projected 1999 revenues: $1.2 billion), management has had no trouble understanding the consolidated results.

Source: Russ Banham, "Better Budgets," *Journal of Accountancy*, February 2000, pp. 37–40.

---

[15] Rick Whiting, "Budget Planning: The Next Generation," *Information Week*, September 25, 2000, p. 163.

10 percent decrease in sales because of a higher-than-expected unemployment in an area, a 5 percent cut in travel expenses across the board, or a supplemental incentive program for high performers. It can see what impact such changes have on the profits and losses and other aspects of the budget.

Recent rapid developments in computer-based online integrated budgeting and planning tools have greatly shortened budgeting processes. It is not unusual for firms to take almost an entire year to prepare budgets without using budgeting-planning software, but firms employing this software can usually complete the same processes in two months or less. Budgeting-planning software also allows integration of various operating and financial functions, frequent updates to reflect changing business conditions, in-depth analyses of likely scenarios, and active involvement of more personnel throughout the organization.

ETHICAL, BEHAVIORAL, AND IMPLEMENTATION ISSUES IN BUDGETING

LEARNING OBJECTIVE 7▶

Discuss the roles of ethics and behavioral concerns in budgeting.

A budget can be successful only if the person responsible for its implementation makes it happen. To encourage persons responsible for budget preparation and implementation to attain the organization's goals efficiently and effectively, firms must consider the numerous ethical and behavioral aspects of budgeting.

Ethics in Budgeting

Ethical issues permeate all aspects of budgeting. A significant amount of information used in budgeting is provided by people whose performance is evaluated against the budget. Employees breach the code of ethics if they deliberately furnish data for budgeting purposes that lead to lower performance expectations.

A budget is also a result of negotiations. Too often people follow this motto: It is better to promise too little and deliver more than to promise too much and deliver less. This might involve negotiating a goal of 12 percent growth in earnings and achieving 14 percent rather than negotiating a goal of 16 percent and delivering 15 percent. The 15 percent actual performance is certainly better for a firm than 14 percent, but when facing a choice between offering a budget with the likelihood of 12 percent growth and one with 16 percent growth, managers usually choose the 12 percent budget because it represents a lower risk to their careers.

Including budget slack, or padding the budget, is the practice of knowingly including a higher amount of expenditure in the budget than managers actually believe is needed. They often justify such practices as insurance against uncertain future events. After all, no one knows exactly how the future will unfold. Budget slacks, however, waste resources and could lead employees to make half-hearted efforts to meet or exceed the budget. In any event, budget padding is not an honest action.

Spending the budget is another serious ethical issue in budgeting. Managers could believe that if they do not use all the budgeted amounts, their future budgets will be reduced. To avoid this, managers could resort to wasteful spending to exhaust the remaining budgeted amount before the end of the period. This wastes precious resources on activities that yield little or no benefit to the firm or acquire unnecessary assets to use up remaining funds. Furthermore, managers waste time on unproductive efforts in trying to use up the budget.

Goal Congruence

Goal congruence is consistency between the goals of the firm and the goals of its employees.

Goal congruence is consistency between the goals of the firm and its subunits and the goals of its employees. A perfect goal congruence is the ideal for which all firms should strive. Realistically, perfect goal congruence almost never exists because resources for satisfying short-term goals of individuals often conflict with those of the firm. For example, employees often desire to earn a high salary with minimum effort, whereas a firm seeks to offer employees low compensation while receiving maximum efforts from them.

Still, a firm's goals must be as consistent as possible with the goals of its employees. A budget devoid of considerations for goal congruence is most likely not to be successful. A budget that aligns the firm's goals with those of its employees has a much better chance to realize successful operations and attain desirable results. One approach that encourages goal congruence is to actively involve all employees throughout the entire budgeting process. Employees are more likely to identify a budget as their own when they have actively participated in the entire budgeting process and the goals of the firm and those of its employees become the same.

Difficulty of the Budget Target

An easily attainable budget target could fail to encourage the employees to give their best efforts. A budget target that is very difficult to achieve can, however, discourage managers from even trying to attain it. Exhibit 9–17 depicts general relationships between the level of employees' efforts and level of difficulty of budget targets. Ideally, budget targets should be challenging yet attainable. But what is a challenging and attainable budget target?

To determine the difficulty level of a budget target, managers must consider the multiple functions a budget serves. A budget allows a manager to convert the organizational goals into budget goals for operating divisions. Budgeting, however, is a planning, coordinating, motivating, controlling, and evaluating tool. For planning and coordinating purposes, budget goals should be set at the level that most managers are likely to attain. Good planning identifies those events most likely to occur. A budget including activities that managers cannot perform because of the target's difficulty is no plan at all and actually undermines the coordination of the budget's function. Firms should expect to achieve goals only if most managers can accomplish the activities and goals as budgeted.

For motivational purposes, the optimal budget target should be set at a level attainable by, say, fewer than half the managers. On the other hand, a budget that allows fewer than half the operations to occur as planned certainly is not a good plan, nor is it a very good guideline for coordinating activities.

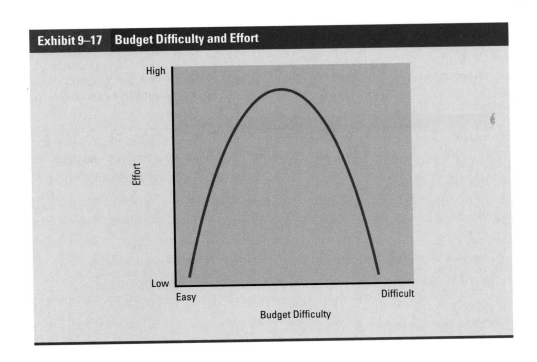

Exhibit 9–17   Budget Difficulty and Effort

Research by Merchant and Manzoni suggests that a highly achievable target, a target achievable by most managers 80 to 90 percent of the time, serves quite well in the vast majority of organizations, especially when accompanied by extra rewards for performance exceeding the target.[16] According to Merchant (1990), the advantages of using a highly achievable budget target include these:

1. Increasing managers' commitment to achieving the budget target.
2. Maintaining managers' confidence in the budget.
3. Decreasing organizational control cost.
4. Reducing the risk that managers will engage in harmful earnings management practices or violate corporate ethical standards. Twenty-nine percent of workers responding to a survey felt pressure to violate the ethical standards of their firms because of overly aggressive business goals.[17]
5. Allowing effective and efficient managers greater operating flexibility.
6. Improving predictability of earnings or operating results.
7. Enhancing the usefulness of a budget as a planning and coordinating tool.

One risk of using highly achievable budgets is that some managers, especially those who are not highly motivated, might not be challenged enough to put forth their maximum performance. Merchant, however, points out that this problem might not be significant because most profit center managers are already highly motivated. Most have risen through the ranks because they perform well and have strong competitive and self-satisfaction drives. More likely than not, profit center managers will continue at the same pace even after they have attained the budget targets. To ensure that managers do not slack off once they have achieved the budget target, some firms provide bonuses for performance exceeding the budget target.

Authoritative or Participative Budgeting

Budgeting processes are either top down or bottom up. In a top-down budgeting process, top management prepares budgets for the entire organization, including those for lower-level operations. This process often is referred to as *authoritative budgeting*. A *participative budgeting* process, on the other hand, is a bottom-up approach that involves the people affected by the budget, including lower-level employees, in the budget preparation process.

Authoritative budgeting provides better decision-making control than does participative budgeting. Top management sets the overall goals for the budget period and prepares a budget for operations to attain the goals. An authoritative budget, however, often lacks the commitment of lower-level managers and employees responsible for implementing it. Furthermore, an authoritative budget does not communicate; it issues or dictates orders. People are likely to resent orders but are more willing to devote extra effort to attain goals they perceive as their own.

A participative budget is a good communication device. The process of preparing it often gives top management a better grasp of the problems their employees face and provides the employees a better understanding of the dilemmas that top management deals with. A participative budget is more likely to gain the employees' commitment to fulfill the budgetary goals.

Unless properly controlled, however, a participative budget can lead to easy budget targets or targets not in compliance with the organization's strategy or budget.

---

[16] Kenneth A. Merchant, "How Challenging Should Profit Budget Targets Be?" *Management Accounting*, November 1990, pp. 46–48; Kenneth A. Merchant, *Rewarding Results: Motivating Profit Center Managers* (Cambridge, MA: Harvard Business School Press, 1989); and Kenneth A. Merchant and J. Manzoni, "The Achievability of Budget Targets in Profit Centers: A Field Study," *The Accounting Review*, July 1989, pp. 539–58.

[17] *The Wall Street Journal*, March 10, 1995, p. A2.

COST MANAGEMENT IN ACTION

What's Wrong with the Budget Process?

A recent survey of Chief Financial Officers (CFOs) by PricewaterhouseCoopers shows that 74 percent of these executives feel that the master budget has one of the highest priorities in the coming years. On a 5-point scale to rank importance, the executives scored the master budget as 4.1. Unfortunately, the executives also reported that the master budget was poorly implemented at their firms (an average score of 2.1 out of 5). Those writing up the study also noted that, for example, Jack Welch, CEO of General Electric, has called the master budget the "bane of corporate America." What are some of the implementation problems these CFOs are concerned about, and how do you think they might address these problems?

An effective budgeting process therefore usually combines both top-down and bottom-up budgeting approaches. Divisions prepare their initial budgets based on the budget guidelines issued by the firm's budget committee. Senior managers review and make suggestions to the proposed budget before sending it back to the divisions for revisions. The final budget usually results from more participation, not enforced negotiations.

Top Management Involvement

To what extent and in what way(s) should top management be involved in budgeting? The answer is complex. For a budget to be effective, top management must be involved and show strong interest in the budget results. Too much involvement, however, can make the budget an authoritative budget and alienate lower managers. The right approach is a good balance of top management involvement with lower-level managers.

The budget review and approval process ensures top management that budget guidelines are being followed. Top management's active involvement in reviewing and approving the proposed budget is an effective way to discourage lower-level managers from playing budget games.[18] The active involvement of top management also motivates lower managers to believe in the budget, be candid in its preparation, and be dedicated to attaining its goals because they know that the boss cares about the budget.

Role of the Budget Department or Controller

The budget department, and in some organizations the controller, stays active throughout the entire budget preparation process examining the accuracy of data in the budget and analyzing it for consistency, and conformity with the organization's budget guidelines and goals. The budget department provides the technicians who put the budget together.

Unfortunately, many of the tasks that the budget department must perform are perceived as negative. At times, budget departments must point out budget slack, excessive inventory, inefficient operations, and other potential problems in budgets. These certainly are not easy tasks, yet they are necessary if a firm is to have an efficient and effective budget for its operations.

Staff members in the budget department should be good communicators. They also must earn a reputation for being fair and impartial and for having personal integrity. A person who possesses such characteristics can offer much as an effective facilitator and coordinator of budgeting.

---

[18] Hofstede examines several budget games that people play. Among them are submitting budgets with easy targets and adding slack to a budget. For details see G. H. Hofstede, *The Game of Budget Control* (New York: Barnes & Noble, 1968).

SUMMARY

An organization's budget is a quantitative plan that identifies the resources and commitments required to fulfill its goal for the budget period. Budget preparation allows management to plan ahead, communicate the plan and goals for the budget period to all divisions, and motivate employees by involving them in setting up plans. A budget also serves as the blueprint for operations, a guideline for controlling operations, and a basis for performance evaluation.

Strategy helps a firm to be more focused in its operations and to take advantage of its strengths and opportunities. A firm carries out its strategy through long-range plans and master budgets. Strategy provides the framework within which the long-range plan is developed. Both strategy and the long-range plan are the starting points in preparing the annual master budget. A successful budget is accepted and supported by the key management. It becomes a personalized budget for the people responsible for implementing the budget; they perceive it as a tool to help them to do a better job, not as a pressure device. A successful budget is also a motivating device and must be technically accurate.

Budgeting processes include the formation of a budget committee; determination of the budget period; specification of budget guidelines; preparation of the initial budget proposal; budget negotiation, review, and approval; and budget revision. The budget committee usually consists of key senior managers; its job is to oversee all budget matters. The committee issues budget guidelines based on plans that rely on the firm's strategy, external and internal factors, and experience gained from implementing the current budget. Based on the budget guidelines, managers of responsibility centers prepare initial budgets and then discuss and negotiate their budget proposals with superiors. The budget committee or the chief executive officer gives final approval of the budget.

The master budget includes sales, production, direct materials, direct labor, factory overhead, selling, and administration expense budgets, and the budgeted cash statement, income statement, and balance sheet.

A service firm prepares a budget following set procedures just as a manufacturing or merchandising firm does. A major difference between budgets for service firms and those for manufacturing or merchandising firms is the absence of a production budget or merchandise purchase budget and its ancillary budgets for service firms. The budgeting procedures and all other budget items are the same for both service and manufacturing or merchandising firms. A service firm must carefully plan its activities for securing the required resources, frequently focusing on the labor force to render the planned services to fulfill the budgeted sales. A budget for a not-for-profit organization often becomes an authorization for its operating activities.

A multinational company should carefully consider in its budget such issues as cultural and language differences, dissimilar political and legal environments, fluctuating monetary exchange rates, and discrepancies in inflation rates of different countries.

Zero-base budgeting requires managers to justify the need for their divisions to engage in any activities to be included in the budget. Activity-based budgeting focuses on the costs of activities or cost drivers to carry out operations. The final budget thus reflects the budget costs of performing various activities. Kaizen budgeting prepares budgets on the basis of operations that are improvements over current practices.

Ethical issues in budgeting include not revealing all information to avoid accepting a higher budget goal, inclusion of budget slack, and spending the budget to avoid having it cut back. Behavioral issues in budgeting encompass the difficulty level of budget targets, drawbacks and advantages of authoritative and participative budgeting processes, the extent of involvement of top management in budgeting, and the role of the budget department or controller in budgeting.

KEY TERMS

COMMENTS ON MANAGEMENT IN ACTION

How to Improve the Budget Process: Warner Lambert, General Electric, and Kmart

A recent survey of CFOs shows that many firms, while they are convinced of the importance of the master budget, are not satisfied with the budget process in their firms. Here are some of the issues the CFOs identify for improvement.

1. Many firms have a budget process that is bottom-up—department managers initiate the process by preparing detailed budgets that are reviewed by top management. Some firms find that a top-down approach is preferable because it places a greater focus on the strategic plans developed by top management and because it is faster and more flexible to execute. Most importantly, it can be more difficult to integrate strategy into the budget process when it has a bottom-up focus. General Electric, in particular, insists that strategic thinking must be integrated throughout the budget process.

2. Many firms use the annual budget process that is not updated for changes during the year. Firms using this approach are not prepared for market and operating changes that require fast response and perhaps a change in strategy. In response, Johnson & Johnson, General Electric, Roche, and other firms use the continuous budget that requires frequent updates of forecasts and re-assessment of competitive factors throughout the year.

3. At some firms there is a problem in that financial managers are not effective in communicating the importance and the benefits of the master budget to department heads. This means that the budget is not fully and properly utilized. Firms like Warner Lambert, General Electric, and Kmart work hard to make sure that financial managers working on the budget are effective at supporting the department heads, and that the budget process is understood and valued throughout the firm.

Source: "Power Planning: An Integrated Business Planning Process," by Richard Harborne, *Strategic Finance*, October 1999, pp. 47–53.

SELF-STUDY PROBLEMS

(For solutions, please turn to the end of the chapter)

1. MASTER BUDGET

Hansell Company's management wants to prepare budgets for one of its products, duraflex, for July 2002. The firm sells the product for $40 per unit and has the following expected sales units for these months in 2002:

April	May	June	July	August	September
5,000	5,400	5,500	6,000	7,000	8,000

The production process requires 4 pounds of dura–1000 and 2 pounds of flexplas. The firm's policy is to maintain a minimum of 100 units of duraflex on hand at all times with no fewer than 10 percent of units on hand at the end of a period to meet the expected sales for the following month. All materials inventories are to be maintained at 5 percent of the production needs for the next month, but not to exceed 1,000 pounds. The firm expects all inventories at the end of June to be within the guidelines. The purchase department expects the materials to cost $1.25 per pound and $5.00 per pound of dura–1000 and flexplas, respectively.

The production process requires direct labor at two skill levels. The rate for labor at the K102 level is $50 per hour and for the K175 level is $20 per hour. The K102 level can process one batch of duraflex per hour; each batch consists of 100 units. The manufacturing of duraflex also requires one-tenth of an hour of K175 workers' time for each unit manufactured.

Manufactured overhead is allocated at the rate of $200 per batch and $30 per direct labor-hour.

Required   On the basis of the preceding data and projections, prepare the following budgets for July 2002:

a.   Sales budget (in dollars).

b.   Production budget (in units).

c.   Production budget for August (in units).

d.   Direct materials purchase budget (in pounds).

e.   Direct materials purchase budget (in dollars).

f.   Direct manufacturing labor budget (in dollars).

2. CASH BUDGET AND INCOME STATEMENT

Hansell Company expects its trial balance on June 30 to be as follows:

HANSELL COMPANY
Budget Trial Balance
June 30, 2002

	Debit	Credit
Cash	$ 10,000	
Accounts receivable	80,000	
Allowance for bad debts		$ 3,500
Inventory	25,000	
Plants, property, and equipment	650,000	
Accumulated depreciation		320,000
Accounts payable		95,000
Wages and salaries payable		24,000
Note payable		200,000
Stockholders' equity		122,500
Total	$765,000	$765,000

Typically, cash sales represent 20 percent of sales and credit sales represent 80 percent. Sales terms are 2/10, n/30. Hansell bills customers on the first day of each month. Experience has shown that 60 percent of the billings will be collected within the discount period, 25 percent by the end of the month after sales, 10 percent by the end of the second month after the sale, and 5 percent will be uncollectible. The firm writes off uncollectible accounts after 12 months.

The term of purchases for materials is 2/15, n/60. The firm makes all payments within the discount period. Experience has shown that 80 percent of the purchases are paid in the month of the purchase and the remainder are paid in the month immediately following. In June 2002, the firm budgeted purchases of $25,000 for dura–1000 and $22,000 for flexplas.

Sixty percent of the factory overhead is variable. The firm has a monthly fixed factory overhead of $50,000, of which $20,000 is depreciation expense. The firm pays all manufacturing labor and factory overhead when incurred.

Total budgeted marketing, distribution, customer service, and administrative costs for 2002 are $600,000. Of this amount, $270,000 is considered fixed and includes depreciation expenses of $150,000. The remainder varies with sales. The budgeted total sales for 2002 are $2 million. All marketing and administrative costs are paid in the month incurred.

Management desires to maintain a minimum cash balance of $40,000. The firm has an agreement with a local bank to borrow its short-term needs in multiples of $1,000 up to $100,000 at an interest rate of 12 percent.

Required

1. Prepare the cash budget for July 2002.
2. Prepare the budget income statement for July 2002.

QUESTIONS

9–1 What is a budget?

9–2 What roles do budgets play in operations?

9–3 Explain the difference between strategic plans and a master budget.

9–4 What are the relationships between master and capital budgets?

9–5 What are a master budget, an operating budget, and a financial budget?

9–6 List some common characteristics of successful budgets.

9–7 What are the primary roles of a budget committee?

9–8 What is the difference between a sales forecast and a sales budget? What is the role of sales forecasting in budgeting?

9–9 The sales budget is the cornerstone of a budget. Do you agree?

9–10 When sales volume is seasonal in nature, certain items in the budget must be coordinated. What are the three most significant items to coordinate in budgeting seasonal sales volume?

(CMA Adapted)

9–11 After completing its sales budget for the budget period, what additional factors does the firm need to consider to complete the materials purchase budget?

9–12 Which two factors determine the amount of factory overhead?

(CMA Adapted)

9–13 What are the major components of a cash budget?

9–14 What are similarities and differences between cash budgets and cash flow statements required for external financial reporting?

9–15 Contrast the budgeting considerations for service organizations and manufacturing companies.

9–16 What are the major differences in the preparation and uses of budgets for a business firm and a not-for-profit organization?

9–17 What is zero-base budgeting?

9–18 Is kaizen budgeting the Japanese term for activity-based budgeting?

9–19 What is slack in a budget? Why is it not unusual to find slack in budgets?

9–20 What is a highly achievable budget? Why do firms prefer such a budget?

9–21 What is the role of top management in participative budgeting?

9–22 Kallert Manufacturing currently uses the company's budget only as a planning tool. Management has decided that it would be beneficial also to use the budget for control purposes. What must the management accountant do for the firm's budgeting and accounting systems to implement this change successfully?

(CMA Adapted)

9–23 Unless Janet DeVolris can find a better way to do her job and ease the constant job pressure she has felt since becoming the purchasing manager of Corkin Manufacturing, a small Midwest manufacturer of specialty tools, she does not think she can last much longer with the firm. Rush orders, last-minute changes, and other operating emergencies seem to be the firm's way of life. One thing she vowed to do differently from her predecessor was not to use expensive overnight services. After six months, she believes that she has relied on overnight shipping even more heavily.

At a recent convention, several suppliers mentioned that Janet's firm rarely takes advantage of the discount terms she worked so hard for them to grant. She was very surprised because the 2/10, n/30 discount terms or better are very good.

Tony Blair, the firm's CEO, recently praised Janet lavishly for her performance for the last six months and gave her a generous raise. Still, she feels frustrated and unfulfilled.

What could Janet do to overcome her frustration?

9–24 Bob Bingham is the controller of Atlantis Laboratories, a manufacturer and distributor of generic prescription pharmaceuticals. He is currently preparing the annual budget and reviewing the current business plan. The firm's business unit managers prepare and assemble the detailed operating budgets with technical assistance from the corporate accounting staff. The business unit managers then present the final budgets to the corporate executive committee for approval. The corporate accounting staff reviews the budget for adherence to corporate accounting policies but not for reasonableness of the line items within the budget.

Bob is aware that the upcoming year for Atlantis could be a difficult one because of a major patent expiration and the loss of a licensing agreement for another product line. He also knows that during the budgeting process, budget slack is created in varying degrees throughout the organization. Bob believes that this slack has a negative effect on the firm's overall business objectives and should be eliminated where possible.

Required

1. Define *budget slack*.

2. Explain the advantages and disadvantages of budget slack from the point of view of (a) the business unit manager who must achieve the budget and (b) corporate management.

3. Bob Bingham is considering implementing zero-base budgeting at Atlantis Laboratories.

   a. Define *zero-base budgeting*.

   b. Describe how *zero-base budgeting* could be advantageous to Atlantis Laboratories in controlling budgetary slack.

   c. Discuss the disadvantages Atlantis Laboratories might encounter in using zero-base budgeting.

(CMA Adapted)

EXERCISES

9–25 AMOUNT OF RAW MATERIALS TO PURCHASE Willard Company is budgeting sales of 100,000 units of its model GS30 small generator for the month of September. Production of one unit of GS30 requires 2 pounds of aluminum and 3 pounds of alloy. The beginning inventory and the desired ending inventory are as follows:

	Beginning Inventory	Desired Ending Inventory
GS30	20,000 units	10,000 units
Aluminum	25,000 pounds	18,000 pounds
Alloy	22,000 pounds	24,000 pounds

Required How many pounds of aluminum and alloy is Willard Company planning to purchase during September?

9–26 PRODUCTION BUDGET Merhendra Company's sales budget shows these projections for the year 2002:

Quarter	Units
First	60,000
Second	80,000
Third	45,000
Fourth	55,000
	240,000

Inventory on December 31, 2001, was budgeted at 18,000 units. The amount of finished goods inventory at the end of each quarter is to equal 30 percent of the next quarter's budgeted sales of units.

Required Determine the number of units to produce for the first two quarters of 2002.

9–27 PRODUCTION BUDGET Shocker Company's sales budget shows quarterly sales for the next year:

Quarter 1	10,000 units
Quarter 2	8,000 units
Quarter 3	12,000 units
Quarter 4	14,000 units

Company policy is to have a finished goods inventory at the end of each quarter equal to 20 percent of the next quarter's sales.

Required What is the budgeted production for the second quarter of the next year?

(CMA Adapted)

9–28 PRODUCTION AND MATERIALS PURCHASE BUDGETS DeVaris Corporation's budget calls for the following sales for next year:

Quarter 1	45,000 units
Quarter 2	38,000 units
Quarter 3	34,000 units
Quarter 4	48,000 units

Each unit of the product requires 3 pounds of direct material. The company's policy is to begin each quarter with an inventory of the product equal to 10 percent of that quarter's sales requirements and an inventory of direct materials equal to 20 percent of that quarter's direct materials requirements for productions.

Required   How many units of the product and how many pounds of direct material are included in the production for the second quarter?

9–29 PRODUCTION AND MATERIALS BUDGETS   Paradise Company budgets on an annual basis. The planned beginning and ending inventory levels (in units) for the fiscal year of July 1, 2002, through June 30, 2003, are as follows:

	July 1, 2002	June 30, 2003
Raw material*	40,000	50,000
Work in process	10,000	20,000
Finished goods	80,000	50,000

*Two units of raw material are needed to produce each unit of finished products. All materials are added at the beginning of production.

Required

1. How many units must Paradise Company manufacture if it plans to sell 480,000 units during the 2002–2003 fiscal year?

2. How many units of raw material must it purchase if Paradise plans to manufacture 500,000 finished units during the 2002–2003 fiscal year?

(CMA Adapted)

9–30 CASH BUDGET   Carla Inc. has the following budget data for 2001:

Cash balance, beginning	$ 20,000
Collections from customers	150,000
Expenses	
Direct materials purchases	25,000
Operating expenses	50,000
Payroll	75,000
Income taxes	6,000
Machinery purchases	30,000
Minimum cash balance desired	20,000

Operating expenses include $20,000 depreciation for buildings and equipment and cash expenditures of $30,000.

Required   Compute the cash financing needs or excess cash available to invest.

9–31 ESTIMATED CASH COLLECTIONS   Ishikawa Corporation is preparing its cash budget for the month of May. The following information is available concerning its accounts receivable:

Estimated credit sales for May	$200,000
Actual credit sales for April	150,000
Estimated collections in May	
For credit sales in May	25%
For credit sales in April	70%
For credit sales prior to April	$ 16,000
Estimated write-offs in May for uncollectible accounts	8,000
Estimated provision for bad debts in May due to credit sales that month	7,000

Required   What are the estimated cash receipts from accounts receivable collections in May?

(CPA Adapted)

9–32 CASH BUDGET Information pertaining to Noskey Corporation's sales revenue includes this:

	November 2002 (Actual)	December 2002 (Budget)	January 2003 (Budget)
Cash sales	$ 80,000	$100,000	$ 60,000
Credit sales	240,000	360,000	180,000
Total sales	$320,000	$460,000	$240,000

Management estimates 5 percent of credit sales to be uncollectible. Of collectible credit sales, 60 percent is collected in the month of sale and the remainder in the month following the sale. Purchases of inventory each month are 70 percent of the next month's projected total sales. Additional units are purchased in the month of sales to meet sales needs. All inventory purchases are on account; 25 percent are paid in the month of purchase, and the remainders is paid in the month following the purchase. The purchase costs are approximately 60 percent of the selling prices.

Required Determine for Noskey

1. Budgeted cash collections in December 2002 from November 2002 credit sales.
2. Budgeted total cash receipts in January 2003.
3. Budgeted total cash payments in December 2002 for inventory purchases.

(CPA Adapted)

9–33 CASH COLLECTION Esplanade Company has the following historical pattern on its credit sales:

70 percent collected in the month of sale.

15 percent collected in the first month after sale.

10 percent collected in the second month after sale.

4 percent collected in the third month after sale.

1 percent uncollectible.

These sales on open account (credit sales) have been budgeted for the last six months of 2002:

July	$ 60,000
August	70,000
September	80,000
October	90,000
November	100,000
December	85,000

Required

1. Determine the estimated total cash collections from accounts receivable during October 2002.
2. Compute the estimated total cash collections during the fourth quarter from credit sales of the fourth quarter.

(CMA Adapted)

9–34 COLLECTION OF ACCOUNTS RECEIVABLE Doreen Company is preparing its cash budget for the month of May. The following information is available concerning its accounts receivable:

Actual credit sales for March	$120,000
Actual credit sales for April	$150,000
Estimated credit sales for May	$200,000
Estimated collections in the month of sale	25%
Estimated collections in the first month after the month of sale	60%
Estimated collections in the second month after the month of sale	10%
Estimated provision for bad debts in the month of sale	5%

The firm writes off all uncollectible accounts at the end of the second month after the month of sale.

Required Determine for Doreen Company for the month of May

1. The estimated cash receipts from accounts receivable collections.
2. The gross amount of accounts receivable at the end of the month.
3. The net amount of accounts receivable at the end of the month.

PROBLEMS

9–35 PURCHASE AND CASH BUDGET D. Tomlinson Retail seeks your assistance in developing cash and other budget information for May, June, and July. At April 30, the company will have cash of $5,500, accounts receivable of $437,000, inventories of $309,400, and accounts payable of $133,055. The budget is to be based on these assumptions:

- **Sales.** Each month's sales are billed on the last day of the month. Customers are allowed a 3 percent discount if payment is made within 10 days after the billing date. Receivables are booked gross; 60 percent of the billings is collected within the discount period; 25 percent is collected by the end of the month; 9 percent is collected by the end of the second month; and 6 percent is likely to be uncollectible.

- **Purchases.** Fifty-four percent of all purchases of material and selling and general administrative expenses is paid in the month purchased and the remainder in the following month. Each month's units of ending inventory equal 130 percent of the next month's units of sales. The cost of each unit of inventory is $20. Selling and general and administrative expenses, of which $2,000 is depreciation, equal 15 percent of the current month's sales.

Actual and projected sales follow:

	Dollars	Units
March	$354,000	11,800
April	363,000	12,100
May	357,000	11,900
June	342,000	11,400
July	360,000	12,000
August	366,000	12,200

Required

1. Determine the budgeted purchases for May and June.
2. Determine the budgeted cash disbursements during June.
3. Determine the budgeted cash collections during May.

(CMA Adapted)

9–36 CASH BUDGET   HyVic Corporation is a retailer that makes all sales on credit. It bills sales twice monthly, on the 10th of the month for the last half of the prior month's sales, and on the 20th of the month for the first half of the current month's sales. The terms of all sales are 2/10, net/30. Based on past experience, accounts receivable are collected as follows:

Within the discount period	80%
On the 30th day	18
Uncollectible	2

HyVic's average markup on its products is 20 percent of the sales price. All sales and purchases occur uniformly throughout the month.

The sales value of shipments for May and the forecasts for the next four months follow:

	Revenues
May (actual)	$500,000
June	600,000
July	700,000
August	800,000
September	400,000

HyVic purchases merchandise for resale to meet the current month's sales demand and to maintain a desired monthly ending inventory of 25 percent of the next month's sales. All purchases are on credit with terms of net/30. HyVic pays for 40 percent of a month's purchases in the month of purchase and 60 percent in the month following the purchase.

Required

1. How much cash can HyVic plan to collect in September from sales made in August?

2. What is the budgeted dollar value of inventory on August 31?

3. How much cash can HyVic plan to collect from accounts receivable collections during July?

4. Determine how much merchandise the firm should purchase during June.

5. Determine the amount that the firm should budget in August for the payment of merchandise.

(CMA Adapted)

9–37 CASH BUDGET   Riley Instruments, a rapidly expanding electronic parts distributor, is in the process of formulating plans for 2002. Samantha Carlson, the firm's director of marketing, has completed her 2002 forecast and is confident that sales estimates will be met or exceeded. The following show the expected growth and provide the planning basis for the other corporate departments:

Forecasted Month	Forecasted Sales	Forecasted Month	Forecasted Sales
January	$1,800,000	July	$3,000,000
February	2,000,000	August	3,000,000
March	1,800,000	September	3,200,000
April	2,200,000	October	3,200,000
May	2,500,000	November	3,000,000
June	2,800,000	December	3,400,000

Bill Stockton, assistant controller, has been given the responsibility to formulate the cash flow projection, a critical element during a period of rapid expansion. The following information can be used in preparing the cash analysis:

- Riley has experienced an excellent record in accounts receivable collection and expects this trend to continue. Sixty percent of its billings are collected in the month after the sale and 40 percent in the second month after the sale. Uncollectible accounts are nominal and will not be considered in the analysis.

- The purchase of electronic parts is Riley's largest expenditure; the cost of these items equals 50 percent of sales. Riley receives sixty percent of the parts one month prior to sale and 40 percent during the month of sale.

- Historically, Riley has cleared 80 percent of accounts payable one month after receipt of purchased parts and has cleared the remaining 20 percent two months after receipt of purchased parts.

- Hourly wages, including fringe benefits, are a factor of sales volume and equal 20 percent of the current month's sales. These wages are paid in the month incurred.

- Selling and general administrative expenses are projected to be $2,640,000 for 2002. The composition of these expenses follows. All are incurred uniformly throughout the year except the property taxes, which are paid in four equal installments in the last month of each quarter.

Salaries	$ 480,000
Promotion	660,000
Property taxes	240,000
Insurance	360,000
Utilities	300,000
Depreciation	600,000
	$2,640,000

- Riley makes income tax payments in the first month of each quarter based on the income for the prior quarter. The firm is subject to an effective income tax rate of 40 percent. Riley's net income after taxes for the first quarter of 2002 is projected to be $612,000.

- Riley has a corporate policy to maintain an end-of-month cash balance of $100,000. Cash is invested or borrowed monthly, as necessary, to maintain this balance.

- Riley uses a calendar-year reporting period.

Required

1. Prepare a pro forma schedule of cash receipts and disbursements for Riley Instruments by month for the second quarter of 2002. Be sure that all receipts, disbursements, and borrowing/investing are presented on a monthly basis. Ignore the interest expense and/or income associated with borrowing/investing.

2. Discuss why cash budgeting is particularly important for a rapidly expanding company such as Riley Instruments.

(CMA Adapted)

9–38 **DIRECT MATERIALS PURCHASES BUDGET AND PAYMENT SCHEDULE** Press Company manufactures and sells industrial components. Its Whitmore Plant is responsible for producing AD–5 and FX–3. Plastic, brass, and aluminum are used in the production of these two products.

Press Company had adopted a 13-period reporting cycle in all of its plants for budgeting purposes. Each period is four weeks long and has 20 working days. The projected inventory levels for AD–5 and FX–3 at the end of the current (seventh) period and the projected sales for these two products for the next three four-week periods follow:

	Projected Inventory Level (in units)	Projected Sales (in units)		
	End of Seventh Period	**Eighth Period**	**Ninth Period**	**Tenth Period**
AD–5	3,000	7,500	8,750	9,500
FX–3	2,800	7,000	4,500	4,000

Past experience has shown that adequate inventory levels for AD–5 and FX–3 can be maintained if 40 percent of the next period's projected sales are on hand at the end of a reporting period. Based on this experience and the projected sales, the Whitmore Plant has budgeted production of 8,000 AD–5 and 6,000 FX–3 in the eighth period. Production is assumed to be uniform for both products within each four-week period.

The raw materials specifications for AD–5 and FX–3 follow:

	AD–5	**FX–3**
Plastic	2.0 lb.	1.0 lb
Brass	0.5 lb.	—
Aluminum	—	1.5 lb

Sales of AD–5 and FX–3 do not vary significantly from month to month. Consequently, the safety stock incorporated into the reorder point for each raw material is adequate to compensate for variations in the sale of the finished products.

Raw materials orders are placed the day the amount on hand falls below the reorder point. Whitmore Plant's suppliers are very dependable, so the given lead times are reliable. The outstanding orders for plastic and aluminum are due to arrive on the tenth and fourth work days of the eighth period, respectively. Payments for all raw materials orders are remitted in the period of delivery. Purchase data and raw materials inventory status follow:

	Standard Purchase Price per Pound	**Purchase Lot (in pounds)**	**Reorder Point (in pounds)**	Projected Inventory Status at the End of the Seventh Period (in pounds)		**Lead Time in Working Days**
				On Hand	**On Order**	
Plastic	$0.40	15,000	12,000	16,000	15,000	10
Brass	0.95	5,000	7,500	9,000	—	30
Aluminum	0.55	10,000	10,000	14,000	10,000	20

Required The Whitmore Plant is required to submit a report to Press Company's corporate headquarters summarizing the projected raw materials activities before each period commences. The data for the eighth period report are being assembled. Determine the following items for plastic, brass, and aluminum for inclusion in the eighth-period report:

1. Projected quantities (in pounds) of each raw material to be issued to production.

2. Projected quantities (in pounds) of each raw material ordered and the date (in work days) the order is to be placed.

3. The projected uses and balance (in pounds) of each raw material at the end of the period.

4. The payments for purchases of each raw material.

(CMA Adapted)

Strategy

9–39 BUDGET REVISION   Mark Dalid founded Molid Company three years ago. The company produces a modulation-demodulation unit (modem) that Mark and several of the firm's major stockholders developed for use with minicomputers and microcomputers. The modem can transmit three times faster than other compatible products. Business has expanded rapidly since the company's inception.

Bob Wells, the company's general accountant, prepared a budget for the fiscal year ending August 31, 2002, based on the prior year's sales and production activity because Mark believes that the sales growth experienced during the prior year will not continue at the same pace. The pro forma statements of income and cost of goods sold prepared as part of the budget process follow:

Pro Forma Statement of Income (in thousands)

Net sales		$31,248
Cost of goods sold		20,765
Gross profit		$10,483
Operating expenses		
Selling	$3,200	
General administrative	2,200	5,400
Income from operations before income taxes		$ 5,083

Pro Forma Statement of Cost of Goods Sold (in thousands)

Direct materials		
Materials inventory, 9/1/2001	$ 1,360	
Materials purchases	14,476	
Materials available for use	15,836	
Materials inventory, 8/31/2002	1,628	
Direct materials consumed		$14,208
Direct labor		1,134
Factory overhead		
Indirect materials	$ 1,421	
General factory overhead	3,240	4,661
Cost of goods manufactured		$20,003
Finished goods inventory, 9/1/2001		1,169
Cost of goods available for sale		$21,172
Finished goods inventory, 8/31/2002		407
Cost of goods sold		$20,765

On December 10, 2001, Mark and Bob met to discuss the first quarter operating results (i.e., results for the period September 1–November 30, 2001). Bob believed that several changes should be made to the original budget assumptions that had been used to prepare the pro forma statements. He prepared the following notes that summarized the changes that had not become known until the first quarter results had been compiled. He submitted the following data to Mark:

a. The estimated production in units for the fiscal year should be revised upward from 162,000 units to 170,000 units with the balance of production being scheduled in equal segments over the last nine months of the fiscal year. Actual first quarter production was 35,000 units.

b. The planned ending inventory for finished goods of 3,300 units at the end of the fiscal year remains unchanged. The finished goods inventory of 9,300 units as of September 1, 2001, had dropped to 9,000 units by November 31, 2001. The finished goods inventory at the end of the fiscal year will be valued at the average manufacturing cost for the year.

c. The direct labor rate will increase 8 percent as of June 1, 2002, as a consequence of a new labor agreement signed during the first quarter. When the original pro forma statements were prepared, the expected effective date for this new labor agreement had been September 1, 2002.

d. Direct materials sufficient to produce 16,000 units were on hand at the beginning of the fiscal year. The plans for direct materials inventory to contain 18,500 units of production at the end of the fiscal year remain unchanged. Direct materials inventory is valued on a first-in, first-out basis. Direct materials equivalent to 37,500 units of output were purchased for $3,300,000 during the first quarter of the fiscal year.

   Molid's suppliers have informed the company that direct materials prices will increase 5 percent on March 1, 2002. Direct materials needed for the rest of the fiscal year will be purchased evenly through the last nine months.

e. On the basis of historical data, indirect materials cost is projected at 10 percent of the cost of direct materials consumed.

f. One-half of general factory overhead and all of selling and general administrative expenses are considered fixed.

After an extended discussion, Dalid asked for new pro forma statements for the fiscal year ending August 31, 2002.

Required

1. Based on the revised data that Bob presented, calculate Molid Company's sales for the year ending August 31, 2002, in (a) number of units to be sold and (b) dollar volume of net sales.

2. Prepare the pro forma statement of cost of goods sold for the year ending August 31, 2002, that Mark Dalid has requested.

3. Bob suggests that the firm should adopt a JIT strategy to better serve customers and to reduce obsolescence costs. He points out that the firm needs to incorporate new manufacturing technologies to maintain its competitive advantage. Mark is reluctant to make changes because he does not want to upset the proven successful business. He knows that any changes cost money, and he does not want to commit fresh capital just to change the business procedures. Bob argues that no additional capital will be needed to fund the changes. He points out that a JIT system maintains no finished goods inventory and no more than the materials needed to produce 100 units of the finished products.

   a. How much will the firm save by changing to a JIT system?

   b. Should the firm follow Bob's suggestion?

   c. What other factors should be considered in making the decision?

(CMA Adapted)

9–40 VARIABLE COSTING PRO FORMA FINANCIAL STATEMENTS Jacqueline Stern is a successful investor whose specialty is revitalizing failed businesses. Her goal is to maximize her profits within the limits of the careful use of external financing, which usually means limiting growth rates and forgoing some potential profit. She believes that this is the key to her success and that unlimited growth

Strategy

can easily lead to fatal financing problems. Jacqueline is once again set to test her approach.

Five years ago, Robert West perfected a technique for joining the edges of laminated plastic parts so that their subsurface layers were not visible. Since subsurface layers are a different color than the surface layer, his edges greatly improved the appearance of the finished product. Robert then designed equipment to use in large-volume production of the edges. His product was unique, and sales and production levels grew rapidly. Rapid growth, however, soon exceeded Robert's ability to manage the firm and to obtain financing. A few months ago, his firm closed, leaving a regional bank holding the plant, equipment, and some inventory.

Jacqueline believes that the product has sales and profit potential and has offered the bank $400,000 in cash plus assumption of the loan for the plant, equipment, and inventory. The bank was only too happy to accept her offer.

Jacqueline has established Edge Company to which she has contributed the acquired assets and $450,000 in cash. Edge Company's statement of financial position at the start of business follows:

THE EDGE COMPANY INC.
Statement of Financial Position
as of January 1, 2003
(in thousands)

Assets	
Cash	$ 450
Accounts receivable	0
Inventory	100
Plant and equipment	2,000
Total assets	$2,550
Liabilities and Equities	
Accounts payable	$ 0
Current portion of long-term debt	90
Long-term debt	1,610
Common stock (no par value)	850
Retained earnings	0
Total liabilities and equities	$2,550

To implement her goal of making conservative use of external financing, Jacqueline has established these financial objectives:

- Paying no dividends, thus keeping all cash generated within the company.

- Issuing no additional capital stock.

- Incurring no new long-term debt while paying $90,000 annually to service current interest and $90,000 of principal annually on the existing bank loan.

- Keeping the cash balance at no less than $50,000.

- Taking advantage of supplier credit but not allowing accounts payable to exceed $100,000.

The bank's loan officer had commented that Robert was unable to control costs and working capital, and Jacqueline agreed. The existing plant and equipment have a capacity of $12,000,000 in annual sales and she plans to hold variable costs at 75 percent of sales to budget a lump sum of $500,000 per year for fixed costs, including both depreciation and interest. Depreciation of plant and equipment is $100,000 per year.

In making her plans, Jacqueline has used 20 percent as the average income tax rate applicable to Edge Company. Because some of the firms she acquires have been in income tax trouble, she makes a point of keeping tax payments current and aims to finish each year with no tax liability on the books.

Customers for products of this kind are notoriously slow payers; however, she is confident that accounts receivable can be kept at 15 percent of annual sales. She also believes that inventories can be maintained at 20 percent of annual variable costs.

Jacqueline has rehired some of Robert's former salespeople, and they believe that Edge Company's first-year sales could easily reach $5,000,000. She believes, however, that managing growth is the most important part of the plan and plans to limit first-year sales to $2,100,000.

Required

1. Determine whether Jacqueline Stern's financial objectives can be achieved by preparing a pro forma income statement in a variable (direct) costing format for the Edge Company for the year ending December 31, 2003, and a pro forma statement of financial position for the Edge Company as of December 31, 2003. Assume that her projections occur and sales are limited to $2,100,000.

2. Without regard to your answer in requirement 1, assume that the following results are from the company's first fiscal year ending December 31, 2003, and that Jacqueline's financial objectives were met.

   • Sales: $2,000,000
   • Net income: $0
   • Cash balance at December 31, 2003: $60,000
   • Accounts payable at December 31, 2003: $100,000
   • Net working capital at December 31, 2003: $470,000

   Compute the maximum amount by which Edge Company could increase dollar sales in its second year (ending December 31, 2004) and still achieve Jacqueline's financial objectives.

3. Do you agree with Jacqueline's strategy of limiting sales growth?

(CMA Adapted)

9–41 BUDGET FOR MERCHANDISE FIRM Kelly Company is a retail sporting goods store that uses accrual accounting for its records. Facts regarding its operations follow:

• Sales are budgeted at $220,000 for December and $200,000 for January, terms 1/EOM, n/60.

• Collections are expected to be 60 percent in the month of sale and 38 percent in the month following the sale. Two percent of sales is expected to be uncollectible and recorded at the end of the month of sales.

• Gross margin is 25 percent of sales.

• A total of 80 percent of the merchandise held for resale is purchased in the month prior to the month of sale, and 20 percent is purchased in the month of sale. Payment for merchandise is made in the month following the purchase.

• Other expected monthly expenses to be paid in cash total $22,600.

• Annual depreciation is $216,000.

Kelly Company's statement of financial position at the close of business on November 30 follows:

KELLY COMPANY
Statement of Financial Position
November 30, 2002

Assets

Cash	$ 22,000
Accounts receivable (net of $4,000 allowance for doubtful accounts)	76,000
Inventory	132,000
Property, plant, and equipment (net of $680,000 accumulated depreciation)	870,000
Total assets	$1,100,000

Liabilities and Stockholders' Equity

Accounts payable	$ 162,000
Common stock	800,000
Retained earnings	138,000
Total liabilities and equity	$1,100,000

Required

1. What is the total of budgeted cash collections for December?

2. How much is the book value of accounts receivables at the end of December?

3. How much is the net income (loss) before income taxes for December?

4. What is the projected balance in accounts payable on December 31, 2002?

5. What is the projected balance in inventory on December 31?

(CMA Adapted)

9–42 **MASTER BUDGET** SecCo manufactures and sells security systems. The company started by installing photoelectric security systems in existing offices and has since expanded into the private home market. SecCo has developed its basic security system into three standard products, each of which can be upgraded to meet the specific needs of customers. SecCo's manufacturing operation is moderate in size; the bulk of the component manufacturing is completed by independent contractors. The security systems are approximately 85 percent complete when SecCo receives them from contractors and require only final assembly in its own plant. Each product passes through at least one of three assembly operations.

SecCo operates in a community that is flourishing. Evidence indicates that a great deal of new commercial construction will take place in the near future, and SecCo's management has decided to pursue this new market. To be competitive, SecCo must expand its operations.

In view of the expected increase in business, Sandra Becker, SecCo's controller, believes that the company should implement a master budget system. She has decided to make a formal presentation to SecCo's president explaining the benefits of a master budget system and outlining the budget schedules and reports that would be required.

Required

1. Explain what benefits can be derived from implementing a master budget system.

2. If Sandra Becker is going to develop a master budget system for SecCo

   a. Identify, in order, the schedules and/or statements that must be prepared.

   b. Identify the subsequent schedules and/or statements to be derived from the schedules and statements identified in requirement 2a.

(CMA Adapted)

9–43 COMPREHENSIVE PROFIT PLAN Palms Manufacturing Company makes two basic products known as cee and dee. Data assembled by the managers follow:

	Cee	Dee
Requirements for finished unit		
Raw material 1	10 pounds	8 pounds
Raw material 2	0	4 pounds
Raw material 3	2 pounds	1 pound
Direct labor	5 hours	8 hours
Product information		
Sales price	$150	$220
Sales unit	12,000	9,000
Estimated beginning inventory	400	150
Desired ending inventory	300	200

	Raw Materials		
	1	2	3
Cost	$2.00	$2.50	$0.50
Estimated beginning inventory in pounds	3,000	1,500	1,000
Desired ending inventory in pounds	4,000	1,000	1,500

The direct labor wage rate is $10 per hour, overhead is applied on the basis of direct labor-hours. The income tax rate of the firm is 40 percent. The beginning inventory of finished products has the same cost per unit as the ending inventory; the work-in-process inventory is negligible.

Factory Overhead Information

Indirect materials	$ 10,000
Miscellaneous supplies and tools	5,000
Indirect labor	40,000
Supervision—fixed	80,000
Payroll taxes and fringe benefits	75,000
Maintenance costs—fixed	20,000
Maintenance costs—variable	10,000
Depreciation	70,000
Heat, light, and power—fixed	8,710
Heat, light, and power—variable	5,090
Total	$323,800

Selling and Administrative Expense Information

Advertising	$ 60,000
Sales salaries	200,000
Travel and entertainment	60,000
Depreciation—warehouse	5,000
Office salaries	60,000
Executive salaries	250,000
Supplies	4,000
Depreciation—office	6,000
Total	$645,000

Required Prepare the following:

1. Sales budget.
2. Production budget.
3. Raw materials purchase budget.

4. Direct labor budget.

5. Factory overhead budget.

6. Cost of goods sold budget with schedule of ending inventory.

7. Selling and general administrative expense budget.

8. Budget income statement.

(CMA Adapted)

9–44 **BUDGET INCOME STATEMENT** The *Metropolitan News,* a daily newspaper, serves a community of 100,000. The paper has a circulation of 40,000, with 32,000 copies delivered directly to subscribers. The rate schedule for the paper is as follows:

Single issue price: $0.75 daily; $3.00 Sunday

Weekly subscription: $7.00 (includes daily and Sunday)

The paper has experienced profitable operations as can be seen from the income statement for the year ended September 30, 2002 (in thousands):

Revenue			
Newspaper sales		$14,000	
Advertising sales		6,430	$20,430
Costs and expenses			
Personnel costs			
Commissions			
Carriers	$3,680		
Sales	1,220		
Advertising	643		
Salaries			
Administration	660		
Advertising	320		
Equipment operators	600		
Newsroom	1,740		
Employee benefits	498	$ 9,361	
Paper		4,830	
Other supplies		1,215	
Repairs		824	
Depreciation		680	
Property taxes		820	
Building rental		480	
Automobile leases		210	
Other		360	
Total costs and expenses			18,780
Income before income taxes			$ 1,650
Income taxes			495
Net income			$ 1,155

The Sunday edition usually has five times as many pages as the daily editions. Direct edition variable costs for 2002–2003 are shown here:

	Cost per Issue	
	Daily	**Sunday**
Paper	$0.30	$1.00
Other supplies	0.15	0.75
Carrier and sales commissions	0.25	0.75
	$0.60	$2.50

The company has scheduled the following changes in operations for the next year and anticipates some increased costs:

  a. The building lease expired on September 30, 2003, and has been renewed with a change in the rental fee provisions from a straight fee to a fixed fee of $300,000 plus 1 percent of newspaper sales.

  b. The advertising department will eliminate the 10 percent advertising commission on contracts sold on a contract basis in the past. The salaries of the four employees who solicited advertising will be raised from $50,000 each to $100,000 each.

  c. Automobiles will no longer be leased. Employees whose jobs require automobiles will use their own and be reimbursed at $0.50 per mile. The leased cars were driven 80,000 miles in 2002–2003, and employees will drive some 84,000 estimated miles next year on company business.

  d. Cost increases estimated for next year:

- Newsprint, $0.04 per daily issue and $0.20 for the Sunday paper
- Salaries:
  Equipment operators, 8 percent
  Other employees, 6 percent
- Employee benefits (from 15 percent of personnel costs excluding commissions to 20 percent), 5 percent

  e. Circulation increases of 5 percent in newsstands and home delivery are anticipated.

  f. Advertising revenue is estimated at $7,500,000 with $5,000,000 from employee-solicited contracts. The firm charges for advertising based on circulation volume.

Required

  1. Prepare a projected income statement for *Metropolitan News* for the 2002–2003 fiscal year using a format that shows the newspaper's total variable costs and total fixed costs (round calculations to the nearest thousand dollars).

  2. The management of *Metropolitan News* is contemplating one additional proposal for the 2002–2003 fiscal year: raising the rates for the newspaper to the following amounts:

    Single issue price: $1.00 daily; $4.00 Sunday

    Weekly subscription: $9.00 (includes daily and Sunday)

The company estimates that the newspaper's circulation will decline to 90 percent of the currently anticipated 2002–2003 level for both newsstand and home delivery sales if this change is initiated. Calculate the effect on the projected 2002–2003 income if this proposed rate increase is implemented.

(CMA Adapted)

9-45 CASH BUDGET Barker Corporation manufactures and distributes wooden baseball bats. The bats are manufactured in Georgia at its only plant. This is a seasonal business with a large portion of its sales occurring in late winter and early spring. The production schedule for the last quarter of the year is heavy to build up inventory to meet expected sales volume.

  The company experiences a temporary cash strain during this heavy production period. Payroll costs rise during the last quarter because overtime is scheduled to meet the increased production needs. Collections from customers are low because the fall season produces only modest sales. This year the company's concern is intensified because prices are increasing during the current inflationary period. In addition, the sales department forecasts sales of fewer than 1 million bats for the first time in three years. This decease in sales appears to be caused by the popularity of aluminum bats.

The Cash account builds up during the first and second quarters as sales exceed production. Barker invests the excess cash in U.S. Treasury bills and other commercial paper. During the last half of the year, it liquidates the temporary investments to meet its cash needs. In the early years of the company, short-term borrowing was used to supplement the funds released by selling investments, but this has not been necessary in recent years. Because costs are higher this year, the treasurer asks for a forecast for December to determine whether the $240,000 in temporary investments will be adequate to carry the company through the month with a minimum balance of $80,000. Should this be insufficient, she wants to begin negotiations for a short-term loan.

The unit sales volume for the past two months and the estimate for the next four months follow:

October (actual)	70,000
November (actual)	50,000
December (estimated)	50,000
January (estimated)	90,000
February (estimated)	90,000
March (estimated)	120,000

The bats sell for $24 each. All sales are made on account. Fifty percent of the sales is collected in the month of the sale, 40 percent is collected in the month following the sale, and the remaining 10 percent in the second month following the sale. Customers who pay in the month of the sale receive a 2 percent cash discount.

The production schedule for the six-month period beginning with October reflects the company's policy of maintaining a stable year-round workforce by scheduling overtime to meet the following production schedules:

October (actual)	90,000
November (actual)	90,000
December (estimated)	90,000
January (estimated)	90,000
February (estimated)	100,000
March (estimated)	100,000

The bats are made from wooden blocks that cost $40 each. Ten bats can be produced from each block. The blocks are acquired one year in advance so they can be properly aged. Barker pays the supplier one-twelfth of the cost of this material each month until the obligation is retired. The monthly payment is $360,000.

The plant is normally scheduled for a 40-hour, five-day work week. During the busy production season, however, the work week may be increased to six 10-hour days. Each employee can produce 7.5 bats per hour. Normal monthly output is 75,000 bats. Factory employees are paid $20 per hour (up $2.00 from last year) for regular time and time and one-half for overtime.

Other manufacturing costs include variable overhead of $2.00 per unit and annual fixed overhead of $1,200,000. Depreciation totaling $300,000 is included among the fixed overhead. Selling expenses include variable costs of $1.20 per unit and annual fixed costs of $360,000. Fixed administrative costs are $720,000 annually. All fixed costs are incurred uniformly throughout the year. The controller has accumulated the following additional information:

a. The balances of selected accounts as of November 30, 2001, are

Cash	$ 96,000
Marketable securities (cost and market are the same)	240,000
Accounts receivable	480,000
Prepaid expenses	36,000
Accounts payable (arising from raw material purchases)	1,800,000
Accrued vacation pay	60,000
Equipment note payable	702,000
Accrued income taxes payable	250,000

b. Interest for December to be received from the company's temporary investments is estimated at $5,000.

c. Prepaid expenses of $28,000 will expire during December, and the balance of the prepaid account is estimated at $42,000 for the end of December.

d. Barker purchased new machinery in 2001 as part of a plant modernization program. The machinery was financed by a 24-month note of $720,000. The terms call for equal principal payments over the next 24 months with interest paid at the rate of 1 percent per month on the unpaid balance at the first of the month. The first payment was made on May 1, 2001.

e. Old equipment, which has a book value of $80,000, is to be sold during December for $75,000.

f. Each month the company accrues $12,000 for vacation pay by charging Vacation Pay Expense and crediting Accrued Vacation Pay. The plant closes for two weeks in June when all plant employees take a vacation.

g. Quarterly dividends of $0.05 per share will be paid on December 15 to stockholders of record. Barker has authorized 10,000,000 shares. The company has issued 7,500,000 shares, and 500,000 of these are classified as treasury stock.

h. The quarterly income tax payment of $250,000 is due on December 15, 2001.

Required

1. Prepare a schedule that forecasts the cash position at December 31, 2001. What action, if any, will be required to maintain a $10,000 cash balance?

2. Without regard to your answer in requirement 1, assume that Barker regularly needs to arrange short-term loans during the November-to-February period. What changes might Barker consider in its business methods to reduce or eliminate the need for short-term borrowing?

(CMA Adapted)

9–46 CASH BUDGET Triple-F Health Club (Family, Fitness, and Fun) is a not-for-profit family-oriented health club. The club's board of directors is developing plans to acquire more equipment and expand the club facilities. The board plans to purchase about $25,000 of new equipment each year and wants to establish a fund to purchase the adjoining property in four or five years. The adjoining property has a market value of about $300,000.

Service

   The club manager, Jane Crowe, is concerned that the board has unrealistic goals in light of the club's recent financial performance. She has sought the help of a club member with an accounting background to assist her in preparing a report to the board supporting her concerns.

The member reviewed the club's records, including this cash basis income statement:

TRIPLE-F HEALTH CLUB
Income Statement (Cash Basis)
For Years Ended October 31 (in thousands)

	2002	2001
Cash revenues		
Annual membership fees	$355.0	$300.0
Lesson and class fees	234.0	180.0
Miscellaneous	2.0	1.5
Total cash received	$591.0	$481.5
Cash expenses		
Manager's salary and benefits	$ 36.0	$ 36.0
Regular employees' wages and benefits	190.0	190.0
Lesson and class employees' wages and benefits	195.0	150.0
Towels and supplies	16.0	15.5
Utilities (heat and light)	22.0	15.0
Mortgage interest	35.1	37.8
Miscellaneous	2.0	1.5
Total cash expenses	$496.1	$445.8
Cash income	$ 94.9	$ 35.7

- Other financial information as of October 31, 2002:
  Cash in checking account, $7,000.
  Petty cash, $300.
  Outstanding mortgage balance, $390,000.
  Accounts payable arising from invoices for supplies and utilities that are unpaid as of October 31, 2002, $2,500.

- No unpaid bills existed on October 31, 2002.

- The club purchased $25,000 worth of exercise equipment during the current fiscal year. Cash of $10,000 was paid as of October 31, 2002.

- The club began operations in 1997 in rental quarters. In October 2000, it purchased its current property (land and building) for $600,000, paying $120,000 down and agreeing to pay $30,000 plus 9 percent interest annually on November 1 until the balance is paid off.

- Membership rose 3 percent during 2002. The club has experienced approximately this same annual growth rate since it opened.

- Membership fee increased by 15 percent in 2002. The board has tentative plans to increase the fees by 10 percent in 2003.

- Lesson and class fees have not been increased for two years. The board policy is to encourage classes and lessons by keeping the fees low. The members have taken advantage of this policy, and the number of classes and lessons has increased significantly each year. The club expects the percentage growth experienced in 2002 to be repeated in 2003.

- Miscellaneous revenues are expected to grow at the same rate as experienced in 2002.

- Operating expenses are expected to increase:
  Hourly wage rates and the manager's salary: 15 percent.
  Towels and supplies, utilities, and miscellaneous expenses: 25 percent.

Required

1. Prepare a cash budget for 2003 for the Triple-F Health Club.

2. Identify any operating problems that this budget discloses for the Triple-F Health Club. Explain your answer.

3. Is Jane Crowe's concern that the board's goals are unrealistic justified? Explain your answer.

(CMA Adapted)

9-47 **ESTIMATED SALES REVENUE** Multiplex Electronics Corporation manufactures custom-designed central processing computer chips for specialized applications. The firm expects to sell 9 million units during the coming year. Total foreign sales are approximately 80 percent of the units sold domestically.

Since the inception of the firm five years ago, the foreign currency exchange rates have been stable. The firm receives $30 per unit and earns a contribution margin of $15 per unit for all units sold. However, financial crises began in September of this year in several countries in the region where the firm exports most of its foreign sales. Consequently, the firm's sales revenue in U.S. dollars has substantially decreased.

For the coming year, the firm expects the exchange rate to be about 60 percent of the level before the devaluation.

Required

1. Estimate the total sales and contribution margin for the coming year if the firm chooses not to alter its selling prices in foreign currencies.

2. Determine the unit selling price for foreign sales for the coming year if the firm desires to receive $30 per unit.

3. Compute the unit selling price for the coming year for all units (for both domestic and foreign markets) if the firm desires to earn the same total amount of contribution margin in U.S. dollars as before the financial crises.

9-48 **SMALL BUSINESS BUDGET** Small businesses usually are the first to feel the effects of a recessionary economy and generally are the last to recover. Two major reasons for these difficulties are managerial inexperience and inadequate financing or financial management.

Small business managers frequently have problems in planning and controlling profits, including revenue generation and cost reduction activities. These important financial methods are especially critical during a recessionary period. The financial problems of small business are further compounded if the firm keeps poor accounting records and is inexperienced in the management of money.

Required

1. Profit planning is critical for the planning and controlling of profits of a small business. Identify key features that should be considered when developing a profit plan.

2. The management accountant can help ensure that good accounting records exist in an organization. Discuss the key features that form the basis for a good accounting system that will support management decisions.

3. Explain how the management accountant can assist an organization in adopting measures to ensure appropriate money management.

(CMA Adapted)

9-49 **ETHICS IN BUDGETING** Norton Company, a manufacturer of infant furniture and carriages, is in the initial stages of preparing the annual budget for 2002. Scott Ford recently joined Norton's accounting staff and is interested in learning as much as possible about the company's budgeting process. During a recent lunch with Marge Atkins, sales manager, and Pete Granger, production manager, Scott initiated the following conversation:

Scott: "Since I'm new around here and am going to be involved with the preparation of the annual budget, I'd be interested to learn how the two of you estimate sales and production numbers."

Marge: "We start out very methodically by looking at recent history, discussing what we know about current accounts, potential customers, and the general state of consumer spending. Then, we add that usual dose of intuition to come up with the best forecast we can."

Pete: "I usually take the sales projections as the basis for my projections. Of course, we have to make an estimate of what this year's closing inventories will be, and that sometimes is difficult."

Scott: "Why does that present a problem? There must have been an estimate of closing inventories in the budget for the current year."

Pete: "Those numbers aren't always reliable since Marge makes some adjustments to the sales numbers before passing them on to me."

Scott: "What kind of adjustments?"

Marge: "Well, we don't want to fall short of the sales projections so we generally give ourselves a little breathing room by lowering the initial sales projection anywhere from 5 to 10 percent."

Pete: "So, you can see why this year's budget is not a very reliable starting point. We always have to adjust the projected production rates as the year progresses and, of course, this changes the ending inventory estimates. By the way, we make similar adjustments to expenses by adding at least 10 percent to the estimates; I think everyone around here does the same thing."

Required

1. Marge Atkins and Pete Granger have described the use of budgetary slack.

    a. Explain why Marge and Pete behave in this manner, and describe the benefits they expect to realize from the use of budgetary slack.

    b. Explain how the use of budgetary slack can adversely affect Marge and Pete.

2. As a management accountant, Scott Ford believes that the behavior described by Marge and Pete may be unethical and that he may have an obligation not to support this behavior. By citing the specific standards of competence, confidentiality, integrity, and/or objectivity from Standards of Ethical Conduct for Management Accountants, explain why the use of budgetary slack may be unethical.

(CMA Adapted)

9–50 **BUDGET REVISION**   Mark Fletcher, president of SoftGro Inc., was looking forward to seeing the performance reports for the month of November because he knew the company's sales for the month had exceeded budget by a considerable margin. SoftGro, a distributor of educational software packages, had been growing steadily for approximately two years; Mark's largest challenge at this point was to ensure that the company did not lose control of expenses during this growth period. When Fletcher received the November reports, he was dismayed to see the large unfavorable variance in the company's Monthly Selling Expense Report that is presented in this problem.

Fletcher called in the company's new controller, Susan Porter, to discuss the implications of the variances reported for November and to plan a strategy for improving performance. Porter suggested that the reporting format that the company had been using might not be giving Fletcher a true picture of the company's operations and proposed that SoftGro revise the budget to correspond with the output level achieved for operation evaluation purposes.

Susan offered to redo the monthly selling expense report for November based on the actual units sold.

Susan discovered the following information about the behavior of Soft-Gro's selling expenses. Using this information and pertinent data from the original monthly selling expense report, she believed that she would be able to redo the report and present it to Mark for his review.

- The total compensation paid to the sales force consists of both monthly base salary and commission; the commission varies with the sales dollars.

- Sales office expense is a mixed cost with the variable portion related to the number of orders processed. The fixed portion of office expense is $3,000,000 annually and is incurred uniformly throughout the year.

- Subsequent to the adoption of the annual budget for the current year, SoftGro decided to open a new sales territory. As a consequence, approval was given to hire six additional salespersons effective November 1, 2001. Susan decided that these additional people should be recognized in her revised report.

- Per diem reimbursement to the sales force, while a fixed stipend per day, is variable with the number of salespersons and the number of days spent traveling. SoftGro's original budget was based on an average sales force of 90 persons throughout the year with each salesperson traveling 15 days per month.

- The company's shipping expense is a mixed cost with the variable portion, $3 per unit, dependent on the number of units sold. The fixed portion is incurred uniformly throughout the year.

Required

1. Cite the benefits of redoing the budget based on the output level achieved to explain why Susan would propose that SoftGro use the revised budget in this situation.

2. Prepare a revised monthly selling expense report for November that would permit Mark to more clearly evaluate SoftGro's control over selling expenses. The report should have a line for each selling expense item showing the appropriate budgeted amount, the actual selling expense, and the monthly dollar variance.

SOFTGRO INC.
Monthly Selling Expense Report
November 2001

	Annual Budget	November Budget	November Actual	November Variance
Unit sales	2,000,000	280,000	310,000	30,000
Dollar sales	$80,000,000	$11,200,000	$12,400,000	$1,200,000
Orders processed	54,000	6,500	5,800	(700)
Salespersons per month	90	90	96	(6)
Advertising	$19,800,000	$ 1,650,000	$ 1,660,000	$ 10,000U
Staff salaries	1,500,000	125,000	125,000	—
Sales salaries	1,296,000	108,000	115,400	7,400U
Commissions	3,200,000	448,000	496,000	48,000U
Per diem expense	1,782,000	148,500	162,600	14,100U
Office expense	4,080,000	340,000	358,400	18,400U
Shipping expense	6,750,000	902,500	976,500	74,000U
Total expenses	$38,408,000	$ 3,722,000	$ 3,893,900	$171,900U

(CMA Adapted)

Service

9–51   BUDGET REVISION   Mason Agency, a division of General Service Industries, offers consulting services to clients for a fee. The corporate management of General Service is pleased with the Mason Agency's performance for the first nine months of the current year and has recommended that its division manager, Richard Howell, submit a revised forecast for the remaining quarter because the division has exceeded the annual plan to date by 20 percent of operating income. An unexpected increase in billed hour volume over the original plan is the main reason for this gain in income. The original operating budget for Mason Agency's first three quarters follows:

MASON AGENCY
2001–2002 Operating Budget

	First Quarter	Second Quarter	Third Quarter	Total Nine Months
Revenue				
Consulting fees				
Management consulting	$315,000	$315,000	$315,000	$ 945,000
EDP consulting	421,875	421,875	421,875	1,265,625
Total consulting fees	$736,875	$736,875	$736,875	$2,210,625
Other revenue	10,000	10,000	10,000	30,000
Total revenue	$746,875	$746,875	$746,875	$2,240,625
Expenses				
Consultant salary	$386,750	$386,750	$386,750	$1,160,250
Travel and related	45,625	45,625	45,625	136,875
General & admin.	100,000	100,000	100,000	300,000
Depreciation	40,000	40,000	40,000	120,000
Corporate allocation	50,000	50,000	50,000	150,000
Total expenses	$622,375	$622,375	$622,375	$1,867,125
Operating income	$124,500	$124,500	$124,500	$ 373,500

When comparing the actual amounts for the first three quarters to the original plan, Richard analyzed the variances and will reflect the following information in his revised forecast for the fourth quarter:

- The division currently has 25 consultants on staff, 10 for management consulting and 15 for EDP consulting, and has hired three additional management consultants to start work at the beginning of the fourth quarter to meet the increased client demand.

- The hourly billing rate for consulting revenues is market acceptable and will remain at $90 per hour for each management consultant and $75 per hour for each EDP consultant. However, due to the favorable increase in billing hour volume compared to plan, the hours for each consultant will be increased by 50 hours per quarter. There is no learning curve for billable consulting hours for new employees.

- The budgeted annual salaries and actual annual salaries, paid monthly, are the same at $50,000 for a management consultant and 8 percent less for an EDP consultant. Corporate management has approved a merit increase of 10 percent at the beginning of the fourth quarter for all 25 existing consultants; the new consultants will be compensated at the planned rate.

- The planned salary expense includes a provision for employee fringe benefits amounting to 30 percent of the annual salaries; however, the improvement of some corporatewide employee programs will increase the fringe benefit allocation to 40 percent.

- The original plan assumes a fixed hourly rate for travel and other related expenses for each billable hour of consulting. These expenses are not reimbursed by the client, and the previously determined hourly rate has proven to be adequate to cover these costs.

- Other revenues are derived from temporary rental and interest income and remain unchanged for the fourth quarter.

- General and administrative expenses have been favorable at 7 percent below the plan; this 7 percent savings on fourth-quarter expenses will be reflected in the revised plan.

- Depreciation for office equipment and microcomputers will stay consistent at the projected straight-line rate.

- Due to the favorable experience for the first three quarters and the division's increased ability to absorb costs, General Service's corporate management has increased the corporate expense allocation by 50 percent.

Required

1. Prepare a revised operating budget for the fourth quarter for Mason Agency that Richard will present to General Service Industries. Be sure to furnish supporting calculations for all revised revenue and expense amounts.

2. Explain why an organization would prepare a revised forecast.

(CMA Adapted)

9–52 **STRATEGY, PRODUCT LIFE CYCLE, AND CASH FLOW** Burke Company manufactures various electronic assemblies that it sells primarily to computer manufacturers. Burke's built its reputation on quality, timely delivery, and products that are consistently on the cutting edge of technology. Burke's business is fast paced: A typical product has a short life; the product is in development for about a year and in the growth stage, with sometimes spectacular growth, for about a year. Each product then experiences a rapid decline in sales as new products become available.

Burke has just hired a new vice president of finance, Devin Ward. Shortly after reporting for work at Burke, he had a conversation with Andrew Newhouse, Burke's president. A portion of the conversation follows.

Andrew: "The thing that fascinates me about this business is that change is its central ingredient. We knew when we started out that a reliable stream of new products was one of our key variables—in fact, the only way to cope with the threat of product obsolescence. You see, our products go through only the first half of the traditional product life cycle—the development stage and then the growth stage. Our products never reach the traditional mature product stage or the declining product stage. Toward the end of the growth stage, products die as new ones are introduced."

Devin: "I suppose your other key variables are cost controls and efficient production scheduling?"

Andrew: "Getting the product to market on schedule, whether efficiently or not, is important. Some firms in this business announce a new product in March to be delivered in June, and they make the first shipment in October, or a year from March, or sometimes, never. Our reputation for delivering on schedule could account for our success as much as anything."

Devin: "Where I previously worked, we also recognized the importance of on-time deliveries. Our absorption cost system set 93 percent on time as a standard."

Andrew: "The key variable that is your responsibility is cash management. It took us a while to recognize that. At first, we thought that profit was the key and that cash would naturally follow. But now we know that cash is the

401

key and that profits naturally follow. Still, we don't manage cash well. Improving our cash management is the main thing we expect from you."

Required

1. Discuss the cash-generating and cash usage characteristics of products in general in each of the four stages of the product life cycle—development, growth, maturity, and decline.

2. Describe the cash management problems confronting Burke Company.

3. Suggest techniques that Devin might implement to cope with Burke Company's cash management problems.

(CMA Adapted)

9–53 CONTINUOUS BUDGET   WestWood Corporation is a woodstove manufacturer located in southern Oregon. WestWood manufactures three models: small stoves for heating a single room, medium-size units for use in mobile homes and as a supplement to central heating systems, and large stoves with the capacity to provide central heating.

The manufacturing process consists of shearing and shaping steel, fabricating, welding, painting, and finishing. Molded doors are custom built at an outside foundry in the state, brass plated at a plater, and fitted with custom etched glass during assembly at WestWood's plant. The finished stoves are delivered to dealers either directly or through regional warehouses located throughout the western United States. WestWood owns the three tractor trailers and one large truck used to ship stoves to dealers and warehouses.

The budget for the year ending February 28, 2002, was finalized in January of 2001 and was based on the assumption that the 10 percent annual growth rate that WestWood had experienced since 2000 would continue.

Stove sales are seasonal, and the first quarter of WestWood's fiscal year is usually a slack period. As a consequence, inventory levels were down at the start of the current fiscal year on March 1, 2001.

WestWood's sales orders for the first quarter ended May 31, 2001, were up 54 percent over the same period last year and 40 percent above the first quarter budget. Unfortunately, not all of the sales orders could be filled due to the reduced inventory levels at the beginning of the quarter. WestWood's plant was able to increase production over budgeted levels, but not in sufficient quantity to compensate for the large increase in orders. Therefore, it has a large backlog of orders. Furthermore, preliminary orders for the busy fall season are 60 percent above the budget and the projections for the winter of 2001–2002 indicate no decrease in demand. WestWood's president attributes the increase to effective advertising, the products' good reputation, the increased number of installations of woodstoves in new houses, and the bankruptcy of WestWood's principal competitor.

Required

1. WestWood's sales for the remainder of the 2001–2002 fiscal year will be much higher than predicted five months ago. Explain the effect this increase will have on the operations in the following functional areas of WestWood.

   a. Production.

   c. Marketing

   b. Finance and accounting.

   d. Personnel.

2. Some companies follow the practice of preparing a continuous budget.

   a. Explain what a continuous budget is.

   b. Explain how WestWood could benefit by preparing a continuous budget.

(CMA Adapted)

9–54 SPREADSHEET APPLICATION Alice Williams, the manager of the financial analysis department, has been asked to forecast the cash position for the Linden Corporation for the third quarter. Alice will use the following pro forma income statement that was prepared by Jerry Miller, a former financial analyst who recently left the company. Jerry prepared the pro forma income statement by using a common spreadsheet package on a microcomputer.

Pertinent information about the company's financial transactions follows:

- All sales are on account, and the accounts receivable have historically been paid and are forecasted to be paid 30 days after the sale.
- All other revenues are presumed to be paid as they occur.
- Cost of goods sold relates to raw materials purchased on account. Accounts payable are settled in 30 days. All other cash expenses are paid as incurred.
- Accrued taxes equal the tax liability and are paid 45 days after the end of the quarter. The second quarter's total tax liability was $95,000.
- Linden is purchasing a $25,000 microcomputer network to be delivered, installed, and paid for in September. Depreciation on this equipment will be based on the straight-line method over five years, with no salvage value at the end of five years. The depreciation expense for this equipment is not currently reflected in the projected expenses.
- In July, Linden will receive $500,000 from a public stock offering of 100,000 shares sold in June.
- On June 10, 2001, the board of directors declared dividends of $75,000 to be distributed on August 15 to the shareholders of record as of June 30.
- The ending cash balance at June 30, 2002, is projected to be $250,000.
- For forecasting purposes, Linden Corporation assumes that all cash flows and transactions consistently occur at the end of each month.

	(A)	(B)	(C)	(D)	(E)
1					
2					
3			**LINDEN CORPORATION**		
4			**2002 Partial Pro Forma Income Statement**		
5			**(in thousands)**		
6		June	July	August	September
7	Revenues				
8	Sales	$230	$250	$260	$290
9	Other revenues	20	10	30	20
10	Total revenue	$250	$260	$290	$310
11	Expenses				
12	Cost of goods sold	$ 80	$ 90	$120	$110
13	Salaries	50	50	50	50
14	Depreciation	40	40	40	40
15	Other	0	10	10	20
16	Total expenses	$170	$190	$220	$220
17	Income before taxes	$ 80	$ 70	$ 70	$ 90
18	Taxes (40 percent)	32	28	28	36
19	Net income	$ 48	$ 42	$ 42	$ 54

Alice is preparing a projected internal cash flow report by referencing the amounts given in the pro forma income statement that Jerry had prepared and the previous financial transactions. Before Jerry left Linden, he gave Alice a brief lesson on forecasting the cash flows by using the spreadsheet package and referencing income statement values. Although Jerry had not developed any specific directions on using this spreadsheet model, he believed that Alice was proficient enough to use it to prepare the cash flow projection. Note that the pro forma income statement is correct. In reviewing the first draft of the following pro forma cash flow statement, Alice observed six errors that are indicated by numbers 1 through 6.

Required

1. The six errors identified on Linden Corporation's third quarter 2002 pro forma cash flow statement displayed here were caused by either incorrect reasoning or spreadsheet logic. Describe the six errors a–f and explain specifically how to correct each error by providing the correct spreadsheet formula using these notations:

Formula	Spreadsheet Formula Notations
BB56	For cell references, column first and row second
= or @	To start formula
+	For addition
−	For subtraction
*	For multiplication
=SUM() or @SUM	For a summation formula
CF	Name for the Cash Flow Report file
IS	Name for the Income Statement file

Use the following format for your answer:

Description of Error	Corrected Spreadsheet Formula
a.	
b.	
c.	
d.	
e.	
f.	

2. List at least three problems inherent in the use of spreadsheet models developed by users who are not trained in the procedural controls of systems design and development.

	(AA)	(AB)	(AC)	(AD)	
51					
52		**LINDEN CORPORATION**			
53		**Third Quarter 2002 Pro Forma Cash Flow Statement**			
54		**(in thousands)**			
55		July	August	September	
56	Beginning cash balance	$250	$735	$735	a.
57	Cash receipts				
58	Sales receipts	250	260	290	b.
59	Other revenue	10	30	20	
60	Equity	500	0	0	
61	Total cash receipts	760	290	310	
62					
63	Cash disbursements				
64	Purchases and expenses	180	190	230	c.
65	Tax payments	95	0	0	d.
66	Dividends	0	75	0	
67	Other (capital purchases)	0	0	25	
68	Total cash disbursements	275	265	230	e.
69	Net cash contribution	485	25	80	
70	Ending cash balance	$735	$760	$1,045	f.

404

(CMA Adapted)

SOLUTIONS TO SELF-STUDY PROBLEMS

1. Master Budget

a.

HANSELL COMPANY
Sales Budget
For July 2002

Budgeted sales in units	6,000
Budgeted selling price per unit	× $ 40
Budgeted sales	$240,000

b.

HANSELL COMPANY
Production Budget (in units)
For July 2002

Desired ending inventory (July 31)	
(The higher of 100 and 7,000 × 0.1)	700
Budgeted sales for July 2002	+ 6,000
Total units needed for July 2002	6,700
Beginning inventory (July 1)	
(The higher of 100 and 6,000 × 0.1)	− 600
Units to manufacture in July	6,100

c.

HANSELL COMPANY
Production Budget (in units)
For August 2002

Desired ending inventory (8,000 × 0.1)	800
Budgeted sales	+ 7,000
Total units needed	7,800
Beginning inventory	− 700
Units to manufacture in August	7,100

d.

HANSELL COMPANY
Direct Materials Purchases Budget (in pounds)
For July 2002

	Direct Materials	
	Dura–1000 **(4 lb. each)**	**Flexplas** **(2 lb. each)**
Materials required for budgeted production (6,100 units of duraflex)	24,400	12,200
Add: Target inventories (lower of 1,000 or 5 percent of August production needs)	+ 1,000	+ 710
Total materials requirements	25,400	12,910
Less: Expected beginning inventories (lower of 1,000 or 5 percent)	− 1,000	− 610
Direct materials to be purchased	24,400	12,300

e.

HANSELL COMPANY
Direct Materials Purchases Budget (in dollars)
For July 2002

	Budgeted **Purchases** **(Pounds)**	**Expected** **Purchase** **Price per Unit**	**Total**
Dura–1000	24,400	$1.25	$30,500
Flexplas	12,300	$5.00	61,500
Budgeted purchases			$92,000

f.

HANSELL COMPANY
Direct Manufacturing Labor Budget
For July 2002

	Direct Labor-Hours per Batch	Number of Batches	Total Hours	Rate per Hour	Total
K102 Hours	1	61	61	$50	$3,050
K175 Hours	10	61	610	$20	12,200
Total			671		$15,250

2. Cash Budget and Budgeted Income Statement

a.

HANSELL COMPANY
Cash Budget
July 2002

Cash Available

Cash balance, beginning		$ 10,000
Add: Cash receipts		
July cash sales	$240,000 × 20% = $ 48,000	
Collections of receivables		
From sales in June		
Collection within the discount period		
	5,500 × $40 × 80% × 60% × 98% = $103,488	
Collection after the discount period		
	5,500 × $40 × 80% × 25% = 44,000	
From sales in May		
	5,400 × $40 × 80% × 10% = 17,280	212,768
Total cash available in July		$222,768
Cash Disbursement		
Materials purchases		
June purchases	($25,000 + $22,000) × 20% × 98% = $ 9,212	
July purchases	$92,000 × 80% × 98% = 72,128	$ 81,340
Direct manufacturing labor		15,250
Variable factory overhead	($200 × 61 + $30 × 671) × 60% =	19,398
Fixed factory overhead	$50,000 − $20,000 =	30,000
Variable marketing, customer services, and administrative expenses		
	[($600,000 − $270,000) ÷ $2,000,000] × $240,000 =	39,600
Fixed marketing, customer services, and administrative expenses		
	($270,000 − 150,000) ÷ 12 =	10,000
Total disbursements		$195,588
Cash balance before financing		$ 27,180
Financing		
Amount to borrow		13,000
Cash balance, July 31, 2002		$ 40,180

b.

HANSELL COMPANY
Budget Income Statement
July 2002

Sales			$240,000
Cost of goods sold*		$22.80 × 6,000 =	136,800
Gross margin			$103,200
Selling and administrative expenses			
Variable		$39,600	
Fixed	$270,000 ÷ 12 =	22,500	62,100
Net income			$ 41,100

*Cost per unit

Direct materials			
Dura–1000	4 lb. × $1.25 =	$ 5.00	
Flexplas	2 lb. × $5.00 =	10.00	$15.00
Direct labor			
K102 labor	0.01 hour × $50 =	$ 0.50	
K175 labor	0.1 hour × $20 =	2.00	2.50
Factory overhead			
Applied based on batch	$200 ÷ 100 =	$ 2.00	
Applied based on direct labor-hour	$30 × 0.11 hour =	3.30	5.30
Cost per unit			$22.80

10

Decision Making with Relevant Costs and Strategic Analysis

After studying this chapter, you should be able to . . .

1   Define the decision-making process and identify the types of cost information relevant for decision making

2   Use relevant and strategic cost analysis to make special order decisions

3   Use relevant and strategic cost analysis in the make, lease, or buy decision

4   Use relevant and strategic cost analysis in the decision to sell before or after additional processing

5   Use relevant and strategic cost analysis in the decision to keep or drop products or services

6   Use relevant and strategic cost analysis to evaluate programs

7   Analyze decisions with multiple products and limited resources

8   Discuss the behavioral, implementation, and legal issues in decision making

Courtesy of Ford Motor Company.

The family sedan segment of the U.S. auto market—especially the Honda Accord, Ford Taurus, and Toyota Camry—experiences an intense level of competition. The Camry and the Taurus have traded places as the top-selling car in the United States.[1] The Camry is now on top, as it has been since 1997. The competition between these two cars illustrates an important cost management issue—striking a balance between product features and price. The two cars do not differ greatly in price, but most analysts argue that the cost and price reductions in the 1997 remake of the Camry brought it to the top of U.S. car sales. In contrast, the remake of the 1996 Taurus added features, cost—and price.

Now we are ready for round two of the match-up. In the 2000 model year, Ford added further improvements to the Taurus, mainly safety features. It added seat belt pretensioners and other design features that improved the Taurus' performance in crash tests. Ford officials believe that safety could become the defining issue for the family sedan in the coming years. Toyota thinks differently; it believes that reliability is still the critical success factor. Honda thinks differently than Toyota and Ford, opting to focus on adding space and a smoother ride in the Accord's redesign.

Toyota, Ford, and Honda are saying that a number of strategic issues are involved in developing a competitive car, including safety features, low-cost manufacturing methods, and a competitive price. In Chapter 5, we focused on product features and design; in this chapter we will discuss how to conduct relevant cost analysis and strategic analysis of decisions about product pricing, selecting cost-effective manufacturing methods, and deciding when to keep or drop a product, among others.

The decision maker has both short-term and long-term objectives for each type of decision. A decision with a short-term objective is one whose effects are expected to occur within about a year from the time of the decision. A decision with a long-term objective is expected to affect costs and revenues for a period longer than a year. Both types of decisions should reflect the firm's overall strategy, but it is often said that the decision maker has a long-term strategy if the focus is primarily on the decision's long-term objectives and a short-term strategy if the focus is on the short term.

Decision makers usually consider both short-term and long-term effects in making the best decision. Although the art and science of decision making has many elements, including leadership, vision, and other characteristics, cost management provides two important resources to improve decisions: relevant cost analysis and strategic cost analysis. Relevant cost analysis has a short-term focus; strategic cost

---

[1] For further reading, see "Ford Bets on Safety, Not Style, for Comeback of Taurus," *The Wall Street Journal*, March 30, 1999, p. B1; and "The Shape of a New Machine," *Business Week*, July 24, 1995; "More Camry for Less Cash," *Business Week*, November 18, 1996, p. 186.

analysis has a long-term focus. Relevant cost analysis and strategic cost analysis are an important part of the financial manager's decision process.

THE DECISION-MAKING PROCESS

In deciding among alternative choices for a given situation, managers employ the five step process outlined in Exhibit 10–1. The first step, and in many ways the most important, is to consider the strategic issues regarding the decision context. This helps focus the decision maker on answering the right question, in part by identifying a comprehensive list of decision options. Strategic thinking is important to avoid decisions that might be best only in the short term. For example, a plant manager might incorrectly view the choice as either to make or to buy a part for a manufactured product when the correct decision might be to determine whether the product should be redesigned so the part is not needed.

The manager's second step is to specify the criteria by which the decision is to be made. Most often the manager's principal objective is an easily quantified, short-term, achievable goal, such as to reduce cost, improve profit, or maximize return on investment. Other interested parties (e.g., owners or shareholders) have their own criteria for these decisions. Therefore, a manager most often is forced to think of multiple objectives, both the quantifiable short-term goals, and the more strategic, difficult-to-quantify goals.

In the third step, a manager performs an analysis in which the relevant information is developed and analyzed, using relevant cost analysis and strategic cost analysis. This step involves three sequential activities. The manager (1) identifies and collects relevant information about the decision, (2) makes predictions about the relevant information, and (3) considers the strategic issues involved in the decision.

Fourth, based on the relevant cost analysis and strategic cost analysis, the manager selects the best alternative and implements it. In the fifth and final step, the manager evaluates the performance of the implemented decision as a basis for feedback to a possible reconsideration of this decision as it relates to future decisions. The decision process is thus a feedback-based system in which the manager continually evaluates the results of prior analyses and decisions to discover any opportunities for improvement in decision making.

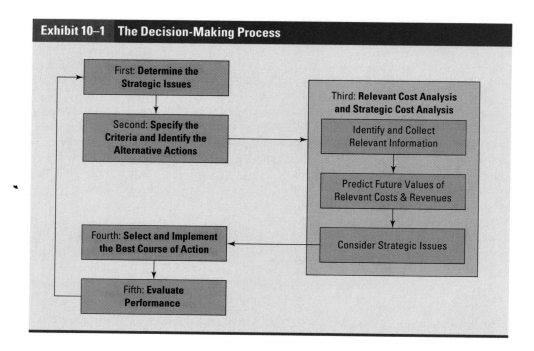

Exhibit 10–1 The Decision-Making Process

RELEVANT COST ANALYSIS

Relevant Cost Information

Relevant costs are costs that will be incurred at some future time; they differ for each option available to the decision maker. A cost that does not differ for each of the decision maker's options is irrelevant because that choice has no effect on the cost. For example, in choosing which new car to buy, a consumer can ignore the cost of licenses and fees as long as these costs are the same for all cars. A cost that has already occurred or has been committed to is also irrelevant; the decision cannot influence these costs. Thus, the cost of the buyer's present car is irrelevant. The only relevant amount for the old car is the future amount—its potential trade-in value. The decision maker's rule is that *only future costs that differ among options are relevant for the decision.* (See Exhibit 10–2.)

A relevant cost can be either a variable or fixed. Generally, variable costs are relevant for decision making because they differ for each option and have not been committed. In contrast, fixed costs often are irrelevant, since typically they do not differ for the options. Overall, variable costs often are relevant but fixed costs are not. So the use of the concept of relevant cost follows naturally from the development of the methods we used in cost estimation, cost-volume-profit analysis, and master budgeting.

Occasionally, some variable costs are not relevant. For example, assume that a manager is considering whether to replace or repair an old machine. If the electrical power requirements of the new and old machines are the same, the variable cost of power is not relevant. Some fixed costs can be relevant. For example, if the new machine requires significant modifications to the plant building, the cost of the modifications (which are fixed costs) are relevant because they are not yet committed.

Assume that the old machine was purchased for $4,200 a year ago, it is depreciated over two years at $2,100 per year, and it has no trade-in or disposal value. At the end of the first year, the machine has a net book value of $2,100 ($4,200 – $2,100). Also assume that the purchase price of the new machine is $7,000 and it is expected to last for two years with little or no expected trade-in or disposal value. The repair of the old machine would cost $3,500 and would be sufficient for another two years of productive use. The power for either machine is expected to cost $2.50 per hour. The new machine is semiautomated, requiring a less-skilled operator and resulting in a reduction of average labor costs from $10.00 to $9.50 per hour for the new machine. If the firm is expected to operate at a 1,000-hour level of output for each of the next two

Relevant costs are costs that will be incurred at some future time; they differ for each option available to the decision maker.

◄**LEARNING OBJECTIVE 1**

Define the decision-making process and identify the types of cost information relevant for decision making.

Exhibit 10–2	**Relevant and Not Relevant Costs: The Car Purchase Decision**

		Cost Classification and Cost Relevance (With examples for the car purchase decision)	
		Committed, or "Sunk" (Generally, in the Past)	Not Committed, Discretionary (Generally, in the Future)
Costs That Differ Among Options		Not Relevant Example: Purchase of Buyer's Guide for the new car	Relevant Costs Example: Price of new car
Costs That Do Not Differ Among Options		Not Relevant Example: Price of old car	Not Relevant Example: American Auto Club membership

years, the two-year total variable costs for power will be 2,000 × $2.50 = $5,000, and labor costs will be $19,000 ($9.5 × 2,000) and $20,000 ($10 × 2,000) for the new and old machines respectively.

Data for Machine Replacement Example

Old machine	
Current net book value	$2,100
Useful life (if repaired)	2 years
Operating cost (labor)	$10 per hour
New machine	
Purchase price	$7,000
Useful life	2 years
Operating cost (labor)	$9.50 per hour

The summary of relevant costs for this decision is in Exhibit 10–3, showing a $2,500 advantage for repairing the old machine. The $1,000 decrease in labor costs for the new machine is less than the $3,500 difference of replacement cost over repair cost ($7,000 − $3,500). Note that the power costs and the depreciation on the old machine are omitted because they are not relevant for the decision.

Exhibit 10–3 Relevant Cost Analysis in Equipment Replacement

	Relevant Costs		Difference
			Replace Minus
	Repair	Replace	Repair
Variable costs (for two years at 1,000 hours per year)			
Labor*	$20,000	$19,000	$(1,000)
Fixed costs (for two years)			
Old machine repair cost	3,500		(3,500)
New machine		7,000	7,000
Total costs	$23,500	$26,000	$ 2,500
Repair cost lower by: $2,500			

*$20,000 = 1,000 hours × 2 years × $10 per hour
$19,000 = 1,000 hours × 2 years × $9.50 per hour

Exhibit 10–4 Relevant Cost and Total Cost Analysis in Equipment Replacement

	Relevant Costs		Total Costs		Difference
	Repair	Replace	Repair	Replace	Replace – Repair
Variable Costs (for two years at 1,000 hours per year)					
Labor	$20,000	$19,000	$20,000	$19,000	$(1,000)
Power			5,000	5,000	0
Fixed Costs (for two years)					
Old machine					
Depreciation			2,100	2,100	0
Repair cost	3,500		3,500		(3,500)
New machine					
Depreciation		7,000		7,000	7,000
Total costs	$23,500	$26,000	$30,600	$33,100	$2,500
Repair cost lower by		$2,500		$2,500	

To show that the analysis based on total costs provides the same answer, Exhibit 10–4 shows the analysis for total costs that includes the power costs and the purchase price of the old machine; neither cost is relevant. The left portion of Exhibit 10–4 is the same as Exhibit 10–3. Note that both analyses lead to the same conclusion. The relevant cost approach in Exhibit 10–3 is always preferred, however, because it is simpler, less prone to error, and provides better focus for the decision maker.

Variable Costs and Activity-Based Cost Drivers

Although most relevant costs for many decisions are variable, the concept of variable cost does not mean only a cost tied to changes in the output level. A variable cost varies directly with changes in a given cost driver, whether it is the number of products produced, the number of batches of product produced, or the number of design features for each product. For example, certain costs that are fixed at the output level (e.g., the cost of setting up machinery) are variable at the batch level because setup costs are incurred with each new batch of product. If we add features to a product, costs increase not only at the output level (additional direct materials and labor) but also at the batch level (increased setup costs) and the product level (increased engineering design costs, inspection and testing costs). In determining the costs that differ for options, managers must consider variable costs in the broadest possible sense as those that might vary at any level of manufacture—units of output, batches, and products.

Consider the decision in Exhibit 10–3 to repair rather than replace the old machine. Assume that the new machine, because of its simpler design, allows the firm to reduce setup time for each batch to 25 percent of the time required for the old machine. Assume further that the average of 1,000 hours of operation per year produces 60 batches of product and that the time required for setup labor is four hours per setup. Of the 1,000 hours, then, 240 hours (60×4) are required for setup and 760 hours $(1,000 - 240)$ are direct labor-hours. For the new machine, the setup time is less, 60 hours (60×1). The analysis of setup costs is as follows:

Setup Costs for New Machine	Setup Costs for Old Machine
$9.50 per hour for labor	$10 per hour for labor
× 60 setups per year	× 60 setups per year
× 1 hour per setup	× 4 hours per setup
× 2 years	× 2 years
= $1,140	= $4,800

Clearly, the new machine saves $3,660 ($4,800 − $1,140) in setup costs for the two-year period as well as $760 in direct labor (760 hours × 2 years × $10 per hr = $15,200 for the old machine versus 760 × 2 × $9.50 per hr = $14,440 for the new machine; $15,200 − $14,440 = $760). The labor savings total is $4,420 ($3,660 + $760) over the two-year period. This more than offsets the excess of the cost of the new machine over the cost of repair, $3,500 ($7,000 − $3,500), for a $920 = ($4,420 − $3,500) net benefit of replacing the machine. See the revised analysis in Exhibit 10–5.

Fixed Costs and Depreciation

A common misperception is that depreciation of facilities and equipment is a relevant cost. In fact, depreciation is a portion of a committed cost (the allocation of a purchase cost over the life of an asset); therefore, it is sunk and irrelevant. There is an exception to this rule: when tax effects are considered in decision making. In this context, depreciation has a positive value in that, as an expense, it reduces taxable income and tax expense. If taxes are considered, depreciation has a role to the extent that it reduces tax liability. The decision maker often must consider the impact of local, federal, and sometimes international tax differences on the decision situation.

Exhibit 10–5 Relevant Costs in Equipment Replacement (including consideration of setup costs)

	Relevant Costs		Total Costs		Difference
	Repair	Replace	Repair	Replace	Replace – Repair
Variable Costs (for two years)					
Labor					
Direct	$15,200	$14,440	$15,200	$14,440	$ (760)
Setup	4,800	1,140	4,800	1,140	(3,660)
Total labor	$20,000	$15,580	$20,000	$15,580	(4,420)
Power			5,000	5,000	0
Fixed Costs (for two years)					
Old machine					
Depreciation			2,100	2,100	0
Repair cost	3,500		3,500		(3,500)
New machine					
Depreciation		7,000		7,000	7,000
Total costs:	$23,500	$22,580	$30,600	$29,680	$ (920)
Replace cost lower by		$ 920		$ 920	

Determining Relevant Costs vs. Strategic Cost Analysis

Determine Relevant Costs	Strategic Cost Analysis
Short-term focus	Long-term focus
Not linked to strategy	Linked to the firm's strategy
Product cost focus	Customer focus
Focused on individual product or decision situation	Integrative; considers all customer-related factors

Other Relevant Information: Opportunity Costs

Managers should include in their decision process information such as the capacity usage of the plant. Capacity usage information is a critical signal of the potential relevance of *opportunity costs*, the benefit lost when one chosen option precludes the benefits from an alternative option. When the plant is operating at full capacity, opportunity costs are an important consideration because the decision to produce a special order or add a new product line can cause the reduction, delay, or loss of sales of products and services currently offered. In contrast, a firm with excess capacity might be able to produce for current demand as well as handle a special order or new product; thus, no opportunity cost is present. When opportunity costs are relevant, the manager must consider the value of lost sales as well as the contribution from the new order or new product.

Another important factor is the *time value of money* that is relevant when deciding among alternatives with cash flows over two or more years. These decisions are best handled by the methods described in Chapter 11. Also, differences in quality, functionality, timeliness of delivery, reliability in shipping, and service after the sale could strongly influence a manager's final decision and should be considered in addition to the analysis of relevant costs. Although these factors often are considered in a qualitative manner, when any factor is strategically important, management can choose to quantify it and include it directly in the analysis.

STRATEGIC COST ANALYSIS

Strategic information keeps the decision maker's attention focused on the firm's crucial strategic goal. Management decisions usually involve several strategic issues. For

Accounting Knowledge and the Use of Opportunity Costs

Research studies have consistently found that decision makers often ignore opportunity costs. For this reason, it is particularly important that the development of decision-making skills place particular emphasis on identifying and incorporating opportunity costs. Interestingly, a recent study found that decision makers with greater expertise in developing comparative income statements appeared to ignore fixed costs more than those with less experience. This was interpreted as resulting in part from the experienced decision makers' strong focus on computing and comparing net income. The problem is that the calculation of accounting net income does not include opportunity costs, thus, a focus on accounting net income could have caused the decision makers to ignore opportunity costs.

Source: Sandra C. Vera-Munoz, "The Effects of Accounting Knowledge and Context on the Omission of Opportunity Costs in Resource Allocation Decisions," *The Accounting Review,* January 1998, pp. 47–72.

example, focusing on the short-term monthly and annual periods should not lead the manager to ignore the long-term strategic factors about markets and production processes. Failing to attend to the long-term, strategic factors could cause the firm to be less competitive in the future. Strategic factors include choices about the nature and amount of manufacturing capacity, product diversity, and product design for cost efficiency.

For example, a strategic decision to design the manufacturing process for high efficiency to produce large batches of product reduces overall production costs. At the same time, it might reduce the firm's flexibility to manufacture a variety of products and thus could increase the cost to produce small, specialized orders. The decision regarding cost efficiency cannot be separated from the determination of marketing strategy, that is, deciding what types and sizes of orders can be accepted.

By identifying *only* relevant costs, the decision maker might fail to link the decision to the firm's strategy. The decision maker also must consider strategic issues. For example, the decision to buy rather than to make a part for the firm's product might make sense on the basis of relevant cost but might be a poor strategic move if the firm's competitive position depends on product reliability that can be maintained only by manufacturing the part in-house. A good indication of a manager's failing to take a strategic approach is that the analysis will have a product cost focus, while a strategic relevant cost analysis also addresses broad and difficult-to-measure strategic issues. The strategic analysis directly focuses on adding value to the customer, going beyond only cost issues.

We now consider the application of the relevant cost analysis and strategic cost analysis to four types of decisions that management accountants often face. For each decision, we develop the cost information that should be used. This cost information includes both relevant cost information and the strategic cost information discussed earlier. The four decisions are as follows: (1) the special order decision, (2) the make, lease, or buy decision, (3) the decision to sell before or after additional processing, and (4) profitability analysis.

SPECIAL ORDER DECISION

COST ANALYSIS

The so-called special order decision occurs when a firm has a one-time opportunity to sell a specified quantity of its product or service. It is called a *special order* because it is typically unexpected. The order frequently comes directly from the customer rather than through normal sales or distribution channels. Special orders are infrequent and commonly represent a small part of a firm's overall business. To make the special order

◀**LEARNING OBJECTIVE 2**

Use relevant and strategic cost analysis to make special order decisions.

decision, managers need critical information about relevant costs, revenues, and any opportunity costs. Consider, for example, the special order situation facing Tommy T-Shirt, Inc. (TTS). TTS is a small manufacturer of specialty clothing, primarily T-shirts and sweatshirts with imprinted slogans and brand names. TTS has been offered a contract by a local college fraternity, Alpha Beta Gamma (ABG) for 1,000 T-shirts printed with artwork publicizing a fund-raising event. The fraternity offers to pay $6.50 for each shirt. TTS normally charges $9.00 for shirts of this type for this size order.

TTS's master budget of manufacturing costs for the current year is given in Exhibit 10–6. The budget is based on expected production of 225,000 T-shirts from an available capacity of 250,000. The 225,000 units are expected to be produced in 200 different batches. The three groups of cost elements are as follows:

1. **Unit-level costs** vary with each shirt printed and include the cost of the shirt ($3.25 each), ink ($0.95 each), and labor ($0.85).

2. **Batch-level costs** vary, in part, with the number of batches produced. The batch-level costs include machine setup, inspection, and materials handling. These costs are partly variable (change with the number of batches) and partly fixed. For example, setup costs are $130 per setup ($26,000 for 200 setups) plus $29,000 fixed costs that do not change with the number of setups (e.g., setup tools or software). Setup costs for 200 batches total $55,000 ($26,000 + $29,000). Similarly, inspection costs are $30 per batch plus $9,000 fixed costs—$15,000 total ($30 × 200 + $9,000). Materials-handling costs are $40 per batch plus $7,000 fixed costs—$15,000 total ($40 × 200 + $7,000).

3. **Plant-level costs** are fixed and do not vary with the number of either units produced or batches. These costs include depreciation and insurance on machinery ($315,000) and other fixed costs ($90,000).

Exhibit 10–7 presents TTS's analysis of the relevant costs. The ABG order requires the same unprinted T-shirt, ink, and labor time as other shirts, for a total of $5.05 per unit. In addition, TTS uses $200 of batch-level costs for each order.

Analysis of Contribution from the Alpha Beta Gamma Order

Sales	1,000 units @ $6.50	$6,500
Relevant costs	1,000 units @ $5.25	5,250
Net contribution	1,000 units @ $1.25	$1,250

Exhibit 10–6	**Master Budget for TTS's Manufacturing Costs** *Expected Output of 225,000 Units in 200 Batches*

Cost Element	Unit-Level Costs		Batch-Level Costs			Plant-Level Costs	
			Variable Costs		Fixed Costs	(all fixed)	
	Amount	Per Unit	Amount	Per Batch			Total
Shirt	$ 731,250	$3.25					$ 731,250
Ink	213,750	0.95					213,750
Operating labor	191,250	0.85					191,250
Subtotal	$1,136,250	$5.05					$1,136,250
Setup			$26,000	$130	$29,000		55,000
Inspection			6,000	30	9,000		15,000
Materials handling			8,000	40	7,000		15,000
Subtotal			$40,000	$200	$45,000		$ 85,000
Machine related						$315,000	315,000
Other						90,000	90,000
Total	$1,136,250	$5.05	$40,000	$200	$45,000	$450,000	$1,626,250

Exhibit 10–7	**Special Order Decision Analysis for TTS**

Cost Type	Unit Costs	Total Cost for One Batch of 1,000 units
Relevant Costs		
Unit-level costs		
Unprinted shirt	$3.25	$3,250
Ink and other supplies	0.95	950
Machine time (operator labor)	0.85	850
Total unit-level costs	$5.05	$5,050
Batch-level costs (that vary with the number of batches)		
Setup		130
Inspection		30
Materials handling		40
Total ($200/batch; $0.20/unit)	0.20	$ 200
Total relevant costs	$5.25	$5,250
Not Relevant Costs		
Fixed batch-level costs ($45,000/225,000)	$ 0.20	
Plant-level costs		
Machine-related costs ($315,000/225,000)	1.40	
Other costs ($90,000/225,000)	0.40	
Total nonrelevant costs	$2.00	
Total cost	$7.25	

The correct analysis for this decision is to determine the relevant costs of $5.25, and then to compare the relevant costs to the special order price of $6.50. The not relevant costs are not considered because they remain the same whether TTS accepts the ABG order. There is a $1.25 ($6.50 – 5.25) contribution to income for each shirt sold to Alpha Beta Gamma, or a total contribution of $1,250, so the order is profitable and should be accepted.

A common **incorrect** analysis of this information focuses on the total unit cost of $7.25 per shirt. If TTS's manager had not recognized that $2.00 of not relevant cost was not affected by the decision, TTS could well have rejected the order on the basis that unit costs ($7.25) exceeded the unit sales price ($6.50).

STRATEGIC ANALYSIS

The relevant cost analysis developed for TTS provides a useful decision regarding the order's profitability. However, for a full decision analysis, TTS also should consider the strategic factors of capacity utilization, short-term versus long-term pricing, the trend in variable costs, and the use of activity-based costing, as follows.

Is TTS Now Operating at Full Capacity?

TTS currently has 25,000 units of excess capacity, more than enough for the ABG order. But what if TTS is operating at or near full capacity; would accepting the order cause the loss of other possibly more profitable sales? If so, TTS should consider the opportunity cost arising from the lost sales. Assume that TTS is operating at full capacity, and that accepting the ABG order would cause the loss of sales of other T-shirts that have a higher contribution of $3.75 ($9.00 – $5.25). The opportunity cost is $3.75 per shirt and the proper decision analysis is as follows:

Contribution from Alpha Beta Gamma order	$ 1,250
Less: Opportunity cost of lost sales (1,000 units × $3.75)	(3,750)
Net contribution (loss) for the order	$(2,500)

Exhibit 10–8   Special Order Decision for TTS under Full Capacity

	With ABG Order	Without ABG Order
Sales		
250,000 units at $9.00		$2,250,000
249,000 at $9.00; 1,000 at $6.50	$2,247,500	
Variable cost at $5.25	1,312,500	1,312,500
Contribution margin	$ 935,000	$ 937,500
Fixed cost (per Exhibit 10–6)	450,000	450,000
Operating income	$ 485,000	$ 487,500
Advantage in favor of rejecting the ABG order		$ 2,500

Exhibit 10–8 shows the effect of accepting the Alpha Beta Gamma order at full capacity, including the irrelevant fixed costs and the irrelevant variable costs; under full capacity, the Alpha Beta Gamma order would reduce total profits by $2,500 due to lost sales.

Excessive Relevant Cost Pricing

The relevant cost decision rule for special orders is intended only for those infrequent situations when a special order can increase income. Done on a regular basis, relevant cost pricing can erode normal pricing policies and lead to a loss in profitability for firms such as TTS. The failure of large companies in the airline, auto, and steel industries has been attributed to their excessive relevant cost pricing because a strategy of continually focusing on the short term can deny a company a successful long term. Special order pricing decisions should not become the centerpiece of a firm's strategy.[2]

Cost Information for Pricing: Competitive Issues

Short-term pricing for special orders uses relevant cost information. For long-term pricing, the firm considers competitive issues as well as cost information. The two following examples illustrate this.

Some firms take a "value" approach to pricing. In what is commonly known as *value-based pricing,* many firms set prices based on the overall value the firm can deliver to the customer, including customer service, assistance with installation and training for the product or service, and finding ways for the product or service to save the customer money.

Some firms "pad" prices to increase margins. Kenneth Merchant and Michael Shields report examples of firms that pad, or overstate, product prices to compensate for the expected large discounts typically granted by the firm's salespersons. The net price received, even after large discounts, is sufficient to meet the firm's profit goals.

In a somewhat similar instance, the Commerce Committee of the U.S. House of Representatives recently studied pharmaceutical firms' apparent practice of increasing prices when their products are subject to increased competition. Although this may seem counterintuitive, the price increase actually makes the drug more attractive to physicians who dispense it. This happens because doctors are reimbursed by Medicare on the basis of the "average wholesale price" (AWP) of the drug, which is typically far less than the price the doctors pay for it. In one example cited, the price to the doctor was less than one-half of the drug's AWP.

Sources: "The Power of Smart Pricing," *Business Week,* April 10, 2000, pp. 160–64; "Chemical Pricing Strategies in Competitive Markets," *Chemical Market Reporter,* New York, November 2, 1998; Kenneth Merchant and Michael D. Shields, "When and Why to Measure Costs Less Accurately to Improve Decision Making," *Accounting Horizons,* June 1993; and "How Drug Makers Influence Medicare Reimbursements to Doctors," *The Wall Street Journal,* September 21, 2000, p. B1.

---

[2]   See John K. Shank and Vijay Govindarajan, *Strategic Cost Management* (New York: Free Press, 1993); and Peter F. Drucker, *Managing for the Future* (New York: Truman Talley Books, 1993), pp. 251–55.

Other Important Factors

In addition to capacity utilization and long-term pricing issues, TTS should consider Alpha Beta Gamma's credit history, any potential complexities in the design that might cause production problems, and other strategic issues such as whether the sale might lead to additional sales of other TTS products.

MAKE, LEASE, OR BUY DECISION

COST ANALYSIS

Generally, a firm's products are manufactured according to specifications set forth in what is called the **bill of materials,** which is a detailed list of the components of the manufactured product. A bill of materials for the manufacture of furniture is illustrated in Chapter 12. An increasingly common decision for manufacturers is to choose which of these components to manufacture in the firm's plant and which to purchase from outside suppliers.

> **◄LEARNING OBJECTIVE 3**
>
> *Use relevant and strategic cost analysis in the make, lease, or buy decision.*
>
> The **bill of materials** is a detailed listing of the components of the manufactured product.

The relevant cost information for the make-or-buy decision is developed in a manner similar to that of the special order decision. The relevant cost information for making the component consists of the short-term costs to manufacture it, ordinarily the variable manufacturing costs, which would be saved if the part is purchased. These costs are compared to the purchase price for the part or component to determine the appropriate decision. Costs that will not change whether the firm makes the part are ignored. For example, consider Blue Tone Manufacturing, maker of clarinets and other reed-based musical instruments. Suppose that Blue Tone is currently manufacturing the mouthpiece for its clarinet but has the option to buy it from a supplier. The following cost information assumes that fixed overhead costs will not change whether Blue Tone chooses to make or buy the mouthpiece:

Cost to buy the mouthpiece, per unit		$24.00
Cost to manufacture, per unit		
Materials	$16.00	
Labor	4.50	
Variable overhead	1.00	
Total variable costs	$21.50	
Fixed overhead	6.00	
Total costs	$27.50	
Total relevant costs		$21.50
Savings from continuing to make		$ 2.50

In this example, the relevant cost to make is $21.50. Since the decision will not affect fixed overhead, the total $27.50 cost is irrelevant. The relevant cost to make is $2.50 less than the purchase cost, so Blue Tone should manufacture the mouthpiece. However, much like the TTS analysis, the make-or-buy analysis for Blue Tone is not complete without a strategic analysis that considers, for example, the quality of the part, the reliability of the supplier, and the potential alternative uses of Blue Tone's plant capacity.

A similar situation arises when a firm must choose between leasing or purchasing a piece of equipment. Such decisions are becoming ever more frequent as the cost and terms of leasing arrangements continue to become more favorable.[3]

To illustrate the lease or buy decision, we use the example of Quick Copy, Inc., a firm that provides printing and duplicating services and other related business ser-

---

[3] The attractiveness of leasing is especially apparent in the case of auto leasing. See "The Business Auto Decision," by Cherie O'Neil, Donald Samuelson, and Matthew Wills, *Journal of Accountancy*, February 2001, pp. 65–73. The lease-or-buy decision can also be aided by specialized computer software, such as Expert Lease Pro (www.autoleasing.com).

vices. Quick Copy uses one large copy machine to complete most big jobs. It leases the machine from the manufacturer on an annual basis that includes general servicing. The annual lease includes both a fixed fee of $40,000 and a per copy charge of $0.02.

The copier manufacturer has suggested that Quick Copy upgrade to the latest model copier that is not available for lease but must be purchased for $160,000. Quick Copy would use the purchased copier for one year, after which it could sell it back to the manufacturer for one-fourth the purchase price ($40,000). In addition, the new machine has a required annual service contract of $20,000. Quick Copy's options for the coming year are to renew the lease for the current copier or to purchase the new copier. The relevant information is outlined in Exhibit 10–9. The lease-or-buy decision will not affect the cost of paper, electrical power, and employee wages, so these costs are irrelevant and are excluded from the analysis. For simplicity, we also ignore potential tax effects of the decision.

The initial step in the analysis is to determine which machine produces a lower cost. The answer depends on the expected annual number of copies. Using cost-volume-profit analysis (Chapter 8 and Exhibit 10–10), Quick Copy's manager determines the indifference point, the number of copies at which both machines cost the same. The calculations are as follows, where Q is the number of copies:

$$\text{Lease cost} = \text{Purchase cost}$$

$$\text{Annual fee} = \text{Net purchase cost} + \text{Service contract}$$

Exhibit 10–9   Quick Copy Lease or Buy Information

	Lease Option	Purchase Option
Annual lease	$40,000	N/A
Charge per copy	0.02	N/A
Purchase cost	N/A	$160,000
Annual service contract	N/A	$20,000
Value at end of period	N/A	$40,000
Expected number of copies a year	6,000,000	6,000,000

Exhibit 10–10   The Lease-or-Buy Example

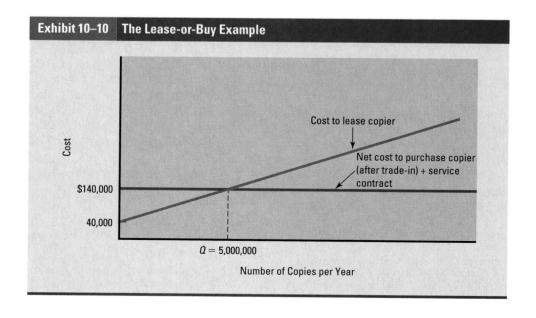

$$\$40,000 + \$0.02 \times Q = (\$160,000 - \$40,000) + \$20,000$$

$$Q = \$100,000/\$0.02$$

$$= 5,000,000 \text{ copies per year}$$

The indifference point, 5,000,000 copies, is lower than the expected annual machine usage of 6,000,000 copies. This indicates that Quick Copy will have lower costs by purchasing the new machine. Costs will be lower by $20,000:

Cost of Lease Minus Cost of Purchase

$$(\$40,000 + \$0.02 \times 6,000,000) - (\$160,000 - \$40,000 + \$20,000)$$

$$= \$160,000 - \$140,000$$

$$= \$20,000$$

In addition to the relevant cost analysis, Quick Copy should consider noncost factors such as the quality of the copy, the reliability of the machine, the benefits and features of the service contracts, and any other factors associated with the use of the machine that might properly influence the decision.

STRATEGIC ANALYSIS

The make, lease, or buy decision often raises strategic issues. For example, a firm using value-chain analysis could find that certain of its activities in the value chain can be more profitably performed by other firms. The practice of choosing to have an outside firm provide a basic service function is called *outsourcing*. Make, lease, or buy analysis has a key role in the decision to outsource by providing an analysis of the relevant costs. Many firms recently have considered outsourcing manufacturing and data processing,

Make or Buy: Human Resources Management

Although the make-or-buy decision is commonly thought to affect parts and components of products, it can also apply to services, including human resource management, internal auditing, security, maintenance and repair, and other service activities performed within the firm. Many firms have chosen to outsource these functions, based in part on the concepts of relevant and strategic cost analysis. For example, to maintain a human resource (HR) function within a firm requires certain fixed and variable costs related to the number of employees. Alternatively, to outsource the function, the firm incurs a fixed fee or a fee that combines fixed and variable elements. The firm can determine the short-term cost of either approach as a basis for deciding between them. The firm also must consider the longer term strategic factors in the decision, as noted in the results of a recent study of the HR policies at 25 large companies. The survey showed that these human resource management functions should not be outsourced:

- Labor/union relations
- Employee relations
- Performance measurement

For example, one human resource manager participating in the study said that his company keeps the employee relations function within the firm but outsources other HR functions. When an employee relations problem arises, he explained, we need "someone from the company who can do something about the problem, and we can't outsource the mechanism that communicates to employees that we care about them."

Source: Charles R. Greer and Stuart A. Youngblood, "Human Resource Management Outsourcing: The Make or Buy Decision," *The Academy of Management Executive,* August 1999, pp. 85–96.

COST MANAGEMENT IN ACTION

Make-or-Buy Strategies: A Survey of U.S. Firms

A recent study of 328 U.S. manufacturing firms revealed that the purchasing managers at most of these firms prefer to purchase parts from outside suppliers rather than to assign the work to an internal manufacturing unit. Factors given as favoring outsourcing include the quality and speed of delivery for the external suppliers, while factors favoring insourcing include concerns for capacity utilization, overhead absorption, employee loyalty, and union contracts. The purchasing managers also tend to prefer to use a number of suppliers in order to develop multiple sourcing relationships. For example, in recent years General Motors (in its U.S. operations) had approximately 3,500 suppliers, while Toyota in Japan had only about 200. How does Toyota keep such a relatively small number of suppliers?

(Refer to Comments on Cost Management in Action at the end of the chapter.)

Contract manufacturing describes the practice of having another firm (sometimes a direct competitor) manufacture a portion of the firm's products.

janitorial, or security services to improve profitability. For example, Eastman-Kodak Corporation has outsourced its data processing requirements, and some airlines are outsourcing food preparation, baggage handling, and reservation systems.

IBM, Texas Instruments, Cisco Systems, and other firms have taken the idea of outsourcing a step further, to what is called **contract manufacturing,** in which another firm manufactures a portion of the first firm's products. When one firm has excess capacity or expertise and the other lacks capacity or know-how, contract manufacturing can be a cost-effective strategy for both firms.[4]

SELL BEFORE OR AFTER ADDITIONAL PROCESSING

COST ANALYSIS

LEARNING OBJECTIVE 4▶

Use relevant and strategic cost analysis in the decision to sell before or after additional processing.

Another common decision concerns the option to sell a product or service before an intermediate processing step or to add further processing and then selling the product or service for a higher price. The additional processing might add features or functionality to a product or add flexibility or quality to a service. For example, a travel agent preparing a group tour faces many decisions related to the features to be offered on the tour, such as side-trips, sleeping quarters, and entertainment that are optional. A manufacturer of consumer electronics faces a number of decisions regarding the nature and extent of features to offer in its products.

The analysis of features also is important for manufacturers in determining what to do with defective products. Generally, they can either be sold in the defective state to outlet stores and discount chains or be repaired for sale in the usual manner. The decision is whether the product should be sold with or without additional processing. Relevant cost analysis is again the appropriate model to follow in analyzing these situations.

To continue with the TTS example, assume that a piece of equipment used to print its T-shirts has malfunctioned, and 400 shirts are not of acceptable quality because some colors are missing or faded. TTS can sell the defective shirts to outlet stores at a greatly reduced price ($4.50) or can run them through the printing machine again. A second run will produce a salable shirt in most cases. The costs to run them through the printer a second time are for the ink, supplies, and labor, totaling $1.80 per shirt, plus the setup, inspection, and materials-handling costs for a batch of product. See

---

[4] See "The Airlines to Labor: Buy in—or Get Bashed," *Business Week*, November 1, 1993, p. 40; also "Farming Out Work—To IBM, DEC, NCR . . .," *Business Week*, May 17, 1993, pp. 92–94.

Exhibit 10–11	Analysis of Reprinting 400 Defective T-Shirts	
	Reprint	**Sell to Discount Store**
Revenue (400 @ $9.00, $4.50)	$3,600	$1,800
Relevant Costs		
Supplies and ink ($.95)	380	
Labor ($.85)	340	
Setup	130	
Inspection	30	
Materials handling	40	
Total relevant costs	$ 920	
Contribution margin	$2,680	$1,800
Net advantage to reprint	$2,680 – $1,800 = $880	
Not Relevant Costs		
Cost of unprinted T-shirt	$ 3.25	$ 3.25
Plant fixed costs per shirt	2.00	2.00

the relevant cost analysis in Exhibit 10–11. Note that the cost of the unprinted T-shirt is the same for both options and is therefore irrelevant.

The analysis shows there is an $880 advantage to reprinting the shirts rather than selling the defective shirts to discount stores.

STRATEGIC ANALYSIS

Strategic concerns arise when considering selling to discount stores. Will this affect the sale of T-shirts in retail stores? Will the cost of packing, delivery, and sales commissions differ for these two types of sales? TTS management must carefully consider these broader issues in addition to the key information provided in the relevant cost analysis in Exhibit 10–11.

PROFITABILITY ANALYSIS

PROFITABILITY ANALYSIS: KEEP OR DROP A PRODUCT LINE

An important aspect of management is the regular review of product profitability. This review should address issues such as these:

- Which products are most profitable?
- Are the products priced properly?
- Which products should be promoted and advertised most aggressively?
- Which product managers should be rewarded?

◀**LEARNING OBJECTIVE 5**

Use relevant and strategic cost analysis in the decision to keep or drop products or services.

These and related issues can be addressed through relevant cost analysis. To illustrate, we use Windbreakers, Inc., a manufacturer of sport clothing. Windbreakers manufactures three jackets: calm (for a light breeze) and windy and gale for harsher weather conditions. Management has requested an analysis of the gale product due to its low sales and low profitability (see Exhibit 10–12).

The analysis of gale should begin with the important observation that the $3.54 fixed cost per unit is irrelevant for the analysis of the current profitability of the three products. Because the $168,000 total fixed costs are unchangeable in the short run, they are irrelevant for this analysis. That is, no changes in product mix, including the deletion of gale, will affect the total fixed costs to be expended in the coming year.

Exhibit 10–12   Sales and Cost Data for Windbreakers, Inc.

	Calm	Windy	Gale	Total
Units sold last year	25,000	18,750	3,750	47,500
Price	$30.00	$32.00	$40.00	
Relevant costs				
Unit variable cost	24.00	24.00	36.00	
Unit contribution margin	$ 6.00	$ 8.00	$ 4.00	
Nonrelevant fixed costs	3.54	3.54	3.54	168,000
Income per unit	$ 2.46	$ 4.46	$ .46	

Exhibit 10–13   Contribution Income Statement Profitability Analysis: Gale Dropped

	Calm	Windy	Total
Sales	$750,000	$600,000	$1,350,000
Relevant costs			
Variable cost	600,000	450,000	1,050,000
Contribution margin	$150,000	$150,000	$ 300,000
Nonrelevant costs			
Fixed cost			168,000
Net income without gale			$ 132,000

The fact that the fixed costs are irrelevant is illustrated by comparing the contribution income statements in Exhibit 10–13, which assumes that gale is dropped, and Exhibit 10–14, which assumes that gale is kept. The only changes caused by dropping gale are the loss of its revenues and the elimination of variable costs. Thus, dropping gale causes a reduction in total contribution margin of $4 per unit times 3,750 units of gale sold, or $15,000, and a corresponding loss in net income. Alternatively,

Benefit: Saved variable costs of gale	$135,000	$(36 × 3,750)
Cost: Opportunity cost of lost sales of gale	(150,000)	$(40 × 3,750)
Decrease in profit from decision to drop gale	$(15,000)	$(4 × 3,750)

Assume that further analysis shows that $60,000 of the $168,000 fixed costs are advertising costs to be spent directly on each of the three products: $25,000 for calm, $15,000 for windy, and $20,000 for gale. The remainder of the fixed costs, $108,000 ($168,000 – $60,000), are not traceable to any of the three products and are therefore allocated to each product as before. Because advertising costs are directly traceable to the individual products, and assuming that the advertising plans for gale can be canceled without additional cost, the $5,000 of advertising costs for gale should be considered a relevant cost in the decision to delete gale. This cost will differ in the future.

Exhibit 10–15 shows that the total contribution margin after all relevant costs for gale is now a net loss of $5,000, providing a potential $5,000 gain by dropping gale because of the expected $20,000 savings in avoidable advertising costs. We can interpret the contribution figures for calm and windy in the same way. The loss in deleting calm or windy would be $125,000 and $135,000, respectively.

In addition to the relevant cost analysis, the decision to keep or drop a product line should include relevant strategic factors, such as the potential effect of the loss of one product line on the sales of another. For example, some florists price cards, vases, and

Exhibit 10–14	Contribution Income Statement Profitability Analysis: Gale Kept			
	Calm	**Windy**	**Gale**	**Total**
Last year's sales	$750,000	$600,000	$150,000	$1,500,000
Relevant costs				
Variable cost	600,000	450,000	135,000	1,185,000
Contribution margin	$150,000	$150,000	$ 15,000	$ 315,000
Nonrelevant costs				
Fixed cost				168,000
Net income with gale				$ 147,000

Exhibit 10–15	Profitability Analysis: Including Traceable Advertising Costs			
	Calm	**Windy**	**Gale**	**Total**
Last year's sales	$750,000	$600,000	$150,000	$1,500,000
Relevant costs				
Variable cost	600,000	450,000	135,000	1,185,000
Contribution margin	$150,000	$150,000	$ 15,000	$ 315,000
Other relevant costs (traceable)				
Advertising	25,000	15,000	20,000	60,000
Contribution after all relevant costs	$125,000	$135,000	$ (5,000)	$ 255,000
Nonrelevant costs (not traceable)				
Fixed cost				$ 108,000
Net income with gale				$ 147,000

other related items at or below cost to better serve and attract customers to the most profitable product, the flower arrangements.

Other important factors include the potential effect on overall employee morale and organizational effectiveness if a product line is dropped. Moreover, managers should consider the sales growth potential of each product. Will a product considered to be dropped place the firm in a strong competitive position sometime in the future? A particularly important consideration is the extent of available production capacity. If production capacity and production resources (such as labor and machine time) are limited, consider the relative profitability of the products and the extent to which they require different amounts of these production resources.

PROFITABILITY ANALYSIS: EVALUATING PROGRAMS

Managers use the concept of relevant cost analysis to measure the financial effectiveness of programs or projects. A good example of such an analysis is the evaluation of the Health and Weight Loss Program, a primary component of the Health Management Program at Kimberly-Clark Corporation in Neenah, Wisconsin.[5] Kimberly-Clark has traced the costs of this program and measured its dollar benefits in three categories: (1) health care savings, (2) sick leave and absenteeism savings, and (3)

◄**LEARNING OBJECTIVE 6**

Use relevant and strategic cost analysis to evaluate programs.

[5] The application is described in Kenneth J. Smith, "Differential Cost Analysis Techniques in Occupational Health Promotion Evaluation," *Accounting Horizons*, June 1988, pp. 58–66.

Exhibit 10–16	Health and Weight Loss Program Income Statement for Kimberly-Clark Corporation	
Revenues		
Health care cost savings		$ 9,416
Sick leave absenteeism savings		4,973
Program fees		2,168
Total revenues		$16,557
Relevant costs		
Program materials		112
Consultant's salary		7,804
Total relevant costs		$ 7,916
Contribution after relevant costs		$ 8,641

program fees for the participating employees. Exhibit 10–16 shows the relevant cost analysis of the profitability of this program.

PROFITABILITY ANALYSIS: SERVICE OFFERING DECISIONS IN A NOT-FOR-PROFIT ORGANIZATION

Triangle Women's Center (TWC) uses relevant cost analysis to determine the desirability of new services. TWC provides several services to the communities in and around a large southeastern city. It has not offered child care services but has received a large number of requests to do so in recent years. Now TWC is planning to add this service. The relevant cost analysis follows. TWC expects to hire a director ($29,000) and two part-time assistants ($9,000 each) for the child care service. TWC estimates variable costs per child at $60 per month. No other costs are relevant because none of the other operating costs of TWC are expected to change. TWC expects to receive funding of $25,000 from the United Way plus $30,000 from the city council. The analysis for the child care service's first year of operation is shown in Exhibit 10–17, which assumes that 20 children, the maximum number, will use the service.

The TWC analysis shows that the child care service will have a deficit of approximately $6,400 in the first year. Now TWC can decide whether it can make up the deficit from current funds or by raising additional funds. Relevant cost analysis provides TWC a useful method to determine the resource needs for the new program.

Exhibit 10–17	Triangle Women's Center Analysis of Child Care Services	
Relevant costs		
Salary of director		$29,000
Salary for two part-time assistants		18,000
Variable costs for 20 children at $60 per month		14,400
Total relevant costs		$61,400
Total funding		
United Way		$25,000
City Council		30,000
		$55,000
Expected deficit in the first year		$ 6,400

Sales Commissions at IBM and Ford Motor Co.

The use of relevant cost analysis in determining product profitability is also important in motivating and rewarding the sales staff. Since the best measure of short-term profitability is *contribution after relevant costs,* this measure should be used for sales commissions to motivate the sales staff to sell the most profitable products, that is, those with the highest contribution margin. The common approach of using sales revenue as a basis for commissions is not consistent with the goal of improving profitability. IBM Corporation recognized the importance of this idea by tying 60 percent of its sales commissions to the **profit** generated by the products sold.

The IBM plan also attends to important strategic factors, such as customer satisfaction. To make sure that salespeople do not simply push for sales of high-margin products, IBM links the remaining 40 percent of their commissions to customer satisfaction. Thus, the compensation plan makes salespeople think like managers—their focus is on profits and customer satisfaction, as is the focus of top management.

Similarly, Ford Motor Co. recently changed the way its sales force is compensated from one based on units sold to one based on profit margins. Previously, salespeople had tended to push the low-price, low-margin vehicles (Escorts and Aspires) to increase volume and save marketing costs. The change has motivated increased sales of the higher margin vehicles (Crown Victorias and Explorers).

Source: "IBM Leans on Its Sales Force," *Business Week,* February 17, 1994, p. 110; and "The Power of Smart Pricing," *Business Week,* April 10, 2000, pp. 160–64.

Relevant Cost Analysis Used Incorrectly by Not-for-Profit Organizations

1. The Massachusetts State Workfare program trains welfare parents to enter the workforce and pays for child care costs incurred during the training period. An analysis of the program showed that the benefits in removing participants from welfare exceeded the costs of supporting the participants during the training period. However, a closer look showed that many of the participants in the training programs would have left welfare, even without the training. Thus, the calculation of relevant benefits was flawed. It assumed that the training program was the only relevant factor in removing the participants from welfare, which turned out not to be the case.

2. The cost/benefit analysis of replacing an existing hospital with a new hospital also used relevant cost analysis incorrectly. The revenue earned by the present hospital was incorrectly counted as a relevant benefit of the new hospital, when only its incremental revenue should have been counted. The revenue of the present hospital is irrelevant because it would have continued if the old hospital had not been replaced.

Source: R. J. Herzlinger and Denise Nitterhouse, *Financial Accounting and Managerial Control for Nonprofit Organizations* (Cincinnati: South-Western Publishing, 1994), p. 468.

MULTIPLE PRODUCTS AND LIMITED RESOURCES

◀**LEARNING OBJECTIVE 7**

Analyze decisions with multiple products and limited resources.

The preceding relevant cost analyses were simplified by using a single product and assuming sufficient resources to meet all demands. The analysis changes significantly with two or more products and limited resources. The revised analysis is considered in this section. We continue the example of Windbreakers, Inc., except that we assume that the calm product is manufactured in a separate plant under contract with a major customer. Thus, the following analysis focuses *only on the **windy and gale products,*** which are manufactured in a single facility.

A key element of the relevant cost analysis is the most profitable sales mix for windy and gale. If there are no production constraints, the answer is clear; we manufacture what is needed to meet demand for both windy and gale. However, when demand exceeds production capacity, management must make some trade-offs about the quantity of each product to manufacture, and therefore, what demand is unmet. The answer requires considering the production possibilities given by the production constraints. Consider two important cases: (1) one production constraint and (2) two or more production constraints.

CASE 1: ONE PRODUCTION CONSTRAINT

Assume that the production of windy and gale requires an automated sewing machine to stitch the jackets and that this production activity is a limited resource: sales demand for the two products exceeds the capacity on the plant's three automated sewing machines. Each machine can be run up to 20 hours per day five days per week, or 400 hours per month, which is its maximum capacity allowing for maintenance. This gives 1,200 (3 × 400) available hours for sewing each month. Assume further that the machine requires three minutes to assemble a windy and two minutes to assemble a gale.

Because only 1,200 hours of machine time are available per month and the gale jacket requires less machine time, more gale jackets can be made in a month than windy jackets. The maximum number of windy jackets is 24,000 jackets per month (1,200 hours times 20 jackets per hour, at 3 minutes per jacket). Similarly, if the sewing machine were devoted entirely to gale jackets, then 36,000 jackets per month could be produced (1,200 times 30 jackets per hour). This information is summarized in Exhibit 10–18.

A continuous trade-off possibility exists for the extreme situations: zero output of windy and 36,000 of gale or 24,000 of windy and zero of gale. These production and sales mix possibilities can be shown graphically; all sales mix possibilities are represented by all possible points on the line in Exhibit 10–19. The line in Exhibit 10–19 can be determined as follows:

$$\text{Slope} = -36,000/24,000 = -3/2$$

$$\text{Intercept} = 36,000$$

The line in Exhibit 10–19 is thus given by

$$\text{Units of gale} = 36,000 - 3/2 \times \text{Units of windy}$$

Exhibit 10–18	**Windbreakers Data for the Windy and Gale Plant** *One Constraint: The Sewing Machine*		
		Windy	**Gale**
Since			
Contribution margin/unit		$8	$4
Sewing time per jacket		3 min	2 min
Then, because sewing time is limited to 1,200 hours per month, we determine the contribution margin per machine-hour			
Number of jackets per hour (60 min/3 min = 20; 60/2 = 30)		20	30
Contribution margin per hour (20 × $8; 30 × $4)		$160	$120
Also, the maximum production for each product, given the 1,200-hour constraint			
For windy: 1,200 × 20		24,000	
For gale: 1,200 × 30			36,000

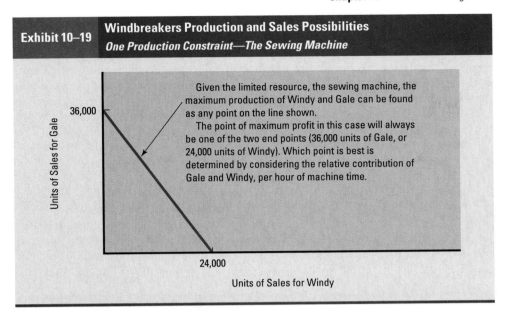

Exhibit 10–19

Windbreakers Production and Sales Possibilities

One Production Constraint—The Sewing Machine

Given the limited resource, the sewing machine, the maximum production of Windy and Gale can be found as any point on the line shown.

The point of maximum profit in this case will always be one of the two end points (36,000 units of Gale, or 24,000 units of Windy). Which point is best is determined by considering the relative contribution of Gale and Windy, per hour of machine time.

Units of Sales for Gale

36,000

24,000

Units of Sales for Windy

To illustrate, assume that Windbreakers is producing 12,000 units of windy so that

$$\text{Units of gale} = 36{,}000 - 3/2 \times 12{,}000 = 18{,}000$$

To see that this production mix (12,000 units of windy and 18,000 units of gale) uses all available capacity of 1,200 hours:

$$\text{Hours for gale} + \text{Hours for windy} = \text{Total hours}$$

$$\frac{\text{Units of gale}}{\text{Number of gales per hour}} + \frac{\text{Units of windy}}{\text{Number of windys per hour}} = \text{Total hours}$$

$$18{,}000/30 + 12{,}000/20 = 1{,}200 \text{ hours}$$

Now that we know the production possibilities, we can determine the best product mix. Note from Exhibit 10–18 that windy has the higher overall contribution margin, $160 per hour (20 jackets per hour × $8 per jacket). Because 1,200 machine-hours are available per month, the maximum total contribution from the production possibilities is to produce only windy and achieve the total contribution of 1,200 × $160 = $192,000 (or $8 per unit × 24,000 units = $192,000) per month. If Windbreakers were to produce and sell only gale, the maximum total contribution margin would be $144,000 per month (1,200 hours × $120 per hour), a $48,000 reduction over the contribution from selling only windy. *Thus, when there is only one production constraint and excess demand, it is generally best to focus production and sales on the product with the highest contribution per unit of scarce resource.* Of course, it is unlikely in a practical situation that a firm would be able to adopt the extreme position of deleting one product and focusing entirely on the other. However, the previous results show the value of considering a strong focus on the more profitable product based on the contribution per unit of a scarce resource.

CASE 2: TWO OR MORE PRODUCTION CONSTRAINTS

When the production process requires two or more production constraints, the choice of sales mix involves a more complex analysis, and in contrast to one production constraint, the solution can include both products. To continue with the Windbreakers case, assume that in addition to the automated sewing machine, a second production activity is required. The second activity inspects the completed jackets, adds labels, and packages the completed product. This operation is done by 40 workers, who can complete the operation for the windy jacket in 15 minutes and for the gale jacket in 5 minutes (because of differences in material quality, less inspection time is required for the gale jacket). This means that 4 (60/15) windy jackets can be completed in an hour, or 12 gale (60/5). Because of the limited size of the facility, no more than 40 workers can be employed effectively in the inspection and packaging process. These employees work a 40-hour week, which means 35 hours of actually performing the operation, given time for breaks, training, and other tasks. Thus, 5,600 hours (40 workers × 35 hours × 4 weeks) are available per month for inspecting and packing.

The maximum output per month for the windy jacket is 22,400 (5,600 hours × 4 jackets per hour). Similarly, the maximum output for the gale jacket is 67,200. All of this information is summarized in Exhibit 10–20.

The production possibilities for two constraints are illustrated in Exhibit 10–21. In addition to the production possibilities for machine time, we show the production possibilities for inspection and packing. The shaded area indicates the range of possible outputs for both gale and windy. Note that it is not possible to produce more than the 22,400 units of windy because all 40 workers inspecting and packing full time would not

Exhibit 10–20	**Windbreakers Data for the Windy and Gale Plant** *The Second Constraint: Inspecting and Packing*		
		Windy	**Gale**
Since			
	Contribution margin/unit	$8	$4
	Inspection and packaging time per jacket	15 min	5 min
Then			
	Number of jackets per hour	4	12
	Contribution margin per hour (4 × $8; 12 × $4)	$32	$48
Also			
	The maximum production for each product, given the 5,600-hour constraint		
	For windy: 5,600 × 4	22,400	
	For gale: 5,600 × 12		67,200

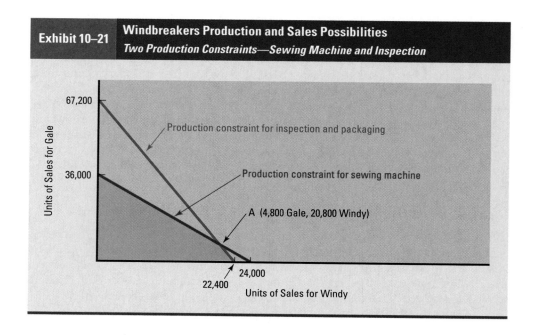

Exhibit 10–21	**Windbreakers Production and Sales Possibilities** *Two Production Constraints—Sewing Machine and Inspection*

be able to handle more than that number, even though the sewing machine is capable of producing 24,000 units. Similarly, although Windbreakers could pack and ship 67,200 units of gale by having all 40 packers work full-time on that jacket, the firm could manufacture only 36,000 units of gale because of limited capacity on the sewing machine.

The production planner can determine the best production mix by examining all of the possible production–sales possibilities in the shaded area, from 36,000 on the gale axis to point A where the constraints intersect, and then to the point 22,400 on the windy axis. The sales mix with the highest contribution must be one of these three points: 36,000 of gale, point A, or 22,400 units of windy. The solution, called the *corner point analysis*, is obtained by finding the total contribution at each point and then choosing the point with the higher contribution. The solution achieved in this manner is for production at point A, 20,800 units of windy and 4,800 units of gale.[6]

The analysis of sales mix and production constraints is a useful way for managers to understand both how a difference in sales mix affects income and how production limitations and capacities can significantly affect the proper determination of the most profitable sales mix.

BEHAVIORAL AND IMPLEMENTATION ISSUES

CONSIDERATION OF STRATEGIC OBJECTIVES

A well-known problem in business today is the tendency of managers to focus on short-term goals and neglect the long-term strategic goals because their compensation is based on short-term accounting measures such as net income. Many critics of relevant cost analysis have raised this issue. As noted throughout the chapter, it is critical that the relevant cost analysis be supplemented by a careful consideration of the firm's long-term, strategic concerns. Without strategic considerations, management could improperly use relevant cost analysis to achieve a short-term benefit and potentially suffer a significant long-term loss. For example, a firm might choose to accept a special order because of a positive relevant cost analysis without properly considering that the nature of the special order could have a significant negative impact on the firm's image in the marketplace and perhaps a negative effect on sales of the firm's other products. The important message for managers is to keep the strategic objectives in the forefront in any decision situation.

◀**LEARNING OBJECTIVE 8**

Discuss the behavioral, implementation, and legal issues in decision making.

PREDATORY PRICING

The Robinson Patman Act, administered by the U.S. Federal Trade Commission, addresses pricing that could substantially damage the competition in an industry. This is called *predatory pricing*, which the U.S. Supreme Court defined in a 1993 decision, *Brooke Group Ltd.* vs. *Brown & Williamson Tobacco Corp.* (B&W), as a situation in which a company has set prices below cost *and* planned to raise prices later to recover the losses from lower prices. This law is relevant for short-term and long-term pricing since it could require a firm to justify significant price cuts. However, the Court in the *Brooke* decision concluded that on the basis of economic theory, predatory pricing does not work and concluded in favor of B&W, the defendant in the case. The Court's reasoning has stood the test of time, because all 37 predatory pricing cases since its

---

[6] The point A, 20,800 for windy and 4,800 for gale, is obtained by solving the two equations:

$$15W + 5G = 35 \times 40 \times 4 \times 60 = 336,000 \text{ minutes}$$
$$3W + 2G = 400 \times 3 \times 60 = 72,000 \text{ minutes}$$

Linear programming, a mathematical method, permits the solution of much larger problems involving many products and production activities. A linear program technique to solve the windy and gale case is shown in Appendix A of this chapter. This technique uses the Solver function of Microsoft Excel.

1993 decision have been found in favor of the defendant. Some economists and lawyers, however, believe that economic theories underlying competition have changed since 1993 and that the plaintiff could prevail in future cases of predator pricing. For example, some lawyers are looking carefully at American Airlines' pricing practices. Its aggressive pricing, especially at the Dallas–Fort Worth airport, has driven some competitors to financial distress.[7]

REPLACEMENT OF VARIABLE COSTS WITH FIXED COSTS

Another potential incentive associated with relevant cost analysis is for managers to replace variable costs with fixed costs. This might happen if mid-level and lower-level managers realize that because they rely on relevant cost analysis, upper management tends to overlook fixed costs. Lower-level managers might choose to replace their assets and other productive resources to reduce variable costs, although this increases fixed costs significantly. For example, a new machine might replace direct labor. The overall costs increase because of the cost of the machine, although variable costs under the manager's control decrease and the contribution margin increases. Management's proper goal is to maximize contribution margin and to minimize fixed operating costs at the same time. Managers should use relevant cost analysis as a tool to maximize contribution and must also develop methods to manage fixed costs.

PROPER IDENTIFICATION OF RELEVANT FACTORS

Another possible problem area of cost analysis is that managers can fail to properly identify relevant costs. In particular, untrained managers commonly include irrelevant, sunk costs in their decision making.[8] Similarly, many managers fail to see that allocated fixed costs are irrelevant. When fixed costs are "unitized" in this manner,

---

Examples of Decision Biases:
Mutual Fund Investors Show "Loss Aversion"

A recent study indicates that mutual fund investors show an unfortunate decision bias when evaluating the returns of individual funds. The average investor is 2.5 times more likely to sell a fund with strong returns than a fund with weak returns (the good news is that they tend to buy strong funds). The researchers call this bias to sell strong funds "loss aversion," and explain it in terms of human emotions: You feel a lot better about selling a winner than you do about selling a loser. From a decision-making point of view, this emotional aspect is unfortunate because the investor simultaneously dumps a winning stock and incurs capital gains taxes on the gain made on the sale.

Source: Robert Barker, "Why Not Lose Those Mutual-Fund Losers," *Business Week,* October 23, 2000, p. 170.

---

[7]   Based on information in "Caveat Predator," *Business Week,* May 22, 2000, pp. 116–18; and "Legend Air, Unable to Get Financing, Suspends Flights," *The Wall Street Journal,* December 4, 2000.

[8]   For a comprehensive coverage of decision-making biases, see John S. Hammond, Ralph L. Keeney, and Howard Raiffa, "The Hidden Traps in Decision Making," *Harvard Business Review,* September–October 1998, pp. 47–58; also D. L. Heerema and R. L. Rogers, "Is Your Cost Accounting System Benching Your Team Players?" *Management Accounting,* September 1991, pp. 35–40 gives useful illustrations of the improper use of relevant cost analysis in the automobile industry, the military, and elsewhere. Prospect theory suggests that people underweight alternatives that are uncertain in comparison to alternatives known to be certain. The theory has been offered as a potential explanation of the tendency people have to include sunk costs in decision making. See D. Kahneman and A. Tversky, "Prospect Theory: An Analysis of Decision under Risk," *Econometrica,* March 1979, pp. 263–92; and Glen Whyte, "Escalating Commitment to a Course of Action: A Reinterpretation," *Academy of Management Review,* 1986, pp. 311–21.

many managers tend to improperly find them relevant. It is easier for these managers to see the fixed cost as irrelevant when it is given in a single sum.

These are illustrations of the pervasive biases present in many managers' decision making. To repeat, effective use of relevant cost analysis requires careful identification of relevant costs, those future costs that differ among decision alternatives, and correctly recognizing sunk costs and unit fixed costs as irrelevant in the short term.

SUMMARY

Relevant cost analysis uses future costs that differ for the decision maker's options. The principle of relevant cost analysis can be applied in a number of specific decisions involving manufacturing, service, and not-for-profit organizations. The decisions considered in the chapter include

- The special order decision for which the relevant costs are the direct manufacturing costs and any incremental fixed costs.
- The make, lease, or buy decision for which the relevant costs are the direct manufacturing costs and any avoidable fixed costs.
- The decision to sell a product before or after additional processing for which the relevant costs are the additional processing costs.
- The decision to keep or drop a product line or service for which the relevant costs are the direct costs and any fixed costs that change if the product or service is dropped.
- The evaluation of programs and projects.
- The decision of a not-for-profit organization to offer a service.

Strategic cost analysis complements relevant cost analysis by having the decision maker consider the strategic issues involved in the situation.

When two or more products or services are involved, another type of decision must be made: to determine the correct product mix. The solution depends on the number of production activities that are at full capacity. With one production constraint, the answer is to produce and sell as much as possible of the product that has the highest contribution margin per unit of time on the constrained activity. With two or more constrained activities, the analysis uses graphical and quantitative methods to determine the correct product mix.

A number of key behavioral, implementation, and legal issues must be considered in using relevant cost analysis. Many who use the approach fail to give sufficient attention to the firm's long-term, strategic objectives. Too strong a focus on relevant costs can cause the manager to overlook important opportunity costs and strategic considerations. Other issues include the tendency to replace variable costs with fixed costs when relevant cost analysis is used in performance evaluation, the pervasive tendency of people not to correctly view fixed costs as sunk but to view them as somehow controllable and relevant.

APPENDIX A

Linear Programming and the Product Mix Decision

This appendix explains how linear programming can be used to solve product mix decisions such as the Windbreakers case illustrated in the chapter. Linear programming is particularly useful when the product mix decision involves three or more constraints since these larger problems are difficult to solve graphically or with the simple corner point analysis explained in the chapter. A number of linear programming tools are available; we use the Solver function of Microsoft Excel because of its wide availability. To access this tool, you simply install it when installing Excel; Solver will appear as an option on Excel's Tool menu.

The first step in using Solver is to enter the data for the problem into an Excel spreadsheet, in the form shown in Exhibit 10–22:

Column A: Shows the product names.

Column B: Solver requires an initial guess at what might be an appropriate solution; for this purpose, we chose the point 10,000 units of windy and 2,000 units of gale; the point should be any of the possible points within the feasible region shown as the shaded area in Exhibit 10–21.

Columns C, D, and E: These contain data entered from the problem information.

Columns F, G, and H: These contain formulas based on the data in columns, C, D, and E; for example, cell F5 contains B5xC5; cell G5 contains B5xD5, and so on.

The second step in using Solver is to enter the parameters as shown in the dialog box in Exhibit 10–22. The dialog box appears by selecting **Solver** from the Tool menu. Note that the target cell is total contribution, located in cell F7, which currently shows the total contribution for sales of 10,000 units of windy and 2,000 units of gale. The "By Changing Cells" section includes those cells representing the total sales of windy and gale, now set at an initial value of 10,000 and 2,000 units, respectively. Then the constraints for sewing time and inspect and pack time are entered in the "Subject to the Constraints" section as shown. Finally, select **Solve** in the dialog box, and the solution appears, as shown in Exhibit 10–23. (See also footnote 6.)

Notice that cells B5 and B6 in Exhibit 10–23 now show the solution values for the two products, and the cells in columns F, G, and H show the total contribution and total use of the two constraints. At this time, it is possible to see any of three possible additional reports, the Answer, Sensitivity, and Limit reports as shown in the dialog box. We have selected only the Answer report for illustration at this time, which is shown in Exhibit 10–24. This report summarizes the initial and final values for the problem data.

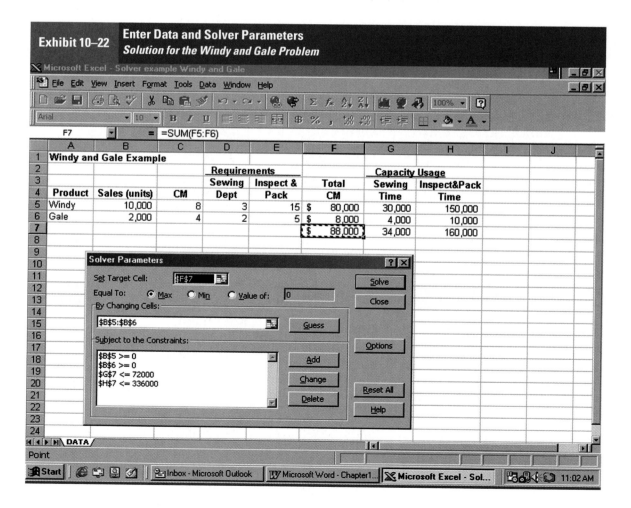

Exhibit 10–22 Enter Data and Solver Parameters
Solution for the Windy and Gale Problem

Exhibit 10–23   Solver Solution for the Windy and Gale Problem

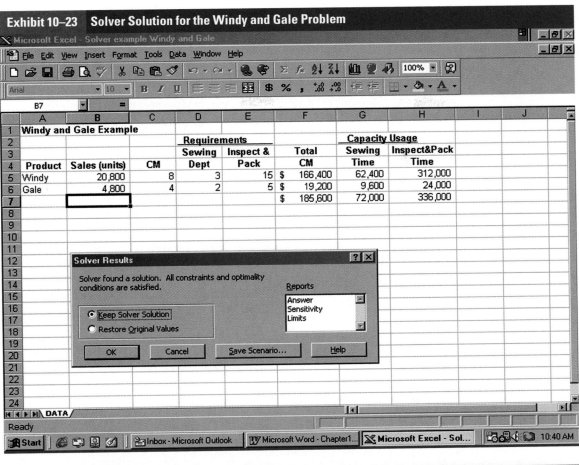

Exhibit 10–24   Solver Solution for the Windy and Gale Problem: Answer Report

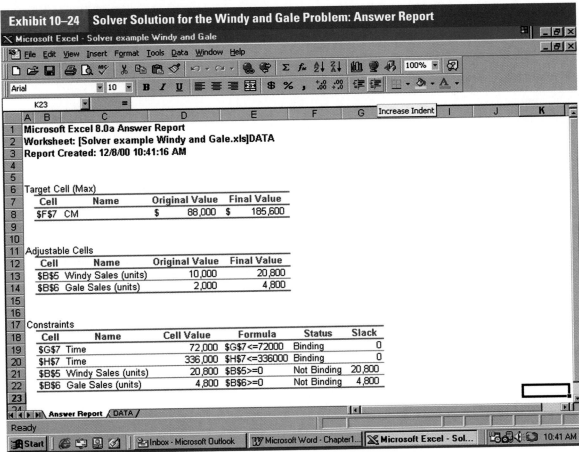

KEY TERMS

Bill of materials   **419**

Contract manufacturing   **422**

Relevant costs   **411**

COMMENTS ON COST MANAGEMENT IN ACTION

Make-or-Buy Strategies: A Survey of U.S. Firms

Toyota Motor Company is able to maintain a small number of suppliers by using two key strategies. First, it develops a hierarchy of suppliers; Toyota deals directly with approximately 200, which are called the *top-tier suppliers*. These 200 suppliers in turn deal with second-tier suppliers who provide products and services to those at the top tier. These second-tier suppliers in turn deal with third-tier suppliers. In this way, Toyota delegates the responsibility for managing the supply function in a way that motivates suppliers at each tier to work effectively with those above and below it in the supply chain. Second, Toyota distinguishes two types of suppliers, general and specialty. Toyota has relatively simple relationships with those in the general category of suppliers but develops close financial and technological ties with the specialty suppliers. The objective is to recognize the strategic importance of the specialty suppliers and to develop strong relationships with them to ensure success.

A recent survey of 328 U.S. purchasing managers showed that they were taking steps to reduce both the number of suppliers and the frequency with which they change suppliers, in effect moving closer to the Toyota model.

Source: Hong Y. Park, C. Surender Reddy, and Sam Sarkar, "Make or Buy Strategy of Firms in the U.S.," *Multinational Business Review*, Fall 2000, pp. 89–97.

SELF-STUDY PROBLEMS

(For solutions, please turn to the end of the chapter.)

1.   SPECIAL ORDER PRICING

HighValu Inc. manufactures a moderate-price set of lawn furniture (a table and four chairs) that it sells for $225. It currently manufactures and sells 6,000 sets per year. The manufacturing costs include $85 for materials and $45 for labor per set. The overhead charge per set is $35, which consists entirely of fixed costs.

HighValu is considering a special purchase offer from a large retail firm, which has offered to buy 600 sets per year for three years at a price of $150 per set. HighValu has the available plant capacity to produce the order and expects no other orders or profitable alternative uses of the plant capacity.

Required   Should HighValu accept the offer?

2.   THE MAKE-OR-BUY DECISION

Assume that HighValu Inc., as described, currently purchases the chair cushions for its lawn set from an outside vendor for $15 per set. HighValu's chief operations officer wants an analysis of the comparative costs of manufacturing these cushions to determine whether bringing the manufacturing in-house would save the firm money. Additional information shows that if HighValu were to manufacture the cushions, the materials cost would be $6 and the labor cost would be $4 per set and that it would have to purchase cutting and sewing equipment, which would add $10,000 to annual fixed costs.

Required   Should HighValu make the cushions or continue to purchase them from the vendor?

3. PROFITABILITY ANALYSIS

Consider again the Windbreakers firm described in the text. Suppose that it determines that dropping the gale product line will release production capacity so that it can manufacture additional units of windy. Assume that, as described in the text, the two production constraints are the automated sewing machine and the inspection and packing operation. The automated sewing machine can make 20 windys or 30 gales per hour. As before, the inspection operation requires 15 minutes for a windy (4 per hour) and 5 minutes for a gale (12 per hour). Currently, 3,750 gales and 18,750 windys are being manufactured and sold. Sales projections show that sales of windy could be increased to 30,000 units if additional capacity were available.

Required

1. If Windbreakers deletes gale entirely, how many units of windy can it manufacture with the released capacity?

2. What is the dollar effect on net income if Windbreakers drops the production and sale of gale and uses the released capacity for windy?

3. What other factors should Windbreakers consider in its decision to drop gale and use the released capacity to produce additional units of windy?

QUESTIONS

10–1 What are relevant costs? Provide several examples for the decision to repair or replace a piece of equipment.

10–2 Define *outsourcing* and explain how the relevant cost analysis model is used in the outsourcing decision.

10–3 List at least four different decisions for which the relevant cost analysis model can be used effectively.

10–4 How does the relevant cost analysis model differ for manufacturing and service firms?

10–5 Define *contract manufacturing* and provide several examples.

10–6 List four to six strategic factors that are often important in the make-or-buy decision.

10–7 Explain what *not relevant cost* means and provide two examples of it.

10–8 Why are variable costs usually more relevant than fixed costs in short-term decision making?

10–9 Give an example of how a firm can decrease variable costs by increasing fixed costs.

10–10 Give an example of how a firm can decrease fixed costs by increasing variable costs.

10–11 How do short-term evaluations affect a manager's incentives and performance?

10–12 List four or five important limitations of relevant cost analysis.

10–13 How do strategic factors affect the proper use of relevant cost analysis?

10–14 List some of the behavioral, implementation, and legal problems to be anticipated in the use of relevant cost analysis.

10–15 How does the presence of one production constraint affect the relevant cost analysis model? Two or more production constraints?

10–16 What is the relationship, if any, between the relevant cost analysis method and cost-volume-profit analysis?

10–17 Explain why depreciation is a nonrelevant cost.

EXERCISES

10–18 SPECIAL ORDER ANALYSIS   Tihon Company recently approached Vander-Meer Corporation regarding manufacturing a special order of 4,000 units of product CRB2B. Tihon would reimburse VanderMeer for all variable manufacturing costs plus 35 percent. The *per-unit* data follow:

Unit sales price	$28
Variable manufacturing costs	13
Variable marketing costs	5
Fixed manufacturing costs	4
Fixed marketing costs	2

VanderMeer would have a retooling cost of $10,000 but otherwise has sufficient plant capacity to manufacture the order. It would incur no marketing costs for this special order.

Required   Should the special order be accepted?

10–19 SPECIAL ORDER: OPPORTUNITY COSTS   Choi Inc. is working at full production capacity producing 20,000 units of a unique product. Manufacturing costs per unit for the product are

Direct materials	$ 9
Direct labor	8
Manufacturing overhead	10
Total manufacturing cost	$27

The unit manufacturing overhead cost is based on a $4 variable cost per unit and $120,000 of fixed costs. The nonmanufacturing costs, all variable, are $8 per unit, and the sales price is $45 per unit.

Sports Headquarters Company (SHC) has asked Choi to produce 5,000 units of a modification of the new product. This modification would require the same manufacturing processes. SHC has offered to share the nonmanufacturing costs equally with Choi. Choi would sell the modified product to SHC for $30 per unit.

Required

1. Should Choi produce the special order for SHC? Why or why not?

2. Suppose that Choi Inc. had been working at less than full capacity to produce 16,000 units of the product when SHC made the offer. What is the minimum price that Choi should accept for the modified product under these conditions?

10–20 PROFITABILITY ANALYSIS, DROPPING A DIVISION   Jackson Financial Services is planning to drop one of its divisions that has a contribution margin of $20,000. In addition, $50,000 of Jackson's corporate overhead is allocated to the division. Of the $50,000, $25,000 can be eliminated if the division is discontinued.

Required   What would be the increase or decrease in Jackson Industries' pretax income by dropping this division?

Strategy

10–21 PROFITABILITY ANALYSIS   Maitax Corporation, located in Buffalo, New York, is a retailer of high-tech products known for their excellent quality and innovation. Recently the firm conducted a relevant cost analysis of one of its product lines that has only two products, RAM and ROM. The sales for ROM are decreasing and the purchase costs are increasing. The firm might drop ROM and sell only RAM.

Maitax allocates fixed costs to products on the basis of sales revenue. When the president of Maitax saw the income statement, he agreed that ROM should be dropped. If this is done, sales of RAM are expected to increase by 10 percent next year; the firm's cost structure will remain the same.

	RAM	ROM
Sales	$180,000	$260,000
Variable cost of goods sold	70,000	130,000
Contribution margin	$110,000	$130,000
Expenses		
Fixed corporate costs	50,000	75,000
Variable selling and administration	18,000	50,000
Fixed selling and administration	12,000	21,000
Total expenses	$ 80,000	$146,000
Net income	$ 30,000	$ (16,000)

Required

1. Find the expected change in annual net income by dropping ROM and selling only RAM.

2. What strategic factors should be considered?

10–22 **RELEVANT COST EXERCISES**

a. **Make or Buy** Murray Inc. manufactures machine parts for aircraft engines. CEO Bucky Walters is considering an offer from a subcontractor to provide 2,000 units of product OP89 for $124,000. If Murray does not purchase these parts from the subcontractor, it must produce them in-house with these costs:

Costs per Unit	
Direct materials	$28
Direct labor	18
Variable overhead	6
Fixed overhead	4

In addition to these costs, Murray would also incur a retooling and design cost of $8,000 to produce part OP89.

Required Should Murray Inc. accept the offer from the subcontractor? Why or why not?

b. **Disposal of Assets** A company has an inventory of 2,000 different parts for a line of cars that has been discontinued. The net book value of inventory in the accounting records is $50,000. The parts can be either remachined at a total additional cost of $25,000 and then sold for $30,000 or scrapped for $2,500. What should it do?

c. **Replacement of Asset** An uninsured boat costing $90,000 was wrecked the first day it was used. It can be either disposed of for $9,000 cash and replaced with a similar boat costing $92,000 or rebuilt for $75,000 and be brand new as far as operating characteristics and looks are concerned. What should be done?

d. **Profit from Processing Further** Almond's Corporation manufactures products A, B, and C from a joint process. Joint costs are allocated on the basis of relative sales value at the end of the joint process. Additional information for Almond's Corporation follows:

439

	A	B	C	Total
Units produced	12,000	8,000	4,000	24,000
Joint costs	$144,000	$ 60,000	$36,000	$240,000
Sales value after joint processing	$240,000	$100,000	60,000	400,000
Additional costs for further processing	28,000	20,000	12,000	60,000
Sales value if processed further	280,000	120,000	80,000	480,000

Required   Should product B be processed further and then sold?

e. **Make or Buy**   Strawn Company needs 20,000 units of a part to use in producing one of its products. If Strawn buys the part from McMillan Company for $85 instead of making it, Strawn could not use the released facilities in another manufacturing activity. Fifty percent of the fixed overhead will continue regardless of CEO Donald Mickey's decision. The cost data are

Cost to make the part	
Direct materials	$35
Direct labor	11
Variable overhead	19
Fixed overhead	20
	$85

Required   Determine which alternative is more attractive to Strawn and by what amount.

f. **Selection of the Most Profitable Product**   Video Company produces two basic types of video games, bash and gash. Pertinent data for Video Company follows:

	Bash	Gash
Sales price	$200	$140
Costs		
Direct materials	56	26
Direct labor	30	50
Variable factory overhead*	50	25
Fixed factory overhead*	20	10
Marketing costs (all variable)	28	20
Total costs	$184	$131
Operating income	$16	$9

*Based on labor hours.

The video craze is at its height so that either bash or gash alone can be sold to keep the plant operating at full capacity. However, labor capacity in the plant is insufficient to meet the combined demand for both games. Bash and gash are processed through the same production departments.

Required   Which product should be produced? Briefly explain your answer.

g. **Special Order Pricing**   Barry's Bar-B-Que is a popular lunch-time spot. Barry is conscientious about the quality of his meals, and he has a regular crowd of 600 patrons for his $5 lunch. His variable cost for each meal is about $2, and he figures his fixed costs, on a daily basis, at about $1,200. From time to time, bus tour groups with 50 patrons stop by. He has welcomed them since he has capacity to seat about 700 diners in the average lunch period, and his cooking and wait staff can easily handle the additional load. The tour operator generally pays for the entire group on a single check to save the wait staff and cashier the additional time. Due to competitive conditions in the tour business, the operator is now asking Barry to lower the price to $3.50 per meal for each of the 50 bus tour members.

Required Should Barry accept the $3.50 price? Why or why not? What if the tour company were willing to guarantee 200 patrons (or four bus loads) at least once a month for $3.00 per meal?

10–23 **MAKE OR BUY** Three Stars Inc. manufactures prefabricated houses. The firm's president, Michelle Brown, is interested in determining whether it would be better to manufacture the doors used in the houses or to buy them from a supplier. The following information, based on production of 500 doors, has been gathered to help determine the best option:

	Costs per Unit
Direct materials	$ 35
Direct labor	50
Variable overhead	10
Fixed overhead	
Administrative salaries	$ 7
Property taxes	2
Insurance	5
Utilities	5
Miscellaneous fixed overhead	6
Total costs	$120

Of the fixed overhead costs, Three Stars could save $5 per unit of miscellaneous fixed overhead if it purchases the doors from a supplier and allocates all other fixed costs elsewhere. The cost to purchase 500 doors would be $55,000.

Required Should Three Stars make or purchase the doors? What is the savings per unit?

10–24 **MAKE OR BUY** (Continuation of 10–23) Three Stars Inc. does not sell as many prefabricated homes in the winter as it does in the spring, summer, and fall. In the winter, builders usually are unable to construct them due to inclement and unpredictable weather. Thus, in the winter months Brown is always faced with the option to close down her facility and lay off her employees or use her facilities for an alternative purpose. The best alternative use involves constructing doors and selling them to retail hardware and home center stores. Last year's financial data for the sale of doors included this information:

Ethics

Revenues	$250,000
Direct costs	225,000
Fixed overhead costs	75,000
Net loss	$(50,000)

Required Should Three Stars continue to manufacture the doors? Include both quantitative and qualitative reasons. What responsibility for providing year-around employment, if any, does Three Stars have to its employees?

PROBLEMS

Strategy

10–25   SPECIAL ORDER ANALYSIS   Hopkins Industries produces high-quality automobile seat covers. Its success in the industry is due to its quality, although all of its customers, the automakers, are very cost conscious and negotiate for price cuts on all large orders. Noting that the auto supply business is becoming increasingly competitive, Hopkins is looking for a way to meet the challenge. It is negotiating with JepCo, Inc., a large mail-order auto parts and accessories retailer, to purchase a large order of seat covers. Much of Hopkins's business is seasonal and cyclical, fluctuating with the varying demands of the large automakers. Hopkins would like to keep its plants busy throughout the year by reducing these seasonal and cyclical fluctuations. Keeping the flow of product moving through the plants at a steady level is helpful in keeping costs down; extra overtime and machine setup and repair costs are incurred when production levels fluctuate. JepCo has agreed to a large order but only at a price of $38 per set. The special order can be produced in one batch with available capacity. Hopkins prepared these data:

Next month's operating information (per unit, for 10,000 units, made in 10 batches of 1,000 each)	
Sales price	$45
Per unit costs	
Variable manufacturing costs	21
Batch-level costs	8
Variable marketing costs	8
Fixed manufacturing costs	6
Fixed marketing costs	3
Special order information	
Sales	2,000 units
Sales price per unit	$38

No variable marketing costs are associated with this order, but Ruby Hopkins, the firm's president, has spent $2,000 during the past three months trying to get JepCo to purchase the special order.

Required

1. How much will the special order change Hopkins Industries' total operating income?

2. How might the special order fit into Hopkins's competitive situation?

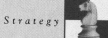

Strategy

10–26   SPECIAL ORDER   BallCards Inc. manufactures baseball cards sold in packs of 15 in drugstores throughout the country. It is the third leading firm in an industry with four major firms. BallCards has been approached by Pennock Cereal Inc., which would like to order a special edition of cards to use as a promotion with its cereal. BallCards would be solely responsible for designing and producing the cards. Pennock wants to order 25,000 sets and has offered $23,750 for the total order. Each set will consist of 33 cards. BallCards currently produces cards in sheets of 132.

Production, marketing, and other costs (per sheet)	
Direct materials	$1.20
Direct labor	0.20
Variable overhead	0.40
Fixed overhead	0.15
Variable marketing	0.10
Fixed marketing	0.35
Insurance, taxes, and administrative salaries	0.10
Costs for special order	
Design	2,000
Other setup costs	5,500

BallCards would incur no marketing costs for the special order. It has the capacity to accept this order without interrupting regular production.

Required

1. Should it accept the special order? Support your answer with appropriate computations.

2. What are the important strategic issues in the decision?

10–27   SPECIAL ORDER   LawnPlus Inc. manufactures lawn fertilizer and because of the quality often receives special orders from agricultural research groups. For each type of fertilizer sold, each bag is carefully filled to have the precise mix of components advertised for that type of fertilizer. LawnPlus's operating capacity is 22,000 one-hundred-pound bags per month, and it currently is selling 20,000 bags manufactured in 20 batches of 1,000 bags each. The firm just received a request for a special order of 5,000 one-hundred-pound bags of fertilizer for $125,000 from APAC, a research company. The production costs would be the same, although delivery and other packaging and distribution services would cause a one-time $2,000 cost for LawnPlus. The special order would be processed in two batches of 2,500 bags each. The following information is provided:

Ethics

Sales and production cost data for 20,000 bags, per bag	
Sales price	$28
Variable manufacturing costs	15
Batch-level costs	4
Variable marketing costs	2
Fixed manufacturing costs	4
Fixed marketing costs	2
Special order	
Sales price	$125,000
Delivery services	$2,000

No marketing costs would be associated with the special order.

Required

1. Should LawnPlus accept the special order? Explain why or why not.

2. What would be the change in operating income if the special order is accepted?

3. Suppose that after LawnPlus accepts the special order, it finds that unexpected production delays will not allow it to supply all 5,000 units from its own plants and meet the promised delivery date. It can provide the same materials by purchasing them in bulk from a competing firm. The materials would then be packaged in LawnPlus bags to complete the order. LawnPlus knows the competitor's materials are very good quality, but it cannot be sure that the quality meets its own exacting standards. There is not enough time to carefully test the competitor's product to determine its quality. What should LawnPlus do?

10–28   MAKE OR BUY; SPECIAL ORDER   Lester-Smith Company manufactures three wood construction components: wood trusses, wood floor joists, and beams. The plant is operating at full capacity. It can produce 200 trusses, 1,000 joists, and 600 beams per month and sells everything it produces. The monthly revenues and expenses for the three products are

Sales revenues	
Trusses	$ 12,000
Joists	40,000
Beams	90,000
Total revenue	$142,000

443

Expenses	
Variable cost	
Trusses	$ 10,000
Joists	24,000
Beams	48,000
Total variable cost	$ 82,000
Fixed cost allocated	
Trusses	$ 4,000
Joists	12,000
Beams	24,000
Total fixed cost	$ 40,000
Total cost	$122,000
Total profit	$ 20,000

Required

1. The firm makes wood trusses mainly to satisfy certain customers by offering a full line of wood components. Lately, it has had a problem making a profit on the trusses and is considering buying them from another manufacturer at $55 a truss. Should the firm buy these trusses or continue to make its own?

2. Lester-Smith has an opportunity to produce an additional 400 beams for a customer at a price of $100 each. If it accepts this special order, the firm cannot produce trusses because the plant will be operating at full capacity. Should the firm accept this special order?

10–29 PROFITABILITY ANALYSIS, SCARCE RESOURCES Santana Company has met all production requirements for the current month and has an opportunity to produce additional units of product with its excess capacity. Unit selling prices and costs for three models of one of its product lines are as follows:

	No Frills	Standard Options	Super
Selling price	$30	$35	$50
Direct materials	9	11	11
Direct labor ($10/hour)	5	10	15
Variable overhead	3	6	9
Fixed overhead	3	6	6

Variable overhead is charged to products on the basis of direct labor dollars; fixed overhead is charged to products on the basis of machine-hours.

Required

1. If Santana Company has excess machine capacity and can add more labor as needed (neither machine capacity nor labor is a constraint), the excess production capacity should be devoted to producing which product or products?

2. If Santana Company has excess machine capacity but a limited amount of labor time, the production capacity should be devoted to producing which product or products?

10–30 SPECIAL ORDER ANALYSIS New Life, Inc., manufactures skin creams, soaps, and other products primarily for people with dry and sensitive skin. It has just introduced a new line of product that removes the spotting and wrinkling in skin associated with aging. It sells these products in pharmacies and department stores at prices somewhat higher than those of other brands because of New Life's excellent reputation for quality and effectiveness.

New Life currently has very low utilization of plant capacity. Two years ago, in anticipation of rapid growth, the company opened a large new manufacturing plant, which has yet to be utilized more than 50 percent. Partly for this reason, New Life has sought new partners and was able, with the help of financial analysts, to locate suitable business partners. The first potential partner identified in this search was a large supermarket chain, SuperValue, which is interested in the partnership because it wants New Life to manufacture an age cream to sell in its stores. The product would be essentially the same as the New Life product but packaged with the SuperValue brand name. The agreement would pay New Life $2.00 per unit and would allow SuperValue a limited right to advertise the product as manufactured for SuperValue by New Life. New Life's CFO has made some calculations and has determined that the direct materials, direct labor, and other variable costs needed for the SuperValue order would be about $1.00 per unit as compared to the full cost of $2.50 (materials, labor, and overhead) for the equivalent New Life product.

Required Should New Life accept the proposal from SuperValue? Why or why not?

10–31 **PROJECT-ANALYSIS, SALES PROMOTIONS** Long Lake Furniture Company makes outdoor furniture from recycled products, including plastics and wood by-products. Its three furniture products are gliders, chairs with footstools, and tables. The products appeal primarily to cost-conscious consumers and those who value the recycling of materials. The company wholesales its products to retailers and various mass merchandisers. Because of the seasonal nature of the products, most orders are manufactured during the winter months for delivery in the early spring. Michael King, founder and owner, is dismayed that sales for two of the products are tracking below budget. The following chart shows pertinent year-to-date data regarding the company's products.

Certain that the shortfall was caused by a lack of effort by the sales force, Michael has suggested to Lisa Buck, financial analyst, that the company announce two contests to correct this situation before it deteriorates. The first contest is a trip to Hawaii awarded to the top salesperson if incremental glider sales are attained to close the budget shortfall. The second contest is a golf weekend, complete with a new set of golf clubs, awarded to the top salesperson if incremental sales of chairs with footstools are attained to close the budget shortfall.

	Glider		Chair with Footstool		Table	
	Actual	**Budget**	**Actual**	**Budget**	**Actual**	**Budget**
Number of units	2,550	4,000	7,100	8,000	3,500	3,300
Average sales price	$80.00	$85.00	$61.00	$65.00	$24.00	$25.00
Variable costs						
Direct labor						
Hours of labor	2.50	2.25	3.25	3.00	0.60	0.50
Cost per hour	$ 9.00	$10.00	$ 9.50	$ 9.25	$ 9.00	$ 9.00
Direct material	$13.00	$15.00	$11.00	$10.00	$ 6.00	$ 5.00
Sales commission	$14.00	$15.00	$10.00	$10.00	$ 5.00	$ 5.50

Required Explain whether either contest is desirable or not.
(**CMA Adapted**)

10–32 **MAKE OR BUY; STRATEGY** GianAuto Corporation manufactures parts and components for manufacturers and suppliers of parts for automobiles, vans, and trucks. Sales have increased more than 10 percent each year based in part on the company's excellent record of customer service and reliability. The industry as a whole has also grown dramatically in recent years as auto manufacturers continue to outsource more of their production, especially to

Strategy

cost-efficient manufacturers such as GianAuto. To take advantage of lower wage rates and favorable business environments around the world, Gian has located its plants in six different countries around the world.

Among the various GianAuto plants around the world is the Denver Cover Plant, one of GianAuto's earliest plants. The Denver Cover Plant prepares and sews coverings made primarily of leather and upholstery fabric and ships them to other GianAuto plants where they are used to cover seats, headboards, door panels, and other GianAuto products.

Ted Vosilo is the plant manager for the Denver Cover Plant, which was the first GianAuto plant in the region. As other area plants were opened, Ted was given the responsibility for managing them in recognition of his management ability. He functions as a regional manager although the budget for him and his staff is charged to the Denver Cover Plant.

Ted has just received a report indicating that GianAuto could purchase the entire annual output of Denver Cover from outside suppliers for $70 million. He was astonished at the low outside price because the budget for Denver Cover Plant's operating costs for the coming year was set at $82 million. He believes that GianAuto will have to close operations at Denver Cover to realize the $12 million in annual cost savings.

Denver Cover's budget for operating costs for the coming year follows:

DENVER COVER PLANT
Budget for Operating Costs
For the Year Ending December 31, 2001
(000s omitted)

Materials		$32,000
Labor		
Direct	$23,000	
Supervision	3,000	
Indirect plant	4,000	30,000
Overhead		
Depreciation—equipment	$ 5,000	
Depreciation—building	3,000	
Pension expense	4,000	
Plant manager and staff	2,000	
Corporate allocation	6,000	20,000
Total budgeted costs		$82,000

Additional facts regarding the plant's operations are as follows:

- Due to Denver Cover's commitment to use high-quality fabrics in all its products, the purchasing department placed blanket purchase orders with major suppliers to ensure the receipt of sufficient materials for the coming year. If these orders are canceled as a result of the plant closing, termination charges would amount to 15 percent of the cost of direct materials.

- Approximately 400 plant employees will lose their jobs if the plant is closed. This includes all direct laborers and supervisors as well as the plumbers, electricians, and other skilled workers classified as indirect plant workers. Some would be able to find new jobs, but many would have difficulty doing so. All employees would have difficulty matching Denver Cover's base pay of $14.40 per hour, the highest in the area. A clause in Denver Cover's contract with the union could help some employees; the company must provide employment assistance to its former employees for 12 months after a plant closing. The estimated cost to administer this service is $1 million for the year.

- Some employees would probably elect early retirement because Gian-Auto has an excellent plan. In fact, $3 million of the 2001 pension expense would continue whether Denver Cover is open or not.

- Ted and his staff would not be affected by closing Denver Cover. They would still be responsible for managing three other area plants.

- Denver Cover considers equipment depreciation to be a variable cost and uses the units-of-production method to depreciate its equipment and the customary straight-line method to depreciate its building.

Required

1. Explain GianAuto's competitive strategy and how this strategy should be considered with regard to the Denver Plant decision. Identify the key strategic factors that should be considered in the decision.

2. GianAuto Corporation plans to prepare an analysis to use in deciding whether to close the Denver Cover Plant. Using the preceding information, identify the relevant and non-relevant costs in this decision.

(CMA Adapted)

10–33 **MAKE OR BUY**   Richard's Specialty Manufacturing (RSM) produces custom vehicles—limousines, busses, conversion vans, and small trucks—for special order customers. It customizes each vehicle to the customer's specifications. RSM has been growing at a steady rate in recent years in part because of the increased demand for specialty luxury vehicles. The increased demand has also caused new competitors to enter the market for these types of vehicles. RSM management considers its competitive advantage to be the high quality of its manufacturing. Much of the work is handmade, and the company uses only the best parts and materials. Many parts are made in-house to control for highest quality. Because of the increased competition, price competition is beginning to become a factor for the industry, and RSM is becoming more concerned about cost controls and cost reduction. It has controlled them by purchasing materials and parts in bulk, paying careful attention to efficiency in scheduling and working different jobs, and improving employee productivity.

Strategy

The increased competition has also caused RSM to reconsider its strategy. Upon review with the help of a consultant, RSM management has decided that it competes most effectively as a differentiator based on quality of product and service. To reinforce the differentiation strategy, RSM has implemented a variety of quality inspection and reporting systems. Quality reports are viewed at all levels of management, including top management.

To decrease costs and improve quality, RSM has begun to look for new outside suppliers for certain parts. For example, RSM can purchase a critical suspension part, now manufactured in-house, from Performance Equipment Inc. for a price of $88. Buying the part would save RSM 10 percent of the labor and variable overhead costs and $54 of materials costs. The current manufacturing costs for the suspension assembly are as follows:

Materials	$166
Labor	68
Variable overhead	112
Fixed overhead	82
Total cost for suspension assembly	$428

Required   Should RSM purchase the part from Performance Equipment? Explain your answer using short-term and long-term considerations.

10–34 **PRICING; PROBABILITIES**   Systems Planners Institute (SPI) is a professional educational association for systems analysts and programmers. The organization has approximately 50,000 members. SPI holds an annual convention each October. Planning for the 2003 convention is progressing smoothly. The convention budget for such items as promotional brochures, fees and expenses for 20 speakers, equipment rental for presentations, the travel and expenses of 25 staff members, consultants' fees, volunteer expenses, and so on is $330,000. This amount does not include hotel charges for meeting rooms, luncheons, banquets, or receptions.

SPI has always priced each convention function separately; that is, members select and pay for only those functions they wish to attend. For each registered function, a member receives a ticket, which he or she surrenders at the function. Members who attend the convention pay a registration fee that gives them the right to attend the annual reception and annual meeting at no additional charge.

The Annual Convention Committee, consisting of volunteer members of SPI, has recommended that SPI consider setting a single flat fee for the entire convention. A registered member would be entitled to attend all functions at the convention under this pricing scheme. Entrance to each convention function would be permitted if the member displays the official convention name badge issued only to registered convention members.

The following table lists the convention functions, percentage of attendees expected at each function, SPI's charge for each function priced separately, and the hotel charges for food service, meeting halls, and rooms. The percentage of persons expected to attend each function is based on past experience and is expected to hold regardless of the pricing plan used.

Function	Percentage of Attendees Participating	Price of Function	Hotel Charge
Registration fee	100%	$50	None
Wednesday reception	100	Free	$25 per attendee
Thursday			
Annual meeting	100	Free	$2,000 for meeting hall
			$25 per attendee
Keynote luncheon	90	$ 40	$25 per attendee
Six concurrent sessions*	70	$ 60	$200 per room or $1,200 in total
Friday			
Plenary session	70	$ 50	$2,000 for meeting hall
Six workshops*	50	$100	$200 per room or $1,200 in total
Banquet	90	$ 50	$30 per attendee

*Attendee selects one session for the fee

The hotel's package of services to SPI and the convention attendees is as follows:

- Three free rooms for convention headquarters and storage.
- Discount of 20 percent on posted room rates for all convention attendees who stay in the hotel during the three-day convention. Attendees are to make room reservations directly with the hotel, and all hotel room charges are the responsibility of the attendees. The types of rooms, posted rate, and the proportion of each type of room taken by attendees follow:

Type	Posted Rate per Night	Percentage Rented
Single	$100	10%
Studio	105	10
Double	125	75
Suite	200	5

- SPI is given credit for one free double room for three days for every 50 convention registrants who stay at the convention hotel. The credit is applied to the room charges of staff and speakers.
- Meeting rooms and halls are free if food is served at the function.
- Meeting rooms and halls for professional sessions are free if 1,000 members register at the hotel.
- Meal costs include all taxes and gratuities.
- The hotel receives all revenue from cash bar sales at the reception and before the luncheons and banquet. The hotel estimates that the average consumption at each of these functions will be one cocktail per attendee at a contribution of $1.50 per cocktail.

If SPI continues to price each convention function separately, the prices given in the previous table apply. Estimated total attendance under this type of pricing scheme is as follows:

Number of Attendees	Probability
1,650	.2
1,900	.3
2,150	.4
2,400	.1

The Annual Convention Committee has estimated the convention attendance for three different single flat fee structures:

Proposed Single Flat Fee	Estimated Number of Attendees
$325	1,600
300	1,750
275	1,900

SPI estimates that 60 percent of the persons who attend the convention will stay in the convention hotel. Furthermore, they will not share hotel rooms (i.e., each attendee will need a room). The average stay at the hotel will be three nights.

Required SPI wants to maximize the contribution from its annual convention. Recommend whether SPI should price each function at the convention separately or charge one of the three single flat fees for the convention. Support your recommendation with an appropriate relevant cost analysis.

(CMA Adapted)

10–35 **MAKE OR BUY, REVIEW OF LEARNING CURVES** Henderson Equipment Company has produced a pilot run of 50 units of a recently developed cylinder used in its finished products. The cylinder has a one-year life, and the company expects to produce and sell 1,650 units annually. The pilot run required 14.25 direct labor-hours for the 50 cylinders, averaging 0.285 direct labor-hours per cylinder. Henderson has experienced an 80 percent learning curve on the direct labor-hours needed to produce new cylinders. Past experience indicates that learning tends to cease by the time 800 parts are produced.

Henderson's manufacturing costs for cylinders are

Direct labor	$12.00	per hour
Variable overhead	10.00	per hour
Fixed overhead	16.60	per hour
Materials	4.05	per unit

449

When pricing products, Henderson factors in selling and administrative expenses at $12.70 per direct labor-hour. All selling and administrative expenses except sales commissions (2 percent of sales) are independent of sales or production volume.

Henderson has received a quote of $7.50 per unit from Lytel Machine Company for the additional 1,600 cylinders needed. Henderson frequently subcontracts this type of work and has always been satisfied with the quality of the units produced by Lytel.

Required

1. If Henderson manufactures the cylinders, determine

   a. The average direct labor-hours per unit for the first 800 cylinders (including the pilot run) produced. Round calculations to three decimal places.

   b. The total direct labor-hours for the first 800 cylinders (including the pilot run) produced.

2. After completing the pilot run, Henderson must manufacture an additional 1,600 units to fulfill the annual requirement of 1,650 units. Without regard to your answer in requirement 1, assume that

   • The first 800 cylinders produced (including the pilot run) required 100 direct labor-hours.

   • The 800th unit produced (including the pilot run) required 0.079 hour.

   Calculate the total manufacturing costs for Henderson to produce the additional 1,600 cylinders required.

3. Determine whether Henderson should manufacture the additional 1,600 cylinders or purchase them from Lytel. Support your answer with appropriate calculations.

(CMA Adapted)

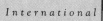
Strategy

International

10–36   SPECIAL ORDER; STRATEGY, INTERNATIONAL   Sommers Company, located in southern Wisconsin, manufactures a variety of industrial valves and pipe fittings that are sold to customers in nearby states. Currently, the company is operating at about 70 percent capacity and is earning a satisfactory return on investment.

Glasgow Industries Ltd. of Scotland has approached management with an offer to buy 120,000 units of a pressure valve. Glasgow Industries manufactures a valve that is almost identical to Sommers' pressure valve; however, a fire in Glasgow Industries' valve plant has shut down its manufacturing operations. Glasgow needs the 120,000 valves over the next four months to meet commitments to its regular customers; the company is prepared to pay $19 each for the valves.

Sommers' product cost for the pressure valve, based on current attainable standards, is

Direct materials	$ 5.00
Direct labor (0.5 hr per valve)	6.00
Manufacturing overhead (1/3 variable)	9.00
Total manufacturing cost	$20.00

Additional costs incurred in connection with sales of the pressure valve are sales commissions of 5 percent and freight expense of $1 per unit. However, the company does not pay sales commissions on special orders that come directly to management.

In determining selling prices, Sommers adds a 40 percent markup to product cost. This provides a $28 suggested selling price for the pressure valve. The marketing department, however, has set the current selling price at $27 to maintain market share.

Product management believes that it can handle the Glasgow Industries order without disrupting its scheduled production. The order would, however, require additional fixed factory overhead of $12,000 per month in the form of supervision and clerical costs.

If management accepts the order, Sommers will manufacture and ship 30,000 pressure valves to Glasgow Industries each month for the next four months. Shipments will be made in weekly consignments, FOB shipping point.

Required

1. Determine how many additional direct labor-hours will be required each month to fill the Glasgow order.

2. Prepare an analysis showing the impact of accepting the Glasgow order.

3. Calculate the minimum unit price that Sommers' management could accept for the Glasgow order without reducing net income.

4. Identify the strategic factors that Sommers should consider before accepting the Glasgow order.

5. Identify the factors related to international business that Sommers should consider before accepting the Glasgow order.

(CMA Adapted)

10–37 **PROFITABILITY ANALYSIS; REVIEW OF MASTER BUDGET, STRATEGY**   RayLok Incorporated has invented a secret process to improve light intensity and manufactures a variety of products related to this process. Each product is independent of the others and is treated as a separate profit/loss division. Product (division) managers have a great deal of freedom to manage their divisions as they think best. Failure to produce target division income is dealt with severely; however, rewards for exceeding one's profit objective are, as one division manager described them, lavish.

The DimLok Division sells an add-on automotive accessory that automatically dims a vehicle's headlights by sensing a certain intensity of light coming from a specific direction. DimLok has had a new manager in each of the three previous years because each manager failed to reach RayLok's target profit. Donna Barnes has just been promoted to manager and is studying ways to meet the current target profit for DimLok.

DimLok's two profit targets for the coming year are $800,000 (20 percent return on the investment in the annual fixed costs of the division) plus an additional profit of $20 for each DimLok unit sold. Other constraints on division operations are

- Production cannot exceed sales because RayLok's corporate advertising program stresses completely new product models each year, although the models might have only cosmetic changes.

- DimLok's selling price cannot vary above the current selling price of $200 per unit but may vary as much as 10 percent below $200.

- A division manager can elect to expand fixed production or selling facilities; however, the target objective related to fixed costs is increased by 20 percent of the cost of such expansion. Furthermore, a manager cannot expand fixed facilities by more than 30 percent of existing fixed cost levels without approval from the board of directors.

Donna is now examining data gathered by her staff to determine whether DimLok can achieve its target profits of $800,000 **and** $20 per unit. A summary of these reports shows the following:

- Last year's sales were 30,000 units at $200 per unit.
- DimLok's current manufacturing facility capacity is 40,000 units per year but can be increased to 80,000 units per year with an increase of $1,000,000 in annual fixed costs.
- Present variable costs amount to $80 per unit, but DimLok's vendors are willing to offer raw materials discounts amounting to $20 per unit, beginning with unit number 60,001.
- Sales can be increased up to 100,000 units per year by committing large blocks of product to institutional buyers at a discounted unit price of $180. However, this discount applies only to sales in excess of 40,000 units per year.

Donna believes that these projections are reliable and is now trying to determine what DimLok must do to meet the profit objectives that RayLok's board of directors assigned to it.

Required

1. Determine the dollar amount of DimLok's present annual fixed costs.
2. Determine the number of units that DimLok must sell to achieve both profit objectives. Be sure to consider all constraints in determining your answer.
3. Without regard to your answer in requirement 2, assume that Donna decides to sell 40,000 units at $200 per unit and 24,000 units at $180 per unit. Prepare a master budget income statement for DimLok showing whether her decision will achieve DimLok's profit objectives.
4. Assess DimLock's competitive strategy.
5. Identify the strategic factors that DimLok should consider.

(CMA Adapted)

Ethics

Strategy

10–38   **MAKE OR BUY; STRATEGY; ETHICS**   The Midwest Division of the Paibec Corporation manufactures subassemblies used in Paibec's final products. Lynn Hardt of Midwest's profit planning department has been assigned the task of determining whether Midwest should continue to manufacture a subassembly component, MTR-2000, or purchase it from Marley Company, an outside supplier. Marley has submitted a bid to manufacture and supply the 32,000 units of MTR-2000 that Paibec will need for 2002 at a unit price of $17.30. Marley has assured Paibec that the units will be delivered according to Paibec's production specifications and needs. The contract price of $17.30 is applicable only in 2002, but Marley is interested in entering into a long-term arrangement beyond 2002.

Lynn has submitted the following information regarding Midwest's cost to manufacture 30,000 units of MTR-2000 in 2001.

Direct material	$195,000
Direct labor	120,000
Factory space rental	84,000
Equipment leasing costs	36,000
Other manufacturing costs	225,000
Total manufacturing costs	$660,000

Lynn has collected the following information related to manufacturing MTR-2000:

- Equipment leasing costs represent special equipment used to manufacture MTR-2000. Midwest can terminate this lease by paying the equivalent of one month's lease payment for each of the two years left on its lease agreement.

- Forty percent of the other manufacturing overhead is considered variable. Variable overhead changes with the number of units produced, and this rate per unit is not expected to change in 2002. The fixed manufacturing overhead costs are not expected to change whether Midwest manufactures or purchases MTR-2000. Midwest can use equipment other than the leased equipment in its other manufacturing operations.

- Direct materials cost used in the production of MTR-2000 is expected to increase 8 percent in 2002.

- Midwest's direct labor contract calls for a 5 percent wage increase in 2002.

- The facilities used to manufacture MTR-2000 are rented under a month-to-month rental agreement. Midwest would have no need for this space if it does not manufacture MTR-2000. Thus, Midwest can withdraw from the rental agreement without any penalty.

John Porter, Midwest divisional manager, stopped by Lynn's office to voice his opinion regarding the outsourcing of MTR-2000. He commented, "I am really concerned about outsourcing MTR-2000. I have a son-in-law and a nephew, not to mention a member of our bowling team, who work on MTR-2000. They could lose their jobs if we buy that component from Marley. I really would appreciate anything you can do to make sure the cost analysis shows that we should continue making MTR-2000. Corporate is not aware of materials cost increases and maybe you can leave out some of those fixed costs. I just think we should continue making MTR-2000."

Required

1. Prepare a relevant cost analysis that shows whether the Midwest Division should make MTR-2000 or purchase it from Marley Company for 2002.

2. Identify and briefly discuss the strategic factors that Midwest should consider in this decision.

3. By referring to the specific ethical standards for management accountants outlined in Chapter 1, assess the ethical issues in John Porter's request of Lynn Hardt.

(CMA Adapted)

10–39 **PROFITABILITY ANALYSIS; LINEAR PROGRAMMING (APPENDIX)**   Home Cooking Company offers monthly service plans to provide prepared meals that are delivered to customers' homes and need only be heated in a microwave or conventional oven. Home Cooking offers two monthly plans, premier cuisine and haute cuisine. The premier cuisine plan provides frozen meals that are delivered twice each month; the premier generates a contribution of $120 for each monthly service plan sold. The haute cuisine plan provides freshly prepared meals delivered on a daily basis and generates a contribution of $90 for each monthly plan sold. Home Cooking's strong reputation enables it to sell all meals that it can prepare.

Each meal goes through food preparation and cooking steps in the company's kitchens. After these steps, the premier cuisine meals are flash frozen.

The time requirements per monthly meal plan and hours available per month follow:

	Preparation	Cooking	Freezing
Hours required			
Premier cuisine	2	2	1
Haute cuisine	1	3	0
Hours available	60	120	45

For planning purposes, Home Cooking uses linear programming to determine the most profitable number of premier and haute cuisine meals to produce.

Required

1. Using the Solver function of Microsoft Excel, determine the most profitable product mix for Home Cooking given the existing constraints and contribution margins.

2. Using the Solver function of Microsoft Excel, determine the most profitable product mix for Home Cooking given the existing contribution margins and all constraints except the preparation time constraint.

(CMA Adapted)

SOLUTIONS TO SELF-STUDY PROBLEMS

1. Special Order Pricing

The key to this exercise is to recognize that the variable manufacturing costs of $130 ($85 material and $45 labor) are the relevant ones and that the fixed overhead costs, since they will not change, are not relevant.

Thus, the correct decision is to accept the offer, since the price of $150 exceeds the variable manufacturing cost of $130. HighValu also should consider strategic factors. For example, will the three-year contract be desirable? Perhaps the market conditions will change so that HighValu will have more profitable uses of the capacity in the coming years. Will the special order enhance or diminish the firm's competitive position?

2. The Make-or-Buy Decision

The relevant costs for this analysis are the outside purchase cost of $15 per set versus the make costs of $10 per set ($6 material plus $4 labor), and $10,000 annual fixed costs.

First, determine the amount of annual savings from the reduction in variable costs for the make option:

6,000 annual sales × ($15 − $10) = $30,000 annual savings

Second, compare the savings in variable costs to the additional fixed costs of $10,000 per year. The net savings, an advantage to make rather than buy, is $20,000 ($30,000 − $10,000).

HighValu also should consider relevant strategic factors, such as the quality and reliability of the supply for the cushion. How will HighValu use the released capacity at its plant? Are any employees' jobs affected?

3. Profitability Analysis

1. To determine the number of windys that can be manufactured if the 3,750 units of gale are no longer produced, we consider the capacity released for each of the two constraints.

For the automated sewing machine: The machine produces 20 windys per hour or 30 gales per hour, so that the number of windys that could be produced from the released capacity of gale is

$$3,750 \times 20/30 = 2,500 \text{ windys}$$

For the inspection and packing operation: The operation requires 15 minutes for windy (4 per hour) and 5 minutes for gale (12 per hour), so the number of windys that could be inspected and packed in the released time is

$$3,750 \times 4/12 = 1,250 \text{ windys}$$

In this case, the inspection and packing is the effective limitation, so that if gale is deleted, the firm can produce *1,250 windys* with the released capacity.

2. If 3,750 units of gale are replaced with 1,250 units of windy, the proper relevant cost analysis should consider the contribution margin of each product:

	Windy	Gale
Unit contribution margin	$ 8	$ 4
Units sold (giving up 3,750 units gale gives 1,250 of windy, per part 1)	1,250	3,750
Total contribution margin	$10,000	$15,000

Thus, the deletion of gale and replacement with windy would reduce the total contribution margin by $5,000 ($15,000 − $10,000).

3. Since the effect on total contribution is significant (as shown in part 2), Windbreakers should continue to make gale. Other factors to consider follow:

   a. At existing sales levels of 18,750 of windy and 3,750 of gale, Windbreakers is operating at full capacity; if there are additional sales opportunities for windy, the firm should consider adding to available capacity so that the current sales of gale can be made plus the additional sales of windy. The analysis of the cost benefit of adding additional capacity is best addressed through the techniques of capital budgeting as described in Chapter 11.

   b. The effect of the loss of gale on the firm's image and therefore the potential long-term effects on the sales of windy.

   c. The long-term sales potential for gale. Will its sales likely exceed the current 3,750 level in future years?

Capital Budgeting 11

After studying this chapter, you should be able to . . .

1 Identify the major steps in the capital budgeting process

2 Select appropriate data for analyzing capital investments including total initial outlays, net cash flows throughout the useful life of the investment, and impact of the final disposition of the investment on cash flow

3 Use capital investment evaluation techniques including the payback period, book rate of return, net present value, and internal rate of return methods to assess capital investments and explain the advantages and limitations of these techniques

4 Identify the underlying assumptions of the discounted cash flow methods and use these methods properly to evaluate capital investments

5 Discuss the relationships between strategic cost management and capital budgeting

6 Identify behavioral factors in capital budgeting decisions

Headquartered in Peoria, Illinois, Caterpillar Inc. is the world's largest manufacturer of construction and mining equipment, diesel and natural gas engines, and industrial gas turbines.[1] A Fortune 100 company with more than $26 billion in assets and ranked number one in its industry, Caterpillar has been growth oriented and focused on the future. Through well-planned capital investments, it responds to changing business climates, reduces costs, improves quality, and strengthens business processes throughout its value chain. Over the last decade, the firm has doubled in size and improved profitability.

One of its capital investments reflects the firm's response to its competitive challenge in the 1980s. Caterpillar suffered three years of consecutive operating losses in the early 1980s that totaled more than $1.1 billion because of the increasing competitive pressures from Kamatsu of Japan and manufacturers in the United States and other countries. The firm began a plant modernization in the early 1980s aiming to acquire modern manufacturing systems, termed plant with a future, to enable it to respond and adjust quickly to changes in demand and in product designs. Caterpillar management analyzed and evaluated the proposals using capital budgeting techniques including net present value, payback period, and internal rate of return. The investments paid off starting in the late 1980s and continued into the next decade. Caterpillar was able to restore profitability and regain its market share.

This chapter presents these and other methods that Caterpillar and many firms, organizations, and individuals use to analyze and evaluate capital investment projects.

> My interest is in the future because I am going to spend the rest of my life there.
>
> CHARLES FRANKLIN KETTERING

> The Indian who sold Manhattan for $24 was a sharp salesman. If he had put his $24 away at 6% compounded semiannually, it would now be $9.5 billion and he could buy most of the now-improved land back.
>
> S. BRANCH WALKER

Businesses and organizations are often required to commit large sums to projects with expenditures and benefits expected to stretch well into the future. Such projects are known as **capital investments**. Examples include the purchase of new equipment, construction of new facilities, development and introduction of new products, the

A **capital investment** requires committing a large sum of funds to projects with expenditures and benefits expected to stretch well into the future.

---

[1] Find out more about the company at its Web site: /www.cat.com/.

Can Olympic Hosts and Sponsors Grab the Gold?

When it comes to being a host city or corporate sponsor of the Olympics, the long-term result can be a boon—or a bust. Host cities not only face possible destruction of their image (e.g., Munich, 1972; Atlanta, 1996), but also they can suffer economic setbacks (e.g., Montreal, 1976). Of course, this is the negative side. Some host cities have benefited enormously from this large investment, enhancing their image and infrastructure and increasing the recognition of corporate sponsors (e.g., Los Angeles, 1984; Seoul, 1988; Barcelona, 1992). How large is the investment made by host cities? For the 1996 games, Atlanta raised an estimated $1.57 billion.

What's the risk of the particular investment? How can hosts and sponsors ensure a gold-medal return? When you go for the gold, you must be prepared for a few risks. Like the athletes who invest years of their lives training to reach the Olympics and encounter risks and returns along the way, host cities and corporate sponsors must invest large amounts and overcome obstacles. These financial sponsors understand these risks, but they also recognize the potential long-term gain, whether to their city's image or its bottom line. "It's hard to allocate the costs and returns, but thanks to the Olympics we got a new bullet train to Tokyo, new expressway, and more sewers," says Shigekazu Nakamura of the 1998 Winter Olympics in Nagano, Japan. He is deputy managing editor of *Shinano Mainichi Shimbun*, the city's largest newspaper. Although these improvements total approximately $12.1 billion, Nagano and Olympic corporate sponsors believe that the long-term return was definitely worth the initial investment. For example, Eastman Kodak Company, a long-time sponsor of the Olympics, believes that its investment in the 1998 Winter Olympics (a minimum of $40 million) is money well spent. "We've always seen an uptick in revenues, in brand awareness [after the Olympics]," says Carl E. Gustin Jr., a senior vice president at Kodak. So, like the Olympic athletes, financial sponsors must be ready for a potential stellar performance or a less-than-fulfilling experience.

Sources: "Sponsorship: The Risks and Rewards of Going for the Gold," *Business Week,* February 9, 1998; "Atlanta's Big Leap," *Business Week,* July 29, 1996; and "A High Hurdle in Atlanta," *Business Week,* May 3, 1993.

installation of computer-based patient records,[2] expansion into new sales territories, and, as the above feature discusses, hosting an Olympic game.

A good capital investment generates cash, decreases cash outlays, or both, over its projected lifetime to earn back the capital committed to the project and a desirable profit. The lack of or poorly executed capital investment can lead to financial hardship, tie up resources for extended periods, curtail opportunities available to the firm, demoralize employees, and vex suppliers and customers. Eventually, the failure to make a good capital investment can doom an organization. Poor capital investments in the late 1990s led to the continuous and considerable drops in the market capitalization of AT&T and forced it to cut its dividends by 80 percent in 2000—the first time since the firm's inception more than 100 years ago. Lack of capital investment or one or a series of poor capital investments often causes the demise of an organization.

Success often results from good capital investments by visionary entrepreneurs. Ford Motor Company grew by leaps and bounds in the early twentieth century as a result of Henry Ford's visionary investment in new manufacturing techniques at the time. Many venture capitalists have profited handsomely by making capital investments in new ideas.

The soundness of capital investment decisions is critical to organizations, whether for profit or not for profit. *Capital budgeting* is the process of identifying, evaluating, and selecting projects that require commitments of large sums of funds and generate benefits stretching well into the future. Sound capital investments are often a result of a careful capital budgeting.

TYPES OF CAPITAL INVESTMENT

Firms make capital investments to acquire assets for various reasons and purposes. In general, they can be classified in three categories.[3]

---

[2]   Leslie A. Kian and Michael W. Stewart, "Justifying the Cost of a Computer-Based Patient Record," *Health-care Financial Management,* 49(7), pp. 58–63.

[3]   Robert Simons, *Performance Measurement and Control Systems for Implementing Strategy* (Upper Saddle River, New Jersey: Prentice Hall, 1999).

1. **Assets to meet regulatory, safety, health, and environmental requirements.** Acquisition of these assets most likely cannot be deferred or rejected without being assessed potentially huge penalties in the future. Costs to acquire these assets are unavoidable costs of doing business.

2. **Assets to enhance operating efficiency and/or increase revenue.** These assets improve or maintain efficient productive capacity or increase revenues. Acquisition of these assets can often be deferred in the short term at the manager's discretion.

3. **Assets to enhance competitive effectiveness.** These assets increase a firm's capacity, allow it to enter new markets, or alter or improve its fundamental operations.

Evaluation criteria and decision procedures for acquiring assets are most likely to differ according to the acquisition's reason or purpose. The extent to which a firm's strategy is applied to asset acquisition decisions also differs according to different needs. For example, the focus of the decision to acquire assets to meet regulatory, safety, health, or environmental requirements is the selection of the most cost-effective way to satisfy the requirements. The firm's strategy plays no role in the decision (other than to continue as a going concern). The firm's strategy plays limited roles in capital investment decisions to acquire assets that enhance operating efficiency and/or increase revenue. Critical factors in this type of investment decisions are likely to be cost-benefit comparisons and availability of funds. Acquisitions of assets that enhance competitive effectiveness are likely to have a significant impact on operating cash flows and profits in the short term and competitiveness in the long term. These assets should be acquired following the firm's strategy. Before acquiring these assets, the proposal should be reviewed considering the firm's strategic goals and the importance of the proposed capital investment in meeting these goals. Because of the strategic impact and substantial costs that such acquisitions often entail, these assets must be subject to a series of tests to ensure that they meet the firm's strategic and financial goals.

CAPITAL BUDGETING PROCESS

A capital budgeting process consists of three successive steps: project identification and definition, evaluation and selection, and monitoring and review.

◄**LEARNING OBJECTIVE 1**

Identify the major steps in the capital budgeting process in capital investment decisions.

Project Identification and Definition

The capital budgeting process begins with project identification and definition. A majority of the firms responding to a survey of capital budgeting practices regarded this step as the most critical and the most difficult for a successful capital investment.[4]

Initial proposals for capital investments often come from the local or branch level. This is especially true for equipment replacement or acquisition of assets to improve efficiency or increase revenue that require only marginal change from current operations. In contrast, higher management often initiates major changes such as construction of new plants, adoption of just-in-time or flexible manufacturing systems, development of new products, and expansion into new territory.

Management must define a clear boundary to an investment project. It must know not only what a project will do but also what it will not do. Lack of a clear definition of a proposed investment project increases the difficulty of estimating revenues, costs, and cash flows. Furthermore, a project without a clear boundary can grow into a huge undertaking that exceeds the firm's available resources.

---

[4] Of the three stages of the capital budgeting process, 51 percent of the firms participating in a survey consider the project identification and definition stage to be the most critical to the success of a capital investment. Forty-four percent of them also consider this step to be the most difficult. James M. Fremgen, "Capital Budgeting Practices: A Survey," *Management Accounting*, May 1973, pp. 19–25.

Evaluation and Selection

Evaluation of a capital investment requires projection of revenues or benefits, costs, and cash flows for the project's entire life cycle. Knowing a project's benefits and costs helps management grasp its impact on the firm's resources and gauge whether the firm can absorb the cost. The benefits and costs include both financial and nonfinancial elements.

Uncertainty about future events often makes estimating the revenues or benefits, costs, and cash flows of a capital investment project a difficult task, especially for those with long lives. Changes in technology; shifts in market demand; actions of other firms in the same or a related industry; and the effects of international, national, regional, and local economies are among the general factors to be considered. In addition, specific factors relating to the project must be identified. Many techniques are available to help make projections. (See Chapter 7 on cost behavior patterns and cost estimation and Chapter 10 on decision making.)

Financial effects are not the only consideration in evaluating and selecting capital investments. A firm undertakes capital investment projects for reasons other than their financial benefits. Among the nonfinancial reasons for committing major capital expenditures are the safety of employees or the public; convenience or comfort of the employees; social concerns; pollution control; legal requirements; contractual commitments; and protection of existing programs, product lines, or market shares.[5]

The critical importance of one or more nonfinancial factors in undertaking a capital investment does not imply that conducting a financial evaluation of the project is unnecessary. Although a firm needs to add pollution abatement equipment to satisfy a legal requirement, it must still perform a financial analysis to identify the equipment's costs and benefits.

Budgeting on Faith or Strategic Investment Analysis

When it comes to investing in new technology, many corporations are known to make the investment decision on faith. The decision of a kitchen unit manufacturer with an established reputation for innovative design to invest heavily in computer-assisted design equipment was based on management's belief that its customers would ascribe high value to the use of sophisticated automatic technology in manufacturing.

Investing in new technology without a formal analysis using a capital budgeting technique is akin to theologians explaining the mysteries of the universe. Faith (capital) budgeting involves the basic assumption that the investment, especially when it is in new technology, differs fundamentally from other capital investments. The investment can so alter a business that its intangible benefits cannot be quantified or fully anticipated. Returns not anticipated or quantifiable cannot be incorporated into capital budgeting models. Traditional capital budgeting techniques such as the payback period, accounting return on investment, or discounted cash flows are of no use and, if used, most likely will lead to underinvestment in new technologies. Not investing in new technology can lead to an inexorable erosion of competitive capability, compounded by market perception that the firm is behind in time and technology—an unacceptable stigma to many managers and CEOs.

Investing in new technology does not have to rely on faith budgeting. All investments involve future events. An investment, whether in a new technology or the addition of a newer and more efficient equipment, should be evaluated on its strategic fit and benefits as well as a formal quantitative analysis. Considerations of strategic fit and benefits can be informal. For example, a medium-size manufacturer and distributor of specialized leisure products adopted MRP, CAD/CAM, and robotized production although these investments failed the company's three-year payback criterion. The firm approved these investments after a long and careful consideration of their informal strategic benefits. Included in its consideration were improvements on product quality, reductions in quality variations, increased manufacturing flexibility, more precise responses to fluctuating demands, increased skill base, and better control and planning.

Sources: Michael Bromwich and Al Bhimani, "Strategic Investment Appraisal," *Management Accounting,* March 1991, pp. 45–48; and John R. Brandt, "Budgeting on Faith," *Industry Week,* 247 (23).

---

[5] Nonfinancial reasons often lead to using urgency as a criterion in capital investment projects. Such a concern is especially prevalent in government projects. For example, a new bridge was rebuilt because the existing one was hazardous. A highway was built because the legislator from the district convinced the Department of Transportation that having a new highway through the area was urgent. For more examples, see "Report to the Congress of the United States by the Comptroller General," *Federal Capital Budgeting: A Collection of Haphazard Practices* (Washington, D.C.: General Accounting Office, 1981).

Monitoring and Review

A successful capital investment requires its continual monitoring and review. Making careful evaluations before selecting an investment is only the first step. As the investment project progresses, situations change, new variables surface, and fresh opportunities arise. The organization needs to be able to modify its original plan, incorporate new developments, and alter the course of action, if necessary, to attain the best results.[6]

DATA FOR CAPITAL BUDGETING

Data used for capital investment decisions differ from those generated for accounting records and reports in two respects: their characteristics and the factors relevant to decisions.

◄**LEARNING OBJECTIVE 2**

Select appropriate data for analyzing capital investments including total initial outlays, net cash flows throughout the useful life of the investment, and impact of the final disposition of the investment on cash flow.

Characteristics of Capital Budgeting Data

The characteristics of the data used for capital budgeting differ from those used for financial reporting purposes in three ways: the data period, the measurement object, and the time horizon. Exhibit 11–1 contrasts data characteristics for capital budgeting and those for financial reporting.

Data Period

Two underlying concepts of financial reporting data are periodicity and accrual basis accounting. *Periodicity* requires firms to record and report accounting data at specified regular intervals: monthly, quarterly, or annually. *Accrual basis* accounting requires firms to include in the period's accounting data and financial statements all figures pertaining to revenues earned and expenses incurred in that period. Receipt or disbursement of cash is not a factor in determining the period in which to include and report the amount.

A capital budgeting process, however, evaluates the investment over its complete life cycle, not in only one accounting period. A decision to introduce a new product, for example, must consider not only the investment required to develop and market the product initially but also the expected revenues and costs during all the years the product is to be on the market. An accrual basis accounting system typically separates the life cycle of the new product into several time periods and focuses on only one period at a time.

Measurement Object

A capital investment budget focuses on cash flows, not on accrual-based revenues and expenses. Thus, a noncash sale in a period is not included in the capital budget for that period if the firm receives no cash from the sale. Similarly, an expense is not included in a capital budget if the firm pays no cash for that expense during that period. In contrast, an accrual-based accounting procedure includes both the noncash sale and the unpaid expense in the period.

Exhibit 11–1	Capital Budgeting and Financial Reporting Data Characteristics	
Characteristic	**Capital Budgeting**	**Financial Reporting**
Data period	Life of the project	Annual
Measurement object	Cash flows	Accrual revenues and expenses
Time horizon	Future events and transactions	Historical events and transactions

---

[6]   Twenty-three percent of the firms participating in the capital budgeting survey conducted by Fremgen consider this stage to be the most critical to the success of an investment.

Time Horizon

Another difference between capital budgeting data and financial reporting data is in the time horizon. Capital budgeting data focus on future transactions and events, but financial reporting data are based on historical transactions and events. A proper financial report records and reports all transactions and events that have occurred during the period and the consequences of past actions. In contrast, historical data are seldom included in capital budgeting and are included only to the extent of their effects on current and future cash flows.

Relevant Factors in Capital Budgeting

The ultimate concern of a firm and its investors is its cash position. The relevant factor in capital budgeting, therefore, is the cash flow affected by the capital investment.

A business firm's managers expect capital investments to improve periodic profits. This interest in profit leads many firms to focus their attention on periodic net income when considering capital investments. Although net income is a measure of profit, overemphasizing its importance can lead to erroneous capital investment decisions because net income is not a good measure of return for such an investment.

Both the periodicity reporting requirement and the arbitrary process involved in determining net income lessen the usefulness of net income as an objective criterion. Net income is the result of applying selected accounting rules and methods to transactions. A period's net income can differ substantially when the firm chooses to follow an alternative accounting rule and use different, yet equally acceptable, accounting methods.

Capital budgeting considers only cash flows. All items affecting cash flows must be incorporated in capital budgeting whether they are accounting revenues or expenses of the period. A noncash item, such as depreciation expense, is included in capital budgeting calculations only to the extent that it affects tax obligation cash flows.

Depreciation expenses are not cash payments and are by themselves irrelevant in capital budgeting. This is true although they are expenses for income determination purposes. A depreciation expense is relevant to a capital budget only because it has an effect on the amount of income taxes the firm must pay for the period. In the same vein, the entire amount of cash paid in a period to purchase an asset is relevant for capital budgeting purposes, although the entire amount might not be an expense for that period in computing net income.

Cash Flows

A capital investment often starts with a cash outflow that is a payment or commitment of funds. Depending on the investment's objectives, its return can decrease cash expenditures, generate cash inflows, or both. Funds also could be needed for additional capital investments during the life of the project.

Cash inflows or *outflows* occur at three stages of the capital investment project:

1. **Project initiation.** Cash flows at this point include
   - Cash outflows to acquire the investment and to begin operations.
   - Cash commitments for working capital needed for the operations.
   - Cash inflow or outflow related to the disposal of the asset being replaced.
2. **Project operation.** Cash flows during the operation of a capital investment include
   - *Outflows for* operating expenditures and additional capital investment after the initial investment.
   - *Commitments for* additional working capital needed in operations.
   - *Inflows of cash* generated by the investment (revenues and cash savings) and cash released from working capital no longer needed in operations.
3. **Final project disposal.** Cash flows at final disposal include
   - Cash inflows or outflows related to the investment's disposal.
   - Cash inflows from the release of working capital no longer committed to the investment.

Determining Cash Flows in Capital Budgeting

Cash received increases the cash available to an organization; cash paid or committed decreases its cash available. The immediate effect that a cash receipt or cash payment or commitment has on cash flows often is referred to as the *direct effect*. An event or transaction often changes a tax-paying organization's tax obligations. The effect that an event or transaction has on the amount of an organization's tax payment for the period is the *tax effect or indirect effect*. The total of the direct effect and the tax effect is the *net effect* on cash flow. Exhibit 11–2 summarizes these effects.

A $10,000 cash revenue *for a for-profit firm* in the 30 percent tax bracket represents a net cash inflow of $7,000, not $10,000, because the additional $10,000 revenues increase its taxes by $3,000. The amount of net cash outflow for a $6,000 payment for expenses is $4,200 because the $6,000 expense decreases the firm's tax expenses by $1,800.

Noncash revenues or expenses can also affect cash flows through tax effects. Because tax liability is figured on accrual-based income, a noncash revenue such as a credit sale does not increase the amount of cash available but does increase taxable income for the period, which increases the amount of cash needed for taxes. Thus, a noncash revenue *decreases*, not increases, cash available to the firm. The amount of the decrease is the increase in taxes resulting from the noncash revenue.

For example, a noncash revenue of $10,000 for a firm in the 30 percent tax bracket reduces, not increases, the amount of cash available to the firm by $3,000. Although the firm receives no cash from a noncash revenue, it nevertheless increases its tax liability by $3,000. Therefore, for a taxpaying organization, *a noncash revenue is a cash outflow*, not a cash inflow.

An increase in expenses, on the other hand, decreases taxable income, which reduces the taxes for the period. A noncash expense, therefore, increases, not decreases, cash flow. Depreciation is a noncash expense that does not require a cash payment in the period in which the expense is recognized. The expense, however, reduces the firm's tax payment for the period. This increases cash available for other uses and results in a cash inflow for the firm.

Activities at various stages of a capital investment differ and have various effects on cash flows. As indicated, cash flows for capital investments occur at the project initiation, during project operation, and at the final disposal.

Project Initiation

Activities at the inception of a capital investment often involve the

1. Acquisition of the investment.
2. Commitment of working capital needed for operating the investment.
3. Disposal of assets replaced.

Effects of Initial Investment Acquisition on Cash Flow

At the initial investment stage, some activities that entail cash outflow include constructing or buying a new facility; purchasing, installing, and testing new equipment; and training personnel. The bulk of the direct cash outflow for an investment usually occurs at its beginning. In capital budgeting, the time when initial cash outflows occur for the acquisition is referred to as *time 0* (or *year 0*).

Exhibit 11–2   Effects of Cash Flow

Direct Effect: Cash receipt, cash payment, or cash commitment

Tax Effect: Changes in tax payments

Net Effect: Direct effect + Tax effect

Investment cash outflows also have tax effects. Acquisition costs to hire or train personnel can be treated as expenses in the period they are incurred. An increase in expense reduces income taxes, and decreases in tax payments reduce cash outflows or increase cash inflows.

Another effect on cash flows derived from the investment is depreciation expense. Depreciation expenses themselves have no immediate cash effect. As a noncash expense that decreases operating (and taxable) income in subsequent periods, the depreciation expense of the investment reduces the tax obligation in subsequent years. A reduction in the tax obligation is a cash inflow for a tax-paying organization. Exhibit 11–3 summarizes the cash flow effects often entailed during a project's initiation stage.

Smith Company manufactures high-pressure pipe for deep-sea oil drilling. The firm is considering the purchase of a milling machine for $500,000. The installation cost will be approximately $5,000. Testing and adjusting before placing the machine in production will cost $10,000. After its expected useful life of four years, disposal costs related to the equipment follows: sale, $100,000 (inflow); machine removal and site cleaning expenses, $20,000 (outflow). The firm uses straight-line depreciation with an estimated salvage value of $75,000 for the investment. The controller expects the firm to be in the 34 percent federal income tax bracket and the state to levy 6 percent income taxes.

The first segment (year 0) of Exhibit 11–4 shows that the initial cash outflow for the investment will be $515,000. The firm uses straight-line depreciation for the equipment.[7] With $75,000 expected salvage value after four years, the total depreciable cost is $440,000 and the depreciation expense for the equipment is $110,000 per year for the next four years, as Exhibit 11–4 shows. The depreciation expense itself has no direct effect on cash flow because the expense requires no cash payment. The depreciation expense, however, does have a tax effect by acting as a tax shield. The

---

Exhibit 11–3	Effects of Investment Acquisition on Cash Flow

Direct Effect (Outflow)
- Cost to purchase, construct, or manufacture buildings and equipment.
- Cost to install and test equipment.
- Cost to hire and train personnel.

Tax Effect (Inflow)
- Decrease in income taxes for acquisition costs treated as expenses.
- Decrease in income taxes due to depreciation on the investment.

---

[7] Most spreadsheet programs can calculate depreciation expense. For example, Microsoft Excel, Lotus, and Quattro Pro calculate depreciation expense using the straight-line depreciation method if you enter (preceded with = for EXCEL and @ for Lotus 1-2-3 or Quattro Pro

$$SLN \text{ (cost, salvage value, number of years)}$$

The function for depreciation expense using sum-of-the-years'-digits method is

$$SYD \text{ (cost, salvage value, number of years, period)}$$

where *period* is the year for which depreciation expense is desired. Enter **1,** for example, if you want to know the depreciation expense for the first year.

The function for depreciation expense using the double-declining balance method is

$$DDB \text{ (cost, salvage value, number of years, period, factor)}$$

where *factor* is the rate at which the balance declines. If factor is omitted, it is assumed to be 2 (the double-declining balance method). In addition, these programs have two other functions, DB and VDB, for calculating depreciation. DB computes an asset's depreciation for a specified period of time using a fixed rate declining balance method. VDB determines an asset's depreciation for any period the user specifies, including a partial period, using the double-declining balance method or another method the user specifies. The keystroke sequences for all depreciation functions are **Insert → Function → Financial.**

To calculate depreciation expenses using other methods such as the ACRS (Accelerated Cost Recovery System) or MACRS (Modified Accelerated Cost Recovery System), refer to the depreciation schedule described for each method in the Internal Revenue Code (see the appendix to this chapter).

Exhibit 11–4	Effects of Asset Acquisition on Smith Company's Cash Flow

Year 0

Cost of equipment	$500,000
Installation cost	5,000
Testing and adjusting	10,000
Total cash *outflow* in year 0	$(515,000)

Year 1 through Year 4

Total cost for depreciation purposes	$515,000
Expected salvage value at the end of useful life	75,000
Total to be depreciated	$440,000
Years of useful life for depreciation purposes	4
Depreciation expense per year, straight-line basis	$110,000
Income tax rate (34% + 6%)	0.40
Total cash *inflow* (tax deduction) each period due to depreciation expense	$ 44,000

Alternative Schematic Form

	Time Period				
Description	Year 0	Year 1	Year 2	Year 3	Year 4
Cost of equipment	$(500,000)				
Installation cost	(5,000)				
Testing and adjusting	(10,000)				
Tax saving on depreciation expense		$44,000	$44,000	$44,000	$44,000
Total	$(515,000)	$44,000	$44,000	$44,000	$44,000

depreciation expense decreases the firm's taxable income and reduces its tax liability. For a for-profit firm in the 40 percent tax bracket (34 percent federal, 6 percent state income taxes), a $110,000 decrease in net income reduces tax liability by $44,000. The firm enjoys this reduced tax liability, a cash inflow, each year of the capital project's life. The reduced tax payment is a cash inflow to the firm.

Effects of Working Capital Commitment on Cash Flow

Working capital is the excess of current assets over current liabilities and is the amount of additional funds needed to meet the requirements of the operations. An investment in plant and equipment often calls for additional working capital to pay for extra payroll and other expenditures, inventories of materials, and supplies required for operations of the investment.

Committing funds to an investment's working capital makes the funds unavailable for other uses. Restricting funds for working capital is a cash outflow in the year the firm commits the funds. The commitment, however, directly affects only cash flow. No tax implications exist because the working capital commitment has no effect on either revenue or expense and, therefore, on taxes.

Not all investments require additional working capital. The amount needed for some operations can even decrease as the result of an investment. The amount of a decrease represents a cash inflow in the period in which the firm reduces its need for working capital. Just-in-time and computer-integrated manufacturing systems are investments that can decrease working capital. Firms investing in these manufacturing systems often reduce their need for inventory—raw materials, work in process, or finished goods. These firms enjoy cash inflows from the reduced working capital because the investment in new manufacturing technologies increases their operating efficiency through reduced inventory levels and other reductions in operating costs.

The milling machine that Smith Company is considering requires $200,000 in addition to increases in accounts payable and other current liabilities to cover inventories needed for operations and accounts receivable expected to arise from the investment. This $200,000 tied up in inventories and accounts receivable will not be available for other uses during operations. Earmarking these funds has the direct effect of increasing the cash *outflow* for the investment in year 0 from $515,000 to $715,000 (see Exhibit 11–5).

Effect of Disposal of the Assets Replaced on Cash Flow

Disposing of unnecessary operating assets has both direct and tax effects on a firm's cash flows as Exhibit 11–6 shows. A firm gains if the net proceeds from disposing of an asset exceed its *net book value* (the difference between its original cost and the amount of depreciation taken on it). Because a gain on the disposal of an asset is taxable, however, the gain's tax liability decreases the firm's net cash inflow from the disposal.

A firm suffers a loss if the net proceeds from disposing of an asset are less than its net book value. A loss reduces the firm's tax obligation. The effect of the disposal on cash inflow is the sum of (1) the net cash proceeds from the disposal and (2) the savings in taxes due to the loss from the disposal. Exhibit 11–7 summarizes the determination of the net effect of asset disposal on cash flow.

The new machine enables Smith Company to dispose of another milling machine acquired seven years ago for $320,000. The accumulated depreciation for the old machine is $200,000 as of the replacement date. A used equipment broker who charges

---

Exhibit 11–5   Direct Effects on Smith Company's Cash Outflow in Year 0

Cost of equipment, installing, and testing	$(515,000)
Working capital needed for operations	(200,000)
Tax effect	0
Net investment (total cash outflow in year 0)	$(715,000)

Exhibit 11–6   Effect of Asset Disposal on Smith Company's Cash Flow

Direct Effect

- **Inflow:** Proceeds from disposal
- **Outflow:** Expenditures for equipment removal and site restoration

Tax Effect

- **Inflow:** Tax effect on loss of the disposal
- **Outflow:** Tax effect on gain of the disposal

Exhibit 11–7   Net Effect of Asset Disposal on Smith Company's Cash Flow

Terminology

Net book value	Original cost – Accumulated depreciation
Net proceeds	Proceeds from disposal – Expenditures for removal and restoration
Gain on disposal	Net proceeds > Net book value
Loss on disposal	Net proceeds < Net book value

Net Cash Effect (Inflow)

For Gain Net proceeds – (Gain on disposal × Tax rate)
For Loss Net proceeds + (Loss on disposal × Tax rate)

a commission of 10 percent of the selling price has found a buyer willing to pay $80,000 for the old machine. Smith Company, however, must pay all removal expenses and estimates that removal will cost about $2,000.

Subtracted from the $80,000 selling price for the equipment are the $8,000 commission for the broker and $2,000 equipment removal expenses. The net proceeds to Smith Company are $70,000. The firm can, however, expect the net cash inflow to be higher than the net proceeds from the sale of the old machine.

Smith Company suffers a loss on the machine's disposal. The firm bought it for $320,000 and has taken $200,000 depreciation on it. This leaves a net cost or book value of $120,000 as of the date of disposal. The firm, however, sold the equipment for only $70,000—a $50,000 loss. This loss decreases taxable income for the period and reduces the firm's income tax liability. At the 40 percent tax rate, the $50,000 loss from the disposal of the old milling machine reduces Smith Company's tax bill by $20,000 (see Exhibit 11–8). The cash inflow from the tax saving, however, occurs at the end of the tax year.

Project Operation

A firm invests in a project to increase revenues, decrease expenses, or both. Changes in revenues or expenses have both direct and tax effects on cash flows. Unlike other types of cash flows that occur perhaps once or twice during the life of the investment, cash flows from operations occur every year or several times during the investment's life.

Increases in sales revenue have direct effects on cash inflows. Smith Company expects its investment to bring in $1,000,000 in cash revenue from increases in production volume in each of the next four years. This investment will have a direct effect of $1,000,000 cash inflow in each of the next four years.

An investment can also increase a firm's activity, expenses, and cash expenditures. Increases in cash expenditures offset the increases in cash from revenues. The $1,000,000 increase in revenues that Smith Company expects from its milling machine investment requires $750,000 cash expenditures for operating expenses of direct materials, direct labor, manufacturing overhead, and selling and administrative expenses. The

Exhibit 11–8   Cash Flows from Smith Company's Disposal of Equipment

Immediate Cash Effect

Selling price		$ 80,000
Expenses related to the disposal of the equipment		
Brokers' commission (10 percent of $80,000)	$8,000	
Equipment removal expenses	2,000	10,000
Net proceeds from the disposal of the equipment		$ 70,000

Cash Effect at End of Year (tax saving from the disposal)

Acquisition cost of the equipment	$320,000
Accumulated depreciation	200,000
Net book value as of disposal date	$120,000
Net proceeds from the disposal	70,000
Loss from the disposal	$ 50,000
Income tax rate	0.40
Income tax saving from the loss on disposal	$ 20,000

Total Cash Effect from Disposal

Immediate cash effect	$ 20,000
Cash effect at end of year	70,000
Total cash inflow from disposal	$ 90,000

net cash inflow from the investment, therefore, is $250,000 per year. At a 40 percent tax rate, the additional $250,000 increases the firm's tax obligation by $100,000. This leaves a net after-tax cash inflow of $150,000 per year before considering the depreciation tax shield for each of the four years of the investment and an additional one-time expenditure in the investment's first year.

In addition, an investment can entail increases in amortized costs and allocated expenses. An investment in plant and equipment also increases the firm's depreciation expenses, thus raising its amortized costs, which are tax deductible. Although depreciation expenses do not take the form of cash payments, they reduce tax liabilities and, therefore, decrease cash *outflows*. You can see this tax effect in Exhibit 11–4, where the savings in taxes from the depreciation expenses of Smith's milling machine investment decrease cash outflows by $44,000 each year for four years. The decreases in cash outflows due to the depreciation expenses increase the cash inflow from the investment to $164,000 and $194,000 in each of the four useful years of the machine as shown in panels A and B of Exhibit 11–9.

Smith Company also expects other additional costs in the first year of operating the new milling machine including expenditures for employee training, work adjustments, and learning effects. The firm expects the total additional costs in year 1 to be $50,000. The net after-tax effect on cash flow of the first year of the investment from these additional expenditures is a cash outflow of $30,000, which reduces the net cash inflow in year 1 from $194,000 to $164,000.

An investment can increase the allocation base of a division and, thus, increase the indirect expenses allocated to it. Suppose that the headquarters allocates its expenses to divisions at a rate of $0.025 per dollar of sales. The investment brings in $1,000,000 of additional sales per year and results in a charge of $25,000 in headquarters expenses to the division each year. The total expenses of the division thus will increase by $25,000 in each of the four years of the investment. The increase in a division's sales, however, does not increase the total costs of the overall company. Looking at the capital investment from the corporate viewpoint, the $25,000 additional charge to the division is not a cash outflow of the firm and, therefore, is not considered in capital budgeting. Also, the tax effect results in no saving because the firm's total expenses remain unchanged.

Panel A of Exhibit 11–9 summarizes the effects of periodic operations on cash flow. Panel B shows an alternative financial approach to determine the same effect. Panel C reports the total effects of initial acquisition activities and periodic operations on the cash flows of each period. Exhibit 11–10 summarizes the determinations of the cash flow effects of various operating items.

Final Project Disposal

Direct Cash Effects The disposal of an investment at the end of its useful life can also affect cash flows. A sale of the investment increases cash inflows. The disposal, however, often requires expenditures either to prepare assets for sale or to clean up and restore the site after the disposal.

Disposal also can decrease the need for personnel. A firm is likely obligated to pay severance or relocation and retraining expenses for employees associated with the operations to be discontinued. These payments or expenses are cash outflows. Anticipating decreasing needs for employees, many firms phase out employees a few years before the final year of an investment by encouraging early retirement, leaving vacated positions unfilled, and transferring the employees to other divisions. Thus, some severance pay, relocation expenses, and retraining costs could occur a few years before the final disposal.

Tax Effects A gain or loss from the disposal of an asset has tax implications for a taxpaying firm as shown forthwith. The firm pays taxes on any gain and receives tax credit benefits for any loss by way of decreased tax liability because of the loss.

Exhibit 11–9   Effects on Cash Flow

Panel A: Effect of Operations on Cash Flows

Effect of cash revenue or expense

Revenues	$1,000,000
Cash operating expenditures	750,000
Increase in cash inflows before taxes	$ 250,000
Income taxes (at 40 percent)	100,000
Increase in cash inflows from operations	$ 150,000

Effect of noncash expense

Depreciation expenses	$ 110,000
Income tax rate	40%
Decrease in cash outflows due to taxes	$ 44,000

Summary of effect on cash flow

From cash revenue or expense	$ 150,000
From noncash expense	44,000
Total cash *inflows* in each period	$ 194,000

Panel B: Alternative Financial Approach to Determine Periodic Cash Flow Effects

Revenues		$1,000,000
Operating expenses		
Cash expenditures	$ 750,000	
Noncash expenditures: Depreciation	110,000	860,000
Operating income before taxes		$ 140,000
Income taxes (at 40 percent)		56,000
Operating income		$ 84,000
Noncash expenditures: Depreciation		110,000
Increase in cash inflow from operations		$ 194,000

Panel C: Total Effect on Cash Flow in Each of the Years

	Time Period				
Description	**Year 0**	**Year 1**	**Year 2**	**Year 3**	**Year 4**
Cost of equipment	$(500,000)				
Installation cost	(5,000)				
Testing and adjusting	(10,000)				
Working capital	(200,000)				$200,000
Disposal of displaced machine	90,000				
Cash inflow from operations (Panel A or B)		$194,000	$194,000	$194,000	194,000
One-time expenditure (net of taxes)		(30,000)			
Total cash inflow (outflow) effect	$(625,000)	$164,000	$194,000	$194,000	$394,000

Exhibit 11–10   Effects of Periodic Operation

Transaction	Effects on Cash Flow
Cash receipts	Amount received × (1 – Tax rate)
Cash expenditures	Amount paid × (1 – Tax rate)
Depreciated initial cost	Tax shield: Depreciation expense × Tax rate
Allocated cost	No effect

Exhibit 11–11	Determination of the Net Effect on Cash Flow of Final Disposal

Cash proceeds from disposal

−

Cash expenditures for preparation, removing, cleaning, and restoration

+

Loss on disposal × Tax rate

or −

Gain on disposal × Tax rate

−

Severance pay and relocation and retraining expense × (1 − Tax rate)

+

Released working capital

=

Net effect on cash flow from final disposal

Released Working Capital   Working capital committed to an investment is no longer needed after the firm terminates it. The funds tied up in investment's working capital will now be available for other uses, and the released working capital is a cash inflow without any tax consequence when the funds are released. Exhibit 11–11 summarizes the procedure to determine the effects of final disposal on cash flows.

Effect of Final Disposal on Smith Company's Cash Flow

Smith Company expects to sell the old milling machine and related equipment at the end of year 4 for $100,000. The estimated salvage value for depreciation purposes, however, is $75,000 (Exhibit 11–4). The cost of removal and cleanup is expected to be $20,000.

The disposal thus has a direct cash inflow of $80,000 ($100,000 − $20,000). The estimated salvage value for depreciation purposes is irrelevant in determining the direct cash effect of the disposal, although it does have a tax effect.

After disposing of the investment, Smith Company can reassign all but 10 employees to other divisions without incurring significant expenses. The firm expects a $150,000 cost for relocation, retraining, and work adjustment for these 10 employees in the investment's last year. This $150,000 is a cash outflow and has a direct effect on cash flow in the year that Smith discontinues the investment.

The net proceeds that Smith Company receives from disposing of the milling machine provide a $5,000 gain for tax purposes ($80,000 net proceeds − $75,000 book value). At the 40 percent tax rate, Smith Company pays $2,000 on this gain. After taxes, Smith has a $78,000 cash inflow from the disposal as Panel A of Exhibit 11–12 shows.

Other cash expenditures also have tax implications. At the 40 percent tax rate, the $150,000 relocation cost to transfer employees decreases the firm's tax liability by $60,000. The relocation expense's net after-tax effect on cash flow is therefore a $90,000 cash outflow, as shown in Panel B of Exhibit 11–12.

Smith Company's $200,000 working capital committed to the milling machine at the investment's commencement is not needed once the investment has been terminated. The release of working capital adds a $200,000 *cash inflow* at the end of year 4, which has no tax effect because a decrease in working capital is not a gain. The addition of the $200,000 cash inflow released from the working capital no longer needed brings the total cash inflow from termination of the investment to $188,000 as shown in Panel C of Exhibit 11–12.

In Exhibit 11–12 you can see the effects of the final disposal of the investment on Smith Company's cash flows. Exhibit 11–13 summarizes the cash flow effects on Smith Company's milling machine investment in each year of its life.

Exhibit 11–12	Effects of Final Disposal on Smith Company's Cash Flow			
		Cash Flows	**Gain**	**Net Cash Flow**
Panel A: Disposal of Machine				
Direct Effect				
Proceeds from sale of machine		$ 100,000		
Machine removal and site cleanup expenses		(20,000)		
Net proceeds from sale of machine			$80,000	$ 80,000
Tax Effect				
Cost of the milling machine		$ 515,000		
Accumulated depreciation		440,000		
Book value of the milling machine			75,000	
Gain on sale of the milling machine			$ 5,000	
Income taxes (at 40 percent)			× 0.40	2,000
Net after-tax cash proceeds from disposal of machine				$ 78,000
Panel B: Other Expenditures				
Direct Effect				
Relocation cost of displaced employees		$ (150,000)		
Tax Effect				
Income taxes (at 40 percent)		60,000		
Net after-tax cash outflow for relocation of employees				$ (90,000)
Panel C: Released Working Capital				
Direct Effect				
Working capital no longer needed				200,000
Total effect of the final disposal on cash *inflow*				$188,000

CAPITAL INVESTMENT EVALUATION TECHNIQUES

Many techniques to evaluate capital investments are available. These are the three most widely used:

1. Payback period.
2. Book rate of return.
3. Discounted cash flow.

Each technique has its merits and shortcomings. None is definitely superior to the others in all aspects. Over the years surveys have found several different capital investment evaluation techniques in use.[8] Furthermore, a firm can use different methods for different types of projects or use more than one method to evaluate a capital investment. Many of the survey's responding firms use at least one secondary technique to supplement the primary analytical method for evaluating capital projects.

Data for Evaluating Investment Capital

In discussing the evaluation of capital investment techniques, we again use data for Smith Company. In addition to the previous investment project, identified as project B, Jennifer O'Clock, the manager, received another investment proposal, identified as project A. Project A also has a four-year expected useful life and requires total initial

◀**LEARNING OBJECTIVE 3**

Use capital investment evaluation techniques including the payback period, book rate of return, net present value, and internal rate of return methods to assess capital investments and explain the advantages and limitations of these techniques.

---

[8] Thomas Klammer, Bruce Koch, and Neil Wilner, "Capital Budgeting Practices—A Survey of Corporate Use," *Journal of Management Accounting Research*, Fall 1991, pp. 113–30.

Exhibit 11–13	Effects of Investment in Project B on Smith Company's Cash Flows (in thousands)				

		Years			
	0	**1**	**2**	**3**	**4**
Initial Investment					
Cost of equipment	$(500)				
Installation cost	(5)				
Testing and adjusting	(10)				
Working capital	(200)				
Disposal of the displaced machine	90				
Operations					
Revenues		$1,000	$1,000	$1,000	$1,000
Operating expenses					
Cash items		$ 800	$ 750	$ 750	$ 750
Noncash item: Depreciation		110	110	110	110
Total operating expenses		$ 910	$ 860	$ 860	$ 860
Operating income before taxes		$ 90	$ 140	$ 140	$ 140
Income taxes (40 percent)		36	56	56	56
Operating income		$ 54	$ 84	$ 84	$ 84
Noncash expense: Depreciation		110	110	110	110
Net cash inflow from operations		$ 164	$ 194	$ 194	$ 194
Final Disinvestment (net of taxes)					
Working capital released					$ 200
Disposal of investment					78
Employee relocation, retraining, or severance pay					(90)
Net effect on cash flow	$(625)	$ 164	$ 194	$ 194	$ 382

investments of $555,000 in year 0. O'Clock expects project A to generate $900,000 of revenue each year for four years. Its operating expense will be $660,000 each year, in addition to depreciation expenses and other allocated headquarters' expenses.

Project A does not require additional working capital and has a salvage value of $60,000 for depreciation purposes. O'Clock expects to sell the investment for $200,000 at the end of year 4. The total expenses for relocation, retraining, and severance pay for the displaced employees and for all other expenses relating to the disposal are expected to be $240,000. Exhibit 11–14 summarizes pertinent data for both projects.

The Payback Period Technique

Investors often ask how long will it take to get their money back when considering investments. The payback period answers this question.

The **payback period** of an investment is the length of time required for the cumulative total net cash inflows from the investment to equal the total initial cash outlays. At that point in time, the investor has recovered the amount of money invested in the project.

> The **payback period** of an investment is the length of time required for its cumulative total net cash inflows to equal its total initial cash outlays.

Determining the Payback Period

The first step in computing a payback period is determining the after-tax cash flows from the investment for each year of the project's life. Exhibits 11–15 and 11–16 present the cash flows for projects A and B, respectively, over their useful lives. The after-

Exhibit 11–14   Data for Projects A and B

Project A

Required initial investment	$ 555,000
Estimated salvage value	$ 60,000
Annual operating data	
Revenues	$ 900,000 per year for four years
Cash operating expense	$ 660,000 per year for four years
Final disposal	
Cash proceeds from disposal	$ 200,000
Employee relocation, retraining, and severance pay	$ 240,000

Project B

Required initial investment	$ 625,000
Estimated salvage value	$ 75,000
Annual operating data	
Revenues	$1,000,000 per year for four years
Cash operating expense	$ 750,000 per year for four years
Other operating data	
Additional cash expenditure	$ 50,000 year 1 only
Final disposal	
Cash proceeds from disposal	$ 100,000
Machine removal and site cleanup	$ 20,000
Employee relocation, retraining, and severance pay	$ 150,000

Company

Depreciation method	Straight-line
Income tax rate	40 percent for combined federal, state, and local taxes

Exhibit 11–15   Payback Period for Project A with Uniform Net Cash Inflows
Total Initial Investment of $555,000

(1)	(2)	(3)	(4)	(5)	(6)	(7)	(8)	(9)	(10)
Period	Revenue	Operating Expenses	Cash Inflows Before Taxes	Depreciation Expense*	Operating Income Before Taxes	Income Taxes (40 percent)	After-Tax Operating Income	Net After-Tax Cash Inflows (4) – (7)	Cumulative Net After-Tax Cash Inflow from Operation
1	$900,000	$660,000	$240,000	$123,750	$116,250	$46,500	$69,750	$193,500	$193,500
2	900,000	660,000	240,000	123,750	116,250	46,500	69,750	193,500	387,000
3	900,000	660,000	240,000	123,750	116,250	46,500	69,750	193,500	580,500
4	900,000	660,000	240,000	123,750	116,250	46,500	69,750	193,500	—
Disposal	200,000†	240,000‡	<40,000>	60,000§	<100,000>	<40,000>	<60,000>	0	—

*Depreciation expense is $123,750 per year [($555,000 – $60,000)/4].

†The selling price of the investment at the end of the fourth year.

‡Employee relocation, retraining, and severance pay, $240,000.

§Salvage value, $60,000.

tax net cash inflows (column 8, Exhibit 11–15) for project A are uniform over the years; the cash inflows for project B (column 2, Exhibit 11–16) are uneven. Although the principle for calculating payback periods is the same, the details in determining payback periods differ for various cash flow patterns.

Exhibit 11–16	Payback Period for Project B with Uneven Cash Flow Returns
	Total Initial Investment of ($625,000)

(1)	(2)	(3)
	Net After-Tax	Cumulative Net After-Tax
Years	Cash Inflow	Cash Inflow
1	$164,000	$164,000
2	194,000	358,000
3	194,000	552,000
4	382,000	

Determining the Payback Period with Uniform Annual Cash Flows

Project A generates revenue of $900,000 each year for four years (column 2, Exhibit 11–15). The cash operating expenses are $660,000 per year, as reported in column 3, in addition to a $123,750 depreciation expense (column 5) per year. The difference between the $900,000 revenue and the sum of the $660,000 cash operation expense and the $123,750 depreciation expense is the operating income before taxes, $116,250 (column 6 of Exhibit 11–15). This amount is taxable. At a total income tax rate of 40 percent, the total income tax on the operating income generated by Project A is $46,500 per year (column 7), and the after-tax operating income is $69,750 in each of the four years (column 8).

The firm expects to terminate Project A after four years. The last row of Exhibit 11–15 shows the effects of transactions relating to the termination. The firm expects to sell Project A's equipment and related assets for $200,000 at the end of its useful life. However, the firm must spend $240,000 in employee relocation, retraining, and severance pay. Thus, the final disposal of Project A will have a $40,000 net cash outflow before taxes. With $60,000 book value for the project at the time of the disposal, the disinvestment's total loss to the firm will be $100,000. A loss of $100,000 for a firm in the 40 percent income tax bracket decreases the taxes by $40,000.

The cash inflow before taxes from operations is $240,000 (column 4), the difference between revenues (column 2) and cash operating expenses (column 3). After paying income taxes (column 7), Project A generates a net after-tax cash inflow of $193,500 (column 9 = column 4 – column 7) from the operations each year. The net after-tax cash inflow (column 9) can also be computed by adding the noncash expense depreciation expenses (column 5) to the after-tax operating income (column 8). Column 10 of Exhibit 11–15 shows the cumulative net cash proceeds starting from the project's first period of operation.

Project A's payback period is the number of periods before the cumulative total cash flow (column 10) equals the project's initial investment. Project A generates $193,500 net after-tax cash inflows each year in the first three years and will have cumulative net proceeds of $387,000 by the end of year 2, which is $168,000 short of the initial $555,000 investment. In the absence of detailed data on cash flow patterns during the year, we assume that revenues and operating expenses flow evenly throughout the year. With the expected net after-tax cash inflows of $193,500 in year 3, the firm needs 0.87 ($168,000 ÷ $193,500) of a year in the third year to generate $168,000 net cash inflows. The payback period of project A, therefore, is 2.87 years, or 2 years and 10.44 months.

Alternatively, the payback period for a capital project with equal cash inflows every year can be determined by dividing the total initial investment by the expected annual cash inflows:

$$\text{Payback period} = \frac{\text{Total initial capital investment}}{\text{Annual expected after-tax net cash inflow}}$$

For project A, the payback period is

$$\text{Payback period} = \frac{\$555,000}{\$193,500} = 2.87 \text{ years}$$

Determining Payback Period with Uneven Annual Cash Flows   Column 2 of Exhibit 11–16 reproduces the information in the last row of Exhibit 11–13 and provides the data for finding the payback period of project B. With uneven net cash inflows, the payback period is the length of time before the cumulative net cash inflows equal the initial cash outlay.

Project B has cumulative net cash inflows of $552,000 by the end of year 3. This amount is $73,000 short of the initial cash investment of $625,000. With the estimated net cash inflow in year 4 of $382,000, it takes 0.19 of a year in year 4 to earn $73,000. The payback period for project B therefore is 3.19 years:

$$3 \text{ years} + \frac{\$73,000}{\$382,000} = 3.19 \text{ years}$$

Evaluation of the Payback Period Technique

Advantages   A major advantage of the payback period technique is that it is easy to compute and to comprehend. A payback period provides a quick estimate of the time needed for the firm to recoup the cash invested.

Many investors consider the length of payback period to be a measure of the investment's risk. The longer an investment's payback period, the riskier it is. This is true for two reasons: First, the farther into the future a payback period is, the more likely the projected revenues and expenses will not be as predicted. Second, the longer to recover the investment, the more likely the product or service will become obsolete or attract competition, making it more difficult to earn cash flows as projected.

A payback period also can indicate the liquidity available to the firm. Cash inflows from a project are available for uses in other projects. A project with a four-year payback period is likely not as liquid as one with a payback period of three years or less.

The payback period technique emphasizes quick payoffs, an important consideration in some instances. Firms in industries with a high obsolescence risk often require short payback periods, as we have witnessed in recent years with investments in high-technology industries such as the computer chip and the personal computer. Short payback periods often become the determining factor for investments in these industries.

Limitations   Among the limitations of the payback period technique are its failure to consider an investment's total profitability and the time value of money. The payback period technique considers cash flows from the initiation of the project until its payback period. This method ignores all cash flows after the payback period.

The second limitation is that the payback period technique disregards the time value of money. It considers only the length of time required to recover the investment regardless of differences in the timing or pattern of cash flows. As long as the payback periods for two projects are the same, the payback period technique considers them equal to the firm, even if one project generates most of its net cash inflows in the early years of the project while the other project generates most of its net cash inflows in the last year of the payback period. The payback period method considers a $5,000 cash inflow in year 5, for example, to be the same as a $5,000 cash inflow in year 1.

To illustrate the effects of these two limitations of the payback period method, assume that a firm must select one of two investments. The expected cash flows for these two projects follow:

Project	Year 0	Year 1	Year 2	Year 3	Year 4	Payback Period
P	$(100,000)	$90,000	$ 5,000	$ 5,000	$80,000	3 years
Q	(100,000)	5,000	95,000	10,000	10,000	2 years

Both projects require the same amount of initial investment. Of the two projects, project Q has a shorter payback period. According to the payback period method, project Q is the preferred investment of the two.

Project Q is the preferred investment, however, only if we can ignore both the amount of the total net cash inflows and their patterns. The payback period technique ignores the fact that project P brings in $180,000 and project Q brings in only $120,000 over the four-year period.

Furthermore, the cash flow patterns show that project P brings in substantially more net cash inflows than project Q in the first year of operations. If the firm invests all cash inflows from investments and earns a 10 percent return, project P has a shorter payback period than project Q (1.71 years versus 1.99 years).[9] If the time value of money is not ignored, the payback period recognizes project P as the better investment of the two.

One common error in using the payback period method is to demand too short a payback period. Companies require short payback periods to maintain a liquid financial position, fulfill the need to finance other investments, manage risk and uncertainty, or to avoid extended projections. Demanding too short a payback period, however, often hampers wise investing by causing firms not to invest in long-term improvements. After all, an investment in hand tools takes a very short time to pay back the initial outlay, while an investment in a new technology—such as a computer-integrated-manufacturing (CIM) system—usually takes years to earn back the investment. A firm that stresses short payback periods in investments and avoids those in projects that require long payback periods most likely do not fare very well in today's competitive global market.

The Book Rate of Return Technique

Determining Book Rate of Return

The book rate of return technique is another common method used to evaluate capital investments. The **book rate of return** is the net income from an investment as a percentage of its book value.

> The **book rate of return** is the average net income from an investment as a percentage of its book value.

$$\text{Book rate of return} = \frac{\text{Average annual net income}}{\text{Investment (book value)}}$$

Both amounts normally appear in financial statements; thus, the amount is often referred to as the *book rate of return*. It is an unadjusted rate of return because the procedure does not adjust for the differences in time value of money of returns received in different periods.

The numerator is the average annual net income from the investment over its useful life. The denominator is either the initial total investment or the average invest-

---

[9] We assume that operating cash flows occur uniformly throughout the year. The estimated payback periods are as follows:

	Project P	Project Q
Initial investment	$100,000	$100,000
Cash inflow in year 1	90,000	5,000
Additional cash inflow needed to pay back the initial investment	$ 10,000	$ 95,000
Cash inflow in year 2		
From operations	5,000	95,000
From interest earned (10%) on the net cash inflow of year 1	9,000	500
Total cash inflow in year 2	$ 14,000	$ 95,500
Therefore, payback periods are		

$$\text{Project P: 1 year} + \frac{\$10,000}{\$14,000} \text{ year} = 1.71 \text{ years}$$

$$\text{Project Q: 1 year} + \frac{\$95,000}{\$95,500} \text{ year} = 1.99 \text{ years}$$

ment (book value) over the useful life of the project. Some companies prefer the original investment because it is objectively determined and is not affected by either the choice of the depreciation method or the estimation of the salvage value. No matter which approach is used in evaluating the investment, the same approach should be used for all investments.

Recall the situation that Jennifer O'Clock faces, as described in Exhibit 11–14. She can expect project A to earn a net income of $69,750 per year:

$$\text{Net income} = \text{Revenues} - \frac{\text{Cash operating}}{\text{expenses}} - \frac{\text{Noncash operating}}{\text{expenses}} - \frac{\text{Income}}{\text{taxes}}$$

$$= \$900,000 - \$660,000 - \frac{\$555,000 - \$60,000}{4} - \$46,500$$

$$= \$69,750$$

The only noncash expense for project A is the straight-line depreciation on the equipment.

The average investment is the average book value for the investment in its accounting records during the investment's life. (See Exhibit 11–17 for project A.)

Project A requires an initial investment of $555,000, and the firm estimates the salvage value after four years to be $60,000. An investment's average in a year is the average of it at the beginning of the year and its balance at the end of the year. According to the accounting records, the amount of investment is $555,000 at the beginning of year 1 and $431,250 at the end of the same year. The average investment for year 1, therefore, is $493,125. The average investment for the life of the investment is the sum of the average investments for each year divided by the number of years. With a total average investment of $1,230,000 over a 4-year period, the average investment over the entire 10-year period is $307,500 ($1,230,000/4).

The book rate of return for project A is therefore 22.68 percent:

$$\frac{\$69,750}{\$307,500} = 22.68 \text{ percent}$$

A firm that uses the straight-line depreciation method can compute the average investment by taking the simple average of the initial investment and its salvage value at the end of its useful life:

$$\text{Average investment} = \frac{\text{Original cost} + \text{Salvage value}}{2}$$

$$= \frac{\$555,000 + \$60,000}{2} = \$307,500$$

This shortcut computation for average investment is not applicable when the depreciation method is not the straight-line method because the decrease in the book

Exhibit 11–17	Smith Company's Average Investment for Project A		
Year	Investment at the Beginning of the Year	Investment at the End of the Year	Average Investment for the Year
1	$555,000	$431,250	$ 493,125
2	431,250	307,500	369,375
3	307,500	183,750	245,625
4	183,750	60,000	121,875
Total			$1,230,000
Average book value = $1,230,000/4 years = $307,500			

Exhibit 11–18	Smith Company's Average Investment When the Firm Uses Double-Declining-Balance Depreciation Method			
Year	Investment at the Beginning of the Year	Depreciation Expense for the Year	Investment at the End of the Year	Average Book Value (investment) for the Year
1	$555,000	$277,500	$277,500	$416,250
2	277,500	138,750	138,750	208,125
3	138,750	69,375	69,375	104,063
4	69,375	9,375	60,000	64,687
Total				$793,125

Average book value (investment) = $793,125/4 years = $198,281

value of the investment is not constant over the years. Exhibit 11–18 shows the determination of the average investment for project A if Smith Company uses the double-declining-balance depreciation method.

Some firms choose to calculate book rates of return on the original total investment. The book rate of return for project A is 12.57 percent if the firm chooses to use the original investment as the denominator.

$$\frac{\$69,750}{\$555,000} = 12.57 \text{ percent}$$

Project A's expected annual net income remains stable throughout its useful life. The average net income thus is the same as its expected annual income. In contrast, the expected net income for project B varies from year to year. The firm, therefore, needs to calculate the average expected net income of project B before computing its book rate of return.

Exhibit 11–13 shows that project B's net incomes over its four-year useful life are $54,000, $84,000, $84,000, and $84,000. The average net income per year is $76,500:

$$\frac{\$54,000 + \$84,000 + \$84,000 + \$84,000}{4} = \$76,500$$

Project B has a book value of $515,000 at its onset and a salvage value of $75,000. The average investment is $295,000:

$$\frac{\$515,000 + \$75,000}{2} = \$295,000$$

The book rate of return is 25.93 percent using the average investment or 14.85 percent using the total initial investment:

$$\frac{\$76,500}{\$295,000} = 25.93 \text{ percent} \qquad \frac{\$76,500}{\$515,000} = 14.85 \text{ percent}$$

Evaluation of the Book Rate of Return Technique

Advantages   The book rate of return technique uses data generated for financial reports. No special procedures are required to generate data to compute the book rate of return. Thus, the cost to generate the data to analyze a capital investment using the book rate of return method is likely to be low comparing to those of other capital investment evaluation techniques. Because managers often are evaluated on the basis of the book rate of return, using the same procedure in both the decision-making stage and the periodic evaluation ensures consistency. The fact that these data are audited using generally accepted accounting principles can add reliability.

In addition, the book rate of return enables decision makers to gauge the capital investment's effect on the financial performance of the division or the firm. The firm can easily measure the impact that the capital investment may have on debt covenants or other contractual agreements.

The book rate of return has an additional advantage over the payback period method because it includes the entire period of an investment in its capital investment analyses. Unlike the payback period method, which uses the data only to the point of recouping the original investment, the book rate of return method considers all net incomes over the entire life of the project and provides a measure of the investment's profitability.

Limitations Like the payback period method, the book rate of return technique ignores the time value of money. Another limitation is its use of accounting numbers in both the denominator and the numerator in determining the book rate of return. Accounting numbers depend on the choice of accounting procedures. Different accounting procedures can lead to substantially different amounts for an investment's net income and book values. For example, Exhibit 11–18 shows that the average book value of Project A is $198,281 when the firm uses the double-declining-balance depreciation method—a $109,219 decrease from the amount shown in Exhibit 11–17.

Net income based on a straight-line depreciation method differs from the net income for the same period using, say, a declining-balance depreciation method. As a result, the calculated book rates of return based on the net incomes using different depreciation methods are different, although nothing except the accounting procedures are different. This condition is undesirable because the result for a capital investment should differ only if its underlying factors vary; the result should not vary because of a change in the accounting procedures.

Also, whereas net income can be a useful measure of the firm's profitability as a whole, cash flows are a better measure of its performance over an investment's life for reasons cited earlier. Furthermore, inclusion of only the book value of the invested asset as the total investment ignores the fact that a project can require commitments of working capital and other outlays.

Neither the payback period nor the book rate of return technique considers the time value of money in evaluating capital investment projects.

We next examine two discounted cash flow techniques that explicitly consider the time value of money.

The Discounted Cash Flow Techniques

The **discounted cash flow (DCF) techniques** evaluate a capital investment by considering equivalent present values of all future net cash inflows from the initial investment.

> The **discounted cash flow (DCF) techniques** evaluate a capital investment by considering equivalent net values of all future net cash inflows from the initial investment.

An investment has cash flows throughout its useful life. A dollar of cash flow in the first year of an investment is worth more than a dollar of cash flow in a later year. A simple addition or subtraction of money received or paid at different points in time to arrive at the total effect of an investment ignores the important consideration of the time value of money. The DCF techniques explicitly consider the time value of money in evaluating capital investments.

Two DCF approaches are in general use: the net present value method and the internal rate of return method. The *net present value (NPV) method* uses a specified discount rate to bring all subsequent net cash inflows after the initial investment to their present values (the time of the initial investment). The NPV method focuses on the dollar amount at the time of the investment.

In contrast, the *internal rate of return (IRR) method* estimates the discount rate that makes the present value of all the subsequent net cash inflows after the initial investment equal the initial cash outlays of the investment. The IRR method's focus is on the rate of return.

Although the focus of these two approaches differ, they are variations of the same concept and use the same factors in evaluating capital investments:

1. The total initial investment.
2. The expected future cash receipts and disbursements.
3. The investor's desired rate of return.

The first two factors have already been discussed. The following section examines issues regarding the third factor, the desired rate of return.

Desired Rate of Return

The desired rate of return is the minimum rate of return the investing firm requires from an investment.

The **desired rate of return** can be defined as the minimum rate of return the investing firm requires from an investment. The minimum rate can be the rate of return the firm would have earned by investing the same funds in the best available alternative investment that bears the same risk. This rate is also referred to as hurdle rate.

Determining the desired rate of return based on the best alternative opportunity available is often difficult in practical terms. Management usually does not know all investment opportunities available to the firm; conducting an exhausting search and examining all opportunities can be very costly or time consuming, or both.

Rather than using the true opportunity cost, firms often use an alternative measure for the desired rate of return. Among the alternative measures of the desired rate of return are

1. Minimum rate of return.

2. Cost of capital.

A firm frequently has a minimum return requirement for all of its investments and considers only capital project proposals that meet it. Among the factors the firm considers in determining the required minimum rate of return are its strategic plan, the industry average, and other investment opportunities.

Cost of capital often ensures that a capital investment project will at least recover the firm's cost in obtaining the necessary funds for the investment. *Statement on Management Accounting No. 4A* by the Institute of Management Accountants defines **cost of capital** as "a composite of the cost of various sources of funds comprising a firm's capital structure."[10] A firm obtains funds by issuing preferred or common stock; borrowing money using various forms of debt such as notes, loans, or bonds; or retaining earnings. The costs to the firm are the returns demanded by debt and equity investors.

The cost of capital is a composite of the cost of various sources of funds comprising a firm's capital structure.

The cost of the debt is the after-tax interest rate on it. If a firm must pay 10 percent interest, for example, to secure a $5,000 loan from its bank, the cost of the debt is 10 percent before considering income tax effects. The cost of the debt is 7 percent if the firm is in the 30 percent tax bracket. Assume now that the firm issued a 10 percent, $5,000 bond and sold the bond for $4,375. The after-tax cost of the bond is 8 percent as computed:

Bond face value	$5,000
Bond interest rate	× 0.10
Interest expense before taxes	$ 500
Income taxes (30%)	− 150
After-tax interest expense	$ 350

$$\text{After-tax cost of bond} = \frac{\text{After-tax interest expense}}{\text{Market value of bond}} = \frac{\$350}{\$4,375} = 8\%$$

The cost of equity securities is the return demanded by shareholders. The cost of a preferred stock is the percentage of the dividend to be paid on it divided by the security's market value. George's Sports, Inc., has an income tax rate of 30 percent and issues 100 shares of $2.40, par $20 preferred stock for $25 per share. The firm's income tax is irrelevant in determining the cost of equities because the returns to shareholders are not tax deductible. The cost of the preferred stock to George's Sports is 9.6 percent, computed as follows:

$$\frac{\text{Dividend per share}}{\text{Market price per share}} = \frac{\$2.40}{\$25.00} = 9.6\%$$

Notice that the dividend rate on the preferred stock is 12% ($2.40/$20). The cost of preferred equity is determined based on the value that investors are willing to pay—

---

[10]   Institute of Management Accountants, *Statement Number 4A: Cost of Capital* (Montvale, N.J., 1984), p. 1.

$25 for shareholders of preferred stocks issued by George's Sports—not on the par value. The cost of common stock is the ratio of the return demanded by shareholders to the market value of the stock. If, for example, George's Sports, Inc., has 100 shares of $10 par common stock outstanding, the market price for this common stock is $200 per share. Investors demand a return of $25 per share on the stock. The cost of the common stock to George's Sports is 12.5 percent:

$$\frac{\text{Return demanded by investors}}{\text{Market price per share}} = \frac{\$25}{\$200} = 12.5\%$$

The cost of capital to a firm is a weighted average of the returns demanded by debt and equity investors. The weighted average is the expected rate of return investors would demand on a portfolio of all the firm's outstanding securities.[11]

As an example, consider a firm in a 40 percent tax bracket for federal and state taxes combined. This firm has a $100,000 bank loan with 12 percent interest; $500,000, 10 percent, 20-year mortgage bond selling at 90; $200,000, 15 percent, $20 noncumulative, noncallable preferred stock with a total market value of $300,000; and 10,000 shares of $1 par common stock that the firm sold for $5 per share. The common stock's current market price is $75 per share. The market demands a return of $15 per share. The weighted cost of capital of the firm is 13.3875 percent, as computed:

	Book Value	Interest or Dividend Rate	After-Tax Rate or Expected Return	Total Market Value	Weight	Weighted Average Cost of Capital
Bank loan	$100,000	12%	7.20%	$100,000	0.06250	0.4500
Bond	500,000	10	6.00	450,000	0.28125	1.6875
Preferred stock	200,000	15	10.00*	300,000	0.18750	1.8750
Common stock	50,000		20.00†	750,000	0.46875	9.3750
Total	$850,000			$1,600,000	1.00	13.3875%

*Total number of shares preferred stock: $200,000 ÷ 20 = 10,000 shares

Market value of per share of preferred stock: $300,000 ÷ 10,000 shares = $30 per share

Dividends per share: $20 × 15% = $3

Expected return on preferred stock: $3 ÷ $30 = 10%

† $15 ÷ $75 = 20%

The Net Present Value Method

Determining the Net Present Value   The **net present value (NPV)** of an investment is the net amount of the present value of future net cash inflows after subtracting the initial investment. The **present value** of a future net cash inflow is its current equivalent dollar value, given the desired rate of return. The present value of $5,000 to be received a year from now by an investor with a 10 percent desired rate of return is $4,545:

$$\$5,000 \times 0.909 = \$4,545$$

where 0.909 is the discount factor for 10 percent in one period. The discount factor can be found in the present value table on page 976. With a 10 percent desired rate of return, receiving $4,545 now or $5,000 a year from now is the same to the investor. To verify, calculate the total amount the investor has on hand one year after receiving $4,545:

Cash received now	$4,545
Interest for one year: $4,545 × 10 % =	455
Total cash on hand one year from now	$5,000

Thus, $4,545 is the present value equivalent of the $5,000 to be received one year from now.

> The **net present value (NPV)** of an investment is the net amount of the present value of future net cash inflows after subtracting the initial investment.
>
> The **present value** of a future net cash inflow is its current equivalent dollar value, given the desired rate of return.

---

[11]   Richard A. Brealey, Stewart C. Myers, and Alan J. Marcus, *Fundamentals of Corporate Finance* (New York: McGraw-Hill Irwin, 2001).

The NPV is the balance of the present value of the expected future net cash inflows after paying for the initial investment.

Present Value of Cash Flow

$$
\begin{array}{cccc}
\text{Net} & \text{Present value} & \text{Present value} & \text{Total net} \\
\text{present} = & \text{of cash} & - \quad \text{of cash} & - \quad \text{initial} \\
\text{value} & \text{receipts} & \text{expenditure} & \text{investment}
\end{array}
$$

The net present value is the amount in current dollars the investment earns after yielding the desired return in each period.

The first step in determining an investment's net present value is to determine the net cash inflow in each year of the investment. The net cash inflows then are converted, based on the desired rate of return, into their present equivalent dollar amounts. The net present value is the remainder after subtracting the total initial cash outlays for the investment from the sum of the present values of all future net cash inflows. These steps summarize the calculation of a project's NPV:

1. Determine net cash inflows in each year.
2. Select the desired rate of return.
3. Find the discount factor for each year based on the desired rate of return selected in step 2.
4. Multiply steps 1 and 3 to determine the present values of the net cash inflows.
5. Total the amount in step 4 for all the years.
6. Subtract the initial investment from the amount obtained in step 5.

A capital project is desirable if it has a positive NPV and undesirable if it has a negative NPV.

Determining NPV with Uniform Net Cash Inflows   Jennifer O'Clock desires to earn a 10 percent after-tax rate of return on investments. These calculations show the determination of the present value of net cash inflows from project A:

$$
\text{Present value of net cash inflows} = \$193{,}500 \times 3.17
$$

$$
= \$613{,}395
$$

The 3.17 is the discount factor for an annuity of four years at 10 percent. An *annuity* is a constant sum received or paid each year for a number of years. The discount factor varies according to the number of years and the rate of the desired return. The present value tables on page 977 present the discount factors for computing present values of annuities.

Project A generates an after-tax net cash inflow of $193,500 each year for four years. The preceding calculation shows that at a 10 percent interest rate, these yearly net cash inflows have a present value of $613,395.

At its beginning, Project A requires an initial investment of $555,000, which is its present value. Subtracting the $555,000 initial investment from the present value of net cash inflows yields $58,395, the NPV of this investment:

$$
\text{NPV of project A} = \$613{,}395 - \$555{,}000 = \$58{,}395
$$

The NPV indicates that a $555,000 investment in project A will earn $58,395 in current dollars for the investor in addition to earning a 10 percent return each year for four years on the $555,000 investment.

Using a Spreadsheet Program to Determine NPV   Most spreadsheet programs offer functions that allow users to calculate present values of cash flows.[12] These functions are:

---

[12]   Keystroke sequences are as follows:
  For Microsoft Excel: Insert → Function → Financial → NPV
  For Quattro Pro: Insert → Function → Financial-Cash Flow → NPV

For both Lotus 1-2-3 and Quattro Pro: @NPV (Rate, Range)

For Microsoft Excel: =NPV (Rate, Range)

where *rate* is the interest rate and *range* refers to the consecutive rows or columns in the spreadsheet that comprise net cash flows of the investment in each of the consecutive years. The first amount specified in *range* is either the amount or the cell of the net cash inflow at the end of the first year. The second amount is either the amount or the cell of the net cash inflow at the end of the second year, and so on. The program returns the present value of the future net cash inflows specified in the *range*. The user then calculates the net present value by finding the difference between the amount returned from the spreadsheet and the initial investment.

The NETPV function in Quattro Pro allows users to enter all cash flows, including the initial cash outflow. The program then returns the net present value:

NETPV (Rate, Range, Initial investment)

Interpretation of NPV An investment that earns the same rate of return as the desired rate of return has an NPV of zero. It will be greater than zero (as in this case) when an investment earns a rate of return higher than the desired rate of return, and a negative amount when the investment earns a return less than the desired rate of return. Project A has an NPV of $58,395. This suggests that project A earns a higher rate of return than the required 10 percent return and is a desirable investment. The investment will earn a 10 percent return on the funds invested plus $58,395 (in current dollars).

Alternative investments exist. The positive NPV of project A simply shows that the return from investing in this project is higher than the discount rate used in the computation. Project A might or might not be the best investment available. Other investment opportunities could yield even higher returns. O'Clock must check alternative investments, such as project B in our example, before she makes the final decision.

Determining NPV with Uneven Cash Inflows Project B has uneven net cash inflows over four years. As a result, the computation of its NPV requires more detailed calculations than those for the NPV of project A. Exhibit 11–19 shows the calculations of project B's NPV. The procedure starts with the after-tax net cash inflows generated each year by the investment during its useful life. These cash flows are then discounted using the present value discount factors on page 976, as shown in the last column of Exhibit 11–19.

The total present value shown in the last column of Exhibit 11–19 tells us that the equivalent total present value of the cash inflows from the investment over the years is $715,920. After subtracting the initial investment, the NPV of project B is $90,920. The positive NPV suggests that project B is also a desirable investment.

Present Value (or Discounted) Payback Period The payback period technique is often criticized for ignoring the time value of money. To avoid this criticism, users of the payback period method can use the present values of net cash inflows from an invest-

Exhibit 11–19 NPV of Project B: An Uneven Cash Flow Example

Years	Net After-Tax Cash Inflow	Discount Factor	Present Value
1	$164,000	0.909	$149,076
2	194,000	0.826	160,244
3	194,000	0.751	145,694
4	382,000	0.683	260,906
Total present value of net cash inflows			$715,920
Less: Initial investment			625,000
Net present value			$ 90,920

The present value payback period or **breakeven time (BET) method** is the span of time required for the cumulative present value of cash inflows to equal the initial investment of the project.

ment to determine its payback period. This payback period is the **present value payback period** that some users refer to as **breakeven time (BET).**

The present value payback period method uses the *present values* of net cash inflows rather than the undiscounted dollar amounts of net cash inflows to determine the payback period. As in the NPV method, the present value of net cash inflows from the investment is estimated using the firm's desired rate of return. The span of time required for the cumulative present value of net cash inflows to equal the initial investment of the project is the present value payback period. The present value payback period of project A is 3.56 years, as calculated in Exhibit 11–20, in contrast to 2.87 years for the simple payback period.

The present value or discounted payback period method has an advantage over the simple payback period method because it considers one dollar today to be more valuable than one dollar in the future. Nevertheless, it suffers the same weakness as the payback period in other aspects. Both methods emphasize quick payoffs and ignore profitability and cash inflows after the payback period.

Internal Rate of Return Method

The internal rate of return (IRR) method is a discounted cash flow method that estimates the discount rate that causes the present value of subsequent net cash inflows to equal the initial investment.

The **internal rate of return (IRR) method** estimates the discount rate that causes the present value of subsequent net cash inflows to equal the initial investment. The NPV of the investment will be zero if we use this estimated rate as the desired rate of return to compute the NPV.

The IRR method evaluates capital investments by comparing the estimated internal rate of return to the criterion rate of return. The criterion can be the firm's desired rate of return, the rate of return from the best alternative investment, or another rate the firm chooses to use for evaluating capital investments.

Determining the Internal Rate of Return

Like the NPV method, the IRR method considers the time value of money, initial cash investment, and all cash flows after the investment. Unlike the NPV method, the computation procedure of the IRR method does not use the desired rate of return to compute the present values of net cash inflows. The IRR method determines an investment's rate of return that makes the present value of net cash inflows after its initiation equal the investment's initial amount and then compares the estimated rate of return with the required rate in assessing the investment's desirability. In using this method, the investor considers the investment's rate of return and how it compares to the firm's desired return.[13]

The computation procedures for IRR vary somewhat with the pattern of net cash inflows over an investment's useful life.

Exhibit 11–20	Present Value Payback Period for Project A			
Year	Net After-Tax Cash Inflow	Discount Factor at 10 Percent	Present Value of Net Cash Inflow	Cumulative Present Value of Net Cash Inflow
1	$193,500	0.909	$175,892	$175,892
2	193,500	0.826	159,831	335,723
3	193,500	0.751	145,318	481,041
4	193,500	0.683	132,161	

Amount needed in year 4 to reach the payback period:

$$\$555,000 - \$481,041 = \$73,959$$

$$\text{Present value payback period} = 3 \text{ years} + \frac{73,959}{132,161} = 3.56 \text{ years}$$

---

[13] The book rate of return method discussed earlier appears to address the same issue; it provides a rate of return on investment. The IRR method, however, considers the time value of money, but the book rate of return method does not. The IRR method also uses cash flows while the book rate of return method uses the net income computed following the accounting rules and procedures the firm chooses to use in estimating the rate of return.

Uniform Cash Flows   The IRR method estimates the discount rate that makes the present value of net cash inflows equal the initial total cash disbursements and commitments. The first step in using the IRR method, therefore, is to determine the investment's total net initial cash disbursements and commitments and its net cash inflows in each year of the investment.

The discount rate that causes the total initial investment and the investment's present value of subsequent net cash inflows to be equal is the IRR of the investment. For an investment with uniform net cash inflows over its life, the IRR is the discount rate that satisfies the following equation:

Total initial investment = Present value of net cash inflows computed using the discount rate

= Annual net cash inflow × Annuity discount factor of the discount rate for the Number of periods of the investment's useful life

Using $A_{r,n}$ to denote the last term in this equation, the equation can be restated as follows:

$$A_{r,n} = \frac{\text{Total initial cash disbursements and commitments for the investment}}{\text{Annual equal net cash inflows from the investment}}$$

where $A_{r,n}$ is the annuity discount factor that makes the present value of the net cash inflows over the investment's life equal the initial investment, n is the number of periods for the project, and r is the discount rate.

The discount rate n,r for the calculated discount factor, $A_{r,n}$, is the interest rate that has the same discount factor as $A_{r,n}$ in the annuity table along the row for n periods, or the one closest to it. This discount rate is the IRR of the investment. To illustrate, the IRR for project A is determined as follows:

$$\$555{,}000 = \$193{,}500 \times A_{r,4}$$

$$\text{Rearrange, } A_{r,4} = \frac{\$555{,}000}{\$193{,}500} = 2.868$$

Using the annuity factor in the present value tables (pp. 976–977) on the four-year row,

$$r \approx 15 \text{ percent}$$

The computed IRR is compared to the firm's required rate of return or some other chosen criterion to assess the investment's desirability. An investment is desirable if the computed IRR exceeds the required rate of return. The computed 15 percent IRR for project A is higher than the 10 percent rate of return that the firm set for this investment. Project A is, therefore, a desirable investment.

When the available annuity table does not have a discount factor reasonably close to the computed discount factor for the project, the IRR method requires an interpolation procedure to estimate the IRR.[14]

---

[14]   To illustrate the interpolation procedure, let's assume that this is the only annuity table available:

n/r	12%	14%	16%
4	3.037	2.914	2.798

The $A_{r,4}$ for project A is 2.868. The annuity table, however, does not have a discount factor of 2.868 for a four-year project. The discount factor is 2.914 at 14 percent and 2.798 at 16 percent. The IRR, which has a discount of 2.868, is between these two discount rates. The following interpolation procedure estimates the IRR:

	Interest Rate		Discount Factor	
At lower rate	14%	14%	2.914	2.914
Target rate		?		2.868
At higher rate	16	—	2.798	—
Difference	2%	?	0.116	0.046

(Footnote continues on next page)

Exhibit 11–21   Present Values of Project B with Interest Rates of 14 and 16 Percent

Year	Net After-Tax Cash Flow	Discount Factor at 16 Percent	Present Value at 16 Percent	Discount Factor at 14 Percent	Present Value at 14 Percent
1	$164,000	0.862	$141,368	0.877	$143,828
2	194,000	0.743	144,142	0.769	149,186
3	194,000	0.641	124,354	0.675	130,950
4	382,000	0.552	210,864	0.592	226,144
Total			$620,728		$650,108

	Interest Rate		Total Cash Flows	
	14%	14%	$650,108	$650,108
		?		625,000
	16		620,728	
Difference	2%	?	$ 29,380	$ 25,108
Internal rate of return				

$$14\% + 2\% \times \frac{\$25,108}{\$29,380} = 15.71\%$$

Uneven Cash Flows   The procedure for estimating the IRR of a project with uneven net cash inflows over the years can involve trial and error and interpolation. The determination of the IRR for project B, as shown in Exhibit 11–21, illustrates this procedure.

The present value of net cash inflows is $650,108 at an interest rate of 14 percent and $620,728 at 16 percent. A 2 percent increase in interest rates from 14 percent to 16 percent decreases the present value of net cash inflows by $29,380. With $625,000 initial investment in the project, the IRR procedure calls for an increase in the interest rate from 14 percent so that the present value of cash flow returns will decrease from $650,108 to $625,000, a decrease of $25,108. The needed increase in the interest rate from 14 percent is 0.855 of the 2 percent increase from 14 percent to 16 percent—an increase of approximately 1.71 percent from 14 percent.

Using a Spreadsheet Program to Determine IRR   Many spreadsheet programs offer easy-to-use functions for estimating internal rate of return. For example, Lotus 1-2-3, Quattro Pro, and Microsoft Excel offer an IRR function to determine internal rate of return. The required inputs for the programs are as follows:

Lotus 1-2-3 and Quattro Pro: @IRR(Estimated rate of return in decimal, Range)

Microsoft Excel: =IRR(Range, Estimated rate of return in decimal)

The user provides a rough starting point for estimating the rate of return.[15] The *range* is the location of the data in the spreadsheet. The first cell of the range is the

---

The difference in discount factors between the interest rates on either side of the target discount factor (2.868), discount factors for 14 and 16 percent, is 0.116. This suggests that an increase of 2 percent in interest rates from 14 percent to 16 percent decreases the discount factor by 0.116.

The interest rate we are looking for has a discount factor of 2.868, a decrease of 0.046 from the discount factor for interest rate of 14 percent. The interest rate, therefore, needs to be increased from 14 percent so the discount factor decreases from 2.914 to 2.868. The needed decrease in the discount factor, 0.046, is 40 percent of the difference in the discount factors between 14 percent and 16 percent. With an increase of 2 percent in interest rates from 14 percent to 16 percent, the discount factor decreases by 0.116. The needed increase in interest rate to decrease the discount factor by 0.046, therefore, is 40 percent of the 2 percent, or 80 percent as shown here:

$$14\% + \left(\frac{0.046}{0.116} \times 2\%\right) = 14\% + \left(0.4 \times 2\%\right) = 14\% + 0.8\% = 14.80\%$$

[15]   Microsoft Excel assumes that the estimated rate of return is 0.1 if none is provided.

initial cash outlay expressed as a negative amount, followed by subsequent net cash inflows.[16]

Using Financial Calculators to Determine NPV and IRR   You can easily determine NPV and IRR using financial calculators. Most financial calculators follow similar keystrokes. We use project B as an example and illustrate keystrokes for three financial calculators. Remember to enter the initial cash outflow as a negative number.

1.   Net present value

Hewlett-Packard HP-10B		Sharpe EL-733A		Texas Instrument BA II Plus	
−625,000	CF₍ⱼ₎	−625,000	CF₍ⱼ₎	CF	
164,000	CF₍ⱼ₎	164,000	CF₍ⱼ₎	2nd	{CLR Work}
				−625,000	ENTER ↓
194,000	CF₍ⱼ₎	194,000	CF₍ⱼ₎		
				164,000	ENTER ↓
194,000	CF₍ⱼ₎	194,000	CF₍ⱼ₎		
				194,000	ENTER ↓
382,000	CF₍ⱼ₎	382,000	CF₍ⱼ₎		
				194,000	ENTER ↓
10	I/YR	10	i		
				382,000	ENTER ↓
	{NPV}		NPV	NPV	
					ENTER
				10	
				↓	CPT

2.   Internal Rate of Return

Hewlett-Packard HP-10B		Sharpe EL-733A		Texas Instrument BA II Plus	
−625,000	CF₍ⱼ₎	−625,000	CF₍ⱼ₎	CF	
164,000	CF₍ⱼ₎	164,000	CF₍ⱼ₎	2nd	{CLR Work}
				−625,000	ENTER ↓
194,000	CF₍ⱼ₎	194,000	CF₍ⱼ₎		
				164,000	ENTER ↓
194,000	CF₍ⱼ₎	194,000	CF₍ⱼ₎		
				194,000	ENTER ↓
382,000	CF₍ⱼ₎	382,000	CF₍ⱼ₎		
				194,000	ENTER ↓
				382,000	ENTER ↓
	{IRR/YR}		IRR	IRR	
				CPT	

---

[16]   Both Microsoft Excel and Quattro Pro offer two additional programs, MIRR and XIRR, for estimating the internal rate of return. MIRR is for situations in which the firm finances the needed cash outflows at a different rate than the expected rate for cash inflows:

=MIRR (Range, Finance rate, Reinvest rate)

XIRR is used when cash flows are not necessarily periodic:

=XIRR (Range, Dates, Estimated rate)

The dates should correspond with the values specified in the range.

Exhibit 11–22	Factors Affecting Results of NVP vs. IRR Analyses

Results from NPV and IRR can differ if projects differ as to
1. Amount of initial investment
2. Net cash flow pattern
3. Length of useful life
4. Fluctuating cost of capital over the project life
5. Results of multiple projects

COMPARISON OF THE NET PRESENT VALUE AND THE INTERNAL RATE OF RETURN METHODS

LEARNING OBJECTIVE 4▶

Identify the underlying assumptions of the discounted cash flow methods and use these methods properly to evaluate capital investments.

Among methods for analyzing capital investments, the discounted cash flow (DCF) methods are the most theoretically sound. The two DCF methods suggest the same answers in most instances. Sometimes, however, the DCF methods yield significantly different results. To use capital budgeting techniques properly, you must recognize situations in which the two DCF methods can reach different conclusions and the reasons for the differences.

Exhibit 11–22 points out that results from analyses using the NPV method and the IRR method can differ when capital investment projects differ in (1) initial investment amounts, (2) net cash flow patterns, or (3) length of useful lives. In addition, these two methods can yield different conclusions in situations with (4) varying costs of capital over the life of a project and (5) results of multiple investments.

Amount of Initial Investment

Although both the NPV and the IRR methods use net cash inflows in evaluating capital investments, they do so differently. The NPV method examines the excess amount of the present value of future net cash inflows generated by an investment over the project's initial investment. The project that has the highest NPV among the investments under consideration is the choice of the NPV method.

The net present value of a project with a large initial investment is more likely to have a higher net present value than one with a small initial investment. Consider two investment projects with these initial investments, years of useful life, and annual net cash inflows:

Project	Initial Investment	Annual Net Cash Inflows	Years of Useful Life	NPV at 10 percent	IRR
P	$5,000	$1,000	10	$1,145	15.13%
Q	1,000	300	10	843	27.38%

Project P clearly has a higher NPV than project Q does. A comparison of the NPVs suggests that project P is the better investment of the two. However, Project Q has an IRR of 27.38 percent while project P has an IRR of only 15.13 percent.

The IRR method favors project Q. Project P has a higher NPV than project Q because P has a much larger investment than project Q, and the NPV method does not consider the difference in the initial investments. The NPV method focuses on the dollar amount of the difference between the present value of the net cash inflows from an investment and the amount initially invested. Once an investment has generated sufficient net cash inflows to pay for itself (earned the firm's desired rate of return), a project that requires a large investment generates a higher amount of NPV than a project that requires a small investment. A $500,000 investment in a project that earns 11 percent return has an NPV of $5,000 if the firm's required rate of return is 10 percent. In contrast, its NPV will be only $500 if the same firm invests $5,000 in another project that earns 20 percent. Notice that the initial investment for project P is five times the amount for Project Q. The net cash inflows of project P, however, are not five times of those of project Q. Nevertheless, the NPV method suggests that project P is the better investment of the two.

A comparison of the net present value of investments requiring substantially different amounts of investment yields no meaningful results. The method should be used only to evaluate investments that are approximately equal in initial investment requirements.

The IRR method uses percentages to evaluate the relative profitability of the investments. The amount of initial investment has no effect on the relative profitability of investments. The IRR method, therefore, is more appropriate to use for assessing investments requiring significantly different amounts of initial investments.

Net Cash Flow Pattern

Firms invest to earn net cash inflows. Not all net cash inflows are the same, however. Variations in patterns of net cash inflows such as the timing, the amount, and the direction of net cash inflows can affect the overall returns on projects and alter capital investment decisions.

Timing and Amounts of Net Cash Flow

Not all investment projects generate cash flows similarly at different points in time. Some projects generate the bulk of their net cash inflows at early stages. Others might not have significant net cash inflows until the last years of the project. Some projects have relatively constant net cash inflows throughout their useful lives. Other projects have rather irregular net cash inflows. Differences in the timing and amount of net cash inflows affect a project's internal rate of return.

Paton Implement Manufacturing Company considers two capital investments in September 2001, project A and project B. Both projects require $100,000 initial investments and have 10 years of useful life. Project A will generate most of its net cash inflows in its early years, while project B will earn the bulk of its net cash inflows toward its completion. Columns 2 and 3 of Exhibit 11–23 contain the expected after-tax net cash inflows for projects A and B, respectively. The cost of capital for both projects is 10 percent.

Project B generates small net cash inflows in its early years. The amount increases, however, over the years. The net cash inflows of project A follow the opposite pattern. At 10 percent cost of capital, project B has a higher net present value than project A. The IRR method suggests the opposite. The internal rates of return are 19.34 percent for project B and 26.18 percent for project A.

Which project is the better investment? The preceding section suggests possible conflicting results from the two DCF methods when projects require different initial investments. However, the two projects, A and B, require the same amount of initial investment.

The two DCF methods involve different assumptions about an investment's earnings of net cash inflows. The NPV method assumes that all net cash inflows from an investment earn the cost of capital or the discount rate employed in calculating its NPV (10 percent in the previous example). In contrast, the IRR method assumes that all net cash inflows from a project earn the same rate of return as its internal rate of return.

Project A has an internal rate of return of 26.18 percent. In arriving at this rate, the IRR method assumes that all of project A's net cash inflows will earn 26.18 percent in each of the subsequent years until the end of its useful life. The $45,000 net cash inflows of project A in year 1, for example, earns the firm $11,781 ($45,000 × 0.2618) by the end of year 2 and $14,865 [($45,000 + $11,781) × 0.2618] by the end of year 3, and so on until the end of project A's useful life.

The internal rate of return of project B is 19.34 percent. Thus, the IRR method assumes that all net cash inflows of project B will earn 19.34 percent in each subsequent year.

Exhibit 11–23	Effects of Patterns of Net Cash Inflows on the Evaluation of Capital Investment Using DCF Methods					
(1) Period	(2) Net After-Tax Cash Inflow of A	(3) Net After-Tax Cash Inflow of B	(4) 10 Percent Factor	(5) Present Value of A	(6) Present Value of B
0	$(100,000)	$(100,000)	1.000	$(100,000)	$(100,000)
1	$ 45,000	$ 13,000	0.909	$ 40,905	$ 11,817
2	39,000	14,800	0.826	32,214	12,225
3	25,000	16,600	0.751	18,775	12,467
4	17,000	20,200	0.683	11,611	13,797
5	23,000	23,800	0.621	14,283	14,780
6	20,000	27,400	0.564	11,280	15,454
7	17,000	35,500	0.513	8,721	18,212
8	15,000	49,000	0.467	7,005	22,883
9	13,000	49,000	0.424	5,512	20,776
10	13,000	43,000	0.386	5,018	16,598
Total	$ 227,000	$ 292,300		$ 155,324	$ 159,009
NPV				$ 55,324	$ 59,009
IRR				26.18%	19.34%

Having earlier net cash inflows and a higher IRR than those of project B, project A raises its IRR in two ways. First, the firm earns returns on the early net cash inflows over a longer period of time than those from the late net cash inflows. Second, all net cash inflows, including the earnings from the net cash inflows of the early years, earn a higher rate of return.

Which rate of return, the internal rate of return of the project or the discount rate employed in the NPV method, is more realistic for the net cash inflows that an investment generates? Earning a certain rate of return on a project does not imply that all net cash inflows of the project also will earn the same rate of return. Yet the IRR method assumes that *all* of a project's net cash inflows earn the *same* rate of return that the project's internal rate of return earns.

The most desirable investment can be a result of a unique investment opportunity, and the high internal rate of return of the project is not likely to be repeated. To expect the net cash inflows of an investment with a high rate of return to earn the same high return is an overly optimistic and most likely an unrealistic assumption.

The IRR method assumes that project B's net cash inflows will earn a lower rate of return in subsequent years than those generated by project A because the internal rate of return of project B is lower, only 19.34 percent. For example, the $13,000 net cash inflow that project B generates is assumed to earn 19.34 percent in each of the subsequent years while the $45,000 generated by project A is assumed to earn 26.18 percent each year until the end of this project. Surely cash available for investment in a given year will not earn a different rate of return because the cash is from a different project.

In contrast, the NPV method assumes that all net cash inflows earn the same rate as the discount rate employed in calculating the project's net present value. The discount rate used by the NPV method usually is the firm's weighted-average cost of capital. This is usually a more conservative and more realistic expectation.

However, the discount rate used to compute NPV might not be the real rate of return that the net cash inflows will earn. To avoid misguided capital investment decisions, management should carefully estimate the rates of return that an investment can be expected to generate.

Changes in Cash Flow Direction

A typical capital investment has net cash outflows in the project's early stage and gen-erates net cash inflows thereafter. In practice, not every capital investment project follows such a neat and uneventful cash flow pattern. After the initial investment, some projects require additional investments that exceed the projects' cash inflows for the same period. These projects then would have a net cash outflow, or negative net cash inflow, for the period. In a survey on capital budgeting practices, Fremgen found that 32 percent of the respondents frequently experienced one or more mixed direc-tions in cash flows.[17] A mixed cash flow pattern can cause projects to have more than one internal rate of return, as the next example demonstrates.

A firm invests $1,323 in a project that will bring in $3,000 in cash proceeds after one year. The project's required cost for equipment disposal and site restoration makes the net effect on cash flow at the end of year 2 an outflow of $1,700.

Exhibit 11–24 shows that the project has two internal rates of return because the cash flow direction changes from a net cash outflow to a net cash inflow and then to a net cash outflow again. The net present value is zero at 10 percent discount rate and again at 16 percent. Theoretically, an investment project can have as many internal rates of return as changes in the direction of net cash flows. The Fremgen survey found that 15 percent of the respondents who used the IRR method had experienced multiple internal rates of return.

Having multiple internal rates of return makes an investment's real rate of return a puzzle. Users should be cautious in applying the IRR method to projects with mixed cash flow directions.

Length of Useful Life

The IRR method considers each additional useful year of a project another year that its net cash inflow will earn a return equal to the project's internal rate of return. As a result, IRR is likely to favor projects with long useful lives.

Assume that Paton Implement Manufacturing Company also considers project C. The investment requirement and expected net cash inflows returns for the first 10 years of project C are the same as those of project A. Project C has a useful life of 15 years. The net cash inflows of the last five years are a mere $1,000 per year, a 1 percent return for a $100,000 investment. Exhibit 11–25 shows that project C's IRR is 26.29 percent. Recall that project A's IRR is 26.18 percent. Project C earns a higher return than project A, although project C earns a mere 1 percent return in each of the last five years of its useful life.

This result is not unique to the IRR method. The NPV method also favors projects with long useful lives as long as the project earns a positive net cash inflow during the additional years. Exhibit 11–25 shows that, although project C earns only a small net

Exhibit 11–24	Investment with Multiple Rates of Return					
(1)	(2)	(3)	(4)	(5)	(6)
Period	After-Tax Net Cash Flow	Discount Factor at 10 Percent	Present Value with 10 Percent Discount Rate	Discount Factor at 16 Percent	Present Value with 16 Percent Discount Rate
0	$(1,323)	1.000	$(1,323)	1.000	$(1,323)
1	3,000	0.909	2,727	0.862	2,586
2	(1,700)	0.826	(1,404)	0.743	(1,263)
NPV			0		0

---

[17]   James M. Fremgen, "Capital Budgeting Practices: A Survey," *Management Accounting*, May 1973, pp. 19–25.

Exhibit 11–25	**Effect of the Length of Useful Life on the Evaluation of Capital Investment Using DCF Methods** *Net After-Tax Cash Inflow*				
Period	Net Cash Inflow A	Net Cash Inflow C	10 Percent Discount Factor	Present Value of A	Present Value of C
0	$(100,000)	$(100,000)	1.000	$(100,000)	$(100,000)
1	$ 45,000	$ 45,000	0.909	$ 40,905	$ 40,905
2	39,000	39,000	0.826	32,214	32,214
3	25,000	25,000	0.751	18,775	18,775
4	17,000	17,000	0.683	11,611	11,611
5	23,000	23,000	0.621	14,283	14,283
6	20,000	20,000	0.565	11,300	11,300
7	17,000	17,000	0.513	8,721	8,721
8	15,000	15,000	0.467	7,005	7,005
9	13,000	13,000	0.424	5,512	5,512
10	13,000	13,000	0.386	5,018	5,018
11		1,000	0.350		350
12		1,000	0.319		319
13		1,000	0.290		290
14		1,000	0.263		263
15		1,000	0.239		239
Total	$ 227,000	$ 232,000		$ 155,344	$ 156,805
NPV				$ 55,344	$ 56,805
IRR				26.18%	26.29%

cash inflow in each of the last five years, its NPV increases from $55,344 to $56,805. As long as the net cash inflow in a year is positive, no matter how small it is, the net present value increases, and the project's desirability improves.

Maintaining an investment ties up resources that the firm could use elsewhere. Even if the project requires no additional out-of-pocket financial outlays in its last years, the firm is paying to continue the project in the form of lost opportunities. The firm could, for example, use the space occupied by the project for other projects, or managers can guide other projects better if they do not have to spend time on this project. With the proceeds from the project's termination, the firm could earn a higher return elsewhere.

Fluctuating Cost of Capital over Project Life

A firm's cost of capital often fluctuates as situations change over the years. A firm might enjoy a low cost of capital when it has access to low-cost funds or the capital market has abundant funds. A firm could face a high cost of capital when it experiences adverse operating results or tight economic conditions. As the firm's financial condition or operating environment changes, its cost of capital could also change. A proper capital budgeting procedure should incorporate changes in the firm's cost of capital or desired rate of return in evaluating capital investments.

The NPV method can accommodate different rates of return over the years. Jennifer O'Clock realizes that the desired rates of return for project B should be different in different years because of several factors relevant to the investment including fluctuations in foreign exchange rates, advances in technology, shifts in market tastes, and changes in the economy. Column 3 of Exhibit 11–26 depicts her desired rate of return at different years. She can still determine project B's NPV by following the same procedure for determining the net present values when there is only one discount rate over the entire period. By using appropriate discount factors for different discount rates, she can determine the net present value of project B as shown in the last column of Exhibit 11–26.

The IRR procedure determines a single rate that reflects the return of the project under consideration. The firm then compares its cost of capital or desired rate of return with the project's single rate of return in assessing the project's desirability. The IRR method cannot easily handle situations with varying desired rates of return.

Results of Multiple Projects

The NPV method evaluates investment projects in dollar amounts while the IRR method evaluates investment projects in percentages or rates. The net present values from multiple projects can be added to determine a single total net present value while percentages or rates of return on multiple projects cannot be added. The total NPV of independent projects is the simple sum of these projects' net present values. If the NPV of a $120,000 investment is $35,000, and the NPV of a $50,000 investment in another independent project is $20,000, the total net present value of investing $170,000 in these two projects is $55,000, the sum of the two net present values. The additivity of net present values makes evaluating multiple investments very convenient.

Internal rates of return of different investments cannot be added to determine the overall internal rate of return of the multiple projects. Investments of $120,000 in one project that earns a 10 percent rate of return and $50,000 in another project that earns a 15 percent rate of return do not make 25 percent the rate of return from the entire $170,000 investment. A change in the composition of projects being considered requires a complete recalculation of the overall IRR.

Exhibit 11–27 compares the two DCF methods. Exhibit 11–28 summarizes factors that could lead the NPV method and the IRR method to reach different conclusions in evaluating the same investment project.

Exhibit 11–26	**Net Present Values of Project B with Different Desired Rates of Return over the Years**			
Year	**Net After-Tax Cash Inflow**	**Desired Rate of Return**	**Discount Factor**	**Present Value**
1	$164,000	0.10	0.909	$149,076
2	194,000	0.12	0.797	154,618
3	194,000	0.13	0.694	134,636
4	382,000	0.15	0.572	218,504
Total PV				$656,834
Initial Investment				625,000
NPV				$ 31,834

Exhibit 11–27	**Comparison of NPV and IRR Methods**
NPV	**IRR**
Not meaningful for comparing projects with different amounts of initial investments	Easy to compare projects with different amounts of initial investments
NPVs of multiple projects are additive	IRRs of multiple projects are not additive
Assumes that cash proceeds can be reinvested to earn the same rate of return as in the computation	Assumes that cash proceeds can be reinvested to earn the same rate as the IRR on that particular project
Allows for multiple discount rates over the years	Allows for only one discount rate for the entire period

Exhibit 11–28	Summary of Factors Affecting Results of Analyses Using the DCF Methods	

Factor	NPV Method	IRR Method
Amount of initial investment	Favors projects with large initial investment	Has no effect
Net cash flow pattern		
• Timing and amount	Has moderate effect	Effects in proportion to the internal rate of return
• Cash flow direction	Has no effect	Can have multiple rates of return for projects with multiple cash flow directions
Length of useful life	Moderately favors projects with long, useful lives	Favors projects with long, useful lives and in proportion to the internal rate of return
Fluctuating cost of capital	Incorporates easily	Incorporates with difficulty
Results of multiple projects	Is the sum of the results of individual projects	Requires recomputation

How a Hospital Justified a Computer-Based Patient Record System

The University of Texas M.D. Anderson Cancer Center in Houston, Texas, has a staff of about 8,000 located in several buildings that include a 518-bed hospital, a 10-story outpatient clinic, and several remote patient care sites. Although it kept some patient information on computer, many records were paper based. Files for repeat patients became unwieldy, requiring regular compiling and thinning. A computer-based patient record (CPR) that integrates financial and clinical information can be an important tool for improving the quality of care and lowering its cost. However, purchasing, implementing, and maintaining a CPR requires a significant investment that management must justify.

The CPR project was the responsibility of an executive team consisting of the vice president for patient care, the vice president for hospital and clinic operations, and the executive vice president for administration and finance. A project steering committee directed the cost-benefit analysis and other aspects of evaluation. A stakeholders group consisting of managers from departments that would be affected by CPR

implementation provided much of the data for the cost-benefit analysis. The chief information officer and the associate vice president of medical information served on all teams and were involved at all levels.

The cost-benefit analysis followed these steps:

- Identified goals for a CPR.
- Determined quantifiable and nonquantifiable benefits.
- Estimated costs.
- Projected costs and benefits over 10 years and calculated the net present value.
- Monitored the results.

The cost-benefit analysis enabled executives to make informed strategic and tactical decisions regarding acquisition and implementation of a CPR.

Based on Leslie A. Kian and Miceael W. Stewart, "Justifying the Cost of a Computer-Based Patient Record," *Healthcare Financial Management,* 49 (7), pp. 58–63.

STRATEGIC COST MANAGEMENT AND CAPITAL BUDGETING

LEARNING OBJECTIVE 5▶

Discuss the relationships between strategic cost management and capital budgeting.

Capital investment is a critical factor in an organization's continued success and should be tailored to its strategy. However, a capital investment can change or reshape an organization's strategy. A capital investment analysis that includes only immediate value-added activities and costs to the firm can be too narrowly focused and fail to capture the full impact of the investment on the firm. A proper analysis of a capital investment should include consideration of the firm's competitive advantage, value chain, and strategic cost drivers.

494

Competitive Strategy and Capital Budgeting

As discussed in Chapter 2, competitive strategy is the way a firm chooses to compete to achieve its goals or mission. A firm can choose a mission to build, to hold, or to harvest. Exhibit 11–29 shows the effect of differences in strategic missions on capital budgeting.

An organization that chooses a build mission often faces many uncertainties, uses evolving technologies, and traverses in environments that change rapidly. Capital budgeting processes in these firms are often less formal, use more nonfinancial or non-quantifiable data, and apply subjective criteria in evaluating investment projects. In contrast, a firm with a harvest mission is more likely to be a mature organization or to have products with mature markets. Its capital budgeting processes are more likely to be formalized, and most of the data for its capital budgeting are likely to be quantifi-able and financial in nature.

Uncertainties often faced by an organization with a build mission can require the firm to adopt a long-term perspective and allow for long payback periods or low hur-dle rates. The long payback periods or low hurdle rates are justified because a firm with a build mission can enjoy a long payoff period if it is successful. However, these projects likely require project approval at a relatively high level of management because of the high risk involved.

A mature market is likely ripe for change. By necessity, a capital investment's pay-back period in such a market needs to be short, and the hurdle rate must be at least the firm's average rate of return. A firm with a harvest mission most likely would not undertake major capital investments. Those capital investments requiring small amounts of funds need only approvals of low level managers.

A firm, however, should never consider its strategic mission as a given in its capital investment analysis. Assuming a continuing stable operating environment can be a fatal mistake. Moreover, a capital investment can help managers redefine strategy, establish new goals, and plan new tactics to reach its goals at a higher level. As a tool for analyzing long-term investment opportunities, capital budgeting is guided by strat-egy and goals, but it is also instrumental in redefining or enhancing the way the firm has chosen to compete. A new manufacturing technology acquired by a harvesting firm with a low-cost competitive position can transform the firm into a different com-petitive position, such as product differentiation with an increased emphasis to build.

Exhibit 11–29	**Strategic Missions and Capital Budgeting**		

| Factor in Capital Budgeting | Strategic Mission | | |
	Build	Hold	Harvest
Formalization of capital expenditure decisions	Less formal DCF analysis	→	More formalized DCF analysis
Capital expenditure evaluation criteria	More emphasis on nonfinancial data (market share, efficient use of R&D dollars, etc.)	→	More emphasis on financial data (cost efficiency; straight cash-on-cash incremental return)
	Longer payback	→	Shorter payback
Hurdle rate	Relatively low	→	Relatively high
Capital investment analysis	More subjective and qualitative	→	More quantitative and financial
Project approval limit at business unit level	Relatively high	→	Relatively low
Frequency of postaudit	Frequent	→	Less frequent

Based on: Vijay Govindarajan and John K. Shank, "Strategic Cost Management: Tailoring Controls to Strategies," *Journal of Cost Management,* Fall 1992, pp. 14–25.

For instance, the adoption of a host of new technologies enabled Levi-Strauss to make individually tailored designer jeans embroidered with the owner's name. Moving into a custom-made market, the firm's most critical factor for the firm's success was no longer cost. Levi-Strauss transformed its market from a commodity market to a custom-made market because of the investment in new information technology.[18]

Value Chain and Capital Budgeting

Critics often charge that conventional capital budgeting techniques render incomplete analyses in today's competitive environment with rapid changes in both technology and the markets. A common criticism is that the conventional capital budgeting techniques are project oriented; they start from the inception of a project, followed by the delivery of goods and services to market, and finish with the disposal of the project at the end of its useful life. Such an analysis, critics argue, fails to capture the full impact of a capital investment at different stages.

Through its activities, a firm adds or creates value and occupies a node in the linked set of value-creating activities from basic raw materials to the ultimate end-use product delivered to the consumer and the final disposals by the end-user. (This process has been defined as a *value chain* in Chapter 2.) Even though a firm can participate in only a segment of the entire value chain, the firm should analyze the impact of its capital investments over the entire value chain.

Shank and Govindarajan conducted a field study and demonstrated the importance of value-chain analysis in capital budgeting.[19] They examined a firm that undertook a conventional capital budgeting analysis, which included only the benefits to the operation where the investment was to be made. The analysis showed no financial gain to the firm and indicated that it should not make the proposed capital investment. However, a value-chain analysis that included impacts to both upstream and downstream operations showed that the investment could save an estimated $33.6 million per year in just one of the firm's locations. The value-chain analysis demonstrated unequivocally the investment's benefit, and the firm changed its decision.

Cost Driver Analysis

Volume frequently is the only cost driver identified in conventional capital budgeting analyses. For many capital investments, however, structural and executional cost drivers can be as critical as, if not more than, volume in determining the investment's success and should be considered.

Structural cost drivers are factors that relate to the firm's strategic decisions on the fundamental structure of the investment such as its technology, scale, product-line complexity, scope of vertical integration, or experience. These structural cost drivers are likely to be found at levels in which the firm chooses to compete (Chapter 2).

A capital investment decision not to invest in a new technology leaves the firm with no choice but to continue operating with the same set of cost drivers. The cost drivers or their levels can differ entirely should the firm decide to invest in new technology. The cost of a business unit with a complex product line is not the same as another one with a product line that is easy to make, service, and sell. McDonnell Douglas Corporation's decision in 1996 not to make the estimated $15 billion investment necessary to compete directly with larger rivals reduced the firm to a minor player in the commercial jet business.[20] A capital budgeting decision can change the

---

[18]   Lawrence P. Carr, William C. Lawler, and John K. Shank, "Cost Analysis for Value Chain Reconfiguration: Adding the Strategic Dimension," Paper presented at 2000 Annual Meeting, Management Accounting Section, American Accounting Association.

[19]   John K. Shank and Vijay Govindarajan, "Strategic Cost Analysis of Technological Investments," *Sloan Management Review*, Fall 1992, pp. 39–51.

[20]   *The Wall Street Journal*, October 29, 1996, p. A3. The firm eventually was acquired by Boeing, its main rival in the United States.

COST MANAGEMENT IN ACTION

Is That Advanced Manufacturing Technology Worth It?

A manufacturer of telecommunications devices is about to review proposals for investment to increase its manufacturing capacity for manufacturing one of its key components. In the past, the proposals vary in the level of technology and the degree of computer integration required for manufacturing process. So far, the firm has minimal experience with advanced manufacturing technology and is using semiauto-mated machines in key parts of its manufacturing process of the components. Over the last several years, company executives have been conscious of the growing competitive pressures that may eventually require investment in advanced manufacturing technology. As a result the firm has been actively seeking out such investment proposals. Many proposals had been reviewed in the last few years. However, no proposals have ever passed the review stage. "The numbers just don't support it," according to one member of the review committee, who has been a staunch advocator of advanced manufacturing technologies.

The firm evaluates all major investment proposals using the net present value method with the estimated long-term (five years) cost of capital as the discount rate. In addition, the firm also uses the payback method in analysis. However, a short payback period is not necessary to justify investment in a project if the project is considered to be among the best in terms of investment proposals. A review of the proposals submitted over the last few years revealed that these proposals ranked consistently higher based upon the net present value method.

You believe that it is critically important for the long-term profitability of the firm to acquire new advanced manufacturing technology. You are of the opinion that the firm will lose its competitive edge, or may not even survive, if it fails to respond to this demand. As the manager of the manufacturing process, who has submitted several unsuccessful proposals for investment in advanced manufacturing technologies, how would you modify your proposal?

firm's structural cost drivers, and the results of structural cost drivers often are the very ones that a capital investment seeks to obtain. A complete capital investment analysis should always include the effects of structural cost drivers.

Executional cost drivers affect a firm's cost position and its ability to work successfully within the economic structure it chooses. Executional cost drivers that are likely to be important include these:

- Workforce involvement (participative management).
- Workforce commitment to continuous improvement.
- Adherence to total quality management concepts.
- Utilization of effective capacity.
- Efficiency of production flow layout.
- Effectiveness of product design or formulation.
- Exploitation of linkages with suppliers and customers throughout the value chain.[21]

In the early 1990s, Motorola derived one of its cost advantages from its ability to reduce defect rates to only three units per million in manufacturing integrated circuits achieved through years of continual capital investments in quality training and process improvements. This example shows the impact of an executional cost driver. The cost advantage led Motorola to enter the business of making billets for fluorescent lamps. Motorola management believed that its quality skills provided a strategic advantage for a successful entry into this new business that uses old technologies.

BEHAVIORAL ISSUES IN CAPITAL BUDGETING

Successful capital budgeting results from the efforts of individuals and teams. Although it is a vital part of corporate decision making, a proper and carefully designed capital investment procedure does not necessarily lead to a successful capital investment because human behavior often plays an important role in such investments.

◀**LEARNING OBJECTIVE 6**

Identify behavioral factors in capital budgeting decisions.

---

[21] Shank and Govindarajan, "Strategic Cost Analysis," p. 47.

A successful manager is often viewed as one who is responsible for a large or growing unit. Large or growing enterprises require capital investments. Furthermore, a new capital asset is visible and is often viewed as "progress" or an "accomplishment." This fact leads many managers to be overly eager to promote capital investments. Firms must carefully contain aggressive managers who overestimate projections in attempting to earn approval for their divisions' capital investments.

Studies have found that escalating commitment is too commonly a phenomenon in capital investments. In an attempt to recoup past losses, a decision maker often considers past costs or losses as relevant in making capital investment decisions. Escalating commitments are even more likely when these managers are also responsible for the negative results of past actions.[22]

Although sunk costs should have no effect on decisions, research in prospect theory has found that they in fact play an important role in influencing the way decisions are framed. Sunk costs should not enter into the computation to determine either the benefits or the costs of a capital investment. The existence of a negative operating result from investments or actions taken in the past could cause subsequent decisions to be framed as a choice between losses, and a positive operating result causes subsequent decisions to be framed as a choice between gains.[23] Decision makers are likely to minimize losses while maximizing gains.

Much-needed capital investments are often not pursued because of the amount of work and time required to secure their approval. Projects that cost less than those that must be approved as a capital investment are undertaken instead. Managers invest in a series of small additions to plants or equipment rather than investing in a major capital project such as computer-integrated manufacturing or flexible manufacturing systems that would vastly improve the firm's competitive advantage. Failure to make necessary capital investments can reduce the firm's competitiveness, erode its market share, and jeopardize its long-term profitability and even survival.

Intolerance of uncertainty often leads managers to require short payback periods for capital investments. Once a project pays for itself, the amount of risk is reduced and the decision is home free. This makes projects with short payback periods the preferred choice to some decision makers, but not all critical capital investments can have a short payback period. Many important projects require a lengthy time to install, test, adjust, train personnel, and gain market acceptance; examples include investments in new manufacturing technologies, new product development, and expanding into new territories, especially a foreign country. Requiring too short a payback period makes the acceptance of such projects very unlikely.

SUMMARY

Capital investment decisions are among the most important that a firm or organization can make. No business firm can survive for long without making sound capital investments. No governmental organization can provide good services to its constituents without carefully considering its capital investments.

Capital budgeting processes include project identification and definition, project evaluation, and monitoring and review. Initial proposals for capital investment often are made at the local or business subunit level. Investments that involve major technology change are more likely initiated at top management level, however.

The capital investment analysis focuses on events that will unfold in the future. In analyzing capital investments, the primary focus is often cash flow. An invest-

---

[22]   Glen Whyte, "Escalating Commitment to a Course of Action: A Reinterpretation," *Academy of Management Review,* 1986, pp. 311–21.

[23]   D. Kanamen and D. Tversky, "Prospect Theory: An Analysis of Decisions under Risk," *Econometrica,* 1979, pp. 263–90.

ment is not a sound one if a firm receives less cash from it than the amount of funds it invests in its project.

Cash outflows in investments occur at three stages: (1) *project initiation* to acquire the investment and begin operations, to provide its working capital, and to dispose of the replaced or disposed assets, (2) *project operation* to cover operating expenditures and any additional investments and to provide additional working capital, and (3) *final project disposal* to dispose of the investment, to restore facilities, and to provide for personnel whose positions have been terminated. An investment generates net cash inflows during its existence through increases in revenues or decreases in expenses. All cash flows for a business firm should be net of tax effects.

Many techniques for analyzing capital investments are available, including undiscounted techniques such as payback period and book rate of return and the discounted cash flow techniques such as net present value and internal rate of return. Exhibit 11–30 summarizes the definitions, computation procedures, advantages, and weaknesses of these techniques.

A capital investment analysis should consider the firm's competitive advantage, the effects of the investment on both upstream and downstream activities in the firm's value chain, and its impact of strategic structural and executional cost drivers.

Exhibit 11–30	Capital Investment Evaluation Techniques			

Technique	Definition	Computation Procedure	Advantages	Weaknesses
Payback period	Number of years to recover the initial investment	*Uniform flow:* $$\frac{\text{Investment}}{\text{Net cash inflow}}$$ *Uneven flow:* Number of years for the cumulative cash flow equal to the investment	1. Simple to use and understand 2. Measures liquidity 3. Allows for risk tolerance	1. Ignores timing and time value of money 2. Ignores cash flows beyond payback period
Book rate of return	Ratio of average annual net income to the initial investment or average investment (book value)	$$\frac{\text{Average net income}}{\text{Investment}}$$ The original total investment or its average book value	1. Data readily available 2. Consistent with other financial measures	1. Ignores timing and time value of money 2. Uses accounting numbers rather than cash flows
Net present value	Difference between the initial investment and the present value of subsequent net cash inflows discounted at a given interest rate	Present value of net cash inflows—initial investment	1. Considers time value of money 2. Uses realistic discount rate for reinvestment 3. Additive for combined projects	1. Not meaningful for comparing projects requiring different amounts of investments 2. Favors large investments
Internal rate of return	Discount rate that makes the initial investment equal the present value of subsequent net cash inflows	Solving the following equation for discount rate i: Present value factor of i × Net cash inflows = Initial investment	1. Considers time value of money 2. Easy for comparing projects requiring different amounts of investment	1. Assumption on reinvestment rate of return could be unrealistic 2. Complex to compute if done manually

APPENDIX A

Modified Accelerated Cost Recovery System (MACRS)

Firms often use different depreciation methods for various depreciable assets and even for the same type of asset. To bring more uniformity into depreciation computations and to encourage businesses to invest in new plant and equipment by allowing them to recover the investment quickly through depreciation, Congress introduced the Accelerated Cost Recovery System (ACRS) in 1981. It was replaced in 1986 by the Modified Accelerated Cost Recovery System (MACRS). As a result, several systems are currently used to determine the depreciation expenses of tangible assets.

Two of the factors that affect the amount of depreciation for an asset are (1) the year it was placed in service and (2) its nature. All assets placed in service after 1986 use MACRS. ACRS is used for assets placed in service after 1980 but before 1987. Assets placed in service before 1981 can use either the straight-line or an accelerated depreciation method. This appendix discusses MACRS only. Publication 534 "Depreciation" from the Internal Revenue Service (IRS) provides detailed information on different depreciation methods.

MACRS assigns all depreciable assets to one of eight classes, referred to as *recovery periods* in the tax law. Exhibit 11–31 describes these classes and their depreciation methods with examples of assets in each class.

MACRS does not use disposable value; MACRS depreciation is calculated based on the entire original cost. With the exception of residential and nonresidential real properties in the last two classes, a half-year convention is used to determine the depreciation for the first year the asset is placed in service, and, if the firm owns the depreciable asset for the entire recovery period, for the year following the end of the recovery period.

A half-year convention allows one-half year of depreciation for the first year the firm places the property in service regardless of when during the year it was actually placed in service. To illustrate, the first-year depreciation for a five-year property would have been 40 percent (200 percent of the straight-line rate) of the original cost without the half-year convention. Because of the half-year convention, the allowable depreciation for the first year is 20 percent whether the asset is placed in service on January 3 or December 3. The depreciation for each remaining year of the recovery period is determined by using the 200 percent declining-balance method. The depreciation for the second year of a five-year property, for example, is 40 percent of the remaining 80 percent, which is 32 percent of the original cost. Exhibit 11–32 shows the depreciation rates for properties other than residential or nonresidential real properties.

Exhibit 11–31	Asset Classes (Recovery Periods) under MACRS	
Class	**Depreciation Method**	**Example**
3-year property	200% declining balance	Light tools and handling equipment
5-year property	200% declining balance	Computers and peripheral equipment, office machinery, automobiles, light trucks
7-year property	200% declining balance	Office furniture, appliances, carpet, and furniture in residential rental property and any asset that does not have an assigned class
10-year property	200% declining balance	Manufacturing assets for food products, petroleum refining, tobacco
15-year property	150% declining balance	Road and shrubbery, telephone distribution plant
20-year property	150% declining balance	Multipurpose farm structures
27.5 year property	Straight line	Residential rental property
31.5 year property	Straight line	Nonresidential real property, office building, warehouse

Exhibit 11–32   MACRS Depreciation Rate

Year	3-year	5-year	7-year	10-year	15-year	20-year
1	33.33	20.00	14.29	10.00	5.00	3.75
2	44.45	32.00	24.49	18.00	9.50	7.22
3	14.81	19.20	17.49	14.40	8.55	6.68
4	7.41	11.52*	12.49	11.52	7.70	6.18
5		11.52	8.93*	9.22	6.93	5.71
6		5.76	8.92	7.37	6.23	5.28
7			8.92	6.55*	5.90*	4.89
8			4.47	6.55	5.90	4.52
9				6.56	5.91	4.46*

*First year of switching to the straight-line method.

Under a special rule, a mid-quarter convention instead of a half-year convention might be required. Residential and nonresidential rental properties use a mid-month convention in all situations. Consult IRS publications or tax professionals for details.

Tax planning is a complex matter. The discussion in this appendix barely scratches the surface. Many issues such as loss carrybacks and carryforwards, qualification for capital assets, state income taxes, and foreign tax credits are not discussed. Always consult a tax professional to ensure that all tax considerations have been included.

KEY TERMS

Book rate of return   476

Breakeven time (BET)   484

Capital investment   457

Cost of capital   480

Desired rate of return   480

Discounted cash flow (DCF) techniques   479

Internal rate of return (IRR) method   484

Net present value (NPV)   481

Payback period   472

Present value   481

Present value payback or breakeven time method   484

COMMENTS ON COST MANAGEMENT IN ACTION

Many benefits of advanced manufacturing technology are often difficult to quantify in dollar amounts or even in numbers. To make matters worse, these benefits, more often than not, are long-term in nature, and the firm will not see immediate tangible results. A large confectionery firm rejected an automated storage and distribution facility because it would not include the benefits that better customer service could provide. Better customer service could have lead to higher sales volume and market share and, eventually, higher profits. Realizing these difficulties, middle managers of a kitchen unit manufacturer, with an established reputation for innovative design, forced an investment in computer-assisted design equipment by exaggerating financial benefits—a practice that should be discouraged and disallowed!

Appraisals of investments in advanced manufacturing technology need to be evaluated in terms of quantitative analysis and strategic consideration. Advanced manufacturing technology can expand the firm product portfolio, enhance corporate image, and increase manufacturing flexibility, in addition to potentially decreasing production time and costs. Firms need to assess both the quantifiable short-term incremental cash inflows and the long-run strategic benefits in judging an investment's merits. In addition to cash flow analysis, an investment proposal can go a long way if it also includes the investment's strategic benefits. A firm manufacturing high-pressure casings decided to convert its manufacturing operations to cell manufacturing. The firm enjoyed such unplanned benefits as a 50 percent reduction in inventory, a 75 percent improvement in quality, substantial reduction in lead times, and flexible machining with overall labor reduction. An electrical switch gear products manufacturer with a sales of $32 million and a total staff of 550 invested in CAD to increase its design capacity in anticipation of a 25 percent growth. The firm's original expectations included reduced lead time in the drawing office and reduced number of employees and WIP inventory. The additional benefits offered more accurate and timely transfer of data which greatly improved the firm's competitive edge and propelled the firm into a new marketing position.

Based on Michael Bromwich and Al Bhimani, "Strategic Investment Appraisal," *Management Accounting*, March 1991, pp. 45–8.

SELF-STUDY PROBLEM

(For solution, please turn to the end of the chapter.)

Capital Budgeting for Expanding Productive Capacity

Ray Summers Company operates at full capacity of 10,000 units per year. The firm, however, is still unable to meet the demand for its product, estimated at 15,000 units annually. This level of demand is expected to continue for at least another four years.

To expand productive capacity to meet the demand, the firm can add equipment costing $580,000. This equipment has a useful life of four years and can be sold for $50,000 at the end of the fourth year. The engineering division estimates that installing, testing, and adjusting the machine will cost $12,000 before it can be put in operation.

An adjacent vacant warehouse can be leased for the duration of the project for $10,000 per year. The warehouse needs $58,000 of renovations to make it suitable for manufacturing. The lease terms call for restoring the warehouse to its original condition on the lease's expiration. The restoration is estimated to cost $20,000. Analysis of current operating data provides this information:

			Per Unit
Sales price			$200
Variable costs			
Manufacturing	$60		
Marketing	20	$80	
Fixed costs			
Manufacturing	$25		
Marketing and administrative	15	40	120
Net income			$ 80

The new equipment has no effect on the variable costs per unit. All current fixed costs are expected to continue with the same total amount. The per-unit cost includes depreciation expenses of $5 for manufacturing and $4 for marketing and administration.

Additional fixed manufacturing costs of $140,000 (excluding depreciation) will be incurred annually if the equipment is purchased. The firm must hire an additional marketing manager to serve new customers. The annual cost for the new marketing manager, support staff, and office expense is estimated at approximately $100,000. The accountant expects the firm to be in the 40 percent tax bracket for combined federal and state income taxes in the next four years. No investment credit is currently in effect. The firm requires a minimum rate of return of 12 percent on investments and uses straight-line depreciation.

Required

1. What is the total investment requirement in year 0?

2. What effect will the acquisition of the new equipment have on net income in each of the four years?

3. What effect will the acquisition of the new equipment have on cash flows in each of the four years?

4. Compute the payback period of the investment.

5. Compute the book rate of return based on the average investment.

6. Compute the net present value.

7. Compute the internal rate of return.

8. Use a spreadsheet to verify your answers for 6 and 7.

9. The firm expects the variable manufacturing cost per unit to increase once the new equipment is in place. What is the most that the unit variable manufacturing cost can increase and allow the firm to still earn the required rate of return on the investment?

QUESTIONS

11–1   What are the major steps in capital budgeting decisions?

11–2   "If I have to name the one most important concern in capital budgeting, I'll say it is the effect on the bottom line." Do you agree? What factor might have led this company executive with more than 20 years of experience to come to this conclusion?

11–3   List cash flows that a hospital is likely to incur after it installs a CAT scanner.

11–4   Name the types of costs required to close a chemical factory after 20 years.

11–5   What is a direct cash effect? Give several examples related to acquiring a new factory.

11–6   What is tax effect? Give several examples related to acquiring a new factory.

11–7   "Book value is nothing but a bookkeeper's figure and is irrelevant in capital budgeting." Do you agree?

11–8   What are the limitations of the payback period technique? Does the present value payback period technique overcome these limitations?

11–9   Does the book rate of return method provide a true measure of return on investment? How about the internal rate of return?

11–10   What should be the decision criterion when using the NPV method to evaluate capital investments? Does the IRR method use the same criterion?

11–11   "Let's be more practical. DCF is not the only gospel. Many managers have become too absorbed with DCF." Can such a statement be justified? Why?

11–12   "Because business executives don't know how to run the numbers, companies are not acting decisively to put these technologies to work. . . . Urgently needed are new cost-benefit formulas and measurements . . . that go beyond the usual return on investment (ROI) evaluations." Do you agree? Why? If you agree, what cost-benefit do ROI evaluations leave out?

11–13   What criterion should be used to choose investment projects for a firm with unlimited funds at a cost of 10 percent to the firm? Can the firm use the same criterion if it has only a limited amount of funds available for investments?

11–14   List at least three important behavioral factors in capital budgeting.

11–15   When do differences in results for the NPV method and the IRR method arise?

11–16   How does the size of the initial investment affect the IRR method and the NPV method?

11–17 "The net present value method weighs early receipts of cash much more heavily than late receipts of cash." Do you agree?

11–18 How can a depreciation expense be relevant in capital investment decisions?

11–19 A firm can alter its desired rate of return from year to year. What factors could have contributed to the changes?

11–20 Should the firm accept the independent projects described here? Why?

    a. A firm's cost of capital is 10 percent and the project's internal rate of return is 11 percent.

    b. A capital project requires $150,000 initial investment. The firm's cost of capital is 10 percent, and the present value of the expected net cash inflows from the project is $148,000.

11–21 How could a firm with a build mission use capital budgeting differently than a firm with a harvest mission? Why might they differ?

11–22 C.W. Yale, president of Hotchikiss, Inc., your client, recently attended a seminar at which a speaker discussed planning and control of capital expenditures, which he referred to as *capital budgeting*. Yale tells you that he is not quite sure he understands that concept.

Required

1. Explain the nature of capital budgeting and identify several of its uses.

2. What are the basic differences between the payback period technique and the net present value method of capital budgeting? Explain.

3. Define *cost of capital*.

4. Financial accounting data are not entirely suitable for use in capital budgeting. Explain.

(CPA Adapted)

EXERCISES

11–23 CASH FLOWS EFFECTS

    a. A hospital paid $50,000 for billing service and had $30,000 in depreciation. The hospital is a not-for-profit organization that pays no income taxes. What effects do these expenses have on the hospital's cash flow?

    b. Warren Elway Sports Shop paid $50,000 for advertising. It also took $30,000 of depreciation on shop equipment and fixtures. On average, the store pays about 20 percent of its income on income taxes. What effects do these expenses have on the store's cash flow?

11–24 BASIC CAPITAL BUDGETING TECHNIQUES

    a. Project A costs $5,000 and will generate annual after-tax net cash inflows of $1,800 for five years. What is the payback period?

    b. Project B costs $5,000 and will generate after-tax net cash inflows of $500 in year one, $1,200 in year two, $2,000 in year three, $2,500 in year four, and $2,000 in year five. What is the payback period?

    c. Project C costs $5,000 and will generate net cash inflows of $2,500 before taxes for five years. The firm uses straight-line depreciation with no salvage value and has 25 percent tax rate. What is the payback period?

    d. Project D costs $5,000 and will generate sales of $4,000 each year for five years. The cash expenditures will be $1,500 per year. The firm uses straight-line depreciation with an estimated salvage value of $500 and has a tax rate of 25 percent.

(a) What is the book rate of return based on the original investment?

(b) What is the book rate of return based on the average book value?

11–25   COST OF CAPITAL

a.   Micro Advantage, Inc., issued a $5,000,000, 20-year bond a year ago at 98 with a coupon rate of 9 percent. Today, the debt is selling at 110. If the firm's tax bracket is 30 percent, what is its after-tax cost of bond?

b.   Micro Advantage, Inc., has $5,000,000 preferred stock outstanding that it sold for $24 per share. The preferred stock has a per share par value of $25 and pays $3 dividend per year. The current market price is $30 per share. The firm's tax bracket is 30 percent. What is its cost of the preferred stock?

c.   In addition, Micro Advantage has outstanding 50,000 shares of common stock that has a par value of $10 per share and a current market price of $170 per share. The expected market return on the firm's common equity is 20 percent. What is Micro Advantage's weighted average cost of capital?

11–26   FUTURE AND PRESENT VALUES

a.   Assume that the Indian referred to in the chapter opener did put away the $24 he received from selling Manhattan and earned 6 percent compounded semiannually. The account had a balance of $9.5 billion as of August 1959. How much would the total amount be on August 2001 if compounded at the same rate? At 8 percent compounded semiannually?

b.   In 2000, Alex Rodriguez signed a 10-year $252 million contract with the Texas Rangers. Assuming equal payments at the end of each year starting from the date of signing, what is the cost of the contract to the owner, whose cost of capital is 12 percent, at the time the contract was signed?

11–27   AFTER-TAX NET PRESENT VALUE AND IRR

a.   eEgg is considering the purchase of a new distributed network computer system to help handle its warehouse inventories. The system costs $60,000 to purchase and install and $30,000 to operate each year, is expected to last four years, and should reduce the cost of managing inventories by $62,000 a year. The firm's cost of capital is 10 percent.

b.   Use the data for eEgg and answer the first two questions by computing the internal rate of return in each case.

Required   What is the net present value under these conditions?

1.   The firm is not yet profitable and pays no taxes.

2.   The firm is in the 30 percent income tax bracket and uses straight-line depreciation with no salvage value.

3.   The firm is in the 30 percent income tax bracket and uses double-declining-balance depreciation with no salvage value.

11–28   BASIC CAPITAL BUDGETING TECHNIQUES, UNIFORM NET CASH INFLOWS   Irv Nelson, Inc., purchased a $500,000 machine to manufacture a specialty tap for electrical equipment. This tap is in high demand, and Nelson can sell all it can manufacture in the next 10 years. The government has exempted taxes on profits from new investments to encourage capital investments. This legislation is not expected to be altered in the foreseeable future. The machine is expected to have 10 years' useful life with no salvage value. Nelson uses straight-line depreciation. The net cash inflow is expected to be $120,000 each year for 10 years. Nelson uses 12 percent in evaluating capital investments.

Required

1. Compute for the capital investment the
    a. Payback period.
    b. Book rate of return based on (a) initial investment and (b) average investment.
    c. Net present value.
    d. Present value payback period.
    e. Internal rate of return.
2. Use a spreadsheet program to verify your answers for requirements c and e above.

11–29   BASIC CAPITAL BUDGETING TECHNIQUES, UNEVEN NET CASH INFLOWS WITH TAXES   Use the same information for this problem as you did for exercise 11–28, except that the investment is subject to taxes and that the net operating cash inflow is as follows:

Year	Cash Inflow
1	$ 50,000
2	80,000
3	120,000
4	200,000
5	240,000
6	300,000
7	270,000
8	240,000
9	120,000
10	40,000

Irv Nelson has been paying 30 percent for combined federal and state income taxes, a rate that is not expected to change during the period of this investment. The firm uses straight-line depreciation.

Required

1. Compute for the project
    a. Payback period.
    b. Book rate of return based on (a) initial investment and (b) average investment.
    c. Net present value.
    d. Internal rate of return.
2. Use a spreadsheet program to find the answers for requirements c and d.

11–30   BASIC CAPITAL BUDGETING TECHNIQUES, UNEVEN NET CASH INFLOWS AND MACRS   Use the data in exercise 11–29 for Irv Nelson, Inc., and MACRS for depreciation for a 5-year property.

Required   Compute for the investment

1. Payback period.
2. Book rate of return based on (a) the initial investment and (b) an average investment.
3. Net present value.
4. Internal rate of return.

11–31   STRAIGHTFORWARD CAPITAL BUDGETING WITH TAXES   Dorothy & George Company is planning to acquire a new machine at a total cost of $30,600.

The machine's estimated life is six years and its estimated salvage value is $600. Dorothy & George Company estimates that annual cash savings from using this machine will be $8,000. The company's cost of capital is 8 percent and its income tax rate is 40 percent. The company uses straight-line depreciation.

Required

1. What is this investment's net after-tax annual cash inflow?

2. Assume that the net after-tax annual cash inflow of this investment is $5,000, what is the payback period?

3. Assume that the net after-tax annual cash inflow of this investment is $5,000, what is the net present value of this investment?

(CPA Adapted)

11–32   CAPITAL BUDGETING WITH TAX AND SENSITIVITY ANALYSIS   Gravina Company is planning to spend $6,000 for a machine that it will depreciate on a straight-line basis over a 10-year period with no salvage value. The machine will generate additional cash revenues of $1,200 a year. Gravina will incur no additional costs except for depreciation. Its income tax rate is 35 percent.

Required

1. What is the payback period?

2. What is the book rate of return on the initial increase in required investment?

3. What is the maximum amount that Gravina Company should invest if it desires to earn a minimum of 15 percent rate of return?

4. What is the minimum annual cash revenue required for the project to earn a 15 percent rate of return?

(CPA Adapted)

11–33   BASIC CAPITAL BUDGETING   Rockyford Company must replace some machinery that has zero book value but a current market value of $1,800. One possibility is to invest in new machinery costing $40,000. This new machinery would produce estimated annual pretax operating cash savings of $12,500. Assume the new machine will have a useful life of four years and depreciation of $10,000 each year for book and tax purposes. It will have no salvage value at the end of four years. The investment in this new machinery would require an additional $3,000 investment of working capital.

If Rockyford accepts this investment proposal, the disposal of the old machinery and the investment in the new one will occur on December 31 of this year. The cash flows from the investment will occur during the next four calendar years.

Rockyford is subject to a 40 percent income tax rate for all ordinary income and capital gains and has a 10 percent after-tax cost of capital. All operating and tax cash flows are assumed to occur at year-end.

Required   Determine

1. The present value of the after-tax cash flow arising from disposing of the old machinery.

2. The present value of the after-tax cash flows for the next four years attributable to the operating cash savings.

3. The present value of the tax shield effect of depreciation at the end of year 1.

4. Which one of the following is the proper treatment for the $3,000 working capital required in the current year?

a.   It should be ignored in capital budgeting because it is not a capital investment.

b.   It is a sunk cost that needs no consideration in capital budgeting.

c.   It should be treated as part of the initial investment when determining the net present value.

d.   It should be spread over the machinery's four-year life as a cash outflow in each of the years.

e.   It should be included as part of the cost of the new machine and depreciated.

(CMA Adapted)

PROBLEMS

Strategy

11–34   EQUIPMENT REPLACEMENT   The management of Devine Instrument Company is considering the purchase of a new drilling machine, model RoboDril 1010K. According to the specifications and testing results, RoboDril will substantially increase productivity over AccuDril X10, the machine Devine is currently using.

The AccuDril was acquired 8 years ago for $120,000 and is being depreciated over its 10 years of expected useful life with an estimated salvage value of $20,000. The engineering department expects the AccuDril to keep going for another three years after a major overhaul at the end of its expected useful life. The estimated cost for the overhaul is $100,000. The overhauled machine will be depreciated using straight-line depreciation with no salvage value. The overhaul will improve the machine's operating efficiency by 20 percent. No other operating conditions will be affected by the overhaul.

RoboDril 1010K is selling for $250,000. Installing, testing, rearranging, and training will cost another $30,000. The manufacturer is willing to take the AccuDril as a trade-in for $40,000. The RoboDril will be depreciated using the straight-line method with no salvage value. New technology most likely will make RoboDril obsolete to the firm in five years.

Variable operating cost for either machine is the same: $10 per hour. Other pertinent data follow:

	AccuDril X10	RoboDril 1010K
Units of output (per year)	10,000	10,000
Machine-hours	8,000	4,000
Selling price per unit	$ 100	$ 100
Variable manufacturing cost (not including machine-hours)	$ 40	$ 40
Other annual expenses (tooling and supervising)	$95,000	$55,000
Disposable value—today	$25,000	
Disposable value—in five years	0	$50,000

Devine Instrument Company's cost of funds is 12 percent, and it is in the 40 percent tax bracket.

Required

1.   Determine the effect on cash flow for items that differ for the two alternatives.

2.   Compute the payback period for purchasing RoboDril 1010K rather than having AccuDril X10 overhauled in two years.

3.   What is the present value of each alternative?

4.   What other factors, including strategic issues, should the firm consider before making the final decision?

11–35 SENSITIVITY ANALYSIS Use the information in problem 11–34 to answer the following questions:

Strategy

Required

1. To what extent can the estimated improvement in machine efficiency be in error and the replacement decision still be a correct financial decision?

2. New technologies developed since the purchase of AccuDril X10 make it possible to overhaul this machine now for $80,000. The overhaul will improve its productivity by 20 percent and reduce the cost of a major overhaul two years from now to $30,000. All overhaul costs will be depreciated using the straight-line method. With either overhaul, the machine will have no salvage value. Either overhaul can be scheduled during regular maintenance and will not affect production. Despite the old saying, "If it ain't broke, don't fix it," should you overhaul it now assuming that no funds are currently available to purchase RoboDril 1010K?

3. Performing the overhaul now also improves product quality. Management believes that the quality improvement is rather subtle and very difficult to quantify. Should the firm overhaul now?

11–36 COMPARISON OF CAPITAL BUDGETING TECHNIQUES Nil Hill Corporation has been using its present facilities at their annual full capacity of 10,000 units for the last three years. However, the company still is unable to keep pace with continuing demand for the product that is estimated to be 25,000 units annually. This demand level is expected to continue at least for another four years. To expand productive capacity and take advantage of the demand, Nil Hill must acquire equipment costing $995,000. The equipment will double the current production quantity. This equipment has a useful life of 10 years and can be sold for $195,000 at the end of year 4 or $35,000 at the end of year 10. Analysis of current operating data provides the following information:

			Per Unit
Sales price			$195
Variable costs			
Manufacturing	$90		
Marketing	10	$100	
Fixed costs			
Manufacturing	$45		
Other	25	70	170
Net income			$ 25

The fixed costs include depreciation expense of the current equipment. The new equipment will not change variable costs, but the firm will incur additional fixed manufacturing costs (excluding depreciation) of $250,000 annually. An additional $200,000 in fixed marketing costs per year is expected. Nil Hill is in the 30 percent tax bracket. Management has set a minimum rate of return of 14 percent before considering capital investments.

Required

1. What effects will the new equipment have on net income in each of the four years?

2. What effect will the new equipment have on cash flows in each of the four years?

3. Compute the investment's payback period.

4. Compute the book rate of return based on the average investment.

5. Compute the net present value.

6. Compute the internal rate of return.

7. Management is unsure of the reliability of the estimated figures for the unit variable cost. What is the maximum deviation allowed for the original decision to remain unchanged if

    a. The change will affect only the variable cost of the additional units to be manufactured by the new machine?

    b. The change will affect the unit selling price of all the units sold by the Nil Hill Corporation?

11–37 REPLACING A SMALL MACHINE: CAPITAL BUDGETING TECHNIQUES AND SENSITIVITY ANALYSIS   Hightec Corporation has a seven-year contract with Magichip Company to supply 10,000 units of XT-12 at $5 per unit. Increases in materials and other costs since signing the contract two years ago make this product a cash drain to Hightec. As the manager of the subsidiary that manufactures and sells XT-12, you have discovered that purchasing a new machine SP1000 would increase productivity and, hopefully, profits. The following is a summary of pertinent information:

	Machine in Use	**SP1000**
Capacity	10,000 units/year	18,000 units/year
Materials	$4.00 per unit	$3.00 per unit
Labor and other variable costs	$1.00 per unit	$0.20 per unit
Maintenance costs	$1.00 per unit	$0.10 per unit

(For simplicity, assume that all revenues and expenses are received and paid at year-end.)

The current machine can be sold for $3,000 today. Its salvage value will be $1,000 if the machine is used for another five years. The new machine costs $100,000, will be depreciated over a five-year life, and will have a net disposal value of $5,000 in five years. The company's cost of capital is 6 percent. If the company decides to keep the old machine, which is fully depreciated, production can continue with it for at least another five years. All machines are depreciated on a straight-line basis with no salvage value. The firm expects to continue to pay approximately 20 percent for both federal and state income taxes in the foreseeable future. At present the Magichip Company is the only user of XT-12.

Required   Compute

1. The effects on the cash flow each year if the new machine is purchased.

2. The net present value of the new machine.

3. The payback period of the new machine.

4. The internal rate of return on the new machine, assuming that the new machine's annual cash inflows were $25,000 and the new machine SP1000 will have no salvage value at the end of its useful life.

5. The internal rate of return assuming that the after-tax cash flow returns for each of the years are

Year 1	$20,000
Year 2	$22,000
Year 3	$25,000
Year 4	$30,000
Year 5	$40,000

6. By how much can the variable costs of the new machine increase (or decrease) and the company be indifferent on the replacement, assuming all the other costs will be as estimated?

11–38 CAPITAL BUDGETING WITH SUM-OF-YEARS'-DIGITS DEPRECIATION Bernie Company purchased a new machine with an estimated useful life of five years and no salvage value for $45,000. The machine is expected to produce net cash inflows from operations, before income taxes, as follows:

1st year	$ 9,000
2nd year	12,000
3rd year	15,000
4th year	9,000
5th year	8,000

Bernie will use the sum-of-the-years'-digits method to depreciate the new machine in its accounting records. Bernie uses 10 percent for evaluating capital investments and is currently in a 24 percent income tax bracket.

Required Compute the

1. Payback period.
2. Net present value.
3. Internal rate of return.

(CPA Adapted)

11–39 WORKING BACKWARD: DETERMINE INITIAL INVESTMENT BASED ON BOOK RATE OF RETURN Bread Company is planning to purchase a new machine that it will depreciate on a straight-line basis over a 10-year period. A full year's depreciation will be taken in the year of acquisition. The machine is expected to produce a net before taxes cash inflow of $6,750 from operations in each of the 10 years. The book rate of return is expected to be 10 percent on the initial increase in required investment. The firm's tax rate is 20 percent.

Required What is the cost of the new machine?
(CPA Adapted)

11–40 WORKING BACKWARD: DETERMINE INITIAL INVESTMENT BASED ON INTERNAL RATE OF RETURN Gene, Inc., invested in a machine with a useful life of six years and no salvage value. It depreciated the machine using the straight-line method; the machine was expected to produce a $20,000 annual cash inflow from operations, after cash expenses but before taxes. Gene has determined that the time-adjusted rate of return on the investment is 10 percent. The firm is in the 20 percent tax bracket.

Required What was the cost of the machine?
(CPA Adapted)

11–41 WORKING BACKWARD: DETERMINE PERIODIC CASH FLOW BASED ON BOOK RATE OF RETURN Dillon, Inc., purchased a new machine for $60,000 on January 1, 2002. The machine is being depreciated on a straight-line basis over five years with no salvage value. The book rate of return is expected to be 15 percent on the initial investment. The machine will generate a uniform cash flow. The firm's tax rate is approximately 25 percent.

Required What is the expected annual before taxes cash flow from operations from this investment?
(CPA Adapted)

11–42 MACHINE REPLACEMENT AND SENSITIVITY ANALYSIS WITHOUT CONSIDERING TAXES Ann & Andy Machine Company bought a cutting machine, Model KC12, on March 5, 2002, for $5,000 cash. The estimated salvage value and estimated life were $600 and 11 years, respectively. On March 5, 2003, Ann, the company CEO, learned that she could purchase a different cutting machine, Model AC1, for $8,000 cash. The new machine would save the company an estimated $750 per year in operating costs compared to KC12. AC1 has an estimated salvage value of $400 and an estimated life of 10 years. The company could get $3,000 for KC12 on March 5, 2003. The company uses the straight-line method for depreciations and 12 percent rate of return.

Required

1. Compute, for AC1, the
   a. Payback period.
   b. Book rate of return using the average investment.
   c. Net present value.
   d. Internal rate of return.
2. Should the firm purchase AC1? Why?
3. What is the minimum (or maximum) savings that AC1 must have without altering your decision in requirement 2?

11–43 VALUE OF ACCELERATED DEPRECIATION   Freedom Corporation acquired a fixed asset for $100,000. Its estimated life was four years, and it had no estimated salvage value. Assume a relevant interest rate of 8 percent and an income tax rate of 40 percent.

Required

1. What is the present value of the tax benefits resulting from calculating depreciation using the sum-of-the-years'-digits method as opposed to the straight-line method on this asset?
2. What is the present value of the tax benefits resulting from calculating depreciation using the double-declining-balance method as opposed to straight-line method on this asset?

(CPA Adapted)

11–44 CAPITAL BUDGETING WITH SENSITIVITY ANALYSIS   Meidi Johnson has owned a medical professional building for the last 20 years. She leased the land from an adjacent medical school 22 years ago for 30 years and had the building constructed. At the end of the lease period, the medical school becomes the sole owner of the land, its improvements, and any structures on the land. The construction took two years. The building is in excellent condition and fully occupied at favorable rental rates. The value of the property has appreciated considerably. Because depreciation is based on the original construction cost, Meidi's taxable income is unusually large.

George Kardell, a commercial real estate broker, has approached Meidi with a proposal from a group of investors. He believes that Meidi can sell the building and the balance of the leasehold at a price that will be profitable to all parties. The sale, if made, would be a cash sale that will provide her with the cash she needs for another project. She is currently negotiating with a bank for financing. The bank is asking for 12 percent interest. Meidi, however, would use 10 percent as her cost of capital if she can sell the building for cash. The potential investor group's cost of capital is 12 percent.

The buyer is in the 30 percent tax bracket. Meidi believes that she has been paying a marginal income tax rate of 40 percent in the last five years, and she expects no change in the next eight years. Unfortunately for her, the tax law in effect since last year eliminates any special tax rate for capital gains earned. This condensed income statement is taken from Meidi's latest tax return.

Income Statement for 2002

Rental revenue		$2,000,000
Expenses		
Operations	$950,000	
Administration	70,000	
Property taxes	280,000	
Depreciation (straight line)	100,000	1,400,000
Net income before taxes		$ 600,000
Income taxes at 40 percent		240,000
Net income after taxes		$ 360,000

The buyer will use the straight-line depreciation method. No change in either rental revenue or expenses is expected.

Required

1. What is the maximum the buyer should pay?
2. What is the minimum selling price Meidi can accept if she has to pay George a 5 percent commission?
3. What is the maximum the buyer would be willing to pay if the purchase is for a MACRS five-year property?

11–45 **CASH FLOW ANALYSIS AND NPV**   Lou Lewis, the president of the Lewisville Company, has asked you to give him an analysis of the best use of a warehouse the company owns.

a. Lewisville Company is currently leasing the warehouse to another company for $5,000 per month on a year-to-year basis.

b. The warehouse's estimated sales value is $200,000. A commercial Realtor believes that the price is likely to remain unchanged in the near future. The building originally cost $60,000 and is being depreciated at $1,500 annually. Its current net book value is $7,500.

c. Lewisville Company is seriously considering converting the warehouse into a factory outlet for furniture. The remodeling will cost $100,000 and will be extremely modest because the major attraction will be rock-bottom prices. The remodeling will be depreciated over the next five years using the double-declining-balance method.

d. The inventory, cash, and receivables needed to open and sustain the factory outlet would be $600,000. This total is fully recoverable whenever operations terminate.

e. Lou is fairly certain the warehouse will be condemned in 10 years to make room for a new highway. The firm most likely would receive $200,000 from the condemnation.

f. Estimated annual operating data, exclusive of depreciation, are

Sales	$900,000
Operation expenses	$500,000

g. Nonrecurring sales promotion costs at the beginning of year 1 are expected to be $100,000.

h. Nonrecurring termination costs at the end of year 5 are $50,000.

i. The minimum annual rate of return desired is 14 percent. The company is in the 40 percent tax bracket.

Required

1. Show how you would handle the individual items in determining whether the company should continue to lease the space or convert it

to a factory outlet. Use the company's analysis form, which is set up as follows:

Item	Description	Net Present Value	Cash Flows in Year					
			0	1	2	3	4	5
a.								
b.								
.								
.								
.								
i.								

Identify any item that is irrelevant.

2. After analyzing all relevant data, compute the net present value. Indicate which course of action, based only on these data, should be taken.

11–46 MACHINE REPLACEMENT WITH TAX CONSIDERATIONS   A computer chip manufacturer spent $2,500,000 to develop a special-purpose molding machine. The machine has been used for one year and will be obsolete after four years. The firm uses straight-line depreciation for this machine.

At the beginning of the second year, a machine salesperson offers a new, vastly more efficient machine. It will cost $2,000,000, will reduce annual cash manufacturing costs from $1,800,000 to $1,000,000, and will have zero disposal value at the end of three years. Management has decided to use the double-declining-balance depreciation method for tax purposes if this machine is purchased.

The old machine's salvage value is $300,000 now and will be $50,000 three years from now; however, no salvage value is provided in calculating straight-line depreciation for tax purposes.

Required   Assume that income tax rates are 45 percent. The minimum rate of return desired, after taxes, is 8 percent. Using the net present value technique, show whether the firm should purchase the new machine.

Ethics

11–47 EQUIPMENT REPLACEMENT   Oilers Company makes a microcomputer desk that it sells for $30 under a contract to a large computer retailer. The company operates one shift in its Ohio plant. The annual normal capacity is 100,000 units.

Oilers pays direct labor at the rate of $8.00 per hour. An employee can produce a desk in 2 hours. Each desk requires 8 board feet of hard board costing $0.25 per board foot. Indirect manufacturing costs (manufacturing overhead) at normal capacity of 100,000 units are described by the following budget line:

Total costs = Fixed costs + Variable cost per unit
Total costs = $25,000 + $0.30/unit

Some years ago, Oilers installed a saw that now has a carrying (book) value of $20,000 and is being depreciated at $2,000 a year. At the time of installation, the saw was expected to have no salvage value at the end of its useful life because that value would equal its dismantling costs.

A sales agent from Whalers Company is encouraging Oilers Company to replace the saw with a numerically controlled one. In addition to being able to perform precision cutting, the new saw also will reduce the time by half to make a desk and reduce the direct labor-hours required to produce one desk from 2 hours to 1 hour. However, because the new saw is more powerful than the present one, utility costs are expected to increase by $0.10 per unit.

The new saw will cost $100,000, including installation and transportation charges. Its estimated useful life is 10 years; it will be depreciated using the straight-line method. At the end of 10 years, the salvage value is estimated to be $10,000.

Whalers Company agrees that if Oilers will buy the saw, Whalers will buy the old one for $4,000 and charge Oilers no dismantling costs. The income tax rate is 40 percent. Oilers management expects a 15 percent return on investment. The loss on the trade-in of the current saw is allowable as an income tax deduction.

Required

1. As financial analyst for Oilers, you are charged with analyzing the purchase of the new saw. In preparing a report for the president, you must determine the following for management's consideration:

   a. The contribution margin per unit under current operating conditions.

   b. The standard overhead rate (applied rate) per unit under current operating conditions.

   c. The budget line for indirect manufacturing costs (manufactured overhead), assuming the purchase and installation of the new saw.

   d. The new saw's manufacturing overhead standard rate (applied rate) is expected to remain the same if normal capacity is 100,000 units.

   e. The contribution margin per unit, assuming the sales price remains unchanged, if the new saw is purchased and installed.

   f. The net additional investment for the new saw, assuming that Oilers decides to purchase and install it.

   g. The expected net additional cash flow per year if the new saw is purchased and installed. Assume that the company sells all that it produces.

2. The firm will be able to lay off approximately half of the hourly production workers currently on its payroll by purchasing and installing the new saw. The plant has been in its current location for more than 50 years. Over 40 percent of the households in this small southeast Ohio town have at least one member who works for the firm. Should the firm purchase the state-of-the-art equipment?

(IMA Adapted)

11–48 **EQUIPMENT REPLACEMENT, MACRS**   VacuTech is a high-technology company that manufactures sophisticated instruments for testing microcircuits. Each instrument sells for $3,500 and costs $2,450 to manufacture. An essential component of the company's manufacturing process is a sealed vacuum chamber where the interior approaches a pure vacuum. The technology of the vacuum pumps that the firm uses to prepare its chamber for sealing has been changing rapidly. On June 1, 1999, VacuTech bought the latest in electronic high-speed vacuum pumps that can evacuate a chamber for sealing in only six hours. The company paid $400,000 for the pump. Recently, the pump's manufacturer approached VacuTech with a new pump that would reduce the evacuation time to two hours.

VacuTech's management is considering the purchase of this new pump and has asked Doreen Harris, the company controller, to evaluate the financial impact of replacing it with the new model. Doreen has gathered the following information prior to preparing her analysis:

- The new pump could be installed on May 31, 2002, and placed in service on June 1, 2002. The pump's cost is $608,000; installing, testing, and debugging it will cost $12,000. The pump would be assigned to the three-year class for depreciation under the Modified

Accelerated Cost Recovery System (MACRS) and is expected to have an $80,000 salvage value when it is sold at the end of four years. Depreciation on the equipment would be recognized starting in 2002, and MACRS rates would be as follows:

Year 1	33%
Year 2	45
Year 3	15
Year 4	7

- The current pump is being depreciated under MACRS and will be fully depreciated by the time the new pump is placed in service. If the firm purchases the new pump, it will sell the current pump for $50,000, its estimated salvage value at the time of purchase.

- At the current rate of production, the new pump's greater efficiency will result in annual cash savings of $125,000.

- VacuTech is able to sell all testing instruments that it can produce. Because of the new pump's increased speed, output is expected to increase by 30 units in 2002, 50 units in both 2003 and 2004, and 70 units in 2005. Manufacturing costs for all additional units would be reduced by $150 per unit.

- VacuTech is subject to a 40 percent tax rate. For evaluating capital investment proposals, management assumes that annual cash flows occur at the end of the year and uses a 16 percent after-tax discount rate.

Required

1. Determine whether VacuTech should purchase the new pump by calculating the net present value at January 1, 2002, of the estimated after-tax cash flows that would result from its acquisition.

2. Describe the factors, other than the net present value, that VacuTech should consider before making the pump replacement decision.

(CMA Adapted)

International

11–49 JOINT VENTURE Perez Group has the opportunity to enter into a joint venture giving it a 49 percent ownership with local investors in an emerging country. The firm would be required to invest the entire $3,000,000 initial outlay needed for the venture and would receive 80 percent of the expected $900,000 yearly profit for 10 years. At the end of 10 years, ownership will be turned over to the local investors. Cost of capital is 10 percent. Perez will accept projects only if its return on investment is more than 20 percent.

Required Should Perez invest in the project?

11–50 RISK AND NPV A new investment opportunity has been submitted to J. Morgan of SparkPlug Inc. It involves taking over a production facility from B.R. Machine Company, which has been running it for the last 20 years. The acquisition will cost $1,500,000, and the after-tax cash flow returns will be $275,000 per year for 12 years. Morgan is unsure, however, about the cost of capital to use in computing this project's NPV. SparkPlug currently uses 12 percent for its cost of capital. Morgan believes, however, that the cost of capital should be 16 percent because of the declining demand for Sparkplug products.

Required

1. Should Morgan accept the project if its cost of capital is 12 percent?

2. If Morgan is correct and uses 16 percent, does that change the investment decision?

11–51 SENSITIVITY ANALYSIS   Griffey & Son operates a plant in Cincinnati and is considering opening a new facility in Seattle. The initial outlay will be $3,500,000 and should produce after-tax net cash inflows of $600,000 per year for 15 years. Due to the effects of the ocean air in Seattle, however, the plant's useful life may be only 12 years. Cost of capital is 14 percent.

Required

1. Will the project be accepted if 15 years' useful life is assumed? What if 12 years of useful life is used?

2. How many years will be needed for the Seattle facility to earn at least a 14 percent return?

11–52 UNEVEN CASH FLOWS   MaxiCare Corporation, a not-for-profit organization, specializes in health care for older people. Management is considering whether to expand operations by opening a new chain of care centers in the inner city of large metropolises. Initial cash outlays for lease, renovations, working capital, training, and other costs are expected to be about $15 million in year 0. The firm expects the cash inflows of each new facility in its first year of operation to equal the total cash outlays for the year. Net cash inflows are expected to increase to $1 million in each of years 2 and 3, $2.5 million in year 4, and $3 million in each of years 5 through 10. The lease agreement for the facility will expire at the end of year 10, and the firm expects the cost to close a facility will pretty much exhaust all cash proceeds from the disposal. Cost of capital for the firm is 12 percent.

Service

Required   Compute the net present value for this venture.

11–53 ENVIRONMENT COST MANAGEMENT   Myers Manufacturing, Inc., wants to build a booth for painting the boxes it makes for small transformers to be used to power neon signs. The company can choose either a solvent-based or a powder paint process. The following table summarizes the costs and investment required by each approach:

	Solvent Paint System	Powder Paint System
Initial investment	$400,000	$1,200,000
Unit paint cost	0.19	0.20
Estimated life in years	10	10
Annual units	2,000,000	2,000,000

The firm will incur additional environmental costs with the solvent paint system but not with the powder paint system. The firm estimates annual environmental costs for the solvent paint system as follows:

	Units	Unit Cost
Monthly pit cleaning	12	$ 1,000
Hazardous waste disposal	183	3,000
Superfund fee	18,690	0.17
Worker training	2	1,500
Insurance	1	10,000
Amortization of air-emission permit	0.2	1,000
Air-emission fee	44.6	25
Record keeping	0.25	45,000
Wastewater treatment	1	50,000

The firm estimates its cost of capital to be 12 percent. Either system is a 10-year property under MACRS. The firm pays a total of 40 percent in income taxes.

Required

1. Without considering environmental costs, what is the difference in cost in today's dollar for the two systems?

2. What is the most the firm is willing to pay for the powder-based system?

(Adapted from German Boer, Margaret Curtin, and Louis Hoyt, "Environmental Cost Management," *Management Accounting* [September 1998], pp. 28–38.)

SOLUTION TO SELF-STUDY PROBLEM

Capital Budgeting for Expanding Production Capacity

1.

Cost of the new equipment	$580,000
Installation, testing, and training	12,000
Renovation cost for the leased warehouse	58,000
Total cash outflow in year 0	$650,000

The total cash outflow for the initial investment is $650,000.

2.

Sales		$200 × 5,000 =	$1,000,000
Cost of goods sold			
Variable manufacturing costs per unit		$ 60	
Fixed manufacturing costs			
Additional fixed manufacturing overhead:			
($140,000 + 10,000)/5,000 units =		30	
Depreciation on new equipment			
(650,000 – $50,000)/4 = $150,000 per year			
$150,000/5,000 units per year =		30	
Manufacturing cost per unit		$ 120	
Number of units		× 5,000	600,000
Gross margin			$ 400,000
Marketing and administrative expenses			
Variable marketing expenses per unit	$ 20		
Number of units	× 5,000	$100,000	
Additional fixed marketing expenses		100,000	200,000
Net income before taxes			$ 200,000
Income taxes			80,000
Net income			$ 120,000

The firm can expect its net income to increase by $120,000 each year in years 1, 2, and 3; net income in year 4 will be $108,000 as computed here:

Net income before restoration expenses		$ 120,000
Restoration expenses	$ 20,000	
Decrease in income taxes	8,000	12,000
Increase in net income in year 4		$ 108,000

3.

	Each of Years 1 to 3	Year 4
Net income after taxes	$120,000	$108,000
Add: Expenses not requiring cash disbursement:		
Depreciation included in fixed costs $30 × 5,000 =	150,000	150,000
Cash inflow from disposal of equipment		50,000
Total cash flow return	$270,000	$ 308,000

Thus, the net cash inflow will be $270,000 each year for the first three years and will be $308,000 in year four.

4.
$$\text{Payback period} = \frac{\$650,000}{\$270,000} = 2.407 \text{ years}$$

Or 2 years and 5 months.

5. Average investment = ($650,000 + $50,000)/2 = $350,000

   Average net income = ($120,000 × 3 + $108,000)/4 = $117,000

   Book rate of return = $117,000/$350,000 = 33.43 percent

6. PV of net cash inflows in year 1 to year 3 at 12%:

$270,000 × 2.402 =	$648,540
PV of net cash inflows in year 4 at 12%:	
$308,000 × 0.636 =	195,888
Total PV of net cash inflows	$844,428
Initial investment	650,000
NPV	194,428

7.

PV of net cash inflows at 25 percent	$653,320	$653,320
Initial investment		$650,000
PV of net cash inflows at 30 percent	598,120	
Difference in PV of net cash inflows	$ 55,200	$ 3,320

Therefore, the internal rate of return is

$$25\% + \frac{\$3,320}{\$55,200} \times 6\% = 25.36\%$$

8. Answers from your spreadsheet should be identical to the answers above (except for rounding).

9. The most the after-tax net cash inflows per year can be

decreased is $194,428/3.037 =	$ 64,020
Add income taxes	42,680
The most that variable cost per year can increase	$106,700

Therefore, the variable cost per unit can increase by $106,700/5,000, or $21.34 per unit, and the firm still will earn 12 percent on the investment.

12

Job Costing

After studying this chapter, you should be able to . . .

1 Describe major choices in designing or selecting product costing systems

2 Describe the strategic role of job costing

3 Contrast job costing and process costing and identify the types of firms that use each system

4 Delineate the flow of costs by using the manufacturing accounts in a job costing system

5 Compute a predetermined factory overhead rate and use it in a job costing system

6 Calculate underapplied and overapplied overhead and dispose of them properly at the end of the period

7 Explain why multiple overhead rates and activity-based cost drivers could be preferred to a single, plantwide overhead rate

8 Apply job costing concepts to service industries

9 Define and explain an operation costing system

10 Account for spoilage, rework, and scrap in job costing

©John Elk/Stock Boston.

Bechtel is a successful global engineering-construction firm that provides premier services to develop, engineer, build, operate, and manage capital projects and facilities worldwide. It has built many world-class projects with advanced technology such as the San Francisco to Oakland Bay Bridge, Hoover Dam, the San Francisco Bay Area Transit System (BART), 1984 Los Angeles Olympic facilities, and Hong Kong's new international airport. In 1995, Bechtel was the first U.S. company to be granted a construction license in China.[1]

In keeping with the firm's mission of continuous improvement and delivering exceptional value to its customers, Bechtel's management philosophy focuses on entrepreneurial approaches, innovative solutions, advanced technology, high-quality projects, and excellent cost management. Bechtel uses job costing and budgeting systems to keep track of a variety of large-scale construction projects. The job costing system provides the firm detailed information about materials, labor, and overhead cost for each construction project.

Part of Bechtel's strategy is to adapt to changes in the e-business environment. For example, when the firm's top management realized in 1999 that online companies were building warehouses and distribution centers, the firm quickly moved to sign huge construction deals with Webvan Group Inc., iMotors.com Inc., and Equinix Inc. In 2000, Bechtel launched a Web marketplace, InfrastructureWorld.com, that seeks to speed the completion of construction projects in established and developing countries.

Product costing is the process of accumulating, classifying, and assigning direct materials, direct labor, and factory overhead costs to products or services. Product costing provides useful cost information for both manufacturing and nonmanufacturing firms for (1) product and service cost determination and inventory measurement, (2) management planning, cost control, and performance evaluation, and (3) strategic and operational decision making.

Many strategic and operational decisions that managers must make are based primarily on information about the cost of products or services, including these decisions:

1. Determining product or service pricing.
   - What is the minimum rate a gas company must charge residential users to cover its costs?
   - How should a restaurant price its menu to cover costs?
2. Assessing the financial effect of adding or deleting a product, division, or subsidiary.
   - Should an automobile manufacturer add an off-road vehicle to its product line?
   - Should a department store close its sporting goods section?

Product costing is the process of accumulating, classifying, and assigning direct materials, direct labor, and factory overhead costs to products or services.

---

[1] For more information about Bechtel, see its website at www.bechtel.com; "Bechtel Gets a New Lift from the Dot-Com Boom," *The Wall Street Journal*, March 1, 2000; "Bechtel, Shell to Erect Border Power Plant in Mexico," *The Los Angeles Times*, June 17, 2000; and "Big Builder Backs Marketplace," *InformationWeek*, September 18, 2000.

3. Deciding to make or buy.
- Should a medical clinic do its own blood tests or purchase services from an outside laboratory?
- Should a toy manufacturing company make or buy some plastic components?

4. Evaluating product, service, or division performance.
- What was last month's printer product line profit for a computer peripheral manufacturing company?
- What profit did the deluxe fishing boat product line make last year for a boat manufacturing company?

Before discussing the uses of cost data for these purposes, we explain how to design and select a good cost system, how cost data are gathered, and how costs are determined.

COSTING SYSTEM DESIGN/SELECTION GUIDELINES

LEARNING OBJECTIVE 1▶

Describe some major choices in designing or selecting product costing systems.

Several different types of product costing systems are available; these include the (1) cost accumulation method—job or process costing systems, (2) cost measurement method—actual, normal, or standard costing systems, and (3) overhead assignment method—traditional or activity-based costing systems.

The choice of a particular system depends on (1) the nature of the industry and the product or service, (2) the firm's strategy and management information needs, and (3) the costs and benefits of acquiring, designing, modifying, and operating a particular system.

Cost Accumulation: Job or Process Costing

In a job costing system, the jobs or batches of products or services are the cost objects. This means that for the purposes of determining product cost, all manufacturing costs incurred are assigned to jobs. In a process costing system, on the other hand, production processes or departments are the cost objects. For example, the metal fabrication department might be one cost center and the assembly department another.

The job costing system usually is used by firms that have a wide variety of distinct products. A job costing system is appropriate in any environment in which costs can be readily identified with specific products, batches, contracts, or projects.

The process costing system, on the other hand, is usually used by firms having homogeneous products. These firms engage in continuous mass production of one or a few products. This chapter describes job costing systems. Chapter 13 discusses process costing systems.

Cost Measurement: Actual, Normal, or Standard Costing

Costs in either a job or process costing system can be measured in their actual, normal, or standard amount. An *actual costing system* uses actual costs incurred for all product costs including direct materials, direct labor, and factory overhead. Actual costing systems are rarely used because they can produce unit product costs that fluctuate from period to period or even from batch to batch. This fluctuation can cause serious problems for decisions concerning pricing, and adding/dropping a product line, and for performance evaluations. Most actual factory overhead costs are known only at or after the end of the period rather than at the completion of the batch of products. Thus, actual costing systems cannot provide accurate unit product cost information on a timely basis.

A *normal costing system* uses actual costs for direct materials and direct labor and normal costs for factory overhead using predetermined rates. Predetermined factory overhead rates are assigned to cost centers based on the predetermined factory overhead application rate and the activity of the cost center. The predetermined factory overhead rate is derived by dividing budgeted annual factory overhead costs by bud-

Cost Measurement Systems

Costing System	Types of Cost Used For		
	Direct Materials	**Direct Labor**	**Factory Overhead**
Actual costing	Actual cost	Actual cost	Actual cost
Normal costing	Actual cost	Actual cost	Applied overhead cost (using predetermined rate(s))
Standard costing	Standard cost	Standard cost	Standard cost

geted volume or activity levels. A normal costing system provides a timely estimate of the cost of producing each batch of product.

A *standard costing system* uses standard rates (costs) and quantities for all three types of manufacturing costs: direct materials, direct labor, and factory overhead. Standard costs are predetermined target costs the firm should attain. Standard costing systems provide good cost control, performance evaluation, and process improvement in many environments. Chapter 12 describes actual costing systems, Chapters 12 and 13 discuss normal costing systems, and Chapters 15 and 16 present standard costing systems.

Overhead Assignment: Traditional or Activity-Based Costing

Traditional product costing systems often allocate overhead to products or jobs using a volume-based cost driver, such as direct labor-hours or dollars. An automated factory environment often requires only a minimal direct labor cost and has a significantly higher fixed factory overhead than an older, labor-intensive factory. Some factory overhead costs are not volume based. For example, machine setup cost is batch based, and product design cost is product based. The traditional volume-based overhead allocation predicated on direct labor-hours or machine-hours can cause serious distortion in product costing by overcosting or undercosting these products.

Activity-based costing systems allocate factory overhead costs to products using cause-and-effect criteria with multiple cost drivers. ABC systems use both volume-based and nonvolume-based cost drivers to more accurately allocate factory overhead costs to products based on resource consumption during various activities. Chapter 4 describes ABC systems; Chapters 12 and 13 discuss traditional costing systems.

Design/Selection Guidelines

Product costing system design or selection is not an easy task. Management accountants follow these guidelines in designing or selecting an appropriate product costing system:

1. **Understand the nature of the business, its products, and the changing manufacturing environment.** Firms with a wide variety of distinct products usually use a *job costing system,* which is applied to low-volume goods and services. Firms with homogeneous products over a significant time period use the *process costing system,* which is applied to high-volume goods when individual units cannot be specifically identified and assigned a cost. In practice, many firms appropriately use job costing for some products or departments and process costing for other products or departments. Automobile manufacturing firms are an example; their products not only have many common features but also have unique features. Automakers cannot use either a pure job costing or a pure process costing system.

A *standard cost system* is suitable when production processes or activities are repetitive. A *normal or actual costing system* is more commonly used by relatively small firms, new firms, or industries that manufacture nonstandard or custom-made products.

Many firms' manufacturing environments are changing rapidly. To provide meaningful information, a product costing system must keep up with the constantly changing manufacturing environment. Many firms change their product costing system from a single volume-based cost driver system to a multiple cost driver ABC system because of changes in their manufacturing environments.

2. Provide useful cost information for management's strategic and operational decision needs. For management cost control purposes, job costing is more suitable than process costing because it provides more focused and timely information. Job costing is also best for the differentiation strategy.

Standard costing systems provide information so that management can control costs better, evaluate performance, and process improvement information than do normal costing or actual costing systems.

Activity-based costing systems provide more accurate product cost information than traditional volume-based costing systems, enabling managers to make various strategic decisions.

3. Consider the cost benefit of acquiring, designing, modifying, and operating a particular system. Because the job costing system focuses more on a detailed level of jobs and cost centers, designing and operating it requires more time and cost than the process costing system.

A standard costing system is more difficult and time consuming to design and update than a typical normal or actual costing system. However, it requires less clerical cost to operate than an actual costing system.

An activity-based costing system is more costly and time consuming to design and update than the traditional volume-related costing system.

A firm can use one product costing system for some purposes, products, or departments and another system for other purposes, products, or departments; the overall integrated costing system must be flexible enough to permit the use of both.

STRATEGIC ROLE OF JOB COSTING

LEARNING OBJECTIVE 2▶

Describe the strategic role of job costing.

Job costing systems provide information for managers to use to make strategic choices regarding products and customers, manufacturing methods, pricing decisions, and other long-term issues. Job costing information is strategically important for a firm for four reasons.

First, a firm competes by using either the cost leadership or the differentiation strategy. If it is following the cost leadership strategy and overheads are complex, the

---

FMI Forms Manufacturers Uses Job Costing

FMI Forms Manufacturers is a machine-intensive printing company that produces business forms. The resources demanded by a specific job depend on the type and amount of paper used and the composition and construction of the business form. All jobs are constrained by the time on a press and a collator capable of producing forms at the required size.

FMI uses a separate factory overhead rate for each machine. Costs of machine operator, support personnel, and supplies are identified directly with presses and collators. Other factory overhead costs, including insurance, supervision, and office salaries, are allocated to machines based on their processing capacity (cost driver is the number of feet of business form per minute), weighted by the maximum paper width and complexity (cost driver is number of colors and/or stations) that they are capable of handling.

When FMI receives a request for a bid on a particular job, it uses a computer software program to determine direct materials costs based on the type and quantity of paper. Then it identifies the least expensive press and collator that are capable of handling the job specifications. Then FMI estimates the total press and collator processing costs by using specific cost driver rates per machine time multiplied by the estimated processing time. The bid price is calculated by adding a standard markup to the total press, collator, and direct materials costs. A higher markup is used for rush jobs and those requiring special features.

Based on information in Jacci L. Rodgers, S. Mark Comstock, and Karl Pritz, "Customize Your Costing System," *Management Accounting,* May 1993, pp. 31–32.

> ### Thomas Jefferson University Hospital Uses Job Costing Information for Drug Cost Evaluation
>
> Thomas Jefferson University Hospital uses a job costing system with each patient as a separate job. The hospital used the system's information to evaluate the cost of using a new cancer chemotherapy drug, Zofran. Although Zofran was a more expensive drug therapy than traditional therapy, the experiment results showed that the use of Zofran did not cost more because patients using it required shorter hospital stays.
>
> Based on information in Carly E. Carpenter, Linda C. Weitzel, Nelda E. Johnson, and David B. Nash, "Cost Accounting Supports Clinical Evaluations," *Healthcare Financial Management,* April 1994, pp. 40–45.

traditional volume-based job costing (which is simpler than either process costing or activity-based costing) provides little help. When a firm is a differentiator, the activity-based job costing can be more appropriate because management focus should be on critical success factors that create differentiation rather than careful cost tracing to a process or department. Note that rather than helping, the traditional volume-based job costing system in many situations can actually hinder development and implementation of a strategy that promotes competitive advantage.

Second, an important strategic issue and a potential ethical issue for job costing involves the decisions the firm makes about the basis for allocating overhead and the proration of overapplied or underapplied overhead. For example, if a firm manufactures products for two types of markets, one of which is price competitive and the other of which is not (e.g., cost-plus government contracts), the manner of overhead allocation involves both strategic and ethical issues. When manufacturing cost-plus products, managers can be tempted to overcost them by choosing an allocation basis or proration method that achieves the desired result.

Third, job costing is suitable for a service firm, especially a professional services firm. Tracing direct costs is not the major issue, and allocating overhead is not complex or difficult. Therefore, the use of job costing facilitates the effective management of a professional services firm.

Fourth, a job cost sheet could be expanded into a strategic balanced scorecard performance report with four dimensions: financial, customer, internal business process, and learning and growth. For example, a company developing a strategic balanced scorecard could include job cost information as a part of both financial measures and internal business process measures.

JOB VERSUS PROCESS COSTING SYSTEMS

Two basic types of product costing systems used in different industries are job costing and process costing. After comparing them, we devote the balance of the chapter to discussing job costing.

Job Costing

Job costing is a product costing system that accumulates costs and assigns them to a specific job. It is typically used by firms with a wide variety of products or services. The production departments of these firms perform tasks that often vary from product to product. Because each product or service can require different operations, the best way to determine the cost of a product or service is to accumulate costs for a job or batch. Therefore, in job costing, the product or service costs are obtained by gathering and assigning costs to a specific job or individual customer order for one or more products. The unit cost of each product or service is calculated by dividing total job costs by number of units produced or served. Job costing is used when the products or

Job costing is a product costing system that accumulates costs and assigns them to a specific job.

services are especially tailored to the customers' needs as in the examples that follow for Topnotch Auto Repair and Sally Industries.

Industries that use job costing are printing shops, shipbuilders, custom furniture-manufacturing plants, contractors, film-producing companies, accounting firms, law firms, advertising agencies, consulting firms, medical clinics, custom-made machine tool or equipment companies, construction companies, and research, engineering, and development services. Each job in these businesses is likely to be different. Examples of companies using job costing systems include Kinko's (www.kinkos.com); Paramount Pictures (www.paramount.com); Jiffy Lube International (www.jiffylube.com); McGraw-Hill/Irwin (www.mhhe.com); Accenture, the new name of Andersen Consulting (www.accenture.com), Kaiser Permanente (www.kaiserpermanente.org), and Hyatt Corporation (www.hyatt.com).

Process Costing

Process costing accumulates product or service costs by process or department and then assigns them to a large number of nearly identical products. Firms continuously mass producing one or a few homogeneous products or services use process costing. It is not economically feasible to track the detailed cost elements applied to each unit. A process costing system accumulates product or service costs by process or department rather than by job or project, as in job costing. Unit product or service cost is calculated by accumulating process costs and dividing the total process costs of the period by the number of units produced or served.

Detergent manufacturing is a suitable business for process costing. Because all boxes of detergent processed during an accounting period are identical, separately recording costs for each unit or batch produced during that period is not needed. The process of finding the average cost of performing each process during the period and then summing these process average costs to arrive at the average cost per box of detergent for the period are much more cost beneficial.

Industries usually employing process costing include chemical plants; food processors; household appliance manufacturers; textile companies; petroleum product manu-

> **Process costing** accumulates product or service costs by process or department and then assigns them to a large number of nearly identical products.

Topnotch Auto Repair Shop

Topnotch Auto Repair Shop in Rowland Heights, California, is a business well suited to job costing. The firm typically performs a wide variety of tasks from changing tires to repairing engines. Although shop personnel are likely asked to do some tasks several times a day, rarely are they asked to do the same task throughout the day. For example, two customers asking for engine tune-ups have different models of cars that vary in their complexity and in the cost of repair. One customer might ask them to rotate the tires on the car. Therefore, it makes more sense for Topnotch to track the costs of repairing each car rather than the total monthly costs of the individual tasks.

Sally Industries Uses Job Costing for Entertainment Robots

Sally Industries, Inc., is a small manufacturer of animatronic figures known as entertainment robots such as E.T., the Extraterrestrial. Because entertainment robots are custom orders, Sally Industries uses a job costing system to help managers make project planning, cost control, performance measurement, and pricing decisions. Each job cost sheet is separated into direct materials, direct labor, and factory overhead. Since Sally Industries is still a small business, it has a relatively simple job costing system that is maintained largely on spreadsheets.

Based on information in Thomas Barton and Frederick M. Cole, "Accounting for Magic," *Management Accounting,* January 1991, pp. 27–31.

Exhibit 12–1 Differences between Job and Process Costing

Job Costing	Process Costing
Costs accumulated by job	Costs accumulated by process or department
Production of wide variety of heterogeneous products or services	Mass production of homogeneous products or services
Unit cost computed by dividing total job costs by number of units produced or served at the end of the job	Unit cost computed by dividing the total process costs of the period by number of units produced or served at end of the period

facturers; paper, lumber, and pulp mills; glass factories; bakeries; wineries; cement factories; and sugar factories. Examples of companies using process costing systems include Royal Dutch Shell Group (www.shell.com), Ford Motor Company (www.ford.com), Coca-Cola (www.cocacola.com), Bethlehem Steel (www.bethsteel.com), International Paper (www.ipaper.com), and Kimberly-Clark (www.kimberly-clark.com).

Comparison of Job and Process Costing Systems

Job costing and process costing have a similar overall purpose, basic set of manufacturing accounts, and flow of costs through manufacturing accounts. The overall purpose of both product costing systems is to properly assign direct materials, direct labor, and factory overhead manufacturing costs to products. Both systems use the same basic set of manufacturing accounts, including Materials Inventory, Work-in-Process Inventory, Factory Overhead, and Finished Goods Inventory. The flow of costs through the manufacturing accounts is basically the same in both systems.

Job costing and process costing have three major differences. First, a job costing system accumulates costs by job; a process costing system accumulates costs by production department. Second, job costing has a wide variety of different products or services; it uses the job cost sheet to accumulate and control costs for a specific job. Process costing has mass production of homogeneous products or services; it uses the production cost report to accumulate and control costs for a particular department. Third, job costing calculates the unit cost by job when each job is completed; process costing calculates the unit cost by department at the end of each accounting period using an equivalent units-of-production concept. Exhibit 12–1 summarizes these three major differences for job costing and process costing.

◀ **LEARNING OBJECTIVE 3**

Contrast job costing and process costing and identify the types of firms that use each system.

JOB COSTING: GENERAL DESCRIPTION

Job Cost Sheet

The basic supporting document in a job costing system is the **job cost sheet**. It records and summarizes the costs of direct materials, direct labor, and factory overhead for a particular job.

The job cost sheet in Exhibit 12–2 is started when the production or processing of a job begins. A job cost sheet has spaces for all cost elements and other detailed data management requires. The job cost sheet follows the product as it goes through the production process; all costs are recorded on the sheet. On completion of production, the total of all costs recorded on the job cost sheet is the total cost of the job. The average cost per unit is determined by dividing the number of units in the job by its total cost.

All costs recorded in a job cost sheet are included in the Work-in-Process Inventory account. The subsidiary accounts to the Work-in-Process Inventory account (such as direct materials, direct labor, and various factory overhead accounts) consist of job cost sheets that include the manufacturing costs incurred during or prior to the

A **job cost sheet** records and summarizes the costs of direct materials, direct labor, and factory overhead for a particular job.

Exhibit 12–2	Job Cost Sheet

Smith Job Shop
Job Cost Sheet

Product	Robot											Job No.	351
Date begun	June 6, 2001											Quantity	20
Date completed	July 15, 2001											Unit Cost	$3.761

		Direct Materials			Direct Labor					Factory Overhead			
Dept.	Date	Requisition Number	Unit	Cost	Date	Hours	Rate	Ticket	Amount	Machine-Hours	Application Rate	Amount	Total Cost
A	6/6	A–4024	20	$1,500	6/6 to 6/25	100	10	A–1101 through A–1150	$1,000	50	10.00	$ 500	$3,000
B	6/26	B–3105	15	400	6/26 to 6/30	60	15	B–308 through B–320	900	60	6.70	402	1,702
C	7/2	C–5051	10	300	7/1 to 7/15	140	12	C–515 through C–500	1,680	35	24.00	840	2,820
Total				$2,200					$3,580			$1,742	$7,522

current period for processing jobs. The total on all job cost sheets equals the total amount on the debit side of the Work-in-Process Inventory account. This amount is the total manufacturing cost to account for. This total is reported on the statement of cost of goods manufactured.

Because a separate job cost sheet is prepared for each job, cost sheets for jobs started but not finished represent a subsidiary ledger that supports the Work-in-Process Inventory Control account. When a job is complete, the appropriate cost sheet is placed in a group of cost sheets representing the cost of goods manufactured.

Direct Materials Costs

When materials are purchased for $2,200, for example, the accountant (1) checks the supporting documents of purchase orders, receiving reports, and invoices and (2) records the purchase amounts in the Receipts column of the subsidiary ledger, the material ledger. These support the following journal entry:

(1)	Materials Inventory	2,200	
	Accounts Payable		2,200

A general ledger control account sums the similar detailed account balances in the related subsidiary ledger. The Materials Inventory account amount is the sum of all direct and indirect materials in the subsidiary ledger.

A product costing system uses materials requisition forms to document and control all materials issued. A **materials requisition form** is a source document that the production department supervisor uses to request materials for production. The production department prepares materials requisition forms to request materials from the warehouse; copies are sent to the accounting department. The warehouse releases the materials based on the requisition. The materials requisition indicates the departments, jobs, and projects charged with the materials used. In an online computer environment, the production department enters this information in computer programs.

A **materials requisition form** is a source document that the production department supervisor uses to request materials for production.

Exhibit 12–3   Materials Requisition Form

MATERIALS REQUISITION FORM   No. A–4024

Job Number	351	Date	June 6, 2001
Department	A	Received by	Tom Chan
Authorized by	Juanita Peres	Issued by	Ted Mercer

Item Number	Description	Quantity	Unit Cost	Total Cost
MI 428	Microprocessors	20	$75	$1,500

Based on the information in materials requisition forms, costs of direct materials issued to production are recorded on the job cost sheet. This document is the source document for determining materials costs for individual jobs. Notice that the materials requisition form in Exhibit 12–3 specifically identifies the job that will use the materials.

For example, Smith Job Shop's department A incurred $1,500 of costs for direct materials for Job 351, with the following journal entry:

| (2) | Work-in-Process Inventory | 1,500 | |
| | Materials Inventory | | 1,500 |

Indirect materials are treated as part of the total factory overhead cost. Typical indirect materials are factory supplies and lubricants. They are recorded in the overhead cost sheet subsidiary ledger and the factory overhead general ledger account. The journal entry to record the issue of an indirect materials cost of $50 to support departments is

| (3) | Factory Overhead | 50 | |
| | Materials Inventory | | 50 |

Exhibit 12–4 describes cost flows for direct materials and indirect materials of transactions (1), (2), and (3) through related general ledger T-accounts, subsidiary ledgers, and various source documents.

◀**LEARNING OBJECTIVE 4**

Delineate the flow of costs by using the manufacturing accounts in a job costing system.

Direct Labor Costs

Direct labor costs are recorded on the job cost sheet by means of a time ticket prepared daily for each employee. A **time ticket** shows the amount of time an employee worked on each job, the pay rate, and the total cost chargeable to each job. Analysis of the time tickets provides information for assigning direct labor costs to individual jobs. Note the typical time ticket form in Exhibit 12–5. The cost of the $1,000 direct labor incurred in Smith Job Shop's department A for Job 351 is recorded by the following journal entry:

| (4) | Work-in-Process Inventory | 1,000 | |
| | Accrued Payroll | | 1,000 |

A **time ticket** shows the time an employee worked on each job, the pay rate, and the total cost chargeable to each job.

In addition to time tickets, clock or time cards are widely used for cost assignment and payroll. The times reported on an employee's time tickets are compared with the related clock cards as an internal check on the accuracy of the payroll computation.

Exhibit 12–4 Materials Cost Flows

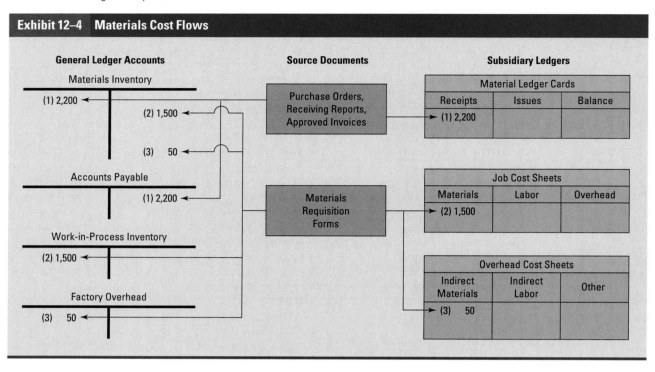

Exhibit 12–5 Time Ticket

TIME TICKET

Employee Number	015	Date	June 6, 2001
Employee Name	Dale Johnson	Job Number	#351
Operation	Assembly	Approved by	Juanita Peres

Time Started	Time Completed	Hours Worked	Rate	Cost
8:00 a.m.	11:00 a.m.	3.00	$10.00	$30.00
Total Cost				$30.00

Indirect labor costs are treated as part of the total factory overhead cost. Indirect labor usually includes items such as salaries or wages for supervisors, inspectors, rework labor, and warehouse clerks. They are recorded in the Indirect Labor column of the overhead cost sheet subsidiary ledger. The following is a journal entry to record the $100 indirect labor cost incurred:

(5)	Factory Overhead	100	
	Accrued Payroll		100

Exhibit 12–6 shows direct labor and indirect labor cost flows through related general ledger T-accounts, subsidiary ledgers, and various source documents.

Exhibit 12–6   Labor Cost Flows

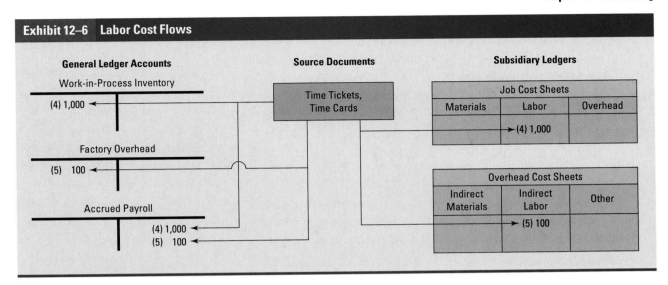

Factory Overhead Costs

Cost allocation is a process of assigning costs to the appropriate products, services, or jobs. **Overhead application or allocation** is a process of assigning overhead costs to the appropriate jobs. Allocation is necessary because overhead costs are not traceable to individual jobs. The three approaches in assigning overhead costs to various jobs are actual costing, normal costing, and standard costing. This chapter discusses the first two approaches. Standard costing is discussed in Chapters 15 and 16.

Overhead application or allocation is a process of assigning overhead costs to the appropriate jobs.

Actual Costing System

An **actual costing system** uses actual costs incurred for direct materials and direct labor and assigns or applies actual factory overhead to various jobs.

Actual factory overhead costs are incurred in an accounting period for indirect materials, indirect labor, and other indirect factory costs, including factory rent, insurance, property tax, depreciation, repairs and maintenance, power, light, heat, and employer payroll taxes for factory personnel. Different firms use terms such as *manufacturing overhead, overhead,* or *burden* in referring to factory overhead.

Indirect materials of $50 and indirect labor of $100 were discussed in transactions (3) and (5), respectively. Other factory overhead costs such as depreciation, utilities, and insurance are accumulated in an overhead cost sheet subsidiary ledger under the Other column. The documents to support these costs include vouchers, invoices, and memos. This journal entry records the actual overhead costs of factory utilities, depreciation, and insurance:

An **actual costing system** uses actual costs incurred for direct materials and direct labor and assigns or applies actual factory overhead to various jobs.

Actual factory overhead costs are costs incurred in an accounting period for indirect materials, indirect labor, and other indirect factory costs, including factory rent, insurance, property tax, depreciation, repairs and maintenance, power, light, heat, and employer payroll taxes for factory personnel.

(6)	Factory Overhead	350	
	Accounts Payable		80
	Accumulated Depreciation—Plant		150
	Prepaid Insurance		120

The actual factory overhead costs applied to various jobs based on allocation bases such as direct labor-hours, number of employees, and square footage are recorded in the Overhead column of the Job Cost Sheets subsidiary ledger. The journal entry to record the overhead application ($50 + $100 + $350 = $500) to job 351 for Smith Job Shop's department A is

(7)	Work-in-Process Inventory	500	
	Factory Overhead Applied		500

Exhibit 12–7 illustrates actual factory overhead and applied factory overhead cost flows through related general ledger T-accounts, subsidiary ledgers, and source documents.

531

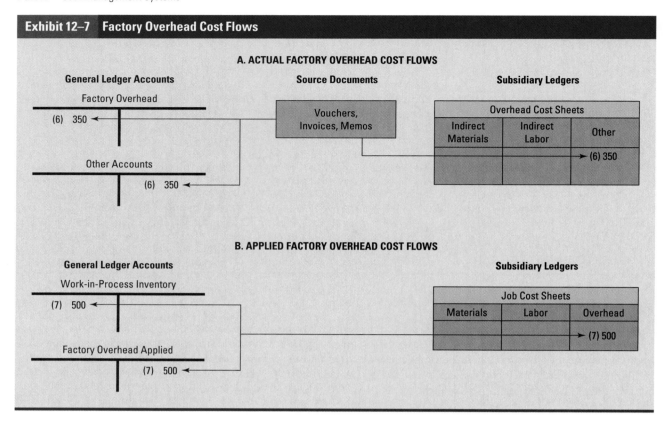

Exhibit 12–7 Factory Overhead Cost Flows

A. ACTUAL FACTORY OVERHEAD COST FLOWS

General Ledger Accounts   Source Documents   Subsidiary Ledgers

Factory Overhead

(6) 350

Vouchers, Invoices, Memos

Overhead Cost Sheets

Indirect Materials	Indirect Labor	Other
		→ (6) 350

Other Accounts

(6) 350

B. APPLIED FACTORY OVERHEAD COST FLOWS

General Ledger Accounts   Subsidiary Ledgers

Work-in-Process Inventory

(7) 500

Job Cost Sheets

Materials	Labor	Overhead
		→ (7) 500

Factory Overhead Applied

(7) 500

Normal Costing System

Normal costing system
uses actual costs for
direct materials and direct
labor and applies factory
overhead to various jobs
using a predetermined
rate basis.

Actual factory overhead costs are not always readily available to most manufacturers at the end of a production process or period, nor can they be easily traced to individual products. In practice, many firms adopt a **normal costing system** that uses actual costs for direct materials and direct labor and applies factory overhead to various jobs using a predetermined rate basis.

The motive for normalizing factory overhead costs is to avoid the fluctuations in cost per unit per period resulting from changes in the volume of units produced during that period. Using a predetermined annual factory overhead rate normalizes overhead cost fluctuations, hence, the term *normal costing*.

We discuss the major reasons for using the predetermined overhead rate and the way it applies or allocates factory overhead costs to the specific jobs in a later section.

Unit Cost Calculation

When a job is complete, the finished products are transferred from the production department to finished goods. The management accountant finds the total cost incurred on the job cost sheet and transfers the total $3,000 cost (Direct materials $1,500 + Direct labor $1,000 + Factory overhead $500) to the Finished Goods Inventory account from the Work-in-Process Inventory account with this journal entry:

| (8) | Finished Goods Inventory | 3,000 | |
| | Work-in-Process Inventory | | 3,000 |

As costs of completed jobs are transferred from the Work-in-Process Inventory account to the Finished Goods Inventory account, the Work-in-Process Inventory account has a balance at the end of the period only if unfinished work exists.

The unit cost for a job ($150) is calculated at its end by dividing the total job cost ($3,000) by the number of units in the job (20).

JOB COSTING: USE OF PREDETERMINED FACTORY OVERHEAD RATE(S)

Need for Using Predetermined Factory Overhead Rate(s)

Overhead costs are not always readily available to most manufacturers at the end of a production process or period, nor can they be easily traced to individual products. Thus, a convenient way for some firms to handle overhead costs is to wait until the end of the accounting period and compute product cost based on actual overhead costs incurred. This procedure is *actual costing*. However, actual costing can cause fluctuations in costs per unit for products produced in different periods due to changes in the number of units produced. Consequently, most firms choose not to use the actual overhead costs incurred to compute manufacturing costs. Instead, these firms determine overhead costs for final cost objects, such as the job or product, using a predetermined overhead rate to apply overhead to the cost object. This latter approach is *normal costing*.

The **predetermined factory overhead rate** is an estimated factory overhead rate used to apply factory overhead cost to a specific job. The amount of overhead assigned to a specific job using a predetermined factory overhead rate is called the **factory overhead applied**. In recent years, companies such as Hewlett-Packard, AT&T, General Motors, American Express, and Weyerhaeuser have used multiple predetermined overhead rates (one for each cost pool) instead of a single overhead rate to apply overhead costs to a specific job or product.

To obtain the predetermined overhead rate(s), follow these four steps:

1. Budget factory overhead costs (one for each cost pool) for an appropriate operating period, usually a year.
2. Select the most appropriate cost drivers for charging the factory overhead costs.
3. Estimate the total amount or activity level of the chosen cost drivers for the operating period.
4. Divide the budgeted factory overhead costs by the estimated activity level of the chosen cost drivers to obtain the predetermined overhead rates.

Some firms favor the use of a predetermined factory overhead rate for at least two reasons. One is to normalize the overhead cost included in each unit of the product. *Normalizing* involves using long-term average unit costs such as annualized overhead

> **Predetermined factory overhead rate** is an estimated factory overhead rate used to apply factory overhead cost to a specific job.
>
> **Factory overhead applied** is the amount of overhead assigned to a specific job using a predetermined factory overhead rate.

Monthly Per-Unit Fixed Factory Overhead Cost Fluctuation at Steece Machine Tools, Inc.

Steece Machine Tools, Inc., has a monthly total fixed factory overhead of $60,000 and variable manufacturing costs per unit of $10 for its only product. The firm produced 50,000 units in January but only 10,000 units in February because it had a large inventory of unsold goods at the end of January. The unit costs would be as follows if actual cost data were used to determine the manufacturing cost per unit:

Month	Production Units	Variable Cost per Unit	Fixed Cost per Unit	Total Unit Cost
January	50,000	$10	$60,000/50,000 = $1.20	$11.20
February	10,000	10	60,000/10,000 = 6.00	16.00

This fluctuation in unit cost certainly does not represent the actual costs to produce the identical products and therefore is not desirable. Predetermined overhead rates are easy to apply and reduce volatility and fluctuations in job costs caused by changes in the production volume and/or overhead costs throughout the year.

rates rather than quarterly or monthly overhead rates to determine overhead costs. This process avoids the fluctuations in cost per unit per period resulting from changes in the volume of units produced in a period.

A substantial portion of factory overhead costs are period costs that remain constant regardless of the units produced, whereas the output level of firms seldom remains the same from period to period. Thus, if the actual overhead cost were used to determine the cost of goods manufactured, the cost assigned to each unit would vary from one period to the next. In periods with low production, the per-unit cost would be high, but in periods with high production, the per-unit cost would be low.

The second reason for firms favoring the use of a predetermined application overhead rate in the costing process is that this procedure allows management to keep product costs current. If, for example, the management of a furniture manufacturing firm wants to know the cost of desks manufactured on completion of a job, the firm's controller can immediately provide the actual materials and labor costs incurred because this information is readily available. The controller, however, usually could not compute the actual per-unit overhead cost of the desks until the end of the accounting period or until some later time when all bills of factory overhead items arrived from the vendors. The costs for overhead elements such as electricity and repair and maintenance, for example, are most likely not available until the end of the period or later. Management certainly would not be satisfied with having to wait until the end of the period to review the manufacturing costs if it wants to bill customers promptly. Use of a predetermined factory overhead rate thus enables the controller to determine the cost of the product immediately.

Cost Drivers for Factory Overhead Allocation

The basis for applying a predetermined overhead rate can be either a volume- or activity-based cost driver measure. The important consideration is that it be closely related to the behavior of the total overhead costs. Otherwise, substantial discrepancies can emerge between the overhead applied and the overhead incurred and, worse, the product cost can be misleading or distorted. The base for applying factory overhead also is called the *cost driver*. The best cost driver choice is the activity or output measure that best represents what drives or causes overhead.

Direct labor-hours, direct labor costs, and machine-hours are among the most frequently used volume-based cost drivers for applying factory overhead. Other activity-based cost drivers include the number of setups, orders, manufacturing cycle time, and inspection hours. The overhead cost driver rate is determined by dividing the estimated total overhead cost by the estimated total units of the cost driver for the relevant period. The proper bases or cost drivers for a labor-intensive firm are probably direct labor-hours, direct labor costs, or some labor-related activity measure. In contrast, if factory overhead costs are predominantly related to the equipment operation, the proper cost driver is probably machine-hours or a related measure. Alternatively, if most overhead costs consist of purchasing, production scheduling, setup, and expediting, the proper cost driver is the number of orders instead of direct labor-hours or machine-hours.

Applying Factory Overhead Costs

LEARNING OBJECTIVE 5▶

Compute a predetermined factory overhead rate and use it in a job costing system.

The predetermined overhead rate usually is calculated at or before the beginning of the year as follows:

$$\text{Predetermined overhead rate} = \frac{\text{Budgeted factory overhead amount for the year}}{\text{Expected level of cost driver for the year}}$$

For example, Smith Lighting Company produces lighting fixtures to fill customers' orders. It has a total budgeted factory overhead cost of $200,000 for the coming year.

Smith's total overhead costs vary directly with the total number of machine-hours worked. Thus, management decided to use the machine-hour as the cost driver for overhead application. Smith has the following budgeted and actual data:

Budgeted annual overhead	$200,000
Expected annual machine-hours	100,000
Actual machine-hours for job 11	3,000
Actual units for job 11	300

Thus, the predetermined overhead rate is

$$\frac{\text{Budgeted overhead}}{\text{Expected number of machine-hours}} = \frac{\$200,000}{100,000} = \$2 \text{ per machine hour}$$

Based on these estimates, the overhead application rate for Smith Lighting Company for the coming year is $2 per machine-hour ($200,000/100,000 hours). The overhead cost applied to job 11 is $6,000, and the overhead cost per lighting fixture is $20:

$$\text{Overhead applied to job 11 is } \$2 \times 3,000 = \$6,000$$

$$\text{Overhead cost per unit of lighting fixture is } \frac{\$6,000}{300} = \$20$$

The applied factory overhead costs are recorded in the Overhead column of the job cost sheets. This journal entry records the application of factory overhead to job 11:

Work-in-Process Inventory-Job 11	6,000	
Factory Overhead Applied		6,000

Firms lacking a Factory Overhead Applied account credit the Factory Overhead account. We use the separate Factory Overhead Applied account to clearly distinguish between actual and applied factory overhead costs.

Using a predetermined overhead rate to apply overhead cost to products causes total overhead applied to the units produced to exceed the actual total overhead incurred in periods when production is higher than expected. On the other hand, in a period with lower-than-expected production, the total overhead charged to the units produced during the period is less than the actual total overhead incurred. If the overhead application rate has been properly determined over a long period of time—usually a complete operating cycle—the amount overapplied should be approximately the same as the amount underapplied. Nevertheless, some differences between the actual amount incurred and the amount applied usually remain. A small difference results in no serious distortions in the cost of goods sold and inventory amounts.

Underapplied and Overapplied Factory Overhead

The total factory overhead applied for a given period is likely to differ from actual overhead cost incurred for the period. Applied overhead can be higher than actual overhead because the actual level of the cost driver exceeded the estimate or because actual overhead was less than expected. When the applied overhead cost, which has been recorded as a credit on the Factory Overhead Applied or Factory Overhead account, is more than the actual overhead cost recorded on the debit side of the Factory Overhead account, we call it *overapplied overhead*. **Overapplied overhead** is the amount of factory overhead applied that exceeds the actual factory overhead cost.

When the applied overhead cost, which has been recorded on the credit side of the Factory Overhead Applied account, is less than the actual overhead cost recorded on the debit side of the Factory Overhead account, the firm has underapplied overhead. **Underapplied overhead** is the amount by which actual factory overhead exceeds the factory overhead applied.

Overapplied overhead is the amount of factory overhead applied that exceeds the actual factory overhead cost.

Underapplied overhead is the amount by which actual factory overhead exceeds the factory overhead applied.

Disposition of Underapplied and Overapplied Overhead

What do we do with the discrepancy between factory overhead applied and the actual amount of overhead incurred? Since actual production costs should be reported in the period they were incurred, total product costs at the end of the accounting period should be based on actual rather than applied overhead.

Underapplied or overapplied overhead can be disposed of in two ways:

1. Adjust the Cost of Goods Sold account.
2. Adjust the production costs of the period; that is, prorate the discrepancy among the amounts of the current period's applied overhead remaining in the ending balances of the Work-in-Process Inventory, the Finished Goods Inventory, and the Cost of Goods Sold accounts.

When the amount of underapplied or overapplied overhead is not a material amount, it generally is treated as a period cost and adjusted to the Cost of Goods Sold. On the other hand, if the amount is significant, it is often prorated.

Adjustment to Cost of Goods Sold

Adjusting to Cost of Goods Sold is the more expedient of the two methods for disposing of overhead discrepancies. The difference between the actual factory overhead incurred and the amount applied to production is disposed of by adding to or subtracting from the Cost of Goods Sold account for the period, whichever is appropriate.

LEARNING OBJECTIVE 6▶

Calculate underapplied and overapplied overhead and dispose of them properly at the end of the period.

Suppose that Smith Lighting Company applied $200,000 of overhead but found at the end of the year that the actual total amount of overhead incurred was $205,000. The $5,000 discrepancy represents underapplied overhead. The appropriate adjusting entry to the Cost of Goods Sold account is

Cost of Goods Sold	5,000	
Factory Overhead Applied	200,000	
Factory Overhead		205,000
To record the disposition of underapplied overhead.		

This entry closes the Factory Overhead and Factory Overhead Applied accounts and increases the cost of the goods sold for the period by $5,000.

To dispose of a variance only in the Cost of Goods Sold account ignores the fact that some portion of current production costs also can be in ending Work-in-Process Inventory or ending Finished Goods Inventory. Closing the variance to the Cost of Goods Sold account is acceptable from a practical point of view when the amount is not material and does not significantly distort the financial results.

If underapplied overhead for Smith Lighting Company is less than 5 percent of net income, this is probably an immaterial amount, and closing the underapplied overhead to the Cost of Goods Sold account is appropriate. After disposal of underapplied factory overhead, the cost of the goods sold for the period increases. On the other hand, disposal of overapplied factory overhead decreases the cost of the goods sold for the period.

Even if the amount of the variance is significant, the underapplied or overapplied factory overhead can still be disposed of in the Cost of Goods Sold account if the difference is a result of some operating characteristics pertaining only to the current period. A variance that is a result of a firm's current operations should be considered an expense in the current period and therefore be treated in the same manner.

Proration among Inventories and Cost of Goods Sold Accounts

Proration is the process of allocating underapplied or overapplied overhead to Work-in-Process Inventory, Finished Goods Inventory, and Cost of Goods Sold accounts.

Proration is the process of allocating underapplied or overapplied overhead to Work-in-Process Inventory, Finished Goods Inventory, and Cost of Goods Sold accounts.

Because factory overhead is one of the manufacturing cost elements that entered into the Work-in-Process Inventory account, underapplied or overapplied overhead affects the value of the work in process, which, in turn, affects the amount transferred out of the Work-in-Process Inventory account and charged to the Finished Goods Inventory account. Eventually, the amount in the Cost of Goods Sold account for the period is also affected because it is determined by the amount in the Finished Goods Inventory account.

If all units placed into production are completed and sold at the end of a period, adjusting for any discrepancy between actual overhead and applied overhead can be accomplished with entries to the Cost of Goods Sold account as just explained. If, on the other hand, all units processed are not completed and/or all units completed are not sold at the end of the period, the adjustment made for underapplied or overapplied overhead affects the Work-in-Process Inventory account and the Finished Goods Inventory account, in addition to the Cost of Goods Sold account. For these ending inventories to reflect the actual cost incurred, the amount of overapplied or underapplied overhead must be allocated to or prorated among the three accounts.

The proration of the variance is based on the current period's applied overhead in the ending inventories of the Work-in-Process Inventory, Finished Goods Inventory, and Cost of Goods Sold accounts at the end of the period. To determine the ratios for the proration, we compute the sum of the applied overhead in the ending inventories of the Work-in-Process Inventory, Finished Goods Inventory, and Cost of Goods Sold accounts at the end of the period. The ratio of each of the components to this sum is the amount of the underapplied or overapplied overhead that should be prorated to the cost of the component.

To illustrate the proration of an overhead variance, assume that Smith Lighting Company's accounts had the following applied overhead balances for the end of period:

Smith Lighting Company Operational Data

Ending Work-in-process inventory	$ 20,000
Ending Finished goods inventory	30,000
Cost of goods sold	150,000
Total factory overhead applied	$200,000
Factory overhead (actual)	$205,000

Suppose that Smith uses the Factory Overhead account to record the actual overhead incurred and the Factory Overhead Applied account to record the application of overhead to the job. The proration of the $5,000 underapplied factory overhead among the Work-in-Process Inventory, Finished Goods Inventory, and Cost of Goods Sold accounts is computed as follows:

Amount	Applied Overhead	Underapplied Percentage of Total	Overhead Prorated
Work-in-process inventory	$ 20,000	10%	$ 500
Finished goods inventory	30,000	15	750
Cost of goods sold	150,000	75	3,750
Total	$200,000	100%	$5,000

The appropriate adjusting entry is

Factory Overhead Applied	200,000	
Work-in-Process Inventory	500	
Finished Goods Inventory	750	
Cost of Goods Sold	3,750	
Factory Overhead		205,000

To record the proration of the underapplied overhead.

Some firms prefer to use the balances of Work-in-Process Inventory, Finished Goods Inventory, and Cost of Goods Sold accounts rather than the applied overhead in the accounts to calculate the percentages.

When a substantial variance between the actual factory overhead incurred and the factory overhead applied occurs, the total manufacturing cost as recorded on the debit side of the Work-in-Process Inventory account is understated (underapplication) or overstated (overapplication). Left unadjusted, the inventory and Cost of Goods Sold accounts would be substantially distorted.

No matter which method is used, underapplied or overapplied overhead is usually adjusted only at the end of a year. Nothing needs to be done about any variances during the year because the predetermined factory overhead rate is based on annual figures. A variance is expected between the actual overhead incurred and the amount applied in a particular month or quarter because of seasonal fluctuations in the firm's operating cycle or other incidental events. Furthermore, an underapplied factory overhead in one month is likely to be offset by an overapplied amount in another month (and vice versa).

ILLUSTRATION OF A JOB COSTING SYSTEM

Thomasville Furniture Industries, Inc. (TFI) (www.thomasville.com), located in Thomasville, North Carolina, has manufactured high-quality home and office furniture for more than a century. TFI's products are made from the finest materials, including hardwoods such as cherry, poplar, maple, elm, mahogany, and oak, and high-quality upholstery materials. The tables and chairs are produced in plants located in and around Thomasville; the upholstered products, such as sofas and chairs, are made in the western part of the state.

The production process for a furniture product requires several steps, including cutting, assembling, and finishing. The materials used in the production of each piece of furniture are described in detail in the *bill of materials*, a list of different materials needed to manufacture a product or part. For example, the bill of materials for TFI's Georgian end table includes 30 different items; a portion of that bill of materials appears in Exhibit 12–8. The table in Exhibit 12–9 is an example.

TFI has hundreds of production jobs in process at any time. For our illustration, we consider simplified, fictitious data from production job X4J-14531 for Georgian end tables. The related transactions, also using fictitious numbers, follow.

Materials Purchased and Used

The eight parts to a Georgian end table include a table top, drawer front panel, side panels, and front apron rail. Each part consists of several materials. The table top, for example, includes five pieces and the drawer front panel includes eight pieces. The table top requires a sheet of $27 \times 21 \times \frac{9}{16}$ inch 5-ply elm.

Assume that the Materials Inventory account has a $10,000 balance on January 1, 2001. This journal entry records the purchase of $25,000 of materials during January:

(1)	Materials Inventory	25,000	
	Accounts Payable		25,000
	To record the purchase of materials.		

Exhibit 12–8 Bill of Materials

Thomasville Furniture Industries, Inc.
Bill of Materials

CHANGES FOR 14521–211

PLANT "T"

STYLE 14531–210 ARTICLE "END TABLE" DATE 1–19–01 SHEET 1 OF 1

LINE		NO. PCS.	DESCRIPTION	FINISH SIZE L	FINISH SIZE W	FINISH SIZE T	FINISH SIZE BS	MULTI	ROUGH SIZE L	ROUGH SIZE W	ROUGH SIZE T	FOOTAGE	SKETCH
1	14531–210 ONLY	1	TOP	26	20	13/16		1	27	21	9/16		
2		1/2	TOP CORE					1	17	47 1/2	3/4		
3		1	TOP CORE SIDE BANDS	47 1/2	2	3/4		1	47 1/2	2	4/4		
4		2	TOP CORE FRT. & BK. BANDS	21	2	3/4		1	21	2	4/4		
5													
6		2	SIDE PANELS	22 3/8	4 15/16	3/4	21 3/8	4	23 7/8	21 3/4	5/8		4/4 POP CORE
7		2	SIDE APRON RAIL	22 3/8	1 7/8	1 7/16	21 3/8	1	23 3/8	2 1/8	8/4		
8		1	BACK PANEL	16 3/8	4 15/16	3/4	15 3/8	4	17 7/8	21 3/4	5/8		4/4 POP CORE
9		1	BACK APRON RAIL	16 3/8	1 7/8	1 7/16	15 3/8	1	17 3/8	2 1/8	8/4		
10		2	FRONT POST	22 3/4	2 1/2	2 1/2		1	23 3/4	2 3/4	3 pcs 5/4		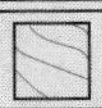
11		2	BACK POST	22 3/4	2 1/2	2 1/2		1	23 3/4	2 3/4	3 pcs 5/4		
12													
13	14531–210 ONLY	1	DRAWER FRONT	14 7/8	3 7/8	3/4		3	16 7/16	16 5/16	5/8		4/4 POP CORE
14		2	DWR. SIDES	20	3	7/16		1	21	3 1/4	5/8		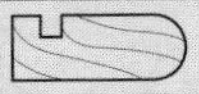
15		1	DWR. BACK	14 11/16	2 7/8	7/16							
16		1	DWR. BOTTOM	14 1/4	19 13/16	3/16		1	15 3/4	20 7/8	R.C.		
17		1	DWR. GUIDE—FEMALE	20 1/2	1 31/32	9/16	19 13/16	1	21 1/2	2 1/4	4/4		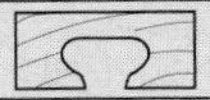
18		1	DWR. GUIDE—MALE	22 1/2	1	1/2		1	23 1/2	1 1/4	4/4		
19		1	DWR. HOWE PULL										
20													

Exhibit 12–8 Continued

21													
22		1	PART. FRT. RAIL BOTT.	16 1/2	1 1/2	3/4	15 3/8	1	17 1/2	1 3/4	4/4		
23		1	DUST FRM. BK. RAIL BOTT.	16 1/2	1 1/2	3/4	15 3/8	1	17 1/2	1 3/4	4/4		
24		2	DUST FRM. END RAIL	20 9/16	1 1/4	3/4	19 9/16	1	21 5/8	1 1/2	4/4		
25													
26		1	FRONT APRON RAIL	16 3/8	1 7/8	17/16	15 3/8	1	17 3/8	2 1/8	8/4		
27		1	TOP FRT. PART. RAIL	16 1/2	1 3/4	3/4	15 3/8	1	17 1/2	2	4/4		
28		1	TOP FRT. PAR. RAIL MLDG.	15 3/8	3/4	3/4		1	16 3/8	1	4/4		
29		1	DWR. BOTT. FILLER MLDG.	15 3/8	3/16	11/16		1	16 3/8	7/16	4/4		
30		2	DWR. END FILLER MLDG.	4 3/8	3/16	11/16		3	16 3/8	7/16	4/4		
31		3	TOP BACK SCREW CLEAT	12	3/4	3/4		1	13	1	4/4		
32													
33													
34													
35		4	PLASTIC FLOOR GUIDES										
36													
37													
38			#14531 – 211 { SAME AS 14531–210 EXCEPT OMIT LINE #1–#13										
39			AND ADD THE FOLLOWING										
40													
41	14531–211 ONLY	1	TOP	26	20	13/16		1	27	21	9/16		
42	14531–211 ONLY	1	DWR. FRONT	14 7/8	3 7/8	3/4		3	16 3/8	13 1/8	5/8		4/4 POP CORE
43													
44													
45													

Exhibit 12–9 Georgian End Table

Assume now that the company has a $5,000 beginning balance in the Work-in-Process Inventory account. During January, the company issued $20,000 in direct materials to its production departments for this job. The use of direct materials is recorded on the credit side of the Materials Inventory account and on the debit side of the Work-in-Process Inventory account:

(2)	Work-in-Process Inventory	20,000	
	Materials Inventory		20,000
	To record the use of direct materials.		

In addition, the company used $3,000 in indirect materials for this job. The issuance of indirect materials to production is recorded on the debit side of the Factory Overhead account and on the credit side of the Materials Inventory account:

(3)	Factory Overhead	3,000	
	Materials Inventory		3,000
	To record the use of indirect materials.		

Labor Costs Incurred

TFI incurred $70,000 in direct labor cost for job X4J-14531. This cost is recorded by debiting the Work-in-Process Inventory account and crediting the Accrued Payroll account:

(4)	Work-in-Process Inventory	70,000	
	Accrued Payroll		70,000
	To record direct labor cost incurred.		

The company also incurred $2,500 in indirect labor costs including the salaries of supervisors, inspectors, and materials handlers. The total indirect labor cost is recorded in the company's books by debiting the Factory Overhead account and crediting the Accrued Payroll account:

(5)	Factory Overhead	2,500	
	Accrued Payroll		2,500
	To record indirect labor cost incurred.		

Actual and Applied Factory Overhead Costs

Unlike direct materials and direct labor, the actual factory overhead is not entered directly into the Work-in-Process Inventory account, as evidenced by the recording of indirect materials and indirect labor costs incurred earlier. The actual factory overhead incurred is recorded on the debit side of the Factory Overhead account. Thus, the debit side of the Factory Overhead account includes indirect materials used, indirect labor incurred, and other factory overhead expenses.

TFI incurred other factory overhead expenses for this job including utilities ($1,000), depreciation on factory equipment ($4,000), and insurance on factory equipment ($500). These amounts are recorded on the debit side of the Factory Overhead account and on the credit side of other appropriate accounts:

(6)	Factory Overhead	5,500	
	Accounts Payable		1,000
	Accumulated Depreciation—Factory		4,000
	Prepaid Insurance		500
	To record actual factory overhead costs.		

TFI applies factory overhead on the basis of direct labor cost. Suppose that the firm estimated its total factory overhead for the year as $30,000,000, and the direct labor cost as $200,000,000. The factory overhead thus was applied at the rate of $0.15 ($30,000,000/$200,000,000) per $1.00 of direct labor costs. The actual direct labor cost for this job was $70,000; therefore the factory overhead applied was $10,500 ($0.15 × $70,000).

The $10,500 factory overhead charged to production is recorded by debiting the Work-in-Process Inventory account and crediting the Factory Overhead Applied account:

(7)	Work-in-Process Inventory	10,500	
	Factory Overhead Applied		10,500
	To record the application of factory overhead to the job.		

Completion of a Job

On completion of a production job, the total production costs of the completed units are transferred from the Work-in-Process Inventory account to the Finished Goods Inventory account. Suppose that TFI had a $5,000 beginning balance in the Finished Goods Inventory account. The company completed $80,000 worth of goods during January 2001. This amount was transferred from the Work-in-Process Inventory account to the Finished Goods Inventory account by crediting the Work-in-Process Inventory and debiting the Finished Goods Inventory account:

(8)	Finished Goods Inventory	80,000	
	Work-in-Process Inventory		80,000
	To record the cost of goods completed.		

Exhibit 12–10 is a cost estimate sheet used by Thomasville Furniture Industries, Inc.

Spoilage sometimes occurs during the manufacturing process. Management accountants must distinguish between normal spoilage and abnormal spoilage because each is treated differently. Normal spoilage occurs under efficient operating conditions and is charged to a specific job or allocated to all jobs. Abnormal spoilage is not expected under efficient operating conditions and is treated as a loss in the period it is detected. Spoilage is discussed in more detail in Appendix A to this chapter.

Exhibit 12–10   Sample Cost Estimate

DATE _____

PLANT _____

SUITE NO. _____   ITEM NO. _____   DESCRIPTION _____

Lumber:	Net Mat'ls	Price	Drawer Stock:	Net Mat'ls	Price
4/4					
4/4					
5/4					
6/4			Total Drawer Stock	→	$
8/4			Carvings:		
Total Lumber	→	$	Total Carvings w/o waste	xxxxxx	
Face Veneer:			Total Carvings Incl. waste 7	→	$
			Cabinet Hdwe.		
			Total Cab. Hdwe. w/o waste	xxxxxx	
			Total Cab. Hdwe Incl. waste 4	→	$
			Hard Board:		
			Total Hard Board	→	$
			Finishing Materials:	→	$
			Mirrors & Glass:		
Total Face w/o waste	xxxxxx		Total M & G w/o waste	xxxxxx	
Total Face Incl. waste 7–8	→	$	Total M & G Incl. waste 2	→	$
Commercial Veneer:			Stone:		
			Total Stone w/o waste	xxxxxx	
			Total Stone Incl. waste 5	→	$
			Trim Hdwe.		
Total Commercial Veneer	→	$			
Glue:		7			
	→	$			
Chipcore:					
			Tot. Trim w/o waste	xxxxxx	
			Tot. Trim Incl. waste 5	→	$
			Packing	→	$
Total Chipcore	→	$	Crating	→	$
Plastic F & B					
Total Plastic F & B w/o waste	xxxxxx				
Total Plastic F & B Incl. waste 5	→	$			
Molded Plastic Parts:					
			Total Material	$	
			Labor Hrs. @ $ /hr.	$	
			Direct Overhead	$	
			Period Overhead	$	
			Factory Cost	$	
Total Mold Plastic w/o waste	xxxxxx		S & A %	$	
Total Mold Plastic Incl. waste 4	→	$	Total Cost	$	
			Chair Seat	$	
			Total Chair Cost	$	

Mechanics of Job Costing

1. Record the costs of direct materials and direct labor used for each job in the Work-in-Process Inventory account.
2. Compute and record the amount of overhead assigned to each job.
3. Determine the job's total cost and unit cost.

Sale of Goods

Assume that TFI sold most of the furniture from job X4J-14531 with a total cost of $70,000 in January 2001. The firm records the journal entry by debiting the Cost of Goods Sold account and crediting the Finished Goods Inventory account:

(9)	Cost of Goods Sold	70,000	
	Finished Goods Inventory		70,000
	To record the cost of goods sold.		

In addition, an entry must record the revenue received from the sale of the goods. Assume that TFI marks up its products at 200 percent of cost. The journal entry to record the sales revenues received from the sale in January 2001 is as follows:

(10)	Accounts Receivable	210,000	
	Sales		210,000
	To record the sale of goods.		

Assume that TFI had the following selling and administrative expenses in January in addition to factory overhead costs:

Advertising expenses	$20,000
Sales commissions	21,000
Office salaries	30,000
Depreciation—Office equipment	2,000
Other administrative expenses	7,000

The first two items are selling expenses; the last three are administrative expenses. The following compound journal entry records these expenses:

(11)	Selling Expenses	41,000	
	Administrative Expenses	39,000	
	Accounts Payable		27,000
	Accrued Payroll		51,000
	Accumulated Depreciation—Office		2,000

Underapplied Overhead

From journal entries (3), (5), and (6), TFI determined that it incurred total actual factory overhead costs of $11,000, but only $10,500 of factory overhead had been applied to Work-in-Process Inventory in journal entry (7). The underapplied overhead amount is

Actual factory overhead	
Indirect materials	$ 3,000
Indirect labor	2,500
Other factory overhead	5,500
Total	$11,000
Applied factory overhead	10,500
Underapplied overhead	$ 500

If we assume that TFI closed the underapplied overhead to the Cost of Goods Sold account, the required journal entry is

(12)	Cost of Goods Sold	500	
	Factory Overhead Applied	10,500	
	Factory Overhead		11,000

Posting Journal Entries to the General Ledger

Exhibit 12–11 shows cost flows through related general ledger T-accounts in the Thomasville Furniture Industries job costing example.

Exhibit 12–11`   General Ledger Accounts for Thomasville Furniture Industries

Materials Inventory		Accounts Payable	
Bal. 10,000	(2) 20,000		(1) 25,000
(1) 25,000	(3) 3,000		(6) 1,000
Bal. 12,000			(11) 27,000

Work-in-Process Inventory		Factory Overhead	
Bal. 5,000	(8) 80,000	(3) 3,000	(12) 11,000
(2) 20,000		(5) 2,500	
(4) 70,000		(6) 5,500	
(7) 10,500		Total 11,000	
Bal. 25,500			

Factory Overhead Applied		Accrued Payroll	
(12) 10,500	(7) 10,500		(4) 70,000
			(5) 2,500
			(11) 51,000

Finished Goods Inventory		Accumulated Depreciation	
Bal. 5,000	(9) 70,000		(6) 4,000
(8) 80,000			(11) 2,000
Bal. 15,000			

Cost of Goods Sold		Prepaid Insurance	
(9) 70,000			(6) 500
(12) 500			

Sales		Accounts Receivable	
	(10) 210,000	(10) 210,000	

Selling Expenses		Administrative Expenses	
(11) 41,000		(11) 39,000	

Schedule of Cost of Goods Manufactured and Sold

Many manufacturing firms periodically prepare a **schedule of cost of goods manufactured and sold** for management use; other firms prepare two separate schedules, a schedule of cost of goods manufactured and a schedule of cost of goods sold. The single schedule shows the manufacturing costs incurred, the change in the work-in-process inventory, the cost of the goods sold, and the change in finished goods inventory during the period. Cost of goods manufactured is the total cost of direct materials, direct labor, and factory overhead transferred from the Work-in-Process Inventory account to the Finished Goods Inventory account during an accounting period.

Exhibit 12–12 displays TFI's January 2001 schedule of cost of goods manufactured and sold. The schedule shows the costs of direct materials, direct labor, applied factory overhead, and cost of goods manufactured carried at normal cost rather than the actual cost. It also shows the normal cost of goods sold before adjustment for the

Schedule of cost of goods manufactured and sold shows the manufacturing costs incurred, the change in the work-in-process inventory, the cost of goods sold, and the change in finished goods inventory during the period.

Exhibit 12–12   Schedule of Cost of Goods Manufactured and Sold

THOMASVILLE FURNITURE INDUSTRIES, INC.
Schedule of Cost of Goods Manufactured and Sold*
For the Month Ended January 31, 2001

Direct materials		
Beginning materials inventory	$ 10,000	
Purchase of materials	25,000	
Total materials available	$ 35,000	
Deduct: Ending materials inventory	(12,000)	
Indirect materials used	(3,000)	
Direct materials used		$ 20,000
Direct labor		70,000
Factory overhead applied		10,500
Total manufacturing costs incurred		$100,500
Add: Beginning work-in-process inventory		5,000
Total manufacturing costs to account for		$105,500
Deduct: Ending work-in-process inventory		(25,500)
Cost of goods manufactured		$ 80,000
Add: Beginning finished goods inventory		5,000
Cost of goods available for sale		$ 85,000
Deduct: Ending finished goods inventory		(15,000)
Normal cost of goods sold		$ 70,000
Add: Underapplied overhead		500
Cost of goods sold (adjusted for underapplied overhead)		$ 70,500

*The figures are fictitious.

Exhibit 12–13   Income Statement

THOMASVILLE FURNITURE INDUSTRIES, INC.
Income Statement*
For the Month Ended January 31, 2001

Sales		$210,000
Cost of goods sold (from Exhibit 12–12)		(70,500)
Gross margin		$139,500
Selling and administrative expenses		
Selling expenses	$ 41,000	
Administrative expenses	39,000	(80,000)
Net income		$ 59,500

*The figures are fictitious.

underapplied overhead and the adjusted cost of goods sold after adjustment for the underapplied overhead. Exhibit 12–13 is the company's income statement.

CONTEMPORARY MANUFACTURING ENVIRONMENT

Plantwide Rate

Many firms have two or more production departments. They can assign factory overhead costs to jobs or products using either a single plantwide overhead rate or a separate departmental overhead rate for each production department.

A **plantwide overhead rate** is a single overhead rate used throughout the entire production facility. It is computed by dividing total plant factory overhead by an activity base or cost driver common to all jobs worked in all departments.

In some production processes, the relationship between factory overhead costs and various cost drivers differs substantially among production departments. For example, some production departments are labor intensive while others are highly automated. It is inappropriate, therefore, for a firm to use a single plantwide overhead application rate for jobs processed by various departments. A labor-intensive department could use a factory overhead application rate based on direct labor while a highly automated department could use an application rate based on machine usage. The use of departmental overhead rates might be required because they produce more accurate overhead cost assignments for individual jobs.

Departmental Overhead Rate

A **departmental overhead rate** is an overhead rate calculated for a single production department. It is computed by dividing total budgeted departmental factory overhead by the budgeted level of a cost driver common to all jobs worked or processed by the department. Firms that use a departmental overhead rate keep separate factory overhead and applied accounts for each department.

The ideal criterion for choosing an allocation base is a cause-and-effect relationship. A plantwide rate is appropriate when all products pass through the same processes or all departments are similar. Departmental rates are appropriate when the converse is true.

Western Furniture Company's practice illustrates the misuse of a single plantwide overhead rate. Assume that this manufacturer has two departments, cutting and finishing. The cutting department is a machine-intensive department, but the finishing department is labor intensive. The company has budgeted the following for the year:

	Cutting Department	Finishing Department	Total
Budgeted overhead	$600,000	$300,000	$900,000
Budgeted labor-hours	10,000	50,000	60,000
Budgeted machine-hours	30,000	3,000	33,000

Assume that the company uses a single plantwide labor-hour overhead rate as the cost driver for overhead allocation. The single predetermined overhead rate is computed as follows:

$$\frac{\text{Budgeted overhead}}{\text{Budgeted labor-hours}} = \frac{\$900,000}{60,000} = \$15 \text{ per labor-hour}$$

During the first week of the year, the company works on two jobs, 1XA3 and 2YQ4. Job 1XA3 is labor intensive, but job 2YQ4 is machine intensive. The company has the following information on the number of labor- and machine-hours required to complete the work:

	Cutting Department	Finishing Department
Job 1XA3		
Labor-hours	100	800
Machine-hours	200	20
Job 2YQ4		
Labor-hours	100	200
Machine-hours	400	40

Exhibit 12–14 shows the factory overhead costs applied to the two jobs using the labor-hour-based plantwide overhead rate. Notice that the overhead allocation is

inaccurate under a single plantwide rate. That is, job 1XA3 uses 220 machine-hours while job 2YQ4 uses 440 machine-hours, yet job 1XA3 has almost three times as much applied overhead. Because more of the overhead (depreciation, maintenance, etc.) relates to the use of machines, job 2YQ4 should be charged more overhead.

To obtain more accurate product costing information, assume that Western Furniture Company decides to use two separate departmental overhead rates for overhead costs, with a machine-hour-based overhead rate for the cutting department and a labor-hour-based overhead rate for the finishing department. The departmental predetermined overhead rates are calculated as follows:

Cutting Department Overhead Rate

$$\frac{\text{Budgeted overhead}}{\text{Budgeted machine-hours}} = \frac{\$600,000}{30,000} = \$20 \text{ per machine-hour}$$

Finishing Department Overhead Rate

$$\frac{\text{Budgeted overhead}}{\text{Budgeted labor-hours}} = \frac{\$300,000}{50,000} = \$6 \text{ per labor-hour}$$

Exhibit 12–15 presents the factory overhead cost assigned to the two jobs using departmental overhead rates.

These calculations show that the applied overhead costs with the single plantwide overhead rate are $4,700 ($13,500 – $8,800) higher for job 1XA3 and $4,700 ($9,200 – $4,500) lower for job 2YQ4 than had the firm used the two departmental overhead rates. Job 2YQ4 requires considerably more machine-hours than job 1XA3, but the overhead cost allocation to jobs with the single rate does not consider these differ-

Exhibit 12–14	**Western Furniture Company's Factory Overhead Allocation Using a Plantwide Overhead Rate**		
		Job	
		1XA3	2YQ4
Cutting department			
$15 × 100		$ 1,500	
$15 × 100			$1,500
Finishing department			
$15 × 800		12,000	
$15 × 200			3,000
Total overhead applied		$13,500	$4,500

Exhibit 12–15	**Western Furniture Company's Factory Overhead Allocation Using Departmental Overhead Rates**		
		Job	
		1XA3	2YQ4
Cutting department: Machine-hours			
$20 × 200		$4,000	
$20 × 400			$8,000
Finishing department: Labor-hours			
$6 × 800		4,800	
$6 × 200			1,200
Total overhead applied		$8,800	$9,200

ences. Using departmental rates, product cost more accurately reflects the different amounts and types of machine and labor work performed on the two jobs.

The departmental overhead allocation is more accurate than the single plantwide overhead for Western Furniture because it makes two improvements: departmental rates and different bases. Prices based on the plant rate are inaccurate and lead to pricing errors. In this case, job 1XA3 is significantly overcharged using the plant rate, resulting in noncompetitive prices. Similarly, job 2YQ4 is underpriced. On balance, Western Furniture is losing 1XA3 business (which is profitable to the firm) and getting too much 2YQ4 business (which is not profitable because the firm's prices are too low). In the long run, the firm will become less and less profitable using these prices.

Cost Drivers and Activity-Based Costing

The recent effort to make U.S. companies more competitive in the world market has created a demand for new cost management systems. Traditional cost accounting systems do a poor job of product costing because they use only volume-based cost drivers. These systems seldom reflect changes in major cost categories that follow increasing plant automation.

Traditional product costing systems allocate overhead to products or jobs using a volume-based cost driver, such as direct labor-hours or dollars. An automated factory environment requires only a minimal direct labor cost and a significantly higher fixed factory overhead than does an older manual factory. Using direct labor-hours or dollars as the cost driver to allocate overhead seriously distorts product costs in an automated factory. In addition, some factory overhead costs are not volume based. For example, machine setup cost is batch based, and product design cost is product based. Thus, traditional volume-based overhead allocation can lead to inaccurate product costing.

Activity-based costing (ABC), assigns factory overhead costs to products or services using cause-and-effect criteria with multiple cost pools. The use of both volume-based and nonvolume-based cost drivers is determined according to the consumption of resources in performing various activities. ABC systems help firms achieve their strategies.

Southern Instruments, Inc., makes specialized instruments for customers to detect water contamination. The company uses multiple cost drivers as overhead allocation bases. Its budgeted overhead cost for each cost pool and cost driver information are shown in Exhibit 12–16.

Suppose that while completing job 5ZN1 with 200 units and job 10XY1 with 800 units, the firm consumed the following resources:

	Job 5ZN1	Job 10XY1
Machine-hours	1,000	4,000
Material handling (pounds)	5,000	15,000
Number of setups	100	100
Number of inspections	200	300

◄**LEARNING OBJECTIVE 7**

Explain why multiple overhead rates and cost drivers could be preferred to a single, plantwide overhead rate.

Exhibit 12–16	Southern Instruments' Overhead and Cost Driver Information		
Overhead Cost Pool	**Budgeted Overhead Cost**	**Cost Driver for This Cost Pool**	**Expected Activity Level**
Power	$ 50,000	Machine-hours	5,000
Materials handling	40,000	Materials weight (lb.)	20,000
Machine setups	60,000	Number of setups	200
Quality control	50,000	Number of inspections	500
Total	$200,000		

The firm uses machine-hours as the single plantwide cost driver to apply overhead costs to job 5ZN1 and job 10XY1:

1. Predetermined overhead rate for the machine-hour cost driver:
   $200,000/5,000 = $40 per machine-hour

2. Overhead costs applied using traditional costing:
   Job 5ZN1 $40 × 1,000 = $ 40,000
   Job 10XY1 $40 × 4,000 = $160,000

The firm's management accountant recently attended an activity-based costing seminar and had proposed the use of multiple cost drivers of machine-hours, materials weight, number of setups, and number of inspections to apply different overhead costs to jobs. Using the ABC approach, the allocation of overhead costs to job 5ZN1 and job 10XY1 involves the following steps:

1. Compute predetermined cost driver rates:
   Power $50,000/5,000 = $10 per machine-hour
   Materials handling $40,000/20,000 = $2 per pound
   Machine setups $60,000/200 = $300 per setup
   Quality control $50,000/500 = $100 per inspection

2. Apply overhead costs to jobs using activity-level and cost driver rates:

	Job 5ZN1	Job 10XY1
Power	$10,000	$ 40,000
Materials handling	10,000	30,000
Machine setups	30,000	30,000
Quality control	20,000	30,000
Total overhead assigned	$70,000	$130,000

Note that the traditional plantwide volume-based overhead method overcosts the high-volume job 10XY1 by $30,000 ($160,000 – $130,000) and undercosts the low-volume job 5ZN1 by $30,000 ($70,000 – $40,000). This overcosting or undercosting could lead management to make incorrect pricing decisions and use false information on the size of gross profits earned.

JOB COSTING FOR SERVICE INDUSTRIES

Job costing is used extensively in service industries such as advertising agencies, construction companies, hospitals, and repair shops, as well as consulting, architecture, accounting, and law firms. Instead of using the term *job*, accounting and consulting firms use the term *client* or *project*; hospitals and law firms use the term *case*, and advertising agencies and construction companies use the term *contract* or *project*. Many firms use the term *project costing* to indicate the use of job costing in service industries.

LEARNING OBJECTIVE 8▶

Apply job costing concepts to service industries.

Job costing in service industries uses recording procedures and accounts similar to those illustrated earlier in this chapter except for direct materials involved (there could be none or an insignificant amount). The primary focus is on direct labor performance. The overhead costs are usually applied to jobs based on direct labor-hours or dollars.

Suppose that Freed and Swenson, a Los Angeles law firm, has the following budget for 2001:

Compensation of professional staff	$ 500,000
Other costs	500,000
Total budgeted costs for 2001	$1,000,000

Other costs include indirect materials and supplies, photocopying, computer-related expenses, insurance, office rent, utilities, training costs, accounting fees, indirect labor costs for office support personnel, and other office expenses.

Freed and Swenson charges overhead costs to clients or jobs at a predetermined percentage of the professional salaries charged to the client. The law firm's recent data show that chargeable hours average 80 percent of available hours for all categories of professional personnel. The nonchargeable hours are regarded as additional overhead. This nonchargeable time might involve training, idle time, inefficiency in resource allocation, and similar factors.

Using these data, the firm's budgeted direct labor costs and budgeted overhead costs are calculated:

1. Budgeted direct labor costs:
   $500,000 × 80% = $400,000

2. Budgeted overhead costs:

Other costs	$500,000
Salary costs for nonchargeable hours:	
$500,000 – $400,000 =	100,000
	$600,000

The predetermined overhead rate is

$$\frac{\text{Budgeted overhead costs}}{\text{Budgeted direct labor costs}} = \frac{\$600,000}{\$400,000} = 150\%$$

Exhibit 12–17 presents relevant data and job costs for the law firm's recent client, George Christatos.

Exhibit 12–17 Job Costing for Freed and Swenson Law Firm

Client: George Christatos

Employee Charges	Hours	Salary Rates	Billing Rates (300 percent)
Partners	10	$80	$240
Managers	20	50	150
Associates	100	20	60
	130		

Total Revenues and Costs for This Client's Job

Service revenues	($240 × 10) + ($150 × 20) + ($60 × 100) = $11,400

Cost of services

Direct labor ($80 × 10) + $ (50 × 20)			
+ ($20 × 100)	= $3,800		
Overhead $3,800 × 150%	= 5,700		
Total costs of services			9,500
Operating income			$1,900

Job Costing at an Advertising Agency

The job costing system used by a New York City advertising agency provided information that assisted management in identifying highly profitable and extremely unprofitable accounts. The advertising agency used its job costing system to discover that a certain account was being served by personnel at a supervisory level while less expensive staff-level personnel would have been adequate. The firm then decided to assign staff personnel to the account, resulting in considerable savings. The job costing system also aided in budgeting costs and revenues for various accounts so that account managers could more effectively manage them. Overall, the system helped the firm improve its planning, control, and performance evaluation processes.

Based on information in William B. Mills, "Drawing Up a Budgeting System for an Ad Agency," *Management Accounting,* December 1983, pp. 47–49.

Gallup Organization, Inc., a firm that provides nationwide opinion polls, developed a job costing system to manage its cost information for 32 cost categories and more than 300 overlapping jobs per year. The system provides timely reports of job costs by cost category (data entry, mailroom, marketing, travel, computer, ballot cost) and by job phase (planning, design, production, report). The job cost report by job phase is illustrated in Exhibit 12–18. The information provided by the firm's job costing system assisted management in estimating costs and bidding more accurately, in controlling cost better, and in increasing profits.

Based on information in Michael A. Kole, "Controlling Costs with a Database System," *Management Accounting*, June 1988, pp. 31–35.

Exhibit 12–18 Gallup Organization's Job Cost Report

JOB BCL2001 MICROCOMPUTERS* Group—LAW Study Director—JAM

Cost Group	Planning	Design	Production	Report	Cost	Percent
Professional salaries	$ 800	$1,000	$1,200	$1,000	$ 4,000	33.3%
Staff salaries	700	800	900	800	3,200	26.7
Direct costs	600	700	800	700	2,800	23.3
Total direct	$2,100	$2,500	$2,900	$2,500	$10,000	
Shared costs	400	500	600	500	2,000	16.7
Total	$2,500	$3,000	$3,500	$3,000	$12,000	

*The figures are fictitious.

Based on information in Michael A. Kole, "Controlling Costs with a Database System," *Management Accounting*, June 1988, p. 33.

OPERATION COSTING

Operation costing is a hybrid costing system that uses job costing to assign direct materials costs and process costing to assign conversion costs to products or services.

Operation costing is a hybrid costing system that uses job costing to assign direct materials costs as well as process costing to assign conversion costs to products or services.

Manufacturing operations whose conversion activities are very similar across high-volume production of several product lines, but whose direct materials used in the various products differ significantly use operation costing. After direct labor and factory overhead conversion costs have been accumulated by operations or departments, accountants use process costing methods to assign these costs to products or services. On the other hand, direct materials costs are accumulated by jobs or batches, and job costing assigns these costs to products or services.

LEARNING OBJECTIVE 9▶

Describe and explain an operation costing system.

Industries suitable for applying operation costing include clothing, food processing, textiles, shoes, furniture, metalworking, jewelry, and electronic equipment. For example, chair manufacturing has two standard operations: cutting and assembling. Different jobs, however, require different wood and fabric materials. Therefore, an operation costing system is well suited for this situation.

Irvine Glass Company manufactures two types of glass for sheets, clear glass and colored glass. Department 1 produces clear glass sheets, some of which are sold as finished goods. Others are transferred to Department 2, which adds metallic oxides to clear glass sheets to form colored glass sheets, which are then sold as finished goods. The company uses operation costing.

Irvine Glass Company finished two jobs: Job A produced 10,000 sheets of clear glass and job B produced 5,000 sheets of colored glass. March manufacturing operations and costs applied to these products follow. No beginning or ending work-in-process inventory existed in March.

Direct materials		
Job A (10,000 clear glass sheets)		$400,000
Job B (5,000 colored glass sheets)		
Materials for clear glass sheets in Department 1	$200,000	
Materials added to clear glass sheets in Department 2	100,000	300,000
Total direct materials		$700,000
Conversion costs		
Department 1		$180,000
Department 2		50,000
Total conversion costs		$230,000
Total costs (Direct materials costs $700,000 + Conversion costs $230,000)		$930,000

Notice in this table that operation costing identifies direct materials by job but that it identifies conversion costs with the two production departments.

The product cost for each type of glass sheet is computed as follows:

	Clear Glass	Colored Glass
Direct materials		
Job A ($400,000/10,000)	$40	
Job B ($300,000/5,000)		$60
Conversion: Department 1 ($180,000/15,000)	12	12
Conversion: Department 2 ($50,000/5,000)		10
Total product cost per unit	$52	$82

Notice in this table that each glass sheet receives the same conversion costs in Department 1 since this operation is identical for the two products. Total product costs are calculated as follows:

Clear glass sheets ($52 × 10,000)	$520,000
Colored glass sheets ($82 × 5,000)	410,000
Total	$930,000

The following journal entries record Irvine Glass Company's flow of costs. Department 1 makes the first entry by recording the requisition of direct materials when job A entered production:

Work-in-Process Inventory: Department 1	400,000	
Materials Inventory		400,000

Department 2 makes the following entry to record the requisition of direct materials when job B enters production:

Work-in-Process Inventory: Department 2	200,000	
Materials Inventory		200,000

Conversion costs are applied in Department 1 with the following journal entry:

Work-in-Process Inventory: Department 1	180,000	
Conversion Costs Applied		180,000

The following entry records the transfer of completed clear glass sheets to finished goods:

Finished Goods Inventory	520,000	
Work-in-Process Inventory: Department 1		520,000

Direct materials $400,000 + Conversion ($12 × 10,000) = $520,000

The following entry records the transfer of partially completed colored glass sheets to Department 2:

Work-in-Process Inventory: Department 2	260,000	
Work-in-Process Inventory: Department 1		260,000

Direct materials $200,000 + Conversion ($12 × 5,000) = $260,000

The following entry records the requisition of the materials by Department 2 when job B enters production:

Work-in-Process Inventory: Department 2	100,000	
Materials Inventory		100,000

Conversion costs are applied in Department 2 with the following journal entry.

Work-in-Process Inventory: Department 2	50,000	
Conversion Costs Applied		50,000

Finally, the completed colored glass sheets are transferred to finished goods.

Finished Goods Inventory	410,000	
Work-in-Process Inventory: Department 2		410,000

Department 2 work-in-process $260,000 + Materials for colored glass $100,000 + Conversions ($10 × 5,000) = $410,000

SUMMARY

Product costing is the process of accumulating, classifying, and assigning direct materials, direct labor, and factory overhead costs to products or services. Product costing provides useful cost information for both manufacturing and nonmanufacturing firms for (1) product and service cost determination and inventory valuation, (2) management planning, cost control, and performance evaluation, and (3) managerial decisions.

Several different product costing systems are available and can be classified as the (1) cost accumulation method—job or processing costing systems, (2) cost measurement method—actual, normal, or standard costing systems, (3) overhead assignment method—traditional or activity-based costing systems. The choice of a particular system depends on the nature of the industry and the product or service; the firm's strategy and its management information needs; and the costs and benefits to acquire, design, modify, and operate a particular system.

Job costing systems provide information for managers to use to make strategic decisions regarding products and customers, manufacturing methods, pricing, overhead allocation methods, and other long-term issues.

Job costing and process costing are two major types of product costing systems. Job costing accumulates costs for specific jobs; it applies to industries with a wide variety of different orders, products, or services. Process costing accumulates cost by processes or departments; it applies to industries with mass production of homogeneous products or services.

Job costing uses several general ledger accounts to control the product cost flows. Direct materials costs are debited to the Materials Inventory account at purchase time and debited to the Work-in-Process Inventory account when production requests materials. Direct labor costs are debited to the Work-in-Process Inventory account when they are incurred. Actual factory overhead costs are debited to the Factory Overhead account when they are incurred. Factory overhead applied using the predetermined factory overhead rate in normal costing is debited to the Work-in-Process Inventory account and credited to the Factory Overhead Applied account. When a job is complete, the cost of goods manufactured is transferred from the Work-in-Process Inventory account to the Finished Goods Inventory account.

The predetermined factory overhead rate is an estimated factory overhead rate used to apply factory overhead cost to a specific job. The application of a predetermined overhead rate has four steps: (1) budget factory overhead costs for an appropriate operating period, usually a year, (2) select the most appropriate cost drivers for charging the factory overhead costs, (3) estimate the total amount or activity level of the chosen cost drivers for the operating period, and (4) divide the budgeted factory overhead costs by the estimated activity level of the chosen cost drivers to obtain the predetermined factory overhead rates.

The difference between the actual factory overhead cost and the amount of the factory overhead applied is the overhead variance; it is either underapplied or overapplied. It can be disposed of in two ways: (1) adjust the Cost of Goods Sold account or (2) prorate the discrepancy among the amounts of the current period's applied overhead remaining in the ending balances of the Work-in-Process Inventory, the Finished Goods Inventory, and the Cost of Goods Sold accounts.

The ideal criterion for choosing an allocation base is a cause-and-effect relationship. A plantwide rate is appropriate when all products pass through the same processes or all departments are similar. In some production processes, the relationship between factory overhead costs and various cost drivers differs substantially among production departments. Then multiple overhead rates with multiple volume-based and nonvolume-based cost drivers based on activity consumption should be used.

Job costing is used extensively in service industries such as advertising agencies, construction companies, hospitals, repair shops and consulting, architecture, accounting, and law firms.

APPENDIX A

Spoilage, Rework, and Scrap in Job Costing

In today's contemporary manufacturing environment, firms adopt various quality improvement programs to reduce spoilage, rework units, and scrap. **Spoilage** refers to unacceptable units that are discarded or sold for disposal value. **Rework** units are units produced that must be reworked into good units that can be sold in regular channels. **Scrap** is the part of the product that has little or no value.

Spoilage

The two types of spoilage are normal and abnormal. **Normal spoilage** occurs under efficient operating conditions; it is uncontrollable in the short term and is considered a normal part of production and product cost. That is, the cost of lost unit costs is absorbed by the cost of good units produced. **Abnormal spoilage** is in excess of the amount of normal spoilage expected under efficient operating conditions; it is charged as a loss to operations in the period detected. Abnormal spoilage is charged to the Loss from Abnormal Spoilage account.

Normal spoilage can be classified as that incurred (1) for a *particular job* and (2) *in common* with all jobs because it relates to the production process in general.

Spoilage cost for a particular job can be reduced by the estimated disposal value or selling price of the spoiled goods. Common spoilage cost is transferred from the particular job cost into the Factory Overhead account. Abnormal spoilage is charged to the Loss from Abnormal Spoilage account.

Suppose during June, Wang Company's job A21 had normal spoilage with the estimated disposal value or selling price of $500 attributable to it, and job B32 had normal spoilage with the estimated cost of $700 due to the general production process failure plus abnormal spoilage of $100. The proper journal entries follow:

Materials Inventory (disposal value or selling price of the spoilage goods)	500	
Work-in-Process Inventory: Job A21		500
Factory Overhead (common normal spoilage cost)	700	
Loss from Abnormal Spoilage	100	
Work-in-Process Inventory: Job B32		800

◀ **LEARNING OBJECTIVE 10**

Account for spoilage, rework, and scrap in job costing.

A **spoilage** is an unaccepted unit that is discarded or sold for disposal value.

A **rework** is a produced unit that must be reworked into a good unit that can be sold in regular channels.

A **scrap** is the part of the product that has little or no value.

A **normal spoilage** is an unacceptable unit that occurs under efficient operating conditions.

An **abnormal spoilage** is an unacceptable unit that should not arise under efficient operating conditions.

Rework

Like spoilage, there are three types of rework: (1) rework on normal defective units for a particular job, (2) rework on normal defective units common with all jobs, and (3) rework on abnormal defective units not falling within the normal range. The cost of rework units is charged to one of three accounts depending on its nature. Normal rework for a particular job is charged to that specific job's Work-in-Process Inventory account. Normal rework common to all jobs is charged to the Factory Overhead account and abnormal rework is charged to the Loss from Abnormal Rework account.

Scrap

Scrap can be classified according to (1) a specific job and (2) common to all jobs. To account for the first type of scrap, reduce the selling price from the Work-in-Process Inventory account. For the second type, reduce the selling price from the Factory Overhead account. Note that accountants do not keep the separate cost incurred to scrap. When the scrap is sold, accountants credit either Work-in-Process Inventory or Factory Overhead account by the selling price of the scrap.

Suppose that Arnold Machine Shop incurred and sold the scrap from a specific job for $100 cash and sold the scrap common to all jobs for $200 cash in July. The proper journal entries follow:

Cash	100	
Work-in-Process Inventory		100
Cash	200	
Factory Overhead		200

KEY TERMS

COMMENTS ON COST MANAGEMENT IN ACTION

ITTFSC Battled Overhead Costs, Billing Delays, and Military Cutbacks

In the early 1990s, ITT's Federal Service Corporation assembled a strike team to reengineer its financial and accounting services. The team decided to replace the firm's 20-year-old mainframe accounting system because of its inflexibility and sluggish performance. The team wanted a system that could easily handle hundreds of concurrent users and process thousands of journal entries in hours rather than in days or weeks. ITT instigated an extensive review of proposals from 40 accounting system vendors and narrowed the list to four for an in-depth review and on-site demonstrations. Based on cost-effective superior functionality, the company decided to install Maxwell Business Systems' Job Cost Accounting/Management Information System (JAMIS).

JAMIS offered a flexible system for modifying ITT's job number structure. ITT cut the waiting period for the internal users dramatically because various department users collect the data themselves and generate reports in a matter of minutes rather than days. Billing, once a labor- and paper-intensive task, became automatic. The system's interactive approach kept ITT's payroll and billing information current and accurate. The new job costing system resulted in a 50 percent reduction in data processing and financial staffing requirements. Billings in the millions of dollars to the federal government could be submitted in days rather than weeks. Now ITT can support the special needs of its government contract and promote service excellence.

Source: "ITT Boosts Financial Productivity, Customer Service," *Management Accounting*, September 1996, pp. 32–33.

SELF-STUDY PROBLEM

(For solution, please turn to the end of the chapter.)

Journal Entries and Accounting for Overhead

Watkins Machinery Company uses a normal job costing system. The company has this partial trial balance information on March 1, 2001, the last month of its fiscal year:

Materials Inventory (X, $3,000; Y, $2,000; Indirect materials, $5,000)	$10,000
Work-in-Process Inventory—Job 101	6,000
Finished Goods Inventory—Job 100	10,000

These transactions relate to the month of March:
a. Purchased direct materials and indirect materials with the following summary of receiving reports:

Material X	$10,000
Material Y	10,000
Indirect materials	5,000
Total	$25,000

b. Issued direct materials and indirect materials with this summary of requisition forms:

	Job 101	Job 102	Total
Material X	$5,000	$3,000	$ 8,000
Material Y	4,000	3,000	7,000
Subtotal	$9,000	$6,000	$15,000
Indirect materials			8,000
Total			$23,000

c. Factory labor incurred is summarized by these time tickets:

Job 101	$12,000
Job 102	8,000
Indirect labor	5,000
Total	$25,000

d. Factory utilities, factory depreciation, and factory insurance incurred are summarized by these factory vouchers, invoices, and cost memos:

Utilities	$ 500
Depreciation	15,000
Insurance	2,500
Total	$18,000

  e. Factory overhead costs were applied to jobs at the predetermined rate of $15 per machine-hour. Job 101 incurred 1,200 machine-hours; job 102 used 800 machine-hours.

  f. Job 101 was completed; job 102 was still in process at the end of March.

  g. Job 100 and job 101 were shipped to customers during March. Both jobs had gross margins of 20 percent based on manufacturing cost.

The company closed the overapplied or underapplied overhead to the Cost of Goods Sold account at the end of March.

Required

1. Prepare journal entries to record the transactions and events. Letter your entries from a to g.

2. Compute the ending balance of the Work-in-Process Inventory account.

3. Compute the overhead variance and indicate whether it is overapplied or underapplied.

4. Close the overhead variance to the Cost of Goods Sold account.

QUESTIONS

12–1   What is the purpose of a product costing system?

12–2   Give three ways that management uses product costs.

12–3   Distinguish between job costing and process costing.

12–4   Explain when companies are likely to use a job costing system or a process costing system. Provide several examples.

12–5   Which product costing system is extensively used in the service industry for hospitals, law firms, or accounting firms? Explain why.

12–6   What document is prepared to accumulate costs for each separate job in a job costing system? What type of costs are recorded in the document?

12–7   Explain how predetermined factory overhead rates are computed and why they are used to apply factory overhead to units of products instead of actual overhead costs.

12–8   What is the role of material requisition forms in a job costing system? Time tickets? Bills of materials?

12–9   What does the statement that accounting for overhead involves an important cost-benefit issue mean? Why is that issue important?

12–10   Describe the flow of costs through a job costing system.

12–11   What do *underapplied overhead* and *overapplied overhead* mean? How are these amounts disposed of at the end of a period?

12–12   Why are some manufacturing firms switching from direct labor-hours to machine-hours as the cost driver for factory overhead application?

12–13   What is a plantwide overhead rate? Under what circumstances is using multiple overhead rates preferred to using a single plantwide overhead rate?

12–14   Explain why overhead might be overapplied in a given period.

12–15   Distinguish between an actual costing system and a normal costing system. What are the components of the actual manufacturing costs and the components of the normal manufacturing costs?

12–16   Factory overhead includes a variety of costs that vary greatly with respect to the production process. What is the best way to choose an appropriate cost driver when applying factory overhead?

12–17   What is the difference between normal cost of goods sold and adjusted cost of goods sold?

EXERCISES

12–18 JOB VS. PROCESS COSTING   Indicate whether job or process costing is more suitable for each of these firms:

1. Food processing
2. Manufacturing textile products
3. Printing shop
4. Automobile repair shop
5. Accounting firm
6. Oil refining
7. Manufacturer of custom-built houses
8. Consulting firm
9. Manufacturer of electronics
10. Cement manufacturer

12–19 BASIC JOB COSTING   Davis Inc. is a job-order manufacturing company that uses a predetermined overhead rate based on direct labor-hours to apply overhead to individual jobs. For 2001, estimated direct labor-hours are 95,000, and estimated factory overhead is $579,500. The following information is for September 2001. Job A was completed during September, and job B was started but not finished.

September 1, 2001, inventories	
Materials inventory	$ 7,500
Work-in-process inventory (All job A)	31,200
Finished goods inventory	67,000
Material purchases	104,000
Direct materials requisitioned	
Job A	45,000
Job B	33,500
Direct labor-hours	
Job A	4,200
Job B	3,500
Labor costs incurred	
Direct labor ($5.50/hour)	42,350
Indirect labor	13,500
Supervisory salaries	6,000
Rental costs	
Factory	7,000
Administrative offices	1,800
Total equipment depreciation costs	
Factory	7,500
Administrative offices	1,600
Indirect materials used	12,000

Required

1. What is the total cost of job A?
2. What is the total factory overhead applied during September?
3. What is the overapplied or underapplied overhead for September?

12–20 JOURNAL ENTRIES   Marita Company uses a job costing system with normal costing and applies factory overhead on the basis of machine-hours. At the beginning of the year, management estimated that the company would incur $1,007,500 of factory overhead costs and use 77,500 machine-hours.

Marita Company recorded the following events during the month of May:

a. Purchased 180,000 pounds of materials on account; the cost was $2.50 per pound.

b. Issued 120,000 pounds of materials to production of which 15,000 pounds were used as indirect materials.

c. Incurred direct labor costs of $240,000 and $50,000 of indirect labor costs.

d. Recorded depreciation on equipment for the month, $15,700.

e. Recorded insurance costs for the manufacturing property, $3,500.

f. Paid $8,500 cash for utilities and other miscellaneous items for the manufacturing plant.

g. Completed job H11 costing $6,500 and job G28 costing $77,000 during the month and transferred them to the Finished Goods Inventory account.

h. Shipped job G28 to the customer during the month. The job was invoiced at 35 percent above cost.

i. Used 7,800 machine-hours during May.

Required

1. Compute Marita Company's predetermined overhead rate for the year.

2. Prepare journal entries to record the events that occurred during May.

3. Compute the amount of overapplied or underapplied overhead and prepare a journal entry to close overapplied or underapplied overhead into cost of goods sold on May 31.

12–21 ACCOUNTING FOR OVERHEAD XYZ Company listed the following data for 2000:

Budgeted factory overhead	$870,000
Budgeted direct labor-hours	60,000
Budgeted machine-hours	20,000
Actual factory overhead	864,500
Actual direct labor-hours	60,500
Actual machine-hours	19,700

Required

1. Assume that XYZ applied overhead based on direct labor-hours. Calculate the company's predetermined overhead rate for 2000.

2. Assume that XYZ applies overhead based on machine-hours. Calculate the company's predetermined overhead rate for 2000.

3. Calculate the overapplied or underapplied overhead if it is applied based on direct labor-hours.

4. Calculate the overapplied or underapplied overhead if it is applied based on machine-hours.

5. Prepare the journal entry to dispose of overapplied or underapplied overhead if XYZ applies overhead based on direct labor-hours. Assume no proration.

6. Prepare the journal entry to dispose of overapplied or underapplied overhead if it is applied based on machine-hours. Assume no proration.

International

12–22 ACCOUNTING FOR OVERHEAD Yamashita Company is a furniture manufacturing firm in a suburb of Tokyo, Japan. It uses a job costing system. It applies factory overhead costs in yen on the basis of direct labor-hours. At the beginning of 2000, management estimated that the company would incur ¥284,000 of factory overhead costs for the year and work 71,000 direct labor-hours.

During the year, the company actually worked 75,000 direct labor-hours and incurred these factory overhead costs:

a. Paid ¥75,400 cash for utilities, power, and other miscellaneous items for the manufacturing plants.

b. Recognized ¥58,000 depreciation on manufacturing property, plant, and equipment for the year.

c. Paid ¥25,000 cash for the insurance premium on manufacturing property and plant.

d. Incurred advertising costs, ¥10,000.

e. Incurred indirect labor costs, ¥54,600.

f. Incurred indirect material costs, ¥53,000.

g. Paid the ¥55,000 salary of the factory superintendent.

h. Accrued sales and administrative salaries, ¥85,000.

Required

1. Compute the firm's 2000 predetermined overhead rate.

2. Compute the amount of factory overhead that should be applied to the Work-in-Process Inventory account for the year.

3. Compute the amount of overapplied or underapplied overhead to be closed into the Cost of Goods Sold account at the end of the year.

4. Check the most recent issue of *The Wall Street Journal* to find the exchange rate between the U.S. dollar and the Japanese yen.

12–23 UNDERAPPLIED OR OVERAPPLIED OVERHEAD   Tyson Company uses a job costing system that applies factory overhead on the basis of direct labor-hours. No job was in process on February 1. During the month of February, the company worked on these three jobs:

	Job Number		
	A23	**C76**	**G15**
Direct labor ($8/hour)	$24,000	?	$8,800
Direct materials	42,000	61,000	?
Overhead applied	?	24,750	6,050

During the month, the company completed and transferred job A23 to the finished goods inventory at the cost of $82,500. Jobs C76 and G15 were not completed and remain in work in process at the cost of $148,650 at the end of the month. Actual factory overhead costs during the month totaled $48,600.

Required

1. Compute the amount of underapplied or overapplied overhead for February.

2. What is the predetermined factory overhead rate?

3. Compute the cost of direct materials issued to production during the month.

4. Prepare a journal entry showing the transfer of the completed job to Finished Goods Inventory.

12–24 APPLICATION AND PRORATION OF FACTORY OVERHEAD   Getaway Company uses a job costing system that applies factory overhead on the basis of direct labor-hours. The company's factory overhead budget for 2000 included the following estimates:

Budgeted total factory overhead	$568,000
Budgeted total direct labor-hours	71,000

At the end of the year, the company's ledger shows these results:

Actual factory overhead	$582,250
Actual direct labor-hours	69,500

The following amounts of the year's applied factory overhead remained in the various manufacturing accounts:

	Applied Factory Overhead Remaining
Work-in-process inventory	$139,000
Finished goods inventory	216,840
Cost of goods sold	200,160

Required

1. Compute the firm's predetermined factory overhead rate for 2000.
2. Calculate the amount of overapplied or underapplied overhead.
3. Prepare a journal entry to prorate overapplied or underapplied overhead to Work-in-Process Inventory, Finished Goods Inventory, and Cost of Goods Sold accounts.

12–25 **REVIEW OF JOB COSTING**   Hogan Company uses a job costing system and applies factory overhead cost to products on the basis of direct labor-hours. Management prepared this overhead budget for 2000:

Direct labor-hours	59,000
Factory overhead	$678,500

During 2000, an economic recession caused Hogan Company to curtail production and the buildup of inventory in its warehouse. The company's ledger shows the following operating data:

Direct labor ($8/hour; 36,000 hours)	$288,000
Inventories, January 1, 2000	
Materials inventory (all direct)	35,000
Work-in-process inventory	198,000
Finished goods inventory	450,000
Inventories, December 31, 2000	
Materials inventory (all direct)	50,000
Work-in-process inventory	125,000
Finished goods inventory	634,000
Cost of goods sold after adjusting for underapplied overhead	987,000

The firm closed underapplied or overapplied overhead directly into the Cost of Goods Sold account. After the adjustment for underapplied overhead, the Cost of Goods Sold account had increased by $18,000.

Required

1. Compute the company's predetermined factory overhead rate for 2000.
2. Determine the actual overhead for 2000.
3. What was the cost of goods manufactured for 2000?
4. What amount of direct materials was purchased during the year?

12–26   ACTIVITY-BASED COSTING, COST DRIVERS

	Overhead Cost Pool			
Overhead Cost Pool	Budgeted Overhead Cost	Budgeted Level for Cost Driver	Cost Driver	Rate
Materials handling	$120,000	3,000 pounds	Weight	$ 40
Machine setup	9,750	325 repetitions	Number of repetitions	30
Machine repair	1,045	5 units	Units of time*	209
Inspections	8,100	135 inspections	Number of inspections	60

Requirements for Job 747	
Materials handling	100 pounds
Machine setups	25 repetitions
Machine repair time	0.5 hour
Inspections	10 inspections

*One unit equals 15-minute intervals.

Required   Use the multiple cost drivers to compute the total factory overhead that should be assigned to job 747.

12–27   OVERHEAD RATE, PRICING

Buckey Associates is an advertising agency in Columbus, Ohio. The company's controller estimated that it would incur $325,000 in overhead costs for 2001. Because the overhead costs of each project change in direct proportion to the amount of direct professional hours incurred, the controller decided that overhead should be applied on the basis of professional hours. The controller estimated 25,000 professional hours for the year. During October, Buckey incurred the following costs to make a 20-second TV commercial for Central Ohio Bank:

 *Service*

Direct materials	$32,000
Direct professional hours ($23/hour)	1,200

Actual overhead costs to make the commercial totaled $14,700. The industry customarily bills customers at 150 percent of total cost.

Required

1.   Compute the predetermined overhead rate.
2.   What is the total amount of the bill that Buckey will send Central Ohio Bank?

PROBLEMS

12–28   APPLICATION AND DISPOSITION OF FACTORY OVERHEAD

Work in process inventory for department 203 at the beginning of period:

Job	Materials	Labor	Overhead	Total
1376	$17,500	$22,000	$33,000	$72,500

Department 203 Costs for 2000:

	Incurred by Jobs			
Jobs	Materials	Labor	Other	Total
1376	$ 1,000	$ 7,000	—	$ 8,000
1377	26,000	53,000	—	79,000
1378	12,000	9,000	—	21,000
1379	4,000	1,000	—	5,000

		Not Incurred by Jobs	
Indirect materials and supplies	$15,000	—	—	$ 15,000
Indirect labor	—	$ 53,000	—	53,000
Employee benefits	—	—	$23,000	23,000
Depreciation	—	—	12,000	12,000
Supervision	—	20,000	—	20,000
Total	$58,000	$143,000	$35,000	$236,000

Department 203 Overhead rate for 2000:

Budgeted overhead	
Variable	
Indirect materials	$ 16,000
Indirect labor	56,000
Employee benefits	24,000
Fixed	
Supervision	20,000
Depreciation	12,000
Total	$128,000
Budgeted direct labor dollars	$ 80,000
Rate per direct labor dollar ($128,000/$80,000)	160%

Required

1. What was the actual factory overhead for department 203 for 2000?

2. What was department 203's underapplied overhead for 2000?

3. Job 1376 was the only job completed and sold in 2000. What amount was included in the cost of the goods sold for this job?

4. What was the amount of Work-in-Process Inventory at the end of 2000?

5. Assume that factory overhead was underapplied in the amount of $14,000 for department 203. If underapplied overhead were distributed between the cost of the goods sold and inventory, how much of the underapplied overhead was charged to the year-end Work-in-Process Inventory?

(**CMA Adapted**)

12–29 **CHOICE OF COSTING SYSTEM**

Required

1. The following is a list of websites for a number of companies. Briefly describe each company and indicate whether it is more likely to use job costing or process costing. Explain why in each case.

   a. New Century Software Inc. at www.newcenturysoftware.com.

   b. Kinko's at www.kinkos.com.

   c. Riverside Cement at www.cement.com.

   d. Paramount Pictures at www.paramount.com.

   e. Evian at www.evian.com.

   f. Ircon International Limited at www.irconinternational.com.

2. Briefly describe two additional companies (and give their websites), one that would use a job costing system and the other that would use a process costing system. Explain why for each company.

12–30 CHOICE OF COSTING SYSTEM

International

Required

1. The following is a list of websites for a number of non–U.S. companies. Briefly describe each company and indicate whether it is more likely to use job costing or process costing. Explain why in each case.

   a. Formosa Plastics Corporation at www.fpc.com.tw.

   b. Zurich Financial Services Group at www.zurich.com.

   c. Toyota Motor at www.global.toyota.com.

   d. Nestle S.A. at www.nestle.com.

   e. Nokia at www.nokia.com.

   f. SAP at www.sap.com

2. Briefly describe two additional non–U.S. companies (and give their websites), one that would use a job costing system and the other that would use a process costing system. Explain why for each company.

12–31 REVIEW OF JOB COSTING; GENERAL LEDGER RELATIONSHIPS Asiana Company is a Malaysian company that manufactures custom-made products. It uses a job costing system to accumulate and record costs for its plant. Factory overhead costs in ringgits (M$) are charged to production on the basis of machine-hours. The following budget information is for 2001:

International

Budgeted total factory overhead	M$4,200,000
Budgeted total machine-hours	300,000

During January, the firm worked on two jobs:

Job 133	
Direct materials	M$27,000
Direct labor	M$33,000
Machine-hours	9,500

Job 243	
Direct materials	M$45,000
Direct labor	M$51,000
Machine-hours	15,500

The beginning and ending inventories follow. Job 133 was completed and sold during the month.

Inventories, January 1, 2001	
Materials inventory (all direct)	M$33,000
Work-in-process inventory (job 133)	M$24,000
Finished goods inventory	0

Inventories, January 31, 2001	
Materials inventory (all direct)	M$26,000
Work-in-process inventory (job 243)	?
Finished goods inventory	0

During January, actual factory overhead costs incurred were M$385,000.

Required

1. Compute the predetermined overhead rate for 2001.

2. What amount of direct materials was purchased in January?

3. What is the cost of goods manufactured for January 2001?

4. What is the balance of the Work-in-Process Inventory at January 31, 2001?

5. What is the total amount of factory overhead applied in January 2001?

6. Compute the amount of overapplied overhead or underapplied overhead.

7. Prepare a journal entry to close overapplied or underapplied overhead to the Cost of Goods Sold account.

8. Check the most recent issue of *The Wall Street Journal* to find the exchange rate between the U.S. dollar and the Malaysian ringgit.

12–32 **SCHEDULE OF COST OF GOODS MANUFACTURED**   Benaline Company uses a job costing system for its production costs. It uses a predetermined factory overhead rate based on direct labor costs to apply factory overhead to jobs. During the month of July, the firm processed three jobs: A12, C46, and M24. A small fire in the administration office during the early hours of August 1 left only these fragments of the company's factory ledger:

Inventories, July 1	
Materials inventory (all direct)	$42,500
Work-in-process inventory (job A12)	54,000
Finished goods inventory	75,000
Inventories, July 31	
Materials inventory (all direct)	?
Work-in-process inventory (job C46 and job M23)	?
Finished goods inventory	96,080
Cost of goods sold, July	102,000
Direct materials purchased, July	25,000
Direct materials issued to production	63,340
Job A12	21,340
Job C46	26,000
Job M23	16,000
Factory labor-hours used ($5.50/hour)	
Job A12	2,800
Job C46	3,800
Job M23	1,700
Indirect labor	900
Other factory overhead costs incurred	
Rent	29,500
Utilities	8,600
Repairs and maintenance	4,600
Depreciation	27,100
Other	6,600

Job A12 is the only job completed during the month; cost of goods manufactured totaled $123,080.

Required

1. Compute the predetermined factory overhead rate.

2. Compute the amount of factory overhead applied during July.

3. Compute the actual factory overhead cost incurred during July.

4. What was the ending balance of the Work-in-Process Inventory account?

5. Compute the amount of overapplied overhead or underapplied overhead.

6. Prepare a schedule of cost of goods manufactured.

12–33   **JOURNAL ENTRIES AND ACCOUNTING FOR OVERHEAD**   Humming Company manufactures highly sophisticated musical instruments for professional musicians. The company uses a normal costing system that applies factory overhead on the basis of direct labor-hours. For 2001, the company estimated that it would incur $120,000 in factory overhead costs and 8,000 direct labor-hours. The April 1, 2001, balances in inventory accounts follow:

Materials inventory	$27,000
Work in process inventory (S10)	10,500
Finished goods inventory (J21)	54,000

Job S10 is the only job in process on April 1, 2001. The following transactions were recorded for the month of April.

a.   Purchased materials on account, $90,000.

b.   Issued $91,000 of materials to production, $4,000 of which was for indirect materials. Cost of direct materials issued:

Job S10	$23,000
Job C20	42,000
Job M54	22,000

c.   Incurred and paid payroll cost of $20,460:

Direct labor cost ($13/hour; total 920 hours)

Job S10	$6,110
Job C20	4,030
Job M54	1,820
Indirect labor	2,500
Selling and administrative salaries	6,000

d.   Recognized depreciation for the month:

Manufacturing asset	$2,200
Selling and administrative asset	1,700

e.   Paid advertising expenses $6,000

f.   Incurred factory utilities costs $1,300

g.   Incurred other factory overhead costs $1,600

h.   Applied factory overhead to production on the basis of direct labor-hours.

i.   Completed job S10 during the month and transferred it to the finished goods warehouse.

j.   Sold job J21 on account for $59,000.

k.   Received $25,000 of collections on account from customers during the month.

Required

1.   Calculate the company's predetermined overhead rate.

2.   Prepare journal entries for the April transactions.

3.   What was the balance of the Materials Inventory account on April 30, 2001?

4.   What was the balance of the Work-in-Process Inventory account on April 30?

5.   What was the amount of underapplied or overapplied overhead?

12–34   **JOURNAL ENTRIES, SCHEDULE OF COST OF GOODS MANUFACTURED**   Apex Corporation manufactures eighteenth-century, classical-style furniture. It uses a job costing system that applies factory overhead on the basis of direct labor-hours. Budgeted factory overhead for 2001 was $1,235,475, and management budgeted 86,700 direct labor-hours. These transactions were recorded during August:

a. Purchased 5,000 square feet of oak on account at $25 per square foot.

b. Purchased 50 gallons of glue on account at $36 per gallon (indirect material).

c. Requisitioned 3,500 square feet of oak and 30.5 gallons of glue for production.

d. Incurred and paid payroll costs of $187,900. Of this amount, $46,000 were indirect labor costs; direct labor personnel earned $22 per hour on average.

e. Paid factory utility bill, $15,230 in cash.

f. August's insurance cost for the manufacturing property and equipment was $3,500. The premium had been paid in March.

g. Incurred $8,200 depreciation on manufacturing equipment for August.

h. Recorded $2,400 depreciation on an administrative asset.

i. Paid advertising expenses in cash, $5,500.

j. Incurred and paid other factory overhead costs, $13,500.

k. Incurred miscellaneous selling and administrative expenses, $13,250.

l. Applied factory overhead to production on the basis of direct labor-hours.

m. Completed goods costing $146,000 to manufacture during the month.

n. Made sales on account in August, $132,000. The cost of goods sold was $112,000.

Required

1. Compute the firm's predetermined factory overhead rate for 2001.
2. Prepare journal entries to record the August events.
3. Calculate the amount of overapplied or underapplied overhead to be closed to the Cost of Goods Sold account on August 31, 2001.
4. Prepare a schedule of cost of goods manufactured and sold.
5. Prepare the income statement for August.

12–35 **PLANTWIDE VS. DEPARTMENTAL OVERHEAD RATE**   Telefax Corporation manufactures a popular fax machine. Cost estimates for one unit of the product for the year 2000 follow:

Direct materials	$200
Direct labor ($12/hour)	240
Machine-hours	20

This fax model requires 12 hours of direct labor in department A and 8 hours in department B. However, it requires 5 machine-hours in department A and 15 machine-hours in department B. The factory overhead costs estimated in these two departments follow:

	A	B
Variable cost	$146,000	$ 77,000
Fixed cost	94,000	163,000

Management expects the firm to produce 1,000 units of the products during 2000.

Required

1. Assume that factory overhead was applied on the basis of direct labor-hours. Compute the predetermined factory overhead rate.

2. If factory overhead were applied on the basis of machine-hours, what would be the plantwide overhead rate?

3. If the company produced exactly 1,000 units during the year, what was the total amount of applied factory overhead in each department in requirements 1 and 2?

4. If you were asked to evaluate the performance of each department manager, which allocation basis (cost driver) would you use? Why?

5. Compute the departmental overhead rates for each department.

12–36   ACTIVITY-BASED COSTING, COST DRIVERS   Southern Metals Company's controller has established these overhead cost pools and cost drivers for 2001:

Strategy

Overhead Cost Pool	Budgeted Overhead	Expected Cost Driver	Activity Level
Machine setups	$117,868	Number of setups	40
Power	341,120	Machine-hours	21,320
Materials handling	85,000	Materials weight	34,000 lb.
Quality control	143,500	Number of units	82,000 units
Other overhead	184,500	Direct labor-hours	14,760 hours
	$871,988		

During March 2001, Southern received an order for 1,500 machine tools and produced them. The order required the following:

Machine setups	7
Machine-hours	3,250
Materials	4,250 lb.
Direct labor-hours	2,750 hours

Required

1. Calculate the predetermined factory overhead rates for cost drivers.

2. What was the total factory overhead assigned to fill the order under the activity-based costing approach?

3. Suppose that a single predetermined factory overhead rate based on machine-hours was used to apply factory overhead. What was the predetermined factory overhead rate? What amount of factory overhead was applied to the order?

4. Which product costing system would you prefer? Why?

5. Identify the implications of your answers to requirements 2 and 3 for the Southern's pricing and product-emphasis strategy.

12–37   ACTIVITY-BASED COSTING, COST DRIVERS   Robert Company manufactures laser printers. It lists the following factory overhead cost drivers:

Strategy

Overhead Cost Pool	Cost Driver	Budgeted Overhead Cost	Budgeted Level for Cost Driver
Quality control	Number of inspections	$ 50,000	1,000
Machine repetitions	Number of repetitions	100,000	1,000
Accounts receivable	Number of invoices processed	650	26
Other overhead cost	Direct labor-hours	30,000	3,000

Robert has an order for 500 laser printers that has the following production requirements:

Number of inspections	25
Number of repetitions	200
Number of invoices processed	250
Direct labor-hours	350

Required

1. What amount of total factory overhead is assigned to the 500 units under the activity-based costing approach?

2. What is the cost per laser printer?

3. If Robert expressed its factory overhead rate in direct labor-hours, how much overhead would it apply to the entire order of 500 laser printers?

4. How do you explain the difference in requirements 1 and 3?

5. Identify the implications of your answers to requirements 1 and 3 for Robert's pricing and product-emphasis strategy.

12–38 **JOURNAL ENTRIES, APPLICATION, AND PRORATION OF OVERHEAD**   Hartford Company uses a job costing system that applies factory overhead on the basis of direct labor cost. Any overapplied or underapplied overhead is allocated between the Work-in-Process Inventory, Finished Goods Inventory, and Cost of Goods Sold accounts. The April 1, 2001, balances in selected accounts were

Inventories, April 1	
Materials inventory (all direct)	$124,000
Work-in-process inventory (job 354)	113,400
Finished goods inventory (job 243)	178,200

Job 354 was the only job in the manufacturing process at the end of March. Job 243 was completed during March but has not yet been sold. These transactions occurred during April 2001:

a. Purchased materials on account, $143,000.

b. Requisitioned materials for use in production.

Direct materials:	
Job 354	$ 23,000
Job 475	?
Job 523	72,500
Indirect Materials	18,700

c. Used the following labor for April according to time cards:

Direct labor	
Job 354	?
Job 475	$102,000
Job 523	36,500
Indirect labor	97,000

d. Recognized depreciation on the factory building and equipment during April, $76,000.

e. Paid rent for the warehouse in cash, $6,500.

f. Paid insurance cost covering the factory operation, in cash, $11,000.

g. Incurred other factory overhead costs, $63,000.

h. Applied $287,500 of factory overhead cost to production on the basis of direct labor cost.

i. Completed and transferred jobs 354 and 475 to the Finished Goods Inventory account. The balance of the Work-in-Process Inventory account on April 30, 2001, was $154,625.

j. Sold jobs 243 and 354 on account during the month. The cost of the goods sold for these jobs was $520,475. The balance of the Finished Goods Inventory account on April 30 showed $254,875.

Required

1. Prepare journal entries for the April transactions.

2. What amount of factory overhead was applied to job 523?

3. Calculate the firm's predetermined factory overhead rate as a percentage of direct labor cost.

4. What was the cost of goods manufactured in April?

5. What was the direct materials cost incurred in April to initiate and complete job 475?

6. What was the direct labor cost incurred in April to complete job 354?

7. What was the balance of the Materials Inventory account on April 30, 2001?

8. Calculate the amount of overapplied or underapplied overhead in April.

9. Prepare a journal entry to allocate overapplied or underapplied overhead among Work-in-Process inventory, Finished Goods Inventory, and Cost of Goods Sold accounts.

12–39 COST DRIVERS; APPLICATION AND PRORATION OF FACTORY OVERHEAD
Northcoast Manufacturing Company, a small manufacturer of parts used in appliances, has just completed its first year of operations. The company's controller, Vic Trainor, has been reviewing the actual results for the year and is concerned about the application of factory overhead. He is using the following information to assess operations:

- Northcoast's equipment consists of several machines with a combined cost of $2,200,000 and no residual value. Each machine has a product output of five units per hour and a useful life of 20,000 hours.

- Selected actual data of Northcoast's operations for the year just ended follow:

Products manufactured	650,000 units
Machine utilization	130,000 hours
Direct labor usage	35,000 hours
Labor rate	$15 per hour
Total factory overhead	$1,130,000
Cost of goods sold	$1,720,960
Finished goods inventory (at year-end)	$430,240
Work-in-process inventory (at year-end)	$0

- Total factory overhead is applied to direct labor cost using a predetermined plantwide rate.

- The budgeted activity for the year included 20 employees, each working 1,800 productive hours, to produce 540,000 units of product. Each employee can simultaneously operate two to four machines, which are highly automated. Normal activity is for each employee to operate three machines. Machine operators are paid $15 per hour.

• Budgeted factory overhead costs for the past year for various levels of activity are shown in the following table:

Northcoast Manufacturing Company
Budgeted Annual Costs for Total Factory Overhead

Units of product	360,000	540,000	720,000
Labor-hours	30,000	36,000	42,000
Machine-hours	72,000	108,000	144,000
Total factory overhead costs			
Plant supervision	$ 70,000	$ 70,000	$ 70,000
Plant rent	40,000	40,000	40,000
Equipment depreciation	288,000	432,000	576,000
Maintenance	42,000	51,000	60,000
Utilities	144,600	216,600	288,600
Indirect materials	90,000	135,000	180,000
Other costs	11,200	16,600	22,000
Total	$685,800	$961,200	$1,236,600

Required

1. Based on Northcoast's actual operations for the past year

   a. Determine the dollar amount of total over/underapplied factory overhead and explain why this amount is material.

   b. Prepare the appropriate journal entry to close out Northcoast's total Factory Overhead account.

2. Vic Trainor believes that the company should use machine-hours to apply total factory overhead. Using the data given,

   a. Determine the dollar amount of total over/underapplied factory overhead if machine-hours had been used as the application base.

   b. Explain why machine-hours would be a more appropriate application base.

(CMA Adapted)

Service

12–40 COSTING IN SYSTEM SELECTION, UNDERAPPLIED OR OVERAPPLIED OVERHEAD   Whittier Clinic is a large, profitable medical complex staffed by doctors who provide a variety of services. It has a net income of $200,000. When a patient goes to an appointment, the doctor fills out a computerized form that lists the services provided the patient during the visit. The clinic mails the patient the completed form with prices noted as the bill.

Required

1. Should Whittier Clinic use a job costing system, or should it try another system? Why?

2. Whittier Clinic's applied overhead was $108,475. The clinic found out, however, that actual overhead was $113,775. Is this overhead underapplied or overapplied? By what amount?

3. What would your answer be if the clinic's applied overhead were $127,850, and actual overhead were $122,950?

4. Should there be a difference between overhead applied and the actual overhead?

5. Using your numerical answer for requirement 2, show with journal entries how you would deal with the underapplied or overapplied overhead amount. Explain why you did it this way and when this procedure should be done.

Service

12–41 BASIC JOB COSTING Daetwyler and Koo CPA firm has the following budget for 2001:

Direct labor (for professional hours charged to clients)	$106,000
Overhead	
Indirect materials	$ 5,000
Indirect labor	75,000
Depreciation—Building	25,000
Depreciation—Furniture	2,500
Utilities	6,000
Insurance	2,400
Property taxes	2,600
Other expenses	1,500
Total	$120,000

The firm uses direct labor cost as the cost driver to apply overhead to clients.

During January, the firm worked for many clients; data for two of them follow:

Davila account	
Direct materials	$ 200
Direct labor	1,500
Jackson account	
Direct materials	$2,690
Direct labor	6,300

Required

1. Compute Daetwyler and Koo's budgeted overhead rate. Explain how this is used.

2. Compute the amount of overhead to be charged to the Davila and Jackson accounts using the predetermined overhead rate calculated in requirement 1.

3. Compute a separate job cost for the Davila and the Jackson accounts.

12–42 JOB COST SHEETS Decker Screw Manufacturing Company produces special screws made to customer specifications. During June, the following data pertained to these costs:

EXCEL

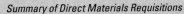

Summary of Direct Materials Requisitions

Department Number	Job Number	Requisition Number	Quantity	Cost per Unit
1	2906	B9766	4,550	$ 1.34
2	2907	B9767	110	22.18
1	2908	B9768	1,000	9.00
1	2906	B9769	4,430	1.35
2	2908	B9770	23	48.00

Summary of Direct Labor Time Tickets

Department Number	Job Number	Ticket Number	Hours	Cost per Unit
1	2906	1056-1168	1,102	$6.50
2	2907	2121-2130	136	8.88
1	2908	1169-1189	151	6.50
2	2908	2131-1239	32	8.88
1	2906	1190-1239	810	6.50

Summary of Factory Overhead Application Rates

Department Number	Basis of Application Rates
1	$3 per direct labor-hour
2	150% of direct labor cost

Decker had no beginning work-in-process inventory for June. Of the jobs begun in June, job 2906 was completed and sold on account for $30,000, job 2907 was completed but not sold, and job 2908 was still in process.

Required

1. Calculate the direct materials, direct labor, factory overhead, and total costs for each job started in June.

2. Perform the same calculations as in requirement (1), but assume that both direct materials quantity used and cost per unit increased by 15 percent and that both direct labor-hours and rate per hour increased by 10 percent.

12–43 **JOB COST DETAILS**   Hannah Cabinets Inc. is a small business that produces wood cabinets. The company collected the following data:

Job order number:	2809		Quantity ordered:	50
Product:	Tiger bookcases		Date started:	10/10/01
Date ordered:	10/03/01		Date wanted:	10/20/01
			Date completed:	10/18/01

	Cutting Department	Assembly Department	Finishing Department
Materials used	$800 (Req. 665)	$160 (Req. 681)	$70 (Req. 688)
Direct labor rate	5.40	6.10	8.00
Direct labor-hours	10	35	18.5
Applied factory overhead	$5 per MH*	80% of DLC†	$3 per DLH‡
Machine-hours	8.25	0	0

*Machine-hour.

†Direct labor cost.

‡Direct labor-hour.

The company uses a 30 percent markup on total factory cost to determine the selling price.

Required

1. Calculate for each department the costs of direct materials, direct labor, applied factory overhead, and total job cost.

2. Calculate the selling price and the gross margin for the job.

Ethics

12–44 **ASSIGNING OVERHEAD TO JOBS**   Aero Systems is a manufacturer of airplane parts and engines for a variety of military and commercial aircraft. It has two production departments. Department A is machine intensive; department B is labor intensive. Aero Systems has adopted a traditional plantwide rate using the direct labor-hour-based overhead allocation system. The company recently conducted a pilot study using a departmental overhead rate costing system. This system used two overhead allocation bases: machine-hours for department A and direct labor-hours for department B. The study showed that the system, which will be more accurate and timely, will assign lower costs to the government jobs and higher costs to the company's nongovernmental jobs. Apparently, the current (less accurate) direct labor-based costing system has overcosted government jobs and undercosted private business jobs. On hearing of this, top management has decided to scrap the plans for adopting the new departmental overhead rate costing system because government jobs constitute 40 percent of Aero Systems' business and the new system will reduce the price and thus the profit for this part of its business.

Required   As the management accountant participating in this pilot study project, what is your responsibility when you hear of top management's decision to cancel the plans to implement the new departmental overhead rate costing system? Can you ignore your professional ethics code in this case? What would you do?

12–45 **PLANTWIDE VERSUS DEPARTMENTAL OVERHEAD RATE**   Rose Bach was recently hired as controller of Empco Inc., a sheet metal manufacturer. Empco has been in the sheet metal business for many years and is currently investigating ways to modernize its manufacturing process. At the first staff meeting Rose attended, Bob Kelley, chief engineer, presented a proposal for automating the drilling department. He recommended that Empco purchase two robots that could replace the eight direct labor workers in the department. The cost savings outlined in Bob's proposal included eliminating direct labor cost and reducing factory overhead cost to zero in the drilling department because Empco charges factory overhead on the basis of direct labor dollars using a plantwide rate.

Empco's president was puzzled by Kelley's explanation of cost savings, believing it made no sense. Rose agreed, explaining that as firms become more automated, they should rethink their factory overhead systems. The president then asked her to look into the matter and prepare a report for the next staff meeting.

To refresh her knowledge, Rose reviewed articles on factory overhead allocation for an automated factory and discussed the matter with some of her peers. She also gathered the following historical data on Empco's factory overhead rates. She also wanted to have some departmental data to present at the meeting and, using Empco's accounting records, estimated the annual averages presented for each manufacturing department in the 1990s.

Historical Data

| | *Average* | | |
Date	Annual Direct Labor Cost	Annual Factory Overhead Cost	Overhead Application Rate
1950s	$1,000,000	$ 1,000,000	100%
1960s	1,200,000	3,000,000	250
1970s	2,000,000	7,000,000	350
1980s	3,000,000	12,000,000	400
1990s	4,000,000	20,000,000	500

| | *Annual Averages* | | |
	Cutting Department	Grinding Department	Drilling Department
Direct labor	$ 2,000,000	$1,750,000	$ 250,000
Factory overhead	11,000,000	7,000,000	2,000,000

Required

1.   Disregarding the proposed use of robots in the drilling department, describe the shortcomings of the system for applying overhead that Empco currently uses.

2. Explain the misconceptions in Bob Kelley's statement that the factory overhead cost in the drilling department would be reduced to zero if the automation proposal were implemented.

3. Recommend ways to improve Empco's method for applying overhead by describing how it should revise its overhead accounting system

   a. In the cutting and grinding departments.

   b. To accommodate the automation of the drilling department.

(CMA Adapted)

12–46 **PLANTWIDE VERSUS DEPARTMENTAL OVERHEAD RATE**   Upton Inc. manufactures a line of home furniture. The company's single manufacturing plant consists of the cutting, assembly, and finishing departments. Upton uses departmental rates for applying factory overhead to production and maintains separate Factory Overhead and Factory Overhead Applied accounts for each of the three departments.

The following predetermined departmental factory overhead rates were calculated for Upton's fiscal year ending May 31, 2002:

Department	Rate
Cutting	$2.40 per machine-hour
Assembly	5.00 per direct labor-hour
Finishing	1.60 per direct labor-dollar

Information regarding actual operations for Upton's plant for the six months ended November 30, 2001, follows:

	Department		
	Cutting	**Assembly**	**Finishing**
Factory overhead costs	$22,600	$56,800	$98,500
Machine-hours	10,800	2,100	4,400
Direct labor-hours	6,800	12,400	16,500
Direct labor dollars	$40,800	$62,000	$66,000

Based on this information and updated projections for the last six months of the fiscal year, Upton revised its operating budget. Projected data regarding factory overhead and operating activity for each department for the six months ending May 31, 2002, follow:

	Department		
	Cutting	**Assembly**	**Finishing**
Factory overhead costs	$23,400	$57,500	$96,500
Machine-hours	9,200	2,000	4,200
Direct labor-hours	6,000	13,000	16,000
Direct labor dollars	$36,000	$65,000	$64,000

Diane Potter, Upton's controller, plans to revise departmental factory overhead rates so that they will more accurately represent efficient operations for the current fiscal year ending May 31, 2002. She has decided to combine the actual results for the first six months of the fiscal year with the projections for the next six months to develop the revised departmental application rates. She then plans to adjust the factory overhead applied accounts for each department through November 2001 to recognize the revised application rates. Diane prepared the following analysis from general ledger account balances as of November 30, 2001:

Account	Direct Materials	Direct Labor	Factory Overhead	Account Balance
Work-in-process inventory	$ 53,000	$ 95,000	$ 12,000	$ 160,000
Finished goods inventory	96,000	176,000	48,000	320,000
Cost of goods sold	336,000	604,000	180,000	1,120,000
	$485,000	$875,000	$240,000	$1,600,000

Required

1. Determine the balance of the factory overhead applied accounts as of November 30, 2001, before any revision for each department.

2. Calculate the revised departmental manufacturing overhead rates that Upton should use for the remainder of the fiscal year ending May 31, 2002.

3. Prepare an analysis that shows how the Factory Overhead Applied account for each of Upton's departments should be adjusted as of November 30, 2001, and prepare the adjusting entry to correct all general ledger accounts that are affected.

(CMA Adapted)

12–47 **OPERATION COSTING** Pomona Company manufactures two sizes of T-shirts, medium and large. Both sizes go through cutting, assembling, and finishing departments. The company uses operation costing.

Pomona's conversion costs applied to products for April were $45,000 for the cutting department, $22,500 for the assembling department, and $15,000 for the finishing department. April had no beginning or ending work-in-process inventory.

The quantities and direct materials costs for April follow:

Job Number	Size	Quantity	Direct Materials
401	Medium	5,000	$20,000
402	Large	10,000	50,000

Each T-shirt, regardless of size, required the same cutting, assembling, and finishing operations.

Required

1. Compute both unit cost and total cost for each shirt size produced in April.

2. Prepare journal entries to record direct materials and conversion costs incurred in the three departments and finished goods costs for both shirt sizes.

12–48 **OPERATION COSTING** Brian Canning Co., which sells canned corn, uses an operation costing system. Cans of corn are classified as either sweet or regular, depending on the type of corn used. Both types of corn go through the separating and cleaning operations, but only regular corn goes through the creaming operation. During January, two batches of corn were canned from start to finish. Batch X consisted of 800 pounds of sweet corn and batch Y consisted of 700 pounds of regular corn. The company had no beginning or ending work-in-process inventory. The following cost information is for the month January:

Raw sweet corn	$5,200
Raw regular corn	2,450*
Separating department costs	1,500
Cleaning department costs	900
Creaming department costs	210

*Included $300 for cream

Required

1. Compute the unit cost for sweet corn and regular corn.
2. Record appropriate journal entries.
3. Post journal entries to T-accounts.

12–49 **SPOILAGE AND SCRAP**   Liu Textile Company's job X12 had normal spoilage with the estimated disposal selling price of $300 in May attributable to this particular job. Its job Y34 had a normal spoilage with the estimated cost of $400 from the general production process failure and abnormal spoilage of $200. The company also incurred scrap due to a specific job and sold it for $80. It also sold the scrap common to all jobs for $120 cash in May.

Required

1. Make the necessary journal entries to record normal and abnormal spoilage costs.
2. Make the necessary journal entries to record both types of scrap sold.

12–50 **SPOILAGE, REWORK, AND SCRAP**   Richport Company manufactures products that often require specification changes or modifications to meet customer needs. Consequently, Richport employs a job costing system for its operations.

Although the specification changes and modifications are commonplace, Richport has been able to establish a normal spoilage rate of 0.025 of normal input. The company recognizes normal spoilage during the budgeting process and classifies it as a component of factory overhead. Thus, the predetermined overhead rate used to apply factory overhead costs to jobs includes an allowance for net spoilage cost for normal spoilage. If spoilage on a job exceeds the normal rate, it is considered abnormal and then must be analyzed and the cause of the spoilage must be submitted to management.

Randa Duncan, one of Richport's inspection managers, has been reviewing the output of job N1192-122 that was recently completed. A total of 122,000 units had been started for the job, and 5,000 units were rejected at final inspection, meaning that the job yielded 117,000 good units.

Randa noted that 900 of the first units produced were rejected due to a very unusual design defect that was corrected immediately; no more units were rejected for this reason. Rejected units were disposed of at an additional cost of $1,200 to Richport.

Randa was unable to identify a pattern for the remaining 4,100 rejected units. They can be sold at a salvage value of $7 per unit.

The total costs accumulated for all 122,000 units of job N1192-122 follow. Although the job is completed, all of these costs are still in the Work-in-Process Inventory account (i.e., the cost of the completed job has not been transferred to Finished Goods Inventory account).

Direct materials	$2,196,000
Direct labor	1,830,000
Applied factory overhead	2,928,000
Total cost of job	$6,954,000

Required

1. Explain the distinction between normal and abnormal spoilage.
2. Distinguish between spoiled units, rework units, and scrap.
3. Review the results and costs for job N1192-122.
   a. Prepare an analysis separating the spoiled units into normal and abnormal spoilage by first determining the normal input required to yield 117,000 good units.

b. Prepare the appropriate journal entries to properly account for job N1192-122 including spoilage, salvage value, disposal, and/or transfer of costs to the Finished Goods Inventory account.

(CMA Adapted)

SOLUTION TO SELF-STUDY PROBLEM

Journal Entries and Accounting for Overhead

1. Journal entries:

a. Materials Inventory ... 25,000
   Accounts Payable ... 25,000
   To record the purchase of direct materials and indirect materials.

b. Work-in-Process Inventory ... 15,000
   Factory Overhead ... 8,000
   Materials Inventory ... 23,000
   To record direct and indirect materials issued.

c. Work-in-Process Inventory ... 20,000
   Factory Overhead ... 5,000
   Accrued Payroll ... 25,000
   To record factory labor incurred.

d. Factory Overhead ... 18,000
   Accounts Payable ... 500
   Accumulated Depreciation—Factory ... 15,000
   Prepaid Insurance ... 2,500
   To record actual overhead costs incurred, including factory utilities, depreciation, and insurance.

e. Work-in-Process Inventory ... 30,000
   Factory Overhead Applied ... 30,000
   To record the application of factory overhead to jobs.

Summary of factory overhead applied
Job 1 ($15 × 1,200) ... $18,000
Job 2 ($15 × 800) ... 12,000
Total ... $30,000

f. Finished Goods Inventory ... 45,000
   Work-in-Process Inventory ... 45,000
   To record the job finished.

Total manufacturing cost for job 101
Beginning inventory ... $ 6,000
Direct materials added ... 9,000
Direct labor incurred ... 12,000
Factory overhead applied ... 18,000
Total ... $45,000

g. Accounts Receivable ... 66,000
   Sales ... 66,000
   To record the total sales revenue of two jobs.
   Cost of Goods Sold ... 55,000
   Finished Goods Inventory ... 55,000
   To record the total cost of goods sold.

Summary of the total cost in shipping orders
Job 100 ... $10,000
Job 101 ... 45,000
Total ... $55,000

Sales = $55,000 × 120% = $66,000

2. Ending balance of the Work-in-Process Inventory account for Job 102:

Direct materials	$ 6,000
Direct labor	8,000
Factory overhead applied	12,000
Total ending balance	$26,000

3. Factory overhead variance:

Actual factory overhead		
Indirect materials	$ 8,000	
Indirect labor	5,000	
Utilities	500	
Depreciation	15,000	
Insurance	2,500	$31,000
Applied factory overhead		30,000
Underapplied factory overhead		$ 1,000

4. To record the disposition of underapplied factory overhead by closing both Factory Overhead and Factory Overhead Applied accounts to the Cost of Goods Sold account.

Factory Overhead Applied	30,000	
Cost of Goods Sold	1,000	
Factory Overhead		31,000

Process Costing

13

After studying this chapter, you should be able to . . .

1   Describe the strategic role of process costing

2   Identify the types of firms or operations for which a process costing system is most suitable

3   Explain and calculate equivalent units

4   Describe the five steps in process costing

5   Demonstrate the weighted-average method of process costing

6   Demonstrate the FIFO method of process costing

7   Analyze process costing with multiple departments

8   Prepare journal entries to record the flow of costs in a process costing system

9   Characterize the impact of the new manufacturing technologies on process costing

10   Account for spoilage in process costing

T he Coca-Cola Company is the world's leading manufacturer, marketer, and distributor of soft drink concentrates, syrups, and soft drinks. Coca-Cola's strategy focuses on both price and differentiation.[1]

Coca-Cola's differentiation strategy is apparent in its positioning: It positions itself as a unique and special product with a young, fresh image equal to none in the soft drink segment; it is a permanent reminder of classic values, of American culture inside and outside the country, and of all things American: entertainment, sports, and youth. Furthermore, its brand is recognized in practically every country in the world. Its exclusive formula makes it unique.

Coca-Cola uses the processing costing system to track product and customer costs such as direct materials, direct labor, and overhead costs incurred in three major processes: (1) concentrate and syrup manufacturing, (2) blending, and (3) packaging. During the first process, mixing water with sugar, colorings, and so on produces concentrates, and adding sweeteners and water to the concentrates produces syrups. In the second process, pure carbon dioxide is added to the blend of syrups and water to produce the beverage. In the third process, a filler injects a precise amount of blending beverage into plastic bottles or cans, and a metal crown or plastic closure seals the package. Process costing information provides useful information for managers to analyze product and customer profitability and to make pricing, product-mix, and process improvement decisions.

In today's globally competitive environment, managers must know product costs to be able to make good decisions. Imagine a large corporation's top manager trying to decide whether to discontinue a product without knowing what it cost to produce. Managers need cost information for setting goals; forming strategy; developing long- and short-term planning; and for control, performance measurement, and decision-making purposes.

Process costing is a product costing system that accumulates costs according to processes or departments and assigns them to a large number of nearly identical products. The typical firm that uses a process costing system employs a standardized production process to manufacture homogeneous and indistinguishable products.

Firms need to set clear goals and form strong strategies to stay competitive. Once they determine strategies, they must put into place the tactics to achieve them and monitor those strategies continuously. Process costing allows monthly or periodic monitoring of the unit costs of any product a firm manufactures. By monitoring and examining these unit costs, managers can determine whether processes need to be

---

[1] For more about the Coca-Cola success story, see its website at www.coke.com; "Coca Cola Co.: Soft Drink Maker Opens $50 Million Plant in China," *The Wall Street Journal,* March 30, 1998; "Coca Cola CEO Speaks to Georgia CPAs," *Journal of Accountancy,* February 1999; and Keith Johnson, "Design Choice: Coke Bottle," *Marketing,* October 7, 1999, pp. 16–17.

improved or tactics need to be changed. Process costing also allows accountants to determine unit costs needed for valuing inventory and the cost of goods sold for external financial reports.

Companies using process costing systems include Royal Dutch Shell Group (www.shell.com), Ford Motor Company (www.ford.com), Coca-Cola (www.coca-cola.com), Bethlehem Steel (www.bethsteel.com), International Paper (www.ipaper.com), and Kimberly-Clark (www.kimberly-clark.com).

STRATEGIC ROLE OF PROCESS COSTING

LEARNING OBJECTIVE 1▶

Describe the strategic role of process costing.

Although the traditional volume-based process costing system can in many situations hinder development and implementation of strategy that promote competitive advantage, the activity-based process costing information helps managers identify where improvements in activities and processes could provide the most benefit to increase company profits.

Process costing systems can provide information for managers to make strategic decisions regarding products, manufacturing methods, pricing decisions, and other long-term issues. Why is process costing information strategically important for a firm?

First, a firm competes by using either a cost leadership or a differentiation strategy. If it is following the cost leadership strategy and has complex overheads, the firm should change its traditional volume-based job costing to an activity-based process costing system to provide useful information to management. For example, Boeing Aircraft once used a job costing system with volume-based direct labor cost as the cost driver. Under this system, production managers had no direct responsibility for controlling factory overhead costs. The company decided to control total costs by changing to an activity-based process costing system.[2] The new process costing system allows factory overhead costs to be assigned to processes regardless of whether managers have direct responsibility for controlling these costs. The new system also produces costs more closely related to activities performed.

An activity-based costing (ABC)/activity-based management (ABM) process costing system helps a firm achieve its low-cost strategy by identifying key activities, drivers, and ways to improve designs and/or processes to reduce cost. For example, potato chip production has three major steps: preparing, processing, and packaging. The preparing steps has four activities: cleaning, selecting, slicing, and shaping. The processing step also has four activities: cooking, frying, salting, and flavoring. For health-conscious customers, the salting activity is a non-value-added activity.

A second important strategic issue is also potentially an ethical issue for process costing because of the decisions the firm makes about (1) the basis for allocating overhead and (2) the proration of overapplied or underapplied overhead. Say, for example, that a firm is manufacturing products for two markets: one is price competitive but the other is not (e.g., cost-plus government contracts); the manner of overhead allocation is both a strategic and an ethical issue. Management could be motivated to overcost the cost-plus products through its choice of an allocation basis or proration method to achieve the desired result.

Third, providing superior customer value is another business strategy for achieving a competitive advantage. One approach is to use value-chain analysis in the process costing system. A firm can apply ABC/ABM, target costing, and life-cycle costing methods to reduce the internal value-chain process costs of research and development, design, production, marketing, distribution, and customer service. For example, Milliken & Co. uses ABC/ABM process costing to sharpen its competitive edge by allowing managers to focus on the actual costs for each process and to reduce non-

---

[2]   Robert J. Bowlby, "How Boeing Tracks Costs, A to Z," *Financial Executive*, November–December 1994, pp. 20–23.

value-added work within a process.[3] A firm can also work with external value-chain stakeholders such as suppliers to reduce its materials-handling costs and customers to improve its production scheduling efficiency.

Fourth, a process costing production cost sheet can be expanded to become a periodic balanced scorecard performance report with four dimensions: financial, customer, internal business process, and learning and growth. The balanced scorecard measures tie directly to a firm's strategy and its critical success factors. For example, a company developing a strategic balanced scorecard could include process costing information as part of both financial measures and internal business process measures.

CHARACTERISTICS OF PROCESS COSTING SYSTEMS

In this section, we identify the types of firms for which a process costing system is most suitable, discuss the concept of equivalent units, present the flow of costs in process costing, and describe the five steps in process costing.

What Types of Firms Should Use a Process Costing System?

Firms having homogeneous products that pass through a series of similar processes or departments use process costing. These firms usually engage in continuous mass production of a few similar products. The work done by the production departments or processes does not vary because all units are essentially the same. Manufacturing costs are accumulated in each process. The departmental production cost report is a key document in tracking production quantity and cost information. Unit product cost is calculated by dividing process costs in each department by the number of equivalent units produced during the period.

The process cost system is used in many industries such as chemicals, oil refining, textiles, paints, flour, canneries, rubber, steel, glass, food processing, mining, automobile production lines, electronics, plastics, drugs, paper, lumber, leather goods, metal products, sporting goods, cement, and watches. Process costing can also be used by service organizations with homogeneous services and repetitive processes such as check processing in a bank or mail sorting by a courier.

◄**LEARNING OBJECTIVE 2**

Identify the types of firms or operations for which a process costing system is most suitable.

Equivalent Units

A manufacturing firm typically has partially completed units at the end of an accounting period. Under the job costing system, these partially completed units are not difficult to handle because job costs are available on job cost sheets.

In a process costing system, however, product costs for partially completed units are not readily available. Because the focus in cost accounting has shifted from jobs to processes or departments, the interest is in the unit cost of performing a certain *process* for a given period. The goal is to find the combined unit cost of all product units processed in that period, including those that are partially complete at either the beginning or the end of the accounting period. Note that by *partially complete*, we mean partially complete for that department; a unit could be complete for a given department but still be in the Work-in-Process Inventory account if this is not the final department.

The calculation of the product cost begins with determining the production cost per unit in each production department. These unit costs are incorrect if the amount of work done on partially complete units is not considered. Therefore, the cost calculations must be adjusted for partially complete units so that all units included in the computations reflect work actually done in the period.

With both complete and partially complete units, we need a way to measure the proper amount of production work performed during a period. An equivalent unit is

◄**LEARNING OBJECTIVE 3**

Explain and calculate equivalent units.

---

[3] James Don Edwards, Cynthia D. Heagy, and Harold W. Rakes, "How Milliken Stays on Top," *Journal of Accountancy*, April 1989, pp. 73–74.

one such measure. The problem of equivalent units arises because we take a continuous process and break it into separate, distinct time periods. The process is continuous, but the reporting is periodic, such as monthly or yearly.

Equivalent units are the number of the same or similar complete units that could have been produced given the amount of work actually performed on both complete and partially complete units.

Equivalent units are the number of the same or similar complete units that could have been produced given the amount of work actually performed on both complete and partially complete units. Equivalent units are not the same as physical units. A firm last month produced 30 television sets of which 20 were complete sets and 10 were partially complete sets (roughly 50% complete). The physical units were 30 sets, but equivalent units were only 25 sets [20 + (10 × 50%)].

The equivalent units should be calculated separately for direct materials, direct labor, and factory overhead because the proportion of the total work performed on the product units in the work-in-process inventories is not always the same for each cost element. Partially complete units are often complete for direct materials but incomplete for direct labor and factory overhead. Examples include chemical or brewing processes that dump direct materials in at the beginning but are not complete until the cooking process, which can extend over hours or days, is finished. Some firms divide costs into direct materials and conversion cost categories. *Conversion costs* are the sum of direct labor and factory overhead costs.

Conversion Costs

For many process industries such as oil refinery, aluminum, paper, chemical, and pharmaceutical, factory overhead and direct labor costs are often combined under conversion costs for the purpose of computing equivalent units of production. Linking these two cost elements is possible because the direct labor cost is not a significant cost element in most process industries.

Many manufacturing operations incur conversion costs uniformly throughout production. The equivalent units of conversion costs are therefore the result of multiplying the percentage of work that is complete during the period by the number of units on which work is partially complete. For example, for 1,000 units estimated to be 30 percent complete in the work-in-process ending inventory, the equivalent units of conversion costs in the period are 300 (the work completed [30 percent] × 1,000 units). However, for 1,000 units 40 percent complete in the work-in-process beginning inventory, the number of equivalent units of conversion work in the current period is 600. Equivalent units, in this case, are calculated by multiplying 1,000 units by the percentage of work remaining to be completed, 60 percent (100 percent − 40 percent = 60 percent).

Firms using nonlabor-based cost drivers (such as machine-hours or the number of setups) for their factory overhead costs find that calculating separate equivalent units of production for factory overhead and direct labor costs is more appropriate.

Direct Materials

Direct materials can be added to the product units gradually in various proportions at discrete points of manufacturing, continuously over production. If the materials are added uniformly, the proportion used for computing equivalent units of direct materials is the same as the proportion for conversion costs. However, if the materials are added all at once, the proportion used in the computation depends on whether the point in the process where the materials are added has been reached.

Exhibit 13–1 illustrates the determination of equivalent units in direct materials for beginning and ending work-in-process (WIP) inventory. The first example assumes that beginning work-in-process inventory has 1,000 product units that are 30 percent complete. The second example assumes that ending work-in-process (WIP) inventory has 1,500 product units that are 60 percent complete. Each example has four materials-adding timing situations: (1) materials are added gradually throughout the process, (2) all materials are added at the beginning of the process, (3) all materials are added at the 40 percent point, and (4) all materials are added at the end of the

| Exhibit 13–1 | Equivalent Units for Direct Materials under Beginning and Ending Inventory | | | | | |

| | | | Equivalent Units This Period* | | | |
Type of Inventory	Physical Units Partially Complete	Percentage of Completion	Materials Added Gradually	All Materials Added at the Beginning	All Materials Added at 40 Percent Point	All Materials Added at the End
Beginning work-in-process inventory	1,000	30%	1,000 × (1 – 30%) = 700	0	1,000 × 100% = 1,000	1,000 × 100% = 1,000
Ending work-in-process inventory	1,500	60	1,500 × 60% = 900	1,500 × 100% = 1,500	1,500 × 100% = 1,500	0

*Equivalent units added to complete the beginning work-in-process inventory during the period, or equivalent units for the ending work-in-process inventory.

process. We will calculate equivalent units (EU) for each example under these four situations.

Example 1: *Beginning* Work-in-Process Inventory, 1,000 Product Units 30 Percent Complete

The four materials-adding timing situations for this example follow:

1. **Direct materials are added gradually and uniformly throughout the process.** EU added during the current period to complete the beginning WIP inventory = 1,000 × (1 – 30%) = 700 units. That is, we must add 700 EU of direct materials during this period to 300 EU of the beginning WIP inventory.

2. **All materials are added at the beginning of the process.** EU added during the current period to complete the beginning WIP = 1,000 × (1 – 100%) = 0 units. That is, if all materials are added at the beginning of the period, we do not need to add any more EU of direct materials to finish the beginning WIP inventory.

3. **All materials are added at the 40 percent point.** EU added during the current period to complete the beginning WIP = 1,000 × (1 – 0%) = 1,000 units. Since 30 percent is smaller than the 40 percent point, we need to add 1,000 EU of direct materials at the 40 percent point.

4. **All materials are added at the end of the process.** EU added during the current period to complete the beginning WIP = 1,000 × (1 – 0%) = 1,000 units. That is, we need to add all 1,000 EU of direct materials at the end of the process.

Example 2: Ending WIP Inventory, 1,500 Product Units 60 Percent Complete

The following shows the four materials—adding timing situations:

1. **Direct materials are added gradually and uniformly throughout the process.** EU for the ending WIP = 1,500 × 60% = 900 units. That is, the WIP ending inventory has 900 equivalent units of direct materials.

2. **All materials are added at the beginning of the process.** EU for the ending WIP = 1,500 × 100% = 1,500 units. Since all materials have already been added at the beginning of the process, the ending WIP inventory has 1,500 equivalent units of direct materials and no more are needed.

3. **All materials are added at the 40 percent point.** EU for the ending WIP = 1,500 × 100% = 1,500 units. Since 60 percent is larger than the 40 percent point, the ending WIP inventory has 1,500 equivalent units of direct materials.

4. **All materials are added at the end of the process.** EU for the ending WIP = 1,500 × 0% = 0 units. Since the ending WIP inventory is only 60% completed, we have not added any EU of direct materials.

Flow of Costs in Process Costing

Flow of costs in process costing is similar to that in job costing except that in process costing, costs flow through different processes or departments. Exhibit 13–2 is a T-account model of direct materials, direct labor, and factory overhead cost flows in a two-department process costing system. Note four key points in this exhibit. First, a separate Work-in-Process Inventory account is used to record costs of each production department. Second, when Department A finishes its work, the costs of the goods completed are transferred to Department B's subsequent Work-in-Process Inventory account for further work. After this further work, the costs of goods completed are then transferred to the Finished Goods Inventory account. Third, direct materials, direct labor, and factory overhead costs can be entered directly into either production department's Work-in-Process Inventory account, not just that of the first department. Finally, starting with the second department (Department B), an additional cost element, *transferred-in-costs* (TI), appears. These are costs of the goods completed in the prior department and transferred into this department during the period.

Boeing Tracks Aircraft Costs with Process Costing

Boeing Company formerly had a job cost accounting system that assigned factory overhead based on direct labor cost. Production managers were almost powerless to control total product cost other than by reducing the direct labor-hours. The company decided to switch to a process costing system in 1994.

Under the new system, unit weighting converts different parts or products to common production units. After the process cost center production unit is calculated, the cost for a particular part is determined by multiplying the cost per production unit times the number of units assigned to that part.

The new process costing system allows factory overhead costs to be assigned to processes for which managers have direct responsibility for controlling costs. The new system also produces costs more closely related to the activities performed.

Source: Robert J. Bowlby, "How Boeing Tracks Costs, A to Z," *Financial Executive,* November–December 1994, pp. 20–23.

Exhibit 13–2   T-Account Model of Flow of Costs for Two Departments in Process Costing

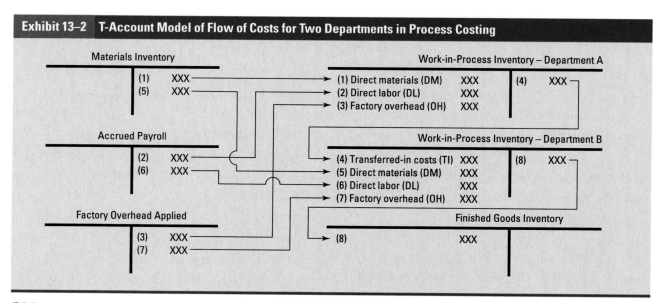

Five Key Steps in Determining Process Costs

1. Analyze physical flow of production units.
2. Calculate equivalent units of production for all manufacturing cost elements.
3. Determine total cost for each manufacturing cost element.
4. Compute cost per equivalent unit for each manufacturing cost element.
5. Assign the total manufacturing costs to units completed and transferred out and units of work in process at the end of the period.

Steps in Process Costing

The key document in a typical process costing system is the production cost report, prepared at the end of each period for a production process or department. The **production cost report** summarizes the number of physical units and equivalent units of a department, the costs incurred during the period, and the costs assigned to both units completed and transferred out and ending work-in-process inventories. The preparation of a production cost report includes these five steps:

Step 1: Analyze Flow of Physical Units

The first step addresses which units were on hand at the beginning of the period, how many units were started or received, which units were completed and transferred out, and which units are in ending work-in-process inventory.

The analysis of physical units includes accounting for both input and output units. *Input units* include beginning work-in-process inventory and all units that enter a production department during an accounting period. *Output units* include units that are complete and transferred out from a production department or are in the work-in-process inventory at the end of a period. (See Exhibit 13–4.)

Step 2: Calculate Equivalent Units

The purpose of calculating equivalent units of production for direct materials, direct labor, and factory overhead is to measure the total work efforts expended on production during an accounting period. The partially complete physical units are converted into the equivalent number of whole units. (See Exhibit 13–5.)

Step 3: Determine Total Costs to Account For

The total manufacturing costs to account for include the current costs incurred and the costs of the units in the work-in-process beginning inventory. (See Exhibit 13–6.) The amount of these costs is obtained from material requisitions, labor time cards, and factory overhead allocation sheets.

Step 4: Compute Unit Costs

The purpose of computing direct materials, direct labor, and factory overhead costs per equivalent unit of production is to have a proper product costing and income determination for an accounting period. (See Exhibit 13–7.)

Step 5: Assign Total Manufacturing Costs

The objective of the production cost report is to assign total manufacturing costs incurred to the units completed and transferred out during the period and the units that are still in process at the end of the period. The total costs assigned in step 5 should equal the total costs to be accounted for in step 3. (See Exhibit 13–8.)

Companies generally divide the five-step production cost report into three parts: production quantity information, unit cost determination, and cost assignment. The first part includes step 1, analyze flow of physical units, and step 2, calculate equivalent units. The second part includes step 3, determine total costs to account for, and

◄**LEARNING OBJECTIVE 4**

Describe the five steps in process costing.

A **production cost report** summarizes the physical units and equivalent units of a department, the costs incurred during the period, and the costs assigned to both units completed and transferred out and ending work-in-process inventories.

step 4, compute equivalent unit cost. The third part includes step 5, assign total manufacturing costs (total costs accounted for).

Process Costing Methods

The **weighted-average method** includes in calculating the unit cost all costs, both those incurred during the current period and those incurred in the prior period that are shown as the beginning work-in-process inventory of this period.

FIFO method includes in calculating the unit cost only costs incurred and work effort performed during the current period.

The two methods used to prepare the departmental production cost report when the firm uses process costing are the weighted-average method and the first-in, first-out (FIFO) method. The **weighted-average method** includes all costs in calculating the unit cost, including both those costs incurred during the current period and those costs incurred in the prior period that are shown as the beginning work-in-process inventory of this period. In this method, prior period costs and current period costs are averaged; hence, the name *weighted average*. The **FIFO method** includes in calculating the unit cost only costs incurred and work effort performed during the current period. FIFO considers the beginning inventory as a batch of goods separate from the goods started and completed within the same period. FIFO assumes that the first work done is to complete the beginning work-in-process inventory. Thus, all beginning work-in-process inventories are assumed to be completed before the end of the current period.

Under the weighted-average method, when a product is started makes no difference; all units completed in the same period or in the ending inventory of that period are treated the same. When this method is used, the status of the product at the end of the period is the only element considered.

On the other hand, the status of the product at both the end and beginning of a period must be considered when the FIFO method is used to determine product costs. That is, the FIFO method looks at the input as well as the output of the production process, whereas the weighted-average method looks only at the output of the production process (completed and transferred out and ending work-in-process inventory).

ILLUSTRATION OF PROCESS COSTING

Basic Data

To illustrate these two process costing methods, assume that Hsu Toy Company has two production departments, molding and finishing. The molding department places a direct material (plastic vinyl) into production at the beginning of the process. Direct labor and factory overhead costs are incurred gradually throughout the process with different proportions. The molding department uses machine-hours as the cost driver to apply factory overhead costs.

Exhibit 13–3 summarizes the molding department's toy units and costs during June of 2001.

Weighted-Average Method

LEARNING OBJECTIVE 5▶

Demonstrate the weighted-average method of process costing.

The weighted-average method makes no distinction between the cost incurred prior to the current period and the cost incurred during the current period. As long as a cost is on the current period's cost sheet for a production department, it is treated as

---

COST MANAGEMENT IN ACTION

Whirlpool Faces Competitive Pressure in the Home Appliance Market

In the late 1980s and early 1990s, the home appliance market, especially that for refrigerators, faced stiff competition. Whirlpool, Maytag, General Electric, and Electrolux tried to be the market leader. Whirlpool took specific steps to achieve this goal. The first step in Whirlpool's plan was to transform its largely domestic operation into a global powerhouse. The second step was to implement cost management techniques to reduce product and asset costs. How did Whirlpool reach its goal? (Refer to comments on Cost Management in Action at the end of the chapter.)

Kunde Estate Winery Uses a Hybrid Product Costing System

Kunde Estate Winery, located in California's Sonoma Valley, uses a hybrid product costing system to determine the cost of a bottle of wine. It traces costs through the various wine-making processes or departments for each job (each lot of grapes).

This hybrid job/process costing system has two major steps. First, the cost of initial harvested grape lots is assigned to jobs based on the amount of grapes allocated to the various types of wine to be produced. Second, it accumulates costs by department and allocates them to each wine batch based on the amount of time the wine spends in each department.

The information provided by the product costing system is useful to managers who must decide how to use the grapes harvested each year to produce different wines.

Source: John Y. Lee and Brian Gray Jacobs, "Kunde Estate Winery: A Case Study in Cost Accounting," *CMA Magazine,* April 1993, pp. 15–18.

Exhibit 13–3	Basic Data for Hsu Toy Company—Molding Department for Month of June 2001	
Work-in-process inventory, June 1		10,000 units
Direct materials: 100 percent complete		10,000
Direct labor: 30 percent complete		1,060
Factory overhead: 40 percent complete		1,620
Beginning work-in-process inventory		$ 12,680
Units started during June		40,000 units
Units completed during June and transferred out of the molding department		44,000 units
Work-in-process inventory, June 30		6,000 units
Direct materials: 100 percent complete		
Direct labor: 50 percent complete		
Factory overhead: 60 percent complete		
Costs incurred during June		
Direct materials		$44,000
Direct labor		22,440
Factory overhead		43,600
Total costs incurred		$110,040

any other cost regardless of when it was incurred. Consequently, the average cost per equivalent unit includes costs incurred both during the current period and in the prior period that carry over into this period through beginning work-in-process inventory. We use the familiar five-step procedure to assign direct materials, direct labor, and factory overhead costs to the cost object, the molding department.

Step 1: Analyze Flow of Physical Units

The first step is to analyze the flow of all units through production. Exhibit 13–4 presents the procedures for this step.

The two sections in Exhibit 13–4 show the two aspects of physical units flowing through production, *input units* and *output units*. This procedure ensures that all units in production are accounted for. Input units include all units that enter a production department during an accounting period or that entered during the prior period but were incomplete at the beginning of the period. These units come from two sources: (1) beginning work-in-process inventory started in a previous period that was partially complete at the end of the preceding period, which is 10,000 units in our example, and (2) work started or received in the current period, 40,000 units in our example. The sum of these two sources, 50,000 units here, is referred to as the number

Units to account for are the sum of the beginning inventory units and the number of units started during the period.

Units accounted for are the sum of the units transferred out and ending inventory units.

of **units to account for,** which is the sum of beginning inventory units and the number of units started during the period.

Output units include those that have been completed and transferred out and those not yet complete at the end of a period. These units can be in one of two categories: the 44,000 units completed or the 6,000 units in the ending work-in-process inventory. The sum of these two categories, 50,000 units, is referred to as the *number of units accounted for.* This number should match the number of units to account for. **Units accounted for** includes the sum of units completed and transferred out and the ending inventory units.

The primary purpose of this first step is to ensure that all units in production are accounted for before we compute the number of equivalent units of production for each production element.

Step 2: Calculate Equivalent Units

The second step in the process costing procedure is to calculate the number of equivalent units of production activity for direct materials, direct labor, and factory overhead. A table of equivalent units, presented in Exhibit 13–5, is based on the table of physical units prepared in step 1 (Exhibit 13–4). Beginning work-in-process inventory units are

---

Exhibit 13–4   Step 1: Analyze Flow of Physical Units—Molding Department

Input	Physical Units
Work-in-Process inventory, June 1	10,000
Units started during June	40,000
Total units to account for	50,000
Output	
Units completed and transferred out during June	44,000
Work-in-process inventory, June 30	6,000
Total units accounted for	50,000

Exhibit 13–5   Step 2: Calculate Equivalent Units—Molding Department
Weighted-Average Method

	Physical Units	Completion Percentage	Equivalent Units Direct Materials	Equivalent Units Direct Labor	Equivalent Units Factory Overhead
Work-in-process, June 1	10,000				
Direct materials		100%			
Direct labor		30			
Factory overhead		40			
Units started	40,000				
Units to account for	50,000				
Units completed	44,000	100%	44,000	44,000	44,000
Work-in-process, June 30	6,000				
Direct materials		100	6,000		
Direct labor		50		3,000	
Factory overhead		60			3,600
Units accounted for	50,000				
Total equivalent units			50,000	47,000	47,600

not included in the calculation of equivalent units because they are completed during the month and are not treated separately under the weighted-average method.

The weighted-average method computes the total equivalent units produced to date. The number of units in production in the current period for each manufacturing production element includes both (1) the units from previous periods that are still in production at the beginning of the current period and (2) the units placed into production in the current period.

In Exhibit 13–5, 44,000 physical units were complete and transferred out of the molding department. These units were 100 percent complete. Thus, they represent 44,000 equivalent units for direct materials, direct labor, and factory overhead. Note that the 44,000 units include 10,000 units placed into production prior to June and completed in June, and 34,000 units (44,000 units – 10,000 units) started and completed in June.

The 6,000 units in ending work-in-process inventory are complete with respect to direct materials because direct materials are added at the beginning of the process. Thus, they represent 6,000 equivalent units of direct materials. However, they are only 50 and 60 percent complete for direct labor and factory overhead, respectively. Therefore, the ending work-in-process inventories represent 3,000 equivalent units of direct labor (6,000 physical units × 50 percent complete) and 3,600 equivalent units of factory overhead (6,000 physical units × 60 percent complete).

From Exhibit 13–5, we calculate the total number of equivalent units as follows:

Completed and transferred out units

\+ Ending work-in-process equivalent units

\= Total equivalent units of production

Combining completed units and ending work-in-process equivalent units, the equivalent units of production for the molding department under the weighted-average method are 50,000 units of direct materials, 47,000 units of direct labor, and 47,600 units of factory overhead.

Step 3: Determine Total Costs to Account For

The third step determines how much money was spent both in the beginning work-in-process inventory and current production for direct materials, direct labor, and factory overhead.

Exhibit 13–6 summarizes the total manufacturing costs to account for. As given in our example data, total manufacturing costs ($122,720) consist of the beginning work-in-process inventory balance, $12,680, plus the current costs added during June, $110,040.

Exhibit 13–6 Step 3: Determine Total Costs to Account For—Molding Department		
Beginning work-in-process inventory		
Direct materials	$10,000	
Direct labor	1,060	
Factory overhead	1,620	
Total		$ 12,680
Current costs added during June		
Direct materials	$44,000	
Direct labor	22,400	
Factory overhead	43,600	
Total costs added		110,040
Total costs to account for		$122,720

Step 4: Compute Unit Costs

For the fourth step in the process costing procedure, we compute the equivalent unit costs of production for direct materials, direct labor, and factory overhead; see Exhibit 13–7. The equivalent per-unit cost for direct materials ($1.08) is computed by dividing the total direct materials cost ($54,000), including the cost of the beginning work-in-process ($10,000) and the cost added during June ($44,000), by the total equivalent units (50,000). Similar procedures are used for direct labor and factory overhead costs. Notice that the total equivalent unit cost of $2.53 can be determined only by adding the unit direct materials cost of $1.08, the unit direct labor cost of $0.50, and the unit factory overhead cost of $0.95.

Step 5: Assign Total Manufacturing Costs

The final step of the process costing procedure is to assign total manufacturing costs to units completed and to units in the ending work-in-process inventory. Exhibit 13–8 summarizes the cost assignment schedule. Various unit numbers come directly from Exhibit 13–5; various unit costs come from Exhibit 13–7. Note that the total costs accounted for in this step ($122,720) should equal the total costs to account for in step 3 (Exhibit 13–6).

Cost Reconciliation

After finishing the five-step procedure, we need to determine whether the total manufacturing costs to account for in step 3 (i.e., total input costs) agree with the total costs accounted for in step 5 (i.e., total output costs). This checking procedure is called the *cost reconciliation*. For example, for Hsu Toy Company's modeling depart-

---

Exhibit 13–7   **Step 4: Compute Unit Costs—Molding Department**
Weighted-Average Method

	Direct Materials	Direct Labor	Factory Overhead	Total
Costs (from Exhibit 13–6)				
Work-in-process, June 1	$10,000	$ 1,060	$ 1,620	$ 12,680
Costs added during June	44,000	22,440	43,600	110,040
Total costs to account for	$54,000	$23,500	$45,220	$122,720
Divide by equivalent units (from Exhibit 13–5)	50,000	47,000	47,600	
Equivalent unit costs	$ 1.08 +	$ 0.50 +	$ 0.95 =	$ 2.53

Exhibit 13–8   **Step 5: Assign Total Manufacturing Costs—Molding Department**
Weighted-Average Method

	Completed and Transferred out	Ending Work-in-Process	Total
Goods completed and transferred out (44,000 × $2.53)	$111,320		$111,320
Ending work-in-process:			
Direct materials (6,000 × $1.08)		$6,480	6,480
Direct labor (3,000 × $0.50)		1,500	1,500
Factory overhead (3,600 × $0.95)		3,420	3,420
Total costs accounted for	$111,320	$11,400	$122,720

ment, $122,720 total manufacturing costs accounted for in step 3 equal the total costs accounted for in step 5.

Production Cost Report

Steps 1 through 5 provide all information needed to prepare a production cost report for the molding department for June. This report is in Exhibit 13–9.

Exhibit 13–9	**Production Cost Report—Molding Department** *Weighted-Average Method*				

Production Quantity Information

	Step 1: Analyze Flow of Physical Units		Step 2: Calculate Equivalent Units		
	Physical Units	**Completion Percentage**	**Direct Materials**	**Direct Labor**	**Factory Overhead**
Input					
Work-in-process, June 1	10,000				
Direct materials		100%			
Direct labor		30			
Factory overhead		40			
Units started	40,000				
Units to account for	50,000				
Output					
Units completed	44,000	100%	44,000	44,000	44,000
Work-in-process, June 30	6,000				
Direct materials		100	6,000		
Direct labor		50		3,000	
Factory overhead		60			3,600
Units accounted for	50,000				
Total equivalent units			50,000	47,000	47,600

Unit Cost Determination

Step 3: Determine Total Costs to Account For	Direct Materials	Direct Labor	Factory Overhead	Total
Work-in-process, June 1	$10,000	$ 1,060	$ 1,620	$ 12,680
Costs added during June	44,000	22,440	43,600	110,040
Total costs to account for	$54,000	$23,500	$45,220	$122,720

Step 4: Compute Unit Costs				
Divide by equivalent units	50,000	47,000	47,600	
Equivalent unit costs	$ 1.08	$ 0.50	$ 0.95	$ 2.53

Cost Assignment

Step 5: Assign Total Manufacturing Costs	Completed and Transferred out	Ending Work-in-Process	Total
Goods completed and transferred out (44,000 × $2.53)	$111,320		$111,320
Ending work-in-process			
Direct materials (6,000 × $1.08)		$ 6,480	6,480
Direct labor (3,000 × $0.50)		1,500	1,500
Factory overhead (3,600 × $0.95)		3,420	3,420
Total costs accounted for	$111,320	$11,400	$122,720

First-In, First-Out (FIFO) Method

Another way to handle inventory in a process costing application is the first-in, first-out (FIFO) method, which assumes that the first units to enter a production process are the first units to be completed and transferred out. The same holds true of the units in inventories. The FIFO method accounts separately for the cost of the units started in the previous period; that cost was carried into the current period through the beginning work-in-process inventory.

LEARNING OBJECTIVE 6▶

Demonstrate the FIFO method of process costing.

Our illustration of the FIFO method of process costing again uses Hsu Toy Company's molding department data (see Exhibit 13–3). Unlike the weighted-average method, the FIFO method does not combine beginning inventory costs with current costs when computing equivalent unit costs. The FIFO method considers the beginning inventory as a batch of goods separate from the goods started and completed within the same period. The costs from each period are treated separately. We follow the same five steps as in the weighted-average method, however, in determining product costs.

Step 1: Analyze Flow Physical Units

The physical flow of product units is unaffected by the process costing method used. Therefore, step 1 for the FIFO method is the same as the weighted-average method in Exhibit 13–4.

Step 2: Calculate Equivalent Units

The FIFO method considers the beginning inventory as a batch of goods separate from the goods started and completed within the same period. The equivalent units in the beginning work-in-process—work done in the prior period—are not counted as part of the FIFO method equivalent units. Only that part of the equivalent units of the beginning work in process to be completed this period is counted.

Two equivalent, alternative procedures are used to calculate equivalent units of production under the FIFO method.

Step 2, Procedure A   The first procedure is to subtract the equivalent units in beginning work-in-process from the weighted-average equivalent units to obtain the FIFO method equivalent units, as shown in the last three rows of Exhibit 13–10. The 10,000 physical units in June 1 work-in-process have 100 percent of direct materials, so they have 10,000 equivalent units of direct materials prior to the current period. However, these units are only 30 percent and 40 percent complete for direct labor and factory overhead, respectively, so they contribute only 3,000 equivalent units of direct labor (10,000 × 30%) and 4,000 equivalent units of factory overhead (10,000 × 40%) prior to the current period. Notice that the $10,000 direct materials cost in the beginning work-in-process inventory is excluded from this calculation. Only current costs added in June are used to compute the equivalent unit cost under the FIFO method.

To calculate the total number of FIFO equivalent units, the following equations are given:

$$
\begin{array}{l}
\text{Completed and transferred out units} \\
\underline{+ \text{ Ending work-in-process equivalent units}} \\
= \text{Weighted-average equivalent units} \\
\underline{- \text{ Beginning work-in-process equivalent units}} \\
= \text{FIFO equivalent units of work done during this period}
\end{array}
$$

Exhibit 13–10 shows that Hsu Toy Company must account for a total of 50,000 units. Of these, 44,000 units are completed and 6,000 units are ending work-in-process inventory that is 100 percent complete for direct materials. The total equivalent units for the period for direct materials under the weighted-average method is

Exhibit 13–10	Step 2: Calculate Equivalent Units—Molding Department
	FIFO Method—Procedure A

	Physical Units	Completion Percentage	Equivalent Units		
			Direct Materials	Direct Labor	Factory Overhead
Input					
Work-in-process, June 1	10,000				
Direct materials		100%	10,000		
Direct labor		30		3,000	
Factory overhead		40			4,000
Units started	40,000				
Units to account for	50,000				
Output					
Units completed	44,000	100%	44,000	44,000	44,000
Work-in-process, June 30	6,000				
Direct materials		100	6,000		
Direct labor		50		3,000	
Factory overhead		60			3,600
Units accounted for	50,000				
Total equivalent units (weighted-average method)			50,000	47,000	47,600
Less: equivalent units in June 1 work-in-process			(10,000)	(3,000)	(4,000)
Equivalent units for work done in June only (FIFO method)			40,000	44,000	43,600

50,000. Of the 44,000 units completed during the period, 10,000 were in the beginning work-in-process inventory. These 10,000 units already had all direct materials added in the prior period. Subtracting 10,000 units from the 50,000 total equivalent units for the period, the FIFO equivalent units for work done only in June for direct materials is 40,000 units. Following the same procedure, equivalent units of production for the molding department using the FIFO method are 44,000 units of direct labor and 43,600 units of factory overhead.

The difference between the weighted-average method and the FIFO method is that under the weighted-average method, the equivalent units of production completed prior to the current period are not subtracted from the total completed units, so equivalent units under the weighted-average method are always as large as or larger than those under the FIFO method.

Step 2, Procedure B An alternative way to determine the equivalent units using the FIFO method is to add equivalent units of work performed in the current period for each component constituting the output. These three components are (1) equivalent units added to complete the beginning work-in-process inventory, (2) units started and completed during the period, and (3) equivalent units of the ending work-in-process inventory. Exhibit 13–11 presents the FIFO equivalent units computation using the second procedure. Notice that under the FIFO method, the equivalent units in the beginning work-in-process inventory from last month's work effort are not added to equivalent units of work performed this month.

For example, the 10,000 units of beginning work-in-process inventory were 30 percent complete for direct labor. Hsu Toy Company completed the beginning work-in-process inventory by adding the remaining 70 percent of the direct labor during the

Exhibit 13–11	**Step 2: Calculate Equivalent Units—Molding Department** *FIFO Method—Procedure B*				

| | | | | Equivalent Units | |
	Physical Units	**Completion Percentage**	**Direct Materials**	**Direct Labor**	**Factory Overhead**
Input					
Work-in-process, June 1	10,000				
Direct materials		100%	10,000		
Direct labor		30		3,000	
Factory overhead		40			4,000
Units started	40,000				
Units to account for	50,000				
Output					
Completed and transferred out					
from work-in-process, June 1	10,000				
Direct materials 10,000 × (1 – 100%)			0		
Direct labor 10,000 × (1 – 30%)				7,000	
Factory overhead 10,000 × (1 – 40%)					6,000
Started and completed					
(44,000 – 10,000) =	34,000	100%	34,000	34,000	34,000
Work-in-process, June 30	6,000				
Direct materials		100	6,000		
Direct labor		50		3,000	
Factory overhead		60			3,600
Units accounted for	50,000				
Equivalent units for work for June only			40,000	44,000	43,600

current period to complete production. In addition, the firm started another 40,000 units in production during the period. Of these 40,000 units, the firm completed the production of 34,000, and the remaining 6,000 were still in the manufacturing process at the end of the period. The firm has completed only 50 percent of the total direct labor to the ending work-in-process inventory, or an equivalent of 3,000 units. To summarize the direct labor spent during the period, the firm spent an equivalent of 7,000 units of direct labor to complete the beginning work-in-process inventory on hand, started and completed 34,000 units, and spent an equivalent of 3,000 units to complete 50 percent of the 6,000 units of ending work-in-process inventory. The total direct labor of the period is equivalent to a production of 44,000 FIFO units.

Step 3: Determine Total Costs to Account For

The total costs incurred to manufacture product units are unaffected by the process costing method used. Therefore, step 3 is the same as the weighted-average method in Exhibit 13–6. It shows that Hsu Toy Company's modeling department has $122,720 total manufacturing costs to account for.

Step 4: Compute Unit Costs

Under the FIFO method, equivalent unit costs are calculated by dividing the costs incurred during the current period by the equivalent units for work completed only during the current period. No cost in the work-in-process beginning inventory is included in determining equivalent unit costs for cost elements. Exhibit 13–12 presents such calculations. The equivalent unit cost for direct materials ($1.10) is computed by dividing the direct materials cost added during June ($44,000) by the equivalent units for work done in June only (40,000). Similar procedures are used for

| Exhibit 13–12 | Step 4: Compute Unit Costs—Molding Department FIFO Method | | | | |

	Direct Materials	Direct Labor	Factory Overhead	Total
Costs (from Exhibit 13–6)				
Work-in-process, June 1				$ 12,680
Costs added during June	$44,000	$22,440	$43,600	110,040
Total costs to account for				$122,720
Divide by equivalent units (from Exhibit 13–10)	40,000	44,000	43,600	
Equivalent unit costs	$ 1.10 +	$ 0.51 +	$ 1.00 =	$ 2.61

direct labor and factory overhead costs. Notice that the total equivalent unit cost of $2.61 can be determined only by adding the unit direct materials cost of $1.10, the unit direct labor cost of $0.51, and the unit factory overhead cost of $1.00.

Step 5: Assign Total Manufacturing Costs

The final step of the process costing procedure is to assign total manufacturing costs to units completed and to units in the ending work-in-process inventory. Like the weighted-average method, the FIFO method assigns the total costs of a period to the units completed, the units transferred out, and the units still in process at the end of the period. Unlike the weighted-average method, however, the FIFO method accounts for different batches of the completed units separately because work performed on different batches could be different.

The manufacturing process for units in the beginning work-in-process overlaps two periods. Thus, units completed from the beginning work-in-process inventory incurred costs prior to the current period as well as during the current period. This fact makes the assignment of total manufacturing costs to units completed during a period a two-part process. In the first part, the total manufacturing cost for units completed from beginning work-in-process is determined. In the second part, the total manufacturing costs for units started and completed during the manufacturing process in the current period are calculated.

Step 5, Part A: Total Cost of Units Completed from Beginning Work-in-Process Inventory

The manufacturing process for units in the beginning work-in-process inventory overlaps two periods. To determine the total manufacturing costs for the units completed from beginning work-in-process, the firm adds the manufacturing costs applied to the units during the current period to the costs from preceding periods already assigned to these units.

The total additional cost incurred in the current period to complete these units is the sum of the equivalent units of each cost element added to complete the element. These are applied to the units in beginning work-in-process and multiplied by the average unit cost for the cost element.

The costs assigned to the 10,000 units of the beginning work-in-process inventory that were completed and transferred out during the current period are calculated as follows:

Work-in-process inventory, June 1, 10,000 units	$12,680
Costs added during June to complete the beginning inventory	
Direct labor 7,000 equivalent units × $0.51	3,570
Factory overhead 6,000 equivalent units × $1.00	6,000
Total for beginning inventory	$22,250

Step 5, Part B: Total Cost for Units Started and Completed   The production cost of units started and completed in the current period can be computed by multiplying the number of units in this category by the cost per equivalent unit of the period.

The number of units started and completed in the period is the difference between the units completed and the number of units in beginning work-in-process. In the molding department example, we compute the units started and completed as follows:

Units completed – Beginning work-in-process = Units started and completed

44,000 units – 10,000 units = 34,000 units

Then the cost assigned to units started and completed is

34,000 units × $2.61 = $88,740

The total costs transferred out are the sum of the total cost from the beginning inventory and the total cost for units started and completed; that is

$22,250 + $88,740 = $110,990

Ending Work-in-Process Inventory   The cost amount assigned to ending work-in-process units is derived by multiplying the average unit costs for the period of each manufacturing cost element by the equivalent units of the ending work-in-process inventory.

The cost of 6,000 units in ending work-in-process inventory of the molding department is computed as follows:

Direct materials, 6,000 equivalent units × $1.10	$6,600
Direct labor, 3,000 equivalent units × $0.51	1,530
Factory overhead, 3,600 equivalent units × $1.00	3,600
Total ending work-in-process inventory	$11,730

Exhibit 13–13 shows that the sum of the costs assigned to goods transferred out and in ending work-in-process inventory equals the total costs accounted for of $122,720.

Cost Reconciliation

Now we need to determine whether the total manufacturing costs to account for in step 3 agree with the total costs accounted for in step 5. Again, step 3 accounts for $122,720 total manufacturing costs; this equals the total costs of $122,720 accounted for in step 5.

Production Cost Report

Steps 1 through 5 provide all information needed to prepare a production cost report for the molding department for June (Exhibit 13–14).

COMPARISON OF WEIGHTED-AVERAGE AND FIFO METHODS

The key difference between the weighted-average and FIFO methods is the handling of partially completed beginning work-in-process inventory units. The FIFO method separates the units in the beginning inventory from the units started and completed during the period. In contrast, the weighted-average method makes no separate treatment of the units in the beginning work-in-process inventory.

The FIFO method separates costs of the beginning work-in-process inventory from the current period costs, and it uses only the current period costs and work effort to calculate equivalent unit costs. As a result, the FIFO method separately calculates costs for units in the beginning inventory and units that were started during the period. In contrast, the weighted-average method uses the calculated average unit cost for all

Exhibit 13–13	**Step 5: Assign Total Manufacturing Costs—Molding Department** *FIFO Method*

	Completed and Transferred out	Ending Work-in-Process	Total
Goods completed and transferred out			
Beginning work-in-process	$ 12,680		$ 12,680
Costs added during June			
Direct materials	0		0
Direct labor (7,000 × $0.51)	3,570		3,570
Factory overhead (6,000 × $1.00)	6,000		6,000
Total for beginning inventory	$ 22,250		$ 22,250
Started and completed			
(34,000 × $2.61)	88,740		88,740
Total costs completed and transferred out	$110,990		$110,990
Ending work-in-process			
Direct material (6,000 × $1.10)		$ 6,600	$ 6,600
Direct labor (3,000 × $0.51)		1,530	1,530
Factory overhead (3,600 × $1.00)		3,600	3,600
Total costs accounted for	$110,990	$11,730	$122,720

Exhibit 13–14	**Production Cost Report—Molding Department** *FIFO Method*

Production Quantity Information

	Step 1: Analyze Flow of Physical Units		Step 2: Calculate Equivalent Units		
	Physical Units	Completion Percentage	Direct Materials	Direct Labor	Factory Overhead
Input					
Work-in-process, June 1	10,000				
Direct materials		100%	10,000		
Direct labor		30		3,000	
Factory overhead		40			4,000
Units started	40,000				
Units to account for	50,000				
Output					
Units completed	44,000	100%	44,000	44,000	44,000
Work-in-process, June 30	6,000				
Direct materials		100	6,000		
Direct labor		50		3,000	
Factory overhead		60			3,600
Units accounted for	50,000				
Total equivalent units (weighted-average method)			50,000	47,000	47,600
Less: equivalent units in June 1 work-in-process			(10,000)	(3,000)	(4,000)
Equivalent units for work performed in June only (FIFO method)			40,000	44,000	43,600

Exhibit 13–14   Continued

Unit Cost Determination

Step 3: Determine Total Costs to Account For	Direct Materials	Direct Labor	Factory Overhead	Total
Work-in-process, June 1				$ 12,680
Costs added during June	44,000	22,440	43,600	110,040
Total costs to account for				$122,720
Step 4: Compute Unit Costs				
Divide by equivalent units (from Step 2)	40,000	44,000	43,600	
Equivalent unit costs	$ 1.10	$ 0.51	$ 1.00	$ 2.61

Cost Assignment

Step 5: Assign Total Manufacturing Costs	Completed and Transferred out	Ending Work-in-Process	Total
Goods completed and transferred out			
Beginning work-in-process	$ 12,680		$ 12,680
Costs added during June			
Direct labor (7,000 × $0.51)	3,570		3,570
Factory overhead (6,000 × $1.00)	6,000		6,000
Total for beginning inventory	$ 22,250		$ 22,250
Started and completed (34,000 × $2.61)	88,740		88,740
Total costs completed and transferred out	$110,990		$110,990
Ending work-in-process			
Direct materials (6,000 × $1.10)		$ 6,600	6,600
Direct labor (3,000 × $0.51)		1,530	1,530
Factory overhead (3,600 × $1.00)		3,600	3,600
Total costs accounted for	$110,990	$11,730	$122,720

units completed during the period, including both the beginning work-in-process inventory and the units started and completed during the period. By conducting a cost-benefit analysis, firms can decide whether to use the FIFO or the weighted-average method.

The weighted-average method generally is easier to use because the calculations are simpler. This method is most appropriate when direct materials prices, conversion costs, and inventory levels are stable. The FIFO method is most appropriate when direct materials prices, conversion costs, or inventory levels fluctuate.

Firms with a cost leadership strategy prefer the FIFO method to the weighted-average method. Calculating costs per unit for each period independent of other periods (which the weighted-average method does not allow) makes the FIFO method preferable for control. The FIFO method also is related more closely to the continuous improvement concept.

Exhibit 13–15 graphically summarizes the difference between the weighted-average and FIFO equivalent units.

Many firms prefer the FIFO method over the weighted-average method for purposes of cost control and performance evaluation because the cost per equivalent unit under FIFO represents the cost for the current period's efforts only. Firms often evaluate department managers' performance on only current period costs without mixing in the effects of performance during different periods. Under the weighted-average method, the costs of the prior period and the current period are mixed, and deviations

Exhibit 13–15 Weighted-Average vs. FIFO Equivalent Units

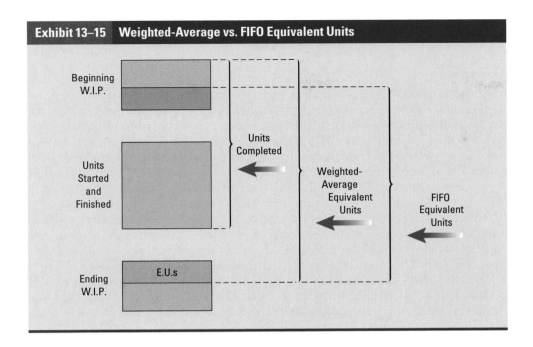

Process Costing in Practice at the U.S. Department of Agriculture (USDA) and in the Pork Production Industry

The USDA's accounting standards manual urges the use of activity-based costing in conjunction with process costing. The USDA also suggests that process costing be used in situations involving a large volume of similar goods or services. An example is the use of process costing to cost the payment of entitlement benefits. The payment of entitlement benefits involves a series of processes: reviewing applications, computing the amount of benefits, and issuing checks. Process costing is well suited for this context.

A recent survey of financial managers in the pork production industry revealed a variety of cost systems used within the industry. Standard cost systems were the most common; job costing and process costing systems were also very common. Pork production can be described in terms of a value chain that includes breeding, nursing, and finishing, among other steps. Job and process cost systems are more often used in the later phases of the pork producer's value chain because the flow of production in lots or groups of swine makes tracking costs using job and or process cost systems more convenient at this phase of the value chain.

Based on information in *U.S. Department of Agriculture Financial and Accounting Standards Manual,* Version 2.0, Chapter 5, Section 5.9 (U.S. Department of Agriculture, October 23, 1997). (http://www.usda.gov/ocfo/fasm/ch05/); and Steve Weiss, "Cost Accounting," presented at the 1998 Pork Financial Management Conference. (www.iowaselect.com/ind_cost.html).

in performance in the current period could be concealed by interperiod variations in unit costs.

The advantage of the weighted-average method is its simplicity, although computers can reduce this advantage. This method is inappropriate when a firm's beginning and ending inventories or manufacturing costs per unit change dramatically from period to period.

PROCESS COSTING WITH MULTIPLE DEPARTMENTS

Most manufacturing firms have multiple departments or use several processes that require a number of steps. As the product passes from one department to another, the cost passes from department to department. The costs from the prior department are called *transferred-in costs* or *prior department costs*. This section discusses the concept of transferred-in costs and describes the weighted-average methods of cost flow assumptions for firms with multiple departments. Appendix B to this chapter describes the use of the FIFO method of process costing for firms with multiple departments.

Transferred-In Costs

Transferred-in costs are costs of work performed in the earlier department that are transferred into the present department.

Transferred-in costs (TI) are costs of work performed in the earlier department that are transferred into the present department. Including these costs is a necessary part of process costing because we treat each department as a separate entity, and each department's production cost report includes all costs added to the product up to that point. If transferred-in costs were not included, each completed unit transferred out of a department would include only the value of the work performed on it by that department. It might help you to think of transferred-in costs as similar to the direct materials introduced at the beginning of the production process. The equivalent units of production of transferred-in costs can be computed in the same manner as direct materials that are added at the beginning of a process. The difference between the direct materials cost and the transferred-in cost is that the former comes from the storeroom while the latter comes from another production department.

The transferred-in cost of work-in-process ending inventory is almost always 100 percent. In this text the equivalent units of the transferred-in cost for ending work-in-process inventory is always assumed to be the same as the number of units in ending work-in-process inventory. Remember that transferred-in costs are treated as if they are added at the beginning of the production process for the department. As units are finished in one department and transferred to a second department for further processing, all transferred-in costs during a period in the second department are carried at one unit cost regardless of the cost flow method used by the previous departments. Because all units in process are complete for prior departments' costs, by definition the number of equivalent units is the number of physical units to account for.

Basic Data

Suppose that Hsu Toy Company's molding department transfers its production units to the finishing department. In the finishing department, direct materials are added at the end of the process. Conversion costs (direct labor and factory overhead) are applied evenly throughout the finishing department's process. The finishing department uses direct labor as the cost driver to apply factory overhead costs.

Data for the finishing department for June 2001 are shown in Exhibit 13–16.

Exhibit 13–16	**Basic Data for Hsu Toy Company—Finishing Department**
Work-in-process, June 1: 14,000 units	
Direct materials: 0 percent complete	
Transferred-in: 100 percent complete	$ 34,250
Conversion: 50 percent complete	7,000
Beginning work-in-process inventory	$ 41,250
Units transferred-in during June	44,000 units
Units completed	50,000 units
Work-in-process, June 30	8,000 units
Transferred-in: 100 percent complete	
Conversion: 50 percent complete	
Costs added during June	
Direct materials	$ 25,000
Conversion	47,000
Transferred-in costs during June	
Weighted-average method	$111,320
FIFO method	110,990

Weighted-Average Method

Follow the familiar five-step procedure as we illustrate the weighted-average method for process costing with multiple departments.

◀**LEARNING OBJECTIVE 7**

Analyze process costing with multiple departments.

Steps 1 and 2: Analyze Flow of Physical Units and Calculate Equivalent Units

The first step is to analyze the physical units of production. The second step is to calculate equivalent units. Exhibit 13–17 summarizes the computation of physical units and equivalent units.

In Exhibit 13–17, the 50,000 physical units that were completed were 100 percent complete. Thus, they represent 50,000 equivalent units for transferred-in, direct materials, and conversion costs. Note that the 50,000 units include 14,000 units transferred from the molding department in May and completed in June, and 36,000 units (50,000 units − 14,000 units) transferred from the molding department and also completed in June.

The 8,000 units in ending work-in-process inventory are 100 percent complete with respect to transferred-in costs because they were 100 percent complete in the preceding department. There is no direct materials component because materials are added at the end of the finishing department. Because ending work-in-process inventory is only 50 percent complete with respect to conversion costs, ending work-in-process inventories represent 4,000 equivalent units of conversion costs (8,000 physical units × 50% complete).

As Exhibit 13–17 shows, the total number of equivalent units is calculated as follows:

> Completed units
>
> + Ending work-in-process equivalent units
> ──
> = Total equivalent units of production

That is, by using the weighted-average method, the equivalent units of production for the finishing department include 58,000 units transferred in, 50,000 units of direct materials, and 54,000 units of conversion.

Exhibit 13–17	Steps 1 and 2: Analyze Flow of Physical Units and Calculate Equivalent Units—Finishing Department				
	Weighted-Average Method				
	Step 1			**Step 2**	
				Equivalent Units	
	Physical Units	**Completion Percentage**	**Transferred-in Costs**	**Direct Materials**	**Conversion Costs**
Input					
Work-in-process, June 1	14,000				
Direct materials		0%			
Transferred-in costs		100			
Conversion costs		50			
Transferred-in	44,000				
Units to account for	58,000				
Output					
Units completed	50,000	100%	50,000	50,000	50,000
Work-in-process, June 30	8,000				
Direct materials		0			
Transferred-in costs		100	8,000		
Conversion costs		50			4,000
Units accounted for	58,000				
Total equivalent units			58,000	50,000	54,000

Steps 3 and 4: Determine Total Costs to Account for and Compute Unit Costs

The third step is to determine the total manufacturing costs to account for, and the fourth step is to compute equivalent unit costs for transferred-in, direct materials, and conversion costs.

Exhibit 13–18 summarizes the total manufacturing costs to account for and unit costs for all cost components. Total manufacturing costs to account for ($224,570) consist of the beginning work-in-process inventory balance, $41,250, plus the current costs added during June, $183,320 ($25,000 + $47,000 + $111,320).

The equivalent unit cost for units transferred in ($2.5099) is computed by dividing the total transferred-in cost ($145,570), including the cost of beginning work-in-process ($34,250) and the cost added during June ($111,320), by the total equivalent units transferred in (58,000). Similar procedures are used for direct materials and conversion costs.

Step 5: Assign Total Manufacturing Costs

The final step of the process costing procedure is to assign total manufacturing costs to units completed and to units in ending work-in-process inventory. Exhibit 13–19 summarizes the cost assignment schedule with $224,574 total costs accounted for in this step 5.

Cost Reconciliation

For the cost reconciliation, the total manufacturing cost to account for in step 3 is $224,570, which does not equal the $224,574 total costs accounted for in step 5. The amount of difference is small, $4, which could be due to a rounding error.

Exhibit 13–18	Steps 3 and 4: Determine Total Costs to Account for and Compute Unit Costs—Finishing Department *Weighted-Average Method*			
Step 3	**Transferred-in Costs**	**Direct Materials**	**Conversion Costs**	**Total**
Work-in-process, June 1	$ 34,250	$ 0	$ 7,000	$ 41,250
Costs added during June	111,320	25,000	47,000	183,320
Total costs to account for	$145,570	$25,000	$54,000	$224,570
Step 4				
Divide by equivalent units (from Exhibit 13–17)	58,000	50,000	54,000	
Equivalent unit costs	$ 2.5099 +	$ 0.50 +	$ 1.00 =	$ 4.0099

Exhibit 13–19	Step 5: Assign Total Manufacturing Costs—Finishing Department *Weighted-Average Method*		
Step 5	**Completed and Transferred out**	**Ending Work-in-Process**	**Total**
Goods completed and transferred out (50,000 × $4.0099)	$200,495		$200,495
Ending work-in-process			
Transferred-in (8,000 × $2.5099)		$20,079	20,079
Conversion (4,000 × $1.00)		4,000	4,000
Total costs accounted for	$200,495	$24,079	$224,574

Production Cost Report

Steps 1 through 5 provide all information needed to prepare a production cost report for the finishing department for June. This report appears in Exhibit 13–20.

Exhibit 13–20	Production Cost Report—Finishing Department
	Weighted-Average Method

Production Quantity Information

	Step 1: Analyze Flow of Physical Units		Step 2: Calculate Equivalent Units		
	Physical Units	**Completion Percentage**	**Transferred-in Costs**	**Direct Materials**	**Conversion Costs**
Input					
Work-in-process, June 1	14,000				
Direct materials		0%			
Transferred-in costs		100			
Conversion costs		50			
Transferred in	44,000				
Units to account for	58,000				
Output					
Units completed	50,000	100%	50,000	50,000	50,000
Work-in-process, June 30	8,000				
Direct materials		0			
Transferred-in costs		100	8,000		
Conversion costs		50			4,000
Units accounted for	58,000				
Total equivalent units			58,000	50,000	54,000

Unit Cost Determination

Step 3: Determine Total Costs to Account For	Transferred-in Costs	Direct Materials	Conversion Costs	Total
Work-in-process, June 1	$ 34,250	$ 0	$ 7,000	$ 41,250
Costs added during June	111,320	25,000	47,000	183,320
Total costs to account for	$145,570	$25,000	$54,000	$224,570

Step 4: Compute Unit Costs				
Divide by equivalent units (from Step 2)	58,000	50,000	54,000	
Equivalent unit costs	$ 2.5099	$ 0.50	$ 1.00	$ 4.0099

Cost Assignment

Step 5: Assign Total Manufacturing Costs	Completed and Transferred out	Ending Work-in-Process	Total
Goods completed and transferred out (50,000 × $4.0099)	$200,495		$200,495
Ending work-in-process			
Transferred-in (8,000 × $2.5099)		$20,079	20,079
Conversion (4,000 × $1.00)		4,000	4,000
Total costs accounted for	$200,495	$24,079	$224,574

JOURNAL ENTRIES AND T-ACCOUNTS FOR PROCESS COSTING

LEARNING OBJECTIVE 8▶

Prepare journal entries to record the flow of costs in a process costing system.

Process costing uses the same general ledger manufacturing accounts as job costing discussed in Chapter 12. However, instead of tracing product costs to specific jobs, we accumulate costs in production departments or other cost centers. Each department has a separate Work-in-Process Inventory account. These journal entries for Hsu Toy Company use weighted-average method data from Steps 3 and 5 of both Exhibit 13–9 (molding department) and Exhibit 13–20 (finishing department). Assume that 50 percent of the conversion costs in the finishing department are direct labor ($47,000 × 50% = $23,500).

The following direct materials were requisitioned and used:

(1)	Work-in-Process Inventory—Molding Department	44,000	
	Work-in-Process Inventory—Finishing Department	25,000	
	Materials Inventory		69,000
	To record direct materials costs added during June.		

The direct labor incurred follows:

(2)	Work-in-Process Inventory—Molding Department	22,440	
	Work-in-Process Inventory—Finishing Department	23,500	
	Accrued Payroll		45,940
	To record direct labor costs incurred during June.		

Factory overhead applied is as follows:

(3)	Work-in-Process Inventory—Molding Department	43,600	
	Work-in-Process Inventory—Finishing Department	23,500	
	Factory Overhead Applied		67,100
	To record the application of factory overhead to departments.		

Transferred-in costs from the molding department follows:

(4)	Work-in-Process Inventory—Finishing Department	111,320	
	Work-in-Process Inventory—Molding Department		111,320
	To record the weighted-average method of the cost of goods completed in the molding department and transferred out to the finishing department.		

Product units finished are as follows:

(5)	Finished Goods Inventory	200,495	
	Work-in-Process Inventory—Finishing Department		200,495
	To record the weighted-average method of the cost of goods completed in the finishing department.		

Exhibit 13–21 represents cost flows through related general ledger T-accounts for Hsu Toy Company.

Exhibit 13–21	General Ledger Accounts for Hsu Toy Company

Materials Inventory

Balance	xx,xxx	(1) 69,000
Balance	xx,xxx	

Work-in-Process Inventory—Molding Department

Balance	12,680	(4) 111,320
(1) DM	44,000	
(2) DL	22,440	
(3) OH	43,600	
Balance	11,400	

Work-in-Process Inventory—Finishing Department

Balance	41,250	(5) 200,495
(1) DM	25,000	
(2) DL	23,500	
(3) OH	23,500	
(4)	111,320	
Balance	24,075	

Factory Overhead Applied

	(3) 67,100

Finished Goods Inventory

Balance	xx,xxx	
(5)	200,495	

Accrued Payroll

	(2) 45,940

EFFECTS OF THE NEW MANUFACTURING ENVIRONMENT

Just-In-Time Systems

In recent years, many firms have adopted just-in-time (JIT) systems to minimize inventories and improve quality control. Under the JIT philosophy, raw materials are received just before they are needed in production. In multiple department situations, production departments assemble goods and subassemblies just in time for the product to be sold. Thus, direct materials inventory, work-in-process inventory, and finished goods inventory are kept at a minimal level.

◀LEARNING OBJECTIVE 9

Characterize the impact of the new manufacturing technologies on process costing.

JIT methodology has three major effects on process costing procedures. First, the difference in unit cost between the FIFO and weighted-average methods is reduced by the decreased inventory units. Second, under JIT, there is much less difference between the number of units completed and the number of units in work-in-process ending inventory. Third, new cost drivers or activity bases (other than direct labor-hours or costs) are needed to assign factory overhead to processes and products because a JIT system replaces most production employees with machines and support personnel. Under JIT, process costing becomes very simple because of reduced inventory. To find the unit cost, we simply divide the total cost of the period by the number of units produced to get a close approximation.

Flexible Manufacturing and Cellular Manufacturing Systems

More manufacturing firms are moving toward flexible manufacturing systems (FMS) and cellular manufacturing systems (CMS). An FMS is an automated production system that produces one or more items in a family of parts in a flexible manner. It uses robots and computer-controlled materials-handling systems to link several stand-alone numerical control machines that quickly and efficiently switch from one production run to another.

The effect of FMS on product costing is similar to that of JIT. Under an FMS environment, process costing is more useful than job costing because more accounting reports are based on time periods rather than the closing of job orders.

A CMS forms a cell containing the machinery and equipment needed to manufacture parts with similar processing requirements. To improve production efficiency, most parts travel in the same direction from one end of a cell to the other. A collection of cells assigned to make a product forms a focused factory. CMS changes the structure of the manufacturing process so that it is by product line rather than process. Under CMS, traditional process costing is less useful than the activity-based costing with cell-level cost pools because activities, not just direct labor- or machine-hours, incur different types of factory overhead.

SUMMARY

Process costing is a product cost system that accumulates costs in processing departments and allocates them to all units processed during the period, including both completed and partially completed units. It is used by firms producing homogeneous products on a continuous basis to assign manufacturing costs to units in production during the period. Firms that use process costing include paint, chemical, oil-refining, and food-processing companies.

Process costing systems provide information so managers can make strategic decisions regarding products and customers, manufacturing methods, pricing options, overhead allocation methods, and other long-term issues.

Equivalent units are the number of the same or similar completed units that could have been produced given the amount of work actually performed on both complete and partially completed units.

The key document in a typical process costing system is the production cost report that summarizes the physical units and equivalent units of a production department, the costs incurred during the period, and the costs assigned to goods both completed and transferred out as well as to ending work-in-process inventories. The preparation of a production cost report includes five steps: (1) analyze physical units, (2) calculate equivalent units, (3) determine total costs to account for, (4) compute unit costs, and (5) assign total manufacturing costs.

The two methods of preparing the departmental production cost report in process costing are the weighted-average method and first-in, first-out (FIFO) method. The weighted-average method includes all costs in calculating the unit cost. It includes those costs incurred in both current and prior periods that are shown as the beginning work-in-process inventory of this period. The FIFO method includes only costs incurred during the current period in calculating equivalent unit cost. It considers the beginning inventory as a batch of goods separate from the goods started and completed within the same period. FIFO assumes that all the beginning work-in-process inventories were completed before other work is performed during the current period.

Under the weighted-average method, when a product is started makes no difference; all units completed in a period are treated the same way. When this method is used, only the status of the product at the end of the period must be known. On the other hand, the status of the product both at the end and at the beginning of a period must be considered when the FIFO method is used to determine product costs. That is, the FIFO method considers input as well as output of the production, whereas the weighted-average method considers only the production output.

Most manufacturing firms have several departments or use processes that require several steps. As the product passes from one department to another, the cost must follow. The costs that come from the prior department are transferred-in costs or prior department costs. Process costing with multiple departments should include the transferred-in cost as the fourth cost element in addition to direct materials, direct labor, and factory overhead costs.

Process costing uses the same manufacturing accounts as job costing discussed in the preceding chapter. Journal entries are essentially the same as in job costing. However, instead of tracing product costs to specific jobs, we accumulate costs in production departments or cost centers.

For firms that adopt either just-in-time or flexible manufacturing systems, choosing between the weighted-average or the FIFO method of process costing is not so important because the new systems reduce inventory units. Such firms also need cost drivers other than direct labor cost to assign factory overhead to products.

APPENDIX A

Spoilage in Process Costing

As discussed in Appendix A to Chapter 12, the two types of spoilage are normal and abnormal. *Normal spoilage* occurs under efficient operating conditions. It is uncontrollable in the short term and is considered a part of product cost. That is, the costs of lost units are absorbed by the good units produced. *Abnormal spoilage* exceeds expected losses under efficient operating conditions and is charged as a loss to operations in the period detected.

◀**LEARNING OBJECTIVE 10**

Account for spoilage in process costing.

Two approaches are used to account for spoilage in process costing systems. The first approach is to count the number of spoiled units, prepare a separate equivalent unit computation with the cost per unit of the spoiled goods, and then allocate the cost to the good units produced. The second approach is to omit the spoiled units in computing the equivalent units of production; the spoilage cost is part of the total manufacturing costs. The first approach provides more accurate product costs because it computes the costs associated with normal spoilage and spreads them over the good units produced. The second approach is less accurate because it spread the costs of normal spoilage over all units—good completed units, units in ending work-in-process inventory, and abnormal spoiled units. This appendix discusses the first approach in detail.

Consider Diamond Company, which has the following data for the current period:

	Units	Cost
Beginning work-in-process inventory	2,000	
Direct materials (100 percent complete)		$100,000
Conversion costs (75 percent complete)		80,000
Units started in the period	8,000	
Costs incurred during the period		
Direct materials		300,000
Conversion costs		405,000
Ending work-in-process inventory	2,000	
Direct materials (100 percent complete)		
Conversion costs (80 percent complete)		
Completed and transferred out	7,000	
Normal spoilage is 10 percent of good production		

Diamond Company uses the weighted-average process costing method. The company inspects all products at the completion point. Using the five-step procedure described in the chapter, we need only add normal spoilage and abnormal spoilage components in calculations.

Step 1. Analyze Physical Units

With 7,000 good production units completed in May, the normal spoiled units total 700 ($7,000 \times 10\%$). The calculation of abnormal spoiled units follows:

Abnormal spoiled units = Beginning work-in-process inventory + Units started
－ Ending work-in-process inventory － Goods completed
and transferred-out units － Normal spoiled units

= 2,000 + 8,000 － 2,000 － 7,000 － 700

= 300 units

Exhibit 13–22	**Diamond Company's Production Cost Report** *Weighted-Average Method*

Production Quantity Information

	Step 1: Flow of Costs		Step 2: Calculate Equivalent Units	
	Physical Units	**Completion Percentage**	**Direct Materials**	**Conversion Cost**
Input				
Work-in-process, May 1	2,000			
Direct materials		100%		
Conversion		75		
Number started	8,000			
Total to account for	10,000			
Output				
Number completed	7,000	100%	7,000	7,000
Normal spoilage (10%)	700		700	700
Abnormal spoilage	300		300	300
Work-in-process, May 31	2,000			
Direct materials		100	2,000	
Conversion		80		1,600
Total accounted for	10,000			
Total equivalent units			10,000	9,600

Unit Cost Determination

Step 3: Determine Total Costs to Account for	Direct Materials	Conversion Costs	Total
Work-in-process, May 1	$100,000	$ 80,000	$180,000
Costs added during period	300,000	405,000	705,000
Total costs to account for	$400,000	$485,000	$885,000

Step 4: Compute Unit Costs			
Divide by number of equivalent units	10,000	9,600	
Equivalent unit costs	$ 40.00	$50.521	$90.521

Cost Assignment

Step 5: Assign Total Manufacturing Costs	Completed and Transferred Out	Ending Work-in-Process	Total
Goods completed and transferred out [(Goods units 7,000 + Normal spoilage 700) × $90.521]	$697,011		$697,011
Abnormal spoilage (300 × $90.521)	27,156		27,156
Work-in-process, May 31			
Direct materials (2,000 × $40.00)		$80,000	80,000
Conversion (1,600 × $50.521)		80,833	80,833
Total costs accounted for	$724,167	$160,833	$885,000

Exhibit 13–23	Diamond Company's FIFO Production Cost Report

Production Quantity Information

	Step 1: Analyze Flow of Physical Units	Step 2: Calculate Equivalent Units	
	Physical Units	**Direct Materials**	**Conversion Costs**
Input			
Work-in-process beginning inventory	2,000	(100%)	(75%)
Started this period	8,000		
Total to account for	10,000		
Output			
Completed	7,000	7,000	7,000
Normal spoilage (10 percent)	700	700	700
Abnormal spoilage	300	300	300
Work-in-process ending inventory	2,000 (80%)	2,000	1,600
Total accounted for	10,000		
Total work done to date		10,000	9,600
Work-in-process beginning inventory		(2,000)	(1,500)
Total work done this period (Total equivalent units)		8,000	8,100

Unit Cost Determination

Step 3: Determine Total Costs to Account For	Total	Direct Materials	Conversion Costs
Work-in-process beginning inventory	$180,000	$100,000	$80,000
Current cost	705,000	300,000	405,000
Total costs to account for	$885,000	$400,000	$485,000
		($300,000/	($405,000/
Step 4: Compute Unit Costs		8,000) =	8,100) =
Cost per equivalent unit	$ 87.50	$ 37.50	$ 50.00

Cost Assignment

Step 5: Assign Total Manufacturing Costs	Total	Direct Materials	Conversion Costs
Units completed (7,000)			
From work-in-process, beginning inventory	$180,000	$100,000	$80,000
Current costs incurred completing units (500)	25,000	0	25,000
Total cost from beginning inventory (2,000)	$205,000	$100,000	$105,000
Normal spoilage (700)	61,250	26,250	35,000
Units started and completed this period (5,000)	437,500	187,500	250,000
Total cost of units completed	$703,750	$313,750	$390,000
Abnormal spoilage (300)	26,250	11,250	15,000
Work-in-process ending inventory		(2,000 × $37.5)	(1,600 × $50)
	155,000	= $75,000	= $80,000
Total costs accounted for	$885,000		

Step 2. Calculate Equivalent Units

Equivalent units for spoilage are calculated in the same way as good units. Following the first approach, all normal and abnormal spoiled units are included in the calculation of equivalent units. Since the company inspects all products at the completion point, the same amount of work is performed on each completed good unit and each completed spoiled unit.

Step 3. Determine Total Costs to Account For

These costs include all costs in the beginning work-in-process inventory and all costs added during the period. The detail of this step is similar to the process costing procedure without spoilage incurred.

Step 4. Compute Unit Costs

The detail of this step is similar to the process costing procedure without any spoilage.

Step 5. Assign Total Manufacturing Costs

This step now includes the costs of good units and spoiled units.

Exhibit 13–22 summarizes the five-step procedure for the weighted-average process costing method, including both normal and abnormal spoilage.

Exhibit 13–23 is the production cost report under the FIFO process costing method. The journal entries for Diamond Company using the FIFO method are

Finished Goods Inventory	703,750	
Work-in-Process Inventory		703,750
To record the total cost of units completed, including the normal spoilage cost.		
Loss from Spoilage	26,250	
Work-in-Process Inventory		26,250
To record the abnormal spoilage cost.		

APPENDIX B

FIFO Method of Process Costing for Firms with Multiple Departments

Now we illustrate the FIFO method of process costing for multiple departments using data from the Hsu Toy Company's finishing department (see Exhibit 13–16).

Steps 1 and 2: Analyze Flow of Physical Units and Calculate Equivalent Units

Exhibit 13–24 summarizes the physical flow units and equivalent units of production for the finishing department.

The physical flow of product units is unaffected by the process costing method used. Therefore, step 1 is the same as with the weighted-average method.

The 14,000 physical units in the June 1 work-in-process inventory have 100 percent of transferred-in costs, so they represent 14,000 equivalent units of transferred-in work. Because the materials are added at the end of the process in the finishing department, zero equivalent units of direct materials for work-in-process inventory are on hand on June 1. The beginning work-in-process inventory is only 50 percent complete with respect to conversion activity, so this department has 7,000 equivalent units of conversion costs (14,000 × 50%).

LEARNING OBJECTIVE 7▶

Analyze process costing with multiple departments.

As Exhibit 13–24 indicates, the total number of equivalent units is calculated as follows:

Completed units
+ Ending work-in-process equivalent units
− Beginning work-in-process equivalent units
= Equivalent units of work completed during this period

Exhibit 13–24	Steps 1 and 2: Analyze Flow of Physical Units and Calculate Equivalent Units—Finishing Department *FIFO Method*				

	Step 1		Step 2		
				Equivalent Units	
	Physical Units	**Completion Percentage**	**Transferred-in Costs**	**Direct Materials**	**Conversion Costs**
Input					
Work-in-process, June 1	14,000				
Transferred-in		100%	14,000		
Direct materials		0		0	
Conversion		50			7,000
Transferred-in	52,000				
Units to account for	66,000				
Output					
Units completed	50,000	100%	50,000	50,000	50,000
Work-in-process, June 30	8,000				
Transferred-in		100	8,000		
Direct materials		0		0	
Conversion		50			4,000
Units accounted for	58,000				
Total equivalent units (weighted-average method)			58,000	50,000	54,000
Less: equivalent units in June 1 work-in-process			(14,000)	(0)	(7,000)
Equivalent units for work done in June only (FIFO method)			44,000	50,000	47,000

That is, equivalent units of production for the finishing department using the FIFO method are 44,000 transferred-in units, 50,000 direct material units, and 47,000 conversion activity units.

Steps 3 and 4: Determine Total Costs to Account for and Compute Unit Costs

Exhibit 13–25 shows the computation of total costs to account for and equivalent unit costs for the finishing department.

The beginning work-in-process inventory has a cost of $41,250. The $182,990 total costs added during June include $110,990 transferred-in costs from the modeling department, $25,000 direct materials costs and $47,000 conversion costs incurred in the finishing department as showing in Exhibit 13–25.

The equivalent unit cost for transferred-in units ($2.5225) is computed by dividing the transferred-in cost during June ($110,990) by the equivalent units for work completed only in June (44,000). Similar procedures are used for direct materials and conversion costs. Notice that the costs of beginning inventory are excluded from this calculation. The calculations use only current costs added in June.

Step 5: Assign Total Manufacturing Costs

The final step of the process costing procedure is to assign total manufacturing costs to units completed and to units in the ending work-in-process inventory. Exhibit 13–26 summarizes the cost assignment schedule.

	Steps 3 and 4: Determine Total Costs to Account For and Compute Unit			
Exhibit 13–25	**Costs—Finishing Department**			
	FIFO Method			

Step 3	Transferred-in Costs	Direct Materials	Conversion Costs	Total
Work-in-process, June 1				$ 41,250
Costs added during June	$110,990	$25,000	$47,000	182,990
Total costs to account for				$224,240
Step 4				
Divide by equivalent units (from Exhibit 13–24):	44,000	50,000	47,000	
Equivalent unit costs	$ 2.5225 +	$ 0.50 +	$ 1.00 =	$4.0225

The costs assigned to the first batch of goods completed and from the 14,000 units of the beginning work-in-process are calculated as follows:

Work-in-process, June 1, 14,000 units	$41,250
Costs added during June to complete the beginning inventory:	
Direct material 14,000 equivalent units × $0.50	7,000
Conversion costs 7,000 equivalent units × $1.00	7,000
Total for beginning inventory	$55,250

The costs assigned to the 36,000 units started and completed during June are calculated:

$$50,000 \text{ units} - 14,000 \text{ units} = 36,000 \text{ units}$$

$$36,000 \text{ units} \times \$4.0225 = \$144,810$$

The total costs completed are the sum of the total costs from beginning inventory and the total costs for units started and completed, that is,

$$\$55,250 + \$144,810 = \$200,060$$

The cost of the finishing department's 8,000 units in ending work-in-process inventory is computed:

Transferred-in: 8,000 equivalent units × $2.5225	$20,180
Conversion: 4,000 equivalent units × $1.00	4,000
Total ending work-in-process inventory	$24,180

In Exhibit 13–26, the sum of the costs assigned to goods completed and ending work-in-process inventory is $224,240. Note that the amount of total costs accounted for in this step 5 should equal the total costs to account for in step 3 (as shown in Exhibit 13–25).

Cost Reconciliation

Now we need to determine whether the total manufacturing costs to account for in step 3 are the same as the total costs accounted for in step 5. Step 3 has $224,240 total manufacturing costs to account for, which equals the total costs accounted for in step 5.

Production Cost Report

Steps 1 through 5 provide all the information needed to prepare a production cost report for the molding department for June. This report appears in Exhibit 13–27.

| Exhibit 13–26 | **Step 5: Assign Total Costs—Finishing Department**
FIFO Method | | | |

	Completed and Transferred out	Ending Work- in-Process	Total
Goods completed and transferred out			
Beginning work-in-process	$ 41,250		$ 41,250
Costs added during June			
Direct materials (14,000 × $0.50)	7,000		7,000
Conversion (7,000 × $1.00)	7,000		7,000
Total from beginning inventory	$ 55,250		$ 55,250
Started and completed (36,000 × $4.0225)	144,810		144,810
Total costs completed and transferred out	$200,060		$200,060
Ending work-in-process:			
Transferred-in (8,000 × $2.5225)		$20,180	20,180
Conversion costs (4,000 × $1.00)		4,000	4,000
Total costs accounted for	$200,060	$24,180	$224,240

| Exhibit 13–27 | **Production Cost Report—Finishing Department**
FIFO Method | | | | |

Production Quantity Information

		Step 1: Analyze Flow of Physical Units		Step 2: Calculate Equivalent Units	
	Physical Units	Completion Percentage	Transferred- in Costs	Direct Materials	Conversion Costs
Input					
Work-in-process, June 1	14,000				
Transferred-in		100%	14,000		
Direct materials		0		0	
Conversion		50			7,000
Transferred-in	44,000				
Units to account for	58,000				
Output					
Units completed	50,000	100%	50,000	50,000	50,000
Work-in-process, June 30	8,000				
Transferred-in		100	8,000		
Direct materials		0		0	
Conversion		50			4,000
Units accounted for	58,000				
Total equivalent units (weighted-average method)			58,000	50,000	54,000
Less: equivalent units in June 1 work-in-process			(14,000)	(0)	(7,000)
Equivalent units for work performed only in June (FIFO method)			44,000	50,000	47,000

(continued)

Exhibit 13–27   Concluded

Unit Cost Determination

Step 3: Determine Total Costs to Account for	Transferred-in Costs	Direct Materials	Conversion Costs	Total
Work-in-process, June 1				$ 41,250
Costs added during June	$110,990	$25,000	$47,000	182,990
Total costs to account for				$224,240

Step 4: Compute Unit Costs

	Transferred-in Costs	Direct Materials	Conversion Costs	Total
Divide by equivalent units (from Step 2)	44,000	50,000	47,000	
Equivalent unit costs	$ 2.5225	$ 0.50	$ 1.00	$ 4.0225

Cost Assignment

Step 5: Assign Total Manufacturing Costs	Completed and Transferred out	Ending Work-in-Process	Total
Goods completed and transferred out			
Beginning work-in-process	$ 41,250		$ 41,250
Costs added during June			
Direct materials (14,000 × $0.50)	7,000		7,000
Conversion (7,000 × $1.00)	7,000		7,000
Total from beginning inventory	$ 55,250		$ 55,250
Started and completed (36,000 × $4.0225)	144,810		144,810
Total costs transferred out	$200,060		$200,060
Ending work-in-process			
Transferred in (8,000 × $2.5225)		$20,180	20,180
Conversion (4,000 × $1.00)		4,000	4,000
Total costs accounted for	$200,060	$24,180	$224,240

KEY TERMS

COMMENTS ON COST MANAGEMENT IN ACTION

Whirlpool Faces Competitive Pressure in Home Appliance Market

The Whirlpool Corporation acquired 47 percent of Philips Electronics' European appliance business unit in 1989 and the remainder in 1991. Whirlpool's European experience puts it far ahead of other U.S. firms such as Maytag, General Electric, and Electrolux in building an integrated global business. Operating income for the first three quarters of 1994 increased to 6.5 percent from 3.6 percent in 1990, and market share increased from 11.5 percent to 13 percent.

Whirlpool's most significant change is in the use of process cost information to improve processes and activities resulting in manufacturing cost reduction. Whirlpool also merged national designers and researchers into pan-European teams that work closely with the company's U.S. designers. This significantly reduced product costs for a series of new Whirlpool products using common "platforms" and processes that allow different models to be built on the same underlying chassis and process.

Whirlpool also reduced asset costs by streamlining Philips' scattered assets. By the end of 1994, it had slashed $400 million in annual costs. Whirlpool closed a surplus plant in Barcelona, trimmed 36 warehouses to 8, and centralized inventory control, chopping Philips' legion of 1,600 suppliers in half. Where Philips had purchased refrigerator power cords from 17 suppliers, Whirlpool buys from two. Together, these changes cut inventories by one-third.

Based on information in Patrick Oster and John Rossant, "Call It Worldpool," *Business Week*, November 28, 1994.

SELF-STUDY PROBLEMS

(For solutions, please turn to the end of the chapter.)

1. Weighted-Average Method versus FIFO Method

Smith Electronic Company's chip-mounting production department had 300 units of unfinished product, each 40 percent complete on September 30, 2001. During October of the same year, this department put another 900 units into production and completed 1,000 units and transferred them to the next production department. At the end of October, 200 units of unfinished product, 70 percent completed, were recorded in the ending work-in-process inventory. Smith Company introduces all direct materials when the production process is 50 percent complete. Direct labor and factory overhead (i.e., conversion) costs are added uniformly throughout the process.

Following is a summary of production costs incurred during October:

	Direct Materials	Conversion Costs
Beginning work-in-process		$2,202
Current costs	$9,600	6,120
Total costs	$9,600	$8,322

Required

1. Calculate each of the following amounts using weighted-average process costing:
   a. Equivalent units of direct materials and conversion.
   b. Unit costs of direct materials and conversion.
   c. Cost of goods completed and transferred out during the period.
   d. Cost of work-in-process inventory at the end of the period.
2. Prepare a production cost report for October 2001 using the weighted-average method.
3. Repeat requirement 1 using the FIFO method.
4. Repeat requirement 2 using the FIFO method.

2. Weighted-Average Method versus FIFO Method with Transferred-In Cost

Reed Company has two departments, a machining department and a finishing department. The following information relates to the finishing department: work-in-process, November 1, 2001, 10 units, 40 percent completed, consisting of $100 transferred-in costs, $80 direct materials, and $52 conversion costs. Production completed for November totaled 82 units; work-in-process, November 30, 2001, 8 units, 50 percent completed. All finishing department direct materials are introduced at the start of the process; conversion costs are incurred uniformly throughout the process. Transferred-in costs from the machining department during November were $800; direct materials added were $720; conversion costs incurred were $861. Following is the summary data of Reed Company's finishing department:

Work-in-process, November 1, 10 units:	
Transferred-in: 100 percent complete	$ 100
Direct materials: 100 percent added	80
Conversion: 40 percent complete	52
Balance in work-in-process, November 1	$ 232
Units transferred in from machining department	
during November	80 units
Units completed during November and	
transferred out to finished goods inventory	82 units
Work-in-process, November 30	8 units
Transferred-in: 100 percent complete	
Direct materials: 100 percent added	
Conversion: 50 percent complete	
Costs incurred during November	
Transferred-in	$ 800
Direct materials	720
Conversion	861
Total current costs	$2,381

Required

1. Prepare a production cost report for November using the weighted-average method.

2. Prepare a production cost report for November using the FIFO method.

QUESTIONS

13–1   What are the typical characteristics of a company that should use a process costing system?

13–2   List three types of industries that would likely use process costing.

13–3   Explain the primary differences between job costing and process costing.

13–4   What does the term *equivalent units* mean?

13–5   How is the equivalent unit calculation affected when direct materials are added at the beginning of the process rather than uniformly throughout the process?

13–6   What is a production cost report? What are the five key steps in preparing a production cost report?

13–7   What is the distinction between equivalent units under the FIFO method and equivalent units under the weighted-average method?

13–8   Identify the conditions under which the weighted-average method of process costing is inappropriate.

13–9   Specify the advantages of the weighted-average method of process costing in contrast to the FIFO method.

13–10 From the standpoint of cost control, why is the FIFO method superior to the weighted-average method? Is it possible to monitor cost trends using the weighted-average method?

13–11 What are transferred-in costs?

13–12 Suppose that manufacturing is performed in sequential production departments. Prepare a journal entry to show a transfer of partially completed units from the first department to the second department.

13–13 Under the weighted-average method, all units transferred out are treated the same way. How does this differ from the FIFO method of handling units transferred out?

13–14 Under the FIFO method, only current period costs and work are included in unit costs and equivalent units computation. Under the weighted-average method, what assumptions are made when unit costs and equivalent units are computed?

13–15 What is the main difference between journal entries in process costing and in job costing?

13–16 What is the difference between process costing and operation costing?

13–17 Describe the effect of automation on the process costing system.

EXERCISES

13–18 **PHYSICAL UNITS**

Required In each case, fill in the missing amount.

1. Work-in-process inventory, February 1	80,000 units
Work-in-process inventory, February 28	?
Units started during February	60,000
Units completed during February	75,000
2. Work-in-process inventory, June 1	?
Work-in-process inventory, June 30	55,000 gallons
Units started during June	75,000 gallons
Units completed during June	83,000 gallons
3. Work-in-process inventory, September 1	5,500 tons
Work-in-process inventory, September 30	3,400 tons
Units started during September	?
Units completed during September	7,300 tons
4. Work-in-process inventory, November 1	45,000 units
Work-in-process inventory, November 30	23,000 units
Units started during November	57,000
Units completed during November	?

13–19 **EQUIVALENT UNITS; WEIGHTED-AVERAGE METHOD** Washington Fisheries, Inc., processes salmon for various distributors. Two departments, processing and packaging, are involved. Data relating to tons of salmon sent to the processing department during May 2001 follow:

		Percent Completed	
	Tons of Salmon	Materials	Conversion
Work-in-process inventory, May 1	1,500	80%	70%
Work-in-process inventory, May 31	2,300	50	30
Started processing during May	6,500		

Required

1. Calculate the number of tons completed and transferred out during the month.

2. Calculate the number of equivalent units for both materials and conversion for the month of May, assuming that the company uses the weighted-average method.

13–20   EQUIVALENT UNITS; WEIGHTED-AVERAGE METHOD   Western Oregon Lumber Company grows, harvests, and processes timber for use as building lumber. The following data pertain to the company's sawmill:

Work-in-process inventory, January 1 (materials: 60 percent; conversion: 40 percent)	25,000 units
Work-in-process inventory, December 31 (materials: 70 percent; conversion: 60 percent)	15,000 units

During the year the company started 150,000 units in production.

Required   Prepare a quantity schedule and compute the number of equivalent units of both direct materials and conversion for the year, using the weighted-average method.

13–21   EQUIVALENT UNITS; FIFO METHOD   Englewood Chemical Company refines a variety of petrochemical products. These data are from the firm's Houston plant:

Work-in-process inventory, September 1	3,000,000 gallons
Direct materials	100 percent completed
Conversion	25 percent completed
Units started in process during September	1,850,000 gallons
Work-in-process inventory, September 30	2,400,000 gallons
Direct materials	100 percent completed
Conversion	80 percent completed

Required   Compute the equivalent units of direct material and conversion for the month of September. Use the FIFO method.

13–22   EQUIVALENT UNITS; FIFO METHOD   Adams Company has the following information for December 1, 2001, to December 31, 2001. All direct materials are 100 percent complete; beginning materials cost $12,000.

Work-in-Process

Beginning balance December 1, 200 units, 9 percent complete	$14,000	Completed 800 units and transferred to finished goods inventory	$140,000
Direct materials	54,000		
Direct labor	34,000		
Factory overhead			
Property taxes	6,000		
Depreciation	32,000		
Utilities	18,000		
Indirect labor	4,000		
Ending balance December 31, 300 units, 11.6 percent complete	22,000		

Required   Calculate equivalent units using the FIFO method.

13–23   EQUIVALENT UNITS; FIFO UNIT COST   Young Company calculated the cost for an equivalent unit of production using the FIFO method.

Data for June 2001

Work-in-process inventory, June 1: 30,000 units	
Direct materials: 100 percent complete	$ 80,000
Conversion: 20 percent complete	24,000
Balance in work-in-process, June 1	$104,000

Units started during June	50,000
Units completed and transferred	60,000
Work-in-process inventory, June 30	
Direct materials: 100 percent complete	20,000
Conversion: 70 percent complete	
Cost incurred during June	
Direct materials	$150,000
Conversion costs	
Direct labor	120,000
Applied overhead	145,000
Total conversion costs	$265,000

Required Compute cost per equivalent unit.

13–24 JOURNAL ENTRIES NYI Corporation manufactures decorative window glass in two sequential departments. These data pertain to the month of August:

	Department 1	Department 2
Direct materials used for production	$ 55,000	$ 32,000
Direct labor	160,000	320,000
Applied factory overhead	340,000	250,000
Costs of goods completed and transferred	850,000	740,000

Required Prepare journal entries to record these events:

1. Incurrence of direct materials and direct labor. Application of factory overhead in department 1.

2. Transfer of products from department 1 to department 2.

3. Incurrence of direct materials and direct labor. Application of factory overhead in department 2.

4. Transfer of complete products from department 2 to finished goods inventory.

13–25 FIFO METHOD Trezevant and Wang, an income tax preparation firm, uses the FIFO method of process costing for the monthly reports. The following shows its March 2001 information:

Service

Returns in process, March 1 (30% complete)	100
Returns started in March	1,100
Returns in process, March 31 (90% complete)	200
Labor and overhead costs for returns in process, March 1	$ 330
Labor and overhead costs incurred in March	$138,000

Required Calculate the following amounts using the FIFO method:

1. Equivalent units.

2. Cost per equivalent unit.

3. Cost of completed returns for the month of March.

4. Cost of returns in process as of March 31.

13–26 EQUIVALENT UNITS; WEIGHTED-AVERAGE METHOD AND FIFO METHOD
Levittown Company employs a process costing system for its manufacturing operations. All direct materials are added at the beginning of the process, and conversion costs are added proportionately. Levittown's production schedule for November follows:

	Units
Work-in-process on November 1 (conversion: 60 percent complete)	1,000
Started during November	5,000
Total to account for	6,000
Completed and transferred out from beginning inventory	1,000
Started and completed during November	3,000
Work-in-process on November 30 (conversion: 20 percent complete)	2,000
Total accounted for	6,000

Required

1. Using the weighted-average method, compute the equivalent units for direct materials and conversion costs.

2. Using the FIFO method, compute the equivalent units for direct materials and conversion costs.

(CMA Adapted)

PROBLEMS

13–27 **SPOILAGE (APPENDIX A); WEIGHTED-AVERAGE METHOD; TRANSFERRED-IN COSTS**   West Corporation is a divisionalized manufacturing company. It manufactures the product Aggregate in one department of the California Division. The direct material is added at the beginning of the process. Labor and overhead are added continuously throughout the process. Shrinkage of 10 to 14 percent, occurring at the beginning of the process, is considered normal. The California Division charges all departmental overhead to the departments and allocates division overhead to the departments on the basis of direct labor-hours. The divisional overhead rate for 2001 is $2 per direct labor-hour. Aggregate is transferred on completion to the Utah Division at a predetermined price where it is used in the manufacture of other products.

The following information relates to production at the California Division during November 2001:

Work-in-process, November 1 (4,000 pounds—75% complete)	
Direct materials	$22,800
Direct labor @ $5 per hour	24,650
Departmental overhead	12,000
Divisional overhead	9,860
Direct materials	
Inventory, November 1, 2000 pounds	$10,000
Purchases, November 3, 10,000 pounds	51,000
Purchases, November 18, 10,000 pounds	51,500
Released to production during November,	16,000 pounds
Direct labor cost @ $5 per hour	$103,350
Direct departmental overhead costs	$52,000
Transferred to Utah Division	15,000 pounds
Work-in-process, November 30, one-third complete	3,000 pounds

West uses the FIFO method for materials inventory valuation and the weighted-average method for work-in-process inventories.

Required

1. Prepare a cost of production report for California Division's production of Aggregate for November 2001, which includes the following:

a. The equivalent units of production by cost factor of Aggregate (e.g., direct material, direct labor, and overhead)

b. The equivalent unit costs for each cost factor of Aggregate.

c. The cost of Aggregate transferred to the Utah Division.

d. The cost of abnormal shrinkage, if any.

e. The cost of the work-in-process inventory at November 30, 2001.

2. California Division intends to implement a flexible budgeting system to improve its cost control of direct labor and departmental overhead. The basis of the flexible budget will be the amount of production of Aggregate that occurs during the budget period in the department. What amount reflects the best measure of production activity for the November 2001 flexible budget? Explain your answer.

(CMA Adapted)

13–28 **WEIGHTED-AVERAGE METHOD**   Ito produces a single model of popular digital watches in large quantities. A single watch moves through two departments, assembly and testing. The manufacturing costs in the assembly department during March follow:

Direct materials added	$137,500
Conversion costs	184,500
	$322,000

The assembly department has no beginning work-in-process inventory. During the month, it started 25,000 watches, but only 23,000 were fully completed and transferred to the testing department. All parts had been made and placed in the remaining 2,000 watches, but only 80 percent of the labor had been completed. The company uses the weighted-average method of process costing to accumulate product costs.

Required

1. Compute the equivalent units and equivalent unit costs for March.

2. Compute the costs of units completed and transferred to the testing department.

3. Compute the costs of the ending work-in-process.

13–29 **FIFO METHOD**   Carolina Pulp Company processes wood pulp for manufacturing various paper products. The company employs a process costing system for its manufacturing operations. All direct materials are added at the beginning of the process, and conversion costs are incurred uniformly throughout the process. This is the company's production schedule for May:

		Percent Completed	
	Tons of Pulp	**Materials**	**Conversion**
Work-in-process inventory, May 1	1,500	100	70
Started during May	5,000		
Units to account for	6,500		
Units from beginning work-in-process, which were completed and transferred out during May	1,500		
Started and completed during May	4,000		
Work-in-process inventory, May 31	1,000	100	60
Total units accounted for	6,500		

The following cost data are available:

Work-in-process inventory, May 1	
Direct materials	$20,750
Conversion	23,470
Costs incurred during May	
Direct materials	$80,000
Conversion	58,880

Required

1. Calculate equivalent units of direct materials and conversion during May. Use the FIFO method.

2. Calculate the cost per equivalent unit for both direct materials and conversion during May. Use the FIFO method.

13–30 **WEIGHTED-AVERAGE METHOD**   Refer to the information in Problem 13–29.

Required   Complete Problem 13–29 using the weighted-average method.

13–31 **WEIGHTED-AVERAGE METHOD**   Yamamoto Company manufactures a single product that goes through two processes, mixing and cooking. These data pertain to the mixing department for August 2001:

Work-in-process inventory, August 1	
Conversion: 80 percent complete	27,000 units
Work-in-process inventory, August 31	
Conversion: 40 percent complete	17,000 units
Units started into production	60,000
Units completed and transferred out	?
Costs	
Work-in-process inventory, August 1	
Material X	$ 64,800
Material Y	89,100
Conversion	119,880
Costs added during August	
Material X	152,700
Material Y	138,400
Conversion	302,520

Material X is added at the beginning of work in the mixing department. Material Y is also added in the mixing department, but not until product units are 60 percent complete with regard to conversion. Conversion costs are incurred uniformly during the process. The company uses the weighted-average cost method.

Required

1. Calculate equivalent units of material X, material Y, and conversion.

2. Calculate costs per equivalent unit for material X, material Y, and conversion.

3. Calculate the cost of units transferred out.

4. Calculate the cost of ending work-in-process inventory.

13–32 **FIFO METHOD**   Jenice Company uses FIFO process costing to account for the costs of its single product. Production begins in the fabrication department, where units of direct materials are molded into various connecting parts. After fabrication is complete, the units are transferred to the assembly department, which adds no material. After assembly is complete, the units are transferred to the packaging department, which packages units for shipment. After the units have been packaged, the final products are transferred to the shipping department. A partially completed production cost report for the month of May in the fabrication department follows:

JENICE COMPANY
Fabrication Department—Production Cost Report
For the Month Ended May 31, 2001

Quantity Schedule	Units
Units to be accounted for	
Work-in-process inventory, May 1 (materials: 100 percent; conversion: 40 percent)	3,000
Started into production	?
Total units to be accounted for	?
Units accounted for as follows	
Transferred to department Y	
Units from the beginning inventory	?
Units started and completed this month	?
Work-in-process inventory, May 31 (materials: 100 percent; conversion: 60 percent)	4,000
Total units accounted for	?

Equivalent Units and Unit Costs	Materials	Conversion	Total
Cost added during May	$172,500	?	?
Equivalent units	?	?	?
Unit Cost	?	?	?
Cost Reconciliation			
Cost to be accounted for			
?			
Cost accounted for as follows:			
?			

The cost incurred in the fabrication department's work-in-process inventory at May 1 is $13,800. The assembly department's production cost report for the month of May shows that the number of transferred-in units is 68,000, costing $393,400.

Required

1. Fill in the missing amounts in the quantity schedule and complete the equivalent units and costs.
2. Complete the cost reconciliation part of the production cost report.

13–33 **WEIGHTED-AVERAGE METHOD** China Pacific Company manufactures a variety of natural fabrics for the clothing industry in a suburb of Shanghai. The following data in Chinese currency called *renminbi* pertain to the month of October 2001.

International

Work-in-process inventory, October 1	25,000 units
Direct materials: 60 percent complete	57,000 renminbi
Conversion: 30 percent complete	45,000 renminbi
Cost incurred during October	
Direct materials	736,000 renminbi
Conversion	1,094,950 renminbi

During October, 175,000 units were completed and transferred out. At the end of the month, 30,000 units (direct materials 80 percent and conversion 40 percent complete) remain in work-in-process inventory.

627

Required   Calculate each of the following amounts using weighted-average process costing.

1. Equivalent units of direct materials and conversion.

2. Unit costs of direct materials and conversion.

3. Cost of goods completed and transferred out during October.

4. Cost of the work-in-process inventory at October 31.

5. Check the most recent issue of *The Wall Street Journal* to learn the exchange rate between the U.S. dollar and the Chinese renminbi.

13–34 **WEIGHTED-AVERAGE METHOD; TRANSFERRED-IN COSTS**   Porter Toy Company has two departments, forming and finishing. Consider the finishing department, which processes the formed toys through hand shaping and the addition of metal. All other direct materials are added at the end of the process in the finishing department. The following summarizes the finishing department's July operations:

	Number of Units
Work-in-process, June 30, 30% complete for conversion costs	4,000
Transferred in during July	21,000
Completed during July	20,000
Work-in-process, July 31, 20% complete for conversion costs	5,000

	Costs
Work-in-process, June 30 (transferred-in costs: $25,000; conversion costs: $5,000)	$ 30,000
Transferred-in from forming department during July	100,000
Direct materials added during July	30,000
Conversion added during July	37,000
Total to account for	$197,000

Required   Calculate each of the following amounts using the weighted-average process costing method:

1. Equivalent units of transferred-in direct materials and conversion.

2. Unit costs of transferred-in direct materials and conversion.

3. Cost of goods completed and transferred out during July.

4. Cost of work-in-process inventory at July 31.

13–35 **PROCESS COSTING METHOD IDENTIFICATION**   Western Auto Products manufactures an expensive car wax compound that goes through three processing departments: grinding, mixing, and cooking. Direct materials are introduced at the start of the grinding process. A partially completed production cost report for the grinding department for the month of May follows:

WESTERN AUTO PRODUCTS
Grinding Department—Production Report
For the Month Ended May 31, 2001

Quantity Schedule	Units
Units to be accounted for	
Work-in-process inventory, May 1 (materials: 100 percent; conversion: 60 percent)	4,000
Started into production	?
Total units to be accounted for	69,000

Units accounted for as follows

	Transferred to mixing department:		?
	Work-in-process inventory, May 31		3,500
	(materials: 100 percent; conversion: 40 percent)		
	Total units accounted for		?

Equivalent Units and Unit Costs	Materials	Conversion	Total
Cost of work-in-process inventory, May 1	$21,600	$?	$?
Cost added during May	?	228,970	?
Equivalent units	?	?	
Unit Cost	?	?	?

Cost Reconciliation

Costs to be accounted for

?

Costs accounted for as follows

?

The mixing department's production cost report reveals that the transferred-in cost for the month of May is $589,500 (materials $360,250 and conversion $229,250).

Required

1. By scrutinizing the partially completed production cost report, identify two ways that indicate whether the company is using the weighted-average cost method or the FIFO cost method.

2. Fill in the missing amounts in the quantity schedule and the equivalent units and unit costs.

3. Complete the cost reconciliation part of the production cost report.

13–36 FIFO METHOD Lester-Smith Company has a department that manufactures wood trusses. The following information is for the production of these trusses for the month of February:

Work-in-process inventory, February 1	10,000 trusses
Direct materials cost: 100 percent complete	$100,000
Conversion: 20 percent complete	$115,000
Units started during February	15,000 trusses
Units completed during February and transferred out	20,000 trusses
Work-in-process inventory, February 29	5,000 trusses
Direct materials: 100 percent complete	
Conversion cost: 40 percent complete	
Costs incurred during February	
Direct materials	$50,000
Conversion	$95,000

 *Ethics*

Required Using the FIFO method, calculate the following:

1. Costs per equivalent unit.

2. Cost of goods completed and transferred out.

3. Cost remaining in the ending work-in-process inventory.

4. Assume that you are the company's controller. The production department's February unit cost is higher than the target or standard cost. If the manager of the first department asks you to do him a favor by increasing the ending inventory completion percentage from 40 to 60 percent to lower the unit costs, what should you do?

Ethics

13–37 **WEIGHTED-AVERAGE METHOD** Refer to the information in problem 13–36.

Required Repeat Problem 13–36 using the weighted-average method.

13–38 **FIFO METHOD; JOURNAL ENTRIES** You are engaged in the audit of the December 31, 2001, financial statements of Epworth Products Corporation. You are attempting to verify the costing of the work-in-process and finished goods ending inventories that were recorded on Epworth's books as follows:

	Units	Cost
Work-in-process (50 percent complete as to labor and overhead)	300,000	$660,960
Finished goods	100,000	504,900

Materials are added to production at the beginning of the manufacturing process, and overhead is applied to each product at the rate of 60 percent of direct labor costs. There was no finished goods inventory on January 1, 2001. Epworth uses the FIFO costing method. A review of Epworth's 2001 inventory cost records disclosed the following information:

		Costs	
	Units	Materials	Labor
Work-in-process inventory, January 1, 2001 (80 percent complete as to labor and overhead)	200,000	$ 200,000	$ 315,000
Started	1,000,000		
Completed	900,000		
Current period costs		1,300,000	1,995,000

Required Prepare a production cost report to verify the inventory balances and prepare necessary journal entries to correctly state the inventory of finished goods and work-in-process, assuming that the books have not been closed.

13–39 **WEIGHTED-AVERAGE METHOD** Hawes House Inc. uses weighted-average process costing in accounting for its production activities. Materials are added at the beginning of the process, and conversion costs are incurred uniformly throughout the process.

October's production records indicate this information:

Quantities	
Beginning work-in-process inventory	1,500 units
Started during October	8,500 units
Completed and transferred out	7,000 units
Ending work-in-process inventory (60 percent complete)	3,000 units

Beginning Inventory Costs	
Direct materials	$ 800
Direct labor	1,000
Factory overhead	440

October Production Costs	
Direct materials	$4,400
Direct labor	9,000
Factory overhead	3,870

Required Prepare a production cost report for Hawes House Inc.

13–40 **WEIGHTED-AVERAGE METHOD; TRANSFERRED-IN COSTS** Choi Corporation manufactures a popular model of business calculators in a suburb of Seoul,

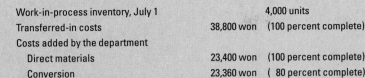

South Korea. The production process goes through two departments, assembly and testing. The following information (in South Korean currency, the *won*) pertains to the testing department for the month of July.

Work-in-process inventory, July 1		4,000 units
Transferred-in costs	38,800 won	(100 percent complete)
Costs added by the department		
Direct materials	23,400 won	(100 percent complete)
Conversion	23,360 won	(80 percent complete)

During the month of July, 15,000 units were transferred in from the assembly department at the cost of 141,700 won, and the mixing department added costs of 194,265 won.

Direct materials	84,125 won
Conversion	110,140 won

During the month, 16,000 units were completed and transferred to the warehouse. At July 31, the completion percentage of work-in-process was as follows:

Direct materials	90 percent
Conversion	60 percent

Required

1. Prepare the production report of the testing department for the month of July using the weighted-average process costing.

2. Check the most recent issue of *The Wall Street Journal* to learn the exchange rate between the U.S. dollar and the South Korean won.

13–41 FIFO METHOD; TRANSFERRED-IN COSTS (APPENDIX B) Wood Glow Manufacturing Company produces a single product, a wood refinishing kit that sells for $17.95. The final processing of the kits occurs in the packaging department. An internal quilted wrap is applied at the beginning of the packaging process. A compartmentalized outside box printed with instructions and the company's name and logo is added when units have 60 percent of the process. Conversion costs consisting of direct labor and applied overhead occur evenly throughout the packaging process. Conversion activities after the addition of the box involve package sealing, testing for leakage, and final inspection. Rejections in the packaging department are rare and can be ignored. The following data pertain to the packaging department's activities during the month of October.

- Beginning work-in-process inventory was 10,000 units, 40 percent complete as to conversion costs.
- In the month, 30,000 units were started and completed.
- Ending work-in-process had 10,000 units, 80 percent complete as to conversion costs.

The packaging department's October costs follow:

Quilted wrap	$80,000
Outside boxes	50,000
Direct labor	22,000
Applied overhead ($3 per direct labor dollar)	66,000

The costs transferred in from prior processing were $3 per unit. The cost of goods sold for the month was $240,000, and the ending finished-goods inventory was $84,000. Wood Glow uses the first-in, first-out (FIFO) method of inventory valuation.

Wood Glow's controller, Mark Brandon, has been asked to analyze the packaging department's activities for the month of October. Mark knows that to properly determine the department's unit cost of production, he must first calculate the equivalent units of production.

Required

1. Prepare an equivalent units of production schedule for the packaging department's October activity. Be sure to account for the beginning work-in-process inventory, the units started and completed during the month, and the ending work-in-process inventory.

2. Determine the October production's cost per equivalent unit.

3. Assuming that the actual overhead incurred during October was $5,000 more than the overhead applied, describe how to determine the value of the ending work-in-process inventory.

(CMA Adapted)

Ethics

13-42 FIFO METHOD Superior Brands, Inc., manufactures a medium-quality rubber cement product that goes through two departments. Cost and production data for the first department are given for June 2001:

Work-in-process inventory, June 1	
Conversion: 40 percent complete	15,000 units
Work-in-process inventory, June 30	
Conversion: 65 percent complete	25,000 units
Started into production	80,000 units
Completed and transferred out	?
Costs	
Work-in-process inventory, June 1	
Direct materials	$ 72,500
Conversion	12,937.50
Costs added during May	
Material A	260,000
Material B	403,750
Conversion	461,437.50

Material A is added at the beginning of work in the first department. Material B is also added in the first department but not until units of product are 50 percent complete with regard to conversion. Conversion costs are incurred uniformly during the process. The company uses the FIFO cost method.

Required

1. Calculate equivalent units of material A, material B, and conversion.

2. Calculate costs per equivalent unit for material A, material B, and conversion.

3. Calculate the cost of units transferred out.

4. Calculate the value of ending work-in-process inventory.

5. Assume that you are the controller of Superior Brands, Inc., and the first department's June unit cost is higher than the target or standard cost. If the manager of the first department asks you to do her a favor by increasing the ending inventory completion percentage from 65 to 80 percent to lower the unit costs, what should you do?

13–43 WEIGHTED-AVERAGE METHOD; TWO DEPARTMENTS An automotive exhaust system manufacturer has two departments in muffler processing, the fabrication and the assembly departments. All materials for the fabrication department were added at the beginning of the process. Data recorded for January 2001 follow:

	Units	Percent Completed	Direct Materials	Conversion
Fabrication department				
Work-in-process inventory, January 1	5,000	50%	$ 15,000	$ 20,000
Transferred to assembly department in January	50,000			
Work-in-process inventory, January 31	3,000	30		
Assembly department				
Work-in-process inventory, January 1 (transferred-in cost: $78,000)	10,000	40		$200,000
Completed and transferred out in January	55,000			
Work-in-process inventory, January 31	5,000	40		
Costs incurred in January				
Fabrication department			$117,500	$310,850
Assembly department				$723,400

Required Calculate the following using the weighted-average method:

1. Equivalent units of direct materials and conversion in the fabrication department.
2. Unit costs of direct materials and conversion in the fabrication department.
3. Cost of goods transferred to the assembly department from the fabrication department in the month of January.
4. Cost of the work-in-process ending inventory in the fabrication department.
5. Equivalent units of transferred-in and conversion in the assembly department.
6. Unit costs of transferred-in and conversion in the assembly department.
7. Cost of goods transferred to finished goods from the assembly department in January.
8. Cost of the work-in-process ending inventory in the assembly department.

13–44 FIFO METHOD; TWO DEPARTMENTS (APPENDIX B) Graybill Company produces plastic photo frames. Two departments, molding and finishing, are involved in the manufacturing. The molding department fills the molds with hot liquid plastic that is left to cool and then opens them. The finishing department removes the plastic frame from the mold and strips the edges of the frames of extra plastic.

The following information is available for the month of January:

	January 1		January 31	
Work-in-Process Inventory	**Quantity (pounds)**	**Cost**	**Quantity (pounds)**	**Cost**
Molding department	None	—	None	—
Finishing department	5,000	$15,000	2,000	?

The work-in-process inventory in the finishing department is estimated to be 25 percent complete both at the beginning and end of January. Costs of production for January follow:

Costs of Production	Materials Used	Conversion
Molding department	$300,000	$50,000
Finishing department	—	40,000

The material used in the molding department weighed 50,000 pounds. The firm uses the FIFO method of process costing.

Required   Prepare a report for both the molding and finishing departments for the month of January. The report should include equivalent units of production (in pounds), total manufacturing costs, cost per equivalent unit (pounds), cost of ending work-in-process inventory, and cost of goods completed and transferred out.

13–45   WEIGHTED-AVERAGE METHOD; FIFO METHOD; TWO DEPARTMENTS   Porter Company manufactures its one product by a process that requires two departments. The production starts in department A and is completed in department B. Materials are added at the beginning of the process in department A. Additional materials are added when the process is 50 percent complete in department B. Conversion costs are incurred proportionally throughout the production processes in both departments.

On April 1, department A had 500 units in production estimated to be 30 percent complete; department B had 300 units in production estimated to be 40 percent complete. During April, department A started 1,500 units and completed 1,600 units; department B completed 1,400 units. The work-in-process ending inventory on April 30 in department A is estimated to be 20 percent complete, and the work-in-process ending inventory in department B is estimated to be 70 percent complete.

The cost sheet for department A shows that the units in the work-in-process beginning inventory had $3,000 in direct materials costs and $1,530 in conversion costs. The production element costs incurred in April were $12,000 for direct materials and $10,710 for conversion. Department B's work-in-process beginning inventory on April 1 was $6,100; it incurred $38,000 in direct materials costs and $24,350 in conversion costs in April.

Department A's cost per unit in March is $14 regardless of which process costing method is used to determine costs. Porter Company uses the FIFO method for department A and the weighted-average method for department B.

Required

1.   Prepare a production cost report for department A.

2.   Prepare a production cost report for department B.

13–46   SPOILAGE; WEIGHTED-AVERAGE METHOD; TRANSFERRED-IN COSTS (APPENDIX A)   JC Company employs a process cost system. A unit of product passes through three departments—molding, assembly, and finishing—before it is completed. The following activity took place in the finishing department during May:

	Units
Work-in-process inventory—May 1	1,400
Transferred in from the assembly department	14,000
Spoiled	700
Transferred out to finished goods inventory	11,200

Direct materials are added at the beginning of the processing in the finishing department without changing the number of units being processed. The work-in-process inventory was 70 percent complete as to conversion on May 1 and 40 percent complete as to conversion on May 31. All spoilage was discovered at final inspection before the units were transferred to finished goods; 560 of the spoiled units were considered acceptable.

JC Company employs the weighted-average costing method. The equivalent units and the current costs per equivalent unit of production for each cost factor follow:

	Equivalent Units	Current Costs per Equivalent Unit
Cost of prior department	15,400	$5
Direct materials	15,400	1
Conversion cost	13,300	3
		$9

Required

1. What is the cost of production transferred to the finished goods inventory?

2. What is the cost assigned to the work-in-process inventory on May 31?

3. If the total costs of prior departments included in the finishing department's work-in-process inventory on May 1 amounted to $6,300, what is the total cost transferred in from the assembly department to the finishing department during May?

4. What is the cost associated with the abnormal spoilage?

(CMA Adapted)

13–47 **CHOICE OF PROCESS COSTING METHOD** Peter Chou is a perfume company that produces a wide line of fragrances for men and women. Each fragrance goes through certain cycles to acquire its desired scent. This information from February includes the production of perfume for Valentine's Day:

Strategy

Work-in-process inventory units (February 1, 2001)	3,750
Percent completed with respect to conversion	50%
Units started in February	41,250
Work-in-process inventory units (February 28, 2001) (50%)	4,000

Required

1. Prepare a schedule of equivalent units for Peter Chou for the month of February. Show the results under both the weighted-average and FIFO methods. Assume that direct materials are added at the beginning of the process.

2. The following costs were incurred to produce the fragrances this month. Calculate the total manufacturing costs and the cost of goods manufactured for February (use FIFO).

	Direct Materials	Conversion Costs	Total
Current cost	$82,500	$452,375	$534,875
Work-in-process inventory (February 1, 2001)	5,250	6,000	11,250

3. How would the answer to requirement 2 change if the weighted-average method were used?

4. If the company has a cost leadership strategy, which process costing method (weighted-average or FIFO) should the company adopt? Why?

13–48   SPOILAGE, WEIGHTED-AVERAGE METHOD; TRANSFERRED-IN COSTS (APPENDIX A)   Romano Foods Inc. manufactures 12-inch Roman Surprise Fresh Frozen Pizzas that retail for $4.69 to $5.99, depending upon the topping. The company employs a process costing system in which the product flows through several processes. Joe Corolla, vice president of production, has had a long-running disagreement with the controller, Sue Marshall, over the way to handle spoilage cost. Joe resists every attempt to charge production with variance responsibilities unless they are favorable. Spoilage costs have not been significant in the past, but, in November, the mixing department had a substantial amount of spoilage. Romano Foods has traditionally treated 10 percent of good output as normal spoilage. The mixing department input 120,000 units of ingredients; inspection rejected 13,000 dough units. Sue is concerned about the abnormal spoilage and wants Joe to take corrective steps. He maintains, however, that the mixing department is operating properly and has prepared the following report to support his contention:

Romano Foods—Mixing Department
Production Cost Report
Month Ended November 30, 2001

Input Units	Total Cost	Good Output Units	Normal Spoilage (10 percent)	Abnormal Spoilage	Good Unit Cost
120,000	$45,360	107,000	12,000	1,000	$ 0.42
Budgeted unit cost					$ 0.435
Actual cost per good unit					0.420
Favorable variance					$ 0.015

Cost Reconciliation

Cost of 107,000 good units @ $0.42 each	$44,940
Abnormal spoilage (charge to purchasing for buying inferior materials): 1,000 units @ $0.42 each	420
Total cost	$45,360

Sue read the report and found out that Joe miscalculated both normal and abnormal spoilage units, and he ignored the normal spoilage in calculating the unit cost.

Required

1. Revise Joe Corolla's production cost report for November 2001 by calculating the correct numbers or amounts for the following:

   a. The number of units of normal spoilage.

   b. The number of units of abnormal spoilage.

   c. The total and per-unit costs of the mixing department's production of good units in November.

   d. The total and per-unit costs of abnormal spoilage.

2. Prepare the journal entry to transfer costs for the mixing department for November to the assembly department.

3. Describe how Joe Corolla's production cost report has shown the performance of the mixing department to be less favorable than that shown in the revised report in requirement 1.

(CMA Adapted)

Strategy

13–49   CHOICE OF PROCESS COSTING METHOD   Kristina Company, which manufactures quality paint to sell at premium prices, uses a single production department. Production begins by blending the various chemicals that are added at the beginning of the process and ends by filling the paint cans. Cans are filled when the mixture reaches the 90 percent stage of completion. The gallon cans are then transferred to the shipping department for crating and shipment. Labor and overhead are added continuously throughout the process. Factory overhead is applied on the basis of direct labor-hours at the rate of $3 per hour.

Prior to May, when a change in the process was implemented, work-in-process inventories were insignificant. The change in the process allows increased production but results in considerable amounts of work-in-process for the first time. The company has always used the weighted-average method to determine equivalent production and unit costs. Now production management is considering changing from the weighted-average method to the FIFO method.

Strategy

These data relate to actual production during the month of May:

	Costs
Work-in-process inventory, May 1	
(4,000 gallons 25 percent complete):	
Direct materials—chemicals	$45,600
Direct labor ($10 per hour)	6,250
Factory overhead	1,875
May costs added:	
Direct materials—chemicals	228,400
Direct materials—cans	7,000
Direct labor ($10 per hour)	35,000
Factory overhead	10,500

	Units
Work-in-process inventory, May 1 (25 percent complete)	4,000
Sent to shipping department	20,000
Started in May	21,000
Work-in-process inventory, May 31 (80 percent complete)	5,000

Required

1. Prepare a schedule of equivalent units for each cost element for the month of May using the weighted-average method and then the FIFO method.

2. Calculate the cost (to the nearest cent) per equivalent unit for each cost element for the month of May using the weighted-average method and the FIFO method.

3. If the company takes a cost leadership strategy, which process costing method (weighted average or FIFO) should the company adopt? Why?

(CMA Adapted)

13–50 **SPOILAGE; WEIGHTED-AVERAGE METHOD; TRANSFERRED-IN COSTS (APPENDIX A)** APCO Company manufactures various lines of bicycles. Because of the high volume of each line, the company employs a process cost system using the weighted-average method to determine unit costs. Bicycle parts are manufactured in the molding department and then are consolidated into a single bike unit in the molding department and transferred to the assembly department where they are partially assembled. After assembly, the bicycle is sent to the packing department.

Cost per unit data for the 20-inch dirt bike has been completed through the molding department. Annual cost and production figures for the assembly department are presented in the schedules that follow.

Defective bicycles are identified at the inspection point when the assembly labor process is 70 percent complete; all assembly materials have been added at this point. The normal rejection for defective bicycles is 5 percent of the bicycles reaching the inspection point. Any defective bicycles above the 5 percent quota are considered to be abnormal. All defective bikes are removed from the production process and destroyed.

Required

1. Compute the number of defective, or spoiled, bikes that are considered to be
   a. Normal.
   b. Abnormal.
2. Compute the equivalent units of production for the year for
   a. Bicycles transferred in from the molding department.
   b. Bicycles produced with regard to assembly material.
   c. Bicycles produced with regard to assembly conversion.
3. Compute the cost per equivalent unit for the fully assembled dirt bike.
4. Compute the amount of the total production cost of $1,672,020 that will be associated with the following items:
   a. Normal spoiled units.
   b. Abnormal spoiled units.
   c. Good units completed in the assembly department.
   d. Ending work-in-process inventory in the assembly department.
5. Describe how to present the applicable dollar amounts for the following items in the financial statements:
   a. Normal spoiled units.
   b. Abnormal spoiled units.
   c. Completed units transferred in to the packing department.
   d. Ending work-in-process inventory in the assembly department.

Assembly Department Cost Data

	Transferred in from Molding Department	Assembly Materials	Assembly Conversion Cost	Total Cost of Dirt Bike through Assembly
Prior period costs	$ 82,200	$ 6,660	$ 11,930	$ 100,790
Current period costs	1,237,800	96,840	236,590	1,571,230
Total costs	$1,320,000	$103,500	$248,520	$1,672,020

Assembly Department Production Data

		Percentage Complete		
	Bicycles	Transferred in	Assembly Materials	Assembly Conversion
Beginning inventory	3,000	100%	100%	80%
Transferred in from molding during year	45,000	100	—	—
Transferred out to packing during year	40,000	100	100	100
Ending inventory	4,000	100	50	20

(CMA Adapted)

SOLUTIONS TO SELF-STUDY PROBLEMS

1. Weighted-Average Method vs. FIFO Method

1. Weighted-average method
   a. Equivalent units
Direct materials: 1,000 + (200 × 100%)	1,200
Conversion: 1,000 + (200 × 70%)	1,140

   b. Cost per equivalent unit
Direct materials: ($9,600/1,200)	$8.00
Conversion: ($2,202 + $6,120)/1,140	$7.30
Total unit costs: $8.00 + $7.30	$15.30

   c. Cost of goods completed and transferred out: $15.30 × 1,000 — $15,300
   d. Cost of work-in-process, 10/31
Direct materials: ($8 × 200 × 100%	$1,600
Conversion: $7.30 × 200 × 70%	$1,022
Total: $1,600 + $1,022	$2,622

2. Weighted-average method production cost report

SMITH ELECTRONIC COMPANY
Chip-Mounting Production Department
Weighted-Average Production Cost Report

Production Quantity Information

	Step 1: Analyze Flow of Physical Units	Step 2: Calculate Equivalent Units	
	Physical Units	Direct Materials	Conversion Costs
Input			
Work-in-process			
beginning inventory	300		
Completion percentage			
Direct materials 0 present			
Conversion 40 percent			
Started this period	900		
Total to account for	1,200		
Output			
Completed	1,000	1,000	1,000
Work-in-process			
ending inventory	200		
Completion percentage			
Direct materials 100 percent		200	
Conversion 70 percent			140
Total accounted for	1,200		
Total work done to date			
(Total equivalent units)		1,200	1,140

Cost Determination

Step 3: Determine Total Costs to Account For	Total	Direct Materials	Conversion Costs
Work-in-process			
beginning inventory	$ 2,202		$2,202
Current cost	15,720	$9,600	$6,120
Total costs to account for	$17,922	$9,600	$8,322

Step 4: Compute Unit Costs		($9,600/1,200)	($8,322/1,140)
Cost per equivalent unit	$15.30	$8.00	$7.30

Cost Assignment

Step 5: Assign Total Manufacturing Costs	Total	Direct Materials	Conversion Costs
Units completed and transferred out	$15,300 ($15.30 × 1,000)		
Work-in-process ending inventory	2,622	(200 × $8) $1,600	(140 × $7.30) $1,022
Total manufacturing costs accounted for	$17,922		

3. FIFO method
   a. Equivalent units:

Direct materials: (300 × 100%) + (1,000 − 300) + (200 × 100%)	1,200
or 1,000 + (200 × 100%) − (300 × 0%)	1,200
Conversion: [300 × (1 − 40%)] + (1,000 − 300) + (200 × 70%)	1,020
or 1,000 + (200 × 70%) − (300 × 40%)	1,020

   b. Cost per equivalent unit

Direct materials: $9,600/1,200	$8
Conversion: $6,120/1,020	$6
Total unit costs = $8 + $6	$14

   c. Cost of goods completed and transferred out

From beginning work-in-process inventory:	
Direct materials: $0 + $8 × 300 × (1−0%)	$2,400
Conversion: $2,202 + $6 × 300 × (1−40%)	$3,282
Total: $2,400 + $3,282	$5,682
Started and completed: $14 × (1,000 − 300)	$9,800
Total cost of goods completed: $5,682 + $9,800	$15,482

   d. Cost of work in process, 10/31

Direct materials: $8 × 200 × 100%	$1,600
Conversion: $6 × 200 × 70%	$840
Total: $1,600 + $840	$2,440

4. FIFO method production cost report

SMITH ELECTRONIC COMPANY
Chip-Mounting Production Department
FIFO Production Cost Report

Production Quantity Information

	Step 1: Analyze Flow of Physical Units	Step 2: Calculate Equivalent Units	
	Physical Units	Direct Materials	Conversion Costs
Input			
Work-in-process beginning inventory	300		
Completion percentage			
Direct materials 0 percent		0	
Conversion 40 percent			120
Started this period	900		
Total units to account for	1,200		
Output			
Completed	1,000	1,000	1,000
Work-in-process ending inventory	200		

Completion percentage			
Direct materials 100 percent		200	
Conversion 70 percent			140
Total units accounted for	1,200		
Total work performed to date		1,200	1,140
Work-in-process beginning inventory	300	0	(120)
Total work performed this period (FIFO equivalent units)		1,200	1,020

Cost Determination

Step 3: Determine Total Costs to Account For Flow	Total	Direct Materials	Conversion Costs
Work-in-process beginning inventory	$2,202		$2,202
Current cost	15,720	$9,600	6,120
Total costs to account for	$17,922	$9,600	$8,322
Step 4: Compute Unit Costs		($9,600/1,200)	($6,120/1,020)
Cost per equivalent unit	$14	$8	$6

Cost Assignment

Step 5: Assign Total Manufacturing Costs	Total	Direct Materials	Conversion Costs
Units completed (1,000):			
From work-in-process beginning inventory	$2,202		$2,202
Current costs incurred completing units	3,480	(300 × $8) = $2,400	(180 × $6) = $1,080
Total cost from beginning inventory	$5,682	$2,400	$3,282
Units started and completed this period	9,800	[$8(1,000 − 300) + $6(1,000 − 300)] = $14(1,000 − 300)	
Total cost of units completed and transferred out	$15,482		
Work-in-process ending inventory	2,440	(200 × $8) = $1,600	(140 × $6) = $840
Total costs accounted for	$17,922		

2. Weighted-Average Method vs. FIFO Method with Transferred-In Cost

1. Weighted-average method

REED COMPANY
Finishing Department
Weighted-Average Production Cost Report

Production Quantity Information

	Step 1: Analyze Flow of Physical Units		Step 2: Calculate Equivalent Units	
	Physical Units	Transferred-in	Direct Materials	Conversion Costs
Input				
Work-in-process, November 1	10 (40%)			
Started this month	80			
Total units to account for	90			(continued)

Output				
Completed	82	82	82	82
Work-in-process, November 30	8 (50%)	8	8	4
Total accounted for	90			
Total work done to date (Total equivalent units)		90	90	86

Unit Cost Determination

Step 3: Determine Total Costs to Account For	Total	Transferred-in	Direct Materials	Conversion Costs
Work-in-process, November 1	$ 232	$100	$ 80	$ 52
Current costs	2,381	800	720	861
Total costs to account for	$2,613	$900	$800	$913

Step 4: Compute Unit Costs		($900/90)	($800/90)	($913/86)
Cost per unit	$29.51	$10.00	$8.89	$10.62

Cost Assignment

Step 5: Assign Total Manufacturing Costs	Total	Transferred-in	Direct Materials	Conversion Costs
Units completed (82):	$2,420 = 82 × $29.51			
Work-in-process, November 30 (8)	193	(8 × $10) = $80	(8 × $8.89) = $71	(4 × $10.62) = $42
Total costs accounted for	$2,613			

2. FIFO method

REED COMPANY
Finishing Department
FIFO Production Cost Report

Production Quantity Information

	Step 1: Analyze Flow of Physical Units		Step 2: Calculate Equivalent Units	
	Physical Units	Transferred-in	Direct Materials	Conversion Costs
Input				
Work-in-process, November 1	10 (40%)			
Started this month	80			
Total units to account for	90			
Output				
Completed	82	82	82	82
Work-in-process, November 30	8 (50%)	8	8	4
Total units accounted for	90			
Total work done to date		90	90	86
Work-in-process, November 1		(10)	(10)	(4)
Total work done this month— FIFO equivalent units		80	80	82

Unit Cost Determination

Step 3: Determine Total Costs to Account For	Total	Transferred-in	Direct Materials	Conversion Costs
Work-in-process, November 1	$ 232			
Current costs	2,381	$800	$720	$861
Total costs to account for	$2,613			

Step 4: Compute Unit Costs		($800/80)	($720/80)	($861/82)
Cost per unit	$29.50	$10.00	$9.00	$10.50

Cost Assignment

Step 5: Assign Total Manufacturing Costs	Total	Transferred-in	Direct Materials	Conversion Costs
Units completed (82):				
From work-in-process, November 1 (10)	$ 232	$100	$80	$52
Current costs added	63			$63 = (6 × $10.50)
Total from beginning inventory	$ 295	$100	$80	$115
Units started and completed (82 − 10 = 72)	2,124	(72 × $10) + (72 × $9) + (72 × $10.5) = 72 × $29.50		
Total cost of units completed and transferred out	$2,419			
Work in process, November 30 (8)	194	(8 × $10) = $80	(8 × $9) = $72	(4 × $10.5) = $42
Total costs accounted for	$2,613			

Cost Allocation

14

Service Departments and Joint Product Costs

After studying the chapter, you should be able to . . .

1 Identify the strategic role of cost allocation

2 Explain the ethical issue of cost allocation

3 Use the three steps of departmental cost allocation

4 Explain the problems in implementing the different departmental cost allocation methods

5 Explain the use of cost allocation in service firms

6 Use the three joint product costing methods

7 Use the four by-product costing methods

Courtesy of General Electric.

In keeping with their firms' mission of continual improvement and superiority in their products and services, General Electric (GE) and many other firms such as Ford Motor Company, Johnson & Johnson, IBM, and Marriott have sought improved methods of providing administrative services within their firms. These administrative services are often called *shared services* because they are shared among the company's operating units. Shared services generally include such transaction-processing services as payroll processing, claims processing, human resources, and many accounting services, among others. The firms named have studied the cost to provide the services and have been alarmed at the relatively high costs, such as $10 or more to process a single vendor invoice. Some firms have chosen to outsource these services or to have the operating units provide the services locally, but, like GE, most firms are centralizing these services to reduce cost, provide a high and standardized level of service quality, and provide a single base of technology for easy use, communication, and future modification.[1]

With the growth of these centralized services, the need for effective methods to allocate the shared costs to the operating units has increased. Generally, the allocation issue arises when cost is shared because of a shared facility, program, production process, or service. The methods used to allocate these common costs to products are explained in this chapter.

This chapter explains methods for allocating common costs to products for two broad types of common costs: (1) the costs of production and service departments shared by two or more individual products and (2) the joint manufacturing costs for products that are not separately identifiable until later in the manufacturing process. An example of the latter is the cost of refining crude oil (the joint cost) into the individual products: gasoline, heating oil, and other products.

We take a strategic perspective in developing these allocation methods and ask key strategic questions: How do the allocation methods we have chosen affect the motivations and behaviors of those in the operating units as well as the service units? Can we use ABC costing principles to develop more accurate methods of cost allocation? Does this service add value or should it be outsourced? The firm's answers to these questions can have a significant impact on its competitiveness and success.

THE STRATEGIC ROLE OF COST ALLOCATION

The strategic role of cost allocation has four objectives:

1. Determine *accurate departmental and product costs* as a basis for evaluating the cost efficiency of departments and the profitability of different products.

---

[1] For more information on company practices, see Ann Triplett and Jon Scheumann, "Managing Shared Services with ABM: *Strategic Finance*, February 2000, pp. 40–45; and "A Day of Reckoning for Bean Counters," *Business Week*, March 14, 1994, pp. 75–76.

2. *Motivate* managers to exert a high level of effort to achieve the goals of top management.

3. Provide the right *incentive* for managers to make decisions that are consistent with the goals of top management.

4. *Fairly determine the rewards* earned by the managers for their effort and skill and for the effectiveness of their decision making.

LEARNING OBJECTIVE 1 ▶

Identify the strategic role of cost allocation.

The first and most important objective requires the cost allocation method to be sufficiently accurate to support effective management decision making about products and departments.

The second objective, motivating managers, means that, to be effective, the cost allocation used must reward department managers for reducing costs as desired. A key motivation issue is whether the manager *controls* the allocated cost. For example, when a department's cost allocation for equipment maintenance is based on the number of the department's machine breakdowns, the manager has an incentive to reduce them and therefore reduce the maintenance costs. On the other hand, when the cost of maintenance is allocated on the basis of a department's square feet of floor space, the manager—who cannot affect the amount of floor space—is not motivated.

The third objective, providing the incentive for decision making, is achieved when cost allocation effectively provides the incentives for the individual manager to act autonomously in a manner that is consistent with top management's goals. For example, a major advantage of cost allocation methods is that they draw managers' attention to shared facilities. The cost allocation provides an incentive for individual and joint efforts to manage these costs and to encourage the managers to use these facilities to improve the performance of their units.

The fourth objective, fairness, is met when the cost allocation is clear, objective, and consistently applied. The most objective basis for cost allocation exists when a *cause-and-effect relationship* can be determined. For example, the allocation of maintenance costs on the basis of the number of equipment breakdowns is more objective and fair than an allocation based on square feet, the number of products produced, or labor costs in the department. The reason is that a cause-and-effect relationship exists between maintenance costs and the number of breakdowns; square feet or labor costs, however, do not have a clear relationship to maintenance costs.

In some situations, cause-and-effect bases are not available and alternative concepts of fairness are used. One such concept is *ability-to-bear*, which is commonly employed with bases related to size, such as total sales, total assets, or the profitability of the user departments. Other concepts of fairness are based on equity perceived in the circumstance, such as *benefit received*, which often is measured in a nonquantitative way. For example, the cost of a firm's computer services might be allocated largely or entirely to the research and development department because the computer is more critical to this department's functioning and this department uses it more than other departments do.

THE ETHICAL ISSUES OF COST ALLOCATION

LEARNING OBJECTIVE 2 ▶

Explain the ethical role of cost allocation.

A number of ethical issues are important in cost allocation. First, ethical issues arise when costs are allocated to products or services that are produced for both a competitive market and a public agency or government department. Although government agencies very often purchase on a cost-plus basis, products sold competitively are subject to price competition. The incentive in these situations is for the manufacturer, using cost allocation methods, to shift manufacturing costs from the competitive products to the cost-plus products. Evidence of this was shown in a 1984 study reported by former Secretary of the Navy John F. Lehman. The study, performed for the Navy by a CPA firm, found that defense contractors' profits on military work were higher than profits on nonmilitary work.

Cost Basis for Governmental Services: The Federal Aviation Agency

The Federal Aviation Agency (FAA), like most federal governmental agencies, must look for ways to reduce costs. Some suggestions include the following:

1. The cost to provide the FAA's services should be determined. For example, no one knows the costs of providing the air traffic control (ATC) system, even though the ATC is approximately 70 percent of the FAA's budget. Based on accurate cost information, users of the ATC could be charged fairly for the services provided.

2. The importance of charging for the use of the ATC system is illustrated by the fact that ATC controllers spend as much time directing a small, twin-engine business jet as a large commercial aircraft. Why not have the airlines pay for each minute that the controller speaks to the aircraft pilots? Perhaps a formula could be devised that would charge the smaller aircraft at a lower rate, using the "ability-to-bear" principle, but the service would not be free to all.

3. The FAA should charge aircraft manufacturers for its licensing and certification services. FAA's David Hinson says FAA engineers spent 125,000 hours on Boeing's 777. There should have been a large fee for this service.

Similar arguments could be made about the nation's interstate highways and coastal and intercoastal navigation systems.

Source: "How to End the Free Ride at the FAA," *Business Week,* May 6, 1997, p. 36.

A second ethical issue in implementing cost allocation methods is the equity or fair share issue that arises when a governmental unit reimburses the costs of a private institution or when it provides a service for a fee to the public. In both cases, cost allocation methods are used to determine the proper price or reimbursement amount. Although no single measure of equity exists in these cases, the objectives of cost allocation identified at the beginning of the chapter are a useful guide.

A good example of the equity issue in cost allocation is the reimbursement of large research universities for what is called *overhead* on research projects sponsored by the government. The payment of overhead is intended to reimburse the university for the cost of facilities and other expenses necessary to maintain the faculty, staff, and equipment for the research. Sometimes what is considered an indirect cost for this purpose is a matter of judgment. For example, in 1990 federal auditors investigated Stanford University; they found that the overhead charges included expenses for the dining and entertainment areas of the university president's home. These costs were denied, the university repaid some of the overcharges, and the overhead rate was reduced by the Office of the Chief of Naval Research.[2]

A third important ethical issue is the effect of the chosen allocation method on the costs of products sold to or from foreign subsidiaries. The cost allocation method usually affects the cost of products traded internationally and therefore the amount of taxes paid in the domestic and the foreign countries. Firms can reduce their worldwide tax liability by increasing the costs of products purchased in high-tax countries or in countries where the firm does not have favorable tax treatment. For this reason, international tax authorities closely watch the cost allocation methods used by multinational firms. The methods most acceptable to these authorities are based on sales and/or labor costs.[3]

---

[2] The dispute was settled by Stanford's payment of $1.5 million to the federal government, a small fraction of the average funding of $200 million per year that Stanford was receiving at the time. Perhaps the most significant effect of the incident was that federal auditors began to challenge the expenses of all research universities, resulting in a significant decline in the average indirect costs the federal government paid in the following years. See "Navy Cuts Indirect Overhead Rate," *The Stanford Observer,* March–April 1991; and Rondald G. Ehrenberg and Jaroslava K. Mykula, "Do Indirect Cost Rates Matter?" National Bureau of Economic Research Working Paper Number 6976 (February 1999).

[3] Eric G. Tomsett, "Allocation of Central Costs in an International Group," *World Tax* (a publication of Deloitte & Touche International), January 1992.

Cost Allocation and Cost Shifting by Federal Reserve Banks and Nonprofit Organizations

FEDERAL RESERVE BANKS REALLOCATE COMMON COSTS TO LESS COMPETITIVE SERVICES

The Monetary Control Act of 1980 required the Federal Reserve (FED) to charge explicitly for certain services, in effect placing Federal Reserve banks in direct competition with large commercial banks for these services. The act also required the FED to price these services based on full cost, including allocated indirect costs. Recent research indicates that the FED responded to the act by both improving the efficiency with which it provides these services and reallocating indirect costs to the less price-competitive services. In this manner, the FED was able to lower the full cost and, therefore, the price of its most price-competitive services.

COST ALLOCATION AND TAXATION OF UNRELATED BUSINESS INCOME AT NONPROFIT ORGANIZATIONS

Nonprofit organizations are exempt from federal income tax except for income from any activities that are unrelated to the nonprofit's exempt purpose. An example is the use of a laboratory for both tax-exempt basic medical research and testing a taxable product for commercial pharmaceutical firms. A concern in these cases is that the tax-exempt nonprofit organization will be able to compete unfairly with for-profit firms because of their tax-exempt status. The key argument is that common costs for the nonprofit's exempt and business activities will be used to "subsidize" the for-profit business (in this case, the taxable product testing). The nonprofit clearly has an incentive to allocate a relatively large portion of the common costs to the business activity to reduce taxes, but current Treasury regulations require that the cost allocation be reasonable. This has led some to argue that common costs should not be allocated in these cases. However, a recent analytical study (using economic models) of the economic productivity of for-profit and not-for-profit firms competing in the same business shows that failure to allocate common costs would lead to economic inefficiency by deterring the nonprofit manager from engaging in economically efficient unrelated businesses. The study supports the Treasury stance, which allows "reasonable" cost allocations.

Based on information in Ken S. Cavalluzzo, Christopher D. Ittner, and David F. Larcker, "Competition, Efficiency, and Cost Allocation in Government Agencies: Evidence on the Federal Reserve System," *Journal of Accounting Research*, Spring 1998, pp. 1–32; and Richard Sansing, "The Unrelated Business Income Tax, Cost Allocation, and Productive Efficiency," *National Tax Journal*, June 1998, pp. 291–302.

COST ALLOCATION TO SERVICE AND PRODUCTION DEPARTMENTS

LEARNING OBJECTIVE 3▶

Use the three steps of departmental cost allocation.

The preceding chapters on activity-based costing (Chapter 4), job costing (Chapter 12), and process costing (Chapter 13) provide a useful context for introducing cost allocation. The processes discussed in those chapters allocated overhead costs either *directly* to products (job costing) or *indirectly* in an allocation first to production departments and then to the products (process costing) or by using production activities (activity-based costing), as illustrated in Exhibit 14–1. Direct allocation pools all overhead into a single amount and allocates overhead using a single rate. In contrast, the departmental approach pools overhead costs in departmental cost pools and allocates overhead from each department to the products using a separate rate, one for each department. The departmental approach is preferred because it more accurately traces overhead costs to the products when different products require different amounts of resources in the various production departments.

The activity-based approach is the most accurate and the most preferred of the three approaches because it identifies cost behavior at the activity level, a much more detailed level of analysis than either the department level, as used in the departmental allocation approach, or plant level, as used in the direct approach.[4] Firms that have not been able to implement an activity-based costing system or cannot use the activity-based approach for cost-benefit or other reasons usually apply the departmental allocation approach. In the following section, we explain the application of the departmental approach.

Departmental Approach

The departmental approach recognizes that the typical manufacturing operation involves two types of manufacturing departments: production departments and service departments. Service departments provide human resources, maintenance, engineering, and other support to the production departments; production departments

---

[4]   For a recent survey of the use of activity-based costing in the allocation of shared facility costs, see Ann Triplett and Jon Scheumann, "Managing Shared Services with ABM," *Strategic Finance*, February 2000, pp. 40–45.

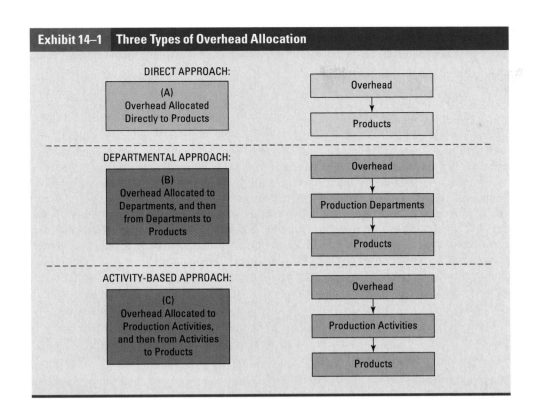

Exhibit 14–1 **Three Types of Overhead Allocation**

DIRECT APPROACH:

(A)
Overhead Allocated
Directly to Products

Overhead
↓
Products

DEPARTMENTAL APPROACH:

(B)
Overhead Allocated to
Departments, and then
from Departments to
Products

Overhead
↓
Production Departments
↓
Products

ACTIVITY-BASED APPROACH:

(C)
Overhead Allocated to
Production Activities,
and then from Activities
to Products

Overhead
↓
Production Activities
↓
Products

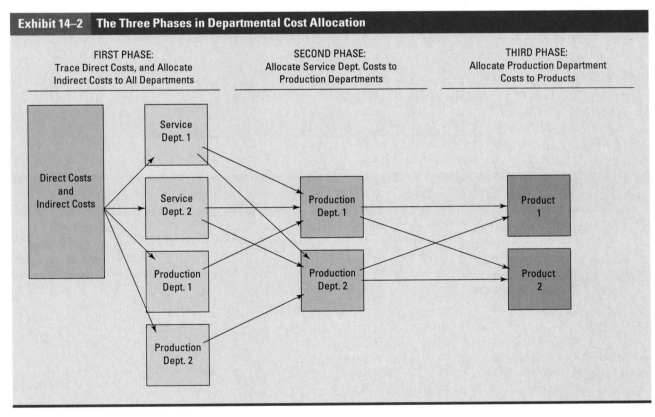

Exhibit 14–2 **The Three Phases in Departmental Cost Allocation**

FIRST PHASE:
Trace Direct Costs, and Allocate
Indirect Costs to All Departments

SECOND PHASE:
Allocate Service Dept. Costs to
Production Departments

THIRD PHASE:
Allocate Production Department
Costs to Products

Direct Costs
and
Indirect Costs

Service
Dept. 1

Service
Dept. 2

Production
Dept. 1

Production
Dept. 2

Production
Dept. 1

Production
Dept. 2

Product
1

Product
2

directly assemble and complete the product. The departmental approach has three phases: (1) trace all direct costs and allocate overhead costs to both the service departments and the production departments, (2) allocate the service department costs to the production departments, and finally (3) allocate the production department costs to the products. These phases are illustrated in Exhibit 14–2.

First Phase: Trace Direct Costs and Allocate Overhead Costs to Departments

The first phase in the departmental allocation approach traces the direct manufacturing costs in the plant to each service and production department that used them and identifies the overhead costs in the plant and allocates them to each of the service and production departments.

For the first-phase allocation, see the information for Beary Manufacturing Company in Exhibit 14–3. Beary manufactures two products and has two manufacturing departments and two service departments. Two types of overhead costs are common to all four departments: indirect labor and indirect materials. Beary uses both labor-hours and machine-hours for allocating the indirect costs.

The first-phase allocation for Beary Company is shown in Exhibit 14–4. Total direct costs of $36,000 are traced to the four departments, and the overhead costs are allocated using labor-hours (for indirect labor) and machine-hours (for indirect materials). The exhibit presents the allocation base information for labor-hour and machine-hour usage. The $25,000 of indirect labor is allocated to the four departments using the labor-hours allocation base. For example, the amount of indirect labor allocated to service department 1 is $3,750 (service department 1's share of total indirect labor, or 15% × $25,000). The allocations of indirect labor costs to the other departments are made in the same way. Similarly, the $5,000 of indirect materials cost

Exhibit 14–3   Data for Beary Manufacturing Company

	Service Department 1	Service Department 2	Production Department 1	Production Department 2	Total Hours	Total Amount
Labor-hours	1,800	1,200	3,600	5,400	12,000	
Machine-hours	320	160	1,120	1,600	3,200	
Direct costs	$1,600	$5,500	$15,500	$13,400		$36,000
Indirect labor	←		Not Traceable		→	25,000
Indirect materials						5,000
						$66,000

Exhibit 14–4   Departmental Allocation, First Phase
Beary Company

		Departments				
Departmental Allocation Bases		**Service 1**	**Service 2**	**Production 1**	**Production 2**	**Total**
Direct labor-hour (DLH)		1,800	1,200	3,600	5,400	12,000
Percent		15%	10%	30%	45%	100%
Machine-hour (MH)		320	160	1,120	1,600	3,200
Percent		10%	5%	35%	50%	100%
First Phase: Trace Direct Costs and Allocate Overhead Costs to Departments						
Direct costs		$1,600	$5,500	$15,500	$13,400	$36,000
Overhead Costs to Departments						
Indirect Labor	DLH	3,750	2,500	7,500	11,250	$25,000
		= 15% × $25,000	= 10% × $25,000	= 30% × $25,000	= 45% × $25,000	
Indirect Materials	MH	500	250	1,750	2,500	$5,000
		= 10% × $5,000	= 25% × $5,000	= 35% × $5,000	25% × $5,000	
Totals for all departments		**$5,850**	**$8,250**	**$24,750**	**$27,150**	**$66,000**

is allocated to the four departments using machine-hours. The amount of indirect materials allocated to service department 1 is $500 (1% × $5,000). The totals for direct costs and allocated indirect costs are $66,000, the same as the total cost to allocate (from Exhibit 14–3).

Service department 1	$ 5,850
Service department 2	8,250
Production department 1	24,750
Production department 2	27,150
Total	$66,000

Second Phase: Allocate Service Department Costs to Production Departments

The second phase allocates service department costs to the producing departments. This is the most complex of the allocation phases because services flow back and forth between the service departments. These are often called **reciprocal flows**. For example, assume that 40 percent (720 hours) of service department 1's 1,800 labor hours are spent serving service department 2. Also assume that 10 percent of service department 2's time is spent serving service department 1. You can see these two reciprocal flows for Beary Company in Exhibit 14–5.

The percentage of service relationships is commonly determined by reference to labor-hours, units processed, or some other allocation base that best reflects the service provided in the departments. At Beary Company, the service flow percentages for each service department are determined according to the labor-hours used for services provided to the other service department and to the production departments. Beary's first service department spends 40 percent of its labor time serving the service department 2 and 30 percent serving each of the two production departments. Service department 2 serves the service department 1 approximately 10 percent of the time, the first production department 30 percent of the time, and the second production department 60 percent of the time.

Accountants use three common methods to allocate costs under the departmental approach: (1) the direct method, (2) the step method, and (3) the reciprocal method.

The Direct Method

The **direct method** is the simplest of the three methods because it ignores the reciprocal flows. The cost allocation is accomplished by using the service flows *only to production departments* and determining each production department's share of that service. For example, for service department 1, the share of time for each production department is 50 percent of the total production department service, determined as follows.

Reciprocal flows represent the movement of services back and forth between service departments.

The **direct method** of cost allocation is accomplished by using the service flows *only to production departments* and determining each production department's share of that service.

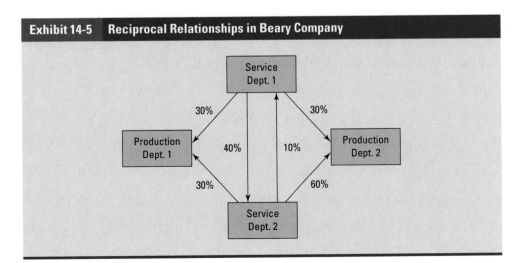

Exhibit 14-5   Reciprocal Relationships in Beary Company

For service department 1:

> Net service to both production departments from service department 1
> = 100% − Time of service to second service department
> = 100% − 40% = 60%
>
> Production department 1's share: 30 percent/60 percent = <u>50 percent</u>
>
> Production department 2's share: 30 percent/60 percent = <u>50 percent</u>

For service department 2:

> Net service to both production departments from service department 2:
> 100 percent − 10 percent = 90 percent
>
> Production department 1's share: 30 percent/90 percent = <u>33.33%</u>
>
> Production department 2's share: 60 percent/90 percent = <u>66.67%</u>

These percentage shares are used to allocate the costs from service departments to production departments, as shown in the second-phase section at the top of Exhibit 14–6. In that panel, for example, $5,850 of service department 1's costs are allocated equally to the production departments; 50 percent each is $2,925. The $8,250 of service department 2's costs are allocated 33.33 percent or $2,750 to production department 1 and 66.67 percent or $5,500 to production department 2. Total costs in production departments 1 and 2 at the end of the first phase allocations are $30,425 and $35,575, respectively.

Exhibit 14-6	**Departmental Allocation Second and Third Phases, Using the Direct Method**
	Beary Company

Second Phase: Allocate Service Department Costs to Production Departments

Direct Method		Production 1	Production 2	Total
Service 1	Service percent to producing departments	30%	30%	
	Allocation percent per direct method	50% = 30/(30 + 30)	50% = 30/(30 + 30)	
	Allocation amount	**$2,925**	**$2,925**	
		= 50% × $5,850	= 50% × $5,850	
Service 2	Service percent to producing departments	30%	60%	
	Allocation percent per direct method	33.3% = 30/(30 + 60)	66.67% = 60/(30 + 60)	
	Allocation amount	**2,750**	**5,500**	
	Plus: First-phase allocation	**24,750**	**27,150**	
		= 33.3% × $8,250	= 66.67% × $8,250	
Totals for Production Departments		**$30,425**	**$35,575**	**$66,000**

Third Phase: Allocate Production Department Costs to Products

	Product 1	Product 2	
Base: labor-hours for each product			
Amount	1,800	1,800	3,600
Percent	50	50	
Machine-hours			
Amount	400	1,200	1,600
Percent	25	75	
Production 1 (labor-hour basis)	**$15,212.50**	**$15,212.50**	
	= 50% × $30,425	= 50% × $30,425	
Production 2 (machine-hour basis)	**$8,893.75**	**$26,681.25**	
	= 25% × $35,575	= 75% × $35,575	
Totals for each product	**$24,106.25**	**$41,893.75**	**$66,000**

Cost Allocation in Hospitals and Health Maintenance Organizations (HMOs)

COST ALLOCATION AND MEDICARE REIMBURSEMENT IN HOSPITALS

A recent study of 105 hospitals found evidence of bias in their cost allocation practices. Since 1983, Medicare has reimbursed hospitals for inpatient services on the basis of specific, prospective rates and for outpatient services on the basis of cost. This reimbursement plan motivates hospitals to allocate as much common cost as possible to outpatient departments instead of inpatient services. The study examined the ratio of cost allocated to outpatient departments relative to total allocated cost for the period 1977 to 1991. Using regression analysis and data for each hospital, the study found a significant upward shift in costs allocated to outpatient departments after 1983.

COST ALLOCATION AND THE FINANCIAL PERFORMANCE OF HMOS

The financial performance of HMOs is under increasing scrutiny by state and federal regulators. Two key performance measures are the *medical loss ratio* (MLR), a statistic that measures the percentage of total HMO premium revenue that is spent on medical care, and the *administrative expense ratio* (AER), which measures the proportion of HMO revenues that are used for administrative costs. Many states require that HMOs report these ratios to potential enrollees. In addition,

Massachusetts has established a minimum MLR of 80 percent for Medicare plans, and Connecticut has established a requirement that the AER be no higher than 20 percent. Faced with these requirements, HMOs are sometimes accused of using cost allocation as a way to achieve the desired ratios. A recent study of the issue included five large HMOs that had widely different MLR and AER values. The study found a large difference in the treatment of allocated costs, especially in the treatment of medical management costs (the cost of the medical director, case managers, and utilization management nurses) and in areas where the cost accounting was unique, such as arrangements with vendors to share certain administrative expenses and arrangements with provider groups (physicians and hospitals) to share certain administrative expenses. All participating HMOs agreed that more detailed and consistent guidance in the area of cost allocation are needed.

Based on information in: Leslie Eldenburg and Sanjay Kallapur, "Changes in Hospital Service Mix and Cost Allocations in Response to Changes in Medicare Reimbursement Schemes," *Journal of Accounting and Economics,* May 1997, pp. 31–51; and Nancy Turnbull and Nancy M. Kane, "The Impact of Accounting and Actuarial Practice Differences on Medical Loss Ratios: An Exploratory Study with Five HMOs," *Inquiry,* The Blue Cross and Blue Shield Association, Chicago, Fall 1999, pp. 343–52.

The third and final phase is much like the first phase. The allocation from production departments to products typically is based on the number of labor-hours or machine-hours used in the production departments that produce the products. For Beary Company, using the direct method, costs are allocated to production department 1 on the basis of labor-hours and to production department 2 on the basis of machine-hours; see the third-phase panel of Exhibit 14–6. Assume that the production of product 1 required 1,800 hours of production department 1's total labor time of 3,600 hours, and thus is allocated 50 percent (1,800/3,600) of the total cost in production department 1. Similarly, assume that product 1 required 400 of the 1,600 machine-hours used in production department 2, it is allocated 25 percent (400/1,600) of the costs of production department 2. Product 2's costs are determined in a similar manner, as shown in Exhibit 14–6. The total cost of $66,000 is allocated as $24,106.25 to product 1 and $41,893.75 to product 2.

The Step Method   The second method to allocate service department costs is the **step method,** so-called because it uses a sequence of steps in allocating service department costs to production departments. In the first step, one service department is selected to be allocated fully, that is, to the other service department as well as to each production department. The department to be allocated fully usually is chosen because it provides the most service to other service departments. At Beary Company, service department 1 provides more service (40%) and it goes first in the allocation. Service department 2 is allocated only to the production departments, in the same manner as the direct method. Overall, this means that the step method provides more accurate allocations because one of the reciprocal flows between the two service departments (the one in the first step) is considered in the allocation, unlike the direct method that ignores all reciprocal flows.

The first phase of the step method (tracing direct costs and initial allocation of indirect costs) is the same as for the direct method as shown in Exhibit 14–4. However, in

> The **step method** uses a sequence of steps in the allocating service department costs to production departments.

the second phase, service department 1, which is in the first step, is allocated to service department 2 and the two production departments. The allocation to service department 2 is $2,340 (40 percent × $5,850). The allocations for the two production departments are determined in a similar manner. Then, in the second step, service department 2 is allocated to the two production departments using the direct method in the same manner as in Exhibit 14–6. The only difference is that the total cost in service department 2 ($10,590) now includes the original cost in service department 2 ($8,250) plus the cost allocated from service department 1 in the first step ($2,340).

The third phase of the step method is completed as in Exhibit 14–6. Using the step method, the total cost allocated to product 1 is $24,008.75 and the total cost allocated to product 2 is $41,991.25, for a total of $66,000.

The **reciprocal method** considers *all* reciprocal flows between service departments through simultaneous equations.

The Reciprocal Method   The **reciprocal method** is the most preferred of the three methods because, unlike the others, it considers *all* reciprocal flows between the service departments. This is accomplished by using simultaneous equations; the reciprocal flows are simultaneously determined in a system of equations.

An equation for each service department represents the cost to be allocated, consisting of the first-phase allocation costs plus the cost allocated from the other department. For Beary Company, the equation for service department 1 is as follows, using the symbol S1 to represent service department 1 and the symbol S2 to represent service department 2.

Allocated S1 Costs = Initial allocation + Cost allocated from S2

$$\text{S1} = \$5,850 + 10\% \times \text{S2}$$

Similarly, the equation for the second service department is as follows:

Allocated S2 Costs = Initial allocation + Cost allocated from S1

$$\text{S2} = \$8,250 + 40\% \times \text{S1}$$

These two equations can be solved for S1 and S2 by substituting the second equation into the first as follows:

$$\text{S1} = \$5,850 + 10\% \times (\$8,250 + 40\% \times \text{S1})$$

$$\text{S1} = \$6,953.13$$

And substituting S1 back into the second equation:

$$\text{S2} = \$11,031.25$$

These values for S1 and S2 are allocated to the producing departments using the percentage service amounts for each department. We illustrate the process for Beary Company in Exhibit 14–8. Note that since the reciprocal method has considered all reciprocal service department activities, the allocation is based on the actual service percentages for each production department. For example, production department 1, which receives 30 percent of service department 1's work, is allocated 30 percent of service department 1's cost, $2,086 (30% × $6,953.13). The allocations are made in a similar manner to the allocation of service department 2's costs and to production department 2.

The third phase analysis in Exhibit 14–8 is done in the same manner as in Exhibits 14–6 and 14–7. The total cost allocated to product 1 is $24,036.25 and for product 2, $41,963.75.

Third Phase: Allocate Department Costs Production to Products

For the third phase of the departmental approach, allocating production department costs to products, review Exhibits 14–6, 14–7, and 14–8. Note that although total costs are the same ($66,000), the amounts allocated to the two products vary. Although these amounts do not vary greatly for Beary Company, wide variations can occur in practice.

Exhibit 14–7 Departmental Allocation, Second and Third Phases Using the Step Method

Second Phase: Allocate Service Department Costs to Production Departments: Using the Step Method

	Service 1	Production 1	Production 2	Total
First Step				
Service 1				
Service percent	40%	30%	30%	
Amount	$ 2,340	$ 1,755	$ 1,755	
	= 40% × $5,850	= 30% × $5,850	= 30% × $5,850	
Second Step				
Service 2				
Service percent		30%	60%	
Allocation percent per direct method		33.33	66.67	
Amount	10,590	3,530	7,060	
	= $8,250 + $2,340	= 33.33% × $10,590	= 66.67% × $10,590	
Plus: First-phase allocation		24,750	27,150	
Totals for production departments		30,035	35,965	$66,000

Third Phase: Allocate Production Department Costs to Products

	Service 1	Production 1	Production 2	Total
Base: labor-hours				
Amount		1,800	1,800	3,600
Percentage		50%	50%	
Machine-hours				
Amount		400	1,200	1,600
Percentage		25%	75%	
Production 1 (labor-hour basis)		$15,017.50	$15,017.50	
		= 50% × $30,035	= 50% × $30,035	
Production 2 (machine-hour basis)		$8,991.25	$26,973.75	
		= 25% × $35,965	= 75% × $35,965	
Totals for each product		$24,008.75	$41,991.25	$66,000

COST MANAGEMENT IN ACTION

Health Care Providers Allocate Cost for Medicare Reimbursement

Since the advent of Medicare in 1966 to cover medical expenses of aged, blind, and disabled individuals, health care providers have been required to use cost allocation methods to receive reimbursement from the federal government for services covered by Medicare. The costs of health care service activities are allocated to the patient revenue-generating services. Some examples of service activities and patient revenue-generating services in a hospital follow:

Patient Revenue-Generating Services

Intensive care unit	Laboratory
Psychiatric care	Radiology
Coronary care	Emergency Room
Surgery	Pharmacy
Anesthesia	

Service Activities

Dietary	Nursing administration
Laundry and linen	Operation of hospital buildings
Admissions	Administrative and general
Social services	Housekeeping

How do hospitals respond to Medicare requirements and allocate the costs of service activities to the patient revenue-generating services? What methods are likely to be preferred?

(Refer to comments on Cost Management in Action at the end of the chapter.)

Exhibit 14-8	Departmental Allocation Second and Third Phases, Using the Reciprocal Method

Second Phase: Allocate Service Department Costs to Production Departments Using the Reciprocal Method

First: Solve the simultaneous equations for Service 1 and Service 2:
  Amount allocated from service 1 $6,953.13
  Amount allocated from service 2 $11,031.25

	Production 1	Production 2	Total
Second: Allocate to producing departments			
Service 1			
Service %	30%	30%	
Allocated amount	$2,086	$2,086	
	= 30% × $6,953	= 30% × $6,953.13	
Service 2			
Service %	30%	60%	
Allocated amount	3,309	6,619	
	= 30% × $11,031	= 60% × $11,031	
Plus: Costs allocated in first phase	24,750	27,150	
Totals for Production Departments	$30,145	$35,855	$66,000

Third Phase: Allocate Production Department Costs to Products

	Production 1	Production 2	Total
Base: Direct labor-hours			
Amount	1,800	1,800	3,600
Percent	50%	50%	
Machine-hours			
Amount	400	1,200	1,600
Percent	25%	75%	
Production 1 (direct labor-hour basis)	$15,072.50	$15,072.50	
	= 50% × $30,145	= 50% × $30,145	
Production 2 (machine-hour basis)	$8,963.75	$26,891.25	
	= 25% × $35,855	= 70% × $35,855	
Totals for each product	$24,036.25	$41,963.75	$66,000

When significant differences exist, a management accountant should consider the value of the reciprocal method, which is more complete and accurate than the others because it fully considers the reciprocal flows between service departments.

Implementation Issues

LEARNING OBJECTIVE 4▶

Explain the problems in implementing the different departmental cost allocation methods.

The four issues to consider when implementing the departmental allocation approach are (1) difficulty in determining an appropriate allocation base, (2) separation of variable and fixed costs (called *dual allocation*), (3) use of budgeted rather than actual amounts, and (4) allocated costs exceeding the outside purchase price.

Difficulty in Determining the Allocation Base Determining an appropriate allocation base and a percentage amount for service provided by the service departments is often difficult. For example, using labor hours could be inappropriate in an automated plant where labor is a small part of total cost. Similarly, square feet of floor space could be inappropriate to allocate certain costs when a great deal of idle space exists. Furthermore, the use of square feet of floor space can have undesirable motivational consequences. For example, if we are allocating plantwide maintenance costs to production departments using floor space as a base, a department has inadequate incentive to limit its use of maintenance expense. Since the actual use of maintenance is unrelated to floor space, if a given department increases its use of maintenance, then the other departments pay for the increase as well, as illustrated in Exhibit 14–9. Here, depart-

Solving for the Reciprocal Allocation Method Using the Solver Function in Microsoft Excel

Solving reciprocal departmental allocation problems can become tedious if three or more departments are involved. In this case, we suggest the use of software programs such as the Solver function in Excel. The following screen capture illustrates how the Solver tool can be used to solve the Beary Company example in the text. Note that the target cell is set to the first phase allocation for S1 and that the constraints include an equality constraint for S2. Note also that the con-

tent of cells B5 and B6 show Solver's solution because this screen capture was taken after the solution was obtained. Before asking Solver to solve the problem for the first time, you will need to enter into B5 and B6 your guess at what the solution might be (it does not have to be close—just something for Solver to start with). For more information on how to use Solver, see Appendix A for Chapter 10, (page 433).

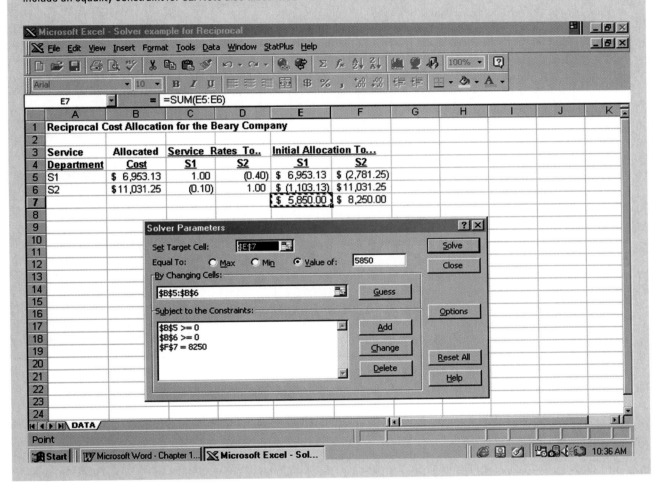

ment A increases its use of maintenance by $6,000 (from panel 2 to panel 3 in Exhibit 14–9), while department B's usage stays the same. The effect of department A's increased usage when allocation is based on square feet is that department B pays one-half of the increased cost. A preferred approach in this example would be to allocate on the basis of maintenance requests in order to achieve the desired objectives of motivation and fairness. Exhibit 14–10 provides some suggested allocation bases that can address some of these difficulties.

Separate Fixed and Variable Costs: Dual Allocation

A preferred departmental allocation approach is dual allocation, which separates variable and fixed costs and traces the variable costs directly to the departments that caused the cost. Tracing variable costs in this way satisfies the allocation objectives of motivation and fairness. However, firms sometimes find that separating the variable

Exhibit 14–9 **Disincentive Effects of Certain Allocation Methods**

	Department A	Department B	Total Maintenance Cost
Panel 1: Basic information			
Square feet of floor space	5,000	5,000	
Average number of maintenance requests	50	50	
Total maintenance costs			$200,000
Panel 2: Maintenance cost allocation in an average month using square feet of floor space			
Allocated maintenance cost	$100,000	$100,000	$200,000

Panel 3: Maintenance cost allocation based on square feet for a month when department A increases usage of maintenance from 50 to 80 maintenance requests, while department B's usage remains the same at 50 requests. Here we assume that maintenance costs are variable with the number of maintenance requests, or $2,000 per request ($200,000/(50 + 50)), so that total maintenance costs increase to $260,000 ($2,000 × [50 + 80]).

	Department A	Department B	Total Maintenance Cost
Allocated maintenance cost:	$130,000	$130,000	$260,000

Exhibit 14–10 **Allocation Bases for Selected Types of Costs**

Personnel-related costs—number of employees

Payroll-related costs (pensions, fringe benefits, payroll taxes)—labor cost

Materials-related costs—materials cost or quantity used

Space-related costs—square feet or cubic feet

Energy-related costs—motor capacity

Research and development costs—estimated time, sales, or assets employed

Public relations costs—sales

Executives' salaries costs—sales, assets employed

Property taxes costs—square feet, real estate or insurance valuation, market value of assets

Source: Institute of Management Accountants, "Allocation of Service and Administrative Costs," *Statement Number 4B* (Montvale, N.J., 1985).

Cost Allocation Should Promote Safety

Organizations of all types incur insurance costs to minimize the potential effect of losses from their liability for injury to employees and customers. These costs are usually allocated to all of the organization's revenue-producing units. The allocation is often made in proportion to the total revenue in each unit, based on the fact that larger units should pay more than the smaller units and that more sales usually means more loss liability. Alternatively, the number of employees in the units can be used in the same way. In other cases, the insurance premium costs are not allocated to the units because unit managers have little control over the occurrence of the losses. In contrast, a common argument currently used is that the insurance costs should be allocated on the basis of loss experience, usually determined over the two or three prior years, to provide a direct incentive for unit managers to reduce product and employee liability losses in their units. Unit managers can do this by consistently reminding employees of the importance of safety in the workplace and offering incentives to enhance workplace safety.

Based on information in: David M. Katz, "Cost Allocation Should Spur Safety," *National Underwriter,* November 9, 1998, pp. 27–30.

and fixed costs of the departments is difficult or uneconomical. The firm then allocates the total costs (both variable and fixed) in the same manner. Because variable costs are not traced, the latter approach based on total cost does not meet the allocation objectives as well as dual allocation.

Budgeted vs. Actual Amounts   When the allocation base is determined from actual amounts (for example, labor-hours incurred in the current period), each department's cost allocation affects the other departments' actual usage of the allocation base. The reason is that each department's actual usage affects total actual usage. Unfavorable incentives arise because one department's usage now affects the amount allocated to the other departments. Exhibit 14–11 continues the example of allocating maintenance costs used in Exhibit 14–9 except that maintenance is allocated on the basis of direct labor-hours. Also, we assume that maintenance costs are both variable and fixed relative to direct labor-hours; there are $100,000 in total fixed costs and a $5 per direct labor-hour variable cost. Exhibit 14–11 shows that department B's allocated costs increased from $100,000 (part 2) to $112,500 (part 3) even though department B did not increase its usage of direct labor-hours or of maintenance requests. The reason for this is that department A reduced its usage of direct labor from 10,000 hours to 6,000 hours. As a result, the $100,000 *total fixed costs in maintenance are allocated over a smaller number of total labor-hours*, thus increasing department B's total cost allocation. The direct labor-hours-based allocation is unfair and unmotivating for department B.

For this reason, using budgeted or predetermined amounts rather than actual amounts for allocating fixed costs is preferable. When budgeted direct labor-hours are used, each department's fixed cost allocation is predictable and is not influenced by the usage in other departments. In contrast, allocating variable costs on the basis of actual usage is preferable, since variable costs can be directly traced to the different users. This is another reason that it is important to separate variable and fixed costs using dual allocation. An important limitation of the use of budgeted rates is that sometimes the budget information could be difficult to obtain. For example, budgeted rates would be difficult to implement when the allocation base varies significantly from period to period or is difficult to predict accurately.

Exhibit 14–11   Disincentive Effects of Actual Usage-Based Allocation Methods

	Department A	Department B	Total Maintenance Cost
Panel 1: Basic Information			
Actual number of direct labor-hours	10,000	10,000	
Budgeted number of direct labor-hours	10,000	10,000	
Average number of maintenance requests	50	50	
Total maintenance costs			$200,000
Panel 2: Maintenance cost allocation in an average month using the number of direct labor-hours			
Allocated maintenance cost	$100,000	$100,000	$200,000

Panel 3: Maintenance cost allocation based on direct labor-hours for a month when department A decreases usage of direct labor-hours from 10,000 to 6,000 hours while department B's usage remains the same at 10,000 hours. Here we assume that maintenance costs have both a variable ($5 per direct labor-hour) and a fixed ($100,000) component. Total maintenance costs decrease to $180,000 (= $100,000 + $5 × (6,000 + 10,000)) and cost/hr is $180,000/16,000 = $11.25

	Department A	Department B	Total Maintenance Cost
Allocated maintenance cost	$67,500	$112,500	$180,000
	= 6,000 hrs	= 10,000 hrs	
	× $11.25	× $11.25	

| Exhibit 14-12 | Cost Allocation Using External Prices | | | | | | |

(A) User Department	(B) Direct Labor-Hours	(C) Direct Labor-Hour Allocation Base	(D) Cost Allocation Based on Labor-Hours	(E) Outside Price	(F) Allocation Base for Outside Price	(G) Allocation Based on Outside Price
A	3,000	30% (3,000/10,000)	$ 300	$ 360	30% (360/1,200)	$300
B	4,000	40% (4,000/10,000)	400	600	50% 600/1,200)	500
C	1,000	10% (1,000/10,000)	100	120	10% (120/1,200)	100
D	2,000	20% (2,000/10,000)	200	120	10% (120/1,200)	100
Total	10,000	100%	$1,000	$1,200	100%	$1,000

Allocated Costs Exceed External Purchase Cost Another limitation of the three departmental methods (direct, step, and reciprocal) is that they can allocate to a department a higher cost than the cost of the service that the department could purchase from an outside supplier. Should the department pay more for a service internally than an outside vendor would charge? To motivate managers to be efficient and to make the right decisions, the allocation should be based on the cost as if each department had to obtain the service outside the firm. Consider the data in Exhibit 14–12 for a firm with four departments that share a common data processing service costing $1,000. Data processing costs are allocated using direct labor-hours in each department as shown in columns (B), (C), and (D) of Exhibit 14–12. The data processing service can also be obtained from an outside firm at the cost shown in column (E).

The direct labor-hours allocation base in this example penalizes department D, which can obtain the service outside the firm for $80 less than the inside cost ($200 – $120), perhaps because of the simplified nature of the requirements in department D. In contrast, department B can obtain the service outside only at a much higher price ($600 versus $400 inside), perhaps because of the specialized nature of the service. In this case, the allocation based on the *outside price* (column G in Exhibit 14–12) is fair to both departments B and D. It is a better reflection of the competitive cost of the service. The question of whether, and under what conditions, the department should be allowed to purchase outside the firm is a different issue, which is addressed in the coverage of management control in chapters 18 and 19.

COST ALLOCATION IN SERVICE INDUSTRIES

LEARNING OBJECTIVE 5▶

Explain the use of cost allocation in service firms.

The concepts presented in this chapter apply equally well to manufacturing, service, or not-for-profit organizations that incur joint costs. For example, financial institutions such as commercial banks also use cost allocation. To illustrate, we use the Community General Bank (CGB), which provides a variety of banking services, including deposit accounts, mortgage loans, installment loans, investment services, and other services. Currently, CGB is analyzing the profitability of its mortgage loan department, which has two main businesses, commercial construction loans and residential construction loans. An important part of the analysis of these loan businesses is determining how to trace or allocate costs to the two businesses.

The cost allocation begins by identifying which departments directly support the two mortgage loan businesses, the loan operations department and the marketing department. The *operations department* handles the processing of loan applications, safekeeping of appropriate documents, billing, and maintaining accounts for both commercial and residential loans. The *marketing department* provides direct advertising, promotions, and customer service for both types of loans.

Other departments support the two loan businesses indirectly by supporting the operations and marketing departments. Two important support departments are the administrative services department and the accounting department. The *administrative services department* provides legal and technical support. The *accounting department* provides financial services, including regular financial reports and the maintenance of customer records. The administrative services and accounting departments provide services to each other as well as to the operations and marketing departments, as illustrated in Exhibit 14–13. Each of the four departments has labor and certain supplies costs that can be traced directly to it. In addition, CGB's human resources department and computer services department provide services to all four departments.

CGB uses the step method to allocate costs from support departments to the loan businesses. See the step method in Exhibit 14–14, which follows the same approach as for Beary Company in Exhibit 14–7. The top of Exhibit 14–14 shows the allocation bases that CGB uses to allocate human resources costs and computer services costs to each department. The allocation base for human resources costs is the number of employees, or the head count, in each department, and the allocation of computer services costs is based on the number of computers in each department. The number of employees and the number of computers in each department are given.

The first phase of the allocation in Exhibit 14–14 shows tracing the totals of $1,560,000 of direct labor and $33,000 for supplies costs to each department as well as the allocation of the human resources costs ($80,000) and computer services costs ($66,000), using the allocation bases head count and number of computers, respectively. The result is that the total cost of $1,739,00 is allocated as follows

Accounting department	$253,700
Administrative services department	381,500
Operations department	623,700
Marketing department	480,100
Total cost	$1,739,000

In the second phase, the accounting and administrative service department costs are allocated to the operations and marketing departments using the step method and the service percentages in Exhibit 14–13. The result is that the $1,739,000 of total cost is now allocated to the operations department ($934,957.50) and the marketing department ($804,042.50).

In the third and final phase, the costs from the operations and marketing departments are allocated to the two businesses, commercial and residential loans. The base

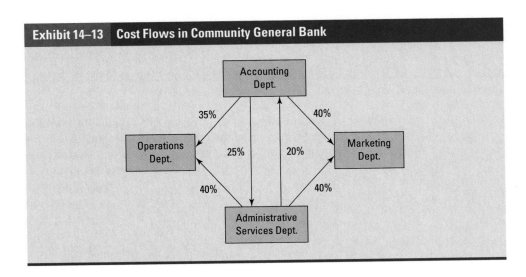

Exhibit 14–13   Cost Flows in Community General Bank

Exhibit 14–14	Use of the Step Method for Cost Allocation at Community General Bank

Departmental Allocation Bases	Departments					Total
	Accounting	**Administrative Services**	**Operations**	**Marketing**		
Human Resources						
Headcount	80	100	160	60		400
	20.0%	25.0%	40.0%	15.0%		100.0%
Computer Services						
Number of computers	60	60	150	30		300
	20.0%	20.0%	50.0%	10.0%		100.0%

First Phase: Trace Direct Costs and Allocate Overhead Costs to Departments

Direct costs (given)						
Labor	$221,000	$399,500	$554,500	$445,000		$1,560,000
Supplies	3,500	8,800	4,200	16,500		33,000
Indirect costs						
Human Resources	16,000	20,000	32,000	12,000	(EG, $12,000 = 15% × $80,000)	80,000
Computer Services	13,200	13,200	33,000	6,600	(EG, $6,600 = 10% × $66,000)	66,000
Totals for all departments	**$253,700**	**$381,500**	**$623,700**	**$480,100**		**$1,739,000**

Second Phase: Allocate Service Department Costs to Accounting and Administrative Costs to Operations and Marketing, Using the Step Method

First step						
Accounting Department	Service percent	25%	35%	40%		
	Amount	$63,425	$88,795	$101,480	(EG, $101,480 = 40% × $253,700)	
Second step						
Administrative services	Service percent		40%	40%		
	Allocation percent per direct method		50%	50%		
	Amount		$222,462.50	$222,462.50	(EG, $222,462.50 = 50% × $444,925)	
Totals for production departments			$934,957.50	$804,042.50		$1,739,000

Third Phase: Allocate Operations and Marketing Costs to Commercial and Residential Loans		Commercial Loans	Residential Loans	Total
Base: Number of banking transactions		15,000	10,000	25,000
	Percent	60%	40%	
Number of loans		900	3,600	4,500
	Percent	20%	80%	
Operations	Number of transactions	$560,974.50	$373,983	
Marketing	Number of loans	$160,808.50	$643,234	
Totals for commercial and residential loans		**$721,783**	**$1,017,217**	**$1,739,000**

that CGB uses to allocate operations department costs is the number of banking transactions handled within operations (15,000 for commercial loans and 10,000 for residential loans) and to allocate marketing costs is the number of loans of either type (900 commercial loans and 3,600 residential loans). The result of the final allocation is that the total cost of $1,739,000 is allocated to the commercial loans department ($721,783) and the residential loans department ($1,017,217), as illustrated for the third phase in Exhibit 14–14.

Cost allocation provides CGB a basis for evaluating the cost and profitability of its services. By taking the allocated operating costs just determined, the cost of funds provided, and the revenue produced by both commercial and residential loans, a prof-

Exhibit 14–15	Profitability Analysis of Mortgage Loans	
	Community General Bank	

	Commercial Loans	Residential Loans
Revenues	$2,755,455	$2,998,465
Less expenses		
Cost of funds	1,200,736	1,387,432
Allocated operating costs	721,783	1,017,217
Contribution	$ 832,936	$ 593,816
Key ratios		
Contribution/revenue	30.23%	19.80%
Cost of funds/revenues	43.58%	46.27%

itability analysis of mortgage loans can be completed. Assume that the commercial loan departments have revenues of $2,755,455 and $2,998,465, respectively, and direct cost of funds of $1,200,736 and $1,387,432, respectively.

The profitability analysis in Exhibit 14–15 shows that the relatively high allocated operating costs of the residential loan department are an important factor in its overall poor performance (only 19.8 percent contribution per dollar of revenue in contrast to more than 30 percent for the commercial loan area). In contrast, the cost of funds appears to be comparable for both types of loans (43.58 percent of revenues for commercial loans and 46.27 percent of revenues for residential loans). The analysis indicates that the bank should investigate the profitability of residential loans and, in particular, the cost of operations and marketing for these loans.

JOINT PRODUCT COSTING

◄LEARNING OBJECTIVE 6
Use the three joint product costing methods.

Firms that have joint products also need cost allocation. These firms produce joint products simultaneously in the same production departments before moving the products to subsequent production departments as separate products. Many manufacturing plants yield more than one product from a joint manufacturing process. For example, the petroleum industry processes crude oil into multiple products: gasoline, naphtha, kerosene, fuel oils, and residual heavy oils. Similarly, the semiconductor industry processes silicon wafers into a variety of computer memory chips with different speeds, temperature tolerances, and life expectancies. Beef and hides are products linked in the meatpacking process; neither of these items can be produced without producing the other. Other industries that yield joint products include lumber production, food processing, soap making, grain milling, dairy farming, and fishing.

Joint products and by-products are derived from processing a single input or a common set of inputs. **Joint products** are products from the same production process that have relatively substantial sales values. Products whose total sales values are minor in comparison to the sales value of the joint products are classified as **by-products.**

A change in market demand or production technology can change the status of a by-product or a joint product. Chips of wood bark are a log-processing by-product because their only use to the manufacturer is to sell them at a token price to a landscaping company to use for mulch. Bark chips would become a joint product, however, if a pharmaceutical company could extract from them a valuable ingredient that raised their value.

Joint products and by-products both start their manufacturing life as part of the same raw material. Until a certain point in the production process, no distinction can be made between the products. The point in a joint production process at which individual products can be identified for the first time is called the **split-off point.** Thereafter, separate

Joint products are products from the same production process that have relatively substantial sales value.

By-products are products whose total sales values are minor in comparison with the sales value of the joint products.

The **split-off point** is the first point in a joint production process at which individual products can be identified.

production processes can be applied to the individual products. At the split-off point, joint products or by-products might be salable or require further processing to be salable, depending on their nature.

Joint costs include all manufacturing costs incurred prior to the split-off point (including direct materials, direct labor, and factory overhead). For financial reporting purposes, these costs are allocated among the joint products. Additional costs incurred after the split-off point that can be identified directly with individual products are called **additional processing costs** or **separable costs.**

> **Additional processing costs** or **separable costs** are those that occur after the split-off point and can be identified directly with individual products.

Other outputs of joint production include scrap, waste, spoilage and defective units. Scrap is the residue from a production process that has little or no recovery value. Waste, such as chemical waste, is a residual material that has no recovery value and must be disposed of by the firm as required. In addition to waste and scrap, some products do not meet quality standards and can be reworked for resale. Spoiled units are not reworked for economic reasons. Defective units are reworked to become salable units.

Methods for Allocating Joint Costs to Joint Products

Joint costs are most frequently allocated to joint products using (1) the physical measure, (2) the sales value, and (3) the net realizable value methods.

The Physical Measure Method

> The **physical measure method** uses a physical measure such as pounds, gallons, or yards or units or volume produced at the split-off point to allocate the joint costs to joint products.

> The **average cost method** uses units of output to allocate joint costs to joint products.

The **physical measure method,** naturally enough, uses a physical measure such as pounds, gallons, or yards or units or volume produced at the split-off point to allocate the joint costs to joint products. The first step is to select the proper physical measure as the basis for allocation. We can use units of input or units of output. For example, if we are costing tuna products, the production of 100 pounds of tuna into quarter-pound cans would have an input measure of 100 pounds and an output measure of 400 cans. When units of output are used, this also is called the **average cost method.**

Assume that Johnson Seafood produces tuna filets and canned tuna for distribution to restaurants and supermarkets in the southeastern United States. The cost of 14,000 pounds of raw, unprocessed tuna plus the direct labor and overhead for cutting and processing the tuna into filets and canned tuna is the joint cost of the process. The flow of production is illustrated in Exhibit 14–16.

The production process starts at point 1. A total $16,000 joint cost ($7,000 direct materials, $5,000 direct labor, and $4,000 overhead) is incurred. Point 2 is the split-off point where two joint products are separated: 2,000 pounds of tuna and 8,000 pounds of canned tuna. The remaining 4,000 pounds of by-products, scrap, and waste are not accounted for. (The appendix to the chapter explains how to account for by-

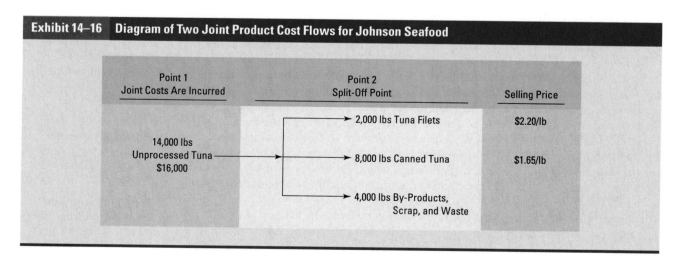

Exhibit 14–16   Diagram of Two Joint Product Cost Flows for Johnson Seafood

Point 1 Joint Costs Are Incurred	Point 2 Split-Off Point	Selling Price
	2,000 lbs Tuna Filets	$2.20/lb
14,000 lbs Unprocessed Tuna $16,000	8,000 lbs Canned Tuna	$1.65/lb
	4,000 lbs By-Products, Scrap, and Waste	

products.) If we use a physical measure method, the joint cost of $16,000 is allocated as shown in Exhibit 14–17.

Based on the physical measure method (pounds in this example), when the joint products reach the split-off point, we can compute the relationship of each of the joint products to the sum of the total units. The joint cost allocated to the products is the average cost per pound of the joint cost, which is $1.60 per pound.

The physical measure used to determine the relative weights for allocating the joint cost should be the measure of the products at the *split-off point*, not the measure when the production of the products is completed. Thus, the relevant measure in the example is the 2,000 pounds of filets and 8,000 pounds of canned tuna.

The production costs per pound for both products follow:

Filet $1.60 per pound = $3,200/2,000 pounds

Canned tuna $1.60 per pound = $12,800/8,000 pounds

Advantages and Limitations   Among the advantages of the physical measure method are that (1) it is easy to use and (2) the criterion for the allocation of the joint costs is objective. This method, however, ignores the revenue-producing capability of individual products that can vary widely among the joint products and have no relationship at all to any physical measure. Each product can also have a unique physical measure (gallons for one, pounds for another) and, hence, the physical measure method might not be applicable. The following method addresses these limitations.

The Sales Value at Split-Off Method

The sales value at split-off method is an alternative and widely used method. The **sales value at split-off method** (or more simply, *sales value method*) allocates joint costs to joint products on the basis of their relative sales values at the split-off point. This method can be used only when joint products can be sold at the split-off point. If we assume that Johnson can sell a pound of filets for $2.20 and a pound of canned tuna for $1.65 and that Johnson has produced 2,000 pounds of filets and 8,000 pounds of canned tuna, the $16,000 joint cost should be allocated between the products as shown in Exhibit 14–18.

The first step in the sales value method (Exhibit 14–18) is to compute the total sales value of the joint products at the split-off point. Note that the sales value is the sales price multiplied by the number of production units, *not the actual number of sales*

> The **sales value at split-off method** allocates joint costs to joint products on the basis of their relative sales values at the split-off point.

Exhibit 14–17 **Physical Measure Method**

Product	Physical Measure	Proportion	Allocation of Joint Cost	Cost per Pound
Tuna filets	2,000 lbs	0.20	$16,000 × 20% = $ 3,200	$1.60
Canned tuna	8,000 lbs	0.80	16,000 × 80% = 12,800	1.60
Total	10,000 lbs	1.00	$16,000	

Exhibit 14–18 **Sales Value at Split-off Method**

Product	Units	Price per unit	Sales Value	Proportion	Joint Cost Allocated	Cost per Pound
Filets	2,000 lbs	$2.20	$ 4,400	0.25	$16,000 × 25% = $ 4,000	$2.00
Canned tuna	8,000 lbs	1.65	13,200	0.75	16,000 × 75% = 12,000	1.50
Total			$17,600	1.00	$16,000	

units. Determining the proportion of the sales value of each joint product to the total sales value is the second step. The final operation allocates the total joint cost among the joint products based on those proportions.

In the Johnson Seafood example, the sales value of filets is $4,400 and of canned tuna is $13,200, a total of $17,600. The proportion of the individual sales values of the products to the total sales value are 0.25 ($4,400/$17,600) for filets and 0.75 ($13,200/$17,600) for canned tuna. The allocated costs are $4,000 to filets and $12,000 to canned tuna.

The production costs per pound for both products are calculated as follows:

Filets $2.00 per pound = $4,000/2,000

Canned tuna $1.50 per pound = $12,000/8,000

Note that filets have a higher unit cost under the sales value method than under the physical measure method. The reason is that filets have a higher sales value. If the sales prices are estimated accurately and no additional processing costs are involved, the sales value at split-off method generates the same gross margin percentage for both filets and canned tuna as shown in Exhibit 14–19.

Advantages and Limitations   The advantages of the sales value method are that it (1) is easy to calculate and (2) is allocated according to the individual product's revenues. This method is superior to the physical measure method because it allocates the joint costs in proportion to the products' ability to absorb these costs. This is an application of the ability-to-bear concept of fairness included in the objectives of cost allocation at the beginning of the chapter.

One limitation of the sales value method is that market prices for some industries change constantly. Also, the sales price at split-off might not be available because additional processing is necessary before the product can be sold.

The Net Realizable Value Method

Not all joint products can be sold at the split-off point. Thus, there is no market price to attach to some products at the split-off point. In these cases, the concept of net realizable value is used. The **net realizable value (NRV)** of a product is the product's estimated sales value at the split-off point; it is determined by subtracting the additional processing and selling costs beyond the split-off point from the ultimate sales value of the product.

> The **net realizable value (NRV)** of a product is the estimated sales value of the product at the split-off point; it is determined by subtracting the additional processing and selling costs beyond the split-off point from the ultimate sales value of the product.

NRV = Ultimate sales value – Additional processing and selling cost

In the Johnson Seafood example, assume that in addition to filets and canned tuna, the firm processes cat food from raw, unprocessed tuna. Assume also that 14,000 pounds of tuna yield at the split-off point 2,000 pounds of filets and 8,000 pounds of canned tuna as before but now an additional 3,000 pounds of cat food. The remaining 1,000 pounds are scrap, waste, and by-products. For cat food the tuna must be processed further for sale to pet food distributors. The additional processing cost is $850 for minerals and other supplements that are important for cat nutrition but that add no weight to the product. The pet food distributors buy the prepared cat food

Exhibit 14–19   Product-Line Profitability Analysis

	Tuna Filets	Canned Tuna
Sales	$2.20 × 2,000 = $4,400	$1.65 × 8,000 = $13,200
Cost of goods sold	$2.00 × 2,000 = 4,000	$1.50 × 8,000 = 12,000
Gross margin	$ 400	$ 1,200
Gross margin percent	9.09%	9.09%

from Johnson at $1.75 per pound and package it into 3-ounce cans for sale to pet stores and supermarkets. Exhibit 14–20 is a diagram of this situation.

Exhibit 14–21 shows the joint cost allocation calculation using the net realizable value method.

If Johnson Seafood sold all products it produced during the period, its gross margin amounts for the products would be as shown in Exhibit 14–22. Note that the gross margin percentage is lower for cat food than for filets because of the additional processing cost of $850.

Advantages and Limitations   The net realizable value method is superior to the physical measure method because, like the sales value at split-off method, it produces an allocation that yields a predictable, comparable level of profitability among the products. The physical measure method might provide misleading guidance to top management regarding product profitability, which can be very frustrating to product-line managers.

However, the net realizable value method can be less objective than the sales value method when the products are not salable at the split-off point, and estimating the sales value at the split-off point is difficult.

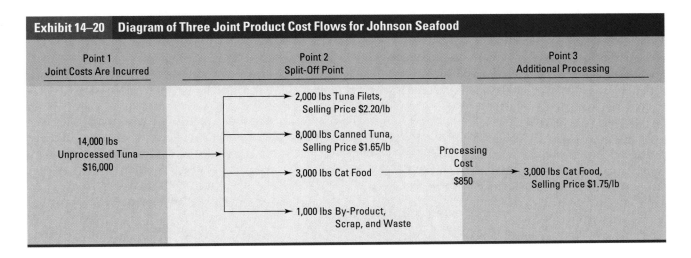

Exhibit 14–20   **Diagram of Three Joint Product Cost Flows for Johnson Seafood**

| Point 1 Joint Costs Are Incurred | Point 2 Split-Off Point | Point 3 Additional Processing |

14,000 lbs Unprocessed Tuna $16,000

→ 2,000 lbs Tuna Filets, Selling Price $2.20/lb
→ 8,000 lbs Canned Tuna, Selling Price $1.65/lb
→ 3,000 lbs Cat Food — Processing Cost $850 → 3,000 lbs Cat Food, Selling Price $1.75/lb
→ 1,000 lbs By-Product, Scrap, and Waste

Exhibit 14–21   **Joint Cost Allocation Using the Net Realizable Value Method**

Product	Pounds	Price	Sales Value	Additional Processing	Net Realizable Value	Weight	Allocated Cost	Total Cost	Cost per Pound
Filets	2,000	$2.20	$ 4,400	—	$ 4,400	0.2	$ 3,200	$ 3,200	$1.60
Canned tuna	8,000	1.65	13,200	—	13,200	0.6	9,600	9,600	1.20
Cat food	3,000	1.75	5,250	$850	4,400	0.2	3,200	4,050	1.35
Total	13,000		$22,850	$850	$22,000	1.0	$16,000	$16,850	

Exhibit 14–22   **Johnson Seafood's Product-Line Profitability Analysis**

	Tuna Filets	Canned Tuna	Cat Food
Sales	$2.20 × 2,000 = $4,400	$1.65 × 8,000 = $13,200	$1.75 × 3,000 = $5,250
Cost of goods sold	$1.60 × 2,000 = 3,200	$1.20 × 8,000 = 9,600	$1.35 × 3,000 = 4,050
Gross margin	$1,200	$ 3,600	$1,200
Gross margin percent	27.27%	27.27%	22.86%

SUMMARY

This chapter introduces the objectives, concepts, and methods of cost allocation. There are two main cost allocation applications—departmental cost and joint product costing. Most important, the objectives and methods for cost allocation are determined based on the firm's strategy. Cost allocation is concerned with strategy in four key ways: (1) to determine accurate departmental and product costs as a basis for evaluating the departments' cost efficiency and profitability of different products, (2) to motivate managers to work hard, (3) to provide the proper incentive for managers to achieve the firm's goals, and (4) to provide a fair basis for rewarding managers for their effort.

Ethical issues often arise in cost allocation when managers must choose between alternative allocation methods. The manager must choose between methods that might decrease the cost of one product, customer, or business unit at the expense of increased costs for another product, customer, or unit.

Departmental cost allocation is performed in three phases: (1) trace all direct costs and allocate overhead to service and production departments, (2) allocate service department costs to production departments, and (3) allocate production department costs to products. The second phase is the most complex. Service department costs can be allocated to production departments using three methods—the direct method, the step method, and the reciprocal method. The three methods differ in the way they deal with service flows among service departments. The direct method ignores these flows, the step method includes some of them, and the reciprocal method includes all. For this reason, the reciprocal method is preferred.

A number of implementation issues arise when applying cost allocation methods including the strategic and ethical issues of the cost allocation. It is also important to allocate variable and fixed costs separately (in a process called *dual allocation*), to use budgeted rather than actual amounts in the allocation, and to consider alternative allocation methods when the result of an allocation to a department is a cost that is the cost at which the department could purchase the item from an outside entity.

The need for cost allocation exists in all types of organizations: manufacturing, service, and nonprofit.

The need for joint product costing arises when two or more products are made simultaneously in a given manufacturing process. The three methods for costing joint products are the (1) the physical measure method, (2) sales value at split-off method, and (3) net realizable value method. The physical measure method is the simplest to use but also has a significant disadvantage. Because the allocation ignores sales value, the gross margins of joint products determined using the physical measure method can differ in significant and unreasonable ways. In contrast, the sales value and net realizable value methods tend to result in similar gross margins among the joint products. The sales value at split-off method is used when sales value at split-off is known; otherwise the net realizable value is used.

APPENDIX A

By-Product Costing

LEARNING OBJECTIVE 7▶

Use the four by-product costing methods.

As defined in the chapter, a by-product is a product of relatively small sales value that is produced simultaneously with one or more joint products. Two approaches are used for by-product costing: (1) the asset recognition approach and (2) the revenue approach. The main difference between these approaches lies in whether they assign an inventoriable value to by-products at the split-off point. The asset recognition approach records by-products as inventory at net realizable values; the value of the by-product is therefore recognized when the by-product is produced. In contrast, the revenue approach does not assign values to the by-products in the period of production but recognizes by-product revenue in the period sold.

Each of the two approaches contain two alternative methods, depending on the way in which by-products are reported in the income statement. The two asset recognition methods follow:

Net Realizable Value Method. This method shows the net realizable value of by-products on the balance sheet as inventory and on the income statement as a deduction from the total manufacturing cost of the joint products. This is done in the *period in which the by-product is produced.*

Other Income at Production Point Method. This method shows the net realizable value of by-products on the income statement as an other income or other sales revenue item. This is done in the *period in which the by-product is produced.*

The two revenue methods follow:

Other Income at Selling Point Method. This method shows the net sales revenue from a by-product sold *at time of sale* on the income statement as an other income or other sales revenue item.

Manufacturing Cost Reduction at Selling Point Method. This method shows the net sales revenue from a by-product sold *at time of sale* on the income statement as a reduction of the total manufacturing cost.

In Exhibit 14–23 we summarize the four major by-product costing methods.

Asset Recognition Methods

To illustrate the asset recognition methods, assume that Johnson Seafood believes that it can make additional profit by taking a portion of the 1,000 pounds of scrap and waste in each batch of unprocessed tuna and reprocessing them to produce a high-quality garden fertilizer. However, the selling price of the fertilizer is expected to be relatively low, 50 cents per pound. Moreover, additional processing and selling costs of 30 cents per pound would be necessary for preparing, packaging, and distributing the product. Since the sales value of fertilizer is relatively low, the firm decides to treat tuna filets, canned tuna, and cat food as joint products and fertilizer as a by-product. Suppose that Johnson sold all production of filets, canned tuna, and cat food, but sold only 400 of the 500 pounds of the fertilizer produced. Exhibit 14–24 shows the cost flows of the three joint products and one by-product.

From Exhibit 14–21, the total sales value of filets, canned tuna, and cat food is $22,850 ($4,400 + $13,200 + $5,250) and the total cost of the goods sold is $16,850 ($3,200 + $9,600 + $4,050). The net realizable value (NRV) of the 500 pounds of fertilizer produced is

$$NRV = \text{Sales value} - \text{Additional processing cost}$$

$$= \$0.50 \times 500 - \$0.30 \times 500$$

$$= \$100$$

Johnson's accounting for the by-product using the asset recognition methods (the net realizable value method and the other income at production point method) appears in Exhibit 14–25.

Exhibit 14–23   A Summary of By-Product Costing Methods

Time to Recognize	Place in Income Statement	
	As Other Income	As a Deduction of Manufacturing Cost
At time of production (asset recognition methods)	Other income at time of production	Net realizable value method; reduction in joint product cost at time of production
At time of sale (revenue methods)	Other income at time of sale	Reduction in cost of joint products at time of sale

Exhibit 14–24 **Diagram of Three Joint Products and One By-Product Cost Flows for Johnson Seafood**

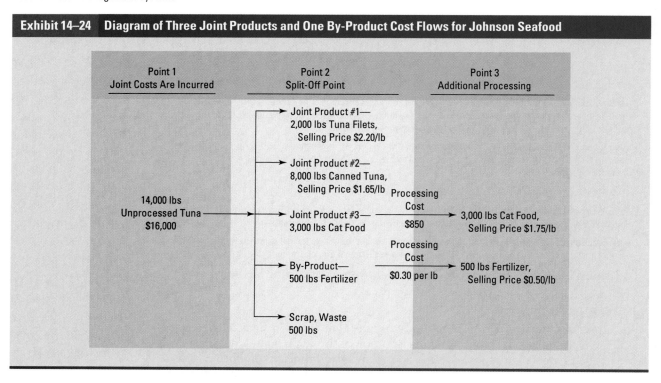

Exhibit 14–25 **By-Product Costing—Asset Recognition Methods**

	Net Realizable Value Method	Other Income at Production Method
Sale of joint products	$22,850	$22,850
Cost of goods sold		
Cost of joint products sold	$16,850	$16,850
Less net realizable value of by-product	(100)	—
Cost of goods sold	$16,750	$16,850
Gross margin	$ 6,100	$ 6,000
Other income at production	—	100
Income before tax	$ 6,100	$ 6,100

Asset recognition methods are based on the financial accounting concepts of asset recognition, matching, and materiality. By-products are *recognized* as assets with probable future economic benefits because a market exists for them. Asset recognition methods also have the preferred effect of *matching* the value of the by-product with its manufacturing cost; when the by-product is sold, its inventory cost is shown as the cost of sales. If the net realizable value of a by-product is *material* (that is, it will have a significant effect on inventory or profit), the asset recognition methods should be used because of the matching concept.

Revenue Methods

Revenue methods recognize by-products at the time of sale. Exhibit 14–26 illustrates the two methods.

Revenue methods are justified on the financial accounting concepts of revenue realization, materiality, and cost benefit. These methods are consistent with the argu-

Exhibit 14-26 By-Product Costing—Revenue Recognition Methods

	Other Income at Selling Point Method	Manufacturing Cost Reduction Method
Sales of joint products	$22,850	$22,850
Cost of goods sold		
Cost of joint products sold	$16,850	$16,850
Less net sales revenue of by-product sold		
($0.50 − $0.30) × 400	—	(80)
Cost of goods sold	$16,850	$16,770
Gross margin	$ 6,000	$ 6,000
By-product revenue	80	—
Income before tax	$ 6,080	$ 6,080

ment that by-product net revenue should be recorded at the time of sale because this is the *point revenue is realized*. Revenue methods are also appropriate when the value of the by-product is *not material*, that is, very small in relation to net income. For *cost-benefit* considerations, many firms use a revenue method because of its simplicity.

KEY TERMS

Additional processing (separable) costs **664**

Average cost method **664**

By-products **663**

Direct method **651**

Joint products **663**

Net realizable value (NRV) **666**

Physical measure method **664**

Reciprocal flows **651**

Reciprocal method **654**

Sales value at split-off method **665**

Split-off point **663**

Step method **653**

COMMENTS ON COST MANAGEMENT IN ACTION

Health Care Providers Allocate Cost for Medicare Reimbursement

The direct method of the departmental approach to cost allocation explained in this chapter has never been permitted for Medicare cost reports. The only permissible method is the step method, which must be performed under Medicare guidelines and audited by a private intermediary (e.g., Blue Cross). A hospital chooses the order in which the step method occurs and the allocation bases (e.g., square feet, pounds of laundry, time spent, number of meals served). The order of the step method and the choice of allocation base are widely recognized to have a significant effect on allocated costs. Hospitals naturally choose methods that favor them in cost reimbursement. Many consultants, authors, and policy makers have called for improved guidance regarding the allocation of costs for Medicare reimbursement. Some have argued that since software tools are readily available to allocate costs using the reciprocal method, Medicare should require this more accurate method.

Source: David T. Meeting and Robert O. Harvey, "Strategic Cost Accounting Helps Create a Competitive Edge," *Healthcare Financial Management*, December 1998, pp. 42–51; and Leslie Eldenburg and Sanjay Kallapur, "Changes in Hospital Service Mix and Cost Allocations in Response to Changes in Medicare Reimbursement Schemes," *Journal of Accounting and Economics*, May 1977, pp. 31–51.

SELF-STUDY PROBLEM

(For solution, please turn to the end of the chapter.)

Joint Product Costing

Northern Company processes 100 gallons of raw materials into 75 gallons of product GS-50 and 25 gallons of GS-80. GS-50 is further processed into 50 gallons of product GS-505 at a cost of $5,000, and GS-80 is processed into 50 gallons of product GS-805 at a cost of $2,000. Exhibit 14–27 depicts this manufacturing flow.

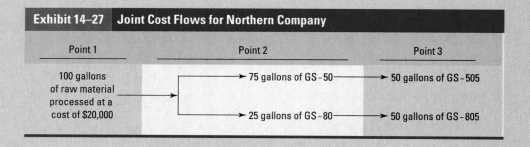

Exhibit 14–27	Joint Cost Flows for Northern Company

Point 1	Point 2	Point 3
100 gallons of raw material processed at a cost of $20,000	→ 75 gallons of GS-50	→ 50 gallons of GS-505
	→ 25 gallons of GS-80	→ 50 gallons of GS-805

The production process starts at point 1. A total of $20,000 in joint manufacturing costs are incurred in reaching point 2. Point 2 is the split-off point of the process that manufactures GS-50 and GS-80. At this point, GS-50 can be sold for $300 a gallon, and GS-80 can be sold for $60 a gallon. The process is completed at point 3—products GS-505 and GS-805 have a sales price of $500 a gallon and $140 a gallon, respectively.

Required   Allocate the joint product costs using each of the three methods: (1) physical measure, (2) sales value at split-off, and (3) net realizable value.

QUESTIONS

14–1   What are the objectives of cost allocation? Which are most important in a retail firm? In a manufacturing firm? In a service firm?

14–2   Explain the difference between joint products and by-products.

14–3   Explain the difference between spoilage, waste, rework, and scrap.

14–4   What are the three methods of departmental cost allocation? Explain how they differ, which is the most preferred, and why.

14–5   What are the three phases of the departmental allocation approach? What happens at each phase?

14–6   Give two or three examples of the use of cost allocation in service industries and not-for-profit organizations.

14–7   What are the four methods used in by-product costing, and how do they differ? Which is the preferred method and why?

14–8   What are the limitations of joint product cost allocation?

14–9   What are the limitations of departmental cost allocation?

14–10   What is the role of cost allocation from a strategic point of view?

EXERCISES

14–11   **COST ALLOCATION, GENERAL**   An organization's service and administrative costs can be substantial, and some or all of these costs usually are allocated to cost objects. Thus, the allocations of service and administrative costs can have a significant impact on product cost and pricing, asset valuation, and segment profitability.

Required

1. What are service and administrative costs?

2. When service and administrative costs are allocated, they are grouped into homogeneous pools and then allocated to cost objects according to some allocation base.

   a. Compare and contrast the benefit and cost criteria for selecting an allocation base.

   b. Explain what the ability-to-bear costs criterion means in selecting an allocation base. Discuss why this criterion has limited use.

(CMA Adapted)

14–12 **BY-PRODUCTS AND DECISION-MAKING STRATEGY** Lowman Gourmet Products produces a wide variety of gourmet coffees (sold in pounds of roasted beans), jams, jellies, and condiments such as spicy mustard sauce. The firm has a reputation as a high-quality source of these products. Lowman sells the products through a mail-order catalog that is revised twice a year. Joe, the president, is interested in developing a new line of products to complement the coffees. The manufacture of the jams and jellies presently produces an excess of fruit liquid that is not used in these products. The firm is now selling excess liquid to other firms as flavoring for canned fruit products. Joe is planning to refine the liquid and add other ingredients to it to produce a coffee-flavoring product instead of selling the liquid. He figures that the cost of producing the jams and jellies, and therefore the fruit liquid, is irrelevant; the only relevant concern is the lost sales to the canneries and the cost of the additional ingredients, processing, and packaging.

Strategy

Required Does this plan make financial and strategic sense?

14–13 **JOINT PRODUCTS** Axe Company produces joint products J, K, and B from a process. This information concerns a batch produced in April at a joint cost of $60,000:

| | | After Split-Off | |
Product	Units Produced	Total Additional Costs	Total Market Value
J	1,000	$20,000	$70,000
K	2,000	10,000	30,000
B	4,000	2,000	7,000

Required How much of the joint cost should be allocated to each joint product using the net realizable value method?

14–14 **JOINT PRODUCTS** Nebraska Corporation manufactures liquid chemicals A and B from a joint process. It allocates joint costs on the basis of sales value at split-off. Processing 500 gallons of product A and 1,000 gallons of product B to the split-off point costs $4,560. The sales value at split-off is $10 per gallon for product A and $14 for product B. Product B requires an additional process beyond split-off at a cost of $2.50 per gallon before it can be sold.

Required What is Nebraska's cost to produce 1,000 gallons of product B?

14–15 **JOINT PRODUCT COSTING; BY-PRODUCTS (APPENDIX)** Malcom Company produces 10,000 units of A, 20,000 units of B, and 10,000 units of C from the same manufacturing process at a cost of $300,000. A and B are joint products; C is regarded as a by-product. The unit selling prices of the products are $25 for A, $10 for B, and $5 for C. None of the products require additional processing. Of the units produced, Malcom Company sells 5,000 units of A, 12,000 units of B, and 8,000 units of C. The firm uses the net realizable value method to allocate joint costs.

Required

1. What is the value of the ending inventory of Product A?
2. What is the value of the ending inventory of Product C?

Service

14–16 **DEPARTMENTAL COST ALLOCATION**   HomeLife Life Insurance Company has two service departments (actuarial and premium rating) and two production departments (advertising and sales). The distribution of each service department's efforts (in percentages) to the other departments is

From	To			
	Actuarial	**Premium Rating**	**Advertising**	**Sales**
Actuarial	—	80%	10%	10%
Premium	20%	—	20%	60%

The direct operating costs of the departments (including both variable and fixed costs) are

Actuarial	$80,000
Premium rating	15,000
Advertising	60,000
Sales	40,000

Required

1. Determine the total cost allocated to the advertising and sales departments using the direct method.
2. Determine the total cost allocated to advertising and sales using the step method.
3. Determine the total cost allocated to advertising and sales using the reciprocal method.

14–17 **DEPARTMENTAL COST ALLOCATION**   Robinson Products Company has two service departments (S1 and S2) and two production departments (P1 and P2). The distribution of each service department's efforts (in percentages) to the other departments is

From	To			
	S1	**S2**	**P1**	**P2**
S1	—	10%	30%	?%
S2	10%	—	?%	40%

The direct operating costs of the departments (including both variable and fixed costs) are

S1	150,000
S2	54,000
P1	50,000
P2	120,000

Required

1. Determine the total cost of P1 and P2 using the direct method.
2. Determine the total cost of P1 and P2 using the step method.
3. Determine the total cost of P1 and P2 using the reciprocal method.

PROBLEMS

14–18   **DEPARTMENTAL COST ALLOCATION; OUTSOURCING**   Wallace Company produces two software products (NetA and NetB) in two separate departments (A and B). These products are highly regarded network maintenance programs. NetA is used for small networks and NetB is used for large networks. Wallace is known for the quality of its products and its ability to meet dates promised for software upgrades.

Strategy

Department A produces Net A, and department B produces Net B. The production departments are supported by two support departments, systems design and programming services. The source and use of the support department time are summarized as follows:

From	To				Total Labor-Hours
	Design	Programming	Department A	Department B	
Design	—	2,000	3,000	5,000	10,000
Programming	600	—	600	800	2,000

The costs in the two service departments are as follows:

	Design	Programming
Labor and materials (all variable)	$26,000	$25,000
Depreciation and other fixed costs	38,000	45,000
Total	$64,000	$70,000

Required

1.   What are the costs allocated to the two production departments from the two service departments using (a) the direct method, (b) the step method (both possible sequences), and (c) the reciprocal method?

2.   The company is considering outsourcing programming services to RJB Services, Inc., for $25 per hour. Should Wallace do this?

14–19   **DEPARTMENTAL COST ALLOCATION**   McKeoun Enterprises is a large machine tool company now experiencing alarming increases in maintenance expense in each of its four production departments. Maintenance costs are currently allocated to the production departments on the basis of labor-hours incurred in the production department. To provide pressure for the production departments to use less maintenance, and to provide an incentive for the maintenance department to become more efficient, McKeoun has decided to investigate new methods of allocating maintenance costs. One suggestion now being evaluated is a form of outsourcing: The producing departments could purchase maintenance service from an outside supplier. That is, they could choose either to use an outside supplier of maintenance or to be charged an amount based on their use of labor-hours. The following table shows the labor-hours in each department, the allocation of maintenance cost based on labor-hours, and the cost to purchase the equivalent level of maintenance service from an outside maintenance provider.

Production Department	Direct Labor-Hours Allocation Base (Percent)	Direct Labor-Hours Allocation Cost	Outside Price
A	20%	$ 90,000	$115,000
B	30	135,000	92,000
C	10	45,000	69,000
D	40	180,000	184,000
Total	100%	$450,000	$460,000

Required

1. As a first step in moving to the outsourcing approach, McKeoun is considering an allocation based on the price of the outside maintenance supplier for each department. Calculate the cost allocation on this basis and compare it to the current labor-hour basis.

2. If McKeoun follows the proposed plan, what is likely to happen to the overall use of maintenance? How will each department manager be motivated to increase or decrease the use of maintenance? What will be the overall effects of going to the new plan?

14-20 **DEPARTMENTAL COST ALLOCATION**   Dundee Corporation distributes its service department overhead costs to product departments. This information is for the month of June:

	Service Departments	
	Maintenance	**Utilities**
Overhead costs incurred	$30,000	$15,000
Service provided to departments		
Maintenance	—	10%
Utilities	20%	—
Producing—A	40	30
Producing—B	40	60
Totals	100%	100%

Required   What is the amount of maintenance department costs distributed to producing department A for June using (1) the direct method, (2) the step method, and (3) the reciprocal method?

14-21 **JOINT PRODUCT COSTING**   Choi Company manufactures two skin care lotions, Smooth Skin and Silken Skin, from a joint process. The joint costs incurred are $540,000 for a standard production run that generates 180,000 gallons of Smooth Skin and 120,000 gallons of Silken Skin. Smooth Skin sells for $2.40 per gallon, while Silken Skin sells for $3.90 per gallon.

Required

1. Assuming that both products are sold at the split-off point, how much of the joint cost of each production run is allocated to Smooth Skin on a net realizable value basis?

2. If no additional costs are incurred after the split-off point, how much of the joint cost of each production run is allocated to Silken Skin on the physical measure method basis?

3. If additional processing costs beyond the split-off point are $1.40 per gallon for Smooth Skin and $0.90 per gallon for Silken Skin, how much of the joint cost of each production run is allocated to Silken Skin on a net realizable value basis?

4. If additional processing costs beyond the split-off point are $1.40 per gallon for Smooth Skin and $0.90 per gallon for Silken Skin, how much of the joint cost of each production run is allocated to Smooth Skin on a physical measure method basis?

(**CMA Adapted**)

14-22 **JOINT PRODUCT COSTING**   Sonimad Sawmill manufactures two lumber products from a joint milling process: mine support braces (MSB) and unseasoned commercial building lumber (CBL). A standard production run incurs joint costs of $300,000 and results in 60,000 units of MSB and 90,000 units of CBL. Each MSB sells for $2 per unit, and each CBL sells for $4 per unit.

Required

1. Assuming that no further processing occurs after the split-off point, how much of the joint costs are allocated to commercial building lumber (CBL) on a physical measure method basis?

2. If no further processing occurs after the split-off point, how much of the joint cost is allocated to the mine support braces (MSB) on a sales value basis?

3. Assume that the CBL is not marketable at split-off but must be planed and sized at a cost of $200,000 per production run. During this process, 10,000 units are unavoidably lost and have no value. The remaining units of CBL are salable at $10 per unit. The MSB, although salable immediately at the split-off point, are coated with a tarlike preservative that costs $100,000 per production run. The braces are then sold for $5 each. Using the net realizable value basis, how much of the completed cost should be assigned to each unit of CBL?

4. Should Sonimad Sawmill choose to process the MSB beyond split-off? What would be the contribution if it did so?

(CMA Adapted)

14–23 **JOINT PRODUCTS**   The Salinas Company produces three products, X, Y, and Z, from a joint process. Each product can be sold at the split-off point or processed further. Additional processing requires no special facilities, and the production costs of further processing are entirely variable and traceable to the products involved. Last year all three products were processed beyond split-off. Joint production costs for the year were $80,000. Sales values and costs needed to evaluate Salinas' production policy follow:  *Strategy*

			If Processed Further	
Product	Units Produced	Sales Value at Split-Off	Sales Value	Additional Costs
X	5,000	$25,000	$55,000	$9,000
Y	4,000	41,000	45,000	7,000
Z	1,000	24,000	30,000	8,000

Required

1. Determine the unit cost and gross profit for each product if Salinas allocates joint production costs in proportion to the relative physical volume of output.

2. Determine unit costs and gross profit for each product if Salinas allocates joint costs using the sales value method.

3. Should the firm sell all of its products after further processing?

4. Salinas has been selling all of its products at the split-off point. Selling any of the products after further processing will entail direct competition with some major customers. What strategic factors does the firm need to consider in deciding whether to process any of the products further?

14–24 **JOINT PRODUCTS; BY-PRODUCTS (APPENDIX)**   Multiproduct Corporation is a chemical manufacturer that produces two main products (Pepco–1 and Repke–3) and a by-product (SE–5) from a joint process. If Multiproduct had the proper facilities, it could process SE-5 further into a main product. The ratio of output quantities to input quantity of direct material used in the joint process remains consistent with the processing conditions and activity level.

Multiproduct currently uses the physical measure method of allocating joint costs to the main products. It uses the first-in, first-out (FIFO) inventory method to value the main products. The by-product is inventoried at its net realizable value, which is used to reduce the joint production costs before they are allocated to the main products.

Jim Simpson, Multiproduct's controller, wants to implement the sales value method of joint cost allocation. He believes that inventory costs should be based on each product's ability to contribute to the recovery of joint production costs. The net realizable value of the by-product would be treated in the same manner that the physical method would.

Data regarding Multiproduct's operations for November 2001 are presented in the following report. The joint cost of production totaled to $2,640,000 for November 2001.

| | Main Products | | By-Product |
	Pepco–1	Repke–3	SE–5
Finished goods inventory in gallons on November 1, 2001	20,000	40,000	10,000
November sales in gallons	800,000	700,000	200,000
November production in gallons	900,000	720,000	240,000
Sales value per gallon at split-off point	$2.00	$1.50	$0.55*
Additional process costs after split-off	$1,800,000	$720,000	—
Final sales value per gallon	$5.00	$4.00	—

*Disposal and selling costs of 5 cents per gallon are incurred to sell the by-product.

Required

1. Describe the sales value method and explain how it would accomplish Jim's objective.

2. Assuming Multiproduct adopts the sales value method for internal reporting purposes, calculate the following:

   a. The allocation of the joint production cost for November 2001.

   b. The dollar values of the finished goods inventories for Pepco–1, Repke–3, and SE–5 as of November 30, 2001.

3. Multiproduct plans to expand its production facilities to further process SE–5 into a main product. Discuss how the allocation of the joint production costs under the sales value method would change when SE-5 becomes a main product.

(CMA Adapted)

Ethics

14–25 JOINT PRODUCTS Alderon Industries manufactures chemicals for various purposes. One process that Alderon uses produces SPL–3, a chemical used in swimming pools; PST–4, a chemical used in pesticides; and RJ–5, a by-product sold to fertilizer manufacturers. Alderon uses the net realizable value of its main products to allocate joint production costs and the first-in, first-out inventory method to value the main products. The by-product is inventoried at its net realizable value, which is used to reduce the joint production costs before they are allocated to the main products. The ratio of output to input of direct material used in the joint process remains consistent from month to month.

Data regarding Alderon's operations for the month of November 2001 follow. During this month, Alderon incurred joint production costs of $1,702,000 in the manufacture of SPL–3, PST–4, and RJ–5.

	SPL–3	PST–4	RJ–5
Finished goods inventory in gallons (November 1, 2001)	18,000	52,000	3,000
November sales in gallons	650,000	325,000	150,000
November production in gallons	700,000	350,000	170,000
Sales value per gallon at split-off	—	$3.80	$0.70*
Additional processing costs	$874,000	$816,000	—
Final sales value per gallon	$4.00	$6.00	—

*Disposal costs of 10 cents per gallon are incurred to sell the by-product.

Required

1. Determine Alderon Industries' allocation of joint production costs for the month of November 2001. Be sure to present appropriate supporting calculations.

2. Determine the dollar values of the finished goods inventories for SPL–3, PST–4, and RJ–5 as of November 30, 2001.

3. Alderon has an opportunity to sell PST–4 at the split-off point for $3.80 per gallon. Prepare an analysis showing whether Alderon should sell PST–4 at the split-off point or process further.

4. As a production supervisor for Alderon, you have learned that small quantities of the critical chemical compound in PST–4 might be present in SPL–3. What should you do?

(CMA Adapted)

14–26 JOINT PRODUCTS; BY-PRODUCTS (REVIEW OF CHAPTERS 8 AND 10) Lond Company produces joint products Jana and Reta, and by-product Bynd. Jana is sold at split-off; Reta and Bynd undergo additional processing. Production data pertaining to these products for the year ended December 31, 2001, were as follows:

	Jana	Reta	Bynd	Total
Joint costs				
Variable				$ 88,000
Fixed				148,000
Separate costs				
Variable		$120,000	$3,000	$123,000
Fixed		90,000	2,000	92,000
Production in pounds	50,000	40,000	10,000	100,000
Sales price per pound	$4.00	$7.50	$1.10	

Lond had no beginning or ending inventories and no materials were spoiled in production. Bynd's net realizable value is deducted from joint costs. Joint costs are allocated to joint products to achieve the same gross margin percentage for each joint product.

Although 2001 performance could be repeated for 2002, Lond is considering operation of the plant at its full capacity of 120,000 pounds. The relative proportions of each product's output with respect to cost behavior and production increases would be unchanged. Market surveys indicate that prices of Jana and Bynd would have to be reduced to $3.40 and $0.90, respectively. Reta's expected price decline cannot be determined.

Required

1. Prepare the following information for Lond Company for the year ended December 31, 2001:

   a. Total gross margin.

   b. Allocation of joint costs to Jana and Reta.

   c. Separate gross margins for Jana and Reta.

2. Compute Lond's breakeven point in pounds for the year ended December 31, 2001.

3. Prepare the following information for Lond Company for the year ending December 31, 2002:

    a. Projected production in pounds for each product at full capacity.

    b. Differential revenues (excluding Reta).

    c. Differential costs.

    d. Sales price per pound of Reta required for Lond to achieve the same gross margin as that for 2001.

(CPA Adapted)

Strategy

14–27 DEPARTMENTAL COST ALLOCATION Marfrank Corporation is a manufacturing company with six functional departments: finance, marketing, personnel, production, research and development (R&D), and information systems, each administered by a vice president. The information systems department (ISD) was established in 2000 when Marfrank decided to acquire a mainframe computer and develop a new information system.

While systems development and implementation is an ongoing process at Marfrank, many basic systems needed by each functional department were operational at the end of 2001. Thus, calendar year 2002 is considered the first year for which the ISD costs can be estimated with a high degree of accuracy. Marfrank's president wants the other five functional departments to be aware of the magnitude of the ISD costs by allocating them in the reports and statements prepared at the end of the first quarter of 2002. The allocation to each department was based on its actual use of ISD services.

Jon Werner, vice president of ISD, suggested that the actual ISD costs be allocated on the basis of pages of actual computer output. He chose this basis because all departments use reports to evaluate their operations and make decisions. The use of this basis resulted in the following allocation:

Department	Percentage	Allocated Cost
Finance	50%	$112,500
Marketing	30	67,500
Personnel	9	20,250
Production	6	13,500
R&D	5	11,250
Total	100%	$225,000

After the quarterly reports were distributed, the finance and marketing departments objected to this allocation method. Both departments recognized that they were responsible for most of the report output, but they believed that these output costs might be the smallest of ISD costs and requested that a more equitable allocation basis be developed.

After meeting with Jon, Elaine Jergens, Marfrank's controller, concluded that ISD provides three distinct services: systems development, computer processing represented by central processing unit (CPU) time, and report generation. She recommended that a predetermined rate be developed for each service based on budgeted annual activity and costs. The ISD costs would then be assigned to the other functional departments using the predetermined rate times the actual activity used. ISD would absorb any difference between actual costs incurred and costs allocated to the other departments.

Elaine and Jon concluded that systems development could be charged on the basis of hours devoted to systems development and programming, computer processing based on CPU time used for operations (exclusive of database development and maintenance), and report generation based on number of pages of output. The only cost they thought should not be included in any of the predetermined rates was for purchased software; these packages usually were acquired for a specific department's use. Thus, Elaine concluded that purchased software would be charged at cost to the department for which it was purchased. To revise the first-quarter allocation, she gathered this information on ISD costs and services:

Information Systems Department Services

| | Estimated Annual Costs | Actual First-Quarter Costs | Percentage Devoted to | | |
			Systems Development	Computer Processing	Report Generation
Wages/benefits					
Administration	$100,000	$25,000	60%	20%	20%
Computer operators	55,000	13,000		20	80
Analysts/programmers	165,000	43,500	100		
Maintenance					
Hardware	24,000	6,000	75	25	
Software	20,000	5,000	100		
Output supplies	50,000	11,500	100		
Purchased software	45,000	16,000*	—	—	—
Utilities	28,000	6,250	100		
Depreciation					
Mainframe computer	325,000	81,250	100		
Printing equipment	60,000	15,000			100
Building improvements	10,000	2,500	100		
Total department costs	$882,000	$225,000			

*All software purchased during the first quarter of 2002 was for the production department.

Information Systems Department Services

	Systems Development	Computer Operations (CPU)	Report Generation
Annual capacity	4,500 hours	360 CPU hours	5,000,000 pages
Actual usage during first quarter, 2002			
Finance	100 hours	8 CPU hours	600,000 pages
Marketing	250	12	360,000
Personnel	200	12	108,000
Production	400	32	72,000
R&D	50	16	60,000
Total usage	1,000 hours	80 CPU hours	1,200,000 pages

Required

1. For ISD, determine the following:

   a. The predetermined rates for each service category: systems development, computer processing, and report generation.

   b. Using the predetermined rates developed in requirement 1a, the amount each of the other five functional departments would be charged for ISD's services provided during the first quarter of 2002.

2. With the method proposed by Elaine Jergens for charging the ISD costs to the other five functional departments, ISD's actual costs incurred and the costs assigned to the five user department might differ.

   a. Explain the nature of this difference.

   b. Discuss whether this proposal will improve cost control in ISD.

3. Explain whether Elaine's proposed method of charging user departments for ISD costs will improve planning and control in the user departments.

4. Assume that a finance manager has suggested outsourcing ISD. What factors should Marfrank consider in deciding whether to outsource ISD functions?

(CMA Adapted)

Strategy

14–28 **DEPARTMENTAL COST ALLOCATION**   Computer Information Services, a computer software consulting company, has three major functional areas: computer programming, information systems consulting, and software training. Carol Birch, a pricing analyst in the accounting department, has been asked to develop total costs for the functional areas. These costs will be used as a guide in pricing a new contract. In computing these costs, Carol is considering three different methods of the departmental allocation approach to allocate overhead costs: the direct method, the step method, and the reciprocal method. She assembled the following data from the two service departments, information systems and facilities:

	Service Department		Production Department			
				Information		
	Information		Computer	Systems	Software	
	Systems	Facilities	Programming	Consulting	Training	Total
Budgeted overhead	$50,000	$25,000	$75,000	$110,000	$85,000	$345,000
Information systems* (hours)		300	1,200	600	900	3,000
Facilities† (thousand square feet)	200		400	600	800	2,000

*Allocated on the basis of hours of computer usage.

†Allocated on the basis of floor space.

Required

1. Using as the application base computer usage time for the information systems department and square feet of floor space for the facilities department, apply overhead from these service departments to the production departments, using these three methods. Use Excel and Solver to determine the allocations.

   a. Direct method.

   b. Step method.

   c. Reciprocal method.

2. Rather than allocate costs, how might Computer InformationServices better assign the information systems department's costs?

(CMA Adapted)

Strategy

14–29 **JOINT PRODUCTS AND BY-PRODUCTS**   Princess Corporation grows, processes, packages, and sells three apple products: slices that are used in frozen pies, applesauce, and apple juice. The outside skin of the apple, which is removed in the cutting department and processed as animal feed, is treated as a by-product. Princess uses the net realizable value method to assign costs of the joint process to its main products. The apple skin by-product is inventoried at its market value, and its net realizable value is used to reduce the joint production costs prior to allocation to the main products. Details of Princess' production process follow:

- The cutting department washes the apples and removes the outside skin. The department then cores and trims the apples for slicing. At this point, each of the three main products and the by-product are recognizable. Each product is then transferred to the next department for final processing.

- The slicing department receives the trimmed apples and slices and freezes them. Any juice generated during the slicing operation is frozen with the slices.

- The crushing department trims pieces of apple and processes them into applesauce. The juice generated during this operation is used in the applesauce.

- The juicing department pulverizes the core and any surplus apple from the cutting department into a liquid. This department experiences a loss equal to 8 percent of the weight of the good output produced.

- The feed department chops the outside skin into animal food and packages it. A total of 270,000 pounds of apples entered the cutting department during November. The following information shows the costs incurred in each department, the proportion by weight (based on pounds) transferred to the four final processing departments, and the selling price of each end product. Assume no beginning or ending inventory of apple slices, applesauce, or juice.

Department	Costs Incurred	Proportion of Product by Weight Transferred to Departments	Selling Price per Pound of Final Product
Cutting	$60,000	—	—
Slicing	11,280	33%	$.80
Crushing	8,550	30	.55
Juicing	3,000	27	.40
Feed	700	10	.10
Total	$83,530	100%	

Required

1. Princess Corporation uses the net realizable value method to determine inventory values for its main products and by-products. For the month of November 2001, calculate each of the following:

   a. Output in pounds for apple slices, applesauce, apple juice, and animal feed.

   b. Net realizable value at the split-off point for each of the three main products.

   c. Cutting department cost assigned to each of the three main products and to the by-product in accordance with corporate policy.

   d. Gross margin in dollars for each of the three main products.

2. Comment on the significance to management of the gross margin dollar information by main product for planning and control purposes as opposed to inventory valuation.

3. List the important issues that Princess faces as a global company. What are its critical success factors? Which key issues arise because Princess operates in several countries? Should any of these issues affect the way Princess allocates costs, as determined in requirement 1?

(CMA Adapted)

14–30   **JOINT PRODUCTS AND BY PRODUCTS**   Goodson Pharmaceutical Company manufactures three main products from a joint process: Altox, Lorex, and

Hycol. Data regarding these products for the fiscal year ended May 31, 2001, follow:

	Altox	Lorex	Hycol
Units produced	170,000	500,000	330,000
Sales value per unit at split-off	$3.50	—	$2.00
Allocation of joint costs*	$450,000	$846,000	$504,000
Separable costs	—	$1,400,000	—
Final sales value per unit	—	$5.00	—

*Joint costs are allocated on the basis of net realizable value, and the net realizable value of any by-product is deducted from the joint costs before allocation.

Altox is currently sold at the split-off point to a vitamin manufacturer. Lorex is processed further after the split-off point and sold as a cold remedy. Hycol, an oil produced from the joint process, is sold at the split-off point to a cosmetics manufacturer.

Arlene Franklin, president of Goodson, is reviewing opportunities to change the processing and sale of these three products. Altox can be refined for use as a high blood pressure medication, but this would result in a loss of 20,000 units. The costs to further process Altox are estimated to be $250,000 annually. The medication would sell for $5.50 per unit. The company has an offer from another pharmaceutical company to purchase Lorex, at the split-off point for $2.25 per unit. Goodson's research department has suggested that the company process Hycol further and sell it as an ointment to relieve muscle pain. The additional processing would cost $75,000 annually and would increase the units of product by 25 percent. The product would be sold for $1.80 per unit.

The joint process that Goodson currently uses also produces 50,000 units of Dorzine, a hazardous chemical waste product that costs the company $0.35 per unit for proper disposal. Dietriech Mills Inc. is interested in using the Dorzine as a solvent; however, Goodson must refine the Dorzine at an annual cost of $43,000. Dietrich would purchase all Dorzine Goodson can refine and is willing to pay $0.75 for each unit.

Required

1. Which of the three main products should Goodson Pharmaceutical Company sell at the split-off point? Which of them should the company process further to maximize profits? Support your answers with appropriate calculations, using a spreadsheet system.

2. Assume that Goodson has decided to refine the waste product Dorzine as a by-product of the joint process in the future and to sell it to Dietriech Mill.

   a. Did Goodson make the correct decision regarding Dozrine? Support your answer with appropriate calculations.

   b. Explain whether the decision to treat Dorzine as a by-product will affect your answer to requirement 1.

(CMA Adapted)

SOLUTION TO SELF-STUDY PROBLEM

Joint Product Costing

The Physical Measure Method

If we use a physical measure method, the joint cost of $20,000 is allocated as shown in Exhibit 14–28.

The production costs per gallon for both products are the same:

Product GS–50: $15,000/75 = $200

Product GS–80: $ 5,000/25 = $200

The Sales Value at Split-Off Method

Assume that Northern Company sold 60 gallons of GS–50 and 20 gallons of GS–80. Then the $20,000 joint cost should be allocated among the products as shown in Exhibit 14–29.

Note that the gallons sold do not figure in the analysis, which is based on *units produced* only. The production costs per gallon for both products are calculated:

Product GS–50 $18,750/75 = $250

Product GS–80 $ 1,250/25 = $ 50

The Net Realizable Value Method

The net realizable values of GS–50 and GS–80 are $20,000 and $5,000, respectively, as shown in Exhibit 14–30. The allocated costs are $16,000 to GS–50 and $4,000 to GS–80.

The costs per gallon for products GS–505 and GS–805 are calculated:

Product GS–505 ($16,000 + $5,000)/50 = $420

Product GS-805 ($ 4,000 + $2,000)/50 = $120

Exhibit 14–28	Physical Measure Method		
Product	**Physical Measure**	**Proportion**	**Allocation of Joint Cost**
GS–50	75 gallons	75%	$20,000 × 75% = $15,000
GS–80	25 gallons	25%	20,000 × 25% = 5,000

Exhibit 14–29	Sales Value at Split-Off Method				
Product	**Units**	**Price**	**Sales Value**	**Proportion**	**Joint Cost Allocated**
GS–50	75	$300	$22,500	93.75%	$20,000 × 93.75% = $18,750
GS–80	25	60	1,500	6.25%	20,000 × 6.25% = 1,250
Total			$24,000	100%	$20,000

Exhibit 14–30	Net Realizable Value Method						
Product	**Production Units**	**Sales Price**	**Sales Value**	**Separable Cost**	**Net Realizable Value**	**Weight**	**Joint Cost Allocated**
GS–50	50	$500	$25,000	$5,000	$20,000	80%	$20,000 × 80% = $16,000
GS–80	50	140	7,000	2,000	5,000	20%	20,000 × 20% = 4,000
Total	100		$32,000	$7,000	$25,000	100%	$20,000

15

The Flexible Budget and Standard Costing

Direct Materials and Direct Labor

After studying this chapter, you should be able to . . .

1   Evaluate the effectiveness and efficiency of an operation and calculate and interpret the operating income variance

2   Develop and use flexible budgets to conduct additional analyses of the operating income variance for control of operations and performance evaluation, as well as calculate and interpret the sales volume and flexible budget variances

3   Set proper standard costs for planning, control, and performance evaluation

4   Identify factors that contribute to an operating income flexible budget variance and analyze and explain selling price variance, direct materials price and usage variances, and direct labor rate and efficiency variances

5   Assess the influence of the contemporary manufacturing environment on operational control and standard costing

6   Recognize behavioral implications in implementing standard costing systems

7   Describe cost flows through general ledger accounts and prepare journal entries for the acquisition and use of direct materials and direct labor in a standard costing system

Founded in 1907 to provide private messenger and delivery services in the Seattle, Washington, area, United Parcel Services (UPS) has become the world's largest package delivery company.[1] Its primary business is the time-definite delivery of packages and documents that UPS guarantees will arrive at times customers specify. In addition to making deliveries throughout the United States, the firm delivers to more than 200 countries and territories. On average, UPS delivers more than 13 million pieces of packages and documents per day worldwide. It generated revenue of more than $27 billion in 1999 and earned a higher profit than its competitors. How does UPS do it?

An early adopter of standards in all phases of its work, UPS has become known for its demand for strict adherence to these standards. Every day each driver of a UPS delivery truck knows the exact number of packages and documents he or she must deliver that day. A long-haul driver is expected to travel a certain distance within the time allowed. UPS customers can track packages on its website to find out the time

---

[1] United Parcel Service Annual Report, 1999. Find out more about the company at its website: /www.ups.com/.

that packages were or will be delivered. Through uses of strict work standards, UPS has been able to deliver as promised and has become one of the best-run companies in the United States.

Standards are performance criteria and goals. All organizations and businesses, be they service, merchandising, or manufacturing firms, for profit or not for profit, can use standards to set performance expectations, evaluate and control operations, motivate employees, and encourage efforts toward their goals. Use of standards allows a manager to identify the cost to manufacture and sell a product or provide a service, to find causes and attributes of cost overruns or efficient operations, and to manage by exception. Manufacturing firms such as Ford, Caterpillar, Toshiba, Siemans, and Thomasville specify the amount of materials and the number of hours to be used to manufacture their products. Retail stores such as The Limited, Wal-Mart, and Target have specific standards for their employees and monitor their adherence to these standards closely. Farmers have standards for the amount of fertilizers to use per acre and the amount of food to feed each pig. This chapter explores the uses of budgets and standard costing systems in operations.

"He who controls the past controls the future."

GEORGE ORWELL

"You can't get caught up in things that you can't control. . . . We cannot control our selling price. We can control our cost of manufacturing. We can control our efficiencies."

STEVEN APPLETON, CEO OF MICRO TECHNOLOGY

Budgets help firms plan and coordinate activities and serve as the bases for control operations and performance evaluation. In this chapter, we turn our attention to how budgets can be used and the roles that standards play in controlling operations and evaluating operating results. Controlling operations assists managers in attaining the budgeted goals they set out to accomplish. Assessing operating results provides feedback to managers and helps them gain insights into the causes that led to the operating results. By learning from the past, managers can, as George Orwell says, control the future.

EVALUATING OPERATING RESULTS

LEARNING OBJECTIVE 1▶

Evaluate the effectiveness and efficiency of an operation and calculate and interpret the operating income variance.

An **effective operation** attains the goal set for the operation.

Two aspects of operations are generally of interest to management in assessing operations: effectiveness in attaining goals and efficiency in carrying out operations.

Effectiveness

An **effective operation** is one that attains or exceeds the goal or goals set for it. A firm that attempts to earn $50 million net operating income for the year and earns $50 million is effective. A student who has a goal of earning a 3.0 grade point average for the semester and receives a 3.25 is effective. A social service organization that has a goal of serving 50,000 hot meals to homeless people and serves 55,000 hot meals has an effective operation.

The firm that had a goal to earn $50 million net operating income for the year but actually has only $49 million is ineffective. The student with a grade point average of 2.75 was not effective, although two part-time jobs may not have been part of the plan when the 3.0 goal was chosen. The social service organization was not effective if it served only 48,000 hot meals when it budgeted to serve 50,000 hot meals, although the food prices increased more than 10 percent over the budgeted amount.

Effective operations are essential in implementing a successful strategy. Ineffective operations render disappointing results, drain cash and other resources, and may lead an organization to its demise. Repeated ineffective operations often force a firm either to abandon or modify its strategy. Intel's effective operations enable the firm to be successful in carrying out its strategy of bringing new computer chips to the market before the competition. Intel has enjoyed high profitability and dominated the market since the mid-1980s. Its failure to be the company that introduced the fastest PC processor to the market in 2000 allowed one of its main competitors to gain 50 percent in market share and might have caused Intel to decide to expand into other markets. A series of setbacks in IBM's operations has forced it to retreat and redirect its strategies several times since the early 1980s. IBM is no longer the computer giant that it once was.

Most organizations have multiple strategic goals. A firm should assess its goals so that management has a clear grasp of the overall effectiveness of operations and the feasibility of attaining the strategic goals.

Some firms measure their effectiveness by analyzing one or a few of their critical success factors. A business firm can assess whether it earns the desired amount of operating income, gains the target market share, introduces new products by the deadlines, or attains the rate of return on net assets as specified in the master budget. School districts can use the average SAT score of their high school graduates as a measure of their effectiveness. Students can assess their effectiveness according to the number of credit hours completed or the grade point average earned.

A master budget delineates the desired operating results for the period and is a common starting point in assessing the effectiveness of operations.

Efficiency

An **efficient operation** wastes no resources. An operation is inefficient if the firm spent more than the necessary amount of resources to complete the tasks. A firm that spent $40,000 to manufacture and sell 10,000 units is efficient if the standard calls for a cost of $4 per unit. The same firm would be inefficient if it cost $50,000 to manufacture and sell the same 10,000 units.

> An **efficient operation** wastes no resources in operations.

Assessments of efficiency are independent of assessments of effectiveness. A firm can be effective in attaining the goal or goals set for its operation, but still be inefficient. Conversely, a firm can be efficient yet ineffective if it fails to attain the goal for its operations. Consider the manufacturing firm just mentioned. If it made and sold 9,000 units in a period when the plan is to manufacture and sell 10,000 units for the period, it was ineffective. It did not meet its sales goal of 10,000 units. If the firm spent $35,000 to manufacture and sell the 9,000 units, it was efficient. The firm was effective if it manufactured and sold 12,000 units and attained the goal of selling 10,000 units during the period. The firm was not efficient, however, if it spent $60,000 to manufacture 12,000 units or $5 per unit instead of the $4 standard cost.

Assessing Effectiveness

An important short-term goal for a company is to earn the budgeted operating income for the period. A company's effectiveness is often measured by comparing the actual amount of operating income earned to the amount in the master budget. The difference between the actual operating income and the master budget operating income is the **operating income variance**—a measure of the effectiveness of the period.

> The **operating income variance** of a period is the difference between the actual operating income of the period and the master budget operating income projected for the period.

Consider the analysis of operations for Schmidt Machinery Company in Exhibit 15–1. The bottom line of column (2) shows that the budgeted operating income for the period is $200,000, while column (1) reports that the firm earned an operating income of $128,000 for the period. The difference is the operating income variance for the period, $72,000 unfavorable [column (3)]. Schmidt Machinery Company was not effective in attaining its goal for the period; its operation fell 36 percent short of its budgeted operating income.

Exhibit 15–1 Comparison of Operating Results with Master Budget

SCHMIDT MACHINERY COMPANY
Analysis of Operations
For October 2001

	(1)		(2)		(3)		(4)	
					Variance			
	Actual Operating Result		Master Budget		Amount		Percent of Master Budget	
Units sold	780		1,000		220	U*	22%	U
Sales	$639,600	100%	$800,000	100%	$160,400	U	20	U
Variable expenses	350,950	55	450,000	56	99,050	F†	22	F
Contribution margin	$288,650	45%	$350,000	44%	$ 61,350	U	18	U
Fixed expenses	160,650	25	150,000	19	10,650	U	7	U
Operating income	$128,000	20%	$200,000	25%	$ 72,000	U	36	U

*U denotes an *unfavorable* effect on the budgeted operating income.
†F denotes a *favorable* effect.

In addition to the operating income variance, Exhibit 15–1 reports the difference between the master budget and the actual operating result for each reported item such as units sold, sales, and others. One notable item is the variance that actual sales deviated from the master budget by 220 units or $160,400—a decrease from the budgeted amount of 22 percent in units and 20 percent in sales dollars.

Exhibit 15–1 also reports that the variable expense incurred in October is $99,050 less than the budgeted amount—a favorable variance. This comparison probably would lead us to conclude that the primary reason for Schmidt's failure to be effective in earning its budgeted net income is the shortfall in sales. The shortfall is so large that even with a good control of expenses, as evidenced by the substantial favorable variance in variable expenses, the firm still suffers a substantial decrease in operating income and, as a result, failed to be effective in earning the budgeted $200,000 in operating income.

That conclusion is only half-correct at best, however, and is misleading. Direct comparisons between the actual amounts incurred and the master or static budget amounts for variable expenses can be meaningless. In this instance, the variable expenses in the master or static budget are for operations at a higher level than that actually achieved. Variable expenses for 780 units should be less than the variable expenses for 1,000 units. Schmidt should not credit its management for having good control of its variable expenses based only on the fact that the variable costs incurred are below the budgeted amount for the period. Differences in the amount for variable expenses for the actual operation and the master budget figure are not measures of effectiveness, nor are they measures of efficiency, as we discuss later.

The operating income variance reveals only whether the firm achieved the budgeted operating income for the period; it does not identify causes for the deviation or help the firm identify courses of action to reduce or eliminate similar deviations in the future. The firm needs to conduct additional analyses to learn the reason for missing the target. An analysis of the efficiency of the operation can shed insights on this question. Flexible budgets play important roles in such analyses.

The Flexible Budget

Budgets are important benchmarks in monitoring and controlling operations and evaluating operating results and performances. Operating conditions, however, are seldom exactly the way they were forecasted when preparing the budgets. As operating conditions change, an organization needs a budget that incorporates these changes. The master or static budget is useful for initial planning and coordinating efforts for the budget period. Assessments of the operations during a period should consider the firm's changed operating conditions and examine the goal set following the preparation of the period's budget. A tool that can help to accommodate an important change in the operation is a flexible budget.

A **flexible budget** is a budget that adjusts revenues and expenses for changes in output achieved. Changes in output (for example, units manufactured or sold for a manufacturing firm, number of patient-days for a hospital, or number of students for a school district) change the firm's revenues and expenses.

Flexible budgets can help management answer many important questions about an operation. The data for Schmidt Machinery Company in Exhibit 15–1 show that the period's operating income is $72,000 below the budgeted amount. On receiving the report, management likely would want to know,

1. Why net income has gone down.
2. Why the expenses have gone from 75 to 80 percent of sales. Can management do something to prevent the same thing from happening next year?
3. Why selling and general expenses have increased $10,650.
4. The reasons for the deterioration in operating results. Is it because of changes in
   a. units sold?
   b. sales price?
   c. sales mix?
   d. manufacturing or merchandising cost?
   e. selling and general expenses?

Flexible budgeting allows management to analyze the operating results and changes in operating conditions in detail and helps to provide this information.

Flexible budgets can differ from the master budget in the number of budgeted output units. Other factors, such as *unit* selling prices and *unit* variable costs, are the same in flexible budgets as in the master budget. The total fixed expenses usually remain the same in both the flexible and the master budgets unless the actual level of operation differs substantially from the planned operation level and the firm had the time to adjust its operation level. Exhibit 15–2 illustrates a flexible budget for Schmidt. As sales units change, the total sales and total variable expenses also change, resulting in a change in the total contribution margin and operating income. The unit selling price, unit variable cost, and total fixed expense, however, remain the same.

With the actual output at 80 percent of the sales level in the master budget, sales, variable expenses, and contribution margin for the flexible budget are 80 percent of the corresponding amounts of the master budget. The fixed expenses remain at the $150,000 level, not 80 percent of the master budget amount. The operating income of the flexible budget also is not 80 percent of the amount of the master budget. The

◄**LEARNING OBJECTIVE 2**

Develop and use flexible budgets to conduct additional analyses of the operating income variance for control of operations and performance evaluation, as well as calculate and interpret the sales volume and flexible budget variances.

The **flexible budget** is a budget that adjusts revenues and costs for changes in output achieved.

Exhibit 15–2 Flexible Budgets for Schmidt Machinery Company

	(1) Flexible Budget at 80 Percent		(2) Flexible Budget at 100 Percent		(3) Flexible Budget at 110 Percent	
Units sold	800		1,000		1,100	
Sales ($800)	$640,000	100.00%	$800,000	100.00%	$880,000	100.00%
Variable expenses ($450)	360,000	56.25	450,000	56.25	495,000	56.25
Contribution margin ($350)	$280,000	43.75%	$350,000	43.75%	$385,000	43.75%
Fixed expenses	150,000	23.44	150,000	18.75	150,000	17.05
Operating income	$130,000	20.31%	$200,000	25.00%	$235,000	26.70%

operating income of Schmidt's flexible budget at the 80 percent output level of the master budget is $130,000. This amount is only 65 percent of the operating income of the master budget ($200,000). Why? The fixed expenses account for the lower operating income percentage because the $150,000 fixed expenses are a much larger proportion of the smaller sales level.

Total sales and total expenses for a flexible budget are calculated using these formulas:

$$\text{Total sales} = \text{Number of units sold} \times \text{Budgeted selling price per unit}$$

$$\text{Total expenses} = \text{Total variable expenses} + \text{Total fixed expenses}$$

$$= (\text{Number of units sold} \times \text{Budgeted variable cost per unit})$$

$$+ \text{Budgeted total fixed expenses}$$

A firm can prepare flexible budgets for different levels of output or activity. In addition, flexible budgets can differ from the master or static budget in the time of preparation and level of detail. A firm can prepare flexible budgets anytime—before, during, or after an operation—but it can prepare a master budget only before operation begins.

Flexible budgets also typically contain fewer details than master budgets, facilitating analysis of selected aspects of an operation. Exhibit 15–3 highlights some of these differences.

Assessing Efficiency

With the help of a flexible budget, we can separate the difference between the operating result and the master budget into two variances: the flexible budget variance and the sales volume variance. The **flexible budget variance** is the difference between the operating result and the flexible budget amount at the actual output level of the period. A flexible budget variance measures efficiency in using input resources to attain the operating results of the period.

Sales Volume Variance

The **sales volume variance** is the difference between the flexible budget and the master or static budget and it measures the effect of changes in units of sales on sales, expenses, contribution margins, and operating income. Column (4) of Exhibit 15–4 shows the sales volume variances for Schmidt's operations in October 2001.

Schmidt Machinery Company sold 780 units during the month. The master budget [column (5)] shows that the firm planned to sell 1,000 units for the period. Column (3) shows the flexible budget at the level of the units sold during the period. Comparing these budgets, we find the sales volume variance to be 220 unfavorable in units and $77,000 unfavorable in operating income [column (4)]. Note that the operating income sales volume variance is the same as the contribution margin sales volume variance. This happens because fixed expenses in the master budget and the flexible budget usually do not change. Thus, an alternative way to compute the operating income sales volume variance is to multiply the difference in units of sales actually sold and in the master (static) budget by the master budget contribution margin per unit.

The **flexible budget variance** is the difference between the operating result and the flexible budget at the actual output level of the period.

The **sales volume variance** is the difference between the flexible budget and the master or static budget, and it measures the effect on sales, expenses, contribution margins, and operating income of changes in units of sales.

Exhibit 15–3	**Comparison of the Master Budget and the Flexible Budget**	
	Master Budget	**Flexible Budget**
Time prepared	Before the period	Before, during, or after the period
Activity levels	Single level	One or more levels
Level of detail	All aspects of operations	Selected aspects

Exhibit 15–4	Assessment of Operating Results with a Flexible Budget

SCHMIDT MACHINERY COMPANY
Analysis of Operations
For October 2001

Data Item for Analysis	(1) Actual	(2) Flexible Budget Variance		(3) Flexible Budget	(4) Sales Volume (Activity) Variance		(5) Master (Static) Budget
Units sold	780	0		780	220	U	1,000
Sales	$639,600	$15,600	F	$624,000	$176,000	U	$800,000
Variable expenses	350,950	50	F	351,000	99,000	F	450,000
Contribution margin	$288,650	$15,650	F	$273,000	$ 77,000	U	$350,000
Fixed expenses	160,650	10,650	U	150,000	0		150,000
Operating income	$128,000	$5,000	F	$123,000	$ 77,000	U	$200,000

Analysis of Operating
Income Variances

Total operating income variance
= $128,000 − $200,000 = $72,000 U

Flexible budget variance
= $128,000 − $123,000
= $5,000 F

Sales volume variance
= $123,000 − $200,000
= $77,000 U

$$\text{Operating income sales volume variance} = \left[\begin{array}{c} \text{Actual} \\ \text{units} \\ \text{sold} \end{array} - \begin{array}{c} \text{Units} \\ \text{budgeted} \\ \text{to be sold} \end{array} \right] \times \begin{array}{c} \text{Master budget} \\ \text{contribution} \\ \text{margin per unit} \end{array}$$

$$= (780 - 1,000) \times \$350$$

$$= \$77,000 \text{ U}$$

The operating income sales volume variance shows that a decrease of 220 units in units sold would have decreased the firm's operating income by $77,000 if the selling price per unit, the variable cost per unit, and the total fixed costs remained at the budgeted amount.

Significant sales volume variances can have serious implications for strategic management. A significant unfavorable sales volume variance can indicate that the market is smaller than the level planned when the firm set its strategy and the goal for the period. The firm might need to modify or abandon its strategy. An insignificant sales volume variance can indicate that the firm's strategy and operating plans are on track to attain its goals. A significant favorable sales volume variance can indicate that the firm needs to pursue a more aggressive strategy or operating goal.

Operating Income Flexible Budget Variance

The **operating income flexible budget variance** is the difference between the flexible budget operating income that would have budgeted for the units sold and the operating income earned during the period. In Exhibit 15–4, the operating income flexible budget variance is the difference in operating income for columns (1) and (3). Column (1) reports the operating income the firm earned from selling 780 units. Column (3) shows the budgeted operating income the firm would have earned if it had budgeted to sell 780 units. The $5,000 difference in operating income is due to the differences in selling price, variable expenses, and/or fixed expenses.

Operating income flexible budget variances measure efficiencies in operations that are primarily internal to the firm. Factors contributing to operating income flexible

The **operating income flexible budget variance** is the difference between the flexible budget operating income for the units sold during the period and the operating income earned during the period.

budget variances include deviations in selling prices, variable costs, and fixed costs. Management is likely to have controls or influences on these factors. Substantial or continuous unfavorable operating income flexible budget variances can diminish the feasibility of the strategy and jeopardize its continuation.

The remainder of this chapter and the next one examine the operating income flexible budget variance in more detail. This detailed analysis isolates the portion of the variance due to differences in selling prices, variable expenses, or fixed expenses. This further examination of the factors contributing to operating income flexible budget variances requires a good understanding of standard costs, so we turn to that topic next.

STANDARD COSTING

LEARNING OBJECTIVE 3 ▶

Set proper standard costs for planning, control, and performance evaluation.

How many strokes should a golfer take to play a course? What should Ford Motor Company's cost be to manufacture an Explorer? How much should Wal-Mart's cost be to sell a hair dryer? How much should a New York City mission's cost be to serve a hot meal to a homeless person?

A golfer uses the par for the course as a gauge for performance. *Par* is the number of strokes a golfer expects to take to cover a course competently; it is the *standard* that the golfer strives to attain. The costs that Ford Motor Company, Wal-Mart, and the New York City mission set for their operations are *standard costs*. A **standard cost** is the ideal predetermined cost a firm sets for an operation; it is the cost the firm should incur for the operation.

A **standard cost** is the cost a firm should incur for an operation.

Standard costs are among the foundations of a firm's planning and control activities. These activities include budget preparation, monitoring and control operations, and performance evaluation. A furniture manufacturer, for example, budgets the dollar amount of direct materials required to produce 5,000 entertainment centers based on the standard usage of direct materials per entertainment center and standard prices of the materials. If the standard calls for 3 square feet of plexiglass for each entertainment center at $15 per square foot, the firm has a materials budget of 15,000 square feet of plexiglass and $225,000 ($15 × 15,000) for producing the planned 5,000 entertainment centers. The firm also uses the $15 price per foot and the 3-foot standard per unit in monitoring manufacturing operations and assessing performance.

Components of a Standard Costing System

A standard cost prescribes what expected performances should be. A complete standard cost for an operation is composed of carefully established standards for each operating cost element, including manufacturing, selling, and administrative expenses. Although the discussions in this and the next chapter focus on standard costing systems for manufacturing operations, these concepts and procedures can also be applied to standard cost systems for other operations.

A manufacturing operation has three manufacturing cost elements: direct materials, direct labor, and factory overhead. This chapter focuses on standard costs for direct materials and direct labor. Chapter 16 discusses the standard cost for factory overhead costs.

Standard costs can vary for different types of standards. Next we discuss the different types of standards that firms use.

Types of Standards

Firms have different expectations as to the proper level at which to set their standards. Differences in expectations lead to two types of standards: ideal and currently attainable.

Ideal Standard

An **ideal standard** demands perfect implementation and maximum efficiency in every aspect of the operation.

An **ideal standard** demands perfect implementation and maximum efficiency in every aspect of the operation. A firm can meet the ideal standard set for its operations when all factors occur as expected or better and the firm performs its operations as prescribed. An ideal standard is forward looking; rarely is it a historical standard.

Suppose that the ideal standard for manufacturing a 4-by-4-foot tabletop calls for cutting one 8-by-4-foot sheet of plywood in half so that each tabletop measures exactly 4-by-4 ft. An ideal standard sets the materials requirement for producing 1,000 tabletops at 500 sheets of plywood. A firm can meet such a standard if all equipment and instruments are in proper working condition, it has no defective plywood, employees cut all pieces perfectly, and all other relevant manufacturing factors are in proper condition and operate as expected.

An ideal standard is not easily attained. During an operation, accidents happen, unexpected events arise, and undesirable circumstances manifest themselves. Perfect performance, however, is not impossible. Today's highly competitive environment and demands for total quality management in all aspects of an operation have made many firms realize the importance of attaining ever higher ideal standards in all operations. This is often referred to as a *continuous improvement strategy*.

At times an ideal standard can be met only if everybody involved, including those performing the task and those in support functions, exert extraordinary efforts throughout the operation. Extraordinary efforts to achieve an ideal standard, while possible, can lead to undue stress over a long period, which, in turn, decreases morale, increases apathetic attitudes among employees, and decreases the organization's long-term productivity. Such concerns have led some firms to adopt ideal standards for their operations only infrequently. Some firms set ideal standards for their operations because they are facing a crisis and need their employees to exert extraordinary efforts.

Firms that use ideal standards often modify performance evaluations and reward structures so that employees are not frustrated by the failure to attain the ideal standard immediately. Firms can, for example, use progress toward the ideal standard rather than deviations from it as the primary factor in its performance evaluation and reward system.

Currently Attainable Standard

A **currently attainable standard** sets the performance criterion at a level that employees with proper training and experience can attain most of the time without extraordinary effort. A currently attainable standard emphasizes normality and allows for some deviations.

Suppose that a firm sets the standard for the plywood to produce 1,000 tabletops at 525 sheets of plywood, although two tabletops can be cut from one sheet. The additional 25 sheets allow for such things as less than ideal input quality, occasional maladjustment of the equipment used in production, and varying experience and skill levels of the personnel involved in the production. With a standard that allows for some deviations, the firm usually can reach a currently attainable standard with reasonable effort.

Selection of Standards

Which standards—ideal or currently attainable—should a firm use in its standard costing system? There is no single answer for all situations. The most suitable standard for a firm is the one that helps it to attain its strategic goals.

For many firms struggling for survival in intensely competitive industries, an ideal standard appropriately motivates employees to put forth their best efforts and allows the firm to be competitive in the market. An ideal standard is not effective, however, if frequent failures to meet the standard discourage employees or lead them to ignore the standards.

Conversely, a currently attainable standard allows for inefficiencies. This allowance is strategically unwise if a firm operates in an intensely competitive environment. A standard that allows 25 additional sheets of plywood conveys to production that it has attained an excellent performance as long as it does not make more than 25 mistakes for every 500 sheets of plywood cut.

A **currently attainable standard** sets the performance criterion at a level that employees with proper training and experience can attain most of the time without extraordinary effort.

Inefficiencies cost the firm and decrease its operating income. Inefficiencies also can negatively affect its competitive position. An ideal standard prescribes a high yet achievable performance. Any deviation from the ideal standard is an imperfection and undesirable to the firm. A world-class firm can ill afford any inefficiency and, most likely, would use ideal standards for its operations.

Today's dynamic and intensely competitive environment requires all organizations to reexamine their standards periodically and to cultivate continuous improvement. New technologies, equipment, and production processes often make existing standards obsolete. Without continuously updating standards, a firm can find survival difficult in a fiercely competitive global economy that demands total quality and high efficiency.

Nonfinancial Measures

Although most measures in standard cost systems eventually are expressed in dollar amounts as costs to the firm, nonfinancial measures often play important roles in standard cost systems. Managers do not manage costs; they manage activities. Losses and profits are the results of activities. Managers must control all activities that are strategically important in meeting the firm's goals. Some activities, such as friendly service, on-time delivery, and high quality, have no financial measures. For example, management at McDonald's considers QSCV (quality, service, cleanliness, and value) to be the foremost factors for its success, yet none of these four factors is reflected directly by a financial measure.

Sources of Standards

Firms often use several sources in determining appropriate standards for their operations. These sources include activity analysis, historical data, standards for similar operations in other firms (a technique known as *benchmarking*), market expectations (target costing), and strategic decisions.

Activity Analysis

As discussed in Chapter 1, *activity analysis* is the process of identifying, delineating, and evaluating the activities required to complete a job, project, or operation. A thorough activity analysis includes all input factors and activities required to complete the task efficiently. The analysis involves personnel from several functional areas including product engineers, industrial engineers, management accountants, and production workers.

Because each product is different, product engineers must specify product components in detail. Based on the firm's facilities and equipment and the product design, industrial engineers then analyze the steps or procedures necessary to complete the task or product. Management accountants work with engineers to complete the analyses.

COST MANAGEMENT IN ACTION

Is Two Minutes and Twenty Seconds Enough for a Brake Part?

At Westinghouse Air Brake Company in Chicago, workers are expected to "feed" a conveyor belt a finished part at fixed intervals. Having done this successfully, the workers in that work cell are rewarded with a $1.50 per hour bonus for that day's work. The bonus, a 12.5 percent increase in pay for the same hours, is a significant boost to the regular pay of $12 per hour and an effective incentive for most workers at the plant.

The speed of the conveyor changes from time to time to reflect changes in customer demand. When demand falls, the rate slows, and vice versa. The firm installed the bonus plan upon the recommendations of consultants and specialists in kaizen (continuous improvement). The bonus plan allowed Westinghouse to improve productivity in the plant by over 10 times the 1991 level. This seems to be a win-win situation for Westinghouse and Westinghouse workers. Do you see any problems?

For example, an activity analysis for preparing a hamburger at a fast-food restaurant starts by assessing the hamburger ingredients and the tasks involved in preparing, cooking, and wrapping it. The analysis specifies the quantities and qualities of onion, lettuce, tomato, pickle, ground beef, buns, and other ingredients. It then determines the tools, steps or procedures, and time needed to chop onions, cut lettuce, slice tomatoes and pickles, cook the hamburger, and wrap it. The analysis specifies the required skill level and experience of the employees, the equipment to be used, and other relevant factors affecting performance. The management accountant adds the cost of the ingredients, the employee wage rates with the required skill levels, the overhead and other relevant cost items to arrive at the total standard cost. The standard for the same operation is likely to vary for different firms because equipment, personnel skill level and experience, operating policies, and other relevant factors will not be the same. For example, the standard for making french fries at McDonald's is likely to differ from the standard for a mom-and-pop burger shop. The mom-and-pop shop could be using 30-year-old equipment and cooking one order at a time every five minutes or so. In contrast, the McDonald's across the street may be using state-of-the-art equipment that can cook 10 orders at a time.

Activity analysis, if properly executed, offers the most precise specification for determining standards. It is time consuming and expensive, however, because each activity needs to be studied individually.

Historical Data

The cost to develop the standards through activity analysis or other alternative methods can be prohibitively high. The high cost of developing standards through an alternative method leaves many firms, especially small businesses, with little choice but to rely on historical data if they want to take advantage of standard costing and flexible budget systems.[2] Historical data for making a similar product can be a good source for determining the standard cost of an operation when reliable and accurate data are available.

By carefully analyzing historical data for manufacturing a product or executing a task, management can determine appropriate standards for operations. A common practice is to use the average or the median of historical amounts for an operation as the standard of the operation. A firm determined to excel, however, would use the best performance in the past as its standard.

Analysis of historical data is usually much less expensive than activity analysis for determining standards. Historical data analysis also has the advantage of including all manufacturing factors relevant to the way a firm operates in determining the standard for the firm. A standard based on the past, however, can be biased and perpetuate past inefficiencies. Furthermore, historical standards are more attainable than ideal standards and are not necessarily consistent with continuous improvements required of many firms in today's worldwide competitive environment.

Benchmarking

Associations of manufacturers often collect industry information and have data available that managers can use to determine operation standards. Current practices of similar operations in other firms, not necessarily firms in the same industry, can also be good guidelines for setting the standard.

In recent years, many world-class firms were not satisfied with using the best operations of firms in the same industry; they have adopted as standards the best operations of any firm. Bath Iron Works, the fourth-largest shipyard in the United States, uses as its standard the benchmarks of the German firm Thyssen for pipe bending, Walt Disney World for preventive maintenance, and L.L. Bean for receipt inspection and paper reduction. IBM's plant in Austin, Texas, uses as benchmarks such plants as

---

2   William C. Lawler and John Leslie Livingstone, "Profit and Productivity Analysis for Small Businesses," *Journal of Accountancy*, December 1986, pp. 190–196.

> ## How Did General Mills Benchmark Changeover Time?
>
> When Stephen W. Sanger, CEO of General Mills was looking to improve efficiency in his production-line changes, he sent technicians to the NASCAR races in North Carolina to watch the pit crews. The technicians applied those techniques and cut the changeover time from five hours to 20 minutes.
>
> Based on *Business Week,* March 26, 2001, p. 76.

Tatung, Sampo, and DTK in Taiwan. For its circuit board manufacturing, Allen-Bradley benchmarks a Hewlett-Packard Company plant in Colorado.

The advantage of using benchmarking is that a firm is using the best performance anywhere as the standard. Using such a standard can help the firm sustain its competitive edge. Data from trade associations or other firms, however, might not be completely applicable to the unique situation in which a firm operates.

Market Expectations and Strategic Decisions

Market expectations and strategic decisions often play important roles in standard setting, especially for firms using target costing (Chapter 5). With a set selling price for which the firm is able or desires to sell the product, the *target cost* is the cost that yields the desired profit margin for the product. It is computed as the difference between the selling price and the desired profit margin of the product. Detailed standards then are determined for manufacturing the product at the target cost.

A firm that has a target selling price of $200 and desires to earn a gross profit margin of 25 percent of the selling price has a target cost of $150. The total standard cost for manufacturing the product then is set not to exceed $150.

Strategic decisions also have effects on a product's standard cost. A strategic decision to strive for continuous improvement (known by the Japanese term *kaizen*) and zero defects require the firm to continuously set the standard for the product at the most challenging level. As another example, the strategic decision to replace a manual drilling machine with a high-precision automatic drilling machine would require the firm to alter the standard for its manufacturing process.

Standard-Setting Procedures

Using one or more of these sources of standards as the starting point, a firm can use either an authoritative or a participative procedure in setting the firm's standard.

An **authoritative standard** is determined solely or primarily by management. In contrast, a **participative standard** calls for active participation throughout the standard-setting process by employees affected by the standard. A firm uses an authoritative process to ensure proper consideration of all operating factors, to incorporate management's desires or expectations, or to expedite the standard-setting process. Firms using an authoritative process in standard setting, however, should keep in mind that a perfect or desirable standard is useless if the employees affected by it do not accept and implement it.

Employee participation in setting the standard means that they will more likely accept it. Participation also reduces the chance that employees will view the standard as unreasonable and increases the likelihood that they will buy into or adopt it as their own. Management needs to be persuasive, however, to ensure that the standards from participative processes will not prevent the firm from achieving its strategic goals or operating objectives.

*An **authoritative standard** is determined solely or primarily by management.*

*A **participative standard** calls for active participation throughout the standard-setting process by employees affected by the standard.*

Establishing Standard Cost

Establishing a standard cost is a joint effort of management, product design engineers, industrial engineers, management accountants, production supervisors, the purchasing department, the personnel department, and employees affected by the standard.

An Exemplary Participative Standard Setting

Merrill-Continental Company, Inc., attributes the successful implementation of its standard cost system to the fact that the standards were essentially designed on the shop floor by the operating supervisors, not by an outside industrial engineering department. The performance standards, as a result, were accepted and used enthusiastically by employees.

Source: Thomas A. Faulhaber, Fred A. Coad, and Thomas J. Little, "Building a Process Cost Management System from the Bottom Up," *Management Accounting,* May 1988, pp. 58–62.

Although not all of them are always involved, they participate at various points in establishing the standard cost. Even in an authoritative standard-setting process, some participation is involved. After all, no management knows everything and better standards are often the result of incorporating input from subordinates before setting the standard.

Costs are the results of activities to create products or render services, and as we have said, activities, not costs, are what managers manage. All standards, therefore, should be established for cost drivers underlying the costs associated with the product or service cost object.

Establishing Standard Cost for Direct Materials

A standard cost for direct materials for a given product has three facets: quality, quantity, and price.

The first step in establishing a standard cost is to specify clearly the quality of the direct materials for the manufacturing process or product. The quality of direct materials permeates all phases of production including the quantity of the direct materials needed in the process, their prices, the time required to process them, and the extent and frequency of supervision needed to complete the process.

Trade-offs are often needed to decide whether to use more expensive, higher-quality direct materials or less expensive, lower-quality direct materials in operations. The marketing department, engineering department, production department, and management accountants need to assess these trade-offs and determine the proper quality of the direct materials required.

Once the quality of the direct materials has been specified, several departments including the industrial engineering department, the production department, and management accountants need to work together to set the standard for the quantity of direct materials for manufacturing the product. Among factors considered in setting quantity standards are product design, cost drivers of manufacturing activities, quality of the direct materials, and the conditions of the production facility and equipment to be used to manufacture the product.

Considerations for setting a price standard include quality, quantity, and, at times, the timing of purchases. In a competitive environment, many companies emphasize long-term relationships with selected suppliers that are reliable in delivering quality materials on time. For a firm that emphasizes long-term benefits and reliability of its supply chain, the price standard needs to be revised only when a change occurs in the underlying long-term factors in determining a price.

Establishing Standard Cost for Direct Labor

Direct labor costs vary for the type of work involved, the product's complexity, employee skill level, nature of the manufacturing process, and type and condition of the equipment used. Considering these factors, the industrial engineering department, production department, labor union, personnel department, and management accountants determine jointly the quantity standard for direct labor.

The personnel department determines the standard wage rate for the type and skill level of employees needed for the manufacturing process. The standard labor rate for either direct or indirect labor includes not only the compensation paid but also the fringe benefits provided to employees and the required payroll taxes associated with wages and salaries. Fringe benefits include health and life insurance, pension plan contributions, and paid vacations. Payroll taxes include unemployment taxes and the employer's share of an employee's Social Security assessment.

Standard Cost Sheet

A **standard cost sheet**
specifies the standard
price and quantity of each
manufacturing cost
element for the production
of one product.

A **standard cost sheet** specifies the standard price and quantity of each manufacturing cost element for the production of one product.

In Exhibit 15–5 is a simplified standard cost sheet for selected manufacturing costs for Schmidt Machinery Company for manufacturing one unit of XV–1. One of the items *not* included in the standard cost sheet is the budgeted variable selling and administrative expense of $50 per unit.

Schmidt's standard cost sheet specifies that the standard cost for one unit of XV–1 is 4 pounds of aluminum at $25 per pound, 1 pound of PVC at $40 per pound, 5 hours of direct labor at $40 per hour, and factory overhead of $36 ($12 + $24) per direct labor-hour.

OPERATING INCOME FLEXIBLE BUDGET VARIANCE

LEARNING OBJECTIVE 4▶

*Identify factors that con-
tribute to an operating
income flexible budget
variance and analyze and
explain selling price variance, direct materials
price and usage
variances, and direct
labor rate and efficiency
variances.*

The **selling price variance**
is the difference between
the total sales revenue
received and the total flexible budget sales revenue
for the units sold during a
period.

Factors that contribute to an operating income flexible budget variance include deviations of selling prices, variable expenses, and fixed expenses from their standard or budgeted amounts. Deviations of fixed expenses are discussed in Chapter 16.

Selling Price Variance

A **selling price variance** is the difference between the total sales revenue received and the total sales revenue in the flexible budget for the units sold during the period. The difference, if any, results from a difference in selling price. Both total sales revenues are for the same number of units: those sold during the period. The total sales revenue received is the product of *the number of units sold* and the actual selling price; the total sales revenue in the flexible budget is the product of *the number of units sold* and the budgeted selling price for these units. Therefore, the difference between these two total sales revenues is the difference between the actual selling price and the budgeted sales price.

Exhibit 15–4 shows that Schmidt Machinery Company sold 780 units of XV–1 for $639,600, or $820 per unit. The budgeted selling price, however, is $800 per unit. At the budgeted selling price of $800 per unit, the total sales revenue in the flexible budget for 780 units is $624,000. The difference, $15,600, occurred because the actual

---

Exhibit 15–5   Standard Cost Sheet

SCHMIDT MACHINERY COMPANY
Standard Cost Sheet

Product: XV–1

Description	Quantity	Unit Cost	Subtotal	Total
Direct materials				
Aluminum	4 pounds	$25	$100	
PVC	1 pound	40	40	$140
Direct labor	5 hours	40		200
Factory overhead (based on direct labor-hours)				
Variable	5 hours	12	60	
Fixed	5 hours	24	120	180
Standard cost per unit				$520

A Standard Cost Sheet of Merrill-Continental Company, Inc.

Product letter			A	B	C
Color			Black	Black	White
Felt			Y	N	Y
Width		Inches	48	48	48
Thickness of rubber		Inches	0.060	0.080	0.060
Roll length		Feet	100	80	100
Package type			1	2	1
Production rate		Feet/Min	6	4	6
Trim loss		Percent	5.0%	5.0%	10.0%
Trim recovery		Percent	2.0%	3.0%	5.0%
Glue usage		Pounds/sf	0.05	0.05	0.10
Materials					
Compound 1	$/lb	0.41	1	1	0
Compound 1	S.G.	1.60			
Compound 2	$/lb	0.41	0	0	1
Compound 2	S.G.	1.58			
Felt 1	$/S.F.	0.06	1	0	0
Felt 2	$/S.F.	0.08	0	0	1
Glue 1	$/lb	0.60	1	0	0
Glue 2	$/lb	0.80	0	0	1
Package 1	$/Each	2.00	1	0	1
Package 2	$/Each	4.00	0	1	0
Labor		$/Hour			
Direct					
Extruder		$10.000	1.00	1.00	1.00
Operator		$6.00	3.00	2.00	3.00
Indirect					
Maintenance		$12.00	0.50	0.50	0.50
Forklift		$8.00	0.30	0.30	0.30
Changeover—Setup					
Line hours		Each	0.50	0.50	0.50
Scrap		S.F. Each	500	500	50

Source: Thomas A. Faulhaber, Fred A. Coad, and Thomas J. Little, "Building a Process Cost Management System from the Bottom Up," *Management Accounting,* May 1988, p. 60.

selling price is $20 per unit higher than the budgeted selling price for the 780 units sold. This is the calculation of the sellings price variance:

$$\text{Selling price variance} = \left[\begin{array}{c} \text{Actual selling} \\ \text{price per} \\ \text{unit} \end{array} - \begin{array}{c} \text{Flexible budget} \\ \text{selling price} \\ \text{per unit} \end{array} \right] \times \begin{array}{c} \text{Units} \\ \text{sold} \end{array}$$

$$= (\$820 - \$800) \times 780 \text{ units}$$

$$= \$15,600 \text{ Favorable}$$

Variable Expense Flexible Budget Variance

The **variable expense flexible budget variance** is the difference between variable expenses incurred and the total variable expenses in the flexible budget for the units sold during the period. This variance is computed based on the standard variable cost per unit, and it reflects the deviation of actual variable expenses from the standard variable expenses for the output of the period (units sold).

The **variable expense flexible budget variance** is the difference between variable expenses incurred and the total variable expenses in the flexible budget for the units sold during the period.

701

Exhibit 15–4 data indicate that Schmidt incurred a total variable expense of $350,950 during the period to produce and sell 780 units of XV–l. On the standard cost sheet in Exhibit 15–5, the standard variable manufacturing expense is $400 per unit, including $140 for direct materials, $200 for direct labor, and $60 for variable manufacturing overhead. For 780 units, the total standard variable manufacturing expense is $312,000. In addition, the standard variable selling and administrative expense is $50 per unit, or $39,000 in total. This brings the total variable expense for manufacturing and selling 780 units to $351,000.

The total actual variable expense incurred in October, $350,950, is $50 less than the standard expense for manufacturing 780 units of XV–1, $351,000. This suggests that the operation met the standards set in the standard cost sheet and that the operation appears to be under control.

Need for Further Analysis of the Variable Expense
Flexible Budget Variance

The variable expense flexible budget variance is the sum of variances of cost elements that constitute the total variable expense. They include flexible budget variances in direct materials, direct labor, variable overhead, and variable selling and administrative expense. Different factors may drive each of these variances. An aggregated total amount, such as the total variable expense flexible budget variance can mask poor performance in one or more of the cost components or operating divisions, especially when there are offsetting materials, labor, manufacturing overhead, or selling and administrative variances, as is true in the operating results of the Schmidt Machinery Company.

Schmidt's operating results for the period show a $50 favorable variable expense flexible budget variance—a small variance that should not be of concern to the management. However, further analyses of the expenses shown in Exhibit 15–6 reveal that Schmidt spent $94,380 for 3,630 pounds of aluminum to manufacture 780 units of XV–1. The standard quantity for aluminum for 780 units of XV–1 is 3,900 pounds, for a

Exhibit 15–6	**Comparison of Actual Variable Expenses and Flexible Budget Variable Expenses**		

SCHMIDT MACHINERY COMPANY
October 2001

Product XV–1
Units Manufactured: 780
Operating Results

Direct materials			
Aluminum	3,630 pounds at $26	$94,380	
PVC	720 pounds at $41	29,520	$123,900
Direct labor	3,510 hours at $42		147,420
Variable factory overhead			40,630
Total variable cost of goods manufactured			$311,950
Variable selling and administrative expenses			39,000
Total variable expense incurred			$350,950

Flexible Budget

Total standard variable cost of goods manufactured:		
Standard variable manufacturing cost per unit (from (Exhibit 15–5)	$400	
Number of units manufactured	× 780	$312,000
Standard variable selling and administrative expenses	780 × $50	39,000
Total standard variable expense		$351,000
Flexible budget variable expense variance		$ 50 F*

*F denotes a *favorable* result.

total cost of $78,000. The amount spent on aluminum exceeds the standard cost allowed by $16,380, or 21 percent. In contrast, the labor and variable overhead variances are favorable. This illustration demonstrates that conducting separate analyses of variances for different costs can prevent offsetting an inefficient use of one resource by efficient uses in one or more other resources. Looking only at the total costs can be misleading.

Direct Materials Variances

The direct materials flexible budget variance is the difference between the total direct materials cost incurred and the total standard direct materials cost for the output of the period (the units of the product manufactured during the period). This variance reflects the overall efficiency in buying and using the direct materials. Attaining efficiency in buying and using materials requires good controls over both the price paid for the materials and the quantity of materials used in the operation. We must analyze the total direct materials variance further into a direct material price variance (PV) and a direct material quantity variance or usage variance (UV) so that the firm can gain a better understanding of the causes of cost variations.

In Exhibits 15–7 and 15–8, we use the Schmidt data to illustrate these analyses. Exhibit 15–7 shows that Schmidt used 3,630 pounds of aluminum at a total cost of

Exhibit 15–7	A Detail Comparison of Actual and Standard Costs

SCHMIDT MACHINERY COMPANY
October 2001

Product XV–1
Units Manufactured: 780
Operating Result

Direct materials			
Aluminum	3,630 pounds at $26	$94,380	
PVC	720 pounds at $41	29,520	$123,900
Direct labor	3,510 hours at $42		147,420
Variable factory overhead			40,630
Total variable cost of goods manufactured			$311,950
Variable selling and administrative expenses			39,000
Total variable expense incurred			$350,950

Flexible Budget

Direct materials			
Aluminum	780 units × 4 pounds × $25 = $78,000		
PVC	780 units × 1 pound × $40 = 31,200		$109,200
Direct labor	780 units × 5 hours × $40 =		156,000
Variable factory overhead	780 units × 5 hours × $12 =		46,800
Total standard variable cost of goods manufactured			$312,000
			39,000
Variable selling and administrative expenses			$351,000
Total flexible budget variable expense	($350,950 – $351,000)		$50 F*

Variances

Direct materials			
Aluminum	$94,380 – $ 78,000 = $16,380 U†		
PVC	29,520 – 31,200 = 1,680 F	$14,700 U	
Direct labor	147,420 – 156,000 =	8,580 F	
Variable factory overhead	40,630 – 46,800 =	6,170 F	
Variable manufacturing cost flexible budget variance		$ 50 F	
Variable selling and administrative expense variance		0	
Variable expense flexible budget variance		$ 50 F	

*F denotes a *favorable* result.
†U denotes an *unfavorable* result.

Exhibit 15–8   Direct Materials—Aluminum Variances, Schmidt Machinery Company

Actual Input at Actual Cost	Actual Input at Standard Cost	Standard Cost for Actual Output
3,630 pounds × $26 = $94,380	3,630 pounds × $25 = $90,750	3,120 pounds × $25 = $78,000

Or

PV = ($26 − $25) × 3,630
    = $3,630 U

UV = (3,630 − 3,120) × $25
    = $12,750 U

PV = $94,380 − $90,750
    = $3,630 U

UV = $90,750 − $78,000
    = $12,750 U

Flexible budget variance
= $94,380 − $78,000 = $16,380 U
= $3,630 U + $12,750 U = $16,380 U

Or
Or

Price Variance:		Usage Variance	
Actual price:	$26	Standard amount allowed (780 units × 4 pounds)	3,120
Standard price	− 25	Actual quantity used	− 3,630
Difference	$ 1 U	Difference	510 U
Actual usage (and purchase)	× 3,630	Standard price	× 25
	$3,630 U		$12,750 U

$94,380 to manufacture 780 units of product XV–1. The standard cost sheet reported in Exhibit 15–5 indicates that the standard cost for one unit of XV–1 is 4 pounds of aluminum at $25 per pound. Exhibit 15–8 shows computations for variances relating to the usage of aluminum to manufacture 780 units of XV–1 during the period.

Total Direct Materials Standard Cost for the Period

The total standard cost for direct materials for the period is based on the unit output of the period. The following steps describe the determination of the total standard cost of direct materials:

   Step 1: Find the total number of output units of the period from the accounting records: Schmidt Machinery Company manufactured 780 units of XV–1 in October.
   Step 2: Note that the standard amount of direct materials to produce one unit is specified in the firm's standard cost sheet. Schmidt's standard cost sheet indicates that it uses 4 pounds of aluminum to manufacture one unit of XV–1.
   Step 3: Calculate the total standard amount of the direct materials for the period by multiplying the two amounts obtained in Steps 1 and 2. Step 1 indicates that the firm manufactured 780 units of XV–1; Step 2 shows that the firm should use 4 pounds of aluminum for each unit of XV–1. The total standard amount of aluminum for the 780 units the company manufactured in October is therefore 3,120 pounds (4 pounds per unit × 780 units).
   Step 4: Find the standard unit cost of the direct materials from the firm's standard cost sheet. Exhibit 15–5 specifies that the cost of aluminum is $25 per pound.
   Step 5: Determine the total standard cost of direct materials for the period by multiplying the amounts from Steps 3 and 4. This is the total amount of direct materials cost in the flexible budget for the units manufactured during the period. At $25 standard cost per pound (Step 4), the total standard cost for the 3,120 pounds of aluminum that Schmidt should have used in the production of 780 units of XV–1 (Step 3) is $78,000 ($25 per pound × 3,120 pounds). Therefore, the total direct materials cost in the flexible budget for the output of the period is $78,000.

Direct Materials Flexible Budget Variance

The **direct materials flexible budget variance** is the difference between the direct materials costs incurred and the total standard cost for the direct materials in the flexible budget for the number of units manufactured during the period. The flexible budget variance for aluminum for Schmidt is the difference between the actual cost for aluminum incurred, $94,380, and the total standard aluminum cost in the flexible budget for the 780 units manufactured during the period, $78,000, or $16,380 unfavorable.

Further Analyses of the Direct Materials Flexible Budget Variance

Price Variance   A **direct materials price variance** is the difference between the actual and the standard unit prices of the direct materials multiplied by the quantity of the direct materials purchased. Schmidt Machinery Company paid $26 per pound to purchase aluminum, but the standard cost sheet (Exhibit 15–5) specifies the standard price to be $25 per pound. The firm paid $1 per pound more than the standard. With a total of 3,630 pounds purchased, the price variance for aluminum for the period therefore is $3,630 unfavorable (Exhibit 15–8).

$$PV_{DM} = (AP_{DM} - SP_{DM}) \times AQ_{DM}$$
$$PV_{Aluminum} = (AP_{Aluminum} - SP_{Aluminum}) \times AQ_{Aluminum}$$
$$= (\$26 - \$25) \times 3,630$$
$$= \$1 \times 3,630 = \$3,630 \text{ Unfavorable}$$

Usage Variance

A **direct materials usage variance** is the product of the difference between the number of units of the direct materials used during the period and the number of standard units of the direct materials that should have been used for the number of units of the product manufactured during the period and the standard unit price of the direct materials. The total standard units of the direct materials that should have been used for the units of the product manufactured are also the flexible budget units for direct materials. Some users call usage variances *efficiency* or *quantity variances*.

Schmidt Machinery Company used 3,630 pounds to manufacture 780 units of the final product XV–1. According to the standard cost sheet (Exhibit 15–5), each unit requires 4 pounds of aluminum. The total standard quantity of aluminum allowed for the production of 780 units is 3,120 pounds (780 units × 4 pounds per unit). This says that the 3,630 pounds of aluminum used in production is 510 pounds more than the total standard quantity allowed for the 780 units of XV–1 manufactured during the period. At the standard price of $25 per pound, the usage variance is $12,750 unfavorable (Exhibit 15–8).

$$UV_{DM} = (AQ_{DM} - SQ_{DM}) \times SP_{DM}$$
$$UV_{Aluminum} = (AQ_{Aluminum} - SQ_{Aluminum}) \times SP_{Aluminum}$$
$$= (3,630 - 3,120) \times \$25$$
$$= 510 \times \$25 = \$12,750 \text{ Unfavorable}$$

Interpreting the Direct Materials Price Variance

A direct materials price variance can result from failure to take purchase discounts, an unexpected price change for the materials, changes in freight costs, variation in grades of the purchased items, or other causes. The purchasing department is often the office most likely to provide an explanation or the responsibility for materials price variances.

Care must be taken in interpreting a price variance. A favorable direct materials price variance could lead to high manufacturing costs if the low-cost materials are of poor quality. Downstream costs such as scrap, rework, schedule disruptions, or field

---

Direct materials flexible budget variance is the difference between the direct material costs incurred and the total standard cost for the direct materials in the flexible budget for the units manufactured during the period.

A *direct materials price variance* is the difference between the actual and the standard unit prices of the direct materials multiplied by the quantity of the direct materials purchased.

A *direct materials usage variance* is the product of the difference between the number of units of the direct materials used during the period and the number of standard units of the direct materials that should have been used for the number of units of the product manufactured during the period and the standard unit price of the direct materials.

services could exceed the price savings from lower materials prices. A firm with a differentiation strategy is most likely to fail when it pursues favorable price variances through purchases of low-quality materials. A firm that competes on low cost also is likely to be doomed if the quality of its products is below the customers' expectations.

Similarly, a firm with a cost-effective purchasing department that has several warehouses full of materials and supplies purchased in bulk at low prices could have a higher total overall cost than a firm that buys in small quantities, as needed, and pays higher purchase prices to maintain only a minimum amount of direct materials on hand. Carrying costs and additional materials-handling costs can cost the firm more than the savings it obtained in purchase prices.

> The **materials usage ratio** is the ratio of quantity used over quantity purchased.

A useful measure for evaluating the performance of purchasing departments, in addition to the traditional price variance, is the **materials usage ratio,** a ratio of quantity used over quantity purchased. A low materials usage ratio suggests that the purchasing department could have made purchases to stock materials, not for the operational needs of the period. Such a move can be costly if the firm considers all costs. The benefit of any favorable price variance should be evaluated along with the cost of inventory storage of the surplus purchases.

Interpreting the Direct Materials Usage Variance

A direct materials usage variance says that the amount of direct materials used in manufacturing processes differed from the amount that should have been used for the operation. This variance measures efficiency in using direct materials. A direct materials usage variance can result from the efforts of production personnel, substitutions of the material for other materials or production factors, variation from standard in the quality of direct materials, inadequate training or inexperienced employees, poor supervision, excess spoilage, or other factors.

Direct Labor Variances

A direct labor flexible budget variance also can be divided into rate (price) and efficiency (quantity) variances. The procedure for additional analysis of the total direct labor variance is similar to the procedure followed for total direct materials variances. Exhibit 15–9 shows the direct labor rate variance and direct labor efficiency variance incurred when Schmidt Machinery Company manufactured 780 units of XV–1.

Exhibit 15–9	**Direct Labor Variances—Schmidt Machinery Company**	
Actual Input at Actual Cost	**Actual Input at Standard Cost**	**Standard Cost for Actual Output**
3,510 hours × $42 = $147,420	3,510 hours × $40 = $140,400	3,900 hours × $40 = $156,000

	Rate Variance (RV)	**Efficiency Variance (EV)**
Or	= ($42 − $40) × 3,510 = $7,020 U	= (3,510 − 3,900) × $40 = $15,600 F
	= $147,420 − $140,400 = $7,020 U	= $140,400 − $156,000 = $15,600 F

Flexible budget variance
= $7,020 U + $15,600 F = $8,580 F

Or

Flexible budget variance
= $147,420 − $156,000
= −$8,580 or $8,580 F

Direct Labor Rate Variance

A **direct labor rate variance** is the difference between the actual and standard hourly wage rate multiplied by the actual direct labor-hours spent in the production. Schmidt Machinery Company paid an average wage rate of $42 per hour during the period and used 3,510 direct labor-hours in production. The standard cost sheet calls for a wage rate of $40 per hour. The firm paid $2 per hour more than the standard hourly rate. With 3,510 total hours actually worked, the total direct labor rate variance is $7,020 unfavorable.

A direct labor rate variance reflects the effect on the operating income of the difference in hourly wage rates for the actual hourly wage rate paid and the standard hourly wage rate specified in the standard cost sheet. A direct labor rate variance could result from the firm's inability to pay the same hourly wage as specified in the standard cost sheet or to use the same skill-level workers as specified in the standard cost sheet.

The personnel department usually is responsible for direct labor rate variances. Production, however, could be responsible for the variance if it chooses to use employees with a different skill level than that specified in the standard cost sheet.

A **direct labor rate variance** is the difference between the actual and standard hourly wage rate multiplied by the actual direct labor-hours spent in production.

Direct Labor Efficiency Variance

The **direct labor efficiency variance** is the difference between the number of hours worked and the number of standard direct labor-hours allowed for the units manufactured multiplied by the standard hourly wage rate. Schmidt Machinery Company spent 3,510 direct labor-hours to manufacture 780 units of XV–1 during the period. The standard cost sheet allows 5 direct labor-hours for 1 unit of XV–1. The total standard hours allowed for 780 units of XV–1, therefore, is 3,900 hours (780 × 5). Thus, Schmidt used 390 fewer direct labor-hours than the total called for to manufacture 780 units. At a standard wage rate of $40 per hour, the total direct labor efficiency (quantity) variance is $15,600 favorable.

A direct labor efficiency variance reflects the effect on operating income of the difference in the number of hours spent to manufacture the output and the total standard number of hours that should have been spent for the units manufactured. Because this difference is a result of the difference in labor-hours, the resulting variance is called a direct labor *efficiency* variance.

A direct labor efficiency variance usually is the responsibility of the production department. Besides the employees' efficiency in carrying out their tasks, however, several other factors—including these—can lead to a direct labor efficiency variance:

The **direct labor efficiency variance** is the difference in the number of hours worked and the number of standard direct labor-hours allowed for the units manufactured multiplied by the standard hourly wage rate.

1. Employees or supervisors are new on the job or inadequately trained.
2. Employee skill levels are different from those specified in the standard cost sheet.
3. Batch sizes are different from the standard size.
4. Materials are different from those specified.
5. Machines or equipment are not in proper working condition.
6. Supervision is inadequate.
7. Scheduling is poor.

Identification of variances helps managers to become aware of deviations from the expected performance. To realize the full benefit of determining and reporting variances, managers should recognize variances in a timely manner.

Timing of Variance Recognition

A direct materials price variance can be identified either at the *time of purchase* or at the *time materials are issued* to production. The difference in the times of reorganizing direct materials price variances also affects the way in which direct materials are recorded in the materials control account. Early recognition of variances such as a price variance identified at purchase allows the firm to be aware early of any discrepancy between the

Exhibit 15-10	Analyzing Materials Variances When the Quantity Purchased and Quantity Used Are Different

Actual Input at Actual Unit Cost	Actual Input at Standard Unit Cost	Standard Cost for Actual Output
Number of units purchased × Actual unit cost of the materials	Number of units purchased × Standard unit cost of the materials	
	Purchase price variance (Based on purchased units)	
	Number of units of materials used × Standard unit cost of the materials	Standard number of units of the direct materials for the units of output manufactured × Standard unit cost of the materials
	Usage variance	

price paid for the purchase and the standard price. Recognizing material price variance at purchase also allows the materials inventory to be carried at the standard cost. Thus, the same materials purchased at different times with different purchase prices carry the same unit cost on the books.

If a direct materials price variance is recorded when the materials are issued to production, the direct materials inventory is carried at actual purchase prices. Deviations of actual prices from the standard may not be known until the direct materials are issued to production. In either case, the costs of direct materials in the work in process are recorded at the standard cost.

If a direct materials price variance is recognized at time of purchase, the purchase price variance is computed based on the actual quantity purchased, not the actual quantity used in the production.[3] Consequently, the quantity actually purchased is used in the price variance computation, while the number of units actually consumed in production is used to compute the usage variance, as shown in Exhibit 15–10.

The analysis of variances for direct labor costs does not need to be divided into two steps because direct labor has no inventory. The number of hours for which employees were paid is always the same as the number of hours worked in production during the period.

EFFECT OF THE NEW MANUFACTURING TECHNOLOGY

LEARNING OBJECTIVE 5▶

Assess the influence of the contemporary manufacturing environment on operational control and standard costing.

Recent advances in manufacturing concept and technology have had great impacts on manufacturing and standard costs. With the introduction of just-in-time (JIT) procedures, automation, manufacturing cells, total quality management, throughput time, and other modern manufacturing concepts and technologies, many firms have changed the focus of their cost control and management. No distinction between units purchased and units used is necessary to compute variances for direct materials for firms that maintain a minimal inventory or that use a JIT system. The quantity purchased in a period by these firms is almost the same as, if not exactly, the amount used during the period.

Furthermore, firms using JIT systems often have less interest in materials purchase price variances. These firms often purchase materials from suppliers under long-term contracts to ensure the reliability of materials deliveries and the quality of materials. The negotiated prices usually avoid short-term fluctuation. JIT firms also emphasize

---

[3] Some writers refer to a price variance computed on the quantity used in production as a *usage price variance*.

the total cost of operations, not just materials purchase costs. Factors such as quality, reliability, and availability often outweigh the purchase cost.

The arrival of new manufacturing technologies such as automation, flexible manufacturing systems, and cluster or cell manufacturing has deemphasized the importance of direct labor variances. Firms that use automated manufacturing systems similar to Hewlett-Packard Company's factory in Fort Collins, Colorado, use little or no direct labor. These firms attach little importance to labor rate and efficiency variances.

Contemporary firms emphasize zero-defect and continuous improvement in quality. The utmost concerns of these firms are to satisfy customers and provide better products than the competition. A well-managed firm is not the one with the lowest unfavorable variances or the highest favorable variances but is the one with happy customers and consistently better products.

The theory of constraints (Chapter 5) emphasizes that the focus on improving a firm's overall efficiency lies in improving throughput time from the beginning of the process through completion and delivery. While decreasing unfavorable labor efficiency variances of nonbottleneck operations might give managers satisfaction, such efforts would not have any effect on overall efficiency.

BEHAVIORAL AND IMPLEMENTATION ISSUES

A standard cost system provides guidance and criteria for operations and performance evaluations. Variances from the standard should be used strictly as inputs to gain a better understanding of the operations and to improve them; variances should never be used to find a scapegoat. Research in organizational behavior has shown that successful operations are often a result of proper rewards. The focus in using a standard cost system should be on influencing behavior through positive reinforcements and appropriate motivation. Seldom does long-term success result from penalties and punishments.

How do managers and employees determine if a standard cost system is affecting the system's success or failure? Their negative perception or motivation because of perceived unreasonable standards, secrecy in setting standards, authoritarian control procedures, poor communication, excessive pressure, inflexibility, uneven reward systems, or excessive emphasis on profits can cause a good standard cost system to fail. Managers or employees with negative perceptions can feel discouraged and adopt protective or defensive behavior or even sabotage the system. These tactics include budget padding, subtle attempts to beat the system, decreases in product and service quality, absenteeism, lackadaisical attitudes, decreased initiative, and sharing trade secrets. On the other hand, managers and other employees who have positive perceptions of a standard cost system show enthusiasm, creativity, and productivity.

The controller and supporting staff are responsible for reporting to all levels of management the results of operations and comparing the operating results with the budgeted goals including variances. The staff is composed of personnel principally concerned with service. The controller and supporting staff should not usurp line authority nor give the impression that they can do so. Staff personnel should not be directed to exercise authority over operating line personnel. Nor should the controller reprimand operating personnel for unfavorable results reflected on performance reports. Any corrective action resulting from either favorable or unfavorable results is strictly a line function. The controller is responsible for designing an effective cost control system. The line executives and supervisors, however, have direct responsibility for implementing cost control.

Not all variances should be treated the same way. The favorable efficiency variance of a *nonbottleneck* operation has little benefit to the firm. An unfavorable direct labor efficiency variance of the same operation does not affect the firm other than in the increased level of manufacturing costs. An unfavorable direct labor efficiency variance in a *bottleneck* operation, on the other hand, can lead to sizable negative

---

Factors that Made Performance Pay Work at Monsanto, DuPont, American Express, and Others

After examining practices in several companies including Monsanto, DuPont, American Express, Xel, Xaloy, GTE, and Black Box, *Business Week* concluded that these factors facilitate excellent performances

- **Setting attainable goals**
- **Setting meaningful goals**   You can neither motivate nor reward by setting targets employees can't comprehend. Complex financial measures and jargon-heavy reports mean nothing to most employees.
- **Bringing employees in**   Give employees a say in developing performance measures and listen to their advice on ways to change work systems.
- **Keeping targets moving**   Performance standards must be constantly adjusted to meet the changing needs of employees and customers. The life expectancy of a performance standard may be no more than three or four years.
- **Aiming carefully**   Know what message you want to send. Make sure the new scheme doesn't reward the wrong behavior.

Source: "Bonus Pay: Buzzword or Bonanza?" *Business Week,* November 14, 1994.

---

ripple effects on the firm's total manufacturing costs and operations. When the unfavorable efficiency variance occurs in an upstream operation that is a bottleneck, the output in all downstream operations might have to be curtailed. A series of unfavorable efficiency variances in bottleneck operations can severely cripple the firm's operation.

COST FLOWS IN GENERAL LEDGERS USING A STANDARD COST SYSTEM

LEARNING OBJECTIVE 6▶

Describe cost flows through general ledger accounts and prepare journal entries for the acquisition and use of direct materials and direct labor in a standard costing system.

Standard costing systems use the same accounts for inventory control and for recording manufacturing cost accounts that other costing systems use. Similar to actual or normal costing systems, standard costing systems have accounts such as Materials Inventory, Accrued Payroll, Factory Overhead, Work-in-Process Inventory, Finished Goods Inventory, and Cost of Goods Sold. Manufacturing costs flow through inventory and manufacturing cost accounts in ways that are similar to cost flows in an actual or normal costing system. One notable difference among these costing systems is that standard costing systems use standard costs instead of actual or normalized costs in inventory accounts.

Standard costing systems add only variance accounts. Most firms have a separate ledger account for each type of variance to identify its source(s) and to gain better operational control. Such firms record discrepancies between costs actually incurred and standard costs for the operation in variance accounts.

When a firm that uses a standard costing system purchases direct materials, it records the purchase as follows:

Debit: Materials Inventory   Total standard cost of the materials purchased
Credit: Cash or Accounts Payable   The amount the firm agreed to pay
                                                                                                    for the purchase

The discrepancy, if any, between the total standard cost and the price the firm actually paid is the *purchase price variance* for the materials. It is recorded in the Materials Purchase Price Variance account (debited for *unfavorable* and credited for *favorable* purchase price variances).

To illustrate, on October 7, Schmidt Machinery Company purchased 3,630 pounds of aluminum at $26 per pound. The term of the purchase is 1/EOM, n/180. The standard cost sheet (Exhibit 15–5) lists the cost as $25. The journal entry for the purchase is as follows:

Oct. 7 Materials Inventory (3,630 × $25)   90,750
    Materials Purchase Price Variance—Aluminum (3,630 × $1)   3,630
      Accounts Payable (3,630 × $26)   94,380
    Purchase of 3,630 pounds aluminum from Dura-Igor Corporation
    at $26 per pound. Terms 1/EOM, n/180; standard price $25 per pound.

The journal entries for issuing direct materials to manufacturing are as follows:

Debit: Work-in-Process Inventory   Standard quantity of materials that should have been used to manufacture the units of product at standard cost

Credit: Materials Inventory   Total amount of materials used at standard cost.

The difference between the amount debited and the amount credited is the *direct materials usage variance* and is recorded (debited for *unfavorable* variance and credited for *favorable* variance) in the Direct Materials Usage Variance account.

On October 9, the production department requested 3,630 pounds of aluminum for the production of 780 units of XV–1.

Work-in-Process Inventory (780 × 4 = 3,120; 3,120 × $25)   78,000
Materials Usage Variance—Aluminum (3,630 – 3,120 = 510; 510 × $25)   12,750
    Materials Inventory (3,630 × $25)   90,750
    Issued 3,630 pounds of aluminum to production for the manufacture
    of 780 units of XV–1. Standard usage is 4 pounds per unit of XV–1.

The total labor wages actually incurred to produce the 780 units is recorded in the Accrual Payroll account (credit), and the total standard direct labor wage for the units manufactured is recorded in the Work-in-Process Inventory account (debit).

Debit: Work-in-Process Inventory   Total number of standard hours for the units manufactured at the standard hourly wage rate

Credit: Accrual Payroll   Total number of hours spent to produce the units at the hourly wage rate actually incurred

The difference between the amount debited (the amount that *should have been incurred* for the units of the product manufactured) and the amount credited (the total amount of direct labor wages actually paid) can result from a difference in either the wage rate or the total number of direct labor-hours. Differences in wage rate actually paid and the standard wage rate are recorded in Direct Labor Rate Variance account. Differences in the number of total hours actually spent in production and the number of total standard hours that should have been spent are recorded in the Direct Labor Efficiency Variance account.

On October 15, Schmidt recognizes that the production department incurred 3,510 hours of direct labor at a cost of $147,420 to complete the production of 780 units of XV–1, or $42 per hour. The standard (Exhibit 15–5) calls for using 5 hours to manufacture one unit of XV–1 at a standard wage of $40 per hour.

Oct. 15 Work-in-Process Inventory (780 × 5 = 3,900; 3,900 × $40)   156,000
    Labor Rate Variance (3,510 × [$42 – $40 =] $2)   7,020
      Labor Efficiency Variance (390 × $40)   15,600
      Accrued Payroll (3,510 × $42)   147,420
    Spent 3,510 direct labor-hours to manufacture 780 units of XV–1.
    Standard cost allows 5 hours per unit of XV–1 at $40 per hour.

When production was complete, the standard cost of the units manufactured is transferred from the Work-in-Process Inventory account to the Finished Goods Inventory account at the standard total product cost.

The standard cost sheet (Exhibit 15–5) specifies that the total standard cost per unit of XV–1 is $520. These journal entries record the completion of manufacturing and transfer of 780 units of XV–1 on October 15:

Oct. 15 Finished Goods Inventory (780 × $520)   405,600
        Work-in-Process Inventory   405,600
     Completed 780 units of XV–1. Standard cost per unit: $520.

Exhibit 15–11 summarizes cost flows through ledger accounts in a standard cost system.

Exhibit 15–11   Cost Flows and Ledger Entries in a Standard Cost System

Materials Inventory

Beginning inventory at standard cost		Units issued to production × Standard price per unit	78,000 28,800
Number of units purchased × Standard price per unit	90,750 28,800		

Materials Price Variance

Unfavorable Variances	3,630 720	Favorable Variances	

Materials Usage Variance

Unfavorable Variances	12,750 2,400	Favorable Variances	

Accrued Payroll

	Actual direct labor hours spent × Actual hourly wage rate	147,420

Labor Rate Variance

Unfavorable Variances	7,020	Favorable Variances	

Labor Efficiency Variance

Unfavorable Variances		Favorable Variances	15,600

Accounts Payable

	Number of units purchased × Actual unit price	94,380 29,520

Work-in-Process Inventory

Beginning inventory at standard cost		Number of units completed × Standard cost per unit	405,600
Standard units of direct materials for the units of product manufactured × Standard direct materials unit price	90,750 31,200		
Standard direct labor hours for the units of the product manufactured × Standard hourly wage rate	156,000		

Finished Goods Inventory

Beginning inventory at standard cost		Actual unit sold × Standard cost per unit
Actual units completed × Standard cost per unit	405,600	

Cost of Goods Sold

Actual units sold × Standard cost per unit	

SUMMARY

Measures of effectiveness and efficiency help managers assess operations. Managers are interested in effectiveness so they can attain the goals set for the operations and in efficiency so they can perform operations with the fewest resources. A commonly used measure of effectiveness is the operating income variance, which is the difference in operating income for master budget and actual results.

An operation is efficient if it wastes no resources. A flexible budget can play an important role in assessing operating efficiency. Using the flexible budget for the operation attained in the period, management can separate the operating income variance into the sales volume and flexible budget variances. The sales volume variance is the difference between the amount in the master budget and in the flexible budget. It measures the effects of changes in sales units on sales, expenses, contribution margins, and operating income. The flexible budget variance is the difference between the actual operating result and the flexible budget result. It measures efficiency in carrying out the operation.

Establishing a standard requires analyzing the operations carefully. A standard can be based on an ideal or one that is currently attainable. A manufacturing operation usually has a standard cost sheet that details the standard quantity and cost for all significant manufacturing elements of the operation. A firm uses activity analysis, historical data, benchmarking, market expectation, or strategic considerations to set standards. Typical standards include those for direct materials and direct labor. By comparing the amount of direct materials and the number of direct labor-hours to the standard amount and number, a firm can identify the materials usage variance and the labor efficiency variance. Exhibit 15–12 summarizes the relationships of these variances. Used properly, these variances can be a powerful tool for controlling operations, identifying factors that might have contributed to favorable or unfavorable operating results, and evaluating performance.

Exhibit 15–12   Hierarchy of Variances

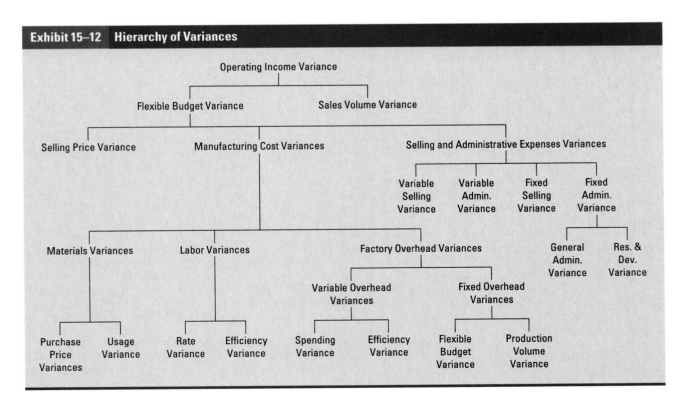

Recent advances in manufacturing technology such as JIT, flexible manufacturing, total quality management, and the theory of constraints have had a significant impact on manufacturing and standard costs including decreased importance of materials purchase price variance, labor variances, and variances in nonbottleneck operations.

Use of a standard cost should focus on influencing behavior and motivation with positive reinforcements rather than imposing penalties and punishments. Unreasonable standards, secrecy in standard setting, authoritarian control, poor communication, inflexibility, unfair performance evaluation, uneven rewards, and excessive emphasis on profits, among other factors, often cause a good standard cost system to fail.

KEY TERMS

Authoritative standard **698**

Currently attainable standard **695**

Direct labor efficiency variance **707**

Direct labor rate variance **707**

Direct materials flexible budget variance **705**

Direct materials price variance **705**

Direct materials usage variance **705**

Effective operation **688**

Efficient operation **689**

Flexible budget **691**

Flexible budget variance **692**

Ideal standard **694**

Materials usage ratio **706**

Operating income flexible budget variance **693**

Operating income variance **689**

Participative standard **698**

Sales volume variance **692**

Selling price variance **700**

Standard cost **694**

Standard cost sheet **700**

Variable expense flexible budget variance **701**

COMMENTS ON COST MANAGEMENT IN ACTION

The Kaizen Productivity Program Saves Jobs, Creates Stress

The improvement in plant productivity brought about by the bonus system and conveyor belt system at Westinghouse Air Brake Company was just what was needed to save the old Chicago plant. Without these improvements, the business would likely have gone overseas. However, the increased demand on workers' attention and effort caused stress. Workers found themselves operating two or more different machines, each of which could operate at a different speed. Workers were usually in constant motion. On the plus side, when the plant was renovated for increased productivity, the machines were located close together, in "U-shaped cells." This allowed the workers to operate the machines more efficiently, and reduced the time required to move parts around the plant.

An unfortunate side effect of the system is that workers often would set aside a half-dozen or more finished parts, in order to have some to "feed" the conveyor belt if there was a distraction or disruption of any kind. The few "extra" finished parts each worker set aside added up to a substantial amount for the plant. Plant managers frowned upon this "hidden" inventory practice and were constantly on the look-out for it.

Source: "Factory Lifts Productivity, But Staff Finds It's No Picnic," by Timothy Aeppel, *The Wall Street Journal,* May 18, 1999, p. A10.

SELF-STUDY PROBLEMS

(For solutions, please turn to the end of the chapter.)

1. Sales Volume and Flexible Budget Variances

Solid Box Fabrications manufactures boxes for workstations. The firm's standard cost sheet and the operating result of October 2002 follows:

	Standard Cost per Unit		Operating Result October 2002
Units			9,500
Sales	$50.00		$551,000
Variable costs			
Direct materials			
5 pounds at $2.4 per pound =	$12.00	48,000 pounds × $3 =	$144,000
Direct labor			
0.5 hour at $14 per hour =	7.00	4,800 hours × $16 =	76,800
Variable manufacturing overhead	2.00		19,000
Variable selling and			
administrative expenses	5.00		55,100
Total variable cost	$26.00		$294,900
Contribution margin	$24.00		$256,100
Fixed costs			
Manufacturing costs	$50,000		$ 55,000
Selling and administrative	20,000		24,000
Total fixed costs	$70,000		$ 79,000
Operating income			$177,100

In preparing the master budget for October 2002, the firm recognized that several costs on the standard cost sheet will change. The sales price will increase by 8 percent. Suppliers have notified the firm that materials prices will increase by 5 percent starting October 1. The labor contract that starts on October 1 will increase wages and benefits by 10 percent. Fixed manufacturing costs will increase $5,000 for insurance, property taxes, and salaries. Fixed selling and administrative expenses will increase as follows: $2,000 in managers' salaries, and $2,000 for advertising during October 2002. The unit sales for October 2002 are expected to be 10,000 units. Solid Box Fabrications uses JIT systems in all of its operations including materials acquisitions and product manufacturing.

Required

1. Prepare the master budget and flexible budgets for 9,500 units and 11,000 units for October 2002.

2. Compute the operating income sales volume variance, operating income flexible budget variance, selling price variance, and variable cost flexible budget variance for October 2002.

3. Determine the direct materials price variance, direct materials usage variance, direct labor rate variance, and direct labor efficiency variance.

2. Direct Materials Price and Usage Variances, Direct Labor Rate and Efficiency Variances, and Journal Entries

Chemical, Inc., has set the following standards for direct materials and direct labor for each 20-pound bag of Weed-Be-Doom:

	Per Bag
Direct materials: 25 pounds XF–2000 @ $0.08	$2.00
Direct labor: 0.05 hour @ $32	1.60

The firm manufactured 2,000,000 pounds of Weed-Be-Doom during December using 2,700,000 pounds of materials and 5,200 direct labor-hours. The firm purchased 3,000,000 lbs. of XF–2000 at $0.075 per pound and incurred a total payroll of $182,000 for direct labor during the month. The firm identifies all variances when it incurs the costs.

Required

1. Compute the price and usage variances for direct materials and the rate and efficiency variances for direct labor.
2. Prepare journal entries to record the company's data.

QUESTIONS

15–1   Tobias Company earned $5 million last year from selling 25,000 units of a special drill that silences sounds annoying dental patients. The master budget calls for sales of 30,000 units and $7.5 million in operating income. The operating income in the flexible budget for 25,000 units, however, is $4.5 million. A member of the operation review committee comments that the firm was neither efficient in its operations nor effective in attaining the operating goal. What is a possible rationale for reaching such a conclusion? Do you agree with this assessment?

15–2   Can a standard cost system be used in job order costing? In process costing?

15–3   Can an organization be effective but not efficient in its operation? Efficient but not effective?

15–4   What is the difference between a standard and a budget?

15–5   What is the difference between a master budget and a flexible budget?

15–6   Do flexible budgets adapt to changes in both inflation rate and activity?

15–7   Verbatim Company's budget for last year included $80,000 for prime costs. The total actual prime costs for the period were $72,000. Can we say that the plant manager has done a better than expected job in controlling the cost if actual production were 80 percent of the budgeted production?

15–8   Which of the following should a firm use as the standard for measuring production efficiencies: engineering standards based on ideal performance, engineering standards based on attainable performance, or recent average historical performance?

15–9   Why does management need to separate direct labor variances into rate variances and efficiency variances?

15–10 The manager of a firm is happy to receive a report that shows a favorable total materials variance of $75. Given that, the manager decides that no more action is needed. Do you agree?

15–11 Which variances would be directly affected by the relative position of a production process on a learning curve?

15–12 Will excess direct labor wages resulting from overtime premiums affect direct labor variances? Which variances?

15–13 Should management feel distressed if all variances for the quarter are unfavorable?

15–14 At the end of its fiscal year, Graham Company had several substantial variances from standard variable manufacturing costs.

Required   Which of the following scenarios is the most justifiable for the firm's allocation of the resulting variances to inventories and cost of sales?

1. Additional cost of raw materials acquired under a speculative purchase contract.

2. Equipment breakdown.

3. Overestimates of production volume for the period resulting from failure to predict an unusual decline in the market for the company's product.

4. Increased labor rates won by the union as a result of a strike.

(CMA Adapted)

15–15 Todco planned to produce 3,000 units of its single product, Teragram, during November. The standard specifications for one unit of Teragram include 6 pounds of material at $0.30 per pound. The firm uses JIT in all operations. Actual production in November was 3,100 units of Teragram. The accountant computed a $380 favorable materials purchase price variance and a $120 unfavorable materials usage variance.

Required Which of the following conclusions do these variances best support?

1. More materials were purchased than were used.

2. More materials were used than were purchased.

3. The actual cost of materials was less than the standard cost.

4. The actual usage of materials was less than the standard allowed.

5. The actual cost and usage of materials were both less than standard.

(CMA Adapted)

15–16 Why do firms using JIT systems often have little interest in materials price variances?

15–17 Identify the effects that new technologies such as JIT, flexible manufacturing systems, and TQM have on standard cost systems.

15–18 Discuss behavioral concerns in establishing and implementing a standard cost system.

15–19 At year-end, how should a firm handle immaterial variances identified?

15–20 Portfolio management is a powerful concept in finance and marketing. The marketing application of the concept is to develop and manage a balanced portfolio of products. Market share and market growth can be used to classify products for portfolio purposes, and the product classifications often are extended to the organizational units that make the product. The market share/growth classifications can be depicted as follows:

Market Growth Rate	Market Share	
	High	**Low**
High	Rising star	?
Low	Cash cow	Dog

The question mark is the classification for products that show high-growth rates but have small market shares, such as new products that are similar to their competitors. A rising star is a high-growth, high-market-share product that tends to mature into a cash cow. A cash cow is a slow-growing established product that can be milked for cash to help the question mark and introduce new products. The dog is a low-growth, low-market-share item that is a candidate for elimination or segmentation. Understanding where a product falls within this market share/growth structure is important when applying a standard cost system.

Required

1. Discuss the major advantages of using a standard cost accounting system.

2. Describe the types of information that are useful in setting standards and the conditions that must be present to support the use of standard costing.

3. Discuss the applicability or nonapplicability of using standard costing for a product classified as a (a) cash cow and (b) question mark.

(CMA Adapted)

15–21 When should journal entries recording variances be posted?

EXERCISES

15–22 **FLEXIBLE BUDGET AND VARIANCES** Schmidt Machinery Company (Exhibit 15–1) manufactured and sold 900 units for $840 each in June. The firm incurred $414,000 total variable expenses and $180,000 total fixed expenses.

Required for the Month of June,

1. Prepare the flexible budget.
2. Compute
   a. The operating income sales volume variance.
   b. The contribution margin sales volume variance.
3. Calculate
   a. The operating income flexible budget variance.
   b. The contribution margin flexible budget variance.
   c. The selling price variance.

15–23 **DIRECT MATERIALS AND DIRECT LABOR VARIANCES** Schmidt Machinery Company (Exhibit 15–6) used 3,375 pounds of aluminum in June to manufacture 900 units. The firm paid $30 per pound during the month to purchase aluminum. On June 1, the firm had 50 pounds of aluminum on hand. At the end of June, the firm only had 25 pounds of aluminum in its warehouse. The firm spent 4,200 direct labor hours in June and the average wage during the month is $42 per hour.

Required Compute for June, Schmidt Machinery Company's

1. Purchase price and usage variances for aluminum.
2. Direct labor rate and efficiency variances.

15–24 **JOURNAL ENTRY** Use the data in Exhibit 15–5. On October 7, Schmidt Machinery Company purchased 720 pounds of PVC at $41 per pound. On October 9, Schmidt's production department requested 720 pounds of PVC for the 780 units of XV–1 to be manufactured.

Required Make the necessary journal entries to record the purchase and the issuance of PVC to production.

15–25 **MATERIALS PURCHASE PRICE** Joseph Company's direct materials costs are as follows:

Standard unit price per pound	$5.00
Quantity purchased (pounds)	2,000
Total standard quantity for units manufactured (pounds)	1,600
Quantity used in production (pounds)	1,800
Materials purchase price variance—favorable	$200.00

Required Compute the following:

1. The actual purchase price per pound (rounded to the nearest penny).
2. The direct materials usage variance.

15–26 **MATERIALS PRICE VARIANCE** SMP Company has the following data from its operations for the month just completed:

Direct materials purchased	30,000 pounds
Direct materials used	28,000 pounds
Total direct materials purchased costs	$90,000
Standard price of direct materials	$3.25 per pound
Direct materials usage variance—unfavorable	$6,500

Required Compute for SMP Company the following:

1. Actual direct materials price per pound.
2. Direct materials price variance.
3. Total standard quantity of direct materials for the operation.

15–27 **MATERIALS PRICE VARIANCE** Rexon Company's direct materials costs for May follow:

Increase in direct materials inventories	2,000 pounds
Direct materials used	60,000 pounds
Cost of direct materials purchased	$220,000
Direct materials usage variance	$ 24,000
Standard quantity of direct materials allowed for May production	54,000 pounds

Required Compute for the month of May the following:

1. Standard cost per pound of the direct material.
2. Total purchases (in pounds) of direct materials during the period.
3. Direct materials price variance.

15–28 **MATERIALS VARIANCES** On June 1, Osbon Company, which has a standard costing system, had 700 gallons of direct material X in its inventory, which were purchased in May for $1.50 per gallon and carried at a standard cost of $1. The following information pertains to direct material X for the month of June:

Number of gallons purchased	1,400
Standard number of gallons allowed for production in June	1,300
Standard cost per gallon	$1.00
Actual cost per gallon in June	$1.10
Direct materials inventory, June 30	600 gallons

Required Compute the materials purchase price and usage variances for direct material X for June.

15–29 **MATERIALS PRICE AND USAGE VARIANCES** Steinberg Company had the following direct materials costs for the manufacturer of product T last month:

Actual unit purchase price	$7.50
Standard quantity allowed for the units of T produced	2,100
Decrease in direct materials inventories	100
Quantity of direct materials used in production	2,300
Standard unit price	$7.25

Required What were Steinberg's direct materials price and usage variances for March?

15–30 **MATERIALS PRICE AND USAGE VARIANCES** Bechtal Company uses a standard costing system to account for its only product. The materials standard per unit was 4 pounds at $5.10 per pound. Operating data for April follow:

Total flexible budget variance for materials	$640 unfavorable
Materials purchase	8,300 pounds
Number of finished units produced	2,000
Increase in direct materials inventory	500 pounds

Required Calculate these:

1. The materials price and usage variances for April.
2. The actual cost of direct materials per pound.

15–31 STANDARD DIRECT MATERIALS COST Agrichem manufactures Insect-Be-Gone. Each bag of the product contains 60 pounds of direct materials. Twenty-five percent of the materials evaporates during manufacturing. The budget allows the direct materials to be purchased for $2.50 a pound under terms of 2/10, n/30. The company takes all cash discounts. Determine the standard direct materials cost for one bag of Insect-Be-Gone.

15–32 MATERIALS PRICE AND USAGE VARIANCES Durable Company installs shingle roofs on houses. The standard materials cost for a type R house is $1,250, based on 1,000 shingles at $1.25 each. During April, Durable installed roofs on 20 type R houses, using 22,000 shingles at a total actual cost of $26,400. The firm maintains no inventory. What are Durable's materials price and usage variances for April?

15–33 MATERIALS USAGE VARIANCE Buckler Company manufactures desks with vinyl tops. The standard materials cost for the vinyl used per Model S desk is $27.00, based on 12 square feet of vinyl at a cost of $2.25 per square foot. A production run of 1,000 desks in March resulted in the usage of 12,600 square feet of vinyl at a cost of $2 per square foot. What was the usage variance resulting from that production run?

15–34 LABOR RATE VARIANCE Erickson Company's direct labor costs for the month of January follow:

Direct labor-hours worked	38,000
Total standard direct labor-hours to manufacture the units	40,000
Total payroll for direct labor	$570,000
Direct labor efficiency variance	$36,000

Required What is Erickson's

1. Standard hourly rate?
2. Direct labor rate variance?

15–35 STANDARD LABOR RATE AND EFFICIENCY VARIANCE Worfel's direct labor costs for the month of January follow:

Direct labor hourly rate paid	$20.00
Total standard direct labor-hours allowed	11,000
Direct labor-hours worked	10,000
Direct labor rate variance	$3,000 favorable

Required Compute these:

1. Standard direct labor rate in January.
2. Direct labor efficiency variance.

15–36 STANDARD LABOR RATE AND TOTAL HOURS Thorp Company's records for April disclosed these data relating to direct labor:

Cost incurred	$10,000
Rate variance	1,000 F
Efficiency variance	1,650 U
Direct labor-hours worked	2,000

Required Compute these for Thorp:

1. Standard direct labor-hour rate.
2. Total standard direct labor-hours for the units manufactured in April.

15–37   **LABOR EFFICIENCY VARIANCE**   Leon Company's direct labor costs for the month of January follow:

Direct labor-hours worked	20,000
Direct labor rate variance—unfavorable	$3,000
Total payroll for direct labor	$252,000
Budgeted units to manufacture	8,000
Budgeted total direct labor-hours	24,000
Units manufactured	7,000

Required   What was Leon's direct labor efficiency variance?

15–38   **LABOR RATE AND EFFICIENCY VARIANCES**   The direct labor standards for producing a unit of targo are 2 labor-hours at $10 per hour. Budgeted production for the period was 1,000 units of targo. The firm manufactured 900 units and spent $19,000 for 2,000 direct labor-hours.

Required   What are the direct labor rate and efficiency variances?

15–39   **LABOR RATE AND EFFICIENCY VARIANCES**   Zajicek Company's direct labor costs to manufacture its only product in October follow:

Standard of direct labor-hour per unit of product	1
Number of finished units produced	10,000
Standard rate per direct labor-hour	$10
Total payroll for direct labor	103,500
Actual rate per direct labor-hour	$9

Required   Determine these for October:

1. Direct labor rate variance.
2. Direct labor efficiency variance.

15–40   **LABOR RATE AND EFFICIENCY VARIANCES**   Use the following information to determine the labor rate and efficiency variances:

Standard labor cost per gallon of output at 20 gallons/hour	$1
Standard labor cost for 8,440 gallons of the actual output	$8,440
Total payroll for direct labor (410 hours at $21.00/hour)	$8,610

15–41   **ACTUAL LABOR HOURS**   Cott Company's direct labor costs follow:

Standard direct labor-hours for the work done	10,000
Standard direct labor rate per hour	$25.00
Actual direct labor rate per hour	$22.00
Direct labor efficiency variance—unfavorable	$27,000

Required   How many total direct hours were worked, rounded to the nearest hour?

15–42   **ACTUAL LABOR HOURS WORKED**   Tubbard Company uses a standard costing system. The following information pertains to direct labor for product B for the month of October:

Standard hours allowed for actual output	2,000
Direct labor rate paid per hour	$22.50
Standard labor rate per hour	$20.00
Labor efficiency variance	$4,000 U

Required   How many total direct hours were worked?

15–43 TOTAL PAYROLL   Tony Company's direct labor costs for May follow:

Standard direct labor rate	$40.00
Standard direct labor-hours	20,000
Total direct labor-hours worked	21,000
Direct labor rate variance—favorable	$63,000

Required   What is Tony's total direct labor payroll for May?

15–44 TOTAL PAYROLL   Susana Corporation's direct labor costs for the month of March follow:

Standard direct labor-hours	12,000
Direct labor-hours worked	10,500
Direct labor rate variance—favorable	$8,400
Standard direct labor rate per hour	$24.00

Required   What was Susana's total direct labor payroll for March?

15–45 STANDARD DIRECT LABOR COST PER UNIT   Saswana manufactures a product that requires three direct labor-hours per unit. Employee benefit costs are treated as direct labor costs. Data on direct labor follow:

Number of employees	25
Number of hours paid weekly per employee	40
Weekly productive hours per employee	35
Hourly wages	$30
Employee benefits	40%

Required   Determine the standard direct labor cost to manufacture one unit of the product.

15–46 ACTUAL AND STANDARD LABOR RATES   Data relating to Max Company's direct labor costs follow:

Standard direct labor-hours for the units manufactured	30,000
Direct labor-hours worked	29,000
Direct labor rate variance—favorable	$17,400
Total payroll	$696,000

Required   Compute Max Company's:

1. Actual direct labor rate.
2. Standard direct labor rate.
3. Direct labor efficiency variance.

15–47 TOTAL DIRECT MATERIALS COST IN FLEXIBLE BUDGET   RedRock Company uses flexible budgeting for cost control. It produced 10,800 units of product during March, incurring a direct materials cost of $13,000. Its master budget for the year has a direct materials cost of $180,000 for 144,000 units.

Required

1. Compute the direct materials cost in the flexible budget for March production.
2. Determine the direct materials flexible budget variance.

(CMA Adapted)

15–48 FLEXIBLE BUDGET AND DIRECT LABOR VARIANCES   Duo Co. has the following processing standards for its clerical employees:

Number of hours per 1,000 papers processed	150
Normal number of papers processed per year	1,500,000
Wage rate per 1,000 papers	$600
Total standard variable cost of processing 1,500,000 papers	$2,700,000
Fixed costs per year	$150,000

The following information pertains to the 1,200,000 papers processed during the year:

Total cost	$915,000
Labor cost	$855,000
Labor-hours	190,000

Required Compute for Duo Co. the following:

1. Expected total cost for the year to process 1,200,000 papers, assuming standard performance.
2. Labor rate variance for the year.
3. Labor efficiency variance for the year.

(CPA Adapted)

15–49 FLEXIBLE BUDGET AND VARIANCES Kermit Company's master budget calls for production and sales of 12,000 units for $48,000; variable costs of $18,000; and fixed costs of $16,000. The firm produced and sold 15,000 units and earned $25,000 operating income.

Required Determine these for Kermit:

1. The amount of operating income in the flexible budget.
2. The operating income flexible budget variance.
3. The operating income sales volume variance.

15–50 SALES VOLUME VARIANCE The following information is available for Mitchelville Products Company for the month of July:

Strategy

	Master Budget	Actual
Units	4,000	3,800
Sales revenue	$60,000	$53,200
Variable manufacturing costs	16,000	19,000
Fixed manufacturing costs	15,000	16,000
Variable selling and administrative expense	8,000	7,700
Fixed selling and administrative expense	9,000	10,000

Required

1. Compute the July sales volume variance and flexible budget variance in contribution margin and operating income.
2. Discuss implications of the variances on strategic cost management.
3. Set up an electronic spreadsheet that will allow the firm to prepare flexible budgets for activities within its relevant range of operation and prepare flexible budgets when sales are
   a. 3,800 units.
   b. 4,100 units.

(CMA Adapted)

PROBLEMS

15–51   STANDARD COSTING SYSTEM   Mark-Wright Inc. (MWI) is a specialty frozen food processor located in the midwestern states. Since its founding in 1982, MWI has enjoyed a loyal local clientele willing to pay premium prices for the high-quality frozen foods prepared from specialized recipes. In the last two years, MWI has experienced rapid sales growth in its operating region and has had many inquiries about supplying its products on a national basis. To meet this growth, MWI expanded its processing capabilities, which resulted in increased production and distribution costs. Furthermore, MWI has been encountering pricing pressure from competitors outside its normal marketing region.

Because MWI desires to continue its expansion, Jim Condon, CEO, has engaged a consulting firm to assist the company in determining its best course of action. The consulting firm concluded that, although premium pricing is sustainable in some areas, MWI must make some price concessions if sales growth is to be achieved. Also, to maintain profit margins, the company must reduce and control its costs. The consulting firm recommended using a standard costing system that would facilitate a flexible budgeting system to better accommodate the changes in demand that can be expected when serving an expanding market area.

Jim met with his management team and explained the consulting firm's recommendations. He then assigned the team the task of establishing standard costs. After discussing the situation with their respective staffs, the management team met to review the matter.

Jane Morgan, purchasing manager, noted that meeting expanded production would necessitate obtaining basic food supplies from sources other than MWI's traditional ones. This would entail increased raw materials and shipping costs and could result in supplies of lower quality. Consequently, the processing department would have to make up these increased costs if current cost levels are to be maintained or reduced.

Stan Walters, processing manager, countered that the need to accelerate processing cycles to increase production, coupled with the possibility of receiving lower-grade supplies, can be expected to result in a slip in quality and a higher product rejection rate. Under these circumstances, per-unit labor utilization cannot be maintained or reduced, and forecasting future unit labor content becomes very difficult.

Tom Lopez, production engineer, advised that failure to properly maintain and thoroughly clean the equipment at prescribed daily intervals could affect the quality and unique taste of the frozen food products. Jack Reid, vice president of sales, stated that if quality cannot be maintained, MWI cannot expect to increase sales to the levels projected.

When the management team reported these problems to Jim, he told it that if agreement could not be reached on appropriate standards, he would arrange to have the consulting firm set them, and everyone would have to live with the results.

Required

1. List for the use of a standard costing system:

   a. Its major advantages.

   b. Its disadvantages.

2. Identify those who should participate in setting standards and describe the benefits of their participation.

3. Explain the general features and characteristics associated with the introduction and operation of a standard costing system that make it an effective tool for cost control.

4. What could the consequences be if Jim Condon, CEO, has the outside consulting firm set Mark-Wright's standards?

(CMA Adapted)

15–52   STANDARD COST SHEET   Singh Company is a small manufacturer of wooden household items. Al Rivkin, corporate controller, plans to implement a standard costing system. He has information from several co-workers that will help him develop standards for Singh's products.

One product is a wooden cutting board. Each cutting board requires 1.25 board feet of lumber and 12 minutes of direct labor time to prepare and cut the lumber. The cutting boards are inspected after they are cut. Because they are made of a natural material that has imperfections, one board is normally rejected for each five boards accepted. Four rubber foot pads are attached to each good cutting board. A total of 15 minutes of direct labor time is required to attach all four foot pads and finish each cutting board. The lumber for the cutting boards costs $3 per board foot, and each foot pad costs 5 cents. Direct labor is paid at the rate of $8 per hour.

Required

1. Develop the standard cost for the direct cost components of the cutting board. For each direct cost component, the standard cost should identify these:
   a. Standard quantity.
   b. Standard rate.
   c. Standard cost per unit.
2. Identify the advantages of implementing a standard costing system.
3. Explain the role of each of the following persons in developing standards:
   a. Purchasing manager.
   b. Industrial engineer.
   c. Cost accountant.

(CMA Adapted)

15–53   STANDARD COST SHEET   ColdKing Company is a small producer of fruit-flavored frozen desserts. For many years, its products have had strong regional sales because of brand recognition; however, other companies have begun marketing similar products in the area, and price competition has become increasingly important. Janice Wakefield, the company's controller, is planning to implement a standard costing system for ColdKing and has gathered considerable information from her co-workers about production and materials requirements for ColdKing's products. Janice believes that the use of standard costing will allow the company to improve cost control, make better pricing decisions, and enhance strategic cost management.

 *Strategy*

ColdKing's most popular product is raspberry sherbet. The sherbet is produced in 10-gallon batches, each of which requires 6 quarts of good raspberries and 10 gallons of other ingredients. The fresh raspberries are sorted by hand before they enter the production process. Because of imperfections in the raspberries and normal spoilage, one quart of berries is discarded for every four accepted. The standard direct labor time for sorting to obtain one quart of acceptable raspberries is 3 minutes. The acceptable raspberries are then blended with the other ingredients; blending requires 12 minutes of direct labor time per batch. After blending, the sherbet is packaged in quart containers. Janice has gathered the following price information:

- ColdKing purchases raspberries for 80 cents per quart. All other ingredients cost 45 cents per gallon.
- Direct labor is paid at the rate of $9 per hour.
- The total cost of materials and labor required to package the sherbet is $0.38 per quart.

Required

1. Develop the standard cost for the direct cost components of a 10-gallon batch of raspberry sherbet. For each direct cost component, the standard cost should identify the following:

   a. Standard quantity.

   b. Standard rate.

   c. Standard cost per batch.

2. As part of the implementation of a standard costing system at ColdKing, Janice plans to train those responsible for maintaining the standards to use variance analysis. She is particularly concerned with the causes of unfavorable variances.

   a. Discuss the possible causes of unfavorable materials price variances, identify the individuals who should be held responsible for them, and comment on the implications of these variances on strategic cost management.

   b. Discuss the possible causes of unfavorable labor efficiency variances, identify the individuals who should be held responsible for them, and comment on the implications of these variances on strategic cost management.

(CMA Adapted)

15–54   FILL IN MISSING DATA   Ohio Valley Precision Machinery Company maintains no inventory and has these data for its fiscal year just ended:

	Actual Operating Result	Flexible Budget Variance	Flexible Budget	Sales Volume Variance	Master Budget
Units	600		a	b	800
Sales revenue	$7,200	d	c	e	$8,800
Variable cost					
Manufacturing	h	$600 F	g	$1,200 F	f
Selling and administrative	i	k	j	l	$1,600
Contribution margin	$2,400	m	n	q	p
Fixed cost	r	v	t	u	s
Operating income	$1,200	x	w	y	$1,400

Required   Find the amounts of the missing items *a* through *y* (there is no *o*).

15–55   FILL IN MISSING DATA   V-Grip Company uses the JIT system in all its operations and has these data for its fiscal year just ended:

	Actual Operating Result	Flexible Budget Variance	Flexible Budget	Sales Volume Variance	Master Budget
Units	b		a	100 F	1,500
Sales revenue	e	$1,600 U	d	c	$37,500
Variable cost					
Manufacturing	h	$1,600 U	f	g	$24,000
Selling and administrative	$4,000	i	3,200	k	j
Contribution margin	l	m	n	p	q
Fixed cost	r	u	s	v	t
Operating income	$1,000	w	$3,600	y	x

Required

1. Find the amounts of the missing items *a* through *y* (there is no *o*).

2. Compute the actual selling price per unit.

15–56   FILL IN MISSING DATA   Paul, Inc., which manufactures "dummy" dolls, misplaced some of its data. Use the following information to replace the lost data:

	Actual	*a*	Flexible Budget	*b*	Static Budget
Units sold	900	*c*	*d*	*e*	825
Revenues	$52,600	$1,300 F	*f*	*g*	*h*
Variable costs	*i*	*k*	*j*	*l*	$23,100
Fixed costs	$10,350	*n*	*m*	*p*	$11,425
Operating income	$22,175	*q*	*r*	*s*	$12,500

Required   Identify or find the missing items *a* through *s* (there is no *o*).

15–57   FILL IN MISSING DATA   Pokeman Bunch, Inc., manufactures PokeMonster figures and has the following data from its operation for the year just completed:

	Actual Results	Flexible Budget Variance	Flexible Budget	Sales Volume Variance	Master Budget
Units sold	1,200	*a*	*b*	*c*	1,000
Revenues	$69,600	*e*	*d*	*f*	$60,000
Variable costs	*j*	*i*	*g*	*h*	$40,000
Contribution margin	*k*	$11,200 U	*l*	*m*	*n*
Fixed costs	*p*	*s*	*r*	*q*	$5,000
Operating income	$5,800	*w*	*v*	*u*	*t*

Required   Find the missing items *a* through *w* (there is no *o*).

15–58   BASIC ANALYSIS OF DIRECT LABOR VARIANCES   Day-Mold was founded several years ago by two designers who developed several popular lines of living room, dining room, and bedroom furniture for other companies. The designers believed that their design for dinette sets could be standardized and would sell well. They formed their own company and soon had all the orders they could handle in their small plant in Dayton, Ohio.

From the beginning, the firm was successful. The owners bought a microcomputer and software to produce financial statements. They thought all information they needed was included in these statements.

Recently, however, the employees have been requesting raises. The owners wonder how to evaluate these requests. At the suggestion of Day-Mold's CPA, who prepares the tax return, the owners have hired a CMA as a consultant to implement a standard costing system. The consultant believes that the calculation of variances will aid management in setting responsibility for labor performance.

The supervisors believe that under normal conditions, the dinette set can be assembled with 5 hours of direct labor at a cost of $20 per hour. The consultant has assembled labor cost information for the most recent month and would like your advice in calculating direct labor variances.

During the month, the firm paid $127,600 direct labor wages for 5,800 hours. The factory produced 1,200 dinette sets during the month.

Required

1. Compute for management's consideration direct labor variances.

2. Provide management with reasons for the variances.

(CMA Adapted)

15–59 **WORKING BACKWARD** Sheldon Company manufactures only one product and uses a standard costing system. During the past month, the manufacturing operations had the following direct labor variances:

Direct labor rate variance	$30,000 F
Direct labor efficiency variance	50,000 U

The firm allows 5 standard direct labor-hours per unit; its standard direct labor-hour rate is $50. During the month, Sheldon spent 25 percent more in direct labor-hours than in the total standard hours allowed for the number of units manufactured.

Required Determine the following for Sheldon Company:
1. The total standard hours allowed for the number of units manufactured.
2. The total direct labor-hours worked.
3. The actual direct labor-hour wage rate.
4. The number of units manufactured.

15–60 **ALL VARIANCES** Funtime Inc. manufactures video game machines. Market saturation and technological innovations caused pricing pressures that resulted in declining profits. To stem the slide in profits until new products can be introduced, top management turned its attention to both manufacturing economics and increased production. To realize these objectives, management developed an incentive program to reward production managers who contribute to an increase in the number of units produced and a decrease in costs.

The production managers responded to the pressure of improving manufacturing in several ways that increased the number of completed units beyond normal production levels. The assembly group puts together video game machines that require parts from both the printed circuit boards (PCB) and the reading heads (RH) groups. To attain increased production levels, the PCB and RH groups began rejecting parts that would have previously been tested and modified to meet manufacturing standards. Preventive maintenance on machines used to produce these parts has been postponed; only emergency repair work is being performed to keep production lines moving. The maintenance department is concerned about serious breakdowns and unsafe operating conditions.

The more aggressive assembly group production supervisors pressured maintenance personnel to attend to their machines rather than those of other groups. This resulted in machine downtime in the PCB and RH groups that, when coupled with demands for accelerated parts delivery by the assembly group, led to more frequent rejection of parts and increased friction among departments.

Funtime operates under a standard costing system. The standard costs for video game machines are as follows:

Cost Item	Standard Cost per Unit Quantity	Cost	Total
Direct materials			
Housing unit	1.0	$20	$ 20
Printed circuit boards	2.0	15	30
Reading heads	4.0	10	40
Direct labor			
Assembly group	2.0 hours	10	20
PCB group	1.0 hour	11	11
RH group	1.5 hours	12	18
Total standard cost per unit			$139

Funtime prepares monthly performance reports based on standard costs. The following is the contribution report for May 2001 when production and sales both reached 2,200 units.

FUNTIME INC.
Contribution Report
For the Month of May 2001

	Budget	Actual	Variance	
Units	2,000	2,200	200	F
Revenue	$400,000	$396,000	$4,000	U
Variable costs				
Direct materials	$180,000	$220,400	$40,400	U
Direct labor	98,000	112,260	14,260	U
Total variable costs	278,000	332,660	54,660	U
Contribution margin	$122,000	$63,340	$58,660	U

Funtime's top management was surprised by the unfavorable contribution to overall corporation profits in spite of the increased sales in May. Jack Rath, the firm's cost accountant, was asked to identify and report on the reasons for the unfavorable contribution results as well as the individuals or groups responsible for them. After his review, Jack prepared the following usage report:

FUNTIME INC.
Usage Report
For the Month of May 2001

Cost Item	Quantity	Actual Cost
Direct materials		
Housing units	2,200 units	$44,000
Printed circuit boards	4,700 units	75,200
Reading heads	9,200 units	101,200
Direct labor		
Assembly	3,900 hours	31,200
Printed circuit boards	2,400 hours	31,060
Reading heads	3,500 hours	50,000
Total variable cost		$332,660

Jack reported that the PCB and RH groups supported the increased production levels but experienced abnormal machine downtime, causing idle time that required the use of overtime to keep up with the accelerated demand for parts. This overtime was charged to direct labor. He also reported that the production managers of these two groups resorted to parts rejections, as opposed to testing and modifying them following former procedures. Jack determined that the assembly group met management's objectives by increasing production while utilizing fewer than standard hours.

Required

1. Calculate these six variances:
   a. Direct material price variance.
   b. Direct material quantity variance.
   c. Direct labor efficiency variance.
   d. Direct labor spending variance.
   e. Selling price variance.
   f. Contribution margin volume variance.

2. Explain the $58,660 unfavorable variance between budgeted and actual contribution margin during May 2001.

3. Identify and briefly explain the behavioral factors that could promote friction among the production managers and between them and the maintenance manager.

4. Evaluate Jack Rath's analysis of the unfavorable contribution results in terms of its completeness and its effect on the behavior of the production groups.

(CMA Adapted)

Strategy

15–61 CHANGES OF STANDARDS NuLathe Co. produces a turbo engine component for jet aircraft manufacturers. It has used a standard costing system for years with good results.

Unfortunately, NuLathe recently experienced production problems. The source for its direct materials went out of business. The new source produces similar but higher quality materials. The price per pound from the old source averaged $7.00; the price from the new source is $7.77. The use of the new materials results in a reduction in scrap that lowers the actual consumption of direct materials from 1.25 to 1.00 pounds per unit. In addition, the direct labor decreased from 24 to 22 minutes per unit because of less scrap labor and machine setup time.

The direct materials problem occurred when labor negotiations resulted in an increase of more than 14 percent in hourly direct labor costs. The average rate rose from $12.60 per hour to $14.40 per hour. Production of the main product requires a high level of skilled labor. Because of a continuing shortage in that skill area, NuLathe had to sign an interim wage agreement.

NuLathe began using the new direct materials on April 1 of this year, the same day the new labor agreement went into effect. The firm had been using standards set at the beginning of the calendar year. The direct materials and direct labor standards for the turbo engine are as follows:

Direct materials 1.2 lbs @ $6.80/lb.	$ 8.16
Direct labor 20 min. @ $12.30 DLH	4.10
Standard prime cost per unit	$12.26

Howard Foster, cost accounting supervisor, had been examining the following performance report that he had prepared at the close of business on April 30. Jane Keene, assistant controller, came into Howard's office. He said, "Jane, look at this performance report. Direct materials price increased 11 percent and the labor rate increased over 14 percent during April. I expected larger variances, but prime costs decreased over 5 percent from the $13.79 we experienced during the first quarter of this year. The proper message just isn't coming through."

"This has been an unusual period," Jane said. "With the unforeseen changes, perhaps we should revise our standards based on current conditions and start over."

Howard replied, "I think we can retain the current standards but expand the variance analysis. We could calculate variances for the specific changes that have occurred to direct materials and direct labor before we calculate the normal price and quantity variances. What I really think would be useful to management right now is to determine the impact the changes in direct labor had in reducing our prime costs per unit from $13.79 in the first quarter to $13.05 in April—a reduction of $0.74."

NULATHE CO.
Analysis of Unit Prime Costs
Standard Cost Variance Analysis for April

	Standard	Price Variance	Quantity Variance	Actual
Direct materials	$6.8 × 1.2 = $8.16	($7.77 − $6.80) × 1.0 = $0.97 U	(1.0 − 1.2) × $6.8 = $1.36 F	$7.77 × 1.0 = $7.77
Direct labor	$12.3 × 0.33 = $4.10	($14.4 − $12.3) × 22/60 = $0.77 U	(22/60 − 20/60) × $12.30 = $0.41 U	$14.4 × 22/60 = $5.28
	$12.26			$13.05

Comparison of Actual Costs

	First Quarter Costs	April Costs	Percentage Increase (Decrease)
Direct materials	$ 8.75	$ 7.77	(11.2)%
Direct labor	5.04	5.28	4.8
	$13.79	$13.05	(5.4)

Required

1. Discuss the advantages of immediately revising the standards and retaining the current standards and expanding the analysis of variances.

2. Prepare an analysis that reflects the impact of the new direct materials supplier and the new labor contract on reducing NuLathe Co.'s costs per unit from $13.79 in the first quarter to $13.05 in April. This analysis should be in sufficient detail to identify the changes due to the direct materials price, the direct labor rate, the effect of direct materials quality on direct materials usage, and the effect of direct materials quality on direct labor usage. The analysis should show the changes in costs per unit due to the following:

   a. Use of the direct materials from new suppliers.

   b. The new labor contract.

(CMA Adapted)

15–62 **STANDARD COST IN PROCESS COSTING; ALL VARIANCES, AND JOURNAL ENTRIES**   Dash Company adopted a standard costing system several years ago. The standard costs for the prime costs of its single product are

Material	(8 kilograms × $5.00/kg)	$40.00
Labor	(6 hours × $8.20/hr.)	$49.20

All materials are issued at the beginning of processing. These operating data were taken from the records for November:

In-process beginning inventory	none
In-process ending inventory	800 units, 75 percent complete as to labor
Units completed	5,600 units
Budgeted output	6,000 units
Purchases of materials	50,000 kilograms
Total actual labor costs	$300,760
Actual hours of labor	36,500 hours
Materials usage variance	$1,500 unfavorable
Total materials variance	$750 unfavorable

Required

1. Compute for November:
   a. The labor efficiency variance.
   b. The labor rate variance.

    c. The actual number of kilograms of material used in the production process during the month.

    d. The actual price paid per kilogram of material during the month.

    e. The total amounts of material and labor cost transferred to the finished goods account.

    f. The total amount of material and labor cost in the ending balance of work-in-process inventory at the end of November.

  2. Prepare journal entries to record all transactions including the variances in requirement 1.

(CMA Adapted)

15–63 JOINT DIRECT MATERIALS VARIANCES Benderboard produces corrugated board containers that the nearby wine industry uses to package wine in bulk. Benderboard buys kraft paper by the ton, converts it to heavy-duty paperboard on its corrugator, and then cuts and glues it into folding boxes. The boxes are opened and filled with a plastic liner and then with the wine.

    Many other corrugated board converters are in the area, and competition is strong. Therefore, Benderboard is eager to keep its costs under control. The firm has used a standard cost system for several years. Responsibility for variances has been established. For example, the purchasing agent has been charged with the raw materials price variance, and the general supervisor has answered for the raw materials usage variance.

    Recently, the industrial engineer and the accountant participated in a workshop sponsored by the Institute of Management Accountants at which there was some discussion of variance analysis. They noted that the workshop proposed that the responsibility for some variances was properly dual. The accountant and engineer reviewed their system and were not sure how to adapt the new information to it.

    The firm has the following standards for its raw materials:

> Standard direct raw materials per gross of finished boxes at $4\frac{1}{2}$ tons of kraft paper at $10 per ton = $45.00

    During May, the accountant assembled the following data about raw materials:

> Finished product: 5,000 gross of boxes
>
> Actual cost of raw materials during month: $300,000 (25,000 tons at $12 per ton)
>
> Direct raw materials put into production (used): 25,000 tons
>
> Benderboard began and finished the month of May with no inventory.

Required Determine the following for Benderboard:

  1. Direct materials price variance.

  2. Direct materials efficiency (usage) variance.

  3. Direct materials joint variance.

(CMA Adapted)

Service

15–64 FLEXIBLE BUDGET AND VARIANCE Phoenix Management helps rental property owners find renters and charges the owners one-half of the first month's rent for this service. For August 2002, Phoenix expects to find renters for 100 apartments with an average first month's rent of $700. Budgeted cost data per tenant application for 2002 follow:

- Professional labor: 1.5 hours at a rate of $20 per hour.
- Credit checks: $50.

Phoenix expects other costs, including a lease payment for the building, secretarial help, and utilities, to be $3,000 per month. On average, Phoenix is successful in placing one tenant for every three applicants.

Actual rental applications in August 2002 were 270. Phoenix paid $9,500 for 400 hours of professional labor. Credit checks went up to $55 per application. Other support costs for August 2002 were $3,600. The average first month rentals for August 2002 were $800 per apartment unit for 90 units.

Required

1. Compute the amount of operating income in August 2002 attributable to flexible budget and sales volume variances.

2. Determine the professional labor rate and efficiency variances for August 2002.

3. What factors should Phoenix consider in evaluating the effectiveness of professional labor?

15–65   ACQUISITION COSTS   Amy Booker is the newly appointed manager of the consumer electronics division of Price Mart, which is among the largest retailers of consumer goods in several U.S. states and in Canada and Mexico. Amy has just come back from a tour of the division's suppliers in several countries including several potential ones in emerging countries.

Ethics

International

Amy is pondering using companies in emerging countries as suppliers for some of Price Mart's most popular electronic products. Switching to these suppliers will greatly enhance the firm's competitive position. By changing, the firm can reduce the purchase cost of a personal cassette player, for example, from $12 to $8. The firm's standard acquisition cost for a cassette player is $11 per unit. Amy's predecessor tried for more than two years and could never meet the standard.

Price Mart relies heavily on data from its standard costing system in performance evaluations. Amy knows that she could become CEO of the company in two years if she performs well.

Two companies, Free Enterprise and Continental Electronic, have agreed to sell up to 1 million personal cassette players at $8, F.O.B. shipping point. Amy, however, is somewhat uncomfortable in doing business with both companies. In its recent annual report, Amnesty International described most of Free Enterprise's workers as prisoners. Continental Electronic is a state-owned company whose president demands as a sales term that an additional 1 percent be deposited in a "scholarship" fund account he has set up at a small bank in New York City.

Required

1. What variances might be reported if Amy purchases personal cassette players from either of these two companies?

2. What ethical issues do Amy and Price Mart face in preparing variance reports?

15–66   PRICE VARIANCE   Applied Materials Science (AMS) purchases its materials from several countries. As part of its cost control program, AMS uses a standard cost system for all aspects of its operations including materials purchases. The standard cost for each material is established at the beginning of the fiscal year and is not revised until the beginning of the next fiscal year.

International

Pat Butch, the purchasing manager, is happy with the result of the year just ended. He believes that the purchase price variance for the year will be favorable and is very confident that his department has at least met the standard prices. The preliminary report from the controller's office confirms his jubilation. This is a portion of the preliminary report:

Total quantity purchased	36,000 kilograms
Average price per kilogram	$50
Standard price per kilogram	$60
Budgeted quantity per quarter	4,000 kilograms

In the fourth quarter, the purchasing department increased purchases from the budgeted normal volume of 4,000 to 24,000 kilograms as a result of the firm's success in a fiercely competitive bidding. The substantial increase in the volume to be purchased forced the purchasing department to search for alternative suppliers. After frantic searches, it found suppliers in several foreign countries that could meet the firm's needs and could provide materials with higher quality than that of AMS's regular suppliers. The purchasing department, however, was very reluctant to make the purchase because the negotiated price was $76 per kilogram including shipping and import duty.

The actual cost of the purchases, however, was much lower because of currency devaluations before deliveries began, which was a result of the financial turmoil of several countries in the region.

Patricia Rice, the controller, does not share the purchasing department's euphoria. She is fully aware of the following quarterly purchases:

	First Quarter	Second Quarter	Third Quarter	Fourth Quarter
Quantity	4,000	4,000	4,000	24,000
Purchase price (per kilogram)	$68	$69	$73	

Required

1. Calculate price variances for the fourth quarter and for the year.
2. Evaluate the purchasing department's performance.

SOLUTIONS TO SELF-STUDY PROBLEMS

1. Sales Volumes and Flexible Budget Variances

1. Master and flexible budgets

	Master Budget	Flexible Budget	
Units	10,000	9,500	11,000
Sales	$540,000	$513,000	$594,000
Variable costs			
Direct materials	$126,000	$119,700	$138,600
Direct labor	77,000	73,150	84,700
Variable manufacturing overheads	20,000	19,000	22,000
Variable selling and administrative expenses	50,000	47,500	55,000
Total variable cost	$273,000	$259,350	$300,300
Contribution margin	$267,000	$253,650	$293,700
Fixed costs			
Manufacturing costs	$ 55,000	$ 55,000	$ 55,000
Selling and administrative	24,000	24,000	24,000
Total fixed costs	$ 79,000	$ 79,000	$ 79,000
Operating income	$188,000	$174,650	$214,700

2. Operating income sales volume variance, operating income flexible budget variance, selling price variance, and variable cost flexible budget variance.

Operating income sales volume variance:
$174,650 − 188,000 = $13,350 Unfavorable

Operating income flexible budget variance:
$177,100 − $174,650 = $2,450 Favorable

Selling price variance = $551,000 − 513,000 = $38,000 Favorable

Variable cost flexible budget variance:
$294,900 − $259,350 = $35,550 Unfavorable

3. **Direct materials price variance, direct materials usage variance, direct labor
    rate variance, and direct labor efficiency variance**

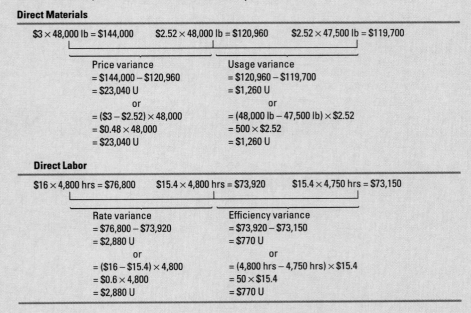

Direct Materials

| $3 × 48,000 lb = $144,000 | $2.52 × 48,000 lb = $120,960 | $2.52 × 47,500 lb = $119,700 |

Price variance
= $144,000 − $120,960
= $23,040 U
  or
= ($3 − $2.52) × 48,000
= $0.48 × 48,000
= $23,040 U

Usage variance
= $120,960 − $119,700
= $1,260 U
  or
= (48,000 lb − 47,500 lb) × $2.52
= 500 × $2.52
= $1,260 U

Direct Labor

| $16 × 4,800 hrs = $76,800 | $15.4 × 4,800 hrs = $73,920 | $15.4 × 4,750 hrs = $73,150 |

Rate variance
= $76,800 − $73,920
= $2,880 U
  or
= ($16 − $15.4) × 4,800
= $0.6 × 4,800
= $2,880 U

Efficiency variance
= $73,920 − $73,150
= $770 U
  or
= (4,800 hrs − 4,750 hrs) × $15.4
= 50 × $15.4
= $770 U

2. Direct Materials Price and Usage Variances, Direct Labor Rate and Efficiency Variances, and Journal Entries

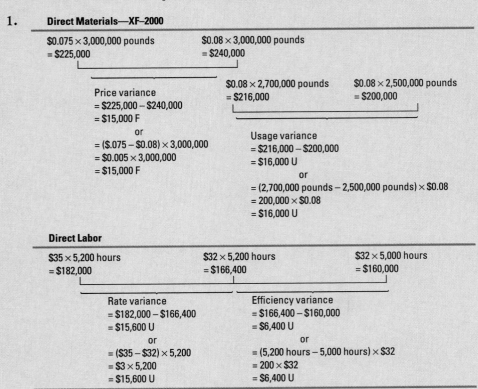

1. **Direct Materials—XF–2000**

$0.075 × 3,000,000 pounds
= $225,000

$0.08 × 3,000,000 pounds
= $240,000

Price variance
= $225,000 − $240,000
= $15,000 F
  or
= ($.075 − $0.08) × 3,000,000
= $0.005 × 3,000,000
= $15,000 F

$0.08 × 2,700,000 pounds
= $216,000

$0.08 × 2,500,000 pounds
= $200,000

Usage variance
= $216,000 − $200,000
= $16,000 U
  or
= (2,700,000 pounds − 2,500,000 pounds) × $0.08
= 200,000 × $0.08
= $16,000 U

Direct Labor

$35 × 5,200 hours
= $182,000

$32 × 5,200 hours
= $166,400

$32 × 5,000 hours
= $160,000

Rate variance
= $182,000 − $166,400
= $15,600 U
  or
= ($35 − $32) × 5,200
= $3 × 5,200
= $15,600 U

Efficiency variance
= $166,400 − $160,000
= $6,400 U
  or
= (5,200 hours − 5,000 hours) × $32
= 200 × $32
= $6,400 U

2.

Materials Inventory (3,000,000 × 0.08)	240,000	
Materials Purchase Price Variance (3,000,000 × 0.005)		15,000
Accounts Payable (3,000,000 × $0.075)		225,000
Purchase 3,000,000 pounds of XF–2000 at 0.075/per pound from Johnson Chemical Suppliers.		
Work-in-Process Inventory (0.08 × 2,500,000)	200,000	
Materials Usage Variance (200,000 × 0.08)	16,000	
Materials Inventory (2,700,000 × 0.08)		216,000
Issued 2,700,000 pounds of XF–2000 for the production of 100,000 bags of Weed-Be-Doom.		
Work-in-Process Inventory (5,000 × 32)	160,000	
Labor Rate Variance (5,200 × 3)	15,600	
Labor Efficiency Variance (200 × 32)	6,400	
Accrued Payroll (5,200 × 35)		182,000
Direct labor wages for the manufacturing of 100,000 bags of Weed-Be-Doom for 5,200 hours at $35 per hour.		

Standard Costing 16

Factory Overhead

After studying this chapter, you should be able to . . .

1   Establish proper standard costs for variable overhead

2   Calculate and interpret a variable overhead flexible budget variance, a spending variance, and an efficiency variance

3   Determine the total standard fixed factory overhead for an operation and the standard fixed factory overhead application rate

4   Compute and interpret the fixed factory overhead total variance, spending (budget) variance, production volume variance, and overapplied or underapplied fixed factory overhead

5   Use two-variance or three-variance procedures to analyze and interpret factory overhead variances

6   Dispose of variances through the financial accounting system

7   Apply a standard cost system to service organizations

8   Describe the effects of recent advances in new manufacturing technologies and rapid changes in operating environments on standard costing systems, and adapt a standard costing system to these changing environments

9   Determine whether to investigate variances

AP/Wide World Photos.

"The third quarter was a difficult period for United. Revenue performance suffered significantly from the operational disruptions we experienced throughout the quarter," James Goodwin, United Airlines chairman and chief executive, said in a recent statement.[1] United (UAL) suffered from thousands of labor and weather-related flight cancellations and delays during the third quarter of 2000 while the airline negotiated a labor contract with its pilots. The earnings per share for the quarter decreased from a profit of $2.89 the previous year to a loss of $1.29.

UAL's operating results experienced this drastic change although the decrease in traffic was only a small percentage of total traffic during the third quarter of 2000. As it is for other companies with high fixed costs, volume is a critical success factor for UAL. Fluctuations in traffic volume at UAL often explain the bulk of changes in operating results. UAL constantly monitors volume variance or passenger-miles variance, which measures the effect that deviations in actual volume (passenger miles) from the budget or planned level have on operation results. The goal to have minimum disruptions to planned operations and to achieve or exceed the expected operation level leads airlines to constantly seek to get that last passenger on board through price restructuring or other maneuvers.

Firms in capital-intensive industries have high fixed costs. These firms often experience wide variations in operating results when the level of operation fluctuates. As a result, management of firms with high fixed costs closely monitors volume variances. This chapter examines production volume and other overhead-related variances that organizations use to monitor operations to gain better control and to improve operating results.

> A man should never be ashamed to own that he has been in the wrong,
> which is but saying in other words, that he is wiser today than yesterday.
>
> JONATHAN SWIFT

Although reporting a variance in a standard costing system is not analogous to saying that something is wrong in the operation, it is true that the most important function of a standard costing system is to help the firm attain a better operating result. In Chapter 15, we discussed the basic concepts of a standard costing system, its applications to direct materials and direct labor, and the recording of standard costs. Building on that material, we examine the application of the standard costing system to variable and fixed overhead. In addition, we examine further the effects that recent advances in manufacturing technologies and rapid changes in operating environments have had on the use of the standard cost system.

STANDARD COSTS FOR FACTORY OVERHEAD

A firm typically has both variable and fixed factory overhead costs. Variable factory overhead costs are for energy, indirect materials, indirect labor, equipment repair, and maintenance. A manufacturing operation can have hundreds of different types of

◀ LEARNING OBJECTIVE 1

Establish proper standard costs for variable factory overhead.

---

[1] "UAL to Post Loss to 3rd Period, Probably for 4th," *The Wall Street Journal,* October 2, 2000, p. A12.

variable factory overhead. As with direct materials or direct labor costs, the amount of variable factory overhead varies with the activity of the firm, and the procedure for analyzing variable factory overhead variances is similar to the procedures for analyzing direct materials or direct labor variances.

Fixed factory overhead costs include salaries for factory managers and plant security guards, depreciation expenses for equipment and factory buildings, and insurance and property taxes for factory buildings and equipment. Because fixed factory overhead has a different cost behavior pattern than variable factory overhead, the procedure for analyzing each is different.

Standard Variable Factory Overhead

Uses of a standard costing system for variable factory overhead include establishing standard variable factory overhead costs, using the standard to monitor and control variable factory overhead costs during operations, and assessing operations based on the standard.

Steps in Establishing the Standard Cost for Variable Factory Overhead

Establishing the standard variable factory overhead cost for an operation involves four steps:

1. Determining the behavioral patterns of variable factory overhead costs.
2. Selecting one or more appropriate activity measures for applying variable factory overhead to cost objects such as products, services, or divisions.
3. Ascertaining the intended level of operation and estimating the total variable factory overhead and the total amount of the selected activity measure.
4. Computing the standard variable factory overhead rate.

Step 1: Determining the Behavioral Patterns of Variable Factory Overhead A manufacturing process often has hundreds of variable factory overhead items. Most variable factory overhead is in small amounts. Although the amount of variable factory overhead changes as the firm's activity changes, not all variable factory overhead items vary at the same rates or with the same activity. For example, the amount of sandpaper that a furniture manufacturer uses will vary primarily with the number of pieces of furniture it manufactured during a period. The amount of oil used for equipment in the factory can be a step function of the units manufactured during the period. If, say, a piece of equipment needs 1 gallon of fresh oil for every 5,000 units, the change in oil cost occurs in discrete steps rather than in direct proportion to the units produced, as it does for direct materials. Exhibit 16–1 illustrates one such overhead pattern. Other variable factory overhead items can have widely divergent variation rates and patterns. The amount of different variable factory overhead also often varies with different manufacturing activities.

Changes in some variable factory overhead costs, however, are not due entirely to changes in manufacturing activity. Some overhead costs change as a result of management decisions. Setup cost is an example of these costs. The manufacture of 10,000 units, for example, might have a total setup cost of $5,000 if the 10,000 units are manufactured in one batch. The setup cost increases to, say, $9,800 if the firm manufactures the 10,000 units in two batches, and to $14,000 for three batches.

In general, the standard variable factory overhead for a manufacturing operation is a function of the number of units manufactured and possibly other activities of the manufacturing processes. The first step in determining standard costs for variable factory overhead is to understand cost behavioral patterns of variable factory overhead costs. Because a number of different activities influence variable factory overhead costs, standard costs for variable overhead should be based on a careful selection of the appropriate activity measures. These activity measures can be volume based or activity based.

Exhibit 16–1	Amount of Oil Needed for a Lathe Machine

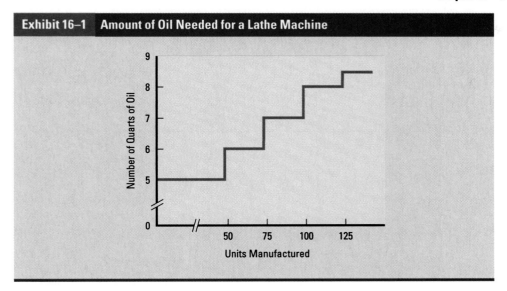

Step 2: Selecting the Activity Measures to Apply Variable Factory Overhead An operation usually has a vast number of variable factory overheads involving many usage patterns. Finding a single activity measure that changes in the same proportion with all the variable factory overhead of an operation is an impossible task. One solution is to use a different activity measure for each variable item that has a different use pattern. Such a solution, however, might not be justifiable in view of its implementation cost.

Many firms use a single activity measure, such as direct labor-hours or direct labor cost, as the activity measure for applying variable factory overhead. This practice is satisfactory so long as the total variable factory overhead is small or it relates to the selected activity measure. The increasing importance of factory overhead and the decreasing amount of direct labor-hours in many operations in recent years, however, have led many firms to reexamine this conventional practice. Their efforts to find more appropriate activity measures have led to increased use of activity-related factory overhead measures.

An activity-based cost measure applies factory overhead to products or services according to the activity level of manufacturing operations. Using activity-based factory overhead cost measures requires identifying activities that cause factory overhead costs to change. Items that change as a result of similar activities are grouped together.

Cooper identifies activities that change the amount of factory overhead as unit-based, batch-based, product-based, and facility-based factory overhead.[2] Unit-based activity measures include machine-hours, direct labor-hours, and units of materials. Batch-based activity measures include the number of times materials and parts are moved during manufacturing, the number of setups, and the number of times that materials and parts are received and inspected. Product-based activity measures include the number of products, number of processes, and number of schedule changes. Facility-based activity measures primarily relate to the size of operations, not production activities.[3]

For simplicity of illustration, the early part of this chapter uses a single activity measure, direct labor-hour. A later example uses multiple activity measures for variable factory overhead. Exhibit 16–2 is the standard cost sheet of Schmidt Machinery

---

[2]   Robin Cooper, "Cost Classification in Unit-Based and Activity-Based Manufacturing Cost Systems," *Journal of Cost Management for the Manufacturing Industry,* Fall 1990, pp. 4–14.

[3]   Robert D. McIlhattan, "How Cost Management Systems Can Support the JIT Philosophy," *Management Accounting,* September 1987, pp. 20–26.

Exhibit 16–2 Standard Cost Sheet

SCHMIDT MACHINERY COMPANY
Standard Cost Sheet

Product Number XV–1

Description	Quantity	Unit Cost	Subtotal	Total
Direct materials				
Aluminum	4 pounds	$25	$100	
PVC	1 pound	40	40	$140
Direct labor	5 hours	40		200
Factory overhead (based on 5,000 direct labor-hours)				
Variable	5 hours	12	60	
Fixed	5 hours	24	120	180
Standard Cost per Unit				$520

Company originally presented as Exhibit 15–5. This standard cost sheet shows that the firm applies variable factory overhead at the rate of $12 per direct labor-hour.

Step 3: Ascertaining the Level of Operation and Estimating the Total Variable Factory Overhead and the Total Amount of the Selected Activity Measure Activity measures for different variable factory overhead items can be diverse. Furthermore, these activity measures might not vary proportionately with changes in operating levels. A firm thus must determine the level of its operation and estimate the total variable factory overhead and the total amount of the selected activity measure at that level of operation before determining the standard variable factory overhead rate.

Schmidt plans to manufacture 1,000 units. At this level of operation, the accountant estimates its total variable factory overhead to be $60,000 and the total amount of the selected activity measure for variable factory overheads, direct labor-hours, to be 5,000 hours.

Step 4: Computing the Standard Variable Factory Overhead Rate The standard variable factory overhead rate is determined by dividing the amount of the selected activity measure into the estimated total variable factory overhead.[4] Schmidt's accountant determines its standard variable factory overhead rate by dividing the total variable factory overhead by the 5,000 direct labor-hours to arrive at the standard variable factory overhead rate of $12 per direct labor-hour.

Exhibit 16–3 summarizes the steps for determining the standard variable factory overhead rate for an operation.

LEARNING OBJECTIVE 2▶

Calculate and interpret a variable factory overhead flexible budget variance, a spending variance, and an efficiency variance.

Analyzing Variable Factory Overhead

To analyze variable factory overhead, management must first determine the total variable factory overhead variance.

Determining the Total Variable Factory Overhead Variance

The **total variable factory overhead variance** is the difference between total actual variable factory overhead incurred and total standard variable factory overhead for the output of the period.

The **total variable factory overhead variance** of a period is the difference between the total variable factory overhead incurred and the total standard variable factory overhead for the output (manufactured) of the period, which is also the flexible budget amount

---

4 An alternative procedure is to use the multiple regression analysis procedure discussed in Chapter 4 to determine the standard variable factory overhead rates. This permits the use of multiple activity measures such as one that includes machine-hours, labor-hours, number of setups, and so forth.

Exhibit 16–3	Steps in Determining the Standard Variable Factory Overhead Rate

Step	Example
1. Determine the behavioral patterns of variable factory overhead.	Management must understand cost behavior patterns.
2. Select the activity measure for applying total variable factory overhead to cost objects.	The firm chose to use direct labor-hours as the basis for determining the amount of variable factory overhead for cost objects and estimated that the total direct labor to manufacture 1,000 units requires 5,000 direct labor-hours.
3. Ascertain the intended level of operation and estimate the total variable factory overhead and the total amount of the selected activity.	The management accountant estimated that the total variable factory overhead to manufacture 1,000 units is $60,000.
4. Compute the standard variable factory overhead rate.	Divide the total variable factory overhead identified in step 3 ($60,000) by the number of direct labor-hours in step 2 (5,000) to obtain the standard variable factory overhead rate ($12 per direct labor-hour).

Exhibit 16–4	Variable Factory Overhead Flexible Budget Variance

SCHMIDT MACHINERY COMPANY
Variable Factory Overhead Flexible Budget Variance
For the Month of October 2001

Total variable factory overhead incurred		$40,630
Total standard variable factory overhead:		
1. Find the number of units manufactured.	780 units	
2. Determine for the units manufactured the standard quantity of the activity measure for applying variable factory overhead.		
a. Find the selected activity measure.	Direct labor-hours	
b. Find the standard quantity of the activity measure for one unit of the product	× 5 Direct labor-hours	
c. Compute the total standard quantity of the activity measure for the units manufactured.	3,900 Direct labor-hours	
3. Find the standard variable overhead rate.	× $12 per direct labor-hour	
4. Compute the total standard variable overhead.		= 46,800
Variable factory overhead flexible budget variances		$6,170 F

of the variable factory overhead for the units manufactured during the period. Some companies refer to the total variable factory overhead variance as the *variable factory overhead flexible budget variance*.

Schmidt Machinery Company used 3,510 direct labor-hours and incurred a total factory variable overhead cost of $40,630 to manufacture 780 units of XV–l during October 2001. The amount of the total variable factory overhead incurred is the sum of the amounts in the subsidiary ledgers of variable factory overhead items.

Exhibit 16–4 shows that the total standard variable factory overhead for units manufactured during the period is $46,800. The procedure to determine the total standard variable factory overhead for a period is similar to the procedures for determining the total standard costs for direct materials or direct labor costs. The only exception is that a substitute activity measure or measures for variable factory overhead costs are used in the procedure instead of quantities of the variable factory overhead items themselves.

Schmidt's accountant determines the total standard variable factory overhead for the units manufactured during October 2001 by first calculating the total standard direct labor-hours allowed for the output of the period, 780 units of XV–1. Direct labor-hours is the activity measure that Schmidt Machinery Company uses to determine the amount of its variable factory overhead for the units manufactured during the period.

Schmidt manufactured 780 units of XV–1 in October 2001. At 5 direct labor-hours for each unit of XV–1 manufactured, the standard direct labor-hours for the units manufactured in October total 3,900. Schmidt's accountant determined its standard variable factory overhead rate to be $12 per direct labor-hour. The total standard variable factory overhead for its operations in October, therefore, is $46,800 (3,900 hours × $12 per hour).

The difference between the total variable factory overhead incurred and the total standard variable factory overhead for the units manufactured is the *variable factory overhead flexible budget variance*. Schmidt Machinery Company incurred a total variable factory overhead of $40,630 in its operations during October 2001. The total standard variable factory overhead for the output of the period as calculated based on the substitute activity measure, direct labor-hours, is $46,800, as determined by the procedure described in step 4. The variable factory overhead flexible budget variance, therefore, is $6,170, favorable ($46,800 – $40,630).

Managers commonly refer to variable factory overhead flexible budget variances as *overapplied* if they are favorable or *underapplied* if they are unfavorable. In October 2001, Schmidt Machinery Company has an overapplied (favorable) variable factory overhead of $6,170.

Further Analysis of the Variable Factory Overhead Flexible Budget Variance

The **variable factory overhead spending variance** is the difference between variable factory overhead incurred and total standard variable factory overhead based on the actual quantity of the substitute activity measure to apply the overhead.

The **variable factory overhead efficiency variance** is the difference between the total standard variable factory overhead for the actual quantity of the substitute activity measure for applying variable factory overhead and the total standard variable factory overhead cost for the units manufactured during the period.

Some firms analyze the variable factory overhead flexible budget variance further into two detailed variances based on the substitute activity measure for applying variable factory overhead. The **variable factory overhead spending variance** is the difference between the variable factory overhead incurred and the total standard variable factory overhead for the actual quantity of the substitute activity measure for applying variable factory overhead. The remainder is the **variable factory overhead efficiency variance**. This variance shows the difference between the total standard variable factory overhead for the actual quantity of the substitute activity measure for applying the overhead and the standard variable factory overhead allowed for the output of the period.

Exhibit 16–5 illustrates this procedure using the October 2001 operating data of Schmidt Machinery Company. Schmidt uses direct labor-hours to apply variable factory overhead to cost objects. Further analysis of its variable factory overhead flexible budget variances thus is based on the number of direct labor-hours.

The procedures to further analyze variable factory overhead flexible budget variances are similar to those for analyzing direct materials or direct labor flexible budget variances. The procedures differ, however, in the activity measure of the cost item being analyzed. Further analysis of the direct materials or direct labor flexible budget variance uses a direct measure of the cost item. In contrast, there is no single direct measure for variable factory overhead because variable factory overhead is the result of many overhead activities: inspection, setup, materials handling, and so forth, each of which can vary with a different activity.

Schmidt Machinery Company used 3,510 direct labor-hours in October 2001. At the standard rate of $12 per hour, the standard variable factory overhead for the actual direct labor-hours during the period is $42,120, shown in point B in Exhibit 16–5. Using this amount, we can separate the variable factory overhead flexible budget variance into two components. The difference between the variable factory overhead incurred, point A, and the total standard variable factory overhead for the actual quantity of the activity measure for applying the variable factory overhead, point B, is the variable factory overhead spending variance. This is $1,490, favorable.

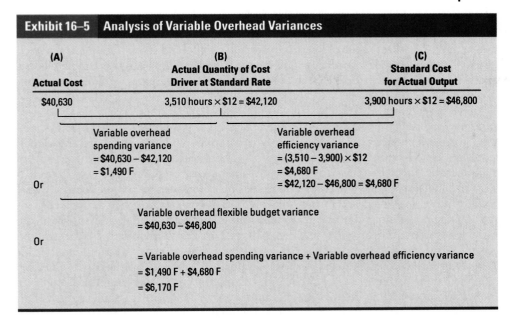

Exhibit 16–5 Analysis of Variable Overhead Variances

(A)	(B)	(C)
Actual Cost	**Actual Quantity of Cost Driver at Standard Rate**	**Standard Cost for Actual Output**
$40,630	3,510 hours × $12 = $42,120	3,900 hours × $12 = $46,800

Variable overhead spending variance
= $40,630 − $42,120
= $1,490 F

Variable overhead efficiency variance
= (3,510 − 3,900) × $12
= $4,680 F
= $42,120 − $46,800 = $4,680 F

Or

Variable overhead flexible budget variance
= $40,630 − $46,800

Or

= Variable overhead spending variance + Variable overhead efficiency variance
= $1,490 F + $4,680 F
= $6,170 F

The difference between point B and the total standard variable factory overhead for the output of the period, point C, is the variable factory overhead efficiency variance, $4,680, favorable.

Differences between Variable Factory Overhead Variances and Direct Materials or Direct Labor Variances

Although the procedures for analyzing variable factory overhead costs are similar to those for analyzing direct materials or direct labor variances described in Chapter 15, implications of variable factory overhead variances may differ for two reasons. First, in addition to varying with volume, the total variable factory overhead cost may vary with activities that change categorically or at intervals such as the number of production runs, number of batches, and the type of products. In contrast, total direct materials or total direct labor costs vary in proportion to changes in production volume.[5]

Second, firms use a single activity measure (cost driver) such as pounds of materials or hours of direct labor to assign direct materials or direct labor costs to cost objects. In contrast, a firm can use two or more activity measures to assign factory overhead costs to cost objects because of the many different overhead activities involved.

Some managers perceive the amount of work needed to maintain a multiple activity measures costing system for detailed identification and measurement of overhead exceeds the benefit derived. As a result, these firms assign factory overhead to cost objects by using a single activity measure such as direct labor-hours, machine-hours, direct material cost, or other easily identifiable factory activities.

When a single activity measure is used for a number of overhead activities, the relationship between factory overhead and the activity measure is not perfect. The amount of factory overhead incurred per machine-hour, for example, can vary from 1 cent to $5, depending on what transpires during the hour measured, although the firm applies, say, $2 of factory overhead per machine-hour to cost objects. The imperfect relationships can have significant effects on the results of variance analysis for factory overhead.

---

[5] Exceptions are firms with guaranteed wages or employment. The guaranteed portions of labor costs are fixed costs.

Interpretation and Implications of Variable Factory Overhead Variances

The imperfect relationships between variable factory overhead items and their substitute activity measures require us to interpret and draw conclusions about variable factory overhead variances with care. The meaning and implications of variable factory overhead variances are not the same as those of their counterparts for direct materials or direct labor variances.

Variable Factory Overhead Spending Variance The counterparts of the variable factory overhead spending variance in direct materials or direct labor are the direct materials price or direct labor rate variances. These variances measure the effect on manufacturing cost of differences between actual unit costs and the standard unit costs. In addition to the effects of cost deviations, however, a variable factory overhead spending variance can contain some or all the effects of quantity deviations.

Assume, for example, that a firm uses machine-hours as the activity measure to apply variable factory overhead. The standard calls for 1 machine-hour with 2 ounces of oil per machine-hour at $2.50 per ounce, or $5 per machine-hour, for the production of 10 units.[6] The firm used 6,000 machine-hours and 12,500 ounces of oil at a cost of $31,250 (2,500 × $2.50) to manufacture 55,000 units during the period just completed.

According to the standard, the manufacture of 55,000 units should have taken 5,500 machine-hours and 11,000 (2 × 5,500) ounces of oil. The accountant calculates variable factory overhead efficiency variances based on the difference in machine-hours because the firm applies variable factory overhead using machine-hours. The operation used 500 machine-hours more than the standard allowed for the manufacture of 55,000 units. At the standard application rate of $5 per machine-hour, the firm has an unfavorable efficiency variance of $2,500 (500 × $5), as shown in panel 1 of Exhibit 16–6. The efficiency variance represents the excess variable overhead cost that the firm would have incurred because of the excess number of machine-hours.

The firm used 12,500 ounces of oil during the operation, an excess of 1,500 ounces over the standard. At the standard price of $2.50 per ounce, the efficiency variance would have been $3,750 unfavorable using the procedure that we used to analyze direct materials usage variances in Chapter 15, as shown in panel 2 of Exhibit 16–6.

In Exhibit 16–6, a part of the variable factory overhead efficiency variance is included in the variable factory overhead spending variance. The difference between the actual quantity of oil used during the operation, 12,500 ounces, and the standard quantity of oil for the actual machine-hours operated, 12,000 ounces, is 500 ounces. At $2.50 standard price per ounce, the 500-ounce excess usage costs $1,250. Both the $1,250 and the $2,500 result from excess usage of oil. The $1,250, however, is included in the variable factory overhead spending variance when the variable factory overhead is analyzed using machine-hours as the activity measure for the overhead. The inclusion of both the price variance and a portion of the efficiency variance in a variable factory overhead spending variance must be considered in interpreting the variance and determining its implications.

Variable Factory Overhead Efficiency Variance

The use of a single activity measure for applying variable factory overhead can render interpretations of variable factory overhead variances difficult because of the imperfect relationship between the chosen activity measure and variable factory overhead.

Each element of variable factory overhead (for example, lubricant, indirect labor, setup materials, or labor) often has a unique activity measure. The use of a single activity measure for all elements of variable factory overhead imperfectly measures the usage (efficiency variance) for many of them. In response, the management

---

[6] The cost of oil is a direct cost if we know that the firm manufactures 10 units per machine-hour and uses 2 ounces of oil per machine-hour. The firm could treat the cost of oil as a direct cost if the cost is significant. However, the cost of oil needed to operate machinery is most likely insignificant and is, therefore, an overhead item.

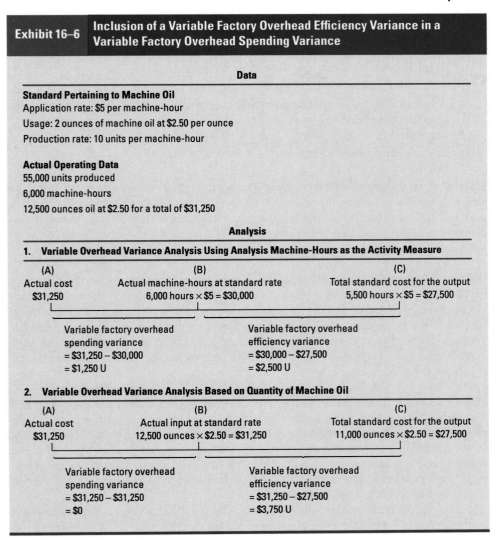

Exhibit 16-6 | **Inclusion of a Variable Factory Overhead Efficiency Variance in a Variable Factory Overhead Spending Variance**

Data

Standard Pertaining to Machine Oil
Application rate: $5 per machine-hour
Usage: 2 ounces of machine oil at $2.50 per ounce
Production rate: 10 units per machine-hour

Actual Operating Data
55,000 units produced
6,000 machine-hours
12,500 ounces oil at $2.50 for a total of $31,250

Analysis

1. **Variable Overhead Variance Analysis Using Analysis Machine-Hours as the Activity Measure**

(A)	(B)	(C)
Actual cost	Actual machine-hours at standard rate	Total standard cost for the output
$31,250	6,000 hours × $5 = $30,000	5,500 hours × $5 = $27,500

Variable factory overhead spending variance
= $31,250 − $30,000
= $1,250 U

Variable factory overhead efficiency variance
= $30,000 − $27,500
= $2,500 U

2. **Variable Overhead Variance Analysis Based on Quantity of Machine Oil**

(A)	(B)	(C)
Actual cost	Actual input at standard rate	Total standard cost for the output
$31,250	12,500 ounces × $2.50 = $31,250	11,000 ounces × $2.50 = $27,500

Variable factory overhead spending variance
= $31,250 − $31,250
= $0

Variable factory overhead efficiency variance
= $31,250 − $27,500
= $3,750 U

accountant can break the variable factory overhead into its elements, choose an appropriate activity measure for each of the cost elements, and calculate the spending and efficiency variances accordingly. Thus, if lubricant, indirect labor, and setup cost are significant variable factory overhead items, we would have a spending variance and an efficiency variance for each of these three elements rather than a single spending variance and a single efficiency variance for all variable factory overhead. The importance of choosing an appropriate activity measure or measures in analyzing variable factory overheads cannot be overemphasized.

Standard Costing for Fixed Factory Overhead

Many firms consider establishing a standard cost for fixed factory overhead an integral part of their standard cost system. One reason is that the GAAP requires the use of full costing for financial reporting. An additional incentive is the mandate to include fixed factory overhead in pricing for federal government procurement. Many genuinely believe that all costs of an operation should be included in the product cost and that fixed factory overhead costs can be assigned to products or operations with reasonable accuracy. Other firms believe that using a standard costing system for fixed factory overhead allows the determination of whether their operations incur fixed factory overheads as expected, the assessment of the effectiveness of their facilities, or the review of the appropriateness of the size of these facilities.

Determining Standard Fixed Factory Overhead Application Rate

Determining the standard fixed factory overhead application rate involves four essential elements:

1. Total *budgeted fixed factory overhead* for the operation.
2. An *activity measure* or measures for applying the fixed factory overhead.
3. The normal level of operations as reflected by the quantity of the activity measure(s) for applying the fixed factory overhead, or the *denominator activity* for the period.
4. The standard fixed factory overhead *application rate*.

Element 1: Total Budgeted Fixed Factory Overhead   Fixed factory overhead items are period expenditures that do not vary with the activity level of the period. Once the activity level has been determined, the total fixed factory overhead for the period remains relatively constant regardless of the level at which the firm operated during the period.

Element 2: Activity Measure(s) for Applying Fixed Factory Overhead   Fixed factory overhead usually is assigned to cost objects via one or more alternative activity measures. Because the total fixed factory overhead does not vary with changes in the activity level in effect no activity measure exists for fixed factory overhead during the period.[7] To include fixed factory overhead in product costs, firms commonly use the same activity measure that they use for the variable factory overhead to apply fixed factory overhead to products or operations.

Elements 3 and 4: Denominator Activity and the Fixed Factory Overhead Application Rate

The **denominator activity** is the desired operating level at the expected operating efficiency for a period, expressed in the quantity of the activity measure for applying fixed factory overhead. A **fixed factory overhead application rate** is the rate at which the firm applies fixed overhead costs to cost objects. A firm determines its fixed factory overhead application rate by dividing the total budget fixed factory overhead for the period by the denominator activity.

Schmidt Machinery Company uses direct labor-hours as the activity measure to apply factory overhead; its normal manufacturing activity level is 1,000 units of product XV–1 per period. With a labor standard of 5 direct labor-hours per unit of XV–1, the denominator activity per period is 5,000 direct labor-hours. Schmidt has a total budgeted fixed factory overhead of $120,000 per period and a denominator activity of 5,000 direct labor-hours. The fixed factory overhead application rate therefore is $24 per direct labor-hour.

Exhibit 16–7 summarizes the steps in determining standard fixed factory overhead application rate for an operation.

Analyzing Fixed Factory Overhead Variances

Although the total fixed factory overhead of a firm can change over a long period, it typically remains relatively stable in the short run. A firm expects the total actual fixed factory overhead for a period to be the same as the budgeted amount, regardless of the level of production attained. Schmidt Machinery Company has a budgeted monthly total fixed factory overhead of $120,000. The budgeted total fixed factory overhead for October 2001, therefore, is expected to be $120,000.

The total flexible budget variance for a variable cost is the difference between the amount incurred for the variable cost and the flexible budget amount for the output of the period. The actual output of a period might or might not be the master budget

---

[7]   Recent studies on activity-based costing reveal that many so-called fixed factory overheads in the past do vary with some activities. For these cost items, firms need to find appropriate activity levels and bases for proper product cost determinations.

Exhibit 16–7	**Steps in Determining Standard Fixed Factory Application Rate**

Step	Example
1. Determine the *total budgeted fixed factory overhead* for the level of operation.	Management decided to manufacture 1,000 units. The budgeted total fixed factory overhead to manufacture 1,000 units is $120,000 per month.
2. Select an *activity measure or measures* for applying fixed factory overhead.	The firm decided to use direct labor-hours as the activity measure for applying fixed factory overhead.
3. Calculate the *denominator activity quantity* for the selected activity measure at the planned level of operation.	At 5 standard direct labor-hours per unit, the firm expected to have a total of 5,000 direct labor-hours, the denominator activity for the period.
4. Determine the standard fixed factory overhead application rate by dividing the amount in Step 1 by the amount in Step 3.	To determine the standard fixed factory overhead rate ($24 per direct labor-hour), divide the amount in Step 1 ($120,000) by the amount in Step 3 identified as the denominator activity (5,000).

amount. In contrast, the total flexible budget variance of a fixed factory overhead is the difference between the fixed overhead amount incurred and the budgeted amount for the period. The budget amount is the same for both the master and the flexible budgets when both the budgeted level of operation and the actual level of operation of the period are within the same range of operations.

Fixed Factory Overhead Spending (budget) Variance   The **fixed factory overhead spending (budget) variance** is the difference between the amount incurred and the amount budgeted for the fixed factory overhead. This variance is the same as the *fixed factory overhead (flexible) budget variance*. Schmidt Machinery Company incurred a total of $130,650 fixed factory overhead in October 2001 (see Exhibit 16–8, point A). The budgeted fixed factory overhead was $120,000 for the month (see Exhibit 16–8, point

The **fixed factory overhead spending (budget) variance** is the difference between the actual amount incurred and the budgeted amount for the fixed factory overhead.

Exhibit 16–8	**Analysis of Fixed Factory Overhead Variances**

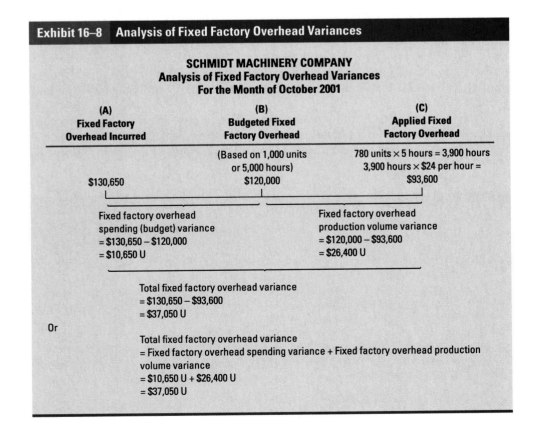

SCHMIDT MACHINERY COMPANY
Analysis of Fixed Factory Overhead Variances
For the Month of October 2001

(A) Fixed Factory Overhead Incurred	(B) Budgeted Fixed Factory Overhead	(C) Applied Fixed Factory Overhead
	(Based on 1,000 units or 5,000 hours)	780 units × 5 hours = 3,900 hours 3,900 hours × $24 per hour =
$130,650	$120,000	$93,600

Fixed factory overhead
spending (budget) variance
= $130,650 – $120,000
= $10,650 U

Fixed factory overhead
production volume variance
= $120,000 – $93,600
= $26,400 U

Total fixed factory overhead variance
= $130,650 – $93,600
= $37,050 U

Or

Total fixed factory overhead variance
= Fixed factory overhead spending variance + Fixed factory overhead production volume variance
= $10,650 U + $26,400 U
= $37,050 U

B). The difference between the total fixed factory overhead incurred (point A) and the budgeted fixed factory overhead for the period (point B) is $10,650, unfavorable. The firm therefore has an unfavorable fixed factory overhead spending (flexible budget) variance of $10,650 for the month (see the calculation on the left side of the middle panel of Exhibit 16–8).

The **fixed factory overhead production volume variance** is the difference between the budget allowance for fixed factory overhead for the period and the applied fixed factory overhead.

Fixed Factory Overhead Production Volume Variance   The **fixed factory overhead production volume variance** is the difference between the budgeted fixed factory overhead for the period and the amount of fixed factory overhead applied to the output (units manufactured) of the period. Fixed factory overhead is applied based on the standard fixed factory overhead application rate to the operation of the period. The operation of the period is measured by the activity measure for applying fixed factory overhead based on the units of output.

A fixed factory overhead production volume variance arises when a firm's actual operating level is not the same as the budgeted level for the period. Schmidt manufactured 780 units of XV–l in October 2001, which, according to the standard cost sheet, requires 3,900 standard direct labor-hours (780 units × 5 hours). At a standard fixed factory overhead application rate of $24 per direct labor-hour, the total standard fixed factory overhead applied to units manufactured in October 2001 was $93,600 (3,900 hours × $24 per hour; see point C in Exhibit 16–8). With a $120,000 budget fixed factory overhead, Schmidt has an unfavorable fixed factory overhead production volume variance of $26,400 for October (see the right side of the middle panel of Exhibit 16–8).

The difference between the budget fixed factory overhead and the fixed factory overhead applied is a production volume variance because the difference is the result of the difference between the number of units manufactured and the budgeted (denominator) volume. The denominator is the number of units the firm budgeted to manufacture during the period. Exhibit 16–9 provides alternative computations for the amounts at points B and C in Exhibit 16–8. This exhibit demonstrates that the production volume variance arises from a difference between the budgeted (denominator) and the actual units of output. The production volume variance is favorable when the firm manufactured more units during the period than the budgeted (denominator) units and is unfavorable when the actual production is less than the budgeted units. No production volume variance exists when the number of units manufactured during the period is the same as the denominator number of units that the firm budgeted (1,000 units).

Some firms view production volume variances as a measure of facility or capacity utilization. A production volume variance reflects capacity utilization because it is the difference between the planned and the actual uses of the firm's facility or capac-

---

Using the Budget as the Denominator in Determining Fixed Overhead Rate

Using the budget as the basis for calculating standard fixed overhead rates requires firms to interpret variances with caution. The budget for many companies reflects the result of a host of assumptions that are likely to include highly speculative economic circumstances and difficult sales forecasts. Furthermore, when budgets are submitted for approval, they are subject to negotiations among superior and subordinate divisions before determining the level of acceptable performance for the budget period. As time goes by, accountants measure actual results and calculate variances to explain what happened. These variances and their explanations might not be relevant but might be difficult to understand because budget assumptions could no longer be valid.

Source: Paul Sharman, "Time to Re-Examine the P&L," *CMA Magazine* 65, no. 7, pp. 22–25.

Exhibit 16–9	**Determinants of a Production Volume Variance**	

(A) Fixed Factory Overhead Incurred	**(B)** Budgeted Fixed Factory Overhead	**(C)** Applied Fixed Factory Overhead
	Budgeted units 1,000	Actual units 780
	× Hours per unit 5	× Hours per unit 5
	5,000 hours	3,900 hours
	× Fixed overhead rate $24	× Fixed overhead rate $24
$130,650	$120,000	$93,600

Fixed factory overhead production volume variance

= (Budgeted units − Actual units) × Standard hours per unit × Standard fixed factory overhead application rate per hour

= (1,000 − 780) × 5 hours × $24 per hour

= $26,400 U

Or

= Underused (overused) capacity in hours × Standard fixed factory overhead application rate per hour

= (Planned level of operation in standard hours − Actual operating level attained in standard hours) × Standard fixed factory overhead application rate per hour

= (5,000 hours − 3,900 hours) × $24

= $26,400 U

ity. Schmidt planned to operate 5,000 direct labor-hours to manufacture 1,000 units. The production of 780 units in October 2001 indicates that the firm operated only at the level of 3,900 direct labor-hours (780 units × 5 standard direct labor-hours per unit). The firm underused its facility by 220 units, or 1,100 hours (5,000 − 3,900). At the standard fixed factory overhead application rate of $24 per hour, the production volume is $26,400 unfavorable (see the bottom panel of Exhibit 16–9). This unfavorable variance indicates that the lower operating level in October 2001 had an implicit cost of $26,400 to the firm.

Total Fixed Factory Overhead Variance   The sum of the fixed factory overhead spending and production volume variances is the total fixed factory overhead variance of the period. This is also the difference between the fixed factory overhead incurred and the standard fixed factory applied to the output of the period. Some firms refer to this amount as the *underapplied or overapplied fixed factory overhead*.

Schmidt Machinery Company incurred $130,650 fixed factory overhead during October 2001 to manufacture 780 units of XV–1. The firm applied $93,600 fixed factory overhead to the 780 units manufactured in October 2001. Schmidt Machinery Company, therefore, has a total fixed factory overhead variance, or underapplied fixed factory overhead, of $37,050 for the period.

Interpretation of Fixed Factory Overhead Variances

Differences in the calculation of variances for fixed factory overhead and for variable factory overhead mandate that the fixed factory overhead variances be interpreted differently. Fixed factory overhead variances, therefore, have different implications from those of variable factory variances.

Fixed Factory Overhead Spending Variance   A fixed factory overhead spending variance can arise when the budget procedure failed to anticipate or incorporate changes in fixed factory overhead. For example, a budget could have inadvertently neglected scheduled raises for factory managers, changes in property taxes on factory buildings and equipment, or purchases of new equipment. A significant fixed factory overhead spending variance that results from an ineffective budget procedure suggests that the firm might need to revise its budgeting process.

An unfavorable fixed factory overhead spending variance can be the result of excessive spending due to improper or inadequate control of operations. Events such as emergency repairs, impromptu replacement of equipment, or the addition of managers for an unscheduled second shift increase fixed factory overhead for the period. Management should investigate the causes of such unfavorable fixed factory overhead spending variances to prevent similar events from occurring in future periods.

When a firm's cost classifications system fails to reflect its cost behavior patterns, fixed factory overhead spending variances arise. Classifying a cost item that is not entirely fixed as fixed overhead would lead to an unfavorable fixed factory overhead spending variance when the actual production is higher than the budgeted production. It would lead to a favorable fixed factory overhead spending variance when the actual production is lower than the budgeted level.

In many operations, no factory overhead item's cost is strictly variable or fixed. A small amount of the fixed factory overhead spending variance that resulted from imprecise classifications of factory overhead items should not alarm management. A large variance, however, should prompt management to investigate the cause of the variance, including reexamining cost behavior patterns of various factory overhead.

Fixed Factory Overhead Production Volume Variance A fixed factory overhead production volume variance reflects the firm's *effectiveness* in attaining the goal set for the period rather than its *efficiency* in controlling costs. Schmidt Machinery Company had a budget to manufacture 1,000 units in October 2001 but manufactured 780 units. As a result, the firm has an unfavorable fixed factory overhead production volume variance of $26,400. Schmidt was ineffective in attaining the goal set for October 2001. In contrast, all other variances discussed so far reflect operation efficiencies.

A fixed factory overhead production volume variance could result from management decisions, an unexpected change in demand for the product, or problems in manufacturing operations, among others. Management could alter the production plan for the period in view of the new market outlook or strategic considerations. It could decide to phase out or increase the production of a product because of knowledge gained about a new technology after the budget was prepared. Or the sales volume since the beginning of the year could suggest a larger or smaller market than expected in the budget. Management, therefore, could decide to step up or reduce production of the product. A fixed factory overhead production volume variance that results from one or more of these causes most likely is beyond the control of factory management.

Unexpected production problems can also be a source of fixed factory overhead production volume variance. Among the production problems a factory might encounter are equipment not functioning properly due to inadequate maintenance or unexpected breakdowns, a product not designed for easy production, or unexpected high labor turnovers. A production volume variance that results from manufacturing problems very likely is the responsibility, either partially or fully, of the factory management.

Alternative Analyses of Factory Overhead Variances

LEARNING OBJECTIVE 5▶

Use two-variance or three-variance procedures to analyze and interpret factory overhead variances.

Not all firms want or need an analysis of factory overhead discussed in such detail as that in the preceding sections, which separated the total variable and the total fixed factory overhead variances into two variances each. Such an analysis is referred as a *four-variance analysis* of factory overhead variances. Alternative ways to analyze various types of factory overhead that are less detailed are the three-variance and two-variance analyses.

Three-Variance Analysis of Factory Overhead Variances

A three-variance analysis of factory overhead variances separates the difference between the total factory overhead incurred and the standard factory overhead costs applied to the operations of the period for both variable and fixed factory overheads into three variances. A three-variance analysis is often necessary because the company's chart of accounts does not separate variable and fixed factory overhead costs or management does not consider a more detailed analysis cost effective.

A three-variance analysis of factory overhead combines the variable factory overhead spending variance and the fixed factory overhead spending (budget) variance and refers to the variance as a *(total) factory overhead spending variance*. The three factory overhead variances from this analysis thus are *factory overhead spending, (variable) factory overhead efficiency, and production volume variances*. The *factory overhead spending variance* is the difference between the total factory overhead incurred and the expected total factory overhead for the operating level at the actual quantity of the activity measure for overhead applications.

Schmidt Machinery Company has an unfavorable (total) factory overhead spending variance of $9,160, which is the sum of a $1,490 favorable variable factory overhead spending variance and a $10,650 unfavorable fixed factory overhead budget variance in the four-variance analysis of factory overhead. Or the firm expects to incur $42,120 in variable factory overhead ($5 variable factory overhead per direct labor-hour for the 3,510 direct labor-hours the firm spent during the period) and $120,000 budgeted total fixed factory overhead for a total factory overhead of $162,120. The firm incurred $171,280 total factory overhead. The $9,160 difference ($171,280 − $162,120) is the factory overhead spending variance for the period, which is unfavorable. Exhibit 16–10 illustrates a three-variance analysis for factory overhead variances.

Computing three variances requires four distinct points, as Exhibit 16–10 shows. Point A is the total factory overhead incurred during the period. Point B is the standard factory overhead applied to the actual quantity of the selected activity measure for applying factory overhead during the period. Point C is the total of the standard variable factory overhead cost and the budgeted total fixed factory overhead for the output of the period. Point D is the total standard factory overhead cost applied to the standard quantity of the selected activity measure for the units manufactured (output) during the period.

The amounts of total fixed factory overhead in points B and C is always the same. Both points represent the budgeted total fixed factory overhead, $120,000 in the example. The only difference between these two points is the amount of the standard variable factory overhead. In point B the standard variable factory overhead is based on the *actual quantity of the activity measure* for applying factory overhead. Schmidt Machinery

Exhibit 16–10	Three-Variance Analysis of Factory Overhead Variances

	(A) Total Factory Overhead Incurred	(B) Total Standard Variable Factory Overhead Rate Applied to Activity Measure Incurred and the Budgeted Fixed Factory Overhead	(C) Total Standard Variable Factory Overhead and the Budgeted Fixed Factory Overhead	(D) Standard Factory Overhead Applied to Output
Variable	$ 40,630	$ 42,120	$ 46,800	$ 46,800
Fixed	+ 130,650	+ 120,000	+ 120,000	+ 93,600
Total	$171,280	$162,120	$166,800	$140,400

Spending variance = $9,160 U

Efficiency variance = $4,680 F

Production volume variance = $26,400 U

Underapplied factory overhead $30,880

Company, which uses direct labor-hours as the activity measure for applying factory overhead, spent 3,510 direct labor-hours in operations during October 2001. At a standard variable factory overhead rate of $12 per direct labor-hour, the total variable factory overhead at point B is $42,120 (3,510 × $12). Adding the budgeted fixed factory overhead of $120,000, the total factory overhead at point B is $162,120.

The difference between points A and B is a factory overhead spending variance. Schmidt has a total factory overhead incurred, identified as point A of $171,280 and point B of $162,120. Its factory overhead spending variance therefore is $9,160, unfavorable.

Point C is the total standard factory overhead for the operation of the period. The total standard variable factory overhead at point C is the product of the standard variable factory overhead application rate and the total standard quantity of the activity measure for applying variable factory overhead for the units manufactured during the period. Schmidt manufactured 780 units of XV–1 during October 2001. With 5 standard direct labor-hours per unit of XV–1 and the application rate of $12 standard variable factory overhead per direct labor-hour, the total standard variable factory overhead for the period was $46,800 (780 units × 5 hours per unit × $12 variable overhead rate per hour). This amount also is the variable factory overhead flexible budget amount. In fact, both the variable and the fixed factory overhead at point C are the flexible budget amounts for the units manufactured during the period. The fixed factory overhead in the flexible budget is $120,000. Thus, the total factory overhead at point C is $166,800.

The difference between points B and C is a factory overhead efficiency variance. Schmidt Machinery Company had $162,120 for point B and $166,800 for point C, and, thus, a favorable factory overhead efficiency variance of $4,680 for its operations during October 2001.

Point D is the total standard factory overhead applied to the output (units manufactured) of the period. The total standard variable factory overhead applied to units manufactured during the period is the same as the flexible budget amount. Schmidt applies a $12 variable factory overhead for each direct labor-hour. For the 780 units manufactured in October 2001, which had total standard direct labor-hours of 3,900, the total variable factory overhead applied was $46,800.

Schmidt Machinery Company budgeted a total of $120,000 fixed factory overhead for the month and applied fixed factory overhead at the rate of $24 per direct labor-hour. The total fixed factory overhead applied to the 780 units of XV–1 manufactured during the period therefore was $93,600 (780 units × 5 hours × $24). The sum of the applied variable factory overhead of $46,800 and the applied fixed factory overhead of $93,600 is the total factory overhead applied to the units manufactured in October 2001, which is $140,400, shown as point D in Exhibit 16–10. The difference between points C and D is a factory overhead production volume variance. For Schmidt's operations during October 2001, this amount was $26,400, unfavorable.

A four-variance analysis requires separately tracking variable and fixed factory overhead and provides a more detailed analysis of an operation. If this additional analysis of variances provides little useful information to management, however, a three-variance analysis is sufficient. A three-variance analysis of factory overhead variances is also used when a firm's cost accounting system makes no distinction between variable and fixed factory overhead.

Two-Variance Analysis of Factory Overhead Variances

A two-variance analysis of factory overhead variances separates the difference between the total factory overhead incurred during the period and the total factory overhead applied to the output of the period into two variances. These two variances are *factory overhead flexible budget variance* and *factory overhead production volume variance*. The factory overhead flexible budget variance also is called a *factory overhead controllable variance*. Exhibit 16–11 is a two-variance analysis of factory overhead variances for the October 2001 factory overhead costs of Schmidt Machinery Company.

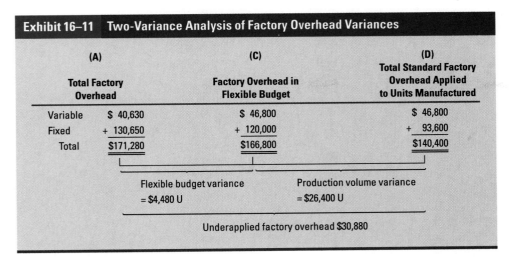

Exhibit 16–11 Two-Variance Analysis of Factory Overhead Variances

	(A) Total Factory Overhead	(C) Factory Overhead in Flexible Budget	(D) Total Standard Factory Overhead Applied to Units Manufactured
Variable	$ 40,630	$ 46,800	$ 46,800
Fixed	+ 130,650	+ 120,000	+ 93,600
Total	$171,280	$166,800	$140,400

Flexible budget variance = $4,480 U   Production volume variance = $26,400 U

Underapplied factory overhead $30,880

Note in Exhibit 16–11 that a two-variance analysis uses three of the four points employed in the three-variance analysis. Point A is the same in all analyses, the total factory overhead incurred during the period. Point C is the factory overhead in the flexible budget for the units manufactured during the period. Point D is the total standard factory overhead applied to the units manufactured during the period. Point B in Exhibit 16–10, the three-variance analysis is not used in two-variance analysis.

The difference between points A and C is a factory overhead flexible budget variance. This variance can also be determined by merging the spending and efficiency variances from the three-variance analysis.

Schmidt Machinery Company incurred a total factory overhead of $171,280 to manufacture 780 units of XV–1 during October 2001. The total standard variable factory overhead to manufacture 780 units of XV–1 is $46,800. The total budgeted fixed factory overhead for the period is $120,000. The total amount at point C, therefore, is $166,800. Schmidt had an unfavorable factory overhead flexible budget variance of $4,480 for its operations during October 2001. Alternatively, we can determine the factory overhead flexible budget variance by combining two of the variances in the three-variance analysis of factory overhead variances, the unfavorable spending variance of $9,160 and the favorable efficiency variance of $4,680.

Summary of Factory Overhead Variances

A firm can separately analyze factory overhead variances for its variable and fixed factory overhead costs, or it can perform the variance analyses without distinguishing the variances from either variable or fixed factory overhead. When variable and fixed factory variances are both separated into two detailed variances, the analysis is a four-variance analysis of factory overhead variances. Exhibit 16–12 illustrates the determination of factory overhead variances using a four-variance analysis. Exhibit 16–13 summarizes the analyses presented earlier for the operations of the Schmidt Machinery Company in October 2001.

A detailed analysis of a variance can assist a firm in isolating different factors that led the operating results to deviate from the budgeted or standard operations. A four-variance analysis for example, shows separately the effects on the operating result of spending on variable overhead items and on fixed overhead items. Knowing these factors can help the firm gain effective control of operations and better assess its performances. Analyses performed at an aggregated level, say identifying only the total variance between the operating result and the budgeted total amount or the total standard cost allowed for the operation, might mask important variations attributable to different causes or in one or more of the individual overhead items that have opposite effects on costs.

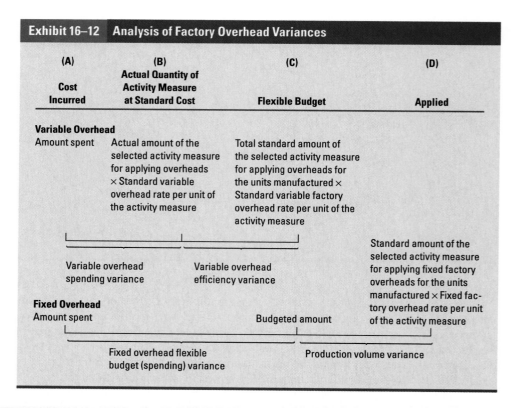

Exhibit 16–12 Analysis of Factory Overhead Variances

(A) Cost Incurred	(B) Actual Quantity of Activity Measure at Standard Cost	(C) Flexible Budget	(D) Applied

Variable Overhead

Amount spent | Actual amount of the selected activity measure for applying overheads × Standard variable overhead rate per unit of the activity measure | Total standard amount of the selected activity measure for applying overheads for the units manufactured × Standard variable factory overhead rate per unit of the activity measure |

Variable overhead spending variance | Variable overhead efficiency variance

Standard amount of the selected activity measure for applying fixed factory overheads for the units manufactured × Fixed factory overhead rate per unit of the activity measure

Fixed Overhead

Amount spent | | Budgeted amount |

Fixed overhead flexible budget (spending) variance | Production volume variance

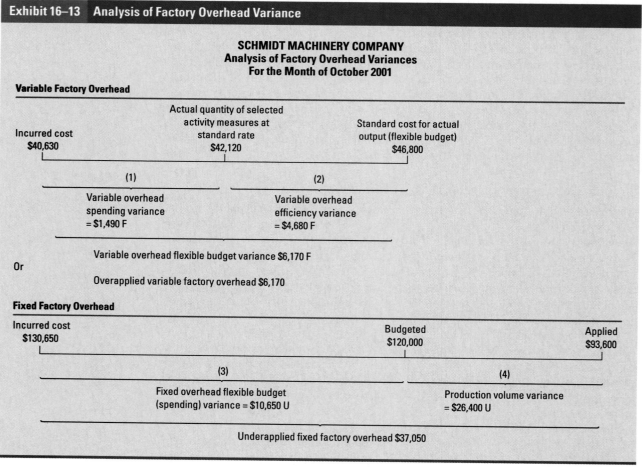

Exhibit 16–13 Analysis of Factory Overhead Variance

SCHMIDT MACHINERY COMPANY
Analysis of Factory Overhead Variances
For the Month of October 2001

Variable Factory Overhead

Incurred cost $40,630	Actual quantity of selected activity measures at standard rate $42,120	Standard cost for actual output (flexible budget) $46,800

(1) Variable overhead spending variance = $1,490 F

(2) Variable overhead efficiency variance = $4,680 F

Variable overhead flexible budget variance $6,170 F

Or

Overapplied variable factory overhead $6,170

Fixed Factory Overhead

Incurred cost $130,650	Budgeted $120,000	Applied $93,600

(3) Fixed overhead flexible budget (spending) variance = $10,650 U

(4) Production volume variance = $26,400 U

Underapplied fixed factory overhead $37,050

A detailed analysis of a variance adds value, however, only if management understands it and is able to use it, the personnel affected by the result can comprehend and accept it, and the firm's costing system supports it. A detailed analysis can be misleading, dysfunctional, or even detrimental if cost items are not properly identified as variable or fixed costs, if the behavioral patterns of the designated activity measure or measures for applying overheads do not represent the behavioral patterns of the underlying overhead costs, or if management or its subordinates do not understand the analysis.

DISPOSITION OF VARIANCES

How should a firm report variances in financial reporting when its actual operating costs differ from the standard cost for the operation? It can dispose of the variance in the period in which the variance occurs. Alternatively, the firm can prorate cost variances among Work-in-Process Inventory, Finished Goods Inventory, and Cost of Goods Sold accounts.

◀**LEARNING OBJECTIVE 6**

Dispose of variances through the financial accounting system.

Variance as a Current Period Savings or Expense

When the amounts of the variances are relatively small, firms often choose to dispose of them at year-end. Firms also can dispose of them at year-end even when the variance amounts are significant. They do so on the ground that the variances of a period are the results of the operations at that period and should therefore be disposed of in the statement that reports that period's operating results.

To dispose of the variances in the period in which they occurred, unfavorable cost variances are added to the total standard cost of goods sold and the unfavorable selling price variances are subtracted from the total flexible budget sales of the period. When the variances are favorable, favorable cost variances are subtracted from the total standard cost of goods sold, and the favorable selling price variances are added to the total flexible budget sales of the period. Exhibit 16–14 illustrates this procedure.

Schmidt Machinery Company sold 780 units. At the budgeted $800 selling price per unit, the total flexible budget sales for the period is $624,000. The firm sold the

Exhibit 16–14	**Income Statement**

SCHMIDT MACHINERY COMPANY
Income Statement
For the Period Ended October 31, 2001

Sales (Exhibit 15–4)	$624,000	
Add: Sales price variance (Exhibit 15–4)	15,600 F	
Net sales		$639,600
Cost of goods sold (at standard)	$405,600*	
Add: Manufacturing cost variances	+ 37,000† U	
Total cost of goods sold		442,600
Gross margin		$197,000
Selling and administrative expenses		69,000
Operating income		$128,000

*Standard manufacturing cost per unit (Exhibit 16–2)	$ 520	
Number of units manufactured and sold	× 780	
Total standard cost of goods manufactured and sold	$405,600	
†Total variable manufacturing cost variance (Exhibit 15–6)	$ 50 F	
Total fixed manufacturing cost variance (Exhibit 16–8)	37,050 U	
Total manufacturing cost variance	$37,000 U	

products for $820 per unit, however, so the $15,600 total favorable selling price variance ($20 per unit × 780 units sold) is added to the total flexible budget sales to arrive at the total sales revenue of $639,000 received during the month.

According to Exhibit 16–2, the standard cost per unit is $520. The total standard cost of the 780 units sold, therefore, is $405,600 ($520 per unit × 780 units). The firm, however, has a $50 favorable total variance for variable manufacturing costs and a $37,050 unfavorable variance for fixed manufacturing costs. The total manufacturing cost variance, $37,000 unfavorable, is added to the standard cost of goods incurred during the period.

Proration of Variance

An alternative to the disposal of variances as a current period cost is to prorate manufacturing cost variances among the cost of goods sold and the ending inventories. Assume that in addition to the 780 units sold with $405,600 in standard costs, Schmidt Machinery Company had $36,400 of work-in-process inventory and $78,000 of finished goods inventory as of the end of October 2001. The firm prorates manufacturing cost variances among ending inventories and the cost of goods sold of the period.[8] The total manufacturing cost variance in October 2001 was $37,000, unfavorable. Exhibit 16–15 shows the proration of the manufacturing cost variances.[9]

Prorations of manufacturing cost variances among ending inventories and the cost of goods sold have the effect of carrying the saving or cost of the efficient or inefficient operations of a period to future periods. When Schmidt Machinery Company sells the finished goods ending inventory in a future period, say 2002, the unfavorable variance added to the finished goods ending inventory of October 2001 will increase the cost of goods sold of 2002 by $5,550. As a result, the operating income of 2002 will decrease by $5,550 because of the unfavorable variance in 2001. If the increase in manufacturing cost resulted from inefficient operations in 2001, reflecting the effect of the inefficient operation in one period in the operating income of one or more future periods is inappropriate. This mixture of performance from one period to another renders analyses and performance evaluations ambiguous.

Prorations of manufacturing cost variances among ending inventories of work-in-process, finished goods, and cost of goods sold are appropriate, however, if the cost variance is the result of inappropriate standards or bookkeeping errors. In these circumstances, management must revise the standard or take action to prevent a recurrence of the same bookkeeping error.[10]

Exhibit 16–15	Proration of Manufacturing Cost Variance			
Accounts	**Cost at Standard**	**Percent of Total**	**Proration of Variance**	**Adjusted Total Cost**
Work in progress—Ending	$ 36,400	7%	$37,000 × 7% = $ 2,590	$38,990
Finished goods—Ending	78,000	15	$37,000 × 15% = 5,550	83,550
Cost of goods sold	405,600	78	$37,000 × 78% = 28,860	434,460
Total	$520,000	100%	$37,000	$557,000

---

[8]   This example assumes that Schmidt carries no materials ending inventories. When materials purchased differ from materials used, however, the proration of the materials price variance should include direct materials ending inventory as well as the direct materials usage variance.

[9]   When different activity measures are used for different cost elements, the proration should be done separately for each cost element based on its activity measure.

[10]   Neither GAAP nor the Internal Revenue Code specifically addresses the issue of proration. Because the total amount of variance is most likely an immaterial amount, firms can use either method to dispose of variances. Many firms, however, prorate variances in financial reports and for tax purposes.

STANDARD COSTING IN SERVICE ORGANIZATIONS

A standard costing system facilitates budget preparation, assists monitoring and controlling operations and performance evaluation, and aids management in making decisions about product pricing and resource management. These benefits are not limited to manufacturing firms. Organizations of all types and in all businesses, including those in service industries, can benefit from using standard costing systems.

In today's highly competitive environment, many service managers and firms in service industries have increasingly recognized the importance of using methods such as product-line planning, productivity monitoring, quality control, and other cost management concepts and techniques in order to run an efficient, competitive, and profitable service organization. To use these methods, managers need costing standards to be able to thoroughly grasp the behavior of cost items in operations, assess and monitor the efficiency and profitability of their organizations, identify deviations in operations, and target areas that need attention.

To best use a standard costing system, an organization must adapt the system to its operating characteristics and objectives. Objectives are likely to differ among various organizations. Some general characteristics, however, distinguish a service firm from a manufacturing or merchandising firm. Among them are the absence of output inventory, labor-intensive products, the predominance of fixed costs, and the lack of a uniform measure for outputs.

Service outputs cannot be stored for use in the future. Vacant service bays in an automobile repair shop today do not increase the service bays available tomorrow. Empty airline seats on a flight do not increase the seats available on the next flight. Vacant hospital beds today do not increase the beds available tomorrow. Thus, service outputs cannot be generated before they are needed; a service output exists only when a customer exists. In contrast, a manufacturer can make products for future deliveries. Consequently, a service firm has no favorable production volume variance. Unfavorable production volume variances, if any, are also the sales volume variances of the period.

People provide services. As a result, most service organizations are labor intensive and incur the bulk of their expenses in salary and wage-related expenditures. With material costs primarily incidental expenses, the major cost items for many service organizations are labor costs and overheads. As a result, labor-related measures such as the labor rate and efficiency variances are much more important than materials variances to managers of service firms. In addition, labor-intensiveness leads service firms to monitor activities and gauge operating results using labor-based measures.

Equipment in service organizations enables staff members to provide better services. Service organizations acquire equipment to (1) replace labor, (2) reduce production costs, (3) improve process efficiency, or (4) improve the quality of services. Cost reduction might not be a service organization's primary goal in acquiring equipment or updating facilities.

New equipment added to a service organization often increases, rather than decreases, its total operating cost and the cost of providing services. A hospital that adds a piece of equipment, for example, improves the quality of treatment it provides; the equipment, however, adds costs to the hospital and ultimately to the patients. A multimedia classroom improves the quality of instruction and increases the cost of that instruction. A simple cost/output ratio often is not a good efficiency measure; if used improperly, it can be detrimental to the ultimate objective of the service organization: to provide better services to customers.

Most costs in service organizations are fixed costs. The bulk of labor costs are for professional personnel who are usually paid monthly salaries. Variations in salaries from one period to the next are few, if any. Other overhead costs often consist of expenses related to facilities and equipment and are fixed in amounts for each time period. The predominance of fixed costs in service organizations increases the importance of monitoring fixed cost variances for profit improvements.

Unlike a manufacturing firm that produces many identical products, a service organization produces outputs that differ in some way. Two patients with similar conditions

◀**LEARNING OBJECTIVE 7**

Apply a standard cost system to service organizations.

who check out of a hospital likely did not receive the same care. The likelihood of two students receiving degrees from the same institution at the same time having received the same education is almost nil.

Furthermore, service organizations often use measures other than units of output to measure their output. Exhibit 16–16 lists some measures of output often used by service organizations. Hospitals use patient-days to measure their product. Colleges and universities use credit-hour production to show their output. These surrogate output measures are seldom perfect indicators of the products of a service organization. Patients or their families are likely to place different values on the same number of patient-days, depending on the results of treatment. A patient who is cured of a disease is likely to be more pleased with the care received than is the family of a patient who died of the same disease although the number of patient-days was identical for both. In addition, the amount

Exhibit 16–16   Surrogate Output Measures of Service Organizations

Type of Organization	Surrogate Output Measure
Airline	Revenue-producing passenger-miles
Hospital	Patient-days
Hotel	Occupancy rate or number of guests
Accounting, legal, and consulting firms	Professional staff hours
Colleges and universities	Credit hours
Primary and secondary schools	Number of students

Standard Cost Sheet for a Hospital

LANCASTER COUNTY HOSPITAL
Standard Cost Sheet for Pediatrics Floor

Direct Expenses	Rate/Price	Amount	Fixed
Salaries and wages			
Supervisors			$4,500
RNs	$15.00 per hour	1.3 hours per patient-day	
LPNs	10.00 per hour	1.7 hours per patient-day	
Nursing assistants	6.50 per hour	0.9 hour per patient-day	
Supplies—Inventory	0.20 per unit	10 units per patient-day	
Supplies—noninventory			300
Pediatrician fees	100 per hour	0.5 hour per patient-day	
Other direct expenses			250
Transferred Expenses			
Housekeeping	5.00 per hour	48 hours + 0.4 hour per patient day + 1.50 hours per patient discharge	
Laundry	0.25 per pound	500 pounds + 15 pounds per patient-day + 30 pounds per discharge + 50 pounds per surgery	
Allocated Expenses			
Personnel	0.08 per hour	242 hours + 3.9 hours per patient-day	
Other administrative and general	3.00 per hour	118 hours + 0.05 hour per patient-day + 1.5 hours per patient discharge	

Source: Based on Table 14 in *Managerial Cost Accounting for Hospitals* (Chicago: American Hospital Association, 1980), p. 97.

How a Hospital Unit Responds to a Performance Report

Date: November 5, 2001
To: Cynthia DeCamp, Hospital Director
From: Stan DeVine, Pediatric Unit Manager
Subject: Direct expenses, October 2001
Direct Labor   Last month, my unit recruited three new RNs at the entry-level pay scale, replacing two retired RNs who had been with us for more than 20 years and were at the top of the pay scale. The average hourly salary for all RNs on the unit was reduced to $14 per hour, resulting in a favorable labor rate variance. The replacements, however, increased my RN nursing hours per patient-day to 1.5 hours, resulting in an unfavorable labor efficiency variance in last month's average daily staffing. To compensate for the increased RN staffing, one LPN was transferred to the Emergency Room, which needs his help. This resulted in both a favorable rate and efficiency variance for LPNs. We expect, however, that the favorable rate variance will be lost in approximately six months when the RNs reach the next pay level. Therefore, I recommend that plans be made to replace one RN with one LPN.

For a period of five consecutive days in the middle of the month, the unit had more than 20 patients and required the use of 48 overtime hours for the nurse assistants, causing an unfavorable rate and efficiency variance for this group.

Supplies—Inventory   Uses of inventory supplies followed the standard level of 10 items per patient-day. However, two brands were changed. The purchasing department informs me that the new brands are less expensive and resulted in a $135 savings last month. Furthermore, the new items appear to be better than the previous brands, and we will continue to use them.

Supplies—Noninventory   The unfavorable quantity variance resulted primarily from purchasing items that had been deferred the last several months. Year-to-date spending on these items, however, still remains favorable.

Pediatrician Fees   The resident pediatrician, Dr. Kiddear, and other staff were required to provide some overtime night-shift service during the period that the patient census was more than 20 patients. Overtime night-shift work is paid at a rate higher than standard, thus causing an unfavorable price variance. The 48 additional hours for overtime night-shift work were responsible for the unfavorable usage variance.

Source: *Managerial Cost Accounting for Hospitals* (Chicago: American Hospital Assn., 1980), pp. 98–99.

---

and type of work performed by a service organization to complete an output unit often varies from one client to the next or from one patient-day to another. The amounts and types of work performed during 30 patient-days of care for two patients with heart-disease can be vastly different although the number of patient-days is identical.

Educational institutions are other service organizations that seldom use their outputs—knowledge learned—as the measure of their output. These institutions frequently cite credit-hour production as the measure of their output. One hundred credit hours of mediocre instruction do not have the same value as one hundred hours of excellent instruction. Intangible attributes, in addition to units of output, play dominant roles in determining the value of outputs from a service organization. These characteristics often lead service firms to rely on input-related measures such as patient-days and the number of credit hours produced to measure and monitor operations.

The differences in operating characteristics for service organizations and typical manufacturing firms create the necessity to modify standard costing systems before applying them to service organizations.

STANDARD COSTING IN THE NEW MANUFACTURING ENVIRONMENT

The new manufacturing environment and the new management techniques emphasize continual improvement, total quality control, and managing activity rather than cost. These emphases have changed product costing, strategic and operational decisions,

LEARNING OBJECTIVE 8▶

Describe the effects of recent advances in new manufacturing technologies and rapid changes in operating environments on standard costing systems, and adapt a standard costing system to these changing environments.

and cost allocation methods, as discussed in the preceding chapters. They also influence the way that a standard costing system and variance analyses are used as management tools, including application to the preparation of flexible budgets, selection of evaluation criteria, and considering the implications of the variances in manufacturing cost elements.

Effect of the New Manufacturing Environment on Flexible Budgeting

Under the conventional approach, flexible budgets are prepared using a single-cost driver for all factory overhead. Exhibit 16–17 is a typical conventional flexible budget for an output of 2,000 units (5,000 direct labor-hours) when the firm has a master budget for an output of 3,000 units (7,500 direct labor-hours) and the firm uses direct labor-hours as the activity measure for assigning factory overhead to cost objects. The firm spent 5,200 direct labor-hours to manufacture 2,000 units. Refer to Exhibit 16–18 for the actual cost during the period and a typical conventional performance report for the operations.

Many firms in new manufacturing environments no longer use a single activity measure, such as direct labor-hours or machine-hours, to determine overhead costs and assign them to cost objects. Recent advances in activity-based costing have led many firms to measure and monitor various types of overhead based on activities that drive overhead cost. These firms also use several activity measures in preparing flexible budgets. The budgeted total factory overhead no longer varies with changes in a surrogate activity measure; instead, it uses the activity that drives the factory overhead. Furthermore, firms often use multiple activity measures for overhead costs.

Exhibit 16–17   **Master Budget and Conventional Flexible Budget**

Cost Function			Flexible Budget 2,000 Units (5,000 direct labor-hours)	Master (Static) Budget 3,000 Units (7,500 direct labor-hours)
Variable	**Fixed**			
$20/unit		Direct materials	$ 40,000	$ 60,000
6/Direct labor-hours		Direct labor	30,000	45,000
2/Direct labor-hours		Indirect material	10,000	15,000
1/Direct labor-hours		Repair and maintenance	5,000	7,500
	$5,000	Receiving	5,000	5,000
	30,000	Engineering support	30,000	30,000
	75,000	Setup	75,000	75,000
		Total	$195,000	$237,500

Exhibit 16–18   **Conventional Performance Report**

	Actual Cost	Flexible Budget	Variance
Direct material	$ 50,000	$ 40,000	$10,000 U
Direct labor	36,000	30,000	6,000 U
Indirect material	11,000	10,000	1,000 U
Repair and maintenance	6,500	5,000	1,500 U
Receiving	3,000	5,000	2,000 F
Engineering support	30,000	30,000	—
Setup	50,000	75,000	25,000 F
Total	$186,500	$195,000	$ 8,500 F

Exhibit 16–19 reflects the preparation of a flexible budget using an activity-based approach. Exhibit 16–20 is a performance report that uses the activity-based cost functions in determining the flexible budget for the product manufactured during the period.

The total manufacturing cost variance for the period changed from $8,500 favorable as reported in the conventional performance report that uses a single activity measure cost function (Exhibit 16–18), to $15,000 unfavorable, derived when using an activity-based flexible budget in preparing a performance report for the period (Exhibit 16–20). Exhibit 16–21 compares these performance reports.

Note in Exhibit 16–21 that variances identified using a conventional approach (single activity measure) can be misleading. Substantial differences are found in variances for the cost items repair and maintenance, receiving, and setups. The conventional approach considers repair and maintenance as a variable cost that varies with direct labor-hours. In contrast, the activity-based approach identifies repair and maintenance as a mixed cost with the variable portion of the cost varying with machine-hours. As a result, the cost variance incurred for repair and maintenance decreases from $1,500 unfavorable to $500 unfavorable. The conventional approach considers both receiving and setups as fixed costs while the activity-based costing approach classifies these two costs as batch-related costs. The net result of these changes in cost variances is a $25,500 total difference in cost variances.

Exhibit 16–19 Cost Functions of Manufacturing Costs

Cost Item	Activity Measure	Cost Function Variable	Fixed	Flexible Budget	Master (Static) Budget
Output	Number of units			2,000 units	3,000 units
Direct labor-hours				5,000 hours	7,500 hours
Machine-hours				300,000 hours	450,000 hours
Number of setups				2 setups	3 setups
Direct materials	Number of units	$20/unit	—	$40,000	$60,000
Direct labor	Number of units	$15/unit	—	30,000	45,000
Indirect materials	Direct labor-hours	$2/direct labor-hours	—	10,000	15,000
Repair and maintenance	Machine-hours	$0.01/machine-hours	$3,000	6,000	7,500
Receiving	Number of setups	$1,500/setup	$500	$ 3,500	$ 5,000
Setup	Number of setups	$25,000/setup	—	50,000	75,000
Engineering support	Per period		$30,000	30,000	30,000
Total				$169,500	$237,500

Exhibit 16–20 Performance Report Using Activity-Based Costing

	Cost Incurred	Flexible Budget	Variance
Direct materials	$ 50,000	$ 40,000	$10,000 U
Direct labor	36,000	30,000	6,000 U
Indirect materials	11,000	10,000	1,000 U
Repair and maintenance	6,500	6,000	500 U
Receiving	3,000	3,500	500 F
Engineering support	30,000	30,000	—
Setup	48,000	50,000	2,000 F
Total	$184,500	$169,500	$15,000 U

Exhibit 16–21	**Comparison of Conventional and Activity-Based Costing Performance Reports**

	Variances		
	Conventional	**Activity-Based**	**Difference**
Direct materials	$10,000 U	$10,000 U	—
Direct labor	6,000 U	6,000 U	—
Indirect materials	1,000 U	1,000 U	—
Repair and maintenance	1,500 U	500 U	$ 1,000
Receiving	2,000 F	500 F	1,500
Engineering support	—	—	—
Setup	25,000 F	2,000 F	23,000
Total	$ 8,500 F	$15,000 U	$25,500

Calculating Variances in the New Manufacturing Environment

In today's new manufacturing environment, not all firms choose to calculate and report all the variances that are usually reported using a conventional standard cost system. Among variances that are no longer computed and reported by some firms are materials price, materials usage, labor efficiency, variable overhead budget, and overhead production volume variances. Chapter 15 discussed materials and labor variances. We now examine overhead variances in a new manufacturing environment.

Overhead Flexible Budget Variance

Using an activity-based costing system enables a firm to calculate overhead variances in more detail for each overhead activity measure as discussed earlier. This system provides an opportunity for more detailed variance analyses that can reveal more of the underlying causes of the variances. Firms should not, however, overemphasize individual overhead variances. The focus should be on the total factory overhead variance, not variances of individual overhead items. An unfavorable setup variance could encourage excessively large production runs. Furthermore, overconcern with unfavorable factory overhead variances could cause minimal inspections or preventive maintenance.

Production Volume Variance

The production volume variance is calculated by multiplying the difference in units manufactured from the units budgeted to be manufactured by the standard fixed factory overhead rate. The standard fixed factory overhead rate is determined by dividing the total budgeted fixed factory overhead by the denominator activity.

Firms should use as the denominator the capacity of the equipment or division that is the constraint of the manufacturing process rather than the operating level of the division or firm. When more than one constraint exists, the denominator should be the smallest capacity among the constrained production processes. Using a nonconstrained activity as the denominator encourages all divisions to manufacture the denominator quantity in order to minimize their production volume variances. The excess units that nonconstrained divisions or equipment manufacture over the production capacity of the constrained divisions or equipment increase work-in-process inventories and consumption of resources; they do not increase the productivity or the operating efficiency of the manufacturing process. Nor do they increase the firm's operating income. In fact, a favorable production volume variance of nonconstrained equipment or divisions has unfavorable effects to the firm; it increases the firm's work and costs of resources for the period.[11]

---

[11] Eliyahu M. Goldratt, *The Goal* (Croton-on-Hudson, N.Y.: North River Press, 1986).

What Effects Does Cell Manufacturing Have on Factory Overhead?

After almost a century of movement toward mass production, use of ever larger machinery, and facility of Henry Ford's assembly line, the National Association of Manufacturers found in 1994 that the majority of factories are now using cell manufacturing. In cell manufacturing, a small team of workers group around manufacturing equipment and make entire products. A single cell makes, checks, and even packages an entire product or component. Each worker performs several tasks, and every cell is responsible for the quality of its products.

The benefits of manufacturing cells include speed, productivity, flexibility, and higher quality. After Gore-Tex adopted cell manufacturing at several of its 46 plants, it cut production time in half and delivered 97 percent, as compared to 75 percent, of the products on time. At both Harley-Davidson and Lexmark, productivity has increased by 25 percent. Harley-Davidson's cell-based plants have experienced substantial improvements in quality, despite the fact that the number of quality inspectors has been cut significantly. Mr. Kathuria, a factory manager at Harley-Davidson, attributed the success of cells to employee satisfaction. Working on an assembly line allows each worker to spend only a few seconds on each product. Few workers would see the finished product. In cells employees see their product from start to finish. As Mr. Kathuria says, "they own the serial number."

However, does cell manufacturing have effect on factory overheads?

A division can achieve a favorable production volume variance by stepping up production activities to increase the number of units manufactured. This favorable production volume variance could be achieved, however, by manufacturing for inventory—a practice in which a JIT firm should never engage. The production volume variance should never be calculated and reported for performance evaluation purposes because it encourages the unwanted behavior of manufacturing for inventory. If calculated, the fixed factory overhead production volume variance should be reported only to top managers. It should never be used to evaluate the performances of lower operating units.

Furthermore, the production volume variance should never be reported alone but should be accompanied by the ratio of units used or shipped to the total units manufactured. So long as the ratio is 1 or very close to 1, any production volume variance can have only long-term implications; it has no significance in short-term evaluation of operations.

INVESTIGATION OF VARIANCES

Identification and report of variances are the first steps in controlling the variances and improving operations. An effective standard costing system requires that management respond properly to variances because one left uncorrected can affect the firm for many periods. Unnecessary corrective action, on the other hand, wastes resources and can cause performance to decline.

◄**LEARNING OBJECTIVE 9**

Determine whether to investigate variances.

Not all variances call for investigation and corrective action. The proper response to a variance depends on the type of standard the firm uses, the firm's expectation, the magnitude and impact of the variances, and the causes and controllability of variances.

Type of Standard

A firm can use either a currently attainable standard or an ideal standard in its standard costing system. Proper actions for variances from these two standards differ. A material variance from a currently attainable standard, either favorable or unfavorable, often requires management's immediate attention.

The same variance from an ideal standard, in contrast, can require no action on the part of management beyond noting improvement in operations as indicated by the magnitude and direction of the variance. So long as the organization is making good progress toward the ideal standard over time, management might not need to take any corrective action, even if the variance is rather substantial in amount.

765

Expectations of the Firm

Firms have different expectations for their operations. A firm experiencing a crisis needs and demands peak performance from all employees. A struggling firm might need to attain the established standards in all cases and allow no exceptions, even if the firm adopts an ambitious ideal standard. In contrast, a highly profitable firm could be satisfied with making steady progress toward its established standard, especially when it uses an ideal standard to communicate its desired ultimate goal to staff members. The firm should not be overly alarmed by minor deviations from the standard. Companies with good management and caring workers, however, care about meeting the standards regardless of whether the firm is struggling or profitable.

Experience can also affect an organization's reaction to a variance. A firm in the early stages of using an ideal standard should not be alarmed by small deviations; a firm further along the path toward an ideal standard might see the same amount of deviation as a setback that requires corrective action.

Magnitude, Pattern, and Impact of a Variance

The magnitude of a variance and its impact on future operations affects the firm's reaction to the variance. Rarely do operating results meet the standards exactly. Small variances are expected, and most of them need no special attention from management unless a pattern develops. A persistent but small unfavorable variance could require management's attention because its cumulative effect on operating results can be quite substantial and reflect deteriorating operations.

A large variance usually catches the attention of management, which usually responds with immediate corrective action. Such a response, however, might not be warranted. A large variance does not require action if it does not represent the underlying operations or if it is a one-time occurrence. A large unfavorable factory overhead efficiency variance identified with direct labor-hours as the base for applying factory overhead might not indicate runaway factory overhead costs if the bulk of factory overhead is driven by activities other than direct labor-hours. Similarly, a large unfavorable direct materials usage variance requires no further action if it is a result of, for example, a poorly adjusted machine that has since been repaired.

Causes and Controllability

The degree to which an organization can control a variance determines whether corrective actions are needed. No action is needed if management has no control over the variance although it has a significant impact on the firm's operations.

Causes of variances can be classified in two categories: random and systematic.

Random variances are beyond the control of management, either technically or financially, and are often considered as *uncontrollable variances*. Standards often are point estimates of the long-term average performance of operations. Small variances in either direction occur in operations, and the firm usually cannot benefit from investigating or responding to them. For example, prices of goods or services acquired in open markets fluctuate with, among other factors, supply and demand at the time of acquisition and the amount of time allowed to acquire the goods or services. These variances are random and require no management action.

Systematic variances are persistent and are likely to recur unless they are corrected. They usually are controllable by management or can be eliminated or reduced through actions of management. Systematic variances that are material in amount require management to take proper corrective action. Among causes for these variances are prediction, modeling, measurement, and implementation. Each of these factors has its own implications for further investigation or for the managerial action to correct the variance. Variances resulting from different sources call for different actions.Exhibit 16–22 classifies variances according to controllability, causes, and actions to be taken.

Random variances are variances beyond the control of management, either technically or financially, that often are considered as uncontrollable variances.

Systematic variances are variances that are likely to recur unless they are corrected.

Exhibit 16–22	Classification of Variances		
Controllability	**Causes of Variances**	**Actions to Be Taken**	**Examples**
Uncontrollable (random)	Random error	None	Overtime wages paid to make up time lost by employees ill with the flu
			Materials lost in a fire
Controllable (systematic)	Prediction error	Modify standard-setting processes	Increase in materials prices faster than expected
	Modeling error	Revise model or modeling process	Failed to consider learning curve effect in estimating product costs
			Not allowing for normal materials lost
	Measurement error	Adjust accounting procedures	Bonus attributed to the period paid, not the period earned
			Costs assigned to wrong jobs
	Implementation error	Take proper corrective actions	Failure to provide proper training for the task

Prediction errors result from inaccurately estimating the amounts of variables included in the standard-setting process. For example, a firm allowed a 5 percent price increase for a direct material when the actual price increased 10 percent, or it expected to have adequate $10-per-hour workers available when a shortage forced it to hire workers at $15 per hour.

Modeling errors result from failing to include all relevant variables or from including wrong or irrelevant ones in the standard-setting process. A modeling error occurs when a firm uses as standards the production rates of experienced workers although most of its workers have little or no experience. The unfavorable direct labor efficiency variance that the firm experienced is a result of the modeling error, not of inefficient operations. The standard of making 100 gallons of output from every 100 gallons of input material is a modeling error when the manufacturing process has a 5 percent normal evaporation rate.

Corrective actions for both prediction and modeling errors require the firm to change its standard for operations.

Measurement errors are incorrect numbers resulting from improper or inaccurate accounting systems or procedures. Including bonuses for extraordinary productivity as a cost of the period in which the bonuses were paid rather than the period in which they were earned is a measurement error. Charging overhead incurred for setups based on direct production labor-hours rather than the number of setups is a measurement error. Corrective actions for measurement errors include redesigning the firm's accounting systems or procedures and properly training cost accountants.

Failure to correct prediction, modeling, or measurement errors would, in the long term, frustrate employees and lead them to focus on showing the best reported results, even at the expense of bettering the firm's overall performance. Employees of firms using standard costing systems that have uncorrected prediction, modeling, or measurement errors often lose confidence in accounting reports.

An **implementation error** is a deviation from the standard that occurs during operations as a result of operators' errors. The unfavorable materials usage variance from using materials of lesser quality than specified by the standard is an implementation error. The direct labor rate or efficiency variance in an operation that assigned workers with a different skill level than the one called for in the standard is an implementation error. The cutting machine that might be set to cut tubes in lengths of 2 feet 9.7 inches instead of 2 feet 10 inches as required is another example of implementation error.

Some implementation errors are temporary and disappear in subsequent periods in a normal course of operation. Other implementation errors could be persistent and reappear until the firm takes proper corrective actions. An incorrectly set cutting machine continues to manufacture products with wrong lengths until the problem is

A **prediction error** is a deviation from the standard because of an inaccurate estimation of the amounts for variables used in the standard-setting process.

A **modeling error** is a deviation from the standard because of the failure to include all relevant variables or because of inclusion of wrong or irrelevant variables in the standard-setting process.

Measurement errors are incorrect numbers resulting from improper or inaccurate accounting systems or procedures.

An **implementation error** is a deviation from the standard that occurs during operations as a result of operators' errors.

corrected. Use of wrong or excessive materials in production, on the other hand, could occur for only one production run.

Among the tools that can help managers keep track of variances and determine the need to investigate variances is the statistical control chart.

Statistical Control Chart

A widely used tool that helps managers identify out-of-control variances is a control chart that plots variances over time (see Exhibit 16–23). A control chart enables managers to grasp the size and the trend, if any, of variances over time. Exhibit 16–23 reflects an upward trend of unfavorable variances in March through June and repeated in September through December. An alert manager would very likely monitor the operations closely starting from, say, April or May. Were corrective actions taken in April or May, the upward pattern of unfavorable variances starting in September might not have occurred. The chart also suggests that the firm tends to have larger unfavorable variances at the end and the beginning of a year. Management needs to examine this phenomenon and determine whether corrective actions are warranted.

Firms often set control limits in control charts. Typically, the two limits are upper and lower. Although the limits in Exhibit 16–23 are equal in distance from the standard cost, they are not necessarily so, especially when it is more costly to the firm to incur unfavorable variances than favorable variances. In such cases, a firm might allow a narrower band for the upper limit than for the lower limit.

Variances within the limits are deemed random variances and no further action is needed unless a pattern emerges.

When the control limits are established using a statistical procedure, the chart is called a **statistical control chart**. A common practice is to set the control limits at ± 3 standard deviations from the standard cost. The control limits, however, vary with the type of standard the firm uses and management expectations.

The chapter Appendix examines a cost-benefit approach in evaluating the decision to investigate variances under uncertainty.

*A **statistical control chart** sets control limits using a statistical procedure.*

Company Practices

Experienced managers usually have a good intuitive feel for whether a variance requires further investigation. Others follow a magnitude rule of thumb, either in dollar amounts or in percentage of variation, to determine whether to further investigate

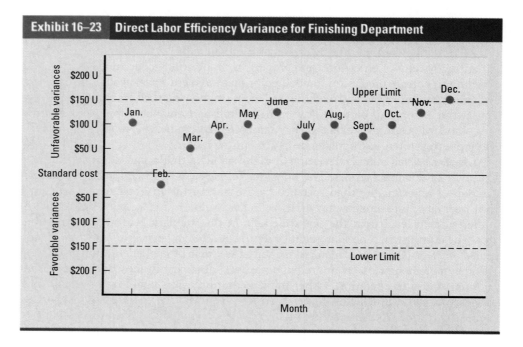

Exhibit 16–23   **Direct Labor Efficiency Variance for Finishing Department**

variances. Often, the cause for a variance is corrected before the variance is reported. Through visual inspections, the operator of a cutting machine might notice that the cuttings are not square as required. The operator could adjust the alignment that caused the improper cutting and correct the problem even before the manager receives the variance report.

The following survey of U.S. managers showed vastly different approaches to investigating direct materials and direct labor variances.

Company Practice for Investigating Direct Material and Direct Labor Variances

	Percent	
	Direct Materials	**Direct Labor**
All variances investigated	6.9%	5.3%
Variances above prescribed dollar limits investigated	34.8	31.0
Variances above prescribed percentage limits investigated	12.2	14.1
Statistical procedures used to select cases for investigation	0.9	0.9
Judgment used to decide whether investigation is needed	45.2	47.8
Variances never investigated	0.0	0.9
Total	100.0%	100.0%

Source: B. Gaumnitz and F. Kollaritsch, "Manufacturing Variances: Current Practice and Trends," *Journal of Cost Management,* Spring 1991, pp. 58–64.

SUMMARY

Establishing standard variable factory overhead for an operation requires determining the cost behavior patterns of overhead cost items, selection of proper measure(s) of activity, and calculation of the overhead application rate. Exhibit 16–24 summarizes an analysis of factory overhead variances.

The variable factory overhead flexible budget variance or the total variable factory overhead variance, shown as (A) in Exhibit 16–24, is the difference between the total variable factory overhead cost incurred during the period and the total standard variable factory overhead for the number of units manufactured. Variable factory overhead spending and efficiency variances are detailed analyses of the total variance. The variable factory overhead spending variance, (B), is the difference between the variable factory overhead incurred and the standard variable factory overhead for the actual quantity of the activity measure for applying variable factory overhead. The variable factory overhead efficiency variance, (C), is the difference between the standard variable factory overhead for the actual quantity of the activity measure(s) for applying variable factory overhead and the standard variable factory overhead for the output of the period. Because of the imperfect association between the activity measure(s) for applying overhead and the variable factory overhead costs, a variable factory overhead spending variance could include both price and usage variances; a variable factory overhead efficiency variance might not measure efficiency in the usage of variable factory overhead items but merely efficiency in use of the activity measure for applying overhead.

Uses of standard costs for fixed factory overhead include establishing the budgeted fixed factory overhead for the operation, selecting one or more activity measure(s) for applying fixed factory overhead, and choosing the denominator activity level for the period as measured by the chosen activity measure. The fixed factory overhead application rate is determined by dividing the quantity of the activity measure at the denominator activity level into the budgeted total fixed factory

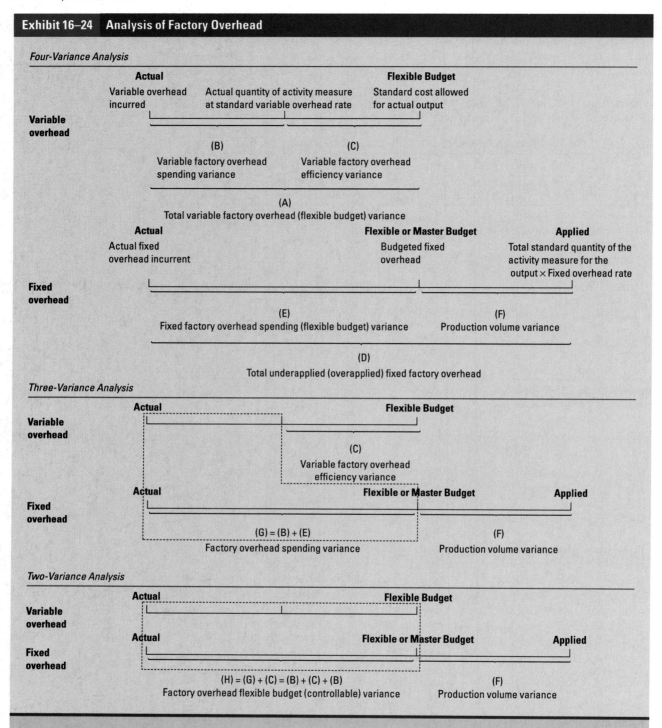

Exhibit 16–24   Analysis of Factory Overhead

Four-Variance Analysis

	Actual		Flexible Budget	
Variable overhead	Variable overhead incurred	Actual quantity of activity measure at standard variable overhead rate	Standard cost allowed for actual output	

(B)
Variable factory overhead spending variance

(C)
Variable factory overhead efficiency variance

(A)
Total variable factory overhead (flexible budget) variance

	Actual	Flexible or Master Budget	Applied
Fixed overhead	Actual fixed overhead incurrent	Budgeted fixed overhead	Total standard quantity of the activity measure for the output × Fixed overhead rate

(E)
Fixed factory overhead spending (flexible budget) variance

(F)
Production volume variance

(D)
Total underapplied (overapplied) fixed factory overhead

Three-Variance Analysis

Variable overhead   Actual — Flexible Budget

(C)
Variable factory overhead efficiency variance

Fixed overhead   Actual — Flexible or Master Budget — Applied

(G) = (B) + (E)
Factory overhead spending variance

(F)
Production volume variance

Two-Variance Analysis

Variable overhead   Actual — Flexible Budget

Fixed overhead   Actual — Flexible or Master Budget — Applied

(H) = (G) + (C) = (B) + (C) + (B)
Factory overhead flexible budget (controllable) variance

(F)
Production volume variance

overhead. Fixed overhead variances include the fixed factory overhead spending (budget) variance and the production volume variance. In Exhibit 16–24, the fixed factory overhead spending variance, (E), is the difference between the actual and the budgeted fixed factory overhead for the period. Neither the actual units manufactured nor the actual level of the activity measure incurred during the period has any effect on the amount of the fixed factory overhead spending variance. The production volume variance, (F), is the difference between the total budgeted fixed factory overhead and the total fixed factory overhead applied to the units manufactured during the period. The difference between the actual and the applied fixed factory overhead (or the sum of spending and production volume variances), (D), also is referred to as *underapplied* or *overapplied fixed factory overhead*.

The variances identified for variable factory overhead and fixed factory overhead can be combined into either three or two variances. The three-variance analysis creates a factory overhead spending variance, (G), by combining variable factory overhead spending and fixed factory overhead spending variances into one variance. The other two factory overhead variances remain intact. The three variances, therefore, are the factory overhead spending variance (G), the factory overhead efficiency variance (C), and the production volume variance (F). The two-variance analysis further combines the factory overhead spending variance, (G), with the factory overhead efficiency variance, (C). The combined variance is the factory overhead flexible budget variance, (H), or factory overhead controllable variance.

A firm can dispose of variances in the income statement of the period in which the variance occurs by charging them to the cost of goods sold. Alternatively, the firm can prorate the variances among the cost of goods sold and ending inventories.

Benefits from using standard costing systems are not limited to manufacturing operations; service firms and other types of operations can also benefit from using them. Because operating characteristics of service firms often differ from those of manufacturing firms, modifications might be needed and emphases could be different when using standard costing in a service organization. Among service organizations' different operating characteristics are the absence of output inventory, the labor-intensive operation, the predominance of fixed costs, and the ambiguity of output measures in service organizations.

Changes in manufacturing environments in recent years have affected the application of standard costing systems. Firms in new manufacturing environments no longer use a single activity measure to measure and apply overhead. An increasing number of firms are using ideal, rather than currently attainable, standards. To be globally competitive, many firms mandate continual improvement and striving for perfection. In addition, these firms do not calculate all variances. The theory of constraints points out that the denominator activity level should be set at the level of the operation's constrained activity.

Whether to investigate variances depends on the type of standard the firm uses, the expectations of the firm, the magnitude and impact of variances, and the causes and controllability of variances. Causes of variances can be random or systematic. Systematic causes include prediction, modeling, measurement, and implementation.

APPENDIX A

Variance Investigation Decisions under Uncertainty

Investigations of variances cost time and money. Firms must weigh the costs of investigation against the benefits in deciding whether to investigate a variance. The purpose of investigation is to determine the states of nature or the underlying cause of the variance. Management can then take proper action.

The states of nature underlying a variance can be either *random* or *systematic*. The alternative actions available to management when facing a variance are either to conduct an investigation or to take no action. With two possible states of nature and two courses of action, there are four combinations, each of which entails a different cost to the firm. These four combinations follow:

IR Investigate and find the reported variance to be a **r**andom fluctuation. No further action is needed.

IN Investigate and determine the reported variance is a result of systematic or **n**onrandom causes. Management then takes corrective action.

NR Do not investigate; the reported variance is a result of random variations.

NN Do not investigate; the reported variance is a result of systematic or nonrandom causes.

Payoff Table

The cost to the firm for different courses of action is likely to be different. Exhibit 16–25 shows the consequences of alternative management action under different states of nature. When the variance is the result of a nonrandom factor, the cost to the firm to correct the variance is C. The cost of correction includes the cost to correct the nonrandom factor that led to the variance and the cost of the variance that the firm continues to experience until the variance is corrected. If management decides not to investigate the reported variance and it is systematic and persistent, the firm then suffers a total cost, L (the present value of all losses the firm will suffer before the next decision time).

The decision not to investigate is correct when the variance is a random occurrence. The firm wastes no resources at all; it will, however, suffer a loss of L if the reported variance is the result of a nonrandom cause.

Management should also estimate the likelihood that the operation is in control or out of control, based on its understanding of the operation. Being in control implies that the reported variance is a random phenomenon. Being out of control suggests that the reported variance is the result of one or more systematic causes. The estimated probabilities of the states of nature enable management to compute the expected costs for each alternative action. The expected costs then serve as the input to the variance investigation decision.

Upon receiving the variance report, management estimates the probability that the reported variance is caused by a random fluctuation at 90 percent. The investigation cost is approximately $1,000. Corrective actions, if needed, will likely cost the firm approximately $5,000, including the loss from the variance that it will continue to incur before the cause is corrected. The firm will suffer losses with a present value of $30,000 if it conducts no investigation but the variance stemmed from a nonrandom cause. Exhibit 16–26 summarizes this information.

Management has a 90 percent chance of finding that the variance is merely a random fluctuation and that the investigation is therefore a waste of time and resources. However, there is a 10 percent chance that the variance results from nonrandom factors that should be corrected to avoid further losses. With the cost of investigation,

Exhibit 16–25	Payoff Table for Variance Investigation	
		States of Nature
Management Action	**Random**	**Nonrandom**
Investigate	—	$I + C$
Do not investigate	none	L

Exhibit 16–26	Decision Based on a Payroll Table		
		States of Nature	
Management Action	**Random** **90%**	**Nonrandom** **10%**	**Expected Value**
Investigate	$1,000	$ 6,000	$1,500
Do not investigate	0	30,000	3,000

$1,000, and the cost of corrective action, $5,000, the firm's total cost will be $6,000 if the investigation finds that the cause of the variance is nonrandom. The expected value of investigation is, therefore, $1,500, as shown in this computation:

$$E(\text{Investigate}) = (\$1,000 \times 90\%) + (\$6,000 \times 10\%) = \$1,500$$

If management decides not to investigate, there is still a 90 percent chance that the variance is random and the firm incurs no cost. There is, however, a 10 percent chance that the variance is a result of nonrandom factors. In this case, the firm is likely to suffer a total loss of $30,000. Thus, the expected cost of not investigating the cause of the variance is $3,000, as shown here:

$$E(\text{Do not investigate}) = (\$0 \times 90\%) + (\$30,000 \times 10\%) = \$3,000$$

The $1,500 expected cost of investigation is lower than the $3,000 cost of not investigating, so the recommended course of action according to the payoff table is to conduct an investigation to find the cause of the reported variance.

Indifference Probability

A payoff table can also be used in determining the maximum level of probability that a nonrandom variance occurred and that management will decide not to investigate the cause of the reported variance. Let p be the probability of a nonrandom variance. Then the probability of a random variance is $1 - p$. Exhibit 16–27 shows the payoff table.

The expected costs of management actions can be represented as follows:

$$E(\text{investigate}) = I \times (1 - p) + (I + C) \times p$$

and

$$E(\text{do not investigate}) = L \times p$$

If the cost of both actions is the same, it makes no difference to the firm which course of action it takes. That is, for management to be indifferent to courses of action (to investigate or not), their expected costs must be equal. At the indifference point,

$$I \times (1 - p) + (I + C) \times p = L \times p$$

Simplifying the equation, we get

$$I + C \times p = L \times p$$

which can be rewritten as

$$p = \frac{I}{L - C}$$

Using the data in Exhibit 16–26, the indifference probability is 4 percent:

$$p = \frac{\$1,000}{\$30,000 - \$5,000} = 4\%$$

The result suggests that the optimal action for management is to conduct an investigation when the probability of nonrandom variance exceeds 4 percent. Our earlier

---

Exhibit 16–27   Use of a Payoff Table to Determine Indifference Probability

	States of Nature	
Management Action	**Random** **$1 - p$**	**Nonrandom** **p**
Investigate	I	$I + C$
Do not investigate	0	L

calculation confirms this conclusion. The probability of nonrandom variance was estimated to be 10 percent, and the payoff table suggests that the recommended course of action is for the firm to investigate the cause of the variance.

KEY TERMS

Denominator activity **748**

Fixed factory overhead application rate **748**

Fixed factory overhead production volume variance **750**

Fixed factory overhead spending (budget) variance **749**

Implementation error **767**

Measurement error **767**

Modeling error **767**

Prediction error **767**

Random variances **766**

Statistical control charts **768**

Systematic variances **766**

Total variable factory overhead variance **742**

Variable factory overhead efficiency variance **744**

Variable factory overhead spending variance **744**

COMMENTS ON COST MANAGEMENT IN ACTION

Firms adopting cell manufacturing have found their factory overheads decreased both in total and in unit cost. At Harley-Davidson, the floor space occupied by the factory was reduced by a third. Gore-Tex decreased the space taken up by the plant by one-quarter. Factors contributing to the need for less space are clustering of equipment and decrease or elimination of work-in-process and finished inventories.

Increased productivity further allows the reduced total factory overhead to be borne by higher volumes and, thus, decreases factory overhead per unit. In 1981, Harley-Davidson took a week to make a cylinder head and turned over its product only 4.5 times a year. In 1994, it took a two-man cell less than three hours to make a cylinder head and the firm turned over its stock 40 times a year.

Based on "The Celling Out of America." *The Economist*, December 1994, pp. 63–4.

SELF-STUDY PROBLEMS

(For solutions, please turn to the end of the chapter.)

1. Analysis of Overhead Variance

Simpson Manufacturing has the following standard cost sheet for one of its products:

Direct materials	5 pounds at	$2	$10
Direct labor	2 hours at	25	50
Variable factory overhead	2 hours at	5	10
Fixed factory overhead	2 hours at	20	40

Factory overhead is to be applied based on direct labor-hours, and the factory overhead rate is determined based on manufacturing 400 units of the product.

The firm has the following actual operating results for the year just completed:

Units manufactured	360	
Direct materials purchased and used	1,800 pounds	$19,800
Direct labor incurred	750 hours	20,250
Variable factory overhead incurred		4,800
Fixed factory overhead incurred		15,800

Before closing the periodic accounts, the balances in selected accounts follow:

Account	Debit (total)	Credit (total)
Work-in-process inventory	$153,000	$134,640
Finished goods inventory	134,640	111,690
Cost of goods sold	111,690	

Required

1. Determine the following:
    a. Total standard variable factory overhead for the period.
    b. Total variable factory overhead applied during the period.
    c. Total budgeted fixed factory overhead.
    d. Total fixed factory overhead applied.
2. Compute the following variances using four-variance analysis:
    a. Total variable factory overhead variance.
    b. Variable factory overhead spending variance.
    c. Variable factory overhead efficiency variance.
    d. Total underapplied or overapplied variable factory overhead variance.
    e. Fixed factory overhead spending variance.
    f. Production volume variance.
    g. Total fixed factory overhead variance.
    h. Total underapplied or overapplied fixed factory overhead variance.
3. Compute the following variances using three-variance analysis:
    a. Factory overhead spending variance.
    b. Factory overhead efficiency variance.
    c. Production volume variance.
4. Compute the factory overhead flexible budget and production volume variances using two-variance analysis.
5. Make proper journal entries for
    a. Incurrence of factory overhead costs.
    b. Application of factory overhead costs to production.
    c. Identification of factory overhead variances assuming that the firm uses the four-variance analysis identified in requirement 2.
    d. Close all factory overhead cost items and their variances of the period if
        (1) The firm closes all variances to the Cost of Goods Sold account of the period.
        (2) The firm prorates variances to the inventory accounts and the Cost of Goods Sold account of the period.

2. Variance Investigation (Appendix A)

David Smiley is the manager of Photobonics Manufacturing. He notices that the operation has had an unfavorable materials efficiency variance of $25,000 in the last few weeks. He is trying to decide whether to investigate this variance. If he does investigate and discovers that the process is indeed out of control, corrective actions will cost the firm $5,000. The cost of an investigation is $2,500. The firm could suffer a total loss of $55,000 if it continues with the operation if it is out of control. Smiley estimates the probability that the operation is out of control to be 60 percent.

Required

1. What are the expected costs of investigating and of not investigating? Should the operation be investigated?
2. At what level of probability that the operation is out of control would Smiley be indifferent as to the course of action to be taken?

QUESTIONS

16–1   Verbatim Company's budget for factory overhead for last year was $80,000. The actual cost for the period is identical to the budgeted amount although the actual production was 90 percent of the budgeted production. Can we say that the plant manager has done a good job in controlling the factory overhead if (a) the firm has only fixed factory overhead or (b) the firm has both variable and fixed factory overheads?

16–2   What is the relationship between the variable factory overhead efficiency variance and the direct labor efficiency variance for firms that use direct labor-hours for applying factory overhead?

16–3   What is the relationship among factory overhead spending variance, variable factory overhead spending variance, fixed factory overhead budget variance, and variable factory overhead efficiency variance?

16–4   What is a factory overhead flexible budget variance?

16–5   "Whether the variance is favorable or unfavorable need not be considered when deciding whether to investigate a variance." Do you agree?

16–6   "As long as the total factory overhead incurred does not vary significantly from the standard cost of the factory overhead required for a given operation, there is no need for further analyses of the factory overhead variance." Do you agree?

16–7   Why do some firms choose to use two-variance instead of three-variance or four-variance analysis of their manufacturing overhead cost variances?

16–8   What is the difference between the applied variable factory overhead and the total variable factory overhead in the flexible budget? Between the applied fixed factory overhead and the total fixed factory overhead in the master budget?

16–9   Would the choice of denominator level affect the amount of fixed factory overhead (flexible) budget variance? Production volume variance?

16–10   Sipple Furniture's annual master budget includes $360,000 for fixed production supervisory salaries at a monthly volume of 500 units. Supervisory salaries are expected to be incurred uniformly through the year. During August, the firm produced 450 units and incurred production supervisory salaries of $29,000. What is Sipple Furniture's supervisory salary's flexible budget variance for August?

16–11   Baxter Corporation's master budget calls for the production of 5,000 units monthly. The master budget includes indirect labor of $144,000 annually; Baxter considers indirect labor as a variable overhead. During April, the firm produced 4,500 units and incurred indirect labor costs of $10,100. What amount would be reported as a flexible budget variance for indirect labor if Baxter prepares a performance report using a flexible budget based on the units produced during the period?

(**CMA** Adapted)

16–12   Can the differences between the actual and the standard factory overhead be separated into price and efficiency variances as can be done when analyzing direct material or direct labor variances?

16–13   List causes that could lead to a variable factory overhead spending variance.

16–14   List causes that could lead to a variable factory overhead efficiency variance.

16–15   List causes that could lead to a fixed factory overhead spending variance.

16–16   List causes that could lead to a production volume variance.

16–17 How do the characteristics of service and manufacturing firms differ? Discuss the effects, if any, that these characteristics could have on the use of a standard costing system by service firms.

16–18 Why do many firms in today's new manufacturing environment no longer compute and report a direct materials price variance?

16–19 What factors should be considered in determining whether to investigate a variance?

EXERCISES

16–20 FACTORY OVERHEAD RATES FLEXIBLE BUDGET AND THREE-VARIANCE ANALYSIS Walkenhorst Company's machining department expects to finish the current year with 42,000 units and is preparing the budget for the coming year using these estimates:

Maximum capacity	50,000 units
Machine-hours per unit	2
Variable factory overhead	$3.00 per hour
Fixed factory overhead	$360,000

The firm decided to prepare the budget at 80 percent of the maximum capacity. The department uses machine-hours as the basis on which to apply factory overhead. The firm spent 85,000 machine-hours and $625,000 in manufacturing overhead to manufacture 42,000 units during the year.

Required Determine for the year

1. The factory overhead application rate.
2. The total flexible budget factory overhead.
3. The production volume variance.
4. The factory overhead spending variance.
5. The factory overhead efficiency variance.
6. The additional information for conducting a 4-variance analysis.

16–21 FACTORY OVERHEAD FLEXIBLE BUDGET AND TWO-VARIANCE ANALYSIS Bush & Co. uses flexible budgets for cost control. During March, Bush produced 10,800 units and incurred $13,000 in total factory overhead, of which $2,500 was for fixed factory overhead.

The master budget for the year called for production of 150,000 units with total factory overhead of $180,000. The total fixed factory overhead in the annual budget was $60,000.

Required Compute the following for March production:

1. Total flexible budget overhead for the units manufactured.
2. All variances, including
   a. Factory overhead spending variance.
   b. Fixed factory overhead production volume variance.
3. Can the firm perform a three-variance or four-variance analysis of factory overhead using the data given? Why or why not?

16–22 FLEXIBLE BUDGET AND VARIANCES FOR DEPRECIATION Somson SuperKlean Service's master budget shows $258,000 for depreciation on equipment. The master budget was prepared at an annual volume of 103,200 chargeable hours. This volume is expected to occur uniformly throughout the year. During September, Somson performed 8,170 chargeable hours, and the firm reported $20,500 for depreciation on equipment.

 *Service*

777

Required

1. Determine the flexible budget amount for depreciation on equipment for September.
2. Compute the spending variance for the depreciation expense on equipment.
3. Calculate the production volume variance for the depreciation expenses.
4. List possible reasons for the spending variance.

16–23 **THREE-VARIANCE ANALYSIS** The following information is available from Swinney Company for its operations in March:

Factory overhead incurred	$20,000
Fixed overhead expenses, incurred	$ 8,000
Fixed overhead expenses, budgeted	$ 9,000
Direct labor hours spent	4,200
Standard direct labor hours for the units manufactured	4,000
Total budgeted direct labor hours	4,500
Standard variable overhead rate per DLH	$ 2.50

Swinney uses a three-variance analysis of factory overhead variances.

Required Compute for Swinney Company

1. The factory overhead spending variance.
2. The variable factory overhead efficiency variance.
3. The factory overhead production volume variance.

16–24 **TWO-VARIANCE ANALYSIS AND APPLIED OVERHEAD** Overhead cost information for Danielson Company for October follows:

Total overhead incurred	$28,800
Fixed overhead budgeted	$ 7,200
Total standard overhead rate per direct labor-hour (DLH)	$ 4.00
Standard variable overhead rate per DLH	$ 3.00
Standard production hours allowed	3,500

Required

1. What is the total factory overhead flexible budget variance?
2. What is the total underapplied or overapplied factory overhead?
3. What is the factory overhead production volume variance?

16–25 **TWO-VARIANCE ANALYSIS OF VARIANCES AND APPLIED OVERHEAD** Information on Conehead Company's overhead costs for May is

Total standard overhead applied	$60,000
Flexible budget overhead for the units produced	54,000
Budgeted total overhead in the master budget for the period	72,000
Overhead incurred	63,000

Required

1. What is the total flexible budget overhead variance?
2. What is the factory overhead production volume variance?
3. What is the total underapplied or overapplied factory overhead?

16–26 **OVERHEAD AT TWO ACTIVITY LEVELS AND FOUR-VARIANCE ANALYSIS** Greenhat Company used a flexible budget system and prepared this information for the year:

	Level of Operation	
	80 percent	**100 percent**
Standard direct machine-hours (MH)	20,000	25,000
Variable factory overhead	$72,000	
Total factory overhead rate per MH	$12.60	

Greenhat applied factory overhead based on the 90 percent capacity level. The standard calls for 2 machine-hours per unit manufactured. During 2001, Greenhat operated 23,000 machine-hours to manufacture 11,300 units. The factory overhead incurred was $12,000 more than the flexible budget amount for the units manufactured, of which $5,000 was due to fixed factory overhead.

Required

1. What is the budget allowance for total fixed factory overhead at 80 percent level of operation? At 100 percent level of operation?

2. What are the standard variable factory overhead rate and the standard fixed factory overhead rate?

3. What is the total factory overhead flexible budget amount for the operation of the period?

4. Using four-variance analysis, compute these for Greenhat Company:

   a. Variable factory overhead spending variance.

   b. Variable factory overhead efficiency variance.

   c. Fixed factory overhead spending variance.

   d. Factory overhead production volume variance.

16–27 **THREE-VARIANCE ANALYSIS** Use the data for Greenhat Company in problem 16–26.

Required Compute the following variances using three-variance analysis:

1. Factory overhead spending variance.
2. Variable factory overhead efficiency variance.
3. Factory overhead production volume variance.

16–28 **TWO-VARIANCE ANALYSIS** Use the data for Greenhat Company in problem 16–26.

Required Compute the following variances using two-variance analysis:

1. Factory overhead flexible budget variance.
2. Factory overhead production volume variance.

16–29 **TWO-VARIANCE ANALYSIS AND DIRECT LABOR VARIANCE** The following information relates to the month of April for Marilyn, Inc., which uses a standard cost system and a two-variance analysis of overhead variances:

Actual total cost for direct labor	$43,400
Total direct labor-hours worked	14,000
Total standard hours for good output	15,000
Direct labor rate variance—unfavorable	$ 1,400
Actual total overhead	$32,000
Budgeted fixed costs	$ 9,000
Normal activity in hours	12,000
Total overhead application rate per standard direct labor-hour	$ 2.25

Required

1. What was Marilyn's direct labor efficiency variance for April?
2. What was Marilyn's factory overhead flexible budget (controllable) variance for April?
3. What was Marilyn's production volume variance for April?

(CPA Adapted)

16–30 **WORKING BACKWARD—TOTAL FACTORY OVERHEAD** Shonburger Company applies factory overhead based on machine-hours (MH) and had a favorable total factory overhead variance of $120,000 for 2001. Additional data pertaining to 2001 follow:

Variable overhead	
Applied based on standard MH for units manufactured	$600,000
Applied to the MH worked	500,000
Fixed overhead	
Applied based on standard MH for units manufactured	$360,000
Budgeted	300,000

Required

1. What is the total overhead incurred in 2001 if the favorable total overhead variance includes production volume variance?
2. What is the total overhead incurred in 2001 if the favorable total overhead variance is defined as the flexible budget overhead variance?

16–31 **ALL FACTORY OVERHEAD VARIANCES** Shateau Job Shop had the following operating data for its operations in 2002:

Budgeted fixed overhead	$20,000
Standard variable overhead (2 machine-hours at $3 each)	$6 per unit
Fixed overhead incurred	$21,400
Variable overhead incurred	$32,500
Budgeted volume (5,000 units × 2 machine-hours)	10,000 MH
Machine-hours spent	9,500
Units produced	4,500

Required Compute these for Shateau Company:

1. Variable factory overhead spending variance.
2. Variable factory overhead efficiency variance.
3. Fixed factory overhead spending variance.
4. Factory overhead production volume variance.
5. Factory overhead spending variance using three-variance analysis.
6. Factory overhead flexible budget variance using two-variance analysis.

16–32 **ABC COSTING** Alden Company uses a two-variance analysis of overhead variances. Its master budget calls for 32 setups during the year to manufacture 6,400 units. Selected data for the 2001 production activity follow:

Budgeted fixed factory overhead costs		
Setup	$ 64,000	
Other	200,000	$264,000
Total factory overhead incurred		$480,000
Variable factory overhead rate		
Per setup		$600
Per machine-hour		$5
Standard machine-hour		30,000 hours
Machine hours worked		35,000 hours
Actual total number of setups		28

Required

1. Compute the factory overhead flexible budget (controllable) variance for 2001.

2. Assume that the firm includes all setup costs as variable factory overhead. The budgeted total fixed factory overhead, therefore, is $200,000, and the standard variable factory rate per setup is $2,600. What is the factory overhead flexible budget (controllable) variance for the year?

3. Assume that the firm uses only machine-hours as the activity measure to apply both variable and fixed factory overhead and includes all setup costs as variable factory overhead. What is the factory overhead flexible budget (controllable) variance for the year?

4. Explain why your answers for 1, 2, and 3 differ.

16–33 THREE-VARIANCE ANALYSIS Tyro Company uses three-variance analysis to determine overhead variances. The following information is taken from its operating data for the year just ended:

Total factory overhead incurred	$15,000	
Fixed factory overhead incurred	7,200	
Budgeted fixed overhead		$8,000
Total hours worked		3,600
Total standard direct labor hours for the units manufactured		4,000
Overhead application rate based on direct labor hour		
Standard variable factory overhead rate		$2.00
Standard fixed factory overhead rate		$2.50

Required Determine the following:

1. The factory overhead spending variance.

2. The factory overhead efficiency variance.

3. The production volume variance.

4. The denominator volume for the master budget.

16–34 FIXED OVERHEAD VARIANCE The annual master budget for Selo Imports includes $324,000 for fixed production supervisory salaries and production volume of 180,000 units. Supervisory salaries are expected to be incurred uniformly throughout the year. The firm spent $28,000 in production supervisory salaries to manufacture 15,750 units in September.

Required Determine the following variances regarding production supervisory salaries that will be included in the performance report for September.

1. The budget (spending) variance.

2. The efficiency variance.

3. The production volume variance.

16–35 THREE-VARIANCE ANALYSIS Savanah Shipping Inc. had the following operating results for its operation in August:

Total standard factory overhead applied	$80,000
Total standard factory overhead for the units manufactured	84,000
Total standard factory overhead for the total hours worked	83,000
Total factory overhead incurred	86,000

Required Compute the following factory overhead variances for Savanah Shipping Inc.

1. The spending variance.
2. The efficiency variance.
3. The production volume variance.
4. The total factory overhead variance.

16–36 FOUR-VARIANCE ANALYSIS Dickey Company had total underapplied factory overhead of $15,000 and unfavorable variable factory overhead spending variance of $6,000 for the year just ended. Additional data follow:

Variable factory overhead	
Applied based on standard direct labor-hours (DLH) allowed	$42,000
Total standard amount based on actual DLH	38,000
Fixed factory overhead	
Applied based on standard DLH allowed	$30,000
Budgeted for the units manufactured	27,000

Required Compute the following for the year:

1. Total variable factory overhead incurred.
2. Total fixed factory overhead incurred.
3. Fixed factory overhead spending variance.
4. Factory overhead production volume variance.

PROBLEMS

16–37 FOUR-VARIANCE ANALYSIS The production budget for Franklin Glass Works for the year ended November 30, 2002, was based on 200,000 units. The standard cost sheet specifies two direct labor-hours for each unit. Total factory overhead was budgeted at $900,000 for the year with a fixed factory overhead rate of $3 per unit. Both fixed and variable factory overhead are assigned to the product on the basis of direct labor-hours. The actual data for the year ended November 30, 2002, follow:

Units manufactured	198,000
Direct labor-hours spent	440,000
Variable factory overhead incurred	$352,000
Fixed factory overhead incurred	$575,000

Required Determine the following for the year just completed:

1. The total number of standard hours allowed for the annual output.
2. The variable factory overhead efficiency variance.
3. The variable factory overhead spending variance.
4. The fixed factory overhead spending variance.
5. The total factory fixed overhead applied.
6. The fixed factory overhead volume variance.

16–38 ALL MANUFACTURING VARIANCES Eastern Company manufactures special electrical equipment and parts. The firm uses a standard costing system with separate standards established for each product.

The transformer department manufactures a special transformer. This department measures production volume in direct labor-hours and uses a flexible budget system to plan and control department overhead.

Standard costs for the special transformer are determined annually in September for the coming year. The standard cost of a transformer at its DeCatur plant for the year just completed is $67 per unit, as shown here:

Direct materials		
Iron	5 sheets × $2	$10
Copper	3 spools × $3	9
Direct labor	4 hours × $7	28
Variable overhead	4 hours × $3	12
Fixed overhead	4 hours × $2	8
Total		$67

Overhead rates were based on normal and expected monthly capacity for the year, both of which were 4,000 direct labor-hours. Practical capacity for this department is 5,000 direct labor-hours per month. Variable overhead costs are expected to vary with the number of direct labor-hours actually used.

During October, the plant produced 800 transformers. This number was below expectations because a work stoppage occurred during labor contract negotiations. When the contract was settled, the department scheduled overtime in an attempt to reach expected production levels.

The following costs were incurred in October:

Direct Material	Purchased	Used
Iron	5,000 sheets at $2.00/sheet	3,900 sheets
Copper	2,200 spools at $3.10/spool	2,600 spools
Direct labor		
Regular time: 2,000 hours at $7.00 and 1,400 hours at $7.20.		
Overtime: 600 of the 1,400 hours were subject to overtime premium. The total overtime premium of $2,160 is included in variable overhead in accordance with company accounting practices.		
Factory overhead		
Variable	$12,000	
Fixed	$ 8,800	

Required

1. What is the most appropriate time to record any variance of actual materials prices from standard?
2. What is the labor rate (price) variance?
3. What is the labor efficiency variance?
4. What is the materials price variance?
5. What is the materials quantity variance?
6. What is the variable overhead spending variance?
7. What is the variable overhead efficiency variance?
8. What is the budget (spending) variance for fixed overhead?
9. What is the factory overhead production volume variance?

(CMA Adapted)

16–39 FOUR-VARIANCE ANALYSIS   Derf Company applies overhead on the basis of direct labor-hours. Each product requires two direct labor-hours. Planned production for the period was set at 9,000 units. Manufacturing overhead is budgeted at $135,000 for the period, of which 20 percent is fixed. The 17,200 hours worked during the period resulted in production of 8,500 units. Variable manufacturing overhead cost incurred was $108,500, and fixed manufacturing overhead cost was $28,000. Derf Company uses four-variance analysis to compute manufacturing overhead.

Required   Compute the following for Derf Company:

1. The variable overhead spending variance for the period.
2. The variable overhead efficiency (quantity) variance for the period.
3. The fixed overhead budget (spending) variance for the period.
4. The factory overhead production volume variance for the period.

(CMA Adapted)

16–40 **FOUR-VARIANCE ANALYSIS**   Able Control Company, which manufactures electrical switches, uses a standard costing system and carries all inventory at standard costs. The standard factory overhead costs per switch are based on direct labor-hours:

Variable overhead	(5 hours at $8/hour)	$ 40
Fixed overhead	(5 hours at $12*/hour)	60
Total overhead		$100

*Based on budget of 300,000 direct labor-hours per month.

The following information is for the month of October:

- The firm produced 56,000 switches, although 60,000 switches were scheduled to be produced.
- The firm used 275,000 direct labor-hours at a total cost of $2,550,000.
- Variable overhead costs were $2,340,000.
- Fixed overhead costs were $3,750,000.

The production manager argued during the last review of the operation that it should use a more up-to-date base for charging factory overhead costs to operations. She commented that her factory had been highly automated in the last two years and has hardly any direct labor. The factory hires only highly skilled workers to set up productions and to do periodic adjustments of machinery whenever the need arises.

Required

1. Compute the following for Able Control Company:
   a. The fixed overhead spending variance for October.
   b. The factory overhead production volume variance for October.
   c. The variable overhead spending variance for October.
   d. The variable overhead efficiency variance for October.
2. Comment on the implications of the variances and suggest any action that the firm should take to improve its operations.

(CMA Adapted)

16–41 **COMPREHENSIVE**   Organet Stamping Company manufactures a variety of products made of plastic and aluminum components. During the winter months, substantially all production capacity is devoted to lawn sprinklers for the following spring and summer seasons. Other products are manufactured during the remainder of the year. Because a variety of products is manufactured throughout the year, factory volume is measured using production labor-hours rather than units of production.

Production volume has grown steadily for the past several years, as the following schedule of production labor indicates:

This year	32,000 hours
1 year ago	30,000 hours
2 years ago	27,000 hours
3 years ago	28,000 hours
4 years ago	26,000 hours

The company has developed standard costs for its several products. It sets standard costs for each year in the preceding October. The standard cost of a sprinkler this year was $4.00, computed as follows:

Direct materials			
Aluminum	0.2 pound	× $0.40 per pound	$0.08
Plastic	1.0 pound	× $0.38 pound	0.38
Production labor	0.3 hour	× $9.00 per hour	2.70
Overhead*			
Variable	0.3 hour	× $1.60 per hour	0.48
Fixed	0.3 hour	× $1.20 per hour	0.36
Total			$4.00

*Calculated using 30,000 production labor-hours as normal capacity.

During February of this year, 8,500 good sprinklers were manufactured. The following costs were incurred and charged to production:

Materials requisitioned for production		
Aluminum	(1,900 pounds × $0.40 per pound)	$ 760
Plastic: Regular	(6,000 pounds × $0.38 per pound)	2,280
Low grade†	(3,500 pounds × $0.38 per pound)	1,330
Production labor		
Straight time	(2,300 hours × $10.00 per hour)	23,000
Overtime	(400 hours × $15.00 per hour)	6,000
Overhead		
Variable	5,200	
Fixed	3,100	8,300
Costs charged to production		$41,670

Materials price variations are not charged to production but to a materials price variation account at the time the invoice is entered. All materials are carried in inventory at standard prices. Materials purchases for February follow:

Aluminum	(1,800 pounds × $0.48 per pound)	$ 864
Plastic		
Regular grade	(3,000 pounds × $0.50)	1,500
Low grade†	(6,000 pounds × $0.29)	1,740

†Plastic shortages forced the company to purchase lower-grade plastic than called for in the standards, which increased the number of sprinklers rejected on inspection.

Required Compute the following:

1. The total variance from standard cost of the costs charged to production for February.
2. The spending or budget variance for the fixed portion of the overhead costs for February.
3. The labor efficiency variance.
4. The labor rate variance (assume that overtime premium is not charged to overhead).

5. The total variable cost variance.

6. The variable overhead spending, efficiency, and flexible budget variances.

7. The factory overhead production volume variance.

8. The materials variances. Also comment on the effects of using materials of different grades.

(CMA Adapted)

16–42 **COMPREHENSIVE**   Cain Company has an automated production process; consequently, it uses machine-hours to describe production activity. The company employs a full absorption costing system. The annual profit plan for the coming fiscal year is finalized each April. The profit plan for the fiscal year ending May 31 called for production of 6,000 units, requiring 30,000 machine-hours. The full absorption costing rate for the fiscal year was determined using 6,000 units of planned production. Cain develops flexible budgets for different levels of activity to use in evaluating performance. A total of 6,200 units was produced during the fiscal year, requiring 32,000 machine-hours. The following schedule compares Cain Company's actual costs for the fiscal year with the profit plan and the budgeted costs for two different activity levels:

CAIN COMPANY
Manufacturing Cost Report
For the Fiscal Year Ended May 31
(in thousands of dollars)

| | | Flexible Budgets for | | |
Item	Profit Plan (6,000 units)	31,000 Machine-Hours	32,000 Machine-Hours	Actual Costs
Direct material				
G27 aluminum	$ 252.0	$ 260.4	$ 268.8	$ 270.0
M14 steel alloy	78.0	80.6	83.2	83.0
Direct labor				
Assembler	273.0	282.1	291.2	287.0
Grinder	234.0	241.8	249.6	250.0
Manufacturing overhead				
Maintenance	24.0	24.8	25.6	25.0
Supplies	129.0	133.3	137.6	130.0
Supervision	80.0	82.0	84.0	81.0
Inspector	144.0	147.0	150.0	147.0
Insurance	50.0	50.0	50.0	50.0
Depreciation	200.0	200.0	200.0	200.0
Total cost	$1,464.0	$1,502.0	$1,540.0	$1,523.0

Required   Compute these:

1. The actual cost of material used in one unit of product.

2. The cost of material that should be processed per machine-hour.

3. The budgeted direct labor cost for each unit produced.

4. The variable manufacturing overhead rate per machine-hour in a flexible budget formula.

5. The manufacturing overhead production volume variance for the current year.

6. The manufacturing overhead spending variance using three-variance analysis of its manufacturing overhead variance for the year.

7. The total budgeted manufacturing cost for an output of 6,050 units.

(CMA Adapted)

Strategy

16–43 REVISING BASE CAPACITY   Yuba Machine Company manufactures nut shellers at its Sutter City plant. Nut processors throughout the world purchase the machines. Since its inception, the family-owned business has used actual factory overhead costs in costing factory output. However, on December 1, 2001, Yuba began using a predetermined factory overhead application rate to determine manufacturing costs on a more timely basis. This information is from the 2001–2002 budget for the Sutter City plant:

Plant practical capacity	100,000 direct labor-hours
Variable factory overhead costs	$3.00 per direct labor-hour
Fixed factory overhead costs	
Salaries	$80,000
Depreciation and amortization	50,000
Other expenses	30,000
Total fixed factory overhead	$160,000

Based on these data, the predetermined factory overhead application rate was established at $4.60 per direct labor-hour.

A variance report for the Sutter City plant for the six months ended May 31, 2002, follows. The plant incurred 40,000 direct labor-hours that represent one-half of the company's expected activity in the master (static) budget.

Variance Report

	Actual Costs	Budgeted Costs*	Variance[†]
Total variable factory overhead	$120,220	$120,000	$ (220)
Fixed factory overhead			
Salaries	$ 39,000	$ 32,000	$ (7,000)
Depreciation and amortization	25,000	20,000	(5,000)
Other expenses	15,300	12,000	(3,300)
Total fixed factory overhead	$ 79,300	$ 64,000	$(15,300)

*Based on 40,000 direct labor-hours.

[†]Favorable (Unfavorable)

Yuba's controller, Sid Thorpe, knows from the inventory records that one-quarter of the applied fixed factory overhead costs remain in the work-in-process and finished goods inventories. Based on this information, he has included $48,000 of fixed factory overhead as part of the cost of goods sold in the following interim income statement:

YUBA MACHINE COMPANY
Interim Income Statement
For Six Months Ended May 31, 2002

Sales	$625,000
Cost of goods sold	380,000
Gross profit	$245,000
Selling expense	44,000
Depreciation expense	58,000
Administrative expense	53,000
Operating income	$ 90,000
Provision for income taxes (40%)	36,000
Net income	$ 54,000

Required

1. Define *practical capacity* and explain why it might not be a satisfactory basis for determining a fixed factory overhead application rate.

2. Prepare a revised variance report for Yuba Machine Company using the expected activity in its master (static) budget as the basis for applying fixed factory overhead.

3. Determine the effect on Yuba's reported operating income of $90,000 at May 31, 2002, if the fixed factory overhead rate was based on the expected activity in the company's master (static) budget rather than on practical capacity.

4. What capacity should the firm use to determine its factory overhead application rate if the firm (a) considers the product a cash cow or (b) is striving to capture market share and to expand the total market size?

(CMA Adapted)

16–44 **VARIABLE OVERHEAD VARIANCES**   Use the data in problem 16–29 for Marilyn, Inc.

Required   Using three-variance analysis, compute the following:

1. The variable overhead spending variance.
2. The variable overhead efficiency variance.

(CMA Adapted)

16–45 **FOUR-VARIANCE ANALYSIS**   Nolton Products developed its overhead application rate from its current annual budget. The budget is based on an expected actual output of 720,000 units requiring 3,600,000 direct labor-hours. The company schedules production uniformly throughout the year.

Nolton produced a total of 66,000 units requiring 315,000 direct labor-hours during May, when its actual overhead costs amounted to $375,000. A comparison of the actual costs with the annual budget and with one-twelfth of the annual budget follows.

Nolton uses a standard costing system and applies factory overhead on the basis of direct labor-hours.

| | Annual Budget | | | | |
	Total Amount	Per Unit	Per Direct Labor-Hour	Monthly Budget	Actual Costs for May 2002
Variable					
Indirect labor	$ 900,000	$1.25	$0.25	$ 75,000	$ 75,000
Supplies	1,224,000	1.70	0.34	102.00	111,000
Fixed					
Supervision	648,000	0.90	0.18	54,000	51,000
Utilities	540,000	0.75	0.15	45,000	54,000
Depreciation	1,008,000	1.40	0.28	84,000	84,000
	$4,320,000	$6.00	$1.20	$360,000	$375,000

Required   Calculate the following amounts for Nolton Products for May 2002. Be sure to identify each variance as favorable (F) or unfavorable (U).

1. Applied overhead costs.
2. Variable overhead spending variance.
3. Variable overhead efficiency variance.
4. Fixed overhead spending variance.
5. Production volume variance.

(CMA Adapted)

16–46 **PRORATION OF VARIANCES**   Butrico Manufacturing Corporation uses a standard costing system to record raw materials at actual cost, record a materials price variance when raw materials are issued to work-in-process, and prorate all variances at year-end. Variances associated with direct materials are prorated based on the balances of direct materials in the appropriate accounts, and variances associated with direct labor and manufacturing overhead are prorated based on the balances of direct labor in the appropriate accounts.

The following Butrico information is for the year ended December 31:

Finished goods inventory at 12/31	
Direct materials	$ 87,000
Direct labor	130,500
Applied manufacturing overhead	104,400
Raw materials inventory at 12/31	$ 65,000
Cost of goods sold for the year ended 12/31	
Direct materials	$348,000
Direct labor	739,500
Applied manufacturing overhead	591,600
Direct materials price variance (unfavorable)	10,000
Direct materials usage variance (favorable)	15,000
Direct labor rate variance (unfavorable)	20,000
Direct labor efficiency variance (favorable)	5,000
Manufacturing overhead incurred	690,000

The firm had no beginning inventories and no ending work-in-process inventory. It applies manufacturing overhead at 80 percent of standard direct labor.

Required Compute these:

1. The amount of direct materials price variance to be prorated to finished goods inventory at December 31.

2. The total amount of direct materials in finished goods inventory at December 31, after all materials variances have been prorated.

3. The total amount of direct labor in finished goods inventory at December 31, after all variances have been prorated.

4. The total cost of goods sold for the year ended December 31, after all variances have been prorated.

(CMA Adapted)

16–47 **WORKING BACKWARD—TWO-VARIANCE ANALYSIS** Beth Company has budgeted fixed factory overhead costs of $50,000 per month and a variable factory overhead rate of $4 per direct labor-hour. The standard direct labor-hours allowed for October production were 18,000. An analysis of the factory overhead indicates that in October, Beth had an unfavorable budget (controllable) variance of $1,000 and a favorable production volume variance of $5,400. Beth uses a two-variance analysis of overhead variances.

Required Compute these:

1. The actual factory overhead incurred in October.

2. Beth's applied factory overhead in October.

3. The amount of budgeted total direct labor-hours.

(CMA Adapted)

16–48 **FOUR-VARIANCE ANALYSIS** Edney Company employs a standard system for product costing. The standard cost of its product is

Raw materials	$14.50
Direct labor (2 direct labor-hours × $8)	16.00
Manufacturing overhead (2 direct labor-hours × $11)	22.00
Total standard cost	$52.50

The manufacturing overhead rate is based on a normal annual activity level of 600,000 direct labor-hours. The firm has the following budgeted annual manufacturing overhead:

Variable	$3,600,000
Fixed	3,000,000
	$6,600,000

Edney spent $433,350 and 53,500 direct labor-hours to manufacture 26,000 units in November. Costs incurred in November include $260,000 for fixed manufacturing overhead and $315,000 for variable manufacturing overhead.

Required Determine these for November:

1. The variable manufacturing overhead spending variance.
2. The variable manufacturing overhead efficiency variance.
3. The fixed manufacturing overhead spending (budget) variance.
4. The manufacturing overhead production volume variance.
5. The amount of under- or overapplied manufacturing overhead.

(CMA Adapted)

16–49 COMPUTE ALL VARIABLE VARIANCES Aunt Molly's Old Fashioned Cookies bakes cookies for retail stores. The company's best-selling cookie is chocolate nut supreme, which is marketed as a gourmet cookie and regularly sells for $8 per pound. This is the standard cost per pound of chocolate nut supremes, based on Aunt Molly's normal monthly production of 400,000 pounds:

Cost Item	Quantity	Standard Unit Cost	Total Cost
Direct materials			
Cookie mix	10 ounces	$0.02/ounce	$0.20
Milk chocolate	5 ounces	0.15/ounce	0.75
Almonds	1 ounce	0.50/ounce	0.50
			$1.45
Direct labor*			
Mixing	1 minute	14.40/hour	0.24
Baking	2 minutes	18.00/hour	0.60
			0.84
Variable overhead†	3 minutes	32.40/hour	1.62
Total standard cost per pound			$3.91

*Direct labor rates include employee benefits.

†Applied on the basis of direct labor-hours.

Aunt Molly's management accountant, Karen Blair, prepares monthly budget reports based on these standard costs. April's contribution report compares budgeted and actual performance:

Contribution Report
April 2002

	Budget	Actual	Variance
Units (in pounds)	400,000	450,000	50,000 F
Revenue	$3,200,000	$3,555,000	$355,000 F
Direct material	580,000	865,000	$285,000 U
Direct labor	336,000	348,000	12,000 U
Variable overhead	648,000	750,000	102,000 U
Total variable costs	1,564,000	1,963,000	$399,000 U
Contribution margin	$1,636,000	$1,592,000	$ 44,000 U

Justine Molly, president of the company, is disappointed with the results. Despite a sizeable increase in cookies sold, the product's expected contribution to the overall profitability of the firm decreased. Justine has asked Karen to identify the reasons that the contribution margin decreased. Karen has gathered this information to help in her analysis of the decrease:

Usage Report
April 2002

Cost Item	Quantity	Actual Cost
Direct materials		
Cookie mix	4,650,000 ounces	$ 93,000
Milk chocolate	2,660,000 ounces	532,000
Almonds	480,000 ounces	240,000
Direct labor		
Mixing	450,000 minutes	108,000
Baking	800,000 minutes	240,000
Variable overhead		750,000
Total variable costs		$1,963,000

Required

1. Explain the $44,000 unfavorable variance between the budgeted and actual contribution margin for the chocolate nut supreme cookie product line during April 2002 by calculating the following variances. Assume that all materials are used in the month of purchase.

   a. Sales price variance.

   b. Materials price variance.

   c. Materials quantity variance.

   d. Labor efficiency variance.

   e. Variable overhead efficiency variance.

   f. Variable overhead spending variance.

   g. Contribution margin volume variance.

2.

   a. Explain the problems that might arise in using direct labor-hours as the basis for allocating overhead.

   b. How might activity-based costing (ABC) solve the problems described in requirement 2a?

   (CMA Adapted)

16–50 COMPARE ACTUAL WITH BUDGETED COSTS   Talbot Company manufactures shirts sold to customers for embossing with various slogans and emblems. Bob Ricker, manufacturing supervisor, recently received the following November production report; the November budget is based on the manufacture of 80,000 shirts.

Ethics

Cost Item	Standard	Actual	Variance
Direct materials	$160,000	$162,000	$ (2,000)
Direct labor	240,000	246,000	(6,000)
Factory overhead	200,000	241,900	(41,900)

November 2002 Production Report

Bob was extremely upset by the negative variances in the November report because he had worked very closely with his people for the past two months to improve productivity and to ensure that all workers are paid their standard wage rates. He immediately asked to meet with his boss, Chris

Langdon. Also disturbed by the November results, Chris suggested that Bob meet with Sheryl Johnson, Talbot's manager of cost accounting, to see if he can gain further insight into the production problems. Sheryl was extremely helpful and provided Bob with the additional information on the annual budget and these actual amounts for November:

Variable Overhead Expenditures

	Annual	Per Unit	November
Indirect material	$ 450,000	$0.45	$36,000
Indirect labor	300,000	0.30	33,700
Equipment repair	200,000	0.20	16,400
Equipment power	50,000	0.05	12,300
Total	$1,000,000	$1.00	$98,400

Fixed Overhead Expenditures

	Annual	November
Supervisory salaries	$ 260,000	$ 22,000
Insurance	350,000	29,500
Property taxes	80,000	6,500
Depreciation	320,000	34,000
Heat, light, telephone	210,000	21,600
Quality inspection	280,000	29,900
Total	$1,500,000	$143,500

- Factory overhead at Talbot includes both variable and fixed components and is applied on the basis of direct labor-hours. The company's 2002 budget includes the manufacture of 1 million shirts and the expenditure of 250,000 direct labor-hours.

- The standard labor rate at Talbot is $12 per hour, and the standard materials cost per shirt is $2.

- Actual production for November was 82,000 shirts.

With these data, Sheryl and Bob analyzed the November variances, paying particular attention to the factory overhead variance because of its significance. Sheryl knows that part of the problem is that Talbot does not use flexible budgeting, and she will be able to explain this to Bob as they analyze the data.

Required

1. By calculating the following four variances, explain the $41,900 unfavorable variance between budgeted and actual factory overhead during the month of November 2002:

   a. Budget volume variance for total factory overhead.

   b. Variable overhead efficiency variance.

   c. Variable overhead spending variance.

   d. Fixed overhead spending variance.

2. Describe the likely behavioral impact of the information provided by the calculations in requirement 1 on Bob Ricker. Be sure to make specific reference to the variances calculated, indicating his responsibility in each case.

(CMA Adapted)

16–51 **INVESTIGATION OF VARIANCE UNDER UNCERTAINTY (APPENDIX A)** The internal auditor of Transnational Company estimates the probability of its internal control procedure being in control as 80 percent. She estimates the costs to investigate at about $20,000 and the cost to revise and improve the internal control procedure as approximately $50,000. The present value of savings from having the new procedure is expected to be $250,000.

Required

1. Construct a payoff table for the firm to use in determining its best course of action.

2. What is the expected cost to the firm if it investigates? If it does not investigate? Should the firm investigate?

3. What is the expected cost of perfect information?

16–52 INVESTIGATION OF VARIANCE UNDER UNCERTAINTY (APPENDIX A)   The manager of MMX Digital must decide whether to initiate an advertising campaign for the firm's newest multimedia computer chip. There has been some discussion among division managers about the chip's market condition. To simplify the discussion and decision, probabilities were assessed by the marketing department regarding a strong market (60%) and a weak market (40%).

The manager, with the help of the marketing staff, has estimated the profits she believes the firm could earn:

Profits with advertising	
Strong market	$10 million
Weak market	4 million
Profits without advertising	
Strong market	8 million
Weak market	5 million

Required

1. Should the firm undertake the advertising campaign?

2. What is the probability level regarding the state of the market that will render the manager indifferent as to the courses of action?

3. What is the maximum amount the firm should pay to obtain the perfect information regarding the state of the market if such information is available?

16–53 INVESTIGATION OF VARIANCE UNDER UNCERTAINTY (APPENDIX A)   A student organization is planning to raise funds by selling flower bouquets on Valentine's Day. The sales booth costs $100, which can be sold to another student organization for $30 after the sales project. The bouquets can be purchased at $7 each and will be sold for $12 each. The cost of having bouquets delivered to the booth is $20 per delivery. Once delivered, no bouquet can be returned.

Required

1. Assume that the organization predicts sales to be 60 units. If actual sales are 48 units, what is the cost of the prediction error?

2. Assume that the organization must place its order in 12-bouquet bundles. With good weather, the organization believes it can sell 100 bouquets, but it will most likely sell 36 if the weather is inclement. A member of the organization majoring in meteorology has predicted, after consulting with meteorologists at the National Weather Bureau and local TV stations, that there is a 60 percent chance of having good weather on Valentine's Day.

   a. Construct a payoff table for the situation the organization faces.

   b. What is the organization's best course of action?

   c. What is the expected value of perfect information?

16–54   INVESTIGATION OF VARIANCE UNDER UNCERTAINTY (APPENDIX A)   Ron Bagley is contemplating whether to investigate a labor efficiency variance in the assembly department. The investigation will cost $6,000; if it finds that the department is operating improperly, corrective action will cost another $18,000. If the department is operating improperly and Ron failed to make the investigation, operating costs from the various inefficiencies are expected to be $33,000. At which probability of improper operation would Ron be indifferent as to investigating and not investigating the variance?

Service

International

16–55   TWO-VARIANCE ANALYSIS   International Finance Incorporated issues letters of credit to importers for overseas purchases. The company charges a nonrefundable application fee of $3,000 and, on approval, an additional service fee of 2 percent of the amount of credit requested.

The firm's budget for the year just completed included fixed expenses for office salaries and wages of $500,000, for leasing office space and equipment of $50,000, and for utilities and other operating expenses of $10,000. In addition, the budget also included variable expenses for supplies and other variable overhead costs of $1,000,000. The firm estimated its variable overhead cost to be $2,000 for each letter of credit approved and issued. The firm approves, on average, 80 percent of the applications received.

During the year, the firm received 600 requests and approved 75 percent of them. The total variable overhead was 10 percent higher than the standard amount applied; the total fixed expenses were 5 percent lower than the amount allowed.

In addition to these expenses, the firm paid a $270,000 insurance premium for the letters of credit issued. The insurance premium is 1 percent of the amount of credits issued in U.S. dollars. The actual amount of credit issued often differs from the amount requested due to fluctuations in exchange rates and variations in the amount shipped from the amount ordered by the importer. The strength of the dollar during the year decreased the insurance premium by 10 percent.

Required

1. Calculate the variable and fixed overhead application rates for the year.

2. Prepare an analysis of the overhead variances for the year just completed.

16–56   COMPREHENSIVE   Allglow Company is a cosmetic manufacturer specializing in stage makeup. SkinKlear, the company's best selling product, protects the skin from the frequent use of makeup. It is packaged in three sizes: 8 ounces, 1 pound, and 3 pounds. It regularly sells for $21 per pound. SkinKlear's standard cost per pound, based on Allglow's normal monthly production of 8,000 pounds, is as follows:

Cost Item	Standard Quantity	Standard Unit Cost	Total Cost
Direct materials			
Cream base	9.0 oz.	0.05/oz.	$ 0.45
Moisturizer	6.5 oz.	0.10/oz.	0.65
Fragrance	0.5 oz.	1.00/oz.	0.50
			$ 1.60
Direct labor*			
Mixing	0.5 hr.	$4.00/hr.	$ 2.00
Compounding	1.0 hr.	5.00/hr.	5.00
			$ 7.00
Variable overhead[†]	1.5 hr.	$2.10/hr.	$ 3.15
Total standard cost per pound			$11.75

*Direct labor dollars include employee benefits.

[†]The firm adds $2.10 per direct labor hour to cover overheads.

Based on these standard costs, Allglow prepares monthly budgets. Following are the budgeted performance and actual performance for May 2002 when the company produced and sold 9,000 pounds of SkinKlear.

Contribution Report for SkinKlear for the Month of May 2002

	Budget	Actual	Variance
Units	8,000	9,000	1,000 F
Revenue	$168,000	$180,000	$12,000 F
Direct materials	12,800	16,200	3,400 U
Direct labor	56,000	62,500	6,500 U
Overhead	25,200	30,900	5,700 U
Total variable costs	$ 94,000	$109,600	$15,600 U
Contribution margin	$ 74,000	$ 70,400	$ 3,600 U

These results did not please Barbara Simmons, Allglow's president; despite a sizeable increase in the sales of SkinKlear, the product's contribution to the overall profitability of the firm had decreased. Barbara has asked Allglow's cost accountant, Brian Jackson, to prepare a report that identifies the reasons that the contribution margin for SkinKlear decreased. Brian gathered the following information to help him prepare the report:

May 2002 Usage Report for SkinKlear

Cost Item	Quantity	Actual Cost
Direct materials		
Cream base	84,000 oz.	$ 4,200
Moisturizer	60,000 oz.	7,200
Fragrance	4,800 oz.	4,800
Direct labor		
Mixing	4,500 hr.	18,000
Compounding—manual	5,300 hr.	26,500
Compounding—mechanized	2,700 hr.	13,500
Compounding—idle	900 hr.	4,500
Variable overhead		30,900
Total variable cost		$109,600

While doing his research, Brian discovered that the manufacturing department had mechanized one of the manual operations in the compounding process on an experimental basis. The mechanized operation replaced manual operations that represented 40 percent of the compounding process.

The workers' inexperience with the mechanized operation caused increased usage of both the cream base and the moisturizer; however, Brian believes these inefficiencies would be negligible if mechanization became a permanent part of the process and the workers' skills improved. The idle time in compounding was traceable to the fact that fewer workers were required for the mechanized process. During this experimental period, the idle time was charged to direct labor rather than overhead. The excess workers could be either reassigned or laid off in the future. Brian is also able to determine that all variable manufacturing overhead costs over standard can be traced directly to the mechanization process.

Required

1. Explain the $3,600 unfavorable variance between the budgeted and actual contribution margin for SkinKlear during May 2002 by calculating the following variances:

    a. Sales price variance.

    b. Materials price variance.

    c. Materials quantity variance.

    d. Labor efficiency variance.

    e. Variable overhead efficiency variance.

    f. Variable overhead spending variance.

    g. Contribution margin volume variance.

2. Allglow Company must decide whether the compounding operation in the SkinKlear manufacturing process that was mechanized on an experimental basis should continue to be mechanized. Calculate the variable cost savings that can be expected to arise in the future from the mechanization. Explain you answer.

(CMA Adapted)

16–57 **VARIANCE ANALYSIS AND REPORT**   Henry Pacer is the general manager of Ace Chemicals division. Following is his division's income statement (in thousands of dollars) for the month just completed:

	Actual	Budget
Sales	$14,005	$12,600
Cost of goods sold	11,605	9,960
Gross profit	$ 2,400	$ 2,640
Other expense	705	640
Operating income	$ 1,695	$ 2,000
Other income	105	200
Pretax income	$ 1,800	$ 2,200
Income taxes	900	1,100
Net income	$ 900	$ 1,100

Henry knew before receiving the statement that sales were above the budgeted amount for the month and that the effect of recent price increases on most products would be realized this month. As you would expect, he was very upset to find that his income results were lower than the budget while his sales were more than 10 percent higher. He has asked the accounting department for an immediate explanation. The accounting department has reviewed the detailed budget and found the following data:

	Sales (in millions of pounds)	Price (per pound)	Cost of Sales (per pound)	Profit (in millions)
Product 1	2,000	$0.600	$0.600	$ 0
Product 2	5,000	0.800	0.650	750
Product 3	7,000	0.200	0.120	560
Product 4	4,000	$1.500	$1.140	1,440
				$2,750

Ace budgeted start-up and obsolescence charges of $110 million per month. The following unfavorable volume variances (in millions of dollars) were included in the budget for November:

Product 1	$100
Product 2	—
Product 3	50
Product 4	100
Total loss	$250

Following is a gross profit report for Ace for the month of November.

Product	Sales (in millions of pounds)	Price (per pound)	Sales (in millions of dollars)	Cost of Goods Sold (in millions of dollars)	Gross Profit (in millions of dollars)	Percent of Gross Profit
1	2,845	$735	$2,091	$1,692	$399	19.1%
2	3,280	$1.023	3,355	3,240	115	3.4
3	7,340	0.195	1,431	991	440	30.7
4	4,320	1.650	7,128	5,400	1,728	24.2
Start-up—Product 2	257	(257)	—	—	—	—
Obsolescence—Product 2				25	(25)	—
Total division			$14,005	$11,605	$2,400	17.1%

These variances (in millions of dollars) were included in cost of goods sold:

	Raw Materials Utility Prices	Performance	Volume	Total
Product 1	$(225)*	$ 12	(20)	$ (233)
Product 2	(222)	82	(600)	(740)
Product 3	(146)	6	(50)	(190)
Product 4	(350)	(224)	(200)	(774)
	$(943)	$(124)	(870)	$(1,937)

*Amounts in parentheses indicate a loss or an unfavorable balance.

Required Provide Henry the appropriate analysis of his business results (net income) for the month.
(IMA Case Adapted)

16–58 **STRATEGIC PRICING; INTERPRETATION OF OVERHEAD VARIANCES** Paste Products manufactures paste sold to commercial customers in 10-gallon metal containers. Always cost conscious, the firm uses a standard costing system revised annually on November 1, the start of the company's fiscal year. Paste Products uses standard costs to evaluate performance and prepares monthly variance reports for this purpose. The revised standard cost card developed for commercial paste for the 2002–2003 fiscal year follows:

Standard Cost for Commercial Paste (one ten-gallon container)			
			Unit Cost
Direct materials			
2 pounds of monocloro	$6.00/pound	$12.00	
1 pound oxotone	$0.80/pound	0.80	
4 gallons of distilled water	$0.30/gallon	1.20	$14.00
Direct labor	0.2 hour	11.00/hour	2.20
Variable overhead			
0.2 hours maintenance	$15.00/hour	$3.00	
0.2 hours supplies	$1.00/hour	0.20	
0.2 hours indirect labor	$18.00/hour	3.60	6.80
Fixed overhead	0.2 hours	$2.00/hour	.40
Total standard cost			$23.40

The composition of Paste Products' fixed factory overhead and its annual budget for the current fiscal year follows:

Factory supervision	$130,000
Contract maintenance	40,000
Utilities	120,000
Property taxes	70,000
Factory depreciation	550,000
Miscellaneous	50,000
Total annual fixed factory overhead	$960,000

The firm purchases all direct materials and indirect supplies from outside vendors on a two-week production lead-time basis. The variable maintenance cost is for maintenance performed by company employees; regular maintenance is under annual contract with the manufacturers of specific equipment. Depreciation is calculated on the straight-line basis. Miscellaneous fixed overhead includes factory insurance and various other items.

Variable manufacturing overhead is considered to vary according to direct labor-hours. Therefore, Paste Products applies both variable and fixed overhead to production on the basis of direct labor-hours. Manufacturing activities and production costs are expected to occur uniformly throughout the fiscal year.

In January 2003, the company was forced to reduce its sales price from $79.95 per 10-gallon container to $49.95 because of aggressive foreign competition. Although the price reduction resulted in increased sales, the income statement for the first six months revealed dwindling profits. Management immediately mandated a product cost reduction program and called on Jill O'Connor, cost accountant, to prepare a report identifying target areas. Jill prepared the following analysis of production costs (for actual production of $1,600,000 units) to determine whether any costs were above standard.

PASTE PRODUCTS
Analysis of Production Cost Variances
For the Six Months Ended April 30, 2003

	Standard Usage at Standard Rates	Actual Usage at Standard Rates	Actual Costs	Quantity (efficiency) Variance	Price (rate) Variance	Total Variance
Direct Materials						
Monocloro	$19,200,000	$19,323,096	$19,387,506	$123,096 U	$64,410 U	$187,506 U
Oxotone	1,280,000	1,278,400	1,246,440	1,600 F	31,960 F	33,560 F
Distilled water	1,920,000	1,921,200	1,857,160	1,200 U	64,040 F	62,840 F
Variable overhead						
Maintenance	4,800,000	4,860,000	4,310,050	60,000 U	549,950 F	489,950 F
Supplies	320,000	324,000	335,400	4,000 U	11,400 U	15,400 U
Indirect labor	5,760,000	5,832,000	5,978,000	72,000 U	146,000 U	218,000 U
				$302,696 U	$ 5,260 U	$357,956 U

	Applied Fixed Overhead	Budgeted Fixed Overhead	Actual Fixed Overhead	Spending Variance	Volume Variance	
Fixed overhead	$640,000	$480,000	$480,000	$160,000 F	0	$160,000 F
						$197,956 U

After completing her analysis, Jill observed that the net production variances were unfavorable in comparison with the budget; however, the fixed overhead volume variance partially offset the variable manufacturing variances. She also observed that the direct labor variances exceeded the standard by almost 15 percent. Investigating further, she learned that the manufacturing plant had been working 10 hours per day, six days per week since late January. Workers are paid time-and-one-half for overtime. She knew that the plant had scheduled overtime, but she was not aware of its magnitude. A closer examination of production records revealed the following facts:

	Regular Production	Overtime Production	Total
Direct labor-hours	268,800	55,200	324,000
Direct labor cost	$3,091,200	$952,200	$4,043,400
Units produced	1,350,000	250,000	1,600,000

Jill plans to use her analysis of production variances as well as additional data that she has accumulated as the basis for her recommendations.

Required

1. To analyze the situation and advise management on the product cost reduction program, Jill O'Connor should determine the number of units that Paste Products had planned to produce in the year. As her assistant, calculate the number of units that Paste Products had planned to produce during its fiscal year beginning November 1, 2002.

2. Jill has decided to revise the variance analysis to reflect the impact that overtime had on direct labor production costs.

   a. Expand the direct labor variance analysis to reveal as much detail about the direct labor costs as possible from the information provided. To do this, separately calculate regular time and overtime variances.

   b. Based on your analysis in requirement 2a, comment on the impact of overtime on Paste Products' direct labor production costs.

3. Jill observed that the fixed overhead volume variance partially offset the variable production variances. She wondered whether Paste Products would benefit by shifting variable costs to fixed costs.

   a. Explain the nature of the fixed overhead volume variance.

   b. Discuss the advantages and disadvantages of shifting variable costs to fixed costs.

4. Discuss the overall impact that the recent change in pricing strategy had on the company.

(CMA Adapted)

SOLUTIONS TO SELF-STUDY PROBLEMS

1. Analysis of Overhead Variance

1.	a.	Units manufactured during the period	360
		Standard direct labor-hours per unit	× 2
		Total standard direct labor-hours for the units manufactured during the period	720
		Standard variable factory overhead rate per direct labor-hour	× $5.00
		Total standard variable factory overhead for the period	$3,600
	b.	The total variable factory overhead applied	$3,600

c.
Budgeted units of production	400
Standard direct labor-hours per unit	× 2
Total standard direct labor-hours for the units budgeted for the period	800
Standard fixed factory overhead rate per direct labor-hour	× $20
Total budgeted fixed factory overhead for the period	$16,000

d.
Total standard direct labor-hours for the units manufactured during the period (from 1a)	720
Standard fixed factory overhead rate per direct labor-hour	× $20
Total fixed factory overhead applied	$14,400

2. a, b, and c.

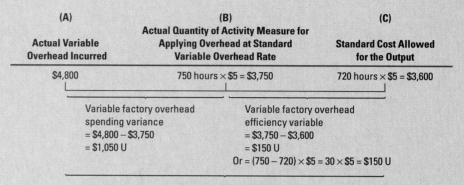

(A)	(B)	(C)
Actual Variable Overhead Incurred	**Actual Quantity of Activity Measure for Applying Overhead at Standard Variable Overhead Rate**	**Standard Cost Allowed for the Output**
$4,800	750 hours × $5 = $3,750	720 hours × $5 = $3,600

Variable factory overhead spending variance
= $4,800 − $3,750
= $1,050 U

Variable factory overhead efficiency variable
= $3,750 − $3,600
= $150 U
Or = (750 − 720) × $5 = 30 × $5 = $150 U

Total variable factory overhead variance
(variable factory overhead flexible budget variance)
= $1,050 U + $150 U = $1,200 U

d. Total underapplied variable factory overhead variance is $1,200.

e, f, and g.

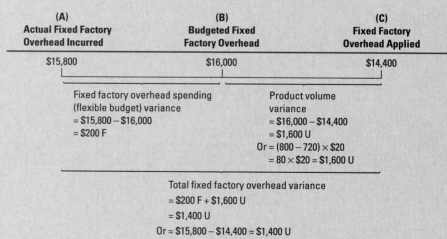

(A)	(B)	(C)
Actual Fixed Factory Overhead Incurred	**Budgeted Fixed Factory Overhead**	**Fixed Factory Overhead Applied**
$15,800	$16,000	$14,400

Fixed factory overhead spending
(flexible budget) variance
= $15,800 − $16,000
= $200 F

Product volume variance
= $16,000 − $14,400
= $1,600 U
Or = (800 − 720) × $20
= 80 × $20 = $1,600 U

Total fixed factory overhead variance
= $200 F + $1,600 U
= $1,400 U
Or = $15,800 − $14,400 = $1,400 U

h. Total underapplied fixed factory overhead variance = $1,400

3. a.
Factory overhead spending variance = Variable factory overhead spending variance + Fixed factory overhead spending variance

= $1,050 U + $200 F = $850 U

b. Factory overhead efficiency variance = Variable factory overhead efficiency variance = $150 U

c. Production volume variance = $1,600 U

4. Factory overhead flexible budget variance = Factory overhead spending variance + Factory overhead efficiency variance

= $850 U + $150 U = $1,000 U

Production volume variance is $1,600 U, the amount identified by both the four-variance or three-variance analysis.

5.

a.

Factory Overhead	20,600	
Cash, Sundry Payable accounts, Prepaid accounts, or Accumulated Depreciations		20,600

b.

Work-in-Process Inventory	18,000	
Factory Overhead Applied		18,000

c.

Factory Overhead Applied	18,000	
Variable Factory Overhead Spending Variance	1,050	
Variable Factory Overhead Efficiency Variance	150	
Production Volume Variance	1,600	
Factory Overhead		20,600
Fixed Factory Overhead Spending Variance		200

d. (1)

Cost of Goods Sold	2,600	
Fixed Factory Overhead Spending Variance	200	
Variable Factory Overhead Spending Variance		1,050
Variable Factory Overhead Efficiency Variance		150
Production Volume Variance		1,600

(2) Ending balances at standard are

Work-in-process inventory ($153,000 – $134,640)	$ 18,360
Finished goods Inventory ($134,640 – $111,690)	22,950
Cost of goods sold	$111,690
Total	$153,000

Account	Cost at Standard	Percent of Total	Proration of Variance	Adjusted Total Cost
Work-in-process, ending	$ 18,360	12%	$2,600 × 0.12 = $ 312	$ 18,672
Finished goods, ending	22,950	15	2,600 × 0.15 = $ 390	23,340
Cost of goods sold	111,690	73	2,600 × 0.73 = $1,898	113,588
Total	$153,000	100%	$2,600	$155,600

Cost of Goods Sold	1,898	
Work-in-Process	312	
Finished Goods	390	
Fixed Factory Overhead Spending Variance	200	
Variable Factory Overhead Spending Variance		1,050
Variable Factory Overhead Efficiency Variance		150
Production Volume Variance		1,600

2. Variance Investigation (Appendix A)

Courses of Action

A_1: Investigate the operation to determine the causes of the efficiency variance.

A_2: Do not investigate the operation.

States of Operation

S_1: The operation is in control.

S_2: The operation is out of control.

Cost and Probability

I = Cost of investigation = $2,500

C = Cost of corrective action, if an out-of-control process is found = $5,000

L = Losses from the operation being out of control and no correction is made = $55,000

P = Probability of the operation being in control = 40%

Payoff Table

	States of Operation	
Management Action	**In Control (random) 0.40**	**Out of Control (systematic) 0.60**
Investigate	$2,500	$2,500 + $5,000
Do not investigate	0	$55,000

1.

$$E(\text{investigate}) = (40\% \times \$2,500) + (60\% \times \$7,500) = \$5,500$$

$$E(\text{do not investigate}) = 60\% \times \$55,000 = \$33,000$$

The expected total cost to the firm will be lower if Smiley investigates the variance and takes proper action to correct the cause of the variance if the operation is found to be out of control.

2. Smiley is indifferent if the probability of in control (P) causes the expected costs of investigation to equal the expected cost of not investigating.

$$\$2,500P + \$7,500(1 - P) = \$55,000(1 - P)$$

$$50,000P = 47,500$$

$$P = 0.95$$

As long as the probability of the operation being in control is 95% or lower, Smiley should investigate the cause of variances.

17

Managing Marketing Effectiveness, Productivity, and Customer Profitability

After studying this chapter, you should be able to . . .

1   Disaggregate sales variance into selling price and sales volume variances

2   Separate a sales volume variance into sales mix and sales quantity variances

3   Explain how market size and market share variances lead to sales quantity variances

4   Describe productivity and the implications of changes in productivity

5   Compute and interpret operational and financial partial productivity

6   Distinguish among productivity change, input price change, and output change

7   Identify the advantages and limitations of applying productivity measures to service firms and not-for-profit organizations

8   Analyze factors affecting revenues and determine net proceeds from customers

9   Describe customer cost categories and identify the costs to serve a customer

10   Conduct customer profitability analysis and determine customer value

When Apple Computer introduced its Apple II computer in the early 1980s, it awed users everywhere by its fantastic feats of technical prowess. Most computer manufacturers at that time either ignored the consumer market or dedicated desktop models to elite professionals or the well to do. Apple Computer almost had the entire consumer market to itself; millions of affordable, user-friendly machines that it turned out were snatched up by consumers, schools, and even teenage hackers. By the time the firm introduced the first Macintosh in 1984, Apple Computer was well on its way to achieving cult status among its users.

Unfortunately, Apple Computer was trapped by success and sacrificed market share for profit margins. In the late 1980s, Apple Computer opted to keep its exclusive right to its operating system instead of licensing it. Throughout the onslaught of PC clones following IBM's introduction of its first personal computer, Apple held fast to its high prices, charging as much as 120 percent more for computers. This was a losing strategy. As Apple's market share dwindled, so did the number of software titles supporting its platform. Decreased availability in application software diminishes willing buyers. A small market discourages software developers from writing new applications, improving existing ones, and adapting software for the product—a vicious cycle. Apple could have at least rivaled Wintel's grip on the market had it licensed its operating system to independent manufacturers early in the race for consumers. Unfortunately, the desire to keep all the profit to itself ignored the importance of market share in its long-term strategy. Its market share has decreased from more than 80 percent to around 4 percent, and Apple has clearly suffered. In the mid-1990s, some analysts even wondered aloud whether the firm could survive in the long term—and all because management was not aware of the importance of market shares.

This chapter contains three separate sections, each of which deals with an important issue affecting the profitability of a firm. The first section examines marketing factors that could cause the operating income of a period to deviate from the amount budgeted. The second section discusses the analysis of productivity changes over the years; this analysis provides important information on the degree of success continuing improvements in operations are achieving. The third section analyzes customer profitability.

PART ONE: MANAGING MARKETING EFFECTIVENESS

A market is the place where a firm earns profits, fulfills its strategic goals, and attains long-term successes. No firm can gain long-term success without marketing effectiveness. A firm is effective in marketing when it accomplishes the following:

- Earns the budgeted operating income,
- Attains the budgeted market share,
- Adapts to market change.

Factors affecting marketing effectiveness include the firm's selling price of products, sales quantity, product mix, market size, and market shares. Variances in any of these factors can prevent the firm from achieving its short-term performance objectives and strategic goals, from desired income, and long-term success. Exhibit 17–1 depicts the components of sales variances.

Differences in the sales revenues earned and the master budgeted amounts is the total sales variance of the period. A sales variance can result from differences in either selling prices or sales volumes. Sales volume variances arise because of sales quantity or sales mix variances. Differences in sales quantity can be the result of market size or market share variances.

SELLING PRICE AND SALES VOLUME VARIANCES

LEARNING OBJECTIVE 1▶

Disaggregate sales variance into selling price and sales volume variances.

A *selling price variance* is the difference between the dollar amount received from the units sold and the budgeted selling price for all units sold. It measures the impacts that differences in actual selling prices and the budgeted selling prices have on operating results. The selling price variance of a period is determined by finding the difference in the total amount of sales earned and the total amount of sales in the flexible budget for the units sold. Alternatively, the selling price variance can be computed by multiplying the difference between the actual and the budgeted selling prices per unit of the product by the number of product units sold. The selling price variance is also the *sales revenue flexible budget variance*.

$$\begin{matrix} \text{Selling} \\ \text{price} \\ \text{variance} \end{matrix} = \begin{bmatrix} \begin{matrix} \text{Actual} \\ \text{selling price} \\ \text{per unit} \end{matrix} - \begin{matrix} \text{Budgeted} \\ \text{selling price} \\ \text{per unit} \end{matrix} \end{bmatrix} \times \begin{matrix} \text{Number of} \\ \text{units sold} \end{matrix}$$

The selling price variance of a period is part of the period's flexible budget variance. The sum of the selling price variance and the total variable cost variance is the flexible budget contribution margin variance for the period.

A *sales volume variance* is the difference between the flexible budget for the number of units sold and the master budget for the period. This variance measures the effect on operating results including effects on contribution margin and operating income when the number of units of one or more products sold differs from the number of units of the product in the master budget for the period. The sales volume variance was introduced in Chapter 15 as part of the analysis of flexible budget variances. Exhibit 15–4 is reproduced here as Exhibit 17–2 to provide a starting point for additional analyses of the sales volume variance.

Schmidt Machinery Company budgeted an operating income of $200,000 from sales of 1,000 units of XV–1 at $800 per unit ($800,000 ÷ 1,000 units); it budgeted a variable expense of $450 per unit ($450,000 ÷ 1,000 units) and a total fixed expense

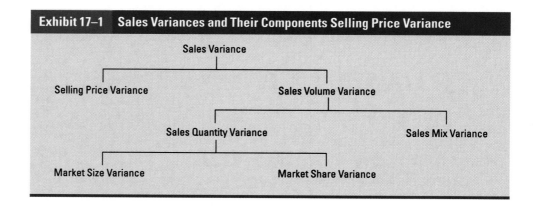

Exhibit 17–1   Sales Variances and Their Components Selling Price Variance

Exhibit 17–2	Actual and Budget Operating Data

SCHMIDT MACHINERY COMPANY
Analysis of Operations
For the Month Ended October 31, 2002

	Actual	Flexible Budget Variances*	Flexible Budget	Sales Volume Variances	Master Budget
Units sold (XV–1)	780	0	780	220	1,000
Sales	$639,600	$15,600 F	$624,000	$176,000 U	$800,000
Variable expenses	350,950	50 F	351,000	99,000 F	450,000
Contribution margin	$288,650	$15,650 F	$273,000	$ 77,000 U	$350,000
Fixed expenses	160,650	10,650 U	150,000	—	150,000
Operating income	$128,000	$ 5,000 F	$123,000	$ 77,000 U	$200,000

*Including both price and efficiency variances.

of $150,000 for the month. The actual operating results show that the firm sold 780 units for $639,600, or an average selling price of $820 per unit. The average actual selling price per unit exceeds the budgeted unit selling price by $20 ($820 – $800). Thus, the firm has a favorable selling price variance of $15,600 ($20 per unit × 780 units sold).

The master budget called for total sales of 1,000 units; but Schmidt sold 780 units. The number of units sold is 220 units fewer than budgeted for the period. At a standard contribution margin of $350 per unit ($800 – $450, or $350,000 ÷ 1,000 units), the decrease in units sold reduces both the total contribution margin and the operating income by $77,000 ($350 × 220 units). This is the contribution margin or operating income *sales volume variance* of the period. It is the difference between the contribution margin (operating income) in the flexible budget for the units sold and the contribution margin (operating income in the master (static) budget) for the period. It is also the product of the difference between the number of units sold and the budgeted number of sales units in the master budget and the budgeted (standard) contribution margin per unit.

$$\begin{array}{l} \text{Sales} \\ \text{volume} \\ \text{variance} \end{array} = \left[\begin{array}{ll} \text{Number} & \text{Number of} \\ \text{of units} - & \text{units in the} \\ \text{sold} & \text{master budget} \end{array}\right] \times \begin{array}{l} \text{Budgeted (standard)} \\ \text{contribution} \\ \text{margin per unit} \end{array}$$

$$= (780 - 1,000) \times \$350 = \$77,000 \text{ U}$$

Several factors can contribute to a sales volume variance, including sales quantity and sales mix variances, which we examine next.

SALES MIX VARIANCE

Most firms have more than one product, and not all of them are equally profitable. Consequently, a period's contribution margin or operating income sales volume variance can result from differences (1) in the number sold, or (2) in the sales mix (the ratio of the number of each product to the entire mix), from their master budget amounts. Thus, two major factors contributing to a sales volume variance are changes in sales mix and in sales quantities. To begin, we consider changes in sales mix.

Assume that, in addition to XV–1, Schmidt Machinery Company carries another product, FB–33. Exhibit 17–3 shows a condensed master budget for the month, and Exhibit 17–4 shows the operating results for November 2002.

◄**LEARNING OBJECTIVE 2**

Separate a sales volume variance into sales mix and sales quantity variances.

807

During November 2002, Schmidt sold 780 units of XV–1 at an average price of $800 per unit ($624,000 ÷ 780 units = $800). This selling price per unit is the same as the price budgeted. The firm also sold 3,220 units of FB–33 at $600 per unit ($1,932,000 ÷ 3,220 units = $600). Again, there is no difference between the budgeted selling price per unit and the selling price per unit at which FB–33 was sold. Thus, the firm had no selling price variance.

Notice that the actual variable expenses *per unit* for both XV–1 and FB–33 (Exhibit 17–4) are the same as those budgeted *per unit* of product (Exhibit 17–3); also, the actual fixed expense is the same as the budgeted amount. There is no variance due to differences in the actual operating expenses from the standard or budgeted amounts. In addition, the total number of units sold, 4,000, is the same as the budgeted number. Thus, there is no sales volume variance. Because the actual selling prices, variable expenses, fixed expenses, and total sales volume are all the same as the budgeted amounts, the actual operating income should be the same as the amount budgeted, yet they are different.

A comparison of the budgeted operating income in Exhibit 17–3 to the operating income of the period in Exhibit 17–4 shows that the firm earned an operating income $15,400 lower than the amount budgeted. With all operating factors—selling prices, variable expenses, total fixed expenses, and total units sold—seemingly the same as those in the master budget, why does the firm have an unfavorable operating income (and contribution margin) variance of $15,400?

Exhibit 17–3 Condensed Master Budget

SCHMIDT MACHINERY COMPANY
Condensed Master Budget
For the Month Ended November 30, 2002

	XV–1 Total	XV–1 Per Unit	FB–33 Total	FB–33 Per Unit	Both Products Total	Both Products Per Unit
Units	1,000		3,000		4,000	
Sales	$800,000	$800	$1,800,000	$600	$2,600,000	$650.00
Variable expenses	450,000	450	960,000	320	1,410,000	352.50
Contribution margin	$350,000	$350	$ 840,000	$280	$1,190,000	$297.50
Fixed expenses	150,000		450,000		600,000	
Operating income	$200,000		$ 390,000		$ 590,000	

Exhibit 17–4 Income Statement

SCHMIDT MACHINERY COMPANY
Income Statement
For the Month Ended November 30, 2002

	XV–1 Total	XV–1 Per Unit	FB–33 Total	FB–33 Per Unit	Both Products Total
Units	780		3,220		4,000
Sales	$624,000	$800	$1,932,000	$600	$2,556,000
Variable expenses	351,000	450	1,030,400	320	1,381,400
Contribution margin	$273,000	$350	$ 901,600	$280	$1,174,600
Fixed expenses	150,000		450,000		600,000
Operating income	$123,000		$ 451,600		$ 574,600

The answer is that the operating income (and contribution margin) variance results from a change in the sales mix. **Sales mix** is the proportion of each product or service to the total products or services. When the firm does not sell the products or services budgeted during a period, the firm has two different sales mixes: budgeted sales mix and actual sales mix. The actual sales units for products XV–1 and FB–33 are not the same as the budgeted amount, although the combined sales volume for the products is the same as that budgeted. XV–1 accounted for 220 fewer units sold during the period than the number budgeted while FB–33 accounted for 220 units sold more than the number budgeted. Differences between sales units and units budgeted for different products contribute to the period's income variance. For a multiproduct firm, selling the same *total* number of units as specified in the master budget does not imply that the flexible budget's operating income will be the same as that in the master budget for the period.

A firm producing multiple products or services includes in its flexible or master budget a separate amount for each product or service that provides a different contribution margin. Thus, even if the total number sold is exactly the same as the number in the master budget, the firm's total contribution margin in the flexible budget will not be the same as that in the master budget if a change occurred in the sales mix. A change in the sales mix can affect the firm's contribution margin and operating income. A product's **sales mix variance** is calculated by multiplying the difference in the sales mix ratios by the number of units of *all* products sold and by the budget contribution margin per unit:

> The **sales mix** of a firm is the proportion of units of each product or service to the total of all unit products or services.

> The **sales mix variance** of a product is determined by multiplying the difference between the actual and budgeted sales mix ratios by the total number of units of all products sold and by the budgeted contribution margin per unit of the product.

$$\begin{matrix} \text{Sales mix} \\ \text{variance for} = \\ \text{a product} \end{matrix} \begin{bmatrix} \text{Actual sales} & & \text{Budget sales} \\ \text{mix ratio for} & - & \text{mix ratio for} \\ \text{the product} & & \text{the product} \end{bmatrix} \times \begin{matrix} \text{Total number} \\ \text{of units of all} \\ \text{products sold} \end{matrix} \times \begin{matrix} \text{Budgeted} \\ \text{contribution} \\ \text{margin per unit} \\ \text{of the product} \end{matrix}$$

A product's sales mix variance measures the effect on the contribution margin and the operating income attributable to the difference between actual and budgeted sales mix ratios. Before computing a sales mix variance, we need to determine the actual sales mix ratio and the budgeted sales mix ratio for each product.

Exhibit 17–5 shows computations of budget and actual sales mixes for XV–1 and FB–33 for November 2002.

The sales mix variances for data in Exhibits 17–3 and 17–4 are as follows:

$$\begin{matrix} \text{Sales mix} \\ \text{variance} = (0.195 - 0.25) \times 4{,}000 \text{ units} \times \$350 = \$77{,}000 \text{ U} \\ \text{of XV–1} \end{matrix}$$

$$\begin{matrix} \text{Sales mix} \\ \text{variance} = (0.805 - 0.75) \times 4{,}000 \text{ units} \times \$280 = \$61{,}600 \text{ F} \\ \text{of FB–33} \end{matrix}$$

Total sales mix variance = \$77,000 U + \$61,600 F = \$15,400 U

The number of units of XV–1 that the firm sold, 780, is 19.5 percent of the total units of all of the firm's product sold during the month. The budget calls for XV–1 to account for 25 percent of the total units sold. Given the 4,000 total units sold and the

Exhibit 17–5	Sales Mix Ratio			
Product	**Budget Units**	**Budget Sales Mix**	**Actual Units Sold**	**Actual Sales Mix**
XV–1	1,000	1,000 ÷ 4,000 = 0.25	780	780 ÷ 4,000 = 0.195
FB–33	3,000	3,000 ÷ 4,000 = 0.75	3,220	3,220 ÷ 4,000 = 0.805
Total	4,000	1.00	4,000	1.00

budgeted contribution margin of $350 per unit of XV–1, the 5.5 percent decrease in sales mix leads to its sales mix variance of $77,000 unfavorable.

Similarly, we can determine that the sales mix variance for FB–33 is $61,600 favorable because the actual sales mix, 80.5 percent, represents more than the budgeted sales mix of 75 percent. The firm's total sales mix variance is the sum of the sales mix variances of all products, which is $15,400 unfavorable for Schmidt Machinery Company.

SALES QUANTITY VARIANCE

The **sales quantity variance** of a product measures the effect of the change in the number of units sold from the number of units budgeted to be sold and is the product of three elements: the difference between the budgeted and actual total number of units sold, the budgeted sales mix of the product, and the budgeted contribution margin per unit of the product.

Another contributing factor to the sales volume variances of firms with multiple products is the difference between the budgeted and the actual sales units. A product's **sales quantity variance** is the product of three elements: (1) the difference in the total number of units budgeted and sold, (2) the budgeted sales mix ratio of the product, and (3) the budgeted contribution margin per unit of the product.

$$\begin{array}{l}\text{Sales} \\ \text{quantity} \\ \text{variance for} \\ \text{a product}\end{array} = \left[\begin{array}{l}\text{Total number} \\ \text{of all product} \\ \text{units sold}\end{array} - \begin{array}{l}\text{Total number} \\ \text{of all product} \\ \text{units budgeted} \\ \text{to be sold}\end{array}\right] \times \begin{array}{l}\text{Budgeted} \\ \text{sales mix} \\ \text{ratio of the} \\ \text{product}\end{array} \times \begin{array}{l}\text{Budgeted} \\ \text{contribution} \\ \text{margin per unit} \\ \text{of the product}\end{array}$$

A sales quantity variance measures the effect of the difference between the number of units sold and the number budgeted. With the focus of a sales quantity variance being the difference between the actual number of units sold and the total number budgeted, we use the budgeted amounts for the other two elements to compute the sales quantity variance.

Notice that the calculation of the sales quantity variance for a product uses the budgeted sales mix and the budgeted contribution margin per unit. However, the difference in amount is the difference between the *total* number of units sold and the *total* number of units budgeted for all of the firm's products.

The previous example for the November 2002 operation of Schmidt Machinery Company had no sales quantity variances because the total number of units sold is the same as the total number budgeted. To illustrate the determination of a sales quantity variance, we examine operating data from another month.

In December 2002, Schmidt sold 1,600 units of XV–1 and 3,400 units of FB–33, all at the budgeted unit selling price, budgeted unit variable expense, and budgeted total fixed expense. Exhibit 17–6 shows the actual operating result of December 2002. With total budgeted sales of 4,000 units, the 5,000 number of total units sold exceeds the number of budgeted units by 1,000.

Exhibit 17–6	Income Statements for Two Products		

SCHMIDT MACHINERY COMPANY
Income Statement
For the Month Ended December 31, 2002

	XV–1	FB–33	Total
Units	1,600	3,400	5,000
Sales	$1,280,000	$2,040,000	$3,320,000
Variable expenses	720,000	1,088,000	1,808,000
Contribution margin	$ 560,000	$ 952,000	$1,512,000
Fixed expenses	150,000	450,000	600,000
Operating income	$ 410,000	$ 502,000	$ 912,000

With no difference between the actual and the budgeted selling prices for both products, no selling price variance exists. The selling price variance shown in the top panel of Exhibit 17–7 confirms this conclusion. The difference between the actual operating income ($912,000 from Exhibit 17–6) and the budgeted operating income ($590,000 from Exhibit 17–3), $322,000 favorable, can thus be attributed to the sales volume variance of the period. The bottom panel of Exhibit 17–7 confirms this result.

The sales volume variance can be separated further into sales mix and sales quantity variances. Following the procedure for calculating the sales quantity variance, we see that Schmidt has a total $297,500 favorable sales quantity variance in December 2002, as shown in Exhibit 17–8.

The total sales quantity variance can help managers examine the effect of changes in the total number of units on operating income. The previous example shows that the firm would have earned $297,500 more in operating income from the 5,000 units sold during the period than the operating income from the budgeted 4,000 units, provided that the firm had maintained the sales mix, contribution margin per unit, and fixed costs that it had budgeted. Exhibit 17–9 verifies this analysis.

Had Schmidt sold the 5,000 units at the budgeted sales mix, it would have sold 1,250 units of XV–1 and 3,750 units of FB–33. With the budgeted contribution margin of $350 and $280 per unit of XV–1 and FB–33, respectively, the firm would have earned a total contribution margin of $1,487,500. After subtracting the budgeted fixed cost of $600,000, the operating income would be $887,500—$297,500 higher than the budgeted operating income of $590,000.

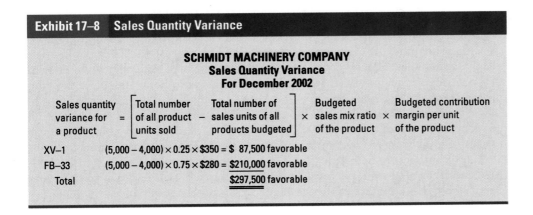

Exhibit 17–7	Selling Price and Sales Volume Variance

SCHMIDT MACHINERY COMPANY
Selling Price and Sales Volume Variances
For December 2002

Selling price variance

XV–1	($800 – $800) × 1,600 = 0
FB–33	($600 – $600) × 3,400 = 0
Total	0

Sales volume variance

XV–1	(1,600 – 1,000) × $350 = $210,000 F
FB–33	(3,400 – 3,000) × $280 = $112,000 F
Total	$322,000 F

Exhibit 17–8	Sales Quantity Variance

SCHMIDT MACHINERY COMPANY
Sales Quantity Variance
For December 2002

$$\begin{array}{c}\text{Sales quantity}\\\text{variance for}\\\text{a product}\end{array} = \left[\begin{array}{c}\text{Total number}\\\text{of all product}\\\text{units sold}\end{array} - \begin{array}{c}\text{Total number of}\\\text{sales units of all}\\\text{products budgeted}\end{array}\right] \times \begin{array}{c}\text{Budgeted}\\\text{sales mix ratio}\\\text{of the product}\end{array} \times \begin{array}{c}\text{Budgeted contribution}\\\text{margin per unit}\\\text{of the product}\end{array}$$

XV–1	(5,000 – 4,000) × 0.25 × $350 = $ 87,500 favorable
FB–33	(5,000 – 4,000) × 0.75 × $280 = $210,000 favorable
Total	$297,500 favorable

Exhibit 17–9   Further Analysis of Sales Quantity Variance

SCHMIDT MACHINERY COMPANY
Further Analysis of Sales Quantity Variance
For December 2002

Product	Budgeted Sales Mix	Total Units at the Budgeted Mix	Contribution Margin per Unit	Total Contribution Margin
XV–1	0.25	5,000 × 0.25 = 1,250	$350	$350 × 1,250 = $ 437,500
FB–33	0.75	5,000 × 0.75 = 3,750	$280	$280 × 3,750 = 1,050,000
Total contribution margin of the total units sold at the budgeted mix				$1,487,500
Budgeted fixed expenses				600,000
Operating income from the sale of the total actual units at the budgeted mix				$ 887,500
Operating income of the master budget				590,000
Sales quantity variance				$ 297,500

The company, however, did not sell its products at the budgeted sales mix in December 2002, as shown here:

Product	Units Sold	Actual Sales Mix	Budgeted Sales Mix
XV–1	1,600	32%	25%
FB–33	3,400	68%	75%
Total	5,000	100%	100%

The firm had sales mix variances for the period. Exhibit 17–10 computes the sales mix and sales quantity variances using a columnar form similar to the form used in Chapters 15 and 16.

Column A in Exhibit 17–10 is the flexible budget for the total number of units sold with the *actual sales mixes* the firm experienced. Column B is the flexible budget for the total number of units sold with the *budgeted sales mixes.* Column C is the master (static) budget for the period.

Schmidt Machinery Company sold 1,600 units of XV–1 and 3,400 units of FB–33 in December. The actual sales mixes in column A are 32 percent and 68 percent for XV–1 and FB–33, respectively.

Column B in Exhibit 17–10 uses the number of units the firm would have sold had the number of total units sold matched the sales mix budgeted. Schmidt sold a total of 5,000 units. According to the budgeted sales mix, 25 percent of the total units sold should be XV–1. Had the firm sold the 5,000 units at this sales mix, the number of units of XV–1 sold would have been

5,000 units × 25 percent = 1,250 units

All three points use the same budgeted (standard) contribution margin per unit. Thus, the only difference between columns A and B is in the sales mix. Column A uses the *actual* sales mix and column B uses the *budgeted* sales mix. The difference in total contribution margin for these two points results from the difference in the sales mix, or the sales mix variance.

The difference between points B and C is the number of total sales units of all products. Point B uses the number of total units of all products sold; point C uses the number of total budgeted sale units of all products. The other two elements in determining the amounts in both points are the same: the budgeted sales mix and the budgeted contribution margin per unit. The difference in amounts between points B and C stems from the difference in the total units: a sales quantity variance.

The sum of the sales quantity variance and the sales mix variance for each individual product and for the firm should be the same as the sales volume variance. The summary in panel 5 of Exhibit 17–10 confirms this result.

MARKET SIZE AND MARKET SHARE VARIANCES

Two factors that contribute to a sales quantity variance are changes in the total market size and in the firm's share of the market. As the total market for its products expands, a firm is likely to sell more units. Conversely, it is likely to be unable to maintain the same sales units when its total market contracts. A *market size variance* measures the effect of the size of the total market for the firm's product on the total contribution margin and the operating income.

◄**LEARNING OBJECTIVE 3**
Explain how market size and market share variances lead to sales quantity variances.

Exhibit 17–10   Sales Mix and Quantity Variances

SCHMIDT MACHINERY COMPANY
Sales Mix and Quantity Variances
For December 2002

Panel 1: Scheme	A	B	C
Total units	Actual	Actual	Budget
Sales mix	Actual	Budget	Budget
Contribution margin	Budget	Budget	Budget

Sales mix variance   Sales quantity variance

Flexible Budget with Actual Sales Mix	**Flexible Budget with Budgeted Sales Mix**	**Master (Static) Budget**
Number of **total units** of all products sold × *Actual* sales mix × Budgeted contribution margin per unit	Number of **total units** of all products sold × *Budgeted* sales mix × Budgeted contribution margin per unit	Total **budgeted units** of sales for all products × Budgeted sales mix × Budgeted contribution margin per unit

Panel 2: Product XV–1	A	B	C
Unit	5,000	5,000	4,000
Sales mix ratio	32%	25%	25%
Contribution margin	$350	$350	$350
	5,000 × 32% × $350	5,000 × 25% × $350	4,000 × 25% × $350
	= 1,600 × $350	= 1,250 × $350	= 1,000 × $350
	= $560,000	= $437,500	= $350,000

Sales mix variance
= $560,000 − $437,500
= $122,500 F

Sales quantity variance
= $437,500 − $350,000
= $87,500 F

Sales volume variance
= $560,000 − $350,000
= $210,000 F

To verify: Sales volume variance
= Sales mix variance + Sales quantity variance
= $122,500 F   + $87,500 F
= $210,000 F

(continued)

Exhibit 17–10   Continued

SCHMIDT MACHINERY COMPANY
Sales Mix and Quantity Variances
For December 2002

Panel 3: Product FB–33	A	B	C
	$5,000 \times 68\% \times \$280$	$5,000 \times 75\% \times \$280$	$4,000 \times 75\% \times \$280$
	$= 3,400 \times \$280$	$= 3,750 \times \$280$	$= 3,000 \times \$280$
	$= \$952,000$	$= \$1,050,000$	$= \$840,000$

Sales mix variance
= $952,000 – $1,050,000
= $98,000 U

Sales quantity variance
= $1,050,000 – $840,000
= $210,000 F

Sales volume variance
= $952,000 – $840,000
= $112,000 F

To verify: Sales volume variance
= Sales mix variance + Sales quantity variance
= $98,000 U   + $210,000 F
= $112,000 F

Panel 4: Both Products	A	B	C
	$\$560,000 + \$952,000$	$\$437,500 + \$1,050,000$	$\$350,000 + \$840,000$
	$= \$1,512,000$	$= \$1,487,500$	$= \$1,190,000$

Sales mix variance
= $1,512,000 – $1,487,500
= $24,500 F

Sales quantity variance
= $1,487,500 – $1,190,000
= $297,500 F

Sales volume variance
= $1,512,000 – $1,190,000
= $322,000 F

To verify: Sales volume variance
= Sales mix variance + Sales quantity variance
= $24,500 F   + $297,500 F
= $322,000 F

Panel 5: Summary

Product	Sales Mix Variance		Sales Quantity Variance		Sales Volume Variance
XV–1	$122,500 F	+	$ 87,500 F	=	$210,000 F
FB–33	98,000 U	+	210,000 F	=	112,000 F
Total	$ 24,500 F	+	$297,500 F	=	$322,000 F

When a firm expands its share of the total market, the number of its total sales units increases relative to those of other firms in the same market. A *market share variance* assesses the effect that changes in a firm's proportion of the total market have on the total contribution margin and the operating income.

When Schmidt's accountant prepared its budget, the firm expected that the total worldwide market for its products, XV–1 and FB–33, would be 40,000 units per month and that it would have 10 percent of the total market. The master budget data for December was reported in Exhibit 17–3. Exhibit 17–6 showed the actual operations for the month. Exhibit 17–8 reported that the firm has a favorable total sales quantity variance of $297,500.

Market Size Variance

A **market size variance** measures the effect of changes in the total market on a firm's total contribution margin and operating income. To capture the effect of changes in the size of the total market, the computation compares the actual and budgeted market sizes and assumes that the firm maintains exactly the same positions in all other factors as specified in the master (static) budget. These other factors include the firm's market share, sales mix, and unit contribution margins. The equation for computing a market size variance follows:

Market size variance measures the effect of changes in the total market size on the firm's total contribution margin and operating income.

$$
\begin{array}{c}
\text{Market} \\
\text{size} \\
\text{variance}
\end{array}
=
\left[
\begin{array}{c}
\text{Actual total} \\
\text{size (in number} \\
\text{of units) of the} \\
\text{market}
\end{array}
-
\begin{array}{c}
\text{Planned total} \\
\text{size (in number} \\
\text{of units) of the} \\
\text{market in the} \\
\text{budget}
\end{array}
\right]
\times
\begin{array}{c}
\text{Planned} \\
\text{market} \\
\text{share in} \\
\text{the budget}
\end{array}
\times
\begin{array}{c}
\text{Weighted-average} \\
\text{contribution} \\
\text{margin per unit} \\
\text{of the budget}
\end{array}
$$

The first term on the right side of the equation is the focus of the variance: the difference between the total actual size (in number of units) of the market and the planned or budgeted size (in number of units) of the market. The second term is the planned or desired market share the firm expected to attain for the period at the time the budget for the period was prepared. The last term in the equation is the weighted-average budgeted contribution margin per unit of all of the firm's products in the same market. This is so because the market size variance deals with the market of all of the firm's products in the market. In our example, Schmidt budgeted sales at a combined total of 4,000 units of XV—1 and FB–33 to earn a total contribution margin of $1,190,000, as shown in Exhibit 17–3. Thus, the budgeted average contribution per unit is $297.50 for the period ($1,190,000 ÷ 4,000 units).

The budgeted total market is 40,000 units, of which the company expected to have a budgeted market share of 10 percent, or 4,000 units. The total market for December 2002 turned out to be 31,250 units—a change in market size. Panel 1 of Exhibit 17–11 shows the calculation of Schmidt's market size variance, $260,312.50 unfavorable.

The total market size of the industry decreased to 31,250 units from the expected 40,000 units. Because Schmidt expected to have 10 percent of the market share, the decrease in market size of 8,750 units (40,000 – 31,250) would have decreased its total sales by 875 units. At an average contribution margin of $297.50 per unit, the total decrease in unit sales would have decreased Schmidt's operating income by $260,312.50.

Exhibit 17–11   Market Size and Market Share Variances

SCHMIDT MACHINERY COMPANY
Market Size and Share Variances
For December 2002

Panel 1: Market Size Variance Calculation:
Difference in market size × Budgeted market share × Average budgeted contribution margin
_____
(31,250 – 40,000) × 10% × $297.50 = $260,312.50 Unfavorable

Panel 2: Market Share Variance Calculation:
Difference in market share × Actual market size × Average budgeted contribution margin
_____
31,250 × (16% – 10%) × $297.50 = $557,812.50 Favorable

Panel 3: Reconciliation of the Market Size Variance, Market Share Variance, and Sales Quantity Variance
_____

Market size variance	$260,312.50 Unfavorable
Market share variance	$557,812.50 Favorable
Sales quantity variance	$297,500.00 Favorable

As the size of the total market for a firm's products changes, its total sales are likely to change with it. When the total market size for a firm's products expands, its total sales are likely to increase. A firm that failed to increase its total sales in proportion to the increase in the total market is not keeping up with the market and is losing its marketing position.

Market Share Variance

Market share variance
compares the firm's actual market share to its budgeted market share and measures the effect of changes in the firm's market share on its total contribution margin and operating income.

The market share of a firm is a function of its market size, core competitors, competencies, and competitive environment. **Market share variance** compares a firm's actual market share to its budgeted market share and measures the effect of the changes in its market share on its total contribution margin and operating income. To determine a market share variance, we need three items: the difference between the firm's actual and budgeted market share, the total *actual market size*, and the weighted-average *budgeted* contribution margin per unit. Notice that the computation uses the *actual*, not budgeted, total market size and the *budgeted*, not actual, weighted-average contribution margin per unit. The product of these three factors—the difference in market share, total actual market size, and weighted-average budget contribution margin per unit—is the market share variance. The equation is

$$
\begin{array}{c} \text{Market} \\ \text{share} \\ \text{variance} \end{array} = \left[\begin{array}{c} \text{Actual} \\ \text{market} \\ \text{share} \end{array} - \begin{array}{c} \text{Budgeted} \\ \text{market} \\ \text{share} \end{array} \right] \times \begin{array}{c} \text{Total actual} \\ \text{number of} \\ \text{units in the} \\ \text{industry} \end{array} \times \begin{array}{c} \text{Weighted-average} \\ \text{budget contribution} \\ \text{margin per unit} \end{array}
$$

Panel 2 of Exhibit 17–11 shows the calculation of the market share variance for Schmidt Machinery Company's December 2002 operations.

Although the total market for the industry decreased to 31,250, Schmidt's total units sold are higher than the budgeted units to sell for the period. As a result, its market share increases from the budgeted 10 percent to 16 percent (5,000 units ÷ 31,250 units = 16 percent). Given the actual total market size of 31,250, the 6 percent increase in the market share would have increased Schmidt's total budgeted units to sell by 1,875. At a budgeted weighted-average contribution of $297.50 per unit, this increase in units would have increased its operating income by $557,812.50.

Reconciliation

Together, the market size variance and market share variance account for the sales quantity variance of the period. Look at panel 3 of Exhibit 17–11 to confirm this result. For December 2002, Schmidt has a favorable market share variance of $557,812.50 and an unfavorable market size variance of $260,312.50. The total of these two variances is $297,500 favorable, which is the sales quantity variance reported earlier.

Exhibit 17–12 calculates market size and market share variances using a columnar form. Remember that market share and market size variances explain the firm's sales quantity variance. The total variance in Exhibit 17–12, the difference between points A and C is the total sales quantity variance for both products, which was shown in Exhibit 17–10 as the difference between points B and C for both products. The left point of Exhibit 17–12, A, is the budgeted total contribution margin the firm would have earned from the number of units it actually sold. Point B of Exhibit 17–10 is the sum of the flexible budget for both products at the budgeted sales mix. Exhibit 17–12 calculates the same amount using market size. Seen from the perspective of the industry's total market size, the total number of units sold by the firm is the product of the industry's total actual market size and the firm's actual market share:

$$31{,}250 \text{ units} \times 16 \text{ percent} = 5{,}000 \text{ units}$$

At A of panel 2, the budgeted weighted-average contribution margin per unit is $297.50 and the total contribution margin from 5,000 units is $1,487,500.

Exhibit 17–12   Market Size and Market Share Variances

SCHMIDT MACHINERY COMPANY
Computation of Market Size and Share Variances Using Columnar Form
For December 2002

Panel 1: Scheme	A	B	C
Total market	Actual	Actual	Budget
Market share	Actual	Budget	Budget
Weighted-average contribution margin	Budget	Budget	Budget

Market share variance   Market size variance

Panel 2: Detail	A	B	C
	Total actual market in units × Actual market share × Budgeted weighted-average contribution margin per unit	Total actual market in units × Budgeted market share × Budgeted weighted-average contribution margin per unit	Budgeted total market in units × Budgeted market share × Budgeted weighted-average contribution margin per unit
	$31,250 \times 16\% \times \$297.50$ = $1,487.500	$31,250 \times 10\% \times \$297.50$ = $929,687.50	$40,000 \times 10\% \times \$297.50$ = $1,190,000

Market share variance
= $1,487,500 − $929,687.50
= $557,812.50 F

Market size variance
= $929,687.50 − $1,190,000
= $260,312.50 U

Sales quantity variance
= $1,487,500 − $1,190,000
= $297,500 F

Point B is the budgeted total contribution margin the firm would have earned had it maintained the budgeted market share. With total market size of 31,250, the firm would have sold 3,125 total units if it had maintained its budgeted market share of 10 percent. At the budgeted weighted-average contribution margin of $297.50 per unit, total contribution would have been $929,687.50. The difference between point A and point B is due entirely to the difference in market share. The difference, $557,812.50, is the market share variance. This variance is favorable because the firm has an actual market share of 16 percent as opposed to only 10 percent budgeted.

Point C is the master budget. The budgeted total of sales in units is the product of the budgeted market size and the budgeted market share:

$$40,000 \times 10 \text{ percent} = 4,000 \text{ units}$$

The only difference between point B and point C (the master budget) is in the total market size. Point B uses the actual market size; point C uses the budgeted market size. The difference, therefore, is a market size variance, which is $260,312.50 in our example. The variance is unfavorable because the actual market size is smaller than the firm anticipated when it prepared the master budget for December 2002.

MARKETING VARIANCES AND STRATEGIC MANAGEMENT

Most businesses have goals to earn higher operating income and increase their market shares by increasing either total sales or sales of higher-margin items. Firms fulfill these and other operating and strategic goals through sales activities. Sales variances, including those for selling price, sales volume, sales mix, sales quantity, market share, and market size, help managers to plan, monitor, and assess the effectiveness of sales activities in attaining budgeted goals. These variances can have a tremendous impact on the firm's strategic planning and implementation, in addition to being important information to be considered in evaluating the performance of managers and divisions.

Strategic Implications of a Selling Price Variance

A price change is a tactical action. A *tactical action* involves few organizational resources, is relatively easy to implement, and can be reversed in a relatively short time. For example, McDonald's decrease of the price of its Big Mac to 99 cents and an airline's temporary reduction of round-trip airfare between Chicago and Paris to $250 are tactical actions. Price decrease is a tool that firms often use as a competitive weapon to expand market shares, (drive out competition), establish market position, implement the strategy of converting the firm into a low-cost provider or implement other desired objectives. Firms can raise prices to implement a differentiation strategy or to take advantage of an expanding market.

Decreasing selling prices to secure a higher sales volume or market share, however, can jeopardize the firm's profitability if the unfavorable selling price variance exceeds the favorable sales volume variance. If the percentage of reduction in selling price per unit is higher than the percentage of increase in sales volume, the firm loses money. Seven-up proved this point with its massive growth by heavily discounting its products in the late 1970s. Profits did not follow from higher volumes, and the firm was eventually acquired by Cadbury Schweppes. Similarly, an increase in total quantity sold might not benefit a firm that sells low-margin items at the expense of high-margin products because the unfavorable sales mix variance is higher than the favorable sales quantity variance.

A firm should consider its current position and the likely reactions of competitors before changing their selling prices. A price change taken by a market leader is likely to cause competitors to immediately do the same. For example, airlines usually reduce their fares in immediate response to competitors' reductions, and pointless price wars follow. As a result, total sales in dollars for all airlines can decrease. The price reduction might not result in an increase in passengers or a change in market share for the firm that first lowered prices. Price reductions that competitors will match make sense only if the firm initiating them has a lower cost structure than its competitors. Unless accompanied by other actions, any gain in market share by the market leader through price reductions is likely to be temporary. A favorable selling price variance experienced by a market leader without meaningful deterioration in its market share suggests that the price increase was a successful tactical action.

A nonmarket leader with a meaningful gain in market share but an unfavorable price variance should assess its ability to sustain this situation. A firm should assess the difference between a favorable price variance and an unfavorable market share variance if it has a favorable selling price variance with a significant loss of market share. An unfavorable selling price variance for a nonmarket leader without a significant gain in market share indicates that the cost reduction is questionable.

A firm should assess the difference between a favorable price variance and an unfavorable market share variance if it has a favorable selling price variance with a significant loss of market share.

A pricing policy is successful if it results in a favorable price variance with no change, an increase in the firm's market share, or an unfavorable price variance with an even greater market share variance. Favorable variances in both price and market share variances can signal unexplored potential.

Strategic Implications of Market Share Variance

A firm that has an unfavorable selling price variance can be following an appropriate strategy if it intends to build its market share to explore market potentials. A favorable market share variance is evidence of the success of such a strategy. In this instance, the firm might place less significance on the overall unfavorable contribution margin or operating income variance as long as it achieves a favorable market share variance. Microsoft followed this strategy in marketing its word processing software, Microsoft Word. WordPerfect was the market share leader in the 1980s, but Microsoft gradually built Word's market share by offering it at low prices and making it easy to use. As Word's market share grew, even dedicated WordPerfect users switched to Word to be compatible with this best-selling product and the Microsoft family of software.

Management should always be alert to declines in a firm's market share. A decrease in market share indicates the erosion of its competitive position and the encroachment of competitors. Ignoring declining market shares can lead to the firm's eventual demise. However, maintaining or increasing market share at the expense of current profit usually is not a wise move.

The wisdom of attaining a favorable market share variance at the expense of unfavorable selling price variances is questionable if the products are in a mature market and is likely devastating for cash cows.

A firm with a differentiation strategy typically does not hold a large share of the market(s)s it serves. The high profitability of its products, however, requires it to monitor its sales quantity and market share. A small change in sales quantity and market share can significantly impact current and future operating income.

The Myth of Market Share

"Jubilant General Motors executives recently announced their May sales figures, showing that GM's share had surged to more than 32 percent of the U.S. car market." This exciting situation stemmed from the reverse of GM's declining market share. From having more than 50 percent of the U.S. car market before the 1980s, GM's market share had declined to approximately 40 percent in the 1980s and to a low of 28.6 in early 1998.

GM regained some lost market share at the expense of profit. To increase sales and increase market share, it began offering 1.9% financing, substantial rebates, and barely profitable lease rates and sold thousands of cars at near cost to rental companies. "As a result, GM's earnings per share is significantly below those of other auto makers. Last year, Ford, with a market share of about 25 percent, earned $978 more in profit than GM on each car sold."

Firm size and market share do not matter—profits do.

Source: Based on Richard Miniter, "Manager's Journal," *The Wall Street Journal*, June 15, 1998.

Expanding in the Face of Declining Market Size

The primary product of Unifi, a North Carolina textile manufacturer, is textured polyester. Polyester's popularity peaked in the early 1970s. The total market decreased by more than 50 percent in 10 years, from a demand of over 1.4 billion pounds in 1975 to 650 million pounds in 1985.

Unifi's chairman, Allen Mebane, saw the shrinking demand for polyester as an opportunity to become a dominant player and spent heavily to purchase state-of-the-art equipment to improve productivity and product quality. Through its investments, Unifi became the low-cost, high-quality producer in the industry and forced out many of its competitors. By 1994 the firm had become the world's largest producer of textured polyester and had more than 70 percent of the U.S. market.

What about profit? Over a recent five-year period, the firm earned an average annual return of 37 percent for its shareholders.

Source: Based on Michael Hitt, R. D. Ireland, and R. E. Hoskisson, *Strategic Management* (St. Paul, MN: West Publishing, 1995), p. 100.

Strategic Implications of Market Size Variance

Misdirected expansion undertaken during periods of declining market size could cause overcapacity, a decline in revenues, or financial distress. Shrinking market sizes, however, do not necessarily result in downsizing, as the experience of textile manufacturer Unifi demonstrates. Indeed, abundant evidence suggested that firms that took action to redefine and expand the market size of their products often experience high profitability. McDonald's expansion in the early 1980s into Japan and Taiwan—countries where people seldom consumed beef products and hated cheese—redefined that firm's total market size. Indeed, McDonald's franchises in Japan and Taiwan have for many years been among its most profitable.

Defining *market* in *market size* is a challenge. Companies expend substantial resources to increase their *share* of a *market*, but they often have difficulty justifying a similar investment to increase market size, although the potential returns from a larger market can substantially exceed those from gaining a few percentages of market share.

PART TWO: MANAGING PRODUCTIVITY

> Productivity is not everything, but in the long run it is almost everything.
>
> PAUL KRUGMAN

LEARNING OBJECTIVE 4▶

Describe productivity and the implications of changes to productivity.

The desire to produce more with less is one of the leading reasons for human progress. Manufacturing productivity has increased in industrial countries by more than 45 times in the last 125 years. As a result, the average number of working hours per year per person has decreased in the United States from more than 3,000 hours to around 1,800 hours. The productivity explosion has paid for the 10 times expansion in education and the expansion of health care. Productivity has become the wealth of nations.[1]

Firms that employ fewer people and use fewer materials, machines, or other production resources than their competitors to manufacture the same product with equal or higher quality enjoy competitive advantages. These firms usually earn higher-than-average returns and command long-term success. For this reason, producing more with less is often a strategic critical success factor for many organizations.

Firms that compete as cost leaders must perform all tasks with fewer resources than their competitors to be successful. Firms competing on differentiation or focus strategies can increase their profit margins by using the same amount of or fewer resources than their competitors. Governments and not-for-profit organizations often require their employees to do more with the limited resources at their disposal. Economists and financial analysts often use the amount of output produced per unit of input to indicate a country's competitiveness and economic well-being. Almost everywhere we look, the ability to do more with less is critically important.

Productivity in USAA

Many firms have improved their productivity continuously over the years. For example, USAA, a financial services firm located in San Antonio, has pursued increases in employee productivity for more than 30 years. The company's financial assets have increased 100 times while the total number of employees has increased by only 5 times.

Source: Based on "Solving the Productivity Puzzle," *The Wall Street Journal,* March 4, 1994.

---

[1] Peter F. Drucker, *Managing for the Future* (New York: Truman Tolley Books, 1993), pp. 93–94.

WHAT IS PRODUCTIVITY?

Productivity is the ratio of what is produced to what is required in producing it.

$$\text{Productivity} = \frac{\text{Output}}{\text{Input}}$$

A firm that spent five days to manufacture 100 units has a productivity of 20 units per day. A social service worker who processed 75 cases over a four-week period has a productivity of 3.75 cases per day. A firm that uses 24.5 pounds of material to manufacture one unit is more productive than a firm that uses 25 pounds of the same materials to manufacture one unit of the same product.

A primary objective in measuring productivity is to improve operations either by using fewer inputs to produce the same output or to produce more output with the same inputs. Improvements in productivity require firms to identify benchmarks or criteria against which to assess their changes in productivity and to determine needed improvements to attain their goals. Among criteria often used are past productivity measures of the firm, of another division of the firm, or of other firms in the same industry; the industry standard; or a benchmark established by top management as the goal for the firm to attain.

MEASURING PRODUCTIVITY

A measure of productivity can be either operational or financial. **Operational productivity** is a physical measure that includes both the input and the output in physical units. **Financial productivity** uses dollar amounts for the input; the output can be a physical measure or a dollar amount. For example, the number of tables made per sheet of plywood indicates operational productivity; the number of tables per dollar cost of plywood reflects financial productivity. Sales revenue per dollar cost of plywood also indicates financial productivity.

A productivity measure that focuses only on the relationship between one input and the output attained is a **partial productivity** measure. The following indicate common partial productivity:

- Direct materials yield productivity such as output/units of materials.
- Workforce productivity such as output per labor-hour or output per person employed.
- Process (or activity) productivity such as output per machine-hours or output per kilowatt hour.

A productivity measure that includes all input resources used in production is **total productivity.** The number of tables manufactured per dollar of manufacturing costs is a total productivity measure because the denominator, manufacturing costs, includes all manufacturing costs incurred to make the tables. Exhibit 17–13 lists different productivity measures.

Exhibit 17–14 is an example of data used to measure productivity; it uses production data for Er-Cat Precision Tool Company in 2002 and 2003 for manufacturing DB2 drill bits. The manufacturing costs include total fixed factory overhead of

Productivity is the ratio of output to input.

Operational productivity is the ratio of output to the number of units of an input factor.

Financial productivity is the ratio of output to the dollar amount of one or more input factors.

Partial productivity is a productivity measure that focuses only on the relationship between one of the inputs and the output attained.

Total productivity is a productivity measure that includes all input resources in computing the ratio of the output attained and the input used to attain the output.

Exhibit 17–13	Productivity Measures

Productivity	Partial productivity
	   Partial operational productivity
	   Partial financial productivity
	Total productivity (financial productivity)

Exhibit 17–14   **Operating Data**

ER-CAT PRECISION TOOL COMPANY
2002 and 2003 Operating Data for DB2
(dollars in 000s)

	2002	2003
Units of DB2 manufactured and sold	4,000	4,800
Total sales ($500 per unit)	$2,000	$2,400
Direct materials (25,000 pounds at $24/pound and 32,000 pounds at $25/pound)	600	800
Direct labor (4,000 hours at $40 per hour and 4,000 hours at $50/hour)	160	200
Other operating costs	300	300
Operating income	$ 940	$1,100

$300,000 per year and variable manufacturing costs consisting of metal alloy (direct materials) and direct labor-hours.

The firm earned $1,100,000 operating income in 2003, a 17 percent increase over the $940,000 earned in 2002. Without examining the operating data in detail, management would probably be very happy with the operating result. The increase in operating income, however, compares unfavorably to the 20 percent increase in total sales. Because fixed costs are the same in both years, the less-than-proportional increase in operating income is a result of a higher-than-proportional increase in the firm's variable costs for direct materials and direct labor.

A multitude of factors, however, could have contributed to the increase in these two costs, including increases in the number of units manufactured and sold; changes in the amounts of the inputs, such as direct materials or direct labor-hours, used in production; and increases in the unit cost of resources. The firm should identify the factors that caused the change in total cost so that management can improve operating income by decreasing manufacturing costs. (Chapters 15 and 16 discuss analyses based on the firm's standard costs for the period to determine the effect of changes in cost elements, such as wage rates, labor-hours, materials prices, and materials usage, on the period's production cost.)

Productivity measurements discussed in this chapter examine the effect of a firm's productivity on its operating income. Increased productivity decreases costs and increases operating income. Changes in the productivity of different resources, however, do not always occur in the same direction or at an equal pace. A firm's productivity or use of direct materials can improve while its productivity for direct labor improves at a slower pace or deteriorates. Worse, productivity of different resources can conflict. For instance, management of a furniture manufacturer can increase materials productivity by reducing waste due to improper cutting, but to do this, employees must spend more labor-hours to cut the boards carefully, resulting in a decrease in labor-hour productivity. Management needs to know the effects of productivity changes on operating income to best use its resources.

Partial Productivity

LEARNING OBJECTIVE 5▶

Compute and interpret operational and financial partial productivity.

A *partial productivity measure* describes the relationship between the output of a period and one required input resource to produce the output.

$$\text{Partial productivity} = \frac{\text{Number of units or value of output manufactured}}{\text{Number of units or cost of a single input resource}}$$

The denominator is the number or cost of a manufacturing factor such as direct materials or direct labor-hours; the numerator is the number of units or the value of the goods or services produced.

Partial productivity of the direct materials for DB2 for the Er-Cat Precision Tool Company in 2002 is 0.16:

$$\text{Partial productivity of DM in 2002} = \frac{4,000}{25,000} = 16\%$$

Partial Operational Productivity

Partial operational productivity reflects the conversion ratio of an input resource to the output. The numerator, the output, is the number of units produced; the denominator is the number of units of input resources used. Exhibit 17–15 presents the partial operational productivity of Er-Cat Precision Company in 2002 and 2003. The partial productivity of 16% for direct materials in 2002 indicates that the firm manufactured 0.16 unit of output for every pound of direct materials used in production.

A comparison of partial productivity over time shows changes in the input resource's productivity. Er-Cat Company's operating results show that the partial productivity of the direct materials decreased over time. The firm manufactured 0.16 unit of DB2 in 2002 but only 0.15 unit of DB2 in 2003 from 1 pound of direct materials, a 6.25 percent decrease in productivity [(0.16 − 0.15) ÷ 0.16 = 0.0625]. Partial productivity of direct labor, however, improved during the same period: 1 direct-hour produced 1 unit in 2002 and 1.2 units in 2003, a 20 percent increase in productivity [(1.2 − 1) ÷ 1 = 0.20].

The changes in productivity can also be examined by computing the amount of input resources that the firm would have used in 2003 had it maintained the 2002 partial productivity, as shown in Exhibit 17–16. In this case, the 4,800 units of DB2

Exhibit 17–15   Partial Productivity

ER-CAT PRECISION TOOL COMPANY
Partial Productivity—Direct Materials and Direct Labor

Product: DB2

	Partial Operational Productivity	
	2002	**2003**
Direct materials	4,000 ÷ 25,000 = 0.16	4,800 ÷ 32,000 = 0.15
Direct labor	4,000 ÷ 4,000 = 1.00	4,800 ÷ 4,000 = 1.20
	Partial Financial Productivity	
	2002	**2003**
Direct materials	4,000 ÷ $600,000 = 0.0067	4,800 ÷ $800,000 = 0.006
Direct labor	4,000 ÷ $160,000 = 0.025	4,800 ÷ $200,000 = 0.024

Exhibit 17–16   Changes in Partial Productivity

ER-CAT PRECISION TOOL COMPANY
Effects of Changes in Partial Productivity of Direct Materials
and Direct Labor in the Production of DB2

Input Resource	2002 Output	2000 Partial Operational Productivity	2003 Output at 2002 Productivity	Input Used in 2003	Saving (Loss) in Units of Input
Direct materials	4,800	0.16	30,000	32,000	(2,000)
Direct labor	4,800	1.00	4,800	4,000	800

manufactured and sold in 2003 would have required only 30,000 pounds of direct materials (4,800 ÷ 0.16). This decreased partial productivity necessitated the use of an additional 2,000 pounds in 2003 (32,000 – 30,000). Similarly, the firm would have spent 4,800 direct labor-hours in 2003 had it had the same direct labor partial productivity in 2003 as in 2002. The firm saved the cost of 800 hours of direct labor (4,800 – 4,000) when its partial productivity in 2003 for direct labor increased from 1.0 to 1.2.

Partial Financial Productivity

LEARNING OBJECTIVE 6▶

Distinguish among productivity change, input price change, and output change.

The bottom panel of Exhibit 17–15 reports the partial financial productivity of direct materials and direct labor. Partial financial productivity indicates the number of units of output manufactured for each dollar the firm spent for the input resource. The 2003 partial financial productivity for direct materials is determined by dividing 2003 actual output (4,800 units) by the actual cost of the year ($800,000). This productivity (0.006 units of DB2 manufactured for every dollar spent on direct materials) indicates that the partial productivity decreased from 2002 to 2003 by 10 percent [(0.0067 – 0.006) ÷ 0.0067].

The partial financial productivity of direct labor is 0.025 for 2002 and 0.024 for 2003, a decrease of 4 percent [(0.025 – 0.024) ÷ 0.025]. This result contradicts the partial operational productivity for direct labor reported earlier (20 percent improvement). These results suggest that, although employee productivity per hour increased, the cost increase due to higher hourly wages more than offset the gain in productivity per hour (see Exhibit 17–17).

Differences in operating results can result from differences in output level, input cost, or productivity. Panel 1 of Exhibit 17–17 shows the analytical framework for determining the effects of each factor. All three factors at point A are 2003 figures: units of output, productivity, and input cost. Point B is the cost to manufacture the 2003 output at the 2002 *productivity* level and 2003 input cost. The only difference between A and B in panel 1, 2, and 3 is for productivity. Thus, the difference between points A and B results from changes in productivity in 2003 and 2002.

The only difference in points B and C is the unit price for the input resource: point B is for 2003 and point C is for 2002. The difference, therefore, in points B and C is the change in input price.

Point D is the cost to manufacture the 2002 *output* at 2002 productivity with 2002 input resource at 2002 unit cost. Recall that point C is the cost to manufacture the 2003 *output* at the 2002 productivity and the 2002 unit cost of the input resource. Any difference in the costs results from the difference in the output levels. Because both points C and D use the same productivity and unit cost of the input resource, the ratio of output to input at these two points is always the same.

The analysis shows that, of the 10 percent decrease in partial financial productivity of direct materials (from 0.0067 to 0.006, Exhibit 17–15), only 6 percent (0.0004/0.0067, Exhibit 17–17) can be attributed to productivity change. The remaining 4 percent (0.000267/0.0067, Exhibit 17–17) reflects the price change per pound of direct materials ($24 in 2002 to $25 in 2003). The total change in partial financial productivity of direct labor is a 4 percent decrease from 2002 (from 0.025 to 0.024, Exhibit 17–15). The partial productivity of direct labor did increase by 16 percent (0.004/0.025, Exhibit 17–17). The 25 percent increase in wages, however, more than offsets any gain in labor productivity. As a result, total direct labor cost increased.

Partial Productivity: Operational versus Financial

Both the numerator and the denominator of a partial operational productivity measure are physical units. Using physical measures makes partial operational measures easy for operational personnel to understand and accept. In addition, an operational productivity measure is unaffected by price changes or other factors, which makes it easier to benchmark.

By focusing on the physical measure of one input resource at a time, a partial operational productivity measure enables management to know how changes in productivity of input resources affect operations. Executives in the auto industry often use

Exhibit 17–17   **Decomposition of Partial Financial Productivity**

ER-CAT PRECISION TOOL COMPANY
Decomposition of Partial Financial Productivity

Panel 1: Framework

	A	B	C	D
Output	2003	2003	2003	2002
Productivity	2003	2002	2002	2002
Input Cost	2003	2003	2002	2002

Productivity Change   Input Price Change   Output Change

Panel 2: Operating Data for Decomposing Financial Partial Productivity

	Actual 2003 Operating Results	2003 Output at 2002 Productivity and 2003 Input Cost	2003 Output at 2002 Productivity and 2002 Input Cost	Actual 2002 Operating Results
Output units	4,800	4,800	4,000	4,000
Input units and costs				
Direct materials	$32,000 \times \$25 = \$\ 800,000$	$30,000 \times \$25 = \$750,000$	$30,000 \times \$24 = \$720,000$	$25,000 \times \$24 = \$600,000$
Direct labor	$4,000 \times \$50 = \ \ \ 200,000$	$4,800 \times \$50 = \ \ \ 240,000$	$4,800 \times \$40 = \ \ \ 192,000$	$4,000 \times \$40 = \ \ \ 160,000$
Total	$1,000,000	$990,000	$912,000	$760,000

Panel 3: Decomposition

	2003 Operation			2002 Operation
	2003 output ÷ (2003 input × 2003 input costs)	2003 output ÷ (2002 input for the 2003 output × 2003 input costs)	2003 output ÷ (2002 input for the 2003 output × 2002 input costs)	2002 output ÷ (2002 input × 2002 input costs)
Direct materials	4,800/$800,000 = 0.006	4,800/$750,000 = 0.0064	4,800/$720,000 = 0.006667	4,000/$600,000 = 0.006667
Direct labor	4,800/$200,000 = 0.024	4,800/$240,000 = 0.0200	4,800/$192,000 = 0.025000	4,000/$160,000 = 0.025000

	Productivity change	Input price change	Output change
Direct materials	0.0060 – 0.0064 = 0.0004 U	0.006400 – 0.006667 = 0.000267 U	0.006667 – 0.006667 = 0
Direct labor	0.0240 – 0.0200 = 0.0040 F	0.02000 – 0.025000 = 0.005000 U	0.025000 – 0.025000 = 0

Panel 4: Summary of Results

Productivity Change from 2002

	Productivity Change		Input Price Change		Output Change		Total Change
Direct materials	0.0004 U	+	0.000267 U	+	0	=	0.000667 U
Direct labor	0.0040 F	+	0.005000 U	+	0	=	0.001000 U

Change as Percent of 2002 Productivity

	Productivity Change		Input Price Change		Output Change		Total Change
Direct materials	6% U	+	4% U	+	0%	=	10% U
Direct labor	16 F	+	20 U	+	0	=	4 U

partial productivity measures to compare labor productivity in the United States to that in Japan as a gauge of their competitive positions in the market. For example, in the early 1980s, auto executives demanded improvements in productivity because Toyota produced one vehicle every 16 to 18 hours in comparison to some U.S. auto manufacturers that produced one car every 40-plus hours.

A partial financial productivity has the advantage of considering the effects of both the cost and quantity of an input resource on productivity. At a management level, the effect of cost, not merely the physical quantity, is a concern. In addition, partial financial productivity can be used in operations that use more than one production factor. Partial operational productivity, on the other hand, can measure only one direct material or type of direct labor at a time.

Limitations of Partial Productivity Analysis

A partial productivity measure has several limitations. First, it measures only the relationship between an input resource and the output; it ignores any effect that changes in other manufacturing factors have on the productivity. An improved partial productivity measure could have been obtained by decreasing the productivity of one or more other input resources. For example, Er-Cat Company could have decided to use less direct labor and more direct materials.

A second limitation is that partial productivity ignores any effect that changes in the production factor have on productivity, for example, a change in the quality of the production factor. The number of labor-hours that Er-Cat used in 2003 might represent a higher skill level than those used in 2002. As a result, the partial productivity of labor increases, but so did the average hourly wage rate. Is it worthwhile, then, for the firm to make the trade-off? Unfortunately, an analysis of partial operational productivity cannot provide an answer.

Third, partial productivity also ignores any effect that changes in the firm's operating characteristics have on the productivity of the input resource. The labor partial operational productivity could have improved because the firm installed high-efficiency equipment. The improvement in labor partial operational productivity can hardly be attributed to increased labor productivity.

Fourth, no efficiency standard is involved in partial productivity measures, and no relationship might exist between a partial productivity measure and the efficiency variance as determined in Chapter 15.

Total Productivity

Total productivity measures the relationship between the output attained and the total cost of all the input resources to produce the output.

$$\text{Total productivity} = \frac{\text{Units or sales value of output}}{\text{Total cost of all input resources}}$$

Total productivity is a financial productivity measure. The denominator represents the total amount of resources used in production. The sum of different resources in their physical measures usually is not meaningful because the resources can include materials, labor, utilities, and other manufacturing factors. Dollars represent a common factor that allows measures for different resources such as materials, labor, and other production factors to be added together.

The first panel of Exhibit 17–18 shows the computation of the firm's total productivity of variable manufacturing costs for 2002 and 2003. The computation of total productivity involves three steps: First, determine the output of each period: 4,000 units in 2002 and 4,800 units in 2003. Second, calculate the total variable costs incurred to produce the output: For DB2, it was $760,000 in 2002 and $1,000,000 in 2003. Third, compute total productivity by dividing the amount of output by the total cost of variable input resources: 0.005263 in 2002 and 0.004800 in 2003. For every dollar of variable cost incurred in 2002, the firm manufactured 0.005263 unit of the output, but in 2003 manufacturing only 0.004800 unit, a decrease of 0.000463 unit or 8.8 percent in productivity [(0.005263 − 0.004800) ÷ 0.005263].

Alternatively, in the numerator, we can substitute total sales revenue for the number of units manufactured to compute the total productivity, as shown in the second panel of Exhibit 17–18. The firm generated $2.6316 in sales for each dollar of variable costs in 2002 but $2.40 in 2003, a drop of $0.2316 in sales, or 8.8 percent [(2.6316 − 2.4000) ÷ 2.6316]. A firm can use the total cost as the denominator to identify productivity of all resources used in operations.

Exhibit 17–18   Total Productivity

ER-CAT PRECISION TOOL COMPANY
Total Productivity for DB2

Panel 1: Total Productivity in Unit	2002	2003
(a) Total units manufactured	4,000	4,800
(b) Total variable manufacturing costs incurred	$760,000	$1,000,000
(c) Total productivity: (a) ÷ (b)	0.005263	0.004800
(d) Decrease in productivity: 0.005263 − 0.004800 = 0.000463 (8.8%)		

Panel 2: Total Productivity in Sales Dollar	2002	2003
(a) Total sales	$2,000,000	$2,400,000
(b) Total variable manufacturing costs incurred	$760,000	$1,000,000
(c) Total productivity: (a) ÷ (b)	$2.6316	$2.4000
(d) Decrease in productivity: $2.6316 − $2.4000 = $0.2316 (8.8%)		

ALCOA Made Safety a Productivity Issue

When Paul O'Neill became CEO of Alcoa, Inc., in June 1987, the Pittsburgh-based firm earned $264 million on sales of $4.6 billion and had 35,000 employees. It was, according to *Business Week*, just another wheezing industrial giant with an unremarkable financial record and a workforce that was biding its time.

O'Neill did not hold his troops to criteria such as profit margins, sales growth rates, or share price appreciation that CEOs commonly use. His singular standard was time lost to employee injuries. In 1987, Alcoa had already outperformed most U.S. manufacturers in this area: Its rate of time lost because of employee injuries was one-third of the U.S. average. Nevertheless, O'Neill believed that "to be a world-class company, it first had to become the safest."

The emphasis on safety fundamentally altered Alcoa's culture. To meet the CEO's targets, managers and even bottom-rung employees began showing initiative instead of mutely waiting for orders. Productivity soon began rising, "Paul came in and got us to do things we never thought we could do," says L. Richard Milner, head of Alcoa's automotive unit.

When O'Neill retired at the end of 2000, Alcoa boasted the industry's safety record. Its rate of time lost for employee injuries is less than one-twentieth of U.S. average. For fiscal-year 2000, the firm had profits of $1.5 billion on sales of $22.9 billion and a payroll of 140,000.

Source: Based on Michael Arndt, "How O'Neill Got Alcoa Shining," *Business Week*, February 5, 2001, p. 39.

Of the two alternative measures of total productivity, the measure of all resources required to manufacture the output units is often used to assess production operations. Achieving higher productivity by making more units is an important first step for a successful firm. To be successful, it must generate higher revenue for each dollar that it spends on resources.

Advantages and Limitations of Total Productivity

Total productivity measures the combined effects of changes in all operating factors. As such, use of a total productivity measure decreases the possibility of manipulating one or two manufacturing factors to improve the measure. The same cannot be said for partial productivity measures. To the extent that partial productivity of direct labor can be improved at the expense of the partial productivity of materials, for example, a manager whose firm measures the partial productivity of direct labor as the primary basis of performance evaluation might not pay due care to minimizing scraps.

By necessity, total productivity is a financial productivity measure. Personnel at the operational level often have difficulty linking financial productivity measures to their day-to-day operations. A deterioration in total productivity can result from increased costs of resources, which could be beyond manufacturing's control. Such ambiguity in the relationship between the performance measure and the reward system could defeat the purpose of having a productivity measurement.

Another consideration in using a total productivity measure is that the basis for assessing changes in productivity could vary over time. For instance, Er-Cat Precision Tool Company assesses the change in productivity in 2003 from 2002 using 2002 as the criterion. The evaluation of the 2002 change in productivity from 2001 would have used 2001 productivity as the criterion. This procedure makes it impossible to compare changes in productivity from 2002 to 2003 to those of changes from 2001 to 2002 because the two measures use different years as the base. One solution to this problem is the use of a constant base year.

In addition, productivity measures can ignore the effects of changes in demand, changes in selling prices of the goods or services, and special purchasing or selling arrangements on productivity.

Changes in demand alter the size of operations. The size of operations can affect total productivity as well as partial productivity for materials, labor or process. Economies of scale often mean that productivity per unit of input differs at various levels of operation.

Increases or decreases in selling prices of the output goods or services change productivity in dollars of output for each unit of input either in part or in total. Management would be pleased to learn that the productivity as measured by the sales revenues per dollar spent on direct materials increased from $4.00 last year to $4.50 this year. The jubilation would not be justified, however, if the firm raised its selling price from an average of $20 per unit last year to an average of $25 per unit this year. The increased selling price alone would have increased the productivity per dollar of direct materials cost from $4.00 to $5.00. The partial productivity of direct materials decreased rather than increased.

Special arrangements in either sales of the output or purchases of input resources also can disrupt the underlying relation between input and output in computing productivity. A special arrangement to sell products at a discount decreases the productivity in dollars of output per input unit. Alternatively, a special purchase of materials increases financial productivity. Neither can be attributed to a loss or gain in productivity.

PRODUCTIVITY IN THE NEW MANUFACTURING ENVIRONMENT

Productivity and Total Quality Management

Too often managers believe that they can attain improvements in quality only at the expense of productivity because of the need for additional resources or decreases in units of good output. The experience of many firms is the opposite; improvements in quality *increase* productivity.

First, quality improvements often decrease waste and spoiled units of the division, downstream divisions, and the firm, and likely decreasing the amount of input resources needed. Improvements in quality at Kangall Manufacturing decreased the rejected units of the total manufactured from 10 percent to 2 percent. The improvement in quality improved the firm's productivity from 1.60 to 1.74.[2]

Second, quality improvements decrease the resources needed in production by decreasing or eliminating rework. Decrease or elimination of rework saves the con-

---

[2] If the firm spent $3,937.50 to manufacture 7,000 units, of which 700 were rejected, its productivity is 6,300/$3,937.50 = 1.6. A decrease in the rejection rate to 2 percent of total units produced would enable the firm to turn out 6,860 good units. The productivity improves to 6,860/$3,937.50 = 1.74 unit per dollar spent.

sumption of materials, production hours, and processes (machine-hours, energy, space). Productivity improves because less input is required to produce output.

Productivity and Business Process Reengineering

Productivity and business process reengineering go hand in hand; these two important approaches can help a firm attain a higher level of profitability and improve competitiveness.

Improving productivity requires determining how a firm can manufacture a product or complete a task with fewer inputs, including materials, time, and facility. Productivity improvement need not be restricted to efforts to reduce the inputs needed for the same output or to increase the level of output from the same input.

A thorough improvement in productivity goes deeper. In efforts to increase productivity, especially in service organizations, firms must identify the task, why it is being done, and whether it needs to be accomplished.[3] These are the same issues that business process reengineering considers. The easiest and perhaps the largest increases in productivity come from redefining the task to be done, especially from eliminating activities and redesigning the processes to perform the task.

Productivity is often computed for all inputs and processes, including both value-added and non-value-added activities. Improving productivity for a non-value-added activity is not a productive use of resources. Non-value-added activities should be eliminated through reengineering, not improved. Productivity should be assessed only on value-added activities. Efforts to improve productivity should focus only on value-added activities.

To be productive is to do better what we already do well. To be competitively productive requires continuous improvement. Continuous improvement entails continuous learning and process reengineering. Only with continuous productivity improvements can a firm remain competitive in the long term.

Finally, productivity improvement is not a synonym for employee layoff or capacity reduction. Although laying off workers and closing plants raises the level of productivity, these methods are one-time shots that do not improve growth rates. When demands increase, the firm might not be able to meet it. The cost of lost profit, yielding opportunities to competitors, and deteriorated competitive position can exceed the benefits of slimming down and restructuring. Boeing benefited from trimming its fat in the early 1990s. As the demand for aircraft rose, however, the firm struggled and failed to keep pace with demand. Production constraints forced Boeing to delay scheduled deliveries in October 1997 and opened opportunities for Airbus, its chief rival.

Productivity and Employee Turnover

Individual employees are important conduits of learning and productivity. When employees leave the company, they take learning with them and productivity can suffer. That is especially true in service firms. Manufacturing firms can mitigate the consequence of employee turnover by automating machinery and improving factory design.

The best companies inspire loyalty and reduce employee turnover by sharing productivity gains with employees. An Atlanta-based fast-food chain, Chick-fil-A, shares store profits with employees on a 50–50 basis. As a result, the firm's employees earn 50 percent more than the competition, and employee turnover is 5 percent a year versus 35 percent for competitors. The firm now has 600 stores—without ever tapping the stock market.

Source: Based on Frederick F. Reichheld, "Solving the Productivity Puzzle," *The Wall Street Journal,* March 4, 1996.

---

[3] Drucker, *Managing for the Future.* p. 98.

PRODUCTIVITY IN SERVICE FIRMS AND NOT-FOR-PROFIT ORGANIZATIONS

LEARNING OBJECTIVE 7▶

Identify the advantages and limitations of applying productivity measures to service firms and not-for-profit organizations.

Service firms and not-for-profit organizations employ more than half of the total workforce in the United States and continue to account for an increasing portion of both the national and global economy. Improving productivity in service firms and not-for-profit organizations is critical for their continued economic progress.

The basic concepts for measuring productivity in service firms and not-for-profit organizations are similar to those used by manufacturing firms. To the extent that a service firm or not-for-profit organization can clearly define and identify its output and the tasks required to attain it as comparable from period to period, organizations can use the procedure discussed for manufacturing operations to examine productivity changes. The productivity change of a shelter for the homeless, for example, can be measured using the ratio of the number of persons housed to the total expenses incurred. An airline can gauge productivity by computing the ratio of paid-passenger-miles to total operating expenses.

Unfortunately, many outputs and required tasks of service firms and not-for-profit organizations cannot be measured precisely. Hospitals often use patient-days to measure their outputs and productivity. Although the number of patient-days can be measured unequivocally, not all patient-days require the same amount of work or generate the same revenue. The level of care needed during a patient-day for an open-heart surgery patient most likely is much higher than that for a normal appendectomy.

Indefinite relationships between the output and input resources required by service firms and not-for-profits often lead their management to measure only financial productivity using dollar amounts for both the numerator and denominator of the ratio. An open-heart patient demands more input resources than does a person having an appendectomy. On the other hand, the open-heart patient's patient-day also generates higher revenue than does the patient-day of an appendectomy patient. Financial productivity can be a good measure for service firms if the relationship between the revenue generated and the cost of the input resources required to generate the revenue is relatively constant and if the dollar amount is a critical factor for the organization. Unfortunately for measurement purposes, dollar amounts can seldom represent a not-for-profit organization's major objective, and revenues of service firms are more likely determined by the quality of the services rendered, not the cost of input resources.

One other difficulty in measuring productivity in a not-for-profit organization is the absence of revenue as the common measure for output. The output of a higher education institution includes the number of students graduated, the total number of credit hours taught, contributions to the advancement of knowledge, and services to the community. It is difficult not only to obtain a clear measure for some of these outputs but also no revenue is attached to most, if not all, of these outputs. Consequently, identifying a revenue-based financial measure of the output of a higher education institution is impossible.

COST MANAGEMENT IN ACTION

Customer Profitability: Is It Better for Web Customers?

An important part of customer profitability is the cost to acquire a new customer. Research at Bain and Company, a consulting firm, has shown that in the consumer electronics industry, obtaining a new customer costs about $56. Based on the contribution from each new customer, these firms are estimated to need more than four years of business from each new customer to break even, but more than half of the new customers will defect before the four-year breakeven point. The numbers are similar for the apparel industry. Many firms are now trying to acquire new customers through the Web. How do you think the Web acquisition affects customer profitability?

PART THREE: CUSTOMER PROFITABILITY ANALYSIS

Firms earn profits from customers, not from manufacturing products. A not-for-profit organization accomplishes its mission by providing services to clients or customers, not from having an efficient operation. Various indicators of a firm's operations, such as manufacturing and marketing variances, can be favorable, yet the firm could suffer operating losses. Until a firm can realize profits from transactions with customers, it has failed to attain the desired goal that it set. A good understanding of profitability of a firm's current and potential customers can help the firm to achieve its goal, raise earnings to a higher level, and strengthen its strategic position. Management accountants, as strategic management partners, can enhance both short- and long-term successes of the organization by providing good customer profitability analyses.

Customer profitability analysis traces and reports customer revenues and customer costs. This process can reveal differences in profitability among customers, provide valuable insights into factors that contribute to the differences, and, by using one or more of the following actions, improve the firm's profitability or the organization's effectiveness in attaining its goals.

> **Customer profitability analysis** traces and reports customer revenues and customer costs.

- Providing better services to highly profitable customers.
- Securing highly profitable customers from competitors.
- Setting prices based on the cost to serve; charging higher prices for expensive services and granting discounts, if necessary, to gain customers requiring low costs to serve.
- Negotiating with customers to reach mutually beneficial levels of services.
- Transforming unprofitable customers into profitable ones through targeted negotiations on price, quantity, product mix, order processing, delivery terms, and payment arrangements.
- Identifying and conceding permanent loss customers to competitors.[4]

Customer profitability analysis includes the assessment of customer revenue, customer cost, and customer value.

Customer Revenue Analysis

A **customer revenue analysis** traces price and cash discounts to customers and identifies financing costs associated with customer revenues. Not all sales dollars contribute equally to a firm's net revenue. Net revenues from customers can differ because of price discounting, sales terms, sales returns and allowances, and the length of time that customer accounts remain outstanding.

Exhibit 17–19 reports revenue-related activities for three major customers of Winsome Office Supply.

> ◀ **LEARNING OBJECTIVE 8**
>
> *Analyze factors affecting revenues and determine net proceeds from customers.*
>
> **Customer revenue analysis** traces selling prices, sales discounts, and cash discounts to customers and identifies financing costs associated with customer revenues.

Exhibit 17–19	Selected Sales Activity, Winsome Office Supply		
	GereCo.	**HomeServ Inc.**	**Advance Tek**
Total sales	$500,000	$480,000	$540,000
Sales discounts	5%	0%	5%
Sales terms			
Payment	2/10, n/30	net 30	2/10, n/30
Delivery	FOB destination	FOB destination	FOB shipping point
Sales returns and allowances	1.0%	0.5%	6.0%

---

[4]   Robert S. Kaplan and Robin Cooper, *Cost & Effect* (Boston: Harvard Business School, Press, 1998), p. 181.

Salespersons grant sales discounts and sales terms to earn business. To earn sales from GereCo. and Advance Tek, the salespersons offered a 5 percent price discount. Both GereCo. and HomeServ paid their accounts within the payment terms specified. In fact, GereCo. paid its account within 10 days to take advantage of the cash discount offered. Advance Tek's accounts were usually overdue, and the firm never took advantage of the cash discount offered. On average, Advance Tek's accounts remained outstanding for three months. Winsome estimates its cost to the firm to be approximately 1 percent per month.

The three customers generate approximately the same amount of total sales. However, an analysis of the net revenues yields a different picture because of differences in sales discounts and sales terms granted to these customers, the magnitude of sales returns and allowances, and the pattern of payments. Exhibit 17–20 illustrates such an analysis.

The net invoice price billed to a customer is the net amount after subtracting sales discounts granted to the customer from the total sales prices. The list price for the sales to GereCo. is \$500.00. The salesperson agreed to a 5 percent price discount. The net invoice amount, therefore, is \$475,000 [\$500,000 − (\$500,000 × 0.05)], but GereCo. was given a sales return allowance of 1 percent of the goods it received or \$4,750 (0.01 × 475.000). The net sales to GereCo. is \$470,250 (\$475,000 − \$4,750), which is the amount it owed Winsome and is the basis for calculating cash discounts if GereCo. pays within 10 days. At 2 percent cash discount as agreed to, the cash discount is \$470,250 × 2% = \$9,405.

Adjustments for a finance charge allow comparisons of net proceeds from firms with different payment patterns. GereCo. pays within 10 days and the funds are, therefore, available to Winsome 20 days earlier than the funds from HomeServ, which pays its accounts in 30 days. Winsome can earn interest on the cash payment received on the 10th day or save the finance charge that the firm might have to pay if the funds were not available until the 30th day. GereCo. remits \$460,845 (\$470,250 − \$9,405) to Winsome on the 10th day. At 1 percent cost of funds per month, the amount of interest earned or finance charge saved for the 20 days is \$3,072 [(\$460,845 × 0.01 × (20 days/30 days)].

The customer revenue analysis shows that the amount of net proceeds to Winsome from sales to HomeServ is the highest of the three customers, although the total amount of sales to it is the lowest. This analysis suggests that HomeServ is the best customer in terms of net proceeds from sales.

Exhibit 17–20	Customer Revenue Analysis, Winsome Office Supply		
	GereCo.	HomeServ Inc.	Advance Tek
Total sales	\$500,000	\$480,000	\$540,000
Less: Sales discounts	(25,000)	—	(27,000)
Net invoice amount	\$475,000	\$480,000	\$513,000
Less: Sales returns and allowances	4,750	2,400	30,780
Net sales	\$470,250	\$477,600	\$482,220
Less: Cash discounts	9,405	—	—
Finance charge*	(3,072)	—	9,644
Net proceeds	\$463,917	\$477,600	\$472,576

*Finance charges:

GereCo.:	Net proceeds on the 10th day: \$470,250 − 9,405 =	\$460,845
	Interest earned for 20 days: \$460,845 × 1% × 20/30 =	3,072
Advance Tek:	\$482,220 × 1% × 2 months =	9,644

Customer Cost Analysis

Chapter 4 points out the importance of identifying cost drivers that change the total production costs when analyzing manufacturing costs. We can apply this valuable tool in analyzing customer profitability. Following a categorization similar to one for manufacturing costs, a **customer cost analysis** classifies costs as follows:

- *Customer unit-level cost—resources consumed for each unit sold to a customer.* Examples include sales commission for each unit sold and shipping cost per unit when the freight term is FOB destination, the freight charge is based on the number of units shipped, and restocking cost per unit for returned products.

- *Customer batch-level costs—resources consumed each time a sale occurs.* Examples include order-processing costs and invoicing costs.

- *Customer-sustaining costs—resources consumed to service a customer regardless of the number of units or batches sold.* Examples are salespersons' travel costs to visit customers, monthly statement processing costs, and late payment collection costs.

- *Distribution-channel costs—resources consumed in each distribution channel the firm uses to service customers.* Examples are operating costs of regional warehouses serving major customers and centralized distribution centers serving small retail outlets.

- *Sales-sustaining costs—resources consumed to sustain sales and service activities that cannot be traced to individual unit, batch, customer, or distribution channel.* Examples are general corporate expenditures for sales activities and salary, fringe benefits, and bonus of the general sales manager.

Exhibit 17–21 reports customer-related activities, cost drivers and their rates, and the cost category of each of the activities of Winsome Office Supply based on the result of a careful study of the firm's selling, administrative, and general expenditures and customer transactions for the last three years. Exhibit 17–22 reports the detailed sales-related activities that Winsome experienced for the sales to the firm's three major customers reported in Exhibit 17–20.

Both customer activity costs, cost categories, and their cost drivers illustrated in Exhibit 17–20 and the detailed customer-related activities reported in Exhibit 17–22

◄LEARNING OBJECTIVE 9

Describe customer cost categories and identify costs to serve a customer.

Customer cost analysis identifies cost activities and cost drivers related to customers.

Exhibit 17–21	Customer-Related Activity, Cost Driver, Cost Rate, and Cost Category	
Activity	**Cost Driver and Rate**	**Cost Category**
Order taking	$30 per order	Customer batch-level
Order processing	$20 per order, and	Customer batch-level
	$1 per item	Customer unit level
Delivery	$100 per trip, and	Customer batch-level
	$1 per mile	Customer batch-level
Expedited order taking, Processing, and delivery (additional costs)	$800 per order	Customer batch-level
Customer visit	$200 per visit	Customer sustaining
Monthly billing:		
First statement	$5 per statement	Customer sustaining
Subsequent reminder	$25 per notice	Customer sustaining
Sales returns and allowance	$100 per occurrence	Customer batch level
Restocking	$5 per item returned	Customer unit level
Sales office		
Salaries and fringe benefit	$100,000 per month	Sales sustaining
Office expenses	$50,000 per month	Sales sustaining

Exhibit 17–22	Customer-Related Activity for Selected Customers, Winsome Office Supply		
	GereCo.	**HomeServ Inc.**	**Advance Tek**
Number of orders	2	20	80
Average number of items per order	400	38	8
Delivery miles	10	15	20
Number of expedited orders	0	0	5
Number of visits by salesperson	1	2	5
Sales returns and allowances			
Number of requests	2	1	10
Number of items per request	3	4	2

Exhibit 17–23	Customer Cost Analysis, Winsome Office Supply		
	GereCo.	**HomeServ Inc.**	**Advance Tek**
Customer unit-level cost			
Order processing	$400 \times 2 \times \$1 = \$800$	$38 \times 20 \times \$1 = \$760$	$8 \times 80 \times \$1 = \$640$
Restocking	$2 \times 3 \times \$5 = 30$	$1 \times 4 \times \$5 = 20$	$10 \times 2 \times \$5 = 100$
Customer batch-level cost			
Order taking	$2 \times \$30 = 60$	$20 \times \$30 = 600$	$80 \times \$30 = 2,400$
Order processing	$2 \times \$20 = 40$	$20 \times \$20 = 400$	$80 \times \$20 = 1,600$
Delivery			
Trips	$2 \times \$100 = 200$	$20 \times \$100 = 2,000$	—
Miles	$10 \times 2 \times \$1 = 20$	$15 \times 20 \times \$1 = 300$	—
Expedited orders	—	—	$\$800 \times 5 = 4,000$
Sales returns and allowances	$2 \times \$100 = 200$	$1 \times \$100 = 100$	$10 \times \$100 = 1,000$
Customer-sustaining costs			
Sales visits	$1 \times \$200 = 200$	$2 \times \$200 = 400$	$5 \times \$200 = 1,000$
Monthly billings	$1 \times \$5 = 5$	$1 \times \$5 = 5$	$1 \times \$5 = 5$
Subsequent reminders	—	—	$2 \times \$25 = 50$
Sales-sustaining costs	0	0	0
Total	$1,555	$4,585	$10,795

provide the basis for analyzing customer costs. Exhibit 17–23 reports customer cost analyses for Winsome's three customers.

As illustrated in Exhibit 17–23, costs to service customers often differ because they do not require the same amount of services and attention. These three customers purchased approximately equal amounts from Winsome. The costs to serve these customers, however, differ substantially, ranging from $1,555 to $10,795. Nevertheless, a customer with a high cost to serve can still be a profitable customer. To evaluate customer profitability, we must bring together customer revenue analysis and customer cost analysis as illustrated in the section on Customer Value Assessment.

Customer Profitability Analysis

LEARNING OBJECTIVE 10 ▶

Conduct customer profitability analysis and determine customer value.

A customer profitability analysis combines customer revenue and customer cost analyses to determine customer profitability and to identify the best actions to improve customer profitability. Exhibit 17–24 illustrates customer profitability analyses for Winsome.

The customer profitability analysis verifies that HomeServ is the most profitable of Winsome's three major customers, although it has the lowest total sales. Although the

Exhibit 17–24 Customer Profitability Analysis, Winsome Office Supply			
	GereCo.	**HomeServ Inc.**	**Advance Tek**
Total sales	$500,000	$480,000	$540,000
Less: Sales discounts	25,000	—	27,000
Net invoice amount	$475,000	$480,000	$513,000
Less: Sales returns and allowances	4,750	2,400	30,780
Net sales	$470,250	$477,600	$482,220
Less: Cash discounts	9,405	—	—
Finance charges	(3,072)	0	9,644
Net proceeds	$463,917	$477,600	$472,576
Customer costs			
Order processing	$800	$760	$ 640
Restocking	75	20	100
Order taking	60	600	2,400
Order processing	40	400	1,600
Delivery			
Trips	200	2,000	—
Miles	20	300	—
Expedited orders	—	—	4,000
Sales returns and allowances	200	100	1,000
Sales visits	200	400	1,000
Monthly billings	5	5	5
Subsequent reminders	0	0	50
Total customer costs	$ 1,555	$ 4,585	$ 10,795
Net customer profit	$462,362	$473,015	$461,781

total sales to Advance Tek are the highest of the three, it yields the lowest net customer profit.

The reasons that GereCo. is not as profitable as HomeServ relate to sales activities. Winsome granted GereCo. much more favorable sales terms than to HomeServ. GereCo. also had a high amount of sales returns and allowances; it returned twice as often as HomeServ did.

Price discounts and sales returns are also among the contributing factors for the low profitability of Advance Tek. Although Advance Tek had the highest total sales, it generated the lowest profit of the three customers. Winsome should be concerned about the much higher returns and the frequency of expediting orders it experienced with Advance Tek. The high return could be a result of the customer's dissatisfaction with Winsome's products. Winsome needs to look into the reason for the high returns before losing the customer to competition. Late payments also add cost to serve Advance Tek; they might also indicate Advance Tek's dissatisfaction with Winsome's sales and services.

Customer Value Assessment

Customer profitability analysis provides valuable information to the assessment of customer values. In addition to considering factors affecting customer profitability, firms also must weigh other relevant factors before determining the action appropriate for each customer. The following are among these relevant factors:

- Customer growth potential, including growth of the customer, the customer's industry, and its cross-selling potential.
- Possible reactions of the customer to changes in sales terms or services.
- Importance of having the firm as a customer for future sales references, especially when the customer could play a pivotal role in bringing in additional business.

SUMMARY

Increasing global competition and rapid changes in technologies require management to be constantly alert to changes in the productivity of input resources as well as opportunities and changes in marketing. Management must be aware of levels and changes in its productive factors, such as materials, labor, energy, and processes. To market effectively, management must be fully informed of the effects of changes in selling prices, sales volumes, sale mixes, market sizes, and market shares on operations and the firm's strategy. Management must monitor the effects of these changes on operating results to be able to take appropriate action at the earliest time.

The sales volume variance reflects the difference in the contribution margin or operating income for the flexible budget amount and the master (static) budget. The sales volume variance for a single product firm is the product of the standard contribution margin per unit of product and the difference in the number of units sold and amount of budgeted sales units. The sale volume variance of firms with multiple products should be separated for analytical purposes into sales mix and sales quantity variances. The product's sales mix variance is the product of three elements: (1) the difference between the actual sales mix (defined as the ratio of the unit of the product to the total units of all products) and the budget sales mix, (2) the total number of units of all products sold during the period, and (3) the product's standard contribution margin. A product's sales quantity variance is the product of three elements: (1) the difference in the number of the firm's total actual and budgeted units, (2) the product's budget sales mix, and (3) its standard contribution margin.

A sales mix variance measures the effect of the difference in the actual and the budgeted mixtures. A product's sales mix variance is favorable if the firm sells more of the product than it budgeted to sell. A sales quantity variance assesses the effect of the difference in the units sold and the number of units budgeted on total contribution margin and operating income.

A sales quantity variance can be separated further into market size and market share variances. The market size variance assesses the effect of changes in the industry's total market size on the firm's total contribution margin and operating income. A market size variance is the product of three factors: (1) the difference between the actual and the budgeted number of total market units, (2) the firm's budgeted market share, and (3) the weighted-average budgeted contribution margin per unit. The market size variance is favorable if the actual total market size is larger than the market size expected when the master budget was prepared. The market share variance measures the effect of changes in the firm's market share on its operating income. Market share is the product of three elements: (1) the total number of units in the market, (2) the difference in the firm's actual and budgeted market share, and (3) the weighted average budgeted contribution margin per unit.

Productivity is the ratio of output to input. Improvements in productivity enable a firm to do more with fewer resources. A productivity measure is often compared to the performance of prior periods, other firms, or a benchmark.

Partial productivity is the ratio of the output level attained to the amount of an input resource used. The higher the ratio is, the better. Partial operational productivity is the required physical amount of an input resource to produce one unit of output. Partial financial productivity is the number of units of output manufactured for each dollar of the input resource spent. A partial financial productivity measure can be separated into changes in productivity, input price, and output. Productivity change is the difference between the actual and the expected amount of input resources to manufacture the output. The input price change accounts for the effects of differences in budgeted (or benchmark) and actual prices for the input resource; the output change variance accounts for the change in cost due to changes in the number of output units.

Total productivity measures the relationship between the output achieved and the total input costs and is usually in financial productivity.

The concepts for measuring productivity in manufacturing firms are also applicable to service firms and not-for-profit organizations. These entities experience limitations in measuring productivity because of imprecise output measures, lack of definite relationships between output and input resources, and absence of revenue for not-for-profits.

Customer profitability analysis traces factors affecting revenues and customer costs to customers to allow management to determine customer profitability and to provide more attentive service to high-profit customers, acquire new high-profit customers, and improve the customer profitability of current ones. Customer profitability analysis include customer revenue analysis, customer cost analysis, customer profitability analysis, and customer value assessment.

KEY TERMS

Customer cost analysis   833

Customer profitability analysis   831

Customer revenue analysis   831

Financial productivity   821

Market share variance   816

Market size variance   815

Operational productivity   821

Partial productivity   821

Productivity   821

Sales mix   809

Sales mix variance   809

Sales quantity variance   810

Total productivity   821

COMMENTS ON COST MANAGEMENT IN ACTION

CUSTOMER PROFITABILITY: RETENTION IS THE KEY

Customer profitability is strongly affected by the overall cost to acquire a new customer. These costs can be as high as $50 or more per customer. When customer retention is low, as it is in some industries, these costs lower overall customer profitability. For example, customer retention in the apparel industry is far higher than in the consumer electronics industry. A number of firms use the Web to acquire new customers, and some do it more effectively than others. For example, America Online, Amazon.com, and Dell Computer have sophisticated programs for identifying potential new customers and for improving the retention of existing customers. Interestingly, studies have shown that Web customers tend to be more loyal; their retention rates are somewhat higher than for traditional customers. Studies show that Web customers are most interested in convenience, not the lowest price, as is commonly thought. When they find a convenient Web source that meets their needs, they tend to consolidate their purchases there. E-loyalty is the road to success for these companies.

Source: Frederick F. Reichheld and Pohil Schefter, "E-Loyalty: Your Secret Weapon on the Web," *Harvard Business Review*, July–August 2000, pp. 105–113.

SELF-STUDY PROBLEMS

(For solutions, please turn to the end of the chapter.)

1. Sales Variance

Springwater Brewery has two main products: premium and regular ale. Its operating results and master budget for 2002 (000s omitted) follow:

	Operating Results of 2002			Master Budget for 2002		
	Premium	**Regular**	**Total**	**Premium**	**Regular**	**Total**
Barrels	180	540	720	240	360	600
Sales	$28,800	$62,100	$90,900	$36,000	$43,200	$79,200
Variable expenses	16,200	40,500	56,700	21,600	27,000	48,600
Contribution margin	$12,600	$21,600	$34,200	$14,400	$16,200	$30,600
Fixed expenses	10,000	5,000	15,000	10,000	5,000	15,000
Operating income	$ 2,600	$16,600	$19,200	$ 4,400	$11,200	$15,600

Pam Kuder, CEO, estimated when she prepared the master budget that total industry sales would be 1,500,000 barrels during the period. After the year, Mark Goldfeder, the controller, reported that the total sales for the industry were 1,600,000 barrels.

Required Calculate the

1. Selling price variances for the period for each product and for the firm.
2. Sales volume variances for the period for each product and for the firm.
3. Sales quantity variances for each product and the firm.
4. Sales mix variances for the period for each product and for the firm.
5. The sum of the sales quantity variance and sales mix variance; also verify that this total equals the sales volume variance.
6. Market size variances.
7. Market share variances.
8. The sum of market size variance and market share variance; also verify that this total equals the sales quantity variance.

2. Productivity Variances

Carlson Automotive Company manufactures fuel-injection systems. It manufactured and sold 60,000 units in 2003 and 64,000 units in 2004 at $25 per unit. In 2003 the firm used 75,000 pounds of alloy TPX–45 at $7.20 per pound and spent 10,000 direct labor-hours at an hourly wage rate of $30. In 2004 the firm used 89,600 pounds of alloy TPX–45 at $6.80 per pound and spent 10,847 direct labor-hours at an hourly wage rate of $32. The total amount for all other expenses remains the same at $450,000 each year. Jerry Olson, CEO, was disappointed that although the total sales increased in 2004, the $195,616 operating income earned in 2004 is only 93 percent of the amount earned in 2003, which was $210,000.

Required Analyze the

1. Operational partial productivity of the direct material and direct labor for both 2003 and 2004.
2. Financial partial productivity of the direct material and direct labor for both 2003 and 2004.
3. Detailed composition of financial partial productivity.
4. Total productivity for 2003 and 2004 as measured in both units and sales dollars.

QUESTIONS

17–1   List important measures in assessing marketing effectiveness.

17–2   What are the components of sales variance?

17–3   Distinguish between a *selling price variance* and a *sales volume variance*.

17–4   What is the difference between a *sales quantity variance* and a *sales volume variance?*

17–5   "As long as a firm sells more units than the number specified in the master budget, it will not have an unfavorable sales volume variance." Do you agree? Why?

17–6 What are the relationships among a selling price variance, a sales mix variance, a sales quantity variance, and a sales volume variance?

17–7 Distinguish between *market size variance* and *market share variance*.

17–8 "A favorable sales quantity variance indicates that the marketing manager has done a good job." Do you agree? Can you give an example in which a market size variance or market share variance results in an indication that is opposite to the one that the sales quantity variance suggested?

17–9 What are the relationships between market size variance, market share variance, sales quantity variance, and sales volume variance?

17–10 An improvement in earnings growth can be achieved at the expense of market share (an unfavorable market share variance). Do you agree?

17–11 What is productivity?

17–12 Discuss why improving productivity is important for a firm that has a strategy to be the cost leader.

17–13 List benchmarks or criteria often used in assessing productivity, and discuss their advantages and disadvantages.

17–14 What is operational productivity? Financial productivity?

17–15 What is partial productivity? Total productivity?

17–16 "A financial productivity measure contains more information than an operational productivity measure does." Do you agree?

17–17 "A total productivity measure encompasses all partial productivity measures." Do you agree?

17–18 "Partial productivity measures should be calculated only for value-added activities." Do you agree?

17–19 Why do manufacturing personnel prefer operational productivity measures to financial productivity measures?

17–20 "An activity productivity measure such as machine-hour productivity is more important in a JIT environment than in a non–JIT environment." Do you agree?

17–21 Which of the following statements is true? (a) The lower the partial productivity ratio, the greater the productivity, (b) productivity improves when partial productivity increases, (c) prices of inputs are incorporated in the partial productivity ratio, (d) the partial productivity ratio measures the number of outputs produced per multiple input, and (e) more than one of the above is true.

17–22 Identify opportunities afforded by customer profitability analysis.

17–23 List factors that a firm should include in conducting a customer revenue analysis.

17–24 Explain customer cost categories.

EXERCISES

17–25 **SALES MIX AND VOLUME VARIANCES** CompuWorld sells two RISC chips, R66 and R100, to small machine tool manufacturers. Pertinent data for 2000 follow:

	Budgeted		Actual	
	R66	**R100**	**R66**	**R100**
Selling price per chip	$50	$160	$55	$155
Variable cost per chip	40	90	43	95
Contribution margin	$10	$ 70	$12	$ 60
Fixed cost per chip	6	30	5	25
Operating income	$ 4	$ 40	$ 7	$ 35
Sales in units	1,200	400	1,000	1,000

Required

1. What is the R66 sales quantity variance?

   a. $ 400 F   d. $3,000 F

   b. $1,000 F   e. $3,600 F

   c. $1,200 F

2. What is the R100 sales mix variance?

   a. $20,000 F   d. $40,000 F

   b. $30,000 F   e. $70,000 F

   c. $35,000 F

3. What is the total sales volume variance?

   a. $10,000 F   d. $22,000 F

   b. $12,400 F   e. $40,000 F

   c. $13,000 F

17–26 **MARKET SHARE, MARKET SIZE, AND SALES VOLUME VARIANCES** C. W. McCall sells a gold-plated souvenir mug; it expects to sell 1,600 units in 2000 for $45 each to earn a $25 contribution margin per unit. Janice McCall, president, expects the year's total market to be 32,000 units. In 2000, the local college won the national hockey championship, and the total market was 100,000 units. C. W. McCall sold 3,000 at $75 each. The variable cost to the firm is $40 per unit.

Required

1. What is the market share variance?

   a. $ 8,000 U   d. $50,000 U

   b. $11,200 U   e. $70,000 U

   c. $40,000 U

2. What is the market size variance?

   a. $ 51,000 F   d. $ 85,000 F

   b. $ 68,000 F   e. $119,000 F

   c. $ 71,400 F

3. What is the firm's sales volume variance?

   a. $ 35,000 F   d. $ 85,000 F

   b. $ 49,000 F   e. $135,000 F

   c. $ 51,000 F

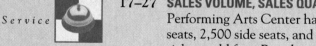

Service

17–27 **SALES VOLUME, SALES QUANTITY, AND SALES MIX VARIANCES** The Varner Performing Arts Center has a total capacity of 7,500 seats: 2,000 center seats, 2,500 side seats, and 3,000 balcony seats. The budgeted and actual tickets sold for a Broadway musical show are as follows:

	Ticket Price	Percentage	
		Budgeted Seats Sold	**Actual Seats Sold**
Center	$60	80%	95%
Side	50	90	85
Balcony	40	85	75

The actual ticket prices are the same as those budgeted. Once a show has been booked, the cost relating to the total number in attendance does not vary.

Required Compute these for the show:

1. The budgeted and actual sales mix percentages for different types of seats.
2. The budgeted average contribution margin per seat.

3. The total sales quantity variance and the total sales mix variance.

4. The total sales volume variance.

17–28 OPERATIONAL PARTIAL PRODUCTIVITY Darwin, Inc., provided the following information for a production factor:

Budgeted production	10,000 units
Actual production	9,500 units
Budgeted input	9,750 gallons
Actual input	8,950 gallons

What is the partial operational productivity ratio of the production factor?

1. 0.97 unit per gallon.
2. 1.02 units per gallon.
3. 1.06 units per gallon.
4. 1.12 units per gallon.
5. none of the above.

17–29 FINANCIAL PARTIAL PRODUCTIVITY AND TOTAL PRODUCTIVITY HFD Corporation makes small parts from steel alloy sheets. Management has some ability to substitute direct materials for direct manufacturing labor. If workers cut the steel carefully, more parts can be manufactured from a metal sheet, but this requires more direct manufacturing labor-hours. Alternatively, HFD can use fewer direct manufacturing labor-hours if it is willing to tolerate more waste of direct materials. HFD provides this information for the years 2001 and 2002:

	2001	2002
Output units	400,000	486,000
Direct manufacturing labor-hours used	10,000	13,500
Wages per hour	$26	$25
Direct materials used	160 tons	180 tons
Direct materials cost per ton	$3,375	$3,125

Required Carry all computations to four digits after the decimal point.

1. Compute the partial financial productivity for both input manufacturing factors for 2001 and 2002.

2. Calculate HFD's total productivity in units for 2001 and 2002.

3. Evaluate management's decision in 2002 to substitute one production factor for another.

17–30 PARTIAL OPERATIONAL PRODUCTIVITY Software Solution (SOS) helps subscribers solve software problems. All transactions are made over the telephone. For the year 2002, 10 engineers, most of whom are recent graduates, handled 100,000 calls. The average yearly salary for software engineers was $45,000.

Starting in 2003, the firm retained and hired only software engineers with at least two years of experience. SOS raised the engineers' salary to $60,000 per year. In 2003, eight engineers handled 108,000 calls.

Service

Required

1. Calculate the partial operational productivity ratio for both years.

2. Calculate the partial financial productivity ratio for both years.

3. Did the firm make the right decision to hire only software engineers with at least two years' experience?

4. List other factors that should be considered in making the decision.

17–31 CUSTOMER REVENUE ANALYSIS JD Company is in the process of analyzing net revenues from customers. The firm has gathered the following data pertaining to two of its major customers. Transworld Services (TS) and Centermin.

	TS	Centermin
Total sales	$800,000	$880,000
Sales discount	12%	15%
Sales terms	1/15, n/45	net 30
Sales returns	0.5%	0.75%

Both firms pay their accounts according to the terms agreed to. In fact, TS pays its accounts within the discount period. The controller estimates that the cost of working capital is approximately 1.5 percent per month.

Required Complete a customer revenue analysis for JD Company.

17–32 **CUSTOMER COST ANALYSIS** Doreen Company has the following customer-related activities for two of its primary customers.

	Jerry Inc.	Donald Co.
Number of orders	10	20
Units per order	500	300
Sales returns		
Number	2	5
Total units returned	40	175
Sales calls	12	4

Doreen sells all of its product at $200 per unit and allows no discount. An analysis of the operating cost for the past 30 months reports the following average costs:

Activity	Cost Driver and Rate
Customer visits	$600 per visit
Order processing	$50 per order
Deliveries	$300 per order
Sales returns	$100 per return and $5 per unit
Sales salary	$100,000 per month

Required Compute the total cost for Doreen Company to service Jerry Inc. and Donald Co.

PROBLEMS

17–33 **MARKET SIZE, MARKET SHARE, WORKING BACKWARD** Triple Delight's sales forecast for 2001 estimated that the firm would sell three cheeseburgers and one fishwich for every four hamburgers sold. The following data were culled from its operation analyses for 2001:

Total operating income variance		
Hamburger	$18,000	Unfavorable
Cheeseburger	50,000	Favorable
Fishwich	10,000	Unfavorable
Sales quantity variance		
Hamburger	14,000	Favorable
Cheeseburger	15,000	Favorable
Fishwich	?	
Sales mix variance		
Hamburger	2,240	Unfavorable
Cheeseburger	4,800	Unfavorable
Fishwich	1,600	Favorable
Fixed costs variances	0	
Market share variance	$ 96,000	Unfavorable
Market size variance	126,000	Favorable
Change in market share	4%	
Fixed cost flexible budget variance	0	

The estimated total volume for the fast-food industry in the region was 2,500,000 units. Industry statistics compiled at the end of 2001 showed 4,000,000 total units sold.

Required Determine the following:

1. Budget weighted-average contribution margin.
2. Budget and actual market shares.
3. Budget and actual total units of sales.
4. Sales quantity variances for fishwich.
5. Budget contribution margin of each product.
6. Actual sales mix of each product.
7. Budget and actual units for each product.

17–34 **FLEXIBLE BUDGET, SALES VOLUME, SALES MIX, AND SALES QUANTITY VARIANCES** Melinda Company has two products, A and B. Melinda's budget for August 2002 follows:

	Product A	Product B	Total
Master budget			
Sale	$200,000	$300,000	$500,000
Variable costs	120,000	150,000	270,000
Contribution margin	$ 80,000	$150,000	$230,000
Fixed costs	100,000	90,000	190,000
Operating income	$(20,000)	$ 60,000	$ 40,000
Selling price per unit	$ 100	$ 50	

On September 1, these operating results for August were reported:

	Product A	Product B	Total
Operating results			
Sale	$180,000	$320,000	$500,000
Variable costs	120,000	140,000	260,000
Contribution margin	$ 60,000	$180,000	$240,000
Fixed costs	100,000	90,000	190,000
Operating income	$(40,000)	$ 90,000	$ 50,000
Units sold	1,900	5,000	

Required

1. Determine for each product the following variances in the contribution margins:

	Product A	Product B
Flexible budget variance	_____	_____
Sales volume variance	_____	_____
Sales quantity variance	_____	_____
Sales mix variance	_____	_____

2. Explain the flexible budget variance using selling price and variable cost variances.

17–35 **FLEXIBLE BUDGET, SALES VOLUME, SALES MIX, AND SALES QUANTITY VARIANCES** Jerry Tidwell, CEO and a major stockholder of Tidwell Company, was unhappy with its operating results in 2000. The company manufactures two environmentally friendly industrial cleaning machines used primarily in automobile repair shops, gas stations, and auto dealerships. The master budget and operating results of the year (000s omitted except for the selling price per unit) follow:

	Master Budget			Actual Result		
	SK–100	SK–50	Total	SK–100	SK–50	Total
Sales	$100,000	$50,000	$150,000	$90,000	$60,000	$150,000
Variable costs	50,000	20,000	70,000	50,000	22,000	72,000
Contribution margin	$ 50,000	$30,000	$ 80,000	$40,000	$38,000	$ 78,000
Fixed costs	20,000	20,000	40,000	30,000	20,000	50,000
Operating income	$ 30,000	$10,000	$ 40,000	$10,000	$18,000	$ 28,000
Unit selling price	$ 100	$ 50				
Units sold				900	1,200	

Required

1. Compute the operating income flexible budget variance, operating income sales volume variance, contribution margin sales quantity variance, and contribution margin sales mix variance for each product and for the firm.

2. Explain to Jerry Tidwell the implications of the variances that you just computed on planning and operational control.

17–36 MARKET SIZE, MARKET SHARE, AND SALES QUANTITY VARIANCES, SINGLE PRODUCT   Prolite Company manufactures one product. Its budget and operating results for 2000 follow:

	Budgeted	Actual
Units sold	90,000	100,000
Unit contribution margin	$ 8.00	$10.00
Unit selling price	$20.00	$21.00

Industry volume was estimated to be 1,500,000 units when the budget was prepared. Actual industry volume for the period was 2,000,000 units.

Required

1. What is the market size variance?
2. What is the market share variance?
3. What is the sales quantity variance?

17–37 MARKET SIZE, MARKET SHARE VARIANCES   Lau & Lau, Ltd., of Hong Kong manufactures two products it sells to the same market. Its budget and operating results for 2000 follow:

	Budgeted	Actual
Unit sales		
Product A	30,000	35,000
Product B	60,000	65,000
Unit contribution margin		
Product A	$ 4.00	$ 3.00
Product B	$10.00	12.00
Unit selling price		
Product A	$10.00	$12.00
Product B	25.00	24.00

When the budget was prepared, industry volume was estimated to be 1,500,000 units. Actual industry volume was 2,000,000 units.

Required

1. What is the budgeted average unit contribution margin?
2. What is the sales volume contribution margin variance for each product?
3. What is the sales mix contribution margin variance for each product?
4. What is the sales quantity contribution margin variance for each product?
5. What is the market size contribution margin variance?

6. What is the market share contribution margin variance?

7. What is the total flexible budget contribution margin variance?

8. What is the total variable cost price variance if the total contribution margin price variance is $50,000 favorable?

9. What is the total variable cost efficiency variance if the total contribution margin price variance is $50,000 favorable?

17–38 SALES VOLUME, SALES QUANTITY, AND SALES MIX VARIANCES I Can't Believe It's Gelatin operates several stores in a major metropolitan city and its suburbs. Its budget and operating data for 2002 follow:

Flavor	Gallons	Budgeted Data for 2002 Selling Price per Gallon	Variable Costs per Gallon	Gallons	Actual Operating Results in 2002 Selling Price per Gallon	Variable Costs per Gallon
Vanilla	250,000	$1.20	$0.50	180,000	$1.00	$0.45
Chocolate	300,000	1.50	0.60	270,000	1.35	0.50
Strawberry	200,000	1.80	0.70	330,000	2.00	0.75
Anchovy	50,000	2.50	1.00	180,000	3.00	1.20

Required

1. Compute these variances for the individual flavors and total sold:

   a. Sales volume.

   b. Sales mix.

   c. Sales quantity.

2. Assess the operation of 2002 based on your analyses.

17–39 MARKET SIZE AND MARKET SHARE VARIANCES Use the data in problem 17–38 for I Can't Believe It's Gelatin. The total market for ice cream, yogurt, and gelatin was expected to be 10 million gallons. The industry group for the area reported that 9,600,000 gallons were sold for the year.

Required Compute the market size and market share variances for I Can't Believe It's Gelatin.

17–40 SALES VOLUME, SALES QUANTITY, AND SALES MIX VARIANCES; WORKING BACKWARD DOA Alive is a group of aspiring musicians and actors who perform in theaters and dinner clubs. It has a matinee and evening show. These operating data pertain to the month of July:

Service

Strategy

Master budget data	
Total operating income	$10,000
Total monthly fixed cost	$39,200
Total number of shows	100
Contribution margin per show: Matinee	$240
Evening	$600
Actual operating results	
Total sales quantity variance	$4,920 U

The actual matinees were 150 percent of the evening shows.

Required

1. Calculate for each type of show and the total

   a. Sales mix variances.

   b. Sales quantity variances.

   c. Sales volume variances.

2. What strategic conclusions can you draw from the variances?

International

Service

17–41 MARKET SIZE AND SHARE VARIANCES TransPacific Airlines (TPA) budgeted 80 million passenger-miles, or 5 percent of the total market for the route, for the year just completed at a contribution margin of 40 cents per mile. The budgeted variable cost is 12 cents per mile.

The operating data for the year show that TPA flew 69.12 million passenger-miles with an average price of 48 cents per passenger-mile. The unexpected financial crises of several countries in the region decreased the total miles flown by all airlines by 10 percent. There is no flexible budget variance for all costs.

Required Assess the effects of the price, sales volume, market size, and market share on the firm's operating results for the year.

17–42 SMALL BUSINESS MARKET SIZE AND SHARE VARIANCES Diane's Designs is a small business run out of its owner's house. For the past six months, the company has been selling two products, welcome signs and birdhouse signs. The owner has become concerned about the company's market effectiveness. The master budget and actual results for the month of March 1999 follow:

Master Budget

	Welcome Signs	Birdhouses	Total
Units	50	25	75
Sales	$1,000	$250	$1,250
Variable costs	900	120	1,020
Contribution margin	$ 100	$130	$ 230
Fixed costs	75	75	150
Operating income	$ 25	$ 55	$ 80

Actual Results

	Welcome Signs	Birdhouses	Total
Units	45	35	80
Sales	$ 675	$420	$1,095
Variable costs	580	270	850
Contribution margin	$ 95	$150	$ 245
Fixed costs	75	75	150
Operating income	$ 20	$ 75	$ 95

The industry budgeted sales for signs is 3,000 and for birdhouses, 200 units. The industry actual sales for signs is 2,550 and for birdhouses, 150 units.

Required

1. Compare Diane's Designs' market share for welcome signs and birdhouse signs.
2. What is the market share variance?
3. What is the market size variance?
4. Explain possible reasons for these variances.
5. How might Diane's Designs improve in the future?

(Contributed by Stacy Armstrong)

17–43 OPERATIONAL PARTIAL PRODUCTIVITY Frisen Communication Inc. manufactures a scrambling device for cellular telephones. The device's main component is a delicate part, CSU10. Unless handled carefully during manufacturing, CSU10 is easily damaged. Once damaged, it must be discarded. Only skilled laborers are hired to manufacture and install CSU10; however, damages still occur. Robotic instruments process all other parts. Frisen's operating data for 2001 and 2000 follow:

	2001	2000
Units manufactured	500,000	600,000
Number of CSU10 used	800,000	825,000
Number of direct labor-hours spent	150,000	200,000
Cost of CSU10 per unit	$156	$135
Direct labor wage rate per hour	$56	$63

Required

1. Compute the partial operational productivity ratios for 2000 and 2001.

2. On the basis of the partial operational productivity that you computed, what conclusions can you draw as to the firm's productivity in 2001 relative to 2000?

17–44 FINANCIAL PARTIAL PRODUCTIVITY Use the data for Frisen Communication Inc. in problem 17–43 to complete the requirements.

Required

1. Compute the partial financial productivity ratios for 2000 and 2001.

2. On the basis of the partial financial productivity ratios you computed, what conclusions can you draw as to the firm's productivity in 2001 relative to 2000?

3. Separate the changes in the partial financial productivity ratios from 2000 to 2001 into productivity changes, input price changes, and output changes.

4. Does the detailed information provided by separating the change of the partial financial production ratio offer any additional insight into the relative productivity for 2000 and 2001?

17–45 TOTAL PRODUCTIVITY Use the data for Frisen Communication Inc. in problem 17–43 to do the following.

Required

1. Compute the total productivity ratios for 2000 and 2001.

2. On the basis of the total productivity that you computed, what conclusions can you draw about the firm's productivity in 2001 relative to 2000?

17–46 OPERATIONAL AND FINANCIAL PARTIAL PRODUCTIVITY In the fourth quarter of 2001 Simpson Company embarked on a major effort to improve productivity. It redesigned products, reengineered manufacturing processes, and offered productivity improvement courses. The effort was completed in the last quarter of 2002. The controller's office has gathered the following year-end data to assess the results of this effort.

	2001	2002
Units manufactured and sold	15,000	18,000
Selling price of the product	$40	$40
Materials used (pounds)	12,000	12,600
Cost per pound of materials	$8	$10
Labor-hours	6,000	5,000
Hourly wage rate	$20	$25
Power (kwh)	1,000	2,000
Cost of power per kwh	$2	$2

Required

1. Prepare a summary contribution approach income statement for each year and calculate the total change in profits.

2. Compute the partial operational productivity ratios for each production factor for 2001 and 2002.

3. Compute the partial financial productivity ratios for each production factor for 2001 and 2002.

4. On the basis of the operational and partial financial productivity you computed, what conclusions can you make about the firm's productivity in 2002 relative to 2001?

5. Separate the changes in the partial financial productivity ratio from 2001 to 2002 into productivity changes, input price changes, and output changes.

6. Discuss additional insight on the relative productivity between 2001 and 2002 from the detailed information provided by separating the change in the financial partial productivity ratios.

17–47 PARTIAL OPERATIONAL AND FINANCIAL PRODUCTIVITY Varceles Design has two alternative approaches, identified as MF and LI, for producing next year's fashion for men. The firm expects the total demand to be 20,000 suits. Varceles can produce the same output with either approach using these combinations of input resources:

	Materials (yds.)	Labor (hrs.)
MF	300,000	100,000
LI	200,000	120,000

The cost of materials is $8 per yard; the cost of labor is $25 per hour.

Required

1. Compute the partial operational productivity ratios for each alternative production approach. Which approach would you select based on the partial operational productivity ratios?

2. Calculate the partial financial productivity ratios for each alternative production approach. Which approach would you select based on the partial financial productivity ratios?

3. Compute the total productivity ratios for each alternative production approach. Which approach would you select based on the total productivity ratios?

Strategy

17–48 DIRECT LABOR RATE AND EFFICIENCY VARIANCES, PRODUCTIVITY MEASURES, AND STANDARD COSTS Textron Manufacturing Inc. assembles industrial testing instruments in two departments, assembly and testing. Operating data for 2000 and 2001 follow:

	2000	2001
Assembly department		
Actual direct labor-hours per instrument	25	20
Actual wage rate per hour	$30	$36
Standard direct labor-hours per instrument	24	21
Standard wage rate per hour	$28	$35
Testing department		
Actual direct labor-hours per instrument	12	10
Actual wage rate per hour	$20	$24
Standard direct labor-hours per instrument	14	11
Standard wage rate per hour	$21	$25

The firm assembled and tested 20,000 instruments in both 2000 and 2001.

Required

1. Calculate the direct labor rate and the efficiency variances for both departments in both years.

2. Compute the direct labor partial operational productivity ratio for both departments in both years.

3. Determine the partial financial productivity for both departments in both years.

4. Compare your answers for requirements 2 and 3. Comment on the results.

5. Do productivity measures offer different perspectives for the firm's strategic decisions from those of variance analysis?

17–49   PRODUCTIVITY AND ETHICS   Janice Interiors installs custom interiors for luxury mobile homes. In its most recent negotiation with the union, the firm proposed to share productivity gains in direct labor equally with the union. In return, the union agreed not to demand wage increases. Most union members, however, are very skeptical about management's honesty in calculating the productivity measures. Nevertheless, union members voted to try the program. Kim Tomas, the management accountant responsible for determining productivity measures, collected these data at the end of 2002:

Ethics

	2002	2001
Number of installations	560	500
Direct labor-hours	112,000	99,000

Steve Janice, the CEO, is very anxious to demonstrate the firm's good intentions by showing the labor union a positive result. He suggests to Kim that some of the direct labor-hours are actually indirect, for example, the hours spent on details are indirect because these hours cannot be allocated to specific types of work. Following his suggestion, Kim reclassifies 12,000 hours as indirect labor.

Required

1. Evaluate whether Steve's suggestion to reclassify some of the direct labor-hours as indirect labor is ethical.

2. Would it be ethical for Kim to modify his calculations?

17–50   CUSTOMER PROFITABILITY ANALYSIS   Spring Company collected the following data pertaining to its activities with selected customers.

	HS Inc.	Adventix	Baldwin
Total sales	$600,000	$750,000	$900,000
Sales discount	2%	3%	2%
Sales terms	2/10, n/30	1/15, n/60	2/10, n/eom
Transportation	FOB shipping point	FOB destination	FOB destination
Sales returns	2%	1%	3%
Number of orders	10	5	50
Units per order	100	250	30
Expedited orders	0	2	5
Sales visits	1	1	2
Number of sales returns	3	4	10

HS pays all accounts within the cash discount period. Baldwin does not take advantage of cash discounts, but it pays within the specified time. Adventix pays half of its account at the end of the allowed time and pays the remainder at the end of the following month. The firm's cost of working capital is, on average, 2 percent per month.

Spring also has gathered the following cost data:

Activity	Cost Driver and Rate
Order taking	$50 per order
Order processing	$75 per order
Deliveries	$300 per delivery
Expedited orders	$500 per order
Restocking	$10 per unit plus $200 per return
Sales visits	$800 per visit

Required Perform a customer profitability analysis for Spring Company.

SOLUTIONS TO SELF-STUDY PROBLEMS

1. Sales Variance

1. Selling price variances (in 000)

Flexible budget sales:

	Master Budget for 2002			Budgeted Selling Price per Unit		Total Units Sold in 2002		Flexible Budget Sales
	Total Sales		Units					
Premium	$36,000	÷	240	=	$150	×	180	=	$27,000
Regular	43,200	÷	360	=	120	×	540	=	64,800

	Premium			Regular		
	Actual	Flexible Budget	Selling Price Variance	Actual	Flexible Budget	Selling Price Variance
Barrels	180	180		540	540	
Sales	$28,800	$27,000	$1,800 F	$62,100	$64,800	$2,700 U

Total selling price variance of the firm = $1,800 F + $2,700 U = $900 U

2. Sales volume variances for the period for each product and for the firm.

Flexible budget variable expenses:

	Master Budget for 2002			Budgeted Variable Expenses per Unit		Total Units Sold in 2002		Flexible Budget Variable Expenses
	Total Variable Expenses		Number of Units					
Premium	$21,600	÷	240	=	$90	×	180	=	$16,200
Regular	27,000	÷	360	=	75	×	540	=	40,500

	Premium			Regular		
	Flexible Budget	Master Budget	Selling Volume Variance	Flexible Budget	Master Budget	Selling Volume Variance
Barrels	180	240		540	360	
Sales	$27,000	$36,000		$64,800	$43,200	
Variable expenses	16,200	21,600		40,500	27,000	
Contribution margin	$10,800	$14,400	$3,600 U	$24,300	$16,200	$8,100 F
Fixed expenses	10,000	10,000	—	5,000	5,000	—
Operating income	$ 800	$ 4,400	$3,600 U	$19,300	$11,200	$8,100 F

Total sales volume variance of the firm = $3,600 U + $8,100 F = $4,500 F

3. Sales quantity variances for the firm and for each product. (See the solution for 4 below.)

4. Sales mix variances for the period for each product and for the firm (000 omitted).

Calculation for sales mixes:

	Budgeted		Actual	
	Total Sales in Units	**Sales Mix**	**Total Sales in Units**	**Sales Mix**
Premium	240	0.40	180	0.25
Regular	360	0.60	540	0.75
Total	600	1.00	720	1.00

Flexible Budget		**Master Budget**
Total units of all products sold × Actual sales mix × Budgeted (standard) contribution margin per unit	Total units of all products sold × Budgeted sales mix × Budgeted (standard) contribution margin per unit	Total budgeted units of all products to be sold × Budgeted sales mix × Budgeted (standard) contribution margin per unit

Premium

$720 \times 0.25 \times \$60 = \$10,800$ $\qquad$ $720 \times 0.40 \times \$60 = \$17,280$ $\qquad$ $600 \times 0.40 \times \$60 = \$14,400$

Sales mix variance = $6,480 U $\qquad$ Sales quantity variance = $2,880 F

Sales volume variance
= $10,800 − $14,400
= $3,600 U

To verify: Sales volume variance
= Sales mix variance + Sales quantity variance
= $6,480 U $\qquad$ + $\qquad$ $2,880 F
= $3,600 U

Regular

$720 \times 0.75 \times \$45 = \$24,300$ $\qquad$ $720 \times 0.60 \times \$45 = \$19,440$ $\qquad$ $600 \times 0.60 \times \$45 = \$16,200$

Sales mix variance = $4,860 F $\qquad$ Sales quantity variance = $3,240 F

Sales volume variance
= $24,300 − $16,200
= $8,100 F

To verify: Sales volume variance
= Sales mix variance + Sales quantity variance
= $4,860 F $\qquad$ + $\qquad$ $3,240 F
= $8,100 F

Total

Sales mix variance $\qquad$ = $6,480 U + $4,860 F = $1,620 U
Sales quantity variance = $2,880 F + $3,240 F = $6,120 F

5. Verification

	Sales mix variance	+	Sales quantity variance	=	Sales volume variance
Premium	$6,480 U		$2,880 F		$3,600 U
Regular	4,860 F		3,240 F		8,100 F
Total	$1,620 U		$6,120 F		$4,500 F

6. Market size variances. (See the solution for 7.)
7. Market share variances (000 omitted).

Weighted-average budgeted contribution margin per unit	
Master budget total contribution margin	$30,600
Master budget total sales units	÷ 600
Total	$ 51

Calculation for Market Shares

Budgeted	Total sales in units 600 ÷ Total sales of the industry 1,500 = 0.40
Actual	Total sales in units 720 ÷ Total sales of the industry 1,600 = 0.45

Calculation for Variances

Actual total market size × Actual market share × Average budgeted contribution margin per unit	Actual total market size × Budgeted market share × Average budgeted contribution margin per unit	Budgeted total market size × Budgeted market share × Average budgeted contribution margin per unit
1,600 × 0.45 × $51 = $36,720	1,600 × 0.40 × $51 = $32,640	1,500 × 0.40 × $51 = $30,600

Market share variance = $4,080 F	Market size variance = $2,040 F

Sales quantity variance
= $4,080 F + $2,040 F
= $6,120 F

---

8. The sum of market size variance and market share variance follows. It verifies that this total equals the sales quantity variance.

Total market size variance	+	Total market share variance	=	Total quantity variance
$2,040 F		$4,080 F		$6,120 F

2. Productivity Variances

1. Operational partial productivity

		2003				2004		
	Output		Input Resource Used	Partial Productivity	Output		Input Resource Used	Partial Productivity
TPX–45	60,000	÷	75,000 =	0.8	64,000	÷	89,600 =	0.7143
Direct labor	60,000	÷	10,000 =	6.0	64,000	÷	10,847 =	5.9002

2. Financial partial productivity

		2003				2004		
	Units of Output		Cost of Input Resource Used	Partial Productivity	Units of Output		Cost of Input Resource Used	Partial Productivity
TPX–45	60,000	÷	$540,000 =	0.1111	64,000	÷	$609,280 =	0.1050
Direct labor	60,000	÷	300,000 =	0.2000	64,000	÷	$347,104 =	0.1844

3. Separation of financial partial productivity

	(A) 2004 Output with 2004 Productivity at 2004 Input Costs	(B) 2004 Output with 2003 Productivity at 2004 Input Costs	(C) 2004 Output with 2003 Productivity at 2003 Input Costs	(D) 2003 Output with 2003 Productivity at 2003 Input Costs
Direct materials	64,000/$609,280 = 0.1050	64,000/$544,000 = 0.1176	64,000/$576,000 = 0.1111	60,000/$540,000 = 0.1111
Direct labor	64,000/$347,104 = 0.1844	64,000/$341,333 = 0.1875	64,000/$320,000 = 0.2000	60,000/$300,000 = 0.2000

	Productivity change	Input price change	Output change
Direct materials	0.1050 − 0.1176 = 0.0126 U	0.1176 − 0.1111 = 0.0065 F	0.1111 − 0.1111 = 0
Direct labor	0.1844 − 0.1875 = 0.0031 U	0.1875 − 0.2000 = 0.0125 U	0.2000 − 0.2000 = 0

Summary of result

	Productivity Change	Input Price Change	Total Change	Change as Percent of 2003 Productivity Productivity Change	Input Price Change	Total Change
Direct materials TPX–45	0.0126 U	0.0065 F	0.0061 U	11.34% U	5.85% F	5.49% U
Direct labor	0.0031 U	0.0125 U	0.0156 U	1.55% U	6.25% U	7.8% U

4. Total productivity

Total productivity in units

	2003	2004
(a) Total units manufactured	60,000	64,000
(b) Total variable manufacturing costs incurred	$840,000	$956,384
(c) Total productivity (a) ÷ (b)	0.071429	0.066919
(d) Decrease in productivity	0.071429 − 0.066919 =	0.00451

Total productivity in sales dollars

	2003	2004
(a) Total sales	$1,500,000	$1,600,000
(b) Total variable manufacturing costs incurred	$840,000	$956,384
(c) Total productivity (a) ÷ (b)	$1.7857	$1.6730
(d) Decrease in productivity	$1.7857 − $1.6730 =	$0.1127

853

18

Management Control and Strategic Performance Measurement

After studying this chapter, you should be able to . . .

1 Identify the objectives of management control

2 Identify the types of management control systems

3 Define strategic performance measurement and show how centralized, decentralized, and team-oriented organizations can apply it

4 Explain the objectives and applications of strategic performance measurement in three common strategic business units: cost SBUs, revenue SBUs, and profit SBUs

5 Explain the role of the balanced scorecard in strategic performance measurement

6 Explain the role of strategic performance measurement in service firms and not-for-profit organizations

©Scott Goodwin Photography.

T alk about some of the most remarkable corporate turnarounds of the last decade! Mobil Oil North America was experiencing profits well below the industry average in the early 1990s, but soon after adopting a new performance measurement system, the firm became profitable. The performance measurement method is one of the most influential in many decades: the balanced scorecard. The same remarkable improvement occurred for CIGNA Property & Casualty Insurance and Chemical Bank when these two firms adopted the balanced scorecard.[1] In these instances, the success of the balanced scorecard is attributed to providing top management a way to effectively communicate strategic initiatives to the large number of managers throughout their firms and to enabling these managers to understand more clearly than perhaps ever before exactly how to implement that strategy. As Kaplan and Norton note (page 7):

> The Balanced Scorecard made the difference. Each organization executed strategies using the same physical and human resources that had previously produced failing performance. The strategies were executed with the same products, the same facilities, the same employees, and the same customers. The difference was a new senior management team using the Balanced Scorecard to focus all organizational resources on a new strategy.

[1] Robert S. Kaplan and David P. Norton, *The Strategy-Focused Organization: How Balanced Scorecard Companies Thrive in the New Business Environment* (Boston: Harvard Business School Press, 2001).

The scorecard allowed these successful organizations to build a new kind of management system—one designed to manage strategy.

Moreover, the balanced scorecard is really a two-way device. Not only does it effectively communicate top management's strategy to the managers who will implement it, but also it provides a framework to consider, critique, and redevelop that strategy. That is, feedback from managers in the field regarding progress on scorecard measures can provide a useful way to continually reexamine the firm's strategy.

This chapter considers the systems used to measure and evaluate performance with a focus on the activities that most effectively help the firm achieve its strategy. We will study several performance systems, including the balanced scorecard. We begin by explaining the broad concepts underlying performance evaluation and control.

PERFORMANCE EVALUATION AND CONTROL

Performance evaluation is the process by which managers at all levels gain information about the performance of tasks within the firm and judge that performance against preestablished criteria as set out in budgets, plans, and goals. Performance evaluation is applied for each of the three management functions: operations, marketing, and finance. In *operations*, the performance evaluation focus is on the activities of production managers and production supervisors who report to them. In *marketing*, the evaluation is applied to the activities of sales executives, sales managers, and individual salespersons. In *finance*, performance evaluation monitors the firm's financing activities, including maintenance of adequate liquidity, management of cash flow, cost of capital, and other financing activities.

Performance is also evaluated at many different levels in the firm: top management, mid-management, and the operating level of individual production and sales employees. In operations, the performances of individual production supervisors at the *operating level* are evaluated by plant managers, who in turn are evaluated by executives at the *management level*. Similarly, individual salespersons are evaluated by sales managers who are evaluated in turn by upper-level sales management, and so on. Often no operating-level employees are involved in financial management, so the performance of financial managers is typically evaluated at the upper-management level only.

Management control refers to the evaluation by upper-level managers of the performance of mid-level managers. **Operational control** means the evaluation of operating-level employees by mid-level managers. Part V covered operational control. Part VI, which begins with this chapter, covers management control.

Operational Control versus Management Control

In contrast to operational control, which focuses on detailed short-term performance measures, management control focuses on higher-level managers and long-term, strategic issues. Operational control has a management-by-exception approach; that is, it identifies units or individuals whose performance does not comply with expectations so that the problem can be promptly corrected. In contrast, management control is more consistent with the management-by-objectives approach, in which long-term objectives such as growth and profitability are determined and performance is periodically measured against these goals.

Management control also has a broader and more strategic objective: to evaluate the unit's overall profitability as well as the performance of its manager, to decide whether the unit should be retained or closed, and to motivate the manager to achieve top management's goals. Because of this broader focus, various objectives for management control generally have multiple measures of performance rather than a single financial or operating measure, as is sometimes true in operational control. Exhibit 18–1 is an organization chart that illustrates the different roles of management control and operational control.

Performance evaluation is the process by which managers at all levels gain information about the performance of tasks within the firm and judge that performance against preestablished criteria as set out in budgets, plans, and goals.

LEARNING OBJECTIVE 1▶

Identify the objectives of management control.

Management control refers to the evaluation by upper-level managers of the performance of mid-level managers.

Operational control means the evaluation of operating level employees by mid-level managers.

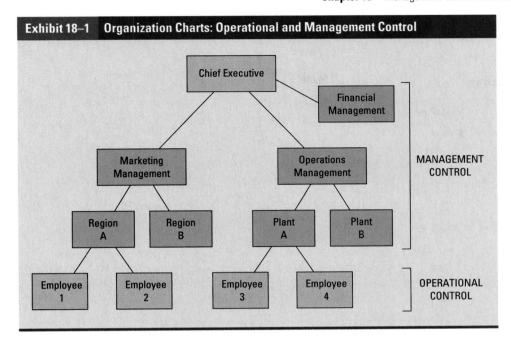

Exhibit 18–1   Organization Charts: Operational and Management Control

Objectives of Management Control

In a management-by-objectives approach, top management assigns a set of responsibilities to each mid-level manager. The nature of these responsibilities and, therefore, the precise nature of top management's objectives depends on the functional area involved (operations, marketing, or finance) and on the scope of authority of the mid-level manager (the extent of the resources under the manager's command).

These areas of responsibility are often called *strategic business units* (SBUs). The concept of a strategic business unit is particularly useful for diversified firms that need performance measures to rationalize and manage the different business units. General Electric Company (GE) is widely cited as pioneering the concept. The GE story is told in two Harvard Business School cases (385–315 and 381–174)[2]; see also Case 1–1 in *Management Control Systems*.[3] The text by Arthur Thompson Jr. and A. J. Strickland III[4] provides a useful discussion of SBUs. An overall discussion of strategic performance measurement is provided by Robert Simons[5] and Kim Langfield-Smith provides a comprehensive survey of the relevant research.[6]

A **strategic business unit** consists of a well-defined set of controllable activities over which the SBU manager is responsible. Generally, managers have autonomy for making decisions and for managing the SBU's human and physical resources. The objectives of management control follow:

1. *Motivate* managers to exert a high level of effort to achieve the goals set by top management.

2. Provide the right *incentive* for managers to make decisions consistent with the goals set by top management.

3. *Determine fairly the rewards* earned by managers for their effort and skill and the effectiveness of their decision making.

> A **strategic business unit (SBU)** consists of a well-defined set of controllable operating activities over which an SBU manager is responsible.

---

[2]   See Cases 385–315 and 381–174 (Boston: Board of Trustees of Harvard University, 1984).

[3]   R. N. Anthony and V. Govindarajan, *Management Control Systems*, 8th ed. (Burr Ridge, Ill.: Irwin, 1993).

[4]   *Strategic Management: Concepts and Cases*, 10 ed. (Burr Ridge, Ill.: McGraw-Hill, 1998), pp. 295–97.

[5]   *Performance Measurement and Control Systems for Implementing Strategy* (Upper Saddle River, N.J.: Prentice Hall, 2000).

[6]   "Management Control Systems and Strategy: A Critical Review," *Accounting Organizations and Society* 12, 22 (1997), pp. 207–32.

A concise summary of top management's objectives is to provide fair compensation to the manager for working hard and making the right decisions, all within the context of autonomous action by the SBU manager. A common mechanism for achieving these multiple objectives is to develop an **employment contract** between the manager and top management that covers each of these points. Assuming that managers act in autonomous self-interest, the contract is designed to provide incentives for them to act independently while achieving top management's objectives and earning the desired compensation. (This is called goal congruence.) The contract specifies the manager's desired behaviors and the compensation to be awarded for achieving specific outcomes by using these behaviors. The contract can be written or unwritten, explicit or implied; some contracts are legal and enforceable by the courts.[7] For clarity and effectiveness, organizations often use explicit written contracts.

An **employment contract** is an agreement between the manager and top management designed to provide incentives for the manager to act independently to achieve top management's objectives.

Employment Contracts

The **principal-agent model** is a conceptual model that contains the key elements that contracts must have to achieve the desired objectives.

An economic model called the **principal-agent model** is a prototype that contains the key elements that contracts must have to achieve the desired objectives. The model sets out two important aspects of management performance that affect the contracting relationship, uncertainty and lack of observability.

> **Uncertainty.** Each manager operates in an environment that is influenced by factors beyond the manager's control—operating factors such as unexpected and unpreventable machine breakdowns and external factors such as fluctuations in market prices and demands. The manager's lack of control means that there is some degree of *uncertainty* about the effectiveness of the manager's actions, independent of the efforts and abilities the manager brings to the job.

> **Lack of observability.** The efforts and decisions made by the manager are *not observable to top management*. The manager generally possesses information not accessible to top management. Because of the manager's independent and unobservable actions, top management is able to observe only the concrete outcomes of those actions, not the efforts that led to these outcomes.

The presence of uncertainty in the job environment and the lack of observability and the existence of private information for the manager complicate the contracting relationship. Ideally, with no uncertainty and perfect observability, the manager and top management would base their contract on the amount of effort the manager is to supply. An observable effort would assure both parties of the desired outcome. However, the presence of uncertainty and the lack of observability mean that the contract between the manager and top management must specifically incorporate both uncertainty and the lack of observability. This can be accomplished by understanding and applying the three principles of employment contracts:

1. Because of uncertainty in the manager's environment, the contract should recognize that other factors inside and outside the firm also influence the outcomes of the manager's efforts and abilities. Therefore, the contract should separate the outcome of the manager's actions from the effort and decision-making skills employed by the manager; that is, separate the performance of the manager from the performance of the SBU.

2. The contract must include only factors that the manager controls. This concept is similar to the first principle, which separates the manager from the SBU; this second principle excludes *known* uncontrollable factors from the contract.

3. Because of uncertainty and lack of observability, a *risk-averse manager is improperly biased* to avoid decisions with uncertain outcomes. In contrast, top manage-

---

[7] For a good overview of the use of contracts in management control, see Kenneth A. Merchant, *Rewarding Results* (Boston: Harvard Business School Press, 1989), especially Chapters 1 and 2.

The Three Principles of Effective Contracting

1. Separate the outcome of the manager's actions from the effort and decision-making skill employed by the manager.
2. Exclude known uncontrollable factors.
3. Make adjustment for the manager's expected relative risk aversion.

Risk Aversion among Mid-Level Managers

Kenneth Merchant illustrates how top management and managers diverge in their risk tolerance with this observation of a profit SBU manager: "We're not restricted by anything the corporation does. We spent millions of dollars trying to build [a new type of product] in the United States. No bank would have gone along with the costs that were adding up, but [the corporation] kept funding it. We failed; we designed something we couldn't manufacture. But I didn't lose my job. Corporate wants us to take risks."

Source: Based on Kenneth A. Merchant, *Rewarding Results* (Boston: Harvard Business School Press, 1989), p. 76; see also Carol Hymowitz, "How Can a Manager Encourage Employees to Take Bold Risks?" *The Wall Street Journal,* January 4, 2000, p. B1.

---

ment would prefer to see some of these relatively risky decisions implemented because of top management's greater tolerance for risk.

In effect, the contract between top management and the manager should recognize the manager's risk aversion and the role of uncertainty: the need to understand and to apply the three principles of contracting.

In the principal-agent model illustrated in Exhibit 18–2, top management supplies compensation to the manager who operates in an environment of uncertainty. The manager supplies effort and decision-making skills as well as a degree of risk aversion. The effect of the effort and decision-making skills on the factors in the environment produces the outcomes. The outcomes are multifaceted, including financial and nonfinancial results: earnings, customer satisfaction, operating efficiency, and so on. The accountant prepares a performance report consisting of financial and nonfinancial measures of the outcomes of the manager's decisions and efforts; the performance report goes to top management, which uses it to determine the manager's pay. In this way, the principal-agent model shows the relationships among the key factors that affect the manager's performance and compensation.

DESIGN OF MANAGEMENT CONTROL SYSTEMS FOR EVALUATION

Developing a management control system involves clearly identifying the who, what, and when for the evaluation. We start with the *who*, that is, who is interested in evaluating the organization's performance? The four recipients of performance reports are: (1) the firm's owners, directors, or shareholders, (2) its creditors, (3) the community or governmental units affected by its operations, and (4) its employees. Each has a different view about what performance is desired.[8]

◀**LEARNING OBJECTIVE 2**

Identify the types of management control systems.

---

[8] For a useful discussion of strategic performance measurement in the context of diverse stakeholders, see Anthony A. Atkinson, John H. Waterhouse, and Robert B. Wells, "A Stakeholder Approach to Strategic Performance Measurement," *Sloan Management Review,* Spring 1997, pp. 25–37.

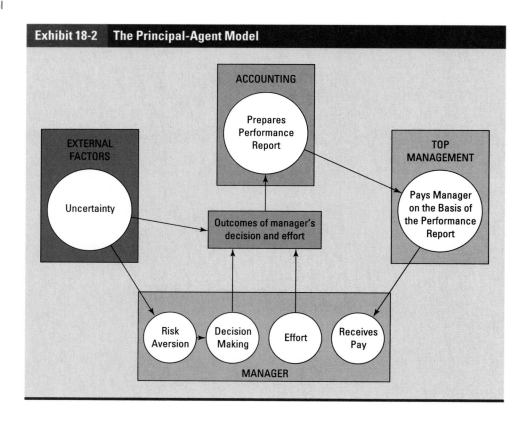

Exhibit 18-2 The Principal-Agent Model

ACCOUNTING

Prepares Performance Report

EXTERNAL FACTORS

Uncertainty

TOP MANAGEMENT

Pays Manager on the Basis of the Performance Report

Outcomes of manager's decision and effort

Risk Aversion

Decision Making

Effort

Receives Pay

MANAGER

The second aspect of management control is *what* is being evaluated. Commonly the evaluation is of the individual manager, to assess the effectiveness and efficiency of the manager's performance. Alternatively, the focus of the evaluation might be the SBU under the manager's control for the purpose of determining whether or not to expand or to divest the SBU. Rather than focusing on the individual manager, the evaluation might be directed to a team of managers. A manager's performance can be compared either with that of other managers or with the manager's own previous performance. Comparison to other managers is common, but comparison to the manager's previous performance is preferable when comparison to others is inappropriate or unfair in some way.

The third aspect of management control is *when* the performance evaluation is conducted. There are two considerations. First, the evaluation can be done on the basis of either *resources input* to the manager or *outputs* of the manager's efforts. The first approach uses the master budget (Chapter 9), while the second uses the flexible budget (Chapter 15). The focus is on inputs when measuring the outputs of the manager's efforts is difficult or the nature and extent of the manager's control over the outputs is not clear. Then the manager's evaluation is performed *ex ante*, that is, before the manager's efforts and decisions have been made. In effect, the manager negotiates with top management for the amount of resources needed. This approach is common in service and not-for-profit organizations for which the outputs are often difficult to measure. In contrast, in manufacturing, where the inputs and outputs are often relatively easy to measure, the *ex post* approach based on actual outputs is more commonly used.

Another timing option is to tie the evaluation to the product life cycle. The life cycle of a product or service is the time from its introduction to its removal from the market. In the early stages of a product's sales life cycle, management focuses primarily on nonfinancial factors such as market penetration and success in developing certain customers. The appropriate performance measures at this time include revenue according to customer class and area, the number of back orders, the number of new customers, and customer satisfaction. As the product achieves market acceptance,

Exhibit 18–3	Sales Life Cycle of Management Control

Stage of Product's Sales Life Cycle	Appropriate Performance Evaluation Measures
Early	Revenue, market penetration
Growth	Profitability, asset management
Mature	Profitability, strategy

profitability and asset management become more important, and the performance measures change. Finally, when the product is in its mature phase—when the nature of the competition is established and the future of the market is clear—the focus on profitability continues with the addition of interest in strategic issues such as customer satisfaction, information regarding product modifications, and potential new markets. Top management must choose the types of performance measures that are appropriate for the sales life cycle stage of the product or service, as illustrated in Exhibit 18–3.

The management accountant first determines the who, what, and when of management control and then designs a system to evaluate it. The systems for management control are of two types, formal and informal. Formal systems are developed with explicit management guidance while informal systems arise from the unmanaged, and sometimes unintended, behavior of managers and employees. Informal systems reflect the managers' and employees' reactions and feelings that result from the positive and negative aspects of the work environment. An example is the positive feelings of security and acceptance held by an employee in a company that has a successful product and offers generous employee benefits.

Informal Control Systems

Informal Systems at the Individual Level

Informal systems are used in firms at both the individual and the group levels. At the individual level, employees' performance is influenced by the individual drives and aspirations they bring to the workplace; these are separate from any incentives and guidance provided by management. Such individual motivators explain performance differences between employees.

Informal Systems at the Team Level

When informal systems exist at the work group or team level, shared team norms, such as a positive attitude to help the firm achieve quality goals or to improve sales, influence the performance of team members. At a broader level, organization-level norms can influence the behavior of teams and of individual employees. For example, some firms have a culture of commitment to customer service (IBM and Wal-Mart); others have a culture devoted to quality (Ford, FedEx) or innovation (Rubbermaid, Hewlett-Packard). Management accountants must consider these informal systems to properly develop control systems that have the desired impact on employees' performance.

Formal Control Systems

Formal Systems at the Individual Level

The three important formal management control systems at the individual employee level are (1) hiring practices, (2) promotion policies, and (3) strategic performance measurement systems. In each system, management sets expectations for desired employee performance. Hiring and promotion policies are critical in all companies and supplement strategic performance measurement systems. Strategic performance measurement systems are the most common method for evaluating managers.

Exhibit 18–4 Systems for Management Control

	INFORMAL SYSTEMS	FORMAL SYSTEMS
INDIVIDUAL	Aspiration Level Personal Drives	Hiring Practices Promotion Procedures STRATEGIC PERFORMANCE MEASUREMENT
TEAMS	Peer Norms Organization Culture	Keiretsu Shared Responsibility

Formal Systems at the Team Level

Little is known about formal systems for management control at the team or group level, although the increased emphasis on teamwork in recent years is likely to produce demand for such systems. Some U.S. companies have adopted the *keiretsu* system of shared responsibility prevalent in Japanese companies, and it is a likely starting place for such a development.[9] The four management control systems are summarized in Exhibit 18–4.

STRATEGIC PERFORMANCE MEASUREMENT

LEARNING OBJECTIVE 3▶

Define strategic perfor-mance measurement and show how centralized, decentralized, and team-oriented organizations can apply it.

Strategic performance measurement is an accounting system used by top management for the evaluation of SBU managers.

Strategic performance measurement is a system used by top management to evaluate SBU managers. It is used when responsibility can be effectively delegated to SBU managers and adequate measures for evaluating the performance of the managers exist. Before designing strategic performance measurement systems, top managers determine when delegation of responsibility (called *decentralization*) is desirable.

Decentralization

A firm is decentralized if it has chosen to delegate a significant amount of responsibility to SBU managers. In contrast, a centralized firm reserves much of the decision making at the top management level. For example, in a centralized multi-store retail

---

The Value of Decentralization at Kids 'R' Us

For certain firms, local knowledge can be critical, as the experience of Kids 'R' Us illustrates. Kids 'R' Us, a retailer of children's clothing, attempted to break into the retail clothing market in Puerto Rico. The objective was to take advantage of the Puerto Rican love for retail shopping; Puerto Ricans spend 55 percent of their disposable income in retail stores. Kids 'R' Us made a big push on back-to-school clothing sales but failed to realize that most Puerto Rican kids wear uniforms to school. In addition, much of the clothing was too heavy and not suitable to the warm Puerto Rican climate. Jeff Handler, the company's marketing director, explained that the firm's central purchasing and planning policies and procedures had caused the errors. Local knowledge was critical for the effective management of the stores in Puerto Rico.

Source: Based on information in *Business Week,* February 28, 1994, p. 8.

---

9 For a recent description of one bank's approach to using team-based performance measures, see Dan Hill, "Cooperation or Competition?" *Strategic Finance*, February 2000, pp. 53–57.

firm, all pricing decisions, product purchasing, and advertising decisions are made at the top management level, typically by top-level marketing and operations executives. In contrast, a decentralized retail firm allows local store managers to decide which products to purchase and the type and amount of advertising to use as well as to make other marketing and operating decisions.

The strategic benefit of the centralized approach is that top management retains control over key business functions, ensuring a desired level of performance. Additionally, with top management involvement in most decisions, the expertise of top management can be effectively utilized, and the activities of the different units within the firm can be effectively coordinated. For many firms, however, a decentralized approach is preferable. The main reason is that top management cannot effectively manage the operations at a very detailed level; it lacks the necessary local knowledge. Decisions at lower levels in the firm must be made on a timely basis using the information at hand to make the firm more responsive to the customer. For example, the retail store manager must often make quick changes in inventory, pricing, and advertising to respond to local competition and changing customer buying habits and tastes.

Although the main reason for decentralization is the use of local or specialized knowledge by SBU managers, other important incentives exist. First, many managers would say that decentralized strategic performance measurement is more motivating because it provides them the opportunity to demonstrate their skill and their desire to achieve as well as to receive recognition and compensation for doing so. Second, because of the direct responsibility assumed by SBU managers, the decentralized approach provides a type of training for future top-level managers. Finally, most managers would agree that the decentralized approach is a better basis for performance evaluation. It is perceived to be more objective and to provide more opportunity for the advancement of hard-working, energetic managers.

Decentralization has a downside as well. It can hinder coordination within the firm. The increased focus on competition also could cause increased conflict among managers, which can lead to counterproductive actions and reduced overall performance.

Types of Strategic Business Units

The four types of strategic business units (SBUs) are cost SBUs, revenue SBUs, profit SBUs, and investment SBUs.

Cost SBUs are a firm's production or support SBUs that provide the best quality product or service at the lowest cost. Examples include a plant's assembly department, data processing department, and shipping and receiving department. When the focus is on the selling function, SBUs are called **revenue SBUs** and are defined either by product line or by geographical area. When an SBU both generates revenues and incurs the major portion of the cost for producing these revenues, it is a **profit SBU**. Profit SBU managers are responsible for both revenues and costs and therefore seek to achieve a desired operating profit. The use of profit SBUs is an improvement over cost and revenue SBUs in

Cost SBUs are production or support SBUs within the firm that have the goal of providing the best quality product or service at the lowest cost.

A **revenue SBU** is defined either by product line or by geographical area.

A **profit SBU** both generates revenues and incurs the major portion of the cost for producing these revenues.

Benefits and Drawbacks of Decentralization	
Benefits of Decentralization	**Drawbacks of Decentralization**
• Uses local knowledge	• Can hinder coordination among SBUs.
• Allows timely and effective response to customers	• Can cause potential conflict among SBUs
• Trains managers	
• Motivates managers	
• Offers objective method of performance evaluation	

many firms because they align the manager's goals more directly with top management's goal to make the firm profitable.

The choice of a profit, cost, or revenue SBU depends on the nature of the production and selling environment in the firm. Products that have little need for coordination between the manufacturing and selling functions are good candidates for cost centers. These include many commodity products such as food and paper products. For such products, the production manager rarely needs to adjust the functionality of the product or the production schedule to suit a particular customer. For this reason, production managers should focus on reducing cost while sales managers focus on sales; this is what cost and revenue SBUs accomplish.

In contrast, sometimes close coordination is needed between the production and selling functions. For example, high-fashion and consumer products require close coordination so that consumer information coming into the selling function reaches the design and manufacturing function. Cost and revenue SBUs could fail to provide the incentive for coordination; in this case, production managers would be focusing on cost and not listening to the ever-changing demands coming from the selling function. A preferred option is to use the profit center for both the revenue and production managers so that both coordinate efforts to achieve the highest overall profit.

When a firm has many different profit SBUs because it has many different product lines, comparing their performance could be difficult because they vary greatly in size and in the nature of their products and services. A preferred approach is to use **investment SBUs,** which include assets employed by the SBU as well as profits in the performance evaluation. Investment SBUs are covered in Chapter 19.

An **investment SBU** includes assets employed by the SBU as well as profits in performance evaluation.

The Balanced Scorecard

Each of the four types of SBUs described above focuses on a critical financial measure of performance. Rather than to focus on financial performance only, some firms use multiple measures of performance to evaluate SBUs, usually in the form of a balanced scorecard. The balanced scorecard provides a more comprehensive performance evaluation, and therefore an evaluation that can be more effective in meeting the evaluation objectives of motivation and fairness. Thus, there are five possible methods to evaluate the performance of an SBU. Most often these methods will be used to evaluate the performance of the manager of the SBU. For example, managers of cost SBUs are expected to meet or exceed targets for cost reduction. Managers of SBUs using the balanced scorecard are evaluated on multiple measures. Sometimes investment SBU performance measures are used in two ways: to evaluate the manager of the SBU and to evaluate the SBU as a business investment. We examine each of these five methods in this and the following chapter.

COST STRATEGIC BUSINESS UNITS

Cost SBUs include direct manufacturing departments such as assembly and finishing and manufacturing support departments such as materials handling, maintenance, and engineering. The direct manufacturing and manufacturing support departments are often evaluated as cost SBUs since these managers have significant direct control over costs but little control over revenues or decision making for investment in facilities.

◀**LEARNING OBJECTIVE 4**

Explain the objectives and applications of strategic performance measurement in three common strategic business units: cost SBUs, revenue SBUs, and profit SBUs.

Strategic Issues Related to Implementing Cost SBUs

Several strategic issues arise when implementing cost SBUs. One is cost shifting, the second is excessively focusing on short-term objectives, and the third is the tendency of managers and top management to miscommunicate because of the pervasive problem of budget slack.

Cost Shifting

Cost shifting occurs when a department replaces its controllable costs with noncontrollable costs. For example, the manager of a production cost SBU that is evaluated on controllable costs has the incentive to replace variable costs with fixed costs. The reason for this is that the manager generally is not held responsible for increases in noncontrollable fixed costs. The net effect might be higher overall costs for the firm, although controllable costs in the manager's department might decrease. Fixed costs go up while variable costs go down. The effective use of cost SBUs requires top management to anticipate and prevent cost shifting by requiring an analysis and justification of equipment upgrades and any changes in work patterns that affect other departments. Top management's attention to cost shifting is particularly important because the foundation of strategic performance measurement systems is an SBU manager who is responsible only for controllable costs. The focus on controllable costs is necessary to achieve the objectives of motivation and fairness. However, as explained earlier, excessive focus on controllable costs can result in dysfunctional cost shifting.

Cost-shifting issues also arise in not-for-profit organizations. For example, many governmental units do not distinguish between direct and indirect costs in their performance reporting. This can lead to poor decision making, as illustrated by the U.S. Forest Service:

> Inappropriate accounting measures allegedly caused the United States Forest Service to cut down trees that an ordinary business would have left standing . . . the Forest Service is not charged for the cost of constructing roads into remote areas to reach the lumber. The Forest Service's response to these measures of its performance is to cut down a great deal of lumber and to construct costly, intricate roads to reach it. The Service already has 342,000 miles of logging roads and plans to build yet another 262,000 by 2040. Critics contend that these roads are constructed to reach increasingly poor quality timber and that they inflict considerable environmental damage. They recommend new measures of its performance that account for the full cost of logging, including the cost of raising the timber, building the roads to reach it, and replacing it.[10]

The Forest Service's failure to identify the full cost of the logging, including the costs of the roads as well as the logging of the trees, caused poor decision making. The costs of the roads were improperly not charged to the Forest Service.

Another incentive for cost shifting in not-for-profit entities is that certain services are reimbursed on a cost-plus basis while others are charged as fixed fees. Cost shifting in this context means allocating joint costs from the fixed-charge to the cost-plus services. The cost shifting can be done in a variety of ways. A number of hospitals, for

---

[10] Regina E. Herzlinger and Denise Nitterhouse, *Financial Accounting and Managerial Control for Nonprofit Organizations* (Cincinnati: South Western Publishing, 1994), p. 419; also, Cox et al., "Responsibility Accounting and Operational Control for Governmental Units," *Accounting Horizons*, June 1989, pp. 38–48, show the results of a survey of 830 governmental units in the United States and Canada with a principal finding that the strategic performance measurement systems in three-fourths of these units did not distinguish between controllable and uncontrollable costs.

example, have shifted the costs of Medicare and Medicaid (fixed-fee) patients to private (cost-plus) patients.[11] Cost shifting undermines the motivation and fairness of the performance evaluation systems within these hospitals.

In a related example, cost shifting can occur *within* the hospital:

> Kevin Schulman, a medical economist at Georgetown Medical School, tells of a hospital where the radiology department decided to save money by sending out only one copy of a report, instead of separate copies to each care provider. It won a hospital efficiency award, while the medical clinic in the same hospital had to hire someone to reproduce that lone report for all the doctors who needed a copy.[12]

The cost shifting was from one department in the hospital to another rather than from one type of patient to another.

Excessive Short-Term Focus

Another strategic issue is the broad concern that many performance measurement systems focus excessively on annual cost figures; this motivates managers to attend only to short-term costs and to neglect long-term strategic issues. This concern is an important reason that cost SBUs should use nonfinancial strategic considerations as well as financial information on costs.[13]

Budget Slack

A third strategic issue in implementing cost-based SBUs is to recognize both the negative and the positive roles of budget slack. **Budget slack** is the difference between budgeted and expected performance. The majority of firms have some amount of slack, evidenced by a budgeted cost target that is somewhat easier to attain than is reasonably expected. Managers often plan for a certain amount of slack in their performance budgets to allow for unexpected unfavorable events. However, a significant amount of slack might result from SBU managers' attempts to make their performance goals easier and therefore indicate an overall lower level of performance than should have been achieved.

The positive view of slack is that it effectively addresses the decision-making and fairness objectives of performance evaluation. By limiting managers' exposure to environmental uncertainty, it reduces their relative risk aversion. The resulting evaluation therefore satisfies fairness, and the reduced risk helps the managers make decisions that are more nearly congruent with the goals of top management.

> **Budget slack** is the difference between budgeted performance and expected performance.

Implementing Cost-Based SBUs in Departments

Production and Support Departments

The two methods for implementing cost SBUs for production and support departments are the discretionary-cost method and the engineered-cost method. These two methods have different underlying cost behavior and a different focus: inputs or outputs. When costs are predominantly fixed, an input-oriented planning focus is appropriate because fixed costs are not controllable in the short term. The planning approach is taken so that top management can effectively budget for expected costs in each cost SBU; the focus is on beginning-of-period planning for expected costs rather than end-of-period evaluation of the amount of costs expended. In contrast, if costs are primarily variable and therefore controllable, an output-oriented approach, based on end-of-period evaluation of con-

---

[11]   See Leslie Eldenburg and Sanjay Kallapur, "Changes in Hospital Service Mix and Cost Allocations in Response to Changes in Medicare Reimbursement Schemes," *Journal of Accounting and Economics*, May 1997, pp. 31–51.

[12]   "Hospitals Attack a Crippler: Paper," *Business Week*, February 21, 1994, pp. 104–6.

[13]   The problems caused by an excessive focus on short-term costs and profits are illustrated in "Corporate Liposuction Can Have Nasty Side Effects," *Business Week*, July 17, 2000, pp. 74–75.

trollable costs, is appropriate. The input-oriented approach is called the **discretionary-cost method** because costs are considered to be largely uncontrollable and discretion is applied at the planning stage. The output-oriented approach is called the **engineered-cost method** since costs are variable and therefore "engineered," or controllable.

Another factor in choosing between discretionary-cost and engineered-cost SBUs is the complexity of the work environment. SBUs that have relatively ill-defined outputs (for instance, research and development) have less well-defined goals and are therefore more likely to be evaluated as discretionary-cost SBUs; SBUs for which the operations are well defined and the output goals are more clearly determined will have engineered-cost SBUs.

Cost behavior in a production SBU is therefore important in choosing the cost SBU method. As explained in Chapter 3, the behavior of an activity measure depends on the level of analysis: the facility, the product, the batch of production, or the unit of production. Similarly, when studying a cost SBU, we must know on which level of analysis it operates. For example, costs in the engineering department are driven primarily by product-level activity measures: the number of new products or product changes. Also, costs in the inspection department are caused primarily by batch-level activity measures: the number of production runs or setups.

Relatively few cost drivers exist at the facility level because most of its costs are fixed and do not fluctuate with changes in production level, production mix, or product. Costs at the facility level have few cost drivers; therefore, most departments at this level are evaluated as discretionary-cost SBUs.

For cost SBUs at the unit, batch, and product levels, managers commonly implement the engineered-cost method based on the appropriate cost driver for that production activity. For example, for the engineering department where the cost driver is at the product level, the engineered-cost method uses the number of engineering changes to new and existing products as the cost driver and evaluates the performance of the engineering department on its costs for each engineering change completed. Similarly, for the inspection department where the cost driver is at the batch level (inspection is done for each batch), the appropriate cost SBU method is again the engineered-cost method, in which management reviews the cost incurred versus the number of batches inspected.

Some production departments are more difficult to classify as batch, product, or facility level. For example, the maintenance department can be viewed as a facility-level activity because much of the demand for maintenance is for plant and equipment that is not influenced by production level (units or batches). However, because the wear on equipment is greater at a higher level of production or for a larger number of batches, batch and unit cost drivers also can be appropriate. The choice of method depends in part on management's objectives. If management wants to motivate a reduction in maintenance use (because of rising costs or of overall budget constraints), the engineered-cost method is appropriate since it rewards cost reduction.[14]

The **discretionary-cost method** considers costs largely uncontrollable and applies discretion at the planning stage; it is an input-oriented approach.

The **engineered-cost method** considers costs to be variable and therefore engineered, or controllable; it is an output-oriented approach.

SBUs for Production and Support Departments

Discretionary-Cost Approach	Engineered-Cost Approach
Costs are mainly fixed, uncontrollable	Costs are mainly variable, controllable
Firms use an input-oriented planning focus	Firms use an output-oriented evaluation focus
Operations are ill-defined	Operations are well-defined
Ex ante, the focus is on planning	Ex post, the focus is on evaluation

---

[14] Note, however, that Robin Cooper and Robert S. Kaplan, in "Activity-Based Systems: Measuring the Costs of Resource Usage," *Accounting Horizons*, September 1992, explain that methods such as the engineered-cost method do not necessarily achieve a reduction in costs unless the supply of resources is reduced following a reduction in the usage of resources.

In contrast, if management is concerned about the low overall serviceability of plant and equipment (due perhaps to a prior lack of maintenance), the discretionary-cost method provides the proper incentive by reducing the maintenance manager's risk aversion and thereby motivating proper additional expenditures on maintenance.

Another option for management control of the engineering department or maintenance department is to treat each of them as profit SBUs and to charge users a price for their services. The effects of using a profit SBU method are added emphasis on cost control and an incentive for the SBU to provide quality service and perhaps seek markets outside the firm.[15]

General and Administrative Departments

Administrative support departments such as human resources, research and development, information technology services, and printing and duplicating are also commonly evaluated as cost SBUs. They seldom have a source of revenue, but the department managers control most of the costs, so the cost SBU method is appropriate. The choice of a discretionary-cost or engineered-cost method for these departments depends on the cost behavior in the department and on management's philosophy and objectives, as explained earlier. The proper choice of method might change over time. For example, when cost reduction is a key objective, the human resources department might be treated as an engineered-cost SBU for a time. Later it might be changed to a discretionary-cost SBU to motivate managers to focus on long-term goals such as the design of new employee bonus systems.

Cost behavior in administrative support SBUs is often a step-fixed cost, as illustrated in Exhibit 18–5. As clerical and/or service support personnel are added, labor costs increase in a step-fixed pattern. Suppose that one clerk is required to process 100 new employee applications per month and that each clerk is paid $1,200 per month. If the firm processes 250 applications per month, it needs three clerks at a total cost of $3,600 per month. If the discretionary-cost method is used, the supervisor of personnel management is likely to have negotiated for three clerks *at the beginning of the year,*

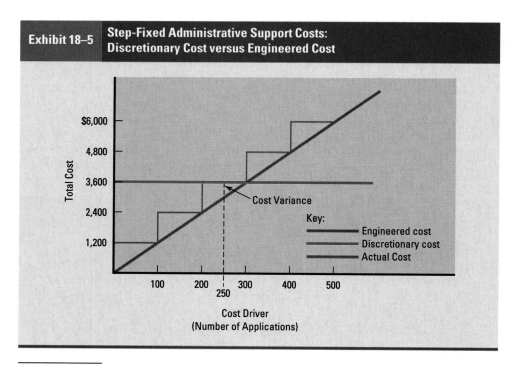

Exhibit 18–5	Step-Fixed Administrative Support Costs: Discretionary Cost versus Engineered Cost

---

15 For example, some hospital departments such as radiology that are commonly viewed as cost SBUs can also be viewed as profit SBUs when management sees their revenue-producing potential. See Ed Egger, "Market Memo: Hospitals Should Look at Radiology as a Profit Center," *Health Care Strategic Management,* February 2000.

and therefore the budget is $3,600 and there is no meaningful *ex post* evaluation. The discretionary-cost method is represented by the horizontal line in Exhibit 18–5.

Recognizing that processing each application in effect costs $12 ($1,200/100), management might choose to use an engineered-cost method that evaluates the personnel department manager by comparing the budget of $3,000 (250 applications times $12 per application) to the actual expenditure of $3,600. Because slack or overcapacity can exist due to the nature of the step-fixed cost, an unfavorable cost variance is likely; only when the operation is exactly at one of the full-capacity points (100, 200, 300 . . .) will there be no variance. Therefore, the interpretation of the cost variances must include both the productivity of labor and the underutilization of labor due to excess capacity.

Outsourcing Cost SBUs

Outsourcing is the term used to describe a firm's decision to have a service or product currently provided by a support department supplied by an outside firm in the future. For example, H. J. Heinz, Eastman-Kodak, and the Vatican in Rome are among the organizations that have chosen to outsource information technology (IT) needs. These firms have found that the use of an outside source is an effective way to obtain reliable service at a reasonable cost without the risk of obsolescence and other potential management problems. It can also enable a firm to gain access to new technologies. The cost of outsourcing is that the firm loses control over a potentially strategic resource and must rely on the outside firm's competence and continued performance.

Outsourcing Allows Firms to Focus on Core Competencies

BP Amoco recently announced a $1.1 billion agreement with PricewaterhouseCoopers (PWC) in which PWC will provide much of the U.S.–based accounting and transaction-processing activities for BP Amoco. The change is expected to reduce BP's accounting costs by 10 to 20 percent. Moreover, it will allow BP to focus on its strategic business plans and core competencies.

Other firms such as Owens Corning, manufacturer of glass fiber, have outsourced the employee time and expense-reporting systems to reduce cost and allow employees to concentrate on core competencies. The Outsourcing Institute (www.outsourcing.com) notes that the outsourcing of services in the United States has tripled in the last five years and explains the cost and strategic reasons for this to continue.

Firms are also seeking to outsource human resources activities to reduce costs and gain competitive edge. David White of Lotus Development Corp. notes, "The human resources function of the not-too-distant future will be a small, high-leveraged, cost-effective internal management consultancy. Most of the functions associated with human resources today will be outsourced or administered by line business units."

Based on information in Charles E. Davis, Elizabeth B. Davis, and Lee Ann Moore, "Outsourcing the Procurement through Payable Process," *Management Accounting,* July 1998, pp. 38–44; "BP Amoco Is Set to Outsource Accounting in $1.1 Billion Deal," *The Wall Street Journal,* November 10, 1999; Tim Kearney, "Why Outsourcing Is In," *Strategic Finance,* January 2000, pp. 34–38; and "Trends in Human Resources Outsourcing," *Management Accounting,* November 1997, pp. 22–27. David White is quoted in *Fortune,* May 13, 1996, p. 176.

COST MANAGEMENT IN ACTION

Outsourcing Information Technology

A number of large firms, including Eastman Kodak, Xerox, and governmental units such as the U.S. Marine Corps and the State of Connecticut are outsourcing significant parts of their information technology (IT) operations. Approximately 20 percent of the largest U.S. firms have already outsourced this operation, according to current estimates, and the trend is for that percentage to increase. Some of the outsourcing is to application service providers (ASPs), which provide a wide range of IT services (e-mail, transaction processing, and more), often over the Internet. In other cases, the IT tasks have been taken over by large consulting firms such as Accenture, IBM, Electronic Data Systems, and Computer Science Corp. Why are these firms outsourcing their IT function? How does outsourcing IT make the firm more competitive? (Refer to Comments on Cost Management in Action at the end of the chapter.)

For this reason, firms analyze this decision thoroughly, select the vendors carefully, and develop precisely worded contracts. Outsourcing is an option increasingly used by many firms for their IT, printing and duplicating, engineering, and other service needs.

Cost Allocation

A pervasive issue when using cost SBUs is how to allocate the jointly incurred costs of service departments, such as IT, engineering, human resources, or maintenance, to the departments using the service. The various cost allocation methods are explained in Chapter 14. The choice of method affects the amount of cost allocated to each cost SBU and therefore is critical in effective cost SBU evaluation. For example, if the cost of maintenance is allocated based on the square feet of space in each production department, the departments with more space have higher costs. The incentives of such an allocation method are not clear because the production departments likely cannot control the amount of space they occupy. Alternatively, if maintenance costs are allocated on the basis of the number of maintenance jobs requested, the production departments can control their allocated maintenance costs by controlling usage.

The criteria for choosing the cost allocation method, as explained in Chapter 14, are the same as the objectives for management control: to (1) motivate managers to exert a high level of effort, (2) provide an incentive for managers to make decisions consistent with top management's goals, and (3) provide a basis for a fair evaluation of managers' performance. For example, when management wants to encourage production departments to reduce the amount of maintenance, allocation based on usage provides the desired incentive. In contrast, if management wants the departments to increase the use of maintenance to improve the serviceability of the equipment, the most effective incentive might be not to allocate the maintenance cost or perhaps to subsidize it in some way.

A useful guide in choosing the cost allocation method, in addition to the three criteria just explained, is to use dual allocation. **Dual allocation** is a cost allocation method that separates fixed and variable costs. Variable costs are directly traced to user departments, and fixed costs are allocated on some logical basis. For example, the variable costs of maintenance, such as supplies, labor, and parts, can be traced to each maintenance job and charged directly to the user department. This approach is both fair and positively motivating. In contrast, the fixed costs of the maintenance department (training, manuals, equipment, etc.) that cannot be traced to each maintenance job should be allocated to the user departments using a basis that fairly reflects each department's use of the service. For example, those departments whose maintenance jobs require more expensive equipment might be allocated a higher proportion of the maintenance department's fixed costs.

To improve on dual allocation, indirect costs could be traced to cost SBUs using activity-based costing (Chapter 4). This approach tends to produce the most accurate cost assignment and therefore would be the most motivating and fairest to the SBU managers.[16]

REVENUE STRATEGIC BUSINESS UNITS

Management commonly uses revenue drivers in evaluating the performance of revenue SBUs. **Revenue drivers** in manufacturing firms are the factors that affect sales volume, such as price changes, promotions, discounts, customer service, changes in product features, delivery dates, and other value-added factors. In service firms, the

Dual allocation is a cost allocation method that separates fixed and variable costs. Variable costs are directly traced to user departments, and fixed costs are allocated on some logical basis.

Revenue drivers are the factors that affect sales volume, such as price changes, promotions, discounts, customer service, changes in product features, delivery dates, and other value-added factors.

---

[16] For an example of how activity-based costing is used to allocate costs for the cost and profit units of an auto retailer, see Jonathan M. Booth and Bala V. Balachandran, "Using ABM to Identify Value: An Automotive Retailer Case Study," *Journal of Cost Management*, September–October 1999, pp. 4–10.

revenue drivers focus on many of the same factors, with a special emphasis on the quality of the service—is it courteous, helpful, and timely?

The marketing department can be viewed as both a revenue SBU and a cost SBU. The revenue SBU responsibility stems from the fact that the marketing department manages the revenue-generating process. The marketing manager must therefore report revenues, typically by product line, and sometimes by sales area and salesperson. Top management uses the revenue reports to assess the performance of the marketing manager in achieving desired sales goals. Often this analysis is performed at a detailed level to determine the separate effects of changes in price, quantity, and sales mix on the overall sales dollars.[17]

The marketing department also can be a cost SBU. In the pharmaceuticals, cosmetics, software, games and toys, and specialized electrical equipment industries, the cost of advertising and promotion is a significant portion of the total cost of producing and selling the product. The marketing department incurs two types of costs: order-getting and order-filling costs. **Order-getting costs** are expenditures to advertise and promote the product. They include samples, demonstrations, advertising and promotion, travel and entertainment expenses, commissions, and marketing research. Because showing how these costs have directly affected sales is often difficult, managers view order-getting costs as a discretionary-cost SBU and focus on planning these expenditures rather than evaluating their effectiveness. In contrast, other firms have developed extensive analyses of order-getting costs to identify the most effective activities for improving sales. Such additional analyses might consist of statistical analyses of general economic data and the firm's sales and operating data, with operational analyses consisting of ratios of sales per salesperson, sales per number of follow-ups on inquiries, and returns and allowances per product and salesperson.

A second category of marketing costs is **order-filling costs**, which include freight, warehousing, packing and shipping, and collections. These costs have a relatively clear relationship to sales volume and as a result, they can often be effectively managed as an engineered-cost SBU. The engineered-cost method could be implemented by developing appropriate operating ratios—average shipping cost per item, average freight cost per sales dollar, and so on.

> **Order-getting costs** are expenditures to advertise and promote the product.

> **Order-filling costs** include freight, warehousing, packing and shipping, and collections.

PROFIT STRATEGIC BUSINESS UNITS

The profit SBU manager's goal is to earn profits. A key advantage of the profit SBU is that it brings the manager's incentives into congruence with those of top management: to improve the firm's profitability. Moreover, the profit SBU should also motivate individual managers because by earning profits, the managers are contributing directly to the firm's success. For these reasons, the profit SBU meets the management control objectives of motivation and decision making explained earlier.

Strategic Role of Profit SBUs

Three strategic issues cause firms to choose profit SBUs rather than cost or revenue SBUs. First, profit SBUs provide the incentive for the desired coordination among the marketing, production, and support functions. The handling of rush orders is a good example. A cost SBU would view a rush order unfavorably because of the potential added cost associated with the disruption of the production process, but a revenue SBU would view it favorably. If they are in separate cost and revenue SBUs, the production manager has little incentive to meet with the marketing manager to coordinate the rush

---

[17]   This is explained in Chapter 17. Also, some marketing managers have a relatively broad view of the responsibility of the marketing function, which includes responsibility for sales and cost of sales. This is suggested, for example, by the Institute of Marketing's definition: "Marketing is the management process for identifying, anticipating, and satisfying customer requirements profitably."

order. In contrast, if the production SBU is a profit SBU, its manager accepts the order if it improves the SBU's profit, a decision consistent with the goals of both the production SBU and top management.

A second reason that firms use profit SBUs rather than cost SBUs is to motivate managers to consider their product as marketable to outside customers. Production departments that provide products and services primarily for other internal departments might find that they can market their products or services profitably outside the firm, or that the firm might be able to purchase the product or service at a lower price outside the firm. For example, American Airlines earns several million dollars per year providing contract maintenance and various other services to other airlines.

The third reason for choosing profit SBUs is to motivate managers to develop new ways to make profit from their products and services. For example, an increasing number of companies find that service contracts (for home entertainment equipment, business equipment, appliances, and so on) provide a significant source of profit in addition to the sale of the product. In the software industry, revenues from providing service and upgrades can be as important as the software's original sales price. Coordination between marketing, production, and design is critical for the success of these efforts, and since many of these contracts are for three years or more, the expected future costs of the service must be carefully analyzed. In a profit SBU, managers have the incentive to develop creative new products and services because the profit SBU evaluation rewards the incremental profits.

The Contribution Income Statement

The **contribution income statement** is based on the contribution margin developed for each profit SBU and for each relevant group of profit SBUs.

A common form of profit SBU evaluation is the **contribution income statement,** which is based on the contribution margin developed for each profit SBU and for each relevant group of profit SBUs. The contribution income statement is illustrated in Exhibit 18–6 for Machine Tools, Inc. (MTI). MTI has two operating divisions, A and B, each of which is considered a profit SBU. The level of detail at which the contribution income statement is developed varies depending on management's needs. For a firm with a limited number of products, the level of detail in Exhibit 18–6 is common. For a firm with several products, a more extensive contribution income statement would be required to provide sufficient detail for management analysis.

This contribution income statement is an extension of the income statement illustrated in Exhibits 10–14 and 10–15 of Chapter 10. Chapter 10 introduces the idea of traceable fixed costs; that is, fixed costs can be traced directly to a product line or pro-

Exhibit 18–6	**Machine Tools, Inc.** *Contribution Income Statement (000s omitted)*						
	Company as a Whole	**Company Breakdown into Two Divisions**		**Breakdown of Division B by Product**			
		Division A	**Division B**	**Not Traceable**	**Product 1**	**Product 2**	**Product 3**
Net revenues	$2,000	$600	$1,400		$400	$700	$300
Variable costs	900	200	700		100	350	250
Contribution margin	$1,100	$400	$ 700		$300	$350	$ 50
Controllable fixed costs	250	100	150	$ 25	25	100	0
Controllable margin	$ 850	$300	$ 550	(25)	$275	$250	$ 50
Noncontrollable fixed costs	400	120	280	20	10	130	120
Contribution by SBU (CSBU)	$ 450	$180	$ 270	$(45)	$265	$120	$ (70)
Untraceable costs	200						
Operating income	$ 250						

duction unit. Exhibit 10–15 shows both contribution margin and contribution margin less traceable fixed costs, **contribution by SBU (CSBU)**. The concept of CSBU is important because it measures *all* costs traceable to, and therefore controllable by, the individual profit SBUs. CSBU is a more complete and fair measure of performance than either the contribution margin or profit.

This chapter expands the contribution income statement by distinguishing controllable and noncontrollable fixed costs. **Controllable fixed costs** are fixed costs that the profit SBU manager can influence in approximately a year or less. That is, the manager typically budgets these costs in the annual budget; some of them involve contractual relationships for a year or less. Examples include advertising; sales promotion; certain engineering, data processing, and research projects; and management consulting. In contrast, **noncontrollable fixed costs** are those that are not controllable within a year's time; usually they include facilities-related costs such as depreciation, taxes, and insurance.

As illustrated in Exhibit 18–6, the firm develops a useful measure of the profit SBU manager's short-term performance by subtracting controllable fixed cost from the contribution margin to determine the **controllable margin**. In contrast, to measure the manager's performance in managing both short- and long-term costs, the CSBU measure is most appropriate since it includes both short-term and long-term fixed costs.

One complication in completing the contribution income statement is that some costs that are not traceable at a detailed level are traceable at a higher level of aggregation. The untraceable costs column in the income statement represents costs traceable to division B but not traceable to any of the product lines. For example, the $25,000 controllable fixed costs might consist of the cost of advertising that was arranged at the division level to benefit all three products, so it is not traceable to any one product.

In addition to providing useful measures of the manager's performance in managing costs, the contribution income statement can be used to determine whether a profit SBU should be dropped or retained, much like our contribution margin analysis in Exhibit 10–15. The analysis is now enhanced because of our ability to distinguish controllable and noncontrollable fixed costs. For example, using the analysis in Exhibit 18–6, MTI can determine that if it drops product 3, the short-term effect will be to reduce profit by $50,000, the amount of the controllable margin. All costs involved in the determination of the controllable margin are avoidable within a period of one year. Taking the longer-term view, suppose that MTI could ultimately save an additional $120,000 of noncontrollable fixed costs by dropping product 3. Then, in the long term, MTI can save a net of $70,000 by dropping product 3, the amount of the contribution by SBU (CSBU) for product 3.

Variable Costing versus Absorption Costing

The use of the contribution income statement often is called *variable costing* because it separates variable and fixed costs. Only variable costs are included in determining the cost of sales and the contribution margin. In contrast, absorption costing is a cost system that includes fixed cost in product cost and cost of sales. Absorption costing is the conventional costing system because it is required by financial reporting standards and by the Internal Revenue Service for determining taxable income.

The advantage of variable costing is that it meets the three objectives of management control systems by showing separately those costs that can be traced to, and controlled by, each SBU. In this section, we see an additional reason for using variable costing: Although net income determined using absorption costing is affected by changes in inventory levels, net income using variable costing is not affected. Exhibit 18–7A and B shows how using absorption costing affects net income.

Panel 1 in Exhibit 18–7A shows the data used in the illustration, including units produced and sold and costs for two periods. Panel 2 shows both the absorption and variable cost income statements for the first of two periods. Two periods are used to

The **contribution by SBU (CSBU)** measures *all* costs traceable to, and therefore controllable by, the individual profit SBUs.

Controllable fixed costs are those fixed costs that the profit SBU manager can influence in approximately a year or less.

Noncontrollable fixed costs are those that are not controllable within a year's time, usually including facilities-related costs such as depreciation, taxes, and insurance.

Controllable margin is determined by subtracting short-term controllable fixed costs from the contribution margin.

Exhibit 18–7A   Comparison of Absorption and Variable Costing

Panel 1 Data Summary	Period 1	Period 2	
Units			
Beginning inventory	0	40	
Price	$100	$100	
Sold	60	140	
Produced	100	100	
Unit variable costs			
Manufacturing	$30	$30	
Selling and administrative costs	$5	$5	
Fixed costs			Per unit
Manufacturing	$4,000	$4,000	$40
Selling and administrative costs	$1,200	$1,200	

Panel 2

Period 1 Income Statement	Absorption Costing		Variable Costing	
Sales (60 × $100)		$6,000		$6,000
Cost of goods sold				
Beginning inventory	$ 0		$ 0	
+ Cost of goods produced	7,000		3,000	
	(= 100 × $70)		(= 100 × $30)	
= Cost of goods available for sale	7,000		3,000	
− Ending inventory	2,800		1,200	
	(= 40 × $70)		(= 40 × $30)	
= Cost of goods sold		4,200		1,800
Less: Variable selling and administrative costs		N/A		300
Gross margin		**$1,800**		
Contribution margin				**$3,900**
Less other costs				
Less: Fixed manufacturing costs	N/A		$4,000	
Less: Selling and administrative costs				
Variable	300		N/A	
Fixed	1,200		1,200	
Total other costs		1,500		5,200
Net income		$ 300		$(1,300)

Recap

Difference in net income = $300 − $(1,300) = $1,600

Difference in ending inventory = $2,800 − $1,200 = $1,600 (or 40 units × $40/unit = $1,600)

show the differences for both possible cases, increasing or decreasing inventory. In the first period, inventory increases; in the second period, it decreases. Exhibit 18–7B shows the comparison of the two income statements for period 2.

In period 1, inventory increases by 40 units because production of 100 units exceeds sales of 60 units. Inventory decreases by the same amount in period 2. Using absorption costing, the unit product cost is $30 variable plus $40 fixed, or $70 per unit in both periods. The $70 unit cost is used to calculate the cost of goods sold on the income statements in periods 1 and 2 for absorption costing. The selling and administrative costs ($5 variable and $1,200 fixed) are deducted after gross margin to determine the net income of $300 in period 1 and $2,300 in period 2.

The variable costing income statement uses variable costing only to determine product cost. The cost of sales and inventory figures are determined using a variable

Exhibit 18–7B	Comparison of Absorption and Variable Costing

Period 2 Income Statement

Sales (140 × $100)		$14,000		$14,000
Cost of goods sold				
Beginning inventory (from period one)	2,800		1,200	
+ Cost of goods produced (for 100 units, same as period 1)	7,000		3,000	
= Cost of goods available for sale	9,800		4,200	
− Ending inventory	0		0	
= Cost of goods sold		9,800		4,200
Less: Variable selling and administrative		N/A		700
Gross margin		**$4,200**		
Contribution margin				**$9,100**
Less: Other costs				
Less: Fixed manufacturing costs	N/A		4,000	
Less: Selling and administrative costs				
Variable	700		N/A	
Fixed	1,200		1,200	
Total other costs		1,900		5,200
Net income		$2,300		$3,900

Recap

Difference in net income = $3,900 − $2,300 = $1,600

Difference in beginning inventory = $2,800 − $1,200 = $1,600

manufacturing cost of $30 per unit. To calculate the total contribution margin, the variable selling and administrative costs of $5 per unit sold are deducted along with the $30 variable cost of sales per unit. The result is a total contribution margin of $3,900 in period 1 and $9,100 in period 2. In variable costing, all fixed costs (both manufacturing fixed cost of $4,000 and selling and administration fixed costs of $1,200) are deducted from the contribution margin, to get a $1,300 loss in period 1 and $3,900 profit in period 2.

The difference in net income in period 1 for absorption and variable costing is $1,600 ($300 profit compared to a $1,300 loss), which is exactly the amount of fixed cost put into the increase in inventory under absorption costing ($1,600 = 40 units × $40 per unit fixed cost). Note that the amount of ending inventory in period 1 differs by $1,600 ($2,800 for absorption cost versus $1,200 for variable costing). This amount is also the difference in net income for variable and absorption costing for both periods 1 and 2, when inventory decreases by 40 units. The useful guide then is that *absorption costing net income exceeds variable costing net income (by the amount of fixed cost in the inventory change) when inventory increases, and variable costing net income is higher than absorption costing net income when inventory decreases.*

The important point is that variable costing is not affected by the change in inventory because all fixed costs are deducted from income in the period in which they occur; fixed costs are not included in inventory so that inventory changes do not affect net income. For this reason, variable costing net income can be considered a more reliable measure and is preferable for use in strategic performance measurement. When absorption costing is used (as is required for financial reporting), the management accountant must use special caution in interpreting the amount of net income and attempt to determine what portion of profit, if any, might be due to inventory changes. This is especially important if net income is used as a basis for performance evaluation, as it is in profit SBUs.

STRATEGIC PERFORMANCE MEASUREMENT AND THE BALANCED SCORECARD

LEARNING OBJECTIVE 5▶

Explain the role of the balanced scorecard in strategic performance measurement.

Cost, revenue, and profit SBUs are widely used methods to achieve strategic performance measurement. A common characteristic of these SBUs in practice is that they use little or no nonfinancial information. However, a complete strategic performance evaluation necessarily attends to all critical success factors of the business, including many nonfinancial factors. A useful approach for a complete strategic performance evaluation is to include both financial and nonfinancial factors for the SBU using the balanced scorecard. The balanced scorecard measures the SBU's performance in four key perspectives: (1) customer satisfaction, (2) financial performance, (3) internal business processes, and (4) learning and innovation. Cost, revenue, and profit SBUs focus on the financial dimension. The main concept of the balanced scorecard is that no single measure can properly evaluate the SBU's progress to strategic success. Rather, multiple measures typically grouped in the four key perspectives provide the desired comprehensive evaluation of the SBU's performance. Moreover, by attending directly to the firm's critical success factors, the balanced scorecard effectively links the performance measurement/evaluation process to the firm's strategy.[18]

A recent survey of 203 firms indicated that customer perspective measures of the balanced scorecard are highly valued by 85 percent of the executives of these firms; 82 percent see the financial measures as highly valuable. Operations perspective measures are highly valued by 79 percent, and employee satisfaction/learning and innovation perspective measures are highly valued by more than 50 percent.[19] These results are strong support for the importance of the strategic approach of the balanced scorecard.

Unfortunately, not all balanced scorecards used by firms are utilized in evaluating and rewarding managers. A recent survey of 60 firms that use the balanced scorecard shows that about 50 percent of them employed the scorecard in evaluating managers, and of those, about 33 percent used it in determining compensation.[20] The reason that scorecards are utilized less often in performance evaluation might be that they are more difficult to compare *across* SBUs. Each SBU has its own scorecard; thus, the scorecard evaluation is more likely based on progress relative to the prior year or to a budget than on the more common, compare-across-all-managers approach.[21] Other implementation issues related to the balanced scorecard for performance evaluation include these:

- Many large firms have installed extensive computer systems called *enterprise resource planning* systems (ERPs). They provide an information system base that stores the detailed information for the balanced scorecard. Firms without an ERP might have difficulty developing and maintaining the data needed for the scorecard. IBM, Oracle, and other vendors offer ERPs; for more information see www.erpsupersite.com.

---

[18] The balanced scorecard concept was developed by Robert S. Kaplan and David P. Norton in a series of articles and books. A representative sample of the most recent publications include *The Strategy-Focused Organization* (Boston: Harvard Business School Press, 2001); "Why Does Business Need a Balanced Scorecard?" *Journal of Cost Management*, May–June 1997, pp. 5–10; "Linking the Balanced Scorecard to Strategy," *California Management Review*, Fall 1996; "Using the Balanced Scorecard as a Strategic Management System," *Harvard Business Review*, January–February 1996, pp. 75–85. The balanced scorecard is a concept similar to the *tableau de bord*, a performance measurement system used in France for several years. The two systems are compared in Marc J. Epstein and Jean-Francois Manzoni, "The Balanced Scorecard and Tableau de Bord: Translating Strategy into Action," *Management Accounting*, August 1997, pp. 28–36.

[19] Christopher D. Ittner and David F. Larcker, "Innovations in Performance Measurement: Trends and Research Implications," *Journal of Management Accounting Research*, 1998, p. 207, citing study by J. H. Lingle and W. A. Schiemann, "From Balanced Scorecard to Strategic Gauges: Is Measurement Worth It?" *Management Review*, March 1996, pp. 56–61.

[20] Ittner and Larcker, "Innovation in Performance Measurement," p. 222.

[21] Note, however, that a recent survey reported that of 214 firms surveyed, 88 percent are considering linking the balanced scorecard to compensation. See Kaplan and Norton, *The Strategy-Focused Organization*, p. 253.

- In contrast to financial data that are subject to financial audit and control systems, much of the nonfinancial information used in the scorecard is not subject to control or audit. Thus, the reliability and accuracy of some of the nonfinancial data could be questionable.

- The performance reviews of managers occur at a regular period—usually every quarter or every year—which fits well with the typical firm's preparation of financial information monthly, quarterly, and annually. In contrast, the nonfinancial information is often prepared on a weekly or daily basis for effective use in operations and decision making. This variance in preparation cycles can complicate the nature and timing of reviews.

- Typically, all financial data used by the cost or profit SBUs are developed internally, using well-developed information systems. In contrast, some of the most valuable nonfinancial information, such as customer surveys, are developed external to the firm, which creates additional issues regarding the timeliness and the reliability of this nonfinancial information.

Whether the balanced scorecard is used for performance evaluation, it is a powerful method to guide managers in achieving the firm's strategic goals and in evaluating its progress to these goals. To contribute to these objectives, Kaplan and Norton have developed the concept of the **strategy map,** which uses the balanced scorecard to describe the firm's strategy in detail by using cause-and-effect diagrams. A simple strategy map is illustrated in Exhibit 18–8. The strategy map links the four scorecard perspectives, showing how measurable goals within each perspective contribute to performance at the next perspective. The map begins with the learning and innovation perspective, which includes the goals—staff competencies, strategy awareness, and technology infrastructure—that are necessary for learning and innovation to take place. The goals contribute directly to the internal business process (operations) perspective, in which the staff apply their competencies and strategic awareness and utilize the technology infrastructure. In a similar way, the goals in the operations perspective support the goals of the customer perspective. The goals within the customer perspective support the financial perspective. As each firm has a different balanced scorecard, so too it has a

A **strategy map** uses the balanced scorecard to describe the firm's strategy in detail by using cause-and-effect diagrams.

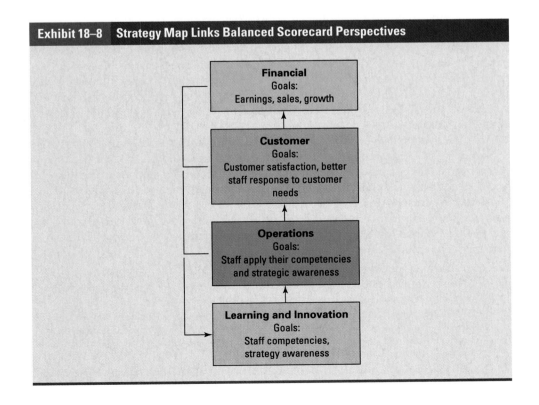

| **Exhibit 18–8** Strategy Map Links Balanced Scorecard Perspectives |

877

Research and Development: Strategically Critical but Difficult to Evaluate

Effective use of research and development (R&D) is an important part of any firm's competitive strategy. Some firms take an "incrementalist" approach to R&D, continually striving to add value to their products and services. Other firms take the opposite approach by looking specifically for "breakthrough" results from R&D. The breakthrough results are those that fundamentally change the nature of the products, the services, and the competition in the industry. An example of a breakthrough result is General Electric's digital X-ray technology, first sold in 1996, which uses digital imaging to replace the conventional film-based technology. An example of a breakthrough approach is Xerox, whose famed Palo Alto Research Facility has been recognized for its significant research accomplishments.

Many firms employ both approaches. Some argue that a firm needs to use both R&D strategies: the incrementalist approach that focuses on continually improving existing products and the breakthrough approach that develops fundamental changes. The incrementalist R&D projects help to keep the current product lines competitive while the breakthrough projects hold the promise of a successful future.

Management of any R&D project is difficult, but breakthrough projects are especially difficult to evaluate because of the extensive uncertainty surrounding them. It is clear, however, that breakthrough projects must be evaluated differently than the incrementalist projects. They require more

patience, and the pressure of short-term cost reports is inappropriate. Nor can these projects be evaluated by comparing the amount spent on research (say, relative to total sales) to that of other firms in the industry. Emphasis must be on the researchers' skills, the funding levels, and other factors that can aid the progress of the research. For example, academic research at Rensselaer Polytechnic Institute shows that the most successful R&D researchers have wide-ranging networks in the research community. The skills of the researchers, the funding level, and the other factors can be evaluated in a balanced scorecard approach.

Recent research involving 75 industrial design managers reported that the firms surveyed use various financial and nonfinancial measures to evaluate new product development, although managers in these firms reported that relatively few of these measures reflect the key aspects of their firms' strategies. Clearly, R&D activities are difficult to evaluate, although they are critical to the strategies of many firms.

Sources: Based on Chris Sandlund, "Paradise Lost?" *Business2.com,* April 3, 2001, pp. 50–53; Julie Hertenstein and Marjorie B. Platt, "Performance Measures and Management Control in New Product Development," *Accounting Horizons,* September 2000, pp. 303–23; Peter Coy, "Research Labs Get Real: It's about Time," *Business Week,* November 6, 2000, p. 51; "R&D by the Numbers," *Business Week,* December 6, 1999, p. 86; and "Getting to Eureka!" *Business Week,* November 10, 1997.

different strategy map. The strategy map is a detailed view of how the firm achieves its strategic goals, showing the interactions between the scorecard's perspectives.[22]

The strategy map also reinforces the idea that financial performance and shareholder value are the ultimate goals for most applications of the balanced scorecard. The other perspectives contribute directly to the ultimate financial goals. Recent research shows that the nonfinancial measures in the other perspectives are in fact good predictors of financial performance.[23] The strategy map also emphasizes the important point that, by describing the firm's strategy in some detail, the balanced scorecard can also be used as a *means for developing strategy* and evaluating progress to achieving strategy.

The use of the balanced scorecard for developing strategy and evaluating progress in achieving it is illustrated by information regarding a food ingredients company taken from a recent study.[24] The firm was actively involved in implementing the balanced scorecard at the time of the study, and management agreed to discuss its strategic goals, the relative importance of these goals (ranked by scorecard perspective), and the key performance measures for evaluating progress toward these goals (see Exhibit 18–9). The firm's perspectives are shown in order of importance from top to bottom in the exhibit.

---

[22] Kaplan and Norton illustrate the strategy maps for several firms, including Mobil and the city of Charlotte, N.C. Kaplan and Norton, *The Strategy-Focused Organization,* pp. 42–43, 139.

[23] See for example, Rajiv D. Banker, Gordon Potter, and Dhinu Srinivasan, "An Empirical Investigation of an Incentive Plan that Includes Nonfinancial Measures," *The Accounting Review,* January 2000, pp. 65–92; and Christopher D. Ittner and David F. Larcker, "Are Nonfinancial Measures Leading Indicators of Financial Performance?" *Journal of Accounting Research,* 1998, pp. 1–35.

[24] This example is adapted from Chee W. Chow, Kamal M. Haddad, and James E. Williamson, "Applying the Balanced Scorecard to Small Companies," *Management Accounting,* August 1997, pp. 21–27.

| **Exhibit 18–9** | **Strategic Goals and Scorecard Measures for a Food Ingredients Company** |

Goals	Measures
Financial Perspective	
Capture an increasing share of market growth.	Company growth versus industry growth
Secure the base business while remaining the preferred supplier to our customers.	Volume trend by line of business; revenue trend line of business; gross margin
Expand aggressively in global markets.	Ratio of North American sales to international sales
Commercialize a continuous stream of profitable new ingredients and services.	Percent of sales from products launched within five years; gross profit from new products
Customer Perspective	
Become the lowest-cost supplier.	Total cost of using our products and services relative to the total cost of using competitive products and services
Tailor products and services to meet local needs.	Cross-sell ratio
Expand those products and services that meet customer's needs better than competitors do.	Percentage of products in R&D pipeline being test-marketed by our customers (percentage of pipeline value)
Increase customer satisfaction.	Customer surveys
Internal Perspective	
Maintain the lowest cost base in the industry.	Our total costs relative to number one competitor; inventory turns; plant utilization
Maintain consistently predictable production processes.	First-pass success rate
Continue to improve distribution efficiency.	Percentage of perfect orders
Build capability to screen and identify profitable products and services.	Change in pipeline economic value
Integrate acquisitions and alliances efficiently.	Revenues per salary dollar
Learning and Growth Perspective	
Link the overall strategy to the reward and recognition system.	Net income per dollar of variable pay
Foster a culture that supports innovation and growth.	Annual preparedness assessment; quarterly reports

We can infer the firm's strategy from reviewing Exhibit 18–9. The firm puts the financial perspective first and emphasizes market growth. This makes sense for a company in a commodity-type industry (food ingredients) where profit margins are small and sales volume is important. Cost control is also important for profitability, as noted in the strategic goals within both the customer and internal perspectives. In effect, the exhibit shows the outline from which a strategy map can be developed. Goals in the learning and growth perspective support the goals in the internal perspective, which in turn support the goals in the customer and financial perspective, as shown by the arrows in Exhibit 18–9.

MANAGEMENT CONTROL IN SERVICE FIRMS AND NOT-FOR-PROFIT ORGANIZATIONS

◄**LEARNING OBJECTIVE 6**

Explain the role of strategic performance measurement in service firms and not-for-profit organizations.

Management control in service firms and not-for-profit organizations is commonly implemented in the form of a cost SBU or a profit SBU. As do manufacturing and retail firms, these organizations choose a cost SBU when the manager's critical mission is to control costs; a profit SBU is preferred when the department manager must

Use of the Balanced Scorecard by Service Firms and Governmental Organizations

The **Mayo Clinic** in Rochester, Minnesota, one of the most prestigious health care providers in the world, recently needed to measure performance in areas beyond the traditional financial and clinical productivity indicators. Various Mayo administrative and operating groups developed a balanced scorecard with six perspectives:

1. Customer satisfaction: internal and external customers.
2. Internal business processes: efficiency of operations.
3. Quality of service.
4. Continuous improvement efforts.
5. Public responsibility and social commitment.
6. Financial performance.

In developing the scorecard, the group learned a number of important lessons. First, its information systems infrastructure had to be improved to deal with the increased expectations developed from the balanced scorecard. Second, the balanced scorecard is really a process rather than a product. It requires continual commitment, critical thought, and an ongoing process of renewal.

Reeling from problems related to hotel overbuilding and the recession in the hospitality industry in the early 1990s, **Hilton Hotels** looked for ways to reevaluate its strategy and

identify underperforming hotels. Hotel management chose the balanced scorecard as a way to integrate all aspects of the business and focus managers on four value drivers, or scorecard perspectives, for the hotel chain:

1. Brand management
2. Revenue maximization
3. Operational effectiveness
4. Customer loyalty

In adopting the balanced scorecard, the **Charlotte, North Carolina**, City Council chose five key perspectives: community safety, transportation, economic development, neighborhoods, and restructuring government.

Sources: Jonathan W. Curtright, Steven C. Stolp-Smith, and Eric S. Edell, "Strategic Performance Management: Development of a Performance Measurement System at the Mayo Clinic," *Journal of Healthcare Management,* January–February 2000, pp. 58–68; Dieter Huckestein and Robert Duboff, "Hilton Hotels," *Cornell Hotel and Restaurant Administration Quarterly,* August 1999, pp. 28–38; Nancy Elliott and Lisa Schumacher, "Charlotte Adopts the Balanced Scorecard," *The American City & County,* October 1998, p. 32; Robert S. Kaplan and David P. Norton, *The Strategy-Focused Organization* (Boston: Harvard Business School Press, 2001).

Exhibit 18–10	Performance Report for the Consumer Loan Department August 31, 2001

Variable costs	
Direct labor	$23,446
Supplies	3,836
Controllable fixed costs	
Supervision salaries	15,339
Advertising	6,500
Fees and services	4,226
Other	766
Noncontrollable fixed costs	
Facilities	650
Data processing	2,200
Other	899
Total costs	$57,862
Operating performance	
Number of accounts at end of month	1,334
Number of new accounts	54
Number of closed accounts	22
Number of transactions processed	1,994
Number of inquiries processed	334

manage both costs and revenues or, alternatively (in a not-for-profit), manage costs without exceeding budgeted revenues.

The most common type of SBU in service firms and not-for-profit organizations is the cost SBU. For example, the performance of a bank's consumer loan department often is monitored as a cost SBU, as illustrated in Exhibit 18–10. Note that the structure of the performance report is much like that of the profit SBU analysis in Exhibit 18–6. The difference is that the focus in Exhibit 18–10 is on costs, which are separated into variable costs such as labor and supplies, controllable fixed costs such as supervision salaries, and noncontrollable fixed costs such as data processing and facilities management. In addition, Exhibit 18–10 includes information regarding certain operating measures critical to the department's success: the number of new accounts, number of closed accounts, number of transactions processed, and number of inquiries handled. This information is used to evaluate department's performance over time and perhaps to compare its performance to that of related departments such as the mortgage loan department. Note that the report does not include the cost of funds provided for the loans since it is assumed that the department manager cannot control either the supply or the cost of those funds.

SUMMARY

The principal focus of management control systems is strategic performance measurement. The goal of top management in using strategic performance measurement is to *motivate the managers* to provide a high level of effort, to *guide them to make decisions that are congruent with the goals of top management*, and to provide a basis for determining *fair compensation* for the managers.

A large number of management control systems are used in practice, including both formal and informal systems and individual or team-based systems. The chapter focuses on one type of formal control system at the individual level, the strategic performance measurement system.

Strategic performance measurement systems are implemented in four different forms, depending on the nature of the manager's responsibilities: the revenue SBU, cost SBU, profit SBU, and investment SBU.

The four types of SBUs are employed in manufacturing firms as well as service firms and not-for-profit organizations. Common cost SBUs in manufacturing firms are production and production-support departments. Cost SBUs often are evaluated as either engineered-cost SBUs or discretionary-cost SBUs. Discretionary-cost SBUs focus on planning desired cost levels; the engineered-cost SBUs focus on evaluation of achieved cost levels.

The marketing department can be either a cost SBU or a revenue SBU, or both. As a revenue SBU, the marketing department has goals for sales growth, as a cost SBU, there are goals for managing order-getting and order-filling costs.

The profit SBU is used when coordination between the marketing and production areas is needed, for example, in handling special orders or rush orders. Evaluation on profit provides the incentive for the departments to work together. Profit SBUs are also used to set a desirable competitive tone. All departments have the profit incentive to compete with other providers of the product or service, inside or outside the firm. The contribution margin income statement is an effective method for evaluating profit SBUs because it identifies each profit SBU's direct costs.

The contribution income statement is sometimes called the *variable costing* statement. It has the benefit of not being affected by changes in finished goods inventory. In contrast, the conventional income statement based on absorption costing is affected by inventory changes.

A key issue in the effective use of strategic performance measurement systems is the integration of strategic considerations into the evaluation. This requires an identification of the firm's critical success factors, and use of appropriate measurement and reporting of these factors, commonly in the form of a balanced scorecard. In many cases, a substantial portion of these factors is nonfinancial, including operating and economic data from sources external to the firm.

The different types of strategic performance measurement are used in service firms, not-for-profit organizations, and governmental units.

KEY TERMS

Budget slack 866

Contribution by SBU (CSBU) 873

Contribution income statement 872

Controllable fixed costs 873

Controllable margin 873

Cost SBU 863

Discretionary-cost method 867

Dual allocation 870

Employment contract 858

Engineered-cost method 867

Investment SBU 864

Management control 856

Noncontrollable fixed costs 873

Operational control 856

Order-filling costs 871

Order-getting costs 871

Performance evaluation 856

Principal-agent model 858

Profit SBU 863

Revenue drivers 870

Revenue SBU 863

Strategic business unit (SBU) 857

Strategic performance measurement 862

Strategy map 877

COMMENTS ON COST MANAGEMENT IN ACTION

Outsourcing Information Technology

The motivation for outsourcing information technology (IT) is twofold. First, it can help to dramatically reduce the firm's overall cost of IT. Second, and perhaps most important, it helps the firm to keep up with advancing technology by partnering with an application service provider or consulting firm with a high level of expertise.

How does it make the firm more competitive? Consultants and analysts disagree on this point. Some argue that IT is a strategic resource in most industries and should be supported within the firm to achieve the desired integration of IT and business strategy. They point to firms such as Wal-Mart that have used IT to improve its strategic goal of low cost and low price. Similarly, ADP, Inc., and Levi Strauss have used IT to improve their competitive position through enhancements in customer service.

Others argue that the question is not *whether* to outsource but *which* of the IT activities to choose to outsource. For example, Xerox has an outsourcing arrangement with Electronic Data Systems (EDS) to handle its operational IT tasks while it maintains a partnership with the software developer Oracle to develop Xerox's strategic goals for IT.

N. Venkatraman, a leading author on IT outsourcing, argues that IT should be viewed as a strategic SBU in either a cost, profit, investment, or service form (for Venkatraman, a "service" SBU puts customer service as top priority). Venkatraman proposes a simple formula for choosing the type of SBU based on two factors: (1) the degree to which the firm needs either operational efficiency or business capability from IT and (2) the degree of risk the firm is willing to bear. A low-risk firm that requires operational efficiency should choose the cost SBU form; a low-risk firm that requires business capability should use a service SBU. In contrast, a firm willing to accept risk and requiring business capability should choose an investment SBU because it will provide the desired long-term perspective for IT.

Sources: Based on David J. Castellani, "ASPs: Changing Information Technology Delivery," *Strategic Finance*, March 2000, pp. 34–37; "The Promised Land for Outsourcing," *Business Week*, July 6, 1998, p. 39; Lawrence Loh and N. Venkatraman, "Diffusion of Information Technology Outsourcing: Influence Sources and the Kodak Effect," *Information Systems Research* 3, No. 4 (1992), pp. 334–58; N. Venkatraman, "Beyond Outsourcing: Managing IT Resources as a Value Center," *Sloan Management Review*, Spring 1997, pp. 51–64; and Tom Groenfeldt, "Who's in the Driver's Seat?" *The Journal of Business Strategy*, January–February 1997, pp. 36–41.

SELF-STUDY PROBLEM

(For solution, please turn to the end of the chapter.)

Discretionary-Cost and Engineered-Cost Methods

C. B. (Chuck) Davis is the manager of the claims processing department for Liberty Life Insurance Co. He has 12 clerks working for him to process approximately 900 claims per month. Each clerk earns a monthly salary of $2,400, including benefits. The number of claims varies somewhat, and, in recent years, it has been as low as 810 and as high as 1,020 per month. Chuck has argued with Liberty officials that his 12 clerks are not enough to handle 1,000 or more claims; he knows from a recent study of his department that it takes a well-trained clerk an average of 121 minutes to process a claim (processing time also varies widely, from as little as a few minutes to as much as several hours, depending on the claim's complexity). While Liberty management agrees that 12 clerks are not sufficient for a month with 1,020 claims, it notes that they are far too many when only 810 claims need to be processed. Management concludes, therefore, that 12 clerks are about right. Assume that each clerk works an eight-hour day except for 40 minutes of break time and that each month has an average of 22 working days. In the most recent month, January, the department processed 915 claims.

Required

1. What type of SBU does Liberty management appear to consider the claims processing department?

2. Assuming that Liberty uses the discretionary-cost method to implement cost SBUs, what is the budgeted cost in the claims department for January?

3. Assuming that Liberty uses the engineered-cost method to implement cost SBUs, what is the budgeted cost in the claims department for January?

4. If you were Chuck Davis, what would you use as a more effective argument to top management in requesting additional clerks?

QUESTIONS

18–1 What is the difference between management control, performance evaluation, and operational control?

18–2 What is strategic performance measurement, and why is it important for effective management?

18–3 Does an effective performance evaluation focus on individual or team performance?

18–4 Explain the difference between informal and formal control systems. What type of control system is strategic performance measurement?

18–5 Name three types of organizational design and explain how they differ.

18–6 What are four types of SBUs, and what are the goals of each?

18–7 Since absorption costing is accepted for financial reporting purposes and variable costing is not, why should we be concerned about the difference between them? What is the difference, and why is it important?

18–8 What are some important behavioral and implementation issues in strategic performance measurement? How does the management accountant deal with these issues?

18–9 What is the role of cost allocation in strategic performance measurement?

18–10 Can strategic performance measurement be used for service firms and not-for-profit organizations? How?

18–11 In what situations is a cost SBU most appropriate? A profit SBU? A revenue SBU?

18–12 How do centralized and decentralized firms differ? What are the advantages of each?

18–13 Can the marketing department be both a revenue SBU and a cost SBU? Explain.

EXERCISES

18–14 **DEPARTMENTAL COST ALLOCATION IN PROFIT SBUs** Elvis Wilbur owns two adjoining restaurants, the Beef Barn and the Fish Bowl. Each restaurant is treated as a profit SBU for performance evaluation. Although the restaurants have separate kitchens, they share a central baking facility. The principal costs of the baking area include depreciation and maintenance on the equipment, materials, supplies, and labor.

Required

1. Elvis allocates the monthly costs of the baking facility to the two restaurants based on the number of tables served in each restaurant during the month. In April the costs were $24,000, of which $12,000 is fixed cost. The Beef Barn and the Fish Bowl each served 3,000 tables. How much of the joint cost should be allocated to each restaurant?

2. In May fixed and unit variable costs remained the same, but the Beef Barn served 2,000 tables and the Fish Bowl served 3,000. How much should be allocated to each restaurant? Explain your reasoning.

Service

18–15 **ALLOCATION OF MARKETING AND ADMINISTRATIVE COSTS; PROFIT SBUs** Snodgrass Academy allocates marketing and administrative costs to its three schools based on total annual tuition revenue for the schools. In 2001 the allocations (000s omitted) were as follows:

	Lower School	Middle School	Upper School	Total
Tuition revenue	$700	$600	$900	$2,200
Marketing and administration	255	218	327	$ 800

In 2002, the middle and upper schools experienced no change in revenues, but the lower school's tuition revenue increased to $1.5 million. Marketing and administrative costs rose to $960,000.

Required

1. Using revenue as an allocation base, how should the costs be allocated for 2002?

2. What are the shortcomings of this allocation formula?

Service

18–16 **ALLOCATION OF ADMINISTRATIVE COSTS** Kuldigs Rental Management Services manages four local apartment complexes of varying sizes and degrees of luxury. Kuldigs' president has observed that the luxurious apartments tend to require more of her staff's time than the simpler units. Kuldigs incurs monthly operating expenses of $15,000, and its president desires a profit of 7 percent, for a total monthly billing of $16,050.

	Units	Average Rent per Unit
Pinnacle Point	100	$720
Whispering Woods	355	540
Hollow Rock	300	425
College Villa	550	340

Required How should the $16,050 be allocated to the four apartment complexes? Explain your answer.

18–17 ALLOCATION OF COMMON COSTS Seven businesses rent offices and suites of various sizes in a 3,500-square-foot office building owned by Bill Luckus. He allocates the utility costs among the tenants according to the square footage rented. Tenants now are balking at this arrangement because last week Dottie's Drapes, a tenant that leases 400 square feet, installed a massive new lighting system and two window-unit air conditioners. The other tenants claim they should not bear the cost of Dottie's use of electricity.

Required How should Bill respond to the tenants' complaints?

18–18 RESPONSIBILITY FOR INEFFICIENCY; ETHICS General Hospital leases its diagnostic equipment from Normed Leasing, which is also responsible for maintaining the equipment. Recently the hospital's MRI machine needed repair and physicians were required to order expensive nonemergency laboratory tests for their patients to diagnose conditions that could have been diagnosed more easily (and less expensively) using the MRI machine. Rather than bill its patients for the entire costs of these tests, the hospital billed the patients for the cost of an MRI and billed the difference to Normed. Normed disputes the charge, claiming that the physicians should have postponed diagnosis of the patients' conditions until the MRI machine could be repaired.

 *Ethics*

Required What issues should be addressed to determine how the charge should be handled properly? How can this situation be prevented? If appropriate, include ethical issues in your response.

18–19 ASSIGNING RESPONSIBILITY Kristen Langdon, the sales manager at a large bicycle manufacturer, has secured an order from a major department store that is due to ship on November 1. She is eager to please the department store in the hope of getting more future business. She asks Bryan Collins, the company's purchasing agent, to procure all necessary parts in time for production to begin on October 10. Bryan orders the parts from reputable suppliers, and most of them arrive by October 7. George Watkins, the production manager, begins production as scheduled on October 10, although the gears that Bryan ordered were delayed because of quality control problems at the manufacturer. Bryan assures George that the gear shipment will arrive before October 16 when those parts are scheduled to be attached to the bicycles. The shipment finally arrives on October 18 after production has been delayed for two days.

Required Which department should bear the responsibility for the two days' downtime? How can similar problems be avoided in the future?

18–20 PROFIT SBUs: ABSORPTION AND VARIABLE COSTING Manzoni Inc. planned and manufactured 300,000 units of its single product in 2001, its first year of operations. Variable manufacturing costs were $40 per unit of production. Planned and fixed manufacturing costs were $900,000. Marketing and administrative costs (all fixed) were $500,000 in 2001. Manzoni sold 150,000 units of products in 2001 at $50 per unit.

Required

1. Determine Manzoni Inc.'s operating income using absorption costing.
2. Determine Manzoni Inc.'s operating income using variable costing.
3. Explain the difference between the operating incomes in requirements 1 and 2.

18–21 **CENTRALIZATION VERSUS DECENTRALIZATION; HEALTH CARE** Doctors Health Care System has integrated health networks in three different regions: northern California, southern Florida, and Oklahoma. These three markets have vast regional differences. Because of the increasing penetration of the U.S. health care market by managed care companies, Doctors Health Care System must create a system that offers continuity of care across the continuum for a set price in order to remain competitive. Its board of directors set the system's goal as being a leader in developing and maintaining integrated health networks that improve the health status of their communities.

Required To meet this goal in the three regions, should the health system's management structure be decentralized or centralized? What are the advantages and disadvantages of each option?

PROBLEMS

Service

18–22 **ALLOCATION OF CENTRAL COSTS; PROFIT SBUs** Whispering Glen Resorts, Inc., operates four resort hotels in the heavily wooded areas of eastern Texas. The resorts are named after the predominant trees at the resort: Oak Glen, Pine Glen, Magnolia, and Pecan Arbor. Whispering Glen allocates its central office costs to each of its four hotels according to the annual revenue it generated. For the current year, these costs (000s omitted) were as follows:

Front office personnel	$ 6,000
Administrative and executive salaries	4,000
Interest on resort purchase	2,000
Advertising	300
Housekeeping	100
Depreciation on reservations computer	80
Room maintenance	80
Carpet-cleaning contract	50
Contract to repaint rooms	40
	$12,650

These are pertinent data relating to the four hotels:

	Pine Glen	Pecan Arbor	Oak Glen	Magnolia	Total
Revenue (000s)	$ 3,000	$ 7,000	$ 9,000	$ 5,000	$ 24,000
Square feet	52,500	75,000	32,500	75,000	235,000
Rooms	150	200	100	250	700
Assets (000s)	$65,000	$110,000	$88,000	$45,000	$308,000

Required

1. Based on annual revenue, how many of the central office costs are allocated to each hotel? What are the shortcomings of this allocation method?

2. Suppose that the current method were replaced with a system of four separate cost pools with costs collected in the four pools allocated on the basis of revenues, assets invested in each hotel, square footage, and number of rooms, respectively. Which costs should be collected in each of the four pools?

3. Using the cost pool system, how much of the central office costs would be allocated to each hotel? Is this system preferable to the single-allocation base system used in requirement 1? Why or why not?

18–23   RESPONSIBILITY FOR WAGE DIFFERENTIAL   Bloomfield University has a staff of five computer repair specialists. During the summer months, the school's computers are used infrequently and thus require very little of the specialists' time. To fully use these employees during the summer, the university reassigns them to the maintenance department, where they assist in the annual cleaning of the classrooms. Because of their relatively high skill level, these employees are paid at a rate of $18 per hour while the maintenance employees, with whom they work in the summer, are paid $11 an hour.

Required   What department should bear the costs of the $7 an hour wage differential for the computer repair workers?

18–24   PROFIT SBUs: COMPARISON OF VARIABLE AND ABSORPTION COSTING   Marshall Company manufactures hair brushes that sell at wholesale for $2 per unit. The company had no beginning inventory in 2001. These data summarize the 2001 and 2002 operations:

	2001	2002
Sales	1,800 units	2,200 units
Production:	2,000 units	2,000 units
Production cost		
Factory—variable (per unit)	$0.60	$0.60
—fixed	$1,000	$1,000
Marketing—variable	$0.50	$0.50
Administrative—fixed	$500	$500

Required   Prepare the following, using a spreadsheet system.

1. An income statement for each year based on absorption costing.

2. An income statement for each year based on variable costing.

3. A reconciliation and explanation of the differences in the operating income resulting from using the absorption costing method and variable costing method.

18–25   PROFIT SBUs: COMPARISON OF VARIABLE AND ABSORPTION COSTING (UNDER- AND OVERAPPLIED OVERHEAD; CHAPTER 12)   Jason Reynolds, Inc. manufactures a specialized surgical instrument called the TDR-11. The firm has grown rapidly in recent years because of the product's low price and high quality. However, sales have declined this year due primarily to increased competition and a decrease in the surgical procedures for which the TDR-11 is used. The firm is concerned about the decline in sales, especially the decline in operating income over the past year. The firm has hired a consultant to analyze the firm's profitability. The consultant provided the following information:

	2001	2002
Sales (units)	2,300	1,900
Production	2,200	1,700
Budgeted production and sales	2,000	2,000
Beginning inventory	850	750
Data per unit (all variable)		
Price	$1,995	$1,885
Direct materials	440	440
Direct labor	255	255
Selling costs	125	125
Period cost (all fixed)		
Manufacturing overhead	$480,000	$480,000
Selling and administrative	160,000	160,000

Required

1. Using the absorption cost method, which Reynold's accountant used to prepare the annual financial statements, prepare the income statements for 2001 and 2002.

2. Using variable costing, prepare an income statement for each period, and explain the difference in net income from that obtained in requirement 1.

3. Write a brief memo to the firm to explain the difference in income between variable costing and absorption costing.

18–26 BALANCED SCORECARD

Required Complete problem 2–22.

18–27 BALANCED SCORECARD

Required Complete problem 2–25.

18–28 BALANCED SCORECARD

Required Complete problem 2–28.

18–29 BALANCED SCORECARD

Required Complete problem 2–37.

18–30 CONTRIBUTION INCOME STATEMENT FOR PROFIT SBUs Majestic Stores, Inc., is an upscale clothing store in New York City and London. Each store has two main departments, Men's Apparel and Women's Apparel. Marie Phelps, Majestic's CFO, wants to use strategic performance measurement to better understand the company's financial results. She has decided to use the profit SBU method to measure performance and has gathered the following information about the two stores and the two departments of the New York City store:

Total net sales	$1,850,000
Fixed costs	
Partly traceable and controllable	120,000
Partly traceable but noncontrollable	100,000
Nontraceable costs	35,000
Total net sales (percent)	
London Store	60%
New York—Men's Apparel	50
New York—Women's Apparel	50
Cost of goods sold—variable (percent of sales)	
London	55%
New York—Men's Apparel	60
New York—Women's Apparel	40
Variable operating costs (percent of sales)	
London	34%
New York—Men's Apparel	24
New York—Women's Apparel	30
Fixed controllable costs—partly traceable (percent of total)	
London	40%
New York total	40
Men's Apparel	45
Women's Apparel	40
Could not be traced	15
Could not be traced to New York or London	20
Fixed noncontrollable costs—partly traceable (percent of total)	
London	50%
New York total	40
Men's Apparel	30
Women's Apparel	10
Could not be traced to either department	60
Could not be traced to London or New York	10

Required   Using this information and a spreadsheet system, prepare a contribution income statement for Majestic, showing contribution for both stores and for both departments of the New York store.

18–31 **CONTRIBUTION MARGIN INCOME STATEMENT FOR PROFIT SBUs; STRATEGY**
Strategy

Music Teachers, Inc., is an educational association for music teachers that had 20,000 members during 2001. The association operates from a central headquarters but has local membership chapters throughout the United States. The local chapters hold monthly meetings to discuss recent developments on topics of interest to members. The association's monthly journal, *Teachers' Forum*, has features about recent developments in the field. The association publishes books and reports and sponsors professional courses that qualify participants for continuing professional education credits. The association's statement of revenue and expense (000s omitted) for the current year follows:

Revenue	$3,275
Expense	
Salaries	$ 920
Personnel costs	230
Occupancy costs	280
Reimbursement to local chapters	600
Other membership services	500
Printing and paper	320
Postage and shipping	176
Instructors' fees	80
General and administrative	38
Total expenses	$3,144
Excess of revenues over expenses	$ 131

The organization's board of directors has requested that a statement of operations be prepared showing the contribution of each profit SBU (i.e., membership, magazine subscriptions, books and reports, continuing education). Mike Doyle was assigned this responsibility and had gathered these data prior to statement preparation:

- Annual membership dues are $100, of which $20 covers a one-year subscription to the association's journal. Other benefits include membership in the association and chapter affiliation. The portion of the dues covering the magazine subscription ($20) should be assigned to the magazine subscriptions profit SBU.

- One-year subscriptions to *Teachers' Forum* are sold to nonmembers and libraries at $30 each. A total of 2,500 of these subscriptions were sold this year. In addition to subscriptions, the magazine generated $100,000 in advertising revenue. The costs for printing and paper and for postage and shipping per magazine subscription were $7 and $4, respectively.

- The books and reports department sold a total of 28,000 technical reports and professional texts at an average unit selling price of $25. Average costs per publication were as follows.

Printing and paper	$4
Postage and shipping	2

- The association offers a variety of continuing education courses to both members and nonmembers. The one-day courses cost $75 each and were attended by 2,400 students in 2001. A total of 1,760 students took two-day courses at a cost of $125 for each course. Outside instructors were paid to teach some courses.

- Salary and occupancy data are

	Salaries	Square Footage
Membership	$210,000	2,000
Magazine subscriptions	150,000	2,000
Books and reports	300,000	3,000
Continuing education	180,000	2,000
Corporate staff	80,000	1,000
	$920,000	10,000

Included in the $280,000 occupancy cost is rent for the books and reports department for an annual cost of $50,000. Personnel costs are an additional 25 percent of salaries.

- Printing and paper costs other than for magazine subscriptions and books and reports relate to the continuing education department.

- General and administrative expenses include all other costs incurred by the corporate staff to operate the association.

Mike has decided to assign all revenue and expense to the profit SBUs on the following basis:

1. Can be traced directly to a profit SBU.
2. Can be allocated on a reasonable and logical basis to a profit SBU.

The expenses that can be traced or assigned to corporate staff as well as any other expenses that cannot be assigned to profit SBUs will be grouped with the general and administrative expenses and not allocated to the profit SBUs. Mike believes that allocations often tend to be arbitrary and are not useful for management reporting and analysis. He believes that additional allocation of the general and administrative expenses associated with the operation and administration of the association would be arbitrary.

Required

1. Prepare a contribution income statement for Music Teachers, Inc.
2. What is the strategic role of the contribution income statement for Music Teachers, Inc.?
3. Mike Doyle is considering the possibility of not allocating indirect or nontraceable expenses to profit SBUs.

   a. What reasons are often presented for not allocating indirect or nontraceable expenses to profit SBUs?

   b. Under what circumstances might the allocation of indirect or nontraceable expenses to profit SBUs be acceptable?

(CMA Adapted)

International

Strategy

18–32 **CONTRIBUTION MARGIN INCOME STATEMENT FOR PROFIT SBUs; STRATEGY, INTERNATIONAL** Stratford Corporation is a diversified company whose products are marketed both domestically and internationally. Its major product lines are pharmaceutical products, sports equipment, and household appliances. At a recent meeting, Stratford's board of directors had a lengthy discussion on ways to improve overall corporate profitability without new acquisitions. New acquisitions are problematic because the company already is heavily leveraged. The board members decided that they needed additional financial information about individual corporate operations to target areas for improvement. Dave Murphy, Stratford's controller, has been asked to provide additional data to assist the board in its investigation. Stratford is not a public company and, therefore, has not prepared complete income statements by product line. Dave has regularly prepared an income statement by product line through contribution margin. However, he now believes that income statements prepared through operating income along both product lines and geographic areas would provide the directors with the required insight into corporate operations. Dave has the following data available:

| | Product Lines | | | |
	Pharmaceutical	Sports	Appliances	Total
Production/Sales in units	160,000	180,000	160,000	500,000
Average selling price per unit	$8.00	$20.00	$15.00	
Average variable manufacturing cost per unit	4.00	9.50	8.25	
Average variable selling expense per unit	2.00	2.50	2.25	
Fixed factory overhead excluding depreciation				$500,000
Depreciation of plant and equipment				400,000
Administrative and selling expense				1,160,000

Dave had several discussions with the division managers from each product line and compiled this information:

- The division managers concluded that Dave should allocate fixed factory overhead on the basis of the ratio of the variable costs per product line or per geographic area to total variable costs.

- Each division manager agreed that a reasonable basis for the allocation of depreciation on plant and equipment would be the ratio of units produced per product line or per geographical area to the total number of units produced.

- There was little agreement on the allocation of administrative and selling expenses, so Dave decided to allocate only those expenses that were directly traceable to the SBU being delineated; that is, manufacturing staff salaries to product lines and sales staff salaries to geographic areas. He used these data for this allocation:

Manufacturing Staff		Sales Staff	
Pharmaceutical	$120,000	United States	$ 60,000
Sports	140,000	Canada	100,000
Appliances	80,000	Europe	250,000

- The division managers provided reliable sales percentages for their product lines by geographical area:

| | Percentage of Unit Sales | | |
	United States	Canada	Europe
Pharmaceutical	40%	10%	50%
Sports	40	40	20
Appliances	20	20	60

Dave prepared this product-line income statement:

STRATFORD CORPORATION
Statement of Income by Product Lines
For the Fiscal Year Ended April 30, 2001

| | Product Lines | | | | |
	Pharmaceutical	Sports	Appliances	Unallocated	Total
Sales in units	160,000	180,000	160,000		500,000
Sales	$1,280,000	$3,600,000	$2,400,000	—	$7,280,000
Variable manufacturing and selling costs	960,000	2,160,000	1,680,000	—	4,800,000
Contribution margin	$ 320,000	$1,440,000	$ 720,000	—	$2,480,000
Fixed costs					
Fixed factory overhead	$ 100,000	$ 225,000	$ 175,000	—	$ 500,000
Depreciation	128,000	144,000	128,000	—	400,000
Administrative and selling expense	120,000	140,000	80,000	$ 820,000	1,160,000
Total fixed costs	$ 348,000	$ 509,000	$ 383,000	$ 820,000	$2,060,000
Operating income (loss)	$ (28,000)	$ 931,000	$ 337,000	$(820,000)	$ 420,000

Required

1. Prepare a contribution income statement for Stratford Corporation based on the company's geographic areas of sales.

2. As a result of the information disclosed by both income statements (by product line and by geographic area), recommend areas on which Stratford Corporation should focus its attention to improve corporate profitability.

3. What changes would you make to Stratford's strategic performance measurement system? Include the role, if any, of the firm's international business operations in your response.

(CMA Adapted)

18–33   **PROFIT SBUs; ANNUAL FINANCIAL REPORTS**   Greg Peterson was recently appointed vice president of operations for Webster Corporation. He has a manufacturing background and previously served as operations manager of Webster's tractor division. The business units of Webster Corporation include divisions that manufacture heavy equipment, process food, and provide financial services.

In a recent conversation with Carol Andrews, Webster's chief financial officer, Greg suggested evaluating unit managers on the basis of the business unit data in Webster's annual financial report. This report presents revenues, earnings, identifiable assets, and depreciation for each business unit for a five-year period. He believes that evaluating business unit managers by criteria similar to that used to evaluate the company's top management is appropriate. Carol has reservations about using information from the annual financial report for this purpose and suggested that Greg consider other criteria to use in the evaluation.

Required

1. Explain why the business unit information prepared for public reporting purposes might not be appropriate for the evaluation of unit managers' performance.

2. Describe the possible motivational impact on Webster Corporation's unit managers if Greg's proposal for their evaluation is accepted.

3. Identify and describe several types of financial information that would be more appropriate for Greg Peterson to use when evaluating the performance of unit managers.

(CMA Adapted)

18–34   CENTRALIZATION VS. DECENTRALIZATION: BANKING   RNB is a bank holding company for a statewide group of retail consumer-oriented banks. RNB was formed in the early 1960s by a group of young investors who believed in a high level of consumer services. The number of banks owned by the holding company expanded rapidly. These banks gained visibility because of their experimentation with innovations such as free-standing 24-hour automated teller machines, automated funds transfer systems, and other advances in banking services.

Service

RNB's earnings performance has been better than that of most other banks in the state. The founders organized RNB and continue to operate it on a highly decentralized basis. As the number of banks owned has increased, RNB's executive management has delegated more responsibility and authority to individual bank presidents, who are considered to be representatives of executive management. Although certain aspects of each bank's operations are standardized (such as procedures for account and loan applications and salary rates), bank presidents have significant autonomy in determining how each bank will operate.

The decentralization has led each bank to develop individual marketing campaigns. Several of them have introduced unique "packaged" accounts that include a combination of banking services; however, they sometimes fail to notify the other banks in the group as well as the executive office of these campaigns. One result has been interbank competition for customers where the market overlaps. The corporate marketing officer had also recently begun a statewide advertising campaign that conflicted with some of the individual banks' advertising. Consequently, customers and tellers have occasionally experienced both confusion and frustration, particularly when the customers attempt to receive services at a bank other than their "home" bank.

RNB's executive management is concerned that earnings will decline for the first time in its history. The decline appears to be attributable to reduced customer satisfaction and higher operating costs. The competition among the banks in the state is keen. Bank location and consistent high-quality customer service are important. RNB's 18 banks are well located, and the three new bank acquisitions planned for next year are considered to be in prime locations. The increase in operating costs appears to be directly related to the individual banks' aggressive marketing efforts and new programs. Specifically, expenditures increased for advertising and for the special materials and added personnel related to the "packaged" accounts.

For the past three months RNB's executive management has been meeting with the individual bank presidents to review RNB's recent performance and seek ways to improve it. One recommendation that appeals to executive management is to make the organization's structure more centralized. The specific proposal calls for reducing individual bank autonomy and creating a centralized individual bank management committee of all bank presidents to be chaired by a newly created position, vice president of individual bank operations. The individual banks' policies would be set by consensus of the committee to conform to overall RNB plans.

Required

1. Discuss the advantages of a decentralized organizational structure.

2. Identify disadvantages of a decentralized structure. Support each disadvantage with an example from RNB's situation.

3. Do you think the proposed more centralized structure is in the strategic best interests of RNB? Why or why not?

(CMA Adapted)

Ethics

18–35 BALANCED SCORECARD; STRATEGIC BUSINESS UNITS; ETHICS Pittsburgh-Walsh Company, Inc. (PWC), manufactures lighting fixtures and electronic timing devices. The lighting fixtures division assembles units for the upscale and mid-range markets. The trend in recent years as the economy has been expanding is for sales in the upscale market to increase while those in the mid-range market have been relatively flat. Over the years, PWC has tried to maintain strong positions in both markets, believing it is best to offer customers a broad range of products to protect the company against a sharp decline in either market. PWC has never been the first to introduce new products but watches its competitors closely and quickly follows their lead with comparable products. PWC is proud of its customers service functions, which have been able to maintain profitable relationships with several large customers over the years.

The electronic timing devices division manufactures instrument panels that allow electronic systems to be activated and deactivated at scheduled times for both efficiency and safety purposes. Both divisions operate in the same manufacturing facilities and share production equipment.

PWC's budget for the year ending December 31, 2001, follows; it was prepared on a business unit basis under the following guidelines.

- Variable expenses are directly assigned to the division that incurs them.

- Fixed overhead expenses are directly assigned to the division that incurs them.

- Common fixed expenses are allocated to the divisions on the basis of units produced, which bears a close relationship to direct labor. Included in common fixed expenses are costs of the corporate staff, legal expenses, taxes, staff marketing, and advertising.

- The company plans to manufacture 8,000 upscale fixtures, 22,000 mid-range fixtures, and 20,000 electronic timing devices during 2001.

PITTSBURGH-WALSH COMPANY
Budget
For the Year Ending December 31, 2001
(amounts in thousands)

	Lighting Fixtures Upscale	Lighting Fixtures Mid-Range	Electronic Timing Devices	Totals
Sales	$1,440	$770	$800	$3,010
Variable expenses				
Cost of goods sold	720	439	320	1,479
Selling and Admin.	170	60	60	290
Contribution Margin	$ 550	$271	$420	$1,241
Fixed overhead	140	80	80	300
Divisional contribution	$ 410	$191	$340	$ 941
Common fixed expenses				
Overhead	48	132	120	300
Selling and admin.	11	31	28	70
Net income	$ 351	$ 28	$192	$ 571

PWC established a bonus plan for division management if the division exceeds the planned product line net income by 10 percent or more.

Shortly before the year began, Jack Parkow, the CEO, suffered a heart attack and retired. After reviewing the 2001 budget, Joe Kelly, the new CEO, decided to close the lighting fixtures mid-range product line by the end of the first quarter and use the available production capacity to grow the remaining two product lines. The marketing staff advised that electronic timing devices could grow by 40 percent with increased direct sales support. Increasing sales above that level and of upscale lighting fixtures would require expanded advertising expenditures to increase consumer awareness of PWC as an electronics and upscale lighting fixture company. Joe approved the increased sales support and advertising expenditures to achieve the revised plan. He advised the divisions that for bonus purposes, the original product-line net income objectives must be met and that the lighting fixtures division could combine the net income objectives for both product lines for bonus purposes.

Prior to the close of the fiscal year, the division controllers were given the following preliminary actual information to review and adjust as appropriate. These preliminary year-end data reflect the revised units of production amounting to 12,000 upscale fixtures, 4,000 mid-range fixtures, and 30,000 electronic timing devices.

PITTSBURGH-WALSH COMPANY, INC.
Preliminary Actual Information
For the Year Ending December 2001
(amounts in thousands)

	Lighting Fixtures Upscale	Lighting Fixtures Mid-Range	Electronic Timing Devices	Totals
Sales	$2,160	$140	$1,200	$3,500
Variable expenses				
Cost of goods sold	1,080	80	480	1,640
Selling and Admin.	260	11	96	367
Contribution Margin	$ 820	$ 49	$ 624	$1,493
Fixed overhead	140	14	80	234
Divisional contribution	$ 680	$ 35	$ 544	$1,259
Common fixed expenses				
Overhead	78	27	195	300
Selling and admin.	60	20	150	230
Net income (loss)	$ 542	$ (12)	$ 199	$ 729

The controller of the lighting fixtures division, anticipating a similar bonus plan for 2002, is contemplating deferring some revenue into the next year on the pretext that the sales are not yet final and accruing in the current year expenditures that will be applicable to the first quarter of 2002. The corporation would meet its annual plan, and the division would exceed the 10 percent incremental bonus plateau in 2001 despite the deferred revenues and accrued expenses contemplated.

Required

1. Outline the benefits that an organization realizes from SBU reporting, and evaluate profit SBU reporting on a variable cost basis versus an absorption cost basis.

2. Why would the management of the electronics timing devices division be unhappy with the current reporting? Should the current performance measurement system be revised?

3. Explain why the adjustments contemplated by the controller of the lighting fixtures division are unethical by citing specific standards in the Institute of Management Accountants' Standards of Ethical Conduct.

4. Develop a balanced scorecard for PWC, providing three to five perspectives and four to six measures of each perspective. Make sure your measures are quantifiable.

18–36 PROFIT SBUs Charleston Manufacturing Company, a maker of building products for commercial and industrial construction, has four divisions:

bathroom fixtures; roofing products; adhesives, paints, and other chemicals; and flooring. Each division is evaluated on its profit as determined by the annual financial report, and the profit figure is used to determine the division managers' compensation. The firm has continued to grow in both sales and profits over the recent years, but top management has observed that it is not growing as fast as other firms in the industry. Moreover, the building products business is experiencing strong overall growth due in part to the rapid increase in construction in the southeastern states where Charleston competes. The firm's CEO is concerned that it is losing ground in the industry at a time of improving opportunities. The CEO believes that the problem might be in the firm's performance measurement system and sets up a task force to determine how the firm should proceed.

Required   You are assigned to lead the task force. What are your suggestions for the CEO regarding Charleston's performance measurement?

Service

18–37   DESIGN OF STRATEGIC BUSINESS UNIT   Hamilton-Jones, a large consulting firm in Los Angeles, has experienced rapid growth over the last five years. To better serve its clients and to better manage its practice, the firm decided two years ago to organize into five strategic business units, each of which serves a significant base of clients: accounting systems, executive recruitment and compensation, client-server office information systems, manufacturing information systems, and real-estate consulting. Each client SBU is served by a variety of administrative services within the firm, including payroll and accounting, printing and duplicating, report preparation, and secretarial support. Hamilton-Jones management closely watches the trend in the total costs for each administrative support area on a month-to-month basis. Management has noted that the costs in the printing and duplicating area have risen 40 percent over the last two years, a rate that is twice that of any other support area.

Required   Should Hamilton-Jones evaluate the five strategic business units as cost or profit SBUs? Why? How should the administrative support areas be evaluated?

18–38   DESIGN OF STRATEGIC BUSINESS UNIT   Martinsville Manufacturing Company develops parts for the automobile industry. The main product line is interior systems, especially seats and carpets. Martinsville operates in a single large plant that has 30 manufacturing processes: carpet dyeing, seat frame fabrication, fabric cutting, and so on. In addition to the 30 manufacturing units, there are six manufacturing support departments: maintenance, engineering, janitorial, scheduling, materials receiving and handling, and information systems. The costs of the support departments are allocated to the 30 manufacturing units on the basis of direct labor cost, materials costs, or the square feet of floor space in the plant occupied by the unit. In the case of the maintenance department, the cost is allocated on the basis of square feet. Maintenance costs have been relatively stable in recent years, but the firm's accountant advises that the amount of maintenance cost is a little high relative to the industry average.

Required   What are the incentive effects on the manufacturing units of the current basis for allocating maintenance costs? What would be a more desirable way, if any, for allocating these costs? Explain your answer.

Service

18–39   DESIGN OF STRATEGIC BUSINESS UNIT   MetroBank is a fast-growing bank that serves the region around Jacksonville, Florida. The bank provides commercial and individual banking services, including investment and mortgage banking services. The firm's strategy is to continue to grow by acquiring smaller banks in the area to broaden the base and variety of services it can offer. The bank now has 87 strategic business units, which represent different areas of service in different locations. To support its growth, MetroBank has invested several million dollars in upgrading its information services function. The number of networked computers and of support personnel has more than doubled in the last four years and now accounts for 13 percent of total operating expenses. Two years ago, MetroBank decided to charge information services to the SBUs based on the head count (number of employees) in each SBU. Recently, some of the larger SBUs have complained that this method overcharges them and that some of the smaller SBUs are actually using a larger share of the total information services resources. MetroBank's controller has decided to investigate these complaints. His inquiry of the director of the information services department revealed that the larger departments generally use more services, but some small departments in fact kept him pretty busy. Based on this response, the controller is considering changing the charges for information services to the basis of actual service calls in each SBU rather than head count.

Required Is the information services department at MetroBank a profit SBU or a cost SBU? Which type of unit should it be, and why? Evaluate the controller's decision regarding the basis for charging information services costs to the SBUs.

18–40 **DESIGN OF STRATEGIC BUSINESS UNIT** Advanced Electronic Devices (AED) is a large manufacturer of electronic parts used in the manufacture of computers, automobiles, and a variety of consumer products. The firm manufactures approximately 3,500 different products each year. Approximately 10 percent of these are new products, and another 10 percent are dropped each year. AED is organized into 16 profit SBUs that cover the main areas of its business and 14 manufacturing support departments, each of whose cost is charged to the profit SBUs on the basis of product cost. The head of engineering, one of the largest support departments, has argued that the current system is dysfunctional. It does not encourage the longer-term type of engineering projects that she thinks are critical to the firm's success. She argues that the longer-term engineering projects will develop the key improvements in the products and production processes that will maintain the firm's "competitive edge."

Required Assess the argument by the head of the engineering department. Is the engineering department currently evaluated as a cost SBU or profit SBU? How do you think the support departments, including engineering, should be evaluated, and how should their costs be charged to the manufacturing departments?

18–41 **PROFIT SBUs: HOSPITALS** Suburban General Hospital owns and operates several community hospitals in North Carolina. One of its hospitals, Cordona Community Hospital, is a not-for-profit institution that has not met its financial targets in the past several years because of decreasing volume. It has been losing market share largely because of the entrance of a new competitor, Jefferson Memorial Hospital. Jefferson has successfully promoted itself as the premier provider of quality care; its slogan is "Patients Come First." To compete with Jefferson, Cordona has developed a new department, guest services, to improve patient relations and overall customer service. Guest services personnel will be positioned throughout the hospital and at major entrances to help patients and their families get where they are going. Guest services will also be visible in the waiting rooms of high-volume areas such as cardiovascular services and women's services to help guide the patients throughout their visit. Cordona's management is wrestling with how to charge guest services to the various profit SBUs in the hospital.

Service

Required What are some different ways to allocate the guest service costs, and what would be the effect of each on the behavior of the managers of the different profit SBUs?

Strategy

18–42 STRATEGY: BALANCED SCORECARD WaveCrest Boats, Inc., located in Kinston, North Carolina, is a large manufacturer of sailboats. The company was founded by brothers Tom and Bill Green, who started it to combine their work and hobby, sailing. The Greens's boats are intended primarily for the first-time boat buyer and accordingly include a number of design features for ease of use. Some of WaveCrest's innovative designs have received the attention of other manufacturers in the industry and of sailing magazine editors. The intended market for the boats is the recreational boating enthusiast and sailing camps and clubs that are looking for a durable and easy-to-use boat.

The sailboat industry can be described as a very cyclical business and depends a great deal on overall economic conditions. Because most customers view sailing as a rather expensive recreational hobby, sales increase when the economy is at its best. The adoption of a boat for racing in a given area and the requirement that competitors use that particular boat to compete have dramatically affected sales.

WaveCrest's plant occupies a single large building plus three smaller buildings for supplies, administration, and other manufacturing uses. The plant has two key manufacturing departments, each with a supervisor. The molding department develops the molds for the boats and produces the fiberglass hull for each boat. The assembly department installs the fittings, rub-rail and other hardware, and packs the mast, sails, lines, and other items for shipment.

WaveCrest is currently manufacturing two boat designs, a 14-foot cat-rigged boat and a 16-foot sloop-rigged boat. The wholesale price of these boats is $2,500 and $4,500, respectively. The plant manufactures an average of 100 of the 14-foot boats and 50 of the 16-foot boats per month. The plant is staffed by six highly skilled workers in the molding department, and five additional employees in the assembly department. Tom and Bill work on marketing and customer relations in addition to boat design and testing. Tom is principally responsible for design and production and has been able to create two promising new designs that the firm is market testing and considering for production, as well as some new ideas for streamlining the production process. Bill is primarily responsible for marketing and customer relations and is on the road much of the time attending boat shows and visiting sailing camps and clubs.

Required

1. Develop what you think is or should be WaveCrest's competitive strategy.

2. The Green brothers are interested in evaluating their performance other than using the financial report. In particular, they want to be able to evaluate their progress toward specific goals in each business area. Because they do not see much of each other as a result of Bill's travel, they also want a way to be more aware of what the other is doing and accomplishing. Someone has suggested the use of a balanced scorecard for this purpose. Based on the firm's strategy, develop three to five perspectives of a potential balanced scorecard and four to six measures for each perspective. Do you think the balanced scorecard will provide the information the brothers are seeking?

SOLUTION TO SELF-STUDY PROBLEM

Discretionary-Cost and Engineered-Cost Methods

1. Liberty management is apparently using a cost SBU for its claims department because it generates no revenues. Since management has chosen not to adjust the number of clerks for the changing number of claims each month, it appears to be using a discretionary-cost method to budget these costs. That is, management has determined it is more effective to provide a reasonable resource (12 clerks) for the claims processing area and not to be concerned directly with the clerks' efficiency, the slack during slow times, or the hectic pace at peak load times. Management's view is that the work averages out over time.

2. If Liberty uses the discretionary-cost method, the budget would be the same each month and would not depend on the level of claims to be processed. The budget would include the costs to provide the number of clerks that management judges to be adequate for the job (12 clerks × $2,400 per month), or $28,800 per month.

3. If Liberty uses the engineered-cost method, each claim that is processed has a budgeted cost based on the average time used as determined by a work flow study. Assume that each clerk works an eight-hour day except for 40 minutes of break time; the number of claims a clerk can process each month (assuming 22 working days) is

$$\frac{[(8 \text{ hours} \times 60 \text{ minutes} - 40] \times 22 \text{ days}}{121 \text{ minutes}} = 80 \text{ claims per month}$$

The cost per claim is thus

$$\$2,400/80 = \$30 \text{ per claim}$$

The engineered-cost budget for January is

$$915 \text{ claims} \times \$30 \text{ per claim} = \$27,450$$

The unfavorable variance for January using the engineered-cost method is $1,350 ($28,800 actual expenditure less $27,450 budgeted expenditure). This unfavorable variance is best interpreted as the cost of unused capacity for processing claims. Since the capacity for processing claims is 80 × 12 = 960 claims, the department has unused capacity of 45 claims (960 − 915 = 45 claims), or approximately one-half of one clerk.

4. Chuck could make the strategic argument that the claims processing department should be staffed for peak capacity rather than for average capacity to ensure promptness and accuracy during the busy months and to provide a better basis for employee morale, which is an important factor in performance during the low-volume months as well.

19

Strategic Investment Units and Transfer Pricing

After studying this chapter, you should be able to . . .

1   Identify the objectives of strategic investment units

2   Explain the use of return on investment (ROI) and identify its advantages and limitations

3   Explain the use of residual income and identify its advantages and limitations

4   Explain the use of economic value added (EVA) in evaluating strategic investment units

5   Explain the objectives of transfer pricing, the different transfer pricing methods, and when each method should be used

6   Discuss the important international tax issues in transfer pricing

The increasing intensity of competition and the growing importance of global trading requirements such as those of the World Trade Organization (WTO) and tax rules in each country are creating new challenges for global businesses. These elements have particularly affected the manner in which global firms evaluate their different business units located throughout the world. In this chapter, we consider how firms evaluate their subsidiaries as strategic business units and how they develop transfer prices for sales between the firm's various units. Differences in accounting practices, tax rates, and foreign exchange rates for different countries seriously affect the evaluation and the transfer prices. According to Bill Gates:

> Microsoft's international business grew really fast once we got rolling overseas. We made a point of moving into international markets as early as possible, and our subsidiaries had a lot of entrepreneurial energy. Giving them the freedom to conduct their businesses according to what made sense in each country was good for customers and profitable for us. Our international business shot up from 41 percent of revenues in 1986 to 55 percent in 1989.
>
> The independence of our subsidiaries extended to their financial reporting, which came to us in a number of different formats driven by a number of different business arrangements and taxation rules. Some subsidiaries accounted for products from our manufacturing corporation in Ireland based on their cost; others used a percentage of customer price as the cost. They'd reconcile the actual sales and profits in different ways. Some of our subsidiaries got a commission on direct sales . . . other subs facilitated direct sales from the parent company, and we reimbursed them on a cost-plus basis. The half dozen or so different financial models gave us a lot of headaches. . . .
>
> "Not knowing any better," as Mike Brown (Chief Financial Officer) likes to say, he and our controller, Jon Anderson, decided to take advantage of the fact that everyone already used PC spreadsheets for other kinds of analysis. They designed a cost-basis profit and loss financial that didn't show any of the inter-company markups or commissions. Mike and Jon showed the new P&L around via e-mail and got quick buy-off on it. When we looked at our subsidiary financials after that, we had a much easier time seeing how we were actually doing, especially when we could pivot the data to see it from angles. . . . One critical aspect is being able to easily control

exchange rate assumptions in any view so you can see results either with or without the effects of exchange rates.[1]

Similarly, the changes in the local currencies of the countries in which they operate can seriously affect global firms such as Goodyear, Caterpillar, and McDonald's. For example, the decline in euro currency in European Union countries during 1999–2000 caused the operating income of these firms to fall by as much as 30 percent.[2] The complexities of evaluating SBUs of these global firms is covered in this chapter.

PART ONE: STRATEGIC INVESTMENT UNITS

Most firms use profit SBUs and investment SBUs to evaluate managers.[3] Profit SBUs are commonly used because of their strong effect on the motivation and goal congruence objectives of SBUs; managers are rewarded for their units' contribution to the firm's total profit. However, firms cannot use profit alone to compare one business unit to other business units or to alternative investments because the other business units and alternative investments are likely to be of different sizes or have different operating characteristics. The desired level of profit for a unit depends on its size and operating characteristics. Thus, although profit alone can be used effectively to evaluate a unit's performance over time, it should not be used to evaluate performance relative to other units or to alternative investments. A method to compare a unit to other units and to alternative investment is needed. The profit per dollar invested for each unit, usually called **return on investment (ROI),** can be used to compare a unit to others or to the profitability of alternative investments. Investment SBUs are based on the concept of return on investment.

Return on investment (ROI) is profit divided by investment in the business unit.

THE STRATEGIC ROLE OF INVESTMENT UNITS

The strategic role of investment SBUs is the same as those of the other SBUs:

1. To motivate managers to exert a high level of effort to achieve the goals set by top management.
2. To provide the right incentive for managers to make decisions consistent with the goals set by top management.
3. To determine fairly the rewards earned by the managers for their effort and skill and the effectiveness of their decision making.

LEARNING OBJECTIVE 1▶

Identify the objectives of strategic investment units

How do investment SBUs achieve these three objectives? The first objective, motivation, can be achieved because the goal to increase return on investment is clear and intuitive and is generally within the manager's control. The second objective, goal congruence, is achieved since return on investment (ROI) is a critical financial performance measure for the firm as a whole. Each successful investment SBU contributes directly to the firm's success. The third objective, fairness of rewards, is achieved because the use of investment SBUs provides a sound basis for comparing the performance of units of different size; profits are measured relative to the amount

---

[1] Bill Gates, *Business @ the Speed of Thought* (New York: Warner Books, 1999, p. 9).

[2] Debra Sparks, "Business Won't Hedge the Euro Away," *Business Week,* December 4, 2000, p. 157; and "The Euro: A Dismal Failure, a Ringing Success," *The Wall Street Journal,* November 2, 2000, p. A29.

[3] The majority of U.S. firms that responded to three recent surveys used either profit SBU or investment SBU strategic performance measurement to evaluate their business units. J. S. Reece and W. A. Cool, "Measuring Investment Center Performance," *Harvard Business Review,* May–June 1978: V. Govindarajan, "Profit Center Measurement: An Empirical Study," working paper. The Amos Tuck School of Business Administration, Dartmouth College, 1994; and A. S. Keating, "Metrics for Division Manager Performance Evaluation," working paper, Simon Graduate School of Business, University of Rochester, March 1996.

of investment. Moreover, ROI contributes to achieving fairness because it is a clear, quantitative measure that managers understand well, and over which they typically have a great deal of control.

The principal measure of investment SBU performance is ROI. In addition, two related measures—residual income (RI) and economic value added (EVA)—are used. We consider each in the following sections.

RETURN ON INVESTMENT

The most commonly used investment SBU measure is ROI, which is a percentage, and the larger the percentage, the better the ROI. ROIs for successful firms range from 10 to more than 50 percent, although each firm's ROI percent must be evaluated by considering its industry average ROI and the economic factors the particular firm faces. Profit is typically determined from generally accepted accounting principles. However, for internal purposes, the firm can choose to use alternative definitions of profit, for example, the variable costing approach explained in Chapter 18.[4]

The amount of investment is often determined by the assets of the business unit based also on generally accepted accounting principles. Alternatively, investment can be measured by the value of the ownership interest, which can be determined from the shareholders' equity on the financial statements of a publicly owned firm. For a nonpublic firm, it can be determined from the amount of total assets less liabilities. When the value of the ownership interest is used for investment, return on investment often is called **return on equity (ROE)**. ROE is of special interest to shareholders and business owners because it is a direct measure of the firm's returns to owners. Because our focus in this chapter is on the performance of managers in meeting top management's goals, we hereafter focus on only ROI. The evaluation of the firm from the viewpoint of the shareholder is considered again in Chapter 20.

◀ **LEARNING OBJECTIVE 2**
Explain the use of return on investment (ROI) and identify its advantages and limitations.

Return on equity (ROE), is the return determined when investment is measured as shareholder's equity.

ROI Equals Return on Sales Times Asset Turnover

We can enhance the ROI measure's usefulness by showing it as the product of two components:

$$ROI = \text{Return on sales} \times \text{Asset turnover}$$

$$ROI = \frac{\text{Profit}}{\text{Sales}} \times \frac{\text{Sales}}{\text{Assets}}$$

Return on sales (ROS), a firm's profit per sales dollar, measures the manager's ability to control expenses and increase revenues to improve profitability. **Asset turnover,** the amount of dollar sales achieved per dollar of investment, measures the manager's ability to increase sales from a given level of investment. Together, the two components of ROI tell a more complete story of the manager's performance and enhance top management's ability to evaluate and compare the different units. For example, research has shown that firms with different operating strategies tend also to have a different mix of return on sales versus asset turnover. Firms with high operating leverage (see Chapter 8) tend to have low asset turnovers and high return on sales; those with low operating leverage and commoditylike products tend to have the highest asset turnovers and the lowest return on sales.[5]

Return on sales (ROS), a firm's profit per sales dollar, measures the manager's ability to control expenses and increase revenues to improve profitability.

Asset turnover, the amount of dollar sales achieved per dollar of investment, measures the manager's ability to increase sales from a given level of investment.

---

[4] Generally accepted accounting principles are the body of accounting rules, methods, and procedures that are set forth as acceptable by the accounting profession for use in preparing financial statements.

[5] ROI based on asset turnover, and return on sales is often referred to as the *DuPont approach* since it was originated by Donaldson Brown, chief financial officer of DuPont Corporation early in the 1900s. See also Thomas I. Selling and Clyde P. Stickney, "The Effects of Business Environment and Strategy on a Firm's Rate of Return on Assets," *Financial Analysts Journal*, January–February 1989; Patricia M. Fairfield and Teri L. Yohn, "Using Asset Turnover and Profit Margin to Forecast Changes in Profitability," presented at the American Accounting Association Annual Meeting, Philadelphia, August 2000.

Illustration of Evaluation Using Return on Investment

Assume that CompuCity is a retailer with three product lines, computers, software, and computer help books. It has stores in three regions, the Boston area, South Florida, and the Midwest. Each store sells only books, computers, and software. CompuCity's profits for the Midwest declined last year, due in part to increased price competition in the computer unit.

Because of this decline in profits, top management uses ROI to study the performance of the Midwest region. Each product line is considered an investment SBU. CompuCity knows that the markups are highest in software and lowest for computers because of growing price competition. Investment in each unit consists of the inventory for sale and the value of the real estate and improvements of the retail stores. Inventory is relatively low in the computer unit since merchandise is restocked quickly from the manufacturers. Inventory is also low in the book unit because about 40 percent of CompuCity's books are on consignment from publishers.

The value of the real estate and store improvements is allocated to each of the three units on the basis of square feet of floor space used. The software unit occupies the largest amount of floor space, followed by computers and books. Panel 1 of Exhibit 19–1 shows the income, sales, and investment information for CompuCity in 2001 and 2002. Panel 2 shows the calculation of ROI, including ROS and asset turnover, for the Midwest region for both 2001 and 2002.

The data in Exhibit 19–1 indicate that CompuCity's ROI has fallen (from 14.4 percent in 2001 to 13.5 percent in 2002) due mainly to a decline in overall return on sales (from 6.1 percent in 2001 to 5.1 percent in 2002). Further analysis shows that the drop in return on sales is due to the sharp decline in ROS for the computer unit (from 4 percent in 2001 to 2 percent in 2002). The computer unit's decline in ROS is likely the result of the increased price competition.

The analysis also shows that software is the most profitable business unit (the highest ROI of 20 percent); this is so primarily because of the relatively high ROS (highest at 10 percent since the markup on software products is relatively high). In

Exhibit 19–1	ROI, Return on Sales, and Asset Turnover for CompuCity *(Midwest Region)*

Panel 1: Income Investment, and Sales for CompuCity

	Income		Investment		Sales	
	2001	**2002**	**2001**	**2002**	**2001**	**2002**
Computers	$ 8,000	$ 5,000	$ 50,000	$ 62,500	$200,000	$250,000
Software	15,000	16,000	100,000	80,000	150,000	160,000
Books	3,200	5,000	32,000	50,000	80,000	100,000
Total	$26,200	$26,000	$182,000	$192,500	$430,000	$510,000

Panel 2: Return on Sales, Asset Turnover, and ROI for CompuCity

	Return on Sales		Asset Turnover		ROI	
	2001	**2002**	**2001**	**2002**	**2001**	**2002**
Computers	4% = 8,000/200,000	2% = 5,000/250,000	4.00 = 200,000/50,000	4.00 = 250,000/62,500	16% = 8,000/50,000	8% = 5,000/62,500
Software	10% = 15,000/150,000	10% = 16,000/160,000	1.50 = 150,000/100,000	2.00 = 160,000/80,000	15% = 15,000/100,000	20% = 16,000/80,000
Books	4% = 3,200/80,000	5% = 5,000/100,000	2.50 = 80,000/32,000	2.00 = 100,000/50,000	10% = 3,200/32,000	10% = 5,000/50,000
Total	6.10% = 26,200/430,000	5.10% = 26,000/510,000	2.36 = 430,000/182,000	2.65 = 510,000/192,500	14.40% = 26,200/182,000	13.50% = 26,000/192,500

contrast, the computer and book units have higher asset turnovers due to the lower required levels of inventory and floor space than the computer unit and the large percentage of consignment inventory for the book unit. ROI has also improved significantly for the software unit because of the decline in investment, due either to a reduction in inventory or a decrease in floor space for software (recall that investment is allocated to the units on the basis of floor space).

Strategic Analysis Using ROI

Use of ROI enables CompuCity to evaluate the managers of the three units and to complete a strategic analysis of the entire firm. CompuCity can set performance goals for managers in terms of both return on sales and asset turnover. The unit managers then have very clear goals to increase sales and reduce costs, reduce inventory, and use floor space effectively. To be effective, the goals should recognize differences in the competitive factors among the units. For example, lower ROS should be expected of the computer unit because of competitive pricing that affects that unit.

Exhibit 19–1 data also reflect the way that competitive factors in the computer unit and business relationships regarding inventory in the computer and book units affect the firm's profitability. This provides a useful basis for an improved strategic analysis: for determining how the firm should position itself strategically. How should CompuCity's competitive approach be changed in view of recent and expected changes in the competitive environment? Perhaps the computer unit should be reduced and the software unit expanded. Which stores in the Midwest are successful, and why? A value-chain analysis might provide insight into strategic competitive advantage and opportunity. For example, CompuCity might find it more profitable to reduce its computer unit and replace it with products that are potentially more profitable, such as printers, pagers, cell phones, fax machines, supplies, and computer accessories.

Overall, ROI provides a useful basis for evaluating not only the unit manager's performance, but also the entire firm's performance.

Use of Return on Investment

For ROI to be useful, income and investment must be determined consistently and fairly:

1. Income and investment must be measured in the same way for each unit. For example, all units must use the same inventory cost flow assumption (FIFO or LIFO) and the same depreciation method.
2. The measurement method must be reasonable and fair for all units. For example, if some units have much older assets than other units have, the use of historical cost-based net book value for assets can significantly bias the ROI measures in favor of the older units.

In the following sections, we consider the measurement issues affecting the determination of both income and investment.

Measuring Income and Investment: Effect of Accounting Policies

Accounting policies regarding the measurement of investments and the determination of income have a direct affect on ROI. The two main types of accounting policies that affect ROI are (1) revenue and expense recognition policies and (2) asset measurement methods. Revenue and expense recognition policies affect ROI by determining when a sale is recognized as revenue and when an expenditure is recognized as an expense. These policies affect the timing of sales and expenses. For example, cash-based accounting systems recognize sales and expenses when the cash is received or disbursed; accrual-based systems recognize sales (and related expenses) when the product or service is delivered or provided. The firm's policy for revenue and expense recognition should be considered carefully since any differences between units might significantly influence the proper interpretation of ROI.

Similarly, the firm has accounting policies for measuring inventory and long-lived assets that affect income and investment:

For Long-Lived Assets

1. **Depreciation policy.** The determination of the useful life of the asset and the depreciation method used affect both income and investment. Larger depreciation charges reduce ROI.
2. **Capitalization policy.** The firm's capitalization policy identifies when an item is expensed or capitalized as an asset. If an item is expensed, the effect reduces ROI.

For Inventory

3. **Inventory measurement methods.** The choice of inventory cost flow assumption (FIFO, LIFO) affects income and the measurement of inventory. Methods that increase cost of goods sold and decrease inventory, as is often the effect with LIFO in times of rising prices, reduce ROI.
4. **Absorption costing** (explained in Chapter 18). The effect of absorption costing creates an upward bias on net income and therefore on ROI when inventory levels are rising and the reverse when inventory levels are falling.
5. **Disposition of variances** (explained in Chapter 16). Standard cost variances can be closed to the cost of goods sold accounts or prorated to the inventory accounts; the choice has a direct effect on income and the inventory balances.

These five measurement issues affect the proper interpretation of net income and investment and, therefore, of ROI.[6] To ensure comparability, all business units must use the same policies. Moreover, when interpreting ROI, top management should consider whether the existing accounting policies have a bias to overstate (or understate) income and investment.[7]

To illustrate the effect of an accounting policy, assume that all units of CompuCity expense all furniture and other items used to display products; these items cost $1,500 per year. Suppose the computer unit decides to capitalize these expenses. What is the

---

Measuring Return on Investment in Employee Training

The cost of training employees can be 15 percent or more of total payroll costs in some firms. These significant expenditures are incurred because of the importance of investing in the job-related abilities of the firm's employees. Since employee training costs are not included on the balance sheet as assets according to generally accepted accounting principles, the training function within a firm is often not viewed as an investment SBU. In contrast, other firms consider training to be one of the most strategically important investments they make and determine an ROI value for it accordingly. Software vendors and consultants assist firms in developing the proper measurements.

Source: Based on Ann P. Bartel, "Measuring the Employer's Return on Investments in Training: Evidence from the Literature," *Industrial Relations,* July 2000, pp. 502–24; and Bill Roberts, "Calculating Return on Investment for HRIS," *HR Magazine,* December 1999, pp. 122–28.

---

[6] Each of the policies also has the effect of either simultaneously increasing income and increasing investment or simultaneously decreasing income and decreasing investment. Since ROI is a ratio that normally is between zero and 1, an increase in income increases ROI although investment also has increased by the same amount, and vice versa.

[7] Frances L. Ayres summarizes the accounting policies that can affect income in "Perceptions of Earnings Quality: What Managers Need to Know," *Management Accounting,* March 1994, pp. 27–29. See also Alfred Rappaport, "Shortcomings of Accounting Numbers," *Creating Shareholder Value* (New York: Free Press, 1986), Chap. 2; Anne Tergesen, "Which Number Is the Real McCoy?" *Business Week,* October 11, 1999, p. 177; Susan Sherreik, "What Earnings Reports Don't Tell You," *Business Week,* October 16, 2000, pp. 201–4.

Exhibit 19–2	**Effect of Capitalizing Certain Costs on ROI for CompuCity** *(Midwest Region)*

Panel 1: ROI Prior to Capitalizing Display Materials (same as Exhibit 19–1)

	Computer Unit	**Book Unit**
Assets	$62,500	$50,000
Income	$ 5,000	$5,000
ROI	8%	10%

Panel 2: Book Unit Expenses Display Costs While the Computer Unit Capitalizes These Costs

	Computer Unit	**Book Unit**
Assets	$64,000 = $62,500 + $1,500	$50,000
Income	$6,500 = $ 5,000 + $1,500	$ 5,000
ROI	10.16% = $6,500/$64,000	10%

effect on ROI? Exhibit 19–2 compares the computer unit to the books unit before the change (in panel 1) and after (in panel 2).

The illustration shows that the decision to capitalize the display costs increased the computer unit's assets, income, and ROI. Although the book unit has the higher ROI when both units expense display costs, the computer unit's decision to capitalize these costs while the book unit does not has caused the computer unit to have the higher ROI.

Other Measurement Issues for Income

In addition to the firm's accounting policies, other effects on income should be considered when using ROI:

1. **Nonrecurring items.** Income can be affected by nonrecurring charges or revenues and then would not be comparable to income of prior periods or of other business units. For example, the high promotion costs for introducing a new product might significantly distort net income in the period involved.

2. **Income taxes.** Income taxes can differentially affect the various units, with the result that after-tax net income may not be comparable. This could be true, for example, if the business units operate in different countries with different tax rates and tax treaties.

3. **Foreign exchange.** Business units that operate in foreign countries are subject to foreign exchange rate fluctuations that can affect the income and the value of investments of these units.

4. **Joint cost sharing.** When the business units share a common facility or cost, such as personnel department or data processing cost, that cost is often allocated to the units on some fair-share basis. For example, the amount of square feet of floor space is used to allocate plant-level costs. (See Chapter 14 for a discussion of allocation objectives and methods.) Different allocation methods result in different costs for each unit, and therefore they affect the units' income.

Each of these effects on income can influence the proper interpretation of ROI and should be considered when using ROI to evaluate investment SBUs.

Measuring Investment: Which Assets to Include?

A common method for calculating ROI is to define investment as the cost of long-lived assets plus working capital.[8] A key criterion for including an asset in ROI is the

---

[8] *Working capital* is defined as current assets less current liabilities. For a discussion of the determination of assets for ROI, see R. N. Anthony and V. Govindarajan, *Management Control Systems*, 8th ed. (Burr Ridge, Ill.: Richard D. Irwin, 1995), pp. 221–39.

degree to which the unit controls it. For example, if the unit's cash balance is controlled at the firmwide level, only a portion (or perhaps none) of the cash balance should be included in the investment amount for calculating ROI. Similarly, receivables and inventory should include only those controllable at the unit level.

Long-lived assets commonly are included in investment if they are traceable to the unit (for shared assets, see the next section). Management problems arise, however, if the long-lived assets are leased or if some significant portion of them is idle. Leasing requires a clear firmwide policy regarding how to treat leases in determining ROI so that unit managers are properly motivated to lease or not to lease, as is the firm's policy. In general, the leased assets should be included as investments since they represent assets used to generate income, and the failure to include them can cause a significant overstatement of ROI.

For idle assets, the main issue is again controllability. If the idle assets have an alternative use or are readily saleable, they should be included in the investment amount for ROI. Also, if top management wants to encourage the divestment of idle

---

Return on Investment at Dell Computer

One of the many factors that has been attributed to the success of Dell Computer is its extensive use of return on investment evaluation. Facing steep price cutting in the computer industry in 1993 and write-offs of $65 million in inventory, Michael Dell decided to recruit savvy top operations and finance managers. As a result, the firm introduced the concept of return on investment, emphasizing the importance of this financial measure to all 10,350 employees. For example, the marketing department began to determine the ROI for each mailing, and managers began to figure the cost of capital tied up in unsold inventory. "We spent 15 months educating people about return on invested capital, convincing them they could impact our future," said chief financial officer Thomas J. Meredith.

Source: Based on Gary McWilliams, "Whirlwind on the Web," *Business Week,* April 7, 1997, pp. 132–36.

Factors Affecting the Proper Interpretation of Return on Investment

Accounting Policies That Affect Return on Investment

1. Revenue and expense recognition policy
2. Inventory and long-lived asset measurement

    Inventory
        Cost flow assumption (FIFO, LIFO)
        Absorption costing
        Disposition of standard cost variances

    Long-lived assets
        Depreciation policy
        Capitalization policy

Other Effects on Income

1. Nonrecurring items
2. Income taxes
3. Foreign exchanges gains and losses
4. Joint cost sharing

Other Effects on Investment

1. Determination of assets to include
2. Joint asset sharing
3. Current cost

assets, including idle assets in ROI would motivate the desired action since divestment would reduce investment and increase ROI. Alternatively, if top management sees a potential strategic advantage to holding the idle assets, excluding idle assets from ROI would provide the most effective motivation since holding idle assets would not reduce ROI.

Measuring Investment: Allocating Shared Assets

When shared facilities, such as a common maintenance facility for the vehicle fleet of different units are involved, management must determine a fair sharing arrangement. As in joint cost allocation (Chapter 14), top management should trace the assets to the business units that used them and allocate the assets that cannot be traced on a basis which is as close to actual usage as possible. For example, the investment in the vehicle maintenance facility might be allocated on the basis of the number of vehicles used in each unit or on their total value.

Alternatively, the required capacity and therefore the investment in the joint facility are sometimes large because the user units require high levels of service at periods of high demand. The assets should be allocated according to the *peak demand* by each individual unit; units with higher peak-load requirements that cause the need for capacity then receive a relatively larger portion of the investment. For example, a computer services department might require a high level of computer capacity because certain users require a large amount of service at certain times.

Measuring Investment: Current Values

The amount of investment is typically the historical cost of the assets.[9] The **historical cost** amount is the book value of current assets plus the net book value of the long-lived assets. **Net book value** is the asset's historical cost less accumulated depreciation. A problem arises when the long-lived assets are a significant portion of total investment because most long-lived assets are stated at historical cost, and price changes since their purchase can make the historical cost figures irrelevant and misleading.

If the relatively small historical cost value is used for investment in ROI, the result is that *ROI can be significantly overstated* relative to ROI determined with the current value of the assets. The consequence is that the use of historical cost ROI can mislead strategic decision makers, since the inflated ROI figures can create an illusion of profitability. The illusion is removed when the assets are replaced later at their current value, and the amount of income might not have been sufficient to support the replacement of the asset at the current higher value.

For example, a firm that enjoys a relatively high ROI of 20 percent based on net book value (e.g., income of $200,000 and net book value of $1,000,000) would find that *if* replacement cost of the assets were four times book value (4 × $1,000,000 = $4,000,000), the ROI after replacement would become a relatively low 5 percent ($200,000/$4,000,000). Strategically, the firm should have identified the low profitability in a timely manner, but use of historical cost ROI can delay this recognition. A proper strategic approach is to use an investment value in ROI that considers replacing the assets at their current market value so that decisions are made on the basis of the current and future profitability of the firm's products and services, not on the basis of their past profitability alone.

In addition to its strategic value, the use of current value helps to reduce the unfairness of historical cost net book value when comparing among business units with *different aged assets*. Units with older assets under the net book value method have significantly higher ROIs than units with newer assets because of the effect of price changes and of accumulating depreciation over the life of the assets. If the old and new assets are contributing equivalent service, the bias in favor of the unit with

Historical cost is the book value of current assets plus the net book value of the long-lived assets.

Net book value is the asset's historical cost less accumulated depreciation.

---

[9] Ninety-nine of 100 firms use historical cost measurement of investment, as reported by Reece and Cool, "Measuring Investment Center Performance," and Govindarajan, "Profit Center Measurement." Of these, 9 of 10 use net book value, and the rest use gross book value.

older assets is unfair to the manager of a unit with newer assets. The difference is also misleading for strategic decision makers. The use of current values helps to reduce this bias since current values are not affected as strongly by age of assets as are historical cost–based net book values.

Measures of Current Values The three methods for developing or estimating the current market values of assets are (1) gross book value, (2) replacement cost, and (3) liquidation value. **Gross book value (GBV)** is the historical cost without the reduction for depreciation. It is an estimate of the current value of the assets. GBV improves on net book value because it removes the bias due to differences in the age of assets among business units. However, it does not address potential price changes in the assets.

The other two approaches, replacement cost and liquidation value, effectively handle both the issues of age of assets and current cost. **Replacement cost** represents the current cost to replace the assets at the current level of service and functionality. In contrast, **liquidation value** is the price that could be received from their sale. In effect, replacement cost is a purchase price and liquidation value is a sales price. Generally, replacement cost is higher than liquidation value.

GBV is preferred by those who value the objectivity of a historical cost number; purchase cost is a reliable, verifiable number. In contrast, replacement cost is preferred when ROI is used to evaluate the manager or the unit as a continuing enterprise because the use of replacement cost is consistent with the idea that the assets will be replaced at the current cost and the business will continue. On the other hand, the liquidation value is most useful when top management is using ROI to evaluate the business unit for potential disposal, and the relevant current cost is the sales value of the assets, or liquidation value.

To illustrate, consider CompuCity's three marketing regions. CompuCity has 15 stores in the Midwest, 18 in the Boston area, and 13 in South Florida. CompuCity owns and manages each store. Exhibit 19–3 shows the net book value, gross book value, replacement cost, and liquidation value for 2002 for the stores in each region.[10]

The stores in the Boston area, where CompuCity began, are among the oldest and are located in areas where real estate values have risen considerably. The newer stores in the Midwest and Florida are also experiencing significant appreciation in real estate values. ROI based on net book value shows the Boston area to be the most profitable. Additional analysis based on GBV, however, shows that when considering that the

Gross book value (GBV) is the historical cost without the reduction for depreciation.

Replacement cost represents the current cost to replace the assets at the current level of service and functionality.

Liquidation value is the price that could be received for the sale of the assets.

Exhibit 19–3	Investment Data and ROI for CompuCity in Its Three Marketing Regions (000s omitted)				
Region	**Income**	**Net Book Value**	**Gross Book Value**	**Replacement Cost**	**Liquidation Value**
Financial data					
Midwest	$26,000	$192,500	$250,500	$388,000	$332,000
Boston area	38,500	212,000	445,000	650,000	1,254,600
South Florida	16,850	133,000	155,450	225,500	195,000
Return on investment					
Midwest		13.51%	10.38%	6.70%	7.83%
Boston area		18.16	8.65	5.92	3.07
South Florida		12.67	10.84	7.47	8.64

[10] The values in Exhibit 19–3 represent the simple average of beginning-of-year and end-of-year values for gross the net book values (beginning and ending values are not shown). Replacement cost and liquidation value are determined as of the point when ROI is calculated. The use of the simple average is a common approach when determining the value of investment using gross book value or net book value in the calculation of ROI. Because income is measured for the entire period, investment is also measured as the average cost of the assets over the entire period.

Boston area stores are somewhat older, the ROI figures for all three regions are comparable, illustrating the potentially misleading information from ROI based on net book value.

Replacement cost is useful in evaluating region managers' performance because it best measures the investment in the continuing business. The ROI figures show that all three regions are somewhat comparable, with South Florida slightly in the lead.

Liquidation value provides a somewhat different answer. The ROI based on liquidation value for the Boston area is very low relative to the other two areas. Because of the significant appreciation in real estate values at the Boston area stores, the liquidation value for the Boston region is quite high. The replacement cost figure is lower than liquidation cost because of the assumption that if CompuCity replaces its stores in the Boston area, they would be located where the real estate values are somewhat lower. The analysis of liquidation-based ROIs is useful for showing CompuCity management that the real estate value of these stores could now exceed their value as CompuCity retail locations. Perhaps the company should sell these stores and relocate elsewhere in areas whose values are near that of the suggested replacement cost figure.

Strategic Issues in Using Return on Investment

In addition to the measurement issues described earlier, two key issues must be considered in using ROI for evaluating investment SBUs: First, use the balanced scorecard to avoid an excessive focus on short-term results. Second, ROI has a disincentive for new investment by the most profitable units.

The Balanced Scorecard: Avoiding Excessive Short-Term Focus

ROI evaluation, much like profit SBUs and cost SBUs, focuses the manager's attention on the current period's costs and revenues, discouraging new investment that would increase long-term profitability, unless a quick and significant improvement in

---

Long-Term versus Short-Term Performance Measurement: Intangible Assets

A useful way to consider the issue of short- versus long-term performance evaluation is to consider financial versus nonfinancial factors as the use of the balanced scorecard does. Using only financial factors such as ROI tends to produce a short-term focus as managers seek to maximize current revenues and reduce current costs. In contrast, the use of nonfinancial measures such as employee training, product development, and customer satisfaction can cause managers to focus on these measures, which will build the base for profitability and strategic success in the long term.

Another way to consider short-term versus long-term performance measurement is to look beyond only physical and monetary assets to intangible assets, which are very real but difficult to measure. For example, employee training is not an asset on the balance sheet, yet it has real value. How is its value measured in dollars as other assets are? Although expenditures on research and development likely bring future benefits, what dollar value can we now place on these benefits? R&D is not typically included in the assets used to measure ROI, nor are training expense and advertising and marketing expense.

Baruch Lev, director of New York University's Project of Research on Intangibles, cites the importance of intangibles in the valuation of companies. For example, he points to AMR Corp, the parent company for both American Airlines and the SABRE flight reservation system. Although American Airlines has many tangible assets (a fleet of jets), SABRE has the key intangible asset: the potential to be used simultaneously by millions of people seeking flight reservations. The result is that, according to Lev's check of market values (in 1996), approximately one-half the value of AMR was due to SABRE.

What makes SABRE so valuable is that it has no practical limit to its use in comparison to the airline's limited physical assets; its jets can make only so many flights in a given day. This explains SABRE's high market value. According to Lev, intangible assets arise from research and development (Merck & Co. Pharmaceuticals), brand development (Coca-Cola), or superior technology (SABRE, AOL Time Warner, and Amazon.com). Were we to focus on ROI based on physical and monetary assets alone, excluding intangible assets, we could not properly evaluate these diverse companies.

Sources: Based on Alan M. Webber, "New Math for a New Economy," *Fast Company*, January–February 2000, pp. 214–24; and Baruch Lev, *Intangibles: Management, Measurement, and Reporting*, New York University Stern School of Business (December 2000). In March 2000, AMR distributed its 83% ownership of SABRE to its shareholders, thereby transforming SABRE into a 100% publicly traded company.

current income occurs. The result, often called *investment myopia,* is that managers tend to avoid new investment because the returns could be uncertain and might not be realized for some time. If the manager is evaluated using current ROI performance, the urgency of meeting the current period's ROI target tends to eclipse efforts to improve long-term profits.[11] The ROI-based incentive is for the manager to reduce research and development spending, advertising, employee training, and productivity improvements in order to improve the current ROI; strategically, however, these decisions might have disastrous long-term effects.

The effects of an excessive focus on short-term results can be addressed by using ROI as *only one part* of an overall evaluation of a strategic investment unit. A good approach is to use a balanced scorecard in which ROI plays an important role in the financial dimension of critical success factors (CSFs). In addition, the balanced scorecard evaluation considers CSFs in the other three dimensions: (1) customer satisfaction, (2) internal business processes, and (3) learning and innovation. The main concept of the balanced scorecard is that no one measure properly evaluates the SBU's progress to strategic success. Moreover, by attending directly to the firm's CSFs, the balanced scorecard effectively links the performance measurement/evaluation process to the firm's strategy. Chapter 18 discusses a food ingredients company's use of the balanced scorecard in strategic performance measurement.

ROI: Disincentive for New Investment by the Most Profitable Units

Business units evaluated on ROI have an important disincentive that conflicts with their achieving the objectives of investment SBUs. ROI encourages units to invest in projects only that earn *higher than the unit's current ROI* so that the addition of the investment improves the unit's overall ROI right away. Thus, the most profitable units have a corresponding disincentive to invest in any project that does not exceed their current ROI, although the project would have a good return. A "good" return can be defined as an ROI in excess of some minimum threshold, for example, 12 percent, based usually on the firm's cost of capital.

The disincentive for new investment hurts the firm strategically in two ways. First, it declines investment projects that would be beneficial. Second, to take advantage of a unit's apparent management skill, ROI evaluation provides a disincentive for the best units to grow. In contrast, the units with the lowest ROI have an incentive to invest in new projects to improve their ROI. Management skills could be lacking in the low-ROI units, however.

The disincentive can be illustrated if we assume that CompuCity's Boston region has an option to purchase for $22,500 a telephone switch that can increase the capacity of its 800 service number and reduce operating costs by $10,000 per year. The switch is expected to last for three years and have no salvage value. Exhibit 19–4 shows the determination of ROI for the purchase of the switch using the straight-line method of depreciation. The ROI for its purchase is 13.33 percent in the first year and 22.22 percent and 66.67 percent in the second and third years, respectively.[12]

Using average net book value, the Boston region's ROI is currently 18.16 percent (Exhibit 19–3). It might not purchase the switch because the first year's return of 13.33 percent is less than the current ROI. Buying the switch would reduce Boston's ROI from 18.16 percent to 17.77 percent [($38,500 + $10,000 − $7,500)/($212,000 +

---

[11] Investment myopia is discussed widely. See, for example, Judith H. Dobrzynski, "A Sweeping Prescription for Corporate Myopia," *Business Week,* July 6, 1992; Kenneth A. Merchant, *Rewarding Results: Motivating Profit Center Managers* (Boston: Harvard Business School Press, 1989), Chap. 4; and John Dearden, "The Case against ROI Control," *Harvard Business Review,* May–June 1969.

[12] Using the discounted cash flow methods explained in Chapter 11, the purchase of the switch has an internal rate of return of approximately 16 percent ($22,500/$10,000 = 2.250; the PV factor for 16 percent and three years is 2.246). As noted in Chapter 11, the discounted internal rate of return provides a summary return for the entire life of a multiyear project in contrast to ROI for which the return increases each year over the life of the project under most depreciation methods.

Exhibit 19–4	ROI for CompuCity Purchase of Switch		
	First Year	**Second Year**	**Third Year**
Depreciation expense (straight-line method)	$7,500 = $22,500/3	$7,500	$7,500
Net book value at year-end	$15,000 = $22,500 − $7,500	$7,500 = $15,000 − $7,500	$0 = $7,500 − $7,500
Average net book value for the year	$18,750 = ($22,500 + $15,000)/2	$11,250 = ($15,000 + $7,500)/2	$3,750 = ($7,500 + $0)/2
ROI	13.33% = $\dfrac{\$10,000 - \$7,500}{\$18,750}$	22.22% = $\dfrac{\$10,000 - \$7,500}{\$11,250}$	66.67% = $\dfrac{\$10,000 - \$7,500}{\$3,750}$

$18,750)] in the first year. In later years, the ROI from the switch would substantially exceed Boston's current ROI, but the manager might not be able to wait for that improvement if strong pressure for current profits exists.

Moreover, from a firmwide perspective, since the return on the switch in each year exceeds the firm's threshold return of 12 percent, the Boston region should purchase it. Thus, a significant limitation of ROI is that it can cause, in conflict with firmwide interests, SBU managers to decline some investments. A useful way to address this limitation is to use an alternative measure of investment SBU profitability, called *residual income*.

◀ **LEARNING OBJECTIVE 3**

Explain the use of residual income and identify its advantages and limitations.

RESIDUAL INCOME

In contrast to ROI, which is a percentage, **residual income (RI)** is a dollar amount equal to the income of a business unit less a charge for the investment in the unit. The charge is determined by multiplying the firm's desired minimum rate of return by the investment amount. Residual income can be interpreted as the income earned after the unit has paid a charge for the funds it needs to invest in the unit.

The RI calculation for CompuCity is illustrated in Exhibit 19–5 using a minimum rate of return of 12 percent. Note that since all three units have an ROI higher than 12 percent, all also have a positive RI. Note too that the unit's ranking on ROI is the same as its ranking based on RI: the Boston area unit has the highest ROI and residual income.

The issues regarding the measurement of investment and income for RI are the same as those discussed for ROI. Because of the effect of different accounting policies and the tendency of net book value to understate investment, the residual income measure must be interpreted carefully. It has the advantage of enabling a unit to pursue an investment opportunity as long as the investment's return exceeds the minimum return set by the firm. For example, using RI, the Boston region would accept the opportunity to purchase the telephone switch described in Exhibit 19–4 because it would contribute to the unit's residual income. The RI in the first year after the investment in the switch would be

$$\$13,310 = (\$38,500 + \$10,000 - \$7,500) - 0.12 \times (\$212,000 + \$18,750)$$

a $250 improvement over the unit's RI without it ($13,060, from Exhibit 19–5).

An additional advantage of RI is that a firm can adjust the required rates of return for differences in risk. For example, units with higher business risk can be evaluated at a higher minimum rate of return. The increased risk might be due to obsolete products, increased competition in the industry, or other economic factors affecting the business unit.

Residual income (RI) is a dollar amount equal to the income of a business unit less a charge for the investment in the unit.

Exhibit 19–5 Illustration of Residual Income for CompuCity

	Income	Average Net Book Value
Financial data		
Midwest	$26,000	$192,500
Boston area	38,500	212,000
South Florida	16,850	133,000
Return on investment		
Midwest	13.51%	
Boston area	18.16	
South Florida	12.67	
Residual income	(minimum rate of return = 12 percent)	
Midwest	$ 2,900 = $26,000 − 0.12 × $192,500	
Boston area	$13,060 = $38,500 − 0.12 × $212,000	
South Florida	$ 890 = $16,850 − 0.12 × $133,000	

Use of Residual Income in Evaluating Federal Programs

A recent project report of the Federal Accounting Standards Advisory Board (FASAB) provides background and perspective for the federal government to consider including the cost of capital in program evaluation. Specifically, the report notes that the inclusion of the cost of capital is consistent with *Federal Financial Accounting Standards Number 4* (managerial cost accounting standards for the federal government), which states that full cost information is desirable in financial reporting by federal programs and projects. The report also explains the calculation of residual income (RI) and its benefits in evaluating federal programs and projects. Particular attention is given to the fact that certain federal regulatory and policy-making activities require small amounts of capital and should

thus have a smaller capital charge. In contrast, agencies with large amounts of assets (for example, with $10 billion or more in assets: The Army Corps of Engineers, General Services Administration, Veterans Affairs; the U.S. Air Force, Army, and Navy; the Departments of the Interior, Agriculture, Energy, and Transportation; and NASA) should have a higher capital charge. The report also notes that the current guidance regarding financial reporting of governmental agencies in Canada and the United Kingdom includes the cost of capital in a manner very much like that of the RI measure.

Source: Based on Federal Accounting Standards Advisory Board, "Accounting for the Cost of Capital by Federal Entities," July 1996 (www.financenet.gov/data/docs/central/fasab/views.txt).

Another advantage is that it is possible to calculate a different investment charge for different types of assets. For example, a higher minimum rate of return could be used for long-lived assets that are more likely to be specialized in use and thus not so readily salable.

Limitations of Residual Income

Although the residual income measure deals effectively with the disincentive problem of ROI, it has limitations. A key one is that because RI is not a percentage, it suffers the same problem of profit SBUs in not being useful for comparing units of significantly different sizes. Residual income favors larger units that would be expected to have larger residual incomes, even with relatively poor performance. Moreover, relatively small changes in the minimum rate of return can dramatically affect the RI for units of different size, as illustrated in Exhibit 19–6. Although both units A and B have the same ROI of 15 percent, the RI amount differs significantly: $300,000 for unit A but only $22,500 for unit B. The difference would be greater for a smaller minimum return.

ROI and RI can complement each other in the evaluation of investment SBUs. The advantages and limitations of each measure are summarized in Exhibit 19–7.

Exhibit 19–6	The Effect of Unit Size and Minimum Desired Rate of Return on Residual Income	
	Business Unit A	**Business Unit B**
Investment	$10,000,000	$750,000
Income	$1,500,000	$112,500
ROI	15%	15%
	= $1,500,000/$10,000,000	= $112,500/$750,000
Residual income, at a minimum desired return of 12 percent	$300,000 = $1,500,000 − 0.12 × $10,000,000	$22,500 = $112,500 − 0.12 × $750,000

Exhibit 19–7	Advantages and Limitations of ROI and Residual Income	
	Advantages	**Limitations**
ROI	• Easily understood • Comparable to interest rates and to rates of returns on alternative investments • Widely used	• Disincentive for high ROI units to invest in projects with ROI higher than the minimum rate of return but lower than the unit's current ROI
Residual income	• Supports incentive to accept all projects with ROI above the minimum rate of return • Can use the minimum rate of return to adjust for differences in risk • Can use a different minimum rate of return for different types of assets	• Favors large units when the minimum rate of return is low • Not as intuitive as ROI • Can be difficult to obtain a minimum rate of return
Both ROI and residual income	• *Congruent* with top management goals for return on assets • *Comprehensive financial measure;* includes all elements important to top management: revenues, costs, and investment • *Comparability;* expands top management's span of control by allowing comparison of business units	• *Can mislead strategic decision making;* not as comprehensive as the balanced scorecard, which includes customer satisfaction, internal processes, and learning as well as financial measures; the balanced scorecard is linked directly to strategy • *Measurement issues;* variations in the measurement of inventory and long-lived assets and in the treatment of nonrecurring items, income taxes, foreign exchange effects, and the use/cost of shared assets • *Short-term focus;* investments with long-term benefits might be neglected

ECONOMIC VALUE ADDED

Economic value added (EVA)[13] is a business unit's income after taxes and after deducting the cost of capital.[14] The idea is very similar to what we have explained as residual income. The objectives of the measures are the same: to effectively motivate investment SBU managers and to properly measure their performance. In contrast to RI, EVA uses the firm's cost of capital instead of a minimum rate of return. The *cost of capital* is usually obtained by calculating a weighted average of the cost of the firm's

◀ **LEARNING OBJECTIVE 4**

Explain the use of economic value added (EVA) in evaluating strategic investment units.

Economic value added (EVA) is a business unit's income after taxes and after deducting the cost of capital.

---

[13] EVA is a registered trademark of Stern Stewart & Co.

[14] G. Bennett Stewart III, "EVA Works—But Not If You make These Common Mistakes," *Fortune,* May 1, 1995, pp. 117–18. See also Marc J. Epstein and S. David Young, "Greening with EVA," *Management Accounting,* January 1999, pp. 45–49; Roger Mills and Carole Print, "Strategic Value Analysis," *Management Accounting (UK),* February 1995, pp. 35–37; Paul Dierks and Ajay Patel, "What Is EVA and How Can It Help Your Company?" *Management Accounting,* November 1997, pp. 52–58; and E. R. Arzac, "Are Your Business Units Creating Shareholder Value?" *Harvard Business Review,* January–February 1986.

The Results Are Coming In: For and Against EVA®

A number of studies have investigated the association of EVA with measures of shareholder value, principally stock price and stock returns. In a 1993 report, Shawn Tully showed that the stock prices of an EVA adopter, the Coca-Cola Company, followed EVA better than either earnings per share or return on equity.

More recently, researchers have found less promising results. A study of 17 Canadian agribusiness firms found little association between EVA and shareholder value for these firms. An econometric study of stock returns for 773 firms from the Business Week 1,000 (for 1988) also found that EVA added only marginally to the information content of accounting earnings. A study of 325 firms from Standard & Poor's 500 and the Business Week 1,000 found that their stock returns have a higher association to residual income and return on investment than to EVA. Another recent study of the use of both EVA and traditional accounting measures in a large New Zealand firm found that the managers' performance appeared to benefit from the EVA evaluation reward process but not necessarily because of the nature of the EVA measure itself. S. David Young, arguing from accounting concepts, states in a recent article that the adjustments to earnings proposed by EVA advocates may not improve EVA over residual income.

Regardless of the controversy, numerous firms in addition to Coca-Cola are enthusiastic about using EVA. For example, the 1998 annual report for Reynolds Metals Company (acquired in 1999 by Alcoa Inc.) reports the company's plans to implement EVA and its progress in achieving this goal. Centura Bank of Rocky Mount, North Carolina, also uses EVA in evaluating performance and determining executive bonuses. The bank explains that EVA has had a significant positive influence on managers' decision making: it offers a stronger focus on tax planning and a more careful analysis of new business plans, among others.

Based on information in Robert McGough, "EVA Pay Plans Aren't a Big Hit in New Study," *The Wall Street Journal,* May 3, 2000, p. C1. "The Real Key to Creating Wealth," *Fortune,* September 20, 1993, pp. 38–50; Calum G. Turvey, Linda Lake, Erna van Duren, and David Sparling, "The Relationship between Economic Value Added and the Stock Market Performance of Agribusiness Firms," *Agribusiness,* Autumn 2000, pp. 399–416: Gary C. Biddle, Robert M. Bowen, and James S. Wallace, "Does EVA Beat Earnings? Evidence on Associations with Stock Returns and Firm Values," *Journal of Accounting and Economics,* 1997, pp. 301–36; S. Riceman, S. Cahan, and M. Lai, "Do Managers Really Perform Better under EVA Bonus Schemes?" working paper, Massey University, Plamerston North, New Zealand, 2000; S. David Young, "Some Reflections on Accounting Adjustments and Economic Value Added," *Journal of Financial Statement Analysis,* Winter 1999, pp. 7–19; and "Centura Banks Promote Sales Culture, Measure Performance by Economic Value Added," *Journal of Retail Banking Services,* Winter 1997, pp. 33–36. See also the reference to EVA in the Centura 1999 annual report at http://www.centura.com/about/news/annrept99/centura.pdf.

two sources of funds: borrowing and selling stock (the cost of capital is defined and explained in Chapter 11). For many firms, the minimum desired rate of return and the cost of capital are very nearly the same, with small differences due to adjustments for risk and for strategic goals such as the firm's desired growth rate. Although RI is intended to deal with the undesirable effects of ROI, EVA is also used to focus managers' attention on creating value for shareholders by earning profits higher than the firm's cost of capital.

Another difference is that EVA users do not follow conventional, conservative accounting policies. For example, these users capitalize expenses that contribute to the company's long-term value. These expenses include research and development, certain types of advertising, and training and employee development usually are expensed according to generally accepted accounting principles. In addition, EVA users often adjust earnings for certain aspects of accrual accounting to make EVA earnings more useful in projecting the firm's cash flows and long-term earnings potential. One adjustment is to use current cost to value inventory for both the balance sheet and its cost of goods sold so that both total assets and earnings are stated in terms of current costs. A second adjustment is that deferred taxes are not considered in determining earnings or liabilities; this provides a more nearly cash-flow–based valuation of earnings. A third adjustment is that goodwill is not amortized against either earnings or assets, again to derive a more nearly cash-flow–based earnings figure.[15]

A number of firms, such as CSX, Coca-Cola, and Briggs & Stratton have adopted EVA in recent years and attribute improvements in profitability to the change. These developments indicate a renewed interest in residual income, with modifications, and some evidence of its usefulness for evaluating investment SBUs.

---

[15] A good source for further information about accrual accounting is J. David Spiceland, James F. Sepe, and Lawrence A. Tomassini, *Intermediate Accounting,* 2d ed. (New York: McGraw-Hill/Irwin, 2001).

PART TWO: TRANSFER PRICING

Transfer pricing is the determination of an exchange price for a product or service when different business units within a firm exchange it. The products can be final products sold to outside customers or intermediate products.

Transfer pricing is one of the most strategic activities in SBU management. It not only directly affects the strategic objectives of the firm (such as the decision of which parts of the value chain the firm should occupy) but also requires coordination among the marketing, production, and financial functions. It affects materials and parts sourcing decisions, tax planning, and, potentially, the marketing of the final and intermediate products. Because significant decision-making autonomy is desirable to enhance the motivation of the business units, setting the transfer price using an arm's-length approach between the units is also desirable. That is, the units should behave as if they were independent businesses. This determination of the transfer price is desirable from both a management perspective and tax purposes, as explained in the next section. The arm's-length approach is not always possible, however, such as when no alternative suppliers exist. The transfer pricing methods explained here include techniques for handling a variety of circumstances.

> **Transfer pricing** is the determination of an exchange price for a product or service when different business units within a firm exchange it.

WHEN IS TRANSFER PRICING IMPORTANT?

Transfers of products and services between business units is most common in firms with a high degree of vertical integration. Vertically integrated firms engage in a number of different value-creating activities in the value chain. Wood product, food product, and consumer product firms are examples. For instance, a computer manufacturer must determine transfer prices if it prepares the chips, boards, and other components and assembles the computer itself. (See Exhibit 2–12 in Chapter 2: Value Chain for the Computer-Manufacturing Industry.) A useful way to visualize the transfer pricing context is to create a graphic such as the one in Exhibit 19–8 that illustrates the business units involved in the transfer of products and services and identifies them as inside or outside the firm, international or domestic. Exhibit 19–8 shows the transfers for a hypothetical computer manufacturer, High Value Computer (HVC), that purchases a key component, the x-chip, from both internal and external suppliers and

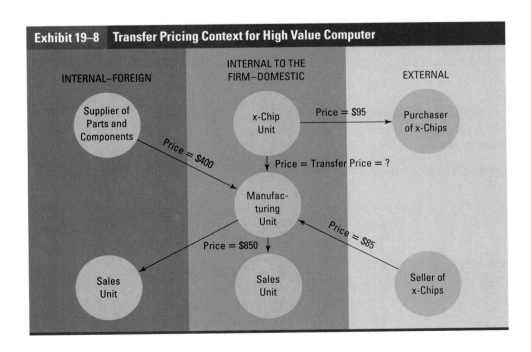

Exhibit 19–8   Transfer Pricing Context for High Value Computer

purchases other components from international sources. The internal unit that manufactures x-chips sells them both internally and externally. The manufactured units are transferred to both internal and external sales units. Where it is known, the transfer price is shown in Exhibit 19–8.

The management accountant's role is to determine the proper transfer price for the internal sales of the x-chip. We begin by considering the objectives of transfer pricing.

OBJECTIVES OF TRANSFER PRICING

LEARNING OBJECTIVE 5 ▶

Explain the objectives of transfer pricing, the different transfer pricing methods, and when each method should be used.

The objectives for transfer pricing are the same as for SBUs: (1) to motivate managers, (2) to provide an appropriate incentive for managers to make decisions consistent with the firm's goals, and (3) to provide a basis for fairly rewarding the managers.

In satisfying these objectives, the transfer price determination also must recognize firmwide strategic goals. For example, an important strategic objective for transfer pricing is to minimize taxes locally and internationally. By setting a high transfer price for goods shipped to a relatively high tax country, the firm can reduce its firm-level tax liability. This would increase the cost and thus reduce the income of the purchasing unit in the high tax country, thereby minimizing taxes there. At the same time, the higher profits shown by the selling unit (as a result of the high transfer price) would be taxed at lower rates in the seller's home country.

Another strategic objective of transfer pricing is to develop strategic partnerships. A relatively high transfer price might also be used to encourage internal units to purchase from an external supplier, to encourage an external business relationship the firm wants to develop because of the supplier's quality, or to gain entrance to a market in a new country. It might also assist a newer or weaker unit to grow or build up a unit for spin-off or sale to outside investors.

International Transfer Pricing Objectives

With the globalization of business, the international aspect of transfer pricing is becoming a critical concern, particularly with tax issues. Other international objectives include minimizing customs charges, dealing with currency restrictions of foreign governments, and dealing with the risk of expropriation by foreign governments. **Expropriation** occurs when a government takes ownership and control of assets a foreign investor has invested in that country. In managing the relationship with any one country, the management accountant attempts to find a strategic balance among these sometimes conflicting objectives.

Expropriation occurs when the government in which a foreign company's investment assets are located takes ownership and control of those assets.

Minimization of Customs Charges

The transfer price amount can affect the overall cost, including the customs charges, of goods imported from a foreign unit. For example, if customs charges are significant on the parts and components imported by the domestic manufacturing unit, High Value Computer's relatively low transfer price on these imports would be beneficial to reduce the amount of customs charges.

Currency Restrictions

As a foreign unit accumulates profits, a problem arises in some countries that limits the amount and/or timing of repatriation of these profits to the parent firm. One way to deal with these restrictions is to set the transfer price so that profits accumulate at a relatively low rate. This objective must be considered with other transfer pricing objectives.

Risk of Expropriation

When a significant risk of expropriation exists, the firm can take appropriate actions such as limiting new investment, developing improved relationships with the foreign government, and setting the transfer price so that funds are removed from the foreign country as quickly as possible.

TRANSFER PRICING METHODS

The four methods for determining the transfer price are variable cost, full cost, market price, and negotiated price. Each has advantages and limitations, and the choice of method depends on a careful consideration of the circumstances.

The **variable cost method** sets the transfer price equal to the selling unit's variable cost. This method is desirable when the selling unit has excess capacity and the transfer price's chief objective is to satisfy the internal demand for the goods. The relatively low transfer price encourages buying internally. This method is not suitable when the selling unit is a profit or investment SBU, however, because it adversely affects the seller's profit.

The **full cost method** sets the transfer price equal to variable costs plus selling unit's allocated fixed cost. Advantages of this approach are that it is well understood and that the information is readily available in the accounting records. A key disadvantage is that it includes fixed costs, which can cause improper decision making (Chapter 10). To improve on the full cost method, firms can use the dual allocation method explained in Chapter 18 or, better yet, the activity-based method described in Chapter 4.[16]

The **market price method** sets the transfer price as the current price of the selling unit's product in the market. Its key advantage is objectivity; it best satisfies the arm's-length criterion desired for both management and tax purposes. A key disadvantage is that the market price, especially for intermediate products, is often not available.

The **negotiated price method** involves a negotiation process and sometimes arbitration between units to determine the transfer price. This method is desirable when the units have a history of significant conflict and negotiation can result in an agreed-upon price. The limitation is that the method can reduce the desired autonomy of the units.

Firms commonly use two or more methods, called *dual pricing*. For example, when numerous conflicts exist between two units, standard full cost might be used as the buyer's transfer price, while the seller might use market price.[17]

The advantages and limitations of the four methods are outlined in Exhibit 19–9.

> The **variable cost method** sets the transfer price equal to the variable cost of the selling unit.
>
> The **full cost method** sets the transfer price equal to the variable cost plus allocated fixed cost for the selling unit.
>
> The **market price method** sets the transfer price as the current price for the selling unit's product in the market.
>
> The **negotiated price method** involves a negotiation process and sometimes arbitration between units to determine the transfer price.

Exhibit 19–9	**Advantages and Limitations of the Four Transfer Pricing Methods**

Method	Advantages	Limitations
Variable cost	• Causes buyer to act as desired, to buy inside	• Unfair to seller if seller is profit or investment SBU
Full cost	• Easy to implement • Intuitive and easily understood • Preferred by tax authorities over variable cost	• Irrelevance of fixed cost in decision making; fixed costs should be ignored in the buyer's choice of whether to buy inside or outside the firm • If used, should be standard rather than actual cost (allows buyer to know cost in advance and prevents seller from passing along inefficiencies)
Market price	• Helps to preserve unit autonomy • Provides incentive for the selling unit to be competitive with outside suppliers • Has arm's-length standard desired by taxing authorities	• Intermediate products often have no market price • Should be adjusted for cost savings such as reduced selling costs, no commissions, and so on
Negotiated price	• Can be the most practical approach when significant conflict exists	• Need negotiation rule and/or arbitration procedure, which can reduce autonomy • Potential tax problems; might not be considered arm's length

---

[16] For an illustration of dual allocation in transfer pricing, see David W. Young, "Two-Part Transfer Pricing Improves IDS Financial Control," *Healthcare Financial Management*, August 1998, pp. 56–65. For an explanation of the use of activity-based costing in transfer pricing, see Robert S. Kaplan, Dan Weiss, and Eyal Desheh, "Transfer Pricing with ABC," *Management Accounting*, May 1997, pp. 20–28, and Gary J. Colbert and Barry H. Spicer, "Linking Activity-Based Costing and Transfer Pricing for Improved Decisions and Behavior," *Journal of Cost Management*, May–June 1998, pp. 20–26.

[17] See a discussion of this issue in *The Wall Street Journal*, April 18, 1997, p. B1, regarding Koch Industries.

Choosing the Right Transfer Pricing Method

The three key factors to consider in deciding whether to make internal transfers, and, if so, in setting the transfer price follow:

1. Is there an outside supplier?
2. Is the seller's variable cost less than the market price?
3. Is the selling unit operating at full capacity?

Exhibit 19–10 shows the influence of these three factors on the choice of a transfer price and on the decision to purchase inside or out.

First: Is there an outside supplier? If not, there is no market price, and the best transfer price is based on cost or negotiated price. If there is an outside supplier, we must consider the relationship of the inside seller's variable cost to the market price of the outside supplier by answering the second question.

Second: Is the seller's variable cost less than the market price? If not, the seller's costs are likely far too high, and the buyer should buy outside. On the other hand, if the seller's variable costs are less than the market price, we must consider the capacity in the selling unit by answering the third question.

Third: Is the selling unit operating at full capacity? That is, will the order from the internal buyer cause the selling unit to deny other sales opportunities? If not, the selling division should provide the order to the internal buyer at a transfer price somewhere between variable cost and market price. In contrast, if the selling unit is at full capacity, we must determine and compare the cost savings of internal sales versus the selling division's opportunity cost of lost sales. If the cost savings to the inside buyer are higher than the cost of lost sales to the seller, the buying unit should buy inside, and the proper transfer price should be the market price.

This three-question analysis is from top management's perspective and is thus the desired outcome of the units making these decisions autonomously. A good approach that preserves much of the units' autonomy is to set clear guidelines regarding top management's objectives in transfer pricing. Unit managers should know that their autonomous action to favor their unit over the interests of the firm as a whole will be viewed negatively in their annual performance evaluation.

Determining the correct transfer price and correct transfer decision can be illustrated using the High Value Computer case (Exhibit 19–8). High Value has the

---

Exhibit 19–10   Choosing the Right Transfer Price

	Decision to Transfer	Transfer Price
First: Is there an outside supplier? If there is **no** outside supply: ⟶	Buy inside	Cost or negotiated price
If there is an outside supply, answer the second question:		
Second: Is the seller's variable cost less than the outside price?		
If it is greater than the outside price, the seller must look for ways to reduce costs ⟶	Buy outside	No transfer price
If seller's variable costs are less than the outside price, answer the third question:		
Third: Is the selling unit operating at full capacity?		
If seller has excess capacity, then ⟶	Buy inside	**Low:** variable cost **High:** market price
If the seller is at full capacity ⟶ And if the contribution of the outside purchase to the entire firm is **greater than** the contribution of the inside purchase ⟶	Buy outside	No transfer price
And if the contribution of the outside purchase to the entire firm is **less than** the contribution of the inside purchase ⟶	Buy inside	Market price

Exhibit 19–11	**Transfer Pricing Example**
	The High Value Computer Company

Key assumptions

The manufacturing unit can buy the x-chip inside or outside the firm.

The x-chip unit can sell inside or outside the firm.

The x-chip unit is at full capacity (150,000 units).

One x-chip is needed for each computer manufactured by High Value.

Other information

Sales price of computer for HVC's computer unit	$850
Variable manufacturing cost of the computer unit (excluding x-chip)	
($400 parts and $250 labor)	650
Variable x-chip manufacturing cost for HVC's x-chip unit	60
Price of x-chip from outside supplier, to HVC computer unit	85
Price of x-chip from HVC's x-chip unit to outside buyer	95

Option 1: X-Chip Unit Sells Outside

High Value manufactures 150,000 computers, using x-chips purchased for $85 from outside supplier; High Value's x-chip unit sells 150,000 units for $95 each to outside buyer.

Contribution Income Statement*
(000s omitted)

	Computer Manufacturing Unit	X-Chip Unit	Total
Sales (price = $850, $95)	$127,500	$14,250	$141,750
Less: Variable costs			
X-chip ($85)	12,750		12,750
Other costs ($650, $60)	97,500	9,000	106,500
Contribution margin	$ 17,250	$ 5,250	$ 22,500

Option 2: X-Chip Unit Sells Inside

High Value manufactures 150,000 computers, using x-chips purchased for $60 (variable cost) from the inside supplier.

	Computer Manufacturing Unit	X-Chip Unit	Total
Sales (price = $850, $60)	$127,500	$9,000	$136,500
Less: Variable costs			
X-chip ($60)	9,000		9,000
Other costs ($650, $60)	97,500	9,000	106,500
Contribution margin	$ 21,000	—	$ 21,000

*It is assumed that fixed costs will not differ for the two options and are excluded from the analysis.

option to purchase the x-chip outside the firm for $85 or to manufacture it. The relevant information is presented in the top portion of Exhibit 19–11. The lower portion of Exhibit 19–11 shows the calculation of the relevant costs for each option.

A comparison of options 1 and 2 in Exhibit 19–11 shows that the firm as a whole benefits under option one when the manufacturing unit purchases the x-chip outside, and the x-chip unit also sells outside. The reason is that the manufacturing unit's $25 savings from internal sales of the x-chip ($85 outside price less $60 variable cost) is less than the x-chip unit's opportunity cost of $35 per unit ($95 outside price less $60 variable cost). In summary, we can answer the same three questions for High Value company in the following way:

First: Is there an outside supplier? High Value has an outside supplier, so we must compare the inside seller's variable costs to the outside seller's price.

Second: Is the seller's variable cost less than the market price? For High Value, it is, so we must consider the utilization of capacity in the inside selling unit.

Third: Is the selling unit operating at full capacity? For High Value, it is, so we must consider the contribution of the selling unit's outside sales relative to the savings from selling inside. Again, for High Value, the contribution of the selling unit's outside sales is $35 per unit, which is higher than the savings from selling inside ($25), so High Value's selling unit should choose outside sales and make no internal transfers.

INTERNATIONAL TAX ISSUES IN TRANSFER PRICING

LEARNING OBJECTIVE 6▶

Discuss the important international tax issues in transfer pricing.

Two recent surveys have found that more than 80 percent of multinational firms (MNCs) see transfer pricing as a major international tax issue, and more than half these firms said it was the most important issue.[18] Most countries now accept the Organization of Economic Cooperation and Development's model treaty, which calls for transfer prices to be adjusted using the arm's-length standard, that is, to a price that unrelated parties would have set. The model treaty is widely accepted, but the way countries apply it can differ. However, worldwide support is strong for an

---

COST MANAGEMENT IN ACTION

Foreign Currency Translation, Transfer Pricing, and Profits

The recent fall in the value of Southeast Asian currencies (the Indonesian rupiah, Thai baht, Malaysian ringgit, and Philippine peso) relative to the U.S. dollar appeared to be an opportunity for some Southeast Asia manufacturers to increase their exports to U.S. retailers and manufacturers. The idea is that the falling currency prices will make the Asian goods less expensive in U.S. dollars, which will increase their appeal in the United States relative to other products and thus increase demand. Nike, which has a number of manufacturing plants in Southeast Asia, says, however, that these currency changes will not have much effect on U.S. prices. Is Nike likely to miss the potential to lower prices and increase U.S. sales? (Refer to Comments on Cost Management in Action at the end of the chapter.)

Transfer Pricing and Tax Avoidance

THE UNITED STATES VERSUS JAPAN

By setting a high transfer price from their factories in Japan to their marketing subsidiaries in the United States, Japanese automakers are able to reduce the profit shown by U.S. subsidiaries and thereby reduce U.S. taxes. Former President Clinton's staff estimated the loss from such transfer pricing abuses to be as high as $15 billion per year. The magnitude of the problem is shown by a recent Internal Revenue Service study of 3,357 foreign-controlled corporations, which found that the majority understated income on their tax returns. According to the study, Japanese companies were the most likely of any of the top 10 U.S. trading partners to use unfair transfer pricing practices.

JAPAN VERSUS THE UNITED STATES

Japan also sees itself as the victim of unfair transfer pricing practices. The Japanese National Tax Administration Agency has charged Coca-Cola Co. with $145 million in additional taxes for 1990–1992 because of alleged transfer pricing abuses. They also charged American International Group, Inc., with $87 million in additional taxes for a transfer pricing disagreement.

The response of the Internal Revenue Service in the United States is that each foreign subsidiary must prove that its transfer price is arm's length; that is, the same price that unrelated parties would have charged.

Source: Based on information in *Business Week,* July 12, 1993, p. 143; and *Business Week,* May 30, 1994, p. 55.

---

[18]   Based on information from two surveys: (1) the Ernst & Young Transfer Pricing Global Survey of 400 MNCs, as reported in the *Ernst & Young Business UpShot,* October 1997; and (2) a survey of 210 companies in the United States, United Kingdom, Japan, Australia, the Netherlands, France, and Germany, as reported in *Accounting Today,* August 21–September 10, 1995.

Survey of Transfer Pricing Practices for Tax Purposes

A recent survey of transfer pricing practices noted some interesting differences in the way firms in different countries determine transfer pricing for international taxation purposes. The survey included 23 firms in the United Kingdom, 14 in the United States, and 8 in Europe. Note the popularity of the cost-plus method in all three areas.

Method	United Kingdom	United States	Europe
Comparable price method	8	2	0
Resale price method	3	4	1
Cost-plus method	9	5	3
Other	3	3	4
Total	23	14	8

Based on information in: Jamie Elliott, "International Transfer Pricing: A Suvey of U.K. and non–U.K. Firms," *Management Accounting (UK)*, November 1998, pp. 48–50.

approach to limit attempts by MNCs to reduce tax liability by setting transfer prices that differ from the arm's-length standard.[19]

The Arm's-Length Standard

The **arm's-length standard** calls for setting transfer prices to reflect the price that unrelated parties acting independently would have set. The arm's-length standard is applied in many ways, but the three most widely used methods are (1) the comparable price method, (2) the resale price method, and (3) the cost-plus method. The **comparable price method** is the most commonly used and the most preferred by tax authorities. It establishes an arm's-length price by using the sales prices of similar products made by unrelated firms.[20] A limitation is that it depends on the availability of comparable and unrelated prices.

The **resale price method** is used for distributors and marketing units when little value is added and no significant manufacturing operations exist. In this method, the transfer price is based on an appropriate markup using gross profits of unrelated firms selling similar products.

The **cost-plus method** determines the transfer price based on the seller's costs plus a gross profit percentage determined by comparing the seller's sales to those of unrelated parties or to unrelated parties' sales to those of other unrelated parties.

Advance Pricing Agreements

Advance pricing agreements (APAs) are agreements between the Internal Revenue Service (IRS) and the firm using transfer prices that establishes the agreed-upon transfer price. The APA usually is obtained before the firm engages in the transfer. The APA program's goal is to resolve transfer pricing disputes in a timely manner and to avoid costly litigation. The program supplements the dispute resolution methods already in place: administrative (IRS), judicial, and treaty mechanisms. Two-thirds of the MNCs in a recent survey indicated that they expected to use APAs in determining their transfer prices.[21]

The **arm's-length standard** says that transfer prices should be set so they reflect the price that unrelated parties acting independently would have set.

The **comparable price method** establishes an arm's-length price by using the sales prices of similar products made by unrelated firms.

The **resale price method** is based on determining an appropriate markup based on gross profits of unrelated firms selling similar products.

The **cost-plus method** determines the transfer price based on the seller's cost plus a gross profit percentage determined by comparing the seller's sales to those of unrelated parties.

Advance pricing agreements (APAs) are agreements between the Internal Revenue Service and the firm using transfer prices that establish the agreed-on transfer price.

---

[19] For further information on international taxation and transfer pricing, see B. J. Arnold and M. J. McIntyre, *International Tax Primer* (Boston: Kluwer Law International, 1995); also S. Crow and E. Sauls, "Setting the Right Transfer Price," *Management Accounting*, December 1994, pp. 41–47.

[20] In this context, *unrelated* indicates that the firm has no common ownership interest.

[21] *Accounting Today*, August–September 1995, p. 10. Also, for a recent survey of advance pricing agreements in 27 different countries, see Susan C. Borkowski, "Transfer Pricing Advance Pricing Agreements: Current Status by Country," *The International Tax Journal*, Spring 2000, pp. 1–16; for U.S. APA procedures, see Steven C. Wrappe, Ken Milani, and Julie Joy, "The Right Transfer Price," *Strategic Finance*, July 1999, pp. 39–43.

SUMMARY

Return on investment (ROI) and residual income (RI) are two of the most commonly used and well-understood financial measures used in business today. Because of the advantage of investment SBUs in motivating managers and in providing a useful basis for top management to compare business units, most firms now commonly use these measures.

ROI, which has the advantages just mentioned has several disadvantages: a short-term focus, the difficulty in determining a unique measure for earnings and investment, and the disincentive for high ROI units to invest in projects with good but not very high returns.

RI is computed as the SBU's earnings less a capital charge based on a minimum desired rate of return. RI solves some, but not all, of the ROI's problems. For example, both have a short-term focus.

The increased interest in the balanced scorecard and in economic value added (EVA) suggest that firms are adapting investment SBUs to include a long-term strategic focus.

The management accountant can serve an important role by overseeing many objectives of transfer pricing: performance evaluation (of management and business units), tax minimization, management of foreign currencies and risks, and other strategic objectives. The common transfer pricing methods include variable costing, full costing, market value, and negotiated price. In setting the transfer price, management considers the availability and quality of outside supply, the internal selling unit's capacity utilization, and the firm's strategic objectives in determining the proper transfer price.

Perhaps the most important aspect in determining a transfer price for international transfers is minimizing international taxes. With the efforts of various international groups each country monitors transfer prices used in international trade. The most common transfer pricing methods used for international trade include the comparable price method, the resale price method, and the cost-plus method. A firm can determine the acceptability (to various countries) of its transfer pricing method by requesting what is called an *advance pricing agreement*.

KEY TERMS

COMMENTS ON COST MANAGEMENT IN ACTION

Foreign Currency Translation, Transfer Pricing, and Profits

Nike is probably correct that U.S. prices for its products and those of its competitors will not change much. The reason is that the cost elements of its products from Southeast Asia affected by the falling local currencies, primarily labor costs, represent only a modest portion of the total product cost. Most of the cost of these manufactured products is for materials, which are imported from the United States and elsewhere outside Southeast Asia. Thus, the effect of the falling Southeast Asian currencies on *total* product cost is likely to be small; Nike estimates it to be 10 percent or less although some currencies have fallen to less than half of their previous value to the dollar.

Moreover, Southeast Asian manufacturers find that they have increased financing costs and sometimes reduced financing availability when the local currency falls and the raw materials from the United States and elsewhere become more expensive. For some of these manufacturers, the total operating and financing cost (in U.S. dollars) might even increase.

From a transfer pricing perspective, the dramatic change in currency value presents real problems in performance evaluation. Should the local manufacturing unit be responsible for costs in U.S. currency or in terms of the local currency? Are the currency fluctuations controllable by the local managers? The answers to these questions are difficult and complex, but many companies expect their local managers to take steps to mitigate the negative effects of currency fluctuations by buying or selling options or other financial instruments, for example.

Source: Based on Jonathan Moore and Moon Ihlwan, "Cheaper Exports? Not So Fast," *Business Week*, February 2, 1998, pp. 48–49.

SELF-STUDY PROBLEMS

(For solutions, please turn to the end of the chapter.)

1. Return on Investment and Residual Income

Selected data from Irol Inc.'s accounting ledger follow:

Sales	$8,000,000
Net book value, beginning	2,500,000
Net book value, end	2,600,000
Net income	640,000
Minimum rate of return	12%

Required

1. Calculate return on investment, return on sales, and asset turnover.
2. Calculate residual income.

2. Proper Transfer Price

Johnston Chemical Company manufactures a wide variety of industrial chemicals and adhesives. It purchases much of its raw material in bulk from other chemical companies. One chemical, T-Bar, is prepared in one of Johnston's own plants. T-Bar is shipped to other Johnston plants at a specified internal price.

The Johnston adhesive plant requires 10,000 barrels of T-Bar per month and can purchase it outside the firm for $150 per barrel. Johnston's T-bar unit has a capacity of 20,000 barrels per month and is presently selling that amount to outside buyers at $165 per barrel. The difference between the T-Bar unit's price of $165 and the outside firm's T-bar price of $150 is due to short-term pricing strategy only; the materials are equivalent in quality and functionality. The T-Bar unit's selling cost is $5 per barrel, and its variable cost of manufacturing is $90 per barrel.

Required

1. Should the adhesive unit purchase T-Bar inside or outside the firm?
2. Based on your answer in requirement 1, what is T-Bar's proper transfer price?
3. How would your answer to requirements 1 and 2 change if the T-Bar unit had a capacity of 30,000 barrels per month?

QUESTIONS

19–1   Explain the advantages of investment SBUs. Why would a firm choose investment SBU evaluation rather than profit SBU or cost SBU evaluation?

19–2   What are the three investment SBU evaluation measures?

19–3   What is return on investment, and how is it calculated?

19–4   What are the measurement issues to consider when using return on investment?

19–5   What are the advantages and limitations of return on investment?

19–6   What is meant by the *arm's-length standard*, and for what is it used?

19–7   What are the components of return on investment, and how is each interpreted and used?

19–8   What are the advantages and limitations of residual income?

19–9   What are the objectives of investment SBU evaluation?

19–10   What is return on equity, how is it calculated, and how is it interpreted?

19–11   What are the three methods most commonly used in international taxation to determine a transfer price acceptable to tax authorities? Explain each method briefly.

19–12   What does *expropriation* mean, and what is the role of transfer pricing in this regard?

19–13   How does the concept of economic value added compare to return on investment and residual income?

EXERCISES

19–14   **INVESTMENT SBUs; THE SALES LIFE CYCLE (REVIEW OF CHAPTER 18)**   The sales life cycle is used to describe the phases a product goes through from introduction to withdrawal from the market. The four phases are (a) introduction, (b) growth, (c) maturity, and (d) decline and withdrawal.

In the introduction phase, the firm relies on product differentiation to attract new customers to the product. In the growth phase, the product attracts competition, although differentiation is still an advantage for the firm. In the maturity phase, competition is keen, and cost control and quality considerations become important. In the final, decline, phase, differentiation again becomes important as do cost control and quality (see Chapter 5 and Chapter 18 for more detail).

Required   At which phases of the sales life cycle, if any, should investment SBU evaluation methods be used, and why?

19–15   **INVESTMENT SBUs; THE COST LIFE CYCLE**   As explained in Chapter 5, the cost life cycle consists of the phases the product goes through within a firm to prepare it for distribution and service. The five phases of the cost life cycle are (a) research and development, (b) design, (c) production, (d) marketing and distribution, and (e) customer service.

The early phases of the cost life cycle are particularly important in that a relatively high percentage (some say as high as 80 percent or more) of the product's life cycle costs are determined at these phases. That is, the downstream costs of manufacturing, service, and repair are a direct consequence of the quality of the design.

Required   At which phases of the cost life cycle, if any, should investment SBU evaluation methods be used, and why?

19–16 RETURN ON INVESTMENT AND RESIDUAL INCOME Consider the following data from Coastal States Financial, Inc. It uses investment SBU evaluation to analyze its two main divisions, mortgage loans and consumer loans (in millions):

	Mortgage Loans	Consumer Loans
Total assets	$2,000	$10,000
Operating income	$400	$1,500
Return on investment	25%	15%

Required

1. Which division is more successful? Why?

2. Coastal uses residual income as a measure of management success. What is the residual income for each division if the minimum desired rate of return is (a) 11 percent, (b) 15 percent, (c) 17 percent? Which division is more successful under each of these rates?

19–17 RETURN ON INVESTMENT; COMPARISONS OF THREE COMPANIES

Required Fill in the blanks:

	Companies in the Same Industry		
	A	B	C
Sales	$1,500,000	$750,000	$_____
Income	200,000	75,000	_____
Investment (assets)	500,000	_____	2,500,000
Return on sales	_____	_____	0.5%
Asset turnover	_____	_____	1.5
Return on investment	_____	1%	_____

19–18 TRANSFER PRICING; DECISION MAKING Daniels Inc., which manufactures sports equipment, consists of several divisions, each operating as a profit SBU. Division A has decided to go outside the company to buy materials since division B informed it that the division's selling price for the same materials would increase to $200. Information for division A and division B follows:

Outside price for materials	$150
Division A's annual purchases	10,000 units
Division B's variable costs per unit	$140
Division B's fixed costs	$1,250,000
Division B's capacity utilization	100%

Required

1. Will the company benefit if division A purchases outside the company? Assume that division B cannot sell its materials to outside buyers.

2. Assume that division B can save $200,000 in fixed costs if it does not manufacture the material for division A. Should division A purchase from the outside market?

3. Assume the situation in requirement 1. If the outside market value for the materials drops $20, should A buy from the outside?

19–19 TRANSFER PRICING; DECISION MAKING Using the information from requirement 1 of problem 19–18, assume that division B could sell 10,000 units outside for $210 per unit with variable marketing costs of $8. Should division B sell outside or to division A?

19–20   **TARGET SALES PRICE; RETURN ON INVESTMENT (ROI)**   Preferred Products, a bicycle manufacturer, uses normal volume as the basis for setting prices. That is, it sets prices on the basis of long-term volume predictions and then adjusts them only for large changes in pay rates or material prices. You are given the following information:

Materials, wages, and other variable costs	$300 per unit
Fixed costs	$200,000 per year
Target return on investment	20%
Normal volume	1,500
Investment (total assets)	$800,000

Required

1.   What sales price is needed to attain the 20 percent target ROI?

2.   What ROI rate will be earned at sales volumes of 2,000 and 1,000 units, respectively, given the sales price determined in requirement 1?

PROBLEMS

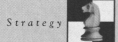

Strategy

19–21   **CALCULATING ROI & RI AND COMPARING RESULTS**   Morgan Industries manufactures die machinery. To meet its expansion needs, it recently (2000) acquired one of its suppliers, Vienna Steel. To maintain Vienna's separate identity, Morgan reports Vienna's operations as an investment SBU. Morgan monitors all of its investment SBUs on the basis of return on investment. Management bonuses are based on ROI, and all investment SBUs are expected to earn a 12 percent minimum before income taxes.

Vienna's ROI has ranged from 14 percent to 18 percent since 2000. The company recently had the opportunity for a new investment that would have yielded 13 percent ROI. However, division management decided against the investment because it believed that the investment would decrease the division's overall ROI.

The 2002 operating statement for Vienna follows. The division's operating assets were $13,000,000 at the end of 2002, a 6 percent increase over the 2001 year-end balance.

VIENNA DIVISION
Operating Statement
For Year Ended December 31, 2002
(000s omitted)

Sales		$25,000
Cost of goods sold		16,600
Gross profit		8,400
Operating expense		
Administration	$2,340	
Selling	3,810	6,150
Income before income taxes		$ 2,250

Required

1.   Calculate the following performance measures for 2002 for the Vienna division:

   a. Return on average investment in operating assets employed.

   b. RI calculated on the basis of average operating assets employed.

2.   Which performance measure (ROI or RI) should Morgan Industries use to provide the proper incentive for each division to act autonomously in the firm's best interests? Would Vienna's management have been

more likely to accept the capital investment opportunity if RI had been used as a performance measure instead of ROI? Explain.

3. What type of strategic performance measurement do you recommend for Vienna Division? Explain.

19–22 TRANSFER PRICING; DECISION MAKING Phoenix Inc., a cellular communication company, has multiple divisions. Each division's management is compensated based on the division's operating income. Division A currently purchases cellular equipment from outside markets and uses it to produce communication systems. Division B produces similar cellular equipment that it sells to outside customers but not to division A at this time. Division A's manager approaches division B's manager with a proposal to buy the equipment from division B. If it produces the cellular equipment that division A desires, Division B would incur variable manufacturing costs of $60 per unit.

Relevant Information about Division B

Sells 50,000 units of equipment to outside customers at $130 per unit.

Operating capacity is currently 80 percent; the division can perform at 100 percent.

Variable manufacturing costs are $70 per unit.

Variable marketing costs are $8 per unit.

Fixed manufacturing costs are $580,000.

Income per Unit for Division A (assuming parts purchased outside, not from division B)

Sales revenue		$320
Manufacturing costs		
Cellular equipment	80	
Other materials	10	
Fixed costs	40	
Total manufacturing costs		130
		190
Gross margin		
Marketing costs		
Variable	35	
Fixed	15	
Total marketing costs		50
Operating income		$140

Required

1. Division A wants to buy 25,000 units from division B at $75 per unit. Should division B accept or reject the proposal?

2. How should division A determine the units to purchase internally and externally that would be in Phoenix Company's best interest?

3. What range will the managers of divisions A and B agree is the best price for each division?

19–23 RETURN ON INVESTMENT; RESIDUAL INCOME Raddington Industries is a diversified manufacturer with several divisions, including the Reigis Division. Raddington monitors its divisions on the basis of both unit contribution and return on investment (ROI), with investment defined as average operating assets employed. All investments in operating assets are expected to earn a minimum return of 9 percent before income taxes.

Reigis's cost of goods sold is considered to be entirely variable; its administrative expenses do not depend on volume. Selling expenses are a mixed cost with 40 percent attributed to sales volume. The 2001 operating statement for Reigis follows. The division's operating assets employed were $15,750,000 at November 30, 2001, unchanged from the year before.

REIGIS STEEL DIVISION
Operating Statement
For the Year Ended November 30, 2001
(000s omitted)

Sales revenue		$25,000
Less expenses		
Cost of goods sold	$16,500	
Administrative expenses	3,955	
Selling expenses	2,700	23,155
Income from operations before tax		$ 1,845

Required

1. Calculate Reigis Steel Division's unit contribution if it produced and sold 1,484,000 units during the year ended November 30, 2001.

2. Calculate the following performance measures for 2001 for Reigis:

    a. Pretax ROI from average operating assets employed.

    b. Residual income calculated on the basis of average operating assets employed.

3. Reigis management is presented the opportunity to invest in a project that would earn an ROI of 10 percent. Is Reigis likely to accept the project? Why or why not?

4. Identify several items that Reigis should control if it is to be fairly evaluated as a separate investment SBU within Raddington Industries using either ROI or RI performance measures.

(CMA Adapted)

19–24 **TRANSFER PRICING METHODS** Lynsar Corporation started as a single plant to produce its major components and then assembled its main product into electric motors. Lynsar later expanded by developing outside markets for some components used in its motors. Eventually, the company reorganized into four manufacturing divisions: bearing, casing, switch, and motor. Each manufacturing division operates as an autonomous unit, and divisional performance is the basis for year-end bonuses.

Lynsar's transfer pricing policy permits the manufacturing divisions to sell either externally or internally. The price for goods transferred between divisions is negotiated between the buying and selling divisions without any interference from top management.

Lynsar's profits for the current year have dropped although sales have increased, and the decreased profits can be traced almost entirely to the motor division. Jere Feldon, Lynsar's chief financial officer, has learned that the motor division purchased switches for its motors from an outside supplier during the current year rather than buying them from the switch division, which is at capacity and has refused to sell to the motor division. It can sell them to outside customers at a price higher than the actual full (absorption) manufacturing cost that has always been negotiated in the past with the motor division. When the Motor Division refused to meet the price that the switch division was receiving from its outside buyer, the motor division had to purchase the switches from an outside supplier at an even higher price.

Jere is reviewing Lynsar's transfer pricing policy because he believes that suboptimization has occurred. Although the switch division made the correct decision to maximize its division profit by not transferring the switches at actual full manufacturing cost, this was not necessarily in Lynsar's best interest because of the price the motor division paid for them. The motor division has always been Lynsar's largest division and has tended to dominate the smaller divisions. Jere has learned that the casing and bearing divisions are also resisting the motor divisions expectation for using actual full manufacturing cost as the negotiated price.

Jere has requested that the corporate accounting department study alternative transfer pricing methods to promote overall goal congruence, motivate divisional management performance, and optimize overall company performance. Three transfer pricing methods being considered follow. The one selected will be applied uniformly across all divisions.

- Standard full manufacturing costs plus markup.
- Market selling price of the products being transferred.
- Outlay (out-of-pocket) costs incurred to the point of transfer plus opportunity cost to the seller, per unit.

Required

1. Discuss the following:

   a. The positive and negative motivational implications of employing a negotiated transfer price system for goods exchanged between divisions.

   b. The motivational problems that can result from using actual full (absorption) manufacturing costs as a transfer price.

2. Discuss the motivational issues that could arise if Lynsar Corporation decides to change from its current policy of covering the transfer of goods between divisions to a revised transfer pricing policy that would apply uniformly to all divisions.

3. Discuss the likely behavior of both buying and selling divisional managers for each transfer pricing method listed earlier, if it were adopted by Lynsar.

(CMA Adapted)

19–25   TRANSFER PRICING ISSUES   Often when transfer prices are based on cost, a supplying division has no incentive to reduce cost. For example, a design change that would reduce the supplying division's manufacturing cost would benefit only downstream divisions if the transfer price is based on a markup of cost.

Required   What can or should be done to provide the supplying division an incentive to reduce manufacturing costs when the transfer price is cost-based?

19–26   TRANSFER PRICING; INTERNATIONAL TAXATION   Hirsch Company has a manufacturing subsidiary in Singapore that produces high-end exercise equipment for U.S. consumers. The manufacturing subsidiary has total manufacturing costs of $1,500,000 plus general and administrative expenses of $350,000. The manufacturing unit sells the equipment for $2,500,000 to the U.S. marketing subsidiary, which sells it to the final consumer for an aggregate of $3,500,000. The sales subsidiary has total marketing, general, and administrative costs of $300,000. Assume that Singapore has a corporate tax rate of 33 percent and that the U.S. tax rate is 46 percent. Assume that no tax treaties or other special tax treatments apply.

International

Required   What is the effect on Hirsch Company's total corporate level taxes if the manufacturing subsidiary raises its price by 10 percent to the sales subsidiary?

19–27   TRANSFER PRICING; DECISION MAKING   Advanced Manufacturing Inc. (AMI) produces electronic components in three divisions: industrial, commercial, and consumer products. The commercial products division annually purchases 10,000 units of part 23-6711, which the industrial division produces for

Strategy

use in manufacturing one of its own products. The commercial division is growing rapidly due to rapid growth in its markets. The commercial division is expanding its production and now wants to increase its purchases of part 23-6711 to 15,000 units per year. The problem is that the industrial division is at full capacity. No new investment in the industrial division has been made for some years because top management sees little future growth in its products, so its capacity is unlikely to increase soon.

The commercial division can buy part 23–6711 from HighTech Inc. or from Britton Electric, a customer of the industrial division, now purchasing 650 units of part 88–461. The industrial division's sales to Britton would not be affected by the commercial division's decision about part 23–6711.

Industrial division	
Data on part 23–6711	
Price to commercial division	$185
Variable manufacturing costs	155
Price to outside buyers	205
Data on part 88–461	
Variable manufacturing costs	65
Sales price	95
Other suppliers of part 23–6711	
HighTech Inc., price	200
Britton Electric, price	210

Required

1. What is the proper decision regarding where the commercial division should purchase the part and what is the correct transfer price?

2. What are the strategic implications of your answer to requirement 1? How can AMI become more competitive in one or more of its divisions?

19–28   **RETURN ON INVESTMENT; RESIDUAL INCOME**   Jump-Start Co. (JSC), a subsidiary of Mason Industries, manufactures go-carts and other recreational vehicles. Family recreational centers that feature go-cart tracks as well as miniature golf courses, batting cages, and arcade games have increased in popularity. As a result, Mason management has been pressuring JSC to diversify into some of these other recreational areas. Recreational Leasing Inc. (RLI), one of the largest firms that leases arcade games to these family recreational centers, is looking for a buyer. Mason's top management believes that RLI's assets could be acquired for an investment of $3.2 million and has strongly urged Bill Grieco, JSC's division manager, to consider the acquisition.

Bill has reviewed RLI's financial statements with his controller, Marie Donnelly; they believe that the acquisition may not be in JSC's best interest. "If we decide not to do this, the Mason people are not going to be happy," Bill said. "If we could convince them to base our bonuses on something other than ROI, maybe this acquisition would look more attractive. How would we do if the bonuses were based on RI using the company's 15 percent cost of capital?"

Mason has traditionally evaluated all divisions on the basis of ROI, which is the ratio of operating income to total assets. The desired rate of return for each division is 20 percent. The management team of any division reporting an annual increase in the ROI is automatically eligible for a bonus. The management of divisions reporting a decline in ROI must provide convincing explanations for the decline to be eligible for a bonus. The bonus for divisions with declining ROI is limited to 50 percent of the amount of the bonus paid to divisions reporting an increase.

The following are the condensed financial statements of JSC and RLI for the fiscal year ended May 31, 2001.

	JSC	RLI
Sales revenue	$10,500,000	—
Leasing revenue	—	$2,800,000
Variable expenses	7,000,000	1,000,000
Fixed expenses	1,500,000	1,200,000
Operating income	$ 2,000,000	$ 600,000
Current assets	$ 2,300,000	$1,900,000
Long-term assets	5,700,000	1,100,000
Total assets	$ 8,000,000	$3,000,000
Current liabilities	$ 1,400,000	$ 850,000
Long-term liabilities	3,800,000	1,200,000
Shareholders' equity	2,800,000	950,000
Total liabilities and shareholders' equity	$ 8,000,000	$3,000,000

Required

1. If Mason Industries continues to use ROI as the sole measure of division performance, explain why JSC is reluctant to acquire RLI. Support your answer with appropriate calculations.

2. If Mason Industries could be persuaded to use RI to measure JSC's performance, explain why JSC would be more willing to acquire RLI. Support your answer with appropriate calculations.

3. Discuss how the behavior of division managers is likely to be affected by the use of

   a. ROI as a performance measure.

   b. RI as a performance measure.

(CMA Adapted)

19–29 **RETURN ON INVESTMENT** Easecom Company manufactures highly specialized products for networking video-conferencing equipment. Production of specialized units are, to a large extent, performed under contract, with standard units manufactured according to marketing projections. Maintenance of customer equipment is an important area of customer satisfaction. With the recent downturn in the computer industry, the video-conferencing equipment segment has suffered, causing a slide in Easecom's financial performance. Its income statement for the fiscal year ended October 31, 2001, follows.

EASECOM COMPANY
Income Statement
For the Year Ended October 31, 2001
(000s omitted)

Net sales	
Equipment	$6,000
Maintenance contracts	1,800
Total net sales	$7,800
Expenses	
Cost of goods sold	4,600
Customer maintenance	1,000
Selling expense	600
Administrative expense	900
Interest expense	150
Total expense	$7,250
Income before taxes	550
Income taxes	220
Net income	$ 330

Easecom's return on sales before interest and taxes was 9 percent in fiscal 2001 when the industry average was 12 percent. Its total asset turnover was three times, and its return on average assets before interest and taxes was 27 percent, both well below the industry average. To improve performance and raise these ratios closer to, or above, industry averages, Bill Hunt, Easecom's president, established the following goals for fiscal 2002:

Return on sales before interest and taxes	11%
Total asset turnover	4 times
Return on average assets before interest and taxes	35%

To achieve Hunt's goals, Easecom's management team considered the growth in the international video-conferencing market and proposed the following actions for fiscal 2002:

- Increase equipment sales prices by 10 percent.
- Increase the cost of each unit sold by 3 percent for needed technology, and quality improvements and for increased variable costs.
- Increase maintenance inventory by $250,000 at the beginning of the year and add two maintenance technicians at total cost of $130,000 to cover wages and related travel expenses. These revisions are intended to improve customer service and response time. The increased inventory will be financed at an annual interest rate of 12 percent; no other borrowings or loan reductions are contemplated during fiscal 2002. All other assets will be held to fiscal 2001 levels.
- Increase selling expenses by $250,000 but hold administrative expenses at 2001 levels.
- The effective rate for 2002 federal and state taxes is expected to be 40 percent, the same as 2001.

These actions were taken to increase equipment unit sales by 6 percent, with a corresponding 6 percent growth in maintenance contracts.

Required

1. Prepare a pro forma income statement for Easecom for the fiscal year ending October 31, 2002, on the assumption that the proposed actions are implemented as planned and that the increased sales objectives will be met. (All numbers should be rounded to the nearest thousand.)

2. Calculate the following ratios for Easecom for fiscal year 2002 and determine whether Bill Hunt's goals will be achieved.

   a. Return on sales before interest and taxes.

   b. Total asset turnover.

   c. Return on average assets before interest and taxes.

3. Discuss the limitations and difficulties that can be encountered in using the ratios in requirement 2, particularly when making comparisons to industry averages.

(CMA Adapted)

Strategy

19–30   STRATEGY; STRATEGIC PERFORMANCE MEASUREMENT   Ajax Consolidated has several divisions; however, only two transfer products to other divisions. The mining division refines toldine, which it transfers to the metals division where toldine is processed into an alloy and is sold to customers for $150 per unit. Ajax currently requires the mining division to transfer its total annual output of 400,000 units of toldine to the metals division at total manufacturing cost plus 10 percent. Unlimited quantities of toldine can be purchased and sold on the open market at $90 per unit. The mining division could sell all the toldine it produces at $90 per unit on the open market, but it would incur a variable selling cost of $5 per unit.

Brian Jones, the mining division's manager, is unhappy transferring the entire output of toldine to the metals division at 110 percent of cost. In a meeting with Ajax management, he said, "Why should my division be required to sell toldine to the metals division at less than market price? For the year just ended in May, metals' contribution margin was more than $19 million on sales of 400,000 units while mining's contribution was just over $5 million on the transfer of the same number of units. My division is subsidizing the profitability of the metals division. We should be allowed to charge the market price for toldine when we transfer it to the metals division."

The following is the detailed unit cost structure for both the mining and metals divisions for the fiscal year ended May 31, 2001:

| | Cost per Unit | |
	Mining Division	Metals Division
Transfer price from mining division	—	$ 66
Direct material	$12	6
Direct labor	16	20
Manufacturing overhead	32*	25†
Total cost per unit	$60	$117

*Manufacturing overhead in the mining division is 25 percent fixed and 75 percent variable.

†Manufacturing overhead in the metals division is 60 percent fixed and 40 percent variable.

Required

1. Explain whether transfer prices based on cost are appropriate as a divisional performance measure and why.

2. Using the market price as the transfer price, determine the contribution margin for both divisions for the year ended May 31, 2001.

3. If Ajax were to institute the use of negotiated transfer prices and allow divisions to buy and sell on the open market, determine the price range for toldine that both divisions would accept. Explain your answer.

4. Identify which of the three types of transfer prices—cost based, market based, or negotiated—is most likely to elicit desirable management behavior at Ajax and thus benefit overall operations. Explain your answer.

(CMA Adapted)

19–31 **TRANSFER PRICING; INTERNATIONAL** Better Life Products (BLP), Inc., is a large U.S.–based manufacturer of health care products; it specializes in cushions, braces, and other remedies for a variety of health problems experienced by elderly and disabled persons. BLP knows that its industry is competitive and hopes to compete through rapid growth, primarily within the United States, where it has a well-established brand image. Because of the competititve industry conditions, BLF is focusing on cost and price reductions as a principal way to attract customers. Because of rising domestic production costs, lower production costs in other countries, and a modest increase in global demand for its products, BLP manufactures some of these products outside the United States. Much of the materials for use by foreign manufacturers is shipped from the United States to the foreign manufacturer, which assembles the final product. In this way, BLP takes advantage of the foreign country's lower labor costs. For this purpose, BLP has formed three divisions, one in the United States to purchase and perform limited assembly of the raw materials; one a foreign division to complete the manufacturing, especially of the labor-intensive components of manufacturing; and one a

Strategy

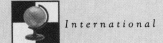

International

marketing and sales division in the United States. Sales of BLP's products are approximately 80 percent in the United States, 10 percent in Canada, and 10 percent worldwide. The foreign divisions tend to focus only on manufacturing because of the specialized nature of the products and because of BLP's desire to have the U.S. sales division coordinate all sales activities. BLP now has 18 U.S. divisions and 23 foreign divisions operating in this manner.

Foreign divisions' shipments to the United States are subject to customs duties according to the U.S. Tariff Code, which adds to BLP's cost of the foreign-based manufacturing. However, the code requires U.S. companies to pay duty on only the value added in foreign countries. For example, a product imported from an Argentine company to BLP pays customs on only the amount of the product's cost resulting from labor incurred in Argentina. To illustrate, a product with $10 of materials shipped from the United States to Argentina that incurs $10 of labor costs in Argentina is charged a tariff based on the $10 of labor costs, not the $20 of total product cost. Thus, for tariff purposes, having as small a portion of total product cost from the foreign country as possible is advantageous to BLP.

BLP division managers, including those of the foreign manufacturing facilities, are evaluated on the basis of profit. Jorge Martinez is the manager of the manufacturing plant in Argentina; his compensation from BLP is based on meeting profit targets.

BLP uses a transfer pricing approach common in the industry to allow each of the company's divisions to determine the transfer pricing autonomously through interdivision negotiations. In recent years, however, top management has played an increased role in such negotiations. In particular, when the divisions determine a transfer price that can lead to increased taxes, foreign exchange exposure, or tariffs, the corporate financial function becomes involved. This has meant that the transfer prices charged by foreign divisions to U.S. sales divisions have fallen to reduce the value added by the foreign country and thereby reduce the tariffs. To avoid problems with U.S. and Argentine government agencies, the transfer prices have been reduced slowly over time.

One effect of this transfer pricing strategy has been the continued decline of the foreign divisions' profitability. Jorge and others have difficulty meeting their profit targets and personal compensation goals because of the continually declining transfer prices.

Required

1. Assess BLP's manufacturing and marketing strategies. Are they consistent with each other and with what you consider to be the firm's overall business strategy?

2. Assess BLP's performance measurement system. What changes would you suggest and why?

International

Ethics

19–32 TRANSFER PRICING; INTERNATIONAL TAXES; ETHICS Target Manufacturing, Inc., is a multinational firm with sales and manufacturing units in 15 countries. One of its manufacturing units, in country X, sells its product to a retail unit in country Y for $200,000. Country X unit has manufacturing costs of $100,000 for these products. The retail unit in country Y sells the product to final customers for $300,000. Target is considering adjusting its transfer prices to reduce overall corporate tax liability.

Required

1. Assume that both country X and country Y have corporate income tax rates of 40 percent and that no special tax treaties or benefits apply to Target. What would be the effect on Target's total tax burden if the manufacturing unit raises its price from $200,000 to $240,000?

2. What would be the effect on Target's total taxes if the manufacturing unit raised its price from $200,000 to $240,000 and the tax rate in country X is 20 percent and in country Y is 40 percent?

3. Comment on the ethical issues, if any, you observe in this case.

19–33 STRATEGIC PERFORMANCE MEASUREMENT: INTERNATIONAL; STRATEGY; SERVICE INDUSTRY   With the multinational company becoming a significant business structure throughout the world, a growing problem is developing in the analysis of the MNC's financial results. When the incidents in this problem occurred, the U.S. dollar was strengthening considerably relative to other currencies. Besides causing economic problems in many developing countries, it also created a problem in the proper evaluation of a multinational's subsidiaries and their contribution to its total results.

International

Strategy

Service

Security System Corporation provides financial services for dealers and consumers in a variety of construction and consumer products areas. The firm is searching for the proper method to evaluate its subsidiaries. Of concern is the subsidiaries' contribution to the company's overall earnings and how to evaluate whether the specific goals developed by the subsidiaries' management have been met.

In search of answers, the company is concerned with the following concepts:

• Analysis of results: In local currency or U.S. dollars?

• Management's explanation of variances: In local currency or U.S. dollars?

• What should the time frames be for comparative data: Plan or forecast?

The firm has six distinctive business segments in the new-residential-housing market: consumer appliance market, commercial nonresidential construction, consumer aftermarket, home furnishing market, automotive market, and capital goods markets. Last year the company achieved 30 percent of its revenues and 35 percent of its earnings from its international subsidiaries. However, years ago when one British pound sterling equaled $2.33 U.S. (whereas now it's one pound = $1.45 U.S.), the firm achieved 35 percent of its revenue—but more significantly, 47 percent of its earnings—from its international subsidiaries. During the past five years, although the U.S. dollar equivalent of earnings from the international subsidiaries has declined from 47 percent of the total to 35 percent, most operations have reported significant, steady gains from year to year in the local currency.

All operations report their monthly financial data to the firm's world headquarters in U.S. dollars. They use the existing exchange rate at the close of business on the last day of the month. The firm reports the exchange based on *FASB 52* accounting guidelines (except for one or two special situations). The comparisons of the monthly financial data are made against a financial plan that uses a predetermined exchange rate for the various months of the year.

Over the past five years, even as the U.S. dollar has steadily strengthened against foreign currencies, the firm has analyzed the financial results of its operations totally in U.S. dollars and then compares its results to a fixed-plan exchange rate.

The firm establishes exchange rates to be used each year, many times optimistically, and then sets an earnings per share target on that basis. If the dollar strengthens even more, the firm misses its targets and prepares statements showing that a particular group missed its planned targets when, in fact, all of the group's operations could have exceeded their local currency plans but are losing on the comparison because of unfavorable exchange rate effects.

Required   How should the firm measure its results to enhance its competitiveness? How can it safeguard its overall EPS target if it uses local currencies in the reporting system? Where does the responsibility for the U.S. dollar attainment of goals lie?
(CMA Adapted)

SOLUTIONS TO SELF-STUDY PROBLEMS

1.   Return on Investment and Residual Income

1.   ROS = Net income/Sales

   = \$640,000/\$8,000,000

   = 0.08

   Asset turnover = Sales/Average investment

   = \$8,000,000/(\$2,500,000 + \$2,600,000)/2

   = 3.137 times

   ROI = ROS × Asset turnover

   = 0.08 × 3.137

   = 25.1%

2.   Residual income = Net income − (Average investment ×
                    Minimum rate of return)

   = \$640,000 − [(\$2,500,000 + \$2,600,000)/2] × 0.12

   = \$334,000

2.   Determining the Proper Transfer Price

1.   Since the T-Bar unit is at full capacity and the contribution on outside sales of \$70 (= \$165 − \$5 − \$90) is higher than the \$60 cost saving of inside production (= \$150 − \$90), the T-Bar unit should sell outside and the adhesive unit should purchase T-Bar for \$150 outside the firm.

2.   Since the T-bar unit is at full capacity and there is an outside market, the best transfer price is market price for T-bar. The relevant market price is the price that the T-Bar unit can charge (assuming it is a reliable, long-term price), \$165. This transfer price will cause the adhesive unit to do the correct thing, that is, to buy outside since the outside price is lower.

3.   If the T-bar unit has excess capacity, it can sell T-Bar both internally and externally. The correct transfer price is then the price that will cause the adhesive unit to purchase internally; that is, any price between variable cost of the seller (\$90) and the outside market price to the adhesive unit (\$150). The units might agree on a price by considering what is a fair return to each unit and in effect split the profit on the sale between them. The actual outcome of the negotiations for the transfer price depends on a number of factors, including the negotiation skills of the two managers.

20

Management Compensation and Business Valuation

After studying this chapter, you should be able to . . .

1   Identify and explain the types of management compensation

2   Identify the strategic role of management compensation and the different types of compensation used in practice

3   Explain the three characteristics of a bonus plan: the base for determining performance, the compensation pool from which the bonus is funded, and the bonus payment options

4   Describe the role of tax planning and financial reporting in management compensation planning

5   Explain how management compensation plans are used in service firms and not-for-profit organizations

6   Apply the two approaches for business valuation: financial analysis and direct valuation

There's no praise to beat the sort you can put in your pocket.

MOLIÉRE

The main issue in this concluding chapter is how to determine management compensation and value the entire company. How do we fairly compensate managers for this success? We have emphasized strategy throughout the book. How do we quantitatively assess the firm's success in achieving its strategy?

Looking at large, publicly held firms, we focus first on a measure of success that many would use: the value of the firm as measured by its market capitalization, that is, the value of its outstanding shares. Fundamentally, all measures of the firm's value are predictions of future performance—an assessment of the future value of the current ownership in the firm. Choosing a method for predicting future value is a difficult task, as Bill Barker, a writer for the Motley Fool says: "I don't think there is any method that anyone will think is the perfect one. If you ask 10 investors what the Holy Grail method would be, you'd get 10 different answers." In this spirit, we consider a number of different valuation methods in this chapter.

We will see that many current valuation methods rely on financial information about the firm's performance, particularly its earnings. Some analysts prefer cash flow measures, and still others prefer total revenues because cash flows and revenues more accurately reflect current operating performance. Another reason is that some of the most valuable firms in the new economy have little or no earnings or cash flows and sometimes unimpressive revenue growth. Consider two of the most successful firms that have large market capitalizations: Amazon.com Inc. and Red Hat Inc. Investors are betting that the intangible assets of these firms—the customer loyalty, innovative products, and marketing—will pay off in future revenues, cash flows, and earnings. Not all analysts agree, however. We will see that valuing a firm is quite a challenge, but it is also one of the most important things for the business and the management accountant to do.[1]

PART ONE: MANAGEMENT COMPENSATION

Recruiting, motivating, rewarding, and retaining effective managers are critical to the success of all firms. Effective management compensation plans are an important and integral part of the determination of a strategic competitive advantage and are important concerns of the management accountant.

◀**LEARNING OBJECTIVE 1**

Identify and explain the types of management compensation.

---

[1] The Motley Fool (*www.fool.com*) is an organization that provides education and information for investors. For more information on Amazon.com, see Walter S. Mossberg, "Amazon.com Still Remains a Web Shopping Model," *The Wall Street Journal*, September 21, 2000, p. B1; Robert McGough and Nick Wingfield, "Amazon or Rashomon: Every Analyst Has Different View of E-Tailer's Prospects," *The Wall Street Journal*, September 27, 2000, p. C1; and "Can Red Hat Stay Red-Hot?" *Business Week*, July 5, 1999.

TYPES OF MANAGEMENT COMPENSATION

Management compensation plans are policies and procedures for compensating managers.

A **salary** is a fixed payment.

A **bonus** is based on the achievement of performance goals for the period.

Benefits include special travel, membership in a fitness club, tickets to entertainment events, and other extras paid for by the firm.

Management compensation plans are policies and procedures for compensating managers. Compensation includes one or more of the following: salary, bonus, and benefits. **Salary** is a fixed payment; a **bonus** is based on the achievement of performance goals for the period. **Benefits** include travel, membership in a fitness club, life insurance, medical benefits, tickets to entertainment events, and other extras paid for by the firm.

Compensation can be paid currently (usually an annual amount paid monthly, twice a month, or weekly) or deferred to future years. Salary and benefits are typically awarded currently; bonuses are either paid currently or deferred, though a wide variety of plans is found in practice.

The compensation plans for high-level managers are generally explained in the firm's proxy statements and must be approved by the shareholders. Base salary usually

---

Wider Use of Bonus Instead of Base Salary: Duracell

In an effort to reduce fixed operating costs, companies are reducing pension and medical benefits for active and retired employees. They are also seeking ways to reduce the basic salary structure, which is primarily fixed cost. If an employee is given a raise, that increase becomes an entitlement and must be paid each year. It is also used to calculate the employee's pension and other company-paid benefits, thus effectively increasing the amount of fixed cost.

Firms can effectively reduce fixed costs by keeping base salary increases to a minimum. In addition, companies are striving to increase the efficiency and productivity of employees at every level, using incentive plans and similar productivity enhancement programs.

A recent survey by William M. Mercer, Inc., shows that firms are moving to extend their stock option plans to lower levels in the organization. For example, Duracell Corp. motivates employees by giving stock options to all full- and part-time employees. "Employees really do have a vested interest in how the company performs, and as we make those hurdles (increase in stock price) there's a real sense of accomplishment," according to Gary Fox, a Duracell manager.

On the other hand, establishing appropriate salary levels and incentive plans is a complex and difficult task. Incentives tend to lose their effect over time as employees begin to consider the incentive as part of the compensation base.

Source: Based on information in *Coopers & Lybrand Executive Briefing,* November 1991; and "At Duracell, an Early Christmas," *Business Week,* September 30, 1996; "Stock Options for the Ranks," *Business Week,* September 7, 1998, p. 22; and Rekita Balu, "Bonuses Aren't Just for the Bosses," Fast Company, December 2000, pp. 74–76.

AT&T CEO Focuses on Pay for Performance

C. Michael Armstrong, CEO of AT&T, wants to make the firm more profitable and quicker to respond to customer needs. A key aspect of his plan is pay for performance. Almost 75 percent of all AT&T executives have their bonuses tied to quantitative goals, including sales, costs, and profits. Also, like their counterparts at other firms such as Kodak, top executives will be required to purchase shares of the company to further align their incentives and goals with those of the firm's shareholders. At AT&T, Armstrong requires executives to purchase stock worth five times their annual salary. A recent study of CEO turnover and executive compensation shows that turnover cannot be explained by total compensation or bonuses, but there is evidence that turnover is lower among those executives that have large stockholdings in their company. Armstrong and Kodak must be right!

Source: Based on information in "New Boss, New Plan," *Business Week,* February 2, 1998, pp. 122–32; and "Money Can't Buy a Loyal CEO," *Business Week,* February 5, 2001, p. 30.

is an annual amount paid throughout the year, although it can also include predetermined future cash payments and/or stock awards. Perks are commonly awarded on an annual basis, although they can include future payments or benefits. Base salary and perks are negotiated when the manager is hired and when compensation contracts are reviewed and renewed. They are not commonly influenced by the manager's current performance, as is bonus pay. A recent study of the top five executives at 1,070 firms in 13 major industries showed that bonus pay is the fastest growing part of total compensation: firms are moving to linking executive pay to performance. The median bonus was 80 percent of salary for the sampled firms, and in some industries, the median bonus was larger than salary. For example, in the financial services industry, the median bonus was 255 percent of the average salary.[2]

STRATEGIC ROLE AND OBJECTIVES OF MANAGEMENT COMPENSATION

The strategic role of management compensation has three aspects: (1) the strategic conditions facing the firm, (2) the effect of risk aversion on managers' decision making, and (3) certain ethical issues.

Design the Compensation Plan for Existing Strategic Conditions

The compensation plan should be grounded in the strategic analysis of the firm: its competitive strengths and weaknesses and critical success factors. As the strategic conditions facing the firm change over time, the compensation plan should also change. For example, the firm's strategy changes as its products move through the different phases of the sales life cycle: product introduction, growth, maturity, and decline (Chapter 5). As a firm's product moves from the growth phase to the mature phase, the firm's strategy also moves from product differentiation to cost leadership. When this happens, the compensation plan should change in response to the new strategy. Exhibit 20–1 illustrates how the mix of salary, bonus, and perks might change as the firm and its products move through different phases of the sales life cycle.

Note in Exhibit 20–1 that the mix of the three parts of total compensation changes as strategic conditions change. For example, in the mature phase of the products' life cycle, when competition is likely to be the highest and the firm is interested in maintaining an established market and controlling costs, a balanced compensation plan of competitive salary, bonus, and benefits is needed to attract, motivate, and retain the

◀ **LEARNING OBJECTIVE 2**
Identify the strategic role of management compensation and the different types of compensation used in practice.

Exhibit 20–1 Compensation Plans Tailored for Different Strategic Conditions*			
Product Sales Life Cycle Phase	**Salary**	**Bonus**	**Benefits**
Product introduction	High	Low	Low
Growth	Low	High	Competitive
Maturity	Competitive	Competitive	Competitive
Decline	High	Low	Competitive

*Key to exhibit: "Competitive" lies between low and high.

Source: Adapted from George T. Milkovich and Jerry M. Newman, *Compensation* (Burr Ridge, Ill.: Richard D. Irwin, 1984), p. 12; also, V. Govindarajan and J. K. Shank present a similar approach based on the Boston Consulting Group's concepts of the three phases: build, hold, and harvest, in "Strategic Cost Management Tailoring Controls to Strategies," *Journal of Cost Management*, Fall 1992, pp. 14–24.

---

[2] *Deloitte & Touche Review*, April 29, 1996, citing a survey by the Conference Board for 1994 compensation. See also David Smith, "The Performance Pay Race," *Management Today (UK)*, November 1999, pp. 70–75.

best managers. In contrast, during the growth phase when the need for innovation and leadership is the greatest, the emphasis is on relatively large bonuses to effectively motivate managers. In effect, top management considers the specific strategic conditions facing the firm as a basic consideration in developing the compensation plan and making changes as strategic conditions change.

Risk Aversion and Management Compensation

The manager's relative risk aversion can have an important effect on decision making (see Chapter 18, "Employment Contracts"). Risk aversion is the tendency to prefer decisions with predictable outcomes over those that are uncertain. It is a relatively common decision-making characteristic of managers. A risk-averse manager is biased against decisions that have an uncertain outcome, even if the expected outcome is favorable.

For example, a risk-averse manager might cancel a planned investment in new equipment that would reduce operating costs if there is a chance that nonoperating costs from installation problems, employee training needs, or other reasons might increase. In contrast, the firm's top management and shareholders might not see the risk of additional nonoperating costs as significant relative to the potential for reduced operating costs. The difference in perspective comes about because the outcome of the decision, while likely to have a relatively small impact on the firm and therefore on top management and shareholders, is likely to directly and significantly impact the manager's bonus..

Compensation plans can manage risk aversion effectively by carefully choosing the mix of salary and bonus in total compensation. The higher the proportion of bonus in total compensation, the higher the incentive for the manager to avoid risky outcomes. To reduce the effect of risk aversion, a relatively large proportion of salary should be in total compensation, with a smaller portion in bonus. Determining the proper balance between salary and bonus must consider all three compensation objectives.

Ethical Issues

Two ethical issues must be addressed when designing and implementing compensation plans: (1) the overall level of compensation and (2) unethical actions that managers might perform to meet goals, such as misrepresenting actual results.

When Is Executive Pay Too High?

There is a common concern that executive pay is too high and that lower-level employees are not properly compensated relative to the very high salaries and bonuses of top executives, particularly during periods of corporate downsizing.[3] High executive compensation is unjust, some argue, and compensation plans are unethical. Others point out that most executives are worth their high compensation because they bring far greater value to the firm than the cost of their compensation. Shareholders and bondholders who see their investments appreciate and attribute this to the executive are likely to see the compensation plans as just and ethical. For example, when a key manager left Wal-Mart, the firm's stock price fell 4 percent on the day of the announcement, indicating the very high importance investors placed on this executive.[4]

---

[3] "Even Executives Are Wincing at Executive Pay," *Business Week*, May 12, 1997, pp. 40–41; "Executive Pay," *Business Week*, April 17, 2000, pp. 100–12; "CEO Pay: The More Things Change . . .," *Business Week*, October 16, 2000, pp. 106–108; Dean Foust, "CEO Pay: Nothing Succeeds Like Failure," *Business Week*, September 11, 2000, p. 46; "Did the CEO Deserve a Raise," *Business Week*, April 24, 2000, p. 32; Pamela L. Moore, "Reliance: Dismal Management, Stellar Pay," *Business Week*, November 22, 1999, p. 145; and Louis Lavelle, "The Artificial Sweetener in CEO Pay," *Business Week*, March 26, 2001, pp. 102–3.

[4] *The Wall Street Journal*, March 29, 1996. Bill Fields, a 25-year veteran of Wal-Mart, left his position as chief of the main discount store business department to accept a similar position at Viacom, Inc. A similar case is reported for Black & Decker, whose stock fell by 8 percent the day Joseph Galli, its chief executive, departed; see "Power Drain," *Business Week*, May 17, 1999, p. 50.

The Internal Revenue Service can deny a firm's right to deduct compensation that it determines to be unreasonable. The U.S. Tax Court analyzes 14 compensation factors to determine whether the compensation is reasonable, including the manager's qualifications, the nature of the work, the size and complexity of the firm, and the prevailing economic conditions.[5]

Unethical Actions

Sometimes the management compensation plan provides an incentive for unethical action. A well-known example is the H. J. Heinz Company, which in 1979 discovered management fraud in many of its divisions.[6] The division managers had been using improper billing, accounting, and reporting practices to transfer income from one fiscal period to another. Their purpose was to achieve a target profit level needed to achieve bonuses. An investigation by the audit committee found that perceived and actual pressures to achieve the goals of Heinz's bonus program were a major reason for the fraud. A lack of top management emphasis on ethics and accounting controls also contributed to the fraud.

Similarly, at one time Sears, Roebuck & Co. paid auto shop employees commissions based on the amount of repair work done. This resulted in charges for work that was unnecessary, and was never done, as well as overcharges for completed work. The discovery of these fraudulent practices in 1992 damaged Sears' auto shop business, requiring Sears to change policies quickly to win back customers. Again, the presence of a very strong motivation due to a compensation plan without compensating accounting controls designed to detect and prevent fraud can lead to unethical behavior.

Objectives of Management Compensation

The firm's key objective is to develop management compensation plans that support its strategic objectives, as set forth by management and the owners. The objectives of

---

Executive Pay Too High?

Nearly three-quarters of Americans believe that corporate bosses are overpaid.

Source: Based on information in Business Week Survey, *Business Week*, September 11, 2000.

High CEO Pay Alienates Lower-Level Managers

A study by researchers at Stanford University and the University of Illinois at Urbana-Champaign found that overpayment of CEOs, relative to industry norms and to the pay levels of lower-level managers, tends to be associated with higher turnover rates of lower-level managers. The implication is that the high CEO pay negatively affects the loyalty and motivation of lower-level managers. Perhaps firms are responding; a recent survey by William M. Mercer, Inc. indicates that to "ease tensions over high executive compensation," firms are beginning to extend stock option plans to a majority of their employees.

Source: Based on information from "Where CEO Pay Really Grates," *Business Week*, October 13, 1997; and "Stock Options for the Ranks," *Business Week*, September 7, 1998, p. 22.

---

[5] The 14 factors are set out in the Tax Court ruling in *Pulsar Components International, Inc.*, v. *Commissioner*, T.C. Memo 1996-129 (3/14/96).

[6] "H. J. Heinz Company, A Case on Ethics in Management," Harvard Business School Case No. 382-034 (Boston, Mass.: Harvard Business School). See also, H. M. Schilit, *Financial Shenanigans: How to Detect Accounting Gimmicks and Fraud in Financial Reports* (New York: McGraw-Hill, 1993); and John A. Byrne, "Smoke, Mirrors, and the Boss's Paycheck," *Business Week*, October 13, 1997, p. 63.

management compensation are therefore consistent with the three objectives of management control as defined in Chapter 18:

1. To motivate managers to exert a high level of effort to achieve the goals set by top management.
2. To provide the right incentive for managers, acting autonomously, to make decisions consistent with the goals set by top management.
3. To determine fairly the rewards earned by managers for their effort and skill and the effectiveness of their decision making.

In Chapter 18 and Chapter 19, these objectives were used to develop performance measurement systems (e.g., cost, profit, and investment SBUs). In this chapter, the objectives are used to develop effective management compensation plans.

The first objective is to motivate managers to exert a high level of effort to achieve the firm's goals. A performance-based compensation plan is best for this purpose. For example, a bonus plan that rewards the manager for achieving particular goals is appropriate. The goals could be financial or nonfinancial, current or long term.

The second objective is to provide the appropriate incentive for managers to make decisions that are consistent with the firm's objectives. The firm's objectives are identified in the strategic competitive analysis from which its critical success factors (CSFs) are derived. CSFs include customer satisfaction, quality, service, product development, and innovation in production and distribution. Firms attend to CSFs by making them part of the manager's compensation.

For example, McDonald's rewards managers who develop its CSFs—quality, service, cleanliness, and value—in addition to the conventional financial performance measures (earnings, growth in sales). International Paper Company includes nonfinancial factors such as quality, safety, and minority employee development as factors in management compensation plans. Research has shown that similar firms with clear strategic goals specified in CSFs include these factors in their compensation plans.[7]

In developing compensation plans, the management accountant works to achieve fairness by making the plan simple, clear, and consistent. Fairness also means that the plan focuses only on the controllable aspects of the manager's performance. For example, compensation should not be affected by expenses that cannot be tied directly to the manager's unit. Similarly, the manager's performance should be separate from that of the unit because economic factors beyond the manager's control are likely to affect the unit's performance. Fairness in this sense is often achieved by basing the manager's compensation on performance relative to prior years or to agreed-on goals rather than on comparison to the performance of other managers.

As a general view, remuneration by fixed salaries does not in any class of functionaries produce the maximum amount of zeal.

JOHN STEWART MILL, ENGLISH PHILOSOPHER
AND ECONOMIST, 1806–1873

BONUS PLANS

As stated earlier, bonus compensation is the fastest growing element of total compensation and often the largest part. A wide variety of bonus pay plans can be categorized according to three key aspects:

- The **base of the compensation,** that is, how the bonus pay is determined. The three most common bases are (1) stock price, (2) cost, revenue, profit, or investment SBU–based performance, and (3) the balanced scorecard.

---

[7] C. Ittner and D. Larcker, "Total Quality Management and the Choice of Information and Reward Systems," *Journal of Accounting Research* (1995 Supplement), pp. 1–34; and R. Bushman, R. Indjejikian, and A. Smith, "CEO Compensation: The Role of Individual Performance Evaluation," *Journal of Accounting and Economics*, April 1996.

- **Compensation pools,** that is, the source from which the bonus pay is funded. The two most common compensation pools are earnings in the manager's own SBU and a firmwide pool based on the firm's total earnings.
- **Payment options,** that is, how the bonus is to be awarded. The two common options are cash and stock (typically common shares). The cash or stock can either be awarded currently or deferred to future years. Stock can either be awarded directly or granted in the form of stock options.

Bases for Bonus Compensation

Bonus compensation can be determined on the basis of stock price, strategic performance measures (cost, revenue, profit, or investment SBU), or the balanced scorecard (critical success factors). For example, when the manager's unit is publicly held, its stock price is a relevant base. When stock price is used, the amount of the bonus depends on the amount of the increase in stock price or whether the stock price reaches a certain predetermined goal. Similarly, when strategic performance measures or CSFs are used, the bonus depends either on the amount of improvement in the measure or on the achievement of a predetermined goal. The bonus can be determined by comparing the stock price, accounting measures, or CSFs for a given manager to that of other managers. The bonus can be determined in three ways. It can be based on a comparison of current performance to (1) prior years, (2) a budget or predetermined target, or (3) the bonus awarded to other managers. By using a budget or a comparison to prior years, firms avoid the influence of uncontrollable factors.[8]

◀ **LEARNING OBJECTIVE 3**

Explain the three characteristics of a bonus plan: the base for determining performance, the compensation pool from which the bonus is funded, and the bonus payment options.

Survey of Executive Pay in the United States and the United Kingdom

A recent survey reports significant differences in compensation practices in the United States and the United Kingdom. The study of the top 10 U.K. firms (based on total sales) indicates that the compensation of their chief executives was 31 percent salary, 30 percent bonuses, and 39 percent long-term incentives such as stock options. The comparable figures for the top 10 U.S. executives are 2 percent, 10 percent, and 88 percent, respectively.

Source: David Smith, "The Performance Pay Race," *Management Today (UK),* November 1999, pp. 70–75.

Linking Rewards to Performance Measures at an Oil Company and Ford Motor Co.

Companies understand that they are more likely to achieve strategic goals if they include them in management compensation. An oil company uses the balanced scorecard as the sole basis for computing incentive compensation. The balanced scorecard–based incentive plan is as follows: 60 percent of executives' bonuses are tied to their achievement of four financial indicators: return on capital, profitability, cash flow, and operating cost. The remaining 40 percent of the bonus is tied to indicators of customer satisfaction, dealer satisfaction, employee satisfaction, and environmental responsibility. The firm's CEO says that linking compensation to the scorecard has helped to align the company with its strategy. "I know of no competitor," he says, "who has this degree of alignment. It is providing results for us."

Ford Motor Company uses a similar idea. The bonus formula that Ford uses for its 5,500 managers worldwide relies on customer satisfaction scores on two surveys of customers, one three months after purchase and the other three years. In 1999 the customer satisfaction score determined 33 percent of the managers' bonuses and in 2000 50 percent.

Source: Based on information in R. S. Kaplan and D. P. Norton, "Using the Balanced Scorecard as a Strategic Management System," *Harvard Business Review,* January–February 1996, pp. 75–85. (Name of actual company disguised by the authors.); Mary Connelly, "Buyers Get Say in Ford Execs' Pay," *Automotive News,* May 1, 2000, p. 97; and Nancy Thorley Hill and Kevin T. Stevens, "Structuring Compensation to Achieve Financial Results," *Strategic Finance,* March 2001, pp. 48–51.

---

[8] For examples of the use of the balanced scorecard in executive compensation, see Robert S. Kaplan and David Norton, *The Strategy—Focused Organization* (Boston, Mass.: Harvard Business School Press, 2001).

Exhibit 20–2	Advantages and Disadvantages of Different Bonus Compensation Bases Relative to Compensation Objectives		
	Motivation	**Right Decision**	**Fairness**
Stock price	(+/–) Depends on whether stock and stock options are included in base pay and bonus (–) Lack of controllability can be unmotivating	(+) Consistent with shareholder's interests.	(–) Lack of controllability
Strategic performance measures (cost, revenue, profit, and investment SBUs)	(+) Strongly motivating if noncontrollable factors are excluded	(+) Generally a good measure of economic performance (–) Typically has only a short-term focus (–) If bonus is very high, creates an incentive for inaccurate reporting	(+) Intuitive, clear, and easily understood (–) Measurement issues: differences in accounting conventions, cost allocation methods, financing methods, and so on
Balanced scorecard (critical success factors)	(+) Strongly motivating if noncontrollable factors are excluded	(+) Consistent with management's strategy (–) Can be subject to inaccurate reporting	(+) If carefully defined and measured, CSFs are likely to be perceived as fair (–) Potential measurement issues, as above

Key: (+) means the base has a positive effect on the objective.
(–) means the base has a negative effect on the objective.

The choice of a base comes from a consideration of the compensation objectives, as outlined in Exhibit 20–2. A common choice is to use cost, revenue, profit, or investment SBUs because they are often a good measure of economic performance; therefore, they are motivating and perceived to be fair. As many firms move to a more strategic approach to cost management, however, the use of CSFs and stock-price-based measures in compensation is likely to increase. Ford Motor Company and International Paper Company, among others, are using CSFs in this way.

Bonus Compensation Pools

A **unit-based pool** is a basis for determining a bonus according to the performance of the manager's unit.

A **firmwide pool** is a basis for determining the bonus available to all managers through an amount set aside for this purpose.

A manager's bonus can be determined by the so-called **unit-based pool** that is based on the performance of the manager's unit. For example, the bonus pool might be determined as the amount of the unit's earnings that are more than 5 percent of the investment in the unit. The appeal of the unit-based pool is the strong motivation for effective managers to perform and to receive rewards for their effort; the upside potential to the individual manager is very motivating.

Alternatively, the amount of bonus available to all managers is often a **firmwide pool** set aside for this purpose. A firmwide pool, for example, might be the amount of firmwide earnings that are more than 5 percent of firmwide investment. Each unit manager's bonus is then drawn from this common pool. General Electric Corporation's bonus compensation plan includes the following in its 1995 Proxy Statement regarding the firm's pool:

> the maximum amount in any year is 10% of the amount by which consolidated net earnings exceed 5% of average consolidated capital investment.

When the bonus pool is unit based, the amount of the bonus for any one manager is independent of the performance of the other managers. In contrast, when a firmwide pool is used, each manager's bonus depends in some predetermined way on the firm's performance as a whole. The sharing arrangements vary widely, although a common arrangement is for all managers to share equally in the firmwide bonus pool. Generally, the firmwide pool provides an important incentive for coordination and cooperation among units within the firm since all managers share in the higher overall firm profits that result from cross-unit efforts. Moreover, those who think executive

Market Value of Employee Stock Options at Leading Firms

The 10 firms with the highest market value of employee stock options as of June 30, 2000, are shown following (all amounts are in billions):

Microsoft	$61.28	Morgan Stanley	21.86
Cisco Systems	55.81	America Online	21.05
Intel	40.85	Oracle	20.19
Yahoo!	30.85	Sun	18.98
Broadcom	26.09	General Electric	18.09

Source: UBS Warburg, reported by Don Clark and Rebecca Buckman, "Microsoft to Resume Buybacks to Provide for Employee Stock Options, Prevent Dilution," *The Wall Street Journal,* August 7, 2000, p. C1. The value of these options changes daily as stock prices change. For example, the value of the Yahoo! options on October 12, 2000, was $14.1 billion, which was less than one-half of their value at June 30, 2000; see "Here Today, Gone Tomorrow," *The Wall Street Journal,* October 16, 2000, p. C1.

Exhibit 20–3	**Advantages and Disadvantages of Different Bonus Pools Relative to Compensation Objectives**

	Motivation	Right Decision	Fairness
Unit based	(+) Strong motivation for an effective manager—the upside potential (–) Unmotivating for manager of economically weaker units	(–) Provides the incentive for individual managers *not* to cooperate with and support other units when needed for the good of the firm.	(–) Does not separate the performance of the unit from the manager's performance
Firmwide	(+) Helps to attract and retain good managers throughout the firm, even in economically weaker units (–) Not as strongly motivating as the unit-based pool	(+) Effort for the good of the overall firm is rewarded—motivates teamwork and sharing of assets among units	(+) Separates the performance of the manager from that of the unit (+) Can appear to be fairer to shareholders and others who are concerned that executive pay is too high

Key: (+) means the pool has a positive effect on the objective.

(–) means the pool has a negative effect on the objective.

pay is too high often argue that pay linked to overall firm performance is preferable since all managers share in this success. We summarize the advantages and disadvantages of each approach to bonus pools in Exhibit 20–3.

Bonus Payment Options

In recent years, the use of different payment options for bonus compensation plans has greatly increased. In the competition for top executives, firms are developing innovative ways to attract and retain the best.[9]

We look at the four most common payment options:

Current bonus (cash and/or stock) based on current (usually annual) performance, the most common bonus form.

Deferred bonus (cash and/or stock) earned currently but not paid for two or more years. Deferred plans are used to avoid or delay taxes or to affect the manager's future total income stream in some desired way. This type of plan can also be used to retain key managers because the deferred compensation is paid only if the manager stays with the firm.

---

[9] "Executive Pay," *Business Week,* April 17, 2000, pp. 100–12; "Executive Pay," *The Wall Street Journal,* special section, April 6, 2000. Compensation practices also change as market conditions change. For example, after the decline in the share values of technology firms in March 2000, these firms shifted to cash-based executive pay; "New Dot-Com Mantra: Just Pay Me in Cash Please," *The Wall Street Journal,* November 28, 2000, p. C1.

Stock options confer the right to purchase stock at some future date at a predetermined price. They are used to motivate managers to increase stock price for the benefit of the shareholders.

Performance shares grant stock for achieving certain performance goals over two years or more.

The current and deferred bonus plans generally focus the manager's attention on short-term performance measures, most commonly on accounting earnings. In contrast, stock options and performance shares focus attention directly on shareholder value. See the advantages and disadvantages of the four plans in Exhibit 20–4.

Exhibit 20–4	**Advantages and Disadvantages of Bonus Payment Options Relative to Compensation Objectives**		
	Motivation	**Right Decision**	**Fairness**
Current bonus	(+) Strong motivation for current performance; stronger motivation than for deferred plans	(–) Short-term focus (–) Risk-averse manager avoids risky but potentially beneficial projects	(+/–) Depends on the clarity of the bonus arrangement and the consistency with which it is applied
Deferred bonus	(+) Strong motivation for current performance, but not as strong as for the current bonus plan since the reward is delayed	Same as for current bonus	Same as for current bonus
Stock options	(+) Unlimited upside potential is highly motivating (–) Delay in reward reduces motivation somewhat	(+) Incentive to consider longer-term issues (+) Provides better risk incentives than for current or deferred bonus plans (+) Consistent with shareholder interests	Same as for current bonus, plus (–) Uncontrollable factors affect stock price
Performance shares	Same as for stock options	(+) Incentive to consider long-term factors that affect stock price (+) Consistent with the firm's strategy, when critical success factors are used (+) Consistent with shareholder interests when earnings per share is used	(+/–) Depends on the clarity of the bonus arrangements and the consistency with which it is applied

Key: (+) means the payment option has a positive effect.
(–) means the payment option has a negative effect.

The Hidden Cost of Stock Options

Many firms use stock options to provide an effective means of manager compensation. The stock options align managers' interests with those of shareholders. The stock option method also has another important benefit: its cost *does not affect net income.* Under current accounting rules, the effect of stock options on net income, determined by the Black-Scholes fair value option pricing model, *need be disclosed only in footnotes* to the financial statements.

For example, the reported earnings of some companies would have been significantly affected if the cost of employee stock options had been included in determining net income as shown here:

Firm	Reported 1999 Earnings per Share	Per Share Earnings (loss) After Stock Options
Yahoo!	$0.01	$(0.06)
Broadcom	0.36	(0.53)
Autodesk	0.16	(0.74)

Source: *Business Week,* September 4, 2000, p. 10.

TAX PLANNING AND FINANCIAL REPORTING

In addition to achieving the three main objectives of compensation plans, firms attempt to choose plans that reduce or avoid taxes for both the firm and the manager. By combining salary, bonus, and perks, accountants can maximize potential tax savings for the firm, and delay or avoid taxes for the manager. For example, many perks (club memberships, company car, entertainment) are deductible to reduce the firm's tax liability but are not considered income to the manager (and therefore not taxed).

In contrast, although salary is a deductible business expense for the firm, it is taxable income for the manager. Bonus plans have a variety of tax effects as outlined in Exhibit 20–5. Tax planning is complex and dynamic, an integral part of compensation planning. Exhibit 20–5 suggests general relationships; a thorough coverage of tax planning is beyond the scope of this text.

◀**LEARNING OBJECTIVE 4**

Describe the role of tax planning and financial reporting in management compensation planning.

Exhibit 20–5   Tax and Financial Report Effects of Compensation Plans

			Tax Effect	
		Financial Statement Effect	On the Firm	On the Manager
Salary		Current expense	Current deduction	Currently taxed
Bonus	Current	Current expense	Current deduction	Currently taxed
	Deferred	Deferred expense	Deferred deduction	Deferred tax
	Stock options—nonqualified plans	Accounting rules encourage but do not require recognition as expense for most stock grants; only footnote disclosure is required	Deduction when exercised	Taxed as ordinary income when exercised
	Stock options—qualified plans	As above	No deduction	Taxed as capital gains when stock is sold if held 18 months from exercise date
	Performance shares	As above	Deferred deduction	Deferred tax
Perks	Certain retirement plans	Current expense	Current deduction	Deferred tax
	Other perks	Current expense	Current deduction	Never taxed

Source: For more on taxation and compensation, see John C. Boma and Michael D. Rosenbaum, "Keep Executives Happy," *Journal of Accountancy,* February 1998, pp. 47–50.

Indexed Options: Improving the Link of Performance to Pay

Many shareholders and analysts as well as Federal Reserve Chairman Alan Greenspan have argued that allowing the improvement in stock prices to result in a large financial reward for executives with stock options is not fair. In many cases, the executive might have had little to do with the improvement in stock price; for example, a general improvement in economic conditions increases all stock values. To link stock options more clearly to executive performance, firms can adopt "indexed options" that link the value of the stock option to whether the stock price meets a predetermined index. The index can be based on the performance of competitors in the firm's industry or on a broad index measure, such as the Standard & Poor's 500 index.

Indexed options can mean more or less total pay for the executive. For example, the data of a study of executive compensation in 1998 indicate that although Jack Welch at General Electric would have benefited from indexed options, Nolan Archibald at Black & Decker would have received much less pay.

Disadvantages of indexed options include the fact that an accounting rule requires companies to charge indexed options against earnings, which is not required for standard options. Some argue that indexed options will hinder firms' ability to attract the best executives.

Source: Alfred Rappaport, "New Thinking on How to Link Executive Pay to Performance," *Harvard Business Review,* March–April 1999, pp. 91–101; and Jennifer Reingold, "An Options Plan Your CEO Hates," *Business Week,* February 28, 2000, pp. 82–84.

Firms also attempt to design compensation plans that have a favorable effect on the firm's financial report. For example, present accounting rules do not require current recognition of the expense for grants of stock or stock options in many compensation cases.[10] This means that the financial report effects of stock-based compensation can be delayed, and earnings can be shown as currently higher than it would be under other types of compensation. A thorough coverage of financial reporting rules regarding management compensation is not attempted here. Exhibit 20–5 provides an overview of the issues.

MANAGEMENT COMPENSATION IN SERVICE FIRMS AND NOT-FOR-PROFIT ORGANIZATIONS

Example of a Service Firm

LEARNING OBJECTIVE 5▶

Explain how management compensation plans are used in service firms and not-for-profit organizations.

Although most compensation plans are used by manufacturing or merchandising firms, an increasing number of service firms, especially financial and professional service firms, are using these plans. A good example is the compensation plan for the architectural and engineering design firm, Short-Elliott-Hendrickson, Inc. (SEH).[11] SEH provides professional services in a variety of markets, each of which is organized as a profit SBU: airport planning, water resources, waste management, municipal services, structural engineering, architecture, and others. SEH has developed a compensation plan for managers of each profit SBU. The plan uses a balanced scorecard approach that focuses on three areas: (1) financial results, (2) client satisfaction, and (3) improvement in the process of developing and providing the services. Management considers the financial results area to be the most important and has developed the following three criteria for evaluating managers and each profit SBU: profitability, efficiency, and collections of accounts receivable.

1. **Profitability** is measured by the *profit multiplier*, the ratio of net revenues to direct labor dollars.
2. **Efficiency** is measured by *staff utilization*, which is determined from the ratio of direct labor-hours chargeable (to clients) to total hours worked less vacation and holiday time.
3. *Collection of accounts* as measured by two ratios:
    a. The percentage of accounts receivable over 90 days, a measure of the ability to collect customer accounts.
    b. Average days of unbilled work outstanding, a measure of the ability to complete assignments and bill promptly for them.

As shown in Exhibit 20–6, SEH's compensation plan is based on three criteria and four measures (two measures for collection of accounts). Note that the water

---

COST MANAGEMENT IN ACTION

When Good Options Go Bad

What does a company do when its stock price falls and its executive stock options are no longer attractive? If the firm does not move quickly, it can lose key executives to other employers that offer a more attractive compensation package. With the inevitable ups and downs of the stock market, firms are likely to face this problem at one point or another; most recently it has affected those in the technology sector. (Refer to Comments on Cost Management in Action at the end of the chapter.)

---

[10]   FASB, *Statement No. 123*, "Accounting for Stock-Based Compensation" (Stanford, Conn.: FASB, 1995).

[11]   Mark Pederson and Gary A. Lidgerding, "Pay-for-Performance in a Service Firm," *Management Accounting*, November 1995, pp. 40–43.

Exhibit 20–6 Management Compensation Plan for the Water Resources Group of SEH Inc.

1. Profit Multiplier (ratio: net revenues to direct labor dollars)		2. Staff Utilization (ratio: chargeable time to total time)		3. Collection of Accounts			
				Percentage of Accounts Receivable > 90 Days		Days Revenue Unbilled	
Actual	88%	Actual	79%	Actual	14%	Actual	50 days
Goal	95%	Goal	83%	Goal	10%	Goal	45 days
Variance	7%	Variance	4%	Variance	4%	Variance	5 days
Multiply by weight of	3	Multiply by weight of	3	Multiply by weight of	2	Divide by goal	45 days
Weighted variance	21%	Weighted variance	12%	Weighted variance	8%	Percent variance	11%
Less	100%	Less	100%	Less	100%	Less	100%
Score	79%		88%		92%		89%

Source: Adapted from Mark Pederson and Gary A. Lidgerding, "Pay-for-Performance in a Service Firm," *Management Accounting,* November 1995, p. 42.

resources group fell short of its target in each of the three areas with scores of 79 percent for the profit multiplier, 88 percent for staff utilization, and 92 percent and 89 percent, respectively, for each of the two measures of collections of accounts. The advantage of this compensation plan is that it clearly places responsibility for financial results on the three criteria that are important to SEH's strategy and is therefore consistent with the objectives of management compensation. The objectives of motivation and correct decision making are achieved since the managers of SEH's profit SBUs have clear, attainable goals consistent with the firm's strategy. The objective of fairness is achieved by focusing on ratios rather than total profits, which increases comparability among managers.

Example of a Not-For-Profit Organization

A good example of compensation-based responsibility accounting in not-for-profit organizations is the bonus arrangement for the manager of the Greensboro, North Carolina, Coliseum. It is a large indoor arena used for sporting events such as basketball (the Atlantic Coast Conference Basketball Tournament) and a variety of musical and other performances. The city owns and manages the Coliseum; it has been running deficits of more than a million dollars per year in recent years.

To address the need to increase revenues, the Greensboro City Council decided to outsource the Coliseum management to a management company for a fee plus a bonus incentive for reducing the deficit. The current Coliseum director proposed forming a management company with himself as director. The proposal included a $175,000 fee to the management company, a $125,000 salary for himself as director, and a bonus that would be available if he were able to generate revenues higher than 80 percent of expenses (i.e., reduce the deficit to less than 20 percent). The current ratio of revenues to expenses is 75 percent.

The city council approved the idea, although the city manager wanted the bonus threshold to be higher (88 percent), and one council member wanted the bonus arrangement to include both a percentage and a specified amount, "If the amount of the deficit is $3 million, I don't want to pay any incentive. If it is $1 million I will."[12]

The management contract is a useful means for Greensboro to achieve its goals for the Coliseum. The director and management company have strong motivation to increase revenues and thereby reduce the city's deficit. As in any type of performance measurement system, however, attention must be given to the measurement issues: How are revenue and expense to be determined?

---

[12] *Greensboro News & Record,* May 29, 1996.

PART TWO: BUSINESS VALUATION

LEARNING OBJECTIVE 6 ▶

Apply the two approaches for business valuation: financial analysis and direct valuation.

In this second part of the chapter, we examine the valuation of the firm as a whole. The goal of strategic cost management is the success of the firm in maintaining competitive advantage, so we must evaluate the firm's overall performance as well as the performance of individual managers.

We take a broad approach to business valuation that includes both the process of evaluating a firm's overall performance and the process of determining an overall value for the firm; ultimately, the objective of the firm's managers is to improve the overall value of the firm.

The two principal approaches for business valuation are financial analysis and valuation. The *financial analysis* approach uses the balanced scorecard, financial ratio analysis, and economic value added as benchmarks. This approach evaluates the firm's overall performance but does not develop a dollar value for it. In contrast, the *direct valuation* of the firm values the firm by estimating its total market value, which can then be compared to the market value for prior periods or for comparable firms.[13]

FINANCIAL ANALYSIS APPROACH

To illustrate the financial analysis approach—using the balanced scorecard, financial ratio analysis, and economic value added—we use EasyKleen Company, a manufacturer of paper products. For relevant information about EasyKleen, see Exhibit 20–7.

The Balanced Scorecard

The use of the balanced scorecard to evaluate the firm is similar to the use of critical success factors in evaluating and compensating the individual manager. When evaluating the firm using CSFs, the management accountant uses benchmarks from industry information and considers how the CSFs have changed from prior years. A favorable evaluation results when the CSFs are superior to the benchmarks and to prior years' performance. For example, assume that EasyKleen has three CSFs, one each from the three key performance categories:

1. Return on total assets (financial performance).
2. Number of quality defects (business processes).
3. Number of training hours for plant workers (human resources).

A target level of performance is set for each CSF based on a study of the performance of the best firms in the industry. The benchmark is set at 90 percent of the best performance in the industry, and EasyKleen is evaluated on its overall performance, as illustrated in Exhibit 20–8.

EasyKleen management sees from the balanced scorecard that the firm met its goal in the financial area but fell short in both the operations and human resources areas. The scorecard is a guide for rewarding managers and for directing attention to achieving desired goals.[14]

---

[13] Some useful references on business valuation are Elizabeth Danziger, "Is Business Appraising for You?" *Journal of Accountancy,* March 2000, pp. 28–33; Frank C. Evans, "Tips for the Valuator," *Journal of Accountancy,* March 2000, pp. 35–41; and Susumu Ueno, "Management Accounting: Creating Corporate Value," (2001) Konan University, Kobe, Japan.

[14] For evidence that institutional investors see the balanced scorecard as useful for business valuation, see the results of an Ernst & Young survey reported by David A. Light, "Performance Measurement: Investor's Balanced Scorecards," *Harvard Business Review,* November–December 1998, pp. 17–20; a recent study by PricewaterhouseCoopers also indicates that institutional investors use measures from all perspectives of the scorecard, not just the financial perspective; see Robert C. Eccles and Harold D. Kahn, "Pursuing Value: The Information Reporting Gap in the U.S. Capital Markets," PricewaterhouseCoopers LLP, 1998.

Exhibit 20–7 Selected Financial Information

EASYKLEEN COMPANY
Summary of Selected Financial Information
For the Year Ended December 31,

Financial Statements	2002	2001
Current assets		
Cash	$ 50,000	$ 40,000
Accounts receivable	100,000	80,000
Inventory	50,000	60,000
Total current assets	$ 200,000	$180,000
Long-lived assets	200,000	210,000
Total assets	$ 400,000	$390,000
Current liabilities	50,000	$ 60,000
Long-term debt	200,000	200,000
Total liabilities	$ 250,000	$260,000
Shareholders' equity	150,000	130,000
Total liabilities and equity	$ 400,000	$390,000
Sales	$1,000,000 (50% credit sales)	
Cost of sales	500,000	
Gross margin	$ 500,000	
Operating expense	300,000	
Operating profit	$ 200,000	
Income taxes	100,000	
Net income	100,000	

Asset Valuation, Total Assets	
Net book value	$ 400,000
Gross book value	550,000
Replacement cost	700,000
Liquidation value	450,000

Other Information	
Depreciation expense	$30,000/year
Current share price	$ 16.25
Number of outstanding shares	50,000
Training expenses	$30,000 (26 hours per worker)
Quality defects	350 ppm (parts per million)
Cost of capital	12%

Cash Flow from Operations	
Net income	$100,000
Depreciation expense	30,000
Decrease (increase) in accounts receivable	(20,000)
Decrease (increase) in inventory	10,000
Increase (decrease) in current liabilities	(10,000)
Total cash flow from operations	$110,000

Financial Ratio Analysis

Financial ratio analysis uses financial statement ratios to evaluate the firm's performance. Two common measures of performance are its liquidity and profitability. *Liquidity* refers to the firm's ability to pay its current operating expenses (usually for a year or less) and maturing debt. The five key measures of liquidity are the accounts receivable turnover, the inventory turnover, the current ratio, the quick ratio, and the cash flow ratio. The higher these ratios the better and the higher the evaluation of the firm's liquidity. The four key profitability ratios are: the gross margin percent, the return on assets, the return on equity, and the earnings per share. The five liquidity ratios and four profitability ratios are explained in other finance and accounting texts but are not covered here. Instead, we show how each of the ratios is calculated for EasyKleen Company in Exhibit 20–9. The information is taken from Exhibit 20–7 and assumes that the benchmark level of performance is 90 percent of the best in the industry.

As Exhibit 20–9 indicates, EasyKleen had a very good year financially. It met six of its nine goals. Profitability is the strongest area; it exceeded three of four ratios substantially; only the earnings per share target was unmet by a small margin. The liquidity goals were largely met, although receivables turnover and cash flow fell short. This points to the need to improve the collection of receivables, which would improve both these ratios. Overall, the financial ratio analysis shows that EasyKleen performed quite well.

Exhibit 20–8	**Balanced Scorecard**

EASYKLEEN COMPANY
Balanced Scorecard
For the Year Ended December 31, 2002

Category	CSF	Target Performance	Actual Performance*	Variance
Financial Operations	Return on total assets	22%	25.3%	3.3% (exceeded)
Operations	Quality defects	300 ppm	350 ppm	50 ppm (unmet)
Human Resources	Training hours	32 hours per employee	26 hours per employee	6 hours (unmet)

*See Exhibit 20–9 for return on assets and Exhibit 20–7 for quality defects and training hours.

Exhibit 20–9	**Financial Analysis**

EASYKLEEN COMPANY
Financial Analysis
For the Year Ended December 31, 2002

Ratio (how calculated)	Benchmark	Actual	Percent Achievement
Liquidity Ratios			
Accounts receivable turnover (Credit sales/Average receivables)	7	5.56 = $500,000/(100,000 + 80,000)/2	79% (unmet)
Inventory turnover (Cost of sales/Average inventory)	8	9.09 = $500,000/($50,000 + 60,000)/2	114% (met)
Current ratio (Current assets/Current liabilities)	2	4 = $200,000/$50,000	200% (met)
Quick ratio (Cash and receivables/Current liabilities)	1	3 = ($50,000 + $100,000)/$50,000	300% (met)
Cash flow ratio (Cash flow from operations/Current liabilities)	2.5	2.2 = $110,000/$50,000	88% (unmet)
Profitability Ratios			
Gross margin percent (Gross profit/Net sales)	35%	50% = $500,000/$1,000,000	143% (met)
Return on assets (Net income/Average total assets)	22%	25.3 = $100,000/($400,000 + 390,000)/2	115% (met)
Return on equity (Net income less preferred dividends/Shareholders' equity)	44%	66.67% = $100,000/$150,000	152% (met)
Earnings per share (Net income less preferred dividends/Weighted—average number of shares outstanding)	$2.15	$2.00 = $100,000/50,000	93% (unmet)

Economic Value Added

As discussed in Chapter 19, economic value added (EVA) is a business unit's income after taxes and after deducting the cost of capital. The cost of capital is usually obtained by calculating a weighted average of the cost of the firm's two sources of funds, borrowing and selling stock. EVA focuses managers' attention on creating value for shareholders. By earning higher profits than the firm's cost of capital, the firm increases its internal resources available for dividends and/or to finance its continued growth. Dividends and growth boost stock price and add shareholder value.

EVA for EasyKleen is determined as follows; *invested capital* is defined for EVA as total assets less current liabilities. Training expenses of $30,000 are added to total assets and back to net income for EVA calculations since training expenses are considered an investment for EVA purposes:

$$\text{EVA} = \text{EVA net income} - (\text{Cost of capital} \times \text{Invested capital})$$

$$= \text{Net income} + \text{Training expenses}$$

$$- 0.12 \times (\text{Total assets} + \text{Training expenses} - \text{Current liabilities})$$

$$= \$100{,}000 + \$30{,}000 - 0.12 \times (\$400{,}000 + \$30{,}000 - \$50{,}000)$$

$$= \$84{,}400$$

The EVA of $84,400 for EasyKleen is a very positive value relative to net income and invested capital. It indicates of the firm's strong profitability and, in particular, its significant contribution to shareholder value.

Major corporations such as Coca-Cola, Quaker Oats, and CSX, use EVA in determining manager compensation to provide a stronger motivation for managers to take actions that add shareholder value.

VALUATION APPROACH

An intuitively appealing performance measure for the firm is its market value. Market value is an objective measure that clearly shows what investors think the firm is worth. It also has the advantage of being consistent with the objective of top management to add shareholder value:

> The essence of corporate strategy is to figure out how the corporation, as intermediary, can add value to the business it oversees. . . . The point here is not that businesses should not be trying to compete effectively in product and service markets; of course they should. But that effort has to be measured not only in terms of its impact on competition in a product or service market, but also in terms of its effect in the market for corporate control (*i.e., in the equity market; stock price*). A company that emphasizes the former at the expense of the latter can find itself in trouble very quickly. . . . Many companies in America are moving quickly and confidently in the wrong direction. They believe that they are becoming leaders in their industries; instead, they are becoming leading targets for raids and proxy fights. . . . To sum up, companies need strategies for competing in two kinds of markets: the familiar product and service markets, and the market for corporate control. Winning in the latter market depends on creating for shareholders superior value that derives from cash flow returns. (emphasis added)[15]

---

[15] T. Copeland, T. Koller, and J. Murrin, *Valuation: Measuring and Managing the Value of Companies* (New York: John Wiley, 1992), pp. 3–26.

Dell Computer and CSX Corporation Benefit from Using Economic Value Added (EVA)

DELL USES ECONOMIC VALUE ADDED TO IMPROVE COMPETITIVENESS

Economic value added (EVA) has enabled a number of firms to significantly improve their competitiveness. Dell Computer was suffering from intense price competition with Compaq Corporation and other competitors in early 1993. It introduced EVA to focus managers and operating employees on their role in improving profitability. For example, the marketing department began to calculate the return on investment for each mailing, and the purchasing department computed the cost of unsold inventory.

EVA HELPS CSX UNIT BECOME MORE PROFITABLE

CSX Corporation's Internodal unit uses trains to carry freight to trucks or cargo ships. In 1988, the unit was unprofitable, as shown by a negative EVA of $70 million. The unit managers were told to bring the EVA up to breakeven before 1993 or the unit would be sold. By 1992, the unit had achieved a positive EVA of

$10 million. This was accomplished by careful attention to the use of assets. A focus on idle assets led unit managers to reschedule certain routes. For example, on the route from New Orleans to Jacksonville, Florida, four locomotives pulled a freight train at 28 mph, arriving four to five hours prior to the time needed to load the trucks or freighters in Jacksonville. By removing one of the four locomotives and using a speed of 25 mph, the train arrived in time for the unloading with an hour to spare. The slow-down and removal of one locomotive was a significant saving to the unit in both capital costs (the locomotive) and operating costs (less fuel required). Looking at all the routes in a similar manner, the Intermodal group was able to achieve significant savings in capital usage and operating costs.

Sources: Based on information from Gary McWilliams, "Whirlwind on the WEB," *Business Week,* April 7, 1997, pp. 132–36; and Shawn Tully, "The Real Key to Creating Wealth," *Fortune,* September 20, 1993, pp. 38–50.

Spin-offs of Business Units: Effect on Market Value and Compensation

WHY THE SPIN-OFF?

Many firms find that spin-offs of business units result in an increase in the market value of these units. The spin-off makes it easier for the market to assess the value of the spun off business since it is difficult for analysts and investors to assess the aggregate value of firms with multiple businesses. Research shows that spun off subsidiaries show better than average growth in sales, income, and capital expenditures. Randall Woolridge of Penn State University finds that business units that are not given much attention by top management tend to suffer and are therefore better spun off.

SPIN-OFFS AND CEO COMPENSATION AT ITT

We see also that management compensation follows the benefits of spin-offs. The total compensation of Rand V. Araskog,

CEO of ITT Corporation, more than doubled in the year that ITT spun off two business units, ITT Industries and ITT Hartford Group. ITT's stock price almost tripled from three years prior. Charles Peck, a senior associate of the Conference Board, a nonprofit business research center in New York, said, "You can make an argument that if a business, through splitting or downsizing, is increasing the earning performance of the company, then the compensation is legitimate. These days, we're going more toward measures of financial performance, rather than the sheer size of the company."

Sources: Based on information from Roger Lowenstein, "Confessions of a Corporate Spinoff Junkie," *The Wall Street Journal,* March 28, 1996; and "Araskog's Piece of ITT Empire Shrinks but Compensation More Than Doubles," *The Wall Street Journal,* April 1, 1996.

As this statement predicts, a public firm that advances its competitive position but fails to achieve acceptance in the market through improved stock price will find itself vulnerable in the market for corporate control. That is, the company might be purchased by investors who see that the market undervalues the firm. Success in the market is achieved by taking a value-oriented approach within the firm—orienting the firm's strategy to shareholder value. This can mean the spin-off of certain business units, financial restructuring, and outsourcing of certain activities.

The concept of adding shareholder value requires a new interpretation of management strategy and the value chain. The role of strategy goes beyond the policies and procedures to achieve competitive advantage. It must also include the overarching objective of adding shareholder value. Similarly, the firm's value chain goes beyond adding value for its customer to adding value also for the shareholders.

Fleet Financial Group: Achieving Strategic Goals versus Improving Shareholder Value

Firms must distinguish between two types of performance: (1) achieving strategic goals and (2) improving shareholder value. While closely related, these two goals are separable; achievement of one does not guarantee achievement of the other. For example, Fleet Financial Group, Inc., began a cost reduction effort in 1993 to improve the firm's competitive advantage with the expectations that stock price would increase and managers would be awarded bonuses on the basis of improved stock price. The cost-reduction plan was a success, but the improvement in stock price, unfortunately, did not follow, nor did the bonuses.

Source: Based on information from *Business Week,* March 18, 1996, p. 34.

| Exhibit 20–10 | EasyKleen Company: Asset Valuation Methods and Values |

EASYKLEEN COMPANY
Asset Valuation Methods and Values

Method	Value
Net book value	$400,000 (from the financial statements)
Gross book value	550,000 (from the financial statements)
Replacement cost	700,000 (estimated, usually by appraisals of experts in commercial real estate)
Liquidation value	450,000 (estimated, usually by appraisals of experts in commercial real estate)

The Market Value Method

The four methods for directly valuing a firm are (1) market value, (2) asset valuation, (3) the discounted cash flow method, and (4) earnings-based valuation. The first method is the most simple and direct. The firm's value is determined by multiplying the number of outstanding shares by the current market price of the shares. For the EasyKleen Company, the value determined is:

$$\text{Number of shares} \times \text{Share price}$$

$$= 50,000 \times \$16.25 = \$812,500$$

The performance of the firm and of its top management can be evaluated by changes either in the firm's share price or its market value. The market value method is the most direct and objective measure of the shareholders' assessment of the firm's performance and its success in creating value for the shareholders.

For nonpublic firms and public firms that have no frequently traded stock a relevant stock price is not available, and one of the three other methods is needed to evaluate the firm.

The Asset Valuation Method

Accountants have four options when using the asset valuation method: net book value, gross book value, replacement cost, and liquidation value (see Chapter 19). An important limitation of the net book value and gross book value methods is that they are affected by the firm's accounting policies, and they can be greatly distorted by the age of the assets. The most desirable valuation is either the replacement cost or liquidation value because they more nearly reflect the actual current value of the assets.

The replacement cost and liquidation value methods have weaknesses, however. Most important, an objective measure for replacement cost or liquidation value rarely exists, since the firm is not likely to be involved in either liquidation or replacement when the valuation is made. The asset values in Exhibit 20–10 show quite a range.

EasyKleen is not considering liquidation, so the replacement cost of $700,000 is likely to be the more useful of the two measures.

The Discounted Cash Flow Method

The discounted cash flow (DCF) method measures the firm's value as the discounted present value of its net cash flows. The DCF is based on the same concepts used in Chapter 11 for capital budgeting decisions. Cash flows a year or more into the future are discounted to consider the time value of money; cash flows in recent periods are more valuable than cash flows in distant periods. Since it is based on cash flows, the DCF method has the additional advantage of not being subject to the bias of different accounting policies for determining total assets and net income, as are the asset valuation and the financial analysis methods. The DCF method is commonly used when the share price is not available or is unreliable.

The DCF method distinguishes two types of value in determining a firm's value. The first is the value of the cash flows for the planning period (usually a three- to five-year period), and the second is the value of the cash flows beyond three to five years. Exhibit 20–11 shows how the method is used for the EasyKleen Company, assuming that the discount rate (the cost of capital) is 12 percent, the planning period is five years, and the net cash flows increase by $10,000 each year and then remain at $150,000 per year for the sixth year and thereafter. Exhibit 20–11 shows that the total discounted value of net cash flows for the first five years is $460,520.

The present values of the cash flows from the sixth year on are determined using the discount factor for an annuity with a continuing life, which is the inverse of the

---

Exhibit 20–11   DCF Valuation of the EasyKleen Company

Years	Cash Flow	Present Value Factor	Present Value of Cash Flows	
1	$110,000	0.893	$98,230	
2	120,000	0.797	95,640	
3	130,000	0.712	92,560	
4	140,000	0.636	89,040	
5	150,000	0.567	85,050	
Total present value of cash flows in the planning period ⟶			$460,520	(A)
6+	$150,000	8.3333	$1,249,995	(B)
Total present value of 6+ year's cash flows ⟶		0.567	708,747	(C) = (B) × .567
Plus: Marketable securities and investments			0	(D)
Less: Market value of debt			200,000	(E)
Value of the firm, shareholder value			$ 969,267	= (A) + (C) + (D) − (E)

The Stock Market Looks at Cash Flows Five Years Out

A study of 30 leading companies by the Alcar Group indicated that 80 to 90 percent of the value of share prices for these companies could be attributed to expected cash flows five or more years out in the form of a forecast of future dividends. The company leaders in the group were Disney, Coca-Cola, and McDonald's, with more than 95 percent of stock price attributed to five-year-plus cash flows. The implication is that investors take a long-term view of the firm when valuing its stock based on a projection of its future cash flows and dividends.

Source: Alfred Rappaport, "CFOs and Strategists: Forging a Common Framework," *Harvard Business Review,* May–June 1992.

discount rate ($1/0.12 = 8.3333$).[16] This gives a discounted value for these six-year-plus cash flows of $1,249,995. To discount this amount back from the beginning of the sixth year to the present, we discount $1,249,995 by the fifth year discount factor (0.567) to arrive at the discounted value of the continuing (six-year-plus) cash flows, $708,747.

To determine the firm's *net valuation*, we now add the discounted value of the planning period cash flows and the discounted value of six-year-plus cash flows to the value of current nonoperating investments such as marketable securities, and we subtract the market value of long-term debt. The net valuation for the firm is then $969,267. This value is somewhat higher than the market value method amount ($812,500) or the replacement cost asset value of $700,000. *If* the cash flow estimates are reliable, the DCF method provides a useful measure in determining the firm's value.

Earnings-Based Valuation

The earnings-based valuation method computes value as the product of expected annual accounting earnings and a multiplier. The multiplier is often estimated from the price-to-earnings ratios of the stocks of comparable publicly held firms. The earnings multiplier has important limitations. The accounting treatment of inventory, depreciation, and other important components of earnings might not be comparable to that of other firms in the industry. When earnings are not comparable for these reasons, determining a relevant and useful multiplier is difficult.

The price-to-earnings ratio measures the amount the investor is willing to pay for a dollar of the firm's earnings per share. If the price-to-earnings ratio is not available for a given firm, an average or representative value is taken from the price-to-earnings ratios of other firms in the industry. This ratio can then be adjusted upward to recognize a firm with future profit potential not recognized in current earnings or vice versa. Assume that the relevant price-to-earnings multiple for EasyKleen is 8.5. Then the value of EasyKleen using this method is determined as follows:

$$\text{Earnings multiplier} \times \text{Earnings}$$

$$= 8.5 \times \$100,000 = \$850,000$$

The earnings multiplier is easy to apply and can provide a useful evaluation of the firm, subject to the limitations noted.[17]

In practice, the management accountant commonly uses two or more of the valuation techniques and evaluates the assumptions in each to arrive at an overall valuation assessment. If the management accountant is confident of the forecasts of net cash flow, a valuation of approximately $900,000 is appropriate and reasonable.

SUMMARY

In this last chapter we discussed management compensation and business valuation. The first part introduces the objectives and methods for compensating managers. The three principal objectives for management compensation, which follow directly from the objectives for management control, are the *motivation* of the manager, the *incentive* for proper decision making, and *fairness* to the manager.

---

[16] Typically, the firm's cash flows are assumed to continue indefinitely, and thus the discount factor for an annuity is used in perpetuity (continuing life). This assumption is consistent with the idea that the firm is an ongoing entity with little or no likelihood of bankruptcy. If a shorter period is desired, the appropriate discount factor from the annuity table can be used for the desired number of years. For example, if the desired period, after the planning period, is from the 6th year to the 20th year, the discount factor is found in the annuity table for 15 years (6 through 20), or 6.811. The factor 6.811 is then used in place of the factor 8.3333 in the analysis in Exhibit 20–11.

[17] See Joel Siegel, Mark Levine, and Adrian Fitzsimons, "Business Valuation Using a Multiplier of Earnings," *The CPA Journal*, May 1997, pp. 81–82.

The three main types of compensation are *salary*, *bonus* and *benefits*. The bonus is the fastest growing part of total compensation and often the largest part. The three important factors in the development of a bonus plan are the base for computing the bonus (strategic performance measures, stock price, and critical success factors), the source of funding for the bonus (the business unit or the entire firm), and the payment options (current and deferred bonus, stock options, and performance shares). The development of an executive compensation plan is a complex process involving these three factors and the three types of compensation, as well as the objectives of management control.

Tax planning and financial reporting concerns are important in compensation planning because of management's desire to reduce taxes and report financial results favorably. Thus, accountants must consider taxes and financial reporting issues when they develop a compensation plan for managers.

Management compensation plans are used in service and not-for-profit organizations as well. The chapter illustrates actual examples for a professional services firm and the Greensboro, North Carolina, Coliseum (see also the self-study problem at the end of the chapter).

The second part of the chapter considers the valuation of the entire firm in contrast to the previous two chapters and the first part of this chapter that focused on the individual manager. The valuation of the firm is important for investors and as one part of an overall assessment of the performance of top management. The two approaches are (1) a financial analysis that focuses on critical success factors and accounting measures and (2) a valuation approach that focuses on market valuation. The four methods for assessing the market value of the firm are the market value of shares, asset valuation, the discounted cash flow method, and the earnings multiplier.

KEY TERMS

Benefits **942**

Bonus **942**

Firmwide pool **948**

Management compensation plans **942**

Salary **942**

Unit-based pool **948**

COMMENTS ON COST MANAGEMENT IN ACTION

When Good Options Go Bad

When a company's stock price falls and its executive stock options no longer look attractive, it has a number of choices. One is to simply reprice the options to a lower price that is more in keeping with the lower market price of the firm's stock. Another choice is to grant new options that have a lower exercise price to replace the old.

Another approach is for the executive to hedge his or her own stockholding or stock options by buying "put" (right-to-sell) options on the firm's stock in the open market. If the stock price falls dramatically, the executive can still sell the stock or exercise the options at the relatively favorable ("put") price. This practice is very much like that engaged in by global firms to hedge their exposure to foreign exchange fluctuations.

The problem with executives hedging their stock holdings and options is that it undermines the principle of pay for performance. Through hedging, the executive can effectively protect against a fall in the stock. Hedging reduces the risk of stock ownership and therefore reduces the incentive for executives to take steps to sustain stock price.

Source: Pallavi Gogoi, "When Good Options Go Bad," *Business Week*, December 11, 2000, pp. EB96–98; Louis Lavelle, "Undermining Pay for Performance," *Business Week*, January 15, 2001, p. 70; and Michael Schroeder and Ruth Simon, "Tech Firms Object as SEC Gets Tougher on their Practice of Repricing Options," *The Wall Street Journal*, February 7, 2001, p. C10.

(For solution, please turn to the end of the chapter.)

Management Compensation Plan

Davis-Thompson-Howard & Associates (DTH) is a large consulting firm that specializes in the evaluation of governmental programs. The lawyers, accountants, engineers, and other specialists at DTH evaluate both the performance of existing programs and the success of potential new government programs. DTH obtains most of its consulting engagements by completing proposals in open bidding for the services desired by governmental agencies. The competition for these proposals has increased in recent years, and as a result DTH's yield (the number of new engagements divided by proposals) has fallen from 49 percent a few years ago to only 26 percent in the most recent year. The firm's profitability has fallen as well. DTH has decided to study its management compensation plan as one step among the many it will take in attempting to return the firm to its previous level of profitability.

DTH has six regional offices, two located near Washington, D.C., and the others near large metropolitan areas where most of their clients are located. Each office is headed by an office manager who is one of the firm's professional associates. The firm's services in these offices are classified into financial and operational audit services, educational evaluation, engineering consulting, and financial systems. The Washington offices tend to provide most of the financial and audit services, and the other offices offer their own mix of professional services. No two offices are alike since each has adapted to the needs of its regional client base. DTH's objective is to be among the three most competitive firms in its areas of service and to increase its revenues by at least 10 percent per year.

DTH's compensation plan awards each office a bonus based on (1) the increase in billings over the prior year and (2) the number of net new clients acquired in the current year. The office manager has the authority to divide the office bonus as appropriate, although these same two criteria are generally used to allocate it to the office professionals. Top management is not aware of any problems with the compensation plan; there have been no significant complaints.

One observation by the CEO might suggest a reason for the firm's decline in yield of proposals. It has been losing out particularly on large new contract proposals that require large staff and a significant professional travel commitment. These are jobs for which it would be necessary to coordinate two or more DTH offices. The CEO notes that DTH has as many regional offices as most of its competitors, which now seem to be winning a larger share of these contracts.

Required

Discuss the pros and cons of DTH's compensation plan. Is it consistent with the company's objectives and competitive environment?

20–1   Identify and explain the three objectives of management compensation.

20–2   Explain the three types of management compensation.

20–3   Explain how a manager's risk aversion can affect decision making and how compensation plans should be designed to deal with risk aversion.

20–4   Explain how management compensation can provide an incentive to unethical behavior. What methods can be used to reduce the chance of unethical activities resulting from compensation plans?

20–5   From a financial reporting standpoint, what form of compensation is most desirable for the firm?

20–6   From a tax-planning standpoint, what form of compensation is least desirable for the manager? For the firm?

20–7   List the three bases for bonus incentive plans; explain how they differ and how each achieves or does not achieve the three objectives of management compensation.

20–8   Identify and explain the five financial ratios used to evaluate liquidity as part of the firm's valuation.

20–9   What are the two types of bonus pools for bonus incentive plans? How do they differ, and how does each achieve or not achieve the three objectives of management compensation?

20–10   List the four types of bonus payment options and explain how they differ. How does each achieve or not achieve the three objectives of management compensation?

20–11   Develop arguments to support your view as to whether executive pay in the United States is too high.

20–12   What are the four valuation methods? Which do you think is superior and why?

20–13   What type of management compensation is the fastest growing part of total compensation? Why do you think this is the case?

20–14   Why do you think it is important for a management accountant to be able to complete an evaluation of the firm separate from an evaluation of individual managers?

20–15   How does the firm's management compensation plan change over the life cycle of the firm's products?

EXERCISES

20–16   **COMPENSATION, STRATEGY, AND MARKET VALUE**   Jackson Supply Company is a publicly owned firm that serves the medical supply needs of hospitals and large medical practices in six southeastern states. The firm has grown significantly in recent years, as the areas it serves have grown. Jackson has focused on customer service and has developed an excellent reputation for speed of delivery and overall quality of service. The company ensures that customer service is each manager's main focus by making it count for 50 percent of the management bonus. The firm measures specific indicators of customer service monthly; progress toward these measures as well as others is used to determine each manager's bonus. In the past several months, top management has noticed that although most managers are meeting or exceeding their customer service goals and receiving bonuses accordingly, the firm's stock price has been lagging while competitive firms' stock prices have been rising steadily.

Required   What modification, if any, should Jackson Supply Company make to its management compensation plan?

Service

20–17   **PERFORMANCE EVALUATION AND RISK AVERSION**   Jill Lewis is the office manager of PureBreds, Inc. Her office has 30 employees whose collective job is to process applications by dog owners who want to register their pets with the firm. There is never a shortage of applications waiting to be processed, but random events beyond Lewis's control cause fluctuations in the number of applications that her office can process.

Alex Zale, the district manager to whom Jill reports, has no way to observe her effort other than to monitor the number of applications that are processed.

Required

1. If Jill is risk adverse, how should Alex compensate her? Why?

For requirements 2 and 3, assume that the correctness of the information is entered into the computers at Jill's office is as important as the volume of processed applications.

2. What are the disadvantages of a compensation package that is influenced by the number of processed applications but not by the correctness of the data input?

3. List at least two ways that Alex could measure how accurately Jill's office is processing the applications.

20–18 PERFORMANCE EVALUATION AND RISK AVERSION   Heartwood Furniture Corporation has a line of sofas marketed under the name NightTime Sleepers. Heartwood management is considering several compensation packages for Amy Johnson, NightTime's general manager. Amy's duties include making all investing and operating decisions for NightTime.

Required

1. Amy is risk neutral and prefers to receive the maximum reward for her hard work. Do you recommend compensation based on flat salary, an ROI-based bonus, or a combination of both? Why?

2. If Amy does not make investing decisions for NightTime, is ROI still a good performance measure? If so, then explain why. If not, suggest an alternative.

3. Heartwood Furniture wants to evaluate Amy by comparing NightTime's ROI to the ROI of Stiles Furniture, which operates in a business environment similar to that of NightTime. Both companies have the same capabilities, but Stiles uses a significantly different manufacturing strategy than NightTime does.

   a. Would evaluating Amy with this benchmark be fair?

   b. Would using residual income instead of ROI offer any advantages?

   c. What are the drawbacks to evaluating Amy using total sales instead of ROI?

20–19 EVALUATING AN INCENTIVE PAY PLAN; STRATEGY   Anne-Marie Fox is the manager of a new and used boat dealership. She has decided to reevaluate the compensation plan offered to her sales representatives to determine whether it encourages the dealership's success. The representatives are paid no salary, but they receive 20 percent of the sales price of every boat sold, and they have the authority to negotiate the boats' prices as far down as their wholesale cost if necessary.  *Strategy*

Required   Is this plan in the dealership's strategic best interest? Why or why not?

20–20 ALTERNATIVE COMPENSATION PLANS   ADM, Inc., an electronics manufacturer, uses growth in earnings per share (EPS) as a guideline for evaluating executive performance. ADM executives receive a bonus of $5,000 for every penny increase in EPS for the year. This bonus is paid in addition to fixed salaries ranging from $500,000 to $900,000 annually.

Cygnus Corporation, a computer components manufacturer, also uses EPS as an evaluation tool. Its executives receive a bonus equal to 40 percent of their salary for the year if the firm's EPS is in the top third of a list ranking the EPS ratios for Cygnus and its 12 competitors.

Required

1. Why are companies such as ADM, Inc., and Cygnus Corporation switching from stock option incentives to programs more like the ones described? What does the use of these plans by the two firms say about each firm's competitive strategy?

2. What are the weaknesses of incentive plans based on EPS?

PROBLEMS

20–21 COMPENSATION; MACHINE REPLACEMENT Choco-Lots Candy Co. makes chewy chocolate candies at a plant in Winston-Salem, North Carolina. Brian Main, the production manager at this facility, installed a packaging machine last year at a cost of $400,000. This machine is expected to last for 10 more years with no residual value. Operating costs for the projected levels of production are $80,000 annually.

Brian has just learned of a new packaging machine that would work much more efficiently in Choco-Lots' production line. This machine would cost $420,000 installed, but the annual operating costs would be only $30,000. This machine would be depreciated over 10 years with no residual value. He could sell the current packaging machine this year for $150,000.

Brian has worked for Choco-Lots for seven years. He plans to remain with the firm for about two more years, when he expects to become a vice president of operations at his father-in-law's company. Choco-Lots pays Brian a fixed salary with an annual bonus of 1 percent of net income for the year.

Assume that Choco-Lots uses straight-line depreciation and has a 10 percent required rate of return. Ignore income tax effects.

Required

1. As the owner of Choco-Lots, would you want Brian to keep the current machine or purchase the new one?

2. Why might Brian not prefer to make the decision that the owner of Choco-Lots desires?

Ethics

20–22 COMPENSATION; BENEFITS; ETHICS DuMelon Publishing Inc. is a nationwide company headquartered in Boston, Massachusetts. The firm's benefits are a significant element of employee compensation. All professional employees at DuMelon receive company-paid benefits including medical insurance, term life insurance, and paid vacations and holidays. They also receive a set reimbursement amount of $100 a day maximum for travel expenses when they conduct business for DuMelon. DuMelon offers a 25 percent match for money the professionals deposit in the company-sponsored 401(k) plan.

These benefits vary, depending on the employee's salary and level in the company. For example, the amount of vacation days increases as a professional is promoted to higher levels. The maximum amount that can be contributed to the 401(k) plan also increases as the employee's salary increases.

When a DuMelon employee attains the position of vice president of a function, such as operations or sales, that person qualifies for a special class of additional benefits: a company car, a larger office with decoration allowances, and access to the executive suite at the Boston office. (The executive suite features a dining room and lounge for the executives' use.) The perks also include total reimbursement for all business travel expenses.

Required

1. Explain the implications for employee behavior and performance of DuMelon's two levels of benefits for professional employees.

2. Suppose that the policy for benefits is not applied strictly at DuMelon. As a result, the following instances have occurred:

   a. The company has occasionally paid the travel expenses of VP's spouses. Company policy is unclear as to whether this is allowed.

   b. Some VPs have special-ordered their company-provided vehicles, which on average costs the company an additional $3,300 for each car.

   c. Passes to the executive suite have been lent to other DuMelon professionals.

   d. Some of the vice presidents have offices that are much larger than those of other vice presidents. No apparent factors determine who gets the larger offices.

   How might this situation affect the behavior of vice presidents and other professionals at DuMelon? What are the underlying implications for cost control of benefits? Use specific examples when applicable.

20–23 **INCENTIVE PAY IN THE HOTEL INDUSTRY**   Jorge Martinez is the general manager of Classic Inn, a local mid-priced hotel with 100 rooms. His job objectives include providing resourceful and friendly service to the hotel's guests, maintaining an 80 percent occupancy rate, improving the average rate received per room to $58 from the current $55, and achieving a savings of 5 percent on all hotel costs. The hotel's owner, a partnership of seven people who own several hotels in the region, want to structure Jorge's future compensation to objectively reward him for achieving these goals. In the past, he has been paid an annual salary of $42,000 with no incentive pay. The incentive plan the partners developed has each of the goals weighted as follows:

Service

Measure	Percent of Total Responsibility
Occupancy rate (also reflects guest service quality)	40%
Operating within 95 percent of expense budget	25
Average room rate	35
	100%

If Jorge achieves all of these goals, the partners determined that his performance should merit total pay of $46,000. They agreed that for the incentive plan to be effective, it should comprise 50 percent of his total pay, $23,000. The goal measures used to compensate Jorge are as follows:

Occupancy goal:	29,200 room-nights = 80 percent occupancy rate × 100 rooms × 365 days
Compensation:	40 percent weight × $23,000 target reward = $9,200 $9,200/29,200 = $0.315 per room-night
Expense goal:	5 percent savings
Compensation:	25 percent weight × $23,000 target reward = $5,750 $5,750/5 = $1,150 for each percentage point saved
Room rate goal:	$3 rate increase
Compensation:	35 percent weight × $23,000 target reward = $8,050 $8,050/300 = $26.83 per each cent increase

Jorge's new compensation plan will thus pay him a $23,000 salary plus 31.5 cents per room-night sold plus $1,150 for each percentage point saved in the expense budget plus $26.83 per each cent increase in average room rate.

Required

1. Based on this plan, what will Jorge's total compensation be if his performance results are

   a. 29,200 room-nights, 5 percent saved, $3.00 rate increase?

   b. 25,000 room-nights, 3 percent saved, $1.15 rate increase?

   c. 28,000 room-nights, 0 saved, $1.03 rate increase?

2. Comment on the expected effectiveness of this plan.

Service

20-24 INCENTIVE PAY FORMULA DEVELOPMENT Use the concepts in problem 20–23 to complete the following requirements.

Required

1. Design an incentive pay plan for a restaurant manager whose goals are to serve 300 customers per day at an average price per customer of $6.88. The restaurant is open 365 days per year. These two goals are equally important. The incentive pay should comprise 40 percent of the manager's $32,000 target total compensation.

2. Calculate the manager's total compensation if the restaurant serves 280 customers per day at an average price of $6.75.

20-25 COMPENSATION POOLS; RESIDUAL INCOME; REVIEW OF CHAPTER 19 Household Products Inc. (HPI) manufactures household goods in the United States. The company made two acquisitions in previous years to diversify its product lines. In 2000, Household Products Inc. acquired glass and plastic producing companies. HPI now (2002) has three divisions: glass, plastic, and paper. The following information (in millions) presents operating revenue, operating income, and invested assets of the company over the last three years.

Operating Revenue	2000	2001	2002
Paper	$12,000	$13,000	$14,000
Plastic	5,000	4,500	4,200
Glass	7,000	7,200	7,400
Operating Income			
Paper	$3,000	$3,200	$3,500
Plastic	500	300	120
Glass	1,100	900	700
Invested assets			
Paper	$7,000	$7,400	$7,900
Plastic	2,000	1,500	1,200
Glass	4,000	4,200	4,800

The number of executives covered by HPI's current compensation package follows:

	2000	2001	2002
Paper	300	350	375
Plastic	40	40	37
Glass	120	140	175

The current compensation package is an annual bonus award. Senior executives share in the bonus pool, which is calculated as 12 percent of the company's annual residual income. *Residual income* is defined as operating income minus an interest charge of 15 percent of invested assets.

Required

1. Use asset turnover, return on sales, and ROI to explain the differences in profitability of the three divisions.

2. Compute the bonus amount to be paid during each year; also compute individual executive bonus amounts.

3. If the bonuses were calculated by divisional residual income, what would the bonus amounts be?

4. Discuss the advantages and disadvantages of basing the bonus on HPI's residual income compared to divisional residual income.

20–26 COMPENSATION; STRATEGIC ISSUES   Mobile Business Incorporated (MBI) is a worldwide manufacturing company that specializes in high technology products for the aerospace, automotive, and plastics industries. State-of-the-art technology and business innovation have been key to the firm's success over the last several years. MBI has 10 manufacturing plants in six foreign countries. Its products are sold worldwide through sales representatives and sales offices in 23 countries. Performance information from these plants and offices is received weekly and is summarized monthly at the Toronto headquarters.

 Strategy

 International

The company's current bonus compensation package focuses on giving rewards based on the utilization of capital within the company (i.e., management of inventory, collection of receivables, and use of physical assets). The board of directors is concerned, however, with the short-term focus of this plan.

Some employees believe that the company's current compensation plan does not reflect its stated goals of maintaining and enhancing its global position through innovative products.

Required   Develop a bonus package that considers MBI's strategic goals and the global environment in which it operates.

20–27 EXECUTIVE COMPENSATION   Wilson & Associates is a medium-size marketing organization specializing in professional promotion and publicity services. The firm's top management believes that it provides quality service as evidenced by the high level of customer satisfaction.

The organization consists of three departments: print media, audio media, and visual media, each of which has a senior director in charge. The company employs 80 clerical staff who are paid on an hourly basis and 30 professional staff who are salaried. A large majority of the employees have an excellent rating in their job skills, and all employees demonstrate above average performance in their job responsibilities. The employees take pride in their achievements, and morale is very good.

Salary ranges are established for different job classifications within the clerical staff (i.e., clerk, clerk typist, secretary, and administrative assistant) and the professional staff (i.e., analyst, manager, and director). A fixed-rate structure is used for all salaries. The company offers no commissions because it does not want its professional staff applying undue sales pressure on its customers. Company management is proud that it does not have to resort to a salary plus commission structure for its professionals to generate sales.

Employees are recognized for superior performances through salary increases and promotions. Management believes that salary increases should be based on merit, and open positions are filled from within whenever possible. Top management contends that highly skilled and motivated employees will improve productivity if they are rewarded with annual merit pay raises and if promotions are based on performance.

Top management announced in November that the amount available for pay increases would be 10 percent of the actual total salary expenditures for 2001. All salary increases would be effective January 1, 2002.

The print media department consisted of 20 clerical and eight professional employees on January 1, 2001. Six clerical employees were added during the year at the rate of about one every two months. Two professionals were added, one on March 1 and one on August 1. Three employees were promoted during the year: two secretaries to administrative assistants and one manager to director. The total actual salary expense for the department without regard for employee benefits and employer tax contributions was $548,000. Therefore, the total amount allocated for wage increases for the print media department in 2002 is designated to be $54,800.

Shortly after the merit pay program was announced, the print media department employees received their year-end evaluation conducted by the employee's supervisor. The senior director met with each supervisor and received all performance reports and then announced the merit pay increase for each employee.

Upon completion of this entire process, several employees complained individually about the inequities of the merit pay program. The senior director was concerned about the employee discontent because the people complaining were some of the highest achievers on the staff. They tended to be at the lower classification levels and were relatively new employees, having been with the company from one to two years. The individuals showed potential and were highly motivated, often working extra hours and assuming additional responsibilities.

The new employees' behavior differed slightly from the employees who had been with the department for a longer period of time. Although highly skilled and competent in their jobs, the veteran employees tended to be reluctant to accept additional responsibility or to work extra hours on a regular basis.

Required

1. Review Wilson & Associates' wage and compensation plan.
   a. Identify and discuss its general strengths.
   b. Identify and explain the shortcomings in the administration of the merit pay increases that are to become effective in 2002, and discuss what effect these shortcomings could have on the group of discontented employees in the print media department.

2. Explain how this compensation program should be revised, if at all.

(CMA Adapted)

Ethics

20–28   EXECUTIVE COMPENSATION; TEAMS; ETHICS   Universal Air Inc. supplies instrumentation components to airplane manufacturers. Although only a few competitors are in this market, the competition is fierce.

Universal uses a traditional performance incentive plan to award middle-management bonuses on the basis of divisional profit. Recently, Charles Gross, chief executive officer, concluded that these objectives might be better served with new performance measures. On January 1, 2001, he assigned his executive team of top-level managers to develop these new measures.

The executive team conducted a customer survey. Although Universal has always prided itself on being on the technological forefront, the survey results indicated technology to be a low priority for customers, who were more concerned with product quality and customer service. As a result, the executive team developed 30 new criteria to measure middle-management performance and directed the controller to develop the necessary monthly reports and graphs to report on these new measures. Then the executive team announced to middle managers that these new indicators would be used to evaluate their performance. The managers were not enthusiastic and complained that some measures were influenced by the performance of other departments that they could not control. Over the next few months, customer complaints increased, and a major customer chose a competitor over Universal.

Upon seeing these results, Charles decided to review the new process. In a meeting with executive and middle managers, he emphasized that the new measures should help balance the company's performance between increased customer value and improved operating process efficiency. He set up two cross-functional teams of executive and middle managers to develop a second set of new measures: one to evaluate new product development and the other to evaluate the customer order and fulfillment process. Both teams are to focus on cost, quality, and scheduling time.

Richard Strong, quality inspection manager, is the brother-in-law of John Brogan, cost accumulation manager. On June 1, John telephoned Sara Wiley, the purchasing manager at Magic Aircraft Manufacturing Inc., one of Universal's major customers. Brogan said, "Listen Sara, we're jumping through all these hoops over here to measure performance, and management seems to be changing the measures every day. It was so easy before, getting a bonus based on the bottom line; now we have to worry about things out of our control based on how the customer perceives our performance. Would you do me a favor? If you have any complaints, please have your people call me directly so I can forward the complaint to the right person. All that really matters is for all of us to make money." In actuality, Richard was the only person to whom John reported the customer complaints that Sara offered.

Required

1. For Universal Air Inc. to remain competitive, it must implement the second set of new performance measures. Identify for the company

   a. At least three customer value-added measures.

   b. At least three process-efficiency measures.

2. Identify at least three types of employee behaviors that Universal can expect by having middle management participate in the development of the second set of new performance measures.

3. Describe what executive management at Universal needs to do to ensure the effectiveness of the cross-functional teams.

4. Referring to the specific standards for ethical conduct by a management accountant (Chapter 1), discuss whether John Brogan's behavior is unethical.

(CMA Adapted)

20–29 **EXECUTIVE COMPENSATION** Jensen Corporation is a holding company with several diversified divisions operating throughout the United States. Jensen's management allows the divisions to operate on an autonomous basis in most areas; however, the corporate office becomes involved in determining some division strategies related to capital budgeting, development of marketing campaigns, and implementation of incentive plans. The area of incentive plans has often been a problem to Jensen because many of the companies it has acquired already had such plans in place. These plans are not easily changed without causing discontent among the managers. Jensen has striven for consistency among its divisions with regard to bonus and incentive plans, but this has not always been achievable.

The restaurant division operates a chain of vegetarian restaurants, Hobbit Hole, in the eastern United States. Jensen acquired it approximately three years ago and has made very few changes to it. The restaurant's reputation was well established and, aside from nominal changes in marketing strategy, the chain has been allowed to operate in much the same manner as it did before its acquisition. In addition to a base salary, Hobbit Hole unit managers participate in the restaurant's profits. This incentive plan was in place when Jensen acquired the chain; although the profit percentage might vary among restaurant units, the overall plans are basically the same. The unit managers are satisfied with this incentive strategy, and Jensen's management does not believe that changes are necessary.

Jensen's motel division was formed 15 years ago when Jensen purchased a small group of motels in the Midwest. Since that time, the division has grown significantly as the company has acquired motels throughout the country using the name Cruise and Snooze Inns. Since its initial motel purchase, Jensen has implemented its own incentive program for unit managers in the individual motels. The incentive program provides annual bonuses based on the achievement of specific goals that are not necessarily finance oriented but pertain to areas such as improved quality control and customer service. This program requires administrative time, but Jensen believes that the results have been satisfactory.

Required

1. Hobbit Hole's restaurant unit managers are covered by a profit participation incentive plan. Discuss the following for this incentive plan:

   a. Its benefits to Jensen Corporation.

   b. The negative behavioral problems that it could cause, if any.

2. The Cruise and Snooze Inns' motel unit managers participate in an incentive program based on goal attainment. Discuss the following for this type of incentive plan:

   a. Advantages to Jensen Corporation.

   b. Disadvantages to Jensen Corporation.

3. Having two different types of incentive plans for two operating divisions of the same company can create problems.

   a. Discuss the behavioral problems that having different types of incentive plans for Hobbit Hole and Snooze Inns could cause Jensen Corporation.

   b. Present the rationale that Jensen Corporation can give to the unit managers of Hobbit Hole and Cruise and Snooze Inns to justify having different incentive plans for two operating divisions of the same company.

(CMA Adapted)

20–30 EMPLOYEE COMPENSATION Kyle Industries operates several large plants that provide the packaging for many consumer products. The company has a progressive compensation system that is market based and competitive with that of similar companies. Every position within Kyle is assigned a grade level from 1 to 30, with 30 being the company's chairman and 1 the lowest-level unskilled position. In assigning the grade levels, Kyle uses the following methodology:

1. The higher-level positions are classified according to the exact titles used by similar firms.

2. The lower-level positions are classified on the following factors:

   a. Formal education attained

   b. Amount of responsibility.

c. Complexity of tasks.

d. Effects of mistakes.

e. Physical difficulty or amount of effort.

3. Salary ranges increase annually according to the rate of inflation.

When Kyle hires employees, they are generally offered a starting salary at the lower end of the position grade level. For an individual with exceptional skills or experience, the offer could be closer to the top of the level. Employees can move through the levels on the basis of performance and merit increases; a promotion moves the employee into a new position level with a higher salary range. Kyle provides various in-house educational programs for its employees and has a tuition reimbursement program.

Susan Henderson, assistant controller for one of Kyle's plants, was hired a year ago at the top level for her position because of her extensive experience in the field. She has just learned that her annual increase will be 3 percent of her salary, the same percentage used to increase all position levels in the current year. Susan believes that her performance merits a larger increase but knows that as long as she remains an assistant controller at the top level, her future salary increases will be similar.

Joe Goldman is an administrative secretary reporting to Kyle's treasurer. Joe has been with the company for several years, earning his current position two years ago through above-average performance. Because Joe has proved to be reliable and efficient, his boss has transferred responsibility for many routine tasks to him. Joe believes that his position should be reevaluated because of these increased duties, but he has not received any encouragement from his boss concerning this.

Peter Connors was recently promoted to supervisor in one of the packaging plants, directing the work of 15 employees. He started at Kyle as a shipping clerk after completing high school and has learned the packaging business on the job by holding increasingly important positions over the years. Many of Peter's cosupervisors are better educated than he is, but lack his experience and frequently turn to him for solutions to their problems. Peter knows that these less-experienced supervisors earn more than he does because of their educational qualifications. Although he is confident that his salary will catch up with the others through merit increases, he does not believe that the company has been entirely fair with him.

Required

1. Describe the incentive effects that Kyle Industries' job evaluation and compensation program is likely to have on Susan Henderson, Joe Goldman, and Peter Connors.

2. Recommend several ways that the firm could improve its evaluation and compensation program to avoid situations similar to those described here.

3. Describe the general conditions that must be present for employees to be motivated to improve their performance under a merit pay system.

(CMA Adapted)

20–31 **BUSINESS VALUATION** Blue Water Sailboats is owned by a partnership of two businesspeople who are friends and avid sailors. At present, they are interested in expanding the business and have asked you to review its financial statements.

Blue Water Sailboats sells approximately 100 to 150 sailboats each year, ranging from 14-foot dinghies to 35-foot cruising sailboats. Their sales prices range from $2,000 to more than $130,000. The company has a limited

inventory of boats consisting primarily of one or two boats from each of the four manufacturers that supply Blue Water. The company also sells a variety of supplies and parts and performs different types of service. Most sales are on credit.

The company operates from a large building that has offices, storage, and sales for some of the smaller sailboats. The larger sailboats are kept in a fenced area adjacent to the main building, and an ample parking area is nearby. This year Blue Water purchased a boat lift to haul boats. The lift has brought in revenues for boat repairs, hull painting, and related services, as well as the boat hauls.

The balance sheet and income statement for Blue Water Sailboats for 1997 through 2001 and for the first eleven months of 2002 follow. The increase in net fixed assets in the recent two years is due to improvements in the building, paving of the parking area, and the purchase of the lift.

The company obtains its debt financing from two sources: a small savings and loan for its short-term funds, and a larger commercial bank, also for short-term loans, but principally for long-term financing. The terms of the loan agreement with the bank include a restriction that its current ratio must remain higher than 1.5.

Required   Evaluate the liquidity and profitability of Blue Water Sailboats using selected financial ratios. Assess the company's overall profitability, liquidity, and desirability as an investment. Use a spreadsheet system to improve the speed and accuracy of your analysis.

BLUE WATER SAILBOATS COMPANY
Comparative Balance Sheet
For the Years Ended December 31,

	1997	1998	1999	2000	2001	2002 (11 months)
Cash	$ 23,260	$ 21,966	$ 18,735	$ 28,426	$ 43,692	$ 31,264
Accounts receivable	99,465	102,834	112,903	125,663	104,388	142,009
Allowance for bad debts	(9,304)	(8,786)	(8,824)	(11,266)	(7,282)	(12,506)
Inventory	35,009	56,784	61,792	67,884	58,994	95,774
Other current assets	11,894	12,894	9,024	11,006	18,923	22,903
Total current assets	$160,324	$185,692	$193,630	$221,713	$218,715	$279,444
Property and equipment	262,195	282,008	299,380	368,565	405,269	498,626
Accumulated depreciation	(65,984)	(93,442)	(122,892)	(158,099)	(187,227)	(226,307)
Total assets	$356,535	$374,258	$370,118	$432,179	$436,757	$551,763
Accounts payable	82,635	78,127	63,346	56,256	40,189	49,544
Taxes payable	11,630	10,983	11,780	14,083	3,738	15,632
Short-term loans	59,876	56,980	37,583	41,093	49,594	76,962
Accrued payroll payable	5,227	4,598	3,649	4,224	4,774	4,779
Total current liabilities	$159,368	$150,688	$116,358	$115,656	$98,295	$146,917
Long-term debt	158,173	172,388	179,490	214,997	229,471	262,258
Partners' equity	38,994	51,182	74,270	101,526	108,991	142,588
	$356,535	$374,258	$370,118	$432,179	$436,757	$551,763

BLUE WATER SAILBOATS COMPANY
Comparative Statement of Income and Cash Flow
For the Years Ended December 31,

	1997	1998	1999	2000	2001	2002 (11 months)
Sales	$767,580	$724,878	$777,480	$929,478	$764,610	$938,857
Returns and allowances	38,379	35,645	40,334	45,998	32,887	46,380
Cost of sales	473,908	441,298	458,015	545,778	453,669	530,597
Gross margin	$255,293	$247,935	$279,131	$337,702	$278,054	$361,880

	1997	1998	1999	2000	2001	2002 (11 months)
Depreciation expense	$ 29,075	$ 27,458	$ 29,450	$ 35,208	$ 29,128	$ 35,563
Interest expense	18,597	19,557	20,998	21,475	24,889	28,993
Salaries and wages	81,923	73,664	77,846	95,764	92,903	99,447
Accounting and legal	9,304	8,786	9,323	11,834	13,108	11,380
Administration expense	79,666	75,234	80,693	96,469	87,995	97,441
Other expense	12,630	18,927	15,763	22,903	18,934	22,662
Total expense	$231,195	$223,626	$234,073	$283,653	$266,957	$295,486
Net income	$24,098	$24,309	$45,058	$54,049	$11,097	$66,394
Cash flow from operations						
Depreciation		$27,458	$29,450	$35,208	$29,128	$35,563
Decrease (increase) in receivables		(22,293)	(4,970)	(3,650)	4,906	(31,556)
Decrease (increase) in inventory		(21,775)	(5,008)	(6,092)	8,890	(36,780)
Decrease (increase) in other current assets		(1,000)	3,870	(1,982)	(7,917)	(3,980)
Increase (decrease) in current liabilities		(8,680)	(34,330)	(702)	(17,361)	48,622
Total		$(1,981)	$34,070	$76,831	$28,743	$78,263

SOLUTION TO SELF-STUDY PROBLEM

Management Compensation Plan

DTH's goal is to increase its business by at least 10 percent a year in a very competitive environment. The compensation plan is consistent with this goal because it rewards increases in revenues and new clients. It is likely, however, that under the current plan, each office is focusing only on the client base in its own region.

A problem occurs when DTH must make proposals that require joint cooperation and participation among two or more offices. The compensation plan does not have an incentive for cooperation. In fact, it could be a distraction and reduce the potential for a substantial bonus for any given office to develop a proposal for a large contract in which other offices might benefit. The cost of the proposal would be borne by the office, and the benefits would accrue to other offices as well as the originating office. The cost of the proposal for large contracts must therefore be shared among the offices in some way, or any one office will not have the incentive to spend the time and money necessary to develop a large proposal.

In addition to sharing the cost of the proposal, DTH should consider having a firmwide proposal development group for these large projects. The individual offices would then be charged for the cost of this group, perhaps in proportion to the fees received from large contracts in that office. Clearly, the firm is losing the larger contracts, and the compensation and proposal development plans must provide the needed incentive for each office to go after them aggressively.

Another alternative is to go to a firmwide compensation pool that would provide a direct and strong incentive for each office to cooperate in developing new business. A disadvantage of this approach is that it would reduce the motivation for each office to seek business in its own region because the revenues from these individual efforts would be shared firmwide.

Another issue concerning the current compensation plan is the office manager's discretion to divide the office bonus among the professionals in the office. Although no one has complained, a lower-level professional is unlikely to complain about the office manager's bonus decisions. The equity of this system should be reviewed to ensure that each office manager is using this discretion in a fair and appropriate way.

Table 1   Present Value of $1

Periods	4%	5%	6%	7%	8%	9%	10%	11%	12%	13%	14%	15%	20%	25%	30%
1	0.962	0.952	0.943	0.935	0.926	0.917	0.909	0.901	0.893	0.885	0.877	0.870	0.833	0.800	0.769
2	0.925	0.907	0.890	0.873	0.857	0.842	0.826	0.812	0.797	0.783	0.769	0.756	0.694	0.640	0.592
3	0.889	0.864	0.840	0.816	0.794	0.772	0.751	0.731	0.712	0.693	0.675	0.658	0.579	0.512	0.455
4	0.855	0.823	0.792	0.763	0.735	0.708	0.683	0.659	0.636	0.613	0.592	0.572	0.482	0.410	0.350
5	0.822	0.784	0.747	0.713	0.681	0.650	0.621	0.593	0.567	0.543	0.519	0.497	0.402	0.328	0.269
6	0.790	0.746	0.705	0.666	0.630	0.596	0.564	0.535	0.507	0.480	0.456	0.432	0.335	0.262	0.207
7	0.760	0.711	0.665	0.623	0.583	0.547	0.513	0.482	0.452	0.425	0.400	0.376	0.279	0.210	0.159
8	0.731	0.677	0.627	0.582	0.540	0.502	0.467	0.434	0.404	0.376	0.351	0.327	0.233	0.168	0.123
9	0.703	0.645	0.592	0.544	0.500	0.460	0.424	0.391	0.361	0.333	0.308	0.284	0.194	0.134	0.094
10	0.676	0.614	0.558	0.508	0.463	0.422	0.386	0.352	0.322	0.295	0.270	0.247	0.162	0.107	0.073
11	0.650	0.585	0.527	0.475	0.429	0.388	0.350	0.317	0.287	0.261	0.237	0.215	0.135	0.086	0.056
12	0.625	0.557	0.497	0.444	0.397	0.356	0.319	0.286	0.257	0.231	0.208	0.187	0.112	0.069	0.043
13	0.601	0.530	0.469	0.415	0.368	0.326	0.290	0.258	0.229	0.204	0.182	0.163	0.093	0.055	0.033
14	0.577	0.505	0.442	0.388	0.340	0.299	0.263	0.232	0.205	0.181	0.160	0.141	0.078	0.044	0.025
15	0.555	0.481	0.417	0.362	0.315	0.275	0.239	0.209	0.183	0.160	0.140	0.123	0.065	0.035	0.020
16	0.534	0.458	0.394	0.339	0.292	0.252	0.218	0.188	0.163	0.141	0.123	0.107	0.054	0.028	0.015
17	0.513	0.436	0.371	0.317	0.270	0.231	0.198	0.170	0.146	0.125	0.108	0.093	0.045	0.023	0.012
18	0.494	0.416	0.350	0.296	0.250	0.212	0.180	0.153	0.130	0.111	0.095	0.081	0.038	0.018	0.009
19	0.475	0.396	0.331	0.277	0.232	0.194	0.164	0.138	0.116	0.098	0.083	0.070	0.031	0.014	0.007
20	0.456	0.377	0.312	0.258	0.215	0.178	0.149	0.124	0.104	0.087	0.073	0.061	0.026	0.012	0.005
22	0.422	0.342	0.278	0.226	0.184	0.150	0.123	0.101	0.083	0.068	0.056	0.046	0.018	0.007	0.003
24	0.390	0.310	0.247	0.197	0.158	0.126	0.102	0.082	0.066	0.053	0.043	0.035	0.013	0.005	0.002
25	0.375	0.295	0.233	0.184	0.146	0.116	0.092	0.074	0.059	0.047	0.038	0.030	0.010	0.004	0.001
30	0.308	0.231	0.174	0.131	0.099	0.075	0.057	0.044	0.033	0.026	0.020	0.015	0.004	0.001	0.000
35	0.253	0.181	0.130	0.094	0.068	0.049	0.036	0.026	0.019	0.014	0.010	0.008	0.002	0.000	0.000
40	0.208	0.142	0.097	0.067	0.046	0.032	0.022	0.015	0.011	0.008	0.005	0.004	0.001	0.000	0.000

Table 2 Present Value of Annuity of $1

Periods	4%	5%	6%	7%	8%	9%	10%	11%	12%	13%	14%	15%	20%	25%	30%
1	0.962	0.952	0.943	0.935	0.926	0.917	0.909	0.901	0.893	0.885	0.877	0.870	0.833	0.800	0.769
2	1.886	1.859	1.833	1.808	1.783	1.759	1.736	1.713	1.690	1.668	1.647	1.626	1.528	1.440	1.361
3	2.775	2.723	2.673	2.624	2.577	2.531	2.487	2.444	2.402	2.361	2.322	2.283	2.106	1.952	1.816
4	3.630	3.546	3.465	3.387	3.312	3.240	3.170	3.102	3.037	2.974	2.914	2.855	2.589	2.362	2.166
5	4.452	4.329	4.212	4.100	3.993	3.890	3.791	3.696	3.605	3.517	3.433	3.352	2.991	2.689	2.436
6	5.242	5.076	4.917	4.767	4.623	4.486	4.355	4.231	4.111	3.998	3.889	3.784	3.326	2.951	2.643
7	6.002	5.786	5.582	5.389	5.206	5.033	4.868	4.712	4.564	4.423	4.288	4.160	3.605	3.161	2.802
8	6.733	6.463	6.210	5.971	5.747	5.535	5.335	5.146	4.968	4.799	4.639	4.487	3.837	3.329	2.925
9	7.435	7.108	6.802	6.515	6.247	5.995	5.759	5.537	5.328	5.132	4.946	4.772	4.031	3.463	3.019
10	8.111	7.722	7.360	7.024	6.710	6.418	6.145	5.889	5.650	5.426	5.216	5.019	4.192	3.571	3.092
11	8.760	8.306	7.887	7.499	7.139	6.805	6.495	6.207	5.938	5.687	5.453	5.234	4.327	3.656	3.147
12	9.385	8.863	8.384	7.943	7.536	7.161	6.814	6.492	6.194	5.918	5.660	5.421	4.439	3.725	3.190
13	9.986	9.394	8.853	8.358	7.904	7.487	7.103	6.750	6.424	6.122	5.842	5.583	4.533	3.780	3.223
14	10.563	9.899	9.295	8.745	8.244	7.786	7.367	6.982	6.628	6.302	6.002	5.724	4.611	3.824	3.249
15	11.118	10.380	9.712	9.108	8.559	8.061	7.606	7.191	6.811	6.462	6.142	5.847	4.675	3.859	3.268
16	11.652	10.838	10.106	9.447	8.851	8.313	7.824	7.379	6.974	6.604	6.265	5.954	4.730	3.887	3.283
17	12.166	11.274	10.477	9.763	9.122	8.544	8.022	7.549	7.120	6.729	6.373	6.047	4.775	3.910	3.295
18	12.659	11.690	10.828	10.059	9.372	8.756	8.201	7.702	7.250	6.840	6.467	6.128	4.812	3.928	3.304
19	13.134	12.085	11.158	10.336	9.604	8.950	8.365	7.839	7.366	6.938	6.550	6.198	4.843	3.942	3.311
20	13.590	12.462	11.470	10.594	9.818	9.129	8.514	7.963	7.469	7.025	6.623	6.259	4.870	3.954	3.316
22	14.451	13.163	12.042	11.061	10.201	9.442	8.772	8.176	7.645	7.170	6.743	6.359	4.909	3.970	3.323
24	15.247	13.799	12.550	11.469	10.529	9.707	8.985	8.348	7.784	7.283	6.835	6.434	4.937	3.981	3.327
25	15.622	14.094	12.783	11.654	10.675	9.823	9.077	8.422	7.843	7.330	6.873	6.464	4.948	3.985	3.329
30	17.292	15.372	13.765	12.409	11.258	10.274	9.427	8.694	8.055	7.496	7.003	6.566	4.979	3.995	3.332
35	18.665	16.374	14.498	12.948	11.655	10.567	9.644	8.855	8.176	7.586	7.070	6.617	4.992	3.998	3.333
40	19.793	17.159	15.046	13.332	11.925	10.757	9.779	8.951	8.244	7.634	7.105	6.642	4.997	3.999	3.333

abnormal spoilage   An unacceptable table unit that should not arise under efficient operating conditions

absolute quality conformance (robust quality approach)   Conformance that requires all products or services to meet the target value exactly with no variation

activity   Composed of actions, movements, or work sequences, it is work performed within an organization

activity analysis   The development of a detailed description of the specific activities performed in the firm's operations

activity-based budgeting (ABB)   A budgeting process that focuses on costs of activities or cost drivers necessary for production and sales

activity-based costing (ABC)   An analysis used to improve the accuracy of cost analysis by improving the tracing of costs to products or individual customers

activity-based management (ABM)   An activity analysis used to improve operational control and management control

activity cost driver   Measures how much of an activity a cost object uses

actual costing system   A costing process that uses actual costs incurred for direct materials and direct labor and assigns or applies actual factory overhead to various jobs

actual factory overhead   Costs incurred in an accounting period for indirect materials, indirect labor, and other indirect factory costs, including factory rent, insurance, property tax, depreciation, repairs and maintenance, power, light, heat, and employer payroll taxes for factory personnel

additional processing costs or **separable costs**   Costs that occur after the split-off point and can be identified directly with individual products

advance pricing agreement (APA)   An agreement between the Internal Revenue Service (IRS) and the firm using transfer prices, that establishes the agreed-upon transfer price

analysis of variance table   A table that separates the total variance of the dependent variable into both error and explained variance components

appraisal costs   Costs incurred in the measurement and analysis of data to ascertain if products and services conform to specifications

arm's-length standard   A transfer price set to reflect the price that unrelated parties acting independently would have set

asset turnover   The amount of sales dollar achieved per dollar of investment; measures the manager's ability to increase sales from a given level of investment

authoritative standard   A standard determined solely or primarily by management

average cost   The total of manufacturing cost (materials, labor, and overhead) divided by units of output

average cost method   A method that uses units of output to allocate joint costs to joint products

balanced scorecard   An accounting report that includes the firm's critical success factors in four areas: (1) financial performance, (2) customer satisfaction, (3) internal business processes, and (4) innovation and learning

basic engineering   The method in which product designers work independently from marketing and manufacturing to develop a design from specific plans and specifications

batch-level activity   An activity performed for each batch of products rather than for each unit of production

benchmarking   A process by which a firm identifies its critical success factors, studies the best practices of other firms (or other units within a firm) for achieving these critical success factors, and then implements improvements in the firm's processes to match or beat the performance of those competitors

benefits   Special benefits for the employee, such as travel, membership in a fitness club, tickets to entertainment events, and other extras paid for by the firm

bill of materials   A detailed list of the components of the manufactured product

bonus   Based on the achievement of performance goals for the period

book rate of return   The average net income from an investment as a percentage of its book value

breakeven point   The point at which revenues equal total cost and profit is zero

budget   A quantitative plan of operations for an organization; it identifies the resources and commitments required to fulfill the organization's goals for the budgeted period

budgeting   The process of preparing a budget

budget slack   The difference between budgeted performance and expected performance

by-products   Products whose total sales values are minor in comparison with the sales value of the joint products

capital budgeting   A process for evaluating an organization's proposed long-range major projects

capital investment   An investment that requires committing a large sum of funds to projects with expenditures and benefits expected to stretch well into the future

cash budget   A budget that brings together the anticipated effects of all budgeted activities on cash

cause-and-effect diagram   A diagram that maps out a list of causes that affect an activity, process, stated problem, or a desired outcome

comparable price method   Establishes an arm's-length price by using the sales prices of similar products made by unrelated firms

computer-aided design (CAD)   The use of computers in product development, analysis, and design modification to improve the quality and performance of the product

computer-aided manufacturing (CAM)   The use of computers to plan, implement, and control production

computer-integrated manufacturing (CIM)   A manufacturing system that totally integrates all office and factory functions within a company via a computer-based information network, to allow hour-by-hour manufacturing management

concurrent engineering   An important new method that integrates product design with manufacturing and marketing throughout the product's life cycle; also called simultaneous engineering

confidence interval   A range around the regression line within which the management accountant can be confident the actual value of the predicted cost will fall

constraints   Those activities that slow the product's total cycle time

continuous budget   A budgeting system that has in effect a budget for a set number of months, quarters, or years at all times

continuous improvement (The Japanese word is *kaizen*.)   A management technique in which managers and workers commit to a program of continuous improvement in quality and other critical success factors

contract manufacturing   The practice of having another manufacturer (sometimes a direct competitor) manufacture a portion of the firm's products

contribution by SBU (CSBU)   A measurement of *all* the costs traceable to, and therefore controllable by, the individual profit SBUs

contribution income statement   Focuses on variable costs and fixed costs, in contrast to the conventional income statement which focuses on product costs and nonproduct costs

contribution margin income statement   An income statement based on contribution margin that is developed for each profit SBU and for each relevant group of profit SBUs

contribution margin ratio   The ratio of the unit contribution margin to unit sales price $(\rho - v)/\rho$

control chart   A graph that depicts successive observations of an operation taken at constant intervals

controllable cost   A cost that a manager or employee has discretion in choosing to incur or can significantly influence the amount of within a given, usually short, period of time

controllable fixed costs   Fixed costs that the profit SBU manager can influence in approximately a year or less

controllable margin   A margin determined by subtracting short-term controllable fixed costs from the contribution margin

conversion cost   Direct labor and overhead combined into a single amount

core competencies   Skills or competencies that the firm employs especially well

correlation   A given variable tends to change predictably in the same or opposite direction for a given change in the other, correlated variable

cost allocation   The process of assigning indirect costs to cost pools and cost objects

cost assignment   The assignment of indirect costs to cost pools and cost objects

cost driver   Any factor that causes a change in the cost of an activity

cost driver analysis   The examination, quantification, and explanation of the effects of cost drivers

cost element   An amount paid for a resource consumed by an activity and included in a cost pool

cost estimation   The development of a well-defined relationship between a cost object and its cost drivers for the purpose of predicting the cost

cost leadership   A competitive strategy in which a firm succeeds in producing products or services at the lowest cost in the industry

cost life cycle   The sequence of activities within the firm that begins with research and development, followed by design, manufacturing, marketing/distribution, and customer service

cost management information   The information the manager needs to effectively manage the firm or not-for-profit organization

cost object   Any product, service, customer, activity, or organizational unit to which costs are accumulated for some management purpose

cost of capital   A composite of the cost of various sources of funds comprising a firm's capital structure

cost of goods manufactured   The cost of goods that were finished and transferred out of Work-in-Process Inventory account this period

cost of goods sold   The cost of the product transferred to the income statement when inventory is sold

cost of quality report   A report that shows the costs of prevention, appraisal, internal, and external failures. An important type of cost of quality report is the quality matrix, which shows the different quality costs for each operating and support function

cost-plus method   A method that determines the transfer price based on the seller's costs plus a gross profit percentage determined by comparing the seller's sales to that of unrelated parties

cost pools   Costs that are collected into meaningful groups

cost SBU   Production or support SBUs within the firm that have the goal of providing the best quality product or service at the lowest cost

costs of conformance   Costs of prevention and appraisal

costs of nonconformance   Costs of internal failure and external failure

costs of quality   Costs associated with the prevention, identification, repair, and rectification of poor quality and opportunity costs from lost production time and sales as a result of poor quality

cost tables   Computer-based databases that include comprehensive information about the firm's cost drivers

cost-volume-profit (CVP) analysis   A method for analyzing how various operating decisions and marketing decisions will affect net income

critical success factors (CSFs)   Measures of those aspects of the firm's performance that are essential to its competitive advantage and, therefore to its success

currently attainable standard   A level of performance that workers with proper training and experience can attain most of the time without extraordinary effort

customer cost analysis   Identifies cost activities and cost drivers related to customers

customer profitability analysis   Process that traces and reports customer revenues and customer costs

customer revenue analysis   Traces selling price, sales discounts, and cash discounts to customers and identifies financing costs associated with customer revenues

CVP graph   Illustrates how the levels of revenues and total costs change over different levels of output

cycle time   The amount of time between receipt of a customer order and shipment of the order

degrees of freedom   Represents the number of independent choices that can be made for each component of variance

denominator activity   The desired operating level at the expected operating efficiency for the period, expressed in the quantity of the activity measure for applying fixed factory overhead

departmental overhead rate   An overhead rate calculated for a single production department

dependent variable   The cost to be estimated

design analysis   A common form of value engineering in which the design team prepares several possible designs of the product, each having similar features with different levels of performance and different costs

desired rate of return   The minimum rate of return the investing firm requires for the investment

differential cost   A cost that differs for each decision option and is therefore relevant

differentiation   A competitive strategy in which a firm succeeds by developing and maintaining a unique value for the product as perceived by consumers

direct cost   A cost conveniently and economically traced directly to a cost pool or a cost object

direct labor cost   The labor used to manufacture the product or to provide the service

direct labor efficiency variance   The difference in the number of hours worked and the number of standard direct labor-hours allowed for the units manufactured multiplied by the standard hourly rate

direct labor rate variance   The difference between the actual and standard hourly wage rate multiplied by the actual direct hours used in production

direct materials cost   The cost of the materials in the product and a reasonable allowance for scrap and defective units

direct materials flexible budget variance   The difference between direct material costs incurred and the total standard cost for the direct materials in the flexible budget for the units manufactured during the period

direct materials price variance   The difference between the actual and standard unit price of the direct materials multiplied by the actual quantity of the direct materials purchased

direct materials usage budget   A plan that shows the direct materials required for production and their budgeted cost

direct materials usage variance   The product of the difference between the number of units of direct materials used during the period and the number of standard units of direct materials that should have been used for the number of units of the product manufactured during the period and the standard unit price of the direct materials

direct method   Cost allocation accomplished by using the service flows *only to production departments* and determining each production department's share of that service

discounted-cash flow (DCF techniques)   A technique that evaluates a capital investment by considering equivalent present values of all future cash flows from the initial investment

discretionary-cost method   Used when costs are considered largely uncontrollable; apply discretion at the planning stage; an input-oriented approach

drum-buffer-rope system   A system for balancing the flow of production through a constraint, thereby reducing the amount of inventory at the constraint and improving overall productivity

dual allocation   A cost allocation method that separates fixed and variable costs. Variable costs are directly traced to user departments, and fixed costs are allocated on some logical basis

Durbin-Watson statistic   A measure of the extent of nonlinearity in the regression

economic value added (EVA)   A business unit's income after taxes and after deducting the cost of capital

effective operation   The attainment of the goal set for the operation

efficient operation   An operation that wastes no resources

employment contract   An agreement between the manager and top management, designed to provide incentives for the manager to act independently to achieve top management's objectives

engineered-cost method   An output-oriented method that considers costs to be variable and therefore controllable

equivalent units   The number of the same or similar completed units that could have been produced given the amount of work actually performed on both completed and partially completed units

executional cost drivers   Factors that the firm can manage in the short term to reduce costs such as workforce involvement, design of the production process, and supplier relationships

expropriation   A foreign government takes ownership and control of assets a domestic investor has invested in that country

external failure costs   Costs incurred to rectify quality defects after unacceptable products or services reach the customer and lost profit opportunities caused by the unacceptable products or services delivered

facility-sustaining activity   An activity performed to support the production of products in general

factory overhead   All the indirect costs commonly combined into a single cost pool in a manufacturing firm

factory overhead applied   The amount of overhead assigned to a specific job using a predetermined factory overhead rate

FIFO method   A process costing method for calculating the unit cost that includes only costs incurred and work effort during the current period

financial budget   A plan that identifies sources and uses of funds for budgeted operations to achieve the expected operating results for the period

financial productivity   The ratio of output to the dollar amount of one or more input factors

Finished Goods Inventory   The cost of goods that are ready for sale

firmwide pool   A basis for determining the bonus available to all managers through an amount set aside for this purpose

first difference   For each variable, the difference between each value and the succeeding value in the time series

fixed cost   The portion of the total cost that does not change with a change in the quantity of the cost driver, within the relevant range

fixed factory overhead application rate   The rate at which the firm applies fixed overhead costs to cost objects

fixed factory overhead production volume variance   The difference between the budgeted allowance for fixed factory overhead for the period and the applied fixed factory overhead

fixed factory overhead spending (budget) variance   The difference between the actual amount incurred and the budgeted amount for the fixed factory overhead

flexible budget   A budget that adjusts revenues and costs for changes in output achieved

flexible budget variance   The difference between the actual operating result and the flexible budget at the actual operating level of the period

flexible manufacturing system (FMS)   A computerized network of automated equipment that produces one or more groups of parts or variations of a product in a flexible manner

flow diagram   A flow chart of the work done that shows the sequence of processes and the amount of time required for each

F-statistic   A useful measure of the statistical reliability of the regression

full-cost method   The transfer price set equal to the variable cost plus allocated fixed cost for the selling unit

functional analysis   A common type of value engineering in which the performance and cost of each major function or feature of the product is examined

goal congruence   The consistency between the goals of the firm and the goals of its employees. It is achieved when the manager acts independently in such a way as to simultaneously achieve top management's objectives

goalpost conformance (zero-defects conformance)   Conformance to a quality specification expressed as a specified range around a target

gross book value (GBV)   The historical cost without the reduction for depreciation

group technology   A method of identifying similarities in the parts of products a firm manufactures, so the same part can be used in two or more products, thereby reducing costs

high-low method   A method using algebra to determine a *unique* estimation line between representative low and high points in the data

histogram   A graphical representation of the frequency of attributes or events in a given set of data

historical cost   The book value of current assets plus the net book value of the long-lived assets

ideal standard   A standard that demands perfect implementation and maximum efficiency in every aspect of the operation

implementation error   A deviation from the standard that occurs during operations as a result of operators' errors

independent variable   The cost driver used to estimate the value of the dependent variable

indirect cost   A cost that is not conveniently or economically traceable from the cost or cost pool to the cost pool or cost object

indirect labor cost   Supervision, quality control, inspection, purchasing and receiving, and other manufacturing support costs

indirect materials cost   The cost of materials used in manufacturing that are not physically part of the finished product

internal accounting controls   A set of policies and procedures that restrict and guide activities in the processing of financial data with the objective to prevent or detect errors and fraudulent acts

internal failure costs   Costs incurred as a result of poor quality found through appraisal prior to delivery to customers

internal rate of return (IRR) method   A discounted cash flow method that estimates the discount rate that causes the present value of subsequent net cash inflows to equal the initial investment

investment SBU   An SBU that includes assets employed by the SBU as well as profits in performance evaluation

ISO 9000   A set of guidelines for quality management and quality standards developed by the International Organization for Standardization in Geneva, Switzerland

job costing   A product costing system that accumulates and assigns costs to a specific job

job cost sheet   A cost sheet that records and summarizes the costs of direct materials, direct labor, and factory overhead for a particular job

joint products   Products from the same production process that have relatively substantial sales values

just-in-time (JIT) system   A comprehesive production and inventory system that purchases or produces materials and parts only as needed and just in time to be used at each stage of the production process

kaizen budgeting   A budgeting approach that explicitly demands continuous improvement and incorporates all the expected improvements in the resultant budget

kanban   A set of control cards used to signal the need for materials and products to move from one operation to the next in an assembly line

learning curve analysis   A systematic method for estimating costs when learning is present

learning rate   The percentage by which average time (or total time) falls from previous levels, as output doubles

least squares regression   One of the most effective methods for estimating costs, found by minimizing the sum of the squares of the estimation errors

life-cycle costing   A management technique used to identify and monitor the costs of a product throughout its life cycle

liquidation value   The price that could be received for the sale of the assets

long-range plan   A plan that identifies which actions are required during the 5- to 10-year period covered by the plan to attain the firm's strategic goal

management compensation plans   Policies and procedures for compensating managers

management control   The evaluation of mid-level managers by upper-level managers

manufacturing cycle efficiency (MCE)   The ratio of processing time to total cycle time

marginal cost   The additional cost incurred as the cost driver increases by one unit

margin of safety   A measure of the potential effect of a change in sales on profit

margin of safety ratio   A useful measure for comparing the risk of two alternative products, or for assessing the riskiness in any given product

market price method   The transfer price set as the current price for the selling unit's product in the market

market share variance   A comparison of the firm's actual market share to its budgeted market share and measurement of the effect of changes in the firm's market share on its total contribution margin and operating income

market size variance   A measure of the effect of changes in the total market size on the firm's total contribution margin and operating income

mass customization   A management technique in which marketing and production processes are designed to handle the increased variety that results from delivering customized products and services to customers

master budget   A plan of operations for a business unit during a specific period

Materials Inventory   The cost of the supply of materials used in the manufacturing process or to provide the service

materials requisition form   A source document that the production department supervisor uses to request materials for production

materials usage ratio   The ratio of quantity used over quantity purchased

mean squared variance   The ratio of the amount of variance of a component to the number of degrees of freedom for that component

measurement errors   Incorrect numbers resulting from improper or inaccurate accounting systems or procedures

merchandise purchase budget   A plan that shows the amount of merchandise the firm needs to purchase during the period

mixed cost   The total cost when it includes both variable and fixed cost components

modeling error   A deviation from the standard because of the failure to include all relevant variables or because of the inclusion of wrong or irrelevant variables in the standard-setting process

multicollinearity   The condition when two or more independent variables are highly correlated with each other

negotiated price method   The determination of a transfer price through a negotiation process and sometimes arbitration between units

net book value   The asset's historical cost less accumulated depreciation

net present value (NPV)   The excess of the present value of future cash flow returns over the initial investment

net realizable value (NRV)   The estimated sales value of the product at the split-off point it is determined by subtracting the additional processing and selling costs beyond the split-off point from the ultimate sales value of the product

network diagram   A flowchart of the work done that shows the sequence of processes and the amount of time required for each

nonconstant variance   The condition when the variance of the errors is not constant over the range of the independent variable

noncontrollable fixed costs   Costs that are not controllable within a year's time, usually including facilities-related costs such as depreciation, taxes, and insurance

non-value-added activity   An activity that does not contribute to customer value or to the organization's needs

normal costing system   A costing process that uses actual costs for direct materials and direct labor and applies factory overhead to various jobs using a predetermined basis

normal spoilage   An unacceptable unit that occurs under efficient operating conditions

operating budgets   Plans that identify resources needed in operating activities and the acquisition of these resources

operating income flexible budget variance   The difference between the flexible budget operating income for the units sold during the period and the actual operating income earned

operating income variance   The difference between the actual operating income of the period and the master budget operating income projected for the period

operating leverage   The ratio of the contribution margin to profit

operational control   The evaluation of operating-level employees by mid-level managers

operational productivity   The ratio of output to the number of units of an input factor

operation costing   A hybrid costing system that uses job costing to assign direct materials costs and process costing to assign conversion costs to products or services

opportunity cost   The benefit lost when choosing one option precludes receiving the benefits from an alternative option

order-filling costs   Expenditures for freight, warehousing, packing and shipping, and collections

order-getting costs   Expenditures to advertise and promote the product

outliers   Unusual data points that strongly influence a regression analysis

overapplied overhead   The amount of factory overhead applied that exceeds the actual factory overhead cost

overhead   All the indirect costs commonly combined into a single cost pool

overhead application or allocation   A process of assigning overhead costs to the appropriate jobs

Pareto analysis   A management tool that shows 20 percent of a set of important cost drivers are responsible for 80 percent of the total cost incurred

Pareto diagram   A histogram of the frequency of factors contributing to the quality problem, ordered from the most to the least frequent

partial productivity   A productivity measure that focuses only on the relationship between one of the inputs and the output attained

participative standard   Active participation throughout the standard-setting process by employees affected by the standard

payback period   The length of time required for the cumulative total net cash inflows from an investment to equal the total initial cash outlays of the investment

performance evaluation   The process by which managers at all levels gain information about the performance of tasks within the firm and judge that performance against preestablished criteria as set out in budgets, plans, and goals

performance measurement   A measurement that identifies items that indicate the work performed and the results achieved by an activity, process, or organizational unit

period costs   All nonproduct expenditures for managing the firm and selling the product

physical measure method   A method that uses a physical measure such as pounds, gallons or yards or units or volume produced at the split-off point to allocate the joint costs to joint products

planning and decision making   Budgeting and profit planning, cash flow management, and other decisions related to operations

plantwide overhead rate   A single overhead rate used throughout the entire production facility

predetermined factory overhead rate   An estimated factory overhead rate used to apply factory overhead cost to a specific job

prediction error   A deviation from the standard because of an inaccurate estimation of the amounts for variables used in the standard-setting process

preparation of financial statements   Requires management to comply with the financial reporting requirements of regulatory agencies

present value   The current equivalent dollar value of a cash flow return, given the desired rate of return

present value payback method or breakeven time (BET)   A method using the span of time required for the cumulative present value of cash inflows to equal the initial investment of the project

prevention costs   Costs incurred to keep quality defects from occurring

prime costs   Direct materials and direct labor that are sometimes considered together

principal-agent model   A conceptual model that contains the key elements that contracts must have to achieve the desired objectives

process costing   A costing system that accumulates product or service costs by process or department and then assigns them to a large number of nearly identical products

product and service costing   In preparing financial statements, management complies with the financial reporting requirements of the industry and of regulatory agencies

product costing   The process of accumulating, classifying, and assigning direct materials, direct labor, and factory overhead costs to products or services

product costs   Only the costs necessary to complete the product (direct materials, direct labor, and factory overhead)

production budget   A plan for acquiring and combining the resources needed to carry out the manufacturing operations that allow the firm to satisfy its sales goals and have the desired amount of inventory at the end of the budget period

production cost report   A report that summarizes the physical units and equivalent units of a department, the costs incurred during the period, and the costs assigned to both units completed and transferred out and ending work-in-process inventories

productivity   The ratio of output to input

product-sustaining activity   An activity performed to support the production of a specific product

profit SBU   An SBU that generates revenues and incurs the major portion of the cost for producing these revenues

profit-volume graph   Illustrates how the level of profits changes over different levels of output

proration   The process of allocating underapplied or overapplied overhead to Work-in-Process Inventory, Finished Goods Inventory, and Cost of Goods Sold accounts

prototyping   A method in which functional models of the product are developed and tested by engineers and trial customers

quality   A product or service that meets or exceeds customers' expectations at a competitive price they are willing to pay

quality circle   A small group of employees from the same work area that meet regularly to identify and solve work-related problems, and to implement and monitor solutions to the problems

random variances   The variances beyond the control of management, either technically or financially, that often are considered as uncontrollable variances

rank-order correlation   A statistic that measures the degree to which two sets of numbers tend to have the same order or rank

reciprocal flows   The movement of services back and forth between service departments

reciprocal method   A cost allocation method that considers all reciprocal flows between service departments through simultaneous equations

reengineering   A process for creating competitive advantage in which a firm reorganizes its operating and management functions, often with the result that jobs are modified, combined, or eliminated

regression analysis   A statistical method for obtaining the unique cost estimating equation that best fits a set of data points

relevant cost   A cost with two properties: it differs for each decision option and it will be incurred in the future

relevant range   The range of the cost driver in which the actual value of the cost driver is expected to fall, and for which the relationship is assumed to be approximately linear

replacement cost   The current cost to replace the assets at the current level of service and functionality

resale price method   A transfer pricing method based on determining an appropriate markup based on gross profits of unrelated firms selling similar products

residual income (RI)   A dollar amount equal to the income of a business unit less a charge for the investment in the unit

resource   An economic element applied or used to perform activities

resource driver   A measure of the amount of resources consumed by an activity

return on equity (ROE)   The return determined when investment is measured as shareholders' equity

return on investment (ROI)   Profit divided by investment in the business unit

return on sales (ROS)   A firm's profit per sales dollar measures the manager's ability to control expenses and increase revenues to improve profitability

revenue drivers   The factors that affect sales volume, such as price changes, promotions, discounts, customer service, changes in product features, delivery dates, and other value-added factors

revenue SBU   An SBU with responsibility for sales, defined either by product line or by geographical area

rework   A produced unit that must be reworked into a good unit that can be sold in regular channels

risk preferences   The way individuals differentially view decision options, because they place a weight on *certain* outcomes that differs from the weight they place on *uncertain* outcomes

robot   A computer-programmed and controlled machine that performs repetitive activities

R-squared   A number between zero and one. Often it is described as a measure of the explanatory power of the regression; that is, the degree to which changes in the dependent variable can be predicted by changes in the independent variable

salary   A fixed payment

sales budget   A schedule showing expected sales in units at their expected selling prices

sales life cycle   The sequence of phases in the product's or service's life in the market—from the introduction of the product or service to the market, to growth in sales, and finally maturity, decline, and withdrawal from the market

sales mix   The proportion of units of each product or service to the total of all unit products or services

sales mix variance   The product of the difference between the actual and budgeted sales mix by the actual total number of units of all products sold and by the budgeted contribution margin per unit of the product

sales quantity variance   The product of three elements: (1) the difference between the budgeted and actual total sales quantity, (2) the budgeted sales mix of the product, and (3) the budgeted contribution margin per unit of the product. It measures the effect of the change in the number of units sold from the number of units budgeted to be sold

sales value at split-off method   A method that allocates joint costs to joint products on the basis of their relative sales values at the split-off point

sales volume or activity variance   The difference between the flexible budget and the master or static budget. A measurement of the effect on sales, expenses, contribution margin, or operating income of changes in units of sales

schedule of cost of goods manufactured and sold   A schedule that shows the manufacturing costs incurred, the change in the work-in-process inventory, the cost of goods sold, and the change in finished goods inventory during the period

scrap   Part of the product that has little or no value

selling price variance   The difference between the total actual sales revenue and the total flexible budget sales revenue for the units sold during a period

sensitivity analysis   The name for a variety of methods used to examine how an amount will change if factors involved in predicting that amount change

split-off point   The first point in a joint production process at which individual products can be identified

spoilage   An unaccepted unit that is discarded or sold for disposal value

standard cost   The cost a firm ought to incur for an operation

standard cost sheet   A listing of the standard price and quantity of each manufacturing cost element for the production of one product

standard error of the estimate (SE)   A measure of the accuracy of the regression's estimates

statistical control charts   Charts that set control limits using a statistical procedure

step cost   A cost that varies with the cost driver, but in discrete steps

step method   A cost allocation method that uses a sequence of steps in allocating of service department costs to production departments

strategic business unit (SBU)   A well-defined set of controllable operating activities over which an SBU manager is responsible

strategic cost management   The development of cost management information to facilitate the principal management function, strategic management

strategic management   The development of a sustainable competitive position

strategic performance measurement   An accounting system used by top management for the evaluation of SBU managers

strategy   A set of policies, procedures, and approaches to business that produce long-term success

strategy map   A device that uses the balanced scorecard to describe the firm's strategy in detail by using cause-and-effect diagrams

structural cost drivers   Strategic plans and decisions that have a long-term effect with regard to issues such as scale, experience, technology, and complexity

sunk costs   Costs that have been incurred or committed in the past, and are therefore irrelevant

SWOT analysis   A systematic procedure for identifying a firm's critical success factors: its internal strengths and weaknesses, and its external opportunities and threats

systematic (controllable) variances   Variances that are likely to recur unless they are corrected

Taguchi quality loss function   Depicts the relationship between the total loss to a firm due to quality defects and the extent of quality defects

target costing   The desired cost for a product is determined on the basis of a given competitive price, so the product will earn a desired profit

templating   A method in which an existing product is scaled up or down to fit the specifications of the desired new product

throughput margin   A TOC measure of product profitability; it equals price less materials cost, including all purchased components and materials handling costs

time ticket   A sheet showing the time an employee worked on each job, the pay rate, and the total cost chargeable to each job

total contribution margin   The unit contribution margin multiplied by the number of units sold

total productivity   A measure including all input resources in computing the ratio of the output attained and the input used to attain the output

total quality management (TQM)   A technique in which management develops policies and practices to ensure that the firm's products and services exceed customers' expectations

total variable factory overhead variance   The difference between total actual variable factory overhead incurred and total standard variable factory overhead for the output of the period

transfer pricing   The determination of an exchange price for a product or service when different business units within a firm exchange it

transferred-in costs   The costs of work performed in the earlier department that are transferred into the present department

trend variable   A variable that takes on values of 1, 2, 3, . . . for each period in sequence

t-value   A measure of the reliability of each of the independent variables; that is, the degree to which an independent variable has a valid, stable, long-term relationship with the dependent variable

two-stage allocation   A procedure that assigns a firm's resource costs, namely factory overhead costs, to cost pools and then to cost objects

underapplied overhead   The amount that actual factory overhead exceeds the factory overhead applied

unit-based pool   A basis for determining a bonus according to the performance of the manager's unit

unit contribution margin   The difference between unit sales price and unit variable cost; it is a measure of the increase in profit for a unit increase in sales

unit cost   The total manufacturing cost (materials, labor, and overhead) divided by units of output

unit-level activity   An activity performed for each unit of production

units accounted for   The sum of the units transferred out and ending inventory units

units to account for   The sum of the beginning inventory units and the number of units started during the period

value activities Firms in an industry perform activities to convert raw material into the final product; includes customer service

value-added activity An activity that contributes to customer value and satisfaction or satisfies an organizational need

value-chain analysis A strategic analysis tool used to identify where value to customers can be increased or costs reduced, and to better understand the firm's linkages with suppliers, customers, and other firms in the industry

value engineering Used in target costing to reduce product cost by analyzing the trade-offs between different types of product functionality and total product cost

variable cost The change in total cost associated with each change in the quantity of the cost driver

variable cost method The transfer price equals the variable cost of the selling unit

variable expense flexible budget variance The difference between the actual variable expenses incurred and the total standard variable expenses in the flexible budget for the units sold during the period

variable factory overhead efficiency variance The difference between the total standard variable factory overhead for the actual quantity of the substitute activity measure for applying variable factory overhead and the total standard variable factory overhead cost for the units manufactured during the period

variable factory overhead spending variance The difference between variable factory overhead incurred and total standard variable factory overhead based on the actual quantity of the substitute activity measure to apply the overhead

weighted average after-tax cost of capital The after-tax cost to the firm of securing funds with a given capital structure

weighted-average method A method for calculating the unit cost that includes all costs, both those incurred during the current period and those incurred in the prior period that are shown as the beginning work-in-process inventory of this period

what-if analysis The calculation of an amount given different levels for a factor that influences that amount

work cells Small groups of related manufacturing processes organized in clusters to assemble parts of finished products

work-in-process inventory Contains all costs put into manufacture of products that are started but not complete at the financial statement date

work measurement A cost estimation method that makes a detailed study of some production or service activity to measure the time or input required per unit of output

work sampling A statistical method that makes a series of measurements about the activity under study

zero-base budgeting A budgeting process that requires managers to prepare budgets from ground zero